Judicial Watch
Because no one is above the law!
Mr. Mark L. Vorce
554 Jean Cir.
Melbourne, FL 32904-5727
MW00666852

What Others Say About Holy Ground

"Just as Scripture reveals its distinction from other writings by showing the raw, naked truth about even its heroes, *Holy Ground* reveals truths that have been glossed over by supporters of Israel. Dr. Grady also demolishes those Christians who try to usurp Israel's rightful place as God's chosen people by revealing the nation's past, present, and future through a detailed examination of the Scriptures as only a real Bible believer can. *Holy Ground* is exceptional and truly stands alone as the definitive work on the subject from the real Bible believer's (AV 1611) point of view."

—Mr. Jack Minor, *World Net Daily* contributing writer; founder JM Publications; internationally known author/editor; served in the USMC under President Ronald Reagan

"This book was inspired by Dr. William Grady's love for God, his love for the Bible, and the Jews. Years of research, travel, study, and writing ability have gone into this classic of Godly literature. It will inform you of Israel from Abraham unto today. Dr. Grady is a great Christian and an outstanding author of many helpful books. Thank you, Brother Grady, for penning this wonderful work concerning God's chosen people."

—Dr. Don Green, sixty years pastor of Parker Memorial Baptist Church, Lansing, Michigan; trained by Dr. J. Frank Norris

"Get ready for an earthquake! *Holy Ground* drew this busy wife and stay-at-home mother into a thrilling account of the political struggle for the modern-day State of Israel. Dr. Grady's case is presented convincingly with breathtaking detail and insight into the underlying spiritual battle being waged for God's covenant people. This packs a punch for any honest reader and leaves one asking the question, "What shall I do then with Israel?"

—Mrs. Laura Barge, Ph.D. physics, Baylor University; former research astrophysicist

From the Afterword to How Satan Turned America Against God
(Volume One of this series)

"Heaven only knows why an unbelieving Jewish scientist in Los Angeles would be recommending a 1,000-page opus written by a Baptist minister in Corryton, Tennessee (though we both hail from New York City). My reasons for doing so follow. First, I consider Bill Grady to be one of the most unusual friends I have known in my eighty-four years. Second, though unable to relate to the spiritual content of this book, I concur wholeheartedly with the author's exceptional grasp of America's current disastrous foreign policy, as well as our growing vulnerability in matters of national security."

—The late Jewish-American physicist, Samuel T. Cohen, assigned to the Manhattan Project at Los Alamos where he helped design "Fat Man," the plutonium bomb detonated over Nagasaki; while working for the RAND Corporation as a nuclear weapon analyst he invented (in 1958) the controversial W70 tactical low-yield thermo-nuclear warhead, officially termed an Enhanced Radiation Weapon (ERW), a.k.a. the "Neutron Bomb"

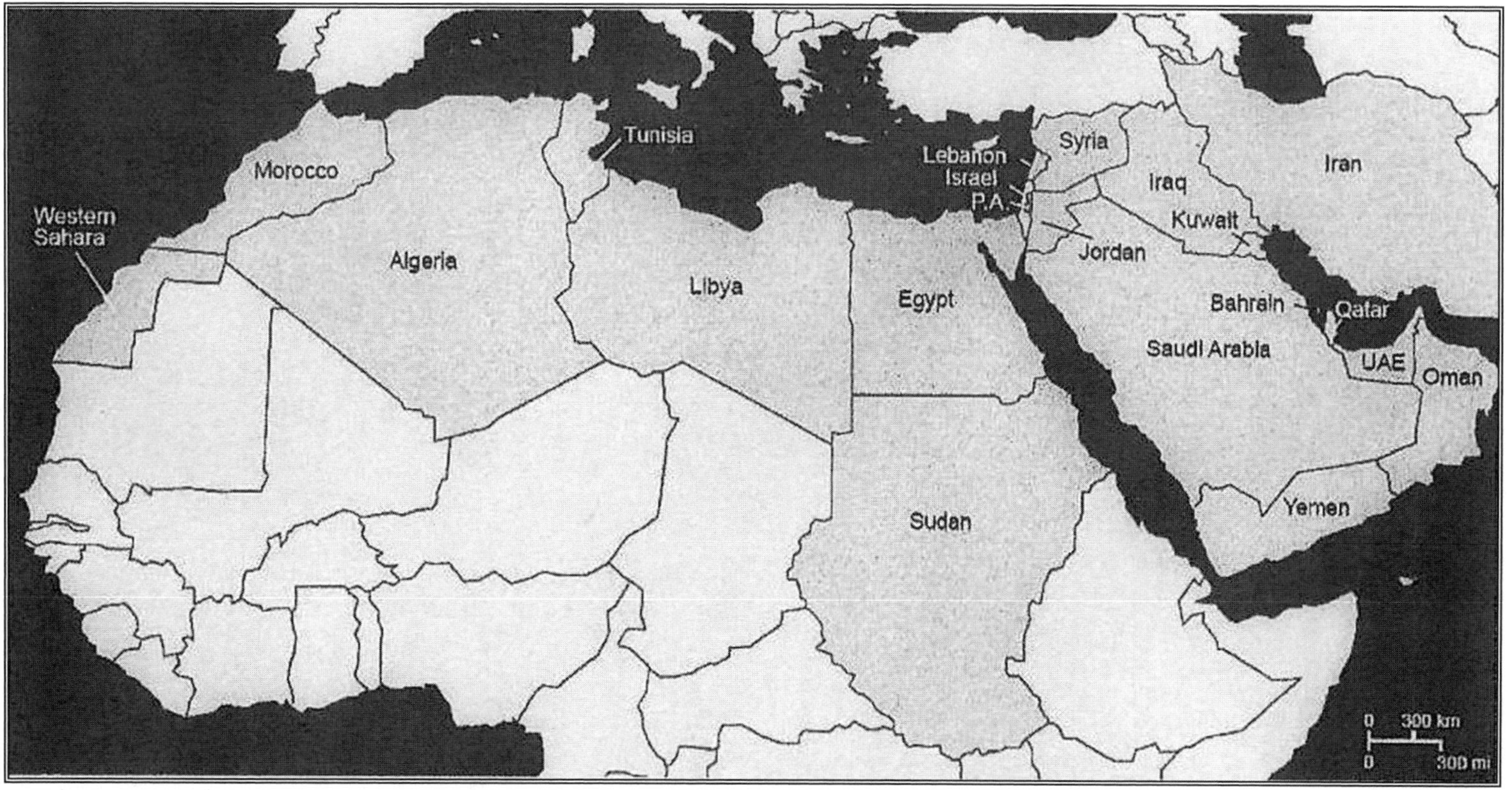

Eretz Israel (8,000 sq. miles) surrounded by the Ummah (7,641,000 sq. miles)

Understanding the Times

Also by William P. Grady:

FINAL AUTHORITY: A Christian's Guide to the King James Bible

WHAT HATH GOD WROUGHT!: A Biblical Interpretation of American History

HOW SATAN TURNED AMERICA AGAINST GOD

GIVEN BY INSPIRATION: A Multifaceted Study on the A.V. 1611 with Contemporary Analysis

UNDERSTANDING THE TIMES
VOLUME TWO

HOLY GROUND

A SCRIPTURAL VIEW OF THE TRUE HISTORY OF THE STATE OF ISRAEL – DEFINED BY A CENTURY OF ANGLO-AMERICAN ANTI-SEMITISM

William P. Grady, Ph.D.

GRADY
PUBLICATIONS, INC.

Copyright © 2017
Grady Publications, Inc.
All Rights Reserved
Printed in the United States of America

DISCLAIMERS

The opinions, arguments, and conclusions contained herein are solely those of the author and do not necessarily reflect the views of the individuals who were featured, interviewed, and/or quoted.

All Scripture is taken from the King James Bible (A.V. 1611), with special emphasis by the author shown in upper case letters.

Every effort has been made to trace all copyright holders; however, if any have been overlooked, the publisher will gladly include the necessary credits in any subsequent reprints or editions.

ISBN 978-0-9628809-4-0
Library of Congress Control Number: 2017901412
First Printing, April 2017

It is the burden of the author to disseminate the truth in this book. No prior permission is required to duplicate up to 3,000 words for non-commercial, non-salable or non-financial purposes. No part beyond this limit may be transmitted in any form or by any means, electronic or mechanical, including photocopying, recording, or by any information storage and retrieval system, without written permission from the publisher.

For information, address:
GRADY PUBLICATIONS, INC.
P.O. Box 6381
Maryville, TN 37802
Phone/Fax: (865) 336-9043
william.grady@gradypublications.com
www.gradypublications.com
Follow us on f and t @ Grady Publications

Dedication

This book is dedicated to the Almighty Jehovah
for His future bride, Israel

"And I will betroth thee unto me for ever; yea, I will betroth thee unto me in righteousness, and in judgment, and in lovingkindness, and in mercies."
(Hosea 2:19)

and

Alvin and Debbie Edwards for inspiring its timely inception

"...for he oft refreshed me and was not ashamed of my chain."
(II Timothy 1:16)

Acknowledgments

"For I know nothing by myself...."
(I Corinthians 4:4)

THE AUTHOR WOULD like to thank the following people for their invaluable contribution to this volume: First and foremost, the precious Lord Jesus Christ for His marvelous sustaining grace (II Corinthians 12:9).

My beloved wife Linda (who lost both of her brothers, George and John Bonnewell, during the writing of this book) for her tireless proofreading, editing, and input (Proverbs 31:11), along with our three children and their families (including thirteen grandchildren) for their prayers, suggestions, encouragement, and patience during our protracted work schedule.

In the technical arena: Tammy Atkins for text design; Tommy and Lori Ray, cover design; Chris Ellison, artwork; Eric Rishell, printing; and Travis McAlister, social media administration.

My research (historical and Biblical) was facilitated by Jack Vandiver, Jr.; Jack Minor; Georges Antonius; Nick Cultrara; Leonard Fogel; Michael Wolsky; Bob Militello; Justin Leisure; Lon Taylor; Vince Massa; Rick Sowell; David Wood; Lisa McCaw; Ed Demarest; my sons, Daniel and Paul; and my history buff grandsons, Joshua Grady and Caleb Branham.

I am also indebted to the professional assistance rendered by the staff of several cultural institutions: Maor Levi, Yad La-Shiryon Museum, Latrun, Israel; Nili Luria, The Israel Museum, Jerusalem; Clay Bauske, Harry S. Truman Library and Museum, Independence, Missouri; Tim Murray, University of Delaware Library, Special Collections (Holocaust Testimonies Project); Brenda Fong, United Nations Photo Library, New York, New York; Ataman Alex Pewnew, Kuban Cossacks Museum,

Howell, New Jersey; Avi Ohayon, Government Press Office, Jerusalem, Israel; Lidia Kafarska, Auschwitz-Birkenau Memorial and Museum, Oświęcim, Poland; Dr. Alexander Shevyrev, Lomonosov Moscow State University, Moscow, Russia; B. A. Lyubnmo, Arkhangelsk Regional Museum, Arkhangelsk, Russia; Ingeborg Weiler, State Museum, Judenburg, Austria; and Stefan Grote, Federal Archives, Koblenz, Germany.

Several individuals and churches rendered financial help to the publication of *Holy Ground*: Austin and Nana Brown; Laura Barge; Alvin and Debbie Edwards; Alan Stiller; Barnabas Williamson; James and Kathy Leichty; Paul Searles; Pete and Laura Kumnik; Hugh and Beverly Anderson; David Moore; Caleb Hickam; Northmont Baptist Church, Statesville, North Carolina; Victory Baptist Church, Hartland, Michigan; Southside Baptist Church, Petersburg, Virginia; Mt. Olivet Baptist Church, Lexington, Kentucky; Silica Springs Baptist Church, Gaffney, South Carolina; Mount Hope Baptist Church, McLeansville, North Carolina; Lighthouse Baptist Church, Eustis, Florida; Charity Baptist Church, Amarillo, Texas; For His Glory Bible Baptist Church, Union, Maine; Rehoboth Baptist Church, Boaz, Alabama; Celina Baptist Temple, Celina, Ohio; and Blessed Redeemer Baptist Church, Mechanicsville, Maryland.

Numerous preachers and other Christians provided miscellaneous support at various stages of the project: Don Green; Keith Gomez; Walter Shepherd; Jerry Rockwell; Randy McAlister; Mike Watkins; Jason Boger; Sam Vallini; Larry Hickam; David Sauls; Ken Anderson; Dave Struble; Harvey Lambert; Bill Whitelaw; Jack Patterson; and especially my own pastor, Tom Hatley, and the warm congregation of Fellowship Baptist Church, Maryville, Tennessee.

Special thanks to David Berkowitz for providing his personal testimony, "From Son of Sam to Son of Hope."

Finally, in addition to the aforementioned museum and university personnel, the author is particularly grateful for those gracious individuals who were featured, interviewed for, and/or quoted in this book, who would not necessarily ascribe to either the thesis or the author's theological views, e.g., Heinrich Pichler; John Frank; Avi Ziv-Tal; Alex Pewnew; Nathalie Basilevsky; and Moshe Saperstein.

Table of Contents

Prologue

"...a little reviving in the midst of our bondage."
(Ezra 9:8)

NEARLY SIX YEARS in the making, *Holy Ground* was published in the wake of three significant dates relative to the State of Israel. On September 28, 2016, former Israeli President and Prime Minister Shimon Peres—the last living patriarch who was present with David Ben-Gurion at Israel's birth—passed away at the age of 93. Dr. Daniel Gordis (author of a dozen books on Judaism and Israel) wrote in the *Bloomberg View*, "...there is no denying the dark clouds overhead. Now, with Peres's death, the curtain is dropping on the Jewish state's founding generation. There's an inescapable sense that, with their last father figure gone – whatever the future may hold – Israelis are entirely on their own."[1]

November 2, 2016, marked the onset of the Balfour Declaration centenary. Israel's sixty-seven-word founding charter was addressed in the name of Arthur James Balfour, then United Kingdom Foreign Secretary, to Lionel Walter Rothschild, a leader of British Jewry, for delivery to the Zionist Federation of Great Britain and Ireland.

On November 8, 2016—after eight years of unprecedented strained US-Israel relations, the direct result of Barack Obama's closet Muslim mindset—Donald Trump trounced Hillary Clinton in the presidential race, becoming America's 45th chief executive on January 20, 2017. The surprise come-from-behind victory by Mr. Trump, a strong supporter of Israel, was reminiscent of that iconic 1948 "Dewey Defeats Truman" headline exonerating Harry Truman's own pro-Israel stand. Within hours of Hillary's concession speech, Israel's Prime Minister Benjamin Netanyahu sent "The Donald" a video greeting:

> President-elect Trump, my friend, congratulations on being elected president of the United States of America. You are a *great* friend of Israel. Over the years you've expressed your support consistently, and I deeply appreciate it. I look forward to working with you to advance security, prosperity, and peace. Israel is grateful for the broad support it receives from the American people. And I am confident that the two of us, working closely together, will bring the great alliance between our two countries, to even greater heights. May G-d bless America, may G-d bless Israel, and may G-d bless our enduring alliance.[2]

That the 2016 election result was a bona fide divine intervention—*the specific answer to millions of Christians' prayers*—there can be no doubt (Jeremiah 33:3). About the time Bibi's video was airing, this author received the following email from a long-time Jewish acquaintance, a gruff, Manhattan-born, one-armed Yom Kippur War veteran living in Israel: "Thank G-d, and thank you, my Christian friends, for restoring my belief in miracles. My wife and I can't stop laughing and crying. And praying." The added blessings of a rescued Supreme Court, a Republican majority in both houses of Congress, and the so-called "nuclear option" (the 2013 back-room Democrat maneuver eliminating the sixty-vote requirement to prevent a filibuster), coming back to bite Harry Reid in the "tuchus" by handing Trump his dream team Cabinet, all coalesced to illustrate Ephesians 3:20, *"Now unto him that is able to do exceeding abundantly above all that we ask or think, according to the power that worketh in us...."*

Like his campaign theme song warned, "You can't always get what you want," Mr. Trump will not satisfy *every* GOP camp, especially Christians. While the Presbyterian president's personal testimony falls short of a born-again experience—e.g., his bizarre views on forgiveness and Christ's person, his unabashed endorsement of the LGBTQIA *ad nauseum* perversion, his "Two Corinthians" faux pas, his praise for Ivanka's conversion to Judaism (i.e., at the expense of Jesus Christ)—his populist, anti-globalist agenda more than meets the scriptural ideal for secular rulers (Romans 13:3-4; I Timothy 2:1-2). Believers can also rejoice in the supportive role of their evangelical vice president, Mike Pence (the very antithesis of Jesuit Tim Kaine), the providential office conforming to the Bible patterns of Joseph, Daniel, and Mordecai.

At the end of the day, given Team Clinton's over-the-top hubris, vitriol, and slander, exacerbated by a steady echo chamber of media bias, negative poll numbers, and "infallible" pundit predictions, Donald Trump was an unknowing surrogate for God's honor; specifically, on matters of right and wrong (see Jeremiah 27:6 and Isaiah 44:28 for more extreme cases). The sudden shock of it all would also resonate with Christians awaiting the surreal and final vanquishing of evil (Daniel 2:44, 45; Revelation 11:15; 19:11-21).

The Trump phenomenon was ultimately about seven things: 1) the LORD putting the focus on Himself (Isaiah 46:5); 2) the open punishment of Bill and Hillary Clinton (Proverbs 28:10); 3) the total repudiation of Barack Obama, who subsequently accused Mr. Putin of doing exactly what *he* did to Israel in *their* 2015 election[3] (Galatians 6:7), then brazenly betrayed Israel with an end-of-term lame duck diplomatic initiative on December 22, refusing to veto a UN Security Council resolution condemning Jewish settlement expansion on the West Bank; 4) the open mockery of the academia-media-celebrity elites (Psalm 2:4); 5) blocking the sure destruction of the United States that would have occurred mainly from anticipated Supreme Court picks; 6) providing a long overdue breath of fresh air to patriotic Americans (Proverbs 29:2), i.e., Hillary's "basket of deplorables," demonized white men in particular; and 7) offering Christians—as a pastor friend of this author put it in his Sunday morning sermon following the election—"a last chance to engage the enemy."[4]

Thus, the most appropriate Scripture to define the surprising Trump victory would be Ezra 9:8, *"And now for a little space grace hath been shewed from the LORD our God, to leave us a remnant to escape, and to give us a nail in his holy place, that our God may lighten our eyes, and give us a little reviving in our bondage."* However, if history is any guide for the future, unfortunately, like the respite under Josiah in II Kings 22 & 23, the Church will fail to profit from this window of opportunity (repeating her anemic response to MacArthur's request for thousands of missionaries to capitalize on Japan's post-WWII disillusionment). And just for the record—to whatever degree euphoric Laodicea *"[does] despite to the Spirit of grace"* (Hebrews 10:29)—the metaphorically deemed *"[T]rump of God"* (I Thessalonians 4:16) could just as easily become America's worst nightmare (Matthew 12:45; II Peter 2:20).

Which leads us to the purpose of this timely book. It is certainly an odd coincidence that the word "trump" appears twice in Scripture (the KJV predominantly)—both times regarding the Rapture (I Corinthians 15:52, I Thessalonians 4:16). Consequently, as the Church Age nears its apostate denouement (II Timothy 3:1 - 4:4; Revelation 3:14-22), the possibilities of a pro-Israel Trump White House (especially moving the embassy to Jerusalem) remain known only to God. However, the best case scenario (a "Debbie Downer" reality check notwithstanding) would be a mere stay of execution, given the prophetic scope of divine wrath in the Great Tribulation, i.e., *"the time of Jacob's trouble...."* (Jeremiah 30:7)

The most conspicuous bellwether of the Jewish/Trump nexus was the December 20, 2016, front cover of *Forbes* magazine featuring the president-elect's Orthodox son-in-law, Jared Kushner, above the telling caption, "THIS GUY GOT TRUMP ELECTED." (Some would argue that the real "hero" of the Trump triumph was another Jew altogether—former New York congressman Anthony Weiner.) According to the exclusive interview, the enigmatic, multi-millionaire father of Trump's two Jewish grandchildren, whose own skyscraper stands three blocks south of Trump Tower (at the uncanny address of "666" Fifth Avenue), employed Facebook micro-targeting and social media as the campaign's key voter outreach strategy. (Ironically, the Jewish-impacted election upset was foreshadowed just six days earlier by the equally "miraculous" Chicago Cubs' World Series win credited to Theo Epstein, the team's Jewish president of baseball operations.)

Yet, herein lies the age-old Jewish conundrum of internecine strife (i.e., "two Jews/three views"). While several powerful Jews stand ready to *help* President Trump "make America great again"—running the gamut from conservative radio talk show hosts, internet news editors, and comedians Michael Savage, Matt Drudge, Michael Medved (maybe the mercurial Mark Levin), and Jackie Mason, through various aides, advisors, and/or friends, like Elliot Broidy; Michael Cohen; Lewis Eisenberg; Stephen Feinberg; Samuel Fox; Alan Garten; Michael Glassner; Lawrence Glick; John Paulson; Steven Roth; Stephen Schwarzman; Mel Sembler; Ronald Weiser; Andrew Weiss; and Allen Weisselberg to key administration appointees, Stephen Mnuchin (Treasury), Stephen Miller (Senior Advisor to the President), Carl Icahn (Regulatory Czar), Boris Epshteyn (Special Assistant to the President), Jason Greenblatt (Special Representative for International Relations), and David Friedman (Ambassador to Israel)—*another* array of Hebrew heavyweights are poised to *oppose* him.

A short list would include: Senators Al Franken, Dianne Feinstein, and Minority Leader Chuck Schumer, aligned with Representatives Steve Israel and Debbie Wasserman Schultz on Capitol Hill (Jewish Democrats in the 113th Congress outnumbering their Republican colleagues twenty-seven to one); Mayor Rahm Emanuel in the vanguard sanctuary city of Chicago; Rahm's brother, Ezekiel (chief architect of the Affordable Care Act) in healthcare reform; Mark Zuckerburg in cyberspace; *New York Times* chairman of the board, Arthur Ochs Sulzberger, Jr., and *CNN* president Jeff Zucker (aided by Wolf Blitzer, David Gregory, Dana Bash, and Jake Tapper), in the fourth estate; Babs Streisand and Sarah Silverman representing Hollywood; Susan Herman in the ACLU; Justices Ruth Ginsburg, Stephen Breyer, and Elena Kagan in the Supreme Court; Chairwoman Janet Yellen and Vice Chairman Stanley Fischer in the Federal Reserve; Hillary's top five campaign donors—Donald Sussman, J. B. Pritzker, Haim Saban, Daniel Abraham, and billionaire atheist George Soros in Wall Street[5]; former presidential advisors, David Axelrod and the unobtrusive, Iranian-born, Valerie Jarrett[6] in the Beltway-based Obama shadow government; plus a slew of assorted antagonists, such as "burnout" Bernie Sanders, Dr. Jill Stein, Mike Bloomberg, and J Street president, Jeremy Ben-Ami, in the "sour grapes" genre.

Considering such unsettling realities, perhaps the most apropos quote would be Prime Minister Netanyahu's musing in his 2000 book, *A Durable Peace: Israel and its Place Among the Nations*—"No one yet knows what awaits the Jews in the 21st century, but we must make every effort to ensure that it is better than what befell them in the twentieth, the century of the Holocaust."[7] Fast forwarding to the eve of Donald Trump's presidency, Jewish author and American diplomat Dennis B. Ross, William Davidson Distinguished Fellow at the Washington Institute for Near East Policy, concurred with this atmosphere of uncertainty, writing in his 2015 bestseller, *Doomed to Succeed*:

> No one predicted the turmoil we are now seeing, least of all the Middle Eastern leaders who have been swept away in its wake or who are now struggling for legitimacy and to define the identity of the region. While humility should be the order of the day in predicting what will unfold in the Middle East, one thing is clear: the U.S.-Israel relationship is going to be buffeted by the transformation that is taking place.[8]

"The secret things belong to the LORD our God...."
(Deuteronomy 29:29)

Foreword

THERE IS A basic mistrust of historians today which has been precipitated by the "revisionist" movement to rewrite history to fit the political position of the culture and the historian. Some historians have a certain political/historical agenda to write history to fit their view of life and history. That is brought about by the fact that the 20th- and 21st-century historians felt that there were things looked at in times past that were skewed by the historian's worldview. Yet, there is an element that escapes the current trend of "revisionist" historians and that is the failure to be honest with the material and documents they encounter. Past historians had a different ethical/moral viewpoint and position than many of the current historians, although that is not intended to put all historians into one basket. There remain historians who are unbiased and unashamed to present history as it is reported and revealed by those reporting the events.

Dr. Bill Grady fits into the last description. There is to be an element of trust and confidence that what is reported in this book, *Holy Ground*, can be trusted and considered an accurate reporting and recording of the events and the persons brought into the discussion. Dr. Grady is an extraordinary historian and theologian. He has done a masterful work in presenting the history of the emergence of Israel from the throes of being *scattered* throughout the world, through the Holocaust of World War II, to the place where they became a nation approximately 2,000 years after the Roman government destroyed Jerusalem in AD 70, which in essence removed the nation of Israel from the historical map.

As a "pre-baby boomer," having lived through nearly two-thirds of what is read in this book, I am appalled at how much information was not made public by the media about the proceedings of the rise of Israel as a nation. This book brings light to so much information that has been, to some degree, withheld from public view. The adage that nothing changes is so true, especially in light of the current political morass in 2016. The media seems to never be on the side of what is right and decent. The anti-Semitism residing in the US was to a large degree kept from the public and handled in the secret chambers of the political process of corrupt and unethical politicians. It is still the same today. This book presents a "fair and balanced" look at the events beginning with the Balfour Declaration through the current status of the nation of Israel.

Many thought that anti-Semitism had disappeared at the end of World War II when the results of the Holocaust were revealed to the public. What is not known by many is that the anti-Semitic politicians have always been around and *will* be around until the dramatic return of the Lord Jesus Christ (Revelation 19:11) to defeat the enemies of God and set the record straight. This long-awaited event could only be hastened by what is perceived as the current events surrounding and centered in the little nation called Israel. The Arab-Israeli struggle can be traced a long way back and will not be settled until the King of kings and Lord of lords appears and brings honesty and integrity to the inhabitants of this weary place called Earth.

Dr. Grady has done an amazing job of digging in the cracks and crevices of history to document the immense struggle which took place over the Balfour Declaration. He demonstrates that the Arab-Israeli conflict is not just as old as the revelation of Scripture, but permeates modern history as well. Many do not realize that the Muslim/Arab problem is not just a current phenomenon. The British have fostered and coddled the Muslim world for a considerable time. This book shows that there is something more sinister about anti-Semitism and should be a must-read for those who see the importance of support for Israel in these "last days."

Some might be amazed, or better, astonished, to find the influence by the Augustinian monk Martin Luther (well-known Reformer) on the German mentality concerning the Jews. The documentation of this is irrefutable and one must wonder at the theology of Martin Luther as well as Dr. Gerhard Kittle, the German theologian who was the *Nazi theologian* and editor of the famous Greek resource by the well-known name, *The Theological Dictionary of the New Testament*. Much blame must be laid at the feet of these two men for propagating the mindset which brought about the atrocities enacted on the Jews by the German government.

Very few are aware of the involvement of the oil industry during WWII. The anti-Semitism that pervaded the development of the petroleum business in Saudi Arabia prior to and during the "Great War" is not known by most who follow the activities that operate even today with the Arab oil industry. The Bible says in Ecclesiastes 1:9, *"The thing that hath been, it is that which shall be; and that which is done is that which shall be done: and there is no new thing under the sun."* The astute observer will see that what is happening in the world in 2016-17, has happened before and will continue to shape the world according to the *"prince of the power of the air"* (Ephesians 2:2).

One cannot imagine the barbarity exercised by the Germans on the Jews and even some POWs. Dr. Grady has given some of the most detailed explanations of the cruelty used by the German government, which was the psyche of Adolf Hitler in practice. It seems as if the Germans delighted in the novelty and creativity they exercised in the killing and torture of the Jews in their captivity.

This foreword is not intended to be a "book review," yet the temptation to do so is tremendous. The things I have read in this book should be read by every Bible believer and teacher who holds to the position that the people of Israel, the Jews, have a place in future world history. The Church has *not* replaced Israel as the Covenant/Replacement theologians try to convince Bible students. The Bible *still* contains the documentation of Romans 9-11, which records what the LORD thinks of the nation of Israel and her place in the future. The place called Palestine is *still* "holy ground" and the serious Bible student and historian cannot avoid the extensive research undertaken by Bill Grady.

I have known Dr. Grady for over twenty-six years. Every book he has written has an element of deep serious commitment to the truth and to an accurate presentation of history. The reader of this tome will not be disappointed with the depth and accuracy of the accounts presented here, nor the desire to reveal the truth and historical record of the people of Israel affected by the Balfour Declaration (which brought about the emergence of Israel as an historical entity again). Yet, it is not written solely as an historical account but has the element of a novel that keeps the attention of the reader to delve deeper into the story.

With these things in mind, my exhortation to the reader is that you need to avail yourself of the contents of this book and be ready for an eye-opening experience that will take you deep into the nearly 100-year process which brought to pass the establishment of Israel as a nation among nations.

Dr. Jerry L. Rockwell
Pastor, Victory Baptist Church
Pierre Part, Louisiana
October 2016

[Editor's note: Dr. Rockwell, a strong advocate of the A.V. 1611, received his initial training in the premillennial, dispensational interpretation of the Scriptures at Dallas Theological Seminary, where he earned an MA in Biblical Studies in 1984.]

Preface

OVER 2,500 YEARS ago, the God of Israel declared in Zechariah 12:2, *"Behold, I will make Jerusalem a cup of trembling unto all the people round about."* While this Old Testament prophecy awaits its primary fulfillment in the Tribulation, that "cup" has already *been* "trembling" for several decades and will continue to do so with a growing intensity. Amid the resultant enveloping culture of global paranoia, Christians pray with jubilant anticipation, *"Even so, come, Lord Jesus."* (Revelation 22:20)

Thus, the latest news from the Middle East is more relevant now than ever. Unfortunately, the history of the Arab-Israeli conflict has been shrouded in confusion, leaving few of God's children with even a moderate grasp of the subject. The purpose for this second installment of *Understanding the Times* is to acquaint the reader with "a scriptural view of the *true* history of the State of Israel." The word "true" implies that most histories of the Jewish State are fallacious. This should come as no surprise, for Satan (*"a liar, and the father of it"*) would obviously focus his greatest attention on any chronicle of the "*Holy* Land," with *confusion* being his forte (John 8:44; I Corinthians 14:33).

In his memoirs, William Tecumseh Sherman wrote that "the truth is not always palatable, and should not always be told."[1] Sir Martin John Gilbert, renowned scholar and official biographer of Winston Churchill, declared, "The history of the world can be divided into two aspects: facts and espionage. The facts are in every history book. Espionage is cloaked and hidden."[2] Thus, many critical events surrounding the creation of the Jewish State have been suppressed, distorted, or censored outright. In their bestselling book *The Secret War Against the Jews*, John Loftus and Mark Aarons ask, "How can free citizens judge the conduct of their elected leaders when one-third of modern history is classified?"[3]

Loftus (a former prosecutor with the US Justice Department) and Aarons (an internationally award-winning investigative reporter) contend, "In order to understand the *what* of modern Israel and its context in the harsh, twisted annals of the Middle East, it is necessary to identify the holes in the history books."[4] The material in this volume will expose many of these unknown "holes."

It will also be discovered, to the dismay of religious sentimentalists, that certain holes have been "plugged" with blatant fantasy. For example, President Richard Nixon "supposedly" came to the aid of Golda Meir in the Yom Kippur War because of a childhood revelation he received from his Bible-reading Quaker grandmother. A typical version states, "One night, she turned to him and gave him a prophecy saying that a day will come when he will have enormous power, and the Jews will need you, and that he must do everything to save the Israeli people." To the contrary (as documented in this work), the *real* hero was a senior White House staffer who singlehandedly orchestrated Israel's miraculous rescue by defying and circumventing the duplicitous and incompetent policy of Secretary of State Henry Kissinger. The president's grandmother would hardly have approved of the hundreds of fascist war criminals that permeated her grandson's political career, Loftus and Aarons stating, "By 1968 Nixon's Nazis had become a permanent fixture of American political life."[5]

Though *Holy Ground* will enlighten many, it will be a disturbing read for others. As the elusive reality of "the *true* history of the *State* of Israel" is revealed, things will only grow *more* disturbing, for all *true* lovers of the "state" (condition) of Israel must acknowledge that, according to the Bible, a secular "state" (government) is the *last* thing Jehovah has planned for His covenant people (don't look for any "Gay Pride" parades in the Millennial Kingdom, etc.).

Yet, such negativity is the *essence* of reality. The Scriptures teach that truth comes at a price; Proverbs 23:23 enjoins, *"Buy the truth, and sell it not."* While Jesus declared in John 8:32, *"And ye shall know the truth, and the truth shall make you free,"* Ecclesiastes 1:18 provides the offsetting principle that *"he that increaseth knowledge increaseth sorrow."* Thus, we discern the spiritual conundrum of "the bondage of truth"—the inescapable fact that sorrow is both the cost for gaining truth and the major benefit of its liberating power, for *"Sorrow is better than laughter."* (Ecclesiastes 7:3)

This holy process also becomes the ultimate means of obeying the inspired exhortation to *"follow his steps,"* our Jewish Saviour and Israel's coming Messiah having fulfilled the inspired profile of *"a man of sorrows, and acquainted with grief."* (I Peter 2:21; Isaiah 53:3) And as the designated spokesman for Church Age believers commanded, *"Be ye followers of me, even as I also am of Christ,"* the Apostle Paul also left us *his* testimony: *"I have great heaviness and continual sorrow in my heart"*; that sorrow being occasioned by his *"kinsmen according to the flesh."* (I Corinthians 11:1 Romans 9:2-3)

As the A.V. 1611 King James Bible remains the final authority on absolute truth, the literary format for this book will ensure a crystal clear presentation by following the scriptural pattern:

"Write the vision, and make it plain upon tables...."
(Habakkuk 2:2)

Introduction

[Author's note for Jewish readers: While the majority of this treatise deals with history, the Introduction was uniquely designed to convey a spiritual overview to Bible-believing Christians (sometimes called "Christian Zionists"). In his Afterward to Volume One of this series, the late Samuel T. Cohen, esteemed Manhattan Project physicist and "Father of the Neutron Bomb," wrote, "Though unable to relate to the spiritual content of this book, I concur wholeheartedly with the author's exceptional grasp of America's current disastrous foreign policy, as well as our growing vulnerability in matters of national security." As stated in his Wikipedia profile (under "Support for Baptist Pastor/Author William P. Grady") the prominent endorsement reflected Cohen's "self-described unusual friendship" with the writer. (Incidentally, "Cohen" being a common Jewish name, the music for "HaTikvah"—Israel's National Anthem—was arranged in 1888 by a Romanian Zionist named Samuel Cohen.) As Hebrews 11:4 says, "he being dead yet speaketh," the sequel to "How Satan Turned America Against God" is recommended in the spirit of Sam's closing remark: "If you are really burdened about the future of America, then apply what you can from this unusual book written by my unusual friend."]

IN 1994 THE New York Times recognized Christian painter Warner Sallman (1892-1968) as the "best-known artist of the century."[1] His most enduring works are the *Head of Christ* and *Christ at Heart's Door*. The latter was Sallman's personal depiction of Revelation 3:20, *"Behold, I stand at the door, and knock."* The conspicuous absence of any outside doorknob or latch was meant to imply that the individual must open his or her heart from within, as Christ will never force His way inside. (Such artistic license is known in the art world as a "created abstraction.") But, is a missing doorknob the *only* explanation why Jesus has to knock? The very thesis of this book is based on an entirely different take on the issue.

The "key" to unlocking the true history of the Jewish state is contained in a subtle, allegorical truth within the context of Revelation 3:20. As the book itself projects *"things which must be hereafter"* (Revelation 1:18), the letters to the seven churches of Asia Minor represent a prophetic profile of the entire Church Age (each church constituting a unique type of a specific period in Church history in chronological order). When a collation is made between the spiritual characteristics ascribed to the sixth and seventh churches, a number of significant differences appear. While the "Philadelphia Age" (c. 1611-1881) reflects the most *fruitful* period of Church history, the "Laodicean Age" (1881 through the present) profiles the *worst* era. Philadelphia is commended for having kept God's word and not denying His name; Laodicea is rebuked for being lukewarm and consumed with materialism. This contrast was forecast in the meaning of their names—"Brotherly Love" versus "Rights of the People."

The most obvious dissimilarity relates to their respective "doors." When Jesus is shown "opening a door" or "knocking on a closed door," the Scripture is employing figurative speech, more specifically, an allegory. In Sallman's private interpretation of Revelation 3:20, the Laodicean door was painted as the entrance to the heart of an unsaved person. While this well-intended portrayal makes "good preaching" by way of devotional application, and has certainly been used with great effectiveness in personal evangelism, it violates the immediate context at verse nineteen. Here, as in the previous six letters where God is addressing the collective members of a particular church period (spiritual or otherwise), the message is directed to the lukewarm Christians of the Laodicean Age. The scriptural evidence that verse twenty applies to backslidden believers (as opposed to the unsaved) is confirmed by cross-referencing the words, *"As many as I love, I rebuke and chasten,"* with Hebrews 12:6-8, *"For whom the Lord loveth he chasteneth, and scourgeth every* SON *whom he receiveth."*

Thus, when the Laodicean door is made to apply to the Church—as it does in the Philadelphia letter—several notable distinctions appear. In the Philadelphia Age, Jesus is sending the Christians out through an open door, an obvious symbol of "liberty." The historical fulfillment of this ancient prophecy was the Bill of Rights' addition to the United States Constitution, securing the widest "open door" in the annals of man's struggle for freedom of conscience—and the paperwork "just happened" to be finalized in a place called Philadelphia (site of the "Liberty" Bell). However, in the Laodicean letter, the *opposite* occurs; the Christians have put Jesus out, closing the door in His holy face! In the last days, the "Church of Jesus Christ" belongs to the apostatized membership. Note how the salutations devolve from the *"church* IN *Philadelphia"* to the *"church* OF *the Laodiceans."* (This same condition was prefigured in III John 10 by the way the godly brethren were treated when Diotrephes *"casteth them out of the church."*)

The emphasis on the individual in the Laodicean appeal, *"if any man hear my voice...I will come in to him, and will sup with him,"* can be seen today by the mass of professing believers "doing their own thing." As the true Church has never been equated with a physical building, the modern church member is only too happy to conform, becoming his *own* church in the process. In September 2011, *USA Today* ran an article entitled "More Americans tailoring religion to fit their needs." According to George Barna, an expert on religion statistics, America is headed for "310 million people with 310 million religions."[2] Barna's profile depicts today's worshiper as decidedly self-oriented: "People say, 'I believe in God. I believe the Bible is a good book. And then I believe whatever I want.'"[3]

In the Philadelphia Age, the Lord freely *"openeth and no man shutteth."* However, in Laodicea, the text implies that a change has occurred; apparently, now He must be *let* in—*"if any man hear my voice, and open the door, I will come in to him."* The solution to this mystery has nothing to do with a missing doorknob. The reason why Jesus can open the Philadelphia door at will is because He has a *key*. Revelation 3:7 states, *"These things saith he that is holy, he that is true, he that hath the* KEY *of David."* Simply put, "Keys open doors."

But this was not just *any* key. Note that it is a *Jewish* key, i.e., *"the key of* DAVID.*"* The cross-reference is Isaiah 22:22, where the immediate context of the preceding verse involves Millennial blessings on Israel, Jehovah declaring about Jesus (through Eliakim) that He will commit the *"government"* (of Isaiah 9:7) *"into his hand."* Thus, the combined spiritual application of Revelation 3:7 reveals that, although the Philadelphia Church Age was predominantly *Gentile* in nature (as with all seven periods beginning at Acts 14:27), the key which opened the door to *that* specific Gentile Age—the greatest of the seven, resulting in America's unparalleled religious liberty—was a *Jewish* key! (This "Hebrew connection" was forecast in Judges 3:25, where the first mention of a "key" in Scripture coincides with the oldest Israeli "covert assassination" in history.)

The illustrations of a Jewish key are legion, starting with Scripture itself. As Philadelphia believers were twice commended for having *"kept the word,"* the era would begin in 1611 with a Jewish book—the King "Jacob" Bible—the English name "James" being a transliteration of the Hebrew name "Yaakov," for "Jacob." Thus, the "Jacobean Age" refers to the period in English and Scottish history that coincides with the reign of King James I of England (1603-1625), encompassing the style of architecture, visual arts, and literature that defined the time.

To the question, *"What advantage then hath the Jew?"* the Apostle Paul replies, *"Much every way: chiefly, because that unto them were committed the oracles of God."* (Romans 3:1-2) Scholarly works, such as Dr. Paul Eidelberg's *The Beginning and End of American Exceptionalism: A Theo-Political Analysis*, document the foundational role of the Mosaic code on US law and education. Thus, the essence of America's Judeo-Christian heritage is conveyed by the adage, "Judaism was the stalk on which the rose of Christianity bloomed."

The emblematic nexus between a "Jewish key" opening a "Gentile door" in "The City of Brotherly Love" is perhaps best illustrated by the selfless sacrifice of the Jewish financier Haym Salomon, who practically bankrolled the entire American Revolution, advancing Congress the incredible sum of $658,007.13. The Hebrew patriot, known as "America's Banker," succumbed to tuberculosis at age forty-five, dying penniless on January 6, 1785. Eulogized as "A banker whose only interest was the interest of his country," Haym was buried by his fellow congregants in the Mikveh Israel cemetery in—Philadelphia.

According to Bible numerology, twelve is the number for Israel (twelve sons of Jacob, twelve tribes, twelve letters in circumcision, etc.). There are twelve letters in "Philadelphia." There are also twelve letters in "Pennsylvania," known as the *Key*stone State (the White House eventually being located on Pennsylvania Avenue in Washington, DC). Having served as the first capital under the First Continental Congress, Philadelphia became the nation's first postwar capital under the Articles of Confederation. (Benjamin Netanyahu, the first Israeli-born Prime

Minister, is a 1967 graduate of Cheltenham High School in suburban Philadelphia.)

In 1790, while touring the colonies to promote ratification of the Bill of Rights, George Washington visited the Hebrew congregation of Yeshuat Israel at the historic Touro Synagogue in Newport, Rhode Island. Upon his departure, America's first president issued a personal letter containing the following prescient words: "May the Children of the Stock of Abraham, who dwell in this land, continue to merit and enjoy the good will of the other Inhabitants, while everyone shall sit in safety under his own vine and fig tree, and there shall be none to make him afraid."[4] Thus, after multiplied centuries of relentless persecution, World Jewry would now find a haven of rest in the United States of America (or, so it seemed to be the case at the time).

This blessing was also destined to be reciprocated, for the tiny fledgling republic would go on to reap the benefit of a "Jewish presence" precisely as promised in Genesis 12:3, *"I will bless them that bless thee...."* Columbia University alumnus, Dr. Eugene Narrett, states, "The one nation, America, the only one in which there has been a far more positive, welcoming and affirming stance toward Judaism, Jews and Israel from its origin was singularly blessed. One could even argue that it was prepared by providence to be a refuge for Jews during the last stages of the exile...."[5] John Adams, the nation's second chief executive, expressed his own appreciation for the legacy of America's Jewish citizenry: "I will insist the Hebrews have [contributed] more to civilize men than any other nation....They are the most glorious nation that ever inhabited this earth....The Romans and their empire were but a bubble in comparison to the Jews....They have...influenced the affairs of mankind more and more happily than any other nation, ancient or modern."[6]

It is against the backdrop of these early Jewish contributions to America that the true picture of Revelation 3:20 may be viewed. The Jewish "key" of Revelation 3:7 reduces the prevailing enigma of the "closed door" to a single thought-provoking question—"Who changed the lock?" Apparently, the key that opened the door in the Philadelphia Age does not fit the door lock in the Laodicean Age. When an estranged wife is determined to keep her husband out of the house, the first thing she does is change the locks. According to II Corinthians 11:2 and Ephesians 5:22-32, the Church is the Bride of Jesus Christ.

Thus, in the Age of Laodicea, the Lord Jesus has been locked out of His own Church by His own apostate Bride!

Even the faithful Philadelphia-minded remnant beset by Laodicean materialism is not without a related scriptural analogy. In Song of Solomon chapter five, the Bridegroom (a picture of Christ), is knocking and entreating at the door of His Bride (a picture of the Church). Unfortunately, having testified, *"I sleep"* (verse two), by the time the drowsy woman opens the door—her fingers and hands dropping with sweet smelling myrrh *"upon the handles of the* LOCK" (verse five)—her beloved has already *"withdrawn himself"* (verse six). The cross-reference is Paul's admonition in Romans 13:11, *"And that, knowing the time, that now it is high time to* AWAKE OUT OF SLEEP: *for now is our salvation nearer than when we believed."*

It is no coincidence that the city of Laodicea just happens to be named after a *woman*—the third-century BC Seleucid queen, Laodice I, namesake of her paternal great-grandmother, Laodice of Macedonia. Furthermore, as if to preview the sordid spiritual unfaithfulness of Christ's Laodicean Bride, it is also no coincidence that the matriarchal Laodice was reputed to have taken the sin of adultery to a whole new level. While married to the renowned Macedonian general, Antiochus, Laodice bore him a son, Seleucus I Nicator (a future general of Alexander and founder of the Seleucid Empire). However, according to the Roman historian Justinus, she later pretended to have discovered in a dream that the child's real father was the "god" Apollo (Genesis 6:1-5; Matthew 24:37).

Of course, this portrayal is not meant to indict all believers in the Laodicean Church Age (nor does it imply that all "professors" are "possessors"). God always has a faithful remnant in every era. Even in corrupt Laodicea, though possessing but *"a little strength,"* a handful of Philadelphia-minded believers continue to *"keep the word"* and *"go out"* for their Lord, content to wait for that glorious day when they *"shall go no more out"* (Revelation 3:8, 10, 12). As implied in the hymn, "I'll Meet You in the Morning," *that* will be the time to "sit down by the river." However, the Laodicean majority has decided to "kick back" now, waging the ultimate feminist revolt in the process, both in type as the unruly Bride of Christ, and in reality as seen by the average unsubmissive wife in the majority of today's Christian homes.

In the aforementioned *USA Today* article, sociologist Robert Bellah introduces "Sheila," a woman who represents the epitome of this modern phenomena: "Sheila says, 'I can't remember the last time I went to church. My faith has carried me a long way. It's Sheilaism. Just my own little voice...It's just try to love yourself and be gentle with yourself. You know, I guess, take care of each other. I think God would want us to take care of each other.'" For the record, "Sheilaism" was identified by the Holy Spirit more than twenty centuries ago when Paul included *"silly women"* in his inspired profile of end-day believers being *"lovers of their own selves."* (II Timothy 3:2,6)

The unanticipated and unrecognized consequence of this outrageous development is conveyed in the subtitle of this volume—*A Century of Anglo-American Anti-Semitism*. As Matthew 5:13 dictates that the actions of the Church will always have a reciprocal effect on the world *("Ye are the salt of the earth...,"* etc.), the rejection of the Jewish Christ by His Gentile Bride precipitated an automatic backlash against His kinsmen *"after the flesh."* While the Lord identified His spiritual oneness with the Church in Acts 9:4 *("Saul, Saul, why persecutest thou me?")*, His indivisible relationship with Israel in the physical realm was similarly relayed in Matthew 25:40—*"And the King shall answer and say unto them...Inasmuch as ye have done it unto one of the least of these my brethren, ye have done it unto me."*

This is not to say that early America was devoid of anti-Semitism; the same applying to Great Britain, as documented in such works as *Trials of the Diaspora: A History of Anti-Semitism in England* by Anthony Julius. However, as Dr. Peter Knight states, "All in all, in the United States in the eighteenth and nineteenth centuries there rarely resulted anti-semitic action comparable to that which was endemic in contemporary European societies."[7] And while it is true that the increase of American anti-Semitism was commensurate with Jewish population growth (primarily from the mid-nineteenth century), the same would have been further affected by the quantity and quality of Christian "salt" (the decline thereof working in tandem with a rise in Jewish anti-Americanism).

The Age of Laodicean apostasy began in 1881 with the Anglo-American eviction of the King "Jacob" Bible in favor of the corrupt *Revised Version*, followed by the *American Standard Version* of 1901—both having come from the Catholic text of *Codex Vaticanus*. By the early 1960s, Supreme Court decisions had outlawed the Jewish Decalogue from the nation's schools (though allowing it to remain in their own chambers). While Christians protested these "terrible developments," they were too "blind" to "see" that *they* were the catalyst (Revelation 3:17-18). For example, the text on Alabama Chief Justice Roy Moore's disputed Ten Commandments monument was taken from the A.V. 1611. However, it does *not* match the wording of the modern versions used in Moore's own place of worship. Thus, before the Ten Commandments were removed from Judge Moore's *court* house they were removed from Judge Moore's *church* house. By the dawn of the twenty-first century, "Sheila" and her *"silly women"* were advocating "Bibles" like the *New International Version* (NIV) with readings such as *"palm tree"* in Jeremiah 10:5 being "improved" to the more "scholarly" (silly) rendering of "scarecrow in a melon patch." This is what Titus 2:5 means when rebellious wives are equated with blaspheming the word of God.

It was, therefore, no coincidence that the first modern wave of Aliyah (Jewish immigration to Palestine) began with the Russian pogroms of 1881. The clock was now ticking as the Church had repudiated its own Bible. However, with the *"King of the Jews"* on the wrong side of the door, it wouldn't be long before His physical brethren would find *themselves* in a "locked out" status also; sadly, in more ways than one. Addressing the suppressed international travesty of European Jews having been denied sufficient immigration visas on the eve of the Holocaust, British Colonel Richard Meinertzhagen wrote, "Nobody loves the Jews, nobody wants them and yet we are pledged to give them a home in Palestine. Instead we slam the door in their faces just at the moment when it should be wide open."[8]

Sadly, according to the acclaimed *Palestine: A Study of Jewish, Arab and British Policies*, "It must be stated as a general principle that the overwhelming majority of the foreign Protestants in Palestine are more or less strongly opposed to Zionism."[9] Yet, ironically, while the average *recognized* "Christian" in the Holy Land would not know the difference between *Laodicea* and *Lowe's* (being Christian in name only), Britain's Jewish High Commissioner in Palestine, Sir Herbert Samuel, made the astute observation in his dispatch of December 8, 1922, "Generally the Christians have become more lukewarm."[10]

Professor Narrett observes that the US also went on to ban the Jews, when "under the tutelage and suasion of its original colonizer, Great Britain, American diplomats shut the doors against Jews in the late 1930s, during the *shoah* (holocaust)."[11] This was bitter irony, indeed, as those sacrosanct lines on the Statue of Liberty—"Give me your tired, your poor, your huddled masses…"—were penned by a young Jewess, Emma Lazarus. According to an article in the Jewish newspaper, *The Forward*, Lazarus believed that "it was the singular destiny of America to secure the fate of the Jews."[12] During those critical years, Zionist leader Chaim Weizmann was constantly appealing to America for the "golden key" that would "open the doors of immigration in Palestine."[13] However, the problem was never about the *key*; it had to do with the *lock*. The history of Anglo-American anti-Semitism is reduced to one question—"Who changed the lock?"

This book will answer that question. The *secular* "locksmiths of Laodicea" (i.e., spawned by the apostate Christians) are multitudinous. Some are household names, like Henry Ford, Joseph Kennedy, Charles Lindbergh, J. Edgar Hoover, Nelson Rockefeller, Richard Nixon, Jimmy Carter, James Baker, Mel Gibson, and Arnold Schwarzenegger. Others may not be as familiar to the Body of Christ, like "Father" Charles Coughlin, Huey Long, James Forrestal, Allen Dulles, and Prescott Bush. Excluding the obvious categories of fascists, Nazis, communists, and Muslims, notable international personalities would include: Arnold Toynbee, Colonel T. E. Lawrence ("of Arabia"), Queen Elizabeth II, the Duke and Duchess of Windsor, Popes Pius XII and Paul VI, and Harry "Jack" Philby of MI5. The craft includes a wide range of artisans and shops, from skinheads, Grand Wizards of the KKK, and the pre-WWII era, pro-Nazi, German-American Bund Party to evangelist Billy Graham, Replacement Theology advocates, and various "Christian skinheads" like conspiracy author Texe Marrs, "African-American" math teacher, Jonas E. Alexis, and the Cecil B. De Mille of our generation—filmmaker wannabe, Pastor Stephen L. Anderson (a.k.a. "Hyper on line one").

The most unusual group would have to be the wide range of so-called "anti-Semitic Jews" (the vast majority of whom are constantly having to explain their "true loyalties," etc.). At the time of the British Mandate, Colonel Meinertzhagen aptly labeled such Jews as "O.T.I." for "Order of Trembling Israelites," though, thankfully, their numbers formed but a small percentage.[14] (During the Holocaust, under the most torturous of mental conditions, Jewish prisoners who chose to extend their lives by collaborating with the SS were labeled Sonderkommandos, German for "special units.") More recently, many of these Jewish "locksmiths," also known as "self-loathing" Jews by their conservative brethren, are especially prevalent within the upper echelon of Israeli society, representing the ruling elites—politicians, judges, journalists, and academics. In the mid-1980s, a movement of Jewish revisionists emerged calling themselves the "New Historians." Challenging traditional views of Israeli history, their leading spokesmen have included Benny Morris, Ilan Pappé, Avi Shlaim, Gabriel Piterberg, Thomas Segev, Baruch Kimmerling, and Simha Flapan. Other proponents of the "Give peace a chance" agenda often align with Noam Chomsky and Norman G. Finkelstein.

As the reader will discover, the locks were changed in three interconnected stages: First and foremost would be the documented, though little-known, record of Anglo-American anti-Semitism itself; next, the perennial efforts to suppress these events by government, media, education, film, and every other relevant venue, while simultaneously promoting Arab propaganda; finally, the perpetual insistence of a two-state solution as a "workable" scenario in the face of the historical record of Palestinian intransigence.

By way of a more specific preview, the ensuing chapters will expose: 1) the most enduring myths of the Arab-Israeli conflict; 2) the consistent suppression of the Jews in Palestine during the British Mandate; 3) the total abandonment of European Jewry before, during, and after the Holocaust; 4) the Vatican's role in facilitating the escape of Nazi war criminals; 5) the concerted effort to defeat the Jewish bid for statehood at the United Nations; 6) the continuous betrayal of Israel by Western espionage; 7) the demand for oil representing the ongoing motive for Arab appeasement at Israel's expense.

Much of this material will apply to Sherman's quote regarding matters that are better left untold. It is the record of how corrupt governments, allied with big business, have been able to orchestrate illegal policies and keep them hidden from their own citizens for decades. It constitutes a rare glimpse into the *real* world. Ultimately, it tells the sad story of how the Jewish people were betrayed by Great Britain and the United States for petrodollars and how the Laodicean apostasy provided the spiritual fuel for this end-day travesty.

As a concluding insightful glimpse into the real history of the Jewish state, the following excerpt from *The Secret War Against the Jews* features three of the most prominent "locksmiths" on record. Having declared about Jack Philby, super sleuth and covert founder of Saudi Arabia, "The untold story of Philby's life is one of the biggest holes in the history of the Middle East,"[15] Loftus and Aarons describe the damage inflicted upon the Jews through the combined efforts of Philby, Ibn Saud (the first King of Saudi Arabia), and their American cohort Allen Dulles (diplomat, lawyer, Wall Street banker, and longest serving Director of the Central Intelligence Agency):

> Between them, these three men built the very foundations of the modern Middle East. They were the architects of the oil weapon, the instigators of war, the manipulators of history. More important, Philby's and Ibn Saud's political and philosophical allegiance was to Nazi Germany, while much of Dulles's profits came from the same source...United by their hatred of Jews, they waged an unremitting campaign against the Zionists and, after 1948, against Israel....
>
> Jack Philby was Ibn Saud's proxy in the secret war to stop Zionist immigration before World War II...He created the oil weapon as an instrument of foreign policy and made presidents and prime ministers bend to his will. He designed the Arab ultimatum: no Jews in Palestine, or no oil for the West.
>
> It was Allen Dulles who delivered on the blackmail by threatening Western oil supplies at the most desperate stage of World War II. While paying lip service to their promises to partition Palestine into Arab and Zionist states, the West, especially the British, slowly strangled the birth of a Jewish homeland through restricted immigration, revised interpretations, and an endless series of committees to study the future of Palestine. At a critical point in history, JACK PHILBY HELD THE KEYS TO PALESTINE IN HIS HAND. THE GATES WERE CLOSED TO THE 6 MILLION JEWS WHO FELL VICTIM TO THE NAZIS.[16] [Author's emphasis.]

The "keys" that Jack held were the keys to the *new* "lock." Given his Pan-Arabist ideology, one might call them—"The keys of Mohammad."

Part I

Struggle for Statehood

1

Palestinian Mythology

"Oriental diplomacy is seldom precise
unless compelled to be so."
(British Foreign Office, 1918)

"Intelligence is a Jewish virtue; intrigue is an Arab vice."
(Colonel Richard Meinertzhagen, 1920)

"A lie is the salt in a man."
(Arab Proverb)

THE AVERAGE PERSON lacks an accurate understanding of the Arab-Israeli conflict primarily due to the prevailing effect of Arab disinformation. In the critical decade prior to the creation of the modern State of Israel, a major outlet for Arab propaganda was actually functioning in the heart of London at the behest of the English foreign policy elite. Begun in 1936 by Dr. Izzat Tannous (a "Christian" Arab), the Palestinian Information Center (PIC) was touted as the first permanent office to put the Arab view before the British public. The PIC was also used as a meeting place where Arab visitors from Palestine could interact socially with their English friends as well as exchange information. The operation was later renamed the "Arab Center," eventually being eclipsed by the more politically sensitive "Arab Office" in the postwar era.

In addition to maintaining a prolific ministry of books, pamphlets, bulletins, letters, and press releases, as well as a monthly newspaper, the main objective of this anti-Zionist organization was establishing personal contact with ranking members of the British Government at Whitehall. In his 1945 memorandum on the Arab Office, John Bennet, a member of the Minister of State's office in Cairo, remarked that "fundamentally what they want the London office for is to build up for the Arabs a position in influential British circles...access to departments, MPs, press and so on."[1]

While these efforts ultimately failed to prevent the formation of a Jewish state, the seeds of Palestinian mythology had been skillfully sown. That a worldwide "famine of truth" was the only projectable "harvest" was conveyed by the words of an Arab proverb common to the *fellahin* (agricultural class): "A lie is the salt in a man."[2] The cumulative effect of this dissemination can be seen today in the pervasive ignorance regarding the true history of the State of Israel. The warning from Orwell's *1984* has finally come about: "The past was erased. The erasure was forgotten. The lie became the truth." Unfortunately, many Christians remain woefully deficient in this area. Paul told the church at Rome, *"Now I would not have you ignorant, brethren,"* likewise exhorting the Philippians, *"whatsoever things are true, whatsoever things are honest, whatsoever things are just...think on these things."* (Romans 1:13; Philippians 4:8) To fulfill these verses, God's children must be diligent to uncover and dispel the pervasive tenets of Palestinian mythology.

According to the online *Merriam-Webster Dictionary*, mythology is "a popular belief or assumption that has grown up around someone or something." The same source defines a mirage as "an optical effect that is sometimes seen at sea, in the desert, or over a hot pavement." Ironically, one rarely makes the connection between the two—that the greatest myths of the twentieth century comprising the so-called "Palestinian Problem" have emanated from a region that is over 75% desert. As if to provide a timely analogy to the delusion of a two-state solution, *Webster's* expanded definition adds, "something illusory and unattainable like a mirage," citing as an example, "A peaceful solution proved to be a *mirage*."

Following the Armistice, Richard Meinertzhagen attended the Paris Peace Conference as a member of the British delegation. He then served as Chief Political Officer in Palestine and Syria from 1919 to 1920 and Military Advisor to the Middle East Department of the Colonial Office from 1921 to 1924. In his book, *Middle East Diary: 1917-1956*, the no-nonsense colonel describes the climate in which the mirage of Palestinian mythology appeared:

> British sympathy is with the Arab and not with the Jew, largely because Zionism, its objects and possibilities, are misunderstood, and because the Arab is surrounded by a halo of picturesque romance. The Arab, his wild, savage nature, his lack of intelligence, his backward state and his connection with the romantic desert will always appeal to the British character in preference to the hard-headed, hard-thinking, practical Jew, bristling with troublesome problems and determined to get that to which he has a right by treaty and covenant. The Arab has not been slow to appreciate this fact and take full advantage of it....[3]

Professor Carroll Quigley referenced this elitist peculiarity in his controversial exposé of British conspiracy history, *The Anglo-American Establishment* (reviewed in volume one of this series):

> The attitude of the Milner Group toward the Arabs and Jews can be seen from some quotations from members of the Group. At the Peace Conference of 1919, discussing the relative merits of the Jews and Arabs, Smuts said: 'They haven't the Arabs' attractive manners. They do not warm the heart by graceful subjection. They make demands. They are a bitter, recalcitrant little people...impatient of leadership and ruinously quarrelsome among themselves....' A few years later, John Dove, in a letter to Brand [Dove's publisher], asked himself why there was so much pro-Arab feeling among the British, especially 'the public school caste,' and attributed it to the Arabs' good manners, derived from desert life, and their love for sports, especially riding and shooting, both close to the heart of the public-school boy.[4]

In another entry over twenty years later, Meinertzhagen reaffirmed his opinion with even more intensity:

> It is remarkable how many British eccentrics are attracted to Arabia or is it that a certain type becomes an eccentric after contact with the Arab?...I suppose a slightly unbalanced mind and a craving for romance or solitude is attracted by the dirt, squalor, dishonesty, inefficiency, laziness, intolerance and unreliability of the Arab, and no doubt the romance of the desert and the nomad has its attractions...I suppose the truth is that a man slightly abnormal is in search of something abnormal and in the Arab and the desert he finds just what he wants, people and places out of the ordinary and

> an atmosphere where his eccentricities find full scope and expansion and where he can with ease become a whale among the smaller fry.[5]

The apex of this affinity occurred on May 6, 2016, the veritable eve of the Balfour Centennial, when Sadiq Aman Khan defeated Zac *Goldsmith* to become the first Muslim mayor of London, marking a political milestone in the Western world. Surprise, surprise, on July 24 the Palestinian Authority announced its plans to sue Great Britain for the Balfour Declaration and the subsequent establishment of a Jewish state. On August 3, a Norwegian national of Somali origin stabbed six people in London, killing a sixty-four-year-old American woman.

The scriptural explanation for this "mysterious desert allurement" is I Samuel 15:23—*"For rebellion is as the sin of witchcraft."* As the greatest concentration of Gentiles in perpetual rebellion against God's covenant people is found in the Middle East, it should come as no surprise that the entire region would constitute one giant mirage, defined by "spells" and "enchantments"—the very fruit of witchcraft. Is it any wonder that the political configuration of the modern Middle East itself is traced to the diabolical 1919 Treaty of Versailles, signed in the "Hall of Mirrors"?

LAWRENCE OF ARABIA

While Jack Philby would become the most destructive of these British "eccentrics" (known as Arabists), it was Lieutenant Colonel Thomas Edward Lawrence who became the face of Arab apologetics, securing his name in history as the celebrated "Lawrence of Arabia." The "Legend of Lawrence" basically centered around his brief liaison role during the overrated Great Arab Revolt against the Ottoman Empire near the end of World War I.

Much of the credit for his initial fame has been attributed to the American journalist, Lowell Thomas, who sensationalized many of Larry's "exploits" in his award-winning screen documentary that played to packed audiences in New York and London. The Public Broadcasting System observed that "the images of *Lawrence in Arabia* captivated a public exhausted by the horrors of the 'war to end all wars'...The romantic and adventurous tales of this 'mysterious blue-eyed Arab in the garb of a prince wandering the streets' were an instant hit."[6]

Lawrence biographer Michael Korda dubbed him the first modern "media celebrity."[7] In essence, he was the "E. T." of Araby.

However, given what is now known about T. E. Lawrence, no better personality could be found to illustrate the true essence of Palestinian mythology. The man behind the myth was eventually exposed by Richard Aldington in his 1955 blockbuster, *Lawrence of Arabia: A Biographical Enquiry*. Aldington, a highly acclaimed author of nearly a hundred works, received a torrent of criticism for having dared to challenge so "hallowed" a reputation as attributed to Lawrence by that time.

Some of the most incriminating material regarding Lawrence surfaced four years later in *Middle East Diary*. Having become intimately acquainted with Lawrence at the Paris Peace Conference, Colonel Meinertzhagen maintained a professional and friendly relationship with his colleague for several years. Lacking any personal animosities, Meinertzhagen corroborates many of Aldington's accusations by simply relating what Lawrence told him in their conversations. The repeated entries acknowledging embellishment, pretense, and outright fraud make "Lawrence of Arabia" one with the mythological race he sought to create. Meinertzhagen's earliest impressions were recorded at the conference:

> He was a shy show-off with little to show, a mass of contradictions and an artist in trying to hide himself in a blaze of limelight. He practised secrecy lit up by publicity; he neither denied nor confirmed many complimentary myths about himself...He is writing a book on his Arabian exploits and admitted to me that though it purports to be the truth, a great deal of it is fancy, what might have happened, what should have happened and dull little incidents embroidered into hair-breadth escapes. He confesses that he has overdone it and is now terrified lest he is found out and deflated. He told me that ever since childhood he wanted to be a hero, that he was always fighting between rushing into limelight and hiding in utter darkness but the limelight had always won. And now he is genuinely terrified at his brazen imagination—all to what purpose? He hates himself and is having a great struggle with his conscience. His self-deception filled him with bitterness.[8]

Writing thirty-five years later, the colonel states:

> Richard Aldington has just published a book exploding the Lawrence Myth. It is a venomous book but true. Lawrence was the victim of his own desire for publicity...I probably knew Lawrence better than any living man...There were no secrets between us and I believe I was the only one of his friends to whom he confided that he was a complete fraud. 'Someday I'll be found out' he said on more than one occasion. Poor little man."[9]

Yet, despite access to such facts, the mirage remains. In 1962, seven years after Aldington's book was published, Columbia Pictures released *Lawrence of Arabia* with Peter O'Toole in the title role. The film was nominated for ten academy awards, winning seven, including Best Picture and Best Director. Today, *Lawrence of Arabia* is considered to be one of the greatest and most influential films in the history of cinema. Steven Spielberg, an "anti-Semitic Jew," called *Lawrence of Arabia* "a miracle," proclaiming the film as his personal all-time favorite. (Spielberg's liberal pro-Palestinian bias was expressed in his own 2005 release, *Munich*, which was strongly condemned by the Zionist Organization of America.)

T. E. Lawrence died on May 19, 1935, at the age of forty-six from injuries sustained in a motorcycle accident near his cottage home in Dorset, England. He left no family behind for, as Meinertzhagen states, "His objection to matrimony was physical contact."[10] In a classic illustration of poetic justice, on that very day in 1916, representatives of Great Britain and France reached a secret accord known as the Sykes-Picot Agreement, by which the majority of Arab lands under Ottoman rule were to be divided into British and French spheres of influence after the war. Seen as a major betrayal to the Arabs (given prior British assurance of territorial sovereignty as compensation for their "revolt"), the pact was subsequently rescinded.

"THE 'MENDACITY' OF HOPE"

By the twenty-first century, Palestinian mythology was alive and well, especially in the United States of America: Michael Bloomberg, the Jewish mayor of New York City, campaigned for a mosque at Ground

Zero (originally named the "Cordoba Project," a subliminal reference to Cordoba, Spain, the first European city conquered by Islam); the reality show "All-American Muslim" followed five "happily adjusted" American Muslim families in Dearborn, Michigan; a Muslim woman from that same city became the first Arab-American to be crowned Miss USA (the former Detroit-area stripper being arrested a year later on a DUI); "The Young Turks" broadcast was touted as the largest online news show in the world; with over 2,500 mosques dotting the land, the former Polish Catholic enclave, Hamtramck, Michigan, became the first American city to allow the Muslim "call to prayer" siren to invade local airwaves (going on to also become the first US city to elect a majority Muslim council); and, most telling of all—an anti-Semitic, bi-racial "African-American" community organizer, whose full name includes three African-Middle Eastern monikers, hailing from the largest Muslim country in the world—occupied the White House for eight years, directing America's "Global War On Terror" along with a triad of hot wars on three Islamic fronts (while simultaneously dodging a wide array of accusers and court challenges that he was really an illegal alien usurper to his office).

Ultimately, a subtle allusion to the "desert" was destined to serve as the portentous sign that significant "change" was just around the next sand dune. The greatest mirage of shifting sands appeared at the beginning of Barry Soetoro Barack Hussein Obama II's first State of the Union address on January 27, 2010. Having expressed his personal disdain for "Hail to the Chief," America's 44th president replaced 175 years of USMC tradition with his own favorite tune—a piano solo of Sting's Arabic melody, "Desert Rose."

"And for this cause God shall send them strong delusion, that they should believe a lie: That they all might be damned who believed not the truth, but had pleasure in unrighteousness."
(II Thessalonians 2:11-12)

2

Eretz Yisrael

"A sad condition was created for the Palestinian
people who were excluded from their homeland."
(Pope John Paul II, October 1980)

"I think that we've had an invented Palestinian people
who are in fact Arabs and who were historically
part of the Arab community."
(Newt Gingrich, December 2011)

*"I will move them to jealousy with those which are
not a people; I will provoke them to anger
with a foolish nation."*
(Deuteronomy 32:21)

THE PHRASE "ERETZ Yisrael" is the English equivalent of the Hebrew ארץ ישראל, meaning "Land of Israel." The term often appears throughout the first five books of the Old Testament and always refers to the physical territory that Jehovah promised to Abraham as the place where his descendents (through Isaac and Jacob) would reside and rule as a nation. Apart from any further discussion involving such related issues as boundaries, other Bible names for the same area, or debate over the intense political ramifications of Eretz Yisrael (especially among Israelis), one fact remains clear from the outset—the land was specifically designated the "Land of Israel," period! The New Testament is also unequivocal on this matter (contrary to the Catholic heresy of Replacement Theology), containing three references to the "land of Israel" in Matthew 2:20-21 and 10:23.

Conversely, the entire Arab-Israeli conflict is built upon one lie—the Jewish State came to power by evicting the "Palestinian people" from *their* ancient homeland, a falsehood that disregards the reality of Eretz Yisrael. The famous British Arabist, Arnold J. Toynbee, presented the myth of a displaced "Palestinian nation" in his foreword to *The Palestine Diary* by co-authors Robert John and Sami Hadawi:

> The story is a tragedy, and the essence of this tragedy is that about 1,500,000 Palestinian Arabs have now become refugees as a result of the intervention of foreign powers in their country's affairs. The might of these foreign powers has been irresistible, and the evicted Palestinian Arabs have been forcibly deprived of their country, their homes, and their property without having been allowed to have a voice in the determination of their own destiny...The tragedy in Palestine is not just a local one; it is a tragedy for the World, because it is an injustice that is a menace to the World's peace.[1]

In his jacket endorsement, Professor Nabih Faris of the American University of Beirut assured the reader that the book would "fill a very serious gap in the history of a unique international controversy."

Of course, the four hundred-year-old King James Bible could never be accepted as "reliable history" by *any* scholar, especially one reared in "Christian" England like Toynbee. The reader will recall from volume one of this series that his uncle, also named Arnold Toynbee, was the undisputed intellectual/philosophical leader among Professor Ruskin's inner circle at Oxford University, eventually forming the "Toynbee Group" in the Cecil Rhodes-Alfred Milner cabal.

The obvious problem with citing the Holy Bible (either Testament) is that it is too politically incorrect for just about everyone—moralizing Gentiles, Israeli politicians, and about 90% of "professing" Christendom. For instance, while Toynbee's claim that the Palestinian Arabs were evicted by the Jews in 1948 is an outright lie (to be dealt with in a later chapter), the earliest recorded history of the area is far more dramatic than that. Originally, Eretz Yisrael was called the "*land of Canaan.*" (Genesis 11:31) However, all that changed when the God of America's Judeo-Christian heritage had Moses command Joshua not to *expel* the original settlers, but to engage in ethnic cleansing! The precise wording for the divinely sanctioned genocide is given in Deuteronomy 20:16, *"But of the cities of these people, which the LORD thy God doth give thee for an inheritance, thou shalt save alive nothing that breatheth."* Joshua never flinched: *"And they utterly destroyed all that was in the city, both man and woman, young and old...with the edge of the sword."* (Joshua 6:21) Even "Allah" is seen as more tolerant than this, the Koran's rule of conquest regarding Christians and Jews stipulating, "Make war...upon such of those to whom the Book [Old Testament] has been given until they pay tribute offered on the back of their hands, in a state of humiliation."[2]

The "Mother of all Myths" regarding a Palestinian displacement implies two historical falsehoods—that a "Palestinian nation" has *ever* existed at all, much less "from time immemorial," and that the Jews only *recently* returned to Palestinian soil after an absence of nearly two millennia, the deduction that *any* return would infer a *prior* habitation being somehow "overlooked." The remainder of this chapter will address these two claims.

THE "PALESTINIAN NATION"

Palestine, a series of three 90-minute documentaries, produced by Thames Television, aired in the United States in late 1979. Journalist John J. O'Conner wrote in the *New York Times*:

> [I]t becomes increasingly clear that a profound and doubtlessly significant change has occurred in this country's televised coverage of Israel and the Palestinians...The crucial point is that the Palestinian cause has risen from a level of near-zero mass press coverage to a point that understandably generates legitimate concern in circles of Israeli support.[3]

The underlying thesis of the landmark British agitprop was that a religio-psychological bond exists between Arab/Muslim "Palestinians" and the land of Palestine, forged by a "continuous presence" spanning several millennia, etc. The mirage of an ancient, continuous "Palestinian nation" is historically indefensible. Even the *World Book Encyclopedia* concedes, "Many peoples have invaded the region, and there has never been an independent Palestinian state."[4]

Bernard Lewis, Cleveland E. Dodge Professor Emeritus of Near Eastern Studies at Princeton University, is a preeminent authority on the history of Islam. Dr. Lewis confirms, "From the end of the Jewish state in antiquity to the beginning of British rule, the area now designated by the name Palestine was not a country and had no frontiers, only administrative boundaries; it was a group of provincial subdivisions, by no means always the same, within a larger entity."[5]

Not only did this area exist without a national identity, but without much of anything else, either. According to the 1937 *Palestine Royal Commission Report*: "In the twelve centuries...since the Arab conquest, Palestine had virtually dropped out of history. One chapter only is remembered—the not very noble romance of the Crusades. In economics as in politics Palestine lay outside the main stream of the world's life. In thought, in science or in letters, it made no contribution to modern civilization. Its last state was worse than its first."[6]

Based on numerous eyewitness accounts, the image of this region can be reduced to three words: "desolate," "silent," and "telling." Such deplorable conditions were caused by centuries of Turkish neglect and misrule.[7] Dr. Carl Voss, founder of the American Christian Palestine Committee, describes the "glories" of the "Palestinian Nation":

> In the twelve and a half centuries between the Arab conquest in the seventh century and the beginnings of the Jewish return in the 1880's, Palestine was laid waste. Its ancient canal and irrigation systems were destroyed and the wondrous fertility of which the Bible spoke vanished into desert and desolation...Under the Ottoman empire of the Turks, the policy of despoliation continued; the hillsides were denuded of trees and the valleys robbed of their topsoil.[8]

Alphonse de Lamartine, a French poet, writer, and politician, traveled to the Holy Land between 1832 and 1833 with his wife and daughter. He related that standing outside the gates of Jerusalem,

> [W]e indeed saw no living object, heard no living sound...I know not whether the plague was the only cause of the emptiness of the roads and the profound silence that reigned within and around Jerusalem; but I think not...Jerusalem, where one would visit one only sepulchre, is itself the tomb of a whole people; but a tomb without cypresses, inscriptions, or monuments, whose stones have been broken up, and whose ashes seem to have covered the earth around it with mourning, with silence, with sterility.[9]

The American satirist, Mark Twain, visited the "Palestinian Nation" in 1867. The experience left him in anything but a humorous mood. Twain took his readers on a Holy Land "reality tour," recording, in his own inimitable style, his utter disillusionment with the "romantic" and "prejudiced" accounts of Palestine:

> Of all the lands there are for dismal scenery, I think Palestine must be the prince. The hills are barren...dull of color...unpicturesque in shape. The valleys are unsightly deserts fringed with a feeble vegetation...The Dead Sea and the Sea of Galilee sleep in the midst of a vast stretch of hill and plain wherein the eye rests upon no pleasant tint...It is a hopeless, dreary, heart-broken land...Palestine sits in sackcloth and ashes. Over it broods the spell of a curse that has withered its fields and fettered its energies...Nazareth is forlorn...Jericho the accursed, lies a moldering ruin...Bethlehem and Bethany, in their poverty and their humiliation, have nothing about them now to remind one that they once knew the high honor of the Saviour's presence...Renowned Jerusalem itself, the stateliest name in history, has lost all its ancient grandeur, and is become a pauper village...Capernaum is a shapeless ruin...Palestine is desolate and unlovely. And why should it be otherwise? Can the curse of the Deity beautify a land? Palestine is no more of this work-day world. It is sacred to poetry and tradition—it is dream-land.[10]

Efraim Karsh is a Professor and Director of the Mediterranean Studies Program at King's College London. He has held various academic posts at Columbia, Harvard, Helsinki, and Tel Aviv Universities, as well as the Sorbonne and the London School of Economics. He has published extensively on Middle Eastern affairs and Soviet foreign policy. Dr. Karsh describes the political structure of the "Palestinian Nation" on the eve of World War I:

> Palestine...did not exist as a unified geopolitical entity...it was divided between the Ottoman province of Beirut in the north and the district of Jerusalem in the south. Its local inhabitants, like the rest of the Arabic-speaking communities throughout the region viewed themselves as subjects of the Ottoman Empire rather than as members of a wider Arab Nation bound together by a shared language, religion, history or culture.[11]

Dr. Karsh's allusion to a "wider Arab nation" is indicative of another debate akin to Palestinian mythology. While the concept of a Palestinian *person* is as baseless as that of a Palestinian *nation*, a similar analysis of "Arabism" will also prove problematic, though in a different area. For example, an honest inquirer will often conclude that the phantom "Palestinian" is really just "an Arab" in political disguise. Assuming this is true, the Arab-Israeli controversy would vanish, as a Palestinian state *already* exists—with *plenty* of vacant land—the Hashemite Kingdom of Jordan. However, the new challenge becomes identifying the essence of a true Arab, a daunting task indeed. At least this was the opinion of "Lawrence of Arabia," who acknowledged in his autobiography, *Seven Pillars of Wisdom*, that the Arabic-speaking people were "as varied as a field full of poppies," having "an equal and essential likeness."[12] The Director of the prestigious Esco Foundation for Palestine comments on this observation:

> Students of Arab life are somewhat troubled in attempting to define what constitutes this 'essential likeness.' They are agreed that the Arabs do not comprise a distinct race or homogeneous stock....One of the reasons for Islam's rapid spread is undoubtedly its complete disregard of the color line. In the term 'Arab' there is a sense of consanguinity, but it is symbolic rather than actual. The amount of 'pure Arab blood' among the people commonly classed as Arab today is insignificant....[13]

Lawrence viewed language as the wider common denominator: "A first difficulty of the Arab movement was to say who the Arabs were. Being a manufactured people, their name had been changing in a sense slowly year by year. Once it meant an Arabian. There was a country called Arabia, but this was nothing to the point. There was a language called Arabic; and in it lay the test."[14] This "language called Arabic" was not a reference to the vernacular, which varies widely by country, but rather to the classic tongue hallowed in the literature and heritage of Islam. Oriental historian, Hamilton Gibb, summarized the matter with the following succinct definition: "To the question 'Who are the Arabs?' there is—whatever ethnographers may say—only one answer which approaches historic truth: All those are Arabs for whom the central fact of history is the mission of Mohammed and the memory of the Arab Empire, and who in addition, cherish the Arabic tongue and its cultural heritage as their common possession."[15]

The word "pan-ethnic," from the Ancient Greek "pan" (entire) and "ethnos" (nation), comes close to defining this illusive status, the *Oxford English Dictionary* stating: "Of or relating to all ethnic groups effecting or embracing people of all ethnic backgrounds." Francis M. Deng, a Senior Fellow at the Brookings Institution, writes:

> Lloyd Binagi [University of Wisconsin] attributes the Arabs' view of their identity to the success of their policy of assimilation through conquest, conversion to Islam, the spread of the Arabic language, and intermarriage. According to Raphael Patai [Jewish ethnographer], the term Arab in the post-Islamic period 'came to denote all the peoples who, after having been converted to Islam, gave up their ancestral languages and adopted Arabic instead.' The evidence of this historical assimilation provides the basis for an argument that anyone can become an Arab simply by adopting Arab culture, speaking Arabic, and, preferably, converting to Islam. A widely accepted definition in the Arab world is that Arabs are those who speak Arabic, are brought up in Arab culture, live in an Arab country, believe in Muhammad's teachings, and cherish the memory of the Arab empire.[16]

While Arab academics often demand the more narrow litmus test of genealogical evidence, historian P. K. Hitti reaffirms that the original Arab invaders were literally thinned out by their own converts:

> Through their intermarriages with the conquering stock they served to dilute the Arabian blood and ultimately to make that element inconspicuous amidst the mixture of varied racial strains....Shortly before the middle of the eighth century a caliph ascended to the Umayyad throne who had been born of a slave mother....His two successors, the last in the dynasty, were also sons of slave women....That the reigning family could no longer boast pure Arab blood was symptomatic of a loosening of moral standards throughout society.[17]

Thus, while the "Palestinian" claim to an unbroken presence in Eretz Yisrael is unquestionably fallacious, changing the approach to an "Arab" identity is also found to be morally ambiguous. Not only does the name "Arab" mean any number of things to as many people, but the repeated specificity that the Zionists stole the "ancient homeland" of these poor folks—whatever you wish to call them—implies that the land had been under their sovereign control from "time immemorial." However, by the epic Battle of Tours in AD 732, the brief era of exclusive "Arab Islamism" was already over. The new power brokers were the Berbers from the West and the Persians from the East. Eventually, the main standard-bearer of Muhammad's legacy would be Turkish. For the record, the greatest evidence exposing the hypocrisy behind the charge that Israel illegally occupied Palestinian lands is the fact that there were no protests from the Arab world, nor from the "Palestinians" themselves, when the West Bank was illegally annexed by Jordan, and the Gaza Strip by Egypt, following the 1948 War.

At least one ranking member of the Palestine Liberation Organization was willing to concede that the mythological Palestinian entity was nothing more than a terrorist ploy. In March 1977, Zuheir Muhsin, head of the PLO's military department, told the Dutch daily *Trouw*, "Yes, the existence of a separate Palestinian identity serves only tactical purposes. The founding of a Palestinian state is a *new* tool in the continuing battle against Israel."[18] Islamic scholar P. J. Vatikiotis affirmed this concession with his reference to "the more chauvinist Arab version of the region's history as having begun with the Arabs and Islam."[19] Thus, we find the further clarifying phrase in the *Palestine Royal Commission Report*, "Palestine—or, more strictly speaking, Syria, of which Palestine had been a part since the days of Nebuchadnezzar," recognizing the region's historical linkage to Arab Syria.[20] This conviction was conveyed, rather nonchalantly, by a Saudi Arabian UN delegate in 1956, who affirmed, "It is common knowledge that Palestine is nothing but Southern Syria." As late as 1974, Syria's President Assad went on record, stating that "Palestine is not only a part of our Arab homeland, but is a principal part of Southern Syria."[21]

PALESTINA

Now while the intrigues of Palestinian mythology are recent, the etymological background is ancient. The English name "Palestine" is derived from the Hebrew word *Pleshet*, meaning, "land of the Philistines."

It defines the coastal area, within Eretz Yisrael, extending from Gaza in the south to Ashdod in the north. (During the 1948 War, "Operation Pleshet" was named for an IDF strike against the Egyptian army in this same locale.) While rendering Pleshet as "land of the Philistines" in Genesis 21:32, Exodus 13:17, and I Samuel 27:1, the KJV translators also employed the more specific regional designation in Joel 3:4, Isaiah 14:29 and 31, and Exodus 15:14, the latter stating that *"sorrow shall take hold on the inhabitants of* PALESTINA.*"* (The modern "Bibles" follow the 1881 Revised Version with "Philistia," losing the latent application to the end-day crisis over "Palestine.")

The district gained its nomenclature from the Philistines, a non-Semitic Aegean strain, originally settled in large numbers along the southern maritime plain during the reign of Ramses III of Egypt (ca. 1190 BC). Some believe that the Philistines originally migrated from Crete (the "Caphtor" of Jeremiah 47:4 and Amos 9:7). This theory is particularly striking when that fellahin proverb ("A lie is the salt in a man") is revisited in the light of an advanced Pauline revelation to Titus in Crete. After citing a local as saying, *"The Cretians are always liars, evil beasts, slow bellies,"* his *inspired* reply to this "intolerant" profiling was, *"This witness is true. Wherefore rebuke them sharply, that they may be sound in the faith."* (Titus 1:12-13) Thus, as with the "legendary" exploits of Lawrence (propagated by Lowell Thomas, Lloyd George, Winston Churchill, et al.), the very origin of the name "Palestine" is appropriately connected to a pack of prevaricators!

The first official usage of "Palestine" began with the Romans in the bloody wake of the Bar Kokhba revolt in AD 135. Intent on removing all traces of Judaism, Emperor Hadrian renamed "Judea" (the main Jewish principality)—"Palestina." He also changed "Jerusalem" to "Aelia Capitolina," while banning circumcision, the Sabbath, the Law, even Judaism itself. Ironically, in view of the new appellation, Jews who fled these repressive measures became the first true "Palestinian" refugees. In their essay, *The Jews in Eretz-Israel/Palestine*, Ruth Kark and Joseph Glass of Hebrew University take it from here, providing a rare and fascinating (though of necessity, somewhat technical) overview of the geopolitical development of the region promoted by Arab mythologists as a continuous, independent "Palestinian Nation":

> By 425 AD, the Byzantine heirs to the eastern part of the Roman Empire had delineated three provinces: Palaestina Prima, which

included the coastal towns, the Judean Hills and the Jewish section of the Jordan Rift; Palaestina Secunda, which comprised the Jezreel Valley, the Galilee and the Golan; and Palaestina Tertia, which consisted of the Negev, Ammon, Moab and Edom. After the Arab conquest in 638, Palaestina Prima was named Jund Filistin. Under the Mamluke (1267-1517) and Ottoman rule, the use of the term Filistin was not resumed. Instead, Ottoman jurisdiction divided the territory between the provinces (*vilayets*) of Sidon (later Beirut) and Damascus. The latter controlled the northern sections of the area east of the Jordan River. Under the 1864 Law of Vilayets the districts (*sanjaks*) of Jerusalem, Nablus and Gaza became a separate administrative unit, called the *mutasariflik* of Jerusalem. In 1873 its rule was transferred directly to Istanbul. In 1906 an administrative boundary was drawn between Sinai and the Ottoman Empire along the Rafah-Taba line. In 1908 the Negev was placed under the Governor of the Damascus province.[22]

At this point, the reader is reminded that this material represents the most complex subject in history. Not only is the area of focus situated on the other side of the world, but the period is both ancient and protracted. For instance, as opposed to studying the American auto industry, *this* "topic" covers a 3,500-year span—in the Middle East—involving the religious, political, and cultural mores of Jews, Arabs, and Christians, among others, with a few archaic British policies of His Majesty's Government (henceforth, HMG) thrown in for good measure (e.g., the *real* "Muhammad Ali" was Muslim Caliph Muhammad Ali Pasha al-Mas'ud ibn Agha, a.k.a. "Father of Modern Egypt," who died in 1848). Also, as stated before, getting to the truth is further hampered by decades of lies and disinformation, perpetrated by the State Department, CIA, MI6, and American Oil, not to mention Satan's interest in keeping the waters muddied (I Corinthians 14:33).

Thus—lest any get "lost in the desert" amidst the *vilayets*, *sanjaks*, *mutasarifliks*, and *Mamlukes*—the gist of this chapter, concerning the history of Eretz Yisrael from the Temple's destruction in AD 70 to the present, may be summarized by four salient waymarks: 1) There has never been a tangible, structural, or political entity known as the Palestinian "anything" within the borders of present-day Israel; 2) The area has been ruled by successive ebb-and-flow waves of foreign powers centered in Rome, Constantinople, Mecca, Cairo, Damascus, Baghdad, and Istanbul. Apart from the Crusader Kingdom of Jerusalem (AD 1099-

1291), the fleeting Mongol invasions of Genghis Khan that hastened its demise, and the brief Napoleonic reign of 1799, "The only Arab domination [i.e., local Arab sovereignty throughout Palestine] since the Conquest in 635 A.D. hardly lasted, as such, 22 years"[23]—or so the Muslim chairman of the Syrian Delegation declared in his address to the Paris Peace Conference; 3) There is no such race as a "*Palestinian* race," the word being a politically correct misnomer. Those who do identify as Palestinian are normally "Arab," but *never* "Palestinian." Yasser Arafat—the most outspoken champion of the "Palestinian People"—was an Egyptian (married to a Roman Catholic, thirty-four years his junior); 4) The actual historic residents of Palestine have comprised an amalgam of Arabs, Greeks, Franks, Turks, Germans, Syrians, Hungarians, Scots, Kurds, Circassians, Egyptians, Bretons, Algerians, Indians, Georgians, Bulgarians, Persians, Russians, Danes, Bosnians, Latins, Motawila, Tartars, Sudanese, Jews, and a few Americans as well; the oldest inhabitants being identified in Scripture as Canaanites, Amalakites, Jebusites, Ammorites, Moabites, Hittites, Perizzites, Hivites, Edomites, and, of course, the Philistines. The 1911 *Encyclopaedia Britannica* cited no less than fifty spoken languages in Palestine by that time,[24] with the 1931 census listing sixty.[25]

"NEXT YEAR IN JERUSALEM!"

The second major lie of Palestinian mythology is that the Jews were gone from the "land of Palestine" for nearly 2,000 years; their late return being dated from the Balfour Declaration of 1917 and the British Mandate of 1922. To the contrary: 1) The dispersions of AD 70 and AD 135 did not expel all of the Jews, the same being true in the earlier deportations of 722 BC and 586 BC; 2) An indigenous Jewish remnant maintained an unbroken presence in the land; 3) This vestige was periodically reinforced through the centuries by waves of Jewish immigrants, usually fleeing persecution elsewhere.[26]

The Anglican scholar, James Parks, speaks to the host of unsung heroes who faithfully *"tarri[ed] by the stuff."* (I Samuel 30:24):

> It was, perhaps, inevitable that Zionists should look back to the heroic period of the Maccabees and Bar-Cochba, but their real title deeds were written by the less dramatic but equally heroic endurance

> of those who had maintained a Jewish presence in The Land all through the centuries, and in spite of every discouragement. This page of Jewish history found no place in the constant flood of Zionist propaganda...The omission allowed the anti-Zionist, whether Jewish, Arab, or European, to paint an entirely false picture of the wickedness of Jewry trying to re-establish a two-thousand-year-old claim to the country, indifferent to everything that had happened in the intervening period. It allowed a picture of The Land as a territory which had once been 'Jewish', but which for many centuries had been 'Arab'.[27]

Loftus and Aarons comment on this "heroic endurance":

> There have always been Jews living in Palestine. During Roman times they numbered in the millions, before they were dispersed by force around the Mediterranean basin. By the nineteenth century there were perhaps 50,000 left, principally in the holy city of Jerusalem, where they formed a slight majority from about 1800 onward. The Arabs called them "the dead ones" and treated them execrably. Jews who wished to pray at the Wailing Wall were forced to enter through the dung gate of the old city, used for the dumping of human waste.[28]

Though traditionally predisposed to Arab demands, HMG acknowledged the historical reality of Eretz Yisrael. One of the more candid affirmations of the Jewish claim was articulated in the formal *Palestine Royal Commission Report* (presented to Parliament in 1937).

> Always, or almost always since the fall of the Jewish State some Jews have been living in Palestine. Under Arab rule there were substantial Jewish communities in the chief towns. In the period of the Crusades and again in the Mongol invasions they were nearly but not entirely blotted out. Under Ottoman rule they slowly recovered. Fresh immigrants arrived from time to time, from Spain in the sixteenth century, from Eastern Europe in the seventeenth. They settled mainly in Galilee, in numerous villages spreading northwards to the Lebanon and in the towns of Safad and Tiberias....There was no schism between those Jews in Galilee and the Moslem and Christian peasants amongst whom they lived...they were equally exposed to the raids of marauding tribesmen...These inroads multiplied as public security deteriorated. Galilee steadily declined. A hundred years

> ago there were only some 4,000 Jews in Safad and some 3,000 in Tiberias....But, small though their numbers were, the continued existence of those Jews in Palestine meant much to all Jewry. Multitudes of poor and ignorant Jews in the ghettos of Eastern Europe felt themselves represented, as it were, by this remnant of their race who were keeping a foothold in the land against the day of the coming Messiah.[29]

Dr. Ernst Frankenstein (1881-1959) was a German-Jewish jurist and authority on international law. Prior to settling in London, he was a member of the Berlin Bar and a legal advisor to the Italian Embassy. He also served as lecturer at the Academy of International Law at The Hague. In his definitive work, *Justice for My People*, Frankenstein presents the Jews' legal claim to Palestine. First he notes that the Jews were the indisputable inhabitants of the land for more than a thousand years until their Roman displacement in AD 70. He then points out that Rome perished without leaving a "legitimate heir." After the Arabs conquered Palestine in 634 a succession of temporary usurpers followed: The Caliphs of Damascus; the Caliphs of Baghdad; the Tulinide Governors of Egypt; back to the Caliphs of Baghdad; then to the Egyptian Ikshidi princes; finally, to the Caliphs of Cairo. After 1071, Palestine was occupied by non-Arab conquerors—the Kurds, the Crusaders, the Mamelukes, and lastly, the Turks.

In 1923, the Ottomans surrendered their rights to the Allied Powers in the Peace Treaty of Lausanne. According to Frankenstein (writing in 1944), "[N]o one owns Palestine as a sovereign in his own right." Great Britain, as the internationally appointed Mandatory Power, was only serving as a temporary, legal trustee for the future sovereign. And of course, there were only two competing claimants: the Jews and the Arab-speaking inhabitants.[30] Citing England's greatest jurisprudence authority, L. F. L. Oppenheim's *International Law*, he states:

> According to the principles of international law the Jews have not lost their rights. They were deprived of their land by the Roman conquest. But though the doctrine of international law, strangely enough, admits the "legality" of conquest, the authorities agree that it is subject to certain conditions. The conqueror must have been in "continuous and undisturbed possession" for a considerable time. But "as long as other Powers keep up protests and claims, the actual exercise of sovereignty is not undisturbed."

> The Jews have never renounced their rights. On the contrary, they have always maintained their protest and claims in the strongest possible form. To maintain the claim to Palestine became a religious duty, and every practicing Jew proclaims it at least twice a year, on the occasion of the Passover and on the Day of Atonement, when he expresses the hope of observing those days as a free man "next year in Jerusalem." The Jews have not even confined themselves to acts of faith, hope and protest. Over and over again they have tried to return to their homeland, individually and collectively, and in spite of persecution and oppression there has always been at least a small Jewish population in Palestine. In the teachings of their religious and philosophical leaders, in the works of their poets, the longing for Palestine and the certainty of once more returning and establishing there a reign of peace and freedom has found most touching expression.[31]

The Arab claim was summarily dismissed as legally inferior. Frankenstein concludes by noting that the ancient Jewish claim received its modern, indisputable endorsement on the international stage, vis-à-vis the Balfour Declaration and the Palestine Mandate, the latter stating in its Preamble: "Whereas recognition has thereby been given to the historical connection of the Jewish people with Palestine and to the grounds for reconstituting their national home in that country...." In the words of Jan Smuts, Field Marshal in Pretoria, South Africa, in 1941, "The promise to Abraham had at last become a part of the international law of the world."[32]

"THAT SMALL NICHE"

While these legal points are sound, many Zionists prefer to press their case in the court of "common sense." The Old Testament enjoins in Isaiah 41:21, *"Produce your cause, saith the LORD; bring forth your strong reasons, saith the King of Jacob."* The prominent Methodist evangelist and educator, Dr. Bob Jones, Sr., would say, "Beware of unreasonable people." Thus, the question begs—Is it unreasonable for a Jew to want to live in Eretz Yisrael? After all, his race *does* exist, so it must have begun *somewhere*. Meinertzhagen answers with a reasonable fact: "The Jews want a Home, not an Apartment."[33] The genetically discredited theory of British Israelism—that all Ashkenazi Jews in

Palestine are really Gentiles descended from the Khazars of medieval Eurasia—deserves no more consideration than any of the other standard claims of anti-Semitic revisionist history.

Isaiah 1:18 says, *"Come now, and let us reason together, saith the* LORD.*"* Is there a more *reasonable* place to search for the roots of Jewish civilization than in Eretz Yisrael? Should the Ugandan terrain from Kaabong to Kabale be preferred to that of Dan to Beersheba? (Most Christians are unaware that "East Africa" was Britain's original proposal for a "Jewish" homeland.) At least *seven* Old Testament texts substantiate that Jehovah covenanted a *specific* parcel of real estate to Abraham's descendants (through Isaac and Jacob) as an "everlasting possession" (Genesis 12:1, 7; 15:18-21; 17:8; 26:2-5; 28:1-4, 13-14).

The fully constituted Jewish "nation" then went on to enter, conquer, and settle the "land of Canaan"—over 2,000 years before Muhammad's birth. King David established Jerusalem as his capital (ca. 1050 BC). Contrariwise, the founder of Islam never stepped foot in the city, though his favorite wife, Aisha, did say that he visited the Temple Mount on one occasion—but only in a *dream* (like Laodice and Apollo). While Jerusalem is cited over 600 times in the Jewish Old Testament, naturally it fails to appear even *once* in the Muslim Koran. Today, pilgrims and tourists are routed past an Islamic "guard shack" to gaze at the massive Western Wall of the Herodian Temple.

There had to be a "reasonable" basis for the League of Nations—with the concurrence of fifty-two leading countries and the formal approval of the United States—to officially recognize the Jewish claim to a national home in Palestine. Western civilization was erected upon a Judeo-Christian dais. Thus, there has always been a propensity, among Christians and Jews alike, to associate Palestine with Jewry. The *Palestine Royal Commission Report* acknowledged: "If Christians have become familiar through the Bible with the physiognomy of the country and its place-names and events that happened more than two thousand years ago, the link which binds the Jews to Palestine and its past history is to them far closer and more intimate."[34]

Many other idiotic contrasts between Jewish and Arab claims could be noted. Modern Israel encompasses roughly 8,000 sq. miles (slightly smaller than New Jersey), while the figure for the twenty-two Arab League nations is estimated at over 6,000,000 sq. miles. However, when the non-Arab Muslim countries of Iran, Pakistan, Afghanistan, and Turkey are factored in, the grand total rises to roughly 7,641,000 sq. miles. This number equates to a land mass over 900 times larger than Israel—the *only* Jewish state within the "community of nations."

In his July 12, 1920, address at Royal Albert Hall, Arthur James Balfour confronted growing Arab resistance to his proposal for a Jewish homeland by issuing a most *reasonable* appeal: "I hope that…they will not grudge that small niche, for it is not more geographically in the former Arab territories than a niche—being given to the people who for all these hundreds of years have been separated from it, but who surely have a title to develop on their own lines in the land of their forefathers."[35] Meinertzhagen lodged his own protest against this inequity, writing in 1938: "[B]e it remembered that the Arabs are the only nation in the world with at least three kings and several sovereign States. The Jews are a nation without a home."[36]

Thus it can be seen that despite Palestinian claims to the land based on religion, perceived historical ties, or *whatever*, that "niche" of 8,000 sq. miles is not indispensable to the survival of Arab-Islamic culture; they still have a little over 7,641,000 miles to play with, much of which is wide open desert. Meinertzhagen summarized the case for "common sense" in 1945, "I believed in the Old Testament prophecy. I believed that Christianity itself depended on a Jewish Palestine…that a people whose history and tradition went back for four thousand unbroken years, a people who gave us the Old Testament, our monotheist religion and Jesus of Nazareth, a people who have contributed so much to art and science: that such people should continue to suffer and be homeless when we could alleviate that suffering and grant that home, was to me a disgrace to civilization."[37]

ETHNOSCAPE

The degree to which Diaspora Jewry maintained an instinctive fixation on their ancient homeland is revealed by a telling example in the *Palestine Royal Commission Report*: "While the Jews had thus been dispersed over the world, they had never forgotten Palestine…Among countless illustrations it is enough to cite the fact that Jews, wherever they may be, still pray for rain at the season it is needed in Palestine."[38] Such enduring commitment to a specific *terra firma* is the defining characteristic of a socio-geographic phenomenon known as an "ethnoscape." According to

Anthony Smith, Professor of Ethnicity and Nationalism in the European Institute, London School of Economics and Political Science, an ethnoscape is "a terrain invested with ethnic significance."[39] (The abstruse sounding concept is analogous to one's periodic return to the "old home place" to recall precious memories.)

Applying the hermeneutical "Law of First Mention," the first time the word "holy" appears in the Bible, the object in question is *dirt*—*"And he said, Draw not nigh hither: put off thy shoes from off thy feet, for the place whereon thou standest is* HOLY GROUND.*"* (Exodus 3:5) As truth is stranger than fiction, the first thing that the "Holy Scripture" labels as "holy" is a parched piece of earth on the Sinai Peninsula—the designation occurring 2,200 years before Muhammad completed his "Holy Koran." From a doctrinal stance, the "ground" was declared "holy" because one day a literal Jewish king will sit upon a literal throne in a literal city atop a literal mountain to receive the literal worship of all who survive a literal Tribulation (constituting the "Kingdom of Heaven" versus the spiritual "Kingdom of God").

After his miraculous healing, Naaman the Syrian showed his gratitude for this heavy truth of "holy dirt" by securing *"two mules' burden of earth"* for his return to Damascus, stating, *"Behold, now I know that there is no God in all the earth, but in Israel."* (II Kings 5:15, 17) However, as the King's own subjects rejected their Messiah in AD 33, another reason was needed to explain why fifty generations of exiles would maintain their fanatical devotion for Eretz Yisrael. Humanly speaking, the "ground" is "holy" to Jews because it has become an ethnoscape—"a terrain invested with ethnic significance."

True to Romans 3:15, history is primarily a survey of warfare, specifically, conflict between *nations*. Due to the expedient use of such impersonal terminology as "England attacked France," the human suffering of international conflict is often veiled behind the fanciful notion that one "clump of hills and trees" is battling another "clump of hills and trees," etc. And yet, ironically, wars *are* fought over "clumps of hills and trees" (Bunker Hill, King's Mountain, Little Round Top, The Wilderness, Cedar Mountain, Argonne Forest, Mount Suribachi, Pork Chop Hill, Hamburger Hill, not to mention Mount Megiddo, yet future). While wars are fueled by the prospect of plunder, the greatest sacrifice on any field will be made in defense of one's homeland. The rationale for dropping two atomic bombs on Japan was a projected casualty list of half-a-million men from an amphibious invasion of the

Nipponese mainland. All things being equal, the home guard will always fight more valiantly than the invader or hired mercenary.

The related scenario of *reclaiming* one's homeland can induce an even greater surge of patriotic adrenaline. In 1689, the Waldensian pastor/general, Henri Arnaud, escorted by 800 parishioners, left the comfort of their temporary Geneva haven, to trek 250 miles across ten mountain peaks in the dead of winter to attack superior Catholic forces outnumbering them 50-1, before finally recapturing their beloved ancient homelands in the valleys of the Cottian Alps. Known as "The Glorious Return of 1689," Napoleon Bonaparte (a Catholic), deemed it "the greatest military campaign of the 17th century." While other worthy examples could be cited for both categories (Thermopylae, Tours, Sterling Bridge, Hastings, Agincourt, Gravelines, Yorktown, Alamo, Antietam, Somme, Stalingrad, Leyte), obviously, the Jews' own incredible defeat of five Arab armies in 1948 was the penultimate "return" of history—the veritable prelude to the Second Advent itself.

Dr. Smith writes in his essay, *Sacred Territories and National Conflict*: "Now, whatever else it may be, nationalism is always an assertion of, or struggle for, control over a piece of territory...What we need, then, is an analysis of the ways in which the members of an *ethnie* or nation become wedded to particular stretches of earth, and how such intense attachments can mobilize large numbers of people and turn ordinary political disputes into bitter national conflicts."[40] That the Jews have been "wedded" to their particular stretch of earth for centuries is demonstrated at every Jewish wedding. Unbeknown to the average Gentile observer, when the jubilant groom stomps on his glass and the guests shout "Mazel tov" ("Good luck")—the crushed goblet serves as an offsetting reminder of the Temple's destruction in Jerusalem. Thus, the "weeping prophet" enjoined his people, *"Ye that have escaped the sword, go away, stand not still: remember the LORD afar off, and let Jerusalem come into your mind."* (Jeremiah 51:50)

An ethnoscape forms when "historical memories" connect with "landscapes and territories." Smith defines this as a "territorialization of memory." Naturally, such a transition can only be forged over the *longue durée*, as mountains and valleys require time to morph into the proverbial "stomping grounds" of several generations (i.e., the soil where *our* fathers toiled; the fields where *our* ancestors fought; the graves where *our* heroes were laid; the hallowed ground where *our* prophets prayed.) "The veneration of an ancestral homeland by the inhabitants and their attachment to its landscapes makes a particular stretch of territory seem part of a community's distinctive character and destiny; without that specific ethnic landscape, the nation would lose much of its meaning and *raison d'être.*"[41]

When Jacob was about to expire in Egypt, he told Joseph, *"Behold, I die: but God shall be with you, and bring you again unto the land of your fathers."* (Genesis 48:21) Mark Twain wrote, "All things are mortal but the Jew; all other forces pass, but he remains. What is the secret of his immortality?" The answer to this question was given in a type nearly 2,700 years ago—*"and the physicians embalmed Israel."* (Genesis 50:2) Following the prescribed mourning period, the *"body* of Israel*"* was removed to the "*land* of Israel," creating the ultimate ethnoscape at the cave of Machpelah. On his own deathbed, *"Joseph took an oath of the children of Israel, saying, God will surely visit you, and ye shall carry up my bones from hence."* (Genesis 50:25)

The patriotic classic, "My Country, 'Tis of Thee," was penned in 1831 by Samuel Smith, a Baptist pastor. The opening stanza contains the phrase, "Land where my fathers died." As a result of this "territorialization of memory," the second stanza follows, "I love thy rocks and rills, thy woods and templed hills." This sequence produces the conviction that one's ethnoscape is under the special watch care of Heaven itself: "Protect us by Thy might, Great God, our King." When this kind of emotional bond is forged, men will "fight to the death" to defend their venerated turf. And Heaven help us if *both* combatants believe in the same God (I Kings 1:25, 39). Less than a generation after Smith's hymn was released, the "rocks," "rills," "woods," and "templed hills" of a sleepy Pennsylvania farm town were soaked with the blood of 50,000 Americans! As the Confederates began their nocturnal retreat on the *4th of July* (thirty-two years to the day that "My Country, 'Tis of Thee" made its public debut in Boston), the hospital wagons carrying the wounded stretched for seventeen miles.

The theme of Lincoln's Gettysburg Address was that the battlefield had already been "consecrated" by the brave soldiers from both armies who gave their "last full measure of devotion," etc. In 1913, the government sponsored a fiftieth anniversary reunion at Gettysburg. From July 1-3, some 53,400 veterans bivouacked in 5,000 tents spread over 280 acres of that historic ground, swapping stories and enquiring about past comrades. The climax of the emotionally charged affair was a reenactment of Pickett's charge. As the mass of Confederate survivors began their surge across the field, the chilling rebel yell was heard once again. Suddenly, an intense groan arose from the Union veterans on Cemetery Ridge. It was then, as one onlooker described, that "the Yankees, unable to restrain themselves longer, burst from behind the stone wall, and flung themselves upon their former enemies...not in mortal combat, but in brotherly love and affection."[42]

Still other patriots have been willing to push the envelope beyond that normal "last full measure of devotion." In the final drama of the First Jewish-Roman War (AD 66-73), 960 Jewish men, women, and children, besieged atop the desert fortress of Masada by 5,000 Roman troops, committed mass suicide rather than surrender *their* ethnoscape. The prevailing "territorialization of memory" from that surreal denouement is seen today as new recruits to the Israeli Defense Forces are sworn in by torchlight on this very site, the ceremony ending with the dramatic words—"Masada shall not fall again!"

Dr. Smith concludes that there are three ways in which territories become sacred to their inhabitants: 1) Whenever the appropriate ethnie is also a "community of believers," linked by a shared religious creed; 2) The accompanying "holy deeds of heroic ancestors" comprising an inviolable heritage of blessing and deliverance; 3) A vision of liberation or utopia, fostering the enduring allurement of a true "promised land" providing peace and good will for all.[43]

A sobering illustration of Jewish resolve was recounted by American pilots who helped airlift munitions to the Israelis during the onset of the 1948 War. The desperate missions were being flown from Czechoslovakia (code-named *Jockstrap*) to Israel (code-named *Oklahoma*). Note the awe they experienced from just a brief glimpse of the emaciated freedom fighters:

> You took on all the gas the plane would hold...From Jockstrap it was an 1,800-mile hop to Oklahoma. A C-46's normal range, with less of a load, was 1,500 miles; and you took off sure of only one thing—you weren't welcome anyplace else. If you landed in Greece, they would impound the airplane and its cargo. If you landed in any of the Arab countries, they would [gruesome details]....But it was when you landed that you realized what it was all about. While you were taxiing up to the apron, the trucks started pulling up. There were men standing in the trucks, new immigrants who would do the

> unloading, and the way they stood there, in their gray caps and shabby clothes, with their haggard unshaven faces, reminded you of newsreels and newspaper photos you had seen not very long ago of similar people riding in similar trucks to their deaths in Nazi concentration camps. The look on them came back to you in your hotel room in Tel Aviv that night. And the thought of making the whole trip back again in a couple of hours didn't seem like such a big deal after all.[44]

When these principles of "holy dirt" are applied to the Arab-Israeli conflict, the Jews are seen to have 3,500 years of "ethnoscape formation" to account for *their* commitment to Eretz Yisrael, while the Palestinians continue to be motivated by myth. Obviously, then, not only has Arab propaganda been directed at the world in general, but toward the individual Palestinian also; for without that "inspirational" link to the land, suicide bombers would be scarce. As the Arab activist Musa Alami put it, "[H]ow can people struggle for their nation, when most do not know the meaning of the word?...The people are in great need of a 'myth' to fill their consciousness and imagination, a myth of which they dream in times of peace and in times of trouble, because it gives their life meaning."[45] While the context of this "myth" relates to the aspiration of a *future* Palestinian State (particularly during the nineteen years of Jordanian quasi-suzerainty), Alami's remark represents an unintentional double entendre regarding the *greater* myth that would disregard 3,500 years of continuous Jewish presence.

"THOSE WHICH ARE NOT A PEOPLE"

As a fitting end to this chapter, the reader will be edified to know that the Holy Spirit anticipated the end-day myth of a "Palestinian people" by over twenty centuries. In late October 2006, Secretary of State Condoleezza Rice, a former board member of Chevron Corporation, declared, "[T]here can be no greater legacy for America than to bring into being a Palestinian State." Opining on these words in his book, *World War III: The War on the Jews*, Dr. Eugene Narrett warns that such a "legacy" would lead America "to destroy itself and plunge the world into chaos on behalf of 'a non-nation and despicable people.'"[46]

In Deuteronomy 32:20-21, the LORD declared about His people: *"I will hide my face from them, I will see what their end shall be...They have moved me to jealousy with that which is not God; they have provoked me to anger with their vanities: and I will move them to jealousy with* THOSE WHICH ARE NOT A PEOPLE*; I will provoke them to anger with a* FOOLISH NATION.*"* (In September 2015, the "official" flag of the so-called non-member/observer "State of Palestine" began flying at the United Nations.)

While the immediate doctrinal application is to the Body of Christ (Romans 10:19, 11:11, and I Peter 2:9-10), the later contemporary fulfillment is striking. In the providence of God, Israel's end-time jealously would be caused by her number one ally, America, vacillating over Muslim oil and being forced to placate the *foolish* Palestinian "nation" in the process—*"those which are not a people."* Thus, according to the judgment bar of history, the tradition of an independent Palestinian political entity is better suited to *One Thousand and One Nights* (*Arabian Nights*)—more specifically—*Ali Baba and the Forty Thieves*.

3

Diaspora to Zionism

"A land without a people for a people without a land."
(Zionist mantra)

"The world saw in this people the uncanny form of one of the dead walking among the living...if the fear of ghosts is something innate...what wonder that it asserted itself powerfully at the sight of this dead and yet living nation?"
(Dr. Leon Pinsker, 1882)

THE BIRTH OF the modern Jewish State was the historical terminus of the late nineteenth-century political ideology known as Zionism. The movement itself was the emotional terminus of the Jews' protracted existence outside Eretz Yisrael, known as the Diaspora ("dispersion"), referenced in Esther 3:8.

The full force of this term implies a stigma of displacement, i.e., Jewry finding itself painfully separated from its ethnoscape, thus, instinctively lamenting—*"How shall we sing the LORD'S song in a strange land?"* (Psalm 137:4) As numerous migrations had predated the Zionist era, the Diaspora likewise began centuries before Titus destroyed Jerusalem in AD 70. The opening verse of Psalm 137 reads, *"By the rivers of Babylon, there we sat down, yea, we wept, when we remembered Zion."* Precipitated by the violent pogroms of Tsarist Russia in 1881, the Zionist revolt was the inevitable repudiation of the social doctrine of "assimilation"—the idea that the "Jewish Question" could be solved by the exiles in each country fading into the majority of the native population.

Apart from the spiritual cause for the Diaspora (conveyed in the Torah and covered in a later chapter), the prevailing social climate was one of surreal anti-Semitism. In 2004, seventeen skeletons were discovered at the bottom of a medieval well in Norwich, England; the grisly find coming ahead of a commercial building project. Scientists using DNA analysis, carbon dating, and bone chemical studies, concluded the remains were members of a single Jewish family, eleven being children. Pictures taken at the site also suggest that the bodies were thrown down the well—headfirst. The most plausible theory is that the victims were either murdered or forced to commit suicide by pogromists in the twelfth or thirteenth century. The bones were put into storage. Today, the spot is marked by the Chapelfield Shopping Centre, featuring eighty shops and seventeen cafés and restaurants.

FUGITIVES AND VAGABONDS

The historical *fact* of the Diaspora was pre-written in Deuteronomy 28:64, *"And the LORD shall* SCATTER THEE AMONG ALL PEOPLE, *from the one end of the earth even unto the other."* It was also anticipated in the words of Cain, an early type of Israel, *"I shall be a* FUGITIVE [one who flees "the law," i.e., "Law of Moses"] *and a* VAGABOND [one who wanders] *in the earth."* (Genesis 4:14)

The dispersion naturally began in the Middle East (Iraq and Egypt) with the exiles who chose not to return to Jerusalem in 538 BC. Several Jewish communities later flourished in both regions. By the final destruction of Jerusalem in AD 135, other waves of refugees had poured into Syria and Yemen and across the Mediterranean into Greece and Italy. Five centuries later, the "Sword of Allah" caused renewed migrations along northwest Africa into Spain.

Ironically, according to Dr. Lewis, "The city of Medina [Islam's second 'holiest' site], some 280 miles north of Mecca, had originally been settled by Jewish tribes from the north."[1] The Jews then added insult to injury by dominating Arabia's economy. However, this would never do, for Medina had become a major Muslim ethnoscape, being the "sacred" birthplace of Abu al-Qasim Muhammad ibn ʿAbd Allah ibn ʿAbd al-Muttalib ibn Hashim himself. Thus, while the Koran permitted the dhimmi (non-Muslims/Jews and Catholics) to remain in most Muslim lands (for tribute), Muhammad's decree, "Two religions may not dwell together on the Arabian Peninsula," signaled a special dispensation for the founder's native land.[2] The ensuing massacre of Arabian Jews, along with the expropriation of their property, became justified as the "will of Allah," the Koran stating, "[S]ome you slew and others you took captive. He made you masters of their *land*, their *houses* and their *goods*...Truly, Allah has power over all things."[3]

Though tolerated elsewhere, non-Muslims were to be ostracized, Muhammad enjoining, "Believers, take not the Jews nor the Christians for your friends."[4] The Dhimma code was an integral part of traditional Sharia law that governed life for heathen subjects in Islamic lands. It also told Muslims how to treat their "infidel inferiors," the main goal being persistent degradation. When Jews approached Muslims, they had to pass on their left, for that was the "side of Satan," etc. They also had to yield the right of way, stepping into the gutter to allow an Arab to pass. If a Jew happened to be riding a horse or an ass, he had to quickly dismount before a follower of Allah.

Confined to their demeaning ghettos, the Jews' daily "existence" included: humiliating dress codes, economic discrimination, extortion on every pretext, religious persecution, petty bullying, and fierce beatings fueled by the vilest slander, all without access to equitable redress in Muslim courts. The British Consulate stated in 1839, "[T]he Jew in Jerusalem is not estimated in value, much above a dog...What the Jew has to endure...is not to be told. Like the miserable dog without an owner he is kicked by one because he crosses his path, and cuffed by another because he cries out...the poor Jew, even in the nineteenth century, lives from day to day in terror of his life."[5]

While Jews in Moslem countries suffered perennial persecution, the *Palestine Royal Commission Report* states that the violence was actually initiated and eclipsed by the "Christians" (i.e. Roman Catholics, as with that twelfth-century well in Norwich):

> From the time when the Roman Empire accepted Christianity, Judaism had always been less tolerantly treated by Christian than by Moslem rulers; and the Jews who had penetrated into Italy and Gaul and, after the fall of the Empire, into Germany and England were exposed to various restrictions and prohibitions which tended to mark them off as a distinct and inferior people. Social factors widened the gulf. In the feudal Europe of the Dark Ages the immigrant Jew could find no place on the land or in the industrial guilds: he inevitably became the middleman, whether merchant or peddler. And, since

> usury was forbidden to Christians by the Church, the Jew inevitably also became the money-lender—an unpopular profession. Jewish life, therefore, tended to be almost exclusively urban, and Jewish energies were directed more and more...into commerce and finance. The Jews took an early share in the banking-system. Some... accumulated fortunes. Christian rulers came to look to them when they wanted money. But, despite their usefulness, they were never liked.[6]

The truth of this resentment is conveyed by the proverb, "The reason Gentiles hate Jews is because Gentiles love money and Jews know how to make it." The report relates that the Jews were also despised because they were "strange looking" and kept to themselves while clinging obstinately to their peculiar faith. And above all else, the convenient justification remained that "on all Jews, in all times and places, lay the guilt of the Crucifixion"[7]:

> This complex of ill-feeling came to a head in...the Crusades. The wrath of the Crusaders fell as much on Jew as on Moslem; and it soon seemed as much an act of piety to kill Jews in Europe as to kill Saracens in the Holy Land. A wave of persecution, increasingly cruel in its methods, spread all over Western Europe. First in England, than in France, Jews were expropriated, tortured, massacred, and finally expelled from the country. For a time there was less brutality in Spain...but in the second half of the 15th century the Inquisition took up its task of scenting out and burning heretics, and in 1492 all Jews who refused to be converted were expelled. Another Jewish migration was thus set going, this time from West to East. The refugees from Southern Europe, especially from Spain, found shelter in the Mediterranean provinces of the Turkish Empire, in the Balkans, in Egypt, in Asia Minor, in Constantinople itself. From this time dates the important settlement of Spanish Jews or *Sephardim* at Salonika.[8]

Most older Americans were weaned on the "glories" of King Ferdinand and Queen Isabella along with their loyal subject, Christopher Columbus. Unfortunately, the history books failed to mention the thousands of Jews and real Christians who suffered the infamous *Auto-da-fé*. (In reference to the 8,800 victims of Torquemada, the official *Catholic Encyclopedia* inanely concedes, "These figures are highly exaggerated...Most historians hold...that the number of persons burnt from 1481 to 1504...was about 2,000."[9])

> In Central Europe and Italy there were massacres of Jews as elsewhere, but no wholesale expulsion. Henceforth…they were kept rigidly apart from Christians, confined to particular quarters of the towns they lived in, known as ghettos, and often obliged to wear a yellow badge to distinguish them from other people. Many…especially in Germany, left their homes and with those expelled from France and England sought refuge on the then only half-developed eastern fringes of an expanding Europe, in Lithuania, Poland and Hungary—a process which continued until a good deal more than half the Jews in the world were congregated in that belt of the country. The Polish kings at first protected them, but the respite was short-lived. With the middle of the seventeenth century came Cossack conquest and, later on, Russian rule. A sort of territorial ghetto, the "Pale of Settlement", was established from the Baltic north of Warsaw to the Black Sea near Odessa to keep the Jews from permeating Russia, and throughout this area the urban ghetto system was imposed.[10]

While the brutality alone was barely imaginable, the same report states, "[M]ore astonishing, perhaps, is the fact that the Jews survived it." Though roughly four million Jews existed in the dawn of the Diaspora, only about one and one-half million could be found in 1700. Yet, they had not been eliminated, either by massacre or conversion. "Judaism, it seemed, was indestructible. And, what it lost in numbers and in wealth from persecution, it gained in intensity."[11]

THE PALE OF SETTLEMENT

The largest number of ghettoized Jews in Imperial Russia was in the "Pale of Settlement" ("pale" from the Latin *palus*, for "stake" or "boundary"). Catherine the Great created the Pale in 1791 as a buffer against further migration into her realm. It comprised about 20% of the landmass of European Russia (equating to modern-day Lithuania, Ukraine, Belarus, Poland, Moldova, and areas in western Russia).

Life in the *shtetls* ("little towns") was unbearable at best. Scores succumbed to poverty and famine. The isolated living quarters also made them soft targets for anti-Semitic violence. The most effective slander throughout the Diaspora was the "blood libel," the claim that Jews murdered children to use their blood in religious rituals. Other historic charges include "well poisoning" and "host desecration." The first *pogrom* (i.e., organized, sanctioned, massacres of Jews) occurred in 1821 in Odessa (modern Ukraine) when fourteen Jews were slain after the death of the Greek Orthodox Patriarch, Gregory V. The word entered common English usage following the wave of anti-Jewish riots throughout southwestern Russia from 1881-1884. The catalyst for this latter outbreak, comprising over 200 incidents, was the assassination of Tsar Alexander II, for which the Jews were falsely implicated.

Ironically, the reality of this dreary existence was conveyed through a lighthearted Broadway musical, the 1964 hit *Fiddler on the Roof.* The original production was the first musical theater run in history to exceed 3,000 performances. *Fiddler* was nominated for ten Tony Awards, winning nine, including Best Musical, score, book, direction, and choreography. (The 1971 film version took three Academy Awards.) The enormous success of this timeless classic speaks to the underlying pathos that arrested the conscience of a relatively carefree American audience. Set in Tsarist Russia in 1905, the story centers around "Tevye, the dairyman" who struggles to maintain his religious traditions while living with his wife and five strong-willed daughters in Anatevka, a shtetl in the Pale. One of the main scenes occurs when the wedding of Tevye's oldest daughter, Tzeitel, is abruptly crashed by a violent pogrom, described by the sympathetic local constable as a "little unofficial demonstration."

The historical context for this "demonstration" was the 1903 Kishinev pogrom where 50 Jews were slain and 500 wounded on the basis of another false accusation, this one being the murder of a Russian Orthodox youth. An article in *The New York Times* reported: "The mob was led by priests, and the general cry, 'Kill the Jews,' was taken up...The Jews...wholly unaware...were slaughtered like sheep...The scenes of horror attending this massacre are beyond description. Babies were literally torn to pieces by the frenzied and bloodthirsty mob. The...police made no attempt to check the terror. At sunset the streets were piled with corpses and wounded. Those who could...fled in terror...the city is now practically deserted of Jews."[12]

Depicting that daily life within "the Pale" was as precarious as "the perch of a fiddler on the roof" (Psalm 107:2), the play ends with the forced eviction and relocation of Anatevka's disconsolate residents. As Tevye schleps out of the village, his pathetic milk cart in tow, the nimble-footed fiddler brings up the rear, playing gaily as he goes.

The character depicted by the constable illustrates that not all Russians were anti-Semitic at heart. The celebrated Baron Peter Nikolayevich Wrangel (1878-1928) is a case in point. Wrangle began his military career as an officer in the prestigious Russian Imperial Guard, the Tsar's personal "Family Regiment." After serving with distinction in both the Russo-Japanese and First World Wars, Wrangel ended his career as the last Commander-in-Chief of the Russian National Army in Russia's Civil War. Unlike many of his peers, he abhorred lawlessness, especially against the Jews. In his memoirs, he stated: "I believe that anything tending to lead to a pogrom, and all propaganda in this direction, is a misfortune for the State, and I will oppose such things by every means in my power. All pogroms demoralize the Army."[13] As the prejudice shown by other Russians had nothing to do with his own convictions, Wrangel argued that "Jewish Communists" likewise "form only a part of the Jewish population, and have perhaps broken with the other part who do not share their Communist views nor accept the Soviet Power."[14] Wrangel describes a pogrom he encountered and dispersed at Stanislavov in July 1917:

> In the hall, leaning against the wall, was an old man with a long white beard all covered with blood...the old man was a Jew, the owner of a shop which had been looted; he had been roughly handled and had escaped death only by a miracle. There were only my orderly and two Hussars near at hand. We went into the street. Pillaging was going on everywhere: windows were being broken, doors smashed in...Fires were smoldering all over the place...An artillery officer I met gave me some men, and I attempted to restore order. Coming upon a group of fugitives engaged in rifling a shop, I struck one of them violently with my fist and felled him to the ground...I called out: "Cossacks, see that this scoundrel is flogged." And the whole lot took themselves off...With the assistance of the gunners, the streets were cleared in two hours...In the side-streets looting still went on. I had done so much shouting that I had lost my voice. With the dawn a squadron of lancers arrived. I commanded the colonel who was with them to put an end to the pogrom, no matter what the cost. He had a few of the pillagers shot down, and order was restored.[15]

In November 1920, General Wrangel saved the lives of 145,693 White Russian soldiers and civilians by evacuating them across the Black Sea in a massive flotilla of 126 ships. He died mysteriously in 1928 while exiled in Brussels, Belgium. (In a series of interviews with Wrangel's daughter, the late Nathalie Basilevsky of Cos Cob, Connecticut, this author was informed that the family believed he was poisoned by a Soviet agent.)

THE "JEWISH QUESTION"

The term "Jewish Question" surfaced in England around the middle of the eighteenth century, eventually spreading to France and Germany. It was essentially a politically correct euphemism for Europe's proverbial "elephant in the room"—the increasingly unpopular debate over Jewish civil liberties. The pertinent legal and economic issues involved disabilities, emancipation, assimilation, and the Jewish Enlightenment. While the Russian Empire remained incorrigible, a fresh spirit of tolerance had enveloped the Continent from the Age of Enlightenment through the Revolutions of 1848.

The new "lawgiver" for this era was the renowned German-Jewish philosopher, Moses Mendelssohn (1729-1786), the Father of Reform Judaism and catalyst for the Jewish Enlightenment. His epoch work, the *Bi'ur* ("explanation")—a German translation of the Pentateuch and other parts of the Old Testament—was regarded as the main bridge between Jewish and German culture. (His grandson, Felix, dubbed the "New Mozart," would expand the movement through music.)

The core ideal of nineteenth-century nationalism envisioned a state for each national group. Thus, for their part, the "stateless" Hebrews were merely expected to become "a little less Jewish." Assimilation ideology was, in the words of the famous German-Jewish poet Heinrich Heine, "the ticket of admission to European civilization," and, one that was "cheap and easily bought."[16] Numbers of pragmatic Jewish parents discerned that Christianity would afford their children "first class" tickets as well—Felix Mendelssohn and Benjamin Disraeli representing two of the more notable "conversions" (Heine's own christening having occurred at age twenty-seven).

To the surprise of many, the ensuing reforms—a.k.a. the "Jewish Emancipation"—resulted in historic integration within European civil society. The House of Rothschild was dubbed the strongest banking family in "Christian" Europe. In 1858, Baron Lionel de Rothschild became the first observant Jew to sit in Britain's House of Commons. A decade later, Benjamin Disraeli became the first (and only) Jewish-born prime minister in England's history. The ghettos *appeared* to be closing. However, as prevailing geopolitics precluded the option of a Jewish state, the only "problem" with assimilation as the final solution to the "Jewish Question" was that it would also become the final solution to the Jew himself; theoretically, he would cease to exist![17]

However, in God's providence, the euphoria was short-lived. As with David's brief and unnatural respite among the Philistines (I Samuel 27-29), a revival of "Jew baiting" returned with a vengeance. Ignited around 1880 by the German agitator and publicist, Wilhelm Marr (a.k.a. the "Father of Modern anti-Semitism," having personally coined the term while rumored to be a Jewish convert himself), the contagion quickly spread, culminating in 1894 with the Dreyfus Affair in France. Bernard Lazare, a Parisian Jewish literary critic, wrote:

> The Jews are no longer confined to their own section of town, the streets where they live are no longer closed off by chains, but they are imprisoned in a hostile atmosphere of suspicion, of latent hatred, of prejudice the more powerful for not being avowed, a ghetto far more terrible than that from which they could escape by exile or revolt. This hostility is generally concealed, but an intelligent Jew has no trouble perceiving it. He senses an obstacle in his path, the wall which his enemies have erected to separate him from those in whose midst he lives.[18]

With three million Jews poised to flee the "Pale of Suffering" between 1880 and 1910, the "Jewish Question" was exactly as Theodor Herzl would later describe—"a hangover of the Middle Ages, of which the modern civilized nations, with the best will in the world, cannot rid themselves."[19] The time had come for a *permanent* solution.

"First Fruits" of Zionism

Oddly enough, Napoleon Bonaparte had already broached "the solution" during his ill-fated Near East campaign in 1799. His invasion of Egypt and Palestine on the eve of the 19th century dated the onset of European rivalry for control of the region. While the French fleet was destroyed by Admiral Nelson at the Battle of the Nile, the victory would be overshadowed by an insignificant appearing, though remarkably prescient, ploy by the Emperor just a few months later.

During the siege of Acre, a notice appeared on the front page of the May 22 *Gazette Nationale ou le Moniteur Universel* (the French government newspaper): "Bonaparte has published a proclamation in which he invites all the Jews of Asia and Africa to gather under his flag in order to re-establish the ancient Jerusalem."[20] The offer also included a pledge to rebuild the Temple. Though ultimately ignored by the Jews (their loyalties remaining with the Anglo-Turkish coalition), the mere fact of Napoleon's clarion call bears an early tacit twofold witness to Europe's recognition of the Jews' claim to Palestine, as well as the existence of an exploitable Jewish ethnoscape.

Within a generation of this proclamation, Hirsch Kalischer, a liberal-minded Orthodox rabbi from the east Prussian town of Toruń (modern-day Poland), was actively promoting a "practical" return to the land. The prevailing religious view held that the long-awaited restoration could only be effected through *supernatural* means, specifically, by the arrival of the Messiah Himself. By 1836, Kalischer had appealed to Asher Meyer Rothschild of Frankfurt and other Jewish philanthropists to underwrite the settling of Jews in Palestine. In 1861 and 1862, he published two pamphlets (*Emunah Yesara* and *Derishat Zion*) reiterating the need for "self-help" and proposing that a society be founded for colonizing Jews in Palestine for the sole purpose of tilling the soil. As a partial result of his collaboration with the *Alliance Israélite Universelle* (Jewish relief agency in France), an agricultural school was formed near Jaffa in 1870 by Charles Netter. Named *Mikveh Israel* ("Ingathering of Israel") the institution bears the distinction of being the first Jewish agricultural school in Palestine.[21]

The next major landmark in agricultural colonization occurred in 1878. Led by Rabbi Yoel-Moshe Salomon, a Jerusalem contingent acquired a plot of land north of Jaffa, founding *Petach Tikvah* ("Door of Hope"/Hosea 2:15). Though the society failed, Edmond de Rothschild revived the work in 1888. Known as the "Mother of the *Moshavot*" ("small cooperative villages"), Petach Tikvah went on to become an important training ground for thousands of pioneers. It is considered the first modern agricultural settlement in Israel.

In the wake of Russia's violent pogroms and the restrictive May Laws (imposed by Alexander III on May 15, 1882), the Jews mostly fled westward (many, all the way to Ellis Island). However, a battered but committed remnant would travel south to Eretz Yisrael. Their epoch-making odyssey became the vanguard of modern Zionism, a.k.a. the "First *Aliyah*" ("ascent" to Israel). Calling themselves *Hovevei Zion* ("Lovers of Zion"), several student activist groups formed to create agricultural colonies in Palestine. The *Bilu* society ("House of Jacob"/Isaiah 2:5), sporting a membership of five hundred students, fostered the prototype of the communal experiment known as the *kibbutz* ("gathering"). In 1882, ten enthusiasts from Kharkov, led by Z. D. Levontin, planted the community of *Rishon LeZion* ("First to Zion"/Isaiah 41:27) on a purchased tract of 835 acres. The colonies of *Rosh Pinah*, *Zichron Ja'acob*, and *Yesod Hama'alah* quickly followed in Galilee. Situated seven miles southeast of present-day Tel Aviv, Rishon LeZion is recognized as the first Zionist settlement forged by volunteers from outside of Israel. The autonomous kibbutz became the all-important seed of Jewish nationalism within the Ottoman Empire.

By 1894, a total of eighteen outposts were functional, their financial aid coming primarily from Edmond de Rothschild who personally began seven additional colonies from 1893-1900. As Zechariah 4:10 cautions, *"For who hath despised the day of small things?"* the literal "first fruits" of the First Aliyah consisted of grapes and oranges. On a technical note, the Jewish population in pre-state Palestine was known as the *Yishuv* ("settlement"); the indigenous Jewish inhabitants being recognized as the "Old Yishuv," while the later Zionist migrations became the "New Yishuv."

Unfortunately, nearly all of the initial settlements were planted in malarial districts as they afforded the best irrigation. Thus, many first-generation pioneers succumbed to the dread disease, known as the "scourge of the Middle East." Yet, the survivors fought on bravely. An early settler, Chaim Chissin, described their attendant hardships:

> I did not have the faintest idea of what it was all about. Still I raised my hoe and started bringing it down on the earth. In a little while, blisters developed. My hands started bleeding and the pain was so excruciating that I had to lay down the hoe. But I immediately felt ashamed of myself. "Is this how you mean to show that the Jews are capable of manual labour?" I asked myself. "Are you

really able to come through this test?" I took new heart and picked up the hoe again, and despite the stinging pain I hoed for two solid hours, though it nearly killed me.[22]

In stark contrast to their marauding Bedouin "neighbors," returning Jews were transfixed by an ethnoscape that transcended their personal suffering. A few lines from a new immigrant in 1810 speak volumes: "Truly, how marvelous to live in the good country. Truly how wonderful to love our country. Even in her ruin there is none to compare with her, even in her desolation she is unequaled, in her silence there is none like her, good are her ashes and her stones."[23]

To the settlers' relief, the swamps were eventually drained, causing the death rate to decline. However, conditions outside the Yishuv were far worse. Jewish mortality from 1922-1925 was 13.62 per thousand while the figure for Muslims was 26.83 per thousand.[24] The cause for this disparity was self-evident; the fellahin villages were literally overrun with filth and disease. Arab farmers supplied their fuel needs by maintaining massive dung hills, sometimes an accumulation of generations. While its more expedient use as fertilizer would not be discovered until the twentieth century, the foul substance did provide an ancillary "benefit"—eye disease being treated with fresh dung and bandages soaked in camel urine! Bathing was not appreciated for its salutary value. Flies swarmed ubiquitously, clustering around the eyes of infants. Children ran amuck barefoot and half-naked.[25] In John Steinbeck's famous World War II dispatches, the Pulitzer and Nobel Prize-winning author summarized the Arab population centers as reeking with the stench of "four thousand years of urine."[26]

"THE WALKING DEAD"

Dr. Judah Leib Pinsker was the most revered Zionist thinker in Russia. Born in 1821 at Tomashov, Poland, Pinsker became a prominent physician in Odessa (Ukraine). In 1882, he anonymously published a German-language pamphlet titled *Auto-Emancipation: An Admonition to His Brethren by a Russian Jew*, urging his kindred to orchestrate their own liberation. His essay concluded with the novel admonition, "Help yourself and God will help you!" For Pinsker, the motivating factor was the feeling of wounded honor. "To be plundered as a Jew, or to be protected as a Jew," he wrote, "is equally shameful and equally painful for the human feelings of the Jew."[27] Pinsker was elected president of the Hovevei Zion in 1884.

The consummate physician, Pinsker was able to skillfully diagnose the pandemic of anti-Semitism. His analysis begins: "The essence of the problem, as we see it, consists in the fact that, in the midst of the nations among whom the Jews reside, they form a heterogeneous element which cannot be assimilated, which cannot be readily digested by any nation."[28] He then explains how and why Jews are different from every other race on earth: "The Jewish people have no fatherland of their own…they have no rallying point, no center of gravity, no government of their own, no accredited representatives. They are everywhere in evidence, and nowhere at home. The nations have *never* to deal with a Jewish *nation*, but always with mere *Jews*."[29] However, it was Pinsker's uncanny perspective on the psychological cause of "Judeophobia" that proved most unnerving to his readers; that Jewry, as a "Diaspora nation," could neither live nor die, and thus—like a ubiquitous apparition—engendered trepidation in the Gentile heart:

> Among the living nations of the earth the Jews occupy the position of a nation long since dead. With the loss of their fatherland, the Jewish people lost their independence, and fell into a decay which is not compatible with existence as an integral, living organism. The state, crushed under the weight of the Roman rule, disappeared from before the eyes of the nations. But after the Jewish people had given up their existence as an actual state, as a political entity, they could nevertheless not succumb to total destruction—they did not cease to exist spiritually as a nation. The world saw in this people the uncanny form of one of the dead walking among the living. This ghostlike apparition of a people without unity or organization, without land or other bond of union, no longer alive…yet moving about among the living—this strange form, hardly paralleled in history, unlike anything that preceded or followed it, could not fail to make a strange, peculiar impression upon the imagination of the peoples. And, if the fear of ghosts is something innate, and has a certain justification in the psychic life of humanity, what wonder that it asserted itself powerfully at the sight of this dead and yet living nation?

> Fear of the Jewish ghost has been handed down and strengthened for generations and centuries. It led to a prejudice which, in its turn...opened the way for Judeophobia...As a psychic disorder it is hereditary, and as a disease transmitted for two thousand years it is incurable. It is the fear of ghosts which, as the mother of Judeophobia, has evoked that abstract, I might say Platonic hatred, thanks to which the whole Jewish nation is wont to be held responsible for the real or supposed sins of its individual members, and to be slandered in so many ways, to be buffeted about so shamefully.[30]

The author then notes the sad reality that Jewrys' unique status of "statelessness" makes any permanent acceptance virtually impossible:

> No people, generally speaking, has any predilection for foreigners... The foreigner has no need to *be*, or *seem* to *be*, a patriot. But as for the Jew, not only is he not a native in his own home country, but he is also not a foreigner; he is, in very truth, the stranger *par excellence.* He is regarded as neither friend nor foe, but as a stranger, of whom the only thing known is that he has no home. People do not care to *confide* in the foreigner, or to *trust* the Jew. The foreigner claims hospitality, which he can repay in the same coin. The Jew can make no such return; consequently he can make no claim to hospitality. He is not a guest, much less a welcome guest. He is more like a beggar; and what beggar is welcome? He is rather a refugee...The Jews are aliens who can have no representatives, because they have no fatherland. Because they have none, because their home has no boundaries behind which they can entrench themselves, their misery also has no bounds. The *general law* does not apply to the Jews, as strangers in the sense of the word. On the other hand, there are everywhere *laws for the Jews*...To sum up what has been said, for the living, the Jew is a dead man, for the natives an alien and a vagrant, for property-holders a beggar, for the poor an exploiter and a millionaire, for patriots a man without a country, for all classes a hated rival.[31]

Dr. Pinsker concludes his exam with the foreboding prognosis that without a state of their own (whether in Palestine or elsewhere), the Jews are doomed to maintain their unique perpetual exile: "The tragic feature of our history is that we can never die nor live. We are not able to die despite the blows of our enemies, and we do not wish to die by our own hand, through apostasy or self-destruction. Neither can we live; our enemies look well to that."[32] He then directs his patients to the only sure remedy he knows—moving beyond their idealistic contentment as the self-perceived "index finger of humanity."[33]

> Therefore we must abandon the delusive idea that we are fulfilling by our dispersion a Providential mission, a mission in which no one believes, an honorable station which we, to speak frankly, would gladly resign, if the odious epithet 'Jew' could only be blotted out of the memory of man. We must seek our honor and our salvation not in illusory self-deceptions, but in the restoration of a national bond of union.[34]

The burden he carried is manifest in his final appeal:

> In the life of peoples, as in the life of individuals, there are important moments which do not often recur, and which, according as they are utilized or not utilized, exercise a decisive influence upon the future of the people...whether for weal or for woe. We are now passing through such a moment. The consciousness of the people is awake. The great ideas of the eighteenth and nineteenth centuries have not passed by our people without leaving a trace. We feel not only as Jews; we feel as men. As men, we, too, would fain live and be a nation like the others. And if we seriously desire that, we must first of all extricate ourselves from the old yoke, and rise manfully to our full height. We must first of all *desire to help ourselves*...Only then will the help of others as well be sure to come...Let "Now or never!" be our watch word. Woe to our descendants, woe to the memory of our Jewish contemporaries, if we let this moment pass by...The proper, the only remedy, would be the creation of a Jewish nationality, of a people living upon its own soil, the auto-emancipation of the Jews; their emancipation as a nation among nations by the acquisition of a home of their own...Help yourselves, and God will help you![35]

Apart from texts like I Thessalonians 2:14-16, which evoke Jewish contrariety with God's chastisement, Christians can relate to Pinsker's analogy of Jewry as an eerie ghost ship, drifting aimlessly upon the seas. While Herod said of Jesus, *"This is John the Baptist...risen from the dead,"* the world fears the Church for emanating the convicting "ghost of Christ," as in the blessed "Holy Ghost"—the Saviour having promised His disciples on the eve of His passion, *"And I will pray the Father, and he shall give you another Comforter...Even the Spirit of truth...and shall be in you. I will not leave you comfortless:* I WILL COME TO YOU.*"* (Matthew 14:2; John 14:16-18)

However, as previously noted, the Laodicean Age has rendered its own class of dense anti-Semites. In his joke book, *Christianity and Rabbinic Judaism*, Jonas Alexis betrays himself as either ignorant of Pinsker's thesis or too ignorant to grasp its plausibility. In an attempt to account for the universal hatred of Jews, Alexis smugly quotes nineteenth-century author, Bernard Lazare, an assimilated French Jew:

> If this hostility, this repugnance had been shown toward the Jews at one time or in one country only, it would be easy to account for the local causes of this sentiment. But this race has been the object of hatred with all the nations amidst whom it ever settled. Inasmuch as the enemies of the Jews belonged to diverse races; as they dwelled far apart from one another, were ruled by different laws and governed by opposite principles; as they had not the same customs and differed in spirit from one another, so that they could not possibly judge alike of any subject, it must needs be that the general causes of antisemitism have always resided in Israel itself, and not in those who antagonized it."[36]

Regarding the subject of "ghosts," Alexis would do well to read Job 4:12-21. With Job as a major type of the Jew in the Tribulation, his "friend," Eliphaz—like Jonas Alexis—steps up to "kick a good man when he's down," though not before having a *really* bad dream: *"Now a thing was secretly brought to me...In thoughts from the visions of the night, when deep sleep falleth on men, Fear came upon me, and trembling, which made all my bones to shake. Then a* SPIRIT *passed before my face; the hair of my flesh stood up."* With the Lord having anticipated the assault on Job's failings, the "spirit" (undoubtedly an angel as per Hebrews 1:7) reminds the Temanite that all mortals (including him) *"dwell in houses of clay, whose foundation is in the dust."* Like Alexis, the message sailed right over his head. The Pharisee (in any Age) is incapable of comprehending, much less caring, that lost men *"are destroyed from morning to evening:* [and] *they perish* FOR EVER *without any regarding it."*

On a final note, the Bible gives its own reason as to why the Jew continues to engender "Judeophobia" in Gentile hearts—even after attaining statehood. As Proverbs 20:6 says, *"Most men will proclaim everyone his own goodness,"* the phenomenon of global anti-Semitism serves as a major embarrassing object lesson to the utter depravity of man. Adolf Hitler's surreal demonstration of "man's inhumanity to man" was the twentieth-century adaptation of Protagoras' fifth-century BC appraisal that "Man is the measure of all things." And yet, having failed to "grudge that small niche" in 1948—without a recurring US veto at the UN—the "Community of Nations" would gladly enable the Palestinian Authority to "drive the Jews into the sea."

The hypocrisy documented in this book corroborates the divine indictment of humanity in Romans 3:12—*"there is none that doeth good, no, not one."* (Jewish readers are referred to Isaiah 64:6, *"But we are all as an unclean thing, and all our righteousnesses are as filthy rags."*) The modern allurement of Middle East oil only amplifies the truth in I Timothy 6:10, *"For the love of money is the root of all evil...."* Thus, from the Diaspora through the Holocaust to Islamic terror in the nuclear age, things remain as Psalm 39:5 says—"EVERY MAN AT HIS BEST STATE IS ALTOGETHER VANITY."

4

Theodor Herzl

"That Herzl looks altogether like a prophet,
like a leader of his people."
(Sultan Abdul-Hamid II)

"Why is it that the best must always fall?
It is because they give to the last ounce of their
strength, and beyond, that they are the best."
(Theodor Herzl)

"In Basle I created the Jewish State. Were I to say this
aloud I would be greeted by universal laughter. But
perhaps five years hence, in any case, certainly fifty
years hence, everyone will perceive it."
(Theodor Herzl, September 1897)

THE MAN REVERED as *Hozeh HaMedinah* ("Visionary of the State") was born on May 2, 1860, in the future co-capital of the Austro-Hungarian Empire. As if to preview his life's work of reconnecting a dislocated people to their land, Theodor Herzl was actually born in the city of "Pest"—thirteen years before its historic linkage with "Buda." His father, Jakob, was director of the Hungaria Bank; his mother, Jeanette, the daughter of a wealthy textile merchant. A prodigy by age five, Theodor learned to read and write after only two weeks of private tutoring.[1] By age nine, he was dreaming about digging a canal across the Isthmus of Panama. His immediate cultural surroundings reflected the prevailing German-Jewish Enlightenment. As wealthy assimilated Jews, the family "neglected" much of their heritage (Herzl's thirteenth birthday was celebrated as a "Confirmation" rather than a traditional Bar Mitzvah).

At the pliable age of seven, Theodor had a stressful experience while attending a Jewish preparatory school. His first exposure to the Biblical account of the Exodus had made a profound impression on his soul. However, when his teacher covered the subject, his indifferent manner betrayed his own disbelief. The child naturally concluded that it was just a nice fairytale. Yet, when Herzl failed to recall the details in a quiz, he received the prescribed "thrashing." He later recalled, "Nowadays many a schoolmaster would like to cane me for remembering that Exodus rather too well."[2] However, the lad was not without a compensating influence. His grandfather, Simon Herzl, was a zealous disciple of Yehuda ben Solomon Hai Alkalai, an acclaimed Sephardic rabbi in Zemun and a major "pre-Herzlian" Zionist.

In 1878, the family moved to Vienna where Herzl entered the University of Vienna, earning a doctor of law degree in 1884. Confronted by a resurgence of anti-Semitism, Herzl resolved to find a scientific explanation for the malady. He began by reading *The Jewish Problem as a Problem of Race, Morals and Culture* by German philosopher Eugen K. Dühring. Herzl was stunned. According to Dühring, Jews were totally worthless, yet "somehow" remained a threat to all. The only solution was an end to the historic emancipation and "a return to the ghetto." Herzl noted in his diary, "An infamous book...If Dühring, who unites so much undeniable intelligence with so much universality of knowledge, can write like this, what are we to expect from the ignorant masses?"[3] In answer to his later reminiscing, "When was it I began to occupy myself with the Jewish question?" Herzl wrote, "Certainly ever since I read Dühring's book."[4]

Herzl joined the German nationalist fraternity *Burschenschaft Albia*, espousing the motto, "*Ehre, Freiheit, Vaterland*" ("Honor, Freedom, Fatherland"). Following the prescribed custom, every member received a new name. A glimpse into Herzl's Jewish awakening may be discerned from his sobriquet—"Tancred, the hero of the first crusade immortalized by [the Italian poet] Tasso as the conqueror of Jerusalem."[5] Herzl's inevitable break with the brotherhood occurred when the members openly supported Herrmann Bahr, a student known for his anti-Semitic rhetoric. While the *Albia* expressed outrage at his resignation, "Tancred" would later recall sardonically, "And so I said farewell to those gallant young fellows."[6]

Through the hectic year of 1884, Herzl received his doctorate in May, joined the Vienna Bar in July, and began his government law practice in August. The pace would only quicken in the years that remained (a mere twenty to be exact). While in college Herzl pursued his first love of writing, specifically, novels, comedies, and dramas. (His personal diary, comprising eighteen handwritten volumes averaging 280 pages each, resides in the Central Zionist Archives in Jerusalem). Gustave Flaubert's dictum depicting literature as "the mystique of those who believe in nothing," held a telling relevance for the many aspiring authors of acculturated Jewry who sought escape from the religious oracles of their elders. Thus, after only a year of composing legal briefs, Herzl quit to become a fulltime playwright, pursuing the *feuilleton* style (short literary essays; light, witty fiction).

In 1889, Herzl married Julie Naschauer, daughter of an affluent Hungarian industrialist. The union produced two girls and a boy. Herzl adored his children, often expressing himself in feuilletons ("The Empty Nursery," "Little Trude's Tears"). "Children are our greatest teachers," he wrote after the birth of his son, Hans. "This little one has given me a tangible, sensuous love of life, for he is my son, my never-ending continuation, the guarantee that I shall forever inherit the earth, forever renewed as my son, my grandson, forever young, forever beautiful and forever strong."[7] Herzl "felt" that strength, proudly recording that Hans, "on his first day pulled my beard so hard it hurt."[8]

The added financial strain of a young family led Herzl to employ his pen in fulltime journalism. Having briefly worked for the *Berliner Tageblatt* and *Wiener Allgemeine Zeitung*, the thirty-one-year-old novice reporter took the prestigious post of Paris correspondent for the *Neue Freie Presse*, the key paper of the Austro-Hungarian Empire. In an early feuilleton, Herzl related a pathetic scene he had viewed at the healing line in Lourdes, France. An elderly Catholic man with failing vision was sprinkling "holy water" between his eyelids—but alas—to no avail. "He tried the same thing a couple of times. Then he gave it up. And as he went away, he heaved a deep and bitter sigh. *He sighed like a Jew!*"[9] Though living the good life of "goyish Jewry," Herzl could not escape his visceral awareness of that distinctive sigh—*"and the children of Israel sighed by reason of the bondage."* (Exodus 2:23)

Herzl's Paris interlude would render five unique incentives for his life's work. First, he was able to view the rise of French anti-Semitism "up close and personal." Of special significance were the anti-Semitic cartoons that appeared weekly in the press, drawn by respected artists like Henri de Toulouse-Lautrec and Caran d'Ache.[10] The experience proved especially ominous given that France had been the center of the Enlightenment. Such disturbing observations led to Herzl's second encounter, occurring in January 1893. Upon receiving an invitation to support the Society to Combat Anti-Semitism in Vienna, Herzl had declined, stating all the philosophical reasons consistent with his assimilationist tradition. This rebuff sparked a heated correspondence between the young reporter and the powerful Jewish industrialist, Baron Friedrich Leitenberger. After enduring all of Herzl's "theories" (twenty-two pages worth), the activist Baron pressed his opponent with a single, stinging rejoinder—"What do you propose to do?"[11] The novel challenge to actually "do" something struck a nerve.

His initial reaction was to start a radical daily to expose anti-Semitism through the power of the printed page. However, subsequent events confirmed a premature timing (particularly the predictable recoil of the *Neue Freie Presse*). Yet, despite the shelved opportunity, the effort had energized Herzl's focus. Though restricted from writing about anti-Semitism, he was certainly free to study the phenomenon. This aroused appetite led to Herzl's third turning point, a thorough review of the lead book that had so inflamed the French against his native people—Édouard Adolphe Drumont's 1886 *La France Juive* (*Jewish France*). Drumont was also the founder of the Antisemitic League of France and the founder/editor of the anti-Semitic newspaper, *La Libre Parole* (*The Free Word*). His thesis mirrored Dühring's—as Jewry constituted "a nation within a nation" dedicated to the destruction of the Christian middle class, their emancipation must be revoked. While *La France Juive* would eventually reach 200 editions, thinking people remained at a loss as to how 40,000 Jews could manipulate a "mere" 37,000,000 Frenchmen. Herzl wrote in June 1895, "I have Drumont to thank for much of the freedom of my present conception of the Jewish question."[12] Yet, he also remained conscious of a superintending providence at work, acknowledging that same month, "Just how I got from the fictional to the practical ideas is already a mystery to me…It all transpired in the unconscious."[13]

The fourth stage in Herzl's metamorphosis occurred on October 19, 1894, at a most inauspicious venue, the Paris studio of Samuel Beer, the famous Jewish sculptor. Beer wanted to make a bust of Herzl, owing to his "noble head and striking features." The focus soon turned to the Jewish question and the rise of anti-Semitism in their hometown of Vienna. "We talked about the fact that it did the Jews no good to become artists and to liberate themselves from the money taint. The curse still sticks to them. We cannot break out of the ghetto."[14]

It was at this time that Herzl experienced the artistic epiphany that would alter his life forever. Before he could walk home, an entire play had formed in his mind; a mere seventeen days later, *The Ghetto* was done (later named *The New Ghetto.*) The plot was an autobiographical tragedy with Herzl's assimilated character dying at the end, a victim of Judeophobia. His parting words were, "Jews, my brothers, they won't let you live until you learn to die...I want out—out of the ghetto!" Though it would be three years before the play was produced, once again, Herzl found himself under an unshakable burden, writing, "The thought that I had to do something for the Jews gripped me ever more forcefully."[15] The Hungarian-born, cosmopolitan, *fin-de-siecle* "Jew" finally came to see that assimilation was a misnomer, for, as he would now say, if enough Jews converted, the anti-Semites would simply change their slurs from "dirty Jew" to "dirty convert."[16]

THE DREYFUS AFFAIR

Herzl's last jolt of Parisian "inspiration" was the 1894 Dreyfus Affair. Alfred Dreyfus was the quintessential assimilated Jew—one who had left his odious heritage in the ghetto, rising to the esteemed rank of captain in the French Army, only to show that *"the last state of that man is worse than the first."* (Luke 11:26) After papers found in the wastebasket of a German military attaché made it *appear* that a French officer was passing intel to the Kaiser, Dreyfus became the immediate suspect. Though later cleared of all charges, being pardoned by the French president himself, Dreyfus had, as a "Jew," performed his greater, traditional duty—serve as a convenient scapegoat whenever and wherever needed. Herzl transports his readers to that emotional scene on January 5, 1895, in the inner courtyard of the *École Militaire*:

> At nine o'clock the great open court was filled with a detachment of troops in square formation: five thousand men in all. In the centre a general sat on horseback. A few minutes after nine Dreyfus

> was led forth...dressed in his captain's uniform. Four men conducted him before the general. The latter said, 'Alfred Dreyfus, you are unworthy to bear arms. In the name of the French Republic I degrade you from your rank. Let the sentence be carried out.' Here Dreyfus lifted his right arm and called out: 'I declare and solemnly swear that you are degrading an innocent man. *Vive la France!*' At that instant the drums were beaten. The officer in charge began to tear from the condemned man's uniform the buttons and cords, which had already been loosened. Dreyfus retained his calm bearing.[17]

After running a gauntlet of his former comrades shouting, "Judas! Traitor!" Alfred Dreyfus, the civilian, was handcuffed and remanded into the custody of the gendarmes. He was then taken to Devil's Island, the notorious penal colony in Guyana, to begin his life sentence in solitary confinement. Some, like Jonas Alexis, naively deny that anti-Semitism was the motive behind the accusation.[18] Though a Zionist in name only who was following the trial as a reporter, Herzl discerned that the degradation of Captain Dreyfus was really a vicarious attack on Jewry as a whole. Dreyfus would merely represent them on Devil's Island—until more "efficient" means could render a *permanent* "solution" to the Jewish question. Herzl wrote in 1899:

> The Dreyfus case embodies more than a judicial error; it embodies the desire of the vast majority of the French to condemn a Jew, and to condemn all Jews in this one Jew. Death to the Jews! howled the mob, as the decorations were being ripped from the captain's coat...Where? In France. In republican, modern, civilized France, a hundred years after the Declaration of the Rights of Man. The French people, or at any rate the greater part of the French...does not want to extend the rights of man to Jews. The edict of the great Revolution has been revoked...Until that time most of us believed that the solution of the Jewish question was to be patiently waited for as part of the general development of mankind. But when a people which in every other respect is so progressive and so highly civilized can take such a turn, what are we to expect from other peoples, which have not even attained the level which France attained a hundred years ago?[19]

Dreyfus had to wait five years for his pardon, and another seven to be exonerated by a military commission. Two years later (1908), while attending a memorial service for a friend, he sustained a gunshot wound to the arm in a foiled assassination attempt. Having taken early retirement due to health issues sustained in prison, the middle-aged patriot returned to active duty on the eve of World War I, surviving frontline action at both Verdun and Aisne (1,000,000 casualties). In November 1918—nearly a quarter century after losing his "buttons and cords"—Lieutenant Colonel Alfred Dreyfus received the *Officier de la Légion d'honneur*, France's highest decoration. He died in Paris (age 75), on July 12, 1935—twenty-nine years to the day of his formal acquittal. On September 13, 1995, a century after the trial, the French military officially acknowledged that Dreyfus had indeed been framed.[20]

En passant, on December 13, 2011, four years before the "Palestine State" flag flew at the UN in New York, it was unfurled at UNESCO, their *Paris*-based organ for education, science, and culture, the French capital teeming with the largest Muslim population in Europe. On November 13, 2015, two days after the EU voted to label Israeli settlement goods, 6 Muslims killed 129 people in the "City of Lights," *chasing President Hollande out of his soccer stadium in the process*.

DER JUDENSTAAT

Herzl would later declare that "the Dreyfus trial…which I witnessed in Paris in 1894, made me a Zionist."[21] Six months after the trial he dispatched a letter to the German-Jewish banker and philanthropist Baron Moritz de Hirsch, one of the wealthiest men alive. The following words of his first paragraph constitute the opening scene of his brief but monumental intervention on behalf of the Jewish people:

> Honored Sir:
>
> When may I have the privilege of visiting you? I wish to discuss the Jewish problem with you. It is not a question of an interview, still less a direct or indirect money matter. I want to discuss with you a Jewish political plan the effects of which will perhaps extend to days when you and I are no longer here.[22]

The key phrase in his opening salvo are the words "Jewish political plan." Till then, the geopolitical notion of a Jewish state was totally foreign to all colonizing strategy. Altruists like Hirsch and Rothschild had shown themselves willing to aid suppressed Jews by underwriting relief settlements in various nations, but always under the prevailing sovereign power. While Hirsch had founded the Jewish Colonization Association to transfer Russian Jews to settlements *in* Argentina, Rothschild's communities likewise existed *in* Ottoman Palestine.

Herzl gained the desired audience in Paris a week later but his fractious host hindered him from articulating his prepared remarks. As with all reform efforts, Herzl was willing to rock the boat alone, while Hirsch was unwilling to face reality; i.e., that the status quo amounted to kicking the proverbial can down the road—the building of a "nation" without a clear title to the "lot" being an exercise in futility. According to Herzl's notes, without radical change the problem would stay the same for all Jews, whether clinging to assimilation or trying infiltration (mere "squatters' rights" colonies lacking legal status):

> You are pariahs! You must forever tremble at the thought that you are about to be deprived of your rights and stripped of your possessions. You will be insulted when you walk in the street. If you are poor, you suffer doubly. If you are rich, you must conceal the fact. You are not admitted to any honorable calling, and if you deal in money you are made the special focus of contempt...The situation will not change for the better, but rather for the worse...There is only one way out: into the promised land.[23]

From his childhood memory of Moses and the Exodus, Herzl understood that the critical prerequisite to any future statehood was a cultural transformation inspired by political leadership. "Throughout the two thousand years of our dispersion we have lacked unified political leadership. I consider this our greatest misfortune. It has done us more harm than all the persecutions. It is this that is responsible for our inner decay...If we only had a unified political leadership...we could initiate the solution of the Jewish question."[24]

For all his efforts, Herzl was branded an unstable visionary, especially by the philanthropic organs of Jewry who insisted on gradual immigration and colonization without legal guarantees. However, the spark of an "idea" had been lit in his soul. "No individual is strong enough or rich enough to transfer a people from one place of residence to another," he wrote, "Only an idea can do it."[25] After his meeting with Hirsch, Herzl began a diary entitled *The Jewish Question*. The opening paragraph reads:

> I have been occupied for some time past with a work which is of immeasurable greatness. I cannot tell to-day whether I shall bring it to a close. It has the appearance of a gigantic dream. But for days and weeks it has filled me, saturated even my subconsciousness; it accompanies me wherever I go, broods above my ordinary daily conversations, looks over my shoulder at my petty, comical journalistic work, disturbs me and intoxicates me. What it will lead to it is impossible to surmise as yet. But my experience tells me that it is something marvelous, even as a dream, and that I should write it down.[26]

Unbeknown to the "stock-exchange Jews," largesse was the *last* thing Herzl wanted, stating that "philanthropy debases the character of our people."[27] For him, the pressing need was a revival of personal character and self respect. "Will they understand the call to freedom and to manhood?" he asks.[28] The inherent power of an ethnoscape would provide the ultimate stimulus: "The Promised Land, where we can have hooked noses, black or red beards, and bow legs, without being despised for it. Where we can live at last as free men on our own soil, and where we can die peacefully in our own fatherland."[29]

Because the Zionist movement was gargantuan in scope, it could only develop in stages. While Eretz Yisrael would ultimately become the only viable "homeland of choice," other regions were initially considered, such as Argentina, Canada, Cyprus, Mesopotamia, Uganda, even Texas. (The Galveston Immigration Scheme imported 10,000 Jews to Texas between 1906 and 1914.[30]) However, one point was never open for debate—that the future ingathering would be sanctioned on a firm legal basis. In Herzl's mind, it could be nothing short of a Judenstaat ("Jewish State").

Having alluded to the "Jewish question" in *The New Ghetto*, Herzl would now pen his magnum opus. Originally forming a sixty-five-page section of his diary, entitled "Address to the Rothschilds," an edited version was published by a Vienna printer in February 1896 under the heading *Der Judenstaat*. (A small English edition appeared in London with the longer title, *The Jewish State, An Attempt at a Modern Solution of the Jewish Question*.) The author's focus offered a detailed plan for mass transport of Jews to Palestine. The Preface begins by humbly acknowledging that Zionism is as old as the Diaspora itself: "The idea which I have developed in this pamphlet is a very old one: it is the restoration of the Jewish State. The world resounds with outcries against the Jews, and these outcries have awakened the slumbering idea." Dividing the work between the passionate and the practical, Herzl explains why the Jews need a State and how to attain one:

> The Jewish question exists wherever Jews live in perceptible numbers. Where it does not exist, it is carried by Jews in the course of their migrations. We naturally move to those places where we are not persecuted, and there our presence produces persecution...I think the Jewish question is no more a social than a religious one, notwithstanding that it sometimes takes these and other forms. It is a national question, which can only be solved by making it a political world-question to be discussed and settled by the civilized nations of the world in council. We are a people, one people...We have honestly endeavored everywhere to merge ourselves in the social life of surrounding communities and to preserve...the faith of our fathers. We are not permitted to do so.
>
> In vain are we loyal patriots, our loyalty in some places running to extremes; in vain do we make the same sacrifices of life and property as our fellow-citizens; in vain do we strive to increase the fame of our native land in science and art, or her wealth by trade and commerce. In countries where we have lived for centuries we are still cried down as strangers, and often by those whose ancestors were not yet domiciled in the land where Jews had already made experience of suffering. The majority may decide which are the strangers; for this, as indeed every point which arises in the relations between nations, is a question of might...In the world as it now is...might precedes right. It is useless, therefore, for us to be loyal patriots...If we could only be left in peace...But I think we shall not be left in peace.[31]

As for particulars, Herzl explains, "Let the sovereignty be granted us over a portion of the globe large enough to satisfy the rightful requirements of a nation; the rest we shall manage for ourselves." He then proposes two agencies to facilitate the plan: "The Society of Jews will do the preparatory work in the domains of science and politics, which the Jewish Company will afterwards practically apply. The Jewish Company will see to the realization of the business interests of departing Jews, and will organize commerce and trade in the new country."[32] The booklet goes on to address a myriad of pertinent issues:

constitutional matters, jurisprudence, political philosophy, agriculture, land purchases, town grids, buildings, labor issues, banking and finance, securities, methods for raising capital, non-transferable goods, promotion of industries, transmigration and group migration, language, rabbis, theocracy restrictions, military power, reciprocity and extradition treaties, even details for a flag. Herzl closes with a psychological appeal to regain a "territorialization of memory":

> I believe that a wondrous generation of Jews will spring into existence. The Maccabeans will rise again. Let me repeat once more my opening words: The Jews who wish will have their State. We shall live at last as free men on our own soil, and die peacefully in our own homes. The world will be freed by our liberty, enriched by our wealth, magnified by our greatness. And whatever we attempt there to accomplish for our own welfare, will react powerfully and beneficently for the good of humanity.[33]

UTILIZING THE JUDENNOT

On April 20, 1895, having swallowed his pride, Herzl decided to send Hirsch a draft copy of *Der Judenstaat*. However, the Baron died that very day. "What a strange coincidence," he noted in his diary, "his death is a loss to the Jewish cause."[34] The less-than-enthusiastic support he was receiving from rank and file Jewry in Vienna and Paris only added to his consternation. Thus, on the timely suggestion of Max Nordau (his closest advisor and future premier administrator), Herzl resolved to test the waters in London. With the aid of Nordau's "Rolodex," a number of important contacts were made.

His initial sponsor was Israel Zangwill, a well-connected journalist and faithful Zionist. Another key endorsement came from Colonel Albert Goldsmid, British Director of Hovevei Zion and founder of the London-based Maccabeans Club. After hearing Herzl's plans he said, "That is the idea of my life."[35] On November 24, 1895, Herzl gave the keynote address for The Maccabeans, representing the first group of any size to hear his Zionist vision. He received a resounding applause and was made an honorary member of the prestigious Jewish society.

Asher Myers, Editor of *The Jewish Chronicle* (the oldest and most widely read Jewish newspaper), was so impressed that he printed an extensive preview four weeks before *Der Judenstaat* was released. Herzl then met with Chief Rabbi Hermann Adler who introduced him to Sir Samuel Montagu, an Orthodox Jewish banker, philanthropist, and Parliament member. Montagu, in turn, endorsed his work to Prime Minister William Gladstone. A timely encounter with Alfred Austin, Poet Laureate of England, resulted in another referral to Gladstone's successor, Robert Gascoyne-Cecil, Marquess of Salisbury. William Hechler, the eccentric Anglican chaplain to the British Embassy in Vienna, learned about Herzl from the Zionist journalist, Saul Landau. Having tutored the now-deceased son of Friedrich I, Grand Duke of Baden, Hechler was able to introduce Herzl to his former patron, who became the first ruling prince to publicly support Zionism. The Grand Duke arranged for Herzl to have a private audience with his nephew, Kaiser Wilhelm II, Emperor of Germany. The apex of these diplomatic missions would occur on May 17, 1901, when Herzl would be ushered into the Yildiz Palace at Istanbul to confer with His Imperial Majesty Abdul-Hamid II, 34th Padishah (Sultan) of the Ottoman Caliphate.

Though not all of the liaisons produced substantive results, the fact that high-profile doors were continuing to open gave Herzl needed credibility. Ironically, the one elusive endorsement, Baron Edmond de Rothschild—the "prize" that everyone viewed as paramount—turned out to be a blessing in disguise. The two finally met in Paris on July 18, 1896. Rothschild should have been receptive as Herzl had the wind at his back. Only five days earlier, a delirious throng of thousands cheered him at the Workingmen's Club in Whitechapel, the heart of eastern European Jewry. While biographer Ernst Pawel called the rally a "turning point" for having "provided the inchoate movement with one of the most effective leaders in modern history," Jakob de Haas described Herzl as "changed into the spear head of a phalanx rebelling against the existing Jewish communal organization."[36] Herzl mused, "I experienced some strange sensations. I saw and heard my legend being born. The people are sentimental; the masses do not see clearly…A light mist is beginning to rise all about me, which may condense into a cloud in which I shall walk…I inwardly made a firm vow to become ever more worthy of their trust and their love."[37] (Unlike T. E. Lawrence, Herzl's "legend" was built on substance.)

Edmond de Rothschild was unmoved. Pawel notes that following their introduction, "Things went rapidly downhill from there."[38] When Rothschild declined Herzl's gracious request to lead the fledgling movement himself, something finally snapped. Dr. Alex Bein, former Director of the Central Zionist Archives, states in his definitive biography, *Theodore Herzl*: "It was a historic decision. By his refusal Rothschild assumed at least as definite a responsibility as he would have done by an acceptance...Rothschild's refusal, which carried with it the refusal of the Hirsch Fund and of the leading London Jews, put an end to the hope that the enterprise might be directed from above."[39] Three days later Herzl told his aide, Jakob de Haas, "There is only one reply to this situation: let us organize our masses immediately."[40]

Though Pawel mentions, "[A]fter the Balfour Declaration, Edmond de Rothschild is said to have admitted that 'Herzl was right and I was wrong,'"[41] the Baron's hesitation became the unforeseen catalyst for Herzl's greatest feat. The following week he wrote another aide, "The day after tomorrow I shall be in Vienna and will call our chief men together for a conference...the first point will be the early convening of a Zionist Congress...My answer to Rothschild is, begin organizing at once."[42] Bein rightly concludes, "the breaking up of negotiations with Rothschild may be designated as the beginning of the new Zionist movement."[43] The Judenstaat would be gained by utilizing "the *Judennot*—the misery of the Jews—which Herzl compared to a head of steam that would drive the engine he had designed."[44]

Herzl began by creating the "Actions Committee," the genesis cell of the new body. As David's fledgling kingdom began in a cave with a handful of Jews who were *"in distress...debt...and discontented"* (I Samuel 22:2), the legal foundation for modern Israel can be traced to a small cadre of faithful early Zionists: "[T]he physician Dr. Schnirer, the lawyer Dr. Kokesch, two engineers Kremenezky and Seidener, the Galician Shakesperian scholar Leon Kellner, Herzl's relative Löbl, the stockbroker from Semlin, and a few others...gathered every Tuesday evening."[45] It was fitting that Dr. Johann Kremenezky, holder of five US patents, had pioneered the electrification of Vienna, for, as the "light" issued forth from that city, other cells began illuminating World Jewry. In his "spare time," Herzl also started a weekly paper to promote these vital developments, naming it *Die Welt* ("The World").

FIRST ZIONIST CONGRESS

At last, the First Zionist Congress was set for August 29-31, 1897, in Basel, Switzerland. It would represent a symbolic parliament for those with Zionist aspirations; a phenomenal display of solidarity. The goal was to showcase the solution to the Jewish problem before the world.

As with Moses, Herzl faced a torrent of unanticipated criticism for his "presumptuousness," *sighing* on October 13, 1896, "No help from anywhere, attacks from everywhere."[46] Many suddenly feared that support for a Judenstaat would impugn the loyalty of Jewish citizens in their countries. The Congress itself had been scheduled for Munich but local rabbinic enmity forced the embarrassing relocation to Basel. Some of his closest supporters questioned the wisdom of ordering such an epochal international conference with only a year to prepare.

Yet, Herzl resolved to press on, declaiming Zionism as "the Jewish people on the march."[47] He alone perceived his unique window of influence—*"for such a time as this."* (Esther 4:14) An example of this aura can be gleaned from an eyewitness account of another speech Herzl would make on October 3, 1898, at the B'nai Zion Association rally in London's Assembly Hall: "The souls of these people were in the hand of this man, and with the breath of his voice, which seldom rose above a low tone, he could do with them whatever he liked."[48]

He was also the only one aware that his *own* window was closing. Given the physical toll of the work, "following his heart" was more than a cliché. On February 12, 1897, Herzl composed a literary testament, noting: "It is proper to be prepared for the end...What I was for the Jews the future generations will judge better than the contemporaneous masses...My name will grow after my death...I have never sold my pen...This last testament may be published."[49]

Though living on borrowed time, Herzl would see the fruit of his labor. On the opening day, some two hundred delegates assembled in the concert hall of the Basel Municipal Casino. They hailed from over twenty nations, including America, England, Russia, Scandinavia, Germany, Austria-Hungry, Holland, Bulgaria, Romania, Belgium, Algeria, and especially, Eretz Yisrael. A group of Christian Zionists, led by Reverend Hechler, was recognized as Dr. Herzl's personal guests. To mark the solemnity of the occasion, delegates were asked to dress appropriately (white tie, frock coat, etc.). Hundreds of letters and telegrams poured in from around the world. The main newspapers of the West were also represented. A huge sign displayed the phrase ZIONISTEN-KONGRESS. A white flag with two blue stripes (inspired by the Talith, the Jewish prayer shawl) and a large gold Star of David hung across the hall's entry, the genius of David Wolffsohn. (In the spirit of Betsy Ross, Lena Harris stitched the flag in the awning shop of her son, Morris, a New York City delegate.) Everyone could sense that an epic event was about to occur. Had not Herzl assured his devotees, "This Congress is to be the great council which must and will be followed by greater acts"?[50] The silence was deafening.

Three taps of the gavel convened the historic event. Dr. Karpel Lippe, dean of the Praesidium and eldest of the Romanian Hovevei Zion delegates, with head covered, uttered the *Shehecheyanu*, to the tears of many: "Blessed art Thou, O Lord our God, King of the Universe, who hast kept us alive and brought us to witness this day."[51] The first order of business was a motion that "a telegram of greeting" be sent to the Sultan of Turkey. Then—Herzl rose—sporting a long black beard and adorned in formal attire, he calmly approached the dais. What followed is described by an eyewitness, author Ben Ami:

> It was extraordinary! What had happened? This was not the Dr. Herzl I had seen hitherto, and with whom I was in discussion as recently as last night. Before us rose a marvelous and exalted figure, kingly in bearing and stature, with deep eyes in which could be read quiet majesty and unuttered sorrow. It is no longer the elegant Dr. Herzl of Vienna; it is a royal scion of the House of David, risen from among the dead, clothed in legend and fantasy and beauty. Everyone sat breathless, as if in the presence of a miracle. And in truth, was it not a miracle which we beheld? And then wild applause broke out; for fifteen minutes the delegates clapped, shouted and waved their handkerchiefs. The dream of two thousand years was on the point of realization; it was as if the Messiah, son of David, confronted us; and I was seized by an overpowering desire, in the midst of this storm of joy, to cry out, loudly, for all to hear: '*Yehi ha-melech!*' Hail to the King![52]

Of course, the Christians on hand (along with the Bible-believing Hovevei of today) would have experienced an overwhelming spirit of ambivalence, especially at such repulsive messianic sentiments. But then again, observing (and surviving) such raw emotion is a major requisite for understanding the true history of the State of Israel.

Herzl, ever the inimitable leader, maintained his composure throughout the ovation. When the applause finally subsided, he began his address by summarizing his life's work in a single, laconic statement: "We are here to lay the foundation stone of the house which is to shelter the Jewish nation." His message contained nothing new, apart from previous speeches and articles. He said that "the wonders of modern methods of communication" enabled Jews to unite in their opposition to renewed anti-Semitism. He encouraged Jewry to recapture its historic identity, "Zionism is the return of the Jews to Judaism even before their return to the Jewish land." The Congress would therefore devote itself to "the spiritual means of reviving and nursing the Jewish national consciousness." To combat their enduring stigma (epitomized by the fraudulent *Protocols of the Elders of Zion*), the Jew's true position would be exposed to all: "We Zionists seek, for the solution of the Jewish question, not an international society, but international discussion...We have nothing to do with conspiracy, secret intervention or indirect methods. We wish to put the question in the arena and under the control of free public opinion."[53]

His focal point was the need for a new modus operandi. While gratitude was shown for the initial agricultural sites in Argentina and Palestine, they were seen as "the opening, and not the closing words of the Zionist movement." Herzl believed that the old methods of slow colonization without legal sanction could never solve the Jewish dilemma. Though a myriad of philosophical differences existed among the delegates, Herzl set forth a single, non-negotiable plank: "The basis can be only that of recognized right, and not of sufferance. We have had our fill of experience with toleration and with the protected Jew. Our movement can be logical and consistent only in so far as it aims at the acquisition of a publicly recognized legal guarantee."[54]

Herzl ended his remarks with an appeal to unity. "And finally, it is the duty of this Congress to see to it that when its sessions have come to an end, we do not relapse into our previous condition of disorganization. We must create here and now an organ, a permanent organ, which the Jewish people has lacked till now."[55] That "organ" was adopted as the Zionist Organization (later, the World Zionist Organization/WZO) with Herzl as its first head. It was also decreed that the Congress would be "the chief organ of the Zionist movement."

The centrality of the Congress has come to be known as the "Basel Declaration." Under the title, "Zionism seeks to secure for the Jewish people a publicly recognized, legally secured home (or homeland) in Palestine for the Jewish people," the four main objectives follow:

> 1) The programmatic encouragement of the settlement of Palestine with Jewish agricultural workers, laborers and artisans;
> 2) The unification and organization of all Jewry into local and general groups in accordance with the laws of their respective countries;
> 3) The strengthening of Jewish self-awareness and national consciousness (*Volksbewusstsein*);
> 4) The preparation of activity for the obtaining of the consent of the various governments...for the fulfillment of...Zionism.[56]

The mood of the last day was stimulated by Basel Rabbi Arthur Cohn (a former Herzl opponent). Representing all orthodox branches, Cohn said that certain remarks had left him with an "unforgettable impression."[57] In the final moments, Dr. Max Mandelstamm (one of the oldest Zionists) requested the dais. After stating his gratitude to all who had attended the event, he shifted the focus to the "courageous man...primarily responsible for this gathering of Jews from all countries taking counsel on the future of our people."[58] As with Herzl's initial appearance, the crowd rose to its feet and issued a thunderous applause. Many stood on tables waving handkerchiefs. Thus, the first meeting of its kind in nearly twenty centuries of Jewish history—a gathering where representatives of Diaspora Jewry had met in a democratic body of their *own*—was gaveled to a close. As a final display of camaraderie, the delegates joined in singing "HaTikvah" ("The Hope"), the future national anthem of the State of Israel.[59]

BEYOND BASEL

On his return to Vienna, Herzl wrote, "If I were to sum up the Basle Congress in a single phrase—which I would not dare to make public—I would say: In Basle I created the Jewish State. Were I to say this aloud I would be greeted by universal laughter. But perhaps five years hence, in any case, certainly fifty years hence, everyone will perceive it."[60]

Fifty-one years later, the world would "perceive" that a flag modeled after Mrs. Harris's was flying over the nascent State of Israel!

However, in the afterglow of Basel, Herzl knew more than anyone that the *real* work had just begun, that same diary entry continuing, "The state exists as essence in the will-to-the-state of a people...The territory is only the concrete basis, and the state itself, with a territory beneath it, is still in the nature of an abstract thing...In Basle I created the abstraction which, as such, is invisible to the great majority."[61] With the sole, "visible" structure of the ZO in place, Herzl would focus on his two critical needs: a Zionist financial institution and legal recognition for the intended Jewish homeland. Though met with many obstacles, he nobly pledged, "At least I know myself; I shall go on until I am stretched out in death."[62] Herzl's resolve stemmed from his belief that the emergence of the delegates themselves had rendered "Der Judenstaat" a fait accompli. They need only perpetuate the reality, i.e., that a "Jewish nation" already existed: "In order to achieve the homeland secured by international law we must first present to the world the evidence of our existence as a people. If the people is there, then the piece of land which it needs comes of itself."[63]

The Second Congress, also in Basel, was attended by 349 delegates (half from Russia), plus 150 journalists. New faces included Herzl's father, Jakob, and a twenty-three-year-old chemistry student from Pinsk, Chaim Weizmann (his successor and Israel's first president). Though the outcome was deemed another successful milestone, further invigorating the Seder benediction, "Next year in Jerusalem," Herzl's quest to obtain a legal sponsor was proving most elusive. And yet, the strategy appeared elementary enough: The Turks were in possession of what the Jews wanted (Palestine); the Turks needed money; the Jews had plenty. By 1881, the phrase "Turkish debt" redounded in European politics. The consolidated figure of 106 million pounds sterling was an embarrassing albatross on the Ottoman Empire. Herzl believed that he could entice the Sultan by offering to restructure the debt (though he had yet to receive the necessary commitments from his Jewish lenders). But first, he would need a European guarantor.

HERZL MEETS THE KAISER

Of the two prevailing powers, England and Germany, Herzl chose the latter (German being the predominant culture of Western Jewry). Through the intercession of Frederick I, Herzl met with Kaiser Wilhelm II at Constantinople on October 17, 1898.

According to the Grand Duke, his uncle was supposedly open to Herzl's idea of a Jewish homeland in Palestine under a German Protectorate and was ready to discuss the matter with his Turkish ally. Having stopped in the Ottoman capital while en route to Palestine on a diplomatic mission of his own, Wilhelm had agreed to receive Herzl before meeting with the Sultan. The hour-long secret audience seemed to go well. In answer to the Kaiser's parting request "tell me in brief what you want me to ask of the Sultan," Herzl replied, "A Chartered Company—under German Protection."[64] The parties then agreed to meet again in Jerusalem two weeks hence. Herzl was ecstatic.

Dr. Herzl arrived in Jaffa harbor on October 26, 1898, for his first and only trip to Eretz Yisrael (a privilege even Moses was denied). The brief stay was packed with emotion and historical relevance. His first stop was the Mikveh Israel Agricultural School. He then toured the Rothschild settlement of Rishon LeZion. Other visits included Ness Ziona and Rehovot. Herzl's group was continually assailed by delirious youth, some weeping, others singing. Bein attributed the scene to "the halo which had gathered around the name of Herzl."[65]

On Friday afternoon, Herzl had an impromptu encounter with Wilhelm during his own stop at Mikveh Israel. The children's choir serenaded the Emperor and his massive entourage with the German Imperial anthem. Bein notes that Herzl "regarded it as a good omen for the forthcoming reception of the deputation."[66] Wilhelm's purpose for the "pilgrimage" was to dedicate the Lutheran Church of the Redeemer in Jerusalem and to visit German settlements. Upon his arrival, the Kaiser was met by a delegation of German Jews. Legend says that as Wilhelm surveyed the neglected, barren landscape, he wiped his brow and asked, "Why is there no shade?" When the Jews answered that they could not plant trees because the Arabs owned the land, the Kaiser said, "Whoever plants the trees will own the land."[67]

However, eclipsing the "omen" of the previous day, the real sign occurred as the Prussian King made his august entry into the Holy

City. Pawel writes, "[S]ince none of the seven gates in Suleiman's massive wall allowed enough clearance for a mounted rider, let alone one who insisted on wearing a spiked helmet, a fifty-foot section had been broken out of the battlements next to the Jaffa Gate to afford the imperial pilgrim access to the holy places without having to humble himself by getting off his horse."[68] What a contrast to Edmund Allenby's meek arrival on December 11, 1917, when the conquering general, an expert rider himself, dismounted *his* steed before that same gate to enter Jerusalem on foot. (Willie eventually did "get down off his high horse" when he abdicated his throne on November 9, 1918.)

Returning to Herzl's activities, upon the end of Shabbat, he toured the Old City with his own retinue. Bein writes "The oriental filth…left him depressed"; while at the Kotel he was robbed of a blessing by "the ugly, miserable, competing beggary." He mused at all the upgrades he could make by preserving the area solely for religious endeavors, creating "a glorious New Jerusalem" in the environs. Only after ascending the Tower of David was he relieved by the ascetic panorama of "the city covered with the first faint twilight of evening."[69]

The next morning, Herzl arrived at the palatial Imperial tent for his much-anticipated summit with the Kaiser. However, the chemistry he felt this time was far removed from the tone in Constantinople. His Excellency certainly "appeared" graceful enough, wearing a gray uniform, turban, and gray gloves. With a riding whip in one hand, he extended the other in a gesture of welcome; though that was about it. Not only was the session short and cool, but Wilhelm's remarks were noticeably noncommittal and obfuscating. To Herzl's appeal for the Jewish ethnoscape—"This is the land of our fathers"—the Kaiser merely replied, "What the land needs above all is water and shade."[70]

Herzl discerned that Wilhelm's approach at the State dinner must have gone south. Indeed, the German ambassador to Vienna would later recount that Abdul-Hamid had kiboshed the subject, leaving his "guest" no apt recourse, given the dictates of Oriental etiquette. In a letter to the Grand Duke of Baden, Herzl lamented, "I can only assume that a hope which was especially dear to me has faded away and that we shall not achieve our Zionist goal under a German protectorate. I am sorrier than I can tell you."[71] And yet, a second, undetected omen had once again pointed to Britain. The date of that failed Jerusalem meeting was November 2, the day on which the Balfour Declaration would be issued nineteen years later. However, before Herzl could cross the Channel, he would have to endure another diplomatic snub.

"NYET!"

Unwilling to give up on the one man who controlled Palestine, Herzl made an even greater leap of faith by asking Russia's Tsar to act as his unlikely interlocutor. Pawel states that "the whole Russian court, with the possible exception of the Archduke Vladimir, regarded Jews as less than human."[72] After some surprising early progress (facilitated by his old ally, the grand duke), Herzl's quixotic request for an audience with Nicholas II dissipated in the fall of 1899. Though the Russians would show renewed interest in 1903, for now the Jews' use of St. Petersburg as an "antechamber to the Holy Land" was a big—"*Nyet!*"

"ENGLAND THE GREAT, ENGLAND THE FREE"

Remaining in Basel, the Third Congress rendered both progress *and* the inevitable seeds of dissension. The main news was that the Jewish Colonial Trust had finally been incorporated to establish a bank for the ZO. (The Anglo-Palestine Bank would open in Jaffa in 1903.) Herzl dismissed the delegates, stating, "Our Congress has been a quiet one. We did not attain to the level of enthusiasm which marked the former Congresses. But as against that, we worked all the more. The Congress has passed out of its boyhood, it has entered the stage of manhood."[73]

Was the opening year of the twentieth century intended to signal the propitious start of a new era of Zionism? Herzl was definitely alive to the spirit of the time. Concerning his diversionary feuilletons, Bein notes, "His favorite subject was the technology of the future and its significance for the individual and social life of man."[74] Upon reading Aaron Bernstein's science books, he even pondered the "Messiah" in terms of electricity: "I said to myself: who knows, perhaps the electric stream is really the Redeemer whom we are awaiting."[75]

In any event, Herzl noted in his diary, "I suddenly realized that we had outgrown Basel. Since then, the idea of London has grown on me. It might give a fresh impetus to the movement."[76] Thus, the Fourth

Zionist Congress was set for London on August 13, 1900, Herzl writing in *Die Welt*, "Political Zionism is going to London, in order to present itself to the English world and to solicit its support—but only its moral and political support, be it well noted."[77] While Herzl was blind to such Old Testament verses as Daniel 12:4—which prophesied that a coming technological revolution would indeed initiate the *"time of the end"* (not to mention Matthew 24:27, which likened the *second* coming of Israel's Messiah to *"LIGHTNING...out of the east"*)—he *was* willing to yield to its *"forces"* (Daniel 11:38).

With his focus on the Gentile world, Herzl delivered his opening address in English (German being the official language of the Congress before shifting to English in the 1930s). He began by describing Britain as the one nation in which "God's old people" was not afflicted with a native anti-Semitism.[78] His message then broke into a grand prophetic utterance, "England the great, England the free, England with her eyes fixed on the seven seas, will understand us. From this place the Zionist movement will take a higher and higher flight, of this we may be sure."[79]

The epic Queens Hall meeting received extensive, mostly favorable press coverage. Herzl suddenly found himself dining with numerous power brokers, including Sir Eric Barrington, private secretary to the current prime minister, Lord Salisbury. (Much of this momentum stemmed from his contacts with Montagu and The Maccabeans). To illustrate the prevailing mood, Herzl and a group of delegates were taken on a Thames cruise. Passing the "Union Jack" at Windsor Castle, the Zionists surprised their hosts by saluting it with a rousing rendition of the "HaTikvah."[80] Herzl's London sabbatical also confirmed that Palestine was *in* and Argentina was *out*, detractor Ernst Pawel writing, "The mystical appeal of Zionism in England, among Jews and non-Jews alike, was rooted in a deep reverence for the Bible, whether as Holy Scripture, prophecy, mythology, or the wellspring of language and literature. There could be no Promised Land other than Palestine, and no ingathering of the exiles anywhere but in the ancestral home."[81]

AT THE SUBLIME PORTE

Yet, in the midst of this new opportunity, Herzl decided to make one last effort at Constantinople. This time, he would employ the Jews' most formidable weapon—*chutzpah*. Assisted by the colorful roving influence peddler, Árminius Vámbéry (hailed by Bismarck as "the best diplomat of modern times"), Herzl would call upon the Muslim Sultan himself. As mentioned, Herzl proposed to exchange Jewish financing for a homeland. But to make a very long story short—it didn't work!

On May 17, 1901, once again the "privileged" newsman was ushered into the presence of nobility, this time, after a *baksheesh* ("fee") of 40,000 francs was paid to the royal bagman. In the ensuing paradox, Herzl the *Jew* engaged a *Muslim* ruler with the *Greek* fable of Androcles and the Lion, stating, "The thorn, as I see it, is the public debt."[82] As Abdul-Hamid distrusted even his closest advisors (sleeping in a different building nightly while sniffing at every food morsel), the paranoiac was incapable of taking Herzl's visit seriously. And so, after a lengthy talk consisting of ambiguities, parlays, and hollow promises, Herzl made his familiar "hat-in-hand" exit. However, the next day he *did* receive a consolation prize—a tie pin with pretty yellow stones.

On this occasion, the Turkish option flopped due to an eleventh-hour funding package brokered by the French (Rothschild himself surreptitiously extracting the thorn).[83] Herzl would hold wealthy Jewry in everlasting contempt: "[F]ifty years from now people will spit on the graves of these men for it, that I should have been almost through with the question of the Sultan, and that I should have been held up because I could not get the miserable money."[84] Yet, despite the appearance of failure, the fact that Herzl had been formally received at the Sublime Porte was a watershed in itself. Even Pawel conceded, "Here, for the first time, a Jew in effect proposed to negotiate with a sovereign government on behalf of the Jewish people as a whole...the Turks merely intended to use him. But in so doing, they implicitly recognized the reality of a secular Jewish nation and his role as its representative. It was a diplomatic recognition of sorts."[85]

Following their encounter, Abdul-Hamid had remarked, "That Herzl looks altogether like a prophet, like a leader of his people."[86] Unfortunately, the "prophet" was quickly wearing thin, recording on January 31, 1901, "The wind blows through the stubble. I feel my autumn approaching."[87] On his forty-first birthday, May 2, 1901, he reflected, "It is nearly six years since I began this movement, which has made me old, tired and poor."[88]

As the leaves began to fall, Herzl's fleeting days maintained their ebb-and-flow routine. The Fifth Congress returned to Basel on

December 26, 1901. Herzl's showpiece was the Jewish National Fund, the ZO's arm for buying land in Israel. Yet things appeared to be stalling. True to the maxim, "The doors of opportunity swing on the hinges of opposition," the first official partisan group formed, calling itself the "Democratic Zionist Fraction." By now, the ideological gap between Herzl's pragmatic Western Jews (controlling the leadership) and Weizmann's stigmatic Eastern Jews (controlling the majority) was reaching the breaking point. The growing distinction pitted political Zionism against the so-called cultural or spiritual brand of Zionism (with language issues in the forefront) advocated by the Odessa sage, Ahad Ha-Am (Asher Ginsberg). Herzl continued to see his pivotal role as "a horseman crossing a frozen river."[89] To complicate matters, he was diagnosed with severe cerebral anemia. Then, it happened...

EPOCH ZO-HMG LINKAGE

In early 1902, Herzl sensed a burst of inspiration that would send him back to the House of Rothschild. However, this time his negotiations would be with the British branch led by Nathan Mayer (younger cousin to Edmond de Rothschild of the French division, Herzl's earlier nemesis). As previously stated, Nathan's father, Lionel, was the first Jewish MP (Parliament member). His selection was no mean feat given the opposition he endured. This legacy—combined with his own milestone as the first Jew in the House of Lords, added to his position as head of the English banking house of Rothschild, Bank of England board of directors member, and president of the United Synagogue in London—made Nathan Rothschild the most powerful Jew in England.

While Nathan had previously rejected Herzl's colonization idea for the same reasons given by his cousin, the proverbial "game changer" had now occurred. After absorbing a small but steady influx of Jewish immigration from 1890 to 1902 (25,000), the British public had suddenly grown anxious over the emerging threat of "cheap labor." In 1902, Whitehall appointed a Royal Commission to study the matter. Herzl was invited to testify, forcing Rothschild, a leading Commission member, to confer with him beforehand. However, on the eve of their summit, Herzl's father died, causing a temporary postponement. Herzl "sighed like a Jew," recording, "How much he has supported me, comforted me...And now I am not at home at the moment when his eyes are closing for ever...How deeply I am indebted to him...He stood there like a tree, and now the tree is no more."[90]

Back from the funeral in Vienna, Herzl met with Rothschild at his London office on July 4. Bein states, "The interview was conducted in a loud tone of voice because Rothschild was hard of hearing; at certain points it was also agitated."[91] Nathan nearly fainted when Herzl shared his prepared remarks for the Commission. As providence allowed, a series of pogroms in Eastern Europe left a mass of victims in its wake (700,000 in Galicia alone). When Herzl informed Rothschild that these destitute *Ostjuden* (Eastern European Jews) would shortly "set themselves in motion" (i.e., toward *England*), Nathan replied, "I wish you would not say that to the Commission. It will lead to restrictive laws." Upon hearing Herzl's defiant reply—"Certainly I shall say it. Most certainly"—Nathan's jaw dropped. Seizing the moment, Herzl resuscitated his would-be patron with the words, "But I have a plan."[92]

"Lord" Rothschild had no choice but to "bow" before realpolitik. Herzl adroitly said, "I would be one of those wicked persons to whom the English Jews ought to raise a monument, because I would be protecting them from an influx of eastern Jews and therefore perhaps from anti-Semitism."[93] Thus, in one of history's greatest ironies, England's richest Jew would rescue Romania's poorest Jews—though only as a means of shielding his own comfortably assimilated British Jews. Affording Herzl with an emergency haven (*anywhere* but here, etc.) would divert the "approaching hordes," sparing Parliament any needless fallout. In his audacity, Herzl had carried the day by holding 60,000 London Jews hostage! Nathan should have seen this one coming, as Herzl's speech at the London Congress broached the impracticality of further Jewish exiles in Britain: "Such immigration would constitute a danger to the Jews already here, as well as to those who might follow. For the latter will import in their pitiful bundles the very thing they are fleeing from, namely, anti-Semitism."[94]

As the two men continued their talk, Herzl's obvious preference for a homeland in Palestine was countered by Nathan's offer of British Uganda. Herzl then agreed to what he saw as an interim concession—potential sites in the Sinai Peninsula, Egyptian Palestine (El Arish), or Cyprus (all under British suzerainty at the time)—as a proving ground and staging area for the eventual move to Eretz Yisrael. In his follow-up letter to Rothschild, Herzl cleared the air for posterity's sake: "To avoid all misunderstanding now and for the future, I wish to make it clear that I have submitted this plan only because you are against Palestine...But apart from this human interest of mine, there exists also a political interest. A great Jewish settlement in the eastern Mediterranean strengthens our position in regard to Palestine."[95]

On the heels of this rapprochement with Nathan de-Rothschild, Herzl appeared before the British Royal Commission on Alien Immigration on July 7th. They would now encounter "Tancred's" unassailable logic. He began by enlightening the commissioners that they had already placed themselves in an untenable position by merely having convened the high-profile conference:

> [T]he Commission must either recommend restrictive legislation or not. If the former, and its recommendations are given effect, then England will break away from the great principle of free asylum to the oppressed which hitherto has been its glory, although the endeavor to keep out the poor, oppressed Jews cannot, I believe, be successful. But if restrictive legislation is not recommended, the mere fact of the Commission having sat will give an impetus to immigration to England.[96]

He then conveyed the obvious point—that the Zionist way was the *only* way out of their "Catch 22" dilemma:

> The Jews of Eastern Europe cannot stay where they are—where are they to go? If you find they are not wanted here, then some place must be found to which they can migrate without raising the problems that confront them here. Those problems will not arise if a home be found for them which will be legally recognized as Jewish. And I do submit that whether the Commission can directly influence that solution of the problem or not, they must not omit to consider it and give it the high value of its opinion.[97]

That last line was particularly relevant, few realizing that the speaker would be gone in less than two years. While Herzl would wait in vain for Nathan and company to do their part, he had attained a major feat. Though the Sinai-El Arish proposal later failed, even Pawel notes that the official dialogue "recognized Herzl as a serious partner in negotiations and constitutes the first formal dealings between the British government and political Zionism."[98] Over the next fifteen years, key players like

Colonial Secretary of State Joseph Chamberlain and Prime Ministers Arthur Balfour and Lloyd George would indeed consider his plan, giving it "the high value of their opinion," the Balfour Declaration being the fruit of that protracted scrutiny.

UGANDA PROPOSAL

By the Sixth Zionist Congress on August 21, 1903 (the largest, with 592 delegates), Herzl was physically and emotionally spent. His last great heartache (and worst debacle) involved the "Uganda Proposal." The British Colonial Office had offered to facilitate and administer a sizable Jewish enclave in British East Africa, specifically, a 5,000-acre tract in the Naivasha Province of Kenya. (Whitehall strategists hoped that a successful colony would underwrite the costly Uganda railroad.)

In Herzl's defense, having endured years of empty promises, he merely viewed it as another stopgap alternative to "nothing." Simply waiting for the inevitable dismemberment of the Ottoman Caliphate was more than a dying visionary could bear. While Palestine would remain the ultimate solution to the Jewish question, a Ugandan colony could conceivably assuage withering conditions in Eastern Europe, the recent deadly Kishinev pogrom in particular. Had not Jacob Bernstein-Kohan, a delegate from Kishinev himself, opined, "[I]n their present circumstances the Jews of Russia would even go to hell"?[99] However, to Herzl's utter consternation, the Russian delegation stormed out of the Congress in protest—apparently preferring Hell over Africa!

Though Herzl's move to study the offer passed by a solid majority, his "victory" nearly split the new movement. As a bizarre example of the prevailing discord, in Paris that December, a deranged Jewish-Russian student, Chaim Luban, tried to assassinate Dr. Max Nordau, Herzl's loyal vice president—at a Hanukkah Ball, of all places. Yelling "Death to the East African," Luban jumped up and fired two shots, leaving Nordau only slightly wounded. After all the rancor, the proposal was summarily dropped when the survey team returned with its data. Stationed in Nyeri, Kenya, at the time, Colonel Meinertzhagen wrote, "The Commission arrived in November 1904 and visited the Uasin Gishu Plateau, but what with elephants by day and lions by night, together with an encounter with Masai warriors in full war regalia, they decided that Kenya was no place for Russian Jewry."[100]

Herzl recorded in his own diary on August 31, 1903, "The great, difficult Sixth Congress is over." Describing a private reception with a few friends after the closing session, he continues, "I said to them, 'I will tell you now what my speech is going to be to the Seventh Congress, if I live till then. By then I shall either have Palestine, or shall have convinced myself of the absolute hopelessness of all further effort.'"[101] He then gave a brief preview of his planned remarks.

Herzl and "His Holiness"

As the new year began, Herzl was so desperate to secure a Jewish state that he traveled all the way to the "Holy See" for help. On January 22, he met with Papal Secretary of State, Merry del Val, who scheduled his audience with the "Holy Father" for January 25. He used the intervening time to confer with King Victor Emanuel III. Back in Vatican City at the appointed hour, Dr. Theodor Herzl, president of the Zionist Organization, was formally received by "His Holiness," Pope Pius X, "Bishop" of Rome, Ruler of the Vatican State, and Head of the Universal, "Holy," and "Apostolic" Roman Catholic "Church."

Though the two spoke at length, the end was never in doubt: "I presented my request briefly but he answered: 'We cannot look with favor upon this movement. We cannot prevent the Jews from going to Jerusalem—but we can never favor it.'"[102] Herzl was then shown the *last* door of his public career, this time, for simply being an "infidel." Pius was clear, "If you come to Palestine and settle your people there, we want to have churches and priests ready to baptize all of you."[103]

"The Worst Horror of All"

In May, Herzl's health took a turn for the worse. He was immediately prescribed six weeks of treatment in Franzensbad (renowned for its mineral springs and radioactive gas baths). Upon arriving, he wrote his closest friend, David Wolffsohn, "I am taking the heart cure here. My mother knows nothing about it, she thinks I'm only here for a rest," but then added, portentously, "Don't do anything foolish while I'm dead."[104] Declaring to Nissan Katzenelenson, "The bell has rung for me," Herzl devoted his last days to Zionism, among other matters, briefing his assistant of yet another possibility for abating Jewry's suffering (a Russian loan brokered by Jewish banker, Jacob Schiff).

His therapy ineffective, Herzl returned to Vienna. On June 3, he left for the nearby alpine area of Edlach, accompanied by his estranged wife, Julie, and his friend, Dr. Nissan Katzenelenson, his eldest child, Pauline, joining them directly. After some encouraging progress, his condition suddenly worsened. The diagnosis was severe bronchial catarrh. Herzl's mother and two younger children were promptly summoned. His suffering was evidenced by his own words: "I always believed that I knew what terror and horror can be. But everything that exists, and everything we can conjure up, is as child's play by comparison with the worst horror of all, with the fight for breath."[105]

On Sunday afternoon, July 3, Herzl's mother finally arrived with his two younger children. Embracing her tenderly, he said, "It's nice, dear mother, to have you here. You're looking well. I'm not looking so well, but that'll soon be over." His signature beard yanked by baby Hans was now heavily streaked with gray. Seeing his son and daughter cheered him greatly; yet, after just a few minutes, he stated, "Well, my dear ones, you saw me, and I saw you. Now go back."[106] Other brief visits followed (Oskar Marmorek and Johann Kremenezky among them). Then, rather suddenly, Herzl soberly announced, "And now, my dear friends, leave me." Bein relates: "At five o'clock Dr. Werner, who had taken his eyes off the patient for a moment to prepare an injection, heard a deep sigh. As he whipped round he saw the head sink on the breast. Herzl was dead."[107] He was just forty-four years of age. His last message to Reverend Hechler had been, "Greet Palestine for me. I gave my heart's blood for my people."[108] This was most apropos, as Herzl is a diminutive of "Herz"—German for "Heart."[109]

THE MEASURE OF THE MAN

Herzl's death came as a total shock to World Jewry, few outside his intimates knowing of his illness. Telegrams of sympathy poured in by the hundreds. As a fitting tribute to his reproach, the word "Zionism" made its first appearance in the *Neue Freie Presse*—in his obituary.[110]

The funeral was in Vienna on July 7. Herzl's will dictated "a burial such as is customary among the poorest classes. No speeches, no flowers." He also asked to be laid in a metal casket next to his father, though—following Joseph's example in Genesis 50:25—only to "remain there until the Jewish people shall transport my remains to Palestine."[111] Upwards of 10,000 mourners followed the simple funeral cortege. (By contrast, 4,000 people passed the casket of Justice Antonin Scalia as it lay upon the Lincoln Catafalque in the Supreme Court's Great Hall.) "Never before had a Jew been accompanied thus to his grave," Bein states. "It was as if the Jewish people had lost its father."[112] Stefan Zweig, an eyewitness, wrote, "At the cemetery, there was a mob scene. The crowds were pressing in on the coffin, weeping, howling, screaming in a wild eruption of despair that turned into a near-riot."[113] After a brief eulogy by David Wolffsohn, thirteen-year-old Hans Herzl read the Kaddish (a ritual prayer of mourning). Though divided in his life, Herzl's mother and wife both fainted at his grave.

Theodor Herzl died on the forty-first anniversary of Picket's charge at Gettysburg—his *own* charge falling short as well. However, unlike the foiled Confederacy, the ZO would prevail to birth the State of Israel. As with all leaders, his critics were legion. Echoing the adage, "The best of men are but men at best," the Russian Zionist, Menachem Ussishkin, paid Herzl the backhanded compliment, "great men have great failings."[114] (The inspired original is Job 32:9, *"Great men are not always wise."*) Owing to his acculturated heritage as an educated, bourgeois Viennese Jew, Herzl's defining "weakness" was his inability to grasp Jewish sentiment as personified in Tevye's "Tradition." (Early on he had even advocated mass conversion to Christianity as the Jews' only hope of survival.[115]) In a related "gotcha question" context, the "Austrian interloper" was also assailed for presuming to lead a movement while not knowing most of its pioneers and history (Leon Pinsker's *Auto-Emancipation*, Hovevei Zion, et al.).

Yet, as Bein painfully notes, "It was said of Herzl that it was his good fortune not to have known the Jewish people: this gave him the courage to act."[116] In 1890—before his foray into Zionism—an idealistic Herzl chose for his life's motto, "To know human beings and to love them just the same."[117] However, only six years later, he groaned, "I have a right to become the greatest of all anti-Semites."[118] (An appropriate anecdote states that when David Ben-Gurion visited Washington, Truman said, "It must be a great honor being Israel's first Prime Minister," whereupon Ben-Gurion reputedly replied, "Mr. President, I am prime minister of 800,000 prime ministers!")

Herzl's diary for March 1, 1896, reads: "The Zionists Birnbaum, Jacob Kohn, and Landau paid me a joint visit and squabbled among themselves...It is downright disheartening to see their petty hostility toward one another."[119] The ultimate victim, Herzl deflected the cause to prolonged persecution: "The ghetto, which was not of our making, bred into us certain anti-social qualities...Our original character cannot have been other than magnificent and proud."[120] The Apostle Paul, a converted rabbi, projected this distinct profile when describing his own race as being *"contrary to all men."* (I Thessalonians 2:15)

The craven cavils against Herzl ranged from having Christmas trees to lacking Hebrew skills. Ironically, given his "modern-day Moses" persona, few realized that the great "Law Giver" was an assimilated Jew himself with plenty of his own baggage (Hebrews 11:24-27). Both were reproved for not circumcising their sons (Exodus 4:24-26). Herzl's main adversary was fellow Jew Ernst Pawel, a New York Life Insurance Company employee who embodied Sam Rayburn's proverb, "Any jackass can kick down a barn, but it takes a good carpenter to build one." While Pawel would demote Bein's work to "hagiography," *Publisher's Weekly* labeled Pawel's own biased *The Labyrinth of Exile: A Life of Theodor Herzl* a "psychobiography."[121]

Ernst spared no shameful diary entry narrating the vice and imprudence of Herzl's collegiate days. While Nordau was wounded by bullets, Herzl suffered a postmortem character assassination. Having "diagnosed" his subject as a sexually repressed misogynist, Pawel's further deviant innuendo—that a "subconscious sexual tension" reputedly existed between Herzl and his most "intimate friend," Heinrich Kana—betrayed his own insatiable lust to defame a dead man's legacy.[122] Pawel concludes, "It is tempting to see his consuming devotion to the Zionist cause as a form of sublimated sexuality."[123]

In less than a decade, Dr. Herzl became the first Jew in twenty centuries to unite the hapless Diaspora on a world stage. Starting as a dandified littérateur and novice reporter with no political connections, Herzl became the consummate diplomat, representing his exiled nation before the German Kaiser, the Ottoman Sultan, the King of Italy, and the Pope, not to mention the Prime Ministers and Foreign Ministers of Germany, Italy, and Austro-Hungary, the Finance and Interior Ministers of Old Russia, the British Colonial Secretary, plus the key religious, social, and financial icons of the day. Even Herzl's greatest blunder, the "Uganda Proposal"—because it represented an official offer from HMG—became the catalyst for the diplomatic process that culminated with the Balfour Declaration. Thus, with all its flaws, the Knesset was literally born in Basel. His last foe, Menachem Ussishkin, conceded: "Herzl brought the Jews unity and courage...Those who came before him carried the ideal in their hearts but only whispered about it in the synagogues...Herzl brought us courage and taught us to place our demands before the whole non-Jewish world."[124]

Like his long-guarded medical "secrets," Herzl's undisclosed financial portfolio was also part of the "grand Zionist conspiracy," etc. Despite his wife's substantial dowry, his many successful plays, and his high paying salary, Herzl, like the Jewish-American patriot, Haym Solomon, died broke, having given everything to Zionism. Only when David Wolffsohn made a national appeal for a special fund for Herzl's family did Jews begin to discern the full measure of his fidelity. "Why is it," Herzl wrote, "that the best must always fall? It is because they give to the last ounce of their strength—and beyond—that they are the best."[125] Though he penned them, Herzl could little understand the future gravity of those words, "and beyond." Sadly, as no amount of "funds" can replace the security of a father's presence, Herzl's greatest sacrifice would be felt beyond the grave—in more ways than one.

A Missing Cinerary Urn

His widow spent the next three years in and out of sanitariums, dying in 1907 at the age of thirty-nine, presumably of heart disease. She was cremated by request. (Pawel speculates that "youthful indiscretions" on Herzl's part may have caused both premature deaths.[126]) Like her mother, Pauline also suffered from mental problems, becoming a promiscuous vagrant and drug addict. The ZO ultimately rejected her repeated embarrassing requests for money. In 1930, she died in a French hospital at age forty from an overdose of morphine.

Hans Herzl, was a manic-depressive who also visited psych wards. Among many life failures, returning from his mother's funeral, the grieving lad left her cinerary urn on the train. Hans also left Judaism, sojourning with Catholics, Anglicans, Unitarians, Quakers, even being immersed as a Baptist.[127] In Bordeaux for Pauline's funeral, he sent a note to the hotel apologizing for the mess he was about to make—then blew his brains out before the service; he was thirty-nine. His macabre note to a local attorney asking that "my body be placed in my sister's coffin, where there is ample room, and have us shipped to Vienna" was not granted; the siblings were interred side by side in Bordeaux.[128]

The youngest Herzl, "Trude" (their pet, born Margarethe), married Richard Neumann, a divorced, wealthy textile manufacturer twenty-six years her senior. Trude also suffered from cyclothymic depression, requiring frequent hospitalizations. The couple had one child, a boy, Stephan Theodor. Fearing for his safety amidst the encroaching Anschluss, they sent him to England in 1935. There he discovered his grandfather's exploits and became an ardent Zionist. Anglicizing his name to Stephen Norman, he enlisted in the British Army at the start of World War II, rising to the rank of captain in the Royal Artillery.

In late 1945 and early 1946, Stephen visited Mandatory Palestine to "see what my grandfather had started." He wrote upon leaving, that he hoped to return soon. That spring he joined the British Economic and Scientific Mission in Washington, DC. He then heard from his former nanny that his parents had perished in the Theresienstadt ghetto near Prague. Martin Gilbert states that Trude died from hunger on March 15, 1943.[129] Overcome with grief, on November 26, 1946, Stephen Theodor Norman—last of the Herzl line—jumped to his death from the Massachusetts Avenue Bridge. He was twenty-seven years old.

MOUNT HERZL CEMETERY

Conforming to his will, in 1949, Herzl's body was flown to Israel and reinterred in Jerusalem. A special commission had carefully selected the site—the summit of a mountain on the city's west side. With the remains of Dr. Theodor Herzl, *Hozeh HaMedinah*, solemnly enshrined at 2,700 feet, the entire mound was destined to be a major Zionist ethnoscape. Thus, a mere two years later, Herzl's unadorned black granite tombstone became the symbolic headstone for Mount Herzl

Cemetery—the official burial ground for the new State of Israel. (The central coast city of *Herzliya* was also named in his honor.)

Over the years, prime ministers, presidents, Knesset members, dignitaries and military heroes have been interred on *Har Herzl* ("Mount Herzl"). In 2006, the remains of Hans and Pauline were interred on their father's mountain, Stephen's body joining them the year after. A crematorium prevented Trude from participating in the disconsolate reunion. Fittingly, the *Yad Vashem* Holocaust memorial stands on the Western slope of Mount Herzl as a monument of its own, honoring the 6,000,000 Jews whose remains can never be found. (*Yad*, "a place," and *Shem*, "a name," from Isaiah 56:5, *"Even unto them will I give in mine house and within my walls a place and a name."*)

As "the truth is not always palatable," the sad "truth" *here* is that Theodor Herzl was a devoted, though unconverted, man who returned to the national identity of his ancient race without the slightest regard to the God of their ethnoscape (much less to the "Jewish Messiah" espoused by Hechler, Christian Zionists, and Messianic Jews). As the founder of *political* Zionism, Herzl was to Israel what John Birch Society founder Robert Welch was to America—an agnostic, secular, super-patriot. In his diary entry for August 18, 1895, Herzl wrote, "God to me is a beautiful, dear old word that I want to preserve...God means to me the Will to Good."[130] In an earlier letter, dated December 27, 1892, Herzl shared his personal thoughts on religion, with his Jewish employer, Moritz Benedikt, editor of the *Neue Freie Presse*:

> I consider religion indispensable for the weak. There are those who, weak in willpower, mind, or emotions, must always be able to rely on religion. The others, the normal run of mankind, are weak only in childhood and in old age; for them, religion serves as an educational instrument or a source of comfort...God is a magnificent symbol for an enormous complex of moral and legal imperatives, the apparent solution to riddles, the answer to all childish questions...which god really makes no difference.[131]

Sadly, given the damage inflicted by that first grade teacher, Herzl was not even afforded the comfort of a supernatural answer to his own childish questions. Cast as the Hebrew icon he once revered, the committed rationalist devolved to view the historical Moses as just another religious "swindler" who "cunningly exploited natural phenomena."[132] When

Jacob lay dying he left his son with the parting assurance, *"Behold, I die: but God shall be with you."* (Genesis 48:21) By contrast, Herzl could only say to his children, "Now go back." Is it any wonder that his entire family descended into despair—left with nothing but a "magnificent symbol" for comfort? Could they have held more hope than he had shown at the death of his own sister, Pauline? "They put my beloved only sister into the cold earth...Now she was to lie all alone, outside the city, in wind and storm and rain...Can it really all be over?...We'll never meet again,"[133] or, when he wrote of his departed father, "[H]e whom I shall never see again"?[134]

In the final analysis, Theodor Herzl was the human instrument of providence who initiated the opening stage of Israel's glorious end-day restoration, pending Jehovah's fearful and glorious culmination—*"the great and dreadful day of the LORD"*—for then, *"the Lord shall be king over all the earth."* (Malachi 4:5; Zechariah 14:9)

> I believe that I shall be named among the great benefactors of mankind. Or is this feeling of mine the beginning of delusions of grandeur?[135]
>
> (Theodor Herzl - June 16, 1895)

> You willed that at your graveside no speeches be made. To us your wish is sacred. But we swear to you that we will keep your name sacred and that it will remain unforgotten as long as a single Jew lives on this earth. In these heavy hours we recall the oath you took at the sixth congress, and we repeat it. *"If I forget thee, O Jerusalem, may my right hand forget its cunning."*[136]
>
> (David Wolffsohn, at Herzl's graveside service)

5

The Balfour Declaration

"But we had Jerusalem when London was a marsh."
(Weizmann to Arthur Balfour, 1906)

"He once told me that 2,000 interviews had gone
to the making of the Balfour Declaration."
(British official speaking of Weizmann)

"Now in the first year of Cyrus king of Persia, that the word of the LORD *by the mouth of Jeremiah might be fulfilled, the* LORD *stirred up the spirit of Cyrus king of Persia, that he made a* PROCLAMATION *throughout all his kingdom, and put it also in* WRITING.*"*
(Ezra 1:1)

IN THE FINAL weeks of Herzl's life, David Wolffsohn cried to a fellow Zionist, "What is to become of us if the doctor is right? And I am afraid he is right."[1] Herzl's death left many orphans across the Diaspora. However, as the old adage goes, "Everything rises and falls on leadership," a Russian chemist took up the mantle of the Austrian journalist. Through the timely role of Dr. Chaim Weizmann, Herzl's experiment would attain a second watershed in twenty years.

At the start of World War I, 12,000 Zionists were running forty agrarian sites in Palestine. By then, Jews had acquired some 400,000 Turkish *dunams* (four dunams to an acre). The overall population grew from 34,000 in 1882 to 90,000 in 1914.[2] Literally coming from the four corners of the earth, the arrivals inspired a renascence of Hebrew as the tongue of choice for their multilingual colonies. Yet, despite this progress (combined with the ZO's growing reputation for diplomacy), the aim of rebuilding a Jewish homeland continued to lack legitimacy. This elusive *sine qua non* (set by the First Congress) was finally secured through two epic documents: the Balfour Declaration issued by HMG on November 2, 1917, and the British Mandate for Palestine, approved by the League of Nations on July 24, 1922.

As early as November 9, 1914 (a week after the Ottomans entered the war), Sir Herbert Samuel, Britain's first Jewish cabinet member, prevailed on Foreign Secretary Edward Grey. With Turkey committed, "it was probable that her empire would be broken up," and thus, "the opportunity might arise for the fulfillment of the ancient aspiration of the Jewish people and the restoration there of a Jewish state."[3] With the Central Powers' defeat, the Ottoman dismemberment *did* become the clear geopolitical factor that permitted these events to unfold.

The resolution assigning Mandatory Palestine to Britain was issued on April 25, 1920, at the San Remo Conference in Italy. The meeting, attended by the Entente Powers, set the terms to be imposed on the vanquished Turks. The "mandate system" was designed by the League to administer non-self-governing terrain. The appropriate mandatory power was to be assigned as a temporary trust to ensure the positive development of the attendant population. This new order was meant to signal the end of British imperialism—the territorial annexation and fiscal dominance based on perceived cultural and racial superiority.

England's postwar claim on Palestine was a foregone conclusion, dating from Maurice de Bunsen's partition committee in 1915. British "boots on the ground" (aided by Jewish intel) would solidify this assertion. The famous charge of the Australian 4th Light Brigade at Beersheba on October 31, 1917 (depicted in the 1987 film "The Lighthorsemen") helped knock Turkey out of the war. Sir Edmund Allenby took Jerusalem on December 9 without firing a shot. The mayor was forced to surrender as the Ottoman 7th Army had retired the night before. (Some allege the defenders grew fearful of the advancing general, having confused "Allenby" with *Allah Nabi*, "Man sent from God"). Speaking to a crowd of Muslims, Christians, and Jews at the Tower of David, Allenby said: "We have come, not as conquerors, but as deliverers. It is our intention to open a new era of brotherhood and peace in the Holy Land."[4] This was five weeks before the Declaration.

With the reluctant private "endorsement" of President Wilson, the Declaration emerged in the form of a letter from British Foreign

Secretary Arthur James Balfour, representing the Government of His Britannic Majesty King George V, to Lord Lionel Walter Rothschild for conveyance to the Zionist Federation of Great Britain and Ireland.[5] Issued as a single sentence—consisting of sixty-seven words, precisely chosen over a ten-month period, through seven drafts by more than a dozen collaborators—the *final* version of this momentous text follows:

> Foreign Office
> November 2nd, 1917
>
> Dear Lord Rothschild,
>
> I have much pleasure in conveying to you, on behalf of His Majesty's Government, the following declaration of sympathy with Jewish Zionist aspirations which has been submitted to, and approved by, the Cabinet.
>
> > 'His Majesty's Government view with favour the establishment in Palestine of a national home for the Jewish people, and will use their best endeavors to facilitate the achievement of this object, it being clearly understood that nothing shall be done which may prejudice the civil and religious rights of existing non-Jewish communities in Palestine or the rights and political status enjoyed by Jews in any other country.'
>
> I should be grateful if you would bring this declaration to the knowledge of the Zionist Federation.
>
> Yours,
> Arthur James Balfour

OLD TESTAMENT HARBINGER

In line with the subtitle of this volume, *A Scriptural View of the True History of the State of Israel*, the reader will note that the epic Declaration was prefigured in the Old Testament book of Ezra—2,453 years *before* it happened!

The book of II Chronicles records the fall of Jerusalem in 586 BC (foretelling the siege by Titus in AD 70). According to the providential order in the A.V. 1611 (unlike the Septuagint or Masoretic Text),

II Chronicles is followed by Ezra, where a Gentile king returns the Jews to their land (like another goy monarch, George V, did in AD 1917).

> *Now in the first year of Cyrus king of Persia, that the word of the* LORD *by the mouth of Jeremiah might be fulfilled, the* LORD *stirred up the spirit of Cyrus king of Persia, that he made a* PROCLAMATION *throughout all his kingdom,* AND PUT IT ALSO IN WRITING, *saying...The* LORD *God of heaven hath given me all the kingdoms of the earth; and he hath charged me to build him an house at Jerusalem, which is in Judah. Who is there among you of all his people? his God be with him, and let him go up to Jerusalem, which is in Judah, and build the house of the LORD God of Israel, (he is the God,) which is in Jerusalem.* (Ezra 1:1-3)

Notice how the Holy Spirit states in verse one that Cyrus not only "*made a* PROCLAMATION *throughout all his kingdom*" (for the Jews' return), but *"put it also in* WRITING,*" exactly* as the Balfour DECLARATION was committed to WRITING in 1917. The account is made even more surreal by the fact that the Lord's agent of providence is named in Isaiah 44:28—some 175 years *before* the event took place.

As an extra "coincidence," Nehemiah comes next, where the Jews begin rebuilding their temple (as they have been doing since 1948). Thus, we discern that contrary to common belief, Persia is a type of *England* in Scripture. (The first beast in Daniel 7 cannot represent Babylon, for all four beasts come up *after* Belshazzar is dead; thus, the animal depicted as Persia is an English "griffin"—a winged lion.[6])

CHAIM WEIZMANN

The main lobbying for the Declaration was done by Chaim Weizmann. Born November 27, 1874, in the shtetl of Motal near Pinsk in Belarus, Chaim studied biochemistry at the Polytechnic Institute of Darmstadt, Germany, and the University of Fribourg, Switzerland, graduating magna cum laude (from the latter) with a PhD in organic chemistry. After working as an assistant lecturer at the University of Geneva, Chaim moved to England in 1904 to become Reader in Biochemistry at the University of Manchester. In 1905, he became a British citizen. He then married Dr. Vera Chatzman, the union producing two sons.

A committed Zionist, Weizmann was now positioned to interact with the powerbrokers at Whitehall. He relates in his autobiography, *Trial and Error*, "There were, at that time, alike in the highest Government posts, and in those of secondary importance, men with a real understanding both of the moral implication of the Zionist movement, and of the potentialities of Palestine. To some extent before my moving to London, but much more afterward, I set myself to discovering these men."[7] As with Herzl, many doors would be opened.

Of the varied "interesting" and "extraordinary personalities" Chaim cites as impacting "Zionist history," Colonel Richard Meinertzhagen topped his list. While certain modern-day critics have sullied the character of this late war hero, Israel's first president eulogized him as a real *mensch*: "He had a magnificent career. He was a man of lion-hearted courage, and had fought on almost every front. He was repeatedly wounded and sent home; I met him during one of these leaves."[8] Richard told how he had once been anti-Semitic himself but changed after "many talks" with a Palestinian Jew, described as being "of great courage and of superior intelligence, devoted to Palestine."[9] (This person was Aaron Aaronsohn, extolled botanist, agronomist, and resistance leader.) Chaim states that Meinertzhagen "became an ardent Zionist...And that not merely in words. Whenever he can perform a service for the Jews or Palestine he will go out of his way to do so."[10]

At the onset of WWI, the brilliant chemist was able to augment his political capital by helping the cause. In 1914, Charles Scott, editor of *The Manchester Guardian*, introduced Chaim to David Lloyd George, Chancellor of the Exchequer (later, Minister of Munitions, 1915-16; Secretary of State for War, 1916; Prime Minister, 1916-22). Another key contact was Mark Sykes, British agent of the secret Sykes-Picot Agreement: "One of our greatest finds was Sir Mark Sykes, Chief Secretary of the War Cabinet...I cannot say enough regarding the services rendered by Sykes...who guided our work into more official channels...If it had not been for the counsel of men like Sykes and Cecil we, with our inexperience in delicate diplomatic negotiations, would undoubtedly have committed many dangerous blunders."[11]

The attitude of the British people was also encouraging: "The tone of public opinion at large...was one of interest, and not unfriendly. The Manchester *Guardian* was with us; the London *Times* was favorably inclined."[12] A small book published by Weizmann, entitled *Zionism and the Jewish Future*, received a positive review in *The Spectator*, Lord Cromer predicting, "The British public will have much more to do with this subject than is apparent now…Before long politicians will be unable to brush it aside as the fantastic dream of a few idealists." For Weizmann, such encounters only confirmed an earlier premonition: "It was gradually borne in on me, even before I had settled in London—that is, before this network of relationships had been created in full—that a decisive period was approaching."[13]

His main ally for this "decisive period" was Arthur James Balfour: Prime Minister, 1902-05; Member of Parliament, 1906-11; First Lord of the Admiralty, 1915-16; and, Secretary of State for Foreign Affairs under Lloyd George during the timely window of 1916-19. Though Balfour—an early Zionist—had maintained his initial preference for Uganda, Chaim is credited with altering his view toward Palestine. The following exchange, from their first visit in 1906, renders an insightful glimpse of the productive "chemistry" they later developed:

> He asked me why some Jews, Zionists, were so bitterly opposed to the Uganda offer…In reply I plunged into what I recall as a long harangue on the meaning of the Zionist movement…I added that if Moses had come into the sixth Zionist Congress when it was adopting the resolution in favor of the Commission for Uganda, he would surely have broken the tablets once again…I looked at my listener, and suddenly became afraid that this appearance of interest and courtesy might be nothing more than a mask…Then suddenly I said: "Mr. Balfour, supposing I were to offer you Paris instead of London, would you take it?"
>
> He sat up, looked at me, and answered: "But, Dr. Weizmann, we have London." "That is true," I said. "But we had Jerusalem when London was a marsh." He leaned back, continued to stare at me, and said two things which I remember vividly. The first was: "Are there many Jews who think like you?" I answered: "I believe I speak the mind of millions of Jews whom you will never see and who cannot speak for themselves, but with whom I could pave the streets of the country I come from." To this he said: "If that is so, you will one day be a force." Shortly before I withdrew, Balfour said: "It is curious. The Jews I meet are quite different." I answered: "Mr. Balfour, you meet the wrong kind of Jews."[14]

Under Dr. Weizmann, a *more* "right" kind of Jew would be spoken for. Though in conflict with Orthodoxy, the Weizmann era of "organic Zionism" resolved to accent the "deeper meaning of Zionism." Eclipsing the Herzlian use of Judennot as the motive for immigration, Chaim would promote the greater need—a release of suppressed potential: "Jewish homelessness was not just a physical discomfort; it was also, and perhaps in larger measure, the malaise of frustrated capacities. If the Jewish people had survived so many centuries of exile, it was not by a biological accident, but because it would not relinquish the creative capacities with which it had been entrusted."[15]

By late 1915, the War Cabinet appeared to favor a Jewish return. University of Wisconsin Professor Horace Kallen (a noted American Zionist), wrote the Foreign Office in December: "I am convinced that a statement on behalf of the Allies favoring Jewish rights in every country…and a very veiled suggestion concerning nationalization in Palestine would more than counterbalance German promises in the same direction."[16] While the anti-Semitic activist, Alison Weir, citing Dr. Sarah Schmidt, would smear Kallen by labeling his private coterie, the *Parushim*, "a secret underground guerilla force determined to influence the course of events in a quiet, anonymous way,"[17] Dr. Mark Raider of the University of Cincinnati had a less paranoid take, calling the patriotic society a "short-lived, semisecret fellowship…made up of men and women devoted to the Zionist cause."[18]

Zionism reacted in January by organizing a Political Committee in London comprising leaders of World Jewry. Chaim's English group, assisted by the American Provisional Committee under Justice Brandeis, would devise an angle to satisfy HMG. A draft of proposals was finalized in October, entitled "Outline of a Program for a New Administration of Palestine and for a Jewish Resettlement of Palestine in accordance with the Aspirations of the Zionist movement."[19] The report was sent to the Foreign Office for review. Finally, in December 1916, after the Second Coalition Government formed around the "Dream Team" of Lloyd George as prime minister and Balfour as foreign secretary, Sykes was charged to formally engage the Zionists.

On February 7, 1917, Sykes met with Chaim and his party (Herbert Samuel, Nathan Rothschild, James de Rothschild, Joseph Cowen, Harry Sacher and Herbert Bentwich) in the home of Dr. Moses Gaster, chief rabbi of London's Sephardic community. Esco notes: "This meeting, to which the leading British Zionists were invited, may be regarded as the first official discussion between Whitehall and the Jews which led to HMG undertaking the responsibility for Palestine."[20] Four main objectives were set forth:

I. International recognition of Jewish right to Palestine;
II. Juridical nationhood for the Jewish community in Palestine;
III. The creation of a Jewish chartered company in Palestine with rights to acquire land;
IV. Union and one administration for Palestine; and
V. Extra-territorial status for the holy places.[21]

Much "discussion" would occur over the final months concerning these and other specifics. Ironically, to Balfour's surprise (and Chaim's chagrin), the worst criticism of the Declaration stemmed from the only Jew in George's government—Edwin Montagu, the powerful secretary of state for India (not to be confused with Samuel Montagu, Orthodox Jewish banker, philanthropist, and MP). On August 8, 1916, Edwin wrote to Eric Drummond, "I view with horror the aspiration for national entity."[22] Montagu, a second generation assimilated Jew and self-described "patriotic Englishman," argued that a Jewish "national home" would constitute a dangerous "dual loyalty" in Britain and elsewhere. Weizmann could only shrug his shoulders, "I made no attempt to conceal from Lloyd George or the others the fact that the rich and powerful Jews were for the most part against us."[23]

Regarding Chaim's claim that the need for an accelerated mass aliyah had become more defined (i.e., by "the malaise of frustrated capacities"), the greater debate, one that would dominate the next three decades, concerned the intended status of the conceded land: Was it to remain *just* a "homeland"—or mature into "statehood?" The potential volatility in this otherwise noble appearing "humanitarian charter" was revealed by the subtly of two words: "[T]he establishment *in* [not "of"] Palestine *of* [not, "as"] a national home for the Jewish people." Carroll Quigley opined, "Probably no document of the wartime period, except Wilson's 14 Points, has given rise to more disputes than this brief statement of less than eleven lines."[24] Meinertzhagen saw it as "a document perhaps intentionally vague."[25] The self-loathing Jewish novelist, Arthur Koestler, whined that "one nation solemnly promised to a second nation the country of a third"[26]; others add that the *third* entity was still part of a *fourth*—Turkey. The abiding, bloody result of this initial Anglo anti-Semitic ploy will be seen throughout this book.

ROMANTIC INCENTIVE

In God's providence, seven factors coalesced to create the Balfour Declaration. The first was the *romantic* incentive. Our story begins in a Manchester laboratory (ca. 1912) where Chaim was experimenting with fermentation. His initial role entailed producing synthetic rubber; with demand rising, a cheaper artificial substitute was needed. This required the manufacture of isoprene and its polymerization into a rubber. The basic raw material for such a process was isoamyl (butyl) alcohol. However, as a by-product of alcohol fermentation, it was not available in large quantities. Chaim proceeded to examine the possibility of making the compounds through microbial fermentation:

> I hoped to find a bacterium which would produce by fermentation of sugar more of this precious isoamyl alcohol than does yeast—one was not yet aware of the fact that isoamyl alcohol is not a fermentation product (of sugar), but is formed by degradation of the small amounts of protein invariably present in a fermenting mash. In the course of this investigation I found a bacterium which produced considerable amounts of a liquid smelling very much like isoamly alcohol. But when I distilled it, it turned out to be a mixture of acetone and butyl alcohol in very pure form.[27]

In early 1916, Chaim received a visit from William Rintoul, chief chemist at Nobel Enterprises, a major explosives firm. Chaim told how he had changed a strain of bacteria-fermented corn into a useful chemical, butyl alcohol, though with the seemingly futile byproduct of acetone (AB Fermentation). *Blown* away—the man told Chaim that his find would greatly interest the military. While the modern relevance of acetone is reduced to nail polish remover, in WWI the same chemical served as the critical colloidal solvent for nitro-cellulose, used to produce cordite, a smokeless explosive powder for military propellant.

Chaim was promptly summoned to the Admiralty and made privy to a dangerous shortage of acetone. Before the war, acetone was made from calcium acetate and imported in small quantities from Germany, Austria, and America. However, with two-thirds of their former suppliers now shooting *at* them, the resultant "shell crisis" threatened Britain with a literal interpretation of the famous novel, *All Quiet on the Western Front.* By May 1915, many guns were firing only four rounds a day.[28] The professor was subsequently drilled at "pointblank range" himself: "Well, Dr. Weizmann, we need thirty thousand tons of acetone. Can you make it?"[29] The query was nearly as intimidating as the inquisitor—First Lord of the Admiralty Winston Churchill.

Given carte blanche by Churchill, the new Director of Admiralty Laboratories correlated his unique anaerobic fermentation process (extracting organisms from cereal and horse chestnuts) with an array of confiscated brewery hardware. Plants rose up in Dorset and Norfolk producing 90,000 gallons of acetone per year. With British grain imports hindered by U-boats, America's entry into the war allowed the nation's farmers to jump in by supplying corn, while distilleries in Terre Haute, Indiana, and Peoria, Illinois, morphed into acetone plants.

By 1917, Britain was making 50 million shells annually. At the Third Battle of Ypres, Sir Douglas Haig fired an initial barrage of 4¼ million rounds—5 tons per yard of the 11-mile front.[30] The rest is history: The Central Powers lost; the Ottoman Empire was dismantled; the Zionist chemist was lionized; and, most importantly, the "door" to Palestine was opened for a Jewish homeland. (Chaim became the first in a long list of prominent 20th-century Jewish scientists involved in cutting-edge ordnance research, the Weizmann Institute of Science in Rehovot, Israel, pioneering the nation's nuclear weapons program.)

In Weizmann's obituary on November 9, 1952, the *New York Times* declared, "Dr. Weizmann refused any monetary reward or a title, and said, 'There is only one thing I want – a national home for my people.' The Balfour Declaration, issued in November, 1917, followed." Lloyd George appeared to concur in his *War Memoirs*, stating that in a 1916 meeting Chaim "explained his aspirations as to the repatriation of the Jews to the sacred land they had made famous. That was the fount and origin of the famous declaration about the National Home for Jews in Palestine…As soon as I became Prime Minister I talked the whole matter over with Mr. Balfour, who was then Foreign Secretary."[31]

STRATEGIC INCENTIVE

Though the eleventh-hour rescue of Britain's acetone crisis is often touted as the obvious "given" cause for the Declaration ("the gift of a grateful nation," etc.), this most certainly was *not* the case, Chaim himself admitting, "I almost wish that it had been as simple as that."[32] Herbert Samuel relates that, as early as his first meeting with Lloyd George in December 1914, "he was preparing a memo on the subject of a Jewish State in Palestine, to present to the Prime Minister."[33]

While Jewish historian Howard Sachar of George Washington University says, "Against this background of Anglo-Zionist cordiality, Weizmann's allusions to a 'British protectorate over a Jewish homeland' struck an increasingly responsive chord among government officials,"[34] at least *six* other factors prevented Chaim from becoming just another *"poor wise man* [who] *by his wisdom delivered the city; yet no man remembered that same poor man."* (Ecclesiastes 9:15) The acetone story—having extra value as it was actually true—provided the perfect smokescreen for these other political realities by fostering and maintaining a sympathetic appeal within the public imagination.

Moved by realpolitik, Lord Curzon told the House of Lords on June 29, 1920, "[T]he chief reason was strategic."[35] Esco relates: "Britain's need for a new Eastern policy after the collapse of her traditional alignment with the Turks was probably the main factor in her decision to support the Zionist policy during WWI."[36] In the past, England had invested heavily in the Ottoman Empire (a.k.a. the "Sick Man of Europe") as a buffer against Imperial Russia. A simple map will reveal Britain's two innate concerns: the Suez Canal, her lifeline to the East; and the pair of narrow straits in northwest Turkey, the Dardanelles and the Bosphorus, affording the Black Sea Fleet access to Mediterranean waters via the Sea of Marmara and the Aegean. The highly sensitive region (inhabited by an equally duplicitous Muslim majority) was situated on the central land route to India, the veritable heart of the Empire; and on the Mediterranean, the shortest sea route to the Asian subcontinent. (Palestine held a military significance even prior to the Suez Canal, being the only land bridge linking the three continents.)

This bond began to falter, however, for as noted earlier, Wilhelm made his own diplomatic debut at the Sublime Porte. The handwriting was on the wall when Turkey backed Germany on August 2, 1914, one day before the outbreak of hostilities. After Turkey committed by attacking Russia in October, Britain had no choice but to declare war on the "aggressor" on November 5. In a speech four days later, Prime Minister Asquith declared that "it is the Ottoman Government and not we who have rung the death-knell of Ottoman Domination, not only in Europe but in Asia."[37] The abortive nine-month Gallipoli fiasco (50,000 Allied deaths) and the inglorious surrender of the British Expeditionary Force in Kut-al-Amara would only stiffen that resolve.

The most sober wake-up call was the initial wave of Arab and Bedouin incursions across the southern Palestine border. A foiled Turkish raid on the Canal itself in early February 1915 confirmed the military's worst fears—that the zone was indeed vulnerable from an overland assault through Palestine. A lead editorial in the Manchester *Guardian* warned that Turkey's loss meant that "the most vital spot in our communications with the East would be exposed to attack from the land, and attack from which the most powerful navy could not possibly secure us."[38] The writer posited the need for a security buffer; and "the only people capable of forming such a state was the Jewish nation."[39]

There was also growing concern that the Kaiser and the "Three Pashas" (Turkey's dictatorial wartime triumvirate) were poised to reconsider Herzl's original request for German suzerainty (a maneuver designed to exploit the Jew's natural aversion to Russia's part in the Triple Entente). To this end, a German-Jewish bund was formed, the V.J.O.D. ("Alliance of the Jewish Organizations of Germany for the Safeguarding of the Rights of the East"). Lloyd George notes that the German General Staff "urged, early in 1916, the advantages of promising Jewish restoration to Palestine under an arrangement to be made between Zionists and Turkey, backed by a German guarantee."[40]

He also said that as late as September 1917 (two months before the Declaration) "the German Government were making very serious efforts to capture the Zionist movement."[41] (The US and Russia would compete for similar favor in 1948.) As Turkish neutrality could no longer serve England's vital Eastern interests, a new "British-friendly" enclave was needed—*fast*; enter one "national home for the Jewish people," a full year before the Armistice. (Not to be outdone, Germany issued a token "Declaration" via the Turkish Grand Vizier on January 5, 1918.) Though the Balfour "niche" was "considerably smaller" than the late Caliphate, its proximity to the Canal would serve HMG well.

MILITARY INCENTIVE

World War I (a.k.a. the "War to End All Wars") produced thirty million combat casualties. With such concomitant side effects as disease, famine, and privation, particularly the influenza epidemic of 1918-19, along with postwar border conflicts in Eastern Europe and the three-year Russian Revolution, the eventual figure rose to *sixty* million.[42]

Things got off with a *bang*. France moved 3,781,000 men in 7,000 trains between August 2-18, 1914, opening her ill-fated attack on Lorraine on August 14. In eleven days, 300,000 men (nearly 25% of their entire force) were dead or wounded; that figure would double.[43] In just two epic battles in 1916 (Verdun and Somme) over 1,700,000 casualties were sustained by both sides! The fire power was so intense that a man died every fifteen seconds. The carnage was only surpassed by the apparent futility of it all, seen by the impasse of trench warfare. Winding over 25,000 miles, the subterranean labyrinth could literally circle the globe. Neither army in "no man's land" could deliver the decisive blow (Germany checked by her own shell shortage, lacking vital raw materials such as cotton, camphor, pyrites, and saltpeter). Thus, the aforementioned title of the War's famous novel—*All Quiet on the Western Front*—actually reflected an official communiqué, i.e., "Nothing new to report." Things were no less surreal on the Eastern Front, Russian General Aleksei Brusilov having lost 1,000,000 men in a single sixty-day campaign in Galicia from June through August 1916.

Lloyd George wrote, "[T]he end of 1916 found the fortunes of the Allies at their lowest ebb."[44] The year's defining debacle proved the war's most ghastly scenario. As truth is stranger than fiction, German General Erich von Falkenhayn concocted a no-win public relations gambit designed to guarantee maximum casualties for *both* armies (his *own* included). Historian General S.L.A. Marshall explains that "he would stage one battle, so terrible in its dimensions, so shattering in its impact on both camps, that governments and peoples would be shocked into making peace on terms short of ruin for Germany."[45] The German "attack," code-named *Gericht* ("place of execution"), would proceed through a narrowly constricted corner of the Western Front.

> [H]e intended to manage the battle. He would keep the area of eruption limited by holding on to the general reserves and keeping

> them at a distance elsewhere...As the forces in the attack became expended, Falkenhayn would release their divisions to the Fifth Army, just enough to keep the battle going but never enough to end it...A more diabolical plan is beyond imagining. [His] object was to get as many people killed as possible.[46]

Because Erich refused to press his advantage, the French were forced to feed reserves into a sinkhole of blood (the resilient and convicting 57-year-old Alfred Dreyfus being among them). Though the insane ten-month "experiment" failed to elicit the intended peace, the Battle of Verdun *did* succeed in the "horrific" department—producing 700,000 casualties, making it one of the most bizarre battles in history!

The Entente Powers naturally felt that their only hope for breaking the stalemate was a major infusion of reinforcements (i.e., America, specifically, her massive production capabilities more so than her manpower). Wilson's avowed isolationism (enforced by a Congress and public in tandem) remained the key obstacle to American aid. In a speech on January 22, 1917, Wilson fantasized that the only way to end hostilities was for both sides to embrace "Peace without Victory." It was also understood that Yanks were ideologically opposed to British imperialism. Thus, while Jewry initially viewed Turkey's defection with optimism—that Herzl's dream would finally be realized—barring specific government intervention to that end, an Allied victory would simply "transfer" Eretz Yisrael to Anglo suzerainty. Another perceived hitch involved assessing the greater "bad guy." American Jews were thought to prefer Wilhelm II to Nicholas II (the "sticks and stones" of Russia's pogroms having "broken more bones" than the racist words of "Hep! Hep!" re-emerging in Germany's fading Emancipation).

British politicians began to assume that influential American Jews could alter the opinion of John Q. Public regarding the war. After all, two of Wilson's closest advisors were powerful Jewish Zionists: Judge Advocate General Felix Frankfurter (later, Justice Frankfurter) and Justice Louis D. Brandeis (Felix's uncle and former chairman of the American Provisional Executive Committee for General Zionist Affairs). In her book, *Against Our Better Judgment*, Alison Weir also denigrates the justices for their "highly unethical" involvement with the *Parushim* (an alleged Zionist cabal), citing Bruce Murphy's claim that "in one of the most unique arrangements in the Court's history...Working together over a period of 25 years, they placed a network of disciples in positions of influence, and labored diligently for the enactment of their desired programs."[47] Yet, one of Weir's own sources, former *New York Times* editor Peter Grose, appears to downgrade Parushim activity as an innocuous subliminal lobby: "The members set about meeting people of influence here and there, casually, and on a friendly basis. They planted suggestions to further the Zionist cause long before official government planners had come up with anything."[48] But then, how could a Bible dunce like Weir know that Jewish surreptitiousness is as old as chapter 13 of Numbers and chapter two of Joshua?

Of course, Eretz Yisrael would be the "key." During the gloomy winter of 1916, Armenian diplomat James Malcom advised Sykes, "You can win the sympathy of certain politically-minded Jews everywhere, and especially in the US, in one way only, and that is, by offering to try and secure Palestine for them."[49] An April 1917 Foreign Office note agreed: "It was supposed that American opinion might be favorably influenced if HMG gave an assurance that the return of the Jews to Palestine had become a purpose of British policy."[50] The naive Brits even thought that, given the coming dissolution of the Tsardom, leading Jewish Bolsheviks, like the Russian-born former Bronx resident, Lev Bronshtein (alias Leon Trotsky), could be "inspired" to dissuade, or at the least stall, the anticipated withdrawal of Imperial forces. At a War Cabinet meeting on October 31, 1917, Balfour said that his forthcoming pro-Zionist declaration would enable HMG "to carry on extremely useful propaganda both in Russia and America."[51]

Thus, as with Abe Lincoln's expedient Emancipation Proclamation, Lloyd George's wartime Balfour Declaration was being advanced (in part) as a *quid pro quo*. Churchill would openly affirm this in a speech before the House of Commons in July 1937: "It is a delusion to suppose this was a mere act of crusading enthusiasm or quixotic philanthropy. On the contrary, it was a measure taken…in due need of the war with the object of promoting the general victory of the Allies, for which we expected and received valued and important assistance."[52] Loftus and Aarons relate, "According to our source from the Foreign and Commonwealth Office, the only reason that the British even made the Balfour Declaration was for foreign propaganda purposes, not for domestic consumption."[53] The authors then add that British intelligence missed the mark, especially regarding the role of the Jewish press (*at that time*), there being "only two Jewish families of any significance among American publishers."[54]

And while the "native" pre-1880 vanguard of 250,000 Jews was primarily German-Ashkenazi—their leaders being highly educated, assimilated, and decidedly anti-Zionist—the later flood of some 3,000,000 immigrants, mostly from the Pale "barely spoke English" and "far from controlling US elections, few of them could even vote."[55] They end by minimizing the ultimate role of Jewish involvement: "The truth is that the support of American Jews was unnecessary. The US military commitment was well under way even before the Balfour Declaration was published."[56]

However, whether exaggerated or less than expected, a degree of Jewish-American clout was clearly used. After Wilson and Brandeis secretly hosted Balfour at the White House on May 10, 1917, Brandeis cabled Louis de Rothschild: "Have had a satisfactory talk with Mr. Balfour, also with our President. This is not for publication."[57] George rightly opined, "There is no better proof of the value of the Balfour Declaration as a military move than the fact that Germany entered into negotiations with Turkey in an endeavor to provide an alternative scheme which would appeal to Zionists."[58] This was the common view in the Fatherland, Samuel Landman (a British Zionist insider) stating, "The fact that it was Jewish help that brought U.S.A. into the War on the side of the Allies has rankled ever since in German—especially Nazi—minds, and has contributed in no small measure to the prominence which anti-Semitism occupies in the Nazi programme."[59]

FINANCIAL INCENTIVE

As the KJV is the *only* English translation that accurately words the eternal fact, *"For the love of money is* THE *root of all evil,"* the world renders its own "amen" via such modern parlance as, "Follow the money," or "If it don't make sense, there's a buck in it." The monetary inducement for the Declaration was the "no brainer," as everything from Sergeant York's bullets to Chaim's chestnuts had to be bought—with *borrowed* monies. That one barrage of 4½ million shells at Ypres cost £22,000,000 alone. (Given "Black Jack" Pershing's crotchet for cavalry, a third of all trans-Atlantic cargo was assigned to horse feed.)

The total estimated costs for all combatants (including shipping losses and mobilization expenses) was a staggering $260 billion which, by one valuation, "represented about six and a half times the sum of all the national debt accumulated in the world from the end of the eighteenth century up to the eve of the First World War."[60] The Carnegie Endowment for International Peace calculated that "the war destroyed over $400 billion of property at a time when the value of every object in France and Belgium was not worth over $75 billion."[61]

The technocrats on both sides not only misjudged the length of the "Great War," but its ultimate cost as well. Assuming that the "other guy" would be picking up the tab, they all suspended the gold standard to fund their costs. This, in turn, waived the automatic limit on the supply of paper money, leading each nation to borrow their way to victory. The House of Rothschild was Europe's predominant financial dynasty, the German poet, Heinrich Heine, writing, "Money is the God of our times, and Rothschild is his prophet."[62] J. P. Morgan & Co. (a.k.a. "The House of Morgan"), the most powerful fiscal institution in America, served as Rothschild's shadow agent. The Allies naturally desired to outbid their opponents for the available cash. The *Palestine Royal Commission Report* states: "In this critical situation it was believed that Jewish sympathy or the reverse would make a substantial difference one way or the other to the Allied cause. In particular Jewish sympathy would confirm the support of American Jewry, and would make it more difficult for Germany to reduce her military commitments and improve her economic position on the eastern front."[63] Lloyd George wrote in *Memoirs of the Peace Conference*:

> It was believed, also, that such a declaration would have a potent influence upon world Jewry outside Russia, and secure for the Entente the aid of Jewish financial interests. In America, their aid in this respect would have a special value when the Allies had almost exhausted the gold and marketable securities available for America purchases. Such were the chief considerations which, in 1917, impelled HMG towards making a contract with Jewry.[64]

"Britain, France and Germany attached considerable importance to the attitudes of Jewry towards them because money and credit were needed for the war," John and Hadawi write. "The international banking houses of Lazard Freres, Eugene Mayer, J. & W. Seligman, Speyer Brothers and M. M. Warburg, were all conducting major operations in the United States, as were the Rothschilds through the New York banking house of Kuhn, Loeb & Co."[65] However, Whitehall also knew that a Russian alliance would not bode well when seeking concessions from Jewish lenders. For, while Turkey was the *visible* barrier to Palestine, Russia was the main snag—being equally opposed by Eastern European Jews with their hatred of Tsarist pogroms and Western assimilated Jews with their habitual bent for German culture.

Jacob Schiff, the German-born senior partner in Kuhn, Loeb & Co., was considered "the most influential figure of his day in American Jewish life."[66] In the April 1915 *Menorah Journal*, he acknowledged: "It is well known that I am a German sympathizer...England has been contaminated by her alliance with Russia...I am quite convinced that in Germany anti-semitism is a thing of the past."[67] Though perhaps not the greatest "prophet" of his day, Schiff knew the banker's Golden Rule, "Whoever has the gold makes the rules." His reputation had also preceded him, the 1906 *Jewish Encyclopedia* stating, "Schiff's firm subscribed for and floated the large Japanese war loan in 1904-1905," the Imperial Russian Navy being sunk in the process.[68] (As noted in the book, *Stateless in Shanghai*, by Liliane Willens, Jews in the Shanghai Ghetto fared better under the Japanese than their European brethren did under Hitler, due in part to that loan.) His Jewish partners, Felix and Paul Warburg, migrated from Hamburg to New York in 1902 to help organize the Federal Reserve System. The siblings were equally antagonized by the climate that would foster the French slur, "Scratch a German and you will find a Hun."

Meanwhile, events were coming to a head. Like Europe's central banks, the Morgan-Rothschild war chest was also nearly spent due to increased Allied demands for credit. However, everything changed on April 6, 1917, with America's dramatic entrance into the conflict—followed eight days later by the War Loan Act extending $1 billion in fiat funds. As it was now only a matter of time before Palestine would be wrenched from Turkey, John and Hadawi confirm that a "*Statement of War Aims in the Near East* was issued under the auspices of HMG directed towards mobilizing American Jewish support to the utmost, and also perhaps to honor the negotiation which had been conducted with the Zionists relative to America's entry into the war. After all, the war had still to be won."[69] The Balfour Declaration debuted four days before the end of the Third Battle of Ypres (500,000 casualties).

About this time, a mundane Bavarian soldier was recovering with his unit in Alsace having survived that epic artillery barrage. Suddenly, however, a new type of "bomb" was seen falling from the sky. At the direction of a British version of the "Palestine Information Center," millions of Declaration leaflets (in Yiddish) were being dropped over "The Fatherland" to sway German-Jewish soldiers. (Copies were also distributed in the Pale.) Parts of the attached message read: "Jerusalem has fallen! The hour of Jewish redemption has arrived...The Allies are giving the Land of Israel to the people of Israel...Stop fighting the Allies, who are fighting for you...Remember! An Allied victory means the Jewish people's return to Zion."[70] There is every likelihood that the news found its way to Lance Corporal Adolf Hitler.

With the Central Powers no longer able to compete, the Armistice was signed on November 11, 1918 (a total of $9.466 million being loaned). As the *Palestine Royal Commission Report* reveals, Lloyd George believed that the Declaration played a key role in these events: "The Zionist leaders (Lloyd George informed us) gave us a definite promise that, if the Allies committed themselves to giving facilities for the establishment of a national home for the Jews in Palestine, they would do their best to rally Jewish sentiment and support throughout the world to the Allied cause. They kept their word."[71] One could also say that in the end, the Jewish money changers got to have their cake and eat it too. For, according to George, as the Tsar's overthrow would enable Germany to transfer several divisions from the Russian front to France before the Yanks could arrive, Britain originally planned to use the Declaration to sublimate the support of Russian Jews for the German war effort (stabilizing Nicholas and his armies in the process):

> Another cogent reason for the adoption by the Allies of the policy of the Declaration lay in the state of Russia herself. Russian Jews had been secretly active on behalf of the Central Powers from the first...by 1917 they had done much in preparing for that general disintegration of Russian society...It was believed that if Great Britain declared for the fulfillment of Zionist aspirations in Palestine under her own pledge, one effect would be to bring Russian Jewry to the cause of the Entente.[72]

However, twelve days before the Tsar's abdication on March 15, 1917, a Provisional Government formed in Russia, its first official act being the repeal of all discriminatory legislation against Jews.[73] Secret talks for a series of American loans totaling $190 million for the new administration of Alexander Kerensky were subsequently initiated on the advice of US Ambassador to Russia David Francis. In his cable to Secretary of State Robert Lansing, Francis noted that "financial aid now from America would be a master-stroke. Confidential. Immeasurably important to the Jews that revolution succeed."[74]

Upon Kerensky's ouster, Lenin took Russia out of the war, signing the Treaty of Brest-Litovsk on March 3, 1918. Unknown to most, the Allies then made the mistake of "throwing good money after bad," deploying 13,000 Anglo-French troops into North Russia and 8,000 American doughboys into Siberia in a failed bid to neutralize the Reds, sustaining 1,000 casualties in the process. While Stalin would have his *own* issues with Soviet Jewry, from a Jewish perspective—one that is often missed in a rush to broad-stroke all "Yids" as "pro-Marxist" more than "anti-Pogrom"—as with the late Hamas terrorist, Yahya "Hold the phone" Ayyash (a.k.a. "The Engineer"), "Little Nicky" would not be evicting anymore shtetls in the Pale (Genesis 12:3).

HISTORICAL INCENTIVE

Though not as pressing, the past also played a role in the Declaration. Britain's main European competitor for Palestine was Catholic France. The Esco study relates: "Prior to the war, the British generally considered it [Palestine], along with Syria, as a sphere of French influence."[75] However, the report also notes, "There was always a party in England which believed that, as a foremost Protestant power, Britain should take a greater interest in the affairs of the Holy Land."[76]

In the post-Reformation era, England shared more with Germany in cultural/spiritual areas than she did with the French. (Even during the Crusades, the focal hero was "Richard the Lion-Hearted.") France was also seen as spiritually bereft, British Prime Minister Herbert Asquith stating that Lloyd George "thinks it will be an outrage to let the Holy Places pass into the possession or under the protectorate of 'agnostic' and 'atheistic' France."[77] The ever politically incorrect Richard Meinertzhagen (descended from a leading Dutch family long-settled in England) remarked, "Our friendship with France, or indeed with any Latin Race, is unnatural and artificial. It can never be permanent."[78] A Meinertzhagen cable to Curzon in 1919 reflects the spirit of Herzl's icy Holy See reception: "It is also known that the Vatican is violently opposed to Zionism, as has already been reported to your Lordship."[79]

Whereas France is revered for "Our Lady of Fatima," England gave humanity the roaring "Monarch of Books"—The Holy Bible, King James 1611 Authorized Version. Even Weizmann pointed to Britain's Christian heritage as the basis for the Balfour Declaration (contrary to that caliber of "modern politics," characterized by a "lack of moral stamina, lack of vision and the principle of living hand to mouth"[80] that would later abandon Jewry): "Those British statesmen of the old school, I have said, were genuinely religious. They understood as a reality the concept of the Return. It appealed to their tradition and their faith."[81] Dr. Sachar writes that "Weizmann's efforts were buttressed by...the mystical veneration with which many devout Anglo-Saxon (or Welsh/Scottish) Protestants regarded the Old Testament traditions, the Children of Israel, and particularly the Holy Land itself."[82] Lord Harlech told Parliament in July 1937 that the primary motivation for the Declaration was the ideal of the restoration of the Jews to their ancient homeland."[83] Meinertzhagen concurred:

> I believed in the Old Testament prophecy...that Christianity itself depended on a Jewish Palestine. I believed that a people whose history and tradition went back for four thousand unbroken years, a people who gave us the Old Testament, our monotheist religion and Jesus of Nazareth, a people who contributed so much to art and science: that such people should continue to suffer and be homeless when we could alleviate that suffering and grant that home, was to me a disgrace to civilization."[84]

ALTRUISTIC INCENTIVE

Howard Temperley of Cambridge wrote, "At a time when justice for oppressed races and small peoples had become an Allied slogan it was at least consistent to include the Jews among those whose wrongs might be righted as an outcome of the War."[85] While the strategic goal of preserving the Suez Canal was the key impetus for the Declaration, pragmatism is not necessarily inconsistent with altruistic impulses. In a memo to Herbert Samuel, Lord Reading explained Lloyd George's attitude: "Your proposal appeals to the poetic and imaginative as well as to the romantic and religious qualities of his mind."[86]

As a statesman and a man of letters, Arthur Balfour strove to identify with both. In addition to promoting his signature doctrine to solidify Britain's artery to the East, he also made repeated, emotional appeals for his countrymen to purge "the ancient stain on our civilization."[87] Dr. Sachar notes, "Yet, in Balfour's case, a genuine vein of Zionist mysticism unquestionably strengthened commitment to the Jewish national home."[88] His biographer agreed, stating, "He had discerned a determination behind the Zionist ideology which appealed to him as a philosopher, and impressed him as a student of history. He became convinced that the revival of the sentiment of Jewish unity was no less worthy of respect than other national movements of the modern world, which were better understood because they sprang from geographically united peoples."[89] In a House of Lords debate, Balfour expressed his conviction regarding the significance of the Jews' aliyah (an appeal not dissimilar in style to George Washington's letter to the Touro Synagogue in Newport, Rhode Island):

> I do not deny that this is an adventure. Are we never to have adventures? I hope your Lordships will never sink to that unimaginative depth, and that experiment and adventure will be justified if there is any case or cause for their justification. Surely, it is in order that we may send a message to every land where the Jewish race has been scattered, a message which will tell them that Christendom is not oblivious of their faith, is not unmindful of the service they have rendered to the great religions of the world, and most of all, to the religion that the majority of your Lordships' House profess, and that we desire to the best of our ability to give them that opportunity of developing, in peace and quietness under British rule, those great gifts which hitherto they have been compelled from the very nature of the case only to bring to fruition in countries which know not their language and belong not to their race? That is the ideal which I desire to see accomplished, that is the aim which lay at the root of the policy I am trying to defend; and, though it be defensible indeed on every ground, that is the ground which chiefly moves me."[90]

SINISTER INCENTIVE

The last incentive is as sorry as the previous one was sentimental; yet, the same players are involved. To begin, the "*Balfour* Declaration" was not even penned by Mr. Balfour. Professor Quigley (of Harvard, Princeton, and Georgetown) confirms: "This declaration, which is always known as the Balfour Declaration, should rather be called 'the Milner Declaration,' since [Alfred] Milner was the actual draftsman and was, apparently, its chief supporter in the War Cabinet."[91]

According to Dr. Quigley, the news was first publicized on July 21, 1937 (seven years after Balfour's death), when Colonial Secretary of State William Ormsby-Gore informed the House of Commons: "The draft as originally put up by Lord Balfour was not the final draft approved by the War Cabinet. The particular draft assented to by the War Cabinet and afterwards by the Allied Governments and by the United States…and finally embodied in the Mandate, happens to have been drafted by Lord Milner. The actual final draft had to be issued in the name of the Foreign Secretary, but the actual draftsman was Lord Milner."[92] Then, in 2000 (twenty-three years after *Quigley's* death), William Rubinstein, a professor at Aberystwyth University in Wales and former president of the Jewish Historical Society of England, asserted in *his* book that the true author was Leopold Amery, Assistant Secretary to the War Cabinet.[93] Finally, to further confuse things, there are *two* "Balfour Declarations"—the latter, dated 1926, confirming the autonomous status of the varied Dominions within the British Empire.

As I Corinthians 14:33 declares, *"For God is not the author of confusion,"* the reader has now arrived at the jumping off point for the subtitle of this volume—*A Century of Anglo-American Anti-Semitism.* Just five years after the Declaration was issued, it was already a matter of "conjecture" as to *why* it was ever issued at all. In a 1922 letter to Churchill about the document's origin, Ormsby-Gore conceded, "Such papers as it has been possible to obtain are very meagre…indeed, little is known of how the policy represented by the Declaration was first given form…only the scantiest records are available."[94]

To comprehend the sinister incentive behind the Balfour Declaration, one must first uncover the cabal that spawned many of its key architects—"The Group" (a.k.a. "The Milner Group" or "Round Table Groups")—the most notorious secret society in the history of Great Britain (covered in volume one of this series.) In his 1,300-page tome, *Tragedy and Hope*, Quigley affirmed: "There does exist, and has existed for a generation, an international Anglophile network which operates, to some extent, in the way the radical Right believes the Communists act…this network, which we may identify as the Round Table Groups, has no aversion to cooperating with the Communists, or any other groups, and frequently does so."[95]

Dr. Quigley's surprise exposé evoked a firestorm for two reasons—his prestigious Ivy League curriculum vitae and his privileged window of access: "I know of the operations of this network because I have studied it for twenty years and was permitted for two years, in the early 1960's, to examine its papers and secret records."[96] His expanded revelation, *The Anglo-American Establishment*, was posthumously released in 1981, the publisher, Stephen Zarlenga, writing:

> On very rare occasions a book appears which forever changes the way in which we perceive the world around us. Within a short while it becomes hard to understand how we could have functioned without the knowledge gained from it. *The Anglo-American Establishment* is such a book. In it Professor Carroll Quigley presents certain "keys" crucial to the understanding of 20th century political, economic and military events – events of the past, present, and future.[97]

With its ideology conceived by the wealthy British socialist John Ruskin at Oxford University in 1870, the movement gained its substantive development under Cecil John Rhodes, followed by Alfred Lord Milner. Typical of all humanist visionaries, one biographer notes, "The government of the world was Rhodes' simple desire."[98] As the founder of Rhodesia wrote to William Stead in 1890: "The key of my idea discussed with you is a Society, copied from the Jesuits as to organization…an idea which ultimately (leads) to the cessation of all wars and one language throughout the world…The only thing feasible to carry this idea out is a secret one (society) gradually absorbing the wealth of the world to be devoted to such an object."[99]

The principle movers and shakers of Cecil's coterie included such "household names" as: Lord Salisbury; Arnold Toynbee; Lord Halifax; Lionel George Curtis; William T. Snead; Reginald Baliol Brett; William Ormsby-Gore; Lord Curzon; Waldorf Astor; Lady Astor; Sir Abe Bailey;

Geoffrey Dawson; Robert Henry Brand; Sir Reginald Coupland; Jan C. Smuts; John W. Wheeler-Bennett; Lord Thomas Brassey; et al. Similar to the alumni of Yale University's Order of Skull and Bones, the tentacles of their clandestine power stretched from Oxford (specifically All Souls, Balliol, and New Colleges), to the control of public opinion via the London *Times*; the recording of their own history via the *Dictionary of National Biography*; the indoctrination of future generations via the prestigious Rhodes Scholarship (William Jefferson Clinton); and, most notably, the direction of foreign policy via the Royal Institute of International Affairs (the Council on Foreign Affairs its US peer). The four-member War Cabinet of 1917-18 consisted of Prime Minister Lloyd George, "assisted" by three Group devotees—Milner, Curzon, and Smuts.

The members who impacted the Declaration include: Lord Milner; Leopold Amery; Nathan Rothschild; Lord Curzon; and, of course, Mr. Balfour. While British Jewry interpreted the Declaration as a mandate for statehood (at least in the foreseeable future), Milner concealed his private interpretation behind a cloak of ambiguity. Addressing the House of Lords on June 27, 1923, he admitted that the *real* purpose for importing Jews into Palestine was—money. "I am not speaking of the policy which is advocated by the extreme Zionists, which is a totally different thing…I believe we have only to go on steadily with the policy of the Balfour Declaration as we have ourselves interpreted it in order to see great material progress in Palestine."[100]

The dissolution of the Ottoman Empire also served to unleash the potential for a measure of Arab nationalism: "Arabism" as the Muslim equivalent of Zionism; i.e., Ibn Saud as the Arab Herzl. Milner's political vision of a British-based commonwealth of nations would therefore have to incorporate a league of Arab states. Thus, in that same speech he declared, "I believe in the independence of the Arab countries, which they owe to us and which they can only maintain with our help. I look forward to an Arab Federation."[101] Of course, looking down the road, the only "problem" was the politically incorrect reality of racial inequality (Steinbeck's "four thousand years of urine" quip). The Group believed that a proportioned influx of Jewish initiative and business acumen would invigorate Palestine, thereby offering the Arab world an appealing "front door" to Western ideas. John Dove, editor of *The Round Table*, wrote:

> If the Arab belongs to the Mediterranean, as T. E. Lawrence insists, we should do nothing to stop him getting back to it…Personally,

> I don't see the slightest harm in Jews coming to Palestine under reasonable conditions. They are the Arabs' cousins...and if Zionism brings capital and labour which will enable industries to start, it will add to the strength of the larger unit which some day is going to include Palestine. But they must be content to be part of such a potential unit.[102]

As Dove's last comment infers, The Group had no intention of *ever* allowing Jewry to secure legal status. Provide economic stimulus for Arab growth? Yes! Attain independence? Never! With reference to Milner's speech, Quigley notes, "He then went on to say that he felt that Palestine would require a permanent mandate and under that condition could become a National Home for the Jews, could take as many Jewish immigrants as the country could economically support, but 'must never become a Jewish state.'"[103] This pecuniary policy was cited in the world's only *inspired* "history" book over 2,500 years ago, Daniel 11:39 stating that the Antichrist will *"divide the land for gain."*

While Quigley wrote, "The Group were never anti-Semitic...In fact, they were very sympathetic to the Jews and to their legitimate aspirations to overcome their fate," he *also* confessed that "this feeling...was rather general and remote," blaming the disconnect on a lack of "real contact with Jews or any real appreciation of the finer qualities of those people."[104] He closes his remarks by recalling that mysterious "desert allurement," affirming that although the powers behind the Declaration were "non-anti-Semitic," they *were* decidedly "pro-Arab": "Their feeling against anti-Semitism was, on the whole, remote and academic. On the other hand, as with most upper-class English, their feeling for the Arabs was somewhat more personal."[105] The Jews' Messiah was not impressed, having previously declared: *"He that is not with me is* AGAINST *me...."* (Matthew 12:30)

CONCLUSION

Having come full circle, a final comment is in order regarding the first of these seven incentives. By now it should be obvious that HMG was more concerned with securing the Suez Canal for Britain than in securing the Holy Land for the Jews. Thus, history confirms that Weizmann's providential role in ending Britain's shell crisis was not *the* catalyst for the Declaration. However, in an instinctive rush to judgment of the romantic, something elementary has been overlooked.

If the flurry of costly production activity that occasioned Chaim's find is to be taken seriously, *could* this timely intervention have tipped the scale in favor of the Allies? While Britain did not award the Declaration *because* of Weizmann, the question begs—Could Britain have awarded it *without* him? Would a paper promising the Jews "a homeland in Palestine" have impressed Turkey if the war had ended according to Wilson's "Peace without Victory" mantra? While the full military effect of Chaim's acetone process may never be known (though his role in the overall Jewish impact on America's entrance into the war cannot be questioned), a contemporary appraisal bears mention. As noted earlier, the esteemed Scottish chemist, William Rintoul, had a propitious encounter with Weizmann two years into the war. What he said regarding Chaim's report constitutes a sentimental witness to the spiritual theme posited in the Introduction of this book:

> One day, in the spring of 1916, I received a visit from Dr. Rintoul, the chief research chemist of Nobel's, the big explosive manufacturers, located at Ardeer, in Ayrshire. What the original purpose of his visit was I do not know. We gossiped about the war, and then the conversation turned to my researches, which I described to him in detail. When I had ended, he said to me, thoughtfully: "You know, you may have the KEY to a very important situation in your hands."[106] (Author's emphasis)

Thus, *the* "key" that opened the door to an Allied victory in World War I was—once again—a *Jewish* key. However, as the rest of *Holy Ground* will document, this event would mark the *last* such usage. For, no sooner had the Declaration been issued than the "Locksmiths of Laodicea" began to repudiate the same. In the future, any and all doors (especially the 1948 UN partition vote) would be "opened" via *forced* entry, using everything from blackmail and targeted assassinations to the threat of nuclear weapons (i.e., "The Samson Option").

6

Little Wrongs

"In short, so far as Palestine is concerned, the Powers have made no statement of fact which is not admittedly wrong, and no declaration of policy which, at least in the letter, they have not always intended to violate."
(Arthur Balfour, 1919)

"Is it fair that Palestine with its undeveloped resources, should be refused progress because its inhabitants are incapable of it?"
(Richard Meinertzhagen, 1920)

"The formation of a Battalion of Jews…in the British Army is an event without precedent…the part played by such a unique unit is assured a niche in history, owing to the fact that it fought in Palestine, not only for the British cause, but also for the Restoration of the Jewish people to the Promised Land."
(John Henry Patterson, 1922)

WHILE THE CABINET was ratifying the final text of the Balfour Declaration, Chaim paced anxiously outside. Finally, the door opened: "Sykes brought the document out to me, with the exclamation: 'Dr. Weizmann, it's a boy!'"[1] The "new father's" response was telling: "Well—I did not like the boy at first. He was not the one I had expected. But I knew that this was a great departure…A new chapter had opened for us, full of new difficulties, but not without its great moments."[2] As with Pharaoh's decree in Exodus 1:22, *"Every son that is born ye shall cast into the river,"* a Whitehall imbroglio had already nearly rendered the newborn dead in the water! "It is no exaggeration to say," Meinertzhagen noted, "that the very people who have undertaken to wean the Zionist child are those who have exerted themselves most to strangle it at birth."[3]

With *"the author of confusion"* (I Corinthians 14:33) on the prowl, the nebulous Balfour Declaration was destined to provoke a climate of mass disorientation. As John 8:44 calls Satan *"a liar and the father of it,"* history confirms that the source of all the trouble was a series of lies and deception perpetrated by the esteemed Government of His Britannic Majesty. Arthur Balfour was *still* trying to clean up the mess in 1922. Doreen Ingrams captured the spirit of the times with her take on Balfour's House of Lords address on the eve of the Mandate's vote by the League of Nations: "He took his stand on the proposition that to do a great right it was expedient to do a little wrong."[4] To the contrary, Dr. Bob Jones, Sr., often said, "It is never right to do wrong to get a chance to do right." Unfortunately, the repercussions from those "little wrongs" would drastically impede the "great right" over the ensuing decades, particularly in that critical five-year "incubation" period.

THE "GREAT ARAB REVOLT"

By 1917, the Milner-led War Cabinet had conjured up their own giant desert mirage by making several disparate promises which they simply could not keep. Two years later, Balfour wrote Lord Curzon, "In short, so far as Palestine is concerned, the Powers have made no statement of fact which is not admittedly wrong, and no declaration of policy which, at least in the letter, they have not always intended to violate."[5]

Like Proverbs 17:4 says, *"A wicked doer giveth heed to false lips,"* the background of this duplicity began with Britain being deceived herself. As late as a year into the war, Whitehall still favored the existence of "Turkey-in-Asia" (an independent though decentralized "empire," as opposed to outright Allied partition). Around this time, the powerful Secretary of State for War Lord Horatio Kitchener had become enamored with a radically diverse plan. (Among his previous "stellar" feats, the Sirdar is remembered for having created the first modern concentration camp during the Boer War, causing 28,000 civilian deaths, mostly women and children.) The new idea was being pitched by Hussein Ibn Ali, Hashemite Sharif of Mecca. (Hashemite

Arabs claim direct or collateral lineage to the "Prophet" Muhammad.) Having passed himself off as the explicit spokesman for the "whole of the Arab Nation without exception,"[6] Hussein offered to incite an empire-wide revolt against the Turks in exchange for a postwar pledge of Arab autonomy—a new empire stretching from Asia Minor to the Indian Ocean and from the Persian frontier to the Mediterranean Sea.

After costly British defeats at Gallipoli and Mesopotamia, the prospect of harnessing Arab cannon fodder in the Middle East theater was a welcome offer indeed. In his zeal to assure Hussein that he was definitely on board, Horatio even hinted at a possible "promotion" for the Sharif, writing in November 1914: "Till now we have defended and befriended Islam in the person of the Turks; henceforward it shall be in that of the noble Arab...It may be that an Arab of true race will assume the Caliphate at Mecca or Medina and so good may come by the help of God out of all evil which is now occurring."[7] (Of course, to imply that the God of Israel would care about enhancing the genetic purity of Islam was indicative of the approaching train wreck.)

While Britain's need to preserve the Canal was always paramount, at this stage it appears that an Arab fix under British suzerainty was being assessed ahead of a Zionist buffer. Reginald Wingate, Governor-General of the Sudan, envisioned "a federation of semi-independent Arab states...linked together by racial and religious bonds, owing spiritual allegiance to a single Arab Primate, and looking to Great Britain as its Patron and Protector."[8] Indeed, the final—and *fatal*—communiqué would contain the inane proviso that "it is understood that the Arabs have decided to seek the advice and guidance of Great Britain only."[9] Efraim and Inari Karsh write in *Empires of the Sand*:

> Given their keen awareness of the colorful mosaic that was the Arabic-speaking communities and their perception of the caliphate in purely religious terms, they viewed this institution as a magic formula that could bring together the disparate elements of the Arabic-speaking peoples, under British tutelage, without creating a unified empire that would endanger Britain's own imperial interests...Yet this caliph was to wield no temporal powers whatsoever, and the promised sovereignty was interpreted "in a generic sense."[10]

Kitchener's clandestine operation would be monitored by his loyal protégés at the Arab Bureau of the Cairo Intelligence Department, Ronald

Storrs, Reginald Wingate, and Gilbert Clayton. (Egypt was declared a British protectorate on December 18, 1914.) The *perceived* conditions of the "Anglo-Sharif alliance" were negotiated in an exchange of letters between Hussein and Sir Henry McMahon, British High Commissioner of Egypt. Throughout their long correspondence, Hussein maintained his specific desideratum—temporal power with definable borders—*in writing*. McMahon held out for the more expedient "spiritual" kingdom. The files of the British Public Record Office also confirm that T. E. Lawrence and St. John "Jack" Philby were applying pressure through a steady barrage of faulty intel reports, inflating both the Turkish threat and the Arabs' fighting prowess.[11]

With the proposed alliance stalled, a 24-year-old Arab deserter would unexpectedly tip the scales in Hussein's favor. (The results of this fateful encounter would reverberate in the desert for decades.) In September 1915, Lieutenant Muhammad Sharif al-Faruqi defected to the Allies (at Gallipoli, of all places) alleging to have critical info for the British High Command. Faruqi was a member of the al-Ahd Arab secret society which, recently merged with the al-Fatat coterie. In his Cairo debriefing, Faruqi claimed that the two groups comprised a massive insurgency network with branches in "every important town or station," commanding the loyalty of "the natives, sedentary and nomads, and all sects." He also insisted that 90% of the Arab officers in the Turkish army were loyal al-Ahd members. His most significant revelation was that both groups had pledged their allegiance to Hussein Ibn Ali and were ready to overthrow the Turks at *his* word.[12]

Well, that was all she wrote! In his official report on Faruqi's interview, Clayton said, "That the attitude of the Shariff is that of the majority of the Arab peoples there can be little doubt."[13] It was time for HMG to pursue another mirage. London was inundated with cables from Cairo. The following excerpt from an October 12 dispatch to Kitchener from Sir John Maxwell (military commander in Egypt) was typical: "A powerful organization with considerable influence in the army and among Arab Chiefs…have made up its mind that the moment for action has arrived…[The] Sharif [of] Mecca, who is in communication with the Arab party…seems uneasy and is pressing for a declaration of policy." The text concludes, "The active assistance which the Arabs would render in return for our support would be of the greatest value in Arabia, Mesopotamia, Syria and Palestine."[14]

While the Foreign Office was weighing this latest issue, the High Commissioner in Cairo was well aware of the prevailing strategy to forestall any territorial commitments. Foreign Secretary Edward Grey, had previously told McMahon: "The simplest plan would be to give an assurance of Arab independence saying that we will proceed at once to discuss boundaries if they will send representatives for that purpose."[15] However, apparently deciding to take matters into his own hands, Sir Henry wired Hussein an "official" promise of his own—the infamous McMahon Pledge of October 24—satisfying nearly all of his demands. With that one precipitous phrase, "I am empowered in the name of the Government of Great Britain to give you the following assurances," the nebulous caliphate had morphed into a bona fide empire with borders! Two days later, Grey was dutifully informed: "In view of the urgency of the matter I seized a suitable opportunity which occurred today of sending a reply to the Sharif of Mecca."[16] McMahon's volte-face was plainly inspired by the "Cairo triumvirate." Karsh concludes, "On the basis of no more than the account of an obscure member of two small secret societies, Cairo had committed HMG to creating a vast empire for the sake of a local potentate."[17]

The "Great Arab Revolt" *finally* began on June 5, 1915. With the tacit approval of the Foreign Office, Sharif Hussein crowned himself "King of the Hejaz" (west of present-day Saudi Arabia). According to Lowell Thomas, "Colonel T. E. Lawrence" was the quintessential swashbuckler who held it all together. However, notwithstanding the action in Peter O'Toole's cinematic version, the highly anticipated desert revolt—equipped, trained, and led by British staff—*flopped*. The Esco study confirms: "The conquest of Palestine and Syria was effected chiefly by the British. The Arabs who assisted Allenby...were a relatively small force. The Syrian and Palestinian Arabs did not contribute to the victory."[18] Lloyd George wrote in his memoirs, "What the Arabs were apt to overlook is the fact that their contribution in the conquest of Palestine and Syria was almost insignificant compared with that of the British Empire."[19] To put things in perspective, during the touted Battle of Aqaba, T. E. accidently shot his camel in the head[20] (not to mention being conspicuously absent at the formal surrender of Damascus, having arrived several hours late).

THE JEWISH LEGION

The dismal showing of the "*Great* Arab Revolt" becomes even more "revolting" when compared to the little-known ("suppressed") Jewish contributions to the war effort. With their entire ethnoscape at stake, scores of Zionist patriots resolved to emulate their ancestors to *"pass over armed."* (Deuteronomy 3:18) Thus, in 1915, the iconic Russians Vladimir Jabotinsky and Joseph Trumpeldor proposed the formation of an all-Jewish regiment to aid in the conquest of Palestine.

Now although General John Maxwell, Commander of the Egyptian Expeditionary Force (EEF), sympathized with the Zionist offer, he had no immediate plans to invade Palestine, nor were foreign nationals allowed in the British military. As an alternative, he suggested that an auxiliary detachment for mule transport be used elsewhere. While Jabotinsky recoiled at associating "mules" with the rebirth of Zion, the more pragmatic Trumpeldor—relating the beast's innate stubbornness to that of his own people—promptly seized the moment, exhorting prospective recruits on March 19, "History is giving us an opportunity which has not been given to us in almost all the centuries of our exile. We will be the first to fight with our blood for the liberation of our land. We will be followed by thousands of other Jews."[21] Nearly 200 Jews (mostly Palestine exiles) volunteered on the spot. The famed "Zion Mule Corps" was now a political reality. Major General Sir Alexander Godley noted the magnitude of the occasion: "Today the English people have entered into a covenant with the Jewish people."[22]

Another 470 joined that the first week. In a major cultural anomaly, the fledgling Jewish trial would be led by a feisty Irish Protestant by the name of *Patterson*. A worldly veteran of the Boer War, Lieutenant Colonel John H. Patterson would become a devoted life-long Zionist. After less than a month of training, 562 "Zion Muleteers" were wading ashore the bloody beaches of Gallipoli (Britain's main debacle of the war). It didn't take long for John's Jews to "forget" their ancillary role. Biographer Denis Brian writes "Although the Zion Mule Corps was officially forbidden to join in the fighting, the men were armed with rifles, bayonets, and ammunition, and soon broke the rule."[23]

Even the mules got in on the action. As the Jews' battle cry was "The sword of the Lord and of Gideon" (Judges 7:20), Patterson called it a "curious coincidence" that the Turks were defeated by a similar providential ruse. Noting that "The Turkish General Staff had not calculated on the Zion mules," he relates how a nocturnal enemy sortie was foiled when the animals suddenly stampeded and "clattered down with clanking chains on the stealthy foe. The Turks undoubtedly took them for charging cavalry, for they poured a volley into them and thus gave away their position. Our men instantly lined the trenches and opened such an intense fire that the Turks were routed."[24]

The commanding general, Sir Ian Hamilton, appraised the Jews' mettle accordingly: "It is a purely Jewish unit (except for Patterson and a few other officers). As far as I know, this is the first time in the Christian era that such a thing has happened. They have shown great courage taking supplies up to the line under heavy fire."[25] Legion chronicler Elias Gilner observed: "The irony of the situation was obvious: what centuries of ethical, self-disciplined living, and the most gruesome persecution could not accomplish, a few mules did. A door to international recognition had been opened."[26]

By August 1917, an all-Jewish *combat* unit was finally approved. The 38th Battalion of Royal Fusiliers became the nucleus of the legendary "Jewish Legion" (the 39th-42nd Battalions forming later, the 39th comprising mostly Jews from America and Canada). Though Patterson proposed that the historic unit be led by a Jew, the Zionists refused his resignation. "There is only one nominee," Jabotinsky said. "Even though he is not a Jew, he must be our colonel, and I hope that one day he will be our general: Patterson."[27] Trumpeldor seconded the nomination, the War Office approved, and Patterson humbly accepted.

The total strength of the Legion—the core of the modern Israeli Defense Force—grew to 5,000 (one-sixth of the British occupation army and half of Faisal's Arab irregulars at median strength). The Foreign Office would later affirm: "Practically the whole available Jewish youth of the colonies, and many of the townsmen of military age, came forward for voluntary enlistment in the Jewish battalions, took the oath to King George V, and were clad in British uniforms."[28]

Jabotinsky's vision was able to see the light of day through a double stroke of providence. First, the most vociferous critic of the proposed experiment, Lord Kitchener himself, was killed by a German U-boat on June 5, 1916—the first anniversary of his celebrated "Arab Revolt." Conversely, the key supporter of the "Jew Army" was none other than Leopold Amery, a member of the infamous Milner Group.

Noting that Amery "wholeheartedly supported a Jewish Legion," Brian adds, "He was also capable of keeping secrets. Not until 1999—forty-four years after his death—was it revealed that he was Jewish."[29]

After a brief training stint in Portsmouth, the 38th Battalion moved to Southampton for embarkation on February 5. The day before their departure, British General Sir Nevil Macready diverted half the troops to London for a symbolic parade (particularly through the Jewish East End). Described by Patterson as "a scene unparalleled in the history of any previous British battalion," 500 legionaries, led by their mounted Irish commander, emerged from the Tower of London bearing both the Union Jack *and* Zionist flag, preceded by the Coldstream Guards band playing the HaTikva.[30] Thousands of Jews and Gentiles cheered and wept together at the sight of their former tailors and merchants marching "shoulder to shoulder, their bayonets dead level," in columns of four abreast, the *Magen David* clearly featured on their uniforms—as Jabotinsky recorded, "each step like a single clap of thunder, clean, proud, and drunk with the sense of a holy mission."[31] The highpoint of the day occurred when Captain and Mrs. Israel Fredman presented the 38th with a *Sefer Torah* (Torah Scroll) to accompany them to Zion.

The Legion arrived at Alexandria, Egypt, on March 1. The next three months were spent in training outside Cairo. With the onset of Passover, Patterson wrote that "history was repeating itself in the Land of Bondage in a Jewish military camp, after a lapse of over three thousand years." He also noted ominously, "I had considerable trouble with the authorities in the matter of providing unleavened bread."[32] Away from the public spotlight in London, the 38th Battalion faced continual discrimination at the hands of General Allenby's EEF. "Hostility to all things Jewish was so open, only those who willfully shut their eyes could fail to see the game that was being played by certain interested parties."[33] Sadly, Edmund Allenby—the same hero who humbly dismounted before the Jaffa Gate—would condone the demeaning anti-Semitism that permeated his subordinates.

In Cairo, such racist acts were justified as "little wrongs" for the "greater right"—appeasing their "loyal" Arab allies.[34] To his credit, John was willing to stand up for his own. "I am always prone to be on the side of the underdog. I was constantly called upon to ward off unfair kicks, aimed at the Jewish Battalion under my command, by certain members of the local Staff of the Egyptian Expeditionary Force."[35] Meinertzhagen shares a typical colorful example: "His Brigadier was a peppery little man who detested Jews. The battalion was inspected and the Brigadier, finding a man with dirty buttons, referred to him as a 'dirty little Jew.' Patterson at once ordered the Battalion to fix bayonets, formed square round the Brigadier and refused to let him out until he apologized, which he did."[36]

The Jewish Legion finally departed for Eretz Yisrael on June 5. As prearranged by the battalion chaplain, Rabbi Falk, trumpets were sounded when the train crossed over to "invade" the Promised Land, the uncanny date being June 6—the future "D-Day" in Europe:

> All through the night, as we sped across the Sinai Desert, seated in our open trucks, we could see the funnel of the engine belching forth a pillar of flame, and we were greatly reminded of the wanderings in this very desert, of the forefathers of these men, who in their night journeys were always guided by a pillar of fire. Nor did the simile cease as dawn broke...then the pillar of flame turned into a cloud of smoke shot up into the still morning air.[37]

Patterson reflected, "[I]t would not surprise me if the historian of the future seized upon this dramatic appearance of the Jewish warrior, fighting for the redemption of Israel under the banner of England, as one of the most interesting episodes of the great World War."[38]

The trip became a spontaneous jaunt into the past. "As we rolled onward, historical places cropped up every few miles and kept us spellbound with interest. Beersheba...the Shephelah...the mountains of Ephraim and of Judea."[39] Detraining in Ludd, the 38th marched to its first bivouac at Surafend, whereupon "the Jewish colonists of Richon-le-Zion, Jaffa, Rechoboth, and all the surrounding colonies, came out in hundreds with flags and banners, on foot, on horseback, and in chariots, to greet us, and show us how much they thought of their brethren who had come all the way from England to help them redeem their country."[40] The Hebrew warriors were in the ultimate ethnoscape.

Once again, the euphoria was short-lived. Patterson notes that on August 12 "we marched off under the walls of Jerusalem, passed the Damascus Gate, skirted the Garden of Gethsemane, and wended our way on to the road which would take us down to Jericho...and the desolation of the Jordan Valley which lay spread out before me."[41] The most flagrant anti-Semitic plot against the Legion was revealed by the inhospitable site of their first extended deployment—seven weeks in the sweltering heat and fever-stricken desolation of *Wadi Mellahah* (a ten-mile rift running a mile to the west of, and roughly parallel to, the Jordan River). According to one Australian veteran, "God need not have troubled to make hell when He had the Jordan Valley."[42]

Situated in the Judean Wilderness, the region remains enveloped in a stagnant fine dust, up to a foot in some places. John recalled that as his men trudged on, "clouds of it arose and choked them, while their feet were actually sucked down at each step, and an effort had to be made to draw the foot out again as if some devil were below, pulling at the sole of their boot...It was about the hottest, most unhealthy, and most God-forsaken place in the universe—in fact, some of my men assured me that they saw the Devil himself there, horns, tails and all!"[43] (The recurring allusions to "Hell" were more prescient than one might realize—Isaiah 34:9, cross-referenced with Revelation 14:10 and Matthew 5:22, 29-30, identifying this sulfuric no man's land as the site of God's literal "Hell on earth" during the Millennium.)

The 38th was also deprived of adequate medical care. The attrition was scandalous, 200 men a week being sidelined from malaria alone.[44] One sick bay report listed 27 officers and 824 enlisted men disabled, nearly 90% of the Battalion.[45] Thus, noting that even "the wild Bedouins...flee from the accursed place in these two dreaded months [August and September]" and that "no British soldier had yet been called upon to endure the horrors of the Mellahah even for a week,"[46] John filed a fourteen-page protest, tantamount to charging GHQ with attempted murder! Brian says "[H]e accused General Louis Bols [infamous Chief Administrator in Palestine, 1919-20] of 'conspiring to have the Regiment wiped out by the Turks by placing it at 1,200 feet below sea level, at the hottest time of the year, at the bottom of the Jordan Valley.'"[47] The irked Irish Zionist remarked, "Knowing that our enemies had already tried to abolish the Battalion, I was reminded of the story of Uriah the Hittite! How terribly we suffered."[48]

Despite these, and other, draconian conditions the men "soldiered on," resolved to support the greater cause. And yet, *any* progress was notable, as the Jews were conspicuously sequestered from occasions for valor in the field. "It almost looked as if our enemies feared we would do well, and our progress would then get noised abroad to the discomfiture of our detractors."[49] Another morale drain was a lack of regimental identity. With over 5,000 Jews "in the system," Allenby repeatedly reneged on his written oath to enact the War Office's stated intent to form a Jewish Brigade. Thus, the 38th and 39th Battalions were shuffled from pillar to post, being "attached" to no less than twelve formations of the British army.[50] John concludes, "[T]he policy adopted by the local staff was to keep us as 'wandering Jews.'"[51]

THE MEGIDDO CAMPAIGN

After having to settle for a number of minor skirmishes along the Mellahah (the extreme right flank of the EEF), the Legion was finally cleared to participate in Allenby's climactic 1918 autumn offensive under the providential command of Major General Sir Edward Chaytor, a Zionist sympathizer and friend of Patterson. The Megiddo Campaign (September 19-25)—fought on the very site of the future apocalyptic Battle of Armageddon—would be the decisive encounter.

On September 19, the Australian and New Zealand Mounted Divisions spearheaded a five-week, 500-mile pincer movement from Jaffa to Syria. As the 38th and 39th set out to augment the campaign strategy, the animated Americans led their "native" brethren in singing "Over There" in Hebrew![52] (Two future Israeli prime ministers and one president were among the group: David Ben-Gurion, Levi Eshkol, and Yitzak Ben-Zvi.[53]) The Legion would pride itself in two key areas.

In the predawn hours of September 22, the 38th Battalion waded across the Jordan in chin-deep water at the strategic Umm esh Shert Ford, routing the entrenched Turks in a ferocious battle. This enabled General Chaytor to rush the 1st Australian Light Horse Brigade into Transjordan to outflank them. Then, while a band of Patterson's men remained at the ford to block the Ottomans' only way of escape, the rest followed Chaytor's mounted eastward advance in a rearguard action, resulting in the capture of Es Salt (ancient Ramoth Gilead) and Amman (Rabbah), effectively ending combat operations in the area.

Unbeknown to the Turks, Allenby had employed the Transjordan expedition as a ruse to divert sizable numbers of the enemy away from his intended invasion route to the west. The Turks suffered 50,000 casualties with Beirut, Aleppo, and Damascus capitulating as a result. (One of the Germans who escaped from Damascus, after being routed from the *Palestinian* front, was a twice-wounded seventeen-year-old sergeant named Rudolf Höss—the future Commandant at *Auschwitz*.)

As this collective stratagem "brought to an inglorious end the Ottoman Empire," John made the astute observation: "It is a curious fact that the whole movement of the British Army in Palestine, which swept the Turks out of the country, was actually pivoted on the sons of Israel, who were once again fighting the enemy, not far from the spot where their forefathers had crossed the Jordan under Joshua."[54] In his address before the Legion, Chaytor went on record, stating:

> I was particularly struck with your good work on the Mellahah front, and by your gallant capture of the Umm Es Shert Ford, and defeat of the Turkish rearguard...for I was then enabled to push my mounted men over the Jordan at that crossing, and so you contributed materially to the capture of Es Salt...the capture of Amman, the cutting of the Hedjaz Railway, and the destruction of the 4th Turkish Army, which helped considerably towards the great victory won at Damascus.[55]

The general was also alive to the scriptural significance of the Palestine theater. When he learned that Colonel Patterson was compiling an official account of the Legion's notable exploits, he sent the following testimonial from New Zealand, on March 9, 1920:

> I hope the history of the 38th Battalion is out by now. So few have heard of the Battalion's good work, or of the very remarkable fact that in the operations that we hope have finally re-opened Palestine to the Jews, a Jewish force was fighting on the Jordan, within a short distance of where their forefathers under Joshua first crossed into Palestine, and all who hear about it are anxious to hear more. I shall always be grateful to you and your Battalion for your good work while with me in the Jordan Valley. The way you smashed up the Turkish rearguard when it tried to counter attack across the Jordan made our subsequent advance up the hills of Moab an easy matter.[56]

Of the many glowing letters John received, the most treasured was written by an old friend on December 11, 1918—three weeks before the man's death. Arriving in early March, the opening line of the posthumous commendation read: "I most heartily congratulate you on leading in what was not only one of the most important, but one of the most dramatic incidents in the whole war." Having lost a boy of his own in the conflict (plus two others wounded), he noted, "To have the sons of Israel smite Ammon 'hip and thigh' under your leadership is something worthwhile." This "letter from the grave" was signed, "Faithfully yours, T. Roosevelt," as in—President Teddy Roosevelt.[57]

In his own appraisal of the Jewish Legion, Harvard alumnus Howard Sachar opined, "It was distinctly more than a token or symbolic force. In truth, its role in the conquest of Palestine eventually signified as much as the ordeal of the early Zionist pioneers, and hardly less than the Balfour Declaration itself, in reinforcing the Jews' claims to their national home. Once achieved under British patronage and the flag of liberation, that armed, self-proclaimed, and militant Jewish bridgehead would not easily be foreclosed."[58]

"MAN-EATERS OF TSAVO"

As defined by his customary toast, "Here's to trouble," Colonel Patterson sustained a career-limiting reputation primarily for opposing the flagrant anti-Semitism he encountered from subordinates and superiors alike.[59] However, though denied the honor of a single promotion or decoration throughout the war, the spirited Irishman would eventually find validation in other venues.

In 1946, Ben-Zion and Cela Netanyahu (parents of Prime Minister Benjamin Netanyahu) named their son Jonathan after Patterson. He was then given the rare favor of being a "goy godfather," holding baby "Yonni" at his bris. He was also honored by having a street named after him in the German Colony neighborhood of Jerusalem.

His most lionized feat would inspire several books, a documentary, and *three* Hollywood films—*Bwana Devil, Killers of Kilimanjaro*, and *The Ghost and the Darkness* (his character portrayed by Robert Stack, Robert Taylor, and Val Kilmer, respectively). With Satan depicted as a *"roaring lion"* in I Peter 5:8, it was fitting that Patterson's ultimate "trophy" became the Chicago Field Museum of Natural History's bloodcurdling "Man-Eaters of Tsavo" permanent exhibit. As David slew a lion and a bear before engaging Goliath, John likewise prepared *himself* for Israel's *modern* enemies—by bagging a pair of nine-foot-long, man-eating lions in British East Africa!

Patterson was originally dispatched to Tsavo in 1898 after a vital railroad project had literally been stopped in its tracks by the carnage of the beasts, some 135 workers eventually being devoured. As the colonel recalled, "Once the lions reached the vicinity of the camps, the roars completely ceased and we knew that they were stalking for their prey. Shouts would then pass from camp to camp: 'Beware, brothers, the devil is coming,' but the warning cries would prove of no avail; and sooner or later agonizing shrieks would break the silence, and another man would be missing from roll call next morning."[60] (The extent and subtlety of Satan's hatred for Jews, along with his ability to manipulate people and events, is revealed by a 2011 University of California study concluding that the victim count was probably "only" thirty-five, thereby casting aspersion on Patterson's integrity, while *The Ghost and the Darkness* has Michael Douglas killing the first lion.)

Despite his secular acclaim, five months before the historic UN Partition vote, Lieutenant Colonel John Henry Patterson, age 79, died penniless in Bel Air, California, and was cremated in obscurity at a local mortuary. However, in accordance with his will, sixty-seven years later his ashes (and those of his wife, Francis) were flown to Israel and reinterred among several of his fellow legionaries north of Netanya. Bibi Netanyahu dubbed him "Godfather of the Israeli military."

"THE MAN WITH THE GOLD"

Despite its abject failure, the "Great Arab Revolt" remains a sacrosanct chapter of Palestine mythology. According to Arab historians, Hussein's rebellion was the natural outcome of an empire-wide "Arab Awakening" that had been stirring for some time. It has also been used to justify "Palestinian" claims of an unfair disenfranchisement regarding the Balfour Declaration ("After all *we* did for *you* in the war," etc.). Yet, the facts speak for themselves.

With a manpower pool in the millions, Hussein could only field "between 10,000 and 20,000 Arab irregulars."[61] When asked about later estimates of 100,000, Lloyd George would simply reply, "Eastern arithmetic is proverbially romantic."[62] As for Faruqi's canard that 90% of the Arab officers in the Turkish army were al-Ahd members ready to mutiny—the *real* figure was only half of 1%.[63] The reason for the dismal Arab showing was simple: the *Ummah* ("Islamic community") never came *close* to endorsing Hussein; as word of "his" revolt spread, the Muslim mood "continued to swing between hostility and disinterest."[64]

In reality, the self-serving Sharif was more devoted to hijacking the Ottoman Empire than in liberating any of its subjects (most of whom did not even want to be liberated—*least* of all by him).

Colonel Meinertzhagen was the EEF intelligence director when the Brits entered Ramleh on December 1. He records a humorous incident that illustrates the degree of Arab "enthusiasm" for Hussein's revolt:

> A large batch of Turkish prisoners were being marched through the village but they were not preceded by their British Guard. The Arabs, thinking it was the return of the Turkish Army, turned out in force, yelling with delight and waving Turkish flags: it was not till the end of the column appeared and they saw British soldiers with fixed bayonets that they realized their mistake and great was their confusion. Their faces fell with a bump and they slank disconsolate to their hovels.[65]

As late as the end of August 1918, a British report stated that "the Muslim population of Judea took little or no interest in the Arab national movement. Even now the Effendi class [Arab professionals], and particularly the educated Muslim-Levantine population of Jaffa, evince a feeling somewhat akin to hostility toward the Arab movement."[66] In a memorandum entitled the "Politics of Mecca," Colonel Lawrence himself stated that "the Arabs are even less stable than the Turks. If properly handled they would remain in a state of political mosaic, a tissue of small jealous principalities, incapable of cohesion, and yet always read to combine against an outside force."[67]

T. E.'s mentor, Arab Bureau Chief David Hogarth, was no more optimistic, writing of "the inability of Arabs themselves to develop any system of imperial administration more adequate than the Patriarchal."[68] Even the royals knew it was all bogus, Hussein's third son, Faisal, later acknowledging at the Paris Peace Conference that "the various provinces of Arab Asia—Syria, Irak, Jezireh, Hejaz, Nejd, Yemen—are very different economically and socially, and it is impossible to constrain them into one frame of government."[69]

Meinertzhagen viewed the idea of Arab nationalism as just another desert mirage, inspired solely by money: "I have dared to tear down this halo and expose the Arab and his so-called government as rotten and never likely to be anything else. I have dared to say that I doubt if an Arab kingdom is any more than a dream, and that Arab National

Feeling is based on our gold and nothing else."[70] While Hussein's initial estimate to the Foreign Office requested a "modest" £50,000 in gold to pay his troops, "unforeseen expenses" bumped that figure to £2,000,000 by the end of the first year alone. (The revised budget also included a personal subsidy *for the Sharif* of £200,000 monthly.)[71]

And yet—after all that gold was paid—HMG *still* could not depend upon Hussein's "Freedom Fighters" if other "opportunities" happened along. "The plundering occupied all the energies of our Bedouins, and Turkish counter-attacks came up unopposed from N. and S.," reported Lawrence.[72] He would also later admit: "Their acquisitive recklessness made them keen on booty, and whetted them to tear up railways, plunder caravans, and steal camels; but they were too free-minded to endure command, or to fight in team."[73] In fact, the campaign was *so* good, T. E. earned another, less flattering, moniker (ignored by Lowell Thomas). Karsh and Karsh note that "nearly half a century later he would still be remembered by bedouins as 'the man with the gold.'"[74]

By the end of the Middle East campaign, "Sonny Boy" Faisal was in charge of the "revolt" (*and* the ever-bulging "war chest"). Neither man trusted the other, as each was so engaged in "liberating the oppressed Arabs from Turkish tyranny," etc., that they both got caught trying to cut their own deals with the Ottoman ruler, Djemal Pasha.[75] The Karshes further note that "the Hashemites's negotiations with their Turkish masters, both prior to the revolt and in its course, were incredible for no other reason than that they underscored the falsehood of their own nationalist pretensions."[76] While Lawrence loved to tout Faisal's dramatic participation in the fall of Damascus, eventually, even he was forced to admit that Faisal was "definitely 'selling us.'"[77]

Ultimately, "Hussein of Hejaz" was just as fake as his pitchman, "Lawrence of Arabia." Yet, in a rare interview with Hogarth in January 1918, the aspiring potentate lowered his guard to "explain" why he had failed to rally the troops and why his postwar prospects seemed to be going nowhere fast: "He admits that Arabs as a whole have not asked him to be their King; but seeing how ignorant and disunited they are, how can this be expected...until he is called?...Who else, he asks, in Arabia, Syria, or Iraq stand enough above his fellows to be King of the whole?...There is, in fact, no one."[78]

THE MCMAHON PLEDGE

A surprise boundary dispute would become the enduring fiasco of the short-lived Anglo-Sharif liaison. The debate focused on the meaning of a single phrase in McMahon's disputable dispatch of October 24, 1915—the so-called "key letter."[79] The exclusory clause *supposedly* dealing with Palestine states: "The two districts of Mersina and Alexandretta and portions of Syria lying to the west of the districts of Damascus, Homs, Hama and Aleppo cannot be said to be purely Arab, and should be excluded from the limits demanded." McMahon then went on to attest: "Subject to the above modifications, Great Britain is prepared to recognize and support the independence of the Arabs in all the regions within the limits demanded by the Sharif of Mecca."[80]

Though Hussein and the Ummah would later insist that the allotted turf comprised Syria, Lebanon, Iraq, and *all* of Palestine (the Arab Rectangle), Britain has always maintained that the portion of central Palestine—west of the Jordan (the Sanjack of Jerusalem)—was *never* an option "owing to its position west of the Ottoman district, or *vilayet*, of Damascus which at the time included the area that was to become the Emirate of Transjordan."[81] While McMahon affirmed this twice (1922/1937), Churchill also concurred in his 1922 White Paper: "This reservation has always been regarded by HMG as covering the vilayet of Beirut and the independent Sanjak of Jerusalem."[82]

The reader will recognize an obvious glitch; Quigley writes, "Much of the controversy arises from the belief that it [the Declaration] promised something to somebody and that this promise was in conflict with other promises, notably with the 'McMahon Pledge' to Sherif Hussein."[83] Thus, from an Arab perspective, the Declaration detached west Palestine from them while the Jews saw the McMahon Pledge exclude east Palestine from them. As they say, "The devil is in the details." No matter *how* much diplomatic circumlocution was tried, Britain never could extricate herself from this political albatross. Though at the time, even Faisal, while contesting the British take on McMahon's verbiage, said that he was "quite prepared to accept…that it had been the original intention of HMG to exclude Palestine."[84]

Yet, the fact remains that London possessed justifiable frustration from a legal standpoint. The Balfour Declaration was approved by the Council of the League of Nations and was therefore binding upon its trustee, England, as the Mandatory power; *no* British letter/pledge could have superseded this prior contractual obligation, even if one *had* been issued. To add insult to injury, though rarely discussed, the Hussein-McMahon correspondence "never culminated in an accepted agreement."[85] It was the inevitable cost for "dealing in the desert." The Karshes state that "in their short-sighted frenzy these officials failed to comprehend that once the genie of the Arab empire was set free, it could not be bottled again."[86] And still *more* lies were to come.

SYKES-PICOT AGREEMENT

In the meantime, while Hussein was being promised the "crescent" moon, Britain was busy making other secret arrangements with her more traditional "Christian" ally. The Milner Group knew that France had long-standing cultural ties with Syria and Lebanon. The only "problem" was that while the Arabs barely tolerated the English—they utterly *despised* the French,

Having made his "deal" with McMahon's authorities, Hussein naturally *assumed* that his future subjects would receive either full independence, or at worst, Arab rule under temporary British suzerainty. However, on December 6, 1917 (just four days after the Declaration), the Muslims were blindsided once again when Turkey's Djemal Pasha "dropped" the proverbial "dime" on the Ententes by floating a copy of a document that Lenin found in the Tsar's files—the "Sykes-Picot Agreement"—a secret Anglo-French accord that nullified the McMahon-Hussein understanding.

On the eve of the fateful McMahon Pledge (over a year into Horatio's schmoozing with Hussein), Foreign Secretary Grey decided that he had better get around to alerting Britain's main ally about the pending deal. The subsequent disclosure was an egregious affront to France as the private Hussein talks had violated both the letter and spirit of the wartime alliance articulated in the September 1914 Declaration of London, obligating the Entente Powers to coordinate all peace terms. Many of the specifics were likewise unacceptable. British concerns in the Middle East clashed with the Council of Ministers, especially in Palestine and Syria. Since the start of the war, France had envisioned direct rule over the Syrian interior and was anathema to the idea of Arab autonomy. The French also felt entitled to the Holy Land itself, having historically defined Palestine as "southern Syria." Foreseeing a conflict, McMahon had lined his ambiguous epistle with "specific" verbiage to allow Paris a little "wiggle room" in the future: "As for those regions lying within those frontiers wherein Britain is free to act without detriment to the interests of her ally, France."

With "King Hussein" naively expecting HMG to present this very territory to *him*, the two allies agreed to resolve their differences posthaste. Colonel Sir Mark Sykes was chosen to represent the interests of Great Britain, while France appointed François Georges-Picot as its chief emissary. By February 1916, the two diplomats had reached an acceptable plan for both nations. In a most unprecedented act, the secret Sykes-Picot Agreement of May 9 and 16, 1916 (the dates of its formal ratification by Britain and France, respectively; Russia and Italy consenting shortly thereafter), was essentially an inter-Allied settlement on the future disposition of the Ottoman Empire—over two years *before* the Ottomans surrendered!

In his acclaimed tome, *The Legal Foundation and Borders of Israel under International Law*, the late Israeli attorney, Howard Grief, states, "The idea that the lands comprising what remained of the dying Ottoman Empire could be secretly attributed to Britain, France, Russia and Italy even before the Empire was defeated and subjugated in World War I was contrary to international law."[87] Among the many dissenters to the Sykes-Picot Agreement (also known as the "Asia Minor Agreement") Brigadier-General George Macdonough, director of military intel in the War Office, remonstrated, "I must confess that it seems to me that we are rather in the position of the hunters who divided up the skin of the bear before they had killed it."[88]

To encapsulate the essentials, Britain was charged with overseeing Arab territories comprising the greatest part of Mesopotamia, most of Transjordan, and southern Palestine, while France would superintend Arab rights in Turkey, Syria, northern Palestine, and the Mosul region of upper Mesopotamia. The Arabian Peninsula (the Hejaz) was to remain independent. In those areas of the Ottoman Empire excluded from the proposed Arab Kingdom, Britain and France would be free to "establish such direct or indirect administration or control as they desire."[89] The main region of British domain, designated the "Red Zone," encompassed southern Mesopotamia, including Bagdad; the northeastern Arabian coast, including Kuwait; and the ports of Acre and Haifa for a rail line from Haifa to Bagdad with easement rights through French Syria. France's "Blue Zone" incorporated Cilicia, Lebanon, and the Syrian coastal strip. (Tsarist Russia basked in her territorial allotments of Istanbul, the Turkish Straits, and the Ottoman Armenian vilayets for all of ten months.)

Palestine naturally became the main obstacle. While the French desired it for cultural pretense, the British required it for military security. And yet, while Britain could not allow another power to control an area of such strategic proximity to the Suez Canal, neither could she appear so presumptuous as to demand exclusive control. The solution was an "ingenious" compromise that divided Eretz Yisrael into three sectors: northern Palestine (Galilee) to the French "Blue Zone"; southern Palestine (Negev) to the Arab Empire "Red Zone"; central Palestine (Gaza to Haifa, west of the Jordan) to be the new "Brown Zone," a Franco/Russian/British condominium for the sole purpose of "securing the religious interests of the Entente Powers."[90]

With the ink from Sykes' signature barely dried on the illegal contract, Whitehall's policy makers were *already* entertaining serious reservations. The degree of backstabbing to date was amazing: Britain betrays France by secretly talking to Hussein; Britain betrays France again by pledging half of her anticipated territory to the Arabs; Hussein betrays Britain by failing to deliver; Britain betrays Hussein by consigning half of his pending "empire" to French suzerainty; and—worst of all—Britain betrays the Jews by ignoring their national aspirations. Incredibly, in addition to Britain, France, and Russia, the eminent international co-op for the truncated Brown Zone included delegates of the Sharif of Mecca—with *no* seats for Zion![91] Little wonder Lloyd George deemed Sykes-Picot "a foolish document."[92]

Britain's growing frustration with her self-inflicted commitment to France was multifaceted. As Kitchener's delusional alliance with Hussein had occasioned the problematic Sykes-Picot Agreement in the first place, the fact that Hussein had technically reneged on his *own* "pledge" made the resultant political debacle all the more bitter. For not only did the McMahon-Hussein "pen pal" fiasco fail to attain the status of a formal treaty (at least two points being tabled, requiring "more detailed consideration" and "further communication")—*had* it prevailed, it would have been annulled by the Sharif's breach of the most elementary reciprocity clause in McMahon's rarely cited postscript of December 14, 1915: "It is most essential that you should spare no effort to attach all the Arab peoples to our united cause and urge them to afford no assistance to our enemies. It is on the success of these efforts and on the more active measures which the Arabs may hereafter take in support of our cause, when the time for action comes, that the permanence and strength of our agreement must depend."[93]

As I Samuel 18:9 states, *"And Saul eyed David from that day and forward,"* Britain "eyed" her future co-trustee differently from Gallipoli and Kut, Sachar writing: "Nevertheless, as the months passed, the prospect of a French military enclave in Palestine, even linked to an Allied condominium, became increasingly unpalatable to London; and all the more so, in the spring of 1917, when Allenby was marshaling tens of thousands of imperial troops for the offensive into the Holy Land."[94] The Foreign Office was also second-guessing its earlier concession to France of the lucrative oil fields of Mosul, an insightful glimpse into the future of "petro politics" in that region.

Consequently, guided by the realpolitik of Prime Minister Asquith's dictum, "Those who are our allies today...may be our competitors tomorrow," Britain's sole perceived "solution" to her dilemma was to engage in even *more* backstabbing.[95] The Sykes-Picot Agreement would simply have to go. Thus, in a special meeting of the War Cabinet in April 1917, a committee report hauntingly noted, "It is desirable that His Majesty's Government should secure such a modification of the agreement with France of May 1916 as would give Britain definite and exclusive control over Palestine."[96]

In keeping with that other adage, "Three strikes and you're out," the French would not survive this third betrayal. President Poincaré acknowledged in his diary on April 17 that "in London our agreements are now considered null and void."[97] Britain's ostensible justification was simple enough; during the War HMG invested 1,400,000 troops and £750,000,000 in the Middle East theater, while French figures were negligible. In a meeting with British and French leaders on December 23, 1919, acting Foreign Secretary Lord Curzon declared matter-of-factly, "When the Sykes-Picot agreement was concluded it was on the hypothesis that France and England would make approximately equal efforts in the matter of men and money in conquering Turkey."[98] The "battle" continued during the Paris "Peace" Conference, Prime Minister Lloyd George reprimanding his French counterpart, Georges Clemenceau, "I wonder if you have any rights to make claims under the agreement, after having refused to take part in the effort that made its execution possible."[99] By then, however, all rhetoric was moot. On February 16, 1919, Sir Mark Sykes died prematurely at the age of 39, the short-lived "agreement" he co-sponsored expiring with him. The 1920 San Remo Conference made it official: Palestine—"*from Dan to Beersheba*"—was now under British control. All that remains to be told is how HMG *really* got in.

THE OPTIMUM MOTIVATION

Britain's claim that France did not "bleed enough" in the Ottoman campaign was more than offset by overall French losses on the Western Front. Besides, men like Sir Henry had already gone on record regarding the matter, his final letter to Hussein of January 25, 1916, stating: "Moreover, when the victory has been won, the friendship of Great Britain and France will become yet more firm and enduring, cemented by the blood of Englishmen and Frenchmen who have died side by side fighting for the cause of right and liberty."[100] The most remarkable outcome of the entire sordid affair—from the McMahon Pledge to the Sykes-Picot Agreement—would be the providential role played by the Balfour Declaration.

Dr. Sachar notes: "[T]he fact of Britain's military predominance was less than an appropriate basis for dealings between wartime allies or for staking any kind of postwar claims to the Holy Land...A more 'idealistic' rationale would still have been preferred...Initially, Whitehall failed to grasp that such a rationale already existed. It had been provided by a rather unlikely source, the Jews."[101] According to noted British historian Sir Charles Webster, "[A] situation had to be created in which the worst features of the Sykes-Picot Agreement could be got rid of without breaking faith...In these circumstances Dr. Weizmann's offer was an attractive one."[102]

As the "Great Arab Revolt" continued to fizzle, and as Whitehall grew increasingly resentful of the Sykes-Picot pipedream, a third factor surfaced in the process—the strong likelihood of a Zionist backlash. In his scathing criticism of the proposed agreement, Sir William Reginald Hall, director of Admiralty Intelligence, warned that "opposition must be expected from the *Jewish interest* throughout the world to any scheme recognizing Arab independence and foreshadowing Arab predominance in the southern Near East."[103] However, this "negative" would prove to be a blessing in disguise, for it became the panacea for the other two perturbations.

In Britain's zeal to follow Lawrence and his Arabians into the dunes, the Jews had been left in the lurch. Sachar writes: "Weizmann and the others, impatient for a public declaration from the War Cabinet [on Zionism], were mystified that support continually fell just short of open commitment. They knew nothing of the prior understanding with France"[104] Chaim later recalled that "months passed before we understood what it was that blocked our progress."[105]

By refocusing on the pathos of "deferred Zionist aspirations," Britain could outmaneuver France—*without* provoking a breach of trust (i.e., saving face by saving Jewry). As Hugh O'Beirne of the Foreign Office stated on March 8, 1916: "It is clear that the Palestine scheme has in it the most far-reaching political possibilities and we should, if I may be allowed to say so, be losing a great opportunity if we did not do our utmost to overcome any difficulties that may be raised by France and Russia."[106] Of course to avoid "the appearance of evil," the Jews would have to *initiate* the move by lobbying Britain for the "historic concession," etc. While Chaim and the Zionists were only too happy to comply, the Government of His Britannic Majesty King George V simply took care of the rest.

Thus, while the aforementioned seven incentives for the Declaration were indeed valid, the *optimum* motivation became the need to rescind the Sykes-Picot Agreement; particularly, the international condominium for the "Brown Zone"—allowing Britain exclusive control over the strategic eastern flank of the Suez Canal. As the French would say, the Balfour Declaration provided the *raison d'être* for England's "alliance" with Zionism.

"The Lord *shore* do move in mysterious ways!"
(Sergeant Alvin York, Valley of the Three Forks
of the Wolf River, Pall Mall, Tennessee)

7

Toward a Mandate

"Demanding everything; conceding nothing."
(Standard Arab negotiating style)

"I created Transjordan with a stroke of a pen
on a Sunday afternoon in Cairo."
(Winston Churchill)

"God granted me success in creating the government
of Transjordan by having it separated from the
Balfour Declaration which included it."
(Emir Abdullah)

THE FIVE-YEAR period between the advent of the Balfour Declaration and its global sanction by the League of Nations was defined by Jews and Arabs jockeying for position: the *former*, striving to nurture their historic diplomatic toehold; the *latter*, lobbying HMG to rescind the deal altogether. Once again, the cause for this conflict was Britain's flagrant duplicity, her touted Declaration having merely served as a convenient smoke screen to occupy Palestine. Five months earlier, Sir Ronald Graham wrote the following to Under Secretary of State for Foreign Affairs Charles Hardinge:

> [I]n view of the sympathy towards the Zionist movement which has already been expressed by the Prime Minister...and other statesmen, we are committed to support it, although until Zionist policy has been more clearly defined our support must be of a general character. We ought therefore to secure all the political advantage we can out of our connection with Zionism and there is no doubt that this advantage will be considerable...I submit...we might meet

> the wishes of the Zionists...Such a step would be well justified by the international political results it would secure.[1]

Britain's Declaration deceit was only exceeded by her air towards Zionism in general. The disdain in Balfour's correspondence to Lord Hardinge on September 24, 1920, was typical: "I enclose a letter from Dr. Weizmann, which shows that this rather unquiet spirit is much distressed about the present situation. Our Jewish friends, who are not always easy to deal with, sometimes get dreadfully perturbed over matters of comparatively small moment."[2] (The "matter" *here* involved whether Jews had adequate drinking water along the northern border.)

Then, having used the Declaration to enter Palestine under false pretenses, Britain would exhibit righteous indignation when faced with the consequences. For example, while everyone knew that a Jewish *state* was the Zionists' end goal (religious Zionists remaining opposed), the word was rarely employed, being the practical equivalent of a hate crime; thus, the Declaration's expedient editing to "National *Home*." However, despite this politically correct precaution, the truth (that Palestine was destined to become "as Jewish as England is English") would still "leak out" occasionally, causing the Arabs to go berserk. (HMG would pay a steep price for ignoring the wisdom of its greatest playwright: "A rose by any other name would smell as sweet.")

For the record, while Chaim was willing to endorse the expedient charade (having little choice as the minority race), in later years both Lloyd George and Balfour would admit that "by the Declaration they always meant an eventual Jewish State."[3] America agreed; on January 21, 1919, a presidential commission issued a report to the Paris Peace Conference, stating that "it will be the policy of the League of Nations to recognize Palestine as a Jewish State as soon as it is a Jewish State in fact."[4] Churchill wrote in the February 8, 1920, *Illustrated Sunday Herald*: "If, as may well happen, there should be created in our own lifetime by the banks of the Jordan a Jewish State under the protection of the British Crown which might comprise three or four millions of Jews, an event will have occurred in the history of the world which would from every point of view be beneficial, and would be especially in harmony with the truest interests of the British Empire."[5]

The *Palestine Royal Commission Report* cleared the air on the matter: "This definition of the National Home [taken from Churchill's 1922 White Paper] has sometimes been taken to preclude the establishment of a Jewish State. But, though the phraseology was clearly intended to conciliate, as far as might be, Arab antagonism to the National Home, there is nothing in it to prohibit the ultimate establishment of a Jewish State."[6] Vladimir Jabotinsky astutely alerted that same body that the framers' *intent* was actually codified in the underrated Introduction, which confirmed British "sympathy with the Jewish Zionist aspirations"—it being common knowledge that such "aspirations" envisioned the eventual establishment of a Jewish *state*.[7]

A second problem may also be traced to the text. While the opening phrase was careful to articulate *only* that "His Majesty's Government view with favour the establishment *in* Palestine of *a national home* for the Jewish people," the related caveat created an impossible scenario—"it being clearly understood that *nothing* shall be done which may prejudice the *civil and religious rights* of existing *non-Jewish* communities in Palestine." Meinertzhagen demurred in 1918: "It is an ambiguous document and can be interpreted in many ways; it does not deny sovereignty to the Jews but I cannot see how a Jewish State can ever be established which would not prejudice the civil and religious rights of the Arabs. The document gives with one hand and denies with the other and to me is disappointing."[8]

As the inevitable friction between Jews and Arabs intensified, Whitehall chose to rely on fanciful optimism. In a memorandum circulated in 1923 by the Duke of Devonshire (Colonial Secretary of State), the answer to Arab criticism over the prevailing McMahon controversy exhibited the epitome of naiveté:

> The Arabs as a whole have acquired a freedom undreamed of before the war. Considering what they owe to us, they may surely let us have our way in one small area, which we do not admit to be covered by our pledges, and which in any case, for historical and other reasons, stands on a wholly different footing from the rest of the Arab countries."[9]

Meinertzhagen (like Micaiah in I Kings 22:8) was a bit more negative, "prophesying" in 1920: "I firmly believe that in twenty to thirty years a Jewish Sovereign State will be established in Palestine. The Arabs will not like that and on all sides they will be attacked and I can see a big upheaval in the Middle East with European States taking sides."[10]

INITIAL DEVELOPMENTS

The first year of the Declaration was shadowed by the turbulent end of WWI. On October 3, 1917, Marshall Allenby formed the Occupied Enemy Territory Administration (OETA) as a wartime governing board for conquered Ottoman lands. Brigadier General Sir Gilbert Clayton was stationed in Cairo as Chief Political Officer. Colonel Ronald Storrs was installed as Military Governor of Jerusalem. No friend of Jacob, Clayton told the Foreign Office on December 20, "The Arabs are still nervous and feel that Zionist movement is progressing at a pace which threatens their interest." He reiterated in January, "[L]ocal Arabs still evince some uneasiness at Zionist activity and fear a Jewish government of Palestine as an eventual result."[11]

To counter growing Arab paranoia, the newly formed Middle East Committee (including, Balfour, Curzon, Sykes, and William Ormsby-Gore) agreed to send a Zionist Commission to Palestine led by Chaim Weizmann. However, the minutes disclose that the *real* motive for the high-profile mission—as seen in the opening statement of purpose—was to apprise World Jewry of "[t]he important political results that had accrued from the declaration of HMG to the Zionists and the need for putting the assurance given in this declaration into practice"[12] (the "Jewish Homeland" was *definitely* up and running, etc.).

This same strategy (to keep those proverbial "cards and letters coming,") was conveyed in a follow-up cable to Sir Reginald Wingate, High Commissioner in Egypt. Along with the standard public relations objective to promote "the establishment of good relations with the Arabs and other non-Jewish communities in Palestine," again, the underlying concern was *perception*: "It is most important that everything should be done to obtain authority for the Commission in the eyes of the Jewish world, and at the same time allay Arab suspicions regarding the true aims of Zionism."[13]

Storrs received the Zionist legation when it arrived in Jerusalem on April 10, 1918. The next morning—while 2,000 Turks were being repulsed by Australian cavalry on the Jericho-Shechem road—Weizmann addressed 5,000 cheering Jews on Mount Scopus (less than two miles from the original *"strong hold of Zion"* taken by David in II Samuel 5:7). Escorted by Ormsby-Gore, Chaim asked that he "convey to Mr. Balfour the thanks...of all Palestinian Jewry for his historical declaration and to General Allenby an expression of assurance of loyalty and regard for his deliverance of Jerusalem thus enabling the establishment of a rule of freedom and justice for all creeds and peoples in Palestine."[14] Later on (while Storrs was engaged in an aid benefit at a Muslim orphanage), two Arabs gave anti-Semitic diatribes, exhorting the "Arab Nation" to "rise up in defense of its land, of its liberty, of its sacred places against those who were coming to rob it of everything."[15] Ron "declined" to challenge the inflammatory rhetoric.

The first "thing" the Jews planned to "rob" from the Arab Nation was *disease*, that same memo to Wingate stipulating, "Should military exigencies permit, foundation of Jewish University, Medical School, to which Jewish world attaches importance and for which large sums are coming in, might be laid."[16] On July 24, 1918, the base stones for Hebrew University were set on Mount Scopus in front of Allenby and his staff, along with Patterson and a contingent of the Jewish Legion. (The humanitarian record of Hadassah Medical Center is legendary.)

One of Weizmann's key contacts was General (later Sir) Wyndham Deedes, a member of Allenby's staff and an ardent Judeophile. Relating, "It was always a relief to go into Deedes' tent," Chaim credits him with revealing "one of the sources of our tribulations." During an early meeting, Deedes handed the Zionist a few sheets of a typewritten text exhibiting exceptionally anti-Semitic rhetoric. Barely completing the first page, he asked what it all meant. "You had better read all of it with care," his friend sternly replied, "it is going to cause you a great deal of trouble in the future." As Chaim goes on to state, "This was my first meeting with extracts from the Protocols of the Elders of Zion," Deedes then added: "You will find it in the haversack of a great many British officers here—and they believe it! It was brought over by the British Military Mission which has been serving in the Caucasus on the staff of the Grand Duke Nicholas."[17] (Written and disseminated by the Tsar's secret police, the fraudulent Protocols constitute the defining "Jewish conspiracy" for world domination.)

PARIS PEACE CONFERENCE

The Armistice went into effect at the 11th hour of the 11th day of the 11th month of 1918. As a final illustration of the insanity of all war, aware that the fighting would cease at the appointed hour, several

Entente units continued firing at the enemy to the last moment—to avoid having to haul away their excess ammunition (the shell shortage no longer in effect). Nearly 11,000 casualties were recorded on that "glorious day" (eleven representing the Bible number for "crisis").

With the Peace Conference set to convene on January 18, 1919, the Zionists wasted no time preparing. Having met with Emir Faisal in Transjordan the previous June, Chaim scored a major publicity coup in London the following January when the pair signed the stunning "Faisal-Weizmann Agreement for Arab-Jewish cooperation." Faisal pledged to accept the Jews and their development of the country *subject* to the protection of Arab farmers, to assure their *own* eventual economic gain. Of course, the Emir left himself a convenient loophole, attaching the laughable codicil: "Provided the Arabs shall obtain their independence as demanded…I shall concur in the above articles. But if the slightest modification or departure were to be made, I shall not then be bound by a single word of the present Agreement."[18]

The year-long gathering, attended by over thirty-two nations, produced two main results: The Treaty of Versailles (signed with Germany on June 28); and, the League of Nations, the first ongoing transnational body "devoted" to world peace. As the fate of Palestine was linked to the forthcoming partition of the Ottoman Empire, a separate dynamic was arranged to resolve that key issue. The process began with the League Council establishing the mandate system to enable the Allies to administrate the non-self-governing territories entrusted to their care. The mandates were essentially colonial "training wheels," Article 22 of the League's Covenant stating:

> Certain communities formerly belonging to the Turkish Empire [Class "A" mandates] have reached a stage of development where their existence as independent nations can be provisionally recognized subject to the rendering of administrative advice and assistance by a Mandatory until such time as they are able to stand alone. The wishes of these communities must be a principal consideration in the selection of the Mandatory.

The mandate allotments (particularly Palestine) became the subject of intense debate within the Supreme Council of the Treaty of Versailles (originally comprising America, Britain, France, Italy, and Japan). Faisal, representing his father and Arab nationalism, demanded an ambiguous autonomy with a "No France Zone" for Syria and Lebanon; the French, wanting nothing to do with him, counter-claimed Syria for their own jurisdiction. The Zionists avoided the Franco-Arab scrap, maintaining their own aspirations vis-à-vis the Balfour Declaration.

KING-CRANE COMMISSION

The King-Crane Commission (initially, the Inter-Allied Commission on Mandates in Turkey) was an American investigation regarding the disposition of non-Turkish territories within the former Ottoman Empire. Convened by President Wilson as a fact-finding mission to determine the political aspirations of those destined to be ruled by the mandate system, the "Inter-Allied" project was a bust from the outset.

First the French withdrew their participation; then the British. Wilson was undeterred. After incurring a long delay, a five-man US delegation led by Henry Churchill King, a liberal theologian, and Charles Crane, a Chicago valve manufacturer and future Arabophile, arrived at Jaffa harbor on June 10, 1919. According to *Foreign Relations of the United States* (FRUS), the foremost reason for their selection was that "the President felt these two men were particularly qualified to go to Syria because they knew nothing about it."[19]

To offset this dangerous naiveté, three veteran technical advisors were included: Professor Albert Lybyer, Dr. George Montgomery, and Captain William Yale. Traversing Syria and Palestine over the next six weeks, the commissioners interviewed numerous delegations from some forty towns and rural centers (the result of over 1,800 petitions). However, by the time the committee reported back in July, the Treaty of Versailles was already signed, with the president headed back to Washington. The Karshes write, "Subsequently, the commission's report had no impact whatsoever on the future of the modern Middle East; indeed, Wilson did not even bother to send it to the deliberations over the Turkish Peace Treaty, which continued after the Paris Peace Conference, and its findings were not made public until 1922."[20]

Alison Weir attributes the delayed release of the King-Crane Commission report to a major Zionist conspiracy led by Justice Brandeis. According to her paranoia, the report was "suppressed" because the recommendations were decidedly at odds with the Zionist agenda.[21] The argument goes that had the League known the paper's inflammatory content at the time—that the Arabs were utterly incensed at their approaching dispossession—"it would have insisted upon a totally different outcome of events."[22] Now, what person who understood the incontestable record of trans-generational Muslim anti-Semitism would possibly anticipate an Arab "Welcome Wagon" basket for *any* Jewish move-ins to Palestine? (Faisal's phony, politically expedient "pact" with Weizmann notwithstanding.)

In reality, the report was an unmitigated disaster. Having imbibed the normal torrent of anti-Semitic rants (particularly by the Syrian Congress), King and Crane decided that the Declaration would never work, being at odds with "Arab self-determination." Their subsequent conclusions—opposed by two of their three appointed consultants (Montgomery and Yale)—proposed: A *single* mandate for Syria and Palestine; a constitutional monarchy under Emir Faisal as the interim government; and, the mandate be given to America. Their worst idea was that "Jewish immigration should be definitely limited, and...the project for making Palestine distinctly a Jewish commonwealth should be given up."[23] Not only was the US unprepared to assume *any* mandate, but President Wilson had already voiced repeated allegiance to the Declaration in terms more extreme than the British model. Thus, the Esco think tank concludes: "In the final analysis, the Report offered nothing in the way of a genuine workable recommendation."[24]

CLANDESTINE ARAB RESISTANCE

After the Paris Peace Conference "was permitted to expire gradually," debate over Turkey shifted to London.[25] The framework for a final settlement was outlined in February 1920 during a meeting of the Supreme Council (now minus America). The Arabs chose this critical juncture to launch a preemptive political strike. On March 7, the Syrian National Congress, led by Hashim al-Atassi, proclaimed Syria—along with Palestine, Lebanon, and Transjordan—a sovereign independent state. The next day, Faisal I was crowned constitutional monarch of the Arab Kingdom of Syria; the defunct sixty-four-day-old Faisal-Weizmann Agreement being so much "romantic Arab arithmetic." Later that month another generic group, the "General Iraqi Congress," announced the "complete independence of Iraq" under Faisal's older sibling Abdullah.[26] The Allies were less than amused.

Faisal's coronation was followed by the deadly Arab riots in Old Jerusalem (April 4-7) during the Islamic festival of *Nebi Musa*. (The holiday exhibits the enduring spiritual ignorance of Muslims; contrary to Deuteronomy 34:5-6, Arab tradition has a Bedouin carrying Moses' body across the Jordan, then burying it at the shrine of *Nebi Musa*, "Prophet Moses.") With the Ottoman collapse, the Arabs pursued their own version of Zionism. The religious rampage was textbook—lives lost, women raped, homes burned, Torah scrolls profaned, tombstones defaced, etc. One eyewitness told a British officer that the first victim "was an old Jew about seventy years of age...his head split open with an Arab's sword, and as soon as he was down he was stoned."[27]

When the smoke cleared, five Jews lay dead, with another 216 wounded, 18 critically. The lead agitator was the infamous Jerusalem-born future Grand Mufti, Haj Muhammad Amin al-Husseini, the most powerful Arab throughout the Palestine Mandate. Though Husseini received a ten-year prison sentence, "somehow" he was able to escape to Transjordan. Meanwhile, the former British officer and decorated WWI hero, Vladimir Jabotinsky, revered as the "Godfather of the Haganah ('The Defense')," was sent to Acre Prison with a heavier sentence—fifteen years hard labor for the "crime" of helping his fellow Jews defend themselves by supplying them "illegal" weapons. (Appeals to Churchill resulted in his subsequent release.)

The seldom-heard British complicity in the massacre speaks to the subtitle of this book. General Louis Bols was the Chief Administrator in Palestine. Disparaging him as "the most rabid anti-Semite he had ever met," Colonel Patterson notes, "As governor of Palestine for thirteen months, Bols packed his administration with anti-Semites who remained in office for years, permeating the Palestinian government with a spirit of antagonism to Zionism."[28] The Arabs observed the flagrant racism shown by the corrupt military regime: The Declaration had yet to be published in Palestine; the Hebrew language was proscribed; discrimination against Jews was tolerated and encouraged; the Jewish Brigade was held in contempt, even barred from Jerusalem during the previous Passover.[29] "This official attitude was interpreted by the hooligan element and interested schemers in the only possible way; namely, that the Military Authorities in Palestine were against the Jews and Zionism, and the conviction began to grow...that any act calculated to deal a death blow to Zionist aspirations would not be unwelcome to those in authority in the Holy Land."[30]

That the "Arab disturbance" was in reality a *British* pogrom ("semi-lawful attack on Jews") is revealed by the facts. As a poignant reminder that the "locks" were changed in Laodicea, within minutes of the eruption, British troops were ordered to *bolt* the city gates. Over the next three days—as Allah's minions went about their rampage, chanting, *"El dowleh ma'ana"* ("The Government is with us")—three culpable acts occurred: Jabotinsky's Self-Defense Corps was kept *out*; wounded and panicked Jews were kept *in*; absolutely *no* British forces were a help from *within*. Patterson says, "It was not until the third day that effective action was taken. In the meantime hell was let loose on these unfortunate people. Even the wretched few who got to the city gates, unless they possessed special permits, were refused permission to escape and were forced to return to the devilries being enacted by the murdering, raping, looting mob. It is a black page in our history."[31]

Colonel Meinertzhagen knew of these telling developments as well, having been appointed Chief Political Officer in Palestine and Syria the previous September. He was also willing to implicate his peers in a pattern that would repeat itself over the next quarter century:

> At Easter, 1920, anti-Jew riots occurred in Jerusalem...I had ample warning that these riots might occur and I warned General Bols and Waters-Taylor [Bols' chief of staff]. I also had ample evidence that Haj al Amin (later, Mufti of Jerusalem) was stirring up the Arab element in Jerusalem encouraged by Waters-Taylor. I warned both Bols and Allenby, neither of whom paid much attention; no precautionary measures were taken in Jerusalem, Waters-Taylor absenting himself in Jericho for the day. I regarded the rioting as a deliberate attempt by the Administration to show H.M.G. the futility of trying to impose Zionism on Palestine.
>
> On April 14th, I addressed a dispatch to Lord Curzon...I criticized the British Administration centered in Jerusalem, I recorded that the officers...are, almost without exception, anti-Zionist in their views and are encouraging the Arabs...The Jews mistrust the British Administration and believe it reflects the policy of Whitehall. The Arabs are encouraged and imagine that by acts of violence they can sabotage Zionism...I considered that these events were an exact replica in miniature of a pogrom...the Arabs were intent on trouble

> and emboldened by a belief that they had the sympathy of the Administration.[32]

After the melee, several Arab notables met in Jerusalem. According to Meinertzhagen, one Aref el Aref incited more trouble: "Fortunately, the British Administration is on our side and we shall not be hurt. My advice, then, is to continue the assault on the Jews." Kamal il Budsiri said, "We shall deliver our country by the sword. We are glad the massacre of the Jews took place and that we have looted them." Fahry il Husseini reminded his dupes that an unbridled Jewish defense would have been costly, "If the Government had allowed the Jews to fight, many of us would have been killed." The Mufti exhorted Hebron's Muslims: "We are proud of our great victory and of the murder of the Jews whom we have killed and the booty we have taken." At a second conference (in the mayor's home) Hafes Ara Tukan said, "This is a great moment; we have succeeded in a great national movement. Now is the time to declare our freedom; we shall meet with no opposition; the British Administration is with us. We must make it appear that our action is against the Jews, but on the day of the revolution we shall destroy the British Administration and with it the Zionists."[33]

Describing Nebi Musa as "the first pogrom under the British flag," Chaim pondered, "I tried to find an answer to a question which was to occupy me for the remainder of my life: Why, from the very word go should we have had to face the hostility, or at best the frosty neutrality of Britain's representatives on the spot?"[34] He *should* have been asking "Who?" as the *main* culprit behind this concerted Arab plot was none other than St. John "Jack" Philby, the renegade MI6 agent. Ironically, Meinertzhagen regarded Philby as his friend. That a Zionist intelligence officer like Richard could be scammed by such a rabid anti-Semite speaks volumes of Philby's skill as the consummate sleuth. To worsen matters, Loftus and Aarons state, "Our sources suspect that, as a young man, Philby had had a number of bisexual adventures in the British public school system, which endeared him forever to the homosexual network within the aristocracy of the empire."[35]

In late 1917, Philby was dispatched to Abd al-Aziz Ibn Saud, Hussein's arch nemesis and the *real* power in the Arabian Peninsula. His mission concerned the Great Arab Revolt. While the Sharif was Britain's designated emir/ally at that time—*opposing* the (Islamic) Ottoman Empire—Ibn Saud, leader of the ultra-fanatical Wahhabi sect, was directing raids against the Sharif's men. Philby was supposed to pressure Saud into backing Hussein. Though Saud passed, Jack experienced a life-changing political epiphany during their encounter:

> According to…several former intelligence officers, Philby and Ibn Saud shared a common hatred of the Jews. When Philby learned of the Balfour Declaration, he took it as a personal affront…He then informed Ibn Saud that they had both been betrayed by England and turned over classified information from the British secret service, including the fact that there would be no Arab nation, only another colonial jewel in the crown…Both men believed themselves brothers in betrayal…Together they would work to end British colonial rule, especially the policy of a Jewish homeland in the Moslem world…From that time onward, Philby was Ibn Saud's private ally in the secret and increasingly vicious war against Zionism…By the time Philby returned to London in 1920, he was already the secret service's first spy against the Jews—a counterweight against the Foreign Office's tendency to be soft on Zionism.[36]

As the reader will discover, the "Philby-Ibn Saud" alliance would play the key role in fomenting Arab resistance against the Zionist agenda.

JERUBBAAL

As the theme of Arab riots and pogroms will continue to resurface throughout this book, an eye-opening Bible study is in order. When the local mob of idolaters surrounded the house of Joash, intent on killing Gideon for tearing down the altar of Baal, the young man's father gave them an answer that stopped them in their tracks: *"And Joash said unto all that stood against him, Will ye plead for Baal? will ye save him? he that will plead for him, let him be put to death whilst it is yet morning: if he be a god, let him plead for himself, because one hath cast down his altar."* (Judges 6:31) The event was so monumental that Gideon was given a second name—*"Therefore on that day he called him Jerubbaal, saying, Let Baal plead against him, because he hath thrown down his altar."* (Judges 6:32)

The lesson in this story exposes the basic fallacy of the Koran and the entire religion of Islam—*"Allah" is powerless to kill his own enemies;*

he has to rely on bloodthirsty sinners to do his dirty work for him. Conversely (with the conquest under Joshua the main exception), when Israel's God wants someone wacked, He is perfectly capable of doing the job Himself. For instance, when the LORD grew weary of Noah's generation, He *drowned them like rats*. When it was time to wipe out the cities of Sodom, Admah, Zeboim, and Gomorrah, He didn't send in a Jihad team; He *burned them to the ground*. Being no respecter of persons, when He got mad at Uzzah for just *touching* the ark, He *shot him through with 220 volts* without anybody's help.

As exhibited by the June 30, 2016, callous murder of Hallel Yaffa Ariel—a thirteen-year-old Israeli girl stabbed to death by a Palestinian thug as she slept in her bed in the West Bank settlement of Kiryat Arba—"Allah" is obviously incapable of going it alone.

SAN REMO CONFERENCE

The Supreme Council (now minus the US) reassembled in San Remo, Italy, on April 19 to complete the treaty with Turkey. "A week or so passed in San Remo while we waited for the Conference to make up its mind about Palestine," Chaim wrote. "As it was almost the last item on the agenda we had little to do except gaze at the sea and discuss things among ourselves. There was always the uneasy feeling that the recent events in Palestine might bring some revision of policy."[37]

An agreement was struck on April 24. The following day a motion naming the mandatories was adopted and recorded in the minutes in the name of the principle Entente Powers. With precise boundaries left unspecified (to avoid further rioting in Faisal's absence), France was assigned the Mandate for Syria (including modern-day Lebanon), while Britain received the Mandates for Mesopotamia and Palestine.

Regarding textual specificity, the Zionists attained a pair of major diplomatic advances in the Preamble alone: the Balfour Declaration was not only inserted, but girded by the landmark clause—"Whereas recognition has thereby been given to the '*historical connection*' of the Jewish people with Palestine and to the grounds for reconstituting their national home in that country." Then, among the manifold duties listed in the 28 articles of the Mandate itself, HMG was entrusted to promote "such political, administrative and economic conditions as will secure the establishment of the Jewish national home" (Article 2) *and* to "facilitate Jewish immigration under suitable conditions" so as to encourage "close settlement by Jews on the land, including State lands and waste lands" (Article 6). The Treaty of Sèvres (also including the Declaration) was signed by the Turks (under protest) on August 10, 1920. Howard Grief notes the significance of these events:

> The legal title of the Jewish People to the mandated territory of Palestine in all of its historical parts and dimensions was first acknowledged and recognized under modern international law on April 24, 1920. That is when the Supreme Council...decided to approve the Balfour Declaration of November 2, 1917, and thereby give international legal effect to its provisions...The Allied Supreme Council decision taken on April 24, 1920, converted the Balfour Declaration, which until then had only been a statement of British Government policy or one of future intentions, into a binding legal document.[38]

World Jewry reacted to San Remo with intense enthusiasm. Mass rallies were held in London and New York. At the London Zionist Conference in July, Justice Louis Brandeis advocated a more guarded optimism: "The work of the great Herzl was completed at San Remo. The effort to acquire the public recognition of the Jewish Homeland in Palestine for which he lived and died has been crowned with success. The nations of the world have done all that they could do. The rest lies with us."[39] (And there was little time to lose, for about this period, Corporal Hitler was discharged from Germany's military and Henry Ford's *Dearborn Independent* began spewing its anti-Semitic poison.)

Several major players lost their jobs in the process. "My offending despatch found Lord Curzon, Lloyd George and Herbert Samuel at San Remo," Meinertzhagen writes. "They acted on my advice within twenty-four hours of its receipt. The military administration fell and with it Bols and Waters-Taylor. Herbert Samuel comes out at the head of a civil administration directly responsible to the Foreign Office, and Palestine is freed from the anti-Zionist policy of its enemies."[40]

On July 1 Sir Herbert Samuel became the first High Commissioner of Palestine. His civil power was a timely development for the incipient Zionist homeland. The specific choice of a British Jew was viewed as Whitehall's reaffirmation of Balfour's tenuous Declaration. Though the well-meaning official would make his mistakes, "The *Yishuv* was overjoyed and hailed Samuel as a second Nehemiah, come to establish the Third Jewish Commonwealth."[41] When the dramatic transition occurred on a railway platform in Jerusalem, General Bols handed his replacement a typed receipt containing the statement, "Received, one Palestine in good order." Samuel signed the slip of paper, but added, "E. & O. E." When Bols asked for the meaning of those letters, Sir Herbert curtly replied, "Errors and omissions excepted."[42]

That same month, victim number three went down the tubes. With their Mandate for Syria firmly in hand, the French marched on Damascus on July 21, effortlessly crushing an Arab force at the battle of Maysalun. Emir Faisal I was promptly deposed and permanently expelled from the country. His "reign" lasting all of 138 days, the so-called Arab State of Syria ceased to exist.

The last casualty was Richard himself (being duly "compensated" for his brave intervention). To save face, Allenby had demanded his reassignment (even threatening to resign). Meinertzhagen, a realist, gracefully conceded, "[A]s a Colonel runs but poor chance against a Field-Marshal of Allenby's caliber, my exit was inevitable from the outset. I have no complaint whatsoever. I have been treated well and justly by all and we have all parted great friends, with I think mutual respect. The future alone can tell whether Allenby or I were right."[43]

[Author's note: While the future *did* exonerate the Colonel's whistle blowing, having devoted much of his long life to Zionism, his legacy would be tarnished—*forty years* after his death—by Brian Garfield's 2007 "exposé," *The Meinertzhagen Mystery* (not dissimilar to Ernst Pawel's scandal sheet and the many *excessive* criticisms of Joan Peters). The litany of allegations range from falsified bird samples (from his ornithologist career) to the murder of his second wife, Anne. Whatever part of Garfield's case may ultimately be upheld, that verdict would *still* leave three essential areas unaffected: Colonel Meinertzhagen's stellar wartime record in intelligence; the consequent historical value of his empirical observations regarding the subject at hand (i.e., a century of Anglo-American anti-Semitism); and, *most* importantly—the aforementioned appraisal of Dr. Chaim Weizmann, the key beneficiary of Meinertzhagen's bold Judeophilia.]

FRANCO-BRITISH BOUNDARY CONVENTION

With Samuel's administration in place, the gates of Palestine officially opened to Jewish immigration in September 1920. Obviously, a sustained policy was essential to building the National Homeland. Norman Bentwich, esteemed British Zionist and legal contributor to the Mandate, held that "in the case of Palestine the Mandatory [was to act] as a trustee for the conscience of the civilized world in order to 'administer that country not simply on behalf of the population which is there, but with a view to helping the people which desire to come there.'"[44] Unfortunately, the Zionists would suffer two serious blows in the final stretch leading to the Mandate's formalization.

Pursuant to the San Remo resolution that the borders of Palestine be set by the Allied Powers, the Franco-British Boundary Convention gathered in Paris on December 23, 1920. The results of this meeting (to establish the northern frontier between Palestine and Syria) would initiate a deceitful process whereby HMG would literally whittle away the prospective Jewish homeland. On the *positive* side, Grief notes: "As a direct result of this Convention, Jewish legal rights and title of sovereignty over most of what had constituted the historical Land of Israel were formally recognized under international law. This recognition specifically covered what is today wrongly called 'the occupied territories' or 'disputed territories' of Judea, Samaria and Gaza, as well as the whole of Transjordan south of the Yarmuk."[45]

On the *negative* side, the Jews suffered a heavy blow to their future security. In November 1918, the ZO had solicited the Foreign Office to set their northern border "from a point on the Mediterranean, between Tyre and Sidon, to a point south of Damascus so as to include both banks of the Litani River and the Hermon Mountain within Palestine."[46] However, at Paris, the Jews lost the fertile region of the southern Litani Valley (present-day southern Lebanon and most of biblical Bashan). The stated cause was profound—France told Britain *they* wanted it for *their* mandate. The results would be vexing for two reasons: First, regarding the noted dismissal of Weizmann's boundary concerns as a "matter of comparatively small moment," the area contained the headwaters of the Jordan and Yarmuk, along with the Banias Springs in Mount Hermon, all vital to irrigation downstream in the Yishuv. Chaim wrote Curzon, "If Palestine were cut off from the Litany, Upper

Jordan and Yarmuk, to say nothing of the eastern shore of Galilee, she could not be economically independent."[47]

The second crisis involved the loss of the strategic Golan Heights; specifically, the northwestern sector. Because the French simply claimed the area for their own mandate (their "rationale" ranging from the Jews killing Christ to the threat of Bolshevik flags on their border), the Zionists would be vulnerable to future Syrian attacks. Also included within this forfeited locale was the village of Banias (site of the Old Testament tribe of Dan). The convention's decision was a political embarrassment to David Lloyd George, given his repeated public commitment to include all of the ancient territories according to the familiar scriptural coordinates—*"from Dan to Beersheba"* (Judges 20:1). As compensation for this aquatic loss, the Jews received *all* of Lake Tiberias (the eastern shore formerly belonging to Syria).

The salient observation here has *nothing* to do with geo-politics or *anyone's* opinion about *anything*. When His Britannic Majesty conspired to sever this *first* portion of Eretz Yisrael, a *deadly* line was crossed; Jehovah God declaring in 797 BC, *"And I will bring again the captivity of my people of Israel, and they shall build the waste cities, and inhabit them; and they shall plant vineyards, and drink the wine thereof; they shall also make gardens, and eat the fruit of them. And I will* PLANT *them upon* THEIR LAND*, and they shall* NO MORE BE PULLED UP OUT OF THEIR LAND WHICH I HAVE GIVEN THEM, SAITH THE LORD THY GOD.*"* (Amos 9:14-15)

With the 1881 *Revised Version* reigning as the nation's celebrated successor for the "archaic" Authorized Version of 1611, it is striking that much of the diplomatic dispute over scriptural borders stemmed from an inability to discern the biblical blueprint itself. After all, even David had to pray, *"Open thou mine eyes, that I may behold wondrous things out of thy law."* (Psalm 119:18) In the minutes of a meeting called by Lloyd George on September 10, 1919, W. M. Gribbon said that "there had been so many different boundaries to Palestine that he doubted whether anyone would agree to recognize any one authority, even Adam Smith [author of *The Historical Geography of the Holy Land*]."[48] Thus, the oriental scholar, David Hogarth, said, "At the Peace Conference, indeed, Mr. Lloyd George had asked for a Palestine restored to its ancient confines of 'Dan unto Beersheba'...But just what, geographically, did the name Dan imply?"[49]

Howard Grief concludes, "The British must be condemned and held liable…for abandoning the historical formula they originally adopted as the legal criterion to fix the northern border."[50] (Of course, with *Dan* being the first sliver of "Holy Dirt" to go, it just so happens that the phrase *"*DIVIDE THE LAND FOR GAIN*"*—foretelling the nadir of this necessary end-day evil—appears in *Daniel* 11:39.)

CAIRO CONFERENCE

The loss of the Golan was child's play compared to what happened next. As previously stated, the Arabist Jack Philby and the anti-Semitic British Secret Service were conspiring in tandem with Ibn Saud to subvert Zionist progress in Palestine. To revisit and analyze a complex scenario, HMG was under pressure to honor two conflicting promises: *one* to Sharif Hussein for an Arab Kingdom in the former Ottoman Empire, via the McMahon Pledge; and *one* to Dr. Weizmann for a Jewish homeland in Palestine, via the Balfour Declaration.

Hussein's three sons—Ali, Abdullah, and Faisal—were the designated emirs for the anticipated caliphate. With Ali (the eldest) positioned to replace his father in the Hejaz, Britain was expected to implement the "Sharifian Solution" to install the other boys on *their* respective thrones—*wherever*. When Faisal flinched in Damascus, events grew more complicated. Upon his ignominious ejection from Syria, the Foreign Office decided to give him Mesopotamia as a "consolation prize." However, the only glitch was that his younger sibling was *already* the appointed emir for *that* slot. And so, *another* kingdom would have to be found, or rather, *founded* for Abdullah.

The time had now arrived for British policymakers to utilize the Declaration's all-important "escape clause." According to *their* take on the ambiguous pledge of a "National Home" for the Jewish people, the intended location of that home had *never* been Palestine *proper*. Contrary to Zionist expectations, HMG had merely viewed with favor its "establishment *in* Palestine." Thus, the decision was made to resolve the thorny issue (along with the Mesopotamia Mandate) at the Cairo Conference of March 12-14, 1921.

The meeting was attended by forty senior British officials from the Middle East theater. Winston Churchill, the new Colonial Secretary, was the moderator. Churchill nicknamed the Cairo attendees his "forty thieves" (a fitting epithet, given the impending decision). Though Colonel Meinertzhagen was away (being on his honeymoon), he could already sense the end. While preparing for his transfer to the Colonial Office, an old War Department friend and colleague, Sir Henry Wilson, had advised him: "You've got to keep Winston on the rails; he might do anything stupid and his military judgment is almost always at fault [e.g., Gallipoli]; he thinks he's the Duke of Marlborough."[51]

When Abdullah came by to request an audience, Churchill agreed to engage him, but only socially. However, if Britain perceived herself as the proverbial "800-lb gorilla" in the room (especially in the Middle East), Abdullah was the "elephant." Everyone knew that he was bivouacked in Amman, having arrived on March 2 with 1,200 troops from Hejaz, intent on liberating Damascus for Faisal. The *last* thing that Whitehall wanted was a French occupation force in Transjordan. Besides, how could they install Faisal in Mesopotamia while leaving Abdullah nothing? In London's opinion, there was only one option. The final decision regarding historic Palestine was *beyond* calamitous: To satisfy Britain's underhanded and unrequited promises to the conniving Sharif, over 75% of the prospective "National Home for the Jewish people" would be forfeited to Abdullah for his royal domain.

JERUSALEM CONFERENCE

Sir Herbert Samuel had invited Winston and his wife, Clementine, to visit Palestine on their return trip to London. On March 24, the Churchills' train was met in Gaza by a massive protest against the Mandate. William Manchester writes, "[T]hey confronted a mob of 150,000 Arabs, whose 'chief cry,' according to a British officer, 'over which they waxed quite frenzied, was: "Down with the Jews! Cut their throats!" Like Haman in Esther 6:6, "Churchill, misunderstanding their fervor, thought they were acclaiming him and waved back cheerfully. Lawrence then translated their chants, and Winston muttered that he was at least grateful that they weren't stoning him."[52] At his next "whistle stop" (in Haifa), ten Jews and five policemen were wounded, with two innocent bystanders killed. The Executive Committee of the Haifa Congress of Palestinian Arabs "greeted" the British Colonial Secretary with a 12,000-word statement denouncing the Balfour Declaration and the proposed Jewish Homeland.[53]

On March 28, Churchill attempted to speak at the Mosque of Omar in Jerusalem, but was shouted down by Arab protestors. He then removed a short distance to the future site of Hebrew University where he planted a symbolic tree to the cheers of Jewish Boy Scouts and Girl Guides. As an omen of things to come, the sapling *broke* in his hand, and with no replacement tree available the befuddled Brit "had to settle for a scrawny palm which wouldn't even grow in that soil."[54]

Meanwhile, given Winston's penchant for *thieves*, Lawrence had "fetched Abdullah to Jerusalem"[55] for another secret three-day meeting, only *this* time it would be all about *him*. The principal attendees were: Abdullah and an aide, Auni Abdul Hadi; Churchill and his assistants, T. E. Lawrence, and Major Hubert Young; and Herbert Samuel and his chief secretary, Colonel Wyndham Deedes.

While Churchill described his guest as a "cheery-faced, shrewd, genial little man," the talks were anything *but* "cheery."[56] Abdullah demanded rule on *both* banks of the Jordan; the Colonial Secretary explained that western Palestine was reserved for the Jews. And as for His Highness "ruling"—*anywhere*—Churchill further explained that London wanted Transjordan as an Arab province of Palestine under an Arab governor directly responsible to the High Commissioner (who happened to be Jewish). Abdullah politely informed his interlocutor that he was not interested in the current "reigning but not ruling" offer; nor could he think of any suitable alternatives at the moment, etc. By day three, a compromise was thankfully reached, Churchill suggesting that "the Emir himself should remain in Trans-Jordania for…six months to prepare the way for the appointment, with his consent, at the end of that time of an Arab Governor under the high Commissioner."[57] An accomplished chess player, Abdullah "reluctantly" accepted the offer (his protracted and eventual independent reign being a foregone conclusion). For his part in this latest show of "Oriental diplomacy," Abdullah agreed to cancel his Syrian campaign and to persuade his daddy to relinquish his nagging claim to western Palestine as well.

As Proverbs 13:16, says *"a fool layeth open his folly,"* the "cheery-faced, shrewd, genial little man" began his "unofficial" reign as Abdullah I, Emir of Transjordan—on April Fools' Day. "Abdullah has promised to work with us and for us," Churchill wrote to Samuel while steaming home. “He must be given a very free hand.”[58] The High Commissioner made a formal visit to Amman later that month, capped by a grant-in-aid of £180,000 for the new regime in July.[59]

Finally, as an apropos conclusion to this “betrayal” at Jerusalem, David Garnett, editor of *The Letters of T. E. Lawrence of Arabia*, reveals that the deed was concluded “in half an hour’s talk at [the] Mount of Olives.”[60] Nearly 2,000 years ago, a former Jewish tax collector recorded, *“And when they had sung a hymn, they went out into the* MOUNT OF OLIVES*...Then cometh* JESUS*...to his disciples, and saith unto them...*THE SON OF MAN IS BETRAYED INTO THE HANDS OF SINNERS.*”* (Matthew 26:30, 36, 45)

HAYCRAFT COMMISSION

On the one-month anniversary of Abdullah’s quasi coronation, Winston discovered that it would take more than a “scrawny palm” on Mount Scopus to root out the Balfour Declaration. Having sown the feckless “land for peace” policy (Arab conciliation at Jewish expense), HMG reaped the fruits of its labor in the Jaffa riots of May 1-7, 1921.

The mayhem occurred after a Labor Day clash between Jewish Communists and regular union groups—Arab terrorists exploiting the fury as a pretense to attack both sides. The Zionist Commission stated, “The most terrible attack was the storming of the immigrants’ houses by a gang of rioters who attacked men, women and children. There is general testimony to the participation of the Arab Police in the riots and of the fanaticism of the murderers.”[61] The victims included a fourteen-year-old girl beaten to death with iron rods. The massacre was followed by Jewish reprisals. This second pogrom in thirteen months resulted in 47 Jewish deaths (including the famous writer, Joseph Brenner) with 146 wounded (Arab casualties totaled 120).

The Haycraft Commission of Inquiry Report (released that November) attempted to give the Arabs a pass. While the violence *was* blamed on “Arab hostility to the Jews,” the report *also* implied that the culprits were incited by flawed British polices and incendiary Zionist rhetoric. According to the *Palestine Royal Commission Report*:

> The report...by Sir Thomas Haycraft, Chief Justice of Palestine, and two officials, revealed to the public for the first time the strength

of the Arab antagonism to the National Home and the reasons for it. 'The fundamental cause of the Jaffa riots and the subsequent acts of violence was a feeling among the Arabs of discontent with, and hostility to, the Jews, due to political and economic causes, connected with Jewish immigration, and their conception of Zionist policy as derived from Jewish exponents.'[62]

Meinertzhagen was more precise: "The acknowledged superiority of Jewish brains and money forces land-owners and business men to realize their impotence to withstand eventual eviction, and they look on Zionism as synonymous with complete Jewish control and possession of land and industrial development in Palestine."[63]

It was here that the High Commissioner embarked upon his first lapse in judgment. As a British Jew administrating a predominantly Arab country, Samuel naturally felt obliged to go the "second mile" in fairness. The problem was that those miles kept adding up, his "strict fairness, often slightly leaning against his own people."[64] In a panicked try at appeasement, he declared a state of emergency, censored the press, and issued an immediate suspension of all Jewish immigration. (A "flotilla" of creaking boats carrying 300 Jews was turned back to Istanbul posthaste.) This cycle of "incited" Arab rioting followed by halted immigration became the norm throughout the Mandate period.

Samuel's greatest error involved Haj Muhammad al-Husseini. He began his term by giving the fugitive terrorist a pardon. Next, Colonel Storrs granted the twenty-six-year-old Islamic neophyte the elevated (invented) title of "*Grand* Mufti of Jerusalem"—the most powerful religious position among Palestinian Arabs to date (the late Kamil al-Husseini, Haj's older brother, was only "Mufti"). Finally, al-Husseini was the duly elected head of the Supreme Muslim Council, enabling him to consolidate both the religious and political power of the land.

Describing Sir Samuel as "one of those delightful men who are too charming and too great a gentleman to be really firm," Meinertzhagen called the Husseini appointment "sheer madness."[65] Convinced that the "Arabs regarded British politeness and sympathy as weakness," he confronted Mr. Churchill over the pending partition of Transjordan:

> I went foaming at the mouth with anger and indignation. Churchill heard me out; I told him it was grossly unfair to the Jews, that it was yet another promise broken and that it was a most dishonest

> act, that the Balfour Declaration was being torn up by degrees and that the...policy of HMG to establish a Home for the Jews in Biblical Palestine was being sabotaged...Churchill listened and said he saw the force of my argument and would consider the question...I'm thoroughly disgusted.[66]

ARTICLE 25

Less than two months after his promise to "consider the question," the "Winston Express" ran plumb off the tracks (the implications of that *other* train experience in Gaza still fresh in his mind). With the Colonial Office preoccupied with the Jaffa riots, a delegation from the "Muslim-Christian Society of Palestine" descended upon London the following August to extract *more* "politeness and sympathy."

The ecumenical anti-Semitic mission was led by Musa Kazim Pasha al-Husseini, former Jerusalem mayor (canned for complicity in Nebi Musa) and powerful head of the Husseini clan. British naiveté on the eve of this event is unreal. Sir John Shuckburgh actually suggested to his colleagues, "In the first place we should bring to their notice and, if necessary, read over to them word by word the whole series of public pronouncements defining British policy in Palestine."[67]

However, in a rare grasp of reality, the Cabinet did acknowledge their untenable "Catch-22" position, their minutes for August 18 stating, "It was not expected that the problem could be easily or quickly solved...On the other hand, it was urged that peace was impossible on the lines of the...Declaration, which involved setting up a National Home for the Jews and respecting the rights of the Arab population. The results of this inconsistency must be to estrange both Arabs and Jews, while involving us in futile military expenditure."[68]

After checking into the posh Hotel Cecil (for their *year-long* stay), Musa and his retinue got down to business. The Husseini negotiating style was simple—"demanding everything and conceding nothing."[69] He began by "demanding": 1) Abrogation of the Balfour Declaration; 2) Return to Ottoman law; 3) Democratic government (i.e., *majority* votes in all legislation; 4) Disarming of the Jews; 5) Suspension of Jewish immigration—*all* of which could be avoided, simply by deporting the "Zionist invaders," etc. As their exasperated hosts tried to explain that practically *none* of the demands were "prudent," the really significant development was that Britain was already tiring of the "Jewish Homeland." (By July 1923, a petition would be signed by eighty Parliament members and sent to the Cabinet Committee, tacitly suggesting that the Declaration be nixed for "injustice to the Arabs.")

With HMG feeling the heat, the timing of the Mandate's final draft was a welcome gift to the Husseini gang, being sent to Whitehall the month of their arrival. The original spirit of the Declaration had been so altered by Cairo that an entirely new clause was needed to empower Parliament with the legal authority for the severance of Transjordan:

> Article 25: In the territories lying between the Jordan and the eastern boundary of Palestine as ultimately determined, the Mandatory shall be entitled, with the consent of the Council of the League of Nations, to postpone or withhold application of such provisions of this mandate as he may consider inapplicable to the existing local conditions, and to make such provision for the administration of the territories as he may consider suitable to those conditions, provided that no action shall be taken which is inconsistent with the provisions of Articles 15, 16 and 18.

The bottom line of this eleventh-hour addendum was that Britain *could*, with the League's approval, deny application of the Declaration to those territories *east* of the Jordan—*if* she deemed it "inapplicable to *existing* local conditions." And, as the Mandate's provisions for the Jewish Homeland *were* later deemed to belong to said designation ("inapplicable to *existing* local conditions," i.e., rabid Arab racism), their total potential allotment was reduced to less than 25% of its initial size—from a little over 120,000 sq. kilometers to some 28,000. Thus, true to Henry Wilson's warning that Churchill "might do anything stupid," Winnie would later boast, "I created Transjordan with a stroke of a pen on a Sunday afternoon in Cairo."[70] (Manchester's less familiar version of this braggadocious quip—"The Emir Abdullah is in Transjordania, where I put him one Sunday afternoon in Jerusalem"—matches the Mount of Olives rendezvous; the "Sunday" notation more accurately the 13th of March in Cairo.)[71]

Dr. Ernst Frankenstein viewed the *protracted* application of Article 25 as a gross miscarriage of justice, remonstrating in 1944:

> But that could have been meant only as a temporary measure. According to the first sentence of the preamble, the Mandatory has been entrusted with the mandate 'for the purpose of giving effect to the provisions of Article 22 of the Covenant of the League of Nations.' This article states the purpose of the mandates system by declaring that 'the well-being and development of such peoples forms a *sacred trust* of civilization.' This sacred trust of developing the whole of Palestine, including Transjordan, has been entrusted to the Mandatory. At the same time Article 2 of the mandate declares him 'responsible for...the development of self-governing institutions.' The Mandatory, therefore, was obliged to develop the people and the land, and in this way to change the '*existing* local conditions,' which had authorized him to exclude Transjordan from the National Home.
>
> In view of what has been achieved in Western Palestine in spite of administrative obstruction, the Government itself should have been able to achieve the same in Transjordan in the same time. In any case, authorization given in Article 25 cannot be construed in the sense that the Mandatory on the one hand may indefinitely postpone or withhold the application of the provisions on the National Home on the ground of *existing* local conditions, while on the other hand he fails to fulfill his obligation to change those conditions. After twenty years of development, or failure of development, the temporary authorization can no longer apply, and Transjordan is due to be re-included in the National Home.[72]

With regard to Ingrams' depiction of Balfour's "little wrongs" justifying a "great right," this latest "little wrong" would inflict the greatest moral vicissitude upon World Jewry since the untimely death of Theodore Herzl—excising nearly 80% of Eretz Yisrael for the Muslim "Hashemite Kingdom of Jordan." Even the *Palestine Royal Commission Report* empathized, "The field in which the Jewish National Home was to be established was understood, at the time of the Balfour Declaration, to be the whole of historic Palestine, and the Zionists were seriously disappointed when Trans-Jordan was cut away from that field under Article 25. This was done...in obedience to the McMahon Pledge, which was antecedent to the...Declaration."[73]

Finally, as bad as this purloining was, the ZO would also have to endure insult to injury. Thanks to "Ali Baba and his Forty Thieves," the new policy of *two* distinct British protectorates under *one* mandate also came with a slight "inequity." While the *Palestine* "British protectorate" would stay under British rule, the *Transjordan* "British protectorate" would be an Anglo-Arab hybrid—existing as a quasi, semi-autonomous Caliphate (like Sharia "no-go zones" in various US cities). Thus the Jews would find that their sacred ethnoscape—the very lands deeded to Reuben, Gad, and Manasseh by Jehovah Himself, not to mention *liberated* by the Jewish Legion—would not only be *off* the table for a reconstituted homeland, but *off* limits for Jews *period*.

Simply put, as Churchill directed Samuel after the Mount of Olives "tea party" that Abdullah "must be given a *free* hand," the Emir was *adamant* that his new kingdom be *Judenfrei* ("*free* of Jews"). And, as truth is stranger than fiction, while Jews were subsequently banned from Transjordan, their Arab neighbors would retain *their* customary rights to enter Palestine *without* passports (encouraging a permanent epidemic of illicit immigration), for as everyone was aware, Jews always create economic development and a higher standard of living.

RETROSPECT

As *all* of the Transjordan region and beyond *could* have been claimed by Zionists as biblical Palestine, Lloyd George somehow being oblivious to Israel's *east-west* boundaries stretching from Mt. Sinai in Horeb to Haran by the Euphrates (Genesis 15:18, Exodus 23:31, II Samuel 8:3, and I Kings 4:21), Article 25 was especially egregious to Weizmann, given his initial "modest" proposal. Unknown to many, when the ZO sent their claims to the Foreign Office in November 1918 (rehearsed in Paris three months later), their expectation of an eastern border fell far short of the Mosaic standard: "In the east a line close to and west of the Hedjaz Railway terminating in the Gulf of Akaba."[74]

Chaim's reasons for doing so were varied. He obviously anticipated the *implications* of the Declaration's weakness (the "Homeland" to be merely "*in* Palestine"). The same would apply to the ubiquitous pressure of the McMahon Pledge—Arnold Toynbee, as early as February 1918 having noted on a Foreign Office telegram, "On the east, Trans-Jordania is bound to fall to the Syrian Arab State."[75] Also, under the sustained heat of battle it was easy to rationalize that "a *quarter* of a loaf" was better than none; besides, there would be plenty of time to expand when the Jewish population was more substantial. Grief offers a more precise motive, noting that the "proposal was made at the time to accommodate Feisal, to give him a corridor along the railway, so as to connect the Hedjaz Kingdom with Damascus."[76]

Inheriting Herzl's heavy mantle, Chaim also saw *his* tenuous role as "a horseman crossing a frozen river." Citing "the hard road which I have had to tread for practically the rest of my life," he elaborates in *Trial and Error*, "I was placed between the hammer and the anvil—between the slow-moving, unimaginative, conservative and often unfriendly British administration, military or civil, and the impatient, dynamic Jewish people, which saw in the Declaration the great promise of the return to them of their own country, and contrasted it resentfully with the administrative realities in Palestine."[77] (HMG was no less irked at the no-win status, Storrs remarking, "Two hours of Arab grievances drive me into the Synagogue, while after an intense course of Zionist propaganda I am prepared to embrace Islam."[78])

Nonetheless, the well-intended pragmatism over Transjordan was as much a breach of Amos 9 as the giveaway of biblical Dan. With much of the Old Testament chronicling God's wrath against His own nation, it behooves this record—"The *True* History of the State of Israel"—to note that Weizmann (as with Dr. Herzl before him) looked to *science* as humanity's ultimate panacea. Once again, the reader is reminded, *"Great men are not always wise."* (Job 32:9). Thus, in 1936, Chaim founded the Daniel Sieff Research Institute in Rehovot, writing a decade later, "I trust and feel sure in my heart that science will bring to this land both peace and a renewal of its youth, creating here the springs of a new spiritual and material life…I speak of both science for its own sake and science as a means to an end."[79] Conversely, the Apostle Paul, a *"Hebrew of the Hebrews,"* trained *"at the feet of Gamaliel,"* elevated Israel's God *above* human wisdom, warning his young protégé in I Timothy 6:20, *"O Timothy, keep that which is committed to thy trust, avoiding profane and vain babblings, and oppositions of* SCIENCE FALSELY SO CALLED.*"* (For obvious reasons, the sacrosanct word "science" is *gone* in all modern versions.)

In Weizmann's defense, he *did* attempt to retract his original claim soon after Faisal was deposed in Syria. On March 1, 1921 (two weeks before Cairo), he wrote Churchill: "In view of the French occupation of Damascus, HMG may now consider…that it could be better for the present at least, to draw no definite eastern frontier short of the desert, but simply to provide special safeguards for the Moslem interests in the

Hedjaz Railway."[80] However, it is always more difficult to reclaim forfeited ground. Thus, having requested but a *portion* of Transjordan, Chaim received *nada*. Instead of gaining the fertile, and largely uninhabited, massive tract of ancient Gilead, the eastern border became the center of the Jordan River. So much for compromise—Ephesians 4:27 warning, *"Neither give place to the devil."*

The timing of Chaim's part in the Transjordan travesty is also significant. In July 1921, the very month before the final draft was submitted to Parliament, the *Twelfth* Zionist Congress convened in Carlsbad, Czechoslovakia—the first *international* forum since the last Congress met in Vienna in 1913. (As previously noted, twelve is the Bible number for Israel.) Dr. Weizmann was elected president of the ZO by an overwhelming majority of the 445 delegates. (Since 1917 he had served as president of the English Zionist Federation.) Thus, while *this* privileged body could now rejoice over a "Jewish Homeland in progress" (the first such Congress to have reached this milestone), Transjordan would constitute Weizmann's first major defeat in office.

At the end of the day, Chapter 32 of the book of Numbers was summarily abrogated by Article 25 of the League of Nations. Little wonder that Isaiah 40:17 reads, *"*ALL NATIONS *before him are as nothing; and they are counted to him less than nothing, and vanity"* (Israel being the sole exception, Numbers 23:9 stating, *"[T]he people shall dwell alone, and shall not be reckoned among the* NATIONS*"*).

WHITE PAPER OF 1922

On July 1, 1922, Mr. Churchill released an official policy statement, known as a "White Paper." (Two other White Papers pertaining to the Palestine Mandate would appear in 1930 and 1939.) Ostensibly prompted by labor riots, the document purported to clarify "the interpretation which His Majesty's Government place upon the Declaration of 1917" (as it applied to the Mandate). As the Husseini party was *still* making its presence felt, they received an advance draft.

The manifesto began by citing Britain's escape clause (as well as a subtle reminder that the Jews' enemies grasped its potential value for them): "They [paranoid Arabs] would draw attention to the fact that the terms of the Declaration referred to do not contemplate that Palestine as a whole should be converted into a Jewish National Home, but that such a Home should be founded '*in* Palestine.'" It then proceeded to placate the Palestine Zionist Executive by assuring that the "Declaration, reaffirmed by the Conference of the Principle Allied Powers at San Remo and again in the Treaty of Sèvres, is not susceptible of change." It also restated that the Jews were "in Palestine as of right and not on the sufferance," thus "a Jewish National Home in Palestine should be internationally guaranteed, and that it should be formally recognized to rest upon ancient historic connection."

The gross inconsistency of the Declaration was also displayed, Churchill affirming on the one hand that Palestine was *never* to become "as Jewish as England is English," while *also* assuring that "with the assistance of Jews in other parts of the world" it would *somehow* "become a centre in which the Jewish people as a whole may take, on grounds of religion and race, an interest and a pride" with "the best prospect of free development and...a full opportunity for the Jewish people to display its capacities."

At this point the *spirit* of the text abruptly changes, projecting an ominous forecast of intolerable immigration policies. After rehearsing the obvious—that "the Jewish community in Palestine should be able to increase its numbers by immigration," it warns—"This immigration cannot be so great in volume as to exceed whatever may be the economic capacity of the country at the time to absorb new arrivals. It is essential to ensure that the immigrants should not be a burden upon the people of Palestine as a whole, and that they should not deprive any section of the present population of their employment."

Then, following the dictum that immigration quotas will be commensurate with available "economic capacity" (available space), a cowardly allusion is made to the planned partition of Transjordan in the most sleight-of-hand manner. Correcting Arab expectations that their "independent national government should be at once established in Palestine," Churchill explains that it can only "be accomplished by gradual stages and not suddenly." Having referenced the McMahon correspondence as the applicable legal authority, the original territorial exemptions were reviewed, *particularly* the denial of the Arabs' claim to *western* Palestine. With the concluding clarification, "The whole of Palestine west of the Jordan was thus excluded from Sir Henry McMahon's pledge," the *inference* remains that Palestine *east* of the Jordan was most assuredly *not*. As Grief states, "This left the clear and unmistakable impression that Palestine east of the Jordan, i.e., Transjordan, would be excluded from the Jewish National Home."[81]

The same diplomatic legerdemain is discernible in Balfour's explanation of Article 25 upon its submission to the League Council.

> Lord Balfour reminded his colleagues that Article 25...provides that the territories in Palestine...east of the Jordan should be under a somewhat different regime from the rest of Palestine...In pursuance of...Article 25...Balfour invited the Council to pass a series of resolutions which modified the mandate...to withdraw from Trans-Jordania the special provisions which were intended to provide a national home for the Jews west of the Jordan.[82]

This was another artful way of saying that the Jewish homeland *itself* was being *withdrawn* from Trans-Jordania, it being "morally inappropriate" to defraud Arabs by forcing them to co-exist with Jewish neighbors endowed with a "somewhat different" legal status.

While the Transjordan policy was anticipated by many, the White Paper of 1922 appeared to make it all official. Weizmann wrote, "The Churchill White Paper was regarded by us as a serious whittling down of the Balfour Declaration. It detached trans-Jordan from the area of Zionist operation...it limited the Balfour Declaration to Palestine west of the Jordan."[83] David Hogarth remarked that the document redeemed the Declaration in "depreciated currency."[84] The *Times* described Palestine without Transjordan as "a travesty on good sense."[85]

However, in the final analysis, while the truncating of Transjordan (with the installation of Abdullah) was certainly *official*, like Tevye's eviction from Anatevka, it was far from *legal*. Grief says that although San Remo did not give *specific* borders, "nevertheless they were assumed to be co-extensive with the historical frontiers of Palestine in accordance with the Lloyd George formula 'from Dan to Beersheba' which undoubtedly included all or portions of Transjordan, extending north and south of the Yarmuk."[86] Winnie's fiat also violated Article 1 of the Franco-British Boundary Convention which set the northern and northeastern lines between Syria and Lebanon on one side and Palestine on the other: "There was no territory in this Convention that was separately and formally designated as Transjordan."[87]

The obvious proof that Transjordan was presumed to be included in the Declaration as part of the Jewish National Home was because it had to be separated *from* Palestine to begin with—vis-à-vis Article 25. Dr. Frankenstein states that Whitehall had initially planned to retain Transjordan within Palestine, but was dissuaded by Abdullah's Amman occupation. "Mr. Churchill, then Colonial Secretary, settled the problems of the Middle East during a conference in Cairo, and the Transjordan question in Jerusalem"; to "drive Emir Abdullah out of Transjordan would have required military intervention, and the cabinet decided not to resort to it."[88] The authority for this is T. E. Lawrence who told L. B. Namier: "The decisions of the Cairo conference were prepared by us in London...It was decided to include Transjordan in Palestine, to make it indistinguishable from Palestine, and to open it to Jewish immigration. Every point was decided at Cairo, as originally settled in London, except the one about Transjordan."[89]

But, not to worry, the Emir *himself* set the record straight in his memoirs. Though Churchill's signature had been the *human* element in the ignoble deal, Abdullah wanted "someone" else to have the *real* praise for giving Transjordan to him: "He [Allah] granted me success in creating the government of Transjordan by having it separated from the Balfour Declaration, which had included it since the Sykes-Picot Agreement had assigned it to the British zone of influence."[90]

Mandate Ratified by League of Nations

Finally—over two years after San Remo—the Palestine Mandate (with Article 25) came up for a League vote on *Saturday*, July 24, 1922, the closing day of the London session. Chaim wrote, "[U]p to the last day we were uncertain of what would happen."[91] He then relates that after a "Hail Mary" stall tactic by the Papal Nuncio was nixed, "Everything went off smoothly, and with the unanimous vote of ratification there ended the first chapter of our long political struggle."[92]

On September 16, the League Council approved the "Transjordan Memorandum" (Britain's request to implement Article 25, excluding Transjordan from provisions applicable to the Jewish homeland). That same month Washington issued its much-delayed endorsement of the Declaration in the form of a Joint Resolution of both Houses of Congress, signed by President Warren Harding (a committed Zionist). Of the special agents of providence who helped sustain the fledgling Zionist movement during that turbulent "first chapter," Meinertzhagen singled out Sir Wyndham Henry Deedes for special recognition:

> Samuel was fortunate in having as his Chief Secretary, Wyndham Deedes, a man of complete integrity and one of the purest Christians I have ever met. His essential character was saintliness and he had a genius for making those he met the better for it. His concern for the Jewish Nation was based on a profound compassion for their suffering and he regarded the establishment of a Sovereign Israel as their just reward.
>
> By his wisdom and scrupulous impartiality he was, more than anyone, responsible for the survival of the Israeli baby which ran a serious risk of death at the hands of its godparents through over-nourishment or strangulation. The infant required very delicate handling during Samuel's Commissionership for many powerful hands were hoping and striving for its death.[93]

"But the midwives feared God, and did not as the king of Egypt commanded them, but saved the men children alive."
(Exodus 1:17)

8

The First Decade

"The Zionists are after a Jewish State...I want the Arabs
to have a chance...I don't want a Hebrew State."
(Lord Curzon, March 1920)

"My first chauffeur was a Jew. He was an excellent driver,
but it never occurred to him to brush me down after I got
out of the car. I stood it for three months and then
I engaged an Arab chauffeur in his stead."
(Colonel Ronald Storrs)

"During the early 1920s, Philby and his secret service
colleagues did everything they could to undercut Zionist
immigration...According to several of our sources, Great
Britain was the first modern country to use its intelligence
service to organize terrorist acts against the Jews."
(John Loftus and Mark Aarons)

THERE WERE INDEED, as Richard Meinertzhagen said, "many powerful hands" hoping and striving for the death of the newborn Jewish National Homeland. Chaim would find the ice on "Lake Herzl" thinner than ever. In the Mandate year alone (1922): Adolf Hitler created his own version of the Boy Scouts, the *Jungsturm* ("Adolf Hitler Boys Storm Troops"), while declaring in an April rally that his "Christian faith" compelled him to be anti-Semitic; Walter Rathenau, Germany's Jewish Foreign Minister, was assassinated by ultra-nationalist military officers who believed he was a literal "Elder of Zion"; hyperinflation required 7,000 *Papiermarks* for 1 US dollar; the Fascist Benito Mussolini became Italy's youngest Prime Minister; Achille Ratti was installed as Pope Pius XI; Vladimir Lenin formed the Union of Soviet Socialist Republics; Joseph Stalin became General Secretary of the Central Committee of the Soviet Communist Party; Harvard President Albert Lowell failed in his bid to impose an admissions quota on Jews; closer to home, Egypt gained independence from Britain, while the Fifth Palestinian National Congress in Nablus approved an economic boycott of Zionists.

With so many dark clouds on the horizon, Jews took solace in the Mandate's pledge that they would not have to face the future alone. Article 4 called for "an appropriate Jewish Agency" to be "recognized as a public body for the purpose of advising and cooperating with the Administration of Palestine in such economic, social and other matters as may affect the establishment of the Jewish national home and the interests of the Jewish population in Palestine." It then specified, "The Zionist organization…shall be recognized as such agency." Thus, hand in hand, the two would work in tandem toward "the establishment of the Jewish National Home"—or, so it certainly *appeared* at the time.

EARLY SELF-GOVERNMENT

The postwar Jewish population in Palestine was roughly 55,000. By 1923, the figure had risen to 92,000 (compared with 600,000 Muslims and 72,000 "Christians"). Of the 37,000 settlers comprising the "Third Aliyah," nearly half hailed from Russia, their traditional status of *persona non grata* having revived in the wake of Lenin's coup d'état.

The vanguard of autonomy was the National Assembly, convened on October 7, 1920. Its 314 elected members were affiliated with twenty different political parties. The Assembly professed to be "the supreme organ in conducting the communal and national affairs of the Jewish people in Palestine and its sole representative internally and externally."[1] The *Va'ad Le'umi*, or JNC (Jewish National Council), was elected as a thirty-six man executive to administrate routine issues such as health, education, welfare, religion, and taxation.

The ultra-Orthodox *Agudath Israel* party (representing 600 families in Jerusalem) protested being forced to join the inclusive JNC. The impasse was solved by a compromise. When the Jewish Community charter was grafted into the 1926 Religious Communities Organization Ordinance, a clause provided that any dissenter could have his name deleted from the register. However, though "united" on paper, the Community remained hampered by social discord due to inter-ethnic "racial profiling." According to Professors Ruth Kark and Joseph Glass, the Ashkenazim viewed their Iberian brethren as lethargic in mind and body, while the Sephardim judged their continental cousins as sycophants and scam artists. Among the others: Yemenites were considered industrious and meek; Maghrabis, poverty stricken; Georgians, healthy workaholics; Bucharans, frequently rich, but lacking scholarship; and the Kurds, too mysterious to stereotype.[2]

The influence of the JNC was later eclipsed by the Palestine Zionist Executive (PZE), a six-man body created during a meeting of leaders in London in July 1920. The new organ designed to function as the quasi-government of Palestinian Jewry. Like its precursor (the Zionist Commission), the PZE (later renamed the Jewish Agency for Palestine) would serve as the main contact for all political interaction with Britain—that "appropriate Jewish Agency" allotted by Article 4—particularly at the office of the High Commissioner of Palestine

However, by decade's end, two key issues would cause the Jewish Agency (JA) to undergo an ideological makeover. The first involved securing greater funding for the homeland. Second, Article 4 required that the "appropriate Jewish agency…secure the co-operation of *all* Jews who are willing to assist in the establishment of the Jewish national home." By January 1927, Weizmann had persuaded his peers to invite non-Zionist Jews into the fold. The Constituent Assembly of the JA was eventually convened in Zurich in August 1929. Chaim was elected president while the noted American lawyer, Louis Marshall, became the council Chair. As they embraced in solidarity, a teary-eyed Albert Einstein passed Chaim a note reading, "On this day the harvest of Herzl and Weizmann is wonderfully reaped." Chaim later recalled, "I felt free from care, I anticipated confidently a future that would witness a great acceleration in the building up of the National Home."[3]

WORKING THE LAND

While the country's industrial growth would see the greater economic results, the agricultural agenda represented the higher *psychological* priority. The JA believed that the best way for Jews to lay claim to the land was to put their roots down, literally (Amos 9:14). What better therapy could await men and women lately brought, as Chaim wrote, from "the hell of the ghetto" to "the threshold of a new life"?[4] Such fidelity to the soil was also consistent with Article 6 enjoining "close settlement by Jews on the land." However, while Article 11 required the Mandatory to "introduce a land system appropriate to…the desirability of promoting the close settlement and intensive cultivation of the land," the Zionists were impeded here as "practically no lands were made available…for Jewish settlement during the first decade."[5]

The lands registered as State Domain at this time was 960,000 dunams (one dunam=quarter acre). While the Arabs were apportioned 397,000 dunams under the Beisan Land Agreement, the Jewish Homeland received 83,000 dunams—65,000 consisting of sand dunes with *zero* agricultural value. Also, two of the concessions, some 60,000 dunams, had already been issued by Ottoman officials before the war. According to the figures of the Palestine Land Development Company, the Jewish National Fund (JNF) was compelled to purchase 92% of its turf from large proprietors (mostly absentee landowners) at exorbitant prices. The total holding of Jewish lands in 1920 was 650,000 dunams; by 1930, that figure had increased to 1,200,000.[6]

There were three main methods to working the land. The Western-styled capitalist farms were primarily devoted to citriculture. The most successful of these were also the oldest settlements—Rishon, Rehovot, and Petach Tikvah. The Institute of Agriculture and Natural Science (called the "Experimental Station") was formed at Rehovot in 1921 to further soil research. The other two approaches were both similar and dissimilar. The large-scale *kibbutz* ("collective") model originated for several reasons. Not only were immigrants hampered by meager fare, but they were also threatened by isolation. Thus, collective farming equated to collective survival. Like Vermont Senator Bernie Sanders, many Jews from the Third Aliyah were also too Socialist-minded to *market* their labor. Their utopian values were forged in the Pale under Joseph Trumpeldor, the most decorated Jewish soldier in Czarist history. His "pep talks" were quite unique:

> [W]e should create a generation that would have no interests and no habits…A wheel is missing – I am the wheel…It is necessary to dig in the soil? I am digging. It is necessary…to be a soldier? I am a

> soldier…I have no face, no psychology, no emotion, I don't even have a name: I am the pure Idea of service, ready for all, not attached to anything; I know only one command: to build.[7]

Sadly, the one-armed former British captain and contributing organizer of the Zion Mule Corps was already gone by this time, having perished on March 1, 1920, while defending the Tel Hai settlement in the Hula Valley of Upper Galilee. His last words are inscribed on a memorial: "It is good to die for our country."[8]

The focal criticism of kibbutz life was a lack of privacy. The cooperative farm was devised as a family-friendly option. Contrary to the communal climate of a kibbutz, the *moshav ovdim* favored a labor settlement. While the *individual* workers continued to pool their resources—buying their equipment and selling their produce "cooperatively"—at quitting time they all repaired to their *individual* dwellings, paid for by their *individual* profits. The Nahalal moshav supported 90 families in the Jezreel Valley. Other successful moshavim followed in the Plain of Sharon and Chefer Valley.[9]

The Esco Foundation believed that three agricultural questions had been settled by the end of the first decade:

> 1) Despite their long separation from the soil, Jews could become good farmers again; 2) Despite its long period of neglect and misgovernment under Arab and Turkish rule, Palestine could be restored to its original fertility; 3) The social concepts of the young Jewish pioneers imbued with labor ideals was an important factor in the success of the agricultural colonies.[10]

FUNDING INDUSTRIAL DEVELOPMENT

Introduced by Herzl in the Fifth Zionist Congress, the JNF was limited by its charter to land purchases only. Other pressing obligations ranged from the basic transitory needs of arriving immigrants such as clothing, housing, equipment, and livestock to the sophisticated demands of public works, utilities, and large agricultural and industrial projects. The question as to *how* the requisite monies should be raised was an early source of contention within the Zionist leadership.

A significant bloc of the more pragmatic-minded Americans, led by Justice Louis Brandeis, advocated "private investment" and "individual project" methods over largesse. Dr. Weizmann was opposed, believing that the coffers of World Jewry should be tapped first. Having prevailed in the debate, he launched the *Keren Hayesod* (Palestine Foundation Fund) in 1920 as the primary financial organ of the National Homeland. Reflecting his personal zeal in soliciting donations, Chaim dubbed himself "King of Shnorrers" (beggars).[11]

Weizmann made his first voyage to America the following year, passing the iconic Statue of Liberty on April 2 (the same day Churchill steamed out of Jaffa Port). Describing his dockside reception as "a pandemonium of people, cars and mounted police," looking like the "whole of New York Jewry," he recalled, "Every car had its horn and every horn was put into action."[12] (Reminiscent of the popular 1960s TV sitcom "Car 54, Where Are You?" the show's star, native New Yorker Joe E. Ross—a.k.a. Patrolman Gunther Toody—was actually a seven-year-old at the time who might have been in that very crowd, born Joseph Roszawikz to immigrant Jews.) He then began a three-month whirlwind tour to introduce his charity to Jewish Americans. Whereas a skeptical Brandeis had set the maximum obtainable amount at five hundred thousand dollars—by year's end over two *million* dollars had come in.[13] ("Ooh! Ooh!" as Officer Toody would say.)

With a growing agricultural base and the Keren Hayesod on solid footing, several ambitious projects were begun. While the "donation route" got off to a good start, the Brandeis group was eventually vindicated; Chaim's five year $150 million goal fell woefully short, only $20 million raised by 1929 (the year the JA was expanded). Still there were no worries as plenty of able Jewish investors were content to follow their God-given instincts to "have their cake and eat it too."

While less than 5% of the population in prewar Palestine was engaged in any form of industrial production, that figure would rise to 14% by 1931. Only 1,235 industrial entities had existed, mostly small and employing few. Working conditions were so primitive that olive factory presses operated by the circumambulation of a blinkered camel or donkey. By 1927, however, the figure had grown to 3,505. Though comprising but 12% of the populace, Jews owned 1,110 of these firms. In 1939, the JA Statistical Department reported that Jews employed

10,968 people at 2,475 sites. Over £2,235,000 in capital was invested, with the value of annual production estimated at £2,510,000.[14]

The dramatic transformation began in 1921, when Nesher, Ltd.'s Portland Cement Company built the nation's first brick factory in Tel Aviv. Then, as the capital flowed in, the factories went up: Palestine Electric Corporation, Ltd., constructing the nation's first power plant in Tel Aviv (other hydroelectric grids following in Haifa and Tiberias); Shemen Oil Press in Haifa, manufacturing oil and soap; Grands Moulins and Matzoth Bakeries in Haifa, producing fifty tons of flour daily; the Rishon le-Zion and Zikhron-Jacob Wineries; and the Palestine Potash Syndicate, extracting minerals from the Dead Sea.[15]

This progress was facilitated by the timely arrival of 70,000 Polish Jews, forming the Fourth Aliyah. With their expertise in construction and mercantilism, the newcomers lead the Yishuv into the modern age of urbanization. After one group built the cities—providing everything from infrastructure to the finished product—the other became the clerks and shopkeepers (both settling in as residents). Between 1924 and 1928, some £4,873,700 was invested in urban growth. Haifa's Jewish population doubled accordingly. Tel Aviv received £2,224,000 of this capital alone.[16] Viewed in 1914 as a "garden suburb" of Jaffa, with only 2,000 residents, a decade later the first all-Hebrew city in modern times sported a population of 34,000; 120,000 by 1935.[17]

The multi-talented Poles were also able to introduce several new industries and/or goods—to the profit of Jew and Arab alike. As Esco notes, under the category "industries…made possible primarily by the knowledge and skill of the new immigrants," Mr. A. P. Clark, manager of the Palestine branch of Barclay Bank, gave the following sample: "Iron bedsteads, biscuits, preserved fruits and fruit juices, cigarettes, refrigerators, aerated waters, knitted goods, concrete pipes, stoves, bathing costumes, praying shawls, neckties, umbrellas, candles, scouring powder, fertilizers, poultry feed, perfumes, matches, lithographic stones, automobile bodies, mirrors, envelopes, toothpaste and insect powder."[18] Clark also noted the significance of artificial teeth, cardboard boxes, hosiery, handbags, and wearing apparel.

The industrial surge fostered a commensurate rise in commerce. In 1920, imports stood at £5,550,000 with exports at £771,700; in 1930, imports were £7,000,000, exports £2,000,000. Clark estimates that from 1919 to 1929 "the amount of capital brought into Palestine *by Jews alone* amounted to no less than £40,000,000." This unique figure, referred to as "invisible exports," enabled the Yishuv to offset an unfavorable trade balance caused by rising demand for consumer goods, along with the requisite raw materials and industrial machinery.

To summarize this era, only one automobile existed in Palestine in 1914; between 1922 and 1931, over 6,400 were imported, mostly from America.[19] The *Histadrut* (Federation of Jewish Labor) was founded in Haifa in December 1920 as the main Jewish trade union. Influenced by the Russian-Jewish Socialist tradition, the membership was open to "all toilers who live by their own labor without exploiting others."[20] The Histadrut served as a mutual aid society offering credit agencies, agricultural cooperatives, consumer and producers' cooperatives, housing cooperatives, manufacturing institutions, and, it's most vital innovation, universal medical coverage, called the *Kupat Cholim* (Sick Fund). It also sought to foster economic security by providing workers with a center of social and cultural enrichment, encompassing everything from education to sports. However, the main responsibility was to maximize Jewish labor on Jewish land. Having begun with a membership of 4,400, the organization claimed 25,000 subscribers by 1927, representing 75% of the Jewish labor force in Palestine.

The JA summarized the rise of Jewish industry in a memorandum to Sir John Hope-Simpson in July 1930. The high points were:

> 1) Jewish industry...was fairly well established, as evidenced by the fact that there was no unemployment and that there had been no failures of any importance...It had absorbed about 33% of the postwar immigration. 2) Jewish industry had filled an economic vacuum and was not dependent on taking away any occupation from Arabs. 3) In order to further the development of industry 'the immigration policy of the Government of Palestine must be *creative*, not *contemplative*; *active*, not *passive*; *bold*, not *timid*.'

The report also clarified that the "willingness and ability of Jewish capitalists to start industries" could only work in tandem with a common sense immigration policy.[21]

HEBREW CULTURE

With over 60 dialects in Palestine, the Mandate recognized Hebrew as one of three official languages (along with Arabic and English). It was the tongue of instruction in nearly all Jewish schools, including the Hebrew University of Jerusalem. In 1919, the Zionist school system, under the auspices of *Vaad Hahinukh* (Board of Education) comprised 94 institutions of all grades, including kindergartens, elementary, secondary, and two teachers' training schools with a total enrollment of over 10,000 students. That figure surpassed 21,000 by 1929.[22]

The schools divided into three categories—General, *Mizrahi*, and Labor—each with its own council to assign teachers and curriculum: 1) General, containing over 60% of the Jewish children, corresponded to "secular" learning centers, though the Tanakh was recognized as the primary text for Jewish *literature* and *history*; 2) Mirzahi, absorbing 33% of the student population, were explicitly Orthodox centers that attempted to blend traditional religious instruction with the essentials of European pedagogy; 3) Labor, the equivalent of trade/agricultural schools, counted for less than 10% of the total national enrollment.[23]

Hebrew University represented the hallmark of the long-awaited Jewish renaissance. With its cornerstone laid in 1918, the institution was formally opened by Lord Balfour in 1925. Dr. Judah L. Magnes served as the first chancellor, then president (1935-48). That inaugural year, 64 regular and 100 non-matriculated students, availed themselves of the three main schools already functional: the Institute of Palestine Natural History, the School of Oriental Studies, and the Department of Bacteriology and Hygiene. The Institute of Mathematics was added the following year. In 1928, a Faculty of Humanities was established, comprised of three departments: Jewish Studies, Oriental Studies, and General Humanities. By 1930, the library contained a quarter of a million volumes, including priceless manuscripts and incunabula. The enrollment that year was 177, with 130 matriculated. In 1932, the first graduating class was honored with the degree of Master of Arts.[24]

The defining literature of the postwar era was a product of the Third Aliyah, known as *chalutziut* ("pioneering idealism"). The leading bards of this genre were Avraham Shlonsky, Uri Greenberg, Yitzchak Lamdan, Avigdor Hameiri, and Yehuda Karni. Sachar notes that the coalesced works depict the immigrant ardor as one "of fevered anguish, of despair mingled with a bitter and cynical hope that a new society ultimately could be resurrected out of a desolated land and a ruined people."[25] Lamdan's semi-biographical poem, *Masada*, used a potent ethnoscape to give the Yishuv a timely vicarious charge.

Ironically, the most telling cultural insight regarding the revived homeland was a religious matter, one that became conspicuous by its absence. Of *all* places—*the* place that received the *least* attention was the Holy City itself. "From its founding, the Zionist Movement had never placed Jerusalem in the forefront of Zionist objectives in Palestine," writes Dr. Yossi Katz, of Bar-Ilan University. "There was a glaring inconsistency between the prominent symbolic position which Jerusalem occupied in the consciousness of both the Jewish people and the Zionist Movement (whose very name derives from one of Jerusalem's sobriquets—Zion) and the lack of actual tangible effort expanded by the Zionist Movement in its eternal capital, Jerusalem."[26]

The main neglect concerned investment capital and land purchase. Two basic causes were responsible for this apparent anomaly, one ideological, the other pragmatic. On the eve of WWI, nearly half of all Palestinian Jews lived in Jerusalem, the great majority identifying as Old Yishuv by conviction. This equated to being ultra-Orthodox, anti-Zionist, and totally bereft of economic incentive due to a longstanding dependence on the *haluka* (religious charity). The unholy recoil against the City of David began with the *Hibat Zion* (pre-Hegelian Zionists) whose leaders brazenly declared, "[W]e have no need either for Jerusalem walls nor for the Temple nor for Jerusalem itself, as the city is not central. What we need is the Land of Israel…Jerusalem has gone rotten and there is no remedy for her."[27] The port city of Jaffa became the focal point for the "New Yishuv"; later, Tel Aviv. The sole exception was Hebrew University (perceived as secular enough, etc.).

Many practical causes also seemed to justify ignoring Psalm 137:5, *"If I forget thee, O Jerusalem, let my right hand forget her cunning."* Politically, the city appeared headed for international status, given the ecumenical character of her religious sites. Thus, any Zionist activity there would elicit immediate scrutiny. (Herzl voiced this in 1896). The agricultural priority also precluded diverting funds to Jerusalem's rocky environs. When the Greek Orthodox Patriarchate's estate went up for sale, the JNF "passed," preferring land in the Jezreel Valley.[28]

This urge for a quick profit through farming also resulted in the ZO neglecting the western range (West Bank). While small tracts were normally available in the Arab hill country of Judea, Samaria, and Galilee, Katz states that the low-lying coastal plains met JNF policy that "prospects for economic success should determine the location of agricultural settlement and preferences accorded to land purchases."[29] He posits that the fourfold demand of modern agriculture—irrigation, mechanization, industrial cultivation, and exportation—was the logical explanation as to why "Jerusalem always came out the loser."[30]

From a spiritual view, such callous disregard for Zion's sacred capital—the mother of *all* ethnoscapes—was symptomatic of the root cause for the Diaspora itself. Lamentations 1:8 says: *"Jerusalem hath grievously sinned; therefore she is removed."* The Jerusalem policy would alter severely in the 1930s, JNF Director Rabbi Meir Berlin confessing in 1942, "We have sinned in the past towards Jerusalem and her daughter."[31] The catalyst for this volte-face on the "City of *Peace*" was renewed Arab furor, peeking with the deadly 1936 revolt.

THE BRITISH TRIANGLE

While the Jews were attempting to put their roots *down* (in the soil and concrete alike), the Arabs were laboring to root them *up*. This pattern was encouraged by Britain's growing reluctance to stay the course. Whitehall was consequently confronted by a triangular dilemma.

First, while the Declaration began as a pretext to secure the Canal, the Mandate bound HMG to a long-haul commitment to the Jewish Homeland. Second, as attested by the High Commissioner of Palestine, though the Arabs were recalcitrant in their opposition—"demanding everything while conceding nothing"—the Jews became the *greater* thorn, primarily because of their "Jewishness." Frankenstein notes:

> A fateful mistake had confided the delicate task of the Palestine Administration to the Colonial Service which was accustomed to rule over more or less subservient 'natives.' The Jews are disturbingly clever and enterprising and, unlike the Arabs, by no means impressed by displays of power and doubtful administrative ability. They even dared to treat British officials as their equals and submit grievances to Ministers of the Crown, to Parliament and League of Nations.[32]

Such effrontery was captured in a remark by Colonel Storrs: "[The Jews] almost forget the difference between themselves and their employers. My first chauffeur was a Jew. He was an excellent driver, but it never occurred to him to brush me down after I got out of the car. I stood it for three months and then I engaged an Arab chauffeur in his stead."[33] The third corner of the British triangle would become the *ultimate* game changer in the escalating Palestine crisis—oil.

The Government likewise divided into three schools of thought. The first party, led by Lloyd George and Balfour, felt a moral obligation to honor the Mandate. The second was directed by Alfred Milner. While "The Group" (to which Balfour also belonged) "professed" affinity with the Jewish *homeland* (though stopping far short of *statehood*), its sinister motives have been previously exposed. The third faction, comprising the majority, continued to promote the "realistic policy" of using the Mandate as a pretense for occupation.

Thus, as the "cantankerous" Jews held His Britannic Majesty's royal feet to the fire "to facilitate the achievement of this object"—i.e., "the establishment in Palestine of a national home for the Jewish people"—the sycophantic Arabs naturally began to get away with murder, *literally*. Rather than man-up to do its ethical and legal duty to Jewry, the Palestine Administration (with the blessing of 10 Downing Street and Parliament) fled to a dream world where the Arab was the *real* victim. Typical were Curzon's words of March, 20, 1920 (the eve of Nebi Musa): "The Zionists are after a Jewish State with the Arabs as hewers of wood and drawers of water. So are many British sympathizers…I want the Arabs to have a chance and I don't want a Hebrew State."[34] To revisit an earlier theme, Frankenstein writes:

> In this struggle against the Jews, the Arabs were natural allies. Arab discontent, instead of being traced back to its economic and social causes, was allowed to grow and was magnified. Arab rebellion, in reality the work of a few hundred who never had more than a few thousand adherents, was—to put it very mildly—not dealt with adequately.
>
> In an age of material and spiritual revolution the members of the ruling class and the adherents of the ruling conviction are confronted with the necessity of either struggling or surrendering. Many, especially of the older generation, do not want either, and try to escape into a better world, if not reality, at least in their dreams.

> At the time of the French Revolution, their paradise was America, the land of the noble red-skins. The escapists of to-day prefer the desert. They faintly remember the tales of the 'Arabian Nights,' they have a nostalgic longing for romance, a morbid predilection for primitivity and backwardness, and hate everyone capable of destroying their escapist paradise by opening it to modern civilization. Their romantic dreams fit excellently into their no less romantic 'realistic policy,' which in a completely changed world tries to uphold the power policy of the past and to bar the way to progress for the sake of unrealistic views.[35]

"ABDULLAH PHILBY"

The blatant Arabist policy of groups two and three would ultimately define the Mandate: Exploit Arab unrest as proof of Jewish guilt to justify curtailed immigration. While Frankenstein put the Arab rebels at "a few hundred" (with "a few thousand" lackeys), the "one" behind it all (as previously noted) was British super sleuth Jack Philby.

Colonel Lawrence and MI6 had engineered Philby's appointment as chief British envoy in Amman seven months after Abdullah became Emir of Transjordan. As Loftus and Aarons show, T. E. and Jack were intent on making Palestine an autonomous Arab state.

> Philby was technically a British diplomat sent to advise what is now the nation of Jordan; in fact, he was the Secret Service head for the entire area including what is now Israel...During the 1920s, Philby and his secret service colleagues did everything they could to undercut Zionist immigration. Philby...organized anti-Jewish propaganda in Palestine...According to several of our sources, Britain was the first modern country to use its intelligence service to organize terrorist acts against the Jews.[36]

The main battle lines were drawn between a pro-Zionist remnant within the Foreign Office and the largely anti-Semitic secret service. "British intelligence agents sponsored waves of Arab terrorism, protests, and propaganda that began to wear down Foreign Office's resolve toward the Jews."[37] In December 1922, Jack and the Emir visited London to attend a series of meetings regarding Palestine. It was here that Philby inaugurated his public relations masquerade with the ZO (henceforth designated WZO for World Zionist Organization). "For the next two decades, Philby courted Weizmann, pretending to be his ally in order to subvert his movement."[38] His dogged duplicity during the talks evoked an early pledge of autonomy for Transjordan, the official ceremony occurring on May, 15, 1923 (barely two years after Abdullah began his "temporary" six-month stint under Samuel). He also elicited the birth of the Arab Legion, "perhaps the crowning achievement of Philby's years in Amman…a force to fight the Jews."[39]

In January 1924, Philby resigned as Britain's main man in Amman. His continued covert support of Ibn Saud's bid for the Hejaz made his presence in Abdullah's Emirate untenable at best. Saud's subsequent victory appeared "inordinately swift": his campaign began in August 1924; Mecca fell two months later; Medina quit in early December 1925, Saud triumphantly entering Jidda a few weeks later.[40] "Philby allegedly played his part in Hussein's defeat by handing over a great deal of intelligence to Ibn Saud, which proved crucial to his successful campaign."[41] The new Emir was so grateful that he appointed Jack to oversee his coronation ceremony.[42] Saud would spend the next seven years subduing the vast territory of central Arabia. "Thus was the kingdom of Saudi Arabia founded by a renegade British spy."[43]

Engaged as a double agent for the Arabs, Philby promptly moved to Saudi Arabia to become Saud's chief financial advisor. After a visit to Jerusalem to see the Grand Mufti, Haj Muhammad Amin al-Husseini, the two formed an enduring bond. Back in the Hejaz, Jack continued to repudiate his Anglo-Saxon heritage. Once, while living in Jidda, he paraded his pet baboons in public to display his social independence from the small attendant European community.[44] Shortly thereafter, the eccentric initiated the final plunge—his full-blown "conversion" to Islam. Saud's offer had been too much to resist: camaraderie with the prestigious Palace entourage; lucrative employment; his own crib; four wives; plus unlimited access to the royal concubines.[45]

On August 7, 1930, Philby made the pilgrimage to Mecca, his final requirement for approval. Upon returning "home," the degenerate, bi-sexual MI6 agent and former Protestant, Harry St. John Bridger "Jack" Philby, received his new Muslim name (from Ibd Saud himself)—*Abdullah*—a.k.a. "Slave of God."[46] (His later, most sinister acts against the Jews will be revealed in the following chapter.)

ARAB RIOTS OF 1929

Herbert Samuel was replaced in 1925 by Lord Herbert Charles Plumer. His three-year rule as High Commissioner was relatively tranquil. To Zion's relief, the philo-Semitic Plumer was genuinely committed to facilitating the Jewish Homeland. As a no-nonsense former Field Marshal, Plumer conducted his non-political regime by the book. His larger-than-life stature had much to do with keeping the peace. Norman Bentwich writes, "Plumer's personality in the country…was worth a battalion; and it was not sufficiently appreciated that, when he left the country, a battalion might be necessary to make up for him."[47]

The point was duly noted when Plumer was replaced by Sir John Robert Chancellor in 1928. Though also a "military man," Lieutenant-Colonel Chancellor was a closet anti-Semite. The main Arab gripe at this time was the restriction on parliamentary rule (an untenable system for a fledgling Jewish minority). Unlike his predecessor, Johnny immediately began to "lend an ear to the complaints of the Arabs."[48] After meeting the Arab Delegation in January 1929, the new Commissioner pledged to revive the stalled representative assembly.

Meanwhile, the proverbial "handwriting" (from Daniel 5:5) was "on the wall" regarding yet another pogrom in the Old City. This time, the Muslim mayhem broke out at the Waqf-controlled Western (Wailing) Wall—a.k.a. The Kotel—shortly before the Jewish holy day of Yom Kippur on September 24, 1928. When the *Shammas* ("beadle" or "sexton") erected the traditional screen to separate the men and women according to strict Orthodox ritual, the Arabs "took offense," complaining that "the status quo had been violated" (the technicality being that the standing Turkish ordinance granting Jews limited access to the Wall contained no provision for appurtenances.)

Then, when an order by the Deputy District Commissioner to remove the barrier was not *promptly* obeyed, the police opted to act. However, their timing could not have been worse, bursting in during *Ne'ilah*—the solemn service ending Yom Kippur. Despite Jewish appeals for tolerance, the screen was carted off, sending shock waves throughout the angry crowd. While the WZO protested to both HMG and the League that their right to worship had been violated contrary to Article 2, the Muslims alerted the Ummah that the Zionists were "plotting to take over the Temple Mount, including the Mosque of Al-Aqsa." And of course, "His Muftiness" was right in the thick of things.

Over the months several harassing actions were enacted near the Wall to distract Jewish devotees: noisy building projects; widening the narrow thoroughfare to expand foot traffic; Muslim "hip-hop" protests called *Zikrs* ("playing the music") employing drums, rattles, and cymbals, accompanied by "holy screaming"; positioning a *muezzin* on a nearby rooftop to issue the call to worship *five* times a day. (As Ecclesiastes 1:9 states *"there is no new thing under the sun,"* when the Jews were rebuilding the walls of Jerusalem in 445 BC, Nehemiah 2:19 names *"Geshem the* ARABIAN*"* as one of *their* main foes.)

Finally, on June 11, 1929, after a lengthy exchange with the law officers of the Crown, the High Commissioner got around to telling al-Husseini that his folks simply had to quit bullying the Jews during their regular prayer times. The Zionist Executive was unimpressed, as this slap on the wrist had failed to render "a comprehensive decision covering the principal matters at issue."[49] While the *Zikrs* stopped, the construction and chanting continued to intimidate Jewish worshipers.

With tempers on the rise, Sir John took a convenient powder (exactly like Waters-Taylor did in 1920 to dodge Nebi Musa). Shortly before his June departure for London, the High Commissioner publicly assured al-Husseini that he would personally lobby the Colonial Office regarding the sensitive Legislative Assembly issue. Later, however, while the Arabist official was dutifully following through on this political promise—all *Hades* broke loose back in Palestine.

On August 15 (the eve of *Tisha b'Av*), a giant rally was held in Tel Aviv by the *Haganah* (the unofficial military of the Yishuv, formed after Nebi Musa). The day after, a local hard-line youth group was allowed to make a peaceful march to the Wall. When they arrived, the Zionist flag was unfurled and a brief speech given. After a two-minute silence, the meeting ended with "HaTikvah." No incidents occurred.[50]

The Arab Executive held a counter-protest on the 17th. According to an official report a frenzied mob of 2,000 Muslims marched through the streets crying, "There is no God but Allah; the religion of Mohammed came with the sword."[51] The paper also confirmed: An "inflammatory speech" was given at the Wall; the Shammas was "hustled and his clothes torn"; his ceremonial table was "upset and broken"; written petitions placed by Jews in the Wall's crevices were "taken out and burnt" along with "prayer books and prayer sheets."[52]

While this chaos was occurring in the Old City, a group of Jewish youths was playing soccer in the Bukharian Quarter of New Jerusalem. During the game, the ball rolled into an Arab's tomato garden. When one of the boys attempted to retrieve it, he was confronted by the property owner and knifed. The neighborhood erupted in violence leaving eleven Jews and fifteen Arabs wounded. As usual, the police were useless (one even managing to get himself hurt). The situation intensified when the victim died on August 20. To exacerbate matters, the large funeral cortege was marred by violent clashes with the police, producing more injuries, including several senior citizens.[53]

By week's end, thousands of self-inflamed Mohammedans were streaming into their "Al-Quds," many concealing pistols and knives. As the Friday afternoon "prayer service" was concluding at the *Haram* (Temple Mount), one of the "worshipers" began yelling—"A religious war is inevitable and we will kill all the Jews."[54] The pogrom ignited like clockwork. After *two hours* of bloodletting throughout the Holy City, British forces were finally ordered to quell the "disturbance." (Of course, all requests by Jews to defend themselves were denied.) The city's outlying districts were invaded on Saturday. In Hebron, sixty Jews (including women and children) were slain, with fifty wounded.

Ben Tzion Gershon, a physician-pharmacist in the Hadassah clinic in Hebron, was renowned for his unbiased compassion. On the riot's first night, an Arab woman went to his home, feigning labor pains. As the good doctor opened the door, a mob of his neighbors stormed in from the shadows, tied him up, and gang-raped his wife. When he pled with his attackers by name, they replied, "If you don't want to see it you don't have to," then gouged out his eyes. The Gershons were then dismembered in front of their two daughters. One of the girls lingered a week before succumbing to her wounds, but not before relating the gruesome story; the other spent the rest of her life in a mental ward.[55]

Similar attacks occurred in Tel Aviv and Haifa. The religious rampage eventually burned itself out on August 29 with a concluding assault on the Jewish quarter in Safed, killing or wounding forty-five additional innocents. According to the *Palestine Royal Commission Report*, the casualty count for the week was 133 Jews dead, with 339 wounded; Arab figures were given at 116 and 232, respectively.[56]

SHAW COMMISSION REPORT

On September 13, 1929, Lord Passfield, secretary of state for the colonies, authorized a four-man Commission of Inquiry to investigate "the immediate causes which led to the recent outbreak in Palestine, and to make recommendations as to the steps necessary to avoid a recurrence."[57] The formal (feckless) delegation, led by Sir Walter Shaw, arrived in Palestine on October 24, 1929.

Over the next two months the men traversed the country soliciting testimony from Jews, Arabs, and government officials alike. The course was predictable. Among several Muslim spokesmen, Haj Amin al-Husseini received special deference.[58] Upon cross-examination, the Mufti admitted that his main source of "enlightenment" for Jewry's real agenda was an Arabic translation of the *Protocols of the Elders of Zion*. (Muslims were merely defending their own interests, etc.) "I understand from this book that the Jews intend to possess this country, Trans-Jordan and other parts of Palestine…and then take possession of the *Haram* area and then restore the Temple."[59] The WZO countered by reminding all that the primary purpose of the Declaration and the Mandate was *supposed* to be establishing the Jewish National Home.

The Shaw Commission Report came out in March 1930. Initially, it appeared to vindicate the Jews, finding that "the outbreak in Jerusalem on the 23rd of August was from the beginning an attack by Arabs on Jews for which no excuse in the form of earlier murders by Jews had been established," while the hits were also accompanied by "wanton destruction of Jewish property."[60] However, the balance of the report placated major Arab concessions, i.e., the *ultimate* cause of the mayhem—without which the officials believed they would *not* have occurred, or would have been limited to local disorder—was "the Arab feeling of animosity and hostility toward the Jews consequent upon the disappointment of their political and national aspirations and fear for their economic future."[61] Among other anti-Semitic conclusions, the Commission opined that the pogrom was *not* premeditated; thus the Mufti's fears *were* partially understandable; and, the police *had* done the best they could, given their limited numbers and resources, etc.

The most telling illation was that "the claims and demands which from the Zionist side have been advanced in regard to the future of Jewish immigration into Palestine have been such as to arouse among the Arabs the apprehension that they will in time be deprived of their livelihood and pass under the political domination of the Jews."[62] This could mean only one thing: Like the 1921 Haycraft Commission, the Shaw Commission of 1930 "recommended a more stringent control of immigration, in accordance with the economic absorptive principle and suggested also that machinery should be devised whereby the non-Jewish interests in Palestine should be consulted."[63]

Thus, the final verdict of what was *supposed* to be a murder inquiry of 133 Jewish men, women, and children was practically a total ban on immigration. "Palestine cannot support a larger agricultural population than it at present carries unless methods of farming undergo a radical change."[64] The Arabs received the Shaw Report "with jubilation as the vindication of their case against the National Home"; *Vaad Leumi* labeled it "one of the most unjust documents which our people have had to face in the course of 2,000 years of persecution."[65] Weizmann took particular exception with a subtle *omission* in the report:

> The report...merely conceded that the Arabs had been the attackers; but it said nothing about the strange behavior of the Palestine administration which during the attacks had issued one communiqué after another representing the riots as 'clashes' between Jews and Arabs. From these communiqués it was made to appear that there were two peoples at war in Palestine, with the British administration as the neutral guardian of law and order. Apart from the gross misrepresentation of the Jewish attitude which such utterances impressed on the world, the implied exoneration of the Arab mobs and their inciters boded ill for the future. I have said that the Haycraft Report of 1921 contained the seed of much of our later troubles. Here were some of the fruits.[66]

HOPE SIMPSON REPORT

The Colonial Office wasted little time prosecuting their latest betrayal of the Declaration. On May 12 an immigration schedule of 3,300 labor certificates, previously approved by the Palestinian Administration, was promptly suspended.[67] Following an immediate Jewish backlash, Sir John Hope Simpson, an authority on agricultural economics, was dispatched to Palestine "to examine on the spot the questions of immigration, land settlement and development."[68] Arriving on May 20, Simpson pursued his fact-finding mission over the next three months.

The much-anticipated Hope Simpson Report was released October 20, 1930. It offered little "hope" for Zionist desires. Based primarily on unreliable aerial surveys of just 10% of the total area, the crux of the 185-page study affirmed: "It has emerged quite definitely that there is at the present time and with the present methods of Arab cultivation no margin of land available for agricultural settlement by new immigrants."[69] Thus, any further Jewish influx would supposedly deprive the "indigenous" rural Muslim base of a decent standard of life (flies, dunghills, camel urine, etc.). He also implied that a curtailed immigration policy was the *moral* thing to do, as Jewry has "had every advantage that capital, science and organization can give them," while the Arabs have "increased with great rapidity and the land available for its sustenance has meanwhile decreased by about one million metric dunams, which have passed into the hands of the Jews."[70]

WHITE PAPER OF 1930

The Zionists were understandably aghast at the Hope Simpson Report. However, at the end of the day (literally), they were reeling from two public relations disasters. At the behest of Prime Minister James Ramsay MacDonald, a twenty-three-page White Paper was also issued by Lord Passfield on October 20. The WZO was curtly told: "It must be realized once and for all that it is useless for Jewish leaders...to press HMG to conform to their policy in regard...to immigration and land, to the aspirations of the more uncompromising sections of Zionist opinion. That would be to ignore the equally important duty of the Mandatory Power towards the non-Jewish inhabitants of Palestine."[71]

While Arab fraud was barely cited, Sachar notes, "[T]he document proceeded to skewer virtually every Zionist hope for the future."[72] After just thirteen years, the Jewish National Homeland seemed to be caput. The same nation that had issued the epic Balfour Declaration, *and* accepted the obligations of the Palestine Mandate had now stated: "There remains no margin of land available for agricultural settlement by the new immigrants, with the exception of such undeveloped lands as the various Jewish agencies hold in reserve."[73]

To MacDonald's shock, a whirlwind of protest erupted from every quarter. London was inundated with letters, telegrams, and petitions. Scathing editorials appeared in the leading newspapers on both sides of the Atlantic. Weizmann resigned from the presidency of both the JA and the WZO in "emphatic protest against a one-sided and unjust criticism of our work."[74] His exit was followed by Felix Warburg's from the JA Administrative Committee and that of Alfred Lord Melchett from the chairmanship of the Council. Baron Edmond de Rothschild registered his solidarity as well. Rabbi Stephen Wise called the White Paper a "great betrayal," while Melchett labeled it a "grotesque travesty" and "an insult to the intelligence of Jewry."[75]

MacDonald's peers were also up in arms. Churchill excoriated the Passfield Paper in the House of Commons. Lloyd George blasted the Prime Minister during a heated parliamentary debate for "breaking the word of England!"[76] In a letter to the *Times*, Stanley Baldwin, Austin Chamberlin, and Leopold Amery indicted the MacDonald Government for making policy opposing the spirit of the Balfour Declaration, the authority of the League of Nations, and the terms of the Mandate "without giving either Jewish or Arab opinion an opportunity to express itself or allowing the voice of Parliament to be heard."[77]

The embattled statesman came to his political senses directly. In a private lunch with Weizmann on November 6, MacDonald agreed to clear the air. Though the White Paper was not *officially* retracted—that would have meant a loss of face—he did perform the next best thing. On February 13, 1931 (a Friday, no less), Jim wrote a personal letter to Chaim "reinterpreting" the toxic text. The salient portion read:

> The obligation to facilitate Jewish immigration and make possible dense settlement of Jews on the land is still a positive obligation of the Mandate, and it can be fulfilled without jeopardizing the rights and conditions of the other part of the Palestine population...His Majesty's Government does not intend to interrupt or prohibit immigrants of any of the various categories.[78]

He closed by reaffirming: "The obligations laid upon the Mandatory are solemn international promises and there is no intention at present, as there was not in the past, of disregarding them."[79] Though not endowed with the status of a Command Paper, the letter was read in the House of Commons and entered into the Hansard. It was also released to the press, transmitted as an official document to the League and sent to the High Commissioner of Palestine. The WZO hailed the MacDonald correspondence for reestablishing the Anglo-Zionist bond. However, though the proverbial "bullet" had been dodged, *everyone* knew that the "gun" was *far* from empty. Esco opined:

> The White Paper of 1930 may be looked upon as containing the germs of repudiation of the Jewish national home policy...From the Administration's manner of handling the situation in its entirety, the Arab leaders could not but have recognized that there were strong forces in the British Government which were more than ready to justify the Arab opposition to the Jewish claims. They could have concluded that their case had been advanced by the use of violence and the strategy of intransigence, and that another try at terror might prove successful.[80]

On February 19, 1931—less than a week after Chaim received his letter—the "cocking of the hammer" was heard again. In his own note to the racist High Commissioner of Palestine, Sir John Chancellor, the Arab Executive President Musa Kazem al-Husseini announced: "I want to assure your Excellency that Prime Minister MacDonald's letter has ruined hope of a policy of cooperation between Arabs and Jews, if there existed such a hope, and has rendered the possibility of understanding between the two parties absolutely impossible."[81] By then, one of Musa's notable cohorts, Islamic fundamentalist Imam Izz al-Din al-Qassam, had made another allusion to the metaphorical handwriting on the wall—the anti-Zionist/British insurgency, known as the "Black Hand." Klaus Mallmann and Martin Cüppers write:

> Al-Qassam reduced the concept of jihad—which previously, as "striving in the way of God," had been a relatively open concept—to the war against unbelievers and declared this militant version to be the authoritative interpretation of the Koran, thereby eliminating any potential for tolerance in one of the world's great religions and providing spiritual cover for any violence.[82]

It was Imam Izz who popularized the belief that seventy virgins awaited Allah's martyrs in Paradise, causing Muslim behavioral patterns to be ideologically charged and permanently radicalized in the process. While the "holy man" would later perfect his own "preaching"—going down in a blaze of glory during a firefight with British police on November 8, 1935—his dual legacy lives on in the Qassam rockets routinely fired at defenseless Israeli villages by the Izz al-Din al-Qassam suicide brigades of Hamas.

While the Jews were subsequently compelled to take matters into their own hands, the legendary *Irgun Zeva'i Le'umi* ("The National Military Organization," also known as "Etzel" or "I.Z.L") was organized that same year to augment the Yishuv's underground security apparatus. Over eighty years later, Arabist Alison Weir would write: "As this colonial project grew, the indigenous Palestinians reacted with occasional bouts of violence; Zionists had anticipated this since people usually resist being expelled from their land."[83]

"The past was erased, the erasure was forgotten,
the lie became the truth."
(George Orwell)

9

Prelude to War

"I regard Henry Ford as my inspiration."
(Adolf Hitler, December 1931)

"The world seemed to be divided into two parts;
those places where the Jews could not live
and those where they could not enter."
(Chaim Weizmann, May 1936)

"At the present moment more than a hundred American
corporations have subsidiaries here [Germany] or
cooperative understandings...I mention these facts
because they complicate things and add to war dangers."
(Ambassador William Dodd, October 19, 1936)

"I can only hope and expect that the other world, which has
such deep sympathy for these criminals will at least be generous
enough to convert this sympathy into practical aid. We, on our
part, are ready to put all these criminals at the disposal
of these countries, for all I care...on luxury ships."
(Adolf Hitler, March 1938)

ON THE URGING of King Faisal, England granted Iraq independence in 1932. As part of the deal, British military bases would remain to secure the strategic Mosul oil fields. Unfortunately for Faisal, his glory was short-lived, the forty-eight-year-old having succumbed to a "heart attack" on September 8, 1933, while on medical leave in Bern, Switzerland. (Some believe he was poisoned.) However, unfolding events in Europe would prove more severe to the Middle East, especially regarding the future Jewish State. In 1934, Adolf Hitler was elected Chancellor of Germany. While the Führer's legacy is the attested murder of six million Jews, what is *not* as widely known is how the Fascist psychopath was bankrolled by a cabal of "civilized" US capitalists; worse yet—how they denied the pitiful victims a route of escape on the very eve of their destruction.

Some of the biggest "holes" in the history books were "punched" between the two World Wars. Professor Antony C. Sutton writes,

> Contemporary academic histories, with perhaps the sole exception of Carroll Quigley's *Tragedy And Hope*, ignore this evidence. On the other hand, it is understandable that universities and research organizations, dependent on financial aid from foundations that are controlled by this same New York financial elite, would hardly want to support and to publish research on these aspects of international politics. The bravest of trustees is unlikely to bite the hand that feeds his organization.[1]

As stated in the Introduction, Allen Dulles, Jack Philby, and Ibn Saud were three of the key architects of Hitler's war and the genocide it spawned. Loftus and Aarons called them "profoundly evil men who bore substantial responsibility for the Holocaust but escaped the judgment of history."[2] While Philby and Saud were rabid anti-Semites, Al was driven by cash, his odious career repudiating the Wall Street adage: "Bulls make money, Bears make money, Pigs get slaughtered."[3] However, as will be seen shortly, with the discovery of Saudi Arabian oil, Dulles would have *no* problem embracing the racist views of his new client. (The same would apply to Wall Street in general.)

"THE GREAT WHITE CASE OFFICER"

The official record has been very kind to Allen Welsh Dulles. His cuddly sobriquet, "The Great White Case Officer," is often evoked in recognition of his many "productive" years in the CIA, etc. He is also credited with prosecuting the intelligence campaign against Hitler. However, Loftus and Aarons note that retired US intel agents hold a far different opinion: "They describe Allen Dulles as one of the worst traitors in American history, an economic version of Benedict Arnold. He was the man who sold his country out for money, blackmailed presidents, and helped to fund Hitler. Our sources say that there was a secret side to Dulles that has never made it into the history books."[4]

Allen and his older brother, John Foster, were high-end corporate lawyers, global finance experts, well-connected State Department envoys, *and* fanatical Roman Catholics. Their long alliance with Jack Philby began in 1921 when the latter was stationed in Transjordan as Britain's intel chief. Philby actually helped Allen break into the spy business by "feeding him timely bits of information."[5] The Dulles boys would amass their fortunes by exploiting the tragedy of WWI to jumpstart the greater profit-making window of WWII ("eliminating" 6,000,000 potential settlers of the future Jewish homeland in the process). Most historians posit that Germany's crushing reparations burden made another war inevitable. However, while the economic chaos set the stage *for* the Fascist transition, it was Dulles and several likeminded "pigs"—from Henry Ford to Prescott Bush—that ultimately supplied the needed stimulus to bring Hitler *onto* that stage.

Under Versailles, Germany was assessed a reparations bill of 132 billion marks (payable in gold or equivalent foreign currency) with a first payment of 20 billion due by May 1921. When the deadline came, the envelope was "light" by 12 billion. In a compromise deal, the 124 billion balance was reduced to a "firm" 50 billion, payable at a rate of 2.5 billion marks per year in interest, plus an annual 0.5 billion toward the remaining principle. To meet these obligations the debtor nation had to maintain a budget surplus *and* a favorable balance of trade.[6]

Now although the London Schedule was "accepted" on paper, the Weimar Republic had no intention of lowering its own expenditures nor the national living standard by raising taxes. As the government had to borrow from the Reichsbank to meet its self-imposed budgetary deficits (inclusive of token reparations payments) the phenomenon of hyper-inflation set in. With the German mark worth 20 to the pound at par, it dropped from 305 to the pound in August 1921 to 1,020 to 1 just three months later. In July 1922, Berlin demanded an emergency moratorium on all cash payments for thirty months. The following January, the mark fell to 80,000 to the pound. That same month, the Reparations Commission voted 3 to 1 (with Britain opposing France, Belgium, and Italy) that Germany was now officially in default.

Two days later, troops from France and Belgium occupied the Ruhr valley. Though only 30 by 60 miles, the area held 10% of Germany's population, producing 80% of her coal, iron, and steel, plus 70% of all rail traffic. When the locals resorted to passive resistance, the mark plunged to 20 *million* to the pound by August. Things having turned ugly (2,500 casualties), the bewildered citizens "celebrated" Christmas 1923 with their currency bottoming out at 20 *billion* to the pound.[7]

The catastrophic slide took the mark from a rate of 50,000 to 1 US dollar in 1921 to 4,210,500,000,000 to 1 in 1923. Housewives hauled their money around in wheelbarrows while shopping. Some had their houses wallpapered with the worthless currency. Postage stamps cost a million marks each. A special medal "marking" the disaster read: "On 1st November 1923 1 pound of bread cost 3 billion, 1 pound of meat: 36 billion, 1 glass of beer: 4 billion." Another illustration depicted patrons at bars ordering a second beer as soon as their first arrived, as the price would double if they waited to reorder. The most telling sign was the slur calling the inflated notes—*Judenfetzen* ("Jew confetti"). Thus, the reparations disaster (along with the fantasy solution put forth by Dulles and his Wall Street cronies) would condition the German populace to yearn for a savior to shield them from the falling confetti.

THE DAWES PLAN

In September 1924, Germany acquiesced to a second compromise schedule called the Dawes Plan, the result of an international cabal of economic experts (i.e., J. P. Morgan) presided over by the American banker Charles G. Dawes. Not only would the annual payment during the first four years drop from 2.5 billion marks to 1 billion (returning to 2.5 in year five), but Germany would also receive $800 million in loans (from Gentile and Jewish bankers alike) to "help revitalize her devastated infrastructure" (i.e., build Hitler's war machine).

Quigley writes, "Using these American loans, Germany's industry was re-equipped with the most advanced technical facilities, and...was able to rebuild her industrial system to make it the second best in the world by a wide margin."[8] The Allies were also requited: "By these loans Germany's creditors were able to pay their war debts to England and the US without sending goods or services. Foreign exchange went to Germany as loans, back to Italy, Belgium, France, and Britain as reparations, and finally back to the US as payments on war debts."[9]

Of course, the "pig in the poke" was that the difference between the lower Dawes payments and the original London Schedule was carried over to the total debt. "Thus Germany paid reparations for five years under the Dawes Plan and owed more at the end than it had owed at the beginning...It is worthy of note that this system was set up by the international bankers and that the subsequent lending of other people's money to Germany was very profitable to these bankers."[10] Dawes received the Nobel Peace Prize in 1925 for his timely "humanitarian" solution to the crisis. (He also became the 30th vice president in 1930.)

Allen and John were also two of the lead culprits in the global gold recycling scam. Supreme Court Justice Art Goldberg reputedly called the Dulles' traitors.[11] Temporarily vacating the State Department, the siblings joined the powerful Wall Street firm of Sullivan & Cromwell. Glen Yeadon writes in *The Nazi Hydra in America*: "In the 1920s-1930s, several Wall Street firms figured prominently in guiding investments into Germany, but almost every deal involved the services of Sullivan and Cromwell."[12] Foster also served as special counsel to the Dawes Committee itself. While Allen was on the board of Schröder Bank in Germany, John was a director of the Nazi-controlled chemical conglomerate, I. G. Farben. Asserting that they "dealt in millions and traded with nations as equals,"[13] Loftus and Aarons note:

> The Dulles brothers were the ones who convinced American businessmen to avoid government regulation by investing in Germany...Nearly 70% of the money that flowed into Germany during the 1930s came from US investors, many of them Sullivan & Cromwell clients...In return for their gold, the American clients received bonds and promissory notes backed by shares of stock in Swiss holding companies that owned stock in German banks. These banks in turn owned the stock of major German corporations, which...owned some of the most valuable industrial patents in the world...American companies, such as Du Pont and General Motors, were more than willing to swap gold for patent rights, at bargain basement prices...The Dulles brothers looked like geniuses. Their "Dawes Plan" of recycling US gold so that Germany could meet its international reparations payments, while rebuilding its domestic industry, was a stunning success, at least for a while...As the biographer of the Dulles family, Leonard Mosley, has noted:

"Financially speaking, it was a mad sort of merry-go-round, but it gave the statesmen a breathing space."[14]

To no one's surprise, the "merry-go-round" was unplugged in 1929 when Germany missed her first payment of 2.5 billion marks. Another bailout was designed—the Young Plan, named after Morgan agent, Owen Young. Though structured with an appealing escalating rate of 1.7 billion marks in 1931, to a peak of 2.4 billion in 1966, the thirty-five year pipedream burst before eighteen months, the entire restitution fiasco having succumbed to the encroaching effect of the New York stock market crash. The final tally for 1924-31 reveals that Germany paid 10.5 billion marks while borrowing 18.6 billion marks abroad. Quigley notes, "Nothing was settled by all of this, but the international bankers sat in heaven, under a rain of fees and commissions."[15]

Wall Street and the Wehrmacht

By the time the confetti hit the fan, the real damage was already done. Thanks to Wall Street, Nazi Germany was now in the throes of a rearmament trajectory destined to produce a second global conflagration, capped by the Final Solution. Few Americans know the shameful (and depressing) role played by their own government in the rise of Adolf Hitler and his *Wehrmacht* (German Armed Forces). The story represents a powerful illustration for the subtitle of this book.

Antony C. Sutton (1925-2002) was a British-born economist, engineer, educator, historian, and author. After studying at London and Göttingen universities, Sutton did his graduate work at UCLA. In the 1960s, he was a Professor of Economics at California State University, followed by seven years as a research fellow at Stanford. While at the Hoover Institute, he authored the three-volume definitive set on technology transfer to the former Soviet Union entitled *Western Technology and Soviet Economic Development*. His barrage of twenty-five pungent exposés on Western perfidy caused the "Eastern Establishment" even *more* consternation than Quigley's works. In his 1976 classic, *Wall Street and the Rise of Hitler*, Sutton cites the array of US corporations and banks that made WWII and the Holocaust a reality: "The contribution made by American capitalism to German war preparations before 1940 can only be described as phenomenal. It was certainly crucial to German military capabilities."[16] On October 19, 1936 (three years after Hitler's rise to power), the US ambassador to Germany, William Dodd, wired President Roosevelt from Berlin:

> At the present...more than a hundred American corporations have subsidiaries here or cooperative understandings. The DuPonts have three allies in Germany that are aiding in the armament business... Standard Oil Company...sent $2,000,000 here in December 1933 and has made $500,000 a year helping Germans make Ersatz gas for war...The International Harvester Company president told me their business here rose 33% a year...Even our airplanes people have a secret arrangement with Krupps. General Motors and Ford do enormous businesses here...I mention these facts because they complicate things and add to war dangers.[17]

Plenty of other household names could be cited under the cloak of "Business is business": Dow Chemical provided large supplies of magnesium for incendiary bombs and miscellaneous explosives; General Electric cartelized Germany's electrical industry; the J. P. Morgan-controlled International Telephone and Telegraph Company made several substantial cash payments to Heinrich Himmler during the war to protect its investment in Focke-Wulf Flugzeugbau AG, an aircraft firm producing fighter planes for use *against* America. While *Luftwaffe* commander Hermann Göring received a death sentence at Nuremburg (cheating the hangman with a potassium cyanide capsule), somebody forgot to prosecute the CEO at Standard Oil of New Jersey for approving the transfer of substantial quantities of high-octane aircraft fuel to Hermann on the eve of Germany's invasion of Poland.[18]

The government's spin was nearly as bad as the treason itself. The claim that US executives were "surprised" by Hitler's plans is absurd. While the postwar Kilgore Committee admitted that "when the Nazis came to power in 1933, they found long strides had been made since 1918 in preparing Germany for war from an economic and industrial point of view,"[19] they were also quick to *qualify* that assertion:

> The United States accidentally played an important role in the arming of Germany. Although the German military planners had ordered and persuaded manufacturing corporations to install modern equipment for mass production, neither the economists nor the corporations seem to have realized to the full extent what that

> meant. Their eyes opened when two of the chief American automobile companies built plants in Germany…to sell in Europe without the handicap of ocean freight charges and high German tariffs. Germans were brought to Detroit to learn the techniques of specialized production of components, and of straight-line assembly. What they saw caused further reorganization and refitting of other key German war plants. The techniques learned in Detroit were eventually used to construct the dive-bombing Stukas…a great deal…was eventually used against the US.[20]

"CAPTAIN OF INDUSTRY"

No spinmeister could explain the un-American track record of famed auto titan Henry Ford (a.k.a. "Captain of Industry"). On October 20, 1922, the *New York Times* wrote that the Dearborn, Michigan, native was financing Hitler's Jew-baiting campaigns in Munich. Ford's early sway over Hitler (twenty-six years his junior) is revealed by the fact that he was the sole American named in *Mein Kampf*: "Jews are the regents of the stock exchange power of the American Union. Every year they manage to become increasingly the controlling masters of the labor power of a people of 120,000,000 souls; one great man, Ford, to their exasperation, still holds out independently there even now."[21]

In addition to lucrative donations, Ford aided his Führer by exports of military hardware—along with "an attitude." While supplying the Wehrmacht with badly needed trucks, he also helped indoctrinate the Nazi cause with his magnum opus, *The International Jew: the World's Foremost Problem*. Having spewed out sixty anti-Semitic issues of the *Dearborn Independent,* Ford repackaged his racism into the four-volume *International Jew* series, selling 10,000,000 copies in America alone, plus millions more via foreign distribution in sixteen languages, including German and Arabic. Henry was so revered in Germany that his portrait adorned the wall behind Hitler's desk at the Nazi Party headquarters in Munich. When asked about the painting by a *Detroit News* reporter, Adolf said, "I regard Henry Ford as my inspiration."[22]

Any doubt about the matter was removed in August 1938, when a German delegation presented Henry with a special 75th birthday gift—"The Grand Cross of the German Eagle" (the nation's highest honor for a non-citizen)—featuring not *one*, not *two*, not *three*, but FOUR

Nazi swastikas! That same year, as Hitler was preparing to occupy Czechoslovakia, the Reich ordered 3,150 trucks from Ford-Werke in Cologne. Detroit was *so* grateful that it expedited the deal by shipping pre-built components.[23] (Though it supplied Hitler with 125,000 wartime vehicles, Ford-Werke was *never* targeted by allied bombers.)

Thus, while the Model T may have "inspired" the Volkswagen, Ford's vitriolic anti-Semitism and vanguard automation efficiency (the latter fashioned after the overhead trolley used by Chicago meat packers) proved the more *lethal* impetus, affording Hitler a "Better Idea" for his Final Solution. In his war trials affidavit, SS physician Friedrich Entress described the efficiency of the Auschwitz crematoria as *am laufenden Band*—"a conveyor belt."[24] Survivor Shlomo Venezia agreed, "Everything happened in a highly organized way, like an assembly belt on which we were the finished products."[25] (While the Ford legacy must include Dearborn's 50,000 Muslims, of the many "shocks" the Bible dunce encountered in Hell, the fact that a *Jew* had depicted the combustible engine in Nahum 2:3-4—*over 2,500 years before Henry's birth*—would have been the ultimate "V8" moment.)

I. G. FARBENINDUSTRIE

In addition to corporate "*work* boots on the ground," another American boost to Germany's illegal rearmament was occasioned by those hefty Dawes Plan loans. According to testimony before the 1946 Senate Committee on Military Affairs, "The Dawes Plan, adopted in August 1924, fitted perfectly into the plans of the German General Staff's military economists."[26] The lion's share of the funds was allocated for the creation of three specific cartels (monopolies) that would dominate prewar Nazi Germany: *Allgemeine Elektrizitäts-Gesellschaft* (German General Electric); *Vereinigte Stahlwerke* (United Steel Works); and American I. G. Chemical (I. G. Farben). Farben would prove the most important, and concerning US-Nazi complicity, the most culpable.

In 1926, *I. G. Farbenindustrie* made the startling report that it had found a way to extract synthetic liquid fuel from coal. The news had major implications for German energy independence, especially *if* another war should "happen" to break out; for though the Fatherland lacked oil, it was rich in natural resources, particularly coal. However, while I. G.

Farben possessed the secret ingredient (*Leunabenzin*), the chemical firm lacked the needed expertise of a petroleum concern to press the advantage. Acknowledging that the "field of petroleum industry is so tremendous," Farben President Carl Bosch told a Reichstag committee that "the consideration of a new production in the fight against these concerns would have been very difficult...and the financial needs...beyond any expectation."[27]

Fortunately for Germany, Standard Oil of New Jersey had panicked at the find. When their research chief, Frank Howard, visited Farben's Leuna works in 1926, he was so awed, he wired Standard's President Walter Teagle: "Based upon observations and discussions today, I think that this matter is the most important which has ever faced the company since the dissolution...This means absolutely the independence of Europe in the matter of gasoline supply."[28] Worried about losing their European markets to synthetic oil, Teagle rushed to Leuna himself, later saying that he "had not known what research meant until I saw it. We were babies compared to the work I saw."[29] (While coal hydrogenation was not competitive with crude, Standard feared that "the nationalistic factor" would eventuate in hydrogenation as the base of a protected industry in nations willing to pay.)

The solution was inevitable—the two behemoths would "share" their unique strengths for the "greater common good," etc. The threat of a shooting war only added to the "wisdom" of the decision, for as Professor Robert Engler alludes, business deals were always easier to slip in under the public relations radar. "The Nazis had recognized the 'very friendly relationships' between the giant corporations while realizing that the German government was not likely to be successful in this quest in view of the international political climate."[30] When pressed by pesky investigative committees, executives could always quote the handy one-liner that "the company cannot constitute itself judge of the rights and wrongs of international problems."[31] (Bill Farish, Standard's wartime CEO, was later grilled as to why his subsidiary was giving Luftwaffe plants fuel refining as late as 1939.)

The expanded structural complexity also ensured that only a fraction of the overall scandal would ever be known. As I Corinthians 14:33 states, *"For God is not the author of confusion,"* Quigley wrote about the diabolical interlocking directorates of German cartels, "This new privately managed monopoly capitalism was organized in an intricate hierarchy whose details could be unraveled only by a lifetime of study."[32]

American I. G. Chemical became Farben's wholly owned US subsidiary. In 1929, Jersey Standard agreed to pay Farben 2% of its stock (546,000 shares/$35 million) for hydrogenation patent rights outside of Germany. As one official described the cozy win-win deal, "The I. G. are going to stay out of the oil business—and we are going to stay out of the chemical business."[33] I. G. Farben became a major shareholder in the Jersey firm, second only to John D. Rockefeller.[34]

After just two years of good ol' "Yankee ingenuity," Germany began to rekindle a measure of her own national pride. In 1931, Friedrich Bergius, inventor of the hydrogenation process, shared the Nobel Prize in chemistry with Carl Bosch. However, for European Jewry, the Standard-Farben marriage would prove a "match made in Hell"—*the* "match" that would light the ovens in Hitler's hellish death camps. Regarding Sherman's two abiding quotes ("The truth...should not always be told" and "War is Hell"), the degree of treason-induced carnage in the Civil War cannot begin to match the horrors of WWII ignited by an army of US firms. Sadly—the facts speak for themselves.

Having rearmed the Rhineland with a bold (and unopposed) stroke in 1936, Hitler sounded the clarion call: "German fuel production must now be developed with the utmost speed. This task must be...executed with the same determination as the waging of a war, since on its solution depends the future conduct of the war."[35] In two years, I. G. Farbenindustrie shot from an autonomous German firm to a Nazified *Judenfrei* industrial arm of the Reich. While American CEOs would betray their own nation in a New York minute, Quigley notes how their Nazi peers (misguided or not), put them to open shame: "German cartel managers were patriotic Germans first and businessmen seeking profits and power second. In most other countries (especially the US), monopoly capitalists are businessmen first and patriots later."[36]

With the concomitant blessings of American I. G. (improved production technologies, better catalysts, higher grade output), Hitler's goal was met on schedule. By the time his Panzers *blitzkrieged* Poland on September 1, 1939 (the very concept of "lightning war" reflecting the Führer's obsession with fuel conservation), fourteen hydrogenation plants were up and running throughout Germany, with six more under construction. By 1940, synthetic fuel production increased to 72,000 barrels per day.[37] Sutton reviews what is now a matter of fact:

> [I]n 1934 Germany produced domestically only 300,000 tons of natural petroleum products and less than 300,000 tons of synthetic gasoline; the balance was imported. Yet, ten years later in World War II, after transfer of the Standard Oil of New Jersey hydrogenation patents and technology to I. G. Farben (used to produce synthetic gasoline from coal), Germany produced about 6½ million tons of oil – of which 85% (5½ million tons) was synthetic oil using the Standard Oil hydrogenation process."[38]

When US forces entered Germany, a Farben report was found in a folder marked "to be destroyed." The incriminating paper reads in part:

> Without lead-tetraethyl [aviation fuel additive] the present method of warfare would be unthinkable. The fact that since the beginning of the war we could produce lead-tetraethyl is entirely due to the circumstances that shortly before the Americans had presented us with the production plants complete with experimental knowledge. Thus the difficult work of development (one need only recall the poisonous property of lead-tetraethyl, which caused many deaths in the USA) was spared us, since we could take up the manufacture of this product together with all the experience that the Americans had gathered over long years.[39]

Depicting the Nazi conglomerate as a "state within a state," Senator Homer Bone told the Military Affairs Committee on June 4, 1943: "Farben was Hitler and Hitler was Farben."[40] What he *didn't* say was that "Farben was Standard and Standard was Farben." However, one review by the US War Department would later go on record, stating:

> Without I. G.'s immense productive facilities, its intense research, and vast international affiliations, Germany's prosecution of the war would have been unthinkable and impossible; Farben not only directed its energies toward arming Germany, but concentrated on weakening her intended victims, and this double-barreled attempt to expand the German industrial potential for war and to restrict that of the rest of the world was not conceived and executed "in the normal course of business." The proof is overwhelming that I. G. Farben officials had full prior knowledge of Germany's plan for world conquest and of each specific aggressive act later undertaken.[41]

Daniel Yergin, former lecturer at Harvard's Business School and John F. Kennedy School of Government, president of Cambridge Energy Research Associates, and Pulitzer Prize-winning author on oil-related issues, reveals the bottom line regarding the key role that synthetic oil played in Hitler's ability to wage war:

> Hydrogenation...provided some 95% of Germany's aviation gasoline. Without those synthetic fuels, the Luftwaffe could not have taken to the air...The synthetic fuels plants were the critical links in the fuel system; in the first quarter of 1944, they provided 57% of total supply—and 92% of aviation gasoline...Altogether, during the Second World War, synthetic fuels would account for half of Germany's total oil production.[42]

STANDARD-FARBEN-BAYER AND ZYKLON B

Finally, the saga's only untold chapter is the cartel's macabre nexus to the Holocaust itself. As the number of hydrogenation plants grew with the onset of war, Hitler directed Farben to tap the death camps for "temporary" slave labor. (Hundreds of Jews were "employed" at Ford Werke.) A giant synthetic fuel and rubber factory sprang up four miles from Auschwitz, the most notorious camp of all. Of its 1,000,000 victims, 300,000 had their nightmare extended at the Farben branch camp, Monowitz *Buna-Werke*.[43] Sleeping on boards, subsisting on barely a thousand calories a day, and subject to constant floggings, the Jews were literally worked to death, often within months. One of the few survivors was a young Italian Jew, Primo Levi (a.k.a. Prisoner 174,517Δ). Levi described Monowitz as a "huge entanglement of iron, concrete, mud and smoke...the negation of beauty...a world of death and phantoms where the last trace of civilization had vanished."[44]

By 1944, one third of Germany's synthetic fuels industry work force was slave labor. The most vile product created by the Standard-Farben hybrid was the Zyklon B gas used in the "showers" at Auschwitz. Farben held the patent. Ironically, the lethal poison, consisting of pure prussic acid (hydrogen cyanide) was sold by the German firm renowned for relieving the common headache—Bayer AG. On a "brighter" note, the personnel at both sites got along "just peachy." After a hard day's work, the men would engage in frequent socializing. In fact, as cited by

Yergin, "Just before one Christmas, the resident I. G. Farben managers at Auschwitz joined men from the local SS in a holiday shooting party. The bag totaled 203 rabbits, one fox, and one wild cat. The head of construction at the Farben complex was 'proclaimed champion hunter' with a bag of one fox and ten rabbits. 'A good time was had by all,' according to the record of the hunt."[45]

OIL IN THE SAND

Meanwhile, though Saud had become the undisputed Emir of Saudi Arabia, by the end of the decade he was broke (the global depression having depleted the realm's lucrative pilgrimage income). The word in the sand was that Saud "could carry his entire national treasury in the saddlebags of a camel."[46] Then, during a timely drive in autumn 1930, "Abdullah" Philby told the Sheik that the answer to his liquidity problems might be under his feet, literally.[47] The New Zealand adventurer Frank Holmes, a.k.a. *Abu Naft* ("The Father of Oil"), had been sniffing around the Arabian peninsula since 1920. His initial finds in Bahrain finally attracted Gulf Oil in 1927. Saud was listening.

In early 1931, Philby introduced his pal to the American philanthropist, Charles Crane, who in turn arranged for a geological survey by the noted engineer, Karl Twitchell. The preliminary results were promising. By October, Standard Oil of California (SOCAL) had acquired Gulf's Bahrain concession, striking oil on May 31, 1932, with major implications for the region. Saud was now happier than ever. SOCAL asked Jack to formally engage "His Majesty Ibn Saud." He was also retained as an advisor, using the extra income to cover the costly Cambridge education of his son, Kim (more about *him* later).

The year-long negotiations proceeded between SOCAL attorney Lloyd Hamilton and Saud's finance minister, Abdullah Suleiman. The final deal, authorizing a sixty-year concession on 360,000 sq. miles, was signed on May 29, 1933. Saud would receive $175,000 in gold (up front), plus $100,000 eighteen months later as a "loan" advance on future royalties. SOCAL secured the initial payment from Guaranty Trust's London office; 35,000 gold sovereigns (filling seven chests) were promptly shipped from the Royal Mint to Saudi Arabia. To avoid needless devaluation in the male-dominated culture, the coins bore the likeness of an English *king* rather than *Her* Majesty, Queen Victoria.[48]

Though early exploration was slow and dispiriting, on March 4, 1938, a gusher was struck at 4,727 ft. in Well 7 (henceforth known as "Lucky 7"). The industry went into shock! Saud received an automatic royal bonus of $500,000. Wasting no time, the Americans built a small city in the sand dunes, named Dhahran. A pipeline connected the oil field to a marine terminal in the coastal niche of Ras Tanura. In April 1939, the Emir led a dramatic cross-desert caravan of 400 cars to Dhahran, "crashing" with his guests in a hastily erected canvas suburb of 350 tents. The purpose for the gala affair was to greet the SOCAL tanker, MS *D. G. Scofield*, as it arrived for the inaugural transport of Saudi oil. Yergin writes, "With appropriate pomp, Ibn Saud opened the valve through which the first trickle of oil flowed out of Saudi Arabia."[49] The date was May 1—the world would never be the same.

With the twist of that tap, His Highness also gained an instant flow of similar "friends" in high places. Loftus and Aarons write, "As will be seen, Jack Philby did more, much more, for US oil companies than obtain the Saudi oil concession. He taught them how to interpret Ibn Saud and his court. The Americans quickly learned that a good dose of old-fashioned anti-Semitism did not go astray in Jidda...he gave the oil men the means to guide, if not control, the mysterious potentates of Arabia."[50] Engler adds, "Oil has brought to its corporate masters the greatest concentration of private wealth and economic power in history. It also brought them into contact with governments and people in every region of the world. Inevitably, the oil corporations have had to formulate and implement polices to guide these relationships."[51]

That last statement was a discreet way of explaining *why* and *how* the oil industry was destined to be *pro*-Arab and *anti*-Israel, for as "fate" would have it, the Jews brought nothing to *this* table. Golda Meir would famously say, "Let me tell you something that we Israelis have against Moses. He took us forty years through the desert in order to bring us to the one spot in the Middle East that has no oil!" Engler expands on the realpolitik of "petrol appeasement":

> Regimes sympathetic to the industry have been backed, regardless of internal political alignments, ideological considerations and, on occasions, the formal position of the American government...With two-thirds of the world's crude reserves in the Middle East, the internationally integrated members of the industry are understandably sensitive to Arab nationalist movements. They have installations,

> long-term commitments, and profit expectations worth billions of dollars. They fear fresh upward demands in royalty percentages and rights, behind which lies the ever present threat of nationalization. Oil wants stability in this region—which means maintenance of the status quo for as long as possible while it races to take out the highly profitable petroleum. Its leaders have been consistent advocates of the appeasement of Middle Eastern feudal rulers.[52]

There would no longer be any question as to which way the sand was blowing when it came to the undisputed "feudal ruler" of the Middle East. The Third Reich promptly established diplomatic relations with Saudi Arabia in 1939. While Emir Saud informed Hitler that he too "hated the English," he showed even more disdain for the Jews, calling them "a race accursed by God according to His Holy Book, and destined to final destruction and eternal damnation."[53] The delighted Führer assured his new ally that he would help him expel the Jews from Palestine and restore the Grand Mufti to power. Secret pledges of munitions were also included along with that ever-popular dangling "caliphate." The implications for Zionism were obvious: "Dulles reported that the utility of a Jewish State...would do nothing but complicate the entry of American oil companies into the region...The Jews were an obstacle to the smooth flow of Arab oil."[54] Thus, as Loftus and Aarons opine, the rarely told "alliance between American oil companies and Saudi Arabia...[was *the*]...indispensable precondition for the war and the Nazi Holocaust."[55]

STANDARD FUEL IN NAZI SUBS

The "alliance" proved especially profitable during the window of opportunity between the blitzkrieg of Poland and the bombing of Pearl Harbor. As Loftus and Aarons reveal, one of the more repugnant and seldom recognized motives for "isolationist" America's "delayed" entry into the war was that her neutral status just *happened* to enable Wall Street to exploit Britain's unavoidable commercial vulnerability:

> American investors structured their multinational holdings to legally make a profit on both sides of the war. As long as the US remained officially neutral, such conduct was technically legal, or at least

offered a plausible defense...British intel watched with chagrin as American competitors moved into their Axis markets. US oil flowed to Germany, Spain, and Italy, while German marks and captured gold continued to pile up in Switzerland."[56]

Of course, this is *not* to say that Anglo-American firms were ever totally disengaged from enemy dealings even *after* their respective governments were formally at war; neutrality just made things less "complicated." After the "sneak" attack on Pearl Harbor (see *Honolulu Advertiser*, front-page headline on November 30, 1941, "Japanese May Strike Over Weekend!"), other, more "discreet," methods of delivery were needed. The following letter was sent to the War Department by Major Charles Burrows of Military Intelligence on July 15, 1941—*when U-boats were sinking Allied ships with impunity*:

> A report has been received from Cleveland, Ohio, in which it is stated that this information is unquestionable, to the effect that the Standard Oil Company of New Jersey now ships under Panamanian registry, transporting oil (fuel) from Aruba, Dutch West Indies, to Teneriffe, Canary Islands, and is apparently diverting about 20% of this fuel oil to the present German government...About six of the ships operating on this route are reputed to be manned mainly by Nazi officers. Seamen have reported to the informant that they have seen submarines in the immediate vicinity of the Canary islands and have learned that these submarines are refueling there. The informant also stated that...Standard Oil...has not lost any ships to date by torpedoing as have other companies whose ships operate to other ports."[57]

Mr. Loftus made the following startling revelation in his highly documented 2011 exposé, *America's Nazi Secret*:

> British SIS reported that Dulles's American clients, including the Rockefellers, were helping the Nazis by laundering oil supplies through neutral countries. When FDR demanded that Justice indict the corporations, DOJ settled for a minor financial penalty. In defense of DOJ, it must be noted that Dulles's corporate cartel did threaten to withhold oil supplies for D-Day unless all charges were dropped.[58]

Thus, one of the biggest "holes" in history is the "unpalatable truth" that while America's military was fighting *against* Germany, her firms and financial institutions were allied *with* Germany. To absorb this *fact* is to feel the truth of Ecclesiastes 1:18—*"he that increaseth knowledge increaseth sorrow."* (On a personal note, the *SS Yorkmar*, a US Merchant Marine ship, was sunk by a U-boat near Murmansk on October 9, 1943, the survivors including this author's twenty-seven-year-old uncle, William F. Grady, a Navy and Coast Guard veteran as well.)

While London was hanging in the balance during the epic Battle of Britain, it was "business as usual" for Jack and his team: "[I]n 1940 there was a three-way deal. Philby represented the Saudi sellers of oil [Caltex since Texaco merged with SOCAL], Allen Dulles represented the Nazi buyers such as I. G. Farben, while Foster Dulles represented the German bankers and Spanish financiers…Through his client, Ibn Saud, a cozy deal could be done to get the Third Reich's hands on Saudi Arabian oil and make lots of money for Dulles's…clients."[59]

For Jewry, however, the Saudi-German-American oil alliance was fraught with peril for everyone knew that "Ibn Saud was…secretly in partnership with the Nazis, who financed his clandestine war against the Zionists in Palestine."[60] Even after Standard came under tighter scrutiny with the end of US neutrality, the King was able to continue his anti-Semitic agenda through blackmail. As Philby would "explain," one potential "danger" was that Saudi oil might "accidently" fall into enemy hands; another was that America's *own* spigot might get turned off, "accidently," of course. Ultimately, Saud's desert gravitas was so good that he was able to extort over $100 million in bribes from FDR and Hitler alike.[61] Ribbentrop even threw in a new Mercedes.[62]

ARAB REVOLT OF 1936-39

With Saud's meteoric rise to fame (backed by Hitler's ideological camaraderie), Allah's point men took their cue to rekindle "Arab Nationalism" (rioting) in Palestine. In 1935, Haj Muhammad Amin al-Husseini, Grand Mufti of Jerusalem, entered his *13th* year as president of the Supreme Muslim Council. He also ruled the Palestine Arab Party (the toughest of six rival sects). To ensure maximum anti-Jewish volatility, the PAB vice president, Arab merchant Alfred Roch, was the most prominent Catholic in town. Every effort was made for the coming insurrection. While Arab "Boy Scouts" patrolled the coast for illegal Jewish immigrants, their fathers joined al-Husseini's Fascist "goon squads." (As the Führer had his "Brown Shirts" and Il Duce his "Black Shirts," the Mufti's "Green Shirts" formed in February 1936.[63])

On the night of April 15, 1936, ten cars were ambushed by Arabs on the Tulkarm-Nablus road between Tel Aviv and Haifa. Two Jews were executed in cold blood. The Arab Uprising of 1936-39 was under way. The next evening two Arabs were slain in retaliation near Petach Tikvah. During one of the funerals in Tel Aviv, a protest led to several assaults on Arab residents. On April 19, Muslims rampaged through Jaffa, destroying property, uprooting crops, and killing three locals.

The High Commissioner responded by condemning the violence, launching an investigation, and imposing a curfew on all major cities. The Grand Mufti responded by condemning the High Commissioner, launching a Muslim conclave, and imposing a national strike and suspension of taxes. The civil disorder decree was issued by the Arab Higher Committee, formed on April 25 as the latest political organ of the Palestinian Arab bloc. As with the Commissioner's predictable "response" (reminiscent of Captain Renault's memorable line in *Casablanca*, "Round up the usual suspects"), the Committee's triad remonstrance was nothing new—demanding an immediate stoppage of all Jewish immigration, land deals, and non-majority governance.

The government rejected all three demands, allowing the "strike" to intensify as planned. Local protests left Jews assaulted and stoned. Even the police were pelted. Dr. Walter Doehle, the German consul general observed, "People speak of a day government and a night government but it is clear that the so-called Arab night government rules most of Palestine by day as well."[64] Arab-on-Arab violence was also common. While Islamic insurgents killed 547 Jews between 1936 and 1939, they also eliminated 494 of their own.[65] The slightest collaboration with the enemy (Jews or British officials) would result in jail time at the local cave or summary execution—ranging from a standard slit throat to the more serious disembowelment.[66] Though arms sales were strictly proscribed, the Arabs were suddenly loaded to the teeth. Eventually, the Brits realized that the new violence was now aimed at them as much as it was against the Jews. "Entire British patrols would often disappear without a trace," wrote German official Franz Schattenfroh.[67] The Commissioner prudently called for backup.

Meanwhile, one Fawzi al-Qawuqji—a Syrian commando who distinguished himself with the Turks in WWI, then as a decorated French intel officer—came out of nowhere to personally lead the guerilla phase of the "strike." The self-appointed generalissimo began training bands of fellahin in the finer points of sabotage and trench warfare with telling results: buildings bombed; roads mined; pipelines punctured; railways damaged; farms and livestock ruined; and—*most* importantly—British soldiers and Jewish settlers killed and wounded. Adding to the chaos, inspired by the Aleppo-born "Arab Garibaldi," thousands of other "freedom fighters" slipped in from Syria and Iraq.[68]

The pressure ratcheted up in June with a letter of protest signed by 1,200 prominent Arabs, including judges and political leaders. When the ploy failed, the Supreme Muslim Council fired off its *own* missive, haranguing HMG in the most abusive manner, invoking the veritable "revenge of God Almighty."[69] For once, local British authorities were *glad* to have the Yishuv on their side. Jews were even empowered as supernumerary police. They were especially lauded for the equitable manner in which they handled the fluid situation. The Esco Foundation delineates their complimentary stratagems as *haganah* (self-defense) and *havlagah* (self-restraint). The first principle meant the Jews "would defend themselves and their settlements against attacks, using arms to do so when necessary"; the second, that "they would not engage in indiscriminate reprisals against the Arabs, and they would not allow themselves to be provoked to counterattacks."[70]

By September, the local Arab economy was tanking. Some 20,000 angry Tommys didn't help any, now more scary to the strikers than the Green Shirts were to the Jews. A face-saving idea was needed, *fast* (i.e., before the orange season passed). Enter stately "peace appeals" from Ibn Saud along with Emirs Abdullah of Transjordan and Ghazi of Iraq. And so, "constrained" by such "impassioned" pleas to "rely on the good intentions of our friend, Great Britain," the Arab Higher Committee issued a petition on October 11, stating their "reluctant" decision "to respond to the appeal of Their Majesties and Highnesses the Arab Kings and Amirs, and to call upon the noble Arab nation in Palestine to resort to quietness and to end the strike and disorders."[71]

Work resumed the next day. Fawzi and his insurgents were allowed to "escape" over Jordan. Apart from a few killings, things seemed to be getting back to normal. The final tally for the latest round of Arab-induced mayhem was 415 Jewish deaths, with over 5,000 Arabs killed and 15,000 wounded.[72] All that remained was the arrival of *another* feckless Royal Commission, to conduct *another* formal study, to issue *another* official report, to produce *another* whitewash. The Arabs did get one consolation; the Labor Schedule approved just 1,850 Jews for the first half of 1937 (about 40% of the prior number confirmed).[73]

PEEL COMMISSION REPORT

The Palestine Royal Commission, headed by Lord Robert Peel, arrived in Eretz Yisrael on November 11, 1936. An array of testimony was submitted in both public and private sessions. After hearing all the standard arguments for and against immigration, the commissioners concluded their two-month inquiry, returning to London in January.

The Peel Commission Report came out in July 1937. Surprisingly, it was anything *but* just "*another* official report." With the Arabs as the clear aggressor—having slain His Majesty's troops, no less—the paper was particularly startling in its lopsided conclusions *against* the Zionists. Once again, Jews would be locked out by Laodicean locksmiths: "From these premises, one might have believed that the Report would recommend that the gates of Palestine be opened wide to Jewish immigration. But the Commission propounded a 'revolutionary' recommendation, as it had been called…the paradoxical conclusion that a very drastic limitation of immigration was required."[74] After crediting the Jews for economic and agricultural advances, being ultimately beneficial to *all* of Palestine, the Report explained why such progress should be ended. The insane bottom line was that the Arabs did not want a better land—*if* it meant *more* Jews.

> There has been a sense of economic rivalry between the races; the Arabs have been alarmed at the business capacity the Jews have shown and the financial resources they can command. But so far…they have not suffered. On the balance the National Home has meant a substantial material gain to them. Not unnaturally they deny it. But, even if they would be persuaded to admit it, we are convinced it would not appreciably weaken their antagonism. Their feeling has been put in some figurative language such as, "You say we are better off: you say my house has been enriched by the strangers who have entered it. But it is *my* house, I did not invite

the strangers in, or ask them to enrich it, and I do not care how poor or bare it is if only I am master in it."[75]

The Jews were now apparently in trouble for doing what they always said they could do—transform wasteland into enhanced living space to facilitate increased immigration. The obvious rub was that *Jewish* land, cultivated by *Jewish* methods, rendered more "absorptive capacity" than *Arab* soil cultivated by *Arab* methods. After crunching the numbers, the Commission gave an ominous forecast: at 60,000 migrants per year, Jewry's population would match the Arab figure by 1947, some 605,000 each; at 30,000 Jews per year, the Arab breathing room would extend to 1960, with a combined total of 1,560,000.

Using such demographics, Peel issued the "logical" posit that the quota for the next five years be capped at 12,000 Jews annually (while maintaining the option of further reductions if needed).[76] Based on projected Arab population growth the ceiling would ensure that Jews remain a *permanent* minority. The official explanation rambled on: "[W]e may say that the principle of economic absorptive capacity, meaning…considerations of economic capacity and these alone should determine immigration, is at the present time inadequate and ignores factors in the situation which wise statesmanship cannot disregard. Political and psychological factors should be taken into account."[77]

Of course, the "only" flaw in Peel's proposal was that it constituted a *total* repudiation of the Jewish National Home inherent in the Palestine Mandate. Thus, the Peel Report ultimately proposed that HMG abrogate the Mandate and submit the land to yet *another* partition. The latest configuration (subject to further tweaking) would limit Eretz Yisrael to the coastal strip from Mount Carmel to south of Be'er Tuvia, Galilee, and the Jezreel Valley, while the new Arab state would encompass the historic central range of Judea and Samaria, along with the Negev. The once prestigious sphere of British influence would shrink to an inspection zone extending from Jaffa to Jerusalem.

To make a long story short (the *Palestine Royal Commission Report* comprising 404 pages), the prophetic conclusion on page 394 begins, "'Half a loaf is better than no bread' is a peculiarly English proverb; and, considering the attitude which both the Arab and the Jewish representatives adopted in giving evidence before us, we think it improbable that either party will be satisfied at first sight with the proposals we have submitted for the adjustment of their rival claims."[78]

Obviously, that axiom could not even apply to the *first* downsizing, the Transjordan truncation having left only a *quarter* of a loaf. Now the quarter would be reduced *again*—by two-thirds. *Really?*

Despite his chagrin, Chaim understood that the Jews were *stuck* (like they remain today); they could either be a minority in *all* of Palestine or a compact Jewish majority in a *part* of the same.[79] However, as the Zionists were about to accept this lesser of two evils, the offer was abruptly tabled by the return of Arab violence. This time, Allah's "holy war" began with the murders in Nazareth on September 26, 1937, of Lewis Andrews, Acting Galilee District Commissioner, and his police escort as the two Christians walked to church on Sunday morning. The government response was finally decisive—martial law was declared, the Arab Higher Committee outlawed, and over 100 Arabs hanged. The Mufti fled to Lebanon disguised as a Bedouin.

VOLKSGEMEINSCHAFT, ENTJUDUNG, JUDENPOLITIK

The tenor of the immigration debate was heightened by events in Nazi Germany. Dr. Peter Longerich, Professor of Modern German History at London's Royal Holloway University and founder of the College's Holocaust Research Center is Germany's preeminent Holocaust authority. A 2010 updated, English edition of his 1998 magnum opus, *Politik der Vernichtung (Politics of Destruction)*, was released under the title of *Holocaust: The Nazi Persecution and Murder of the Jews*.

Oxford University Press states, "Longerich argues that anti-Semitism was not a mere by-product of Nazi political mobilization or an attempt to deflect the attention of the masses. Rather, from 1933 onwards, anti-Jewish policy was a central tenet of the Nazi movement's attempts to implement, disseminate, and secure National Socialist rule."[80] In his opening section ("Racial Persecution, 1933-1939") Longerich employs three German concepts to encapsulate the six-year prewar period of Adolf Hitler's *twelve*-year "Reich."

The first of these conveyed the ultimate goal of Hitler's utopian kingdom-builders. "The basic aim of the Nazi movement was a racially homogeneous national community, *Volksgemeinschaft*, in which the potential for creative energy inherent in the German people could at last come to fruition and where the German people could achieve full self-realization."[81] Thus, the *Volkswagen*, or "people's car," became Hitler's version of his mentor's "Model T."

The *means* to this end comprised the second term—removing all things "non-Aryan." However, the best Nordic minds despaired of devising a credible eugenics-based litmus test (i.e., exactly *what* blood components represented "true Aryanism"). Thus, the Reich opted for a less scientific method—ridding that disparate element despised by *all* "loyal" Germans. Since "everyone" knew that the Jews were behind WWI and the reparations, and even now were on the cusp of launching another war, etc., the time had come for the Fatherland to recapture its intrinsic cultural identity via a panacean remedy: *Volksgemeinschaft* would be attained by pursuing *Entjudung*—"the removal of the Jews."

Encompassing the landmark decision itself, the third word involved the requisite *political* means. *Judenpolitik* ("Jewish policy") became a Nazi euphemism for the party's long-term plans regarding the "Jewish Question." Judenpolitik faced two initial tasks. First, it was incumbent to formulate a working model that defined the targeted foe. Because classification by *race* was deemed too elusive, Hitler chose *religion*. A decision was made in April 1933 that the legal term "non-Aryan descent" would apply to any person who had *a* Jewish parent *or* grandparent; the parent or grandparent was presumed to be Jewish if he or she belonged to the Jewish faith.[82] (This early codification would be meticulously enlarged by 1935.) The second aim was to pressure Jewry into *voluntary* emigration—vis-à-vis anti-Semitic legislation effectively disenfranchising them from German society. Contrary to popular belief, Hitler was *not* dying to *kill* the Jews in *his* country (not *yet* anyway); he *was* dying to place them in everyone *else's* country, especially as the "exit fee" (Reich Flight Tax, a.k.a. "Atonement Contribution") usually equated to whatever assets remained after *Aryanization* (expropriation). Longerich writes, "[E]migration, itself the very goal of NS [National Socialist] anti-Jewish policies, was now being used as a pretext to secure assets for the state."[83]

Thus, during the prewar years, German Jewry experienced three phases of intense racial bias: 1) The March 1933 upheaval and April 1 boycott, precipitating the nation's first Judeophobic statutes; 2) The revived spring and summer violence of 1935 spawning the Nuremberg Laws; 3) The brutal excesses in the summer and fall of 1938, culminating in the watershed pogrom of November 9, known as *Kristallnacht* ("Night of broken glass"). With the fledgling National Socialist German

Workers' Party (NSDAP, i.e., Nazi Party) flying by the seat of its pants (promising much, but delivering little), a growing anti-Jew agenda would also serve as a convenient smokescreen.[84]

After just a month on the job, the new Führer got the ball rolling on March 7, instituting regional boycotts against Jewish merchants. (Convinced that World Jewry was behind the growing international criticism of his rogue regime, Hitler planned to use the bans to stifle this resistance.) Launched in the Rhine-Ruhr district, the terror quickly spread to Central Germany, covering Frankfurt, Mecklenburg, and Berlin, The drive ended with a mass coordinated boycott on April 1 (*Nazi* boycotts, employing special "greeters" at the doors). Aryan businessmen were also being pressed to terminate their dealings with Jewish traders. Loans were denied to "Jew-sh-t" firms, along with advertising, government contracts, and other routine accommodations.

In the ensuing wave of racist fiats, civil servants and legal professionals (including judges) of "non-Aryan" descent were flushed from the system. Similar measures were soon applied to all the non-manuals (accountants, academics, physicians, pharmacists, dentists). By late April, a "campaign against un-German thinking" was fueling book burnings in the Reich's leading universities. Jewish children in state-funded schools were threatened and bullied (by students and teachers alike). As Jewish culture was also deemed *verboten*, Party goons disrupted concert and theatrical performances by Jewish artists. Jews were excluded from sporting clubs and associations. On Shabbat, they were dragged out of their Synagogues and beaten at will. The dead were not even exempt as Jewish cemeteries were desecrated.[85]

The next period of abuse occurred in mid-1935. Judenpolitik now entailed banning "racial miscegenation" between Jews and Aryans; reducing non-Aryans to provisional, second-class citizenship; and further destabilizing the Jewish economy. These steps were later incorporated under the infamous Nuremberg Laws enacted on September 15, 1935. The signature statute was the Law for the Protection of German Blood and Honor to "regulate the problems of marriage between 'Aryans' and 'non-Aryans.'" A "new and improved" designation for "Jewishness" was hastily supplied by Interior Ministry wizards Bernhard Lösener and Franz Medicus. According to the First Ordinance of the Reich Citizenship Law of November 14, 1935 (as delineated by Dr. Raul Hilberg), "non-

Aryans" would now be segregated by the following two-fold, mind-boggling criteria:

> Everyone was defined as a Jew who (1) descended from at least three Jewish grandparents (full Jews and three-quarter Jews) or (2) descended from two Jewish grandparents (half-Jews) and *(a)* belonged to the Jewish religious community on September 15, 1935, or joined the community on a subsequent date, *or (b)* was married to a Jewish person on September 15, 1935, or married one on a subsequent date, *or (c)* was the offspring of a marriage contracted with a three-quarter or full Jew after the Law...had come into force (September 15, 1935), *or (d)* was the offspring of an extramarital relationship with a three-quarter or full Jew and was born out of wedlock after July 31, 1936...the presumption remained that the grandparent was Jewish if he or she belonged to the Jewish religious community.
>
> Defined *not* as a Jew but as an individual of "mixed Jewish blood" was (1) any person who descended from two Jewish grandparents (half-Jewish), but who *(a)* did not adhere (or adhered no longer) to the Jewish religion on September 15, 1935, and who did not join it at any subsequent time, *and (b)* was not married (or was married no longer) to a Jewish person on September 15, 1935, and who did not marry such a person at any subsequent time (such half-Jews were called *Mischlinge* of the first degree), and (2) any person descended from one Jewish grandparent (Mischling of the second degree).[86]

The Nuremberg Laws (and similar edicts) had essentially rendered the Jews stateless refugees within their own country. Israeli historian Avraham Barkai estimates that by early 1938, 60-70% of Jewish firms existing in 1933 were no longer run by their original owners.[87] The list of demoralizing ordinances seemed endless: *barred* from dating and/or intermarriage with Aryans; *barred* from employment in commerce, law, government, agriculture, journalism, education, medicine, and the arts; *barred* from schools and universities; *barred* from union halls, libraries, concerts, theaters, cinemas, museums, circuses, restaurants, gardens, parks, beaches, swimming pools, municipal baths, barber shops, boulevards, street cars and trains; *barred* from visiting dozens of towns and villages; *barred* from owning real estate; *barred* from peak hour shopping; *barred* from using public telephones; *barred* from obtaining driver's licenses; *barred* from the military; *barred* from raising the swastika; *barred* from owning firearms; and finally, *barred* from choosing non-

Jewish names for their own newborns. (Hitler was especially absorbed with choosing names for Jewish children.[88])

In time, the majority of Germany's goy population acquiesced to their Führer's "wisdom": Aryan children shied away from Jewish playmates; integrated youth groups disbanded; neighbors no longer visited or even spoke; public greetings ceased; friendships and love affairs ended. All was gloom and doom. And yet—for all their bigoted hubris—the Jews' oppressors could not conceal their *own* inferiority complex. For example, while Jews, long viewed as cultural barbarians, were being kept from museums and art galleries, some of Europe's finest paintings were passing from Jewish ownership to the private stores of Hitler and Göring.[89] (See 2015 film, *Woman in Gold*) When the Justice Ministry proposed removing Jewish names of expropriated firms so the new owners could sell their goods without these "reminders of the supremacy of Jewish business sense in the German market,"[90] the pragmatic "Thanks, but no thanks" reply by the would-be beneficiaries was that many established names [like Rosenthal] had become the "epitome of quality."[91]

ÉVIAN CONFERENCE

The only "problem" with Hitler's plan for Jewish *emigration* was an embarrassing shortage of *immigration* certificates outside of the Reich. Although the victims were always *free* to go, they had to have a place *to* go. By 1938, the entire "Community of Nations" had absorbed only 150,000 German Jews, a mere quarter of the country's total Jewish population. Added to the 185,000 Austrian Jews from the *Anschluss*, 635,000 Jews in the Greater Reich *still* had nowhere to run. Thus, the futility of Peel's 12,000 annual permits is apparent. David Wyman, Chair of the David S. Wyman Institute for Holocaust Studies relates: "Until the Nazis blocked the exits in the fall of 1941, the oppressed Jews of Europe might have fled to safety. But relatively few got out, mainly because the rest of the world would not take them in."[92]

Now this is *not* to imply that the world's civilized nations made *no* "attempt" to assuage the plight. With the international press reporting over two hundred suicides a day in Vienna, Roosevelt grew pressured to act. Thus, on March 22, 1938, he invited delegates from thirty-three countries to conduct a humanitarian conference for the emergency rescue of political refugees from Germany and Austria. The designated governments included twenty Latin American republics, plus Britain, France, Belgium, The Netherlands, Italy, Switzerland, Denmark, Norway, Sweden, Canada, Australia, New Zealand, and South Africa.

The "refugee conference" was set for July 6-15 at the luxurious *Évian-les-Bains* resort on the French shore of Lake Geneva. (Nearly forty private and volunteer groups would also be represented.) And to put everyone at ease, the White House invitation specified that *no* country "would be expected or asked to receive a greater number of emigrants than is permitted by its existing legislation."[93] FDR was also quick to assure his *own* constituents, telling reporters that *no* increase in US quotas would occur. The main goal was to send a strong signal that freedom-loving nations would never condone oppression, etc.

Hitler was incensed with the blatant hypocrisy. During a particular tirade at Königsberg on March 25, he scored a public relations coup, reminding all that *Germany* was ready to do *its* part in the crisis. "I can only hope and expect that the other world, which has such deep sympathy for these criminals, will at least be generous enough to convert this sympathy into practical aid. We, on our part, are ready to put all these criminals at the disposal of these countries, for all I care, even on luxury ships."[94] Around that time, 3,000 Jews a day waited in vain for visas at the US consulate in Vienna, while 10,000 applications lay unanswered at the Australian embasy.[95] Chiune Sugihara (Japan's Vice-Consul in Lithuania) was the rare exception, ultimately saving 6,000 Jews by handwriting illegal travel visas 18 hours a day—tossing the last ones from his departing train the afternoon his office closed.

The Führer had thrown down the gauntlet, knowing full well that Évian would be nothing more than window dressing. Roosevelt was so opposed to his own idea that he declined to send a member of the government to represent him. Instead, the US delegation was led by Myron C. Taylor, one of the president's Wall Street friends. Two days before the event began, *New York Times* columnist Anne McCormick wrote, "It is heartbreaking to think of the queues of desperate human beings around our consulates in Vienna and other cities waiting in suspense for what happens at Évian...Can America live with itself if it lets Germany get away with this policy of extermination?"[96] Though barred from the proceedings, over 200 reporters would publicize the apathetic spirit that unfolded at the balmy "Pearl of Lake Geneva."

With Italy and South Africa refusing to attend (more beach chairs to go around), the envoys divided their time between sunbathing, socializing, and speechmaking. As to the actual "business" at hand, the meeting was summed up in a succinct statement by historian Arthur Morse, "[O]ne after another the nations made clear their unwillingness to accept refugees."[97] Comprising both the fifth largest landmass *and* lowest population density in the world, Australia brazenly announced, "As we have no real racial problem, we are not desirous of importing one."[98] Then, adding insult to injury, Dr. Weizmann (of *all* people) was denied a speaking slot (the result of collusion between Taylor and Britain's chief emissary, Michael Palairet). Golda Meir recalled her chafe at being in "the ludicrous capacity of the 'Jewish observer from Palestine,' not even seated with the delegates but with the audience, although the refugees under discussion were my own people."[99]

The trajectory of collective apathy begun at Évian was captured in the convicting title of a research work by Canadian historians Irving Abella and Harold Troper—*None is Too Many: Canada and the Jews of Europe, 1933-1948*. (In 2015, the liberal government of Justin Trudeau, a.k.a. "the best white-guy Bhangra dancer on earth," declared that it would accept 35,000 *Syrian* refugees, listing "members of the LGBT community" among its prioritized groups.) Kenya's governor committed to twenty-five families per year, *but* only of "the right type, i.e., nordic from Germany or Austria."[100] The Dominican Republic constituted the stellar exception, offering to take 100,000 refugees for settlement in agriculture. (Though the tiny third-world nation was unable to meet its well-meant, albeit unrealistic goal, falling "short" by 99,528, it is notable, based on Genesis 12:3, that in 2012, Santo Domingo had the ninth-largest economy in Latin America, the second-largest in the Caribbean, *and* the region's largest tourist revenues.)

By contrast, the *sole* concession made by the mighty USA—custodian of the iconic Statue of Liberty and host of the touted conference itself—was a pledge to honor (for the first time) its full legal annual quota of 27,370 visas for Germany and Austria. It was easy for FDR to extol this "magnanimous" gesture, as the actual number of *processed* certificates was generally "held to about 10% of the already small quota limits."[101] In a related travesty, the unused quotas from one country (the annual total for all being 154,000) could not be used by refugees from other nations. (When two petitions with 365,325 signatures arrived at the White House asking that unused quotas be filled by Jews, they were promptly placed in "File 13."[102])

In a final, face-saving move led by Taylor (against British dissent), the Intergovernmental Committee on Refuges (ICR) was founded with permanent headquarters in London. The reader can guess the ultimate value of this worthless agency. (Hint: The press was quick to note that Évian spelled backwards is "naive.") The *Daily Herald* mocked the event, stating, "If this is coming to the help of the refugees, then what would the nations do if they meant to desert them?"[103] Two weeks after the meeting ended, Henry Ford received his special birthday gift from the Führer. The sad reality was that every Jew in Germany and Austria *could* have escaped the threat of Hitler's ovens if the nations at Évian had committed to just 20,000 refugees each. Meinertzhagen could only sigh, writing on July 24, 1938, "We have frittered away one of the greatest opportunities we have ever had," concluding, "The action of H.M.G. in Palestine is very near to that Hitler in Germany."[104] (Ironically, the site of the polluted affair has come to be identified with a chic product label promoting "natural spring water.")

"The Hebrew Hammer"

The Roosevelt administration was able to ride out the crisis due to an epic rise of anti-Semitism on the home front. Wyman states, "During the decade before Pearl Harbor, more than a hundred anti-Semitic organizations had pumped hate propaganda throughout American society."[105] A major bigot of this era was Charles E. Coughlin, an outspoken Catholic priest. Coughlin held a weekly radio broadcast in Royal Oak, Michigan, just up the road from Henry Ford. His racist rants drew about 30,000,000 listeners and 8,000 letters per week.

On a lighter note, while Ford and the "Reverend" were filling the Motor City with *their* agenda, a Detroit Tigers first baseman (who also *happened* to be named Henry) was getting some notoriety of his own. Henry (Hank) Benjamin Greenberg, born *Hyman* Greenberg (a.k.a. "Hammerin Hank," "The Hebrew Hammer," even "Hankus Pankus"), became the sport's first Jewish superstar. With Hank batting .339 in 1934 (his second season), Detroit climbed from fifth place to a shot at the pennant. Suddenly, however, as the race was closing dramatically, a religious controversy burst on the scene. Raised in New York City by

Romanian immigrant parents in an Orthodox home, the 6' 4", 215 lb. "nice Jewish boy" faced a crisis of conscience when two games fell on Rosh Hashanah *and* Yom Kippur. The rabbis sensed a dilemma. Though Hank was gaining points for Jews with the goyim, should he play on High Holy Days? The fans argued: "Rosh Hashanah comes every year, but Detroit hasn't won a pennant since 1909!"

After much soul-searching, Hank employed his own solution: on Rosh Hashanah, he went to the *stadium* to *play*—hitting two homeruns as Detroit *beat* Boston, 2-1; on Yom Kippur, he went to the *synagogue* to *pray*—meditating as Detroit *lost* to New York, 5-2. After the win, the *Detroit Free Press* ran "Happy New Year" in Hebrew on the morning front-page; after the loss, poet Edgar Guest wrote, "We shall miss him on the infield and shall miss him at the bat. But he's true to his religion—and I honor him for that." Though Hank's name received a "good cussin'" by a less gracious majority at Navin Field, his brethren at Congregation Shaarey Zedek gave their Jewish giant a standing ovation. (Detroit won the pennant but lost the World Series to St. Louis in seven.) Conversely, to Adolf Hitler's delight, the 1936 US Olympic team would shame the nation's integrity by participating at Munich *despite* the fact that Germany's 30,000 Jewish athletes were disqualified for lacking "*weltanschaulich* [ideological] fitness."[106]

Hank led the Tigers to their first World Series title in 1935, becoming the first Jew to be voted Most Valuable Player in either league. Pankus would attain many accolades throughout his celebrated career. In 1940, he earned MVP again. He joined the likes of Lou Gehrig and Joe DiMaggio as a member of the American League All-Star team in 1937—repeating this feat in 1938, 1939, 1940, and 1945. In 1954, he became the first Jewish player elected to the National Baseball Hall of Fame in Cooperstown, New York. The legendary Ted Williams, known as "The Greatest Hitter Who Ever Lived," considered Hank his personal idol.[107] In 1998, a ninety-minute documentary was released entitled "The Life and Times of Hank Greenberg." He was even featured on a US postage stamp in 2006.

However, some maintain that the Jewish slugger was also subjected to a "Hall of *Shame*." On September 19, 1937, "Hammerin Hank" hammered the first homer into the center bleachers at Yankee Stadium. With any number of European relatives in harm's way, he had more than one motive for hitting home runs, stating, "[I]f I, as a Jew, hit a home run, I was hitting one against Hitler."[108] In 1938, Hank was on the cusp of passing Babe Ruth's all-time season homerun record of 60. When the nail-biting race ended, many of his family and fans cried "foul." Citing recent analysis at *Retrosheet.org*, Howard Megdal wrote in his 2010 *New York Times* article, *Religion Aided a Home Run Chase and May Have Led to its Failure*:

> Evidence has finally been published that seems to resolve a 72-year-old mystery. When Hank Greenberg of the Detroit Tigers made a run at Babe Ruth's season home run record, falling two short with 58 in 1938, was he pitched around because he was Jewish? It is impossible to know what was in pitchers' hearts, but it is also impossible to ignore the statistical record. In short, the American League didn't seem exactly thrilled with Greenberg's pursuit...Greenberg received many more walks as he chased Ruth in 1938 than he did in the rest of his career...the way pitchers handled Greenberg early in the season was clearly different than the way they approached him as Ruth's record came into view. Greenberg had four three-walk games in the final two months of the 1938 season, three in September.[109]

Though Hank would endure years of racial epithets from fans and players alike ("Hey, *Mo*!" for Moses; or, "Throw him a pork chop—he can't hit that," etc.), occasionally confronting his abusers as well (once rumored to have called out the entire Yankee bench), he personally dismissed the intentional walk theory, a credit to his overall humility.

During World War II, he interrupted his career to serve his country with the Army Air Force in the China-Burma-India theater. Following his honorable discharge in 1945, *Captain* Greenberg rejoined the Tigers. After twelve seasons with Detroit, Hank's contract was sold to the Pirates in 1947, his last year in the sport. (To put it in his native Bronx vernacular—"Greenboig" retired in "Pittsboig.")

Henry Greenberg's daydreams of "hitting homers against Hitler" became Henry Ford's worst nightmare—the automaker's nemesis morphing into a Jewish version of Jessie Owens. And yet, Hank's "uncanny" drive would generate a most ironic historical feat. The "Hebrew Hammer" hit his first career homerun in his opening start on May 6, 1933—*62 days after Hitler came to power.* Then, in his first game after four years of war, Hank slammed one out of Briggs Field on July 1, 1945—*62 days after Hitler shot himself.* His jersey number was formally retired by the Tigers organization in 1983. Ironically, given the macabre statistic of 6,000,000 murders that paralleled his career, Hank's number was *5*—the scriptural numeric for *death*.

THE "LONG ISLAND EXPRESS"

The largest prewar anti-Semite movement in the US was the American National Alliance, a.k.a. the German-American *Bund* ("bond"). With 250,000 members spread over 65 chapters, inclusive of nearly every major city, the group's main focus was the heavily German section of Manhattan known as Yorkville (ironically named after Sergeant York).

The dual agenda of this racist society was to intimidate Jewish Americans while projecting a favorable view of Nazi Germany. The first goal was attained by identifying with "all things Adolf Hitler"—Nazi uniforms, swastikas, jackboots, etc.; the second goal was pursued by identifying with "all things George Washington"—protecting America from Marxist infiltration, i.e., "Jews," vis-à-vis the Russian Revolution, manipulation of world markets, the Great Depression, labor unions, etc. (A huge picture of the first president was displayed before 20,000 American Nazis at the controversial Madison Square Garden rally on Washington's birthday, February 20, 1939.)

The Bund was led by Fritz Kuhn, a German-born American who served with the Bavarian infantry in WWI. Built on American ideals (pragmatism, hustle, "bigger is better"), his creation was essentially Americanized Fascism. Of particular concern to Germany was Kuhn's propensity for drawing unwanted attention. The Bund actually tried to exclude Jewish citizens from serving in the government, a portion of their loony request reading: "A petition for an amendment to the Constitution of the United States, to elect and appoint none but Aryans to Public Office and Supreme, Federal, State, and Municipal Courts. The United States of America is a White Gentile Nation. The founders of the republic who gave us our nation, were Aryan men."[110] The sect was *so* radical that Hitler himself refused to endorse their activities.

To maintain its Prussian image, Khun operated 28 military camps from Long Island to Los Angeles. The largest (and weirdest) of these facilities was Camp Siegfried, a 45-acre compound located on Long Island, N.Y., at Yaphank. In his best-selling work, *As America Has*

Done To Israel, John McTernan states, "The largest Nazi rallies outside of Germany took place at Camp Siegfried…ground zero for the Nazis in the US. Of all the fascists groups in America, the Bund was the worst, and Camp Siegfried was the heart of the Bund."[111] Not content with barracks and parade grounds, the Bund Führer pushed the envelope in 1937 by forming, with the approval of the politically-correct, "brain-dead" township, an adjacent little Nazi village called "German Gardens." This latest "in your face" project had a street grid with actual names such as Hindenburg, German, Göring, and Goebbels Streets, *and*—most astounding of all—Adolf Hitler Street![112]

The first mass rally at Siegfried was held on September 25, 1935, with 5,000 US Nazis on hand. The finale was a hideous torchlight parade after sundown. On September 1, 1936, over 12,000 Bundists descended on their Long Island ethnoscape. By August 1937, the number had doubled to 30,000. In the wake of Évian, Nazi-American hauteur was off the chart. One month after FDR's "do-nothing conference," Fritz held his "no-nonsense conference," featuring *plenty* of open commitment. When the satanic assembly convened on Sunday morning, August 14, 1938, over 40,000 right hands snapped out in a collective *Sieg Heil* ("Hail Victory") salute! ("All those in favor of gun control, raise your right hands.") The largest Nazi rally outside of Germany was being held on US soil. To the shock of everyday New Yorkers (an oxymoron in itself), whole trains were being rented by the Bundists to shuttle their Brooklyn and Manhattan delegates. The sixty-mile run to Yaphank was dubbed the "Camp Siegfried Special."[113]

Three weeks later, Israel's God opted to send Kuhn, Ford, Dawes, Coughlin, Rockefeller, Taylor, Roosevelt, the Babe, the Dulles boys, and the entire country on a rail ride of their own—one they would *never* forget. Psalm 83:4, 15 says, *"They have said, Come, and let us cut them off from being a nation; that the name of Israel may be no more in remembrance…So persecute them with thy tempest,* AND MAKE THEM AFRAID WITH THY STORM.*"*

On September 4, 1938, a meandering weather depression off the African coast moved to the Cape Verde Islands, then turned due west. By September 18, "the storm" (hurricanes not receiving personal names until 1950) was a Category 5 hurricane churning toward America. Two days later, it veered away from Florida and headed north as a Cat 3—its intense 50 mile-wide, sky blue "*eye*" fixed eerily on Long Island. By early morning on September 21, it was moving with intense acceleration. At 3:00 p.m., "The Great New England Hurricane of 1938" *roared* ashore with a 30-foot surge at the inconceivable speed of 70 miles per hour! The force of impact registered on seismographs as far away as Alaska. Given that most hurricanes normally travel less than 20 mph, the New York phenomenon was aptly nicknamed "The Long Island Express."[114]

The epicenter for the impending catastrophe was the sleepy seaside village of Bellport, where Coast Guard officials logged a barometric pressure of 27.94 inches (946 millibars). With Camp Siegfried a mere six miles inland, the fast-moving storm would represent Jehovah's *own* blitzkrieg for Kuhn's storm troopers. Within minutes, that "*eye*" was over Adolf Hitler Street, peering down on the *remnants* of German Gardens. Those liberal township officials were nowhere in sight; they (and everyone else) were running for their lives. Mayor LaGuardia's wife got stranded on the second floor of their flooded summer cottage in Northport and had to be rescued.[115] More than fifty locals died outright. Winds atop the Empire State Building were clocked at 120 mph (enough to blow King Kong back to Skull Island). Pat McGrady of *The New York Times* wrote, "We saw roofs floating without walls, walls without roofs, whole houses afloat...We saw bodies clad only in shoes and socks. The wind had blown off the rest of the clothing."[116]

Everything else is history. After *pulverizing* the general locale, the "Long Island Express" pulled out to make its other scheduled stops: *Connecticut*, 3:30 p.m.; *Rhode Island*, 3:45 p.m.; *Massachusetts*, 5:00 p.m.; *Vermont*, 6:00 p.m.; *New Hampshire*, 7:00 p.m.; *Maine*, 8:00 p.m.; finally dissipating over *Montreal* near 10:00 p.m. The composite damage was surreal. Having traversed some 300 miles in seven hours, the "no name" hurricane killed over 700 people, while injuring 1,800; damaged or destroyed 24,000 houses and buildings, leaving 63,000 homeless; felled over a billion trees, "flooding" the lumber market; downed 20,000 miles of telephone and power lines, igniting hundreds of deadly fires; ruined 25,000 cars and trucks; sank or wrecked 6,000 fishing boats and recreational watercraft, along with scores of docks, boardwalks, piers, and marinas; washed away hundreds of miles of rail tracks and numerous bridges, derailing several *trains* in the process; and, last but not least, slaughtered some 1,600 livestock and 750,000 chickens. Total damages were nearly $300 million (*billions* in today's dollars). While a ticket on the "Camp Siegfried Special" was $0.25, the "Long Island Express" cost America *roughly* $1,000,000 per mile!

The "Great Hurricane of 1938" (a.k.a. "The Great New England Hurricane"), was the most powerful storm to make landfall along America's northeast coast in over two centuries. It also marked the first time that an entire *region* was decimated by a sole disaster. McTernan adds an ominous postscript: "The coastline was dramatically altered by this collision with the powerful storm surge. Not only was Long Island's coastline altered, but all of southern New England's as well."[117] On September 22, the Heaven-sent aberration shared coast-to-coast front-page headlines with the fast-approaching "storm" in Czechoslovakia. With her tacit Anglo-American desertion, vis-à-vis the September 29 Munich Accord, another 300,000 Jews were put in Hitler's death grip. About the time Nazi troops were occupying the Sudetenland in early October, a homeless man was spotted in Boston Common wearing a sandwich sign reading: "For $0.25 I'll listen to your story of the hurricane."[118] Everyone seemed to have one to tell.

WHITE PAPER 1939

On November 9, 1938, Britain announced plans to host yet another stupid meeting of Arab and Jewish leaders (Saint James Conference). The next day, emboldened by Neville Chamberlain's appeasement and FDR's empty words regarding the Czechoslovakian front, Reich Propaganda Minister Dr. Joseph Goebbels unleashed his *Kristallnacht* ("Night of Broken Glass") upon Germany's unsuspecting Jews. (On a technical note, though Göring and Himmler were also blindsided by Joe's "unauthorized" act, Hitler had privately ordered the attack.)[119]

In the ensuing national pogrom, at least 20,000 Jews were arrested and sent to concentration camps where many died; 195 synagogues were burned; over 800 shops were destroyed, with 7,500 looted. The insurance claims for the glass alone totaled six million Reichsmark. The "official" death toll of 36 was off by 55.[120] The victims were then assessed a fine of one billon Reichsmark for having "instigated" the disturbance. (The affair "supposedly" stemmed from the November 7 assassination of Ernst vom Rath, a minor official at the German embassy in Paris, by a seventeen-year-old Jewish immigrant, Herschel Grynszpan.)

Back in the good ol' USA, Father Coughlin justified the atrocity as a "defense mechanism" against Jewish inspired Marxism.[121]

Meanwhile, Hitler's patience with "the other world" was wearing thin. In October 1938, 15,000 Polish Jews were simply rounded up and dumped at the Polish border. The door was closing fast. London knew well what European Jewry would encounter if denied an eleventh-hour escape. Morse relates, "A message to the British Foreign Office in 1938 confirmed the daily deaths at Buchenwald, adding that relatives of the victims were required to pay 3 marks ($1.20) for their ashes."[122]

On April 20, 1939, six months after his "Peace in our time" speech, Neville cleared the air before the Palestine committee of the Cabinet: "If we must offend one side, let us offend the Jews rather than the Arabs."[123] In a letter to his sister on July 30, 1939, he confided, "[N]o doubt Jews aren't a loveable people; I don't care for them myself."[124] As late as 1951, seven years *after* Auschwitz was liberated, Foreign Secretary Anthony Eden wrote his private assistant, "If we must have preferences, let me murmur in your ear that I prefer Arabs to Jews;" the man then noted in *his* diary, "Unfortunately, A. E. is immovable on the subject of Palestine. He loves Arabs and hates Jews."[125]

In a secret cabinet memo dated January 18, 1939, Colonial Secretary Malcolm MacDonald explained why Britain was *morally* obligated to rescind the "repressive" Declaration. "Arab detestation of the Jewish invasion into Palestine being what it is, it would be wholly wrong to suggest that this large Arab population should one day in their own native land and against their will come under the rule of the newly arrived Jews."[126] Thus, as showcased at Évian, history confirms that the door to Jewish immigration was slammed shut by HMG *before* the doors to Hitler's "showers" were ever sealed.

Having overseen several weeks of "full, free and frank discussions" among both Arab and Jewish delegations, the Secretary rendered his verdict on May 17. While Peel's plan was deemed impractical, the 1939 MacDonald White Paper endorsed the creation (within ten years) of a new independent State, neither Jew nor Arab, but "Palestinian." Further land sales to Jews were strictly verboten. Finally, and most tragically, the attendant immigration statute would seal the fate of untold thousands of Jewish refugees—unless, of course, the Arabs were willing to "intervene" on their behalf. The relevant portion reads:

> Jewish immigration during the next five years will be at a rate which, if economic absorptive capacity permits, will bring the Jewish population up to approximately one third of the total population of the country...For each of the next five years a quota of 10,000 Jewish immigrants will be allowed...as a contribution towards the solution of the Jewish refugee problem, 25,000 refugees will be admitted as soon as the High Commissioner is satisfied that adequate provision for maintenance is ensured...After the period of five years, no further Jewish immigration will be permitted unless the Arabs of Palestine are prepared to acquiesce in it.[127]

So there you have it! While Jewish ashes were going for "a buck, twenty" in Buchenwald—less than four months before Hitler's panzers would be squashing Polish cavalry—HMG made a royal pledge to: 1) Approve 10,000 immigrants per year for five years "*if* economic absorptive capacity allowed"; 2) Approve 25,000 more "as soon as the High Commissioner was satisfied"; and, 3) Halt further arrivals "*unless* the Arabs of Palestine were prepared to acquiesce." And some wonder *why* the cradle of the KJV was bombed *57 nights straight*, killing 40,000 and wrecking 1,000,000 homes—as if the words *"And I will...curse him that curseth thee"* no longer applied. (Genesis 12:3)

The logic for so blatant a tergiversation was that the Mandate's framers "could not have intended that Palestine should be converted into a Jewish State against the will of the Arab population of the country."[128] The *real* motive was strategic. As in WWI, Britain felt that pacifying the Arabs was necessary for preserving the Empire, especially at the Canal. In a candid meeting with Jews at the St. James Conference, MacDonald said that, in the event of war, "the security of British forces in the Middle East and lines of communication with India and the Far East" were paramount and that a "continuation of the estrangement in Palestine" would not only menace British interests but could cause "a good deal of unrest among the Moslems of India."[129]

Thus, in twenty-two short years, the landmark Balfour Declaration had devolved to a permanent Arab veto over *any* Jewish immigration beyond 1944. (For the record, by April 1, 1944, the very height of the Holocaust, only about 50,000 Jews had entered the country, leaving 25,000 certificates unfilled.) The Jewish Agency vowed, "It is in the darkest hour of Jewish history that the British Government proposes to deprive the Jews of their last hope and to close the road back to their

Homeland. This blow will not subdue the Jewish people. The historic bond between the people and the land of Israel cannot be broken. The Jews will never accept the closing to them of the gates of Palestine nor let their national home be converted into a ghetto."[130]

Chaim was so hot that he told the British Secretary of State *to his face* that he was *worse* than Hitler! Historian Bernard Wasserstein describes the dressing-down MacDonald received while hosting a "tea party" in his own home: "The conversation reached its crisis when Dr. Weizmann, in analyzing the Government's new policy, said that at least in Hitler one found the virtue of an absolutely frank brutality, whereas Mr. MacDonald was covering up his betrayal of the Jews under a semblance of legality."[131] When Malcolm whimpered that "he knew that the Jews had been calling him a hypocrite and a coward," Chaim shot back—"I have never called you a coward."[132]

Finally, it would behoove the reader to interpret this historic betrayal by the spiritual thesis presented in the Introduction. Because the Church always affects the world (Matthew 5:13), while the Christians in the Laodicean Age have kept Jesus locked out of his own Church, the *secular* locksmiths (i.e., British and American foreign policy makers) have *likewise* kept His brethren after the flesh from entering Eretz Yisrael. (Remember that, by 1922, the Ormsby-Gore letter to Winston Churchill revealed that HMG was already questioning the purpose of the Balfour Declaration.) As the following two chapters will show, the full force of this racist agenda would transfix European Jewry during the Holocaust years.

"THE VOYAGE OF THE DAMNED"

It was fitting that four days before the White Paper appeared, the ill-fated MS *St. Louis* left Hamburg, Germany, for Cuba, carrying 937 Jewish refugees (over 400 women and children among them). The diesel-powered ocean liner represented the exact type of "luxury ship" sardonically cited by Hitler. However, as things turned out, the cruise would morph into "The Voyage of the Damned" (the title of a 1974 book by Gordon Thomas and Max Morgan-Witts, and a film in 1976).

Despite having purchased all necessary certificates, the travelers were subjected to a marathon sequestration in Havana Harbor, only to be denied entrance to the country. They were then barred from Canada and America. As the *St. Louis* drifted off Miami, the Coast Guard shadowed the ship with orders to stop any Jews from swimming to land.[133] The ultimate tragedy was that 734 Jews already possessed US immigration vouchers. The problem was that the preapproved papers would not be good for ninety days, entailing a three-month Cuban layover.

When the American Jewish Joint Distribution Committee asked the State Department that the victims be given their citizenship early, the request was "rebuffed unqualifiedly."[134] The ship returned to Europe, docking at Antwerp on June 17. The traumatized exiles were later absorbed by several Continental nations (a further mockery of the US for having taken *none*). Hitler's spin organ, *Der Weltkampf*, wasted no time exploiting the moment: "We are saying openly that we do not want the Jews while the democracies keep on claiming that they are willing to receive them—and then leave the guests out in the cold! Aren't we savages better men after all?"[135] Scholars believe that 25% of these Jews died in the Holocaust. Redolent of Longfellow's "ships that pass in the night," about the time the *St. Louis* had left Hamburg, the *D. G. Scofield* was exiting Dhahran with that first load of Arab oil. (For the record, a mere twenty years later, the Cuban people would "reap the whirlwind" of Fidel Castro.)

ISRAEL BALINE

A final story from the prewar years is apropos. While those doughboys from the 39th Battalion were teaching their comrades to sing "Over There" in Hebrew, a Jewish soldier was penning a song of his own back in the States. Born Israel Baline in 1888 in Mohilev, Russia, his family immigrated to New York City five years later. Having changed his name, "Irving" was drafted in 1917 and was processed through the same Army base as Alvin York. Ironically, the pair even trained at Camp Upton in *Yaphank*, New York—a dozen years before Camp Siegfried would defile the same locale (Upton closing in 1921).

As dictated by providence, the Jewish prodigy wrote a most inspiring tune in 1918, yet kept it filed away for twenty years. In 1938, the manager of a popular female vocalist asked Irv if he had any patriotic material she could use for her radio program on the twentieth anniversary of Armistice Day. He gave her a slightly revised form of the song he wrote back in Upton—a simple, forty-word prayer for divine protection in uncertain times. While the *performer* would have been oblivious to any scriptural realities (being a traditional Catholic), the *performance* became her signature song, as well as an enduring hymn.

On November 11, 1938, *two days after* Kristallnacht—Jewry being deserted by the "free world," with the US the *most* complicit—a radio audience of millions thrilled as Kate Smith belted out Irving Berlin's classic, "God Bless America." As the song quickly became the country's "second National Anthem," Berlin would credit his immigrant mother for instilling those three sacred words into his heart.

10

The Real "Final Solution"

"These are as yet mere rehearsals. Much worse is to come."
(Theodore Herzl, Vienna, July 15, 1895)

"As a general rule, Jews…magnify their persecution."
(Reginald Leeper, British Foreign Office, April 21, 1940)

"1½ million Jews who were living in Eastern Poland have simply disappeared…nobody knows how and where."
(David Kelly, British Swiss Legation, November 19, 1941)

"We have already opposed the idea of a general appeal to the German Government suggesting that they should unload all Jews under their control on the Allies. German acceptance would raise insuperable difficulties."
(Ian Henderson, British Foreign Office, April 19, 1943)

"It is my duty to describe something beyond the imagination of mankind."
(Bergen-Belsen dispatch, April 15, 1945)

THE TWENTY-FIRST Zionist Congress opened in Geneva on August 16, 1939, under the shadow of the White Paper. The mood of the 539 delegates went from gloom to doom with the signing of the Molotov-Ribbentrop Pact on August 23. Dr. Weizmann addressed the anxious throng in Yiddish the next evening: "It is with a heavy heart that I take my leave…There is a darkness all around us and we cannot see through the clouds…My heart is overflowing." Turning to the Poles, he cried: "God grant that your fate be not that of the Jews in the neighboring countries."[1] As the session ended with the "HaTikvah," Monty Penkower wrote: "All were sadly aware that they were soon to be cut off from each other. With the abyss yawning before them, they might well never meet again."[2] Chaim would later confirm: "Most of our Polish friends we never saw again."[3]

They would not have long to wait. On September 2, the day after Hitler invaded Poland, two Jews were shot dead. The bullets, however, were not from Nazi rifles—the victims died when a British coastal vessel fired on an "illegal" immigration ship, the *Tiger Hill*, as it landed 1,400 Jews from Poland and elsewhere on a Tel Aviv beach! (The majority escaped detention by mixing with the crowd on shore.) With England declaring war on September 3, Wasserstein notes, "These were probably the first hostile shots fired by British forces after the German attack on Poland."[4] The travesty was an omen of the future; a pungent insight to both the current chapter title and subtitle of this book. For, as the reader will learn, a scenario *more* bizarre than the escape being foiled by *Brits* was that the "humanitarian mission" was facilitated by *Nazis* working in tandem with *Zionists* in Palestine.[5]

"THE FINAL SOLUTION"

Adolf Hitler is the second-most written about subject in history, his ideological nemesis—Jesus Christ, King of the Jews—being first (John 21:25). The reason for this literary "distinction" will soon be apparent. When attempting to conceptualize the horrors of the Bergen-Belsen sick camp (superintended by Josef Kramer, a.k.a. "The Beast of Belsen"), a British *Gazette* reporter coined the phrase: "The story of that greatest of all exhibitions of 'man's inhumanity to man.'"[6]

The British anti-tank unit that liberated Belsen on April 15, 1945, encountered the stench of *10,000* unburied corpses, many in advanced decay. (14,000 others would die later, with thousands more found in burial pits.) The living cannibalized the dead; the rats ingested both.[7] The veteran war correspondent struggled to begin his dispatch: "It is my duty to describe something beyond the imagination of mankind."[8] Lying somewhere in that acre of carnage were the bloated, emaciated remains of a shorn, tattooed fifteen-year-old Jewess whose thirty-two-month race against death was ended by a typhus epidemic three weeks shy of rescue. Her name was Anne Frank. Dr. Raul Hilberg wrote, "Himmler and Goebbels explained that the 'Final Solution' was a task that could not have been postponed, because in world history there was only one Adolph Hitler and because the war had presented to the German leadership a unique opportunity for 'solving the problem.'"[9]

The term "Final Solution" was an evolving Nazi euphemism for the eventual systematic genocide of European Jewry—i.e., *die endlösung der Judenfrage* ("*the* Final Solution of the Jewish question"). Other verbal camouflage included: "resettlement in the East" (transfer of Jews to death camps in Poland); "special Aktions" (gassings); "installations" and "bathhouses" (gas chambers); and "corpse cellars" (crematoria). However, as will be documented directly, the expression also constituted a macabre "double entendre" that is rarely entertained.

The salient developments equated with the *traditional* usage of the epithet begin on September 21, 1939. At the behest of *SS-Reichsführer* (General of the Army) Heinrich Himmler (a.k.a. "The Loyal Heinrich"), chief of the German Police in the Reich Ministry of the Interior, *SS-Gruppenführer* (Major-general) Reinhard Heydrich (a.k.a. "The Hangman"), first director of the newly formed Reich Security Main Office (RSHA), circulated a secret memo to his principals in Berlin titled: "Jewish question in the occupied territory."

In accord with the German-Soviet Treaty, Stalin invaded Poland on September 15, absorbing the eastern expanse into the USSR (Hitler remaining over the rest). The western portion (comprising the four executive districts of Wartheland, Silesia, Danzig-West Prussia, and East Prussia) became the "Incorporated Eastern Territories" (annexed to the Reich for future German settlement). The remaining Polish interior (intended as a transitory dumping ground for Jews and Poles alike) was named the *Generalgouvernement* ("General Government"). Heydrich's historic communiqué addressed the Final Solution in two steps: "Distinction must be made between: 1. The final aim (which will require extended periods of time) and 2. the stages leading to the fulfillment of this final aim (which will be carried out in short periods)." It also broached the ghetto concept: "For the time being, the first prerequisite for the final aim is the concentration of the Jews from the countryside into the larger cities…to be carried out speedily."[10]

The "scientific" rationale for the coming storm was the perennial Aryan need for *Lebensraum* ("living space"). As early as January 27,

1932, the future Führer told the Industry Club at Düsseldorf that "in order to survive a people must turn its strength outward."[11] For the initial stage, 600,000 Jews from the Incorporated Eastern Territories (plus 400,000 from the Greater Reich) would be ejected and crammed into ghettos within the General Government (primarily the Lublin district) as a "Jewish Reservation"; Reich and ethnic Germans (the so-called "German Diaspora," scattered mostly throughout Eastern Europe, the Balkans, and the Soviet Union) would then be repatriated, pursuant to Hitler's Lebensraum agenda. (A massive eviction of ethnic Poles, starting with political undesirables, would follow, Hitler having vowed "to rid the territory of the Reich of Jews and Polacks."[12])

SS-Obersturmbannführer (Lieutenant Colonel) Adolf Eichmann (a.k.a. "the desk murderer" and "the accountant of death") was entrusted with the pertinent logistics. Renowned for his bureaucratic prowess, organizational skills, and personal initiative (once even paying a rabbi for Hebrew lessons[13]), Eichmann promptly took over Gestapo Section IV-B-4 (Jewish Affairs and Evacuation) of the Reich SS Security Department. Ironically nicknamed by his schoolmates "the little Jew" (for his looks and dark complexion),[14] Adolf's killing "territory" would eventually encompass sixteen nations.

In the wake of "Operation Barbarossa" (Hitler's June 1941 surprise Russian incursion), special mobile paramilitary death squads called *Einsatzgruppen* ("task forces") were deployed to "carry out executive measures against the civilian population."[15] Within days thousands of Jews were being systematically shot at point-blank range, their bodies falling into graves dug by their own hands. On July 31, Reichstag President Hermann Göring told Heydrich to fix the Jewish problem "in the most favorable way, given present conditions" ("Keep doing what you can, *until* things improve").[16] Reinhard's rolling hit men obliged, shooting 500,000 over the next four months as building started on the world's first death camps. Hitler's vanguard murder modus debuted in Chełmno, Poland, that December. Thanks to the latest "innovation" (carbon monoxide), 1,000 Jews could now be gassed daily.

The January 20, 1942, Berlin Wannsee Conference provided further syncretization to expedite the Final Solution. Heydrich presided over the "august gathering" of various government ministers (forming an enlarged web of co-conspirators, or "blood kit").[17] Eleven million European Jews (excluding Britain and the neutral states) would now be "involved in this Final Solution."[18] Five additional killing centers were built within the borders of Poland: Bełżec, Sobibór, Treblinka, Majdanek, and Auschwitz. By war's end 6,000,000 Jews, comprising 3,000,000 men, 2,000,000 women, and 1,000,000 children, would be *permanently* "resettled." On a positive note, as the "Reich" itself fell short by 988 years, the Final Solution missed about 5,000,000 targeted victims (pursuant to God's promise in Jeremiah 30:11; 46:28).

DARK THESIS

In a speech (prepared by Eichmann), Heydrich announced at Wannsee: "Instead of emigration there is now a further possible solution to which the Führer has already signified his consent—namely deportation to the east."[19] Those first three words speak to one of the least known and most egregious facets of the Holocaust tragedy—that *emigration* was Hitler's *original* solution to the "Jewish question."

This fact was revealed in a May 24, 1934, memo to (then-Security Chief) Heydrich from an aide: "Jews must be deprived of their potential for a life—not only in the economic sphere. Germany must be a land without a future for them. Only the old generation should be allowed to die here in peace, but not the young, so that the incentive to emigrate remains."[20] Raul Hilberg, the world's preeminent authority on the Holocaust (also known as the *Shoah*, "catastrophe"), attests in his definitive trilogy, *The Destruction of the European Jews*: "[A]s the anti-Jewish regime intensified, unusual and extraordinary efforts were made to reduce Europe's Jewish population by mass emigration...The Jews were not killed before the emigration policy was exhausted."[21]

It was also Hitler's preference well into the war itself. Dr. Bernard Wasserstein, Professor of History at the University of Chicago, writes: "During the early part of the war German policy was not opposed to Jewish emigration. On the contrary, the Germans favored, encouraged, and even promoted Jewish movement out of the Reich as well as from certain occupied areas."[22] After the fighting began, Helmut Wohlthat, Nazi State Department Minister, assured Britain that Germany had every intention of continuing to release as many Jews as possible. As late as May 1941, Göring ordered that emigration be "stepped up in spite of the war, in so far as this was humanly possible."[23] Unbeknown to many, before Eichmann was placed over "Jewish Affairs and *Evacuation*," he directed the "Reich Central Office for Jewish *Emigration*" (the earlier posting made on January 18, 1939). Apart from Hitler's abject racism (fueled by the neo-pagan "theology" of the Thule Society), he possessed two main motives for deporting Jews—expropriation and infiltration. Regarding the former, the Reich Flight Tax (1931-43) and the Jewish Atonement Payment (1938-40) yielded two billion Reichsmark alone (the legalized plunder being justified as "recovered stolen property.") Dr. Hilberg writes:

> The combined yield during the fiscal year 1938 (*ℛℳ* 841,000,000) represented nearly 5 percent of the total revenues (*ℛℳ* 17,690,000,000) of that year. Fiscal 1938 (April 1, 1938, to March 31, 1939) was a year of mobilization. The shortage of funds was "critical." As the finance minister collected the Jewish money, it was poured immediately into armament spending...the two billion Reichsmark constituted the greatest profit registered by the Reich in the entire European destruction process.[24]

Thus, the reader is confronted with the unpalatable truth that the sizable revenue collected from the small percentage of Jews fortunate enough to emigrate aided Hitler's ability to wage war, thereby contributing *indirectly* to the deaths of their loved ones left behind.

The Nazis also viewed the Jews' relocation—*anywhere*—as a strategic bonus (similar to Castro's 1980 Mariel boatlift). Dr. Bryan Mark Rigg (a Baptist proselyte to Judaism) writes, "Hitler claimed that in getting rid of the Jew, Germans were justified in allying themselves even with Satan."[25] On July 3, 1920, the Führer wrote a supporter:

> I cannot reproach a tuberculosis bacillus for doing something that means destruction for a human being but life for the bacillus itself; I am no less compelled and legitimated in conducting the battle against tuberculosis by annihilating its cause, because my very existence depends on it. Over thousands of years, the Jew is becoming and has become a racial tuberculosis affecting many peoples. To fight him means to remove him.[26]

Twenty-two years later, Hitler told a private gathering: "The same battle that Pasteur and Koch had to fight must be led by us today. Innumerable sicknesses have their origin in one bacillus: the Jew."[27] Himmler concurred: "Anti-Semitism is exactly the same as delousing.

Getting rid of lice is not a question of ideology; it is a matter of cleanliness."[28] (SS doctors even recorded the size of inmates' head lice.) Reich Foreign Office Press Chief Paul Schmidt concluded: "The Jewish question is no question of humanity, and it is no question of religion; it is solely a question of political hygiene."[29]

As if inspired by the medieval siege tactic of catapulting plague-infected corpses over castle walls, Hitler believed that any "body-politic" naive enough to absorb his "Jewish germs" (described in *Mein Kampf* as "a moral pestilence...worse than the Black Plague"[30]) would become that much weaker in their future ability to oppose him. Thus, the extirpation of exportable Jews would be analogous to destroying perfectly good stockpiles of WMD. To summarize the Nazi mindset: Germany's *gain* (emigration) would be the world's *loss* (immigration).

However, to Hitler's frustration (not to mention European Jewry's), the Allies apparently shared his prognosis of a potential "Semitic pandemic." While America refused to increase its meager and grossly unused immigration quotas, Britain followed suite in Palestine. The White House feared Congress; Whitehall feared Islam. Meanwhile, a genuine "Mexican standoff" was occurring in October 1938. Poland-bound *German* trains, carrying Jews of *Polish* nationality were being checked at the border, while German-bound *Polish* trains with Jews of *German* nationality were reciprocating Hitler's "generosity."[31] Then, in a dramatic turn of events three months later, the Führer made an 11th-hour attempt to *scare* the world into opening their gates—by stating *exactly* what he intended to do. Normally cloaking the Final Solution in a shroud of euphemisms, on January 30, 1939 (the sixth anniversary of his power grab), Hitler boldly addressed the Reichstag:

> And there is one thing that I should like to state on this day, memorable perhaps for others as well as us Germans. In the course of my life I have very often been a prophet and was generally laughed at for it. During my struggle for power it was in the first instance Jewish people who laughed at my prophecies that I would someday assume the leadership of the state and thereby of the entire nation and then, among many other things, achieve a solution of the Jewish problem. Their laughter was uproarious but I think that for some time now the Jews have been laughing on the other side of their faces. Today I will be a prophet again: if international Jewish financiers within Europe and abroad should succeed once

more in plunging the nations into a world war, then the consequences will be not the Bolshevization of the world and therewith a victory of Jewry, but on the contrary, the annihilation of the Jewish race in Europe.[32]

Incredibly, Hitler repeated this threat in *another* speech on September 1, 1939. Hilberg concurs that the rhetoric was designed to force more emigration: "The tactical intention of...Hitler's speech on 30 January, is clear: by means of the threat of annihilation the pressure of expulsion upon the German Jews was to be heightened and the willingness of foreign powers to receive them extorted through a form of blackmail."[33] As late as mid-1940, Himmler revealed a rare glimpse of the Reich's reluctance to implement Hitler's rant. In a memo to his Führer on May 25, the future Shoah triggerman relates that "an inner conviction" led him to reject "the Bolshevist methods of the physical extirpation (*Ausrottung*) of a people as un-German and impossible."[34]

Yet, despite these explicit warnings, the Allies remained oblivious. With the prospect of *normal* emigration to *normal* destinations fading, Heydrich wrote to Ribbentrop on June 24, 1940, "therefore a territorial Final Solution is necessary."[35] As Lincoln initially favored sending America's Negros to Liberia, SS officials were considering deporting *all* of Europe's Jews to the marshy island of Madagascar.[36] Hopefully, France would cede her extensive African colony to Germany primarily for Jewish immigration (plus a naval base). Hitler ordered the Navy to avail the historic evacuation. In reality, the plan called for Madagascar to morph into a Nazi Alcatraz so that European Jewry could be held as hostages to ensure the concerted conduct of her "racial comrades" in America; i.e., sustained neutrality.[37] (The pipedream eventually fizzled, being contingent upon an Anglo-German pact.)

Thus, in a morbid way, one could say that "business" was so bad at Eichmann's *first* job (emigration) that he was forced to "moonlight" with a *second* (extermination). However, tenacity being a core German trait, to Adolf's "credit," he refused to quit. Wasserstein notes, "In the absence of any welcoming gesture from the Allies, Eichmann's office took advantage of the Zionists' desire to organize illegal immigration to Palestine from central Europe. According to Zionist agent, Ehud Avriel, Jewish Agency representatives who applied to Eichmann's office for exit permits for Jewish emigrants 'were treated like preferred customers.'"[38] Longerich cites two Nazi records from 1937 and 1938 showing Hitler's support of Jewish emigration to Palestine.[39] In fact, a unique "export-import arrangement" between Germany and the Jewish Agency for Palestine already existed from 1933 to 1939.

The Aryan-Jewish hybrid served as an incentive to facilitate a fast-track to emigration by permitting the entrants to salvage more of their wealth. According to the *Haavara Transfer Agreement*, an emigrating Jewish "capitalist" was allowed to contract a German exporter for the transfer of his "goods" to Palestine (merchandise he was resigned to repurchase at inflated prices). The exporter was paid in Reichsmark from his client's blocked account. Palestine importers would then pay for the cargo in local currency, liquidating the immigrant's investment. Hilberg relates, "Haavara-transfers, including goods purchased with Reichsmark in Germany by emigrants themselves, totaled over 100 million Reichsmark and facilitated the emigration of about 36% of the 50,000 Jews who entered Palestine from the Old Reich."[40]

Unfortunately, as previously shown, the Reich Immigration Bureau was powerless to shield its helpless "clients" from *Allied* bullets (i.e., along Israel's coastline). As early as December 1938, Foreign Minister Ribbentrop apprised his French counterpart, Georges Bonnet: "[W]e all wanted to get rid of our Jews but…the difficulties lay in the fact that no country wished to receive them."[41] Wasserstein concludes: "That the great majority of Jews failed to emigrate was primarily due to the extreme reluctance of all countries to admit them."[42] An end to Hitler's "grace period" was inevitable. On July 31, 1941, Reichstag President Hermann Göring signed the following order for Heydrich:

> Complementing the task already assigned to you in the directive of January 24, 1939, to undertake, by emigration or evacuation, a solution of the Jewish question as advantageous as possible under the conditions at the time, I hereby charge you with making all necessary organizational, functional, and material preparations for a complete solution of the Jewish question in the German sphere of influence in Europe.[43]

And then it happened. One day toward the end of summer (Longerich says September or October[44]), Eichmann was summoned to Heydrich's office where the RSHA chief told him: "I have just come from the Reichsführer [Himmler]: the Führer has now ordered the physical annihilation of the Jews."[45] On October 23, Himmler gave the decree closing the gates to all further emigration. Thus—with nowhere to "catapult" the Jews—a previous utterance by Nazi Friedrich Uebelhoer, was about to transpire: "In the end...we must burn out this bubonic plague."[46] (Hamburg's Jews were promptly deported to Łódź, ostensibly to provide replacement housing for German victims of Allied bombing.) Hilberg comments on this ominous Judenpolitik:

> The expulsion and exclusion policy was adopted by the Nazis and remained the goal of all anti-Jewish activity until 1941. That year marks a turning point in anti-Jewish history. In 1941 the Nazis found themselves in the midst of a total war. Several million Jews were incarcerated in ghettos. Emigration was impossible. A last-minute project to ship the Jews to the African island of Madagascar had fallen through. The 'Jewish problem' had to be 'solved' in some other way. At this crucial time, the idea of a 'territorial solution' emerged in Nazi minds. The 'territorial solution,' or 'the Final Solution of the Jewish question in Europe,' as it became known, envisaged the death of European Jewry. The European Jews were to be killed.[47]

Though Hitler's preference for emigration would *pass*, his prophecy of extermination would *come* to pass. Goebbels' diary entry for March 27, 1942, reads: "Not much will remain of the Jews...A judgment is being visited upon the Jews [which is] barbaric...The prophecy which the Führer made about them for having brought on a new world war is beginning to come true in a most terrible manner."[48] Hitler revisited his pesticide theme yet again on September 30, 1942: "At one time, the Jews of Germany laughed about my prophecies. I do not know whether they are still laughing or whether they have already lost all desire to laugh. But right now I can only repeat: they will stop laughing everywhere, and I shall be right also in that prophecy."[49]

The world's greatest crime would now be wrought by four distinct hierarchical groups working in tandem under a single Führer: military, party, industry, and the ministerial bureaucracy. However, as Hilberg opines, though a deliberate, systematic, and coalescent effort from the start, the entire affair was destined to follow an arbitrary trajectory:

> The process of destruction unfolded in a definite pattern. It did not, however, proceed from a basic plan. No bureaucrat in 1933 could have predicted what kind of measures would be taken in 1938,

> nor was it possible in 1938 to foretell the configuration of the undertaking in 1942. The destruction process was a step-by-step operation, and the administrator could seldom see more than one step ahead...The engine of destruction was a sprawling, diverse and, above all, decentralized process.[50]

And so, even *more* "unpalatable" than corporate America's wartime complicity with Nazism is the revolting reality that, at the end of the day, the Final Solution of the Jewish question was *finalized* by the Allies themselves; in death camp parlance—by "having limited all routes of escape to the crematoria chimneys." Germany never could have murdered her six million victims without two main accomplices: the United States and Great Britain. Goebbels' diary entry for December 13, 1942, reads: "I believe both the English and the Americans are happy that we are exterminating the Jewish riffraff."[51]

Hitler was not about to let the Allies escape the inexorable verdict of history. As early as 1939, the "prophet" was positioning them to share in the inevitable common guilt, stating in his January 30 speech: "It is a shameful example to observe today how the entire democratic world dissolves in tears of pity but then, in spite of its obvious duty to help, closes its heart to the poor, tortured Jewish people."[52] Hilberg notes: "This was not an idle accusation; it was an attempt to drag the Allied powers into the destruction process as passive but willing accomplices."[53] Longerich adds: "But the threat of extermination contained one further perspective: if it remained ineffective, that is, if emigration made no significant progress and in the event of war the Western powers could not be restrained from intervening, the locus of 'guilt' for a further intensification of the German persecution of the Jews was, in the view of leading National Socialists, already clear."[54]

Thus, to turn the well-known historical phrase on its head, the *ultimate* double entendre of the *real* Final Solution can be summarized by a simple rhetorical question. As the legendary Jewish actor Charlie Chaplin would have asked in the spirit of *The Great Dictator*—"What's a Führer to do?" When French Prime Minister Pierre Laval was grilled about his willingness to deport Jews from the unoccupied zone, he retorted: "Well, what am I to do? I offered these foreign Jews to the Allies, but they didn't take them off my hands."[55] Randolph Paul, a senior US Treasury official, concurred with the thesis, venting a similar sarcasm in December 1943: "I don't know how we can blame the

Germans for killing them when we are doing this. The law calls it *para-delicto*, of equal guilt."[56] As a dying inmate told Elie Wiesel in Auschwitz: "I have more faith in Hitler than in anyone else. He alone has kept his promises, all his promises, to the Jewish people."[57]

BRITISH TREACHERY

The shocking story of Anglo-American resistance to the rescue efforts of the Reich Central Bureau for Jewish Emigration answers the *key* question posed in the Introduction—"Who changed the locks?" The degree of moral culpability can only be exceeded by the apathy shown *after* the Final Solution was known to be underway. When eyewitness reports from German-occupied Poland reached the Foreign Office in April 1940, Under-Secretary Reginald Leeper said, "As a general rule Jews are inclined to magnify their persecutions."[58] Ten days later, 167,000 Jews were *locked up* in the Łódź Ghetto. By December 1941, the Jews' "paranoia" had magnified significantly. David Kelly of the British Legation in Switzerland, quoted a Polish informant: "About 1½ million Jews who were living in eastern (recently Russian) Poland have simply disappeared altogether; nobody knows how and where."[59]

To begin with *Anglo* resistance, hundreds of Jewish males of German or Austrian birth living in England when the war started were branded "enemy aliens" and confined to local internment camps. By mid-1940, over 8,000 additional Jewish subjects were deported overseas, mainly to Canada and Australia.[60] British disruption of "illegal" Jewish migration has also been attested in several venues. On the diplomatic front, as most Jews desired to reach Palestine, the Foreign Office tried to "head them off at the pass" by pressing the nations in southeast Europe to seal all likely escape routes.[61] The Admiralty was then coaxed to stop vessels carrying Jews in the Mediterranean.[62] Conducted under the aegis of the "Contraband Control Service," the controversial practice was in contravention of international law. While ships and cargo were liable to forfeiture, their captains and crews could face fines and/or prison.

Because most commandeered vessels were in no shape to return to their embarkation point, the "fugitives" were sent to detention camps (e.g., Cyprus and Mauritius). Many were "privileged" to do their time in Haifa's *Atlit* facility. Thus, in one of the most disconcerting scenes imaginable, men and women, boys and girls, seniors and infants, all fleeing Nazi camps, suddenly found themselves surrounded by *British* barbed wire and machine gun towers—in Eretz Yisrael. Several of the enervated arrivals had already endured Dachau and Buchenwald.[63]

As foreshadowed by the *St. Louis* debacle, several public relations disasters would haunt HMG throughout the war. On October 3, 1939, 1,100 Jews departed Vienna via the Danube aboard the riverboat *Uranus*. When the voyage was halted by ice, the exiles were marooned in Kladovo, Yugoslavia. All aid requests were ignored by the British. When the American Jewish Joint Distribution Committee attempted to send food and medicine, the Colonial Office asked the Foreign Office to refuse the request, citing Middle East "security concerns." Though the supplies eventually arrived, the Kladovo group was confined in a camp near Belgrade. Following the German occupation of Yugoslavia in April 1941, all 915 internees were summarily murdered.[64]

Another needless tragedy occurred in 1940 when a small Bulgarian schooner, *SS Salvador*, left Burgas with 327 Jews. The vessel wrecked in a storm near Istanbul on December 12, killing 223, including 66 children. The 125 survivors were returned to Hitler. On August 5, 1944, four tiny ships attempting to move 1,500 exiles from Romania to Turkey were engaged by German gunboats just after midnight. The *SS Mefkura*, carrying 295, with 100 children, capsized in the attack. The hapless passengers were machine-gunned in the water; five survived.[65] (Other accounts claim the vessel was sunk by a Russian submarine.)[66]

On September 3, 1940, another four-ship flotilla taking 3,600 Jews from Prague, Vienna, and Danzig steamed down the Danube "under the Swastika flag."[67] At the Romanian Black Sea port of Tulcea, the human cargo was moved onto three small Greek boats of Panamanian registry and the Palestine voyage resumed. However, by the time the rickety convoy limped into Haifa Bay in mid-November, the Colonial Office had decided to reroute the entire party to Mauritius via the French ocean-liner, *SS Patria*. With all appeals for asylum denied, the imminent prospect of being hauled 4,000 miles from their beloved ethnoscape to a squalid prison camp off the southeast coast of Africa sparked a tragic application of the old adage, "Desperate times call for desperate measures." At 10 a.m. on November 25, with half of the Jews already transferred onboard, a powerful blast gutted the *Patria's* hull, killing 267 and injuring 172; a dozen British policemen also died.

In an attempt to merely disable the vessel to preclude its departure, the Haganah had planted a bomb. Unfortunately, the well-intentioned saboteurs had miscalculated the amount of powder required. The 12,000-ton liner sank in fifteen minutes. After protracted litigation, the survivors were given asylum in Palestine; however—the proviso only applied to those who were on the *Patria* when the blast occurred. The 1,580 non-boarded Jews (including 621 women and 116 children) were promptly deported to Mauritius. The *Zionist Review* labeled the policy an "act of inhumanity...which mocks at justice, wisdom, and humanity," whereupon Sir John Shuckburg of the Colonial Office inanely noted, "The Jews have no sense of humor and no sense of proportion."[68] When the 1,310 detainees were later asked (in 1945) where they wanted to go, 81% chose Palestine and were returned to Haifa in August. Wasserstein observes, "The survivors...thus reached their destination five years after beginning their odyssey."[69]

Of the sundry maritime disasters of this era, the *MV Struma* is the definitive case. The 180-ton Romanian ship was chartered to transport 769 Jews from Constanta to Haifa. The plan was to reach neutral Turkey, then await immigration certificates to Palestine. However, from its ill-fated launch on the Black Sea on December 12, 1941, the trip was an unmitigated disaster. Under normal conditions, the seventy-eight-year-old former cattle barge could hold 100 people; with 769, a leaky hull, defective motor, and only two lifeboats, the *Struma* was the quintessential "accident waiting to happen." After three days at sea, the ship lost power off Istanbul and had to be towed into port.

While repair efforts were begun, Turkey caved to British pressure, prohibiting all disembarkation. According to a Royal Navy report, conditions aboard the *Struma* were "appalling."[70] Imagine 769 people having to share *one* lavatory and *one* small kitchen. Other "amenities" included: *no* provisions; *no* fresh water; *no* clean air; *no* sane sleeping quarters; and *no* medical supplies (many contracting dysentery). For ten agonizing weeks the exiles stayed sequestered in their floating rust bucket, sustained solely by local Zionist charities. The JA begged that their stranded brethren be allowed into Eretz Yisrael, even pledging £6,000 to underwrite the cost. Yet, the Colonial Office and Palestine Government remained united against the plea (despite the telling fact that 10,000 immigration vouchers for 1941 were still unfulfilled).

The Turks finally ordered the *Struma* and her passengers back to Romania. However, by now the ship's engine was deemed un-repairable. Nonetheless, on February 23, the crippled *Struma* was towed through the Bosphorus to the Black Sea, then cast adrift beyond Turkish territorial waters. As the doomed Jews faded from view, witnesses recalled seeing banners in Hebrew and English, reading: "SAVE US!"[71] With the *Struma* "dead in the water," a Russian sub surfaced near dawn and fired a single torpedo. Though the explosion was heard along the coast six miles away, there were *no* attempts at rescue. Consequently, 428 men, 269 women, and 70 children were lost, only two making it to shore. Incredibly, Sir Harold MacMichael, High Commissioner in Jerusalem, concluded: "The fate of these people was tragic, but the fact remains that they were nationals of a country at war with Britain, proceeding directly from enemy territory. Palestine was under no obligations toward them."[72] Wasserstein notes:

> More than any other single event of the war years the *Struma* episode aroused Palestinian Jewish hostility to the British and Palestine Governments. The disaster may, indeed, have marked a psychological watershed for the *Yishuv*, destroying the last vestiges of the special relationship between Britain and Zionism inaugurated by the Balfour Declaration."[73]

CALLOUS US IMMIGRATION POLICY

Whereas Britain's "locksmiths" focused their efforts on sealing the Jews' escape routes in Europe, their American counterparts ensured that no "kike" would slip past the Statue of Liberty—no matter *who* penned her famous inscription. On October 28, 1936, Franklin Roosevelt was slated to speak at "Lady Liberty's" Golden Jubilee. The previous week, John Dewey wrote the president, "Fifty years ago, at the Statue, this country was spoken of as an asylum of the oppressed...Today this tradition is in danger of being completely discarded. The gates have been closed to immigrants...We urge you to declare...that this country will...re-establish the proud principle it once maintained as an asylum for political and religious refugees."[74] In his subsequent remarks on Ellis Island, FDR would only say, "For over three centuries a steady stream of men, women and children followed the beam of liberty which this light symbolizes...fired anew by the dream of a better life in America...Within this present generation that stream from abroad has largely stopped."[75]

Of course, the veteran politician knew better than to open *that* can of worms. The reason *why* the stream of European immigrants, *Jews* in particular, had slowed to a trickle was because the *source* of the flow—US immigration policy—had become increasingly plugged by xenophobia-induced legislation. Ultimately, Jews in harm's way on the Continent were denied safe haven in America because Roosevelt was more worried about his *own* survival at the polls. Conscience never had a chance when met by realpolitik: the sizable voter-bloc that feared the Jew; the "honorable" members of Congress who feared the voters; and the tenuous occupant of the White House who feared *both* groups, particularly Capitol Hill. In 1938, four national polls revealed that 71%-85% of the public opposed raising quotas to shelter Jews.[76]

The cause for such atypical callousness is attributed to four factors: 1) the cumulative effect of US-bred anti-Semitism; 2) job competition after the Depression; 3) induced paranoia over Communist infiltration and espionage, notably by Russian Jews; and, 4) widespread ignorance regarding the true plight of European Jewry. Ironically, at the height of the Holocaust itself, mini-pogroms were actually breaking out in *this* country. With the "New Deal" being spun by Ford and Coughlin as the "Jew Deal," synagogues and Jewish cemeteries were desecrated, swastikas appeared in conspicuous areas, and anti-Semitic literature was openly distributed. While the worst violence occurred in the urban Northeast (New York City and Boston, in particular), a gang of hoodlums in the nation's heartland accosted a twelve-year-old Jewish boy, painting a Star of David with the word "Jude" on his chest.[77]

Throughout FDR's unprecedented tenure, Jewish immigration was minimized in two ways. First, there were no emergency increases to the already meager figures allotted to each country. The Quota Act of 1921 adopted the first numerical restrictions on European immigrants; 3% of the foreign-born of each nationality residing in the US as per the 1910 census, with a maximum annual of 355,000 immigrants. (The original "anti-refugee" position was the anti-*Catholic* American Nativist Movement begun in the 1830s.) In 1929 (Stock Market Crash), the figure was cut to 153,774. Over half this total (83,574) was conveniently "wasted" on the United Kingdom and Ireland, while the turf across the Channel—*Eichmann's* future "quotas"—got to divvy up the rest: Germany-Austria, 27,370; Poland, 6,524; Italy, 5,802; The Netherlands, 3,153; France, 3,086; Czechoslovakia, 2,874; Soviet Union, 2,784; Norway, 2,377; Belgium, 1,304; Denmark, 1,181; Hungary, 869; Yugoslavia, 845; Romania, 295; and Bulgaria, 100.[78]

The second, more unconscionable ploy was to *keep* the minimum *to* a minimum, *especially* with Jews. According to the Immigration and Naturalization Service, a total of 476,930 refugees representing all faiths entered America from 1933 to 1943; Jews accounted for 165,756, with roughly 138,000 having escaped persecution. Yet, Morse notes, "During this ten-year period, United States immigration quotas could have permitted the entry of 1,500,000 aliens. Thus the number of Jews entering the US during this period approximated only 10% of the total number of immigrants permissible under law."[79]

When the quotas were *reduced* during the critical window between Pearl Harbor and VE Day (to 27,000 from Axis-controlled nations), the Jews' dismal percentile stayed unchanged. Wyman notes, "Thus 90% of those quotas, nearly 190,000 openings, went unused while the mass murder of European Jewry ran its course."[80] Most of the wartime Jewish immigrants (as high as 40% in 1942-43) had already reached safety in the Western hemisphere and were merely upgrading to their ultimate preference.[81] (That a Jew could reach the West at *all* was no mean feat, given the degree of US pressure upon Latin governments to preserve "hemispheric security"[82]; a joke in light of that region's reputation for U-boat refueling stations and Nazi asylums.)

The heavily anti-Semitic US State Department sent hundreds of thousands of Jews to their deaths by many bureaucratic measures. As a sign of things to come, the immigration saga began with the American sponsor confronted by an intimidating visa application—one that would extend *over four feet* in length by July 1943.[83] Six copies of the double-sided "form" were duly required. Then, while the *SS* could "process" 20,000 Jews in 24 hours at Auschwitz, the *INS* claimed it needed nine *months* for a *single* application. Ironically, the very Jews *most* in need—those biding their time under Nazi occupied regimes—were automatically assured the *least* assistance, classified as "enemy aliens." Under the applicable "relatives rule," any applicant with a parent, child, spouse, or sibling staying in German, Italian, or Soviet territory would be subject to the highest scrutiny (judged "guilty until proven innocent"). The refugee would then have to "prove" that he or she would represent a "positive benefit" to America as well. The most ludicrous procedure concerned section 7(c) of the 1924 Immigration Act, requiring the prospective citizen to submit a police affidavit affirming his good character for the previous five years. Morse writes:

> Although the notion of a Jew dropping by police headquarters to receive a certificate of good character from his oppressors may strike the reader as a particularly sardonic touch of bureaucracy, State Department files refer repeatedly to this requirement and its importance...One wonders whether the State Department lawyers ever had an opportunity to read the dispatches from Germany describing police treatment of the Jews.[84]

Treasury Department lawyers ultimately launched a covert review of State Department procedures, declaring afterward: "If anyone were to attempt to work out a set of restrictions specifically designed to prevent Jewish refugees from entering this country it is difficult to conceive of how more effective restrictions could have been imposed than have already been imposed on grounds of 'security.'"[85]

In December 1945, a *New York Times* article on America's immigration laws agreed: "The United States, once the haven of refuge for the oppressed peoples of Europe, has been almost as inaccessible as Tibet."[86] Citing the iconic Liberty Island effigy, Morse concludes, "The lamp remained lifted beside the golden door, but the flame had been extinguished and the door was *padlocked*."[87] (Author's emphasis)

THE GENESIS OF GENOCIDE

On February 20, 1939, a baby was born blind, retarded, and missing a leg and portions of both arms. The father, Richard Kretschmar, a farm laborer in Leipzig, petitioned Chancellor Hitler to authorize a "merciful death" for his severely handicapped son. The benchmark request was "reluctantly" approved. The child was promptly put to death on July 25 by the Führer's own physician, Karl Brandt. The "creature" (as Brandt called his patient) is believed to have been given Luminal in the form of a dissolving tablet, inducing unconsciousness, death occurring three to five days later.[88] Thus, as borne out by history, five-month-old Gerhard became the "genesis of genocide."

Within days of this procedure, Hitler announced a seminal program for "euthanizing" children. To facilitate the obviously low-profile agenda, a front group was formed under the imposing title: "Reich Committee for the Scientific Registration of Severe Illnesses with Hereditary or Predisposed Causes." Upon the parents' approval, the deformed child would be sent to one of thirty so-called "specialist children's clinics" to be killed by tablets, needles, or starvation. The program dispatched 5,000 boys and girls, Aryan and Jewish alike.[89] It is sadly ironic that the name of the child who formed the spearhead of Hitler's devilish movement is derived from the Germanic element *ger* for "spear" (the Führer himself retaining a cultic infatuation *with* and rumored stewardship *of* the so-called "Spear of Destiny"[90]).

The systematic murder of adults naturally followed, beginning with psychiatric inmates, primarily in the annexed areas of Poland, but also in the *Altreich* ("Old Reich," i.e., territories under Nazi control prior to 1938). According to a rare document from October 1939, Hitler covered his euthanasia team by officially directing them to grant "a merciful death" to those who were, "as far as mankind can judge, terminally ill."[91] The new buzz phrase was, "Life not worth living may be unworthy of life." Suddenly, hordes of mental patients, especially non-ethnic Germans, were being "mercifully" *shot* all over the place.

In late November, inmates from two clinics were sent to Fort VI (a concentration camp in Posen) and asphyxiated with carbon monoxide in a sealed room. Longerich observes: "This was the first National Socialist mass murder to be carried out using poison gas."[92] Starting in 1940, *SS-Sturmbannführer* (Major) Herbert Lange (future chief of Chelmno death camp) introduced a fleet of gas vans to expedite the killing. According to declassified CIA papers, the technology was formatted to mass murder by *SS-Standartenführer* (Colonel) Walther Rauff, an official at the Criminal Technical Institute of the RSHA.[93] The earliest models had the disarming words *Kaisers Kaffee Geschäft* ("Kaiser Coffee Company") painted on their sides.[94] As the Jews vanished, the facilities were occupied by SS units, used as prisons or army barracks, or offered to German arrivals in need of housing.

In the Old Reich, a program was begun called "Aktion T4" (named after the central euthanasia Berlin office address, *Tiergartenstrasse 4*). SS Major *Christian* Wirth (future Bełżec Commandant) was a key T4 administrator. Initially, two locations were used, one in Brandenburg prison, the other in Grafeneck Mental Hospital in Württemberg. A trial gassing occurred at Brandenburg in January 1940. As a chilling precursor, over a dozen dazed patients were led into a gas chamber disguised as a *shower*. Death followed within minutes. After a search for gold teeth, the bodies were cremated. Other sites went up in Bernburg and Hadamar. The Nazi criteria for "mercy" soon included the blind, deaf, epileptic, even slow learners. In August 1941, the T4 program was abruptly ended due to protests from citizens and clergy alike (though some crowded Catholic asylums desired the "service"[95]). The total victim count is estimated at 70,000.[96] Longerich concludes:

> [T]he Chancellery of the Führer...had developed a process through which a large number of people had been murdered in procedures that had been centrally directed, were ostensibly under scientific control, and were bureaucratically managed in the minutest detail...T4 can be seen as a model for the 'Final Solution'...The systematic murder of some 4,000 to 5,000 Jewish patients represents an important 'bridge' between 'euthanasia' and the later annihilation of the whole Jewish population.[97]

For the record—the Führer's own cousin, Aloisia Veit—died by carbon monoxide in December 1940 in a Vienna "medical institute."

EINSATZGRUPPEN

In the first twenty-one months of the war, only about 30,000 Jews had succumbed to Nazi terror. Apart from T4, this was normally due to *Einzelaktionen* ("short violent outbursts against individual Jews," i.e., pogroms), mostly during the Polish occupation. Some were immolated in their synagogues, the majority shot or hanged. The survivors were subjected to looting, public humiliation, beatings, and rape.[98]

Operation Barbarossa (June 1941) marked the critical watershed of the Final Solution. Over five million Jews were living under the Soviet flag. In the wake of the incursion, four Einsatzgruppen units began a methodical slaughter of Communist officials, Polish military officers, intelligentsia, clergy, partisans and saboteurs, Gypsies, Asians, mental patients, the terminally ill, "asocials" (homosexuals, prostitutes, carriers of sexually transmitted diseases, the chronically unemployed), and—*any* Jewish male civilians. The growing death swath comprised northeastern

Poland, Estonia, Latvia, Lithuania, the Ukraine, White Russia, and the western regions of the Russian Republic. An SS report from October 1941 noted that "the cleansing operations being carried out by the security police, in accordance with basic instructions, have as their objective the total elimination of the Jews."[99] Thus, before the *Jews* were ever brought to the *killers* (in the camps), the *killers* were brought to the *Jews* (in the fields). By November, 500,000 had *already* been "eliminated," with a further "cleansing" of 900,000 occurring the following year.[100] Yet, despite these horrific statistics, against the backdrop of the stereotypical "death camp," historians have labeled this initial phase of the Final Solution, the "Overlooked Holocaust."

The Einsatzgruppen were deployed by the RSHA as Hitler felt such a task (removing the "Jewish-Bolshevik intelligentsia") was too much for the army alone.[101] The Führer salved the Wehrmacht's wounded honor by giving General Alfred Jodl (Chief of Army Operations) a simple analytical premise: "[T]he Jewish-Bolshevist intelligentsia, hitherto the 'oppressor' of the people must be eliminated," whereupon Jodl gave the corollary order, "[A]ll Bolshevist chiefs and commissars are to be neutralized immediately."[102] The key clause in the Army-RSHA accord stated: "[W]ithin the framework of their instructions and upon their own responsibility, the Sonderkommandos are entitled to carry out executive measures against the civilian population."[103]

In a further eleventh-hour accommodation, the Hangman's death squads would be *tolerated*, not only in army group rear, but in the corps areas along the front as well. Hilberg notes, "This concession was of great importance to the Einsatzgruppen, for the victims were to be caught as quickly as possible. They were to be given no warning and no chance to escape."[104] As seen in Hitler's March speech, Barbarossa would transcend normal military victory to utter annihilation: "If we do not see it in those terms, then whilst we may beat the enemy, in 30 years we will be faced once more by the Communist foe."[105] (This resolve extended to Russian POW camps where thousands of Jewish soldiers were routinely executed.)[106]

First blood flowed within a week when 2,000 Jews were shot in Białystok, Poland, on June 27 ("Red Friday"). Another 7,000 murders occurred in Lwów three days later. Kishinev was taken by German and Romanian units on July 17. While 50 Jews died there in the 1903 pogrom (the setting for *Fiddler on the Roof*), 10,000 others were shot by summer's end (the Jewish population of 65,000 eventually falling to

13,000). However, like the Final Solution itself, the precursor stage was a work in progress. "Not until after the launching of the military campaign were specific directives issued in writing as well as orally," Hilberg relates. "These orders taken together do not reveal a preconceived plan. They do indicate an evolving policy with ever widening effect."[107] This "evolving policy" was partially caused by the fact that, for all their goose-stepping bravado, the perpetrators were really cowards and bullies at heart.

"ETC."

While most SS men "understood" that "the Jews" were the *real* targets and that innocent Jewish women and children would eventually have to die as well, this was never *directly* conveyed beforehand. The rationale lay somewhere between an instinctive desire on the *leaders'* part to maintain plausible deniability and the psychological need on the *followers'* part to psych themselves up to such an abysmal task.

Hilberg cites the latter: "That uneasiness was the product of moral scruples that were the lingering effect of two thousand years of Western morality and ethics...[T]he bureaucracy wanted to cloak its deeds, to conceal them not only from all outsiders but also from the censuring gaze of its own conscience."[108] Longerich elucidates the "wink-wink" angle: "What emerges from all this is the impression of a degree of vagueness in the ways orders were issued to *Einsatzgruppen*. A manner...in which the subordinate was supposed to recognize the 'meaning' behind the words intuitively is familiar from National Socialist anti-Jewish policy from 1933 onwards, in particular in cases where the orders had something criminal about them."[109] The only candor given was that their task required "firmness" and "severity" as it entailed a life-and-death struggle between two "world views."[110]

On July 2, 1941, Heydrich circulated a memo to the Higher SS and Police Commanders recapping his verbal orders to the Einsatzgruppen on invasion eve. Under the title "Executions," the list of "those to be executed" encompassed "all functionaries of the Comintern (and all professional Communist politicians of any kind); People's Commissars; Jews in Party and state posts; other radical elements (saboteurs, propagandists, snipers, assassins, agitators, etc.)."[111]

With the key "Jewish-Bolshevik" nexus in place, Longerich relates that Heydrich would then entrust his junior officers "to shoot the Jews under one pretext or another, whether under the heading of state and Party functionaries, or agitators, or propagandists, or merely, 'etc.'"[112] Other related equivocations enjoined Einsatzgruppen chiefs to help locals initiate the "self-purification process" and to do so "invisibly" (doublespeak for inciting pogroms with discretion).[113] Thus, the basic idea was to incite a trickle-down "intuitive initiative" in the periphery.

The opening executions focused on males suspected of Communist sympathies. However, at an SS meeting on July 8 in Białystok, Himmler reputedly said, "[E]very Jew must in principle be regarded as a partisan."[114] Hitler didn't help any by adding a week later, "[S]hoot dead everyone who so much as blinks at you."[115] Jewish men were liquidated under every imaginable pretense: arson; dissemination of anti-German literature; looting; sabotage; refusal to work; support for partisan groups; black market dealings; even the threat of plague.[116]

The most sustained *raison d'être* for killing Jews was "security." Himmler wrote, "We had the moral right vis-à-vis our people to annihilate this people which wanted to annihilate us."[117] It also provided an "invisible" incentive for the Wehrmacht to join in the slaughter. After a particular sortie in Rudensk, a divisional commander ordered extra patrols, stating: "[W]e have to ensure that the Jews are…removed from the villages. We are continually finding that they are the only support that the partisans have for surviving now and over the winter. Their annihilation must…be carried out uncompromisingly."[118] Reprisals were another useful ploy. When a single militia member was shot in an ambush near Pinsk, 4,500 Jews were killed in retaliation.[119]

Once again, the Nazis' ongoing need for exculpation speaks to their cowardly nature; plagued by such massive crimes—*any* viable excuse would do. But the *really* heavy Sword of Damocles was the killing of women and children. While Jewesses were occasionally shot as enemy collaborators, the majority (with their young) were generally "driven into the marshes" (after their husbands' executions).[120] But, when Himmler was in Minsk in August, he alerted Otto Bradfisch (Chief of *Einsatzkommando* 8): "[T]there is an order from the Führer for the shooting of all Jews. This order must be followed, however difficult that may be for us."[121] To illustrate the mental gymnastics involved, he told an audience of high-ranking party officials in October 1943: "I did not assume to have the right to exterminate the men—in other words kill them or have them killed—and have the avengers personified in the children to become adults for our children and grandchildren."[122]

The greatest challenge remained the sheer size of the mission itself. Overrun by the number of victims, SS officials hired local muscle by exploiting the Pale's perennial anti-Semitism. Significant pre-invasion collusion with various émigré groups succeeded in blaming Jewish provocateurs for Soviet occupation crimes. Another, tangible incentive was a share in the victims' belongings. The combined number of mercenaries in the Baltic and Ukrainian fronts was about 300,000.[123]

On July 10, half of the residents in the Polish village of Jedwabne murdered the other half in a night of sheer terror. Led by the mayor, the Catholic mob used rifles, bats, and knives to dispatch their 1,600 Jewish neighbors. The survivors were corralled in a barn and burned alive. Longerich indicts the German Security Police.[124] In his report of a similar rampage by Lithuanian partisans in Slutsk, Heinrich Carl, the Regional Commissioner, described it as being carried out with "what amounted to sadism"; he ended by imploring, "Please grant me only one wish: 'Protect me from this police battalion in [the] future."[125] An officer of the Polish underground wrote in 1942:

> The peasants…are hunting down the Jews in the countryside; they bring them to the towns or sometimes they kill them on the spot. Generally speaking, Jews are treated as if they were wild animals; the people here are driven into a kind of psychosis, and disinhibited by the German example, they forget that the Jews are human beings; they treat them like rabid dogs, rats, or other vermin, which have to be exterminated in any way possible."[126]

The Nazis called this a *Judenjagd* ("Jew hunt"). Ethnic Germans were also known to get a little "sideways" on occasion. Concerning an Aktion in southern Ukraine, Ernst Biberstein, former Chief of Einsatzkommando 6, related after the war: "We were actually frightened by the bloodthirstiness of these people."[127] A militia in Transnistria killed 28,000 Jews in the winter of 1941-42 alone.[128]

"WE SEE THINGS NO ONE HAS EVER SEEN BEFORE"

The mechanized mayhem continued unabated at a satanic pace. Nearly 1.5 million Jews were ultimately liquidated under the auspices of less than 3,000 Einsatzgruppen—an astounding average of 2,000 victims per day, seven days a week, for over a hundred weeks! (On a technical note, the four main Einsatzgruppen units were augmented by Himmler's Order Police, Security Police, and Waffen-SS.)

The modus operandi was routine: get drunk; enter targeted village behind advancing Wehrmacht units; round up all Jews; march into woods; confiscate belongings; make victims dig their own graves; rape younger women; shoot, bury, and go on. Goebbels wrote in his diary on Valentine's Day 1942, "The Führer once more expressed his determination to clean up the Jews in Europe pitilessly. There must be no squeamish sentimentality about it...We must hasten this process with cold ruthlessness."[129] *SS-Hauptscharführer* (Sergeant) Felix Landau wrote, "Here we see things no one has ever seen before...We stand and look on."[130] One witness recalled Jews in the Lithuanian village of Virbalis being "placed alive in anti-tank trenches about two kilometres long and killed by machine guns. Lime was sprayed upon them and a second row of Jews was made to lie down. They were similarly shot." [The procedure was repeated six times.] "Only the children were not shot. They were caught by the legs, their heads hit against stones and they were thereupon buried alive."[131] (Lithuania's Archbishop, Vincentas Brizgys, remained silent to avoid alienating Hitler.)[132] Another bloody scene was described by a German engineer:

> I saw one family of about six, all already stripped naked and waiting for the order to get down into the grave. Next to the father was a boy of ten or twelve years old. He placed a hand on the boy's head and pointed the other towards heaven and said something to the boy, who I could see was trying to keep back his tears. The man's wife was standing near an old woman with snow-white hair, either her mother or the mother of her husband, who held a baby in her arms, singing softly to it and stroking it.
>
> Then came the order, "Next ten!" and the family began moving round the mound of earth to climb into the grave...Then the next were called out to make themselves ready, that is, to take off their clothes. And then I heard shooting and believed that everything was

> over...I walked round the grave and saw a few people still moving. Not all the shots had killed. An S.S. man sat on the edge of the grave, with one leg crossed over the other...I called out, "Look, they're not all dead!" to which he replied, "Ach! Tonight the grave will be filled up with rubbish and it'll all be finished."[133]

Though veteran SS were willing to obey, they required artificial stimulants. Polish journalist Kazimierz Sakowicz noted in his diary on August 2, 1941: "Today about four thousand people were...shot by eighty executioners. All drunk."[134] (Sakowicz was later shot as well.) The daily encounters defied reality. Einsatzkommando 4a struck the Ukrainian ghetto in Zhitomir at 4 a.m., on September 19, 1941, killing the entire population of 3,145 Jews.[135] Another 10,000 Ukrainian Jews died in a cemetery in Stanislawow on October 12.[136] During a related event in Mostovoye, children were tossed alive onto funeral pyres. In a reprisal Aktion in Odessa on October 25, a warehouse packed with the living and the dying was "sent flying into the air" by explosives. In November, 11,000 Jews awaiting execution in the Romanian village of Bogdanovca were being quartered in pigpens (built for a maximum of 7,000 animals). On December 21, 5,000 of the ill and infirm were moved to stables, covered with straw, doused in gasoline, and then set ablaze. Meanwhile, in the Crimean capital of Simferopol, the Eleventh Army insisted that all shootings end by Christmas to enable the soldiers to celebrate Christ's birth without Jews or Gypsies present.[137]

In August 1942, a botched burial in Slonim, Belarus, spawned a 37-mile "quasi-zombie walk" (Matthew 27:53). "Because of the killers' drunkenness, many victims were left for a whole night, breathing and bleeding...some of these Jews dragged themselves, naked and covered with blood, as far as Baranowicze. When panic threatened to break out among the inhabitants, native auxiliaries were dispatched to round up and kill these Jews."[138] After another revenant episode in 1941, the White Russian Commissioner General, Wilhelm Kube, enjoined Reich Commissar Heinrich Lohse, "The burial of seriously wounded people who could work themselves out of their graves was such a disgusting business that it ought to be reported to Göring and Hitler."[139]

Some 12,000 Jews were shot in Stanislaw, Ukraine, on October 12, 1941, known as "Bloody Sunday." In a mammoth Aktion in Borisov on October 20, Stanislav Stankievich (a.k.a. "The Butcher of Borisov") killed 8,000 Jews in one day, perfecting what he called the "sardine method." After his victims were made to lie head-to-toe atop one another, they were shot through in pairs to save ammunition; the wounded were then covered with a thin layer of dirt and suffocated beneath another double layer of corpses. (The process went on all day: a layer of dirt; two layers of bodies; a layer of dirt.) Loftus and Aarons add, "After the war the worst part of the atrocities was discovered. The bodies of the smallest children had no wounds. Apparently, to save the price of a bullet, Stankievich buried the babies alive."[140]

On November 30 (another "Bloody Sunday"), 10,000 Jews were dispatched in Riga. The war's worst massacre was in late September 1941, when 34,000 Kiev Jews were killed over two days at Babi Yar ravine. With so many humans shot in rapid fire, a higher percentage than normal survived the initial blast. Thus, in one chilling report, a Hungarian soldier described a shallow grave of 7,000 Jews "heaving like a living sea."[141] Another recalled that "the earth was moving long after, because wounded and still alive Jews were still moving. One girl was crying: 'Mammy, why do they pour sand into my eyes?'"[142]

The most surreal accounts were preserved by the actual survivors. On August 14, 1942, SS units surrounded the ghetto of Zagrodski (near present-day Belarus). Among the five hundred families marked for execution were Rivka Yosselevska and her small daughter, wearing her Shabbat dress. The next evening trucks hauled the victims to a large ditch a few miles away. The following excerpts are from Rivka's testimony at the trial of Adolf Eichmann in Jerusalem, May 8, 1961:

> We saw naked people lined up...Some of the young people tried to run, but they were caught immediately, and...shot right there. It was difficult to hold on to the children...we were anxious to get it all over...we all trudged along to come nearer to the place...to the end of the torture of the children...we were already undressed...our father did not want to undress; he remained in his underwear...When it came to our turn, our father was beaten...they tore the clothing off the old man and he was shot...they took my mother...and shot her too...then there was my grandmother, my father's mother standing there; she was eighty years old and she had two children in her arms...And there was my father's sister...she was shot on the spot...my younger sister...went up to the Germans with one of her friends...she asked to be spared...He looked into her eyes and shot the two of them. They fell together in their embrace...Then my second sister was shot and then my turn came.

> We were already facing the grave. The German asked, 'Whom do you want me to shoot first?' I did not answer. I felt him take the child from my arms. The child cried out and was shot immediately...he aimed the revolver at me...and shot...I fell...into the pit amongst the bodies; but I felt nothing...I thought I was dead...Then I felt that I was choking; people falling over me. I tried to move and felt that I was alive and...could rise. I was strangling. I heard the shots and I was praying for another bullet to put an end to my suffering, but I continued to move about...I tried to save myself, to find some air...then I felt that I was climbing towards the top of the grave above the bodies. I rose, and I felt bodies pulling at me with their hands, biting at my legs, pulling me down, down. And yet with my last strength I came up on top of the grave...so many bodies were lying all over...not all of them dead, but in their last sufferings; naked; shot, but not dead. Children crying, 'Mother,' 'Father'...."[143]

To Rivka's surprise, the Germans had vanished. Though shot in the head, she managed to literally escape from the grave. "I was naked, covered with blood, dirty...with the excrement from other bodies which was poured on me...I was searching among the dead for my little girl, and I cried for her—Merkele was her name—Merkele!"[144] She then encountered two other woman survivors along with several children. Stumbling along, they heard others cry in panic, "Pull me out from amongst the corpses, I am alive, help!"[145]

The SS later returned to finalize the mass interment. Though all the children were shot, for some reason Rivka and the remaining women were ignored. The Nazis then left for good. Yet, for Rivka and her companions, survival became a fate worse than death: "We went on to the grave...envying those who were dead already and thinking what to do now...Blood was spurting from the grave in many places, like a well of water...I was digging with my fingernails, trying to join the dead...but the grave would not open...I cried out to my mother, to my father, 'Why did they not kill me?...I have no one to go to. I saw them all being killed. Why was I spared?"[146] After laying "stretched out on the grave, three days and three nights," Rivka was found and sheltered by a caring farmer. She was later reunited with Jews hiding in the forest, where she survived till Soviet forces arrived in summer 1944.[147]

To end this section with another illustration of the theme, "What's a Führer to do?" the SS viewed the inevitable percentage of Jews that eluded their grasp as just one more form of victory—vis-à-vis Russia's "gain." An operational report for September 22, 1941, stated: "Therein may be viewed an indirect success of the work of the Security Police, for the movement of hundreds of thousands of Jews free of charge—reportedly most of them go beyond the Ural—represents a notable contribution of the solution of the Jewish question *in Europe*."[148]

Wannsee Conference

One of the main topics of debate among Holocaust pundits involves a single German word—*Führerentscheidung* ("Führer decision"). While a glaring correlation between the first six letters with the last four speaks to Proverbs 10:7, *"the name of the wicked will rot,"* the concept applies to the ongoing efforts by scholars to fix the proximate date when Hitler *himself* "pulled the trigger" for the Final Solution.

Ironically—for being the most written about man in history—an unequivocal written order that would document Hitler's infamous legacy has *never* been found (and may well have *never* existed). It was, as Himmler told the SS in Posen in October 1943, "an unwritten, never-to-be-written page of our glory in history."[149] The enduring euphemism will also be seen to represent, more precisely, the final *version* of the Final Solution, at least four stages having occurred.

As hindsight is always 20/20, it is often hard to grasp a real-time radicalization of the fluid events that killed 6,000,000 men, women, and children in some 42 months. Hitler's Lebensraum program always consisted of three parts: 1) seize new land; 2) eject undesirables (Jews and Slavs); 3) repatriate ethnic Germans. From 1933 to 1939, the Führer made every effort to push the Jews out of Germany. Following Poland's dismemberment, Jews and Poles from the newly incorporated territory were sent eastward into the General Government, enabling displaced Germans to return home. The Jews were marked with yellow stars and confined to ghettos, their presence always viewed as a *temporary* measure, pending the next "territorial development."

The first option was the ill-fated Madagascar Plan. The next try began with Barbarossa. The prefatory executions of 1,400,000 Jews in freshly conquered lands gave Hitler two benefits: the assuaging of Bolshevik resistance and the commensurate expansion of Lebensraum. Yet, as late as the fall of 1941, the plan for the Final Solution of the Jewish question was *still* substantially different from its ultimate display.

The key to a proper understanding of German intentions at this time was Hitler's belief of an imminent Soviet collapse, followed by the end of the war itself. It was then that the Reich's *third* choice of a Final Solution would occur: the ultimate eastbound transfer of *all* European Jewry—*over the Urals*—to be slowly worked and/or starved to death under draconian conditions in postwar Siberian captivity.[150]

The policy was known as "extermination through labor." The Reich Ministry of Food planned to pillage enough provisions (mostly from the fertile "Black Earth Zone" in Central Russia) to starve 30 million people to death.[151] As the General Government's Jewish population continued to defy sustainable levels (removals from western and central Europe having begun that spring), Governor-General Hans Frank was assured that "relief" (his *own* eastbound transports) was just around the corner.[152] However, a serious incident occurred in October.

In a meeting with Alfred Rosenberg, Reich Minister for the Occupied Eastern Territories, Frank was told that at the time, there was no chance "for the implementation of resettlement plans of this kind"[153] (the obvious problem being war-related rail moratoriums). Another factor was the growing logjam of Reich Jews within the incorporated territory, primarily in Łódź. Longerich writes, "From that point onwards the government of the General Government began to think about a 'Final Solution' of the 'Jewish question' in their own territory."[154] Thus, that same month, construction began on Himmler's first *stationary* death camp in Bełżec. (Chelmno, the vanguard gas van facility in the incorporated territory, was also ramping up at this time.) The main criteria for staying in the ghetto was one's ability to exhibit (and sustain) a competitive edge in the workplace; an age restriction of 16-32 was frequently set as well. (The new "extermination through labor" policy gave the Nazis yet another pretext for killing inmates, those now expendable, being unfit for the "work program," etc.[155])

With the likelihood of gassings in the General Government viewed as a logistical matter (ghettos being emptied for new arrivals, from the Reich in particular), the "Hangman" and his henchmen continued to pursue the Final Solution for European Jewry in occupied Russian land. Accordingly, on November 29, Heydrich invited fifteen high-ranking party functionaries, state secretaries, and SS officers to an RSHA summit on December 9 at a posh villa on the shore of Berlin's Wannsee Lake. The proposed agenda would focus on appropriate Judenpolitik for the approaching final Aktion. (Off the record, the meeting would also serve as another "indirect" stratagem to expand the ring of "verifiable complicity" should anything go wrong in the future—like Nuremberg.[156]) However, two portentous events caused an abrupt six-week delay of the meeting: Marshal Zhukov's Moscow counter-offensive on December 6, sending the German 6th Army reeling from its first defeat, and Japan's assault on Pearl Harbor on December 7, triggering America's declaration of war four days later.

Adolf Hitler made a felicitous speech on December 12, referencing his "prophecy" an incredible fourth time. Goebbels noted the day after, "As regards the Jewish question, the Führer is resolved to make a clean sweep. He prophesied to the Jews that if they were to bring about another world war, they would bring about their own destruction as a result. This was not empty talk. The world war is here, the destruction of the Jews must be the necessary consequence."[157]

On January 20, the one-day conference was assembled by Reinhard Heydrich. As the sole extant copy of the minutes reveals, the historic conclave was a key segue to the Final Solution. Heydrich told his pals, "After appropriate prior approval by the Führer, emigration as a possible solution has been superseded by a policy of evacuating the Jews to the East." He then set the bar at 11 million deportees; Hitler's sweep would now encompass England and Ireland, as well as Jews from the neutral powers of Spain, Switzerland, Sweden, Portugal, and Turkey. Longerich cites the passage anticipating Jewry's grand finale:

> As part of the development of the Final Solution the Jews are now to be put to work in a suitable manner under the appropriate leadership. Organized into large work gangs and segregated according to sex…Jews fit for work will be led into these areas as road-builders, in the course of which, no doubt, a large number will be lost by natural wastage. The 'remainder who…inevitably survive' will, 'since they are the ones with the greatest powers of endurance', 'have to be dealt with accordingly' to prevent their becoming 'the germ cell of a new Jewish regeneration'. Initially the Jews were to be taken to 'transit-ghettos', from which they were to be 'transported further toward the East.'[158]

With Hitler increasingly peeved (especially after Stalin's reciprocal exile of the Volga Germans to Siberia), Heydrich continued "going through the motions." Only a week before Wannsee, the Commissars General in Brest-Litovsk, Zhitomir, Nikolayev, Dnepropetrovsk, and Kiev were told to organize ghettos so that "Jews from the Old Reich could be accommodated in the course of 1942."[159] However, a more "immediate" remedy was already being floated. Near the adjournment, General Government State Secretary Josef Bühler said that his regime would "welcome it if the Final Solution to this question could begin in the General Government, because…the problem of transportation does not play a decisive role here and because these measures will not be obstructed by issues involving labor deployment."[160]

Bühler's offer that the Final Solution could begin *in* the General Government is telling. In an earlier meeting on December 16, Frank told his staff what his superiors in Berlin had just informed him: "Why are people making such a fuss? We can't do anything with them…liquidate them yourselves!" Frank then declared: "We must annihilate the Jews wherever we find them…in order to maintain here the whole structure of the Reich…We can't shoot these 3.5 million Jews, we can't poison them, but we will be able to intervene in a way that will somehow lead to their successful extermination."[161] Whereas the word *Vernichtung* ("annihilation") originally meant destroying the Jews' disproportionate economic and political *power* in Europe, it now meant eliminating their existence as a people. The Catholic Goebbels wrote in his diary on March 27, 1942, "Thank God the war means that we now have a whole series of possibilities that were denied to us in peacetime. We must exploit these possibilities."[162] Longerich closes:

> [T]he Wannsee Conference took place at a watershed. The original plan, for which concrete steps had already been taken, for the comprehensive deportation and annihilation of the Jews in camps in the occupied Soviet territories ('road-building' as a synonym for forced labor in inadequate conditions) was still being adhered to. However, at the same time it had become clear that the precondition for this, an impending victory, could not be expected at least in the short term…During this critical period, the deportation to the occupied Soviet territories increasingly became a fiction, while mass murder in the General Government increasingly became reality.[163]

Upon America's entry into the conflict, National Socialist Germany found herself in a true world war. The "prophet" would now have to be proved. Besides, the "hostage deterrent" was no longer viable.[164] Thus, the fourth and *final* version of the Final Solution was initiated.

CHELMNO

On the Monday morning that President Roosevelt delivered his famous line declaring the previous day as "a date which will live in infamy," a far more sinister event was unfolding in the European theater. While December 7, 1941, began with Japanese Zeros delivering 450 bombs on Pearl Harbor, the day would end with German lorries delivering 700 Jews to an isolated site thirty miles from Łódź—Chelmno-on-Ner (Ner River). All were dead within 24 hours. Though the fatalities at Pearl were over triple this amount, the eventual death toll at Chelmno would far exceed this number. Hilberg gives a low estimate of "over 150,000"[165]; Gilbert suggests 360,000.[166] The largest group comprised nearly all of the last Jews in Łódź (Poland's second-largest city).

Unlike the initial mechanized shooting squads, Chelmno became the prototype of the stationary death camp (the first extermination center in history), using carbon monoxide as the instrument of choice. Oddly enough, Himmler's incentive for making the change was to find a more "humane" execution modus—for the *killers*, that is. Heinrich's wake-up call came just weeks into the action when one of his favorite officers, *SS Obergruppenführer* (General) Erick von dem Bach-Zelewski, told him, "Look at the eyes of the men of this Kommando, how deeply shaken they are. These men are finished for the rest of their lives. What kind of followers are we training here? Either neurotics or savages."[167] An August trip to Russia pushed Himmler over the edge. The *Reichsführer* was invited to witness the murder of 100 Jews in Minsk, his first such exposure. "Heini-Himmler" (as he was privately called by the SS, given his lack of combat experience—Heini" meaning "a little boy who's afraid of everything") was visibly shaken by the proceedings. Staring at the ground with each volley, he was upset that the two females in the group had not died immediately.

Despite the Führer's advice to "Grit your teeth and think revenge," Himmler concluded that shooting so many folks up close, particularly women and children, was too much of a psychological burden for his soldiers, especially as many were "family men," etc. On September 27, 1941, an SS officer wrote his wife: "I am in a very gloomy mood.

I must pull myself out of it. The sight of the dead (including women and children) is not very cheering."[168] In another letter, he assured his kiddos: "I have already told you about the shooting, that I could not say 'no' here...But you can trust your Daddy. He thinks about you all the time and is not shooting immoderately. So that's our life."[169]

In a bizarre effort to assuage the stress, Einsatzkommando 4a would "confine itself to the shooting of adults while commanding its Ukrainian helpers to shoot children."[170] Monsignor Szepticki, metropolitan of the Greek Catholic Church in Lvov, testified that he heard the confession of a distraught young man who had slain seventy-five Jews in one night.[171] Auschwitz Commandant Rudolf Höss wrote in his prison memoirs of "many suicides among the ranks of the SS Special Action Squads."[172] Even Bach-Zelewski wound up undergoing emergency stomach surgery from his constrained participation.[173]

Himmler's initial attempt to find a more sane way of killing Jews "fell short" of the desired end. In September 1941, twenty-five mental patients were moved from a local sanatorium in Minsk to a wooden bunker in the forest. As a medical team stood by, the site was dynamited.[174] With portions of victims hanging *from* the trees—as wild-eyed survivors tore *for* the trees—the "imbecilic" experiment was terminated. At another asylum in Mogilev, a second group of human guinea pigs was subjected to poison gas (directed by former T4 technicians under a follow-up program abbreviated 14f13).[175] The lethal fumes flowed into the sealed room via tubes connected to the exhaust pipe of a police truck parked outside. Since all were killed quite effortlessly, gas would now replace guns; T4 veteran Herbert Lange (assisted by Christian Wirth) became the logical choice to oversee the Chelmno camp.

Nearly 100 SS officials, gendarmes, and local Poles were engaged in the daily routine at Chelmno. (One of the more "renowned" staffers was *SS Oberwachtmeister* [Staff-Sergeant] Bruno *Israel*, a German Protestant "Christian" from Łódź.[176]) Under the guise of "resettlement in the East," Polish Jews would arrive by train at the small village of Powiercie. From here they were marched a mile through the woods to Zawadki, spending the night locked in a mill (sometimes a church). In the morning trucks took them to the hamlet of Chelmno where they entered a deserted, Neo-Gothic manorial estate (a.k.a. "the Castle").

An officer declared that they would have to shower and have their clothes disinfected prior to resuming their trek. The group undressed in a heated room, then proceeded down a long corridor with signs reading *Zum Bad* ("To the bath"). Reaching the end of the hall they exited the building and were shoved up a ramp into a large gray van, ostensibly for a quick commute to the bathhouse. However, when the twin hermetically sealed rear doors locked behind them, the ninety-plus riders, standing naked and shoulder to shoulder, were hauled to a trench in Rzuchowski Forest. They couldn't know that their designated driver for the morning "shower shuttle" was wearing the SS uniform of the *Totenkopfverbande* ("Death's-Head Units"), emblazoned with the identical emblem ascribed to by Yale University/Skull and Bones alumni, Presidents George H. W. Bush and George W. Bush.

When the lorry reached the ditch, the driver would activate the generator in the cab (sometimes doing so before leaving). This began the flow of carbon monoxide through a pair of tubes into the exhaust pipe under the carriage, discharging the fumes through a vent in the floor. Of course, the "brave" Aryan wasted no time bailing out for his *own* safety. It was then, according to the testimony of Szlamek Bajler, a *Juden Kommando* ("Jewish grave-digger") and one of few Chelmno escapees, that "frightful screaming, shouting and banging against the sides of the van could be heard."[177] A local Polish girl recalled: "[Y]ou had to put your hands to your ears, you couldn't stand it...End of the world, such were those cries."[178] If all went according to schedule, the group would die in about 15 minutes (on occasion, it took *hours*).[179]

Major Lange utilized three of Rauff's gassing vans, known as *sonderwagens* ("special cars"). Commenting on his exploratory usage of these vehicles in the earlier T4 campaign, Longerich writes, "Lange's unit therefore represented an important organizational link between the systematic mass murder of the disabled and handicapped and that of the Jews."[180] From October 1941 to July 1942, nearly 100,000 people in the Eastern territories perished in twenty of the rolling gas chambers. Residents of Chelmno (appropriately pronounced with a silent "C") called them "black hells."[181]

The overworked engines would often falter. Other problems bordered on the bizarre, like the time one driver got "embarrassingly lost" in a nearby city.[182] Another incident with an ironic twist involved a Pole who, while assisting in the loading process, was inadvertently locked in with the Jews and began to panic. The SS decided it was not prudent to reopen the door "just for him," etc.[183] The greatest glitch would result from putting too much "pedal to the metal"; Nazi doctor August

Becker wrote, "The application of gas is usually not undertaken correctly. In order to come to an end as fast as possible, the driver presses the accelerator to the fullest extent. Thus the persons executed die by suffocation and not by dosing off as planned."[184]

After shining a light through two peepholes, the driver would give the thumbs-up. Five minutes later, the doors would be opened by eight Juden Kommandos who removed the dead (at times, the dying) amidst a stifling effusion of noxious fumes. (It was not unusual for some Jew to go into shock upon finding his own wife or child.[185]) The amount of vomit, excrement, and facial distortion would reveal how "smoothly" things had run. The bodies were promptly rifled for valuables. Then, a second eight-man detail would meticulously arrange the corpses in the ditch to maximize space. However, according to Professor Konnilyn Feig, so many bodies were interred that "the ground over the graves began to ferment and heave, necessitating the destruction of the entire forest."[186] The SS later resorted to a complex system of funeral pyres.

"We Don't Want To Die!"

Of Chelmno's third-of-a-million victims, the most arresting scene was the September 1942 arrival of two special trains from Łódź. Nearly all of the 15,685 passengers were under age ten or over sixty-five. The SS had decreed that the weaker be expelled to house new and stronger bodies, capable of fostering the ghetto's unique status as a Wehrmacht production hub. The eviction charge fell upon the controversial Nazi-appointed head of the "Jewish Elders," Chaim Mordechai Rumkowski (a.k.a. "King of the Jews").[187] Resigned to his untenable role (similar to the religious leaders in Matthew 2:4), Chaim reasoned: "I have to perform this bloody operation myself; I simply must cut off the limbs in order to save the body. I have to take away children, because otherwise others will also be taken."[188] In his *outré* (and legendary) speech to the parents over their imminent parting, he implored:

> A severe blow has befallen the ghetto. They [the SS] are asking from it the best that we possess—[our] children and old people. I have not had the privilege of having a child of my own and therefore I devoted the best of my years to children. I lived and breathed together with the children. I never imagined that my own hands

> would have to deliver the sacrifice to the altar. In my old age, I must stretch out my hands and beg: "Brothers and sisters, give them to me! Fathers and mothers, give me your children."[189]

As the youngsters were loaded onto trucks, they cried—*"Mir viln nisht shtarbn!* ("We don't want to die!").[190] Upon their arrival at the Castle, as most were too small to climb into the gas vans alone, they were tossed in like so many ragdolls.[191] (Rumkowski and his own family would die at Auschwitz on August 28, 1944.)

About 1,000 (six to nine vanloads) were gassed on a "normal" day. To keep things interesting, others would make the one-way ditch trip as well; the gravediggers themselves were never quite "out of the woods," being quartered in the Castle cellar on a "nightly basis" only. The head guard was a sadist called "Big Whip." At quitting time he would pursue his favorite ritual—shooting eight of the sixteen Juden Kommandos in the head.[192] Survivors recalled inscriptions on the walls: "No one leaves this place alive"; "Whoever can, should save himself"; "When people are taken to work, they are being shot."[193] The historical graffiti was even short-lived; on April 7, 1943, Chelmno Castle was razed to hide Nazi crimes. Eichmann toured the site the previous autumn. Like Heini's revulsion at Minsk, the macho "desk murderer" shared the same during his pre-trial grilling in Jerusalem:

> I followed the van and then came the most horrifying sight I've ever seen...The van drove up alongside a long pit, the doors were opened and the bodies thrown out; the limbs were still supple, as if...still alive. They were thrown into the pit. I saw a civilian pulling out teeth...then I took off. I rushed to my car and departed and said no more. I was through. I had had it. A white-coated doctor said that I ought to look through the peephole and see what went on inside the vans. I refused. I couldn't speak. I had to get away. Frightful, I tell you. An inferno. Can't do it. I can't do it.[194]

THE STONES CRY OUT

Jesus rebukes the Pharisees in Luke 19:40, *"I tell you if these should hold their peace, the* STONES *would immediately cry out."* While the SS were able to destroy Chelmno, the indirect (and totally unforeseen) proof of their deeds would later bear witness in a most bizarre setting.

In 1939, the Jewish population of Łódź was 233,000, second only to Warsaw. As expected, the local Jewish cemetery records reflect the longstanding Jewish presence. From its opening in 1892 to the eve of WW II, 180,000 gravesites were made, on which were affixed 65,000 tombstones, and other markers.[195] Viewed as Europe's largest Jewish burial ground, the 105-acre tract represents a symbolic, macabre lapidarium that validates the Hitlerian genocide in various particulars.

The site underwent a 25% expansion with the secret burial of the 43,411 Jews who died in the Łódź ghetto. (Some were executed *in* the cemetery.) Miroslaw Wojalski writes, "The ghetto area, now called the 'Ghetto Field' remains a witness to the holocaust—the Nazi policy of extermination of the Jewish nation."[196] A total of 877 Jews were still alive at the city's liberation on January 19, 1945, only because the Red Army arrived earlier than expected. Five pre-dug pits preserved along the eastern wall bear solemn witness to their providential reprieve.

Today, less than 200 Jews live in Łódź. Thus, the record-sized graveyard continues to morph into an abysmal, unkempt jungle of indescribable atrophy—a final, silent testimony to the historical reality and ongoing effect of the Shoah in Łódź. (Similar conditions prevail in Warsaw and other prewar Jewish population centers in Poland.)

AKTION REINHARD

Inaugurated on the eve of Wannsee, Chelmno was the opening salvo of *Aktion Reinhard*, the codename for Hitler's liquidation of the Jews in the General Government (primarily at Bełżec, Treblinka, and Sobibór). As the appellation implies, the special operation was named after Reinhard Heydrich. However, the event that occasioned the kudos would be less than desirable from the honoree's perspective.

On September 29, 1941, the RSHA chief was made Deputy Reich Protector of Bohemia and Moravia (the part of Czechoslovakia taken into the Reich on March 15, 1939). With Himmler stating that he now expected his T-4 veterans to employ "superhuman-inhuman" effort, Reinhard would prove especially proficient in "protecting" his realm from Jews.[197] Between March 26 and April 7, 1942, four transports of girls and young women (about 3,800) were dispatched to Auschwitz-Birkenau (some of the earliest arrivals at the new camp). By late June, the number of deported Slovakian Jews would reach 50,000.[198]

However, at the *height* of his momentum (eight meetings with Himmler, in seven days, at three sites), the Hangman got a little "hung up" himself while exiting Prague on May 27 to confer with Hitler in Berlin. As depicted in the 2016 film, *Anthropoid* (the operation's name), as his Mercedes 320 Convertible B was negotiating a curve, a British-trained Slovak unit fired an anti-armor hand grenade, wounding Heydrich and his driver. After days of lingering with a damaged diaphragm, spleen, and lung, the 6'4'' Aryan died on June 4 from septicemia (a bacterial blood infection, caused by strands of horsehair from the upholstery embedded by the blast).

Two days before entering eternity—with "Loyal Heinrich" by his side—the Catholic psychopath turned philosophical, citing a line from one of his father's operas entitled, *Amen:* "The world is just a barrel-organ which the Lord God turns himself. We all have to dance to the tune which is already on the drum."[199] It would appear that Hedyrich's "sentimental doggerel" (as biographer Callum MacDonald called it), "reflect[ing] a staggering evasion of personal responsibility [by its] appeal to fate and predestination,"[200] would indict God Himself for those Russian mental patients being blown to Kingdom come.

Following an elaborate funeral in Prague, a second service was held in the Reich Chancellery on June 9 with Himmler giving the eulogy. While a "mournful" Führer laid Heydrich's decorations on his casket pillow, privately he "extolled" him as an *idiot*, having remarked on the day of his death: "Since it is the opportunity which makes not only the thief but also the assassin, such heroic gestures as driving in an open, unarmored vehicle or walking about the streets unguarded are just d----d stupidity, which serves the country not one whit. That a man as irreplaceable as Heydrich should expose himself to unnecessary danger, I can only condemn as stupid and idiotic." [201]

To honor his fallen protégé, Himmler said in his eulogy: "Within a year we will definitely have completed the mass migration of the Jews; then no more will migrate."[202] Longerich notes, "[I]n the second half of April or early May…the Nazi regime definitively abandoned the idea of a 'reservation' in the eastern area of the General Government or the occupied Eastern territories which had increasingly become a fiction given the mass murder that was already under way."[203]

By the end of 1942, Aktion Reinhard was well on *track*—some 1,274,166 General Government Jews being railroaded through the Reich's new string of death camps (leaving only 298,000 to go.)[204] In the wake of this momentous progress, the *greater* Aktion would then produce a "clean sweep" of Continental Jewry *in situ* (i.e., no longer just in Germany, Poland, and Russia, but in every other domain as well, conquered and allied governments alike). And with the main ghettos of the Polish interior dissolving, the Jews from Central and Western Europe would henceforth move directly to the camps.

WHAT WAS KNOWN AND WHEN

Arthur Morse writes, "'We really didn't know what the Nazis were doing at the time' is a familiar refrain in contemporary American discussions of the murder of six million Jews and of the specific events which preceded their final journey to the gas chambers."[205]

On June 22, 1944, Walter Garrett of the British news agency, *Exchange Telegraph*, delivered a firsthand report of the atrocities at Auschwitz to no less of a ranking official than Allan Dulles, director of the US Office of Strategic Affairs in Geneva. The highly credible dossier was co-authored by escapees Rudolf Vrba and Alfréd Wetzler. Breakouts from Auschwitz were rare, the corpse of a captured inmate being propped up on a chair with a sign reading: "I am here again!"[206] The "Great White Case Officer" read the cable in his presence. "He was profoundly shocked," Garrett recalled. "He was as disconcerted as I was and said: 'One has to do something immediately.'"[207] (The news was forwarded to the State Department the following day.)

In reality, by mid-1944, the Vrba-Wetzler report was already old news. Three months earlier, the Polish General Staff Headquarters in London gave the OSS an equally precise, two-page report compiled by an anonymous Polish source.[208] (From 1943-44, female inmates in Ravensbrueck sent twenty-seven encrypted letters, *written in urine*, exposing SS medical experiments; due to acid reaction with the paper, the urine became invisible, requiring the recipients to heat up the letters.)[209] Earlier yet, on January 19, 1942, while en route to his grave-digging assignment at Chelmno, Szlamek Bajler escaped out a bus window, reaching Polish officials in Warsaw. Under the pseudo-name Yakov Grojanowski, Bajler gave a detailed paper on the gassings. Excerpts from the "Grojanowski Report" appeared in the June 1, 1942, edition of *Liberty Barricade* (a bi-weekly underground periodical). Thus, Dulles and his hacks were well aware of "Big Whip and company"—two full years *before* Garrett's "shocking" exposé.

Within four months of the Einsatzgruppen offensive, the *Jewish Telegraphic Agency* cited eyewitnesses from the Ukrainian city of Kamenets-Podolsk that on August 27-28, 1941, "between 7,500 and 15,000 Jews had been killed and their corpses were floating down the Dniestr river." Historian Randolph Braham dubbed it: "The first five figure massacre of the Nazis' Final Solution."[210] The October *Jewish Chronicle* stated that thousands died in the Ukraine. The next month it confirmed that 33% of the Jewish population in Bessarabia was gone. In December, a report by the Board of Deputies of British Jews and the Anglo-Jewish Association detailed the Babi Yar carnage.[211]

The Gentile press also went on record with the "shocking" news (albeit via spotty coverage, given the implications regarding human nature). Both the *New York Post* and the *New York Times* recounted the Kamenets-Podolsk tragedy on October 23 and 26, respectively. In a prescient editorial on December 5, the *New York Herald Tribune* wrote: "[T]he sum of it all indicates that the fate reserved for the Jews by the Nazis is worse than a status of serfdom—it is nothing less than systematic extermination." Thomas Mann, a German exile novelist, detailed the atrocities via a series of BBC programs in December 1941 and January 1942.[212] On June 2, 1942, another BBC broadcast aired a Polish report that began: "From the day that the Russo-German war broke out, the Germans embarked on the physical extermination of the Jewish population on Polish soil, using Ukrainian and Lithuanian Fascists for this job." An estimate of 700,000 victims was included.[213]

The London *Daily Telegraph* made a further innovative distinction between *persecution* and *extirpation* on June 25 and 30. The first story began, "More than 700,000 Polish Jews have been slaughtered by the Germans in the greatest massacres in the world's history," giving "the most gruesome details of mass killings even to the use of poison gas." The sequel headline stated: "More than 1,000,000 Jews killed in Europe." The paper then made the bold claim (as Dulles would have read) that Hitler's goal was "To wipe the race from the European continent." The *New York Times* reprinted the material on June 30 and July 2.[214] On August 10, 1942, *Newsweek* informed its readers that trainloads of Warsaw Jews were vanishing into a "black Limbo."[215] By January 1943, the *New York Times* (and other major American papers) would run arresting headlines like: "Two-thirds of Jews held in Poland slain; only 1,250,000 said to survive of 3,500,000 once there."[216]

Even the Reich press would give occasional "food for thought." As late as May 20, 1942, the *Strassburger Nueste Nachrichten* cited Nazi Robert Ley: "We have to fight the Jews to the very last consequence. It is not enough to isolate the Jewish enemy of mankind; the Jew must be destroyed." On June 14, Goebbels was quoted in his own weekly, *Das Reich*: "The Jews will pay with the extermination of their race in Europe and perhaps beyond."[217] But then, Dulles was never beholden to any media outlet for *his* information, being privy to the vast pool of diplomatic and intel communiqués. As noted earlier, on November 19, 1941, David Kelly informed Frank Roberts in the Foreign Office: "I have just heard...that 1½ million Jews...living in Eastern Poland have simply disappeared altogether; nobody knows how and where."[218]

While Gerhard Kretschmar was the Führer's spearhead, the *Allies'* earliest diplomatic corroboration of a plan to kill all European Jews came from a young lawyer—Gerhart Riegner (World Jewish Congress agent in Geneva). Dr. Riegner, a Berlin native, learned the sober news on August 1, 1942, during a secret rendezvous in Lausanne with an anonymous Reich industrialist (later identified as Eduard Schulte.)[219] As the owner of a firm employing ranking Nazis, Schulte had regular Chancellery access. It was there that he first heard the order discussed, whereupon he resolved to intervene by using Riegner as his conduit to the free world. Thus, it would appear that at the 11th hour, providence had entrusted the thirty-year-old Zionist with a preview of the greatest mass murder in history. On August 8, the following text was presented at the American Consulate in Bern for immediate transmission to WJC co-founder and President Rabbi Stephen Wise in New York:

> Received alarming report that in Führer's Headquarters plan discussed and under consideration all Jews in countries occupied or controlled Germany number 3-½ to 4 millions should after deportation and concentration in East at one blow be exterminated to resolve once for all Jewish question in Europe *Stop* Action reported planned for autumn Methods under discussion including prussic acid *Stop* We transmit information with all necessary reservation as exactitude cannot be confirmed *Stop* Informant stated to have close connections with highest German authorities and his reports generally speaking reliable *Stop* Riegner.

Though exhibiting some inaccuracies (the plan no longer "under consideration," nor mandating all Jews be killed "at one blow"), the cable did represent the Reich's first avowal that the traditional pogrom would be eclipsed by Continental genocide. To inform his Whitehall contacts (particularly MP Sydney Silverman), Riegner copied in the British consulate with the added directive, "Inform and consult New York."[220] This proved fortunate, as Washington nixed the news, given the "fantastic nature of the allegations."[221] Leland Harrison, US Ambassador to Switzerland, dismissed it as "a wild rumor inspired by Jewish fears."[222] Dr. Wise heard the report on August 28 from the WJC's London branch. When he appealed to Undersecretary of State Sumner Welles, the rabbi was told to "cool his jets," pending official confirmation, etc. With five death camps up and running, the amount of subsequent attestation was exceeded only by the degree of further obfuscation and obstruction. By November, the enveloping Shoah was so out there that even the "Holy See" confessed: "The mass execution of Jews continues...tens of thousands...killed by poison gas in chambers...prepared for that purpose...Reports...Germans are making use of their corpses in plants manufacturing chemical products."[223]

PRESSURE MOUNTS

The rest of 1942 witnessed a series of protests in America and Britain over what modern spinmeisters now insist was an unknown tragedy at the time. The WJC held a press conference in London on June 29, stating that the Nazis had made Eastern Europe a "vast slaughter house for Jews."[224] On July 21, 20,000 people filled Madison Square Garden to condemn the "unknown tragedy" (thousands more keeping vigil outside). The speakers included Rabbi Wise, Governor Herbert Lehman, Mayor Fiorello La Guardia, and AFL President William Green. President Roosevelt sent his pledge that the American people "will hold the perpetrators of these crimes to strict accountability in a day of reckoning which will surely come." A similar cable from Churchill read, "The Jews were Hitler's first victims." Two days later, a moment of prayer was observed in the House of Representatives.[225]

By August, over two hundred Anglo groups were pressing HMG to do *something* on the Jews' behalf.[226] On October 7, the House of Lords announced the formation of a UN commission to explore war crimes.

Ironically (yet predictably), Lord Chancellor Simon made just a glancing reference to the persecution of *Jews*.[227] Not only was England hesitant to imply that Jews impacted official policy, she was also paranoid at drawing attention to her own reticence to avert the crisis vis-à-vis the 1939 White Paper. British Jewry recoiled in the public arena. Meanwhile, the US State Department received an affidavit from Dr. Paul Guggenheim, noted attorney and professor at the Graduate Institute of International Studies in Geneva, confirming Riegner's assertions. His five-point analysis began: "There exists an order of Hitler demanding the extermination (*Ausrottung*) of all Jews in Germany and in the occupied countries up to December 31, 1942."[228] Wise was summoned to Washington on November 24 where Welles showed him the affidavit and said: "I regret to tell you, Dr. Wise, that these confirm and justify your deepest fears." He then added grimly, "There is no exaggeration. These documents are evidently correct."[229]

A day of mourning was held by World Jewry on December 2, 1942. Services, radio programs, and a ten-minute work halt occurred in New York City. Press coverage was broad and positive, the *New York Times* calling the Nazis "homicidal maniacs." In the more tenuous European climate, the event had an added twist of moroseness similar to a scene from the American Civil War. During the Federal assault at Cold Harbor, Virginia, 7,000 men were killed or wounded in one eight-minute period. Prior to the charge, soldiers sewed name tags inside their coats; one fatalistic youth made an advance diary entry: "June 3. Cold Harbor. I was killed."[230] Morse says, "One million Jews, doomed to die at Auschwitz from the effects of prussic acid, were among those who observed the day of mourning on December 2, 1942."[231]

Within days, Wise led a delegation to the Oval Office. Roosevelt was handed a twenty-page synopsis of the Final Solution entitled *Blue Print for Extermination*. The cover letter warned that "unless action is taken immediately, the Jews of Hitler Europe are doomed."[232] FDR forfeited any future claims of "plausible deniability" by replying: "The government of the United States is very well acquainted with most of the facts you are now bringing to our attention. Unfortunately we have received confirmation from many sources. Representatives of the United States government in Switzerland and other neutral countries have given us proof that confirms the horrors discussed by you."[233]

The Allies finally relented, issuing their first joint statement on December 17, acknowledging Nazi war crimes *specifically* aimed at Jews. The declaration (citing eleven nations) was read in the House of Commons by Anthony Eden. It began: "The German authorities...are now carrying into effect Hitler's oft-repeated intention to exterminate the Jewish people in Europe."[234] The shocking disclosure continued: "From all the occupied countries Jews are being transported in conditions of appalling horror and brutality to Eastern Europe. In Poland...the principal Nazi slaughterhouse, the ghettos established by the German invader are being systematically emptied of all Jews except a few highly skilled workers required for war industries. None of those taken away are ever heard of again."[235] After denouncing "this bestial policy of cold-blooded extermination," Eden ensured that "those responsible for these crimes shall not escape retribution."[236] James de Rothschild then arose with immense dignity and spoke for five minutes, tears flowing from his eyes. A Gentile member from London's East End was so moved that he enquired if the body might rise to express its collective empathy with the Jewish people. Sir Henry Channon commented in his diary that "the House as a whole rose and stood for a few frozen seconds. It was a fine moment, and my back tingled."[237] Eden noted in his own journal: "It had a far greater dramatic effect than I had expected...Lloyd George said to me later: 'I cannot recall a scene like that in all my years in Parliament.'"[238]

BERMUDA CONFERENCE

In the wake of the Allies' formal censure of the Shoah—a quasi admission that it not only existed, but that it had done so for some time—both the White House and Whitehall were flooded with letters and petitions demanding a humanitarian intervention. Roosevelt consequently announced that an emergency Anglo-American Refugee Conference would be held in Hamilton, Bermuda, April 19-29, 1943.

While many pro-Jewish Americans welcomed the news, a cynical minority—jaded by Évian—could only envision *more* "fun in the sun." They would not be disappointed, the *London Observer* reporting: "Here are the leisurely beach hotels of the Atlantic luxury island, where well-dressed gentlemen assemble to assure each other in the best Geneva fashion that really nothing much can be done."[239] Like the omen that

"Évian" spelled backwards was "naive," Wasserstein notes, "[T]he British and American delegates gathered on the island of Bermuda in the 'Horizons Hotel': the name, however, was soon belied in the sessions of the conference, as the prospect of havens for large numbers of refugees receded from sight."[240] The most telling sign was the "Bermuda *Triangular*" coincidence that the ten-day meeting convened amidst Easter, Passover, *and* Adolf Hitler's birthday.

Mirroring Évian, American leadership at Bermuda was a joke. The first three men offered the "honor" instinctively declined (Myron Taylor, Supreme Court Justice Owen Roberts, and Charles Seymour, president of Yale University). Only a week before, Princeton President Harold W. Dodds agreed to serve as chairman. Wasserstein notes: "Dr. Dodds, the chief US delegate, was said to have 'cheerfully admitted that he had had such little warning of his appointment that he knew nothing about refugees until after he had arrived."[241] Of course, ten days at any good "leisurely beach hotel" would be *plenty* of time to bone up on such a "light" subject; besides, it wasn't as if the issue was serious or anything—just the most heinous act of genocide in history!

Though dupes like Dodds were clueless, the powers that be (State Department and Foreign Office) knew *exactly* what was happening. With only Yanks and Brits calling the shots (contrary to Évian), the resultant skullduggery was appalling. Dr. Wyman states, "On British insistence…Britain's Palestine policy would not be discussed at the conference."[242] Also unlike Évian, only five journalists were approved, having limited access to the mostly private talks. On a "positive" note, in his opening remarks Dodds assured all: "The problem is too great for solution by the two governments here represented."[243]

The irony of ironies at Bermuda was that the subject everyone *assumed* to be paramount—rescuing Jews from Hitler—*somehow* fell through the cracks. The three main objectives were: 1) Outline steps to encourage neutral countries to absorb more escaped refugees; 2) Seek temporary shelter in, and transportation to, UN territories in Europe and Africa; and 3) Convene an early meeting of the Intergovernmental Committee on Refugees (ICR) to implement the resolutions reached at Bermuda.[244] The insidious nuance was the generic rescue of "refugees" *per se*—as opposed to *Jewish* refugees in *particular*.

While the Foreign Office cautioned that the crisis could not be handled as "a wholly Jewish problem,"[245] Washington piously agreed, stating that the "refugee problem should not be…confined to persons of any particular race or faith."[246] With Palestine off the table, a dozen remote islands were proffered as sanctuaries for the "non-sectarian fugitives," British Guiana and Mindanao being among them. And to further ensure that absolutely *nothing* was done, the very Semitic race that bequeathed the inspired Decalogue upon Western civilization would now be done in by another slate of "Ten Commandments" inspired by the satanic State Department. Morse enumerates:

> The Americans were instructed *not* to limit the discussion to Jewish refugees; *not* to raise questions of religious faith or race in appealing for public support or promising U.S. funds; *not* to make commitments regarding shipping space for refugees; *not* to expect naval escorts or safe-conducts for refugees; *not* to delay the wartime shipping program by suggesting that homeward-bound, empty transports pick up refugees en route; *not* to bring refugees across the ocean if any space for their settlement was available in Europe; *not* to pledge funds, since this was the prerogative of Congress and the President; *not* to expect any changes in the U.S. immigration laws; *not* to ignore the needs either of the war effort or of the American civilian population for food and money; and *not* to establish new agencies for the relief of refugees.[247]

The delegation from the land of the A.V. 1611 followed by adding three *more* "nots," for a total of "*Thirteen* Commandments" (the Bible's numeric for sin and rebellion): "The British would *not* consider a direct appeal to the Germans, would *not* exchange prisoners for refugees *or* lift the blockade of Europe for the shipment of supplies."[248] The opening British proviso also became the first of seven recommendations issued at the end of the meeting, specifically "that no approach be made to Hitler for the release of potential refugees."[249] The explanation behind this clear Anglo stipulation constitutes one of the most stunning revelations of this book. The main reason why HMG would not even *consider* direct talks with Hitler over the release of refugees was simple—he would probably approve!

THE "TRANSFER OF ODIUM"

The paper trail for this disturbing accusation is both extensive and incriminating. On January 20, 1943, the Colonial Office notified the State Department about "certain complicating factors" concerning the escalating refugee crisis: "There is a possibility that the Germans or their satellites may change over from the policy of extermination to one of extrusion, and aim as they did before the war at embarrassing other countries by flooding them with alien immigrants."[250]

In a meeting on March 27, 1943, between Roosevelt, Secretary of State Cordell Hull, Under Secretary Welles, and Anthony Eden, Britain's Secretary of State for Foreign Affairs, Eden advised his American colleagues to "move very cautiously about offering to take all Jews out of a country."[251] He then warned, most candidly: "Hitler might well take us up on any such offer, and there simply are not enough ships and means of transportation in the world to handle them."[252] Ian Henderson of the Foreign Office echoed a similar audacious strain at Bermuda: "We have already opposed the idea of a general appeal to the German Government suggesting that they should unload all Jews under their control on to the Allies. German acceptance would raise insuperable difficulties"[253] Five days later, Britain's chief negotiator, Richard Law, said that "if Hitler accepted a proposal to release millions of unwanted persons, we might find ourselves in a very difficult position…he might say, 'Alright, take a million or two million.' Then because of the shipping problem, we should be made to look exceedingly foolish."[254] (Law obviously "forgot" that Hitler's offer included carriage—luxury ships, in fact.)

Many later comments also concur. In October 1943, a State Department official reiterated, "There are grave objections to a direct approach to the German Government to request the release to us of these people…The net result would be the transfer of odium from the German to Allied Governments."[255] A. G. Randall of the Foreign Office Refugee Department warned on Christmas Eve: "Once we open the door to adult male Jews to be taken out of enemy territory, a quite unmanageable flood may result. (Hitler may facilitate it!)"[256] Wasserstein notes that the "flood threat" was at 10%: "By December 1943 British Intel reports indicated that 90% of Poland's 3,300,000 Jews were dead."[257] The minutes of a May 31, 1944, meeting of the Cabinet

Committee on Refugees state: "There seemed to be some danger that an indication that we might negotiate through a Protecting Power with the German Government might be followed up, and lead to an offer to unload an even greater number of Jews on our hands."[258]

After ten days of "deliberations" at Bermuda, the esteemed body rendered *one* fiat for the entire crisis: 21,000 fugitives in *Spain*, 4,000-5,000 being Jews from Central Europe, would be relocated to North Africa.[259] Thus, while Birkenau was being fitted with forty-six cutting-edge furnace muffles, placing its overall cremation capacity at 4,756 bodies per day, the sole Anglo-American action to ameliorate the Final Solution was to shift 5,000 *non-threatened* Jews from neutral Spain to a pair of small refugee camps in Moslem Morocco![260] Still, Eden told the Cabinet that the conference was a "marked success."[261] However, in their private report to the Foreign Office, the delegates themselves acknowledged, "[S]o far as immediate relief to refugees is concerned, the conference was able to achieve very little."[262] Myron Taylor remarked: "The Bermuda Conference was wholly ineffective, as I view it, and we knew it would be."[263] Welles summed up the ICR accordingly: "The final results amounted to little more than zero."[264]

In retrospect, Law's fear that Britain might find herself "in a very difficult position" and thus made to look "exceedingly foolish" was initiated in 1938 when Nazi Propaganda Minister Goebbels issued his brazen calculated taunt to the world's freedom loving democracies: "If there is any country that believes it has not enough Jews, I shall gladly turn over to it all our Jews." Morse adds, "There were no takers."[265] Thus, while the Allies were able to avoid a "transfer of odium" in the short run, they would bear their own yellow star of ignominy through the ages (the indelible *stain* of Eden's "*marked* success"). When Law was asked in 1965 to share his Bermuda memories, he said: "It was a conflict of self-justification, a façade for inaction. We said the results of the conference were confidential, but in fact there were no results that I can recall."[266] (Though unnoticed at the time, the A.V. 1611 had *already* determined "His Lordship's" inglorious legacy, Job 3:25 stating that *"the thing which I greatly* FEARED *is come upon me."*)

The delegates offered varied excuses for their dismal results. Some warned that Axis agents would exploit any expansion of immigration by infiltrating the new arrivals. Others argued that diverting military resources, particularly shipping, could undermine the war effort. It was even hinted that Hitler might retaliate with more killings. The shipping argument was especially absurd, Wyman asking: "Even if one accepts Eden's contention that transportation was not available, can anyone doubt that Jews would have *walked*, if necessary, across the Balkans and out through Turkey?"[267] He then confirms: "In reality, ample shipping existed. Neutral vessels crossed the Atlantic throughout the war…American troopships, lend-lease and other cargo vessels could also have carried thousands…clearing neutral European countries of fugitives and opening…a continuing exodus from Axis territory."[268]

Citing the *Norwegian Journal of Commerce and Shipping*, Morse adds that enough vessels existed to carry at least 50,000 Jews a month from the Balkans to Palestine or other Mediterranean ports. He then provides the politically incorrect postscript: "A private study in Britain… included a reference to the fact that the Allies always managed to find shipping to transport thousands of Moslems on their annual pilgrimage to Jidda, while simultaneously denying the availability of ships for Jews in flight."[269] Wyman concurs: "The real problem as far as Eden and the British were concerned was not ships. It was the immense pressure that the release of thousands of Jews from Europe would place on the British policy of placating the Arabs by strictly limiting Jewish immigration into Palestine."[270]

The seemingly feckless revival of the ICR was actually a crafty scam to deflect further inquiries about Jews. Wyman writes, "[T]he ICR took on the appearance of a capable international organization, the logical body to assume responsibility for the refugee problem. The State Department then used it as a byway to which it could divert rescue proposals with full confidence that little or nothing would come of them."[271] Appeals for Jews would now get the following pat reply:

> I assure you that the plight of the unfortunate victims of Axis tyranny is a matter which has been, and is, receiving the careful and sympathetic attention of this Government…the Conference at Bermuda has examined in detail every possibility for the relief and sufferings of the persecuted people of occupied Europe. Steps are now being taken to put into effect the recommendations made by the Conference.[272]

Rabbi Israel Goldstein remarked acerbically: "The job of the Bermuda Conference apparently was not to rescue victims of Nazi terror, but to rescue our State Department and Foreign Office."[273] The *Jewish*

Chronicle concluded: "And so the greatest tragedy in modern history must go on…the ghost of Évian walks abroad."[274]

The reader will note that the Bermuda Conference constitutes the third and most egregious Anglo-American betrayal of the Jewish people. First, Wall Street created Hitler and his Wehrmacht. Then, the dual effect of Évian and the White Paper of 1939 blocked all routes of escape for Europe's Jews on the eve of WWII. However, it was the "well-dressed gentlemen" on that "Atlantic luxury island" who gave the Führer his greatest birthday present—doing *nothing* while having *incontrovertible* proof that the Shoah was fully underway! Ironically, Bermuda also served as the headquarters for Allied censorship, one of the main outlets for gaining the latest news of Hitler's atrocities.[275]

WARSAW GHETTO UPRISING

The timing of Bermuda would coincide with yet another significant milestone—the April 19 launching of the Warsaw Ghetto Uprising, the largest revolt of the Holocaust (not to be confused with the Warsaw Uprising of the Polish Resistance Home Army, August-October 1944).

The Warsaw Ghetto was established on October 16, 1940, by the aforementioned Catholic German Governor-General of the Polish General Governorate, Hans Michael Frank (a.k.a. "King Frank"). In accord with Heydrich's order, Warsaw's entire Jewish population of 350,000 was relocated to a 1.3 sq. mile slum. Of the city's 1,800 streets, 73 were allotted to the ghetto. Thus, 30% of Warsaw's 1.3 million residents would now have to "live" in 2.4% of its area.[276] An eyewitness wrote: "Try to picture one-third of a large city's population moving through the streets in an endless stream, pushing, wheeling, dragging all their belongings from every part of the city to one small section, crowding one another more and more as they converged…appalling chaos…the tremendous hubbub of half a million uprooted people."[277]

Furthermore, given minimal preparation time (a ploy by their new taskmasters) and having little or no storage options, the Jews were forced to leave most of their belongings. These items, along with abandoned properties and businesses, were promptly expropriated. Over 4,000 houses on both sides of the ghetto walls were confiscated while 112,000 commercial entities were reduced to 3,000.[278]

The ghetto system constituted the third phase of Hitler's fourfold answer to the "Jewish question." When *degradation* failed to attain *deportation* ("no takers," etc.), *detention* in the ghettos facilitated *destruction* in the camps. It also represented the third stage of Eichmann's *modus operandi* for reaching his Führer's ultimate goal: *definition* (resolving who is a Jew); *expropriation* (of Jewish assets); then *concentration* (in ghettos). The Polish capital naturally had the nation's largest ghetto (the greatest in all of Nazi-occupied Europe as well), expanding with new arrivals to nearly 500,000 at its peak.

Following a month of rising bedlam and fear, the ghetto was finally sealed on November 16. The newly erected walls surrounding the urban prison stretched for eleven miles, standing ten to twenty feet high, topped with glass and barbed wire. Even here, Jews had to wear their stars and adhere to the nightly curfew (7 p.m.-7 a.m.). Hilberg writes, "The ghetto was a captive city-state in which territorial confinement was combined with absolute subjugation to German authority."[279] A letter from the Jewish Labor Bund described the site as "one big concentration camp" where Jews were sequestered from the world.[280] However, as depicted by a member of the Swiss medical mission—with a mortality rate *forty* times higher than the rest of the city—that original assessment would morph into "one big *cemetery*."[281] Over 100,000 Jews would die from starvation, disease, and random killings.

The key to German control of all ghettos was utilizing the historic *Judenrat* ("Jewish Councils," ranging from twelve to twenty-four ruling elders). Prior to the war, the main responsibilities incumbent upon Jewish leaders concerned synagogues, orphanages, religious schools, hospitals, and cemeteries. Under the occupation, Judenrats functioned as the central liaison organ between Nazis and Jews. Empowered by a Jewish police force, the Council enacted numerous German directives; the most odious involved informing, seizures, collection of taxes and fines, confiscation of valuables, food distribution (beset by a bureaucratic pecking order), and selections for labor and/or deportations. While desirous to alleviate suffering when possible, the Judenrat rarely failed to enact the most callous SS demands. Hilberg notes, "Thus the Jewish leadership both saved and destroyed its people, saving some Jews and destroying others, saving the Jews at one moment and destroying them at the next."[282] (Though unforeseen at the time, these Jewish auxiliaries comprised the vanguard of the coming *Sonderkommandos*.)

For the first eighteen months, ghetto occupants were exploited through a variety of debilitating slave labor venues. As early as February 1940, Governor Frank praised the Jews' work ethic, stating in a press interview: "They work very well, yes, they are even eager about it."[283] The following September he told a conference of his main division chiefs: "We can teach the Poles neither the energy nor the ability to take the place of the Jews. That is why we are forced to permit these skilled Jewish laborers to continue in their work."[284] Even children grasped the nexus between labor and life. When an SS officer in the Polish town of Sandomierz seized a three-year-old girl for deportation, the child begged for mercy, displaying her hands and affirming that she could work—the pathetic effort being in vain.[285]

As the Reich Flight Tax had enabled Hitler to launch his war, Hilberg notes: "[T]he army emerged as the most important purchaser of ghetto products, crowding out other buyers."[286] For all their lauded efforts, the Jews were compensated with a shrinking food supply, described as "below prison level." Frank was unabashed, stating in April 1941, "I'm not remotely interested in the Jews. Whether they have something to eat or not is the last thing on earth I care about."[287] Together with a growing typhoid epidemic (due to insufficient soap, coal, and *Jewish* "living space," worsened by latrines with fecal piles three feet high), the inevitable denouement began: impaired digestion; shrinkage of vital organs; abnormal weigh loss; and withered skin. Julian Fliederbaum, a ghetto doctor, gave the attendant symptomology:

> Active, busy, energetic people are changed into apathetic, sleepy beings, always in bed, hardly able to get up to eat or go to the toilet. Passage from life to death is slow and gradual, like death from physiological old age. There is nothing violent, no dyspnea, no pain, no obvious changes in breathing or circulation. Vital functions subside simultaneously. Pulse rate and respiratory rate get slower and it becomes more and more difficult to reach the patient's awareness, until life is gone. People fall asleep in bed or on the street and are dead in the morning. They die during physical effort, such as searching for food, and sometimes even with a piece of bread in their hands.[288]

Mass deportations to Treblinka death camp began on July 23, 1942. As an added indignity (and reassurance of the trip's feigned purpose,

Dr. Theodor Herzl
Hozeh HaMedinah

The Basel Casino, site of the First Zionist Congress, held December 1896. "In Basel I created the Jewish State."

Inset: Lieutenant-Colonel Alfred Dreyfus, whose unjust, anti-Semitic military trial sparked Dr. Herzl's vision concerning a Jewish homeland

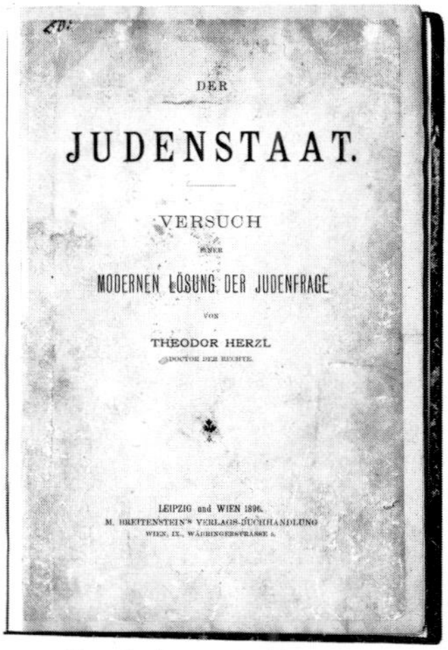

DER

JUDENSTAAT.

VERSUCH

EINER

MODERNEN LÖSUNG DER JUDENFRAGE

VON

THEODOR HERZL

DOCTOR DER RECHTE.

LEIPZIG und WIEN 1896.

M. BREITENSTEIN'S VERLAGS-BUCHHANDLUNG

WIEN, IX., WÄHRINGERSTRASSE 5.

Der Judenstaat title page (German edition, 1896)

An early Zionist Congress in Basel, Switzerland (date in dispute, Ernst Pawel/1896; Alex Bein/1897)

Theodor Herzl in Eretz Yisrael, October 1898; gains international prestige by meeting with Kaiser Wilhelm II in Jerusalem

Herzl with children, Hans, Trude, and Paulina (c. 1900), all of whom (along with their mother) would meet tragic deaths

Herzl's funeral cortege of 10,000 mourners, Vienna, July 7, 1904
"Why is it that the best must always fall?"

Julie Naschauer Herzl, c. 1889

At Trois Rois Hotel, Basel, 1901

Entombed atop Mount Herzl
(Marco Plassio)

Arthur James Balfour, United Kingdom Foreign Secretary, penned the original text of the Balfour Declaration (a ploy to initiate a quid pro quo Jewish-American lobby for US entry into WWI). The final draft, of debatable authorship (Alfred Milner, per Carroll Quigley; Leopold Amery, per William D. Rubinstein), was officially addressed in the Foreign Secretary's name to Walter Rothschild, a leader of British Jewry, for delivery to the Zionist Federation of Great Britain and Ireland.

Alfred Lord Milner, 1st Viscount Milner; British statesman, colonial administrator; leader of the Round Table movement, a secret society begun by Cecil Rhodes

Leopold "Leo" Charles Maurice Stennett Amery; crypto-Jewish journalist and politician; Colonial Secretary; First Lord of the Admiralty; member of the Milner Group

Lionel Walter Rothschild, 2nd Baron Rothschild of Tring; scion of the Rothschild family; banker; Member of Parliament; eminent zoologist

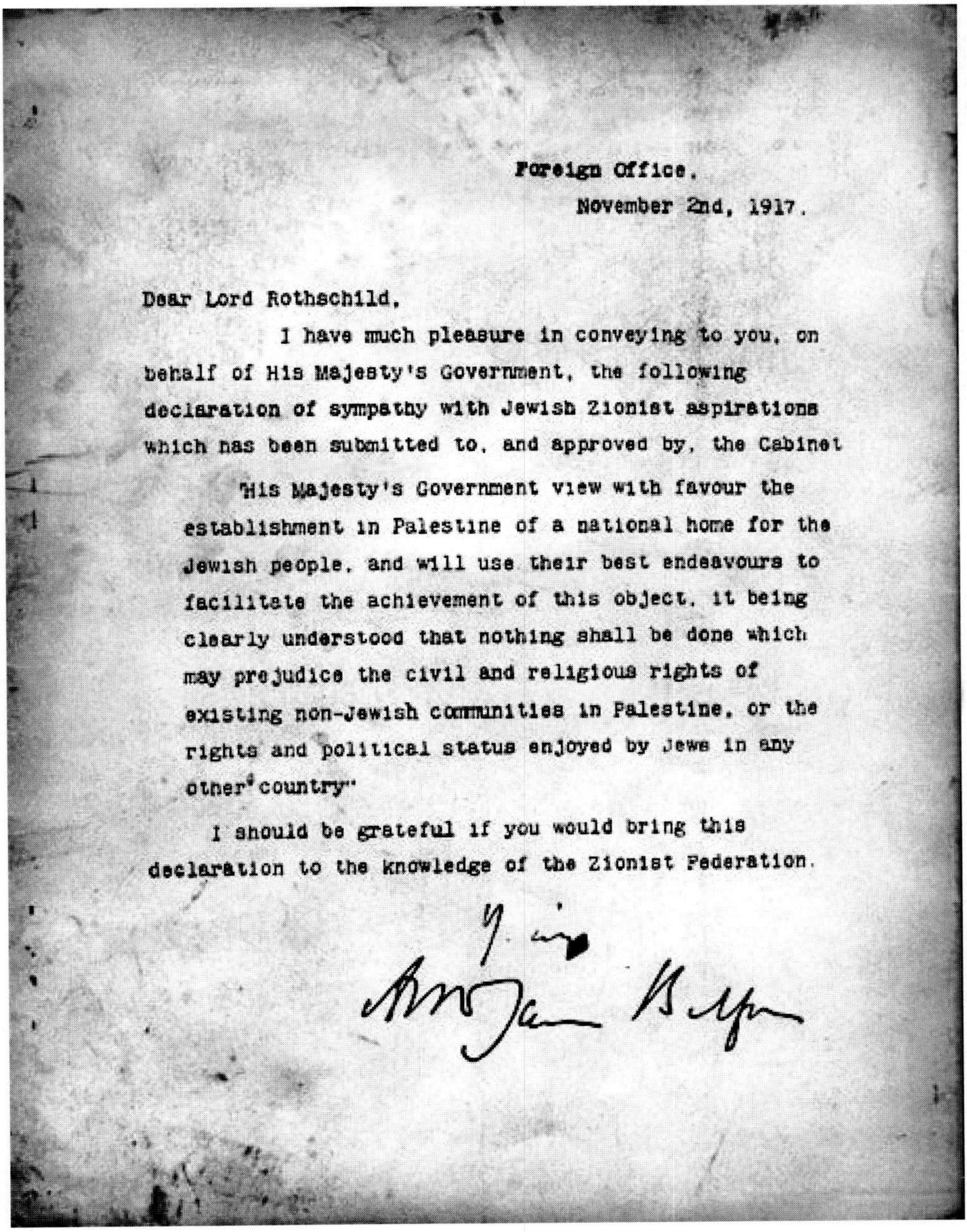

Foreign Office,
November 2nd, 1917.

Dear Lord Rothschild,

I have much pleasure in conveying to you, on behalf of His Majesty's Government, the following declaration of sympathy with Jewish Zionist aspirations which has been submitted to, and approved by, the Cabinet

"His Majesty's Government view with favour the establishment in Palestine of a national home for the Jewish people, and will use their best endeavours to facilitate the achievement of this object, it being clearly understood that nothing shall be done which may prejudice the civil and religious rights of existing non-Jewish communities in Palestine, or the rights and political status enjoyed by Jews in any other country"

I should be grateful if you would bring this declaration to the knowledge of the Zionist Federation.

Yours sincerely,
Arthur James Balfour

The Balfour Declaration

General Edmund Allenby entering the Old City of Jerusalem on foot, December 11, 1917

Ze'ev Jabotinsky, "We do not have to apologize for anything," and Joseph Trumpeldor, "It is good to die for one's country," co-founders of Zion Mule Corps, forerunner of the Israel Defense Forces

Colonel John H. Patterson, Irish Protestant Zionist, Commander of the Jewish Legion (38th-42nd Battalions of the Royal Fusiliers)

Patterson leading his soldiers through London's East End, February 4, 1918, the day of their deployment to Palestine

The Jewish Legion at the Western Wall on Temple Mount

Patterson's Tsavo Lions on exhibit at Field Museum, Chicago, Illinois *(Getty Images)*

Karl Marx, atheistic Jew, father of modern Communism, 1875

Vladimir Lenin, lately discovered to have Jewish ancestry

Lev Bronstein, alias Leon Trotsky, Lenin's "left-hand" man

The Russian Imperial Romanov family, slain (upon Lenin's directive) in Ipatiev House, Yekaterinburg, July 17, 1918

Yakov Yurovsky, "Lutheran Jew" who led the Cheka execution squad

American doughboys enter Vladivostok, August 1918, in a failed bid to retain Russian forces on the field following the October Revolution of 1917

Baron Peter Wrangel, Commander-in-Chief of anti-Bolshevik White Army; opposed anti-Semitism; poisoned by OPGU agent, April 1928

Author in front of captured British Mark V tank, Arkhangelsk, Russia

Harry St. John Bridger "Jack" Philby, a.k.a. Sheikh Abdullah, c. 1922; British Arabist; colonial intel operative; key adviser to King Ibn Saud; converted to Islam in 1930

CIA Director Allen Welsh Dulles, mass corruption from reparations to ratlines *(Central Intelligence Agency)*

Baseball card for Moe Berg, multi-lingual MLB catcher and OSS spy during WWII

Camp Siegfried, Yaphank, NY, ground zero for The Great Hurricane of 1938 *(Bettmann/Getty Images)*

German-American Bund parade along E. 86th St. in Manhattan, October 30, 1939 *(Library of Congress)*

Hitler hosting the Grand Mufti, November 28, 1941 *(Hulton Archive/Getty Images)*

Heinrich Himmler reviews Muslim Waffen SS division *(Bundesarchiv Bild 146-1986-012-21/o.Ang)*

Roll call of Jews imprisoned following Kristallnacht, Buchenwald concentration camp, November 1938

Maria "Masha" Bruskina, a seventeen-year-old Jewess, hanged along with fellow partisans in Minsk, Belarus, October 1941

Jewish women awaiting execution near Liepāja, Latvia, forced to undress and pose, December 1941

Einsatzgruppen soldier shooting a mother and child during a Judenaktion, Ivangorod, Ukraine, 1942

Children from Łódź Ghetto rounded up for deportation to Chelmno death camp, central Poland, September 1942

Jewish man leaping to his death during Warsaw Ghetto Uprising, April 1943

Arbeit Macht Frei ("Work makes free") sign over main entrance at Auschwitz I, 50-acre administrative HQ of the tri-partite SS facility *(Author's Collection)*

Crematorium I, partially reconstructed after WWII *(Author's Collection) Inset:* Zyklon B gas pellets

Gas chamber, Crematorium I; maximum capacity of 800, smallest in Auschwitz *(Author's Collection)*

Nighttime in Planet Auschwitz, *"...at even thou shalt say, Would God it were morning! for the fear of thine heart..."* (Deuteronomy 28:67)

Inmates pouring concrete for ceiling of underground dressing rooms adjacent to gas chamber in Crematorium II, Birkenau

Infamous "Gate of Death," Auschwitz II - Birkenau; macabre extermination center; nearly 1,000,000 Jews murdered on 500 acres; depicted as *anus mundi* ("anus of the world"), a former inmate stating, "There was no God at Auschwitz. There were such horrible conditions that God decided not to go there." *(Author's Collection)*

Arrival and selection of Hungarian Jews, June 1944, over 400,000 dying in next two months, victims of callous Allied immigration policy *(Auschwitz Album)*

Roman Catholic SS Captain Dr. Josef Mengele, heinous "Angel of Death," rat-lined to "peaceful" retirement in South America

Dazed women *"with child and...them that give suck"* (Luke 21:23) going to the "showers" within minutes of their arrival at the Judenrampe *(Auschwitz Album)*

The long, sad walk to eternity, Crematoria II & III having operated at road's end, to the left and right, respectively *(Author's Collection)*

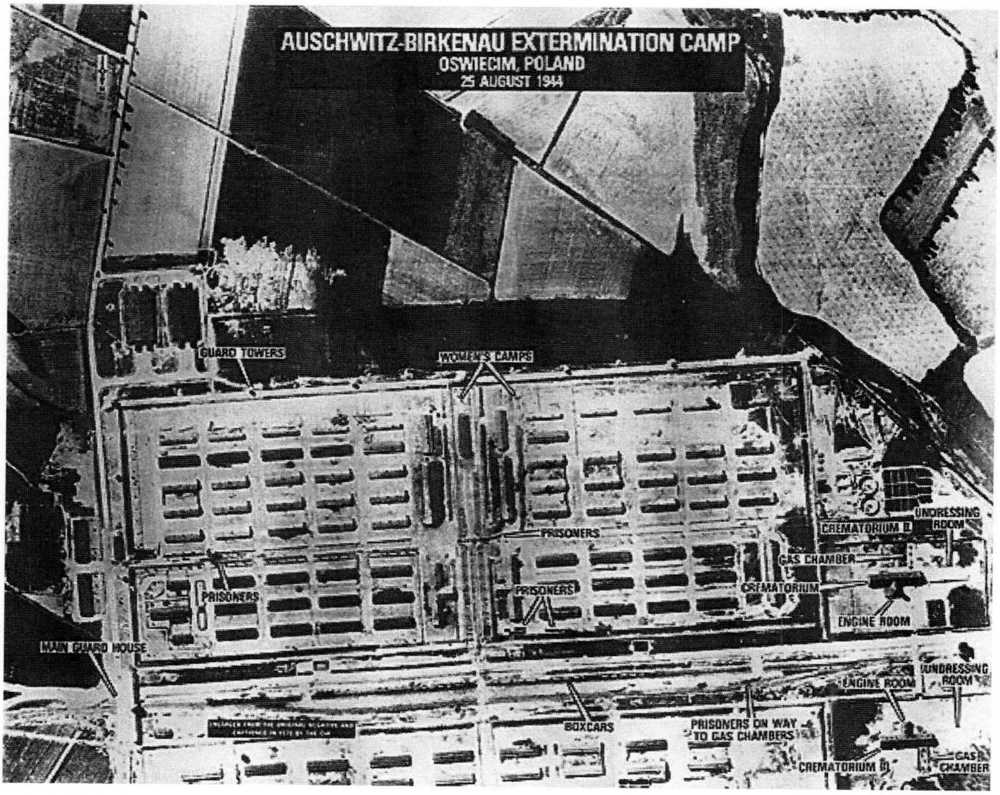

USAAF aerial reconnaissance photo showing boxcars and Jews walking to the open gate of Crematorium II *(National Archives and Records Administration/RG 263: Auschwitz; 19-08)*

Ruins of Crematorium II; steps *"down to the chambers of death"* (Proverbs 7:27); dressing area in forefront; oven rooms visible in distance *(Author's Collection)*

Author with Auschwitz survivor, John Frank, 98842Δ; rescued mothers with a single infant (or child) on the Judenrampe by employing a ruse to pass the little one "temporarily" to another woman with several already in tow; recalled Dr. Mengele's "death stare"

Viennese Jew/Soviet double agent Richard Kauder (a.k.a. Fritz Klatt) bled Wehrmacht on Eastern Front via Abwehr spy ring "Max and Moritz," saving the Yishuv from genocide; procured Israel's first weapons in early 1948 from Czechoslovakia *(Avi Ziv-Tal)*

Radio messages dispatched from second story of import-export firm, Sophia, Bulgaria *(Avi Ziv-Tal)*

Luftwaffe photo of deployed dummy Russian tanks

The real armor being rushed to defend Stalingrad

General Konstanin Rokossovsky (far left) interrogates Field Marshal Friedrich von Paulus (far right) upon his epic surrender of the German 6th Army at Stalingrad, January 31, 1943. Deceived by Klatt, von Paulus stated, "I was sure that you were in Moscow." Rokossovsky simply smiled. This event is regarded as the turning point of World War II.

Jewish Lieutenant Lydia Litvyak, a.k.a. "The White Rose of Stalingrad," Russia's all-time top-scoring female fighter ace; shot down at age twenty-three during the Battle of Kursk, August 1, 1943

British lorries transferring repatriated Cossacks across Mur River to Soviet Zone in Judenburg Austria, June 1945 *(Stadtmuseum Judenburg)*

Dr. Heinrich Pichler, Austrian native and career UN diplomat, shows author train trestle in Oberdrauburg where, as a child, he observed Gulag-bound Cossacks jumping to their deaths in the Dura River. Code-named "Operation Keelhaul," Alexander Solzhenitsyn called this travesty "the last secret of World War II."

Steel mill in Judenburg where elements of the 15th Cossack Cavalry Corps were cremated by SMERSH officials. Surreal glimpse into the psyche of an Anglo-American anti-Semitism capable of deserting European Jewry, exhibited by the Allies' own post-Holocaust genocide —the Yalta-spawned forcible (illegal) repatriation of some 2,200,000 Russian nationalists who fought for Hitler to oust Stalin *(Author's Collection)*

Chased by flamethrowers, Keelhaul survivor, Ataman Alex Pewnew, curator of the Kuban Cossacks Museum, Howell, New Jersey, stands before painting "Betrayal of Cossacks at Lienz, Austria, June 1945" *(Author's Collection)*

Lone German POW plot, Finns Point National Cemetery, Pennsville, New Jersey, holding the remains of three anti-Bolshevik Russians who chose suicide at Fort Dix over return to USSR *(Author's Collection)*

King Ibn Saud, founder of Saudi Arabia, confers with FDR aboard the USS Quincy on the Great Bitter Lake, Suez Canal, February 14, 1945 *(Library of Congress)*

British soldier at work in Bergen-Belsen, where over 10,000 unburied corpses were found and subsequently interred in mass graves, Anne Frank *(inset)* among them

Security badge of Samuel Cohen, Manhattan Project physicist who worked on "Fat Man," plutonium bomb detonated above Nagasaki, August 9, 1945, effectively ending war. "I will say that regarding nuclear weapons, Jews, by far and away, have had a disproportionate effect on their development and the policies of their use." *(Los Alamos National Laboratory/ Wartime Staff Badge Photos)*

Greta Zimmer Friedman, the young woman whose image in this iconic "V-J Day in Times Square" picture brought closure to America, was a Holocaust refugee from Austria. *(Alfred Eisenstaedt/Getty Images)*

Execution of former Auschwitz commandant, Rudolf Höss, near Crematorium I, April 16, 1947

Author with Jack Vandiver, Jr., of the famed 42nd "Rainbow" Division, instruments of retribution at Dachau, April 29, 1945

Chimney memorial, Radegast train station, Łódź, Poland, declares in Hebrew, Polish, and English, "Thou Shalt Not Kill" *(Author's Collection)*

Monument near 51 Postra St. to Warsaw Ghetto fighters forced to flee through the sewers *(Author's Collection)*

Adolf Eichmann at his war crimes trial in Jerusalem, 1961; hanged on June 1, 1962, in Ramla *(Israel Government Press Office)*

"Wall of Death" memorial, Auschwitz I *(Author's Collection)*

Plaque in Oświęcim cemetery honoring 38 British POWs who died in bombing of Monowitz (Auschwitz III), August 3, 1944 *(Author's Collection)*

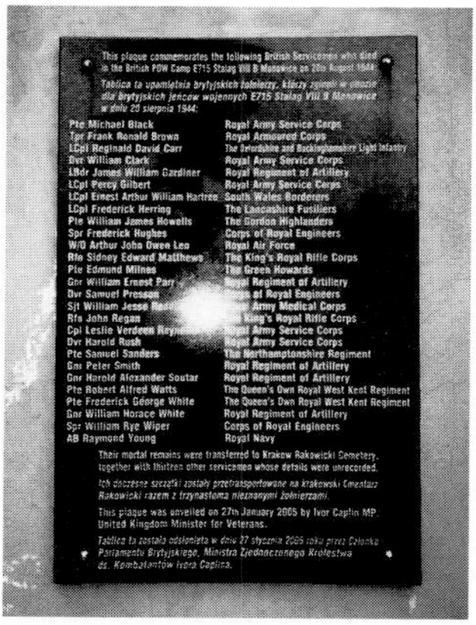

The Jewish Cemetery in Łódź *(Author's Collection)*

"resettlement for labor"), passengers had to buy their own rail tickets (one-way). The last transport left the *Umschlagplatz* on September 21, Yom Kippur. In less than sixty days, 300,000 Jews had vanished. The returning empties were called *Judenzug* ("Jew trains.") The victims included the family of renowned Polish piano virtuoso Wladyslaw Szpilman. Of the many poignant accounts, the Warsaw orphans' bears telling. While "King Chaim" sent *his* children out of Łódź, Dr. Janusz Korczak, founder and longtime director of the Dom Sierot orphanage, refused an offer of amnesty (ostensibly for his medical expertise) to personally escort *his* beloved charge of 192 little ones, ultimately—as Szpilman wrote—"into the next world." Hillel Seidman, archivist of Warsaw's Junenrat, captured the pathos of the last assembly:

> And so a long line is formed in the front of the orphanage on Slisks Street. A long procession, children, small, tiny, rather precocious, emaciated, weak, shriveled and shrunk. They carry shabby packages, some have school books, notebooks under their arms. No one is crying. Slowly they go down the steps, line up in rows, in perfect order and discipline, as usual. Their little eyes are turned towards the doctor. They are strangely calm; they feel almost well. The doctor is going with them, so what do they have to be afraid of? They are not alone, they are not abandoned.
>
> Dr. Korczak busies himself with the children with a sober earnestness. He buttons the coat of one child, ties up a package of another, or straightens the cap of a third. Then he wipes off a tear which is rolling down the thin little face of a child...Then the procession starts out. It is starting out for a trip from which—everybody feels it—one never comes back. All these young, budding lives...And all this is marching quietly and orderly to the place of their untimely doom. The children are calm, but inwardly they must feel it, they must sense it intuitively. Otherwise how could you explain the deadly seriousness on their pale little faces? But they are marching quietly in orderly rows, calm and earnest, and at the head of them is Janusz Korczak.[289]

Szpilman adds, in *The Pianist*:

> He told the orphans they were going out into the country, so they ought to be cheerful...When I met them in Gesia street the smiling children were singing in chorus...Korczak was carrying two of the

> smallest infants…I am sure that even in the gas chamber, as the Cyclon B gas was stifling childish throats and striking terror instead of hope into the orphans' hearts, the Old Doctor must have whispered with one last effort, 'It's all right, children, it will be all right,' so that at least he could spare his little charges the fear of passing from life to death.[290]

WAIST-HIGH HUMAN WASTE

The second phase of deportations began on January 18, 1943. This time, the Jews reacted with a token armed resistance lasting three days (a prelude to the main uprising). In retaliation, the Nazis massacred 1,000 victims in the main square on January 21. The transports were halted after a few days; only 5,000 Jews were removed.

By spring, barely 60,000 were still alive. Rumors began to circulate that the last transports would resume shortly. On April 19, Himmler launched an offensive to liquidate the ghetto. The date was chosen as Hitler would turn fifty-four the next day. Not to be outdone by the surprise appeasement of the Bermuda conferees, Heinrich's birthday gift for his beloved Führer would be the total extirpation of Warsaw's Jewish population.[291] However, as April 20 was also the start of Passover, the Jews decided to give Hitler a present of their own.

With nothing to lose, the fateful revolt began when a handful of Jewish guerrillas ambushed the SS phalanx with small arms fire, Molotov cocktails, and light bulbs filled with sulphuric acid. After six hours, the bewildered Nazis retreated. The next morning 850 troops reentered the ghetto (followed later by 3,000 veteran Waffen SS, SD, and Police, with 2,000 Ukrainian, Latvian, and Lithuanian auxiliaries), to face off against 750 ill-equipped men, women, and teenagers.[292] The end was never in doubt. Charles Lawliss states, "One of the survivors, Alexander Donat, wrote that the uprising was undertaken 'solely for death with dignity, and without the slightest hope of victory in life.'"[293] On April 21, a wireless operator tried to send a message but was cut off after four lines; the text ended—"Save us."[294]

For twenty days the Jewish Fighting Organization (ZOB) waged a brave, though futile battle, employing a labyrinth of bunkers, cellars, rooftops, and drainpipes. Women were seen firing pistols with both hands. SS General Jürgen Stroop ordered the ghetto torched, calling it the "only and ultimate way to defeat the rabble and scum of the earth and bring them above ground."[295] The house-by-house destruction was horrific. The enemy arsenal included bombs, machine guns, howitzers, flamethrowers, gas grenades, and dogs. Mothers and children leaped to their deaths from infernos, sprayed by bullets in midair. Hundreds of charred, bloodied bodies provided a feast for the rats, cats, dogs, and crows. The wounded were killed or tortured to give up their comrades.

The most graphic scene epitomizing the desperation would give new meaning to the term "*underground* resistance." As the juggernaut tightened, many of the ZOB were forced to retreat through the municipal sewer system. The maneuver required them to shuffle along in single file—*waist high in noxious human waste*—one hand resting on the shoulder in front, the other on the wall for balance. The strong ammonia caused temporary blindness for some. One partisan recalled his two-day trek in *lip*-high sewage: "Thirst was the worst handicap. Some even drank the thick, slimy sewer water. Every second seemed like months."[296] (The 2011 Polish film, *In Darkness*, tells the story of Leopold Socha, a Catholic sewer worker in the city of Lwów, who hid ten Jews in the sludge; as recounted in *The Girl in the Green Sweater*, the 2012 memoir of survivor Krystyna Chiger, the surreal ordeal lasted fourteen months.) Simhah Rotem, the head ZOB courier, wrote:

> It was ten o'clock at night and pitch-dark in the sewers…there was neither day nor night…The central sewer…is about two meters high and the sewage streams in a mighty flow. There is one more difficulty: the side channels are small and we sometimes had to crawl on our bellies…It was no pleasure to flounder in excrement, to smell the stench, but we had no choice.[297]

Near the end, others chose self-destruction over surrender or capture. One poor soul put four shots into his own mother, though she continued to move.[298] Mordechai Anielewicz, the celebrated twenty-three-year-old ZOB Commander, along with his girlfriend and several staff members, committed suicide in the headquarters bunker at 18 Mila Street.[299] (A bronze monument marking the spot near 51 Postra Street, where the last insurgents escaped on May 10, depicts a sewage canal rising vertically with disembodied hands climbing to freedom.)

Ironically, the most significant ghetto-related suicide occurred in England. Shmuel Zygielbojm, a member of the Warsaw Jewish Council, had been smuggled abroad to describe the Nazi occupation. He later joined the London-based Polish National Council (Poland's exiled parliament). His testimony played a key role in the landmark BBC program reporting the deaths of 700,000 Jews. Zygielbojm grew cynical over the Allies' apathy to the Jewish suffering in his land. He became even more disillusioned by the news that his wife and children had been executed. On May 12, 1943 (thirteen days after the Bermuda Conference adjourned), the forty-eight-year-old patriot killed himself as a protest to the greater tragedy of Anglo-American deceit. In his suicide note to the Polish president and prime minister, Shmuel wrote:

> I cannot be silent. I cannot live while the remnants of the Jewish population of Poland, of whom I am a representative, are perishing. My friends in the Warsaw ghetto died with weapons in their hands in the last heroic battle. It was not my destiny to die together with them but I belong to them and in their mass graves. By my death I wish to make my final protest against the passivity with which the world is looking on and permitting the extermination of the Jewish people. I know how little human life is worth today, but as I was unable to do anything during my life, perhaps by my death I shall contribute to breaking down the indifference of those who may now at the last moment rescue the few Polish Jews still alive...I bid farewell to everybody and to everything that was dear to me and that I have loved.[300]

The ghetto's last transmission read: "The world of freedom and justice is silent and does nothing."[301] At precisely 8:15 p.m. on May 16, the Great Synagogue on Tlomachie Street (situated outside the walls) was blown up, symbolically ending the short-lived revolt. General Stroop wrote in his journal: "The Warsaw Ghetto is no more." The unofficial tally of Germans killed ranges from seventeen to over a hundred. The Jews suffered 7,000 dead, with 56,000 (i.e., everyone left) "recaptured," 7,000 being shot, with 21,000 sent to Treblinka and Majdanek. Gilbert adds, "Another of those who probably perished in the Warsaw ghetto uprising was Yakov Grojanowski, the man who, in January 1942, had brought the news of the Chelmno death camp to Warsaw."[302] Nearly the entire ghetto was razed with the notable exception of the Roman Catholic Church of Saint Augustine. Nożyk Synagogue, the sole surviving prewar shul (located in the Small Ghetto), was spared by the Nazis as a place to stable their horses.

Finally, similar to the phenomenon of deserted Jewish cemeteries, in the aftermath of Germany's surrender, the conspicuous absence of 350,000 former residents returning to re-inhabit their city testifies against the proponents of Holocaust denial theory. Agnieszka Haska, of the Polish Center for Holocaust Research, comments accordingly: "In the former Ghetto area—there was no-one to come back. The empty space became a symbol not just of the despoilment of the material traces of the Ghetto but also of its inhabitants—a tangible sign of the Annihilation of the Jews."[303]

"I looked on my right hand, and beheld, but there was
no man that would know me: refuge failed me;
no man cared for my soul."
(Psalm 142:4)

11

The Camps

"I live in crazy times."
(Anne Frank)

"I do not want the concentration camps to be transformed into sanatoria. Terror is the most effective political weapon…I need people who act severely and do not even begin to think when they have to kill someone…A conscience is a Jewish creation."
(Adolf Hitler)

"Planet Auschwitz—a forlorn, damned, and desolate world."
(Rolf Hochhuth, German playwright)

"There was no God in Auschwitz. There were such horrible conditions that God decided not to go there."
(Libusa Breder, Auschwitz survivor)

ACCORDING TO DANIEL Goldhagen's 1997 book, *Hitler's Willing Executioners* at least 10,005 *lagers* ("camps") of all kinds existed throughout the Reich. The total number of known ghettos and forced labor camps designed specifically for Jews exceeded 1,600. The SS also operated 52 main concentration camps, augmented by 1,202 *aussenlagers* ("satellite facilities").[1]

In 2013, the US Holocaust Museum quadrupled Himmler's "lager archipelago" to 42,500 camps! Curator Hartmut Berghoff told the *New York Times*, "The numbers are so much higher than what we originally thought."[2] In January 2005, the Bonn government had initiated the "long-awaited" (delayed) declassification of Hitler's secret archive at the Red Cross International Tracing Service in Bad Arolsen. Over sixteen miles of shelves, storing fifty million pages, note the deaths of seventeen million Nazi victims (Jews and Gentiles alike).

In March 1933—two months after Hitler became Chancellor—Dachau opened outside Munich as Germany's first concentration camp. (Rudolf Höss, future commandant of Auschwitz, started his "career" there.) Another *fifty* like institutions emerged that inaugural year. Buchenwald, one of the larger lagers on German soil, began in July 1937. The director's wife, Ilse Koch (a.k.a. "The Witch of Buchenwald"), reputedly made lampshades out of inmates' skin. Thomas J. Dodd, Executive Trial Counsel at Nuremberg, caused a stir with Exhibit No. USA-254—a *shrunken head* from Buchenwald.[3]

In one of the lesser-known atrocities, seventy-three American POWs (including many Jews) succumbed to malnutrition, exhaustion, and disease at the Berga-an-der-Elster subterranean arms factory (Buchenwald satellite). Ravensbrück camp for women and children began in May 1939. Inmates at Wöbbelin reportedly slept on "sheets" of barbed wire. The Niederhagen facility served as Himmler's private lager, commissioned to develop the environ of Wewelsburg Castle (dubbed the future "Center of the World" after the "Final Victory"). Multitudes would also suffer and die in such places as Mauthausen-Gusen, Stutthof, Sachsenhausen-Oranienburg, Neuengamme, and Natzweiler-Struthof (the only camp opened in present-day France).

However, as noted earlier, the Shoah was primarily consigned to six unique "extermination centers." Despite thirty months of war and the onset of mass murder, roughly 75% of Hitler's future victims were still alive in January 1942. One year later, the same percentage were dead.[4] Designed for secrecy and instantaneous death, all six sites were located in Poland due to the nation's vast rail system and thinly populated, densely wooded terrain. The "death camp" was the *twelfth* and *final* step in the Nazi plan to extirpate European Jewry. Longerich gives the following succinct synopsis of the preceding eleven stages:

> Definition of Jews, deprivation of their rights, and expropriation; concentration in transition camps and ghettos; deportation; deliberately engineered high mortality rate in the phase of concentration and deportation; selection of those 'fit to work'; murder of those "unfit"

> for work or those not needed for work via mass executions or by means of gas; "extermination through work"; strict secrecy; systematic covering of traces.[5]

Raul Hilberg reduces the Final Solution to six parts: "Definition; Dismissals of employees and expropriations of business firms; Concentration; Exploitation of labor and starvation measures; Annihilation; [and] Confiscation of personal effects."[6]

With Chelmno as the vanguard, this chapter will survey Bełżec, Sobibór, Treblinka, and Majdanek, concluding with an expanded study of the largest and most infamous death camp of all—Auschwitz.

BEŁŻEC

While US cities were celebrating St. Patrick's Day (March 17) 1942, Bełżec opened under SS Major Christian Wirth (a.k.a. "The Wild Christian" and "Christian the Terrible"). Sadly, the "luck of the Irish" was nowhere around. Jan Karski, an underground courier, wrote, "The common report was that every Jew who reached it, without exception, was doomed to death."[7] (Rudolf Reder would be the *only* survivor.)

On April 1—the first night of Passover—15,000 Jews from Lvov were led to the slaughter. By the time Bełżec closed nine months later, 434,500 Jews had experienced "concentrated death" on a barren, barbed wire-enclosed plot of ground just 1.5 miles square. Bełżec was the first camp to employ *stationary* gas chambers. However, this "innovation" was offset by a lack of crematoria—the bodies burned in open pits, or simply thrown into mass graves. As at Chelmno, the earth would eventually heave (particularly in summer), requiring special units to disinter and burn scores of partially decomposed remains.

The SS used ingenious methods to disguise their real agenda. Upon arrival, prisoners encountered orchestra music and potted geraniums. However, like the victims themselves, the charade was short-lived. Bełżec's worst nightmare was the recurring deficiency of their Diesel engines. After hundreds of naked men, women, and children had been herded and crammed into one of the six carbon monoxide chambers (ostensibly for baths and disinfection), the killing apparatus would often fail, leaving the terrorized throng in the ultimate state of suspended animation—sometimes for *hours*. One of the most graphic accounts of this ordeal was given by Kurt Gerstein, a rare SS officer who protested the atrocities (later dying under suspicious conditions). His depiction of what he called "the corpse factory" follows:

> For a number of men there still flickers a lingering hope, sufficient to make them march without resistance to the death chambers. The majority know with certainty what is to be their fate. The horrible, all-pervading stench reveals the truth. Then they climb some small steps and behold the reality. Silent mothers hold their babies to their breasts, naked; there are many children of all ages. They hesitate, but nevertheless proceed toward the death chambers, most of them without a word, pushed by those behind, chased by the whips of the SS men.
>
> A woman of about forty curses the chief of the murderers, crying that the blood of her children will be on his head. Wirth...strikes her across the face with five lashes of the whip and she disappears into the chamber. Many pray...The SS men squeeze people into the chambers...About seven to eight hundred people in an area of about a hundred square yards. The doors close, the rest of the transport stands waiting, naked...
>
> But the Diesel engine is not functioning...fifty minutes pass by; seventy minutes. The people in the death chambers remain standing. Their weeping is heard...Only after two hours and forty-nine minutes does the Diesel finally begin to work. Twenty-five minutes pass by. Many have already died, as can be seen through the small window. Twenty-eight minutes later a few are still alive. After thirty-two minutes all are dead...Jewish workers open the doors on the other side...The dead, having nowhere to fall, stand like pillars of basalt.
>
> Even in death, families may be seen standing pressed together, clutching hands. It is only with difficulty that the bodies are separated in order to clear the place for the next load. The blue corpses, covered with sweat and urine...babies and bodies of children, are thrown out. But there is no time! A couple of workers are busy with the mouths of the dead..."With gold to the left—without gold to the right," is the order. Others search in the private parts of the bodies for gold and diamonds.[8]

SOBIBÓR

Sobibór death camp operated forty-three miles southeast of Warsaw. SS Captain Franz Paul Stangl (a.k.a. "The White Death") was the first commandant. Over 150,000 Jews perished there from May 1942 to October 1943, cattle cars crammed full of disoriented humans arriving daily from a variety of occupied lands.

The standard deception followed. An impressive-looking official in a white physician's smock told the people that they were at a "transit camp" and would have to "bathe" before going on to their "work assignments." The men were parted from the women and children. All were told to undress and surrender any valuables; women were shorn.[9] The groups were then herded along a 650-foot-long, barbed wire-enclosed path, a.k.a. "The Road to Heaven"—unaware that they were actually *"going down to the chambers of death."* (Proverbs 7:27) About 15,000 people daily were "disinfected" in five carbon monoxide chambers. (When Himmler visited Sobibór in July 1943, 300 Jewesses from Majdanek were gassed in his honor.[10]) The bodies were sprinkled with lime and buried in pits; or burned in open-air pyres, the bones then ground to powder to supply the Fatherland with fertilizer. Other items that joined the daily ten-car, Germany-bound trainload of contraband included shoes, clothing, and bags of women's hair.[11]

While most Jews were gassed on arrival, some were spared (usually for about three months) to aid with the treachery, as well as to render personal services to their captors (cleaning, laundry, shining boots, even playing music and making jewelry). Doris Bergen of Toronto University notes that because no SS man would trust a razor-wielding Jew, the Jehovah's Witnesses became the Nazis' barbers of choice.[12] Known as *Sonderkommandos* ("special units") this fraternity would pay a high price for its tenuous stay of execution. As illustrated by the homicidal maniac, "Big Whip" (John 19:1), Germans loved torturing "the help"—in *any* camp. *SS Helferin* ("Female SS Helper") Irma Grese (a.k.a. "The Hyena of Auschwitz") had a penchant for flaying the breasts of buxom women with her whip, then "swaying rhythmically and foaming at the mouth" during the requisite surgery.[13] SS Sergeant-Major Otto Moll (another Auschwitz "celebrity") chose twenty of the most attractive Jewess arrivals from one transport, stood them in a row, stark naked, then used them for target practice.[14]

Among several creative diversions called *Sportmachen* ("to make sport"), inmates were ordered to strike the Alsatian guard dogs, causing the incensed beasts to retaliate.[15]Entrants in "Swim-Frog" had to tread water, croaking like a frog, until drowning from fatigue.[16] Others had their trouser bottoms sewn up and rats thrown in[17]; if they dared to move, they were beaten.[18] A special favorite was the Nazi version of *Fiddler on the Roof*, called the "SS parachute game"—Jews with umbrellas pushed off buildings.[19] (On one occasion, 90 women in Auschwitz were tossed from a third-floor window into a courtyard below.[20]) Mock weddings were held before gassings.[21] To celebrate Hitler's birthday in 1942, a Jew was shot every two minutes for nearly two hours.[22] Salamo Arouch, a Greek-born Jewish boxing champion outlived his entire family at Auschwitz by beating over 200 fellow gladiators in bloody SS bouts.[23] As literal "fights to the finish," losers rarely survived in (or out of) the ring. Salamo's story was made into the 1989 movie, *Triumph of the Spirit* (the first filmed at Auschwitz).

In addition to the emotional toll of viewing the daily gassing of their friends and neighbors, Sonderkommandos would observe the SS at their worst, especially toward the weak and helpless. Children had their skulls crushed, while babies would be torn from their mothers' arms and split down the middle by their legs, or tossed into the air for target practice. Among various items unearthed by Israeli archeologists at Sobibór, a "Mickey Mouse" pin was particularly telling.[24] The worst psychological blow was the guilt caused by their own complicity. "A cruel and accursed fate has compelled us to take part in the extermination of our people," wrote former Auschwitz Sonderkommando, Filip Müller. "And yet, whoever wanted to stay alive had to ignore the detestable reality and the conditions under which he was forced to live, however violently he loathed them."[25]

Sobibór's "claim to fame" was the daring daylight revolt of October 14, 1943. As dramatized in the 1987 award-winning British television film, *Escape from Sobibór*, the plot was conceived in three weeks and led by a Soviet-Jewish POW, Alexander "Sasha" Pechersky. Though hindered by several last-minute obstacles, the core group was able to overpower a pre-selected list of SS and Ukrainian guards, enabling the entire body of 600 to make a run for the woods. Unfortunately, amidst the ensuing confusion, many of the 400 who actually got out, exited on the wrong side and were cut down by land mines. Yet, over 100 Jews eventually reached freedom, some thirty-five (including Sasha) surviving the war.[26] When the smoke cleared, eleven SS were dead, plus thirty-eight Ukrainian casualties. Two days later, a humiliated Reichsführer ordered Sobibór razed to the ground.

According to survivor Thomas Blatt, the last thing a Jew would see at the end of the "Road to Heaven" was a Star of David at the entrance to the gas chamber.[27] When conveying her own assessment of "Himmler's Paradise," historian Konnilyn Feig (a Lutheran) stated, "[T]he words in Revelation 6:8 seem to provide an accurate description of Sobibór: *'And I looked, and behold a pale horse: and his name that sat on him was Death, and Hell followed with him. And Power was given unto them over the fourth part of the earth, to kill with sword, and with hunger, and with death, and with the beasts of the earth.'*"[28] (Oddly enough, though the demon-possessed Catholic CEO of the Final Solution drew his "spiritual energy" from a deep addiction to the occult, the name "Himmler" just *happens* to be derived from the Middle German word *Himmel*—meaning "Heaven.")

TREBLINKA

Some 800,000 Jews perished at Treblinka from July 1942 to October 1943, inspiring the infamous nickname, "Big Factory of Death."[29] On a "normal" day, thirteen gas chambers utilizing carbon monoxide could asphyxiate 25,000 humans; 30,000 on an "exceptional" day.[30]

Working conditions left much to be desired. Franz Stangl, the second commandant (formerly of Sobibór), abhorred the "indescribable smell" of the hellhole. Feig gives his two main issues as "the thousands of decomposing, putrefying bodies" and "the gas chamber waiting area, where the women defecated from fear...."[31] Newcomers often went into shock as they confronted mounds of decaying bodies. Little wonder Stangl strove to preserve his own "sanity" by customizing an onsite retreat with gardens, orchestra music, plenty of booze, even a small zoo.[32] (There is no record of Dr. Korczak's orphans visiting the zoo prior to their gassing.) Stangl's assistant (later, successor), Kurt Franz (a.k.a. "a sadist of exquisite cruelty"), trained his St. Bernard dog "Barry" to attack his victims' genitals and buttocks.[33] (After a brief and peaceful retirement, Barry grew ill and was himself "euthanized" in 1947.)[34]

However, as with the Einsatzgruppen, the greatest stimulus for hard liquor was the stress of having to view the ghastly pandemonium that preceded the stench. (Feig notes that even Stangl "detested what was happening…"[35]) Like Sobibór, a Star of David adorned the gas chamber, along with a heavy, dark curtain from a synagogue, stating in Hebrew: "This is the gate through which the righteous pass."[36] With that "gate" sealed behind them, some had to stand for thirty minutes before *passing*; still others were known to *pass* the whole night before the engine was even started.[37] Yankel Wiernik, a Treblinka escapee, depicts a typical scene, Ukrainian guards Ivan and Nicholai presiding:

> I suffered most when I looked at the little ones walking beside their mothers, or at the others walking alone, who had no thought of the quick and cruel death impending. Their eyes were wide with fear and wonder…When they saw the stoney faces of their parents, however, they kept silent and prepared for whatever might come. They remained stock still or nestled against one another or cuddled up to their parents, awaiting the ghastly end. Suddenly the entrance doors would swing open. Ivan would appear with thick gas pipe, a meter long. Nicholai was with him, swinging a sword. At a signal the victims would be driven in, clubbed and lashed without mercy. To this day the fearful screams of the women and the crying of the children ring in my ears. There was despair and agony in the screams…
>
> Into the chamber of twenty-five square meters 400 to 500 people were jammed. The congestion was unbelievable. The victims carried in the children, somehow hoping thus to save them from death. On their way to die they were beaten and driven by truncheons and gas pipes. Dogs were set upon them; barking, they threw themselves upon the victims. Everyone, eager to escape the blows and the dogs, rushed screaming into the lethal chamber. The stronger pushed the weaker. But the tumult did not…endure. The doors closed with a clang on the packed chamber. The motor was connected with the inflow apparatus and switched on. In twenty-five minutes, at the most, all lay dead. But they did not really lie, for they had no room to fall. They died standing, their legs and arms entangled. There were no more screams. Mothers and children were clasped in death's embrace…No one was more beautiful or ugly—all were suffocated, yellowed by gas.[38]

Lacking crematoria, Treblinka's "earth moving" problems would make R. G. LeTourneau roll over in *his* grave. The soil eventually contained 700,000 bodies—a volume of 69,000 cubic meters weighing 35,000 tons (equal to a mid-sized battleship.[39]) Stangl describes an especially ghoulish scene: "One of the pits overflowed. They had too many corpses in it and putrefaction had progressed too fast, so that the liquid underneath had pushed the bodies on top up and over and the corpses had rolled down the hill...oh God, it was awful."[40] But then things *always* went "downhill" when bodies had to be disinterred for burning. In March 1943, Himmler gave the insane order to retrieve and burn every corpse in Treblinka. Wiernik recounts the dreadful task:

> Whenever a grave is opened, a terrible stench polluted the air, as the bodies were in an advanced stage of putrefaction...[W]omen burned easier than men. Accordingly, corpses of women were used for kindling the fires. The sight was terrifying, the worst that human eyes have ever beheld. When corpses of pregnant women were cremated, the abdomen would burst open, and the burning of the fetus inside the mother's belly would become visible.[41]

On August 2, 1943, over 700 Sonderkommandos staged an uprising of their own. Estimates vary from 200 to 600 reaching the forest, with as many as 60 surviving the war.[42] Three months later, the camp was blown up and the terrain covered with a farmhouse and pine trees.

MAJDANEK-LUBLIN

Majdanek, the Nazis' second-largest camp, was originally established in 1940 as a combination labor/POW facility. Karl-Otto Koch was the first of five commandants. Despite its highly visible, urbanized setting (on the eastern outskirts of Lublin), the installation of gas chambers and crematoria in September 1942 gave Majdanek a tri-fold agenda. (Gas vans, hangings, and mass shootings were also widely employed.)

Professor Bergen writes, "The SS men in Majdanek were known as sadists who enjoyed killing children in front of their mothers and forcing prisoners to engage in deadly 'sports.'"[43] Female guards were no less cruel, telling Jewish mothers that their little ones were going to the "rose garden" (gas chamber).[44] One such child was the ten-year-old prodigy, Irena Szyldkraut (a.k.a. "The Polish Shirley Temple"[45]). Journalist Edgar Snow called Majdanek "the most brilliant success in perverting the very virtues of a once great people into the service of a machinery of crimes almost too monstrous for the human mind to accept."[46] Due to deficient records, the total number of Jewish victims is uncertain; estimates (including sub-camps) range from 60,000 to 100,000, making Majdanek the least destructive of the death camps.

In the first week of November 1943, some 50,000 Jews were executed in ditches during an area-wide slaughter known as *Aktion Erntefest* ("Operation Harvest Festival").[47] The sheer number of victims compelled the killers to revert to shooting. Two loudspeaker trucks helped drown out the gunfire with music. However, as the slain had significantly impacted the local labor force (albeit slave), Lublin's merchants were said to have "lost the ground under their feet."[48] Even Governor Frank acknowledged in a conference, "[W]e can tell the agencies of the Reich that the taking away of the Jews has led to tremendous difficulties in the labor field."[49] It is noteworthy that the killers were also hit in the purse, the SS having gained a considerable kickback from the exploited revenue, particularly their own entrepreneurial ventures operating within the camps. Hilberg writes:

> Even in the SS enterprises and the munitions-producing armament plants, the Jews had to 'disappear,' and indeed, few lived to see the light of day. That was the price for the 'final solution' in Poland. What about the profits? Not much could be placed on the plus side of the balance sheet…The Polish Jews were annihilated in a process in which economic factors were truly secondary.[50]

Thus, the Ministry for Eastern Occupied Territories decreed, "Economic questions should not be considered in the solution of the Jewish question."[51] A Harvest Festival survivor gave the following eyewitness account of the Poniatowa camp liquidation:

> We undressed quickly and, our arms uplifted, went in the direction of the ditches we had dug ourselves. The graves which were two metres deep were full of naked bodies…My little daughter was quaking with fear, and asked me to cover her eyes. I embraced her head; my left hand I put on her eyes while in my right I held her hands. In this way we lay down, our faces turned downwards. Shots

> were fired; I felt a sharp pain in my hand, and the bullet pierced the skull of my daughter…I was utterly shaken…I realized that I was still alive, and expected another bullet to hit me, but I did not move…Apparently I made the impression of being dead…[After lying still for several hours the woman was finally able to raise her head in the twilight.]…I glanced at my daughter. Her face was usually oval, but now it was round and as pale as a sheet. With my lips I touched her back and hair, and her little hand slipped out of my hand.[52]

PLANET AUSCHWITZ

[WARNING! As the Jews naively entered Auschwitz under the disarming banner—*ARBEIT MACHT FREI* ("Work makes you free")—the reader has likewise arrived at the present chapter, *totally* oblivious to the horror that awaits within.]

From summer 1940 to winter 1944, approximately 1.1 million men, women, and children (90% Jews), perished at *Konzentrationslager Auschwitz* (Concentration Camp Auschwitz) under the fiendish plenipotentiary rule of SS-*Obersturmbannführer* (Commandant) Rudolf Franz Höss (oddly, no alias and often confused with Deputy Führer Rudolf Hess). The list of minority victims included 70,000-75,000 ethnic Poles, nearly 21,000 Gypsies, about 15,000 Soviet POWs, and 10,000-15,000 of various nationalities.[53]

Located thirty-five miles west of Krakow, the most lethal Nazi camp has been depicted in a variety of ways. Modern Holocaust denial notwithstanding, the voluminous historical record presents Auschwitz as "The World's Largest Cemetery Without Graves." Raul Hilberg labeled it "a symbol for the Jewish catastrophe in Europe."[54] With more deaths attributed to Auschwitz than the combined American and British losses of World War II, Tadeusz Borowski, an ethnic Polish survivor, classed it "the bloodiest battle of the war."[55] Gazing through her cattle car window at "people without hair…walking like lunatics," Violette Fintz (newly arrived from Rhodes) remarked to her mother, "I think we've come to a lunatic asylum."[56] Upon viewing his first "special Aktion" (a gassing at 3:00 a.m.), SS physician Johan Kremer stated, "By comparison, Dante's Inferno seems almost a comedy."[57] Another doctor, Heinz Thilo, said, "[W]e are located here in '*anus mundi,*' the 'anus of the world.'"[58]

When struggling to describe the chilling death rattle of several hundred suffocating Jews, Müller wrote, "It was as if Judgment day had come."[59] Another rare former Sonderkommando, Shlomo Venezia, recalled, "[Y]ou feel as if you've lost your bearings, as if you're on another planet."[60] The German playwright, Rolf Hochhuth, was more precise, dubbing it "Planet Auschwitz, a forlorn, damned, and desolate world."[61] Libusa Breder, a Jewess survivor, concluded: "There was no God in Auschwitz. There were such horrible conditions that God decided not to go there."[62] Zalmen Gradowski, who died in the revolt on October 7, 1944, testified from the grave via a posthumous manuscript, defining Auschwitz as "a lifeless island…the residence of death."[63] Dr. Jonathan Webber, contributing editor to the definitive photographic treatise *Auschwitz: A History in Photographs*, conceded: "We don't have a word in our language to adequately describe what this place is."[64] However, to the "Roman (Catholic) Triumvirate" of Hitler, Himmler, and Höss, Auschwitz became the veritable epicenter for the Final Solution to the Jewish question. Making a home for her husband and five children—under a cloud of smoke and ashes from Crematorium I—the "First Lady of Planet Auschwitz," Frau Hedwig Höss, reputedly said: "Here I want to live until the end of my days."[65]

Upon visiting Auschwitz as a naive teenager in 1972, this author has remained at a loss to convey the macabre experience of having traversed the greatest crime scene in history. Only now, however, the painful memories of glass-enclosed piles of shoes, luggage, pots and pans, toiletries, eyeglasses, artificial limbs, and women's hair have been exacerbated by four decades of intermittent follow-up research, capped by a second, extended visit in 2013. But then, no amount of "study" can invalidate the truism of German author Martin Walser: "What Auschwitz was is known only to its inmates and to no one else."[66] The conundrum here is that despite a wealth of extant testimony, a vicarious glimpse into Planet Auschwitz (or any other camp) remains elusive for one basic reason, evidential clarity has been compromised by the fact that most inmates could barely process their *own* hypnagogic ordeal at the time, much less fully assimilate the same upon a return to reality. Zdenka Fantlova relates accordingly:

> Auschwitz was such a terrible shock for me that my memories of it and everything I experienced appear to be shrouded in a veil of mist. During my entire stay there it felt as though someone had hit me on the head. For a long time I was unable to comprehend what I had experienced was reality. I stopped thinking and feeling. That was the only help given us by nature to preserve our health.[67]

While students may *read* Nobel Laureate Elie Wiesel's account of SS thugs tossing babies into fiery ditches, alive—*comprehending* such horror is another matter—the witness having barely survived himself: "[S]omehow I did not lose my mind."[68] Planet Auschwitz defined the adage, "Truth is stranger than fiction," the scene within constituting a ubiquitous phantasmagoria. For instance, after being "touched by an *angel*" whistling symphonic arias at the selection ramp (the demon-possessed Catholic physician, SS Captain Josef Mengele, a.k.a. the "Angel of Death"), scores of Jews headed to the "showers" would suddenly find themselves trudging "to the accompaniment of light operatic music played by girls dressed in blue and white."[69] Some might catch a glimpse of a soccer match, Borowski recalling: "Between two throw-ins in a soccer game, right behind my back, three thousand people had been put to death."[70] Moving gingerly between rows of electrified triple-barbed wire, the paranoid chattel may have gained added security from the skull and bones signs: "WARNING! DANGER OF DEATH." ("What irony," Wiesel notes. "Was there here a single place where one was *not* in danger of death?"[71])

The last proof of their commandant's "true concern" would have been the International Red Cross truck parked conspicuously nearby (sometimes following the column[72]). Little did they know that the contrived vehicle had just delivered the poison gas to dispatch them.[73] As the inevitable screams and wails erupted from beneath the fake showerheads (perforated plates mounted on wooden blocks), Sonderkommandos were already hauling their personal effects to "Canada," the camp's main warehouse comprising thirty-five huts. (With the moniker derived from the inmates' perception of that nation being a "land of plenty," it also represents a rebuke of Canada's callous immigration slogan: "None is too many.") Finally, could any Jewesses have *possibly* imagined that the very locks of their hair would be destined for a multitudinous array of manufactured products ranging from felt, yarn, fabric, stockings, and socks to ignition mechanisms for bombs[74] and insulation material for submarines?[75]

ARBEIT MACHT FREI

Outsiders viewed Planet Auschwitz through a kaleidoscope of their own. Unlike most camps, Auschwitz was situated astride a factory complex sporting a moderate population center. The now-famous sign (copied from Dachau) atop the main gate—ARBEIT MACHT FREI—made area residents ponder, "Free from *what*?" How could so *many* daily arrivals be accommodated there? Auschwitz was big, but it wasn't *that* big. The math didn't add up.

The strange smell and periodic "ash showers" that plagued the area (especially in high winds) were troubling as well. Adolf Barthelmäss, a rail worker living in nearby Babice recalled that his flat reeked with a "sweetish odor, and the windows were covered with a bluish film."[76] Then there were those "slightly" foreboding 15-foot-high pillars of flame, belching from the four 50-foot-high chimneys, visible 24/7 from nearly 12 miles away![77] No wonder SS official Pery Broad stated that whenever commuter trains passed by Auschwitz, "The passengers usually rose from their seats and went to the windows."[78]

The secrecy was so strict that not even a "king" could just drop by. During one try at satisfying his curiosity, Hans Frank had his staff car stopped and diverted due to an "epidemic" in the camp, etc.[79] Even years after the war, morbidity refused to die as "prospectors" could be seen excavating the burial areas in search of missed treasure.[80] On August 1, 1984, a group of Polish Carmelite nuns opened a convent just outside the walls of Auschwitz I—in the very two-story building the SS used to store their deadly Zyklon B gas! (After nearly a decade of controversy, the sisters vacated the unholy ground in July 1993.)

The name "Auschwitz" is the Germanized form of *Oświęcim*, a drab eastern Upper Silesian town of 12,000 in the immediate locale. Historian Robert-Jan van Pelt writes, "Its name seems unassimilable. Before we have recovered from its harsh and repulsive beginning (*Ausch*), we are hit by its violent and sarcastic end (*witz*)."[81] Situated astride the confluence of the Vistula and Sola rivers, the ancient Jewish community had existed as a center for Judaism since 1549.

On April 27, 1940, Himmler ordered that the existing fifty-acre Polish army cantonment at Auschwitz be refurbished into a concentration camp for Polish resistance members. Nearly 200 private firms were contracted for the project. Ethnic Poles were evicted from the designated "Zone of Interest"; many were arrested and exiled, some executed. The entire Jewish population of 7,000 was scattered to area ghettos in Sosnowiec, Będzin, and Chrzanów. Over 90% of these would soon return "home," only to be gassed at Konzentrationslager Auschwitz. The first transport of political prisoners (728 Poles from Tarnow) arrived on June 14, 1940. On December 24, the first of five Christmas Eves behind barbed wire, the SS erected a lighted tree on the main square—under which they placed the bodies of prisoners who had either died during work or frozen to death during roll call.[82]

Following Operation Barbarossa, an expected entry of Soviet POW labor slated to renovate Oświęcim for Aryan colonization (Himmler's personal eastern fiefdom), led Reich planners to expand the complex to the nearby village of Brzezinka. With the area rich in fresh water, coal and lime, I. G. Farben would also harness the anticipated human energy for a synthetic rubber factory. However, by January 1942, the "Russkies" were a no-show (due to the Moscow debacle). In the words of van Pelt, the sprawling 425-acre complex was "quite literally a site in search of a mission."[83] Himmler opted to use the dormant area to expedite the Final Solution. Thus, though a concentration camp per se, Auschwitz metastasized into a matrix of multi-purpose facilities.

The original, semi-pristine Auschwitz I primarily served as the *Stammlager* ("General Administrative Headquarters"), originally housing mostly Polish insurgents for slave labor. As the Jews did not begin arriving until February 1942, the vast majority would perish at the obscure Auschwitz II-*Birkenau* ("birch forest") site two miles away. (Seweryna Symaglewska described her former residence as "a swamp fenced off by electrified wires."[84]) Finally, the gargantuan Farben plant housing 2,000 prisoners in the nearby town of Monowitz, was designated Auschwitz III-Monowitz (or "Buna," for its rubber product). Monowitz-Buna was the largest of forty-five "equal opportunity" slave labor satellite camps, exploiting Jews and goyim alike via numerous venues (farming, brickyards, construction, quarries, coalmines, armaments). Of the 35,000 inmates processed at Monowitz, about 25,000 died.[85] The prisoner count for all three sites would grow from 25,000 at the start to 105,000 in August 1944. Thus—to the exploitable advantage of Holocaust deniers—

the history of "Auschwitz" can appear complex at times, as circumstances and procedure not only frequently changed, but the recorded details and activity in one camp (Auschwitz I) can easily be confused with the corresponding policy (or lack thereof) at another (Auschwitz II or III).

Birkenau played a unique role in Hitler's plans as the goal was not *immediate* death for all. Enter Dr. Mengele's infamous selections on the *Judenrampe* ("Jew ramp"). Whereas the elderly and the visibly weak, plus nearly all mothers with children under fourteen, were sent to the *left* for immediate gassing, the "unselected" (about 25%) passed to the *right* for slave labor. During an inspection of children (as related by survivor, Dr. Bertold Epstein) a rod was set at four feet, three inches.[86] Kazimierz Smolen, an ethnic Pole survivor and longtime director of the Auschwitz Museum, stated: "Children who had passed under the rod would be gassed. Small children, knowing only too well what was waiting them, tried hard to push out their necks when passing under the rod, in the hope to escape gassing."[87]

Hundreds of dwarfs and children, especially twins, would escape the gas only to die in Mengele's laboratory (at Crematorium II). In one of his more notorious experiments, the veins of Gypsy twins were sewn together to make a set of artificial Siamese twins; in another, involving a one-year-old triplet, Mengele reputedly conducted a "postmortem" *while the child was still alive* (albeit under anesthesia).[88] Also, while sodomites were required to wear pink triangles, adolescent boys were secretly abused by salacious capos.[89] Wiesel affirms, "[T]here existed here a veritable traffic of children among homosexuals."[90]

While the selection process was specifically designed for Jews, all prisoners entering Birkenau's labor force received a personal registration number. Originally sown on the uniform, beginning in 1943 the numeric was tattooed on the inmate's left forearm (a process unique to Auschwitz). Some 405,000 prisoners of both sexes, from nearly every country in Europe were branded, half of whom eventually perished.[91] In addition to Jews (the largest group, hailing from as far away as Norway and Greece), the consortium included: political prisoners (mostly Poles); police prisoners (legitimate criminals); correctional prisoners; Soviet POWs; Catholic priests; and *asoziales* ("asocial elements"), primarily Romanian Gypsies (targeted for intransigence), prostitutes, sodomites, and Jehovah's Witnesses.

Jews had a small triangle added to their tattoos (ironically, the ancient Christian symbol of the Trinity). The import of this minute racial distinction readily became apparent. Though unaware of their tenuous fate, Jews who evaded Mengele's initial ramp-side caprice would be intentionally worked to death via the draconian SS policy of *Vernichtung durch Arbeit* ("Extermination through labor"). Heydrich alluded to this at Wannsee, stating: "As part of the development of the final solution the Jews are now to be put to work...as road-builders, in the course of which...a large number will be lost by natural wastage."[92] An obvious mockery of "Arbeit macht frei," "Vernichtung durch Arbeit" gave Himmler the dual "advantage" of subjecting his catatonic captives to a prolonged death while squeezing them for maximum profit. Hitler said:

> I do not want...the concentration camps to be transformed into sanatoria. Terror is the most effective political weapon. Everybody supports undertaking something against us, until he learns about what awaits him at a concentration camp...I need people who act severely and do not even begin to think when they have to kill someone...A conscience is a Jewish creation....[93]

Former inmate Yisrael Gutman wrote: "It was under the unremitting oppression of the concentration camps that the Nazi concept of absolute power over a captive population came closest to full implementation."[94] Recalling the collective mindset as being "killed in our spirit long before our anonymous death,"[95] fellow survivor Primo Levi adds, "It is in this way that one can understand the double sense of the term 'extermination camp.'"[96] Hannah Arendt, a German-American political theorist, concurred, stating: "[T]he concentration and extermination camps of totalitarian regimes serve as laboratories in which the fundamental belief of totalitarianism that everything is possible is being verified."[97]

Thus, the bottom-line philosophy at Planet Auschwitz was simple—"*Anything* goes." Gutman elaborates: "Destruction through work assumed two main forms: (1) work as punishment in the comprehensive terror system, involving humiliation, brutal treatment, and physical abuse, and (2) backbreaking labor without even the simplest work tools, performed by prisoners living in conditions below subsistence-level...."[98] The results were inevitable: "Every day in the life of a prisoner was filled with unbearable tension and superhuman effort, emotional turmoil and terror, continuing without respite for months on end."[99] Thus, workers rarely received any tools. While buildings often had to be torn down *by hand*, the replacement structures went up similarly.[100] Jews in road construction would move loads of earth or gravel to a site several hundred feet away using their shirts and overcoats as baskets. Other men were harnessed to "roller-wagons," large carts used for hauling everything from food, clothing, and building materials to latrine waste and corpses. Jewish women were also driven to an early grave through various tasks: building dikes and other earthworks; dredging ponds in waist-high water, (regardless of the season); even pulling plows on local SS farms.[101]

"SECRETORY CATASTROPHES"

The prisoners' daily routine was precisely what the Führer prescribed. Rising in the morning (the opening gong sounding anywhere from 3:00-4:30 a.m., depending on the calendar), the first challenge after rolling out in their tattered, louse-infested, blue-gray striped denim uniforms and ill-fitted wooden clogs (intentionally designed for discomfort) was simply surviving the initial trip to the toilet.

The camp's plumbing logistics defied all logic, averaging one latrine hut for every 7,000 inmates (7,800 per wash barrack). Each of the 18 communal outhouses was essentially a single concrete open sewer (118 ft. x 3 ft.), enclosed by a shed. The word "privy" was a cruel misnomer; there were no "shame walls" and no commodes, just staggered holes with a single horizontal beam providing the sole back support. The elongated trench was accessed from separated walkways on one side or the other (i.e., the only way in or out was at the opposite ends). Thus, given an overall floor space of 1,745 sq. ft., each prisoner had a grand total of 0.2 sq. ft. of toilet space.[102] As an acclaimed architectural authority, Dr. van Pelt presents a stunning perspective:

> Imagine 7,000 inmates at sunrise, suffering from diarrhea or dysentery, trying to enter, find an unoccupied place, defecate, manage not to fall into the sewer, and get out in the 10 or so minutes allocated by the camp's regulations to such necessities. Assuming that 150 inmates could find a place at one time, and also assuming that all 7,000 inmates were to move their bowels in the morning, it would require 46 successive 'seatings,' with all the traffic jams involved...One sewer, supplied with an anemic supply of water and with a drop of

only 1.6 percent, could never flush the discharge of 7,000 people in such a short time. The result was a secretory catastrophe."[103]

Females naturally suffered worse; Wanda Okon recalled, "The greatest tragedies in the camp were experienced by the Jewish women."[104] Höss wrote in his memoirs: "They stumbled through the area like ghosts, completely without will, and had to be literally pushed everywhere by others until one day they just quietly died. These walking corpses were a terrible sight."[105] Camp physician Gisella Perl, lived to testify: "There was one latrine for thirty to thirty-two thousand women…We stood in line to get in to this tiny building, knee-deep in human excrement. As we all suffered from dysentery, we could rarely wait until our turn came, and soiled our ragged clothes, which never came off our bodies, thus adding to the horror of our existence by the terrible smell which surrounded us like a cloud."[106]

With many a wealthy Jewess having entered the camp wearing a luxurious fur coat, survivor Isabella Leitner, relates, "Summer and winter we have but one type of clothing. Its name is 'rag'…The lice are having an orgy in our armpits, their favorite spots."[107] Many of the later Hungarian arrivals were spared this ordeal, forced instead to "go around without any clothes whatsoever."[108] Halina Birenbaum told how women with diarrhea would relieve themselves in soup bowls or coffee pans and then hide the soiled utensils under the mattress until the contents could be smuggled out to the latrine.[109] (Anne Frank encountered these identical hardships during her brief sojourn from early September 1944 to her late October transfer to Bergen-Belsen.)

Like Wiesel's sardonic remark, Levi and Müller expressed their own disdain for placards promoting hygiene; the former citing, "After the latrine, before eating, wash your hands, do not forget,"[110] the latter, "One louse may be your death."[111] Shoah scholar Terrence Des Pres opined that the excreta itself became the psychological game changer: "How much self-esteem can one maintain, how readily can one respond to the needs of another, if both stink, if both are caked with mud and feces?"[112] With the loss of one's innate human dignity, the SS would "reach the orgasmic peak of their potential domination…Spiritual destruction became an end in itself, quite apart from the requirements of mass murder."[113] Martin Gilbert quotes Leon Szalet regarding Jews being ordered to drink out of unflushed toilets: "'The men could not bring themselves to obey this devilish order…They only pretended to drink. But the block-führers had reckoned with that; they forced the men's heads deep into the bowls until their faces were covered with excrement...[T]he victims almost went out of their minds—their screams...sounded so demented."[114]

ROLL CALL AND THE DAILY ROUTINE

The next hurdle was enduring the morning roll call, a volatile ordeal that could drag on anywhere from two *hours* to two *days*.[115] To illustrate, the first recorded death at Auschwitz occurred on July 6, 1940 (after just three weeks of operation), when an inmate keeled over during a *nineteen*-hour muster (held in reprisal for an escape the day before). The unfortunate harbinger, David Wongczwski, just happened to be a Jew. In a similar punitive assembly that October, 120 dead and unconscious victims had to be removed from Roll Call Square.[116]

With only weak coffee for breakfast (plus any leftover crumbs from the previous evening's miniscule ration of stale bread), the slaves would march out of camp in rows of five, borne along by the force of the prison orchestra—"the voice of the Lager."[117] Comprised of both Aryans and Jews (with a female group in the women's camp), their repertoire included everything from foxtrots and tangos to the *Tancredi Overture*, a morbid throwback to Herzl's fraternity days.[118] Often made to entertain at various SS social affairs, Jewish musicians reputedly had the highest suicide rate, apart from Sonderkommandos. (The "Shoah music" in Terezin was the epitome of this tragic waste.)

The rest of the day was fairly routine—*eleven hours of continuous physical, mental, and emotional abuse*—with a thirty-minute lunch break consisting of rotten potato soup. In addition to engaging the standard "four horsemen"—exhaustion, hunger, cold, and sickness—the atrophied apparitions would also be assailed by sadistic torture; periodic selections of the weakening, known as *Muselmänner* (Muslim), named for the position they collapsed into from exhaustion; and summary executions (i.e., "Not fit to work; not fit to live"). The selections were often on Jewish holidays—*especially* Yom Kippur.[119]

Among a myriad of threats, it was not uncommon for guards to shoot Jews just for a citation or some extra vacation days, claiming the prisoner had "tried to escape," etc.[120] In another ordeal, the handle of a shovel was placed on a victim's throat so the capo could jump on the opposite ends with both feet. Inmates who received a public flogging had to count the number of each lash—in *German*.[121] (Though twenty-five was supposedly the prescribed maximum, some Jews were known to count as high as seventy.)[122] Then, as "the band played on," the returning slaves were obliged to parade in cadence, many bearing the added load of dead comrades, so their pedantic captors could square the morning count. Obviously, evening roll call was more strenuous, especially in winter. On December 24, 1941, despite temperatures below freezing, the inmates had to endure Pope Pacelli's Christmas Eve homily (also in German); 42 prisoners "swooned in the spirit."[123]

After muster, the inmates got to finish off (or horde) their daily food portions (1,300-1,700 calories) comprising 350 grams of "sawdust bread" (with some margarine), "smelly marmalade," or "putrid sausage," a half liter of coffee, and a liter of watery turnip soup.[124] (Those doing hard labor received larger portions.) Dr. Perl recalled the soup: "There were pieces of wood, potato peeling and unrecognizable substances swimming in it."[125] Denied a minimal caloric intake, the body would compensate by burning the energy stored in its own fatty tissue. When the reserve ran out, the muscle mass would begin to deteriorate, which lowered the body's resistance, inducing organ damage. Of the many debilitating diseases (typhus, prurigo, dysentery, phlegmon, malaria), starvation diarrhea claimed the most lives.[126] On a "positive" note, with Mengele in charge, the camp hospital became known as the "crematorium waiting room."[127]

Their meals done, the inmates would prepare for the evening portion of their dreary existence. After a final latrine stop, the last battle was securing a sleeping "berth" in the packed wooden "barracks" (WWI-era prefab horse stables sitting on bare earth). Two to three prisoners would share each of the three-tiered, wooden-plank bunks. On occasion, the total count would exceed fifteen, causing the rickety structure to implode in a twisted mass of splinters and bodies.[128] While Ecclesiastes 5:12 states, *"The sleep of a labouring man is sweet...,"* there was *nothing* "sweet" about Planet Auschwitz (apart from the sickly-sweet piquancy of Zyklon B). Originally designed for 52 animals, the makeshift stalls would billet as many as 800 humans, the straw used for mattresses.[129] Wiesel called it "the antechamber of hell...."[130] Borowski noted, "If the barrack walls were suddenly to fall away, many thousands of people, packed together, squeezed tightly in their bunks, would remain suspended in mid-air. Such a sight would be more gruesome than the medieval paintings of the Last Judgment."[131] Survivor John Frank stated how his *blockführer* would assuage space problems by assigning the guards a quota of 100 bludgeoning deaths per night![132] Venezia infers that men occupying the *lower* bunks would experience their *own* "secretory catastrophes."[133]

According to van Pelt's calculations, one's private space equated to all of 11 sq. ft., or 53 cu. ft.—the size of a shallow grave.[134] This dark analogy was realized on a nightly basis as prisoners would often expire while "resting" in their cramped, cold, damp, fetid, windowless, roof-leaking, rat-infested, disease-ridden "cribs." Some actually had better odds of seeing the dawn by spending a night in Block 11's penal medieval standing cell, likened to immurement ("walling in"). Then, the end of *one* man's suffering would inevitably trigger a new level of pain for *another*. The dense dwelling often prevented an expeditious extraction of the corpse, causing, as van Pelt put it, a "forced intimacy between the living and the dead."[135] Thus, one can see how a *real* nightmare—*like sleeping with a cadaver*—would inspire the nocturnal meditation, *"Would God it were morning!"* (Deuteronomy 28:67) By mid-1944, "burned-out" Sonderkommandos were spending *their* nights in the crematoria attics—staring at the cinerary urns containing the detritus of departed goys (made available to relatives at bargain prices).[136]

"NA, GIB INHEN SCHON ZU FRESSEN!"

In the evolution of death at Planet Auschwitz, eight homicidal gas chambers were used: the initial experimental operation in the cellars of Block 11 at Auschwitz I; the former morgue at the original camp incinerator (henceforth designated Crematorium I); the two converted cottages situated among the peripheral Birkenau Woods at Auschwitz II (i.e., Bunkers I and II); the four combination gassing-crematoria facilities, also at Birkenau (Crematoria II, III, IV, and V). Bodies at the cottages were incinerated in massive pits, the process being replicated whenever the crematoria ovens were overloaded or undergoing repair.

As previously noted, the cutting-edge Zyklon B (prussic acid) pesticide was the special wartime "contribution" of the Rockefeller Standard Oil-I. G. Farben alliance. This chemical was first employed in Auschwitz as a disinfectant for barracks and clothing. Potency levels ranged from A to F: Strength "D" was the normal dosage for lice, mice, or rats; "E" was for resistant vermin, i.e., roaches.[137] However, in a landmark experiment on September 3, 1941—involving *human* organisms—600 Soviet POWs and 250 hospital patients were asphyxiated in Block 11 using level "B." (To illustrate the "intuitive-initiative" approach, this climacteric test was ventured in the Commandant's absence by Captain Karl Fritzsch.)[138] One eyewitness testified: "I saw people clutching hair in their fists which they had torn from their own heads or those of others. I saw people locked in a tight embrace. I saw fingers that had been bitten through."[139]

A lethal dose equated to one milligram per kilogram of body weight. In a postwar affidavit, Höss estimated that only 13 lbs (in six 1-kg cans) were needed to gas 1,500 people.[140] The poison was emitted and would spread when the crystals came in contact with air. The accompanying odor reeked of burning metaldehyde, rendering a bitter-sweet taste. The victims experienced excessive throat irritation and unbearable pressure in the head. When the cyanide penetrated the lungs it abruptly paralyzed the respiratory center. The official cause of death was internal suffocation from a breakdown in the process of oxygen exchange between the blood and tissues.[141]

The mortuary of the "old" incinerator was promptly improvised to harness the promising new technology. Though small by later "industry" standards (the 835 sq. ft. cavity capable of murdering "only" 1,000 humans per twenty-minute cycle), it nonetheless became the first provisional gas chamber in the camp's dark history. Höss was elated, writing in his memoirs: "[T]he gassings had a calming effect on me…I was always horrified by the death by firing squads…Now I was at ease. We were all saved from these bloodbaths…."[142] Following a successful six-month trial run, the enhanced procedure was exported to Birkenau, just as the first Jewish transports were beginning to arrive.

To the demented Nazis, the uncanny fact that a former pesticide would now be used to exterminate "Jewish vermin" was conceptualized as an ideological bonus. In the 1940 propaganda film, *Der Ewige Jude* ("The Eternal Jew"), purporting to explain the Jews' evil role in history, audiences in Germany and Nazi-occupied Europe viewed repeated scenes of rats and Jews juxtaposed.[143] The same SS orderlies who took their fumigation training at *Degesch* (the Hamburg bug control firm with the Zyklon B patent) would now apply their honed skills to the Final

Solution.[144] Note how Höss makes the consummate Freudian slip when describing the gassing procedure in his prison memoirs: "Those Jews selected for *extermination* were brought as quietly as possible...The levers locking the door were then quickly shut tight. *Fumigators* who were on stand-by outside then immediately emptied the Zyklon B down through special shafts that opened into outlets in the ceiling...."[145] (Author's emphasis)

Two local vacant cottages (owned by evicted peasants) were promptly transformed into makeshift gas chambers (windows filled in, interior walls removed, and special airtight doors installed). Over the next year, 175,000 Jews were asphyxiated in these cozy-appearing facilities. Bunker I, a.k.a. "Little Red House" (brick exterior), was activated on March 20; Bunker II, a.k.a. "Little White House" (white plaster exterior), debuted on June 30.[146] (They would be anything *but* a "little house on the prairie.") Höss wrote: "In the spring of 1942 hundreds of people in the full bloom of life walked beneath the budding fruit trees of the farm into the gas chamber to their death, most of them without a hint of what was going to happen to them."[147]

The dead were initially moved to nearby ditches by small carts on special tracks. However, as one survivor reported, the corpses swelled by summer and a "black, evil-smelling mass oozed out and polluted the ground water in the vicinity."[148] The decomposing, maggot-infested remains were painstakingly exhumed and incinerated 2,000 at a time on pyres of wood; later in pits. Bunker I was dismantled, with II provisionally deactivated as Himmler's four state-of-the-art combined gas chamber-crematoria fired up between March and June 1943. The timing was critical, as all five other death camps would be closed by November 1943. The opening program was capped on "a bright March morning" by the gassing and burning of 8,000 Jews from Krakow.[149]

The killing routine was as follows: After a Judenrampe selection for death, the victims were immediately marched to the "showers" (the elderly and disabled taken by trucks). There, a contingent of fellow-Jewish "attendants" (Sonderkommandos) calmly ushered them down the stairs into the cellar changing rooms, women and children normally going first. Various signs read: "To the Baths" and "To Disinfection." They were then told to undress and hang their clothes on special numbered coat hooks along the wall. (Jews at the bunkers disrobed in the woods.) An SS official persistently coached them to remember their number to expedite their departure; some received soap and towels. Finally, they entered the heated gas chamber to await the men (always the smaller number). Höss, a former Catholic altar boy, recalled "little children...clutching a toy as they went into the gas chamber."[150] After the last males were pushed inside, the sealed door was screwed shut with iron bolts. Historian Marcello Pezzetti gives the gassing capacities of Crematoria II & III as exceeding 1,500 each (the smaller IV & V at 1,200[151]). Other estimates have reached 2,000.[152]

If the "Red Cross" truck was running late, guards would heighten the tension by flicking the lights on and off. The monocled *SS Hauptscharführer* (Sergeant-Major), Otto Moll (a.k.a. "Cyclops"), would then issue his infamous order—*"Na, gib inhen schon zu fressen!"* ("All right, give them something to chew on!").[153] When the rooftop hatch opened, pea-sized chalky pellets of diatomaceous earth, soaked in prussic acid, were sprinkled down four perforated hollow induction shafts by an SS "disinfector" in a gas mask. As the lethal fumes slowly floated upwards, the much-anticipated shower became a sauna of terror. Within ten to twelve minutes the bedlam was over. Nazi doctor Johann Kremer later testified: "Shouting and screaming of the victims could be heard...it was clear that they fought for their lives."[154] The peephole would confirm the quiet—*everyone* was gone.

The ventilation system was activated next. After another twenty minutes, the go-ahead was given to extract the remains for cremation. Jewish historian Franciszek Piper writes, "In cases of great congestion, many of the dead were found half-squatting, their skin colored pink with occasional red or green spots. Some foamed at the mouth, others bled from the ears."[155] The bodies were often found in heaps; children and elderly at the bottom. To escape the rising fumes, the stronger would mount the weaker in a futile effort to reach the last pockets of air. Describing the deaths of 800 women, Dr. Kremer recalled: "Being an anatomist I had seen many horrors, had dealt with corpses, but what I then saw was not to be compared with anything ever seen before."[156] Venezia concurred, "The sight that lay before us when we opened the door was terrible; nobody can even imagine what it was like...bodies were so entangled and twisted together – legs here, heads there...in a pile more than three feet high, sometimes four feet or more."[157] As the corpse attendant labored to explain, the task was dreadful because:

> [T]heir death had been anything but gentle. It was a foul, filthy death. A forced death, difficult and experienced differently by each of them...I find it difficult to speak of those visions of the gas chamber. You could find people whose eyes hung out of their sockets because of the struggles the organism had undergone. Others were bleeding from everywhere, or were soiled by their own excrement, or that of other people. Because of the effect that their fear and the gas had on them, the victims often evacuated everything they had in their bodies. Some...were all red, others very pale, as everyone reacted differently. But they had all suffered in death. People...imagine that the gas was thrown in, and there you were...victims die. But what a death it was!...You found them gripping each other—everyone had desperately sought a little air. The gas was thrown onto the floor and gave off acid from underneath, so everyone tried to find some air, even if each one needed to climb on another until the last one died."[158]

(The reader will recall Dr. Herzl's deathbed remarks: "I always believed that I knew what terror and horror can be. But everything that exists, and everything we can conjure up, is as child's play by comparison with the worst horror of all, with the fight for breath.")

While Filip Müller was also reticent to revisit *his* memories of sloshing through similar workplace conditions ("blood, excrement, urine, vomit, everything"[159]), a sacred impromptu vow compelled him to testify. On March 7, 1944, the chamber was packed with Slovakian Jews from the agitprop "Family Camp," lately imported from Theresienstadt (Terezin), the ghetto where Trude Herzl died. Aware of their doom, the throng sang the Slovak national anthem, then broke out in a final defiant rendition of "HaTikva," prompting Müller to record: "[T]hey were glancing into the future, but it was not a future which they would be allowed to see."[160] Amazingly, this eyewitness account would not have seen the light of day had it not been for what happened next. Overcome with despair, Müller, a native Czech himself, resolved to join the victims as his dying testament of solidarity. "I thought that here I would remain undiscovered until the gas chamber was full, when it would be locked."[161] Yet to his utter shock, a group of young women accosted him with a lecture to the contrary: "*We* must die, but you still have a chance to save your life...perhaps you'll survive this terrible tragedy and then you must tell everybody what happened."[162]

With only minutes to spare, their chief spokesperson entrusted him with a last request on a personal level:

> '[T]his gold chain round my neck: when I'm dead, take it off and give it to my boyfriend Sasha. He works in the bakery. Remember him to me. Say "love from Yana". When it's all over, you'll find me here.' She pointed at a place next to the concrete pillar where I was standing. Those were her last words...Before I could make an answer to her spirited speech, the girls took hold of me and dragged me protesting to the door of the gas chamber. There they gave me a last push which made me land bang in the middle of the SS men.[163]

Müller then concludes:

> During the removal of the corpses...I went to the pillar near which the girls had talked to me. There I found Yana...She lay where she had said she would. I took off the necklace, pocketed it and left the room. As soon as I returned to the camp...I found Sasha in the bread store...When I handed him the gold chain and delivered his sweetheart's farewell greetings, the tears ran down his bronzed, scarred face.[164]

As the bodies were dragged to the anteroom, Sonderkommandos had two immediate jobs: cut the women's hair and search the corpses, removing spectacles, dentures, prostheses, *especially* gold fillings, plus any valuables concealed within body orifices. With the extraction racket raking in over twenty-five pounds of gold per month, the penalty for missing a filling was being kicked into the furnace.[165] The bodies in Crematoria II & III were loaded onto electric freight elevators (seven to ten at a time), then taken up to the main floor for burning. The smaller chambers in Crematoria IV & V were built above ground for financial reasons. (While there is no evidence for the Shoah's worst canard—the *routine* making of soap from the fat of Jewish corpses—at least two reports exist of this occurring on a local and limited basis.)[166]

When pressed, 2,500 corpses could burn every 24 hours in each of Crematoria II & III, plus 1,500 daily in IV & V.[167] Jan Hartman, a Jewish Czech youth recalled, "[T]here was the smell of human flesh being burnt, a certain smell, it was in the air...the air was not clean: you were breathing the dead."[168] The "mopping up" phase required that the chambers be ventilated and whitewashed for the next arrivals, the

Jews' personal effects be sent to "Canada," then their bones ground to powder and strewn with their ashes on fields (as fertilizer) or dumped in local waterways.

Holocaust deniers (like Steven Anderson) insist that a body could not be cremated in 25 minutes because *modern* mortuaries require two hours. Thus, 1,000,000 Jews could not have passed through the 52 ovens of Auschwitz, etc. To *"answer a fool according to his folly"* (Proverbs 26:5, as marvelously cross-referenced with Romans 11:25), these self-conceited fools forgot seven things: 1) the SS was not held to ICCFA standards; 2) three bodies (sometimes more) were burned together; 3) no cremation caskets were used; 4) after 25 minutes—the partially incinerated bones having fallen from the chamotte grid to the ash collection channel below to smolder for another 20 minutes—new bodies were packed in alongside the preceding remains; 5) the victims were normally emaciated, 50% being women and children; 6) tens of thousands were consumed in open air pits; 7) far from "Jewish lies" (Anderson), these facts were corroborated by the Auschwitz Construction Agency (*Bauleitung*), J. A. Topf engineers, and Commandant Rudolf Höss himself.[169]

MARTIN LUTHER

The hefty, highly negotiated, and later (with Jews burning), vehemently disputed contract for constructing the four crematoria at Birkenau was awarded to J. A. Topf und Söhne ("and Sons"), manufacturers of heating equipment in Erfurt, Germany. It is not without historical significance that the famous German reformer, Martin Luther, imbibed his deleterious anti-Semitism at the University of Erfurt. Dr. Luther's pivotal role in sparking the Vatican-smashing Protestant Reformation notwithstanding, the former Augustinian monk must also bear the blame for taking his nation's racist ideology to a whole new level. The same preacher who gave *Rome* the "95 Theses"; *Germany*, the Luther Bible; and *Christianity*, "A Mighty Fortress is Our God" and "Away in a Manger," *also* gave the anti-Semitic world a 65,000-word diatribe dubbed *About the Jews and Their Lies*. Among several invectives, Luther called the Jews "thirsty bloodhounds and murderers of all Christendom," loathing their presence "like a plague, pestilence [and] pure misfortune in our country."[170] Under the title, "I shall give you my sincere advice," his seven-point rant recommended:

> First, to set fire to their synagogues or schools and to bury and cover with dirt whatever will not burn, so that no man will ever again see a stone or cinder of them. This is to be done in honor of our Lord and of Christendom...Second, I advise that their houses also be razed and destroyed...Third, that all their prayer books and Talmudic writings be taken from them...Fourth, that their rabbis be forbidden to teach henceforth on pain of loss of life and limb...Fifth, that safe conduct on the highways be abolished completely for the Jews. For they have no business in the countryside...Sixth, that usury be prohibited to them, and all cash and treasure of silver and gold be taken from them and put aside for safekeeping...Seventh, putting an ax, a hoe, a spade, a distaff, or a spindle into the hands of young, strong Jews and Jewesses, letting them earn their bread in the sweat of their brow...."[171]

Then Dr. Luther "lovingly" concludes:

> I ask that our rulers...act like a good physician who, when gangrene has set in, proceeds without mercy to cut, saw, and burn flesh, veins, bone, and marrow...If this does not help we must drive them out like mad dogs, so that we do not become partakers of their abominable blasphemy and all their other vices and thus merit God's wrath and be damned with them. I have done my duty. Now let everyone see to his. I am exonerated...May Christ, our dear Lord, convert them mercifully and preserve us steadfastly and immovably in the knowledge of him, which is eternal life. Amen."[172]

With Luther representing a transitional trajectory within the historical anti-Semitic cycle of *conversion*, *expulsion*, and *destruction*, Hilberg summarizes: "The missionaries of Christianity had said in effect: You have no right to live among us as Jews. The secular rulers who followed had proclaimed: You have no right to live among us. The German Nazis at last decreed: You have no right to live."[173] When Hitler denounced the Jews in Deutschland, he invariably struck a familiar cord. "The picture of the Jew encountered in Nazi propaganda and Nazi correspondence had been drawn several hundred years before. Martin Luther had already sketched the main outlines of that portrait, and the Nazis, in their time, had little to add to it."[174] Thus, when Julius Streicher, publisher of the racist tabloid *Der Stürmer* ("The Attacker"), was asked at Nuremberg about the prevalence of other anti-Jewish literature, he replied: "Anti-Semitic publications have existed in Germany for centuries...Martin Luther would very probably sit in the defendants' dock today...In the book *The Jews and Their Lies*...Luther writes that the Jews are a serpent's brood and one should burn down their synagogues and destroy them."[175]

In late 1945, a conclave of Lutheran churchmen in Stuttgart issued a Protestant *mea culpa*, confessing: "[W]e are bound to our people not only in a community of suffering but also in a solidarity of guilt. With heavy pain we say: Through us, unending misfortune was brought to many countries and nations."[176] Despite the clerical tears, in 1951, German lawyer Henry Picker published transcripts of the Fürher's casual wartime dialogue, known colloquially as *Hitler's Table Talk*—an unsettling throwback to Luther's own posthumous sayings, released in 1566 as *Colloquia Mensalia* ("Divine Discourses at his Table").

The impact of Luther's legacy may be aptly illustrated by two notable Germans. After twelve years of service as a Lutheran pastor, Ernst Biberstein became the leader of Einsatzkommando 6. At Nuremberg, "Reverend" Biberstein was condemned to hang for the murder of 2,500 Jews near Rostov. However, his sentence was commuted to "*life* imprisonment"; twelve years later, Ernst was out and about, even making a brief return to the "pulpit." He died in 1986.

The *other* Nazi was far more influential. In 1938, he went from being an interior *decorator* to *director* of *Referat Deutschland* (the main Foreign Office division involving Jewish affairs). In May 1940, he was made Foreign Minister liaison to the SS. He was also the main Reich delegate to the Wannsee Conference. His personal record of the minutes (found in 1947) is the *only* copy to survive the war. Then, as *Unterstaatssekretär* ("Under-Secretary of State") at the German Foreign Ministry, his main task was coercing reluctant German allies to surrender their Jewish populations for deportations to the camps.

In his treatise, *The Wilhelmstrasse: A Study of Nazi Diplomats Under the Nazi Regime*, Dr. Paul Seabury attests that this individual "played a decisive role in facilitating negotiations with the Bulgarian, Hungarian, Rumanian, and Slovakian regimes during 1942, which led to mass deportations of Jews from these countries...."[177] The mystery Nazi was also charged with "spreading disinformation and propaganda throughout the Middle East."[178] Once considered Reich Minister for Foreign Affairs Joachim von Ribbentrop's right-hand man, the overly ambitious bureaucrat "fell from grace" in the spring of 1943. After living out the war in confinement, he died of a "heart attack" in Berlin on May 13, 1945, at the age of 49. His name was—Martin Luther.

TOBY & JOHN

This author was privileged to have personally made the acquaintance of two Jewish survivors of Auschwitz-Birkenau (one by happenstance, the other through a scheduled interview arranged by a mutual friend). Their names were—Toby and John.

Nearly half-a-century after surviving Himmler's "destruction through work" program, Toby, a vibrant, kind-hearted Jewess, was spending her golden years (ca. 1990) *cleaning tables and mopping floors at a fast-food restaurant in Crown Point, Indiana.* On break, she would lean on a mop and relate stories from her former existence in the lager. However, it was painfully obvious that few of the patrons were interested. In their rush to devour more calories in one *meal* than she was previously allotted in two *days*, the junk food junkies had rendered themselves oblivious to "Toby's tattoo." (This author and his family gratefully indulged in the fleeting window of learning.)

John M. Frank, a longtime resident of Newark, Delaware, was born Judel Mejer Foimczyk on July 23, 1925, in Pruzany, Polesie, Poland. On the night of February 2, 1942, sixteen-year-old Judel, his parents, four sisters, and two (of three) brothers, detrained from their cattle car at the Judenrampe in Auschwitz. John and his three oldest sisters went to the right; the rest *departed* leftward. His new "name" for the next three years was 98842, along with that telltale triangle. (The girls would all die in three months.) Among the many experiences Mr. Frank shared in our two meetings in 2002, he showed the most gravity when recalling the gaze of Dr. Mengele—describing it as "that solid stare, the death stare." (Having arrived a year before Mengele, John's contact would have been during the Angel's recurring camp selections; other physicians included Hans König, Heinz Thilo, and Fritz Klein.)

A different memory was conveyed with considerable pathos—his unwonted method of saving certain Jewish mothers on the ramp. As noted, women with small children or infants were condemned on site. Whenever John would observe a mother with just one, he would get her to let him "play" with the child momentarily. He would then use a pretense to pass the tyke to a different woman with several children already in tow. Only later would the hysterical parent make the ambivalent find that her life had been spared by John's timely ruse.[179] Martin Gilbert refers to this activity, in camp parlance, as "children to the old."[180] (Borowski adds that other, less-devoted mothers, when sensing danger, would *try* to abandon their little ones.[181])

"PRECIOUS MEMORIES"

The more one studies Planet Auschwitz, the more bizarre that hellish world becomes. As Ecclesiastes 12:12 states, *"of making many books there is no end,"* the burden of this author can be likened to a triage nurse—What *should* be told and what should *not.* A similar exasperation was expressed by the inspired writer in Hebrews 11:32, *"And what shall I more say? for the time would fail me to tell of..."* (the focus here being on Israel's *triumphs* rather than her *tragedies*).

Yisrael Gutman writes in *Anatomy of the Auschwitz Death Camp*, that 25,000 to 30,000 inmates were killed by phenol injections to the heart.[182] In the same book, Andrzej Strzelecki states that Himmler sent the salvageable clothes of gassed Jews (minus the yellow stars) to resettled Germans for *Christmas* presents; Soviet troops found seven *tons* of abandoned women's hair; and that a caravan of baby strollers bound for the "Father Land," being pushed five abreast from "Canada" to the local train depot, took over an *hour* to pass.[183] Shlomo Venezia recalls in *Inside The Gas*: a capo named *Goliath*; inmates hiding coins and valuables by ingesting, passing, and later retrieving them (often, more than once); Jews bartering gold teeth for hunks of bread; maneuvering amidst 2,000 asphyxiated corpses releasing a cacophony of flatulence; a baby girl at her mother's breast in the gas chamber—having miraculously survived by gaining insulation through the strength of her sucking—being taken out and *shot* upon discovery.[184]

Tadeusz Borowski bequeathed *his* readership the following "precious memories": a small, one-legged girl being tossed into a truckload of dead arrivals headed for the ovens; 28,000 naked women stampeded out of the barracks in a delousing procedure; the ground floor "cultural section" in Block 24, comprising a library, museum and concert hall, with the camp brothel (hypocritically employing "asocial whores") occupying the second floor; other females being artificially inseminated, injected with typhoid and malaria germs, and operated upon in various crackpot experiments in Block 10; the cannibalizing of corpses, especially raw brains; a Sonderkommando grieving over family photos he received—having found them in the pocket of his own father after dutifully pointing him to the "showers"; a Nazi's parting advice to an elderly Jew who naively requested a word with the commandant, "Look here, old man! In half an hour you'll be talking with the top commandant! Only don't forget to greet him with a *Heil Hitler!*"; a dying SS officer, shot by a bold Jewess in a rare prison revolt, crying out, "O God, my God, what have I done to deserve such suffering?" (Perhaps the most unusual part of Borowski's memoirs, *This Way for the Gas, Ladies and Gentlemen*, is the fact that the work was published posthumously, the Gentile survivor having taken his *own* life on July 1, 1951—*by opening a gas valve.*)[185]

Finally, Filip Müller's story, *Eyewitness Auschwitz*, includes: nearly suffocating in the back of a truck beneath a crushing load of corpses toppled during a jarring ride; stoking bodies with a pitchfork to make them burn better; 2,500 corpses roasting in a pit as the "tongues of a thousand tiny blue-red flames were licking at them"; the decapitated remains of Oświęcim's "terminated" German mayor going up the chimney as well; Muselmänners exercising their only liberty by choosing the time, method, and even nickname of their suicidal deaths, "going to the wire"; clotheslines strung across the crematoria hair-drying loft, displaying, like so much dripping laundry, pegged tresses of women's hair of every color and hue; SS officers spending their Sunday afternoons truncheoning dozens of Jewish men to death in the courtyard of Block 11 for such "infractions" as wearing an ill-fitting cap, displaying spectacles with thick lenses, or simply having a nose deemed too long; 20,000 inmates shot in the nape of the neck before the "Black Wall of Death"; a mother with her daughter *begging* to be shot first, only to have the sadist circle the pair (seeking a target on so small a body), ultimately denying the plea *at point blank range.*[186]

As most of these shooting victims were partisans (including women and children) of the Polish resistance, the following eyewitness account by former prisoner, Dr. Boleslaw Zbozien, is provided in memoriam of the 75,000 ethnic Poles who also perished at Auschwitz.

> Sometime, I cannot remember the exact date, we encountered Palitzsch [opprobrious non-commissioned officer, Gerhard Palitzsch,

> a.k.a. "The greatest b-----d of Auschwitz"] on the streets of the camp at Auschwitz. Before him, he was driving a man and a woman. The woman was carrying a small child in her arms, and two larger children, around four and seven years old, walked next to her. The entire group was walking toward Block 11...As long as I live, the scene that played out before our eyes will remain engraved in my memory.
>
> The man and woman did not resist when Palitzsch stood them before the Wall of Death. It all took place in the greatest calm. The man held the hand of the child who stood on his left side. The second child stood between them; they both held his hand. The mother clasped the youngest to her breast. Palitzsch first shot the baby in the head. The shot to the back of the head exploded its skull...and induced massive bleeding. The baby struggled like a fish, but the mother only held him more firmly to herself. Palitzsch next shot the child standing in the middle. The man and the woman...continued to stand without moving, like statues. Later, Palitzsch struggled with the oldest child, who would not allow himself to be shot. He threw him to the ground and shot him at the base of the head while standing on his shoulders. He then shot the woman, and at very last, the man. This was the greatest monstrosity...After that, although many executions were carried out, I did not watch them.[187]

Before leaving Planet Auschwitz, a final, sad story is apropos. As dawn broke on a gray summer morning in August 1943, 2,000 Jews, the vanguard of the liquidation of the nearby Sosnovits and Będzin ghettos, were herded into the courtyard of Crematorium V. Müller's eyewitness remarks follow: "Facing them was the red-brick building with its two forbidding chimneys belching forth the smoke and the fumes of the fires of hell."[188] Arriving from only twenty-five miles away, the pitiful group was *more* than aware of their imminent demise. The exceptional number of menacing guards bore added witness to the same. Contrary to the normal ruse, there were no pep talks about showers and the like, only a terse order to disrobe where they stood.

Resigned to their fate, they began to undress themselves and their children "as though with every garment they were discarding a little of their lives, those lives which for most of them had, in any case, consisted of nothing but want and privation. Many were fighting back their tears, afraid that their children might be alarmed or start asking questions...The children too were looking around sad-eyed."[189] Finally—all were ready. "Husbands and wives embraced, caressing their children and trying to comfort each other. Disappointed with a world that had turned its back on them, they used their last few minutes to search their souls and think about their lives which, however wretched they might have been, still seemed more desirable than the death which now awaited them."[190] Then—at the very nadir of their collective tragedy—a solitary unassuming Jew ignited the surprise denouement, briefly reversing the role of captor and victim:

> Suddenly from among the crowd a loud voice could be heard: an emaciated little man had begun to recite the Viddui [deathbed confessional prayer]. First he bent forward, then he lifted his head and his arms heavenward and after every sentence, spoken loud and clear, he struck his chest with his fist. Hebrew words echoed round the yard: '*bogati*' (we have sinned), '*gazalti*' (we have done wrong to our fellow men), '*dibarti*' (we have slandered), '*heevetjti*' (we have been deceitful), '*verhirschati*' (we have sinned), '*sadti*' (we have been proud), '*maradti*' (we have been disobedient). 'My God, before ever I was created I signified nothing, and now that I am created I am as if I had not been created. I am dust in life, and how much more so in death. I will praise you everlastingly, Lord, God everlasting, Amen! Amen!'
>
> The crowd of 2,000 repeated every word, even though perhaps not all of them understood the meaning of this Old Testament confession. Up to that moment, most of them had managed to control themselves. But now almost everyone was weeping. There were heart-rending scenes among members of families. But their tears were not tears of despair. These people were in a state of deep religious emotion. They had put themselves in God's hands. Strangely, the SS men did not intervene, but let the people be."[191]

The presiding *Oberscharführer* ("platoon sergeant")—having recovered from his own momentary shock—was now glaring at his watch impatiently. The drama, however, was not over yet. The reader will recall the special day of sorrow by World Jewry the previous year. As Morse related, "One million Jews, doomed to die at Auschwitz from the effects of prussic acid, were among those who observed the day of mourning on December 2, 1942." And so, taking things to the next and final level, having ended the Viddui, the condemned prisoners proceeded to recite their *own* funeral dirge. "The prayers had reached a climax: the crowd was reciting the prayer for the dead which traditionally is said only by surviving relatives for a member of the family who has died. But since after their death there would be nobody left to say the Kaddish for them they, the doomed, recited it while they were still alive." He concludes, "And then they walked into the gas chamber. Zyclon B crystals extinguished their lives while life in the camp and in the Sonderkommando went on as usual."[192]

RESCUE *VERSUS* STATEHOOD

In the wake of Bermuda, the plight of Europe's Jews was exacerbated by a disconcerting (albeit typical) split within American Zionism. Irgun veteran, Peter Bergson (born Hillel Kook), representing the Joint Emergency Committee for European Jewish Affairs (JEC), advocated an immediate Allied rescue mission. The American Jewish Congress (AJC) mostly endorsed the Biltmore Program (birthed at the May 1942 Biltmore Conference in New York), arguing that all lobbying efforts remain focused on the anticipated postwar struggle for statehood.

The timing of this dispute could not have been worse, for as Wyman notes regarding Biltmore, "This was the first time the American Zionist movement had explicitly advocated a Jewish state in Palestine. It constituted a basic shift from the previous position, which accepted indefinite postponement of the statehood goal while concentrating on building up the Jewish community in Palestine."[193] Undaunted, Bergson convened the Emergency Conference to Save the Jewish People of Europe (July 20-25) at the Hotel Commodore in Manhattan, drawing an impressive 1,500 delegates. Proclaiming that European Jewry was "caught between the hammer of the enemy's brutality and the anvil of democracy's indifference," the invigorated "Bergsonites" resolved to confront their pragmatic brethren in both the public and political arenas.[194] The opposition, led by Rabbi Abba Silver (backed by Wise and Weizmann), countered with the American Jewish Conference at the Waldorf Astoria (August 29 - September 2). Iowa Senator Guy Gillette, a committed Zionist, quoted a frustrated colleague, "I wish these d----d Jews would make up their minds…."[195]

Bergson then persuaded Eleanor Roosevelt to give her husband a copy of the "Findings and Recommendations of the Emergency Conference." The president returned the report on August 16 with a note: "I do not think this needs any answer at this time. FDR."[196] With Évian and Bermuda to his "credit," the curt reply represented FDR's "third strike." On October 6 (three days before Yom Kippur), 400 Orthodox rabbis "chased" him out of the Oval Office. In town to participate in a "Pilgrimage for Rescue," the delegation (conspicuous with their beards, long black coats, and chanting), somberly marched from Union Station to the Capitol. As the president was "unavailable" due to "pressure of other business" (having slipped away just hours before to attend the "critical" swearing-in ceremony of forty Yugoslavs into the US Army Air Force), Vice President Wallace and several congressmen received the distinguished deputation.[197]

Bergson and the JEC were ultimately derailed by the Zionist-heavy AJC. As the Allies promoted victory in Europe as the most expeditious remedy for the Shoah, the Zionists concurred, choosing a future homeland for the survivors as the greater priority. Wyman writes, "An unavoidable conclusion is that during the Holocaust the leadership of American Zionism concentrated its major force on the drive for a future Jewish state in Palestine. It consigned rescue to a distinctly secondary position."[198] Thus, as the Holocaust was *induced* by Western democracies sealing their borders to European Jews, it was ironically *extended* by American Jews blocking military intervention.

FDR & THE WRB

Although the president was unwilling to make any substantive commitment to a rescue plan for European Jews—given the political animal that he was (i.e., his ability to feel the heat from pro-Jewish factions, specifically, a forthcoming emotionally charged Rescue Resolution)—he did manage *one* cosmetic concession. On January 22, 1944, FDR headed Congress off at the pass by issuing Executive Order 9417, creating the imposing War Refugee Board (WRB).

Treasury Secretary Henry Morgenthau's assistant, John W. Pehle, was made Executive Director. The presidential fiat directed the State, Treasury, and War Departments to render whatever assistance the WRB required to implement its agenda "to take all measures within its power to rescue the victims of enemy oppression who are in imminent danger of death and otherwise to afford such victims all possible relief and assistance consistent with the successful prosecution of the war."[199]

Of course, those *last eight words* would provide Roosevelt's regime with plenty of wiggle room to pursue business as usual.

Theoretically, the WRB was to prosecute an extensive rescue plan, working in tandem with private Jewish agencies. Wyman relates, "Its main contours included (1) evacuating Jews and other endangered people from Axis territory, (2) finding places to which they could be sent, (3) using psychological measures (especially threats of war-crimes trials) aimed at preventing deportations and atrocities, and (4) shipping relief supplies into concentration camps."[200] In reality, the agency's accomplishments would fall woefully short, thwarted by negligible funding and bureaucratic encumbrance (some natural, most contrived). Secretary Morgenthau, the Jews' main ally (denounced as "that d----d Jew in the Treasury") was continually hamstrung by mid-level State Department officials.[201]

FDR's War Department also proved consistently uncooperative. Regarding America's "partners," while Russia refused to participate, the British were obstructive. Revisiting a familiar theme concerning the latter, Morse remarks: "The possibility of mass rescue threatened England's Palestine policies; the vision of Jews streaming to Palestine seemed to upset Whitehall more than the vision of Jews walking to their death in the gas chambers."[202] Yet, the President was covered, Wyman stating, "Roosevelt took little interest except as a source of occasional favorable publicity."[203] Meanwhile, as one group of refugees would later bemoan, "For two years there has been only one phrase on everyone's lips, 'When are the Americans coming?'"[204]

LAST CHANCE FOR REDEMPTION

From April 1943 to March 1944, "only" about 150,000 Jews had died in the new Birkenau crematoria. That figure would triple in eight months. An omen of things to come, in May a rail spur line was laid right into the camp itself, passing through the notorious "Death Gate."

By early 1944, Hungary was poised to repudiate her Axis alliance. While Miklos Horthy had previously repulsed Hitler's lust for Jewish deportations (primarily out of economic concerns[205]), his cohorts now hoped that "clemency and benevolent treatment" might be garnered from the Allies "because of their hospitable attitude towards Jewry."[206]

German forces promptly occupied the country in March. With the formation of a new "Hitler-friendly" government (under the titular quisling, Dominik Sztojay), Eichmann set out to make up for lost time.

The Hungarian Aktion was unique in several particulars. While the nation's Jews (like the Franks in Holland) were able to survive until mid-1944, they died in Hitler's last year of power. Hungary was the only place where the Nazis *knew* the war was lost when they invaded, Göring declaring to Goebbels, "[I]n the Jewish question we are so locked in that there is no escape left for us."[207] The furious pace would be typified by Revelation 12:12,*"for the devil…knoweth that he hath but a short time."* Hungary's Jews also possessed the clearest insight to their impending doom. Lastly, at such a late hour, the Führer's final stab at the Final Solution would be acted out before the entire world.

Thus, in the bitterest of ironies, the *highest* number of Jews would be slaughtered in the *shortest* amount of time at the *precise* moment when the Allies had the *greatest* amount of technical wherewithal to intervene (via precision bombing sorties). Hilberg concludes: "The success of these operations, in the twilight of the Axis, says much about the Germans, who began the venture, about the Hungarians, who were drawn into it, about the Jews, who suffered it, and about the outside powers, who stood by and watched it come to pass."[208]

While the Allies sat on their hands, the standard prelude of repressive ghettoizing began in earnest. In April, Riegner dispatched his second historic cable, this time warning that Hitler intended to annihilate all of Hungarian Jewry. He told of seeing 10,000 Budapest Jews (old and young) crowded into a brickyard with no sanitary facilities, many dying on their feet.[209] Requests for immediate sanctuary in America were denied, being "contrary to prevailing immigration quotas." That over 100,000 German POWs were currently quartered in the USA only aggravated the imminent slaughter of nearly 300,000 Jewish civilians by the government of those very prisoners.

Roosevelt did manage to send a letter denouncing the atrocities and threatening postwar repercussions. Meanwhile, the WRB's laughable "strategy" was reduced to urging the Pope to threaten his Nazi "parishioners" with excommunication from the Church.[210] Having already abandoned hundreds of his *own* priests at Auschwitz,[211] Pius XII (as Cardinal Carlo Salotti put it) was not *about* to violate his rule for "impos[ing] upon himself, in word and deed, the most delicate reserve" (i.e., avoiding the "slightest appearance of partiality"), *especially* on behalf of several hundred thousand "Christ-killers."[212]

When the pro-Reich Arrow Cross party in Veszprém "persuaded" the Franciscans to conduct a Mass of thanksgiving for the Jews' expulsion, the "humble" friars obliged (yet under "protest").[213] More to the point, resulting from the earlier (fall 1942) secret negotiations between Germany and Cardinal Luigi Lavitrano, Archbishop of Palermo, Pius XII consented to a bona fide gag order. Aarons and Loftus write in *Unholy Trinity*, "On the eve of the Final Solution...the Lavitrano Mission had agreed to compromise with the Nazis. In return for easing religious persecution in the East, the Vatican would become neutral in favour of the Germans. For the rest of the war, the Pope never discussed Nazi atrocities against the Russians, nor was the word 'Jew' ever mentioned in any Papal pronouncement."[214] Correctly anticipating that the volume of papal silence would only grow "louder" in the ensuing Shoah, the War Department noted on October 27, 1942, "A certain modus vivendi seems to have been established in this sense as the result of the Commission of Cardinal Lavitrano."[215]

In a pitiful attempt to save their own skin, thousands of Jews were sprinkled into the Roman faith in the air-raid shelters of Budapest.[216] As usual, while ubiquitous Pacelli apologists keep their Catholic readers on life support, history confirms how the actual participants felt. When Sándor Török, president of the Society of Christian Jews in Hungary, proposed to Cardinal Jusztinián Serédi that Communion be denied to gendarmes, policemen, functionaries, or railroad men who collaborated with the SS in the deportations, the exasperated prelate threw his biretta on the floor and replied: "If His Holiness, the Pope, is doing nothing against Hitler, what can I do in my narrow confines?"[217]

And so—once again—left with no viable alternative (consistent with his demonic ideology), the Führer was "constrained" to trigger the final stage of the Final Solution. From May 15 to July 9, German and Hungarian police crammed and sealed 437,000 Jews into 147 "Holocaust trains" for their three-day odyssey to Planet Auschwitz (the number of occupants marked in chalk on the outside of each car.[218]) The hellish pace required three to four transports per day; 3,000 to 3,500 Jews per train; 70 to 90 per car—with two communal buckets, one for water, the other for excrement.[219] Echoing *Night* author Wiesel's observation, a survivor recalled: "When we arrived in Birkenau, such a smell of burning flesh wafted towards us that in the groups arriving at night, who not only smelt the stench but saw the flames rising from the crematoria, many committed suicide at once."[220]

Despite repeated oven malfunctions caused by corpse overload, between 250,000 and 300,000 Hungarian Jews were gassed or shot within a forty-six day period (massive burning pits taking up the slack).[221] One of the more disconcerting scenarios occasioned by the Hungarian influx was the interminable foot traffic along the path to the crematoria causing lengthy delays at each site.[222] With the killing frenzy reaching 10,000 Jews daily, the Little White House had to be reactivated. The Allies were astounded, having erroneously anticipated a moderation of anti-Semitic policy given the Reich's imminent defeat.

"Blood for Goods"

Although the Nazis displayed a frenetic resolve to *finish* the Final Solution, they were not totally oblivious to their own impending demise. For instance, as deteriorating supply lines caused a commensurate shortage of plasma for wounded Germans (the Red Cross ruse coming back to haunt them), numbers of arriving Hungarian Jewesses were spared long enough to "give" blood for the Fatherland in hefty quantities, Dr. Perl recalling women lying faint on the ground with "deep rivers of blood flowing around their bodies.[223] In a further unprecedented (and equally humiliating) move, a severe drop in military production forced Hitler to approve an emergency *westbound* transfer of 100,000 Hungarian Jews from Auschwitz to German labor camps.[224] However, the most telling proof of Axis desperation appeared in April 1944 when Eichmann offered to *ransom* Hungary's remaining Jews for badly needed war supplies.

Under the catchy slogan, "*Blut gegen Waren*" ("Blood for Goods"), the Commissioner for Jewish Affairs literally proposed swapping one million Jews for two million bars of soap, eight-hundred tons of coffee, two hundred tons of cocoa, eight hundred tons of tea, and ten thousand trucks.[225] The antithesis of fellow German Oskar Schindler's selfless purchase of 1,200 Jews, Eichmann's spiel to his Jewish agent in Budapest, Joel Brand, was: "I am ready to sell you a million Jews. Goods for blood—blood for goods. What do you want to save? Virile men? Grown women? Old people? Children? Sit down and talk."[226]

When Brand asked about guarantees, the Nazi replied: "When you come back from Istanbul and tell me that the offer has been accepted, I will dissolve Auschwitz and move 10 percent of the promised million to the border. You take over the 100,000 Jews and deliver for them afterwards one thousand trucks. And then the deal will proceed step by step. For every hundred thousand Jews, a thousand trucks. You are getting away cheap."[227] He also "promised" that the trucks would be used "only on the eastern front" (a caveat bound to inspire Stalin).[228]

In their second (and last) meeting on May 15, Eichmann reaffirmed his pledge that if the money came in—"*Dann spreng ich Auschwitz in die Luft*" ("Auschwitz would be blown up"). During the talks, Isaac Sternbuch, representing the Swiss affiliate of *Vaad Hahatzala* (a New York-based rescue committee), floated a cash offer of five million dollars for 300,000 Jews (about $17 per person). The Jews would go out at the rate of 15,000 per month, in return for monthly installments of $250,000. (A smaller deal pitched 100 tractors for 1,200 rabbis.[229])

To make a long (and macabre) story short, by now the reader should have little problem guessing the extent of any *serious* Anglo-American counteroffers. Not only was the scheme rejected out of hand (forfeiting the standard negotiating tactic of "taking the matter under consideration"—a stalling move which could have saved many), but the "messenger was shot" as well, the British blocking Brand's return from Cairo (effectively sealing the fate of his family and countrymen).

A perfunctory gesture did occur in August, however. With 91% of US immigration quotas for occupied European territories unfilled (equating to 55,000 unused for the year), FDR "graciously" opened the gates for a "whopping" 982 fugitives (89% Jewish) to resettle in Fort Ontario, New York (thirty-five miles northwest of Syracuse). Over 100 of these had suffered at Dachau or Buchenwald. (Ironically, the token group, diverted from *Oświęcim* solely by political expediency, arrived via a special overnight *train* at their dreary, isolated American refugee camp, situated near the town of *Oswego*.[230]) To Eichmann's "credit," he never quit trying to "perfect the art of the deal." From August 1944 to as late as April 1945 (a month before VE Day), some 17,000 Jews stayed in "storage" at a labor camp in Austria—in his own words, "put on ice" for later use as "human goods" for cash.[231]

RAOUL TO THE RESCUE

Amidst the rank hypocrisy, a single noble soul rose to the fore. Raoul Wallenberg, a Swedish-born, thirty-year-old University of Michigan alumnus—with a *strain* of Jewish ancestry—left a lucrative banking career in Haifa to avail his talents to the WRB office in Stockholm.

By summer 1944, only 200,000 Jews were still alive in Budapest (450,000 having perished at Auschwitz). With the blessing of King Gustaf V, Raoul was given full diplomatic status as Third Secretary of the Swedish legation in Budapest. Arriving at the capital in July, he promptly organized a special branch for the shelter and relief of Jews. Of course, the Wolverine's modalities would be a bit "unorthodox." In addition to bribing corrupt officials, every pretense was employed to secure provisional passports for Jews with "any" ties to neutral Sweden (personal or commercial). The document (bearing legal seals and the Swedish triple crown insignia) affirmed that the bearer was awaiting entry to Sweden and was thereby under the protection of that government in the interim. With the Gestapo watching his every move, Raoul secured thirty-two apartment houses for his growing charge.

Working tirelessly, Raoul Wallenberg eventually rescued at least 20,000 Jews from deportation and certain death.[232] Unfortunately, following the Soviet "liberation" of the city, the selfless humanitarian disappeared within Stalin's gulag archipelago. Among an international array of posthumous acclaim, Morse notes that a local street in Budapest was named in Raoul's honor; he then adds:

> But the Israelite Congregation of Pest, where the Swedish houses had been located, paid him a quiet tribute which included these words:…'We shall never forget him and shall be forever grateful to him and the Swedish nation, because it was the Swedish flag which warranted the undisturbed slumber of thousands of Jews in the protected houses. He was a righteous man. God bless him.'[233]

The solemnity of the occasion was undoubtedly heightened by its remarkable proximity to the birthplace of Theodore Herzl. Nearly a half-century earlier—in keeping with Abdul-Hamid's observation, "That Herzl looks altogether like a prophet"—the Zionist founder had appraised a Viennese pogrom in 1895 with the chilling forecast: "These are as yet mere rehearsals. Much worse is to come."[234]

BOMBERS OVER BIRKENAU

Through summer 1944, the Allies maintained a conspicuous resistance to any means of slowing the Shoah. As trainloads of Jews continued to pass through the "Gate of Death," the "Gate of Palestine" stayed shut. While thousands of innocent men, women, and children were spending their last conscious moments in abject fear, Christopher Eastwood of the Colonial Office warned the Foreign Office on July 28, "We are afraid that we may be on the verge of a flood of refugees."[235]

When the Jewish Agency solicited emergency aid for insurgents in Axis territory, Britain refused. Requests for anti-Nazi radio and leaflet propaganda threatening postwar repercussions were also denied. An offer that Jewish volunteers from Palestine parachute into Europe to engage in espionage and sabotage was spurned as well.[236] Yet on July 11, the ever vacillating Churchill wrote Eden, "There is no doubt that this is probably the greatest and most horrible crime ever committed in the whole history of the world, and it has been done by scientific machinery by nominally civilized men in the name of a great State and one of the leading races of Europe."[237]

Meanwhile, the report by escapees Rudolf Vrba and Alfréd Wetzler had reignited a bold proposal (one no longer easily dismissed). In May, Jewish leaders in Budapest asked the Allies to bomb the rail lines to Poland. The week after, Rabbi Michael Weissmandl and Mrs. Gisi Fleischmann of the Slovak Jewish Resistance turned up the heat. As the WRB now had a detailed map of the camp, the pair made a fervid plea to the world to "bombard the death halls in Auschwitz."[238] While the RAF had dodged the issue in 1943, claiming "distance logistics," the capture of airfields at Foggia and Brindisi in southern Italy had closed the range to 600 miles, rendering the objection moot.

Still, the Allies refused to target any camps. Adding insult to injury, British and American pilots were ordered to avoid bombing US-owned firms in Germany. While Cologne got clobbered, the Ford plant remained noticeably unscathed, even serving as a civilian air raid shelter. (Incredibly, as some pilots "muffed it," following the war, "Allan Dulles' clients demanded, and received, Allied compensation for bomb damage to their factories in Germany."[239])

The callous refusal to bomb Birkenau was compounded by the sorrow of Jewish parents whose patriotic children were either killed or wounded in various Anglo-American operations. Born on Israel's first kibbutz to Shuel and Devorah Dayan, Moshe later lost an eye to a Vichy sniper on June 8, 1941, while serving as a British scout in the Syria-Lebanon campaign. Chaim and Vera Weizmann's younger son, twenty-five-year-old Flight Lieutenant Michael Oser Weizmann, an RAF reserve volunteer, was shot down over the Bay of Biscay on February 11, 1942; his body was never recovered.

On July 3, Colonel Harrison Gerhardt, an aide to Assistant Secretary of War John McCloy, sent his boss a memo regarding a new WRB petition. His words are arresting: "I know you told me to 'kill' this but since those instructions, we have received the attached letter from Mr. Pehle. I suggest that the attached reply be sent."[240] (The proposed draft comprised an elaborate list of pilot excuses, from "tactical challenges" to "psychological burdens.") On July 4 (another sad irony), McCloy defended his decision, parroting his "Cliff's Notes": "The War Department is of the opinion that the suggested air operation is impracticable. It could be executed only by the diversion of considerable air support essential to the success of our forces now engaged in decisive operations and would in any case be of such very doubtful efficacy that it would not amount to a practical project."[241] Three days later, the USAF initiated a series of *ten* bombing raids on a complex of Nazi oil plants—on the very outskirts of Auschwitz!

In a letter to the WJC on August 14, over a month into the aerial campaign, McCloy reiterated: "After a study it became apparent that such an operation [bombing Auschwitz] could be executed only by the diversion of considerable air support…."[242] Wyman notes, "On Sunday, August 20, late in the morning, 127 Flying Fortresses, escorted by 100 Mustang fighters, dropped 1,336 500-pound high-explosive bombs on the factory areas of Auschwitz, *less than five miles* to the east of the gas chambers."[243] With regard to "practicality," that same month, Hitler's assembly line efficiency reached a high one-day quota of 24,000 cremations (roughly 1,000 corpses per hour).[244]

For the record, according to a previously unpublished private conversation taped in 1986 between McCloy and Morgenthau's son, Henry II, the ninety-one-year-old former assistant war secretary intimated it was the president who had ultimately squelched the bombing request: "I remember talking one time with Mr. Roosevelt about it, and he was irate. He said, 'Why, the idea! They'll only move it down the road a little way.'"[245] In a 1994 oral history interview with the US Holocaust Museum, Benjamin Ferencz, former US Army Chief Prosecutor at the Einsatzgruppen Trial, said that FDR's top Jewish advisor, Samuel Rosenman had agreed with the decision.[246]

From July through November 1944, more than 2,800 bombers struck targets near Auschwitz; over 100,000 Jews died in Birkenau in the weeks following the August 20 flyby. An incredible aerial photograph taken on August 25 shows a group of Jews marching toward the open gate to Crematorium II. However, to McCloy's "credit," the camp *was* bombed on September 13; well, *sort of*. During an intense raid by 96 B-24 Liberators on the adjacent industrial area, another photo captured a cluster of eight high-explosive bombs falling on Birkenau—*by mistake*. (Auschwitz I was also hit in the accidental strike.) When the smoke cleared, the damage was minimal: fifteen SS men killed and twenty-eight seriously wounded; the inmates sustained forty killed (twenty-three being Jews) and sixty-five injured.[247]

Sadly, the fluke payload represents one of the few "prayers" answered at Planet Auschwitz. Survivor Olga Lengyel recalled how many of her comrades had longed for the sorties, believing, "If the Allies could blow up the crematory ovens! The pace of the extermination would at least be slowed."[248] Wyman writes: "Two sisters, Hungarian Jews who were in Birkenau when the Auschwitz industrial areas were hit, told of the prisoners in their section praying for the bombers to blast the gas chambers. They were more than ready to die for that."[249] Wiesel adds, "[W]e no longer feared death. Every bomb that hit filled us with joy, gave us renewed confidence."[250]

David Wyman earned an AB in history at Boston University and a PhD in history at Harvard. He contends that the crematoria could have easily been disabled by a squadron of twenty British Mosquitoes, as the fast-flying aircraft excelled at low-altitude precision bombing. In fact, while the Jews received nothing but excuses as to why innocent civilians could not be saved, a similar mission had already occurred in February when nineteen de Havilland Mosquitoes bombed the prison in Amiens, France, enabling French resistance fighters to escape. "The first two waves of attack struck with such accuracy, smashing the main wall and shattering the guardhouses, that the last six planes did not bomb."[251] Wyman also cites survivor and former pilot Herbert Loebel, who noted that night raids (needing little, if any fighter escort) would have been ideal given the crematoria's highly visible flames.[252]

Although the military could not justify the "diversion" of bombing missions "merely" to save Jewish civilians, McCloy *did* make exceptions for "more serious" matters. While the German town of Rothenberg was spared for its medieval architecture, Kyoto, the ancient capital of Japan, received a pass for being a major cultural center.[253] The 2014 Hollywood film, *The Monuments Men*, documents the true story of a WWII platoon sanctioned by FDR to enter Germany to recapture artistic masterpieces stolen by the Nazis. As revealed in an older film, *Miracle of the White Stallions*, while Jews at Auschwitz were sleeping in stables, General Patton was given the official thumbs up for "Operation Cowboy"—diverting the US Third Army's Second Cavalry to rescue 1,200 *horses*, including 150 Lipizzaners, from advancing Soviet troops. Hilberg writes, "It is characteristic that the Jews in Auschwitz were hoping that an air raid might destroy the killing installations, while the Germans were consoled by the thought 'that the Allied airmen knew and avoided the camp.'"[254]

Ultimately, after Eichmann's offer to dynamite Auschwitz was unrequited, followed by the Allies' refusal to bomb the camp themselves—the impatient Jews took matters into their own hands. On October 7, a group of Sonderkommandos staged an uprising, killing several SS guards (forcing one into an oven *alive*). Over 450 inmates died. While details are scarce, Crematorium IV was disabled. After an inquiry, four Jewesses were tortured and hanged in the women's camp on January 6, 1945, for having smuggled gunpowder from the Union munitions factory to their male counterparts. With the noose around her neck, Roza Robota, the twenty-three-year-old ringleader, assured the crowd that "vengeance would come." The message *Hazak V'amatz* ("Be Strong and Brave") was found scrawled on the wall of her cell.[255]

"MISCARRIAGES OF HELL"

Meanwhile in Berlin, the Justice Ministry, oblivious to reality, met on November 16, 1944, to consider widening the circle of "mercy" killings to include—believe it or not—*ugliness*. The actual minutes read: "During various visits to the penitentiaries, prisoners have always been observed who—because of their bodily characteristics—hardly deserve the designation human; they look like miscarriages of hell…It is planned that they too shall be eliminated…photos should be submitted that show the deformity."[256]

No telling *what* they would have done with the King of the Jews: *"For he shall grow up before him as a tender plant, and as a root out of a dry ground: he hath no form nor comeliness; and when we shall see him, there is no beauty that we should desire him."* (Isaiah 53:2)

THE END OF AUSCHWITZ

By late 1944, the Soviet 60th Army of the First Ukrainian Front was rapidly approaching the Vistula River. One of the last transports to pass through the "Death Gate" arrived from Holland on September 6. (It is believed that Anne Frank and her family were aboard that train.)

With the end in sight, the lager became a beehive of activity: 65,000 labor-worthy prisoners were funneled back to Germany for extended exploitation (e.g.,1,000 barefoot women sent to Gross-Rosen to dig anti-tank ditches in the snow); 3,824 inmates in quarantine were killed; dozens of empty wooden barracks were dismantled and sent west; Canada's coffers were shipped back as well; incriminating documents and prisoner lists were burned; most of the remaining Sonderkommandos were "eliminated" from the realm of potential witnesses; the cremation pits were cleaned out and covered with sod; last of all, the costly incinerators were disassembled and removed.[257]

The last roll call in Konzentrationslager Auschwitz was taken on January 17, 1945. Some 67,012 male and female inmates were counted (divided almost evenly between I, II, & III). Dr. Mengele, fiendish files in hand, hightailed it for Berlin. Over the next four days, the SS beat their own hasty (though orderly) retreat, hauling 58,000 prisoners along in staggered intervals (the rest were left, deemed unfit to travel). The only "orchestral accompaniment" on *this* ignominious occasion was the ominous *booms* of Soviet artillery. The opening leg required a death march through roughly forty miles of blowing snow to the rail yards at Gliwice and Wodzisław Śląski. Many of the half-dead Jews were forced to carry their tormentors' baggage. Wiesel recalled the SS shouting, "Faster, you tramps, you flea-ridden dogs!"[258]

As expected, the evacuation route was quickly littered with corpses. The captives either dropped dead from exhaustion or were put out of their misery beforehand. One local recalled later: "A woman in advanced pregnancy fell out of line. She held herself up by the stomach against a transformer wall. The column went by and did not stop. An SS man...pushed the woman to the curb...The prisoner was lying on her back in the snow. The SS man shot her in the face with his pistol and a second time in the stomach...She was young...around twenty-five."[259] Those who survived the trek would then make the shocking discovery that the train ride *out* of Planet Auschwitz would be even *more* harrowing than the *inbound* transport had been. The passengers (including Anne Frank) were routed via Bohemia and Moravia to their final destinations (Mauthausen, Dachau, and Buchenwald for the men; Ravensbruck and Bergen-Belsen for women)—*in open freight cars in the dead of winter.* Denied food and water, approximately 15,000 perished in the final nightmare.[260]

Back at Birkenau, the SS were ordered to kill all remaining prisoners. However, in a final burst of uncharacteristic panic, the Nazis decided to put their *own* escape first. Though still they were able to attain several "vital" last-minute goals, i.e., shooting 200 Jewesses and dynamiting the shells of Crematoria I and II on January 20; torching Canada on January 23; and blowing Crematorium V at 1 a.m. on January 27.[261] Venezia adds, "Nine thousand persons, mainly the sick, remained in the Auschwitz complex. The guards posted in the camp nonetheless still had time to kill another 700 Jews on the eve of what would have been their liberation."[262] As a parting picture of the demonic force behind the entire Shoah—200 of these last victims were *burned alive* inside their barracks at the Fürstengrube sub-camp.[263]

On the morning of January 27, 1945 (a Sabbath, no less), the first scouts from the Soviet 100th Lvov Infantry Division (led by Major General Fyodor Krasavin) reached Monowitz on the Planet's eastern periphery. The main body arrived at Auschwitz-Birkenau around noon where moderate resistance was encountered from retreating German forces. The Red Army overran the garrison, losing 300 men in the process. Both camps were liberated by 3 p.m.[264] However, what they found inside was staggering (even by Gulag standards). In addition to 9,000 emaciated zombies wandering amidst hundreds of corpses, the Russians uncovered what the Nazis were forced to abandon in their hasty exodus: 43,525 pairs of shoes; 348,820 pieces of men's clothing; 836,525 items of women's and children's clothing; countless toothbrushes, eyeglasses, and other personal items; 460 artificial limbs; and 7 tons of women's hair, bagged for shipment to the Reich's nationalized *upholstery* industry. (See: "Heydrich's horsehair.")

THE FINAL ILLUSTRATION

Recalling the exhuming and burning of bodies, Eli Wiesel wrote, "Thus, for the first time in history, Jews were not only killed twice but denied burial in a cemetery."[265] This dark act is not without precedent. In 1428, Rome was so livid with Protestant, John Wycliffe, that Pope Martin V had his corpse disinterred, burned, and his ashes cast into the River Swift. Israel's God revealed His *own* capacity to afflict the dead when He judged idolatrous Judah by having the bones of *her* kings, priests, prophets, and inhabitants taken from *their* graves and spread before the sun, moon, and stars as *fertilizer* for the earth (Jeremiah 8:1-2). However, the most bizarre contemporary case will astound you.

The deep-seated anti-Semitism of HMG was revealed during the little-known German occupation of the Channel Islands. While Jews on the English mainland were beyond Hitler's reach, three Jewesses on Guernsey Island were arrested by British bobbies and duly turned over to the SS. Initially deported to France, Auguste Spitz, Marianne Grunfield, and Therese Steiner landed in Auschwitz (via Łódź) where they were gassed upon arrival. In his book, *The Jews of the Channel Islands and the Rule of Law, 1940-1945*, David Fraser affirms that the locals were "complicit" in the "persecution of the Jews."[266] A British report in August 1945 affirms: "When the Germans proposed to put their anti-Jewish measures into force, no protest whatever was raised by any of the Guernsey States Officials, and they hastened to give the Germans every assistance."[267] And so—like the "coincidental" timing of Chelmno and Pearl Harbor—the following account is included as a sober example of what the world would call "poetic justice."

As previously related, the USAAF dropped over thirteen hundred 500-pound, high-explosive bombs on the Monowitz-Buna complex on August 20, 1944. A multinational labor force of 22,000, augmented by 7,000 registered inmates, comprised the vulnerable cannon fodder below. With Jews constituting the majority of the latter, the detainees *also* included a unique detachment of 1,400 British POWs (primarily North African veterans designated E715, a sub-camp of the Stalag VIII B POW camp in Lamsdorf, Germany). Calling themselves "Kriegies," slang for *Kriegsgefangenen* ("prisoners of war"), the men received enhanced treatment due to their status under the Geneva Convention.

Many Kriegies were appalled at the open, incremental barbarism inflicted upon Jews. (Most estimates place the number of Monowitz deaths from exhaustion, disease, shooting, hanging, and selection for gassing at between 23,000 to 25,000.)[268] Some even attempted to succor Jews on occasion. However, according to Joseph Robert White, a Post-Doctoral Fellow at the Center for Advanced Holocaust Studies:

> [O]ther POWs openly harbored 'benign' antisemitic attitudes in camp and afterward...Some referred to...Monowitz as the 'Jew Camp,' while others accepted the notion that Jews were too powerful in the economy...During World War II, British antisemites saw Jews as money-grubbers, black-marketeers, and draft dodgers. POWs in E715 were working-class young men who grew up during a rare period of anti-Jewish incidents in their nation's recent past, particularly in London's East End.[269]

Arthur Dodd was a British POW in E715 on that fateful Sunday in August. In his memoir, *Spectator in Hell*, Dodd describes the key moment of that half-hour raid, along with the surrealistic aftermath:

> The date was 20 August 1944. Early in the afternoon, as the men were enjoying themselves, they were interrupted by the air-raid sirens and as the camp was now being bombed on a regular basis, the men made their way to the brick-built shelters, entered via a sloping ramp and closed off by steel doors...Just as the doors were shut, they heard an almighty swishing sound followed by a tremendous explosion. The ground shook and the far end of the shelter caved in as it took a direct hit. Inside the shelter were some 150 POWs and nearly all were at least injured in some way...Severe injuries eventually pushed the number of deaths up to 38...The dead men were laid out for each survivor to pay his respects. Two days later a small service was held and the bodies were loaded onto a truck draped in the Union Jack flag. They were taken to the local parish cemetery in Oswiecim and buried beside a wall in a communal grave...On 13 September 1944, the common grave was hit by a bomb dropped by the USAF during its bombing of the Farben works. It was completely destroyed.[270]

Killed in their bomb shelter—*blasted* from their burial site—the Kriegies' final whereabouts are inscribed on a stone memorial tablet in the Oświęcim burial ground: "Their mortal remains were transferred to Krakow Rakowicki Cemetery."

"For I speak to you gentiles...Be not highminded, but fear:
For if God spared not the natural branches, TAKE HEED
LEST HE ALSO SPARE NOT THEE. *Behold therefore*
the goodness and severity of God: on them which fell,
severity; but toward thee, goodness, IF *thou continue*
in his goodness: OTHERWISE THOU ALSO
SHALT BE CUT OFF."
(Romans 11:13, 20-22)

12

The Jews and WWII

"In heaven Allah; on earth Hitler."
(Egyptian Brotherhood Battle Cry)

"Get rid of the Jew for heaven's sake!"
(Hitler, on Richard Kauder)

"I will say that regarding nuclear weapons, Jews,
by far and away, have had a disproportionate effect
on their development and the polices for their use."
(Sam Cohen, "Father of the Neutron Bomb")

"This is truly the last secret, or one
of the last of the Second World War."
(Alexander Solzhenitsyn, on "Operation Keelhaul")

TWO OFFICIAL FLIGHTS from Rome arrive together at Derna, Libya, on June 29, 1942. The lead plane makes an emergency crash landing, killing the pilot's barber and chef. After the second aircraft taxies to a halt, a magnificent white Arabian charger is led from the cargo hold onto the tarmac; his name is Atlantico. On June 6, 1944, while the US Army's 29th Infantry Division is engaged in the epic D-Day invasion (the twenty-four-year-old future father-in-law of this author being among them), a twenty-four-year-old Jewess operative is preparing to cross the Hungarian border into Nazi-occupied territory (having parachuted into Yugoslavia in March). Three years earlier, a twenty-four-year-old blond Jewish beauty queen (Miss Hungary 1936) was being smuggled *out* of the same country by a shadowy

Croatian Roman Catholic priest (later to become the premier Vatican agent for aiding thousands of Nazi war criminals in fleeing the Continent). On October 16, 1944, a German-Arab commando team, comprised of two native Muslims and three Palestinian-born Germans, hits the silk over Jericho to foment sabotage and smuggle weapons for jihad. Representing a multi-regional undertaking, the SS provocateurs are equipped with submachine guns, dynamite, radios, a duplicating machine, and a German-Arabic dictionary. Lastly, three "German" soldiers, having duly surrendered to Allied forces, are sent abroad to a US internment camp where they meet a most untimely death on June 29, 1945.

To explain—the steed belonged to the lead pilot, Italy's delusional dictator, Benito Mussolini (a.k.a. "Il Duce"), who *had* planned to ride him into Cairo with great panache after an expected Axis win at El Alamein.[1] With Benito partial to "spit and shine," 200 drums of black shoe polish were also onboard so his goose-stepping storm troopers could gloss their jackboots for the parade[2]—one that never took place—Montgomery's providential defeat of Rommel having stopped Hitler's secret plan to finalize the Shoah in Eretz Yisrael itself.

The youthful intelligence agent was Budapest native Hannah Szenes, one of thirty-two volunteers from Palestine who dropped into harm's way (boot polish on their *faces*) to rendezvous with the Hungarian-Slovak resistance (any auxiliary aid afforded Jewish refugees being done on their *own* time, etc.). While the German-Arab mission was aborted (three of the saboteurs being caught[3]), Hannah was seized by Hungarian gendarmes and tortured for months in a failed bid to extract her accomplices' names. Standing before a German firing squad on November 7, 1944, the brave woman went to her death refusing a blindfold.[4]

The other Jewess—having eluded the Hungarian Aktion at Auschwitz—retired in 1997 after a fifty-year reign in Hollywood as the "celebrated" Zsa Zsa Gabor, dying at the ripe old age of 99.[5] While the Tinseltown tart is remembered for having married nine times (her mother and two sisters bringing the family total to twenty-two), thirty-two streets in Israel bear the name Hannah Szenes (a.k.a. "Joan of Arc of Israel"). Her remains repose on Mount Herzl.

Finally, another burial site solves the mystery of those three strange deaths in 1945. According to its own literature, the tiny Civil War-era Finns Point National Cemetery near Pennsville, New Jersey, contains an isolated plot holding the remains of thirteen German POWs who died during their detention at Fort Dix. The only "problem"—as revealed by the headstones—is that three of those "Germans" were *Russians.* Unbeknown to 99% of the American public, 2nd Lt. Ignat Nasarenko, 2nd Lt. Feoktist Kalinin, and Pvt. Felip Sbotow[6] were three of some 2,000,000 Soviet patriots sent to their deaths (or exile) by Franklin Roosevelt and Winston Churchill at the Yalta Conference via the clandestine atrocity code-named "Operation Keelhaul." At the time of their capture or surrender to US and British forces, the Russians were fighting with Germany—though for the sole, stipulated goal of ousting Joseph Stalin. The trio chose suicide an hour from the "Jersey Shore" over forced repatriation "back in the U.S.S.R."

These illustrations represent but a fraction of the untold history of World War II—specifically, the integral machinations among the participants themselves—Jewish, Arab, German, Soviet, British, American, and Vatican. The current chapter highlights five of the most redacted subjects from this nebulous period, much of which relates to Jewry: 1) Hitler's secret plan to annihilate the Jews in Eretz Yisrael; 2) decisive Jewish contributions to the war; 3) Allied-Vatican evacuations of Nazi war criminals; 4) the *almost* Anglo-German rapprochement; and 5) the Anglo-American *Russian* Holocaust.

THE SHOAH TO THE YISHUV

The year 1942 found the Continent under Nazi occupation (a swastika even flying from the Eiffel Tower), America preoccupied with retaliation in the Pacific, and England standing virtually alone, her capital in ruins. Hitler could now focus his inordinate (and insatiable) lust on two immediate objectives—Russian oil and *more* Jewish blood.

As the British blockade deprived Germany of fuel from Venezuela and Iran, the Reich was forced to rely on European energy, primarily from Romania. By late 1941, Hitler had sustained dual critical setbacks—petroleum projections at the Ploesti refineries were deemed unsustainable and Barbarossa had stalled at Moscow (a sobering first for the "invincible" Wehrmacht). Following several Soviet counteroffensives through the winter, Germany renewed its Eastern incursion, only this time securing the vast Baku oilfields in Azerbaijan was deemed a strategic imperative. (Baku produced 161,000,000 barrels of oil in 1940, 72% of all Soviet output.[7]) But then, to Hitler, "gas" was just a means to a "better" *end* (as in the *Final* Solution).

Assuming that Russia would surrender and the fuel depots would be secured, to orchestrate the war's boldest pincer movement—*encircling the Yishuv itself*—one army would advance over the Caucasus while the other would arrive via Cairo. While gaining the Suez Canal would be a tactical bonus, Hitler shared his greater, *ideological* motive with Himmler and Heydrich in October 1941: "It is good if the fear that we will exterminate the Jews precedes us. The attempt to found a Jewish state will be a failure."[8] A Nazi Fifth Column in Palestine, comprising several hundred members of the NSDAP, stood ready to welcome their Führer.[9]

Hitler intended to exploit anti-British sentiment along both invasion routes. The *Abwehr* (Reich intel-gathering agency run by Admiral Wilhelm Canaris) had long monitored Arab reaction to the rise of National Socialism in Germany. Self-identifying with the ignominy of Versailles, the Islamic world grew enchanted with the Führer's jingoism. Karl Kossak-Raytenau, special correspondent for the Nazi paper *Der Angriff*, quoted a Palestinian agent in 1938: "We Arabs follow Germany's rise with great interest and affection, because...before Hitler came to power, Germany found itself in a similar situation to the one we Arabs face in Palestine."[10] The Reich was also viewed as having overcome the world's economic chaos, particularly chronic unemployment. Two years earlier, Germany's envoy in Jaffa, Timotheus Wurst, opined, "[I]n the eyes of many Arabs, Adolf Hitler is without a doubt simply the most important man of the 20th century."[11] Egypt's Muslim Brotherhood (the plague of the 21st century) grew from 800 members in 1936 to 200,000 in 1938.

The Arabs' cultish emulation of Hitler provoked an ill-fated *coup d'état* of the London-backed Iraqi regime of Regent Abd al-Ilah on April 1-2, 1941; the pro-Nazi Rashid Ali installed as prime minister. The British counterattack began on April 18. With the strategic Mosul oil fields at stake, Hitler was forced to assist his hapless cohorts in their precipitant Anglo-Iraqi War. On May 3, he ordered that "everything possible be done with regard to military support."[12] Thus, on May 11, the Luftwaffe roared into Mosul with 24 heavy fighters and bombers. The commander, Major Axel von Blomberg (the former war minister's son), was assigned to raise a German-led Arab Brigade comprising volunteers from Iraq, Syria, Palestine, and Saudi Arabia.[13]

What went down the next day would constitute an augur regarding Hitler's immediate plans for the Yishuv. As the delirious Baghdadis cheered the low altitude sortie from the streets and rooftops below—a few of Ishmael's kinfolk got a little "wild" (Genesis 16:12). When von Blomberg's Heinkel He 111 bomber landed, the highly regarded squadron leader was found dead at the controls, having sustained a fatal headshot during the customary barrage of celebratory gunfire.

SONDERSTAB F

Undeterred, Hitler issued Directive No. 30 on May 23, stating that an experimental German-Arab military mission code-named *Sonderstab F* ("Special Staff F") would deploy to render covert support to the "Arab Freedom movement…our natural ally against the British in the Middle East." The operation was designed to work "in conjunction with an offensive against the Suez Canal…."[14]

In their highly documented work, *Nazi Palestine: The Plans for the Extermination of the Jews in Palestine*, Stuttgart-based Professors Klaus-Michael Mallmann and Martin Cüppers concur: "The Arabs were clearly viewed as a fifth column of the Third Reich."[15] An internal report described the mutant unit as fielding "specially selected German troops and men from the Eastern countries, who are all Mohammedan…."[16] Hitler outlined the three-fold task of Sonderstab F as follows: 1) advise and support Iraqi military; 2) establish liaison with anti-British forces outside Iraq; 3) foster experience and intelligence for the Wehrmacht.[17] Meanwhile, the Luftwaffe mission was scrubbed after two weeks due to unforeseen logistical challenges. Upon the German retreat, a ceasefire was brokered in Baghdad by British officials on May 31. Prince Abd al-Ilah (uncle to six-year-old Faisal II, grandson of Faisal I) was promptly restored to his regency.

The Führer's plan to invade Palestine was reaffirmed three weeks later in Directive No. 32, entitled: "Preparations for the Period after Barbarossa." Again, the focus was a two-theater thrust: "The struggle against the British positions in the Mediterranean and in Western Asia will be continued by converging attacks launched from Libya through Egypt, from Bulgaria through Turkey, and in certain circumstances also from Transcaucasia through Iran."[18] Other excerpts include:

> In view of the expected British reinforcement of the Near and Middle East, especially for the defense of the Suez Canal, a German operation from Bulgaria through Turkey will be planned, with the aim of attacking the British position on the Canal from the East also...If the Soviet collapse has created the necessary conditions, preparations will be made for the dispatch of a motorized expeditionary force from Transcaucasia against Iraq.[19]

That ominous phrase—"motorized expeditionary force"—should raise some flags by now.

Under the heading "Exploitation of the Arab Freedom Movement," the order elaborates: "The situation of the English in the Middle East will be rendered more precarious, in the event of major German operations, if more British forces are tied down at the right moment by civil commotion or revolt."[20] Then, as all relevant "military, political, and propaganda measures to this end must be closely coordinated during the preparatory period," the paper's author (General Walter Warlimont) declares, "I nominate Special Staff F, which is to take part in all plans and actions in the Arab area...."[21] It concludes: "The Chief of the High Command of the Armed Forces will specify the duties of Special Staff F...."[22] Though unknown then, the providential Moscow debacle would deter Hitler's salacious goal to posture Sonderstab F at the Suez Canal, i.e., adjacent to "Ground Zero" for the Final Solution.

"THE MOST IMPORTANT ARAB QUISLING"

The epitome of Arab fidelity was seen five months later when the "exalted" Haj Muhammad Amin al-Husseini, *exiled* Grand Mufti of Jerusalem (lately slumming in Damascus, Beirut, and Baghdad), made a special pilgrimage to Berlin (via Istanbul and Rome). An MI6 report named him "the most important Arab Quisling in German hands."[23]

The historic November 28, 1941, "audience" (photo-op) between Führer and fugitive nearly ended before it began, however. According to one eyewitness, given the "behavioral peculiarities" of the host, Hitler refused al-Husseini's invitation to join him in a customary opening round of java. Announcing with *great* agitation that he did not permit "anyone at all to drink coffee in the headquarters" (notwithstanding the

German etymology of *Kaffeeklatsch*), Hitler stormed out of the room leaving his mortified guest in astonishment.

After regaining his composure (no doubt repeating to himself, "The enemy of my enemy is my friend"), "Herr Whack Job" returned and gave al-Husseini a glass of lemonade.[24] The Muslim sycophant proceeded to assure his hero that the Arab world absolutely *adored* him—yada, yada, yada! Hitler reciprocated by pledging to end the despised Anglo-Zionist occupation of Palestine, asserting that, after Russia's defeat (allowing the Wehrmacht into the Middle East via the Caucasus), "Germany would have no further imperial goals of its own and would support Arab liberation." He then gave the best news of all, "Germany's objective would then be solely the destruction of the Jewish element residing in the Arab sphere under the protection of British power."[25] As a special bonus, the Mufti was given the distinct impression that he would get to engineer the destruction: "I expressed to Herr Hitler for an explicit undertaking to allow us to solve the Jewish problem...The answer I received was: The Jews are yours."[26] (Hitler's parting gift of a *bullet proof vest* would serve as a token of his personal fidelity.)

Obviously, the Führer's virulent anti-Semitism was his most "endearing" trait. While the two may have clashed on coffee, *both* saw Jewry as a loathsome pestilence needing extermination, al-Husseini writing, "The Jews can be compared to disease-carrying insects. If they are far away, one can believe them to be peaceful creatures, but if a person is stung by them and afflicted with the illness, then only radical remedies can help."[27] He also loved evoking the embarrassing political pressure that Hitler kept on the Allies: "It would be wise to send the Jews as a gift to the people who defend the Jews. With the Jews in their country, they would then quickly join our ranks."[28]

The Grand Mufti was quite the social butterfly during his extended Berlin stay (residing in a *vacated* Jewish mansion[29]). In June 1942, he told the Reich envoy to Iran, Erwin Ettel, "Germany is the only country in the world that does not hesitate to fight the Jews on its own soil; rather, it has uncompromisingly declared war on world Jewry. In this conflict with the Jews, the Arabs feel the closet connection with Germany."[30] He gave a similar spiel to Foreign Minister Ribbentrop in May 1943: "Thanks to our common interests, the friendly Arab people have without any hesitation taken the side of the Axis powers in this defensive battle against communism and against the Anglo-Saxons.

The Arabs are waiting for their friends, the Axis powers and their allies, to provide the solution to the world's Jewish problem."[31]

Al-Husseini was also quite adept at name-dropping, citing his petrodollar-connected pal, Ibn Saud, who stated in 1939: "All Arabs and Mohammedans throughout the world have great respect for Germany, and this respect is increased by the battle that Germany is waging against the Jews, the archenemy of the Arabs."[32] On November 2, 1943, he received a special telegram from Himmler, ending with the words, "I am sending you on the anniversary of the infamous Balfour declaration my hearty greetings and wishes for the successful pursuit of your struggle until the final victory."[33]

Consequently, given the magnitude of such a potential alliance, the British Foreign Office commissioned a major research study in 1942. The final report essentially confirmed all of the preceding testimony:

> Parallels are often drawn between German and Arab history, and German unification is held up as a model for the anticipated Arab unification. German promises are accepted with absolute confidence, and the concern repeatedly expressed by leading Germans, including the Führer himself, for the current situation of the Arab people has greatly strengthened the positive feelings toward the German people.[34]

The obvious nexus was anti-Semitism: "The struggle against Zionism and thus against the Jews is an undertaking that is approved by every Arab and supported to the extent it is possible. The Jews are seen as the mortal enemy."[35] The advent of radio technology became the primary tool for winning Arab hearts and minds in the Middle East.[36] In his book *Oil, Blood and Sand*, Robert Baker devotes an entire chapter to this medium entitled "Invasion on Kilocycles."[37]

The evidence for this premise was ubiquitous across the Ummah: Hitler and Mussolini's pictures in shop windows; pro-Nazi graffiti in the villages; German flags and swastikas displayed on Muhammad's birthday (drawing salutes from "neutral" Arab police); local greetings of "Heil Hitler" or "Heil Rommel" (code names used when discretion required, the Führer's being *Haddsch Numur*—"The Tiger").[38] In their military primer, *The Secret War of the Middle East*, Arab-American siblings, Youssef H. Aboul-Enein, CDR USN, adjunct military professor and chair of Islamic studies at the Dwight D. Eisenhower School for Resource Strategy and National Security, and Basil Aboul-Enein, a former USAF captain, concluded: "The Arab Nationalist movement amounted to nothing more than a shapeless, fragmented, counter position to British imperialism, imported to the Arab East via Berlin and Rome for Nazi and Italian Fascist aspirations."[39]

With the mood in Palestine projecting a morbid parallel to the Filipinos' longing for Douglas MacArthur, Himmler aide Walter Schellenberg noted in December 1942, "The extraordinary pro-German attitude of the Arabs is due primarily to the fact that they 'hope Hitler will come' to drive out the Jews…Rommel has become a legend…Thus, all Arabs today long for the arrival of the Germans; they continually ask when the Germans will come."[40] In 1938, articles began to appear in Arab periodicals comparing Hitler to Muhammad himself. Ettel wrote on February 2, 1941: "For months the embassy has received notifications from various sources…that throughout the country, clerics are…speaking to believers about old secret prophesies and dreams indicating that God has sent the twelfth imam to the world in the form of Adolf Hitler."[41] The Muslim Brotherhood adopted the battle cry: "In heaven Allah; on earth Hitler."[42] (In Syria: "No more 'Monsieur,' no more 'Mister'—God in Heaven; on earth Hitler!"[43])

Still more egregious was how the Nazis tried to exploit the Islamic aberration to advance their own Middle East agenda. On May 15, 1943, Himmler actually authorized a "Koran study," hoping to find passages to exploit showing that Hitler *was* "foretold and called to complete the work of the Prophet."[44] The results were less than negligible. The propaganda ministry was also busy ensuring that Muslims only viewed edited portions of *Mein Kampf*—the original featuring some *serious* anti-Arab rhetoric. (The first complete Arab translation did not appear until 1960 in Beirut.[45])

While the "Holy" Koran failed to identify Hitler as the "12th Imam" (Israel's number, no less), the Holy Bible naturally has the answer. With Adolf Hitler (12 letters) constituting the main forerunner of the Antichrist—that ultimate anti-Semite, assimilated Jew (Daniel 11:37) connected to the familiar 666—the Führer's original NSDAP number just *happened* to be 555 (the triple numeric for death).

PANZERS AT THE PYRAMIDS

In the wake of the Bagdad fiasco and the greater trial at Moscow, the Wehrmacht gained a badly needed boost in early 1942 from the sustained advance of the famed *Panzerarmee Afrika* (Afrika Korps) led by Field Marshal Erwin Rommel (a.k.a. "The Desert Fox"). Rommel's renown across the Maghreb was so intimidating that Sir Claude Auchinleck (a.k.a. "The Auk"), Britain's Commander-in-Chief Middle East, actually cautioned his staff that the prodigious, near mythical German "could become a bogeyman for our troops, simply because they talk about him so much."[46] (The Brit was a little insecure as well, his memo concluding: "PS, I'm not jealous of Rommel."[47])

On June 20, the "bogeyman" captured the heavily fortified Libyan port of Tobruk in one day. Churchill called it one of the "bitterest moments of the entire war."[48] In the ensuing battle at the Egyptian seaport town of Mersa Matruh, Rommel seized 6,000 prisoners in 48 hours. Though only 20% of the total taken at Tobruk, it was over twice the size of his entire scaled-down force. As no man is an island, "The Fox" was able to monitor "The Auk's" movements thanks to an Italian spy planted in the US embassy. Recruited for his expertise as a locksmith, the Italian Military Intelligence (SIM) agent broke into the office of Colonel Norman Fiske, military attaché in Cairo, and copied the Black Code (a cipher used by US military diplomats worldwide.[49])

At 3:00 a.m. on July 1, Rommel began his climacteric month-long engagement against the British Eighth Army led by General Auchinleck. The decisive clash would occur near a dilapidated rail station called El Alamein—a mere sixty miles from Alexandria. Rising from their desert bases, Rommel's scout planes buzzed everything from Pompey's Pillar in the heart of the city to the Suez Canal itself. King Farouk and his ministers "strangely" declined to do *anything* for the "defense" of their own country. (The nation's 50,000 Italian residents were also "unavailable," given that a giant welcome festa was being prepared for their "great equestrian leader, Il Duce.") On a highly debated point, the sybaritic Farouk was *not* bound by the 1936 Anglo-Egyptian Treaty to declare war on British enemies (though he *did* retain the option to strike back if attacked himself).[50] Seized by the prospect of "panzers at the pyramids," British military and civilian officials in Cairo burned thousands of documents (the inglorious date being dubbed "Ash Wednesday").

And as the smoke was rising, Axis propaganda leaflets were dropping (some 1,100,000 to date.[51])

To say that the normally stoic British were in the *throes of panic* would be an understatement: evacuation plans were underway; refugees jammed major arteries; the Royal Navy fled Alexandria for the calmer waters of Port Said, Haifa, and Beirut; His Majesty's gold reserves went to Khartoum (causing banks their own sieges); and while plans were underway to blow the Nile's dams, rumors spread that bridges were going up across the Tigris and Euphrates for a mass exodus to Persia.[52] The chaos was conjured by Jewish author Daniel Yergin in an allusion rife with symbolic undertone: "Allied personnel were being squeezed into cattle trains for a hasty evacuation."[53]

British *flight* naturally induced the offsetting recoil of Jewish *fright* and Arab *delight*. Pictures of Churchill and Roosevelt were covered by images of Rommel and Hitler; imams whipped their devotees into frenzies at area mosques; mobs ran the streets chanting, "Rommel, Rommel, Rommel!"; the fellahin declined to honor mandatory-specific grain quantities for Jewish buyers (prepaid orders being a no-brainer); thousands of Arabs in the British army (especially in Palestine) deserted with their weapons; widespread sabotage was reported.

In *The Forgotten Ally*, Dutch-born Canadian-American writer Pierre van Paassen asserts that Arab peasants in Palestine were advised to sell their land to Jews, as they would soon be getting it back.[54] Mallmann and Cüppers relate the most foreboding sign of all—a profane, generic reversal of the first Passover Eve: "[S]ecret chalk marks appeared on Jewish houses overnight. No one was able to explain them initially, but eventually it was revealed that the Arabs, confident of Rommel's arrival and the resulting change of government, had already staked their claims to the Jews' property."[55] Arabs grew emboldened as German and Italian bombers flew sorties over Mandate terrain, Haifa and Tel Aviv absorbing twenty-five raids in July and August alone.[56] Thus, the inevitable "disturbances" began anew, a prelude to the coming bloodbath.[57] Ironically, as guns were banned, numbers of Jews procured *cyanide* as their option of last resort.[58]

Thus, on July 13, an optimistic Himmler authorized the RSHA to issue his long-anticipated secret order reassigning the dread Einsatzgruppen to shadow the final German thrust into Palestine. As the saying goes, "If it ain't broke, don't fix it," the key passage in the mission directive reflects the identical command structure and operational latitude employed by the mechanized murder squads that "successfully" killed 1.4 million Jews in Soviet territory:

> With the approval of the Reichsführer-SS and the chief of the German police, the deployment of the SS unit with Afrika Korps will be regulated as follows: The SS Einsatzkommando receives its technical instructions from the chief of the security police and SD and carries out its assignments under its own responsibility. It is entitled, within the scope of its mission, to take executive measures against the civilian population on its own authority.[59]

Loosely interpreted, the phrase "executive measures against the civilian population" equated to the imminent cold-blooded murder of 500,000 Jewish men, women, and children residing in the Yishuv.

The handpicked unit (viewed as an advance force with a surge to follow) comprised seven SS officers and seventeen noncommissioned officers and men. Himmler personally chose Waffen-SS Lieutenant Colonel Walther Rauff (a.k.a. "Father of the Mobile Gas Chamber") to lead the strike. Mallmann and Cüppers relate, "They were to be deployed first in Egypt and then, after the conquest of Egypt, in neighboring Palestine, where they would doubtless have been engaged first and foremost in the mass murder of the Jewish population."[60] As in Eastern Europe, quislings would sell out cheap for pogroms.

> As numerous reports had long attested, a vast number of Arabs, in some cases already well organized, were ready to serve as willing accomplices of the Germans in the Middle East. Immediately after the panzer army's arrival in Africa, the central task of Rauff's Einsatzkommando—the implementation of the Holocaust in Palestine—would have been quickly put into action with the help of those collaborators.[61]

Professor Howard Sachar of Harvard concurs: "The Reich's objective then would…be…the destruction of Palestine Jewry."[62]

On July 20, two notable flights occurred—one *landing*, the other *departing*. (The respective moods onboard would become the hallmark ambiance on the runways at Las Vegas.) As Rauff was arriving in Tobruk to receive "from Field Marshal Rommel the necessary instructions for the deployment,"[63] Mussolini was leaving for Rome in dejection. Three weeks into El Alamein, Rommel was being vexed by overextended supply lines. Fuel trucks based in Tripoli used more gas getting to the front and back then they could carry. More critical (and puzzling) was the precipitant spike in maritime cargo being sunk by the British (6,339 gross register tons in July to 50,562 in August[64]).

This was particularly humiliating for Italy's dictator, having always viewed the Mediterranean as *mare nostrum* ("our sea"). You might say that Benito couldn't win for losing. At 2:45 p.m. on June 29—the very day he and Atlantico stepped foot (and hoof) into Libya—the Italian freighter *Diana*, en route to resupply the Afrika Korps, was sunk by the British submarine *HMS Thrasher*, 100 miles north of Tobruk. Meanwhile, *Colonel* Rauff was relegated to a Rommel staffer (the pragmatic Desert Fox, averse to Hitler's deleterious anti-Semitism, being "conveniently" occupied 300 miles eastward). However, despite Erwin's snub, the RSHA unit was redeployed on July 29 from Berlin to a staging area in Athens to await the anticipated breakthrough.

THE FÜHRER GETS A CAKE

While the North African theater was strategic, securing the vast Baku oil fields—the key to both defeating Russia *and* sustaining the Wehrmacht—trumped increasing Churchill's "disgrace" by occupying Mosul and the Suez. Consequently, the Don offensive, code-named *Fall Blau* ("Case Blue") was renewed on June 28, 1942.

The opening strategy was for Army Group South to punch through the south Russian steppes to capture the Caspian crude. Army Groups North and Center would maintain their own respective drives along the massive Eastern Front. And should Rommel capture Cairo, Afrika Korps would transition on to Mosul, leaving Rauff and his thugs in Palestine. Within a month, however, the ever-meddling Führer stunned his generals by issuing Directive No. 45, splitting Army Group South in two; Group B would now divert eastward to attack Stalingrad, while Group A would continue through the Caucasus alone. Many believe that the Bohemian corporal was psycho enough to target Stalingrad just for being the namesake of his nemesis. (See Battle of Smolensk for his *first* costly meltdown, delaying Germany's arrival at Moscow.)

Both advances got off to a good start. By late July, the Sixth Army had reached the outskirts of Stalingrad. Three weeks later, the swastika was raised on Mount Elbrus, highest peak in the Caucasus. In preparation for the final phase, a new German-Arab battalion was dispatched with Sonderstab F to the Azerbaijani village of Salino. The propaganda tool (the "brain" child of al-Husseini), comprised four Muslim companies totaling 800, augmented by 5,200 Germans.[65]

Since January 1942, the SS had been recruiting and training a consortium of Turkistani, Caucasian, and Tatar legions. The ethnic insignia on their Nazi uniforms featured a crescent moon, mosque, and crossed scimitars.[66] "The armed deployment of the legions should not only save German blood," concluded Army Group South's commander, "but also serve as a political weapon to subvert and weaken the enemy's resistance."[67] Speaking for the Crimean Tatars (10% being in the Wehrmacht), the Mullah of Simferopol stated: "It is an honor for us to be able to fight under the Führer Adolf Hitler, the greatest man of the German nation."[68] Mallmann and Cüppers opine: "In the event of an advance over the Caucasus, the commandos of Einsatzgruppe D, moving with the German army, would no doubt have begun to arrest and murder the Jews living in that area as well."[69]

With victory in sight, the Baku attack was set for September 25. The general staff was so confident that they presented their Führer with a custom cake decorated in the shape of the Caucasus. Newsreel footage shows Hitler slicing the piece with BAKU spelled out in chocolate cream for himself. However, aware that one rarely gets to "have his cake and eat it too," upon finishing his treat, Hitler soberly reminded his officers—"Unless we get the Baku oil, the war is lost."[70]

In less than sixty days the tide would turn against Germany on both fronts. Like the Midianites learned 3,200 years ago with *their* foiled invasion of Eretz Yisrael, Hitler was about to taste a *Jewish* "cake" baked by the *ultimate* "Cake Boss," Judges 7:13 stating: *"And when Gideon was come, behold, there was a man that told a dream unto his fellow, and said, Behold I dreamed a dream, and, lo, a* CAKE *of barley bread tumbled into the host of Midian, and came unto a tent, and smote it that it fell, and overturned it...."* (And for some heavenly "icing on the cake," the Scripture address of 7:13 just *happens* to match both the month and day of Himmler's order deploying the Einsatzgruppen to Palestine.)

THE BEGINNING OF THE END

The first barley cakes tumbled out of the sky on the night of October 25, when Soviet planes attacked the strategic German airfield at Armavir, Russia, destroying grounded aircraft, substantial fuel depots, and critical oil drilling equipment.[71] The defeat was particularly humiliating for the Wehrmacht, as the enemy "bombers"—forty primitive Polikarpov Po-2 crop dusters—were "manned" by eighty young *female* volunteers, many still in their teens!

Officially designated the 588th Night Bomber Regiment, the Nazis called them *Nachthexen* ("Night Witches"), as the whooshing noise of their plywood and canvas biplanes echoed a witch's broomstick. The gutsy gals would idle their motors, drop their two-bomb payloads while in stealth glide mode, then, hopefully, restart them to make their daring escape. The women flew eight to eighteen sorties per night, carrying no parachutes, guns, radar, or radios in their open cockpits (only maps and a compass). All told, the legendary aviators conducted 30,000 missions in four years, dumping 23,000 tons of bombs on thousands of enemy positions. They were so effective that any Nazi who downed a "witch" won an Iron Cross. Thirty of the eighty-woman regiment died in action. Lydia Litvyak, Russia's "top scoring female fighter ace of all time,"[72] died in a dog fight at age twenty-three; Lieutenant Litvyak—a.k.a. "White Rose of Stalingrad"—was Jewish.

The Germans were ultimately stopped from taking Baku due to the deprivation they endured in their bitter six-month siege of Stalingrad. At the battle's apex (late November to late January), the Wehrmacht lost a quarter of a million men (one per second), a thousand panzers, eighteen-hundred pieces of artillery, an entire Luftwaffe fleet of transport craft, and untold quantities of military supplies. (Several million metric tons of US lend-lease supplies had also reached the Red Army via the "Persian Corridor," the emergency overland route opened by the Anglo-Soviet occupation of Iran in August 1941.)

The loss of the Sixth Army—one of the greatest military blunders in history—was the strategic turning point of the war. As confirmed by Sir Basil Liddell Hart (dean of military historians), given the Führer's predisposition to "Stalinitis," all that sugar from the Baku cake was the *last* thing he had needed: "'Stalingrad' was an inspiring symbol for the Russians, and a hypnotic symbol for the Germans—especially for their

Leader. It hypnotised Hitler into a state in which he lost sight of strategy, and lost all regard for the future. It became more fatal than Moscow—because its name meant more."[73] (Thus, Admiral Raeder's ingenious blueprint for a combined naval and panzer assault on Alexandria and the Suez Canal was ignored in this stupor.[74])

Undaunted (though now quite desperate), Adolf Hitler—undisputed champion and defender of blonde-haired, blue-eyed Aryans everywhere—issued an *unthinkable*, "sacrilegious" edict on February 10, directing the prestigious Waffen-SS to form an all-Islamic SS division of Bosnian devotees in Croatia.[75] Appropriately numbered the "13th SS Mountain Division," the satanic entity received a unique name, chosen and conferred upon them by the Führer himself—"Handschar" (local word for curved Arab scimitar). Himmler supervised the design and production of a special fez for his Tatar recruits. A cooking class was even developed so German food preparers could be versed in Allah's dietary laws.[76] (The Nordic "gods" must have rolled over in their graves.) Heinie also fretted that his boys might be bullied by their "Christian" comrades, writing: "I forbid jokes and facetious remarks about Muslim volunteers."[77] In a January 1944 pep rally, Himmler told his Mohammedan hordes:

> We have the same aims...For 200 years Germany has not had the slightest...friction with Islam...Now we Germans and you in this division, you Muslims, share a common feeling of gratitude that God—you call him Allah, but it's the same—has sent our tormented European nations the Führer, the Führer who will rid first Europe and then the whole world of the Jews, these enemies of our Reich... also your enemies...from time immemorial."[78]

Regarding the North African campaign, after General Auchinleck ceased offensive operations on July 31, the initial engagement was judged a stalemate. Following a brief respite, the decisive Second Battle of El Alamein commenced on October 23. This time, the British Eighth Army had a new commander—Field Marshal Bernard Law Montgomery (a.k.a. the "Spartan General"). Ironically, Montgomery was a second cousin to Jack Philby, as well as the best man at his controversial wedding to Dora Johnson in 1910.[79]

While "Monty" would show himself to be a major improvement over the "Auk," eventually commanding a numerical edge of 5-1 as well (though no threat to the crafty "Desert Fox"), once again, the key factor would be fuel for Rommel's panzers. By November 11, Afrika Korps was in full westward retreat. The epic oscillation of Reich fortunes was captured in a pair of letters from Rommel to his wife. In his upbeat June 28 update regarding a July vacation in Italy, Erwin had advised, "Get passports!" Two weeks after El Alamein, the dejected spouse wrote, "Shortage of petrol! It's enough to make one weep."[80]

The Rommels were forced to postpone their trip, due primarily to the stellar accomplishments of British cryptologists. With the breaking of the German radio code, Mussolini's tankers were being sunk with impunity. (An old WWII joke goes: Q. Why does the new Italian Navy use glass-bottomed boats? A. So they can steer clear of the *old* Italian Navy.) Churchill articulated the watershed moment accordingly: "Before Alamein we never had a victory. After Alamein we never had a defeat."[81] William Manchester wrote in his posthumous biography of Churchill: "The Battle of Britain and the Battle for Egypt were two sides of the same coin. Neither would survive if the other fell."[82]

The Germans would make their last stand in Tunisia. However, with the amphibious landings of Anglo-American forces in Morocco and Algeria on November 8, the end was never in doubt. Out of gas (in more ways than one), Rommel was airlifted to Hitler's headquarters on March 9. Colonel Rauff, having arrived in Tunis on November 24, was evacuated to Naples on May 9 with his entire staff. The Axis forces surrendered four days later, yielding 275,000 prisoners.

While Sonderstab 4 was providentially barred from the Yishuv, Colonel Rauff stayed on in Tunisia to the last moment, doing what he could under less than ideal conditions. With George C. Patton in the vicinity, the French resident-general, Jean-Pierre Esteva, was reluctant to sanction the slaughter of Tunisia's sizable Jewish community. Thus, apart from a few scattered murders, the "only" contribution Rauff was able to make in his brief five-month sojourn was a sprawling network of Jewish slave-labor camps (thirty in Tunis alone), most building redoubts on the main defense line. The laborers numbered about 3,000 initially; 4,500 by January.[83] Mallmann and Cüppers conclude: "If the conditions in the bridgehead had been more favorable and less consideration necessary for the Italian allies, Rauff would doubtless have been ready to engage in mass murder in Tunisia as well—or so his earlier actions strongly suggest."[84]

JEWISH WARTIME CONTRIBUTIONS

Three essential truths coalesce to introduce the subject of Jewish contributions to World War II: 1) They were diverse, disproportionate, and decisive; 2) The Jews continued to render their assistance despite the treatment afforded them by the very governments they were laboring to save; 3) Their aggregate value has been largely ignored, understated, or denied outright by Western revisionists.

Such injustice was nothing new for Jews, going back to Bible times. After Joseph helped one of Pharaoh's officers, Genesis 40:23 says, *"Yet did not the chief butler remember Joseph, but forgat him."* Ecclesiastes 9:15 tells about a poor man who used his wisdom to deliver a city, *"yet no man remembered that same poor man."* And though Mordecai had literally saved King Ahasuerus' life, Esther 6:2 relates that the deed went unrecognized for years. While entire books could be written on the subject of Jewish participation in WWII, the present section will survey but a sample of these heroic exploits.

The Allies' pat response to the Jews' entreaties to stop the Holocaust was that ending the war was the best way to end the same. So, the Jews set out to make it happen; the despised, nationless race would help their temporary domicile attain *her* imposing and elusive goal. (Someone said that the reason Hitler suffered from depression was because he couldn't face reality—though *right* about a "master race," he had, "unfortunately," picked the *wrong* one.)

Consider the decisive North Africa campaign. By now, the reader is aware that the Suez Canal represented the strategic solar plexus of His Britannic Majesty's global defense system. Pierre van Paassen writes:

> It took the war, and above all, Rommel's grave and long-lasting threat to inter-Empire and inter-Allied lines of communication to set in strong relief the value of the settlement of half a million Jews in Palestine—that is to say, in the immediate vicinity of the most vital arteries of the British world system. Jewish Palestine contributed more effectively to the repulse of the Axis advance upon Syria, Iraq, Egypt, and the Suez Canal...than the fifty times larger populations of the Arab countries combined.[85]

Unlike their pro-Nazi Arab neighbors, the Jews in Mandatory Palestine were committed to Britain—in spite of their despised status. Ben-Gurion expressed the Jewish rationale: "We must fight the war as if there were no white paper and fight the white paper as if there were no war."[86] On the eve of the war, Weizmann assured Chamberlain that the Jews would be there for him: "The Jewish Agency has recently had differences in the political field with the Mandatory Power. We would like these differences to give way before the greater and more pressing necessities of the time. We ask you to accept this declaration in the spirit in which it is made." The snobby prime minister managed a reticent response: "You will not expect me to say more at this stage than that your public-spirited assurances are welcome and will be kept in mind."[87] Mallmann and Cüppers add: "Just four months after the German attack on Poland, the Jewish Agency was able to present a list with the names of 134,000 Palestinian Jews who had declared their readiness to serve in the British army. Within a very short time, every second Jewish man and 20,000 Jewish women of the Yishuv had reported for military service."[88]

Yet, when Chaim lobbied for the redeployment of the Jewish Legion, Chamberlain refused, stating that such a move would only further antagonize the Arabs. The politically sensitive Brits went so far as to experiment with a ludicrous kind of affirmative action; despite an overwhelming swell of Jewish volunteers (fifteen for every one Arab), only an equal number of Jewish and Arab recruits could serve in noncombat units. However, with Rommel knocking at the gates of Cairo, the British came to their senses, reluctantly approving the emergency formation of special Jewish infantry battalions.[89]

By late 1942, 18,800 Palestinian Jews were in the British military (1,600 of these in the RAF and 400 in the RN).[90] The majority manned exclusive Jewish battalions, 25% assigned to frontline combat positions.[91] Another 24,000 served as paramilitary police auxiliaries.[92] In the spirit of their ambidextrous ancestors, as exhibited in Nehemiah 4:17—*"every one with one of his hands wrought in the work, and with the other hand held a weapon"*—the Jews' multifarious contributions included: battlefield engineers and demolition experts; pilots, bombardiers, and observers; thousands of technical personnel among the ground crews of Egyptian airdromes; weather data from the Hebrew University Meteorological Department; fully manned anti-aircraft stations in Palestine; one hundred speed boats from the Jewish Coast Guard patrolling the hazardous Mediterranean shores between Cyprus, Palestine, Egypt, and Libya; radar and wireless operators; scouts and interpreters; intelligence and reconnaissance; sabotage, espionage, commando and suicide squads;

and Jewish mothers (a.k.a. "chicken soup"), serving with their daughters in the medical corps.

The groundwork for much of the guerrilla activity was laid in 1936 by the legendary British Christian Zionist (Plymouth Brethren), Major-General Orde Charles Wingate, founder, trainer, innovator, and leader of the equally celebrated "Special Night Squads" (their forte being "going outside the wire"). Affectionately known in the Yishuv as *HaYedid* ("The Friend"), Wingate was recalled to London in 1939 due to intense Arab political pressure.

As with their predecessors in 1917, the Jewish legionaries served nobly. In June 1942, one thousand Palestinian Jews led by Major Felix Liebman (fighting with the Free French Brigade) successfully covered a critical retreat by the British Eighth Army at the village of Bir Hacheim. Only forty-five Jews were still alive when relief came on July 2.[93] Van Paassen shares an exhilarating, though rarely told postscript:

> The Jews stumbled into the open, looking like so many tortured ghosts. General Koenig of the Free French walked up to Major Liebman and embraced him. '*Vous avez tenu bon, jusqu'au bout*, you held out till the end,' he said. Then tears choked the Frenchman's voice. The Jews were given water, and the Major informed them that they were to accompany the French column. The siege was over. French soldiers were loading the remaining equipment on trucks. A flock of Spitfires sailed by, the pilots waving their helmets. One Jewish soldier took down the blue and white flag of Zion, rolled it up, and was about to place it in its holder when General Koenig saw him and asked him a question. 'We are not permitted to fly that flag,' explained Major Liebman. 'It's against regulations…' '*Pardon*,' said Koenig, 'I am in command here. *Je m'en fous pas mal des régulations*, I don't care a d--n about regulations…That flag goes on my car in front, next to the tricolor. That's where it belongs. *Nous sommes victorieux, tous les deux*, we have both come through victoriously!' And turning to his men, the French officer shouted: '*Legionnaires! Le drapeau juif! Salut!* Legionnaires, the Jewish flag! Salute!'[94]

The Jews' *non*-military support has been even less known and appreciated. Writing as a popular war correspondent (rather than a rigorous historian), Van Paassen observed: "When Britain's fate hung in the balance and when Rommel boasted that as far as he was concerned it was all over...the little land of Palestine placed at the disposal of the British Empire and its armies in the Near East an industrial apparatus of seven thousand factories, large and small."[95] By 1943, 63% of the Jewish labor force was dedicated to the British defense effort.[96] The highly significant and surprising role of the Jews' manufacturing base is shown by the commensurate rise of production revenue—from 14 million dollars in 1941 to 32.4 million in 1942.[97] "When Montgomery himself said privately that only a miracle could save him...Jewish Palestine was part of that miracle. Jewish Palestine was one of the imponderables that turned the tide against Hitler at the moment when he and almost the whole world least expected it."[98]

With its own supply lines jeopardized, the British Eighth Army would be sustained by the coalesced resources of Jewish industry and agriculture. Geographically speaking, with Afrika Korps pressing from the west, the Yishuv would have Monty's back—in the most literal sense. Thus, while millions of Jews were being abandoned to their deaths in Europe, the God of Abraham, Isaac, and Jacob mercifully ordained that the Jews of Eretz Yisrael would *"furnish a table in the wilderness"* (Psalm 78:19) for Chamberlain's beleaguered "Desert Rats." The supernatural spread included

> bandages, pharmaceutical articles, ether, sulfanilamide, benzoic acid, nicotinic acid, vitamin B complex, ascorbic acid (vitamin C), insulin, alkaloids, microscopic stains...precision instruments...135,000 pairs of boots per month, fruit, vegetables, wheat, wine, X-ray apparatus, 25,000 tons of cement per month, soap, chocolate, spare parts for automobiles and trucks, sandbags, timber, tents, linen uniforms, and buses taken from the Palestinian transportation system...laboratory equipment, electrical appliances, meat, especially mutton; photographic material, water pipes, stationery, typewriters, burr drills, steel helmets, three million dollars' worth of processed diamonds for cutting tools... matches...glassware and crockery, bedding, mattresses, maps, sheet metal, parachutes, disinfectants, oil burners, armored cars, cranes, five hundred ambulances, wire, shovels, water pails, cutlery, hammers, saws, nails, screws, saddles, camels, mules, horses...railway equipment and steel....[99]

FROM BLETCHLEY PARK TO LOS ALAMOS

Students of World War II generally agree that the secret code-breaking operation at Bletchley Park proved to be one of the decisive factors accelerating the Axis defeat. The 55-acre manorial estate located in Milton Keynes, Buckinghamshire, housed the main British decryption center known as the Government Code and Cypher School (GCCS).

The exceptional data produced from the Bletchley decrypts earned the famous code name "Ultra." Bletchley alumnus Sir Harry Hinsley, official historian of British wartime intelligence, believed that Ultra intercepts shortened the war by two to four years and that without them the outcome would have been uncertain.[100] Ultra intel enabled MI6 to locate and destroy half of Mussolini's tankers.[101] Thus, General Auchinleck opined, "[B]ut for Ultra, 'Rommel would have certainly gotten through to Cairo.'"[102] Bletchley's main feat was breaking the German "Enigma" system. The odds of hacking the labyrinthine code were roughly one hundred and fifty million, million, million against![103]

Now, what is *not* so widely known (a nice way of saying—*hardly known at all*), is that the core group at Bletchley comprised some 150 Jewish men and women, many hailing from nearby Oxford and Cambridge. (Though 2% of the staff, Jews represented less than 0.5% of Britain's population.)[104] In the late twenties, Jewish scientist Charles Proteus Steinmetz predicted, "There will come about an age of small and independent nations whose first line of defense will be knowledge." (Steinmetz was highly qualified to address this topic; despite a hunchback and hip dysplasia due to genetically inherited dwarfism, he excelled in electrical engineering, devising mathematical theories, pioneering the development of alternating current, facilitating the expansion of America's electric power industry—all while earning 200 patents.) Richard Deacon writes in *The Israeli Secret Service*:

> It was Steinmetz who encouraged Jewish scientists in Germany and elsewhere to acquire this specialized knowledge, if necessary by espionage, subterfuge and cunning, if they wished to see the Jews survive as a free people. It was through Steinmetz's teaching, his constant urging for the quest for knowledge that Jewish intellectuals came to be brought to work on the decoding of enemy signals in World War II. They were among the people who decoded German signals…known as the Enigma Chain."[105]

In his 2005 article for the *Journal of the Jewish Historical Society of England*, "Breaking the Codes: Jewish personnel at Bletchley Park in WW2," Martin Sugarman provides a detailed list of the key Jewish cryptologists, as well as a number of biographical highlights. It should be axiomatic by now that these unassuming folk represented some of the most intelligent people in the United Kingdom. Among other academic disciplines, they specialized in ancient and oriental languages, advanced mathematics, ciphers, statistical analysis, probability theory, and, last but not least—chess.[106]

Irving John "Jack" Good (born Isidore Jacob Gudak) was so intellectually endowed, he was able to precipitate the cracking of the Enigma code by perfecting a technique that came to him in a dream![107] (Conversely, in March 1943, Adolf Hitler temporarily sidelined his liquid-fueled V-2 rocket program after experiencing a nightmare that the weapon failed to cross the English Channel.[108]) The work of Cambridge math professor Max Newman helped create "Colossus," the world's first operational electronic computer.[109] (Meanwhile, another Jewish cryptographer, Colonel William Friedman, led the US Army team that broke Japan's codes via "Operation Magic.")

To view the entire cryptology operation in its inevitable Hebrew context, the Victorian Bletchley Park mansion itself was originally owned by a prominent British-born Jewish financier and politician, Sir Herbert Samuel Leon. The Jews' unique eavesdropping contribution was a throwback to II Kings 6:12, where the servant told King Benhadad of Syria, *"Elisha, the prophet that is in Israel, telleth the king of Israel the words that thou speakest in thy bedchamber."* The first Nazi code cracked by Ultra was the cipher which enabled MI6 to monitor the murders of the Byelorussian Einsatzgruppen, though sadly, doing nothing to intervene.[110] (The words of John 8:32, *"And ye shall know the truth and the truth shall make you free"*—spoken by a *Jewish* rabbi and recorded by a *Jewish* fisherman—were carved into the wall of the original lobby of the US Central Intelligence Agency.)

While Jewish prodigies were busy serving the Allied cause at Bletchley Park, a kindred operation was underway across "the pond" in Los Alamos, New Mexico. Though "Ultra" definitely *shortened* the war, "Little Boy" and "Fat Man" officially *ended* the same. Here again, a Jewish brain trust would prove to be the power behind the historic twin blasts in Japan.

Continuing the tradition begun at the Weizmann Institute of Science in Rehovot, the main scientists that forced Emperor Hirohito to *his* knees were: Albert Einstein ("Father of the Atomic Age," Nobel Laureate in Physics); J. Robert Oppenheimer ("Father of the Atomic Bomb," director at Los Alamos); Edward Teller ("Father of the Hydrogen Bomb"); Samuel T. Cohen ("Father of the Neutron Bomb"); John von Neumann ("World's Smartest Human"); Stanislaw Ulam (co-inventor of H-Bomb); Leo Szilard (Manhattan Project creator; first to envision a nuclear chain reaction); Otto Robert Frisch (co-authored Frisch-Peierls paper drafting first theoretical mechanism for detonating an A-Bomb); Rudolph Peierls (assembled "Little Boy" by hand); Samuel Abraham Goudsmit (ALSOS chief charged to assess Nazi ability to build an A-Bomb, proposed concept of electron spin); Arnold Kramish (predicted date of first Soviet H-Bomb detonation); Victor Fredrick Weisskopf (developed nuclear structure theory, "Clouded Crystal Ball"); Eugene Paul Wigner (pioneered theory of symmetries in quantum mechanics, Nobel Laureate in Physics); Hans Bethe (head of Theoretical Division at Los Alamos, Nobel Laureate in Physics); Niels Henrik David Bohr (first to apply quantum theory to nuclear structure, Nobel Laureate in Physics); Felix Bloch (developed nuclear magnetic resonance, Nobel Laureate in Physics); Richard Feynman (founded quantum electrodynamics theory, Nobel Laureate in Physics); and Emilio Gino Segrè (fled Italy due to Mussolini's anti-Semitism laws, A-bomb group leader, discovered technetium, astatine and antiproton, a sub-atomic antiparticle, Nobel Laureate in Physics).

Sam Cohen worked on "Fat Man" (plutonium bomb detonated over Nagasaki). In 1958, he invented the controversial W70 warhead (Neutron Bomb). He states in his memoirs, "I will say that regarding nuclear weapons, Jews, by far and away, have had a disproportionate effect on their development and the polices of their use."[111] Concerning the Manhattan Project, he attests: "Rarely, when some of us at the lab discussed our project and its meaning did we dwell very much on the profound moral aspects…This is not to imply that many of us did not do so privately (I never did). However, when two or more of us got together we never doubted openly that we were doing the right thing for a righteous cause. We were Americans whose country was at war with detestable enemies."[112]

After relating that many Jews were at Los Alamos and that most had lost loved ones in the Shoah, Cohen acknowledged that his peers "harbored precious little affection for the Nazis. They had a vindictive and even barbaric compulsion to complete the project in time to bomb Germany...Undoubtedly nuclear bombing Germany would have made many scientists at Los Alamos, especially the Jews, including myself, deliriously happy."[113] Of course, this was not to be (though technically, they only missed Berlin by 91 days). Sam then went on to drop a bomb of his own—relating an eyewitness piece of the past that you will *never* see on the History Channel. The setting was the hastily assembled meeting of the scientific staff to hear Oppenheimer deliver the first news about one of the "units," reported to have been "dropped over Japan." Not one person knew if the "unit" had even detonated.

> He arrived very late and entered the theater from the rear, strode down the aisle while all of us rose and cheered him, stomped our feet and in general behaved like a pack of bloodthirsty savages welcoming back their conquering warriors...When Oppenheimer was able to finally quiet down the mob, he set about telling us what little was known about the results of the bombing. There was one thing he knew for sure: the 'Japs' (not Japanese) didn't like it. More howling, foot stomping, and the like. Then he got to the nub of the matter: While we apparently had been successful, and his chest was practically bursting with pride, he did have one deep regret, that we hadn't completed the Bomb in time to use against the Germans. That really brought down the house. This had to be the most fascinating, to say nothing about being the most historic, speech I've ever heard. Apart from those who were there, I don't recall ever meeting anyone who had heard of it.[114]

Looking into the future, another Jewish fisherman wrote in AD 60, *"But the day of the Lord will come as a thief in the night; in the which the heavens shall pass away with a great noise, and* THE ELEMENTS SHALL MELT WITH FERVENT HEAT, *the earth also and the works that are therein shall be* BURNED UP.*"* (II Peter 3:10) Well, if a Jewish King (i.e., the Lord Jesus Christ) is going to melt the elements in the not-too-distant future, should it surprise anyone that His brethren "after the flesh" would have a similar propensity for all things nuclear? As the Führer would have said—"It's in the genes!"

MOE

While two-time MVP Hall of Famer Hank "The Hebrew Hammer" Greenberg became baseball's first Jewish superstar, Morris "Moe" Berg was considered a third-rate, back-up catcher during most of his fifteen seasons in the majors. Yet, the lesser esteemed "Berg" was easily the brightest Jewish athlete in the history of American sports.

Born March 2, 1902, in New York City to poor Russian immigrants, Berg went on to graduate *magna cum laude* from Princeton University, mastering Latin, Greek, French, Spanish, Italian, German, Japanese, and Sanskrit. After matriculating at the Sorbonne, the erudite catcher earned a second degree at Columbia Law School, finishing second in his class. He then passed the New York State bar. Among several extracurricular activities, Moe read ten newspapers a day while gaining notoriety as a successful radio quiz show contestant. "Casey" Stengel (somewhat nearer the *other* end of the cerebral spectrum) called Berg "the strangest man ever to play baseball."[115]

Thus, given his "less than stellar" baseball credentials, eyebrows raised in 1934 when Moe was selected (ahead of even Hank) to tour Japan with a group of All-Stars the likes of Babe Ruth, Lou Gehrig, Jimmie Foxx, and Charlie "Lefty" Gomez. Well, as events unfolded, while Japanese fans were swarming "the Babe" for photos, "the Berg" was busy taking his own pictures—elsewhere. Years before Hank Greenberg would serve in the Pacific as a squadron leader of the Twentieth Bomber Command, Moe had already made *his* contribution to America's aerial campaigns in that theater. Under the heading "'Moe' Berg: Sportsman, Scholar, Spy," the official website for the US Central Intelligence Agency provides "the rest of the story":

> Berg's entrance into the field of intelligence began when he, Babe Ruth, Lou Gehrig and other baseball greats formed an all-star team and traveled to Japan in the mid-1930s for exhibition games. Proficient in Japanese, Berg talked his way into one of the tallest buildings in Tokyo. He climbed to the rooftop alone and used a movie camera to film the capital city's shipyards. Reportedly, the US used Berg's footage to plan bombing raids over Tokyo in World War II.
>
> Following the attack on Pearl Harbor in 1941, Berg initially joined the White House's new Office of Inter-American Affairs but left for the Office of Strategic Services (OSS) in 1943. He became

> a paramilitary officer and carried out various intelligence operations in Europe, including parachuting into Yugoslavia to evaluate resistance groups there. By 1945 Berg had been tasked to determine whether Nazi Germany was close to having a nuclear weapon. Using his language skills and charm, he managed to locate and chat with Werner Heisenberg, a top physicist in the Third Reich. Berg accurately determined that the answer was "no." Berg stayed with the OSS until it dissolved in 1945. Afterward, he served on the staff of NATO's Advisory Group for Aeronautical Research and Development."[116]

Moe was offered the Medal of Freedom Award in 1946 but declined to accept due to the sensitive nature of his wartime exploits. After passing his later years in a blur of enigmatic activity, the lifelong bachelor died on May 29, 1972, at age seventy from injuries sustained in a fall. According to a nurse at the Bellville, New Jersey, hospital where he expired, his last words were: "How did the Mets do today?"[117] While Moe's medal is now at the Baseball Hall of Fame in Cooperstown (his sister having accepted it posthumously), his baseball cards may be viewed at the CIA Museum in Langley, Virginia.

THE MAX FACTOR

The Bible declares that *"in the last days...evil men and seducers shall wax worse and worse,* DECEIVING AND BEING DECEIVED.*"* (II Timothy 3:1, 13) Adolf Hitler remains the quintessential fulfillment of this specific prophecy. However, while most people recognize the first two correlations—that the Führer was *evil* personified (6,000,000 Jewish victims in 42 months) and that his vileness was compounded by the *deception* he used ("To the bath," etc.)—few know the story of how Hitler himself was ultimately taken in (*and* out) by a fraud of epic proportions. Colonel James Milano, a US intelligence agent, described the perpetrator as "practically omnipotent, a genuine magician."[118]

While Americans generally view the European phase of WWII through the prism of Hollywood films like *The Longest Day*, *Saving Private Ryan*, and *Band of Brothers*, the fact remains that 70% of the German divisions were lost on the *Eastern* Front (four of every five Wehrmacht soldiers dying *there*). To Hitler's perpetual derision, the one man who, probably more than anyone else, hastened the *Götterdämmerung* ("catastrophic collapse") of the Third Reich (via the Russian theater), just *happened* to be—a full-blooded *Jew.*[119]

Richard Joseph Kauder was an unassuming, thirty-nine-year-old fledgling Budapest publisher of Hungarian German-language tourist guides when the Nazis "recruited" him as a spy in January 1940. The unlikely prospect of a Jew working for the Abwehr was triggered by a confluence of three factors. First, with the paranoid Germans wanting to monitor their newest ally, Bulgaria, Kauder's proficiency in Balkan dialects was naturally appealing. He also came highly commended by his closest friends (who, unknown to him, had joined the Abwehr themselves): Harry-Peter Smolka-Smollett, his Jewish business partner; Lieutenant Colonel Otto Hatz, a senior intelligence officer in the Hungarian army; Momotaro Enomoto, a journalist for the Japanese paper, *Mainishi Shimbun*; and Ilya Longa, his initial, unnamed Russian patron. However, at the end of the day, Richard's German handlers, Colonel Rudolf Graf von Marogna-Redwitz and Major Roland von Wahl Welkrish, simply "made him an offer he couldn't refuse." His widowed mother, Laura, was to remain in Vienna under "protective custody." (Hitler would rue the day he picked on *this* Jewish mama.)

The following afternoon, Richard Kauder received a new German passport under the alias "Fritz Klatt." Two months later, he was already settled into an apartment at 55 Skobolev Street, Sofia, Bulgaria. He was instructed to lease office space for a front export-import business, hiding his covert operation on the second floor. The sensitive project was code-named "Max and Moritz" (ironically, after one of Hitler's favorite children's books written by Wilhelm Busch).[120]

All messages involving Russia and the Ukraine were designated "Max"; Middle East intel (mostly British North African activity) carried the heading "Moritz." While the former moved from Sofia (code-named "Schwert") to Vienna ("Vera"), the latter originated at the Spanish embassy in Ankara, Turkey ("Anker"), being forwarded to Vienna via Sofia. All dispatches were transmitted in encrypted German code. The radio personnel in Vienna were highly trained Abwehr agents who operated Enigma. Now, what the reader is about to learn is that the Führer not only would have to suffer the *enigma* that his "impregnable" codes were breached by those "subhuman" Jews at Bletchley Park—but the added *stigma* that a *second* group of Jews was destined to use the Enigma—against *him* (II Samuel 23:21).

In early October 1940, Enomoto asked Richard to accompany him to Greece for an overdue weeklong "vacation." The men stayed at the Alexandria Hotel near Salonika Port (home to then-sixteen-year-old future Sonderkommando, Shlomo Venezia). During a night stroll, the friends slipped onto a Soviet commercial ship to meet a mysterious stranger whom Enomoto would only refer to as the "Director General." A gregarious, multi-lingual Russian approached Kauder, introducing himself as Ivan. Then, "comrade" Ilya Longa stepped out of the shadows. The course of WWII was about to be dramatically altered. Though Kauder would not discover the Russian's true identity until after the war, the purpose for the nocturnal rendezvous was clear—a fresh job offer had presented itself—one that he readily embraced. Eight months before Barbarossa, the Soviets had flipped "Fritz" to become their most effective double agent. Kauder's new boss was the notorious Jewish KGB agent, General Nahum Isaakovich Eitingon (coordinator of fellow Jew Leon Trotsky's assassination).

According to Eitingon, Kauder would be the undisputed chief of operations. "You will conduct all communication. You will be in charge and will be the only person authorized to talk to the Germans."[121] Following the Nazi incursion, the modus operandi for Max and Moritz was simple. The KGB assembled a team of "White Russians," led by former Ukrainian general Prince Anton Vasilievich Turkul (Longa's mentor) to feed the Abwehr a steady flow of intel regarding Soviet activity. It was vital that the reports be variegated, convincing—and above all else—dead-on accurate, given the enemy's penchant for meticulous verification. Then, after gaining the Germans' confidence, "Max" could impact key battles by inserting just the *right* amount of *wrong* information (disinformation) at the pivotal moment.

In the definitive Kauder biography, *Enigma Named Max*, Israeli author and retired IDF Colonel, Avraham Ziv-Tal writes, "Their goal was to obtain maximum credibility at minimum costs and therefore, kept up a steady stream of credible, accurate intelligence that would cause minimal damage to the Soviet forces, while concealing information that they were not interested in exposing."[122]

TWO RICHARDS

Kauder's first significant victory of the operation produced Hitler's first defeat of the war—the winter catastrophe at Moscow. Prior to the battle, Vera had received several reports from Schwert affirming that the Soviets were severely "undermanned." An excerpt from the October 12, 1941, transmission stated, "Stavka [Russian Military High Command] has given clear orders to preserve manpower. We have a severe shortage of soldiers and each one is extremely valuable."[123] After a six-week slugfest through 1,242 miles in record temperatures (reaching -50° F), a German reconnaissance unit caught its initial glimpse of the Kremlin's glittering spires on December 2. Four days later, the German 6th Army learned a new Russian word, *maskirovka* ("deception"). Far from short-handed, Marshal Zhukov launched a surprise counterattack—*reinforced with fifteen newly arrived Soviet divisions* (well equipped for winter combat). Within weeks, the decimated, half-frozen, and "undermanned" *Nazis* had already retreated 125 miles to the west.

Regarding the Max factors at work, having signed a non-aggression treaty with Japan on April 13, 1941, Stalin grew anxious over her intentions after Hitler's own breach of the Molotov-Ribbentrop Pact only two weeks later. Which agreement would Tokyo honor? Would the "Japs" (as Oppenheimer would say) advance *Hokunshin* ("north") toward the Soviet eastern border, primarily Mongolia and Manchuria, or move *Nanshin* ("south"), attacking Anglo-American colonies, primarily Pearl Harbor? The Führer was also getting antsy, hoping for a Hokunshin strike to draw Russia into a two-front war like himself. By autumn 1941, RSHA chief Walter Schellenberg (Himmler's aide) authorized "Max" (Turkul and Kauder) to tap their Japanese sources for an answer.[124] Turkul's main contact was a German-Russian "journalist" Richard Sorge, a veteran GRU spy.[125] (Kauder would also have access to Sorge via Isono Kiyosho, an obscure Tokyo reporter.)[126]

Sorge worked with a highly placed Nipponese agent, Hotsumi Ozaki (also posing as a reporter). In time, the pair gained the trust of Major General Eugen Ott, Germany's envoy to Japan. Between late August and early September, Ozaki learned (from the prime minister's own inner circle) that Japan had opted for Nanshin. Maintaining his cover, Ozaki duly informed Ott and Sorge, whereupon the men passed the disappointing news to Hitler through their separate channels.

Of course, Koba (Stalin's moniker) also got the news—*freeing him to rush his Mongolian divisions across Siberia to Moscow.* Dr. Stewart Goldman of the National Council for Eurasian Research writes:

> On August 25-26, Sorge drafted this message to Moscow: 'Invest [Ozaki's alias] was able to learn from circles closest to [Prime Minister] Konoye...that the High Command...discussed whether they should go to war with the USSR. They decided not to launch the war within this year, repeat, not to launch the war this year.' At an Imperial conference September 6, the decision to advance southward was reconfirmed...On September 14 Sorge reported even more emphatically to Moscow that 'in the careful judgment of all of us here...the possibility of launching an attack, which existed until recently, has disappeared...There can be absolutely no doubt about this.' Only then did the Soviet High Command undertake a massive transfer of forces from east to west.[127]

Sir Basil Liddell Hart confirms:

> A fundamental factor in the failure of the invasion was the invaders' miscalculation of the reserves that Stalin could bring up from the depths of Russia. In that respect the General Staff and its Intelligence Service were as much deceived as Hitler. The fatal error is epitomized in one pregnant sentence of [Franz] Halder's diary in mid-August: 'We underestimated Russia: we reckoned with 200 divisions, but now we have already identified 360.'[128]

According to recently declassified US intelligence files, Sorge sent his intel to Berlin via Turkul's associate, "Fritz Klatt."[129] Thus, while Richard *Sorge* delivered the *truth* to Stalin in early *September*, the *other* Richard fed Hitler a flow of *half-truths* from *October* onward. For, while the previously cited Max report of October 12 was *technically* correct—at the time—a relieved Stalin would now have ten weeks to prepare his Moscow "welcoming committee." Aarons and Loftus conclude, "Hitler did not know it, but the tide of the war was turning against him forever. The Turkul network was a cancer from which the Third Reich would never recover."[130] (Incidentally, it was no coincidence that the date of this turning point just *happened* to correspond to the opening of Germany's first death camp at Chelmno.)

"GET RID OF THE JEW FOR HEAVEN'S SAKE."

The Jewish writer of Psalm 137:5 declared, *"If I forget thee, O Jerusalem, let my right hand forget her cunning."* Richard Kauder would later inform his British interrogators that he had sent roughly 12,000 Max and 3,000 Moritz reports.[131] His most lethal deception after Moscow led to the previously cited German fiasco at Stalingrad.

In the summer of 1943, Max advised that Stavka was anticipating a renewed strike against Moscow and was marshalling its remaining forces in a defensive posture. In reality, Stalin knew that Germany's objective was the Caspian oil fields. Thus, when Hitler took the bait, issuing Directive 32—splitting Army Group South to humble Stalingrad enroute to the Caucasus—over 1,000,000 Soviet troops and thousands of tanks were discretely moved from Moscow to Joe's patronymic town. As an added precaution, Max alerted Abwehr on November 4 that the Soviets would attempt an 11th-hour counterstrike against Army Group Center near the Rzhev salient (outside Moscow), effectively neutralizing sizable German reinforcements in the process.

The surprise Red attack began November 19. The end was inevitable. Ziv-Tal relates: "On January 31, 1943, when Paulus arrived to submit the Sixth Army's instrument of surrender in Stalingrad, he was generally surprised to see Marshal Rokossovsky [Soviet Central Front Commander]. 'I was sure that you were in Moscow….' Rokossovsky, neatly shaved and meticulously dressed for a historical photograph, couldn't help but smile."[132] The key inference here is that the Max factor derailing of Hitler's Stalingrad offensive foiled his greater objective of capturing the Caspian oil fields, thereby saving the Yishuv from the imminent incursion of Sonderstab F from the north.

While Sorge and Ozaki were convicted of espionage and hanged in Japan on November 7, 1944, Fritz Klatt would continue to outwit his Nazi masters to the end. Having studied the "enigma named Max" for twelve years, Ziv-Tal confirms, "Recent research claims that the Soviets successfully deceived the Germans in approximately 140 regional offensives and conducted several dozens of specific strategic deceptions such as those in Moscow and Stalingrad."[133] Kauder's routine of reporting phantom Soviet deployments to various fronts was reinforced by engineer battalions assembling entire mock divisions by night, complete with: hundreds of "tanks" made of tin, rubber, and wood;

phony air strips; pre-recorded radio chatter; smoke screens; and sporadic anti-aircraft fire. German aerial reconnaissance was fooled every time. In summer 1943, Max intel and related diversionary tactics enabled the Russians to achieve their surprise counterattack at the Battle of Kursk—the greatest armor engagement in military history.[134]

Admiral Canaris' rivals within the Nazi-dominated SDA eventually tipped Hitler that a "Jew" was running his Sofia spy ring. The Führer went apoplectic, ordering the Gestapo—"Get rid of the Jew for heaven's sake. I refuse to allow a single Jew to be a part of the National-Socialist intelligence service…."[135] However, by this late hour (mid-1943), Wehrmacht doyens like General Heinz Guderian were in open rebellion against the sacrosanct dogma of *Führerprinzip*, ("Leadership Principle"), a Nazi euphemism for sycophant. Thus, Guderian's response to the Führer's decree was simple: "The network is the most important one that we have. Interfering with its activity is a criminal act."[136] By now, Richard had also come under the protection of one of Hitler's most trusted advisors, Colonel Kurt Jahnke, Chief of the Jahnkebureau (Ribbentrop's personal intelligence service).[137]

The volatile impasse was resolved by having Fritz continue his mission, but "under the radar." On June 22, 1944, the third anniversary of Barbarossa, Stavka launched its own surprise attack, "Operation Bagration," nearly destroying Army Group Center at the "Belarusian Balcony." This was Germany's *greatest* defeat in the east, sustaining over 500,000 casualties (worse than Verdun in 1916). Ziv-Tal writes, "It was clear to all that the Germans had once again been deceived."[138]

The last Max report was on February 13, 1945. Aarons and Loftus note: "Every branch of Nazi intelligence, including General Guderian at Hitler's highest headquarters, depended on Klatt. It appears that he may have been the one mysterious Jew in the SS intelligence service who received Honorary Aryan status."[139] Even SS General Walter Schellenberg was willing to give credit where credit was due, describing Kauder as the head of a global "information network [that] went through various countries and penetrated every stratum of society. He furnished quick and exact reports from the senior staffs of the Russian Army…."[140] The co-authors conclude: "Max was the most successful, and most closely guarded, intelligence operation of Nazi Germany…It would not be an exaggeration to say that the 'Fascist Jews" of the Max network did more to defeat the German Army than all of the Western intelligence services combined."[141]

While Richard's mother outlasted her house arrest, her two sisters and one brother shared the fate of Herzl's daughter and son-in-law in Theresienstadt.[142] As for the 50,000 Jews who happened to encompass Kauder's base of operations, Michael Bar-Zohar reveals in *Beyond Hitler's Grasp: The Heroic Rescue of Bulgaria's Jews*, "[A]stonishingly, not one Bulgarian Jew ever left the country."[143] (Prior to his execution in 1944 for conspiring in the July 20 plot against Hitler, Colonel Rudolf Graf von Marogna-Redwitz, a Catholic, rescued twelve Jewish lives at Richard's request.[144])

When Kauder approached the Allies after the war, he was foolishly rebuffed as a "despicable Bolshevik."[145] Nonetheless, though working for Moscow until his death in 1952, he kept General Reinhard Gehlen (Dulles agent) apprised of his intel. He would also become a valuable ally to the Zionists, especially during the 1948 War of Independence.

GO FIGURE!

When forward units of the 42nd and 45th Infantry Divisions of the US 7th Army reached Dachau on April 29, 1945, they were met by a ghastly death train with forty roofless boxcars holding 2,300 Jewish corpses (recent Buchenwald arrivals). After finding more gore inside, several of these red-blooded GIs (many still in their teens) simply "lost it" as the SS guards tried to surrender. ("Heil Hitler" salutes were particularly unwise.) This author was privileged to interview a 91-year-old former member of the famed "Rainbow (42nd) Division" who shared his own eyewitness account of the retribution that flared on that bloody Sunday afternoon. The number of SS killed remains unclear, estimates ranging from 50-500; Patton would later dismiss all charges.

Yet, one fact *is* clear. In the spirit of Phinehas—that Hebrew vigilante and grandson of Aaron the High Priest, who vented *his* righteous indignation by skewering a fornicating couple—several livid Americans made their *own* abrupt, high-profile "statement," devoid of political correctness. And while the LORD (called *"a man of war"* in Exodus 15:3) was not only similarly unwilling to prosecute His own, but rather rewarded Phinehas *"because he was zealous for his God..."* (Numbers 25:13), let the record state that the reprisals *pale* alongside the Allied-Vatican-Wall Street intrigues that permeate this chapter.

For example, eight days after Dachau's liberation, Germany formally surrendered. Having perpetrated the Final Solution of the Jewish question, the Third *Reich* (Nazi Millennium) suffered its own premature denouement, imploding after only *twelve* years (the Jews' number). Ironically, in his postwar trial, former Governor Hans Frank opined before an international court: "A thousand years will pass and still this guilt of Germany will not have been erased."[146] However, as events later unfolded, there was *plenty* of guilt to go around.

The enormity of the prevailing ecopolitics (the Shoah as the nadir) can be illustrated by simple math. According to the history books, the "War to make the World Safe for Democracy" *supposedly* began because *one* sovereign nation, Poland, was occupied by the Axis dictator, Adolf Hitler. Then, after six years of bloodletting, rendering 35,000,000 deaths, the fleeting euphoria of V-E Day marked the start of a paradoxical transition wherein the *original* victimized nation was deeded over to the Allies' dictator, "Uncle Joe" Stalin—along with *nine* other countries (East Germany, Hungary, Czechoslovakia, Romania, Bulgaria, Albania, Estonia, Latvia, and Lithuania). The so-called "Iron Curtain" (Warsaw Pact) coalition (scrawled on a napkin) would stand for nearly half a century (a.k.a. the Cold War). The total death count (including famine) attributed to democide in the Stalin era (1922-53) is roughly 50,000,000. As the saying goes—"Go figure!"

RATS AND RATLINES

In the unincorporated community of Suitland, Maryland (just southeast of DC), a massive, subterranean repository exists, holding twenty vaults (each an acre in size) crammed floor to ceiling with most of the classified archives of the Federal government. Among an extensive labyrinth of non-indexed files and documents pertaining to WWII and the Cold War the sordid tale of US Holocaust complicity lay dormant for twenty-five years. The evidence was unearthed by the diligent efforts of John J. Loftus, a GS-13 Supervisory Trial Attorney for the US Department of Justice Office of Special Investigations.

As a former Army intelligence officer holding some of the highest security clearances in the nation (Q, S, CIA Codeword, and NATO COSMIC), Mr. Loftus completed two years (1977-79) of unrestricted research within the Suitland caverns while engaged in the arrest, prosecution, and deportation of Nazi war criminals. While the content of Loftus' first book, *The Belarus Secret* (1982), spawned an Emmy award-winning interview on *60 Minutes* (followed by the 1985 made-for-TV movie, *Kojack: The Belarus File*), his subsequent exposés, *Unholy Trinity* (1992) and *The Secret War Against the Jews* (1994), both co-authored with Mark Aarons, and *America's Nazi Secret* (2010), have only exacerbated the consternation of surviving culprits from Foggy Bottom to Vatican Square. Thus, the US Census Bureau website reassures one and all: "The last of the vaults was destroyed by fire in the mid 1990s and demolished. The vaults, however, live on in the popular imagination, fueled by conspiracy theorists and an episode of the television series, The X-Files."[147] As with Britain's cowardly censure of the conservative Jewish American author and radio host, Michael Savage, *The Secret War Against The Jews* remains banned by *Her* Majesty's Government.[148] (Much of the following synopsis is cited from Loftus' highly acclaimed *and* highly criticized revelations.)

Constituting one of the war's great ironies, while the Allies consistently refused to help Europe's Jews escape the Final Solution, they *did* help the Jews' killers flee the crime scene. Many Nazis were secreted all the way to America, some even finding employment within the government itself. And, to the oft-expressed chagrin of the Irish Catholic Loftus, on *this* occasion, "All roads led *from* Rome"—the Eternal City having served as the hub of this human contraband. In May 1947, a classified State Department report affirmed: "[T]he Vatican…is the largest single organization involved in the illegal movement of emigrants…."[149] Colonel Hans Rudel, the decorated Luftwaffe ace who became a global spokesman for postwar neo-Nazism, said in 1970: "In Rome itself, the transit point of the escape routes, a vast amount was done. With its own immense resources, the Church helped many of us to go overseas…in quiet and secrecy…."[150]

The opening line of *Unholy Trinity: The Vatican, The Nazis, and Soviet Intelligence* reads accordingly: "Unholy Trinity is the story of the Vatican's underground Nazi-smuggling networks, code-named 'Operation Ratline.'"[151] A "ratline" is a rope ladder that dangles from the top of a ship's mast (the last place of safety when a vessel is about to sink). The expression was originally coined by the Office of Strategic Services (OSS) as a generic intelligence term for the maze of escape routes used by downed American airmen in occupied Europe. However, the nautical word found its ultimate idiomatic usage as a double entendre in conjunction with 30,000 *Nazi* rats abandoning the sinking *SS Reich*[152] (half of whom would enter the US illegally[153]).

As the facts now speak for themselves, the standard moral spin for having aided and abetted Hitler's henchmen is that many of the vanquished Nazis, along with their former collaborators, were deemed invaluable for what was thought to be, *at the time*, an inevitable military showdown between America and the Soviet Union. The Vatican "State" was especially wary of growing Communist influence in Western Europe. Being estranged as a wayward daughter since AD 1054 was bad enough, but now the "child" was grown, Red, and after her "Mama's moolah." (See *The Vatican Billions*, Avro Manhattan.)

Viewing fascism as the lesser of two evils, "His Holiness" Pius XII "reluctantly" entered into a clandestine alliance with British and US intelligence to defeat the "Russian Horde," etc. The Vatican Information Service (VIS) became the Holy See's equivalent of the CIA. The Catholic lay group, *Intermarium*, played a lead role in VIS intrigue. Meaning "between the seas," Intermarium became the code name for the papal plan to create a Catholic federation of all nations bordering Russia "from the Baltic to the Aegean"—a renewed Holy Roman Empire to expedite the USSR's demise (i.e., eliminate Rome's nearest competitor for global dominion). The oversight for the new spy apparatus was given to a pro-Commie cleric, Vatican Under Secretary of State Monsignor Giovanni Montini (the future Pope Paul VI).

The prospect of a hasty postwar rapprochement with Germany to initiate World War III against Russia was not at all shocking to Allied insiders. Before his execution at Nuremberg, Foreign Minister Ribbentrop asserted that he—together with a former British prime minister (Ramsay MacDonald) *and* a future king (Edward Windsor)—had nearly concluded a secret Anglo-German accord in the 1930s.[154] On the war's eve, Nazi intel officers Kurt Jahnke and Admiral Canaris had plotted to overthrow the Führer to form an anti-Bolshevik alliance with Britain.[155] (The Reich's anti-Hitler faction was code-named Black Orchestra.) Wehrmacht veterans instinctively preferred a deal with HMG to attack Stalin, rather than pursue Hitler's Soviet pact to invade Poland, then everyone else (including England and America). Thus, detached from reality, Hitler was genuinely surprised when Britain and France declared war on *him* for "merely" securing a staging area in *Slavic* Poland for his coming invasion of *Communist* Russia.

Regarding subsequent olive branches (Rudolf Hess' controvertible parachuting into Scotland among them), Loftus and Aarons confirm, "According to SS records, captured by the Soviet and U.S. armies, the secret Nazi negotiations continued throughout the war."[156] Churchill admitted that he had told Lord Montgomery "to be careful in collecting the German arms, to stack them so that they could easily be issued again to the German soldiers."[157] The key players laboring to unite Berlin and the West were SS Intel Director Walter Schellenberg and Basel OSS Chief Allen Dulles (acting on his own).

Forty assassination attempts on the "beloved" Führer indicate how so-called "saner" elements within the Reich were thinking, which leads to the main problem with that loaded postulate about needing "Nazis" for Stalin; there were *two* categories of defeated Germans from which to draw—regular Wehrmacht forces and Waffen-SS war criminals. The enduring Allied stigma is that Rome's ratlines were overrun with the latter—the worst vermin in history. And to top it off, hundreds of high-profile Germans (like Eichmann) were "ratlined" out to perpetual underground asylum in South America and elsewhere with *no* intended participation in *any* anti-Soviet Cold War activities.

To give a brief sketch of this complex and multi-staffed operation, the Nazi "rats" in question were hiding among the millions of DPs ("Displaced Persons") in the Western Occupation Zones of Germany, Austria, and Italy. Most were not even German but rather Central and Eastern European quislings (leaders of fascist puppet regimes, municipal officials, police chiefs, members of auxiliary police—*all* having aided the Shoah). The main ratline sponsors were Dulles and the de facto US intel chief in postwar Italy, Lieutenant James *Jesus* Angleton. The hands-on smuggling was initiated by Titular Bishop Alois Hudal, rector of Pontificio Santa Maria dell'Anima (seminary for German priests in Rome). A former professor of Old Testament at the University of Graz and Consultor to the Holy Office, Hudal was also a hard-line, anti-Semitic, card-carrying Nazi.

One of "Big Al's" first clients was a personal friend—Walter Rauff. When German forces in Italy surrendered on April 29, 1945, Rauff was issued a false passport in the name of Carlo Comte. Though arrested by legitimate American authorities the day after, within hours a priest arrived, securing his transfer to a US Army Hospital. After his subsequent release and interrogation by S Force Verona (an OSS intelligence unit), the SS gas van specialist was allowed to repose (hunker down) "in the convents of the Holy See."[158]

Señor Comte showed his gratitude by helping to organize and finance the Bishop's ratline for other Nazis waiting in the wings. Entrants received counterfeit money and all necessary credentials, including an International Red Cross Passport (genuine or forged). Avro Manhattan, prolific author and world-renowned authority on Catholic intrigue, related in *The Vatican's Holocaust*: "The Vatican campaign of protective secretiveness was maintained, owing to the fact that Vatican City was considered a sovereign state…Vatican City meanwhile became a veritable beehive of bureaucratic operations, mostly centered upon paperwork. Birth certificates, visas, passports, and similar other such documentations were manufactured, prepared, and delivered with professional efficiency."[159] According to reliable sources, the "rats" would scurry from Rauff in Milan, to Hudal in Rome, then on to Archbishop Giuseppe Siri in Genoa, where they boarded ships and sailed away to their new lives in South America.[160]

Many other death camp celebs were likewise aided. While Gustav Wagner was deputy commander at Sobibór, his former superior, Franz Paul Stangl, was running Treblinka. When the two mass murderers crossed paths in Graz, Austria, in 1948, they proceeded on to Rome together, eventually singing Hudal's praises in Brazil.[161] John Demjanjuk (one of Wagner's guards at Sobibór) escaped to Cleveland, Ohio, where he retired as an auto worker at Ford Motor Company. (How fitting!) In 1986, John was deported to Israel, where he received a death sentence for war crimes, though it was overturned by the Israeli Supreme Court in 1993. (After returning to the Buckeye state, he was deported to Germany in 2009, where he was convicted again, dying on March 17, 2012, while his sentence was under appeal.)

Alois Brunner, the tactician who expedited the corralling and deportations of Europe's Jews, also absconded via Hudal's ratline. The Simon Wiesenthal Center credits Brunner with 128,500 victims.[162] Adolf Eichmann (Brunner's superior) was undoubtedly the highest ranking beneficiary of the Bishop's "ministry" (though the "Little Jew" was later caught in Argentina and hanged in Israel). Wiesenthal testified, "During my search for Eichmann I found out that many [Nazis] were living in monasteries, equipped by Hudal with false documents…."[163] (Rauff himself died "peacefully" in Chile in 1984.)

THE USTASHI

Another major Vatican co-conspirator was the Bosnian Franciscan, Krunoslav Draganović, Secretary of the Croatian Institute of San Girolamo in Rome (and succourer of Zsa Zsa Gabor). The Rolodex of this "reverend" stretched from Klaus "The Butcher of Lyon" Barbie to Joseph "The Death Angel" Mengele.

Known to his US handlers as the Vatican's "DP Resettlement Chief,"[164] the Croat's real forte was smuggling Nazi collaborators.[165] Scores of Ukrainian fugitives traveled down his ratline, the most notorious being Home Security and Police Minister Mykola Lebed, a cold-blooded killer of thousands (including Wiesenthal's mother). Lebed was the highest-ranking war criminal ever to enter the US (dying in Pittsburgh in 1998).[166] In one of the most sensational ratline episodes, an entire Ukrainian Waffen SS division (11,000 men, many with family) escaped by the personal intervention of Pius himself.[167]

Draganović was a loyal supporter of the *Ustashi*, the genocidal goon squad in Hitler's breakaway Yugoslavian regime of Croatia. Under the brutal administration of the Roman Catholic sadist, Dr. Ante Pavelić, *Poglavnik* ("leader") of the Independent State of Croatia, some 40,000 Jews, 50,000 gypsies, and 800,000 Orthodox Serbs were dispatched in the most barbaric medieval fashion. That equates to *forty times* the fatality count of the Spanish Inquisition and St. Bartholomew's Day Massacre *combined.*

The next time some bigoted Catholic tries to dismiss his heinous heritage as a "thing of the past," have him explain: 250 peasants buried alive in the Serbian district of Bjelovar; 2,000 children gassed in Bosanska; a father and son crucified together on the front door of their home in Mliniste; mothers and children impaled on the same stake in Gorevac; a mother in Kosinj forced to hold the basin catching the blood of her four sons as their throats were slit; an expectant mother having her unborn child surgically replaced with a *cat* in the Jasenovac death camp; 1,360 prisoners having their throats cut by one guard during an all-night throat-slitting contest (also at Jasenovac); not to mention dismemberments; beheadings; crowns of thorns; special graviso knives for throat-cutting prowess; necklaces of tongues and eyes; holding cells with ankle-deep blood; plus 10,000 other atrocities condoned by Zagreb Archbishop Aloysius Viktor Stepinac, who "prayed" at the opening of Croatia's

Parliament in February 1942 for "the Holy Ghost to descend upon the sharp knives of the Ustashi."[168]

The worst carnage was at the extermination center near the village of Jasenovac. Jews arriving in need of medical care were brought to the "hospital" where they were summarily eviscerated by a deranged Ustashi in a physician's smock (Ljubo Miloš).[169] The commandant was a Franciscan monk, "Father" Miroslav Filipović. Other hieratic killers included Dr. Branimir Zupanic; Srecko Peric; the Jesuit, Dr. Dragutin Kamber;[170] and one *really* wild Franciscan—Bozidar Bralow, known for dancing around dead Serbs with his "constant companion," a loaded machine gun.[171] Manhattan notes, "The Nazis, who for a time were posted in Croatia, were so horrified at the Ustashi atrocities that they set up special commissions to investigate them."[172]

In April 1941, the Poglavnik had a private audience with Pius. After the war, Pavelić and his retinue slipped in and out of Vatican safe houses while hundreds of Ustashi were extracted from teeming DP camps and sent down the ratline. Ante was often seen being chauffeured around Rome in a Vatican limo with diplomatic plates. After getting his Red Cross Passport from Draganović, "The Butcher of the Balkans" sailed from Italy on September 13, 1947, arriving in Buenos Aires on November 6 as "Pablo Aranyos."[173] (In 1998, his mentor, Cardinal Archbishop Stepinac, was beatified by John Paul II).

THE BELARUS SECRET

A particularly pesky chapter of the emerging ratline scandal concerns the hundreds of former Nazi collaborators from Byelorussia (present-day Belarus) who entered the US illegally between 1948 and 1950, later becoming naturalized citizens, many settling down in South River, New Jersey (hometown of NFL legend Joe Theismann).

Unknown to Congress and the public, the State Department had created its own shadow version of the newly formed CIA to privately recruit, import, and employ the capos of nearly all former Nazi puppet regimes ("from the Baltic to the Aegean") in a grandiose scheme to foment instability within the Soviet bloc. The catalyst for America's growing Russophobia was a flow of ominous reports from one of Dulles's prized "trophies," General Reinhard Gehlen, former German Intelligence Chief of FHO (Foreign Armies East). Thus, at the urging of Dulles and Secretary of State George Marshall, President Truman's National Security Council issued the watershed directive, NSC 10/2, creating the Office of Policy Coordination (OPC) on June 18, 1948.

Frank Wisner, a charismatic Wall Street lawyer (Dulles crony) was made executive director. Paul Nitze labeled the new organ, "The Department of Dirty Tricks."[174] The OPC directory listed goals such as "propaganda, economic warfare, preventative direct action including sabotage, anti-sabotage, demolition and evacuation measures...subversion against hostile states, including assistance to underground resistance movements, guerrillas and refugee liberation groups, and support of indigenous anti-Communist elements in threatened countries of the free world"[175]; and later, "political assassination."[176]

Thus, a covert anti-Communist operation would be trained, financed, and sustained behind the Iron Curtain via a parallel nexus of émigré front organizations in America (Radio Liberty, Radio Free Europe, NCFE, Captive Nations, AMCOMLIB, Crusade for Freedom). Loftus elucidates one of the most incongruent moments in US history:

> After Truman's surprising defeat of Dewey, America actually had two CIA's. There was the official CIA that worked for President Truman and the Democrats. The other CIA, the OPC, worked for Allen Dulles and the defeated Republicans under cover of the State and Justice Departments. The official CIA hunted Nazis, the other recruited them for the State Department's OPC.[177]

Once again, the problem with such anti-Red rhetoric was that many of the "freedom fighters" (political warfare operatives) being organized in the US cut their teeth devouring thousands of Jews in the Shoah, particularly with the Einsatzgruppen in Byelorussia, the heart of the Pale.[178] (Their "spare time" was spent in the Waffen-SS Belarus Brigade fighting Americans.) The reader will recall how Stanislav Stankievich, the Nazi-appointed mayor of Borisov used the "sardine method" to kill 7,000 Jews in a single day. The man who buried Jewish babies alive to save bullets became a naturalized American citizen on March 8, 1969, residing in Richmond Hill, New York.[179]

Emanuel Jasiuk, the puppet administrator of Kletsk, who could only manage 5,000 murders in *his* 24-hour pogrom, retired as a respectable US citizen in the adjacent Garden State. Dr. Vitold Tumash, quisling mayor of Minsk—the capital and municipal nerve center for the Byelorussian genocide—wound up running the Slavic desk at the New York City Public Library. Having overseen the deaths of 42,000 Jews in the Minsk Ghetto, SS General Franz Kushel, chief of the Nazi-controlled Byelorussian police, received *his* American visa on May 18, 1950, later opening a White Russian social club in Brooklyn.[180] Finally, as former president of the Byelorussian Central *Rada* (Council), Radislaw Ostrowsky was the most influential collaborator of all. Yet, he too was later privileged with US status. Ostrowsky moved to Jersey in 1956 where he lived undisturbed until his death on October 17, 1976 (eight days shy of his 90th birthday.)[181]

While Europe's Jews were denied entry into America for want of Nazi affidavits "proving" they would be a "positive benefit," Loftus recaps the certifiable behavior of the refugees who *were* approved by the OPC: "In all, about two-thirds of the approximately 375,000 Jews who lived in Byelorussia before the Nazi invasion were swallowed up by the Holocaust."[182] As Wisner's superior, George Kennan, Director of Policy Planning at the State Department, implied in a wartime memo that "plausible deniability" was the *only* way to survive: "[T]he degree of relative guilt which such inquiries may bring to light is something of which I, as an American, prefer to remain ignorant."[183] Incredibly (and representing a topic of its own) Kennan and the rest of the so-called "Wise Men" had to extend their ostrich mentality to a revival of post-Holocaust pogroms induced by Wisner's anti-Semitic agents (old habits being hard to break, etc.).[184]

Francis Cardinal Spellman—the most powerful prelate in America—was, naturally, in the thick of émigré intrigue. In May 1947, his New York office (a.k.a. "The Little Vatican") helped deliver a petition from 5,000 Ukrainian Catholics in the US Zone in Austria to the State Department.[185] Francis also played a critical role in the furtive 1948 CIA-Vatican talks for laundering ten million dollars in American aid ("black currency") to help defeat Communist candidates in Italy's elections. As usual, there was just one hitch, Christopher Simpson writing in *Blowback*, "[A] substantial part of the funding for clandestine activities in Italy came from captured Nazi German assets, including money and gold that the Nazis had looted from the Jews."[186] Spellman would also prove adept at promoting Rome's Judephobic agenda, especially the internationalization of Jerusalem.[187]

Among other milestones (separation of Church and State notwithstanding), "His Gray Eminence" was the first priest to officiate a Mass (i.e., "mess") in the White House (February 17, 1937)[188] and the first Vatican-appointed Military Vicar of the US Armed Forces (December 11, 1939).[189] And like Giovanni Montini—and thousands of other "celibate fathers"—*Francis* was also widely rumored to have been a closet sodomite.[190] (Broadway chorus *boys* reputedly called him "Cardinal Franny.") Under Spellman's authority as head of the New York Archdiocese, Archbishop Stepinac High School opened in White Plains as an all-boys academy in 1948—three years *after* Stepinac's participation in the Croatian genocide. (In 2002, Stepinac High joined the *long* list of Catholic institutions embroiled in clerical sex abuse.)

Vatican ratlines were also used for evacuating plundered assets. According to Loftus and Aarons, "[T]he vast bulk of the wealth of the Nazi empire quietly disappeared before the end of World War II, only to reappear within a decade in the hands of the same men who financed Hitler's war against the Jews."[191] The problem may be summarized in three points: 1) 1920s and '30s—US companies invested heavily in Germany to gain exclusive advantages (primarily monopolies and taxes); 2) 1930s and '40s—These same entities (with their Reich partners) panicked under Hitler's policies and began plotting with Rome to extricate their assets; 3) 1940s and '50s—The crimes were hidden under the guise of "national security." Over 7,000 train trucks of machinery and industrial equipment were "evacuated" from Hungary to Western Germany ahead of advancing Red forces (undoubtedly the same cattle cars used in the Hungarian Aktion).[192]

The greatest "transfer of assets" concerns the famous vanishing of over $2.5 billion in Nazi gold. "The *Guinness Book of Records* lists the missing Reichsbank treasure as the greatest unsolved bank robbery in history…According to our source, the bulk of the treasure was simply shipped a very short distance across Austria and through the Brenner Pass into Italy. Dulles's contacts were waiting at the Vatican."[193] Like the "human traffic," a sizable portion of the precious metal went to Argentina for "safe keeping."[194] From there, only "the Shadow knows" where it went (the culprits having taken their secrets to the grave)—though "the Holy See's own shares portfolio," via The Institute for the Works of Religion (Vatican Bank, founded in 1942), would "reap a handsome dividend" from fees and commissions, along with her own hefty prewar Reich investments.[195] (The mystery intensified in 2015 with the find of a subterranean WWII-era train tunnel under the 13th-century Ksiaz Castle near Walbrzych, Poland.)

Suffice it to say that, while Exodus 28 has the precious metal in the vestments of the Levitical priesthood, "Father" Draganović was known as "the *golden* priest."[196] And while the "first Pope" said in Acts 3:6, *"Silver and gold have I none...,"* the Vatican Bank remains the only global financial institution with the competitive edge of diplomatic immunity (a role model for the audit-proof US Federal Reserve).[197]

As a final insult to Holocaust victims, like the "Great Arab Revolt," the Dulles-Wisner pipe dream of an anti-Soviet Cold War émigré army utilizing thousands of known Nazi collaborators turned out to be a colossal flop. Simpson writes, "[T]he CIA's Nazi utilization programs never did produce the practical benefits to the United States that their sponsors once claimed they would."[198] The cause was twofold.

First, though the danger of Communist expansion had always existed, General Gehlen's forecast of an imminent massive invasion of Western Europe was woefully inaccurate. "[T]he estimates of Soviet military power that Gehlen provided to the Americans were simply wrong and grossly overstated both the Soviets' ability and their desire to fight."[199] The "Motherland" lost 27,000,000 offspring in her war against the "Fatherland" (including 12,000,000 soldiers). This was nearly the entire generation of 1923 who were 18 years old at the time of Barbarossa. The Nazis wasted 1,700 cities, 6,000,000 homes, 70,000 villages, 30,000 factories, 61 electric plants, 40,000 miles of track, 90,000 bridges, and millions of cattle and sheep.[200] Victor Marchetti, CIA analyst of Soviet capabilities, explained the conflict of interest: "Gehlen had to make his money by creating a threat we were afraid of...so we would give him more money to tell us about it...The agency loved Gehlen because he fed us what we wanted to hear...We used his stuff constantly, and fed it to everybody: the Pentagon; the White House; the newspapers. They loved it, too. But it was hyped up Russian boogeyman junk, and it did a lot of damage to this country."[201]

Second, CIA files disclose that, by 1951, OPC's capture rate for US assets exceeded 98%.[202] Thus, by 1959, Langley "somehow" had lost *every* courier, safehouse, and intel network behind the Iron Curtain.[203] And while many of the touted "Nazi scientists" arriving in America via "Operation Paperclip" were found to be more *Nazi* than *scientist*, numbers of the brighter minds kept "popping up" in Moscow.[204] The mystery was later traced to a nexus of Soviet moles that had penetrated everything from Gehlen's cabal and Wisner's Euro-American émigré network to the Vatican itself. In 1967, one of its key plants defected to Tito's Red regime in Yugoslavia; only later would the Allies learn that "Father" Draganović, was not only a Marxist, but a double agent as well, having worked for German intelligence.[205]

The greatest surprise of the entire ratline affair was Harold Adrian Russell "Kim" Philby (code name *Stanley*), son of Mohammad "Jack" Philby. In the early 1960s, MI6 made the embarrassing find that their celebrated veteran agent had been spying on *them* for years (*Stan* having become the proverbial "man behind the [Iron] curtain," the one they should have been paying attention to). John Cairncross (one of Kim's "co-workers") sent over *6,000* classified documents to Moscow from Bletchley Park.[206] Having gutted the entire OPC program as its chief British counterpart,[207] Philby defected to Moscow in 1963. Two years later, Wisner blew his brains out at his Maryland farm. Recalling Wisner's reaction to the botched Hungarian Revolt in 1956, CIA veteran Tom Braden said, "That's when he first went nuts."[208] Thus, as seen by America's growing skinhead craze, Wiesenthal rightly opined, "Nazi criminals were the principal beneficiaries of the Cold War."[209]

On a positive note, Wisner's nucleus of émigré paramilitary companies (trained at Fort Dix, New Jersey, as "Labor Service units") later morphed into America's legendary Green Berets, the Special Forces motto—*De Oppresso Liber* ("From Oppression We Will Liberate Them")—reflecting the original OPC mission statement.[210]

"TRACE THE MONEY"

Representing a last Cold War "kick in the pants" reality check, *every* epic development—from John Kennedy's inspiring June 26, 1963, "Ich bin ein Berliner" greeting to Ronald Reagan's June 12, 1987, bravado, "Mr. Gorbachev, tear down this wall!"—*must* be viewed through the unsettling prism of Professor Antony Sutton's incontrovertible trilogy on treasonous technology transfer to the former Soviet Union, *Western Technology and Soviet Economic Development* (published in 1968 by the prestigious Hoover Institute).

According to Rush Limbaugh's "Kook Test," Dr. Sutton would fall under the classification of "conspiracy kook" for *daring* to challenge the status quo.[211] Sutton exposed the myth of "Soviet technology" in his testimony before Subcommittee VII of the Platform Committee of the Republican Party in Miami Beach, Florida, on August 15, 1972:

> In a few words: there is no such thing as Soviet technology. Almost all—perhaps 90-95%—came directly or indirectly from the US and its allies. In effect the US and the NATO countries have built the Soviet Union, its industrial *and* its military capabilities. This massive construction job has taken 50 years. Since the Revolution in 1917 it has been carried out through trade and the sale of plants, equipment and technical assistance.[212]

The flip side of this travesty is that the Communists paid for their technology with capital generated from their exports of raw materials (timber, mining) harvested by the slaves in Stalin's "gulag archipelago." Thus, Martin Gilbert's thesis, "The history of the world can be divided into two aspects: facts and espionage," is really only two-thirds true—the missing element of *greed* being misconstrued as "conspiracy history." Like the old spy told Loftus, "Forget the ideology. Trace the money."[213] But, then again, history being "*His* story," the despised A.V. 1611 has had the answer all along: *"For the love of money is the root of all evil...."* (II Timothy 6:10)

THE BIGGEST RAT

The subject is often debated as to whether the biggest rodent of all was able to exchange a hangman's rope for a Vatican ratline. In 2009, the famous "Hitler skull fragment" (with bullet hole)—held in Moscow for decades as the centerpiece of Stalin's "Hitler memorabilia" collection—was finally subjected to DNA testing. It turned out to be that of a female under the age of forty (and *not* Eva Braun).

In the wake of this disclosure, the definitive treatise for the most sensational conspiracy theory ever was posited in 2011 by military historian Simon Dunstan and international journalist Gerrard Williams in *Grey Wolf: The Escape of Adolf Hitler*. Through nearly 300 pages of meticulous documentation, the work makes a *semi*-compelling case that Adolf Hitler—along with his beloved dog Blondi, Eva Braun, Martin Bormann, Hermann Fegelein, and six trusted SS officers—fled by U-boat to a remote valley enclave in Argentina. After a five-year project involving seventeen trips abroad, dozens of interviews with supposed eyewitnesses and access to lately declassified Soviet archives, the authors contend that the Führer went on to enjoy an easy life in Patagonia until his death on February 13, 1962. Yet, even the Publisher's Note calls the thesis "almost too horrible to contemplate," before giving the discreet disclaimer, "This book raises many intriguing questions, but it does not conclusively settle the issue."[214]

While such a theory may well remain, as the publisher suggests, "a mystery that will never be solved," one thing *is* certain, *if* the "Grey Wolf" *did* make it to South America, the quality of his flickering life would have been nominal at best. Siegfried Knappe was a decorated Wehrmacht officer. After the war he immigrated to the States with his wife, settling near Xenia, Ohio. In 1992, he wrote his memoir, *Soldat: Reflections of a German Soldier, 1936-1949*. Major Knappe was a regular in the *Führerbunker* during the Reich's death throes of late April 1945. His final impression of the one behind the Final Solution reads like Proverbs 13:15—*"the way of transgressors is hard."*

> I was shocked by his appearance. He was stooped, and his left arm was bent and shaking. Half of his face drooped, as if he'd had a stroke, and his facial muscles no longer worked. Both of his hands shook and one eye was swollen. He looked like a very old man, at least twenty years older than his fifty-six years...Hitler said goodbye, shook my hand again, and disappeared in the direction of Goebbels's quarters. Although his behavior had not been lethargic, his appearance had been pitiful. Hitler was now hardly more than a physical caricature of what he had been. I wondered how it was possible that in only six years, this idol of my whole generation of young people could have become such a human wreck. It occurred to me then that Hitler was *still* the living symbol of Germany—but Germany as it was now. In the same six years, the flourishing, aspiring country had become a flaming pile of debris and ruin.[215]

With less than 36 hours to live, Adolf Hitler's last will and testament was dictated and signed at 4:00 a.m. on April 29, 1945. Having nominated a slate of new cabinet members, the Führer's final word in what would constitute his last written statement on earth bears witness to his relentless, demented fixation: "Above all I pledge the leadership of the nation and its followers to the scrupulous observance of the racial laws and to implacable opposition to the universal poisoner of all peoples, international Jewry."[216] (As a postscript, one of these "universal poisoners" who eluded Hitler's wrath was Mirko *Rat*, an engineer from Budapest who went on to become a valued member of MI6; his grandchildren live in Israel today.)

THE *PASSING* OF PIUS

Eugenio *Maria* Giuseppe Giovanni Pacelli (a.k.a. Pope Pius XII), has been universally criticized for not openly condemning the Shoah. One spaced-out nun wrote, "The fact is that His Holiness became a victim of public opinion in order to protect those who were victimized. 'Thousands of Roman Jews would have been captured by Nazi troops on October 16, 1943, had it not been for the prudent politics of the Vatican,' wrote Carlo Sestieri, a well-known Jew…."[217] On a more "serious" matter, Pacelli did manage to publicly excoriate the "worldly" consumer products that American GIs were introducing to his parishioners (Coca-Cola, gum, movies, *Reader's Digest*, etc.).[218]

To exacerbate matters, the Roman Curia was technically responsible for Hitler's dictatorial powers in the first place, vis-à-vis the July 1933 Vatican-Reich Concordat (drafted by Cardinal Secretary of State Pacelli for his predecessor, Pius XI) and subsequent dissolving of the Catholic Centre Party. Hitler saw the treaty as his private pass for genocide, calling it "especially significant in the urgent struggle against international Jewry."[219] However, by December 1942, El Papa had apparently had enough. And so, with all of civilized humanity holding its breath (especially Jews headed to the "showers"), Pius "lowered the boom" (on Christmas Eve, no less): "Humanity owes this vow to those hundreds of thousands who, without any fault of their own, sometimes only by reason of their nationality or race, are marked down for death or gradual extinction."[220]

Wow—*what* a slap! The Führer must have been shaking in his jackboots. Instead of a bold and unequivocal statement on the Nazi genocide, the Pontiff managed to whimper one ambiguous sentence that somehow avoided any reference to the words "Jew," "non-Aryan," "German," or "Nazi." Award-winning journalist John Cornwell took issue with this latest rendering of "most delicate reserve," writing in *Hitler's Pope*: "It was to remain the fullest extent of his protest and denunciation for the rest of the war. It is not merely a paltry statement. The chasm between the enormity of the liquidation of the Jewish people and this form of evasive words is shocking."[221]

This is not to imply that Pius did *nothing* to slow the Shoah; to the contrary, Cornwell notes, "[T]he Pope was in the habit during the war of conducting a form of exorcism to cast out the devil that he assumed inhabited the soul of Hitler—which he did in the dead of night in his private chapel in the papal apartments."[222] Jesus' question in Mark 3:23 has never been more apropos—*"How can Satan cast out Satan?"*

Of all the Jewish blood on Pacelli's hands, the transports from his own backyard remain in a class of their own. The saga began on September 27, 1943, when the SS placed an exorbitant ransom of 50 kilograms of gold upon the heads of the 7,000 victims in central Rome. While the Vatican offered to *loan* the Jews 15 kg, all of the necessary funds came in, with many of the local non-Jewish residents chipping in as well. (The final total was 80 kg.) Raul Hilberg writes:

> In certain basic respects the Italian approach to anti-Jewish persecutions was similar to the Italian attitude toward the war. The Italians wanted to keep up with their powerful German ally; they strove, above all, to be taken seriously, like the Germans...in the end the Italians did not match the Germans in expenditure of ferocity and the shedding of blood. Quite unlike the German Nazis, the Italian Fascists committed themselves in words without fulfilling themselves in deeds, for in their hearts the Italians had no use for the Germans and the German way of life.[223]

With the gold in Berlin, Eichmann suddenly changed his mind and reinstated his deportation decree. On the dark and rainy early morning of Saturday, October 16, the first 1,000 Jews were herded from Rome's old ghetto area to a gathering point at the *Collegio Militare*, not a half-mile from St. Peter's Square. Cornwell's account is riveting:

> [T]he trucks filled with men, women, and children were finding their way through the heavy downpour, many with difficulty, to the bleak barracks of the Collegio Militare. Some trucks passed the boundary of St. Peter's Square, driven deliberately by that route, it has been said, so that the SS soldiers who had been drafted into Rome for the roundup could catch a glimpse of the famous church. The Jews, it has also been said, called out for the Pope to help them as they

> passed along the perimeter of the square. Eyewitness accounts are full of pathos. An Italian journalist reported: 'The eyes of the children were dilated and unseeing. It seemed as if they were asking for an explanation for such terror and suffering'...[Another recounted] 'I saw in their terror-stricken eyes, in the faces grown pale as if with pain, and in their little quivering hands that clung to the sides of the truck, the maddening fear that had overtaken them.'[224]

There is no record of any parting "blessing" from the famous papal balcony. When the German envoy, fearful of local reprisals, asked Vatican Secretary of State Luigi Maglione to solicit Pacelli's help, the Cardinal gave a stock reply, "The Holy See would not wish to be put in a situation where it was necessary to utter a word of disapproval."[225] The entraining of Rome's Jews began at dawn on October 18. Some 1,256 deportees were boarded sixty to a car. At 2:05 p.m., the train departed Tiburtina station, crossed the Tiber, then headed north.

Five days later, 1,060 men, women, and children were gassed at Planet Auschwitz (149 men and 47 women detained for slave labor). Just fifteen survived the war. Settimia Spizzichino, the sole female and former guinea pig for Mengele, was sent to Bergen-Belsen where she was found sleeping under a pile of corpses (any of which could have been Anne Frank). Due to increased political pressure, "only" 1,084 additional Jews went to Birkeanu.[226] Once again, Italy's tempered anti-Semitism was attributed more to being "anti-Germany" and "anti-Mussolini" (not to mention the Jews' role in the national economy).

On Thursday, October 9, 1958, "His Holiness" Pius XII—the so-called (as per the Vatican's website) Bishop of Rome, Vicar of Jesus Christ, Successor of the Prince of the Apostles, Supreme Pontiff of the Universal Church, Primate of Italy, Archbishop and Metropolitan of the Roman Province, Sovereign of the State of Vatican City, and Servant of the Servants of God—*dropped into Hell* around 3:50 a.m. The official cause of death was ruled a "circulatory phenomenon."[227] With 12 being the Bible number for Israel, the fact that the Shoah Pope (a.k.a. "Hitler's Pope") would presume to bear the Jews' numeric in his official title (Pius XII) speaks volumes of the Vatican's unscriptural, anti-Semitic heresy of Replacement Theology (i.e., that the Catholic Church replaced Israel) forecast in John 11:48.

Notwithstanding a plethora of high-profile, pro-Pacelli apologists (e.g., Jesuit historian Charles Gallagher; Fulbright Scholar Sister Margherita

Marchione; Catholic lawyer Ronald Rychlak; Protestant author Gordon Thomas; even a rare *Jewish* exception like Golda Meir's politically expedient eulogistic remarks[228] that simply prove the rule), the A.V. 1611—rightly divided—repudiates *every* definitive doctrine of the Catholic Church (Ex. 20:4-5; Psa. 49:7, 69:8-9; Matt. 1:14, 8:38-39, 13:55-56, 15:3, 16:23, 23:9; Lk. 1:46-47, 5:21; Jn. 3:3, 6:63, 17:11; Acts 1:24, 6:7, 8:14, 10:25-26; Rom. 4:6; I Cor. 1:2; II Cor. 5:8; Gal. 2:11, 16, 21; Eph. 2:8-9; Col. 2:8; I Tim. 2:5, 3:2, 4:1-6; II Tim. 1:9; Tit. 3:5; Heb. 1:3, 9:24-28, 10:10-14; I Pet. 2:5, 9).

While John Paul II issued a quasi-endorsement of evolution in 1996, Pope Francis (the first Jesuit pope) opened Heaven to sodomites and atheists in 2013. Moving from heresy to murder, the Bible states that *"by their fruits ye shall know them."* (Matthew 7:20) Whereas Hitler's killing spree lasted four years, the track record of his church—being *"drunken with the blood of the saints, and with the blood of the martyrs of Jesus"* (crusades, inquisitions, dungeons, iron maidens, *auto-da-fés*, racks, stakes, gibbets)—has continued unabated for over a millennium (Revelation 17:6). Thus, the KJV translators identified the Pope as "The Man of Sin." (For the record, this author is an ordained Baptist minister with a charge in I Timothy 4:1-6 that transcends all political correctness, having *nothing* to do with "religious bigotry."[229])

With two chapters in the New Testament (Revelation 17 & 18) describing the end-time, cataclysmic destruction of the Vatican State (a.k.a. "MYSTERY, BABYLON THE GREAT, THE MOTHER OF HARLOTS AND ABOMINATIONS OF THE EARTH"), the papal corpse itself would provide a most graphic illustration of the "Great Whore's" coming judgment. Apparently, Pius had developed an aura of supernatural fragrance (Psalm 45:8). John Guest, a British banker and author who met Pacelli during the war, recalled being mesmerized by a "pervading scent" that emanated from the Pontiff's person: "Not a scent in the worldly sense," he explained, "not sweet or exciting in any way, but a cool, very clean, smell...A sort of delicious early-morning dewy smell that could almost be described as the sudden absence of all other smells...Possibly it is imagination; possibly sympathetic nervous affection of the nose when one's other senses are highly stimulated; possibly even, it is the genuine and original 'odour of sanctity.'"[230]

However, Pacelli's posthumous fragrance (caused by a botched embalming) would be anything *but* a "delicate reserve," serving as a morbid reminder of what the Sonderkommandos encountered daily in the crematoria. Having stated, "So *passed* one of the most remarkable pontiffs in the history of the papacy, his memory *fragrant* with esteem" (author's emphasis), Cornwell gives—the *rest* of the story:

> The good doctor…had taken charge of the embalming, experimenting with a new method and leaving the intestines in place; in consequence, the corpse began to rot immediately in the autumn heat. As the hearse paused outside St. John Lateran, a series of dreadful farts and eructations was heard to issue from the coffin, a result, apparently, of rapid fermentation. During the lying-in-state in St. Peter's, the dead Pope's face turned gray-green and then purple, and the stench was so overpowering that one of the attendant guards fainted. A final indignity, his nose went black and fell off before interment.[231]

OPERATION KEELHAUL

While the following material does not relate to Jews directly, it was included to demonstrate the degree of moral depravity exhibited by the so-called "good-guys" in the war—specifically, in the political realm. As such, it affords circumstantial evidence for the subtitle of this book.

It has been estimated that the average young person in America reads only *six sentences* about the Holocaust in *twelve years* of school.[232] At the college level, the topic will normally re-surface under the anti-Semitic genre of "Holocaust denial."[233] For those privileged few with a basic knowledge of the subject, the added evidence that the Allies abandoned the Jews before, during, and after the fact, rates second only in shock value to the genocide itself. But there is more.

While discussing this issue, this author will often ask: "What would you think upon learning that Franklin Roosevelt (with Churchill's blessing) sanctioned a *second* (albeit smaller) genocide of 'only' 2,000,000 men, women, and children—complete with roundups, cattle cars, deception, camps, slave labor, torture, executions, even crematoria?" The iconic Russian dissident and Nobel laureate, Alexander Solzhenitsyn, cited this Allied cover-up in his trilogy, *The Gulag Archipelago*: "It is surprising that in the West, where political secrets cannot be kept long, since they inevitably come out in print or are disclosed, the secret of *this* particular act of betrayal has been very well and carefully kept by the

British and American governments. This is truly the last secret, or one of the last, of the Second World War."[234]

The thought that a US chief executive could be compared to Hitler sounds preposterous; yet, their political careers reveal many uncanny parallels. For example, Hitler became chancellor of Germany on January 30, 1933—Roosevelt's fifty-first birthday. The two men not only held their power for the identical *amount* of time, but over the identical *period* as well. While Roosevelt was inaugurated for his first of four terms on March 4, 1933, the Führer received *his* dictatorial powers a few weeks later via the Enabling Act. Both anti-Semites died in the *twelfth* year of their "reigns"; FDR on April *12*, 1945, Hitler, eighteen days later. When the war began, Stalin was with Hitler; when it ended, he was with Franklin. In 1939, Hitler gave Koba a third of Poland; in 1945 Roosevelt gave him the *whole* country. While Germany's dictator transgressed via the sin of *commission*—having *murdered* the Jews—America's president committed the sin of *omission*—having *abandoned* the Jews; James 4:17 states, *"[T]o him that knoweth to do good, and doeth it not, to him it is sin."*

So, *why* should anyone be shocked that FDR would sign the death warrants of *another* mass of innocents? (The bizarre difference here being that the victims would perish in peacetime, going to *their* graves *after* he entered his.) Known as "Operation Keelhaul," the act involved the forced (illegal) repatriation, by the Anglo-American governments, of two million anti-Bolshevik insurgents from within the USSR who fought *with* Germany in a desperate gambit to oust Stalin's hated regime. With the tenuous pact stipulating that no Russian would be compelled to fight against the Western allies, the consortium included disgruntled POWs; émigré groups; the Russian Liberation Army (ROA); and transient Cossack Cavalry Corps (including family). Non-engaged Soviet displaced persons were also part of Keelhaul.[235]

Stalin's worst nightmare began within weeks of the surprise German attack, the Nazis themselves taken aback by two unexpected events. While millions of starving peasants welcomed the Wehrmacht as liberators, numerous Red Army units apparently couldn't *wait* to surrender. In the first eight months of Barbarossa, over 4,000,000 Russians felt "disinclined" to bleed for Stalin's *red* flag, opting for a *white* one instead. (This figure exceeded the entire invasion force.) Stalin cited the embarrassing scenario in Secret Order No. 0019: "There are many elements on all fronts who even run to meet the foe and throw away their weapons on their first contact with him."[236] (Of course, he "forgot" to mention such relevant tidbits as his army having only *one* disposable weapon per every *two* soldiers, or that his 1937-38 purge of 30,000 officers would have diminished any *esprit de corps*.)

The Battle of Stalingrad affords a dual case of both soldierly umbrage and savagery by the NKVD ("People's Commissariat for Internal Affairs," a law enforcement agency and KJB precursor). While Stalin hacks were executing 13,500 of their own troops (a figure higher than a division), over 50,000 Russian citizens were fighting in German uniforms with the Sixth Army.[237] Sven Steenberg writes, "[I]n the fall of 1942, about 800,000 to 900,000 members of Russia's various nationalities were bearing arms against their own government, without Hitler's having knowledge of the fact."[238] Many came from German POW camps (the officer corps, exclusively Wehrmacht). Hart relates, "By the end of 1943 a Russian company was a common sight in a German battalion."[239] Thus, giving new meaning to the expression "fog of battle," the student of WWII is left to ponder the following three-ring circus: 1) Western powers, constrained by circumstances, embracing Hitler's spurned ally as their own; 2) Britain, willing to let bygones be bygones (i.e., London's rubble), negotiating with a cabal of German officers intent on assassinating their Führer; 3) White Russians, sporting Nazi eagles, invading their own ethnoscape.

To summarize a complex scenario, in the war's closing months, one in ten "German" POWs was found to represent some element of the anti-Stalinist insurgency. The largest percentages were either ROA volunteers of General Andrey Vlasov (decorated hero of the Battle of Moscow) or Cossack tribal units loyal to General Pyotr Krasnov. Having interrogated hundreds of Soviet prisoners, the Foreign Office compiled a uniform profile: The men were mostly poor, humble, illiterate, and politically ignorant. They had suffered terribly under Stalin and desired asylum in the West; most feared death if returned.[240]

When the "Big Three" met at Yalta, February 4-11, 1945, Marshal Stalin insisted that the "traitors" be promptly repatriated for "rehabilitation." As FDR went through the motions of enlightening his ally that "such was not the American way, etc.," Stalin reminded his terminally ill co-conspirator that several thousand US and British POWs "liberated" by Red Army forces were currently in *Soviet* hands. For their part, Franklin and Winnie knew that Koba was capable of anything. Only the week before, a Russian sub in the Baltic sank the former German hospital ship MV *Wilhelm Gustloff*, killing 9,343 people (including 5,000 children)—a fatality count over three times the *Lusitania* and *Titanic* combined! Thus, after a few more rounds of Vodka, the secret codicil (already in the works for *months*) was formally ratified on Sunday, February 11. After all, what the leader of Russia did with his *own* kind was certainly *his* business, etc. When the Foreign Office enquired if the *quid pro quo* deal should be publicized and registered with the UN, Thomas Brimelow replied on February 19, "STRONG objection. This agreement must remain secret."[241]

Tantamount to legalized murder, some 2,272,000 Russians were subsequently repatriated from numerous DP camps in Europe, Britain, and even the US.[242] On a technical note, though the truth will never be known, NKVD records claim that five-and-a-half million Russians were actually returned, 20% given death sentences or 25 years in the Gulag (a *virtual* death sentence—just prolonged), 45% getting 5-10 years.[243] While many of the victims, particularly within the ROA and Committee for the Liberation of the Peoples of Russia (KONR) leadership were former collaborators in the Shoah (or at least anti-Semitic), most were not.[244] (Yet, it must also be noted that the Czars routinely employed Cossack muscle to prosecute their pogroms.)

The sick truth is that neither Roosevelt nor Churchill could have cared *less* about separating the wheat from the chaff. With the ink barely dry on the protocol, Britain's prime minister wired Stalin on February 17, "I pray that you may long be spared to preside over the destinies of your country, which has shown its full greatness under your leadership."[245] (In his speech at Missouri's Westminster College thirteen months later, the hypocritical "prayer warrior" would coin the now-famous "Iron Curtain" moniker when explaining how Stalin went on to "preside over the destinies" of several *other* countries as well.) In an earlier memo anticipating the verdict, Foreign Office Assistant Legal Advisor Patrick Dean wrote: "In due course all those with whom the Soviet authorities desire to deal must be handed over to them, and we are not concerned with the fact that they may be shot or otherwise more harshly dealt with than they might be under English law."[246]

The Anglo-Russian historian, Count Nikolai Tolstoy (head of the senior branch of the prominent Tolstoy family), released two tomes exposing the repatriation atrocity—*The Secret Betrayal* (1977) and *The Minister and the Massacres* (1986). In a personal letter to this author in

2004, the scion related, "I have collected a great deal of fresh material since *The Minister and the Massacres* was published, which I hope one day to publish in another book." Ironically, the framework for the Yalta accord was drafted the previous October by Soviet Foreign Minister Molotov and his British counterpart Anthony Eden in a secret Moscow conference code-named—*Tolstoy*.

"THE SOVIETS WERE CREMATING THE COSSACKS"

The two-year implementation of Operation Keelhaul (1945-47) evoked an array of heart-wrenching scenes. American historian George Fisher called the reparations "an indelible blot on the West's tradition of ready asylum for political exiles."[247] The attendant pathos included the naiveté which prompted the initial surrenders; the resultant panic once the betrayal was known; the revulsion of many Allied commanders at having to consign their captives to certain death; the inevitable tumult at transfer points; and the many suicides throughout. While some Cossacks were wrenched from the arms of their wives and children, other families were returned together.

In late May 1945, an entire community of 7,000 Cossacks held by the British 78th Infantry in Oberdrauburg, Austria, was dispatched to Stalin's henchmen in Judenburg. Dr. Heinrich Pichler, an Austrian native and career UN diplomat, was an eyewitness to this travesty. At age eleven, Pichler was staying on his uncle's farm in the center of the Cossack camp. In August 2002, this author interviewed Dr. Pichler at his home in Oberdrauburg. He told how trainloads of Cossacks were forced to slow down when crossing the Drau River (due to bad bridge conditions). This afforded numbers of desperate families an alternative to "Uncle Joe." Sitting at his kitchen table (about 100 yards from his uncle's farmhouse), Pichler shared his childhood memories:

> We, as children, obviously were following this thing and, together with my cousins were eyewitnesses. Many Cossacks who were coming from Lienz were jumping into the river! We saw it with our own eyes. It was a very, very sad tragedy how the whole thing was handled. It was handled very brutally by the British...Most of the general public, including my former colleagues, don't know much about this tragedy and they don't want to know...It was a position

> taken at Yalta...The sad thing was, there were men, women, and children all together...The older émigrés were also handed over to the Russians, which was not part of the original agreement...Most of them were killed.[248]

Alexander Pewnew was sixteen years old when his whole settlement of 20,000 Cossacks in the Peggetz cantonment near Lienz, Austria, was betrayed to the Soviets on June 1, 1945. Alex was able to escape and eventually emigrate to America. In 1986, he was elected Ataman over the remnant of the Cossack nation (outside of Russia) and appointed curator of the Cossack Museum in Howell, New Jersey. In a 2002 interview with this author, Ataman Pewnew stated:

> Tanks were all around us. Big American trucks were brought in to transport us to the small train depot a short distance away. The British soldiers were beating the people, who were crying hysterically. There was blood all over. Even two- and three-month-old babies were thrown into the trucks. Some of the troops were even cursing at us in Russian...I managed to get away by the River Drau. My sister was caught but before she could be put on a truck, the British called it quits for the day...Our parents took us into the mountains...The British were constantly searching the mountains. Sometimes they would fire their guns in the air while calling for the Cossacks to come out. They even fired flame throwers at us...So many innocent people were sent out to their deaths while the British and US governments knew what was happening...They said we were traitors to our government. We were *not* traitors. We didn't have a legitimate government to betray. When twenty to thirty million people disappeared from the earth in Russia under Stalin, how can you say you would support a government like that? They betrayed their own people![249]

The official terminus for the XVth Cossack Cavalry Corps was the Soviet Zone in Judenburg (district capital of the Austrian state of Styria). British lorries delivered the "cargo of misery" to officials of Soviet Military Counter-Intelligence (SMERSH) poised at the halfway point of the Mur River bridge. From there they were taken to a nearby steel mill. While common soldiers were generally processed to the Gulag, most of the officers were dispatched within earshot of their "delivery drivers." British guards also testified of hearing singing prior to the executions. Corporal Edward Stewart described his recollection as "the finest male choir I had ever heard."[250] Within days of the Cossacks' arrival, the townsfolk were transfixed by a mysterious development. According to survivors' accounts cited by Tolstoy:

> The factory had begun to operate! Smoke was rising from the factory chimneys, but all the workers remained unsummoned at home...Scouts were sent out. Their report was regarded as absurd and incredible and nobody believed it, the Soviets were cremating the Cossacks...However, they swiftly came to accept it as soon as work began again for the settlement and after the whole town was oppressed by the stench of burning human flesh.[251]

Austrian historian Dr. Siegfried Beer calculated: "Between the 28th of May and the 8th of July about 50,000 persons had been handed over, 35,000 of them were Cossacks."[252] Among the leading Moscow show trial executions, General Vlasov was hanged on August 1, 1946, in Lubyanka Prison while Ataman P. N. Krasnov and Major General Helmuth von Pannwitz (*German* Commander of the XVth Cossack Cavalry Corps) were hanged in Lefortovo Prison in January 1947.

The most bizarre repatriation junkets embarked from POW camps in the good ol' USA, principally Fort Dix, New Jersey; Camp Opelika in Alabama; Idaho's Camp Rupert; and of *all* places—Camp Patrick "Give me liberty or give me death" Henry in Newport News, Virginia. On June 29, 1945, a major riot erupted at Fort Dix when 154 Russians refused to board their Soviet-bound ship. The desperate men fought with fists, mess kits, and clubs made from furniture. Armed guards at Pier 51 had to restrain curious New Yorkers as the press learned of the story.[253] A tenuous truce was brokered after seven prisoners were wounded by machine gun fire. Thanks to Yankee ingenuity, the problem was solved the next day when a sergeant had the bright idea to neutralize the inmates by mixing barbiturates in their coffee. After falling asleep, the men were promptly loaded onboard unawares.[254]

As the Soviet vessel steamed past "Lady Liberty," only 151 prisoners were accounted for; the other three were found hanging by their belts from the rafters of their barracks. It was later learned that the entire group had planned a mass suicide.[255] As related in this chapter's introduction, the three Russians were discretely buried in the German POW plot at Finn's Point National Cemetery in Pennsville.

A sober postscript showing the futility of covering sin (Proverbs 28:13) was another heinous act which drew a barrage of unwanted publicity to the remote five-acre cemetery. According to Salem County Prosecutor Ron Epstein, on May 8, 1997, the caretaker, William Reese, was fatally shot in his basement office not far from the Russian graves he meticulously manicured for two decades. The perpetrator was Andrew Cunanan, a twenty-seven-old California sodomite who had already slain three others. Fleeing the scene in Reese's pickup, the spree killer would make national headlines, including the FBI's "Ten Most Wanted" list. After driving to Miami Beach, Cunanan murdered the high-profile sodomite fashion designer, Gianni Versace, on July 15. Eight days later he shot himself when confronted by police.

Finally, it was fitting that the first exposé of the Anglo-American repatriations conspiracy would be authored by a Jew. Julius *Epstein* was an Austrian émigré who fled Europe in 1938, settling in New York City. Ironically, the focal transit point of Judenburg just happens to mean "Jews Castle," after the adjacent medieval fortress—Castle *Eppenstein*. While a research associate at the Hoover Institution at Stanford University, Epstein labored many years to secure the elusive evidence for his incontestable 1973 work, *Operation Keelhaul: The Story of Forced Repatriation*. He concludes:

> The final and definitive record – three volumes strong – of the whole American-British forced repatriation operation was compiled by the Army and classified Top Secret on September 18, 1948. It bears the unmistakable title: 'Forced Repatriation of Displaced Soviet Citizens – Operation Keelhaul.' Its secret file number is 383.7-14.1... Keelhauling was the most atrocious punishment in the old British and Dutch navies [*hauling* the offender under the boat's keel by ropes, from one side to side]. Most of those subjected to it were dead when they were fished out of the water. Therefore, the very choice of this word by U.S. military authorities to designate forced repatriation does not leave any doubt that they knew its true character.[256]

IL DUCE UPSTAGED—LITERALLY

This final section was included as dark humor to illustrate the ultimate judgment of God Almighty upon the enemies of His covenant nation;

as King David wrote, *"Fret not thyself because of evildoers, neither be thou envious against the works of iniquity. For they shall soon be cut down like the grass, and whither as the green herb."* (Psalm 37:1-2)

Benito Mussolini was always intrigued with the movies. In April 1937, he opened the nation's premier film studio in Rome, *Cinecittà* ("Cinema City"). Known as "Hollywood on the Tiber," the hub of Italian cinematography made nearly 300 movies in just the first six years. In October 1937, the Irish Catholic American television and film producer, Hal Roach, sent shockwaves through the *real* Hollywood (a predominantly Jewish institution) by announcing his intention to form an American-Italian film production partnership with Vittorio Mussolini, twenty-one-year-old son of the local dictator. The new venture was appropriately called RAM ("Roach and Mussolini") Productions. However, viewed as collaboration with the enemy, the fascist-capitalist hybrid disappeared in a vortex of bad publicity before Germany could even occupy the Sudetenland.

While Hal dropped back to punt, refocusing on his more familiar projects (*Laurel and Hardy*, *The Little Rascals*, *Topper*, et al.), Benito continued to daydream about *his* favorite dictum: *Il cinema è l'arma più forte* ("Cinema is the most powerful weapon"). Besides, as a "Dictator/Director," Il Duce could make as many films as he wanted (especially ones about himself), and it didn't matter whether anyone liked them or not. According to IMDb, Benito Mussolini actually had fourteen titles professionally credited to his name—ten being films or documentaries about—*you guessed it*—Benito Mussolini!

As Jesus asked in Matthew 6:27, *"Which of you by taking thought can add one cubit unto his stature?"* the 5 ft. 6 in. psychotic no doubt employed fantasy as an escape mechanism for his lifelong struggle with the psychological phenomenon known as the "Napoleon complex" (or "short man syndrome"). In addition to his ships being blown out of the water, one should not ignore the "stellar" role of the Royal Italian Armed Forces as a whole (i.e., WWII-era humor: "Italian tanks have one forward gear—and three reverse"; see "Giuseppe" in *Sahara*, starring Humphrey Bogart and "Lulu Belle" the tank).

In September 1940, Field Marshal Rudolfo Graziani was poised for a rare victory (nothing short of capturing Alexandria *and* the Suez Canal together) when General Archibald Wavell, British commander of the vastly outnumbered Army of the Nile, literally saved the day with a herd of camels, horses, and donkeys. (The British hired a contingent of

Bedouin day laborers to have their animals drag large planks to kick up the sand, effectively deceiving Italian aerial reconnaissance, which caused Rudy to halt his advance.[257]) Then, there was the time that Hitler had to deploy a team of Wehrmacht airborne and Waffen-SS commandos to rescue his hapless ally from the embarrassing house arrest imposed on him by his own king, Victor Emmanuel. He even had to endure the Allied bombing of his beloved Cinecittà Studios. As Italian Foreign Minister Ciano said, "The Germans have loved us without respecting us."[258]

One of the most revealing (and hilarious) episodes began on August 28, 1941, when Il Duce accompanied the Führer in his FW 200 Condor, the *Immelmann III*, on a 600-mile flight to the Ukrainian city of Uman. (The occasion was a public relations inspection tour of the newly-arrived Italian Expeditionary Corps in Russia.[259]) Other dignitaries on board included Heinrich Himmler, Foreign Minister Ribbentrop, the Reich Press Chief Otto Dietrich, and Italy's envoy to Germany, Filippo Anfuso. The entire excursion went fine—that is—*until* Mussolini stunned his host during the return leg by asking if *he* could fly them home. While Hitler reluctantly agreed, he prudently ordered his pilot, Hans Baur, to remain vigilant at the controls. With Benito settled in the cockpit, Adolf nervously returned to his *Führersessel* ("special leader's seat").

Well, sure enough, it wasn't long before the Condor began making several steep banks and other wild aerial maneuvers. The genetics-conscious passengers must have been trying *real* hard not to dwell on the fact that just the previous month, Captain *Bruno* Mussolini—twenty-three-year-old son of their current quasi-pilot—had died when the Piaggio P.108 bomber prototype he was test-flying *crashed into a house*. Himmler reputedly wondered if the whole episode was a Soviet plot to assassinate Hitler.

After roughly an hour, to everyone's relief, Benito relinquished the controls. In his book, *Hitler and Mussolini*, Santi Corvaja records Anfuso's account: "When the time came to land, Hitler's pilot...told the Duce that landing was not such a good idea. Mussolini turned and saw the convulsed faces of the passengers, who having so far avoided death at the hands of the Soviets did not want to die because of an Italian, however famous he may have been."[260] (Not about to forfeit a badly needed ego boost, Il Duce had his aide release a joint press statement from the Axis leaders confirming that *he* had "personally" piloted the Führer and his entourage back from the front.)

Now the question remains—was this shameful experience weighing on Benito's mind as he prepared to land at Derna on that fateful 29th day of June? As he went skidding along the runway, did he feel jinxed in some way by his paisano's public lack of confidence in his flying skills? No one will ever know for sure. However, though his "momentary" lapse of judgment cost him a barber and a chef, at least his horse, flags, band instruments, and shoe polish did arrive intact on the *second* plane. In any event, it was that return flight to Rome that *really* took the starch out of Il Duce's signature black shirt. Bradley Lightbody writes in *The Second World War: Ambitions to Nemesis*:

> To conserve his meagre supplies, Rommel pulled back to the safety of his defensive positions...The Axis forces had no choice but to dig in...Mussolini, who had waited for three weeks in Libya to lead the victory parade, returned to Rome and took to his bed complaining of amoebic dysentery. One of his less than loyal ministers remarked: 'It is a less commonplace disease. It's called humiliation.'[261]

Apparently, Mussolini had failed to learn from Kaiser Wilhelm's haughtiness at the Jaffa Gate.

As an appropriate object lesson, representing *all* of Satan's dupes, Benito Mussolini would pay a high price for his sins—four in particular: 1) his "Pact of Steel" aiding and abetting Adolf Hitler, creator of the Final Solution; 2) his own accountability for the 8,000 Italian Jews eventually deported to the camps, despite his more tolerant, *pragmatic* strain of anti-Semitism; 3) affording al-Husseini substantial financial support for Axis-friendly cells in Palestine[262]; 4) the blasphemous presumption to impersonate Jesus Christ by riding into the Holy Land on his own white horse (Revelation 19:11).

Thus, as the saying goes, "The party in Hell has been canceled due to fire"—2 years, 10 months, and 24 days after *Heydrich's* assassination; 45 days after *Rommel's* suicide; 2 days before *Hitler's* suicide; 3 days before *Goebbels'* suicide; 1 year, 5 months, and 12 days before *Göring's* suicide; 1 year, 11 months, and 19 days before *Höss'* execution; and 17 years, 1 month, and 4 days before *Eichmann's* execution—the Roman Catholic thug, Benito Amilcare Andrea Mussolini, alias "Il Duce," was summarily *shot* at point-blank range by irate Italian partisans near Lake Como on April 28, 1945.

And for an added bonus, given Mussolini's predilection for the "self-documentary" genre, his own citizens were *more* than happy to oblige. The following day he was posthumously cast in the lead role of his last film. The collective black and white (non-audio) archival footage (lasting all of about ten minutes) scans the bloody, bullet-ridden "disrespected" corpses of Benito, his longtime whore, Claretta Petacci, and three other associates, lying in the gutter in Milan's Piazzale Loreto. The now-famous curtain call shows the group being hoisted upside-down by their heels from the roof of an Esso gas station, drawing a standing ovation from the 5,000-plus "fans" in attendance (Esther 7:10). The closing scene elicits two compelling messages: The unconventional scaffold was itself a fitting testimony to the *fuel* Mussolini failed to provide Rommel. Far from being exterminated in Eretz Yisrael, the fact that Jewish code breakers were ultimately responsible for Mussolini's ignominious end bears profound witness to the meaning of Jacob's name—"one who takes by the heel or supplants" (Genesis 25:26).

However, in traditional fairy-tale style, the "tragedy" *does* have a happy ending. While Il Duce's movie aspirations tanked, his faithful horse, believe it or not, did go on to make it in the "big time," all the way to Hollywood...well...sort of. According to an August 1, 1952, article in the *Geneva Daily Times* of New York, it appears that good ol' Atlantico—not quite ready for the pasture yet—was able to land a job at Cinecittà Studios! "Immediately after the war, the 20-year-old horse was bought by a movie company and used in several films."[263]

Like Absalom's mule who "went away" in II Samuel 18:9, leaving *his* owner hanging from a tree, Atlantico discovered there was life after Mussolini. In an earlier story (dateline October 20, 1950), *The Sydney Morning Herald* confirmed from down under that the "star" was not affiliated with any two-bit spaghetti Westerns, either: "Benito Mussolini's old white horse appeared as an actor in the Rome-made film, *Quo Vadis* [Latin for "Where are you going?"]."[264] For what it's worth, *Quo Vadis*, filmed at Cinecittà for Metro-Goldwyn-Mayer, was nominated for eight academy awards, earning $30 million at the box office to become the highest grossing US film of 1951!

"A horse is a horse, of course, of course..."

13

Statehood

"You can have vengeance, or you can have a country,
but you cannot have both."
(Rockefeller to Ben-Gurion agent, November 1946)

"The people of this nation know Mr. Truman
for the nincompoop he is."
(Chicago Daily Tribune, June 10, 1948)

"Dewey Defeats Truman"
(Chicago Daily Tribune, November 3, 1948)

"God put you in your mother's womb so you
would be the instrument to bring the rebirth
of Israel after two thousand years."
(Rabbi Herzog to Truman, May 1949)

"Is it of the Jews, one of the most ancient peoples,
who can say, as few if any others can, that they won
independence in the year 5708 of their history?"
(Associated Press, 1967)

THE THREE-YEAR period between VE Day, May 8, 1945, and the end of the British Mandate, on May 15, 1948, comprised the critical transition from the Balfour Declaration to partition and statehood in Eretz Yisrael. On November 29, 1947, the United Nations General Assembly (UNGA) approved Resolution 181 recommending the adoption and implementation of its "Plan of Partition with Economic

Union," designed to create independent Arab and Jewish States with a "Special International Regime" for Jerusalem. At 8:00 a.m. on May 14, 1948, HMG lowered the Union Jack in *Yerushalayim*. At 4:00 p.m., David Ben-Gurion, chairman of the Provisional Government (WZO and Jewish Agency), read the Declaration of Independence of the State of Israel over live radio from the Tel Aviv Museum. Finally, at 12:00 a.m., the Yishuv morphed into a legitimized sovereign entity. This momentous event could not have happened but for a series of provocative confrontations—the catalyst being a most peculiar summit on a saltwater lake in February 1945.

Following Roosevelt's participation at Yalta, the president flew from the Crimean peninsula to the Suez Canal Zone to rendezvous with King Ibn Saud aboard the USS *Quincy*, anchored in the Great Bitter Lake. The five-hour series of talks was arranged by Secretary of State Edward Stettinius, Jr., primarily on behalf of American oil interests. Former CIA Case Director Robert Bauer writes:

> Contemporary historians and other commentators tended to treat the meeting as an aside, and even modern historians are apt to give it short shrift. Yalta is where the action was. The war was winding down. Europe needed to be rebuilt: Germany and Japan, to be shaped into pacifist nations. But it was on the *Quincy*, not at Yalta, that the energy cornerstone of America's postwar industrial machine was laid.[1]

When Saud arrived (via the USS *Murphy*), he spurned the commodore's offer of his private cabin, opting to crash on deck in an improvised canvas tent. (Muammar Gaddafi's bid for a similar crib in New York's Central Park in 2009 was denied by city officials.) Among the emir's retinue were seven live sheep (negotiated down from his original request of 100). Roosevelt believed he could use his "personal charm" (as he had with Stalin) not only to secure renewed US oil and landing rights on the Arabian peninsula, but shore up Jewish votes as well by coaxing Saud to adopt more flexibility on Zionism. (Was *he* ever in for a shock!) When Saud refused to consider further Jewish immigration to Palestine (much less statehood), the president gingerly mentioned that "three million Jews had been murdered in Poland alone," whereupon the Muslim bluntly replied: "[T]here must be room for three million more!"[2] Nearly falling out of his wheelchair, FDR promptly assured his guest that: "He would do nothing to assist the Jews against the Arabs and would make no move hostile to the Arab people, nor would his government change its policy [on] Palestine without full and prior consultation with both Jews and Arabs."[3] Official US policy would now be *pro*-Arab "neutrality."[4]

Back on Capitol Hill, Roosevelt told Congress, "On the problem of Arabia, I learned more about that whole problem – the Moslem problem, the Jewish problem – by talking with Ibn Saud for five minutes than I could have learned in an exchange of two or three dozen letters."[5] He then reaffirmed his pledge to Saud in a letter dated April 5, signed in his "capacity as Chief of the Executive Branch of the Government…."[6] However, about the time "His Highness" was showing off his official Oval Office keepsake, *another* chief executive was already calling the shots. Reflecting upon FDR's April 12th death, David Niles, a Zionist Jew and presidential advisor, opined: "There are serious doubts in my mind that Israel would have come into being if Roosevelt had lived."[7] Though he was probably right, the vacancy would not have ensured a Jewish state if it was filled by another political trimmer. Happily, as Five-Star General of the Army Douglas MacArthur would attest, Harry S. Truman—a.k.a. "Give 'Em H--l Harry"—was anything *but* your typical poll-conscious elected official.

TRUMAN VS. ATTLEE

President Truman inherited three pressing emergencies: Japan and the atomic bomb; the presence of Soviet Armed Forces in Eastern Europe; and the prickly Arab-Jewish crisis. Margaret Truman believed that the Palestine imbroglio was her father's greatest challenge.[8]

The first clash on the Jews' behalf would pit the new president against his British counterpart (also newly installed), Prime Minister Clement Attlee. Truman's focus was the deplorable treatment of Shoah survivors in Europe. As Saud implied, Adolf Hitler left the Continent bereft of massive Jewish population centers; the gruesome tally numbered 2,800,000 *Polish* Jews, 800,000 *Soviet* Jews, 450,000 *Hungarian* Jews, 350,000 *Romanian* Jews, 243,000 *Czechoslovakian* Jews, 180,000 *German* Jews, 110,000 *Dutch* Jews, 80,000 *Greek* Jews, 65,000 *French* Jews, 60,000 *Austrian* Jews, 50,000 *Yugoslavian* Jews, 25,000 *Belgian* Jews, and 10,000 *Italian* Jews.[9] (While FDR did little to slow the demise of the first six million Jews, the other five million were undoubtedly saved by America's providential entry into the war.)

Upon Germany's surrender, the Allies could no longer feign ignorance or hide behind pressing wartime priorities. However, with upwards of 3,000 Holocaust survivors daily entering Central Europe from the East, Britain maintained her stringent Palestine immigration embargo. Thus, by late 1946, some 250,000 Jews were crammed into DP camps in West Germany alone.[10] In uncanny fashion, these former victims of SS terror found themselves in renovated concentration camps, making it "a psychologically intolerable ordeal."[11]

For his part, Dwight D. Eisenhower, military governor of the US Occupation Zone, insisted that "the refugees" be *repatriated* to their countries of origin—i.e., back to the greatest crime scenes in history, seething with anti-Semitic former Nazi collaborators. Incredibly, pogroms had already revived in Poland.[12] And with "Uncle Joe" as the *real* "man behind the (Iron) curtain," Hitler's escapees faced a most untenable dilemma. During the war, they were abused by the *Germans* for being *Bolsheviks*; afterward, by the *Soviets* for being *capitalists*. Jews who returned East hoping to regain factories or farms learned that "communization" was the new Russian equivalent for "expropriation."[13] Any dissenters would also find that Stalin's gulags were no less intimidating than Hitler's lagers (*far* worse in the winter).

NUREMBERG

Jewish exiles were also plagued with growing despondency on the political front. As previously noted, the Cold War had relegated the Shoah to secondary status behind the greater priority of Soviet Communism. Thus, the acclaimed Nuremberg War Trials (November 20, 1945 to April 13, 1949) devolved to feckless exhibitions.

After fifteen drafts, the High Court was empowered to try the defendants—*not* for the near-total destruction of European Jewry—but for the more generic, politically correct charge of "Crimes Against Humanity." Stating that an "all-encompassing roster of perpetrators would fill a multivolume directory," Hilberg renders a shortlist of nearly 400 perpetrators who were formally implicated in said "crimes."[14] While tens of thousands of Nazis were slipping down ratlines, 177 scapegoats were eventually corralled by the International Military Tribunal. Their collective claim of innocence was typical, moving defense lawyer Helmut Becker to say, "Everybody has saved the few survivors, nobody has killed the many dead."[15]

With six million murders to avenge, twenty-five defendants received the death penalty; thirty-five were found not guilty; ninety-seven received prison sentences ranging from time served to twenty-five years; twenty were given life. (Most terms were later reduced.)[16] Of the twenty-four civilian executives tried in the I. G. Farben trial, ten walked; the rest averaged about three years each. Billionaire Nazi industrialist Alfried Krupp—the only defendant to have his assets seized—did thirty-six months and then received a full refund.

Ten prominent Nazis were hanged on October 16, 1946: military leaders Wilhelm Keitel and Alfred Jodl; political officials Joachim von Ribbentrop, Wilhelm Frick, Alfred Rosenberg, Hans Frank, Fritz Sauckel, Julius Streicher, and Artur Seyss-Inquart; and *finally*, one of the few high-ranking SS officers to die for the Shoah, RSHA director *SS Obergruppenführer* Ernst Kaltenbrunner. (Himmler took cyanide after his capture, Göring doing the same the night before his scheduled execution.) Other notable hangings—resulting from the Einsatzgruppen trial, the ninth of twelve US Military trials known as the "Subsequent Nuremberg Trials"—included four Einsatzgruppen chiefs, seven doctors, and SS official Oswald Pohl.

A smattering of camp administrators, capos, guards, doctors (even nurses) were also tried and executed at various Allied and/or national tribunals, e.g., Auschwitz-Krakow, Dachau, Majdanek, Mauthausen-Gusen, and Hamburg-Ravensbruck. (On July 15, 2015, 94-year-old Oskar Gröning, a.k.a. "The Bookkeeper of Auschwitz," was convicted by a German court as an accessory to the murder of 300,000 Hungarian Jews at Birkenau; the former SS officer in charge of collecting the arrivals' effects received a four-year sentence, though any jail time remains doubtful due to the lengthy appeal process.)

HANNS AND RUDOLF

In a rare case of poetic justice, a German-born Jew and British soldier, Hanns Alexander, was able to track down and capture Rudolf Höss. As chronicled in the amazing book, *Hanns and Rudolf: The True Story of the German Jew Who Tracked Down And Caught the Kommandant of Auschwitz*, by Thomas Harding, the author's great-uncle, Captain Howard Harvey "Hanns" Alexander, and twenty-five other British soldiers, apprehended Höss (disguised as a gardener) on March 11, 1946, at a farm in Gottrupel, Germany.

Ironically, the SS chief was given up by his own wife. With Hedwig Höss and her children in British custody, the captain flushed the covey with an ingenious ruse. Harding backed a steam engine up to the jail and told the former chatelaine that she had ten minutes to write down her husband's location or else he would deport their fifteen-year-old son, Klaus, to *Siberia*—the old man never had a chance.

Meanwhile, back at the farm, when Höss heard the knock on that dark snowy night, he opened the door but insisted he was Franz Lang. When Harding attempted to identify him by his SS tattoo he discovered that it had been removed. He then noticed that Höss was wearing his wedding ring. Being German, Harding knew that it was customary for couples to engrave their initials on their bands. When he demanded the ring, Höss refused, only to relent after the Nazi hunter brandished a knife. The Catholic 'fessed up on the spot. After allowing his mostly Jewish unit several minutes to "interrogate" Rudy with axe handles (specifically brought along for the occasion), Harding had the reprobate thrown into a lorry and trucked to a nearby prison.

Höss made his debut at Nuremberg on April 15, 1946, where he calmly gave a detailed account of his crimes. On April 16, 1947, the quondam Kommandant of Konzentrationslager Auschwitz was hanged on location from the one-person gallows in the shadow of Crematorium I—a stone's throw from the cozy family cottage. His last request was that his wedding ring be given to Hedwig.

"TO GET TOO MUCH AT THE HEAD OF THE QUEUE..."

Living conditions in postwar Germany also pointed to Palestine as Jewry's only hope of spatial recovery. Dr. Gerhard Peters, managing director of Degesch Corporation, whose Zyklon B "product" killed one million Jews at Auschwitz, was initially convicted in 1949 of "aiding in manslaughter" and given five years, but after several appeals was found not guilty by a local magistrate in 1955 due to changes in the law. The most prominent Farben personnel to be convicted—Otto Ambros, Heinrich Bütefisch, Walter Dürrfeld, Fritz Ter Meer—were all later elected to directorate boards of new German corporations. (Otto eventually served as a US Department of Energy consultant and a paid advisor for W. R. Grace and Company.)[17]

German Jews who attempted to recover Aryanized property, or appropriate indemnification and other reparations, received little help from Allied agencies. Hilberg writes: "Though initially concerned with depriving Germany of its war industries and external assets, the Western coalition soon began to look upon the West German industrial complex as a potential bulwark against the Soviet Union."[18] On day one of the Farben trial, Judge James Morris commented to Prosecutor Josiah DuBois: "We have to worry about the Russians now; it wouldn't surprise me if they overran the courtroom before we get through."[19] Then, ironically, for much of the Jewish possessions that remained on European soil, there were no living owners and no surviving heirs. With heirless property routinely falling to the government, few of these tangible resources found their way to Jewish communities and/or relief organizations.[20] To Bohn's credit, the equivalent of $70 billion was eventually paid to Shoah survivors in *compensation*. Germany's willingness to pay triggered Genesis 12:3, with the resultant economic stimulus enabling the funds to continue.

On June 22, 1945, President Truman appointed Earl Harrison, dean of the University of Pennsylvania Law School, to investigate the Jews' conditions in Europe, particularly the DP camps. Harrison submitted his report in August. After confirming their appalling status, he attested: "The desire to leave Germany is an urgent one...They want to be evacuated to Palestine now, just as other national groups are being repatriated to their homes...it is morally wrong and politically indefensible to impose obstacles to the entry of Palestine now of any Jews who wish to go there." The study "strongly recommended, as 'the only real solution,' the quick evacuation of all non-repatriable Jews in Germany and Austria, who wish it, to Palestine."[21] Truman immediately set out to remediate their suffering. According to David McCullough, Pulitzer Prize-winning author of *Truman*, the president

> wanted to do what was right for the hundreds of thousands of European Jews, survivors of the Holocaust, who had suffered such unimaginable horrors. His sympathy for them was heartfelt and deep-

> seated...Politics and humanitarian concerns and foreign policy were all closely, irrevocably intertwined. Yet for Truman unquestionably, humanitarian concerns mattered foremost. His sympathies were naturally with the underdog, but he was influenced too by a lifelong love of ancient history, his own remarkable grasp of the whole complicated chronicle of the Fertile Crescent. For Truman, Palestine was never just a place on the map. [Citing White House Counsel Clark Clifford]...his own reading of ancient history and the Bible made him a supporter of the idea of a Jewish homeland in Palestine...He did not need to be convinced by Zionists...I remember him once talking about the problems of displaced persons, 'Everyone else who's been dragged from his country has someplace to go back to,' he said. 'But the Jews have no place to go.'[22]

Having ameliorated the hardships in the teeming camps, Truman's next move was to challenge Britain's intolerable immigration policy. Though the new Labour government was naturally more empathetic to the Zionists (via their ideological linkage to the Histadrut), Attlee was ultimately constrained by fiscal realities. To put it bluntly, His Britannic Majesty's Government was nearly *broke*.[23] With 25% of the national wealth consumed by the war, the remaining hard currency would barely cover 40% of existing bills. Thus, in Whitehall's view, it was now more imperative than ever to preserve Britain's most important overseas resource—her vast Middle East oil holdings (Iran, Iraq, Kuwait, and Qatar). While the wells seemed bottomless, the main threat (for disruption) concerned the hundreds of miles of pipelines traversing multiple frontiers. And of course, the only way to keep the Arabs happy was to keep the Jews unhappy (i.e., barred from Eretz Yisrael). And should the Brits show insensitivity to such matters, Moscow would gladly exert its hegemony in the area (especially since the French had been lately maneuvered out of Syria and Lebanon.[24])

On August 31, 1945, Truman wrote Attlee, urging that 100,000 Jewish DPs be allowed to flee to Palestine pronto. "The main solution appears to lie in the quick evacuation of as many as possible of the non-repatriable Jews who wish it to Palestine. If it is to be effective, such action should not be long delayed."[25] The prime minister was so taken aback by Truman's effrontery that he delayed his answer for over two weeks. The reply then proposed that only a third of that number be squeezed into two camps in *Muslim North Africa*. Attlee's bottom line was typical: "In the case of Palestine we have the Arabs to consider as well as the Jews, and there have been solemn undertakings... given by your predecessor, yourself, and Mr. Churchill...It would be very unwise to break these solemn pledges and so set aflame the whole Middle East."[26] Harry was *not* amused.

In a speech before Parliament on November 15, Secretary of State for Foreign Affairs Ernest Bevin exacerbated the impasse by relating the stereotypical Jewish propensity "to get too much at the head of the queue..."[27] to demand aid. "Is it 'getting too much to the head of the queue' if, after the slaughter of six million Jews, the remnant of a million-and-a-half appeal for shelter in their homeland?" the normally tranquil Weizmann rejoined four days later in a speech before the Zionist Organization of America Convention at Atlantic City. "What [a] sorry epitaph the new declaration of policy seeks to write over the graves of the six million of our dead!"[28] He also reminded his audience that there had been a time when "Jews had the highest priority in the queues which led to the crematoria of Auschwitz and Treblinka."[29]

Meanwhile, in a follow-up appeal to the White House, Attlee tried a stalling tactic, proposing that a joint Anglo-American committee investigate the crisis. Truman jumped on the offer, stipulating that Palestine be the sole destination.

THE ANGLO-AMERICAN COMMITTEE OF INQUIRY

The Anglo-American Committee of Inquiry consisted of six Americans, led by Judge "Texas Joe" Hutcheson, and six Brits led by Sir John Singleton. The participants represented a diverse group of diplomats, scholars, and politicians. Their four-month itinerary took them from New York and Washington to London, Europe, Cairo, and Palestine, conducting dozens of briefings, hearings, and interviews.

In London, Leopold Amery made an impassioned plea for partition, reminding the Committee that "as a young official he had been responsible for the final draft of the Balfour Declaration."[30] To the Jews' dismay, Albert Einstein appeared to equivocate in his endorsement of Jewish nationalism. Weizmann was the first Jewish spokesman in Palestine. Though over seventy and nearly blind, the patriarch delivered a spirited overview of the historic controversy. The Arab Higher Committee made the inane charge that Jews "in their present attitude in

Palestine are nothing but the embodiment of Nazism."[31] The committee then divided into groups and inspected various DP camps in the American, British, and French occupation zones in Germany, Austria, Italy, Czechoslovakia, Poland, and Greece.[32] When scores of Shoah survivors were surveyed as to their preferred destination, over 85% replied, "Eretz Yisrael." Dr. Michael Robert Marrus of the University of Toronto writes in *The Unwanted*:

> The Jews in Central Europe had little desire to return to their countries of origin, often seen as a graveyard for the Jews. With more authority than the Harrison inquiry, the committee reported that the Jewish DPs wanted desperately to go to Palestine. Of 138,320 Jewish DPs enumerated in the British, American and French zones (the Soviets did not permit entry to the committee), 118,570 declared Palestine their preferred destination.[33]

The emissaries spent April in Lausanne collating their data. The *Report of the Anglo-American Committee of Enquiry Regarding the Problems of European Jewry and Palestine* was released on May 1, 1946. Less than one hundred pages, it exposed the intolerable physical and psychological abuse of Europe's Jewish remnant, juxtaposed with the prevailing anti-Semitism. Concluding, "We know of no country to which the great majority can go in the immediate future other than Palestine," the committee unanimously recommended the immediate release of 100,000 immigration certificates.[34] Motions regarding Palestine proper were indecisive; though preferring a unified state to partition, they divided over the obvious snag of which race would run the country, conceding: "In neither case would minority guarantees afford adequate protection for the subordinated group."[35] In summary, the bipartisan board proposed that 100,000 Jewish DPs be sent to Palestine now; subsequent unhindered Jewish immigration (though not to exceed the Arab population); and, the Mandatory authority remain in the interim (the need of a further permanent solution being implied).

Attlee was stymied by an advance copy of the paper, particularly its support of Truman's request of 100,000 certificates. The president was ecstatic. On April 27, Bevin cabled Washington, begging the White House to delay release of the report pending further dialogue. To Whitehall's dismay, on May 1, Harry not only published it on the spot, but also voiced his approval. Baron Francis-Williams, Bevin's friend and biographer, later disclosed that Truman's words "threw Bevin into one of the blackest rages I ever saw him in."[36]

Once again Attlee delayed, calling for further talks to assess financial liabilities for said humanitarian project. While Truman reluctantly agreed, Attlee ultimately refused to honor an earlier pledge to follow any unanimous proposal. To exacerbate matters, Bevin "set Truman's teeth on edge" by ascribing the president's intervention as a political tactic to gain Jewish votes in New York.[37] Ernest also told a Labour party gathering that the US favored the transfer of 100,000 Jews into Palestine because "they did not want too many of them in New York."[38] When he later sailed to America, the former dockworker and labor leader learned that the stevedores in the port of New York had refused to handle his luggage.[39] As things turned out, the foreign secretary was extremely fortunate that this was his *worst* experience; thanks to MI5, a Sternist plot to kill Bevin *by an aerial bombing of the Foreign Office* was detected and averted.[40]

ALIYAH BET

In the wake of Attlee's initial resistance, the Jewish Agency reactivated its illegal immigration program code-named *Aliyah Bet* ("Immigration B," i.e., unofficial immigration). Shaul Avigur, a veteran human smuggler, was resettled in Paris to serve as director.

The main goal of Aliyah Bet, also called *Ha'apala* ("ascension"), was psychological—to maximize public awareness of the flight and plight of Jewish refugees. The interception and re-internment of thousands of traumatized Holocaust survivors was meant to embarrass Britain by exposing her own ongoing callous complicity in the Final Solution. As the audiovisual display at the Clandestine Immigration and Naval Museum in Haifa remarks: "There is no precedent in human history for a people who seeks to sneak into its own homeland."[41]

While Colonel Patterson's famed Jewish Legion was not allowed to remobilize until late in WWII, the men went on to serve a far more relevant task by facilitating the escape of postwar refugees. With the covert support of French agents, the first wave of several hundred Jews was smuggled out of the American Zone in autumn 1945. The fugitives were trucked over mountain passes to the French and Italian coasts, then placed on ships bound for Palestine. Others just walked.

By early 1946, the system was processing over a thousand "illegals" per month. Known as *Ma'apilim* ("to brave one's way to the land of Israel"), the boat of choice was usually an Italian coastal vessel of prewar vintage. To thwart the attempted entries Britain deployed a formidable naval blockade augmented by 80,000 land-based troops. The alien transports were routinely stopped and boarded by armed members of the Royal Navy (RN). Deadly resistance was not uncommon, the passengers eventually being subdued, removed, and deported to squalid detention facilities in Cyprus. (British ships were frequently sabotaged by Haganah underwater demolition teams.)

The most disconcerting terminus was the Atlit Detention Camp (south of Haifa), where over 3,500 Shoah survivors found themselves crammed into a twenty-two-acre lager of long wooden barracks, enclosed by high barbed wire fences and machinegun towers—only now—within Eretz Yisrael itself! Imagine the surreal *déjà vu* encounter as each new transport of men, women, and children was sent to the "disinfection building" for a mandatory "shower." Afterward, the inmates were segregated by gender (including families); issued a board, pillow, and blanket (a one-meter gap between beds); subjected to stringent roll calls and head counts; then assigned to various work.[42]

Only five of sixty-three maritime embarkations between 1945 and 1948 reached Palestine unmolested. The refugee population in Cyprus quickly burgeoned to 26,000.[43] Thus, the Jews concluded their pathetic circuit from *concentration* camp to *death* camp to *displaced persons* camp, and finally, to the *detention* camp. The protracted publicity was telling. When the *Beauharnais* was towed into Haifa harbor, the defiant exiles unfurled a banner reading: "We survived Hitler. Death is no stranger to us. Nothing can keep us from our Jewish homeland. The blood be on your head if you fire on this unarmed ship."[44]

In the end, fifty-eight Aliyah Bet "defeats" spelled a pyrrhic victory for His Majesty's Britannic persona. As Sachar writes, "Its impact on world opinion and the British taxpayer turned out to be the Jews' most effective weapon."[45] The Hungarian-British writer, Arthur Koestler, observed: "The fate of the 100,000 began to act on world opinion like a pebble throne into a pond. Its ripples soon grew into waves which threatened to drown Britain's prestige and economic future."[46]

BEGIN VS. BEVIN

While Ben-Gurion decried the Anglo-American Committee Report for skirting Jewish statehood, the fact that Whitehall had refused to issue the certificates did not bode well for occupation troops in Palestine. Attlee & Bevin had thrown down the gauntlet and the Yishuv's paramilitary forces were *more* than willing to pick it up. On May 12, 1946, the following warning was issued over *KOL Israel* ("The Voice of Israel"), the Haganah's underground radio station in Tel Aviv:

> Present British policy is based on an erroneous assumption: Britain, in evacuating Syria, Lebanon, and Egypt, intends to concentrate her military bases in Palestine and is therefore concerned to strengthen her hold over the mandate, and is using her responsibility to the Jewish people as a means to that end. But this double game will not work... We would therefore warn publicly His Majesty's Government that if it does not fulfill its responsibilities under the mandate—above all with regard to the question of immigration—the Jewish Resistance Movement will make every effort to hinder the transfer of British bases to Palestine and to prevent their establishment in this country.[47]

British officials had every reason to take such a threat seriously. On November 6, 1944, three months after the failed assassination attempt against Palestine High Commissioner Sir Harold MacMichael, Britain's minister-resident in Cairo, Lord Walter Moyne, was gunned down as he left his residence by two members of the ultra-violent Stern Gang. (The shooters were eventually arrested, tried, and hanged.) Later, on October 31, 1945, the Haganah blew-up railway lines in 153 locations, completely disrupting the system. The band had even managed to infiltrate the British Palestine Police with agents of their own elite intelligence service, the *Shai* ("Information Service").[48]

As previously related, the variegated militias in the Yishuv encompassed a wide range of tactical philosophy. Established in 1920, the Haganah became the largest underground military unit of the Jewish Resistance Movement. The group split in 1931 over its founding principle of *havlagah* ("restraint"). Believing that "the best defense is a good offense," Vladimir Jabotinsky formed the *Irgun Zvai Leumi* (IZL), or *Etzel* ("National Military Organization"), on the credo that "every Jew has a right to enter Palestine." The Irgun's insignia featured a hand gripping a rifle over a map of Palestine—*including* Transjordan—with the motto *Rak Kach* ("Only Thus"). In 1940, the *Lehi* ("Stern Gang") split away from IZL in order to continue fighting the British *during* the war. Finally, on the notable date of May 15, 1941, the Haganah high command sanctioned its own elite attack unit called the *Palmach* ("Strike Force"). The primary motivation for this decision was the impending Axis invasion of Palestine.

On the night of October 10, 1945, the Palmach gave HMG a serious wakeup call—breaking into Atlit and freeing over 200 detainees! On June 17, 1946, Haganah forces blew ten of eleven bridges joining Palestine to her neighbors, effectively isolating the country. The British retaliated by launching "Operation Agatha" on *Saturday*, June 29 (henceforth known as "Black Sabbath"), a two-week, nationwide, block-by-block, house-by-house, basement-to-attic, cordon and search of Jewish homes and businesses. Not even schools and hospitals were spared. Startled patients had their casts broken off by soldiers looking for weapons.[49] The Jewish Agency reacted by directing the Haganah to divert their energies to illegal immigration, whereupon the ultra militant Lehi picked up the slack, committing over one hundred acts of mayhem between September 1946 and May 1948. However, the lion's share of the violence would stem from the Irgun, led by one who quickly became Ernest Bevin's worst nightmare.

While David Ben-Gurion (destined to become Israel's first prime minister) was the anticipated successor to the ailing Dr. Weizmann, the bespectacled, Polish-born Holocaust survivor, Menachem Begin (another future prime minister), was the gutsy commando who would ensure that a Jewish state materialized—*period.* His guerrilla tactics were similar to those of the legendary Confederate general, Nathan Bedford Forrest, i.e., "*anything* goes," if it works, etc. (Begin once evaded a British dragnet by disguising himself as a bearded Rabbi.)

Over the next eighteen months Irgun and Lehi forces pressed the offensive, coordinating twenty-five assaults on British and Arab targets. The growing incident count chased His Majesty's troops into confined quarters (dubbed "Bevingrad" by the city's Jews). In autumn 1946, a report from the Jaffa-Tel Aviv district advised London that "morale both with officers and ordinary soldiers is particularly low."[50] How ironic that the persecutors of Jews were now finding themselves restricted to their *own* "ghettos." Another dispatch noted the "uncomfortable hours erecting barbed wire and even more uncomfortable hours living behind it."[51] The fight also went beyond the borders of Palestine. On October 31, 1946, the British embassy in Rome was blown up, killing three. Yet Menachem would reserve his boldest strike for a most felicitous moment indeed.

MORRISON-GRADY REPORT

By summer 1946, Attlee and Bevin were ready to renegotiate their highly unpopular Palestine policy. Truman sent a special three-man cabinet committee to London, led by Dr. Henry F. Grady. Britain's team was chaired by Deputy Prime Minister Herbert Morrison. The two bodies conducted intense talks for five weeks. Morrison proposed a unitary federal trusteeship with Jewish and Arab provinces granted quasi-independence under British suzerainty, Jerusalem and the Negev remaining subordinate to London. While Arabs and Jews would elect their own legislatures, the High Commissioner would retain authority over customs, police, defense, diplomacy, and the judiciary.

The so-called "Cantonization Plan" was highly disadvantageous to the Jews, leaving them with only 17% of Eretz Yisrael—their *worst* offer yet. The Zionist province would include about two-thirds of the coastal plain, the Jezreel Valley and most of eastern Galilee. The only "plus" was the motion to admit 100,000 immigrants the first year after the plan began. The High Commissioner would then consider further certificates based on the old ploy of "economic absorptive capacity."

The British were particularly motivated to maintain control of the Negev due to their recent exodus from Egypt. Contrary to Truman's known bent, Grady co-endorsed the federative solution, the final report concluding optimistically: "We believe this plan provides as fair and reasonable a compromise between the claims of Arabs and Jews as it is possible to devise, and that it offers the best prospect of reconciling the conflicting interests of the two communities."[52] However, a week before the proposals were announced to Parliament, Whitehall was given a graphic illustration of said "conflicting interests," rendering the Morrison-Grady Report dead on arrival.

KING DAVID HOTEL BOMBING

In a spectacular daylight raid on July 22, 1946, over a dozen IZL operatives dressed as Arabs entered the prestigious King David Hotel in Jerusalem carrying 225 kilograms of explosives hidden in milk churns. The six charges were planted in the basement directly under the wing housing the administrative headquarters of the British Secretariat in Palestine. The ensuing explosion at 12:37 p.m. collapsed the entire western half of the southern portion of the hotel.

The next day the headline story in *The Palestine Post* (renamed *The Jerusalem Post* in 1950) described the carnage accordingly: "When the billowing smoke started to drift off into the sunny, cloudless sky, there was a huge, gaping chasm where the six-storey corner had been. Wounded troops and civilians, their clothes spattered with blood, their faces covered with white dust and streaked with blood, staggered out of the wreckage dazed by shock."[53] The attack caused 91 deaths and 46 injuries, including 15 Jewish casualties. (The *Post* itself would be blown to pieces by Arab insurgents on February 1, 1948). Despite several telephone warnings, all were ignored (and later denied) by the British. In another article on July 23 the paper recounted:

> According to one report, an anonymous woman caller telephoned to the switchboard operator at the King David and told him that the building must be evacuated as there would be an explosion 'in a few minutes.' About 12:35, *The Palestine Post* was told, also by a woman, in English, that the Government offices were about to be blown up, and that the people there had been warned to evacuate the building. A mysterious woman caller telephoned the French Consulate General and said, 'In a few minutes there will be an explosion in your neighborhood. We suggest that you open all your windows.' This was done and no one was hurt there.[54]

The strike represented the apex of Jewish defiance to HMG in Eretz Yisrael. The bombing inflamed public opinion against Bevin and Attlee. In similar fashion, the Jewish Agency and Vaad Leumi united to "express their horror at the dastardly crime perpetrated by the gang of desperadoes who…shed the innocent blood of Government officers and other citizens, British, Jewish and Arab." The joint declaration concluded: "The Yishuv in Palestine is called upon to rise up against these abominable outrages."[55] Ben-Gurion and the Haganah, absolved of any complicity, also felt compelled to denounce Begin and the Irgun as a "terrorist organization." Weizmann voiced ambivalent sentiments.

As expected, a wave of restrictions was renewed against Jewish civil liberties. On July 31 (the day Morrison-Grady hit Parliament), the *Post* reported: "Nearly 20,000 British troops and Palestine Police were engaged here today in the most intensive and complete search operation ever undertaken in Palestine or perhaps in any other part of the world, with the object of finding members of terrorist gangs."[56]

LONDON CONFERENCE

While British reaction to Morrison-Grady was naturally positive (despite the blast), the other key players remained opposed, Truman and the Zionists wanting partition, the Arabs, a *Palestinian* state. Harry would later write, "I studied the plan with care, but I was unable to see that anything would come out of it except more unrest."[57]

Nonetheless, Jewish and Arab leaders were invited to London for yet *another* conference on September 19, 1946. The prospects were less than inviting. Truman cabled Attlee on August 7: "The opposition in this country to the plan has become so intense that it is now clear that it would be impossible to rally in favor of it sufficient public opinion to enable this Government to give it effective support."[58] The Zionist Executive rejected the offer outright, while the Palestinian Arabs deferred to show without their exiled Mufti (currently in Cairo).

The truncated gathering convened with only British and Arab attendees (the latter from outside of Palestine). After two days of one-sided Arab rants, the hosts suspended the embarrassing anti-Semitic convention, ostensibly for "additional study." On October 1, a desperate Attlee reached out to Chaim and other Zionists in private. However, his "new" offer was only for protracted trusteeship, lasting up to ten years ("hopefully" ending in self-rule, etc.). Two days later, Attlee received an advance copy of Truman's annual greeting to American Jewry on Yom Kippur. Once again, Britain's leader was aghast, begging for a reprieve. Harry refused. On October 4, the president not only advocated immediate Jewish entry into Palestine, but partition over federation as well. Bevin accused Truman anew of chasing Jewish votes, whining,

"In international affairs, I cannot settle things if my problem is made the subject of local elections."[59]

Twenty-Second Zionist Congress

Seven long years had passed since Dr. Weizmann bade his uneasy farewell to the Polish delegates at the last Zionist Congress in Geneva. When the Twenty-Second Congress convened in Basel on December 9, 1946, the depleted ranks sadly confirmed his foreboding, Chaim noting that "the great fountains of European Jewry had been dried up."[60] The new dominant voting blocs hailed from America and Palestine (led by Rabbi Abba H. Silver and Ben-Gurion, respectively).

The prevailing mood of this unique Congress—the first in the postwar era and the last before statehood—was utter distrust of the British and a radical resolve. Weizmann wrote, "[O]ne feature was common to all of them: the conviction of the need for fighting against British authority in Palestine—or anywhere else, for that matter."[61] Chaim's routine appeal for diplomacy consequently fell on deaf ears. The critical vote on whether delegates should be sent to the London Conference on Palestine (set to resume in January) was denied by a slim margin—a tacit repudiation of Weizmann himself. Any doubt was removed by the fact that he was not reelected to his traditional post as ZO president (the office remaining conspicuously vacant). "I left the Congress depressed," Chaim wrote, "far more by the spirit in which it had been conducted than by the rebuff I had received."[62] However, though "put out to pasture," the Zionist warhorse would yet supply a timely intervention at the critical hour of Israel's bid for statehood.

Britain Solicits UN Intervention

Following yet another failed proposal (a.k.a. the "Bevin Plan"), Ernest finally threw in the towel, announcing on February 14, 1947, that he would seek the advice of the United Nations to resolve the Mandate crisis. Colonel Meinertzhagen decried the decision as "the complete abdication of Britain's moral influence in the world and an equally complete admission of failure."[63] In the interim, Begin and the IZL kept the pressure on, blowing up the Goldschmidt House Officers Club in Jerusalem on March 1 (killing seventeen British officers and injuring twenty-seven). Nearly 2,000 relatives of civilian staff were evacuated to England (the rest hunkering down behind barbed wire).

On April 2, 1947, Trygve Halvdan Lie (*what a name*), the first UN Secretary General, received a letter from Sir Alexander Cadogan, asking that "the question of Palestine" be placed on the agenda of the next session of the General Assembly (rather than the smaller Security Council). The First Special Session of the UNGA convened on April 28 at its temporary headquarters located in Flushing Meadows, New York. However, before the Norwegian Lie could comply, *another* unsettling demonstration of Zionist resolve occurred in Palestine.

ACRE PRISON BREAK

The ancient fortress city of Acre (or *Akko*) stands at the northern extremity of Haifa Bay in Israel's northern coastal plain. The Apostle Paul passed through there (*Ptolemais*) on his way to Jerusalem (Acts 21:7). During the Mandate, the citadel served as a jail. It was the most guarded lockup in Palestine, sporting thick high walls and bordered on the east and north by a deep moat, and on the west by the sea.

In the spring of 1947, some 400 Arabs and 120 Jews were confined at Acre. The majority of the Jewish prisoners were members of the Haganah, Irgun, and Lehi. On April 16, four IZL men were hanged[64] (with another four to follow). The executions prompted an ingenious escape plan; the "break*out*" would be precipitated by a "break-*in*."

Begin timed the operation for May 4, just hours before the UNGA was scheduled to convene in New York. Around 2:00 p.m., a command jeep carrying a bemedaled "British" captain (Dov Cohen) led a convoy of "British" lorries, complete with standard camouflage colors, straight to the fortress gates. Two of the vans proceeded through the market area to a Turkish bath situated below a vulnerable portion of the southern wall. An Irgun demolition team disguised as telephone technicians entered the joint, hauling their ladders and "equipment" to "repair a faulty electrical line." The men wore Engineering Corps uniforms, sported English haircuts, and even walked with a military gait. They then scaled the roof of the Basha bagnio (adjacent the prison wall) and affixed explosive charges to the cell windows. At 4:22 p.m., the facility was rocked as a gaping hole was ripped through the south facade. The Jewish inmates then began to extricate themselves using additional TNT previously smuggled in.

When the smoke cleared, three members of the thirty-four-man strike force were dead (including Cohen). Six escapees and three British guards were also killed. According to the *Palestine Post*, 251 prisoners got out. The total included 20 select IZL and 7 Lehi fighters, 93 regular Jewish inmates, and 131 Arabs. The action was universally acclaimed by the foreign press as "the greatest jail break in history." Conservative MP Oliver Stanley stood in the House of Commons and questioned what action HMG was planning to take "in light of the events at Acre Prison which had reduced British prestige to a nadir."[65]

UN Special Committee on Palestine

After two weeks of debate within the GA, an eleven-nation committee of enquiry was appointed on May 13. Designated the United Nations Special Committee on Palestine (UNSCOP), the organ comprised folk from Australia, Canada, Czechoslovakia, Guatemala, India, Iran, the Netherlands, Peru, Sweden, Uruguay, and Yugoslavia. The members were charged to investigate the crisis and "make recommendations under Article 10 of the Charter concerning the future of Palestine."

On May 26, UNSCOP held its first session. The group then journeyed to Palestine in mid-June to conduct five weeks of hearings and achieve a general understanding of the problem. The Arab Higher Committee boycotted the Commission. While the Mufti's adherents staged numerous anti-Semitic demonstrations in the larger cities, the Zionists stayed the course with their carefully reasoned arguments. The diplomats were also able to observe firsthand both the tension and determination that permeated the Yishuv.

The "Sergeants Affair"

Soon after the Acre break, several of the Jewish escapees and commandos were captured. After much controversial litigation, three Irgun members were hanged in the early morning of July 29. The next day—in what became known as the "Sergeants Affair"—two British sergeants, seized eighteen days earlier, were hanged from eucalyptus trees in retribution. As Begin put it, "We repaid our enemy in kind."[66]

On the night of July 31, livid British troops and police held a lethal pogrom in Tel Aviv. Similar riots broke out in Britain. Meinertzhagen wrote: "The real men responsible for the killing of those two sergeants are the politicians who sit in Downing Street, the Government of this country and ultimately the British public. All my sympathy is with the Jews who have been driven by apathy, anti-Semitism and broken promises into a state of exasperation. If I were a Jew I should be a terrorist, a violent one, and I would aim at Whitehall."[67]

Exodus 1947

The UNSCOP mission would also coincide with the definitive tragedy of the Aliyah Bet era. On July 11, 1947, a battered 1,800-ton former Chesapeake Bay ferry, the *SS President Warfield*, sailed from Marseilles, France, with 4,515 Jews (including 655 children, many being orphans) headed for Palestine. Most were Shoah survivors. The ship drew a British naval "escort" the moment it left French waters.

In a solemn open sea ceremony on July 17, the vessel was renamed *Exodus 1947*. The blue and white Zionist flag with the Star of David was hoisted amidst repeated choruses of "HaTikvah." The following night, the overcrowded steamer (built for 400 travelers) was rammed by two destroyers twelve miles from Palestine (i.e., in international waters). It was then boarded by sailors and royal marines. Two teenage orphans and the ship's chief mate (Bill Bernstein, an American Aliyah Bet volunteer) died in the ensuing melee. With broom sticks, potatoes, and cans of kosher meat no match for guns, truncheons, and teargas, over 150 Jews and crewmembers suffered various injuries as well.[68]

The damaged boat was towed to Haifa Port. Ruth Gruber, a Jewish-American journalist, recorded the unfolding pathos:

> The voices of thousands of people floated to us on the quay. They were singing "HaTikvah," the Hebrew hymn of hope…The ship looked like a matchbox that had been splintered by a nutcracker. In the torn, square hole, as big as an open, blitzed barn, we could see a muddle of bedding, possessions, plumbing, broken pipes,

> overflowing toilets, half-naked men, women looking for children. Cabins were bashed in; railings were ripped off; the lifesaving rafts were dangling at crazy angles.[69]

As UNSCOP men stared in disbelief, within 24 hours the exhausted human cargo was transferred onto three deportation vessels, *ostensibly* for internment in Cyprus. However, while the island jail was bad enough (Gruber depicting the place as "a twentieth century purgatory, circumscribed…by two walls of barbwire whose architecture had come from Dachau and Treblinka…"), Bevin privately told Sir Alan Cunningham, High Commissioner of Palestine, to punish the French by returning the "illegals" to them.[70] Code-named *Operation Oasis*, the spent Jews arrived at Port-de-Bouc in southern France, August 2.

To the Limeys' dismay, despite meager rations, various maladies, and a severe heat wave, the desperate passengers refused to disembark, declaring: "None but dead men will be landed here."[71] French authorities prudently declined to remove them. Pining away in the ships' holds (described as "floating cages"), the refugees ratcheted up the pressure by announcing a hunger strike. The stalemate dragged on for over three weeks. Finally, on August 22, amidst worldwide outrage, Bevin redeployed his pathetic flotilla to Hamburg, Germany. According to the *Palestine Post*, the first "Liberty" ship (SS *Ocean Vigour*) carrying 1,400 Jews, was met on a "cage-lined dock" by "more than 1,000 British troops armed with machine guns, rifles, tommyguns, tear-gas pistols, steel-tipped truncheons and high-pressure hosepipes."[72] All were promptly dragged off their ships and hauled to detention camps in the British occupation zone near Lübeck.

London's hope that the *Exodus* affair had dampened the spirits of the Ma'apilim was dashed within weeks when the 700-ton *Af-Al-Pi-Chen* sailed from Formia, Italy, with 434 passengers. Although the vessel was intercepted by two RN destroyers (a passenger, *Noah* Goldfarb, killed in the process), the mission's main feat was the subliminal message of Jewish resolve conveyed in the ship's name. Representing the first post-*Exodus* launch, the Italian-owned *Michael Parma* (formerly the LCT R 147, a Canadian tank landing craft used in the Allied invasion of North Africa) was intentionally renamed the *Af-Al-Pi-Chen* (roughly translated "Nevertheless," or "In spite of it all"). When the Jews were facing opposition in the post-captivity era, Nehemiah relates: "NEVERTHELESS *we made our prayer unto our God…."* (Nehemiah 4:9) In 1968, the *Af-*

Ai-Pi-Chen became the centerpiece of the Clandestine Immigration and Naval Museum.

UNSCOP RECOMMENDS PARTITION

The 52nd (and last) UNSCOP session met in Geneva on August 31, 1947. Their report unanimously endorsed eleven guidelines. The most important of these proposed that "the Mandate for Palestine shall be terminated at the earliest practicable date"; "independence shall be granted in Palestine at the earliest practicable date"; and, "the problem of the distressed European Jews, of whom approximately 250,000 are in assembly centers, will be dealt with as a matter of extreme urgency for the alleviation of their plight and of the Palestine problem…."[73]

The key statute regarding partition, "Recommendation XII. THE JEWISH PROBLEM IN GENERAL," came under the heading: "Section B. Recommendation approved by substantial majority." The final tally for their "Plan of Partition with *Economic Union*" was as follows: seven member nations—Canada, Czechoslovakia, Guatemala, the Netherlands, Peru, Sweden, and Uruguay—voting for *partition*; three countries—India, Iran, and Yugoslavia—proposing *federation*; Australia's delegate was the lone abstention.

The boundary proposals were fairly standard: Jerusalem under international jurisdiction (residents free to choose citizenship in either the Arab or Jewish state); Arab territory to encompass western Galilee, the hill country of central Palestine, and the coastal plain between Ashdod and Egypt's border; the Jewish allotment comprising "everything" else—roughly *11%* of the original Balfour designation! Also, certain land within the proposed Jewish state sporting large Arab populations (Jaffa and Acre) received the deleterious status of "Arab enclaves."[74] Britain and the US would co-administrate a two-year transition period (not to exceed three years) under the aegis of the UN. Jewish immigration would proceed at 6,250 certificates per month. Finally, labeling the proposal a "*qualified* partition," the UNSCOP majority report decreed that "economic unity" would require that the Jewish state ante up a financial subsidy to the Palestinian state.[75]

As usual, the longsuffering Zionists took the "grin and bear it" approach, while the Arab League "lost it," threatening war if the UN *dared* to sanction the proposal. On September 23, the GA referred the matter to the Ad Hoc Committee on the Palestinian Question (comprising all member nations). Fourteen meetings followed over twenty-four days. While oil-conscious Britain remained a lame duck participant, Russia increasingly stole the spotlight after Andrei Gromyko's May announcement endorsing the "aspirations of the Jews to establish their own State."[76] On October 9, Truman learned that the Arab League Council had authorized its constituent nations to deploy troops on the Palestine border. Two days later, Herschel Johnson, US representative to the GA's Palestine Committee, voiced the president's personal endorsement for partition. Moscow followed on October 13.

On November 25, upon incorporating a few minor territorial modifications, the Palestine Committee approved an amended partition plan 25-13, with 19 abstentions. Under the final draft, the Arab state would encompass 4,500 sq. miles, 804,000 Arabs and 10,000 Jews, while the Jewish state would consist of 5,500 sq. miles, 538,000 Jews, and 397,000 Arabs.[77] The stage was now set for the concluding vote by the full plenary General Assembly.

TRUMAN VS. "THE STRIPED-PANTS BOYS"

Throughout this critical time, a third major confrontation was playing out on behalf of the Zionists. President Truman found himself compelled to oppose much of his own administration, particularly Secretary of Defense James Forrestal and Secretary of State George C. Marshall. The former haberdasher from Independence, Missouri, had nothing but contempt for the so-called "Eastern establishment" (a.k.a. "The Wise Men"), especially their pro-oil, anti-Semitic policies:

> I had carefully read the Balfour Declaration, in which Great Britain was committed to a homeland in Palestine for the Jews. I had familiarized myself with the history of the question of a Jewish homeland and the position of the British and the Arabs. I was skeptical, as I read over the whole record up to date, about some of the views and attitudes assumed by the "striped-pants boys" in the State Department. It seemed to me that they didn't care enough about what happened to the thousands of displaced persons who were involved. It was my feeling that it would be possible for us to watch out for

the long-range interests of our country while at the same time helping these unfortunate victims of persecution to find a home.[78]

Naval Secretary James V. Forrestal (a fanatical Catholic) became America's first Secretary of Defense in September 1947. The former president of Wall Street behemoth Dillon, Read & Co. (one of Hitler's main banks) was also the ringleader of a coterie of State Department and intelligence officials, conspiring with the likes of John and Allen Dulles, St. John "Jack" Philby, King Saud, and the US oil lobby (ARAMCO in particular) against the Zionists' bid for statehood. Forrestal's key allies were General of the Army George C. Marshall and Under Secretaries of State Dean Acheson and Robert Lovett.

By 1947, America's petroleum giants controlled 42% of Middle Eastern reserves (primarily in Saudi Arabia, though also in Kuwait, Bahrain, and Iraq).[79] As the Saudi-US relationship blossomed, Arab output grew from 21.3 million barrels in 1945 to 142.9 million in 1948. "The prestige and hence the influence of the United States is in part related to the wealth of the Government and its nationals in terms of oil resources," Forrestal wrote, adding, "Indeed, the active expansion of such holdings is much to be desired."[80] Jim lectured the pro-Zionist, Clark Clifford: "You just don't understand. There are four hundred thousand Jews and forty million Arabs. Forty million Arabs are going to push four hundred thousand Jews into the sea. And that's all there is to it. Oil—that is the side we ought to be on."[81] With the looming "Red menace" sealing the argument, Truman's biographer wrote: "When his Secretary of Defense, Forrestal, reminded him of the critical need for Saudi Arabian oil, in the event of war, Truman said he would handle the situation in the light of justice, not oil."[82]

The president had to overcome a last-minute barrage of internal opposition just to reach the preliminary October 11 endorsement of Herschel V. Johnson, his own deputy representative to the United Nations. In a speech to the UN on September 17, 1947, George Marshall implied that Washington was reluctant to endorse partition. Five days later, Loy Henderson, director of the State Department's Middle East section, sent a memorandum to Marshall arguing against partition. In light of the ubiquitous intolerance across the *Ummah*, Henderson had the gall to say of the Zionists: "They recognize the principle of a theocratic racial state and even go so far in several instances as to discriminate on grounds of religion and race...."[83]

Forrestal was no less hypocritical (given the political machinations of his own church), stating that "no group in this country should be permitted to influence our policy to the point where it could endanger our national security."[84] The Joint Chiefs of Staff concurred, positing on October 10 that Jewish statehood would threaten US access to Middle Eastern oil while enabling Russia to attain regional hegemony. However, even after Johnson's pledge was secured, Forrestal refused to yield. Citing the *Forrestal Diaries*, Loftus and Aarons write that on November 6, the Secretary of Defense

> buttonholed J. Howard McGrath, senator from Rhode Island and Democratic National chairman. Forrestal repeated his arguments that 'no group in this country should be permitted to influence our policy to the point where it could endanger our national security.' McGrath was not encouraging; he 'replied by saying that there were two or three pivotal states which could not be carried without the support of people who were deeply interested in the Palestine question. I [Forrestal] said I would rather lose those states in a national election than run the risks which I felt might develop in our handling of the Palestine question.'[85]

While genuinely committed to Zionist aspirations, Truman was also pragmatic enough to remind the "striped-pants boys" that he had hundreds of thousands of pro-Jewish supporters, though virtually no Arabs, among his voting constituents.[86]

ALARMING TEST VOTE TRAJECTORY

For the main partition resolution to pass in the UNGA, a two-thirds majority was necessary. The Zionists received a providential wakeup call by observing the voting margins of three preliminary resolutions that were passed by the Ad Hoc Committee on November 24 and 25. As the membership of the Committee and Assembly were identical (comprising all member nations) the final percentages were revealing.

The first resolution represented a two-portion, Arab-backed motion to stall the partition by referring the Palestine question to the International Court of Justice. Both parts (requiring simple minorities) were defeated, the first by a vote of 25-18, with 11 abstentions, the second, 21-20, with

13 abstentions. Thus—less than one week before the final show down—the Zionists *barely* overcame the second challenge with only 51% of the vote (abstentions ignored). The last ballot determined if the Ad Hoc Committee would refer the measure to the UNGA (i.e., back to itself) for review. On Tuesday, November 25, the "Plan of Partition with Economic Union" passed by a margin of 25-13, with 17 abstentions, any discrepancy totals here and afterward being attributable to absenteeism. Here, the victory margin was 65%—*one* vote short of the needed two-thirds majority. However, more "yes" votes would still be needed should any abstainers switch to a "nay," or if any "yeas" flipped. With the UNGA poised to begin its debate the following day, the Jews were suddenly operating on borrowed time.

BEN-GURION VS. "ROCKY"

The opening talks on the Ad Hoc partition resolution ended late Wednesday without a final vote. As the following day happened to fall on Thanksgiving, Dr. Osvaldo Aranha, the Zionist-leaning UNGA president from Brazil (nudged by the Truman delegation) declared a holiday adjournment until Friday morning.[87] Though falling short of Harry's executive turkey pardon, the Jews had a stay of execution.

About this time, a news flash from Jerusalem announced that Dr. Isaac Herzog, Chief Rabbi of Mandate Palestine, had "wept openly" before the Western Wall, imploring Jehovah: "I pray to you God, to open the gates of heaven to beating Jewish hearts from one end of the globe to the other on this most crucial day of Jewish history since the destruction of the Temple."[88] The UN delay was a welcome birthday present for Dr. Chaim Weizmann who turned seventy-three on November 27. That crisp autumn day would rewrite the book on "getting out the vote"—David "Don Ben-Gurion" would make Nelson Aldrich Rockefeller "an offer he couldn't refuse."

According to the initial Ad Hoc voting pattern, several Central and South American nations (i.e., pro-Vatican) had vacillated in favor of the Arabs.[89] On the second part of the first sub-committee resolution, six voted *against* the Israeli position (Argentina, Brazil, Columbia, Cuba, El Salvador, and Haiti), while five abstained (Bolivia, Ecuador, Honduras, Mexico and Nicaragua). In their *best* showing—the generic procedural vote (sending the measure to the UNGA)—five abstentions remained

(Argentina, Columbia, El Salvador, Honduras and Mexico) along with one absentee nation (Paraguay). Thus, Truman told Acting Secretary of State Lovett to intensify US pressure on the Latin bloc.[90]

However, as Ben-Gurion knew well the anti-Semitic cabal within the Truman administration, he decided to procure his own hedge against the uncertain Latino vote, as well as the number of recent surprise abstentions by various Western nations. To shore up the former, the Zionists paid an impromptu visit to the one American who carried the ultimate clout in that part of the world, Nelson Rockefeller.

In July 1940, FDR appointed Rockefeller to the new position of Coordinator of Inter-American Affairs (CIAA)—ostensibly a cultural/intelligence post to further the standing and security of the US in the southern hemisphere. Of course, Rocky would use it to further his *own* security (i.e., fuel sales to Nazi Germany via neutral Spain). Thus, his *government* staff would exploit the war by "coordinating" (cornering) the Latin market for his *corporate* staff (the region's raw materials being monopolized in the process). While Britain and other capitalist nations in Europe were being denied a legitimate piece of the action, Loftus and Aarons relate, "All through the war, at least while Rockefeller was in charge, everything the Germans wanted in South America they got, from refueling stations to espionage bases."[91] After all, this was the *least* he could do, given that Farben held the second-largest share of the Rockefeller-controlled Standard Oil Company.

Brazil was the only Latin country to field a major military force in WWII, while eleven of the twenty republics (led by Argentina) did not even *declare* war against Germany.[92] Meanwhile (on Rocky's watch), these same fascist governments were quick to ban Charlie Chaplin's misguided propaganda film, *The Great Dictator*, because of its Hitler parody.[93] Then, to exacerbate matters, in 1944 Nelson was promoted to Assistant Secretary of State for Latin American Affairs. One of his "stellar accomplishments" here was to coax the "Magnificent Seven" to declare war on Hitler *no later than* February 1, 1945 (to qualify for UN membership). Argentina, the *numero uno* haven for "rat-liners," would stall until late April—two weeks before Germany surrendered. In June 1945, Rockefeller was a member of the American delegation at the UN Conference on International Organization at San Francisco. His main job now was to "coordinate" the Latin blocs, etc. The self-serving envoy was canned by the new president three months later.

According to Loftus and Aarons, British, American, and Israeli intelligence insiders confided that Rockefeller played a significant, albeit *involuntary*, role in the United Nations vote concerning Israel:

> Ben-Gurion had already accumulated more than enough ammunition against Rockefeller and had decided that he could not take any chances with an indirect approach. There was no time for a British-style media campaign. The Latin American votes were needed in three days. Our American sources insist that the Jews simply laid their cards on the table for Nelson to read and 'blackmailed the h--l out of him.'[94]

The authors' Israeli contact identified Ben-Gurion intel director (and future pioneer Mossad chief) Reuven Shiloah, as the mastermind of the eleventh-hour shakedown. For Nelson, the timing could not have been worse. In a landmark civil case just two months earlier, Federal Judge Charles Clark ruled: "Standard Oil can be considered an enemy national in view of its relationships with I. G. Farben after the United States and Germany had become active enemies."[95]

Rocky coolly examined the incriminating dossier. The contents were *devastating*—his Swiss bank records with Germany; his signed correspondence forming the Reich cartel in South America; transcripts and wiretaps of his conversations with Nazi agents during the war; plus, plenty of ratline complicity with Allen Dulles.[96] Nixon's future vice president then issued a staggering counteroffer: "You can have vengeance, or you can have a country, but you cannot have both."[97] To guarantee the Hispanic bloc, the Jews would have to drop their pursuit of Nazi money and war criminals, especially in the "region of interest." (Naturally, cohorts, like the Dulleses, Pius XII, the Vatican Bank, et al., would also be exempt.) Loftus and Aarons conclude:

> According to our Israeli informant, whose account was corroborated by several other sources in the intelligence community whom we interviewed subsequently, Ben-Gurion's representative was heartsick. Counter-blackmail had not been in the game plan. He made a telephone call to try to obtain guidance. It took several hours before the reply came: 'Yes.' There really was no choice but to give Rockefeller whatever he wanted. On behalf of the still-unborn state of Israel, the promise was formally given to let the Nazis go free. The men who murdered the Jews of Europe were effectively given amnesty, except for the unlucky few who had already been punished.[98]

When the General Assembly resumed deliberations on Friday morning, the partition resolution was still in jeopardy. In fact, upon his arrival, Dr. Aranha told reporters that if a vote were taken then, partition would lose.[99] With Rocky working the phones, another nail-biting adjournment was adopted at 4:38 p.m. by a vote of 25-15. The historic denouement was set to break forth on the Jewish Sabbath.

UN Resolution 181

The final UNGA vote was on Saturday, November 29. Surprisingly to many, Resolution 181 passed by 33-13 with 10 abstentions, a decisive margin of 72%. In the three-day interim, eight countries went from abstaining to affirming, while the nays remained at 13. Apart from Cuba and Greece, all dissenting votes were either Arab or Asian.[100] Given the Herzlian metaphor of "skating on thin ice," it was apropos that the cavernous gray building had formerly housed an ice rink.

Rockefeller had assured Ben-Gurion's private delegation: "Don't worry, every country in Latin America will either vote in favor of Israel or abstain."[101] As numerous Western intelligence officers have confirmed, the power broker delivered the goods—and *then* some. While every Latin member (except Cuba) either voted *for* Israel or abstained, there were two important perks as well. After abstaining from the Ad Hoc vote on Tuesday, Haitian delegate Antonio Vieux had affirmed on Wednesday: "[T]he representative of the Republic of Haiti, in accordance with his Government's views, will vote *against* the partition of Palestine."[102] Yet, on Saturday, Haiti moved into the "yea" column. Also, whereas Paraguay was *away* for the Tuesday vote, her representative returned to endorse UN 181.

While the eminent Jewish historian Howard Sachar acknowledged: "The pivotal bloc of votes in favor of the resolution—not less than 40 percent of the United Nations membership—ultimately was cast by the Latin American delegations," he naively adds, "Zionist pressure here was minimal. Nor was the intercession of the United States anywhere apparent in the Latin American stance."[103] Even pro-Palestinian authors Robert John and Sami Hadawi knew better, citing the *New York Times* of November 30: "British officials felt that the postponement of the vote on Friday had made partition a certainty, since delay had permitted the United States to gain time to bring certain Latin-American republics into line with its own views."[104]

With the UNGA sanction, Zionism had *finally* achieved Theodore Herzl's sole non-negotiable—"[T]he creation of a home for the Jewish people in Palestine to be secured by public law." However, the higher-than-expected margin of victory ultimately proved a bittersweet win for Ben-Gurion and his people. Because some Western nations which had previously abstained changed to a "yea" (specifically France, the Netherlands, and New Zealand), at the end of the day the Latin bloc was *not* the decisive factor. Loftus and Aarons write: "In effect, the extra votes for passage in the UN were bought with the blood of 6 million Jewish victims of the Holocaust."[105] To Ben-Gurion's credit, over the next twelve years (while he was either prime minster or defense minister) the Government of Israel kept its part of the deal. The agreement was not breached until 1960 when the Mossad received special permission to extract Adolf Eichmann from Argentina.

Finally, as a pitiful postscript, having sponsored the epic Balfour Declaration on November 2, 1917, HMG would end the Palestine Mandate thirty years later to the month—choosing *abstention* as "the better part of valor"—joining the likes of Argentina, Ethiopia, and Yugoslavia (behind the *yeas* of Haiti, Liberia, and Russia). The final tally follows: *For* – Australia, Belgium, Bolivia, Brazil, Byelorussian S.S.R., Canada, Costa Rica, Czechoslovakia, Denmark, Dominican Republic, Ecuador, France, Guatemala, Haiti, Iceland, Liberia, Luxembourg, Netherlands, New Zealand, Nicaragua, Norway, Panama, Paraguay, Peru, Philippines, Poland, Sweden, Ukrainian S.S.R., Union of South Africa, U.S.S.R., United States of America, Uruguay, and Venezuela; *Against* – Afghanistan, Cuba, Egypt, Greece, India, Iran, Iraq, Lebanon, Pakistan, Saudi Arabia, Syria, Turkey and Yemen; *Abstained* – Argentina, Chile, China, Columbia, El Salvador, Ethiopia, Honduras, Mexico, Yugoslavia, and last, but not least, the United Kingdom; *Absent* – Thailand.

ARABS THREATEN THEIR OWN "FINAL SOLUTION"

It is both uncanny and ironic, that Jews and Arabs essentially share the same self-defining word to describe the nadir of their collective trauma. The Hebrew word *Shoah*—Jewry's equivalent of the Holocaust—has been rendered by various synonyms, "catastrophe" being among them. For Muslims, *Nakba* Day—meaning "Day of the Catastrophe"—is observed around the date of Israel's Independence.

As the UNGA was about to vote on 181, Jamal al-Husseini, vice president of the Arab Higher Committee (AHC), issued the following threat: "We are solidly and permanently determined to fight to the last man against the existence in our country of any Jewish state, no matter how small it is. If such a state is to be established, it can only be established over our dead bodies."[106] Obviously, a mere 11% of the original Balfour designation was 11% too much. In a concomitant circular, Jamal brashly evoked the infamous phrase coined by his cousin's departed mentor: "The Arabs have taken into their own hands the final solution of the Jewish problem. The problem will be solved only in blood and fire. The Jews will soon be driven out."[107] Thus, the initial Arab response to the Partition Resolution—apart from rejecting it themselves—was an outbreak of pogroms, in many cases condoned (and even facilitated) by the local British authorities.

In the early hours of November 30, a bus carrying twenty-one commuters from Netanya to Jerusalem was riddled by bullets and grenades near the Arab village of Faja. A woman seated behind the driver died instantly, thus becoming the first fatality in the War of Independence. After killing four more and wounding five, the Muslims struck a second bus, causing four casualties.[108] The Arab Higher Committee set a three-day strike ("riot") for December 2-4. Attacks were subsequently launched on Jewish quarters in Jerusalem, Haifa, and Jaffa: bombs tossed into cafes; Molotov cocktails thrown at shops; and car bombs exploded in streets. Jews in Acre were assaulted by their Arab cellmates. British records confirm that 207 Jews and 220 Arabs were killed in the first six weeks following the partition vote.[109]

Even Ben-Gurion had to "duck" on December 7 when his jeep blew a tire in enemy territory. (The new Haganah commander for Jerusalem, Yehoshua Globerman, was killed the next day in the same area.)[110] On December 11, Britain reaffirmed that the Mandate would end on May 14, 1948. Back in October, a Muslim gang met in Lebanon to form the "Arab Liberation Army" (ALA), an irregular pan-Arab invasion force for the coming "defense of Palestine."[111] General Ismail Safwat Pasha, an Iraqi, was put in charge. By February, 3,000 ALA mercenaries had infiltrated Palestine (via Syria), the number pushing 8,000 by April.

The bid to survive was daunting, the Jews being vulnerable in three theaters: twenty-seven isolated Negev kibbutzim; thirty-three colonies in Arab areas; and 100,000 people (one-sixth of the Yishuv) besieged in Jerusalem. The ancient capital was Israel's unique dilemma—*geographically* separated, while *spiritually* inseparable. The enemy's main strategy was ambushing commuter and commercial traffic on the Tel Aviv-Jerusalem highway. A macabre evening ritual at the Egged bus station pictured life in the Holy City. As the daily convoy of steel-plated, eight-ton vehicles ground to a halt before the anxiously waiting crowd, the wounded were the first to exit; the deceased, last.[112]

The ebb-and-flow action was horrific on all fronts. On January 14, 400 Arabs beset the Kfar-Etzion commune north of Hebron. The entire force was neutralized by less than thirty Jewish marksmen who had anticipated the attack route. The next day, a contingent of thirty-five IZL reinforcements from Jerusalem were surprised by a superior Arab force and mowed down to the last man. A British officer later said that "he found the body of one of the fighters with a stone, his last weapon, in his hand."[113] On February 16, another ALA force of 300-500 stormed kibbutz Tirat-Zvi in eastern Galilee. This time, sixty Arabs were killed and 100 wounded, compared to only one Jewish fatality.

The worst tragedy of the six-month Arab-Israeli conflict occurred on April 13, 1948, when a ten-vehicle medical caravan en route to Hadassah Hospital atop Mount Scopus was ambushed with landmines, rifles, machine guns, grenades, and fire bombs, causing the deaths of seventy-seven doctors, nurses, and scientists, including Dr. Chaim Yassky, the hospital director. The Arabs would later try to justify the massacre by spreading an inflated version of Jewish actions at Deir Yasin.[114] (Though not one of Israel's better moments,[115] thankfully, the Irgun atrocity was the exception to the rule.) Many Hadassah victims were burned alive, their remains reduced to ashes. Regarding the others, journalist Daniel Greenfield reported, "The barbarity of the attack was then followed by snapshots of the dead, who in some cases had been decapitated, being sold as postcards as yet another reminder that the enemy was operating on a whole other notion of morality."[116] More shameful is the fact that the *five-hour, daylight* assault happened *less than 600 feet from a British military post.* At three different times British vehicles drove right past the bloodletting with total apathy.[117]

The only place where Jews and Arabs co-existed in peace and harmony was the government insane asylum in Jerusalem. Jacques de

Reynier, the French delegate of the International Red Cross, made the pitiful entry in his diary, *"Vive les fous!"* ("Long live the nuts!")[118]

THE BRITISH "SERGEANT YORK"

The turning point came on April 6 when Haganah forces launched their first offensive, "Operation Nachshon," ending the Jerusalem blockade. Other victories followed in Haifa, Jaffa, Safed, and Tiberias. With one month to independence, Jewish casualties were estimated at 875 dead and 1,858 wounded (Arab figures being 967 and 1,911, respectively). These late ground-sweeping actions would prove to be the key factor in the IDF's ability to withstand the May 15 invasion.

About this time Colonel Meinertzhagen personally entered the fray (unofficially, that is). According to his diary for April 23, 1948 (a Passover Seder), upon his arrival in Haifa (from Arabia) a full scale, shore-line battle was underway between Arabs and Jews. Describing his actions as "grossly irregular behaviour" (his unit only responsible to protect Government stores), the Zionist marksman promptly slipped away unawares and dug in with twenty Haganah fighters at the front:

> My first shot was a bull's-eye and there was a cheer from the Haganah as the man rolled over and writhed about on the sand. I crept forward to a better position and found I could take the Arabs in the flank; which I proceeded to do. Two more paid the penalty. The Haganah kept up with me and between us we got five more...There were now some twenty Arabs firing at us, at ranges between 300 and 600 yards; so we crept on and bagged four more...About an hour later, after we had disposed of all the Arabs in front of us, a Coldstream officer came along, asked who the [blank] I was and on recognizing me, he ordered me back to the ship, which I had to obey; but it mattered little as by then I had fired all my 200 rounds. So off I went, rather sheepishly, and without further incident got aboard... Altogether I had had a glorious day. May Israel flourish![119]

"CHAM"

James Forrestal used the anticipated unrest to launch his own counteroffensive against the tenuous US support for partition. For although Resolution 181 had cleared the General Assembly, it was still vulnerable to a derailment in the Security Council, comprising the so-called "Big Five"—America, Britain, France, China and Russia. (The eventual alignment here would surprise many.)

The anti-Truman forces mobilized a challenge based on "national security." Thus, a Defense Department leak informed the Associated Press that "US military observers were opposed to partition, on the grounds that it might put Russian troops in the Mediterranean within minutes of flying time from the Suez Canal and American Middle East oil concessions."[120] The argument appeared rational enough—Why *else* would Moscow endorse partition if not to forge her own alliance with the pro-Commie Jews? Bogus British intelligence continued to feed Forrestal's paranoia that "the Zionists' immigration and arms-smuggling traffic were part of a wider Soviet-inspired campaign."[121]

However, unbeknown then, Rocky was not the *only* victim of Ben-Gurion's "bargaining" skills. According to two former Israeli agents, the wily Jew told Stalin that the price for his continued silence regarding the still secret Max-Turkul network in Eastern Europe was a complete reversal of his former position on Palestine.[122] Loftus and Aarons write: "There is evidence that Ben-Gurion's blackmail worked. Suddenly, in 1947, the Soviet Union became one of the leading proponents of partitioning Palestine into Arab and Jewish states."[123]

As Team Forrestal maintained its full-court press through the winter and spring, Truman was increasingly aware of his fall re-election bid. (Forrestal, a closet Republican by now, was privately backing Dewey.) The potential of a Soviet-Israeli nexus was proving an easy scare tactic to exploit. So was the threat of a costly US military commitment. Under Secretary of State Robert Lovett provided a policy paper concluding that partition was unworkable; Dean Rusk and Loy Henderson concurred. Facing pressure from George Marshall, on February 17, Truman reluctantly approved a State Department proposal to invoke the conciliatory powers of the Security Council.[124] Partition would be scrapped for a UN trusteeship. Harry did insist, however, that he be shown a final copy of any speeches to be given.[125]

The pile-on began a week later. During a Security Council review of the first monthly progress report of the Palestine Commission, Ambassador Warren Austin (a former Vermont Republican senator) asked his fellow delegates to consider whether an imminent threat to world peace existed due to the pending partition. Ironically, of the major powers that had originally supported the November decision, only Communist Russia continued to hold the line.[126] With the anti-partition cabal on the ascendancy and Truman appearing to weaken, Zionist lobbying efforts intensified. The president would later recall:

> Jewish pressure on the White House did not diminish following the partition vote in the U.N. Individuals and groups asked me, usually in rather quarrelsome and emotional ways, to stop the Arabs, to keep the British from supporting the Arabs, to furnish US soldiers, to do this, that, and the other. I think I can say that I kept my faith in the rightness of my policy in spite of some of the Jews...As the pressure mounted, I found it necessary to give instructions that I did not want to be approached by any more spokesmen for the extreme Zionist cause.[127]

About this time, Weizmann had made a 6,000-mile journey from Palestine just to see the president. Though Truman was initially adamant that not even the ailing "grand old man of the Zionist party" would be accommodated, he was eventually persuaded by his long-time Jewish army pal and former business partner from Kansas City, Eddie Jacobson. Pointing to an equestrian statue of Andy Jackson on a table in the Oval Office, Jacobson won the day by telling Truman that just as *he* had a hero in Jackson, he *also* had a hero—in Weizmann.[128]

Truman and Weizmann respected one another. As the president related, he was not able to pronounce "Chaim" at their first encounter. "So I called him 'Cham.' He liked it. He was a wonderful man, one of the wisest people I think I ever met...a leader, one of the kind you read about."[129] The pair had secretly met in the White House on November 19, just before the pivotal UN vote. Spreading a map on Truman's desk, the brainy acetone inventor had mesmerized the WWI vet and former Missouri farmer with the agricultural potential in the Negev.[130]

On the night of March 18, 1948—with a new Gallup Poll showing that, regardless of what Truman did in Palestine, he would no doubt lose in November—the "little doctor" was quietly ushered into the White

House through the East Wing to avoid reporters. According to both, the forty-five-minute talk was mutually beneficial. Harry wrote, "I felt that he had received a full understanding of my policy and that I knew what it was that he wanted."[131] Chaim likewise: "The President was sympathetic personally, and still indicated a firm resolve to press forward with partition."[132] Though dismissed at the Twenty-Second Congress, Dr. Weizmann had risen to the occasion at the critical hour of decision. The pendulum was swinging back toward the Jews.

TRUMAN BLINDSIDED

Now while Harry and "Cham" were having their timely chat, Forrestal and his allies were completing what amounted to a *fait accompli* of their own. For on the very next day (March 19), despite the president's explicit order that he screen all major Security Council speeches, Austin announced that the US was officially reversing its position on Palestine. Ostensibly, because war was "certain" upon the Brits' departure, he asked the council to suspend the partition plan. The pertinent details called for the UNGA to reconvene in emergency session to replace Resolution 181 with a temporary trusteeship for Palestine under the UN Trusteeship Council, effective May 15.

The Zionists were enraged. Rabbi Silva told the Security Council that Austin's recommendation was a "shocking reversal" and a "final capitulation" to Arab threats. Karsh writes, "America's apparent retreat from partition was seen as effectively signaling the demise of the idea and a huge step toward the ultimate goal of Palestine's immediate transformation into an Arab state."[133]

In the most unthinkable scenario, America's president did not even learn of the debacle until he glanced at the morning paper. To say that Truman was furious would be an understatement. At 7:30 a.m., he phoned Clark Clifford at his home and told him to come to the White House immediately. Harry noted on his calendar: "This morning I find that the State Dept. has reversed my Palestine policy. The first I know about it is what I see in the papers! Isn't that h--l? I'm now in the position of a liar and a double-crosser. I never felt so low in my life. There are people on the 3rd and 4th levels of the State Dept. who have always wanted to cut my throat. They are succeeding in doing it."[134] Clifford wrote: "Truman was in his office as disturbed as I have ever seen him." He was particularly disheartened about his promise to Weizmann, stating: "He must think I'm a sh----s."[135]

THE LAST CONFRONTATION

The president was now referring to his antagonists as the "striped pants *conspirators*."[136] While American Jewry fretted, Harry quietly planned his political revenge. The man who dropped two A-bombs on Japan was not *about* to be intimidated by a pair of his own cabinet members. He began by sacking and replacing Loy Henderson with the pro-Zionist John Hilldring, telling Judge Sam Rosenman, "I have Dr. Weizmann on my conscience." Sachar opines, "There was a certain pathos in Truman's eagerness to regain Weizmann's respect."[137]

By spring, momentum for a "temporary trusteeship" was all but dead due to insane Arab demands. "A strange lethargy overtook the United Nations," recalled Guatemalan delegate, Jorge Granados.[138] On May 12, following an all-night deliberation, Israel's *Minhelet HaAm* ("People's Administration") voted 6-4 to reject a last-minute request by the State Department to postpone a declaration of independence to "avert certain annihilation." In New York at the time, Weizmann endorsed the decision by telephone after reportedly exploding in Yiddish, "What are they waiting for, the idiots?" He then placed an immediate call to Truman requesting further diplomatic pressure.[139]

Consequently—with His Majesty's Government packed and ready to depart (along with scores of Arab civilians) and five Muslim nations preparing to invade—the only "plot" that remained was to smother the newborn state by withholding formal US recognition. (By now the Security Council had declined to intervene.) Thus, the time had now arrived for the politically neutral Five-Star General of the Army, George C. Marshall—one of the most popular and respected postwar figures in America—to give *Harry* the proverbial "what for."

At 4 p.m. on Wednesday, May 12—exactly fifty hours to Israeli statehood—George Catlett Marshall and Robert Abercrombie Lovett (accompanied by two officials from State) marched into the Oval Office. Truman was seated behind his famous plaque, "The Buck Stops Here." Clifford and two aides rounded out the participants. The under secretary began by criticizing the Jewish Agency and then launched into a lengthy pitch for trusteeship. In the course of his remarks, Lovett chose a most indelicate idiom, saying that a premature recognition of the Jewish state would be analogous to "buying a *pig* in a poke."[140] Marshall followed by assuring his "commander-in-chief" that the military was not prepared to intervene on Israel's behalf in the likely event of war. He concluded by asserting that America should endorse UN trusteeship while deferring any decision on recognition.

Truman then directed that his White House counsel brief the secretary on the president's bias for recognition. "'As I talked,' Clifford recalled, 'I noticed the thunder clouds gathering—Marshall's face getting redder and redder.'" Marshall then remonstrated, "'I don't even understand why Clifford is here. This is not a political meeting,'" to which the president calmly replied, "'General, he is here because I asked him to be here.'"[141] Clifford's presentation took about fifteen minutes, during which he explained the Balfour Declaration, revisited the tragedy of the Shoah, and validated the Zionists' claim by quoting Deuteronomy 1:8, *"Behold, I have set the land before you: go in and possess the land which the LORD sware unto your fathers, Abraham, Isaac, and Jacob, to give unto them and their seed after them."*

Well, the general had certainly heard enough. After trashing "Clark's" position, Marshall flexed his political muscle and looked right at Truman. Clifford writes: "Speaking with barely contained rage and more than a hint of self-righteousness, he made the most remarkable threat I ever heard anyone make directly to a President: 'If you follow Clifford's advice and if I were to vote in the election, I would vote against you.'... Everyone in the room was stunned."[142] McCullough states that the remark, regarded by Clifford as "the sharpest rebuke *ever* for him," coming from "the great one of the age," brought the meeting to a 'grinding halt.'"[143] Instead of pledging his support for a Jewish state, the secretary of state left Truman in a *different* state: "There was really a state of shock," Clark recalled. "The President, I think, was struck dumb by it...There was this awful, *total*, silence." Truman attempted to defuse the situation, feigning that he was "inclined to agree with General Marshall, but thought it best they all sleep on the matter."[144] The president now had less than two days to make the most important decision of his life. Marshall's rejoinder fell short of an explicit threat to resign. To incur his wrath over Israel would send Dewey to the White House come November. Harry would have to rise to the maxim displayed on his other famous office sign—"If you can't take the heat, stay out of the kitchen."

A BAR OF RUSTED IRON

On Thursday afternoon, May 13, a contingent of His Majesty's troops vacated the Jewish Quarter of Old Jerusalem, marching upon the ancient cobblestones to the skirl of British bagpipes. Suddenly, the last detachment veered up a twisting alley, stopping in front of No. 3 Or Chayim Street, home to Rabbi Mordechai Weingarten, senior resident of the venerable district. Co-authors Larry Collins and Dominique Lapierre write in *O Jerusalem!*:

> Lost in his thoughts, he hesitated a moment at the knock on his door. He got up, put on his black vest and jacket, adjusted his gold-rimmed spectacles and his black hat, and stepped into the courtyard. There before Weingarten stood a middle-aged British major wearing the yellow-and-red insignia of the Suffolk Regiment. From his right hand dangled a bar of rusted iron almost a foot long. With a solemn gesture he offered it to the elderly rabbi. It was a key, the key to Zion Gate, one of the seven gates of the Old City of Jerusalem. 'From the year 70 A.D. until today,' he said, 'a key to the gates of Jerusalem has never been in Jewish hands. This is the first time in eighteen centuries that your people have been so privileged.'
>
> Weingarten extended a trembling hand to accept the key. Jewish legend held that on the night the Roman Emperor Titus destroyed the Temple, its despairing priests had thrown the keys of Jerusalem to heaven crying 'God henceforth be thou the guardian of the keys.' Now the improbable agent of their return to Jewish hands stood to attention and saluted. 'Our relations have not always been easy,' he said, 'but let us part as friends. Good luck and goodbye.' 'Blessed art Thou, O Lord,' murmured Weingarten, 'Who had granted us life and sustenance and permitted us to reach this day.' Then, addressing the Englishman, he said, 'I accept this key in the name of my people.'[145]

As the major and his troops departed the Quarter (their presence being immediately filled by privy members of the Haganah), a menacing cacophony replaced the fading Celtic pipes—the sound of Arab guns.

DECLARATION OF INDEPENDENCE

The next morning, May 14, Sir Alan Cunningham, Britain's last High Commissioner of Palestine, quit Jerusalem in his bullet-proof Daimler limousine. All remaining troops, civilians, and civil servants followed close behind, ending nearly three decades of British suzerainty. (The timing was none too soon as 128 Jewish men and women would be massacred at Kfar Etzion the following day—*after their surrender*.)

With the Red Cross flag replacing the Union Jack over Government House, the Battle for Jerusalem commenced. Here and elsewhere, Haganah and Irgun forces scrambled to occupy whatever official buildings and control posts not already ceded to the Arabs. (On a technical point, Britain's *military* rule ceased on June 30 with their evacuation of Haifa harbor.)

By 4:00 p.m., some 350 invited guests were assembled at the Tel Aviv Art Museum (formerly the home of Tel Aviv's first mayor, Meir Dizengoff; today, Independence Hall). Standing before a large, framed portrait of Theodore Herzl, flanked by two Star of David flags, David Ben-Gurion gaveled the meeting to order, prompting a spontaneous singing of "HaTikvah." The prime minister-designate then spent the next *twelve* minutes reading the Declaration of Independence live over the first "legal" broadcast of *Kol Yisrael.* After a reciting of the *She'Hecheyanu* blessing by Rabbi Yehuda Fishman, the parchment was signed by twenty-five of the thirty-seven members of the Provisional State Council (eleven of the missing signatories being "detained" in besieged Jerusalem).

With the signing completed, the crowd rose to its feet as the Israel Philharmonic Orchestra played "HaTikvah." Ben-Gurion then concluded the historic occasion with the words: "The State of Israel is established! This meeting is adjourned!" Stella Yollin, a Holocaust survivor who rode the last train from Łódź to Auschwitz, and later shared the same barrack with Anne Frank at Bergen-Belsen, described the euphoria that erupted outside: "Everyone was dancing in the streets with joy. We were all dancing in the streets all night long. We were so happy."[146] In a candid endorsement of Israel's unequivocal legitimacy, the Associated Press rightly observed: "Is it of the Jews, one of the most ancient peoples, who can say—as few if any others can—that they won independence in the year 5708 of their history?"[147]

AMERICA RECOGNIZES ISRAEL

Back in the Beltway—at the very moment the Declaration was being read in Tel Aviv—Clifford was on the phone with Eliahu Epstein, head of the Jewish Agency's Political Department in Washington, asking that a letter be rushed to Truman before 12 a.m., formally requesting that the United States recognize the new Jewish state.

This was in tandem with an overnight letter just arrived from Weizmann petitioning the same. Clark writes: "Even without a clear signal from Lovett and Marshall, I felt we had to set in motion the machinery for recognition, in the event that a favorable decision was made." After hanging up in a spirit of euphoria, Epstein suddenly rang back in a panic: "We've never done this before, and we're not quite sure how to go about it." Clark then relates that he referred Epstein to "two of the wisest lawyers in Washington, David Ginsburg and Benjamin Cohen…strong supporters of the Zionist cause. Working together with me during the rest of the morning, Epstein and his team drafted the recognition request."[148]

The ensuing pace was so intense that when Eliahu's aide, Harry Zinder, drove off with the finished papers, the name of the new country was left blank. Because it was yet to be determined (most assuming "Judea"), Epstein had simply typed "the Jewish State." However, when only moments later he heard on his shortwave radio that "Israel" would be the name, he immediately dispatched a second courier to overtake Zinder with the update. (See the uncanny parallel of Ahimaaz and Cushi in II Samuel 18:22-29.) Clark writes: "Two blocks from the White House, Zinder, sitting in the car Epstein had provided, crossed out with a pen the words "Jewish State" and inserted the word "Israel." Zinder then proceeded to my office. It was the first time I had heard the name of the new state."[149] (In 1949, Epstein, as Eliahu Elath, became the first Israeli ambassador to America.)

Meanwhile, the discerning Marshall must have had a few restless moments of his own, having "slept on the matter." Around 4:00 p.m., Lovett called Clark: "I have talked to the General. He cannot support the President's position, but he has agreed that he will not oppose it."[150] With George sulking, Lovett promptly rang Truman to confirm that the general had finally recanted. The game of "Chicken" was over; with two hours to go, Marshall *flinched*. As the clock ticked down, Truman was heard to murmur at 5:16 p.m., "The old Doctor will believe me now."[151] Finally—at the stroke of midnight (once again, *twelve* being Israel's number)—the British Mandate terminated and the *Medinat Yisrael* ("State of Israel") was officially proclaimed by David Ben-Gurion. And, exactly eleven minutes later, at 6:11 p.m. EST, Truman's press secretary, Charlie Ross, beckoned the White House press corps into the West Wing and read the following *de facto* recognition of the new Jewish State:

> Statement by the President: This Government has been informed that a Jewish state has been proclaimed in Palestine, and recognition has been requested by the Provisional Government thereof. The United States recognizes the provisional government as the de facto authority of the new State of Israel. Signed: Harry Truman. Approved, May 14, 1948.

From a scriptural perspective, this magnanimous action would constitute America's finest hour (the "striped-pants boys/conspirators" notwithstanding). That the president's courageous stand for Jewish statehood came to fruition at 6:11 p.m. (specifically scrawled on the press release) bears testimony to the words of another selfless politician preserved in Nehemiah 6:11, *"Should such a man as I flee?"* Truman's near-solo feat was the stellar exception to the prevailing rule of Anglo-American anti-Semitism. For a brief, though ineffable moment, the "locksmiths" had met their match—*one* Missourian following the homespun wisdom of *another*—"Always do right. This will gratify some people and astonish the rest" (Mark Twain).

Nearly everyone at the United Nations was "astonished" to hear of Truman's action—*especially* the US diplomats who were busy garnering votes for a resolution on trusteeship. McCullough writes:

> The American delegation at the United Nations was flabbergasted. Some American delegates actually broke into laughter, thinking the announcement must be somebody's idea of a joke. Ambassador Austin, the only one of the delegation who had been notified in advance and only at the last moment, was so upset he went home without telling any of the others. At the State Department, meantime, Marshall had dispatched his head of U.N. affairs, Dean Rusk, by plane to New York to keep the whole delegation from resigning."[152]

In one of the weirder moments, when Cuba's envoy, Guillermo Belt, *took off* for the podium to announce his nation's withdrawal from the UN, he had to be physically restrained by the Americans, press officer Porter McKeever literally sitting on his lap.[153] Of course, beyond Flushing Meadows, massive celebrations were spreading throughout Jewish neighborhoods in all five boroughs ("We're just wild about Harry," etc.). In the wake of mass criticism, Truman wrote: "I was told that to some of the career men of the State Department this announcement came as a surprise. It should not have been if these men had faithfully supported my policy...I wanted to make it plain that the President of the United States, and not the second or third echelon in the State Department, is responsible for making foreign policy."[154]

The May 15 front-page headline of the *Palestine Post* read: "STATE OF ISRAEL IS BORN." As with the November 29 partition vote, May 15 fell on the Sabbath. However, of far greater import, the fact that the first diplomatic recognition of Israel occurred in the *eleventh* minute of her existence revealed that *"the times of the Gentiles..."* (Luke 21:24) were now about to end ("eleven" representing the scriptural numeric for crisis or disintegration, i.e., American Airlines Flight 11 striking the first of the Twin Towers on September 11 in New York City, 11 letters, New York the 11th state in the Union, etc.). And so, with the Muslim hordes "almost" as enraged as Truman's cabinet, the following cablegram was dispatched from the Secretary-General of the League of Arab States to the Secretary-General of the United Nations on that first day of Israel's renewal:

> The recent disturbances in Palestine further constitute a serious and direct threat to peace and security within the territories of the Arab States themselves. For these reasons, and considering that the security of Palestine is a sacred trust for them, and out of anxiousness to check the further deterioration of the prevailing conditions and to prevent the spread of disorder and lawlessness into the neighbouring Arab lands, and in order to fill the vacuum created by the termination of the Mandate and the failure to replace it by any legally constituted authority, the Arab Governments find themselves compelled to intervene for the sole purpose of restoring peace and security and of establishing law and order in Palestine.[155]

The prospect of an imminent Israeli military defeat was the last solace in the Forrestal camp. As five Arab armies, *trained and equipped with modern British weapons*, were precipitating the nascent state's first "crisis"—invading from the south, east, and north—a secondary *Post* headline read: "Egyptian Air Force Spitfires Bomb Tel Aviv; One Shot Down."[156] For the record, while Russia granted *de jure* recognition to Israel two *days* later, Britain's sanction did not arrive until two *years* later (April 27, 1950). Israel's *greatest* enemy, the so-called "Holy See," did not establish diplomatic relations with Tel Aviv until 1993! And a host of anti-Semitic naysayers like Alison Weir, Henry Cattan, Pitman Potter, Quincy Wright, Jeremy Hammond, et al., *still* do not believe that the partition resolution was legally effective or binding on the Palestinian people.[157] Like the Old Testament prophet wrote in Ezekiel 18:2, *"The fathers have eaten sour grapes...."*

GENESIS 12:3

As the Lord declared, *"And I will bless them that bless thee, and curse him that curseth thee,"* Truman and Forrestal would each experience their own unique payback. For Harry, it was that iconic photo (taken at the St. Louis train station when he was returning from Independence to Washington) showing the jubilant president displaying a copy of the *Chicago Tribune* from November 3, prematurely stating: "DEWEY DEFEATS TRUMAN." (The Republican-leaning paper had called Harry a "nincompoop" in an editorial on June 10, 1948.[158])

Despite having slumped to a 36% standing in the polls that spring, Harry "squeaked by" in November, garnering 303 electoral votes to the popular New York governor's 189. Only weeks before, a *Newsweek* poll of fifty Washington journalists revealed that not *one* of them believed that Truman could win.[159] Comedian Bob Hope sent the incumbent president a one-word congratulatory telegram: "Unpack." For what it's worth, the "nincompoop" was also voted *Time* magazine's "Man of the Year" for 1948 (having won in 1945 as well).

As for James Forrestal, his "striped breeches" split within months. Just prior to the election the popular columnist, Drew Pearson, had exposed the highly unethical Forrestal-Dewey alliance. By late December, Truman also learned that his defense secretary was experiencing "a total psychotic breakdown...characterized by suicidal features."[160]

Forrestal was subsequently "asked" to tender his resignation, whereupon he complied on March 29. Four days later, he was confined to the mental ward at Bethesda Naval Hospital.

In the early hours of May 22, 1949—one week after the first anniversary of the State of Israel—Forrestal fell to his death from a window near his room on the 16th floor. He reportedly tied his dressing gown sash to a radiator, knotted the other end around his neck, and jumped (the cord breaking in the process). In his final days, Forrestal was allegedly heard "screaming that the Jews and Communists were crawling on the floor of his room seeking to destroy him."[161] Though many conspiracy theorists believe that Forrestal's "suicide" was something more sinister (Weir even implying a possible Zionist plot[162]), a "curse" by any other name is *still* a curse; i.e., "If you mess with the Jew, God will mess with you!" Thus, having messed with Israel, James *Forrestal* morphed into *Forrest* Gump (Daniel 4:33).

Should any doubt remain, America's first supercarrier, the USS *Forrestal*—completed in 1954 by 16,000 engineers, draftsmen, and builders as the Navy's highest honor to its former secretary—later went on to experience her *own* ignoble demise. While in the Gulf of Tonkin on July 29, 1967 (just after the Six-Day War), a "stray voltage" triggered a freak missile launch from an F-4 Phantom parked on the runway, hitting an armed A-4 Skyhawk (piloted by future senator, Lt. Cmdr. John McCain). In the ensuing fiery chain reaction, 134 men were killed with 161 injured; 21 aircraft were also lost in the $72 million accident. On the uncanny date of September 11, 1993, the CV-59 was decommissioned and stricken from the Naval Vessel Register. All subsequent efforts to donate the historic carrier for use as a museum or memorial were, oddly, declined. On October 22, 2013, the 1,063 foot, 80,000-ton USS *Forrestal* (now known as the "USS Forrest Fire"), built for $217 million ($2 billion today), was sold to a Texas scrap yard for *one* penny! Conversely, the official website for the Nimitz-class USS *Harry S. Truman* (CVN 75) currently describes the president's legacy as "the finest aircraft carrier in the fleet."[163]

Harry Truman was the last chief executive in modern times elected without a college degree. He was also the last White House occupant who was not a millionaire. To be sure, Truman would make his share of political blunders. And though Baptist by *profession*, "Brother Truman's" notorious profanity, dancing, poker playing, bourbon drinking, and

Masonic affiliation (plus several aberrant doctrinal remarks) place him *way* outside of a scriptural testimony (I John 2:15). His secular biographer was more gracious, stating that "he was only a reasonably good Baptist as the term was understood in Grandview."[164] Describing himself as a "Lightfoot Baptist" in a letter dated March 19, 1911, to his future wife, Bess Wallace, the worldly-wise suitor candidly acknowledged: "I am not very strong as a Baptist."[165]

On the other hand, Truman's personal integrity was legendary (an anomaly in politics). As presidential pensions did not exist then, the Trumans spent their golden years living on Harry's military stipend from World War I. And, like fellow veteran Alvin York, he declined several lucrative commercial endorsements rather than compromise the dignity of his office. (This author's late father—a former security provider at Margaret Truman Daniel's Manhattan apartment building—having observed and conversed with the retired president during his occasional visits, once remarked: "Truman was so honest he probably never took a postage stamp from the White House.")

At the end of the day, despite his many shortcomings (both sacred and secular), Harry S. Truman was *familiar* enough with the Bible (having read it through a dozen times in his youth) to know *where* the Jews belonged; *discerning* enough to sense his providential role in the prophetic window; and *courageous* enough to hazard his political career to bring the miracle to fruition. He was at least truer to the scriptural view of Israel than his British nemesis, Foreign Secretary Bevin, whose own *Baptist* affiliation[166] cast him as the *key* "Laodicean locksmith" in the closing phase of Israel's struggle for statehood (Luke12:48). Thus, when Yitzhak HaLevi Herzog, Chief Rabbi of Israel, visited the White House on May 10, 1949, he stunned Truman by saying: "God put you in your mother's womb so you would be the instrument to bring the rebirth of Israel after two thousand years." David Niles remarked, "I thought he was overdoing things, but when I looked over at the President, tears were running down his cheeks."[167]

And those were not the last tears that he would shed over Eretz Yisrael. On May 8, 1951, Prime Minister David Ben-Gurion visited Washington to present Truman with a Menorah for his 67th birthday. Ten years later, the two senior statesmen met again at Ben-Gurion's Waldorf suite. (Harry was now retired; the prime minister, serving his second term.) Ben-Gurion's account of their final encounter is a fitting conclusion to this opening section of *Holy Ground*:

At our last meeting, after a very interesting talk, just before [the President] left me – it was in a New York hotel suite – I told him that as a foreigner I could not judge what would be his place in American history; but his helpfulness to us, his constant sympathy with our aims in Israel, his courageous decision to recognize our new state so quickly and his steadfast support since then had given him an immortal place in Jewish history. As I said that, tears suddenly sprang to his eyes. And his eyes were still wet when he bade me goodbye. I had rarely seen anyone so moved. I tried to hold him for a few minutes until he had become more composed, for I recalled that the hotel corridors were full of waiting journalists and photographers. He left. A little while later, I too had to go out, and a correspondent came to me to ask, "Why was President Truman in tears when he left you?"[168]

"Thou tellest my wanderings: put thou my tears into thy bottle: are they not in thy book?"
(Psalm 56:8)

PART II

Survival through Statehood

14

The War of Independence

"...lead me to the rock that is higher than I. For thou hast been a shelter for me, and a strong tower from the enemy."
(Psalm 61:2-3)

"Each of us, in his own way, believes in the 'Rock of Israel' as he conceives it."
(David Ben-Gurion, May 1948)

"There is a way which seemeth right unto a man, but the end thereof are the ways of death."
(Proverbs 14:12)

"Of the Rock that begat thee thou art unmindful, and hast forgotten God that formed thee."
(Deuteronomy 32:18)

"...and that Rock was Christ."
(I Corinthians 10:4)

ISRAEL'S DECLARATION OF Independence was immediately followed by her War of Independence. The undeniable supernatural deliverance of the *latter* was conspicuously inconsistent with a shameful policy decision involving the *former*. The final wording of the Declaration was approved by the *Moetzet HaAm* ("People's Council") in a hurried ninety-minute session at the Jewish National Fund building in Tel Aviv on May 14. (The meeting adjourned at 3:00 p.m., *one* hour before the historic proclamation was read over the airwaves by David

Ben-Gurion.) The two remaining issues concerned borders and religion. After agreeing to delete the specific perimeters prescribed by the United Nations, the framers zeroed in on the Yishuv's last order of business—*whether or not God's name would appear in the concluding section of the document.*

The contested draft proposed: "Placing our trust in 'the Almighty' we affix our signatures to this Proclamation," etc. While Rabbi Moshe Shapira wanted the more personal "God of Israel" (or "the Almighty and Redeemer of Israel"), the secularist Aharon Zisling decried *any* allusion to deity, arguing for his side that "God died with their families in the Shoah." In the end, Ben-Gurion prevailed upon his colleagues to adopt "Rock of Israel" as the most expedient compromise, a most ironic contradiction, given that the same government had named their new nation "Israel," meaning "Prince with GOD" (Genesis 32:28).

Incredibly—with *five* (the death number) Arab armies poised on Israel's borders—the phrase was seen as duplicitous enough to satisfy believers and atheists alike. Such a "Rock" could be conveniently interpreted as referring to God *or* Eretz Yisrael. As the first prime minister reasoned: "Each of us, in his own way, believes in the 'Rock of Israel' as he conceives it."[1] Ben-Gurion would have been wiser to have heeded the warning in Proverbs 14:12, *"There is a* WAY *which seemeth right unto a man, but the end thereof are the ways of death."*

Dr. Eliezer Segal, professor of religious studies at the University of Calgary, writes: "I personally find it hard to imagine that an enthusiastic Bible scholar like Ben-Gurion would have been taken in by his own non-theological interpretation of 'Rock of Israel.'"[2] He then cites David's usage in II Samuel 23:3, which reads in the KJV: *"The God of Israel said, the* ROCK OF ISRAEL *spake to me, He that ruleth over men must be just, ruling in the fear of God."* While the document's English translation (by Moshe Sharett, Israel's second prime minister) referenced in nearly all official records, rendered the generic "rock" as "Almighty God," the more literal (and politically correct) "Rock of Israel" was "set in stone" by a Knesset vote in 1962.

With Herzl's portrait behind him as he read, Ben-Gurion's pragmatism was at least consistent with the founder. As previously cited, Herzl shared his view of religion in a letter to his Jewish boss, "I consider religion indispensable for the weak…God is a magnificent symbol for an enormous complex of moral and legal imperatives, the apparent solution to riddles, the answer to all childish questions. Which religion, or which god, really makes no difference...."

The tragic irony of May 14, 1948, is that the architects of the new Jewish state were *religious* enough to ensure that the signing ceremony ended by Shabbat, yet *secular* enough to bar God's name from the parchment. As if to illustrate the resultant stench in God's nostrils, the tightly packed hall consigned the transmitter conveying the obnoxious snub to a toilet just off the museum's main gallery (Amos 4:10; 5:21).[3] As previously noted, the nation's first president, Dr. Chaim Weizmann believed that science would be Israel's panacea, stating in 1946, "I feel sure that science will bring to this land both peace and a renewal of its youth, creating here, the springs of a new material and spiritual life."[4]

Fortunately for apostate Israel, the applicable prerecorded attitude of the God of Abraham, Isaac, and Jacob toward *"oppositions of* SCIENCE *falsely so called"* affirmed: *"If we believe not, yet he abideth faithful: he cannot deny himself."* (I Timothy 6:20; II Timothy 2:13) As the following chapters in this second section of *Holy Ground* reveal, the LORD would enable His covenant nation to *survive* one war after another—*whether they believed in Him or not*!

OVERVIEW

The 1948 War began unofficially with the internal Palestinian revolt following the passage of UN Resolution 181 on November 30, 1947. It is vital to remember that the Arab League unanimously rejected the resolution despite the fact that it offered the Palestinians 87% of Mandatory Palestine (leaving the Zionists with only 1/6 of 1% of the designated "Arab World"). Unwilling to acknowledge *Jehovah's* existence, the State of Israel was ultimately attacked by eight distinct belligerents unwilling to recognize *them*: two domestic terror cells, the Holy War Army (HWA) and the Arab Liberation Army (ALA); five external nation armies, Egypt, Transjordan, Syria, Lebanon, and Iraq; plus a token Saudi auxiliary detachment under Egyptian command.

As previously noted, the two-part catastrophic encounter was named "al-Nakba." The invasion phase (May 15, 1948-March 10, 1949) consisted of three stages (first fruits, main harvest, and gleanings) divided by two feckless UN ceasefires. On December 11, 1948, the General

Assembly adopted Resolution 194, defining principles for reaching a final settlement and returning "Palestinian refugees" to their homes. The last armistice was signed with Syria on July 20, 1949. The War of Independence was the costliest crisis in Israel's history, resulting in 6,373 killed (including 2,400 civilians), roughly 1% of the population, with five times as many wounded. Total military expenditures were nearly $500 million.

ARMS EMBARGO

When a reporter asked David Dinkins to recall his initial impression upon becoming the first black mayor of New York City, he insisted that his experience was not the vicarious dilemma of a dog that had finally caught the car he was always chasing, i.e., "*Now* what do I do?" The tiny State of Israel *was* faced with this reality.

On December 5, 1947, George Marshall declared an arms embargo on all combatants in the expanding Middle East crisis. Having pushed the envelope with his surprise endorsement of Israel, Harry was ill-prepared to reverse the Marshall doctrine. (At least such pre-election acquiescence showed that his earlier magnanimity was not solely about votes). According to divine providence, President Truman was now in the role of King Darius, who, being hamstrung by similar political realities, had to pass a sleepless night before enquiring, *"O Daniel...is thy God, whom thou servest continually, able to deliver thee from the lions?"* (Daniel 6:20) Of course, modern Israel was a *long* way from serving Jehovah. Thus, once again, while Laodicea's political locksmiths took their cue from their apostate religious counterparts—keeping the Jewish Saviour out in the cold—the LORD Himself would intervene, for *"hath he said, and shall he not do it? or hath he spoken, and shall he not make it good?"* (Numbers 23:19)

The rank hypocrisy of contrived US "neutrality" was that the Arabs had already been armed to the teeth by the British[5] vis-à-vis an annual military subsidy of £2,000,000.[6] Thus, Britain's own "embargo," imposed in February 1948, was equally disingenuous. Furthermore, as Loftus and Aarons document, certain German POWs (i.e., hardcore, Jew-hating Nazis) still being "held" in Egypt were somehow "escaping" and finding their way into Palestine via Muslim ratlines "where they became instructors for the Arab units."[7]

Arabist Alison Weir inanely states, "Zionist military units…before the UN vote…had acquired massive weaponry…were better equipped and had more men under arms than their opponents."[8] She then cites the equally biased Kathleen Christison: "America's diplomats…knew from the beginning that the Arabs were certain losers in their war with Israel. Every source confirmed the overwhelming military superiority of the Israelis over their Arab opponents."[9]

However, as we have already seen, the two most powerful officials in the Truman administration were predicting the very opposite. While Defense Secretary Forrestal told Clark Clifford: "Forty million Arabs are going to push four hundred thousand Jews into the sea."[10] General Marshall went on record, warning, "militarily the Jews were embarked on a very risky venture in Palestine, and should the tide turn against them, there was nothing to guarantee help from the United States."[11]

CLANDESTINE OPERATIONS

This was not the first time that Jews were deprived of weapons in their own ethnoscape. I Samuel 13:19 says, *"Now there was no smith found throughout all the land of Israel: for the Philistines said, Lest the Hebrews make them swords of spears…."* During the Mandate, Yishuv leaders had to think outside the box in matters of homeland security.

Yosef Avidar, director of Israel's covert military production, once camouflaged a subterranean ordnance plant as a kibbutz right under the Brits' noses. Situated adjacent to a Royal army base (between Nes Ziona and Rehovot), the audacious operation, code-named the Ayalon Institute, manufactured more than two million 9 mm bullets from 1945 to 1948 (importing millions of lipstick tubes from British cosmetic concerns for the more particular nine-millimeter rounds). In fact, the ruse was so effective that British officers actually took their uniforms to the kibbutz laundry.[12] ("No tickee, no shirtee!") To keep their patrons away, the Jews even ran a pick-up/delivery service.

In another instance, Chaim Slavin, the Russian-born electrical engineer regarded as the father of Israel's military industries, learned that the British were dumping outdated cordite (five-year shelf life) into the

Mediterranean. Reminiscent of the other Chaim's acetone experiments which ensured the production of cordite in World War I, Leonard Slater writes: "Slavin sent down divers to bring it up, then put a roomful of young women to work with impoverished machines made of razor blades to chop up the congealed chunks and dry out the explosive [Slavin later relating], 'It was a great victory.'"[13]

The main hub for illicit exports at this time was Milan, Italy. France would also prove a generous source of weapons procurement[14] (as with Israel's initial purchase of ten Hotchkiss "H-39" light tanks). The Haganah Secret Service (forerunner to Shin Bet, the Israel Security Agency or ISA) appointed Yehuda Arazi to oversee the Italian arms-smuggling operation. British officials would later learn (to their chagrin) that Arazi had acquired much of his hardware (including gas) from them, having disguised himself as part of the respectable anti-Communist Polish Anders émigré group. Arazi's men were also adept at salvaging sunken armaments, including shells and guns.

To circumvent the Admiralty's blockade, the Zionists set up a small, unobtrusive navy of their own, run by an intel front in Tangier (across from Gibraltar).[15] By the end of 1947, 193 Bren guns, 1,500 rifles, 378 sub-machine guns and over a million rounds of ammo had been acquired by Haganah and Irgun Ops.[16] However, while such meager stores had been adequate for containing locals, a major spike of firepower would be needed to meet the threat of five Arab armies.

With his back to the wall, Ben-Gurion made several trips to the United States to recruit powerful Jews willing to underwrite an illegal gunrunning operation to Palestine. His prime contact was Manhattan industrialist Rudolf Goldschmid Sonneborn, scion of a wealthy German-Jewish family from Baltimore. The two men, acquaintances since 1910, initially enlisted seventeen likeminded American Zionists for the secret mission.[17] Known as the "Sonneborn Institute," the expanded coterie would eventually purchase, then bootleg—at great personal risk—enough stockpiles of weapons, ammo, and explosives, including machinery for an indigenous small arms industry, to help counterbalance the British-backed Arab Legion. Sometimes the contraband was detected and confiscated. One of the more publicized snafus occurred on January 3, 1947, at Jersey City's Pier F on the New York waterfront ("I coulda been a contendah!"). After a crate marked "Used Industrial Machinery" was dropped and damaged while being loaded aboard the *SS Executor*, several tins designated "TNT Corps of Engineers, U.S. Army" were found during the repair. The FBI impounded 190 tons of the high explosives bound for Palestine.[18]

Another sort of stateside covert Zionism was performed by Hillel Kook, the senior Irgun officer outside of Palestine. Traveling under the alias of "Peter H. Bergson," his mission was to mobilize financial aid for the expansion of paramilitary units in Eretz Yisrael. Kook and his team (known from the late 1930s as "Bergsonites," or "Bergson Boys") also employed a vigorous lobbying campaign on behalf of Jewish statehood, remaining under the radar by utilizing a labyrinth of ambiguous front organizations (Committee for a Jewish Army of Stateless and Palestinian Jews, American League for a Free Palestine, Hebrew Committee for National Liberation, Emergency Committee for the Rescue of European Jewry, et al.). Their public venues enlisted the support of various celebrities such as Frank Sinatra, Dean Martin, Edward G. Robinson, Leonard Bernstein, and Marlon Brando.[19]

CZECH GUNS VIA RICHARD & ROBERT

Jilted by the West, Ben-Gurion was ultimately forced to procure his first and most significant weapons cache from behind the descending Iron Curtain. (Israel's future would be secured by Golda Meir's early 1948 cross-country fund raising tour in America, procuring fifty-million dollars in Jewish contributions.) It was fitting that the source was Czechoslovakia, given her betrayal by Britain and later Nazi occupation. (As late as 2012, a UN resolution to make "Palestine" a non-Member Observer State was voted against by the Czech Republic—the sole European country, and one of only nine to do so, against 138 yeas and 41 abstentions.)

In late November 1946, two young Jews arrived in Vienna from Paris. The men were Haganah intelligence agents Georg Überall (later known as Ehud Avriel) and future six-term Jerusalem mayor, Theodor "Teddy" Kollek (a.k.a. "The greatest builder of Jerusalem since Herod"[20]). Their original assignment was transporting Jewish refugees from Austria to Palestine. Their first contact was Harry-Peter Smolka-Smollett, a *London Times* correspondent in Austria and childhood friend of Teddy. To avoid the British, the men agreed to hold their meetings at the Esquire

Club, a popular watering hole in the American district of Vienna. At their next conference, Smolka-Smollett showed up with a British officer, introducing him as Ludwig "Lev" Hoch, a Czech Jew. Hoch was an interrogator for the local MI6 office and would navigate the cadre through British checkpoints in the capital.

Smolka-Smollett then recommended that Kollek and Überall meet another well-connected friend recently settled in Salzburg. Shortly thereafter, the four Zionists conferred with the man at a Salzburg eatery. The next day they visited local refugee facilities. After several weeks of shuttling between Vienna and Salzburg, Kollek finally broached his greater burden during a discussion at the Esquire—acquiring arms for Palestine. While Smolka-Smollett quickly ruled out Austria, Hoch hinted that they should try the Czechs, noted for their munitions expertise (lately exploited by Nazi Germany). When Kollek and Überall asked how they might do this, Smolka-Smollett had a ready reply; he told them to ask their newfound colleague in Salzburg.

About this time (February 1947), David Ben-Gurion burst on the scene, ostensibly to tour DP camps. However, his real purpose was to see "the Jew from Salzburg." Before Ben-Gurion departed, "Richard" assured him of his personal commitment to the struggle ahead. In a follow-up talk with Kollek and Überall, the man lifted a letterhead from his wallet bearing the emblem of the nationalized *Zbrojovka Brno* (ZB) arms plant in Czechoslovakia—signing his full name on the back—Richard Joseph *Kauder*. He then handed the paper to Kollek, saying, "Give this to Otto Šling in Brno and tell him that I asked him to help you." Šling, a Bohemian Jew, had originally sent the stationery to Kauder (via Smolka-Smollett) with the attached message: "Give this to Richard and tell him that if he needs anything, I will be happy to help. Tell him to write 'Kauder' on the back of the paper and I will know that it is from him."[21] In his book, *The Hitler Kiss: A Memoir of the Czech Resistance*, Radomir Luza writes: "As secretary of the regional committee of the Communist Party in Brno, Šling decided the affairs of everyone in and around the city…."[22] Ziv-Tal affirms, "This was the first step towards the arms deal with the Czech Republic."[23]

Having saved both the Yishuv from genocide and the Continent from Nazification through his Max network as "Fritz Klatt," Richard Kauder would now do his part to rescue the pending Jewish state from impending annihilation. According to Aarons and Loftus, Richard's compatriot for his final achievement was the MI6 officer, Lev Hoch. To summarize an intricate narrative, after Hoch escaped the Nazis in Slovakia, he availed his services to the French Resistance, then the French Foreign Legion, and finally, to the British, only to land in a prison camp in England on a skewed charge of insubordination. By now he had changed his name to "Robert Maxwell." However, it was here that he had a providential encounter with another political detainee, Vladimír Clementis, an ethnic Czech communist and former parliament member. Through a series of further developments, Robert was able to join the British army, rise to lieutenant, win the Military Cross for bravery (rescuing a platoon trapped by Germans), finally, parlaying his skill in foreign languages (especially Russian) into a job with MI6—all while keeping his Zionist aspirations under wraps.[24]

In 1946, Robert was shocked to learn that MI6 was preparing to oust the postwar Slovakian government of Foreign Minister Jan Masaryk. Why would Whitehall want to blindside the only democratic nation in the Eastern bloc with barely a 30% Communist vote? The intel came from British super-sleuth Kim Philby (Moscow's best-kept secret). At Stalin's order, the double-agent told his MI6 superiors that the Kremlin was secretly calling the shots in Prague and that Masaryk had to go. (Of course, in reality, Comrade Stalin was incensed at the Czech social democracy with its free trade unions and other political embarrassments.) Then, "oddly" enough, Philby endorsed the unpalatable Vatican-backed, anti-Communist, former Nazi quisling, Dr. Ferdinand Ďurčanský (listed as a UN Category A war criminal.)[25]

Losing most of his family in the Holocaust, Robert must have recoiled at the thought of the British installing a fascist Catholic thug over his beloved homeland. He therefore seized the moment, apprising his old cellmate of the approaching putsch. The plot was subsequently exposed by the non-Red Czech Security Service. While the hard-line Slovenian communists attained a successful countercoup in the parliament (Philby's plan all along), Vladimír Clementis, the more moderate vice-minister of foreign affairs, became the new Foreign Affairs Minister in March 1948. (Ďurčanský would later take a ratline to Argentina).[26] Loftus and Aarons provide the anticipated finale:

> Maxwell had watched the buildup of Arab arms from France, the US, and Britain with secret horror. He knew that Truman's arms embargo tolled the death knell for the Jews of Palestine. In return

> for saving his native country from Ďurčanský's civil war, Maxwell begged the Czechs for weapons for his adopted country, Israel. He wanted Clementis to send guns to Ben-Gurion, when no one else in the world would supply them.[27]

The authors then corroborate Ziv-Tal's "Maxwell-Max" nexus:

> There is considerable evidence that Maxwell's Czech strategy was coordinated by Ben-Gurion's secret double agent inside Soviet intelligence. In fact, it is almost certain that in the aftermath of the Communist coup, Maxwell was supported by another secret Zionist agent, an Austrian Jew. It was, say our sources in the intelligence community, Richard Kauder, code-named Klatt, the head of the Max network. At the end of 1947 Kauder helped a team of Zionist intelligence agents to travel to Prague, where they quickly made contact with the Czech government through his local sources from the Max network. By early 1948 they had concluded the first of a series of crucial arms deals with the Czech authorities, thanks to Maxwell's warnings about the Ďurčanský plot.[28]

British historian Richard Deacon also alludes to Kauder's role:

> In the early stages Czechoslovakia was earmarked as the most promising source of supply for arms, not only because it was an arms-producing country, but because at that time it was freer from Soviet domination than any of the other Soviet bloc countries of Eastern Europe. Nevertheless it still required Secret Service style activities to plan the purchase of such arms. The Palestinian Jews were helped by a former German Jew who had been one of a number of such Jews specially recruited by Admiral Canaris as agents for his *Abwehr* (German Secret Service)....[29]

Ziv-Tal states that the initial shipment constituted "four crates of Bren machine guns," the cargo proceeding to southern Italy by rail, then to northern Africa and Palestine by ship. The author concludes with a heart-pounding postscript that perfectly illustrates the aforementioned theme of God's unconditional personal commitment:

> Surprisingly enough, the Americans did find out about the deliveries but decided to turn a blind eye to them and allow them to proceed. The story was as follows: the Bren machine guns came

> with English-language manuals. Someone brought one of the manuals to the DP camp in Bad Gastein in search of someone who spoke English and could translate the manual into Yiddish. He approached a Jewish American sergeant who conversed with the refugees in fluent Yiddish. The sergeant agreed to translate the manual and informed his commander, who allowed him to proceed and promised to remain silent.[30]

Ziv-Tal repeated the same account to this author during a 2014 interview in Jerusalem. Upon the successful trial run, a consignment of 200 MG-34 machine guns, 4,500 P-18 rifles, and 50,400,000 rounds of ammunition in early 1948 marked the beginning of "Operation Balak"; plenty more would follow, from bayonets to German Spitfires and Messerschmitts. Ben-Gurion later opined, "Without these weapons, it's doubtful whether we could have won. The arms deal with the Czechs was the greatest assistance we received."[31] Sadly, while Clementis' timely pipeline saved Israel, it took his life in return. For defying Koba, the Slovakian patriot was condemned in a show trial and hanged on December 3, 1952. (Otto Šling was also executed on this date.) Loftus and Aarons conclude: "But for a few brave hours in 1948, Maxwell's friends in the Czech government had done what no other nation on earth was courageous enough to do. They had, for the first time in two thousand years, given the Jews a fair fight."[32]

GLUBB PASHA

On May 15, 1948, the nascent State of Israel absorbed a massive, though maladroit, pincer movement across a divergent array of fronts under the tacit command of Emir Abdullah Hussein. As decided in the final pre-invasion haggling, the key players had reluctantly chosen Abdullah's plan to annex Jewish territories as the lesser of two evils over an independent Palestinian state ruled by the Grand Mufti of Jerusalem. (The reader will recall that following the Allied victory in WWI, the Sharif's sons, Feisal and Abdullah, had expected to receive a Hashemite Empire based in Syria, only to wind up with the consolation kingdoms of Iraq and Transjordan, respectively.)

While the Egyptian Expeditionary Force (EEF) entered the Negev with tanks and aircraft from the south (their bombers striking Tel Aviv within hours), Syrian and Lebanese units descended on the Galilee region from the north. An Iraqi force of two infantry and one armored brigade crossed the Jordan to assault Jewish settlements in northern Samaria. The 6,000-man Arab Legion of Transjordan, considered to be the strongest army of the multi-national invasion force, hazarded *the* quintessential (though dangerously impractical) "holy" mission—holding the West Bank to conquer Jerusalem, including the ancient Jewish Quarter in the Old City. Sachar writes: "Abdullah's decision to engage in hostilities was influenced…by a deeply rooted, almost visceral yearning for the city of Jerusalem, with all its Moslem historical associations."[33] (Abdullah's father, Hussein bin Ali, King of Hejaz, was interred near the Temple Mount in 1931.)

Representing one of the most shocking twists of the war, the leader of this highly symbolic *Muslim* attack on *Jerusalem* was the revered kahuna of the 4,000-man Arab Legion—Sir John Bagot Glubb—a decorated former lieutenant-general of the British army (Royal Engineers) whose numerous awards include: Knight Commander of the Order of the Bath (KCB), Companion of the Order of St. Michael and St. George (CMG), Distinguished Service Order (DSO), Officer of the Most Excellent Order of the British Empire (OBE), and a Military Cross (MC). The son of an army officer and a graduate of the Royal Military Academy himself, Glubb was severely wounded in France during World War I. He later became an ardent Arabist, resigning his commission in 1926. Four years later, King Abdullah hired him to help organize the Arab Legion (Transjordan being a British protectorate at the time). In 1939, "Glubb Pasha," as he was now affectionately known ("Pasha," title for a Turkish officer of high rank), was appointed supreme commander of the Legion.

An author as well, his twenty-one books include such "classics" as *A Soldier with the Arabs*, *Britain and the Arabs*, *Arabian Adventures: Ten Years of Joyful Service*, *The Story of the Arab Legion*, *The Great Arab Conquests*, *A Short History of the Arab Peoples*, *The Empire of the Arabs*, and, last but not least, *The Life and Times of Muhammad*—hailed by the *Los Angeles Times* as, "The best popular life of the Prophet of Islam available in the English language."[34] Benny Morris labeled the soldier/scholar as "the Hashemite's obedient and loyal retainer and the Arabs' most successful general."[35] That such an eminent British personage would play the dominant role in an *illegal* invasion of the new Jewish state (receiving knighthood in his later years) speaks to the irremediable, anti-Semitic corruption of HMG.

However, while Glubb chose to lend his unethical support as a *retired* British officer, the cream of his officer corps consisted of thirty-eight *active* British officers as well.[36] Colonel Richard Meinertzhagen noted in his diary on May 18, 1948:

> The Transjordan Frontier Force, officered by British officers, is in action on the Judean Highlands...Never in the history of England has there been such a shameful abdication after years of shilly-shallying, no policy and no decision beyond those prompted by anti-Jewish sentiment...I am thoroughly ashamed of our Government, our Press, our people and my religion.[37]

Four days later, a week into the "Arab" invasion, the following remonstrance appeared in the *London Times* under the signature of Lyall Wiles, MP (Member of Parliament):

> British missions are training and re-equipping Arab armies in Saudi Arabia and Iraq; the British air mission is still functioning in Iraq; the Arab Legion is wholly subsidized by us and is commanded by 38 British officers...every tank and aeroplane now being used by the Arabs has been supplied by the United Kingdom."[38]

The full story of British complicity is rarely heard. As late as March 1948, Britain had renewed her Anglo-Transjordan alliance with Abdullah.[39] According to Glubb, Bevin supported the impending Transjordanian invasion as "the obvious thing to do..." (i.e., to secure the land rejected by the dumb Palestinians), while also cautioning against any encroachment of land allotted to the Jews.[40] However, as revealed in a secret memo on February 8, 1948, by Bernard Burrows, head of the Foreign Office's eastern department—*off* the record, Whitehall privately hoped that Glubb Pasha would *go a little further*:

> It is tempting to think that Transjordan might transgress the boundaries of the United Nations Jewish State to the extent of establishing a corridor across the Southern Negev joining the existing Transjordan territory to the Mediterranean and Gaza. This would have immense strategic advantages for us, both in cutting the Jewish State...off from the Red Sea and by extending up to

the Mediterranean the area in which our military and political influence is predominant....[41]

A distinction had also evolved over the term "Arab territory" now including designated Jewish land containing an Arab majority.[42] Meinertzhagen wrote on July 28, 1948: "A quarter of a million pounds has been paid to Transjordan this week as a subsidy for their invasion of Palestine. Without this subsidy Abdullah could not possibly maintain the Arab Legion in Palestine...."[43] So, to check this Anglo-Arab subterfuge, led by *their* Philistine champion, the Zionists would draft their *own* soldier of fortune—a fellow Jew by the name of *David.*

DAVID MARCUS

David Daniel "Mickey" Marcus was born on George Washington's birthday (February 22) in 1901, on the poverty-stricken Lower East Side of Manhattan, the fifth child of Romanian immigrants, Mordecai and Leah Marcus. When David was eight years old, his father died. Deprived of modern "bully-free zones," Mickey learned to box in order to survive the tough streets. He was nicknamed after his main hero, his older brother, Mike (a.k.a. "Big Mike," or "Mick" for short).

Having applied himself academically, Mickey entered West Point when Douglas MacArthur was superintendent. While continuing to hit the books, he also "hit" various classmates, winning the intercollegiate welterweight boxing championship in his junior year. His biographer, Ted Berkman, writes of the 130-pound southpaw: "That left was already a campus legend, suggesting Ira Gershwin's memorable phrase, 'Li'l David was small—but Oh my!'"[44] Marcus graduated with honors in 1924. While on his first assignment (on Governor's Island in New York Harbor), he began to study law at night. In 1927, he married a teacher, Emma Chaison. He later resigned his regular commission to stay in New York, earning a doctorate from Brooklyn Law School.

His amazing multifaceted career began in 1934 when Mayor Fiorello LaGuardia appointed the energetic Prohibition prosecutor to be the first Deputy Commissioner of Correction. At age thirty-four, he became the Honorable Judge David Marcus (the youngest magistrate on the bench), filling a temporary appointment to Manhattan's Fifth District. In 1940, he was sworn in as New York City Commissioner of Correction. While famous for busting bad guys, most notably playing a key role in the trial and deportation of Salvatore Lucania (a.k.a. "Lucky Luciano"), Marcus was also known for his benevolence, once buying a coat for a shabbily dressed Irish longshoreman-turned-aspiring pugilist, James Braddock (a.k.a. the "Cinderella Man").[45] His exploits were so pronounced that his character was portrayed by John Garfield in the 1938 film, *Blackwell's Island*, making him a genuine legend in his own time (though this would not be his last "biopic").[46]

Maintaining a reserve commission, Mickey utilized his legal expertise by joining the Judge Advocate General's Corps (JAG). Following Pearl Harbor, he was recalled to active duty as divisional judge advocate and commander of the Army Ranger School in Hawaii (training 8,000 men for combat). Over the months, Colonel Marcus also engaged in every wartime conference (Cairo, Dumbarton Oaks, Quebec, Yalta, Potsdam), interacting with Roosevelt, Truman, Churchill, Atlee, Chiang Kai-shek, Zhukov, Molotov, and Stalin.

In May 1945, Mickey became US Secretary-General in occupied Berlin (third highest policy maker for America.[47]) The man of many hats was described as "a legal wizard, organizer, trouble shooter, and all-around answer to a military administrator's dream."[48] General John Hilldring called him "the keenest mind in the Pentagon."[49] He was also appointed chief of planning for the Civil Affairs Division of the War Department and, providentially, chief of the Pentagon's War Crimes Division (the no-win task of choosing the lawyers, prosecutors, and judges for the war crimes trials)—personally attending Nuremberg.[50]

In one of his more "unconventional" (and unauthorized) moves, Mickey snuck away from his mundane desk responsibilities to finagle a high-altitude parachute jump with the 101st Airborne on D-Day. Remarkably, it was the former Ranger commander's *first* jump![51] After leading a dozen firefights, once wiping out a six-man German machine gun nest while armed only with his automatic weapon, Mickey was located by Major General Maxwell Taylor who asked him, "What the h--l are *you* doing here?" With his insouciant reply, "Oh, just looking around," the AWOL colonel was sent *back* to Washington for a "stern" reprimand. In his debriefing, Mickey said, "I won't deny personal gratification in fighting against Hitler…."[52]

"LA LA LA"

In late 1947, Ben-Gurion had an aide ask Marcus to recommend a US officer to serve as Israel's chief military advisor. At the time, Mickey was ensconced in his own Manhattan law practice. Berkman writes:

> Might he have embarked on such an Odyssey for freedom anywhere? Given a similar impetus of personal experience, very possibly. But the fact is that the call came from the Jews of Palestine; and for this particular cause, a multitude of forces and motivations within Mickey dovetailed, almost as if some unseen hand had molded his life to prepare him for his role at this special crossroad of history.[53]

Unbeknown to Ben-Gurion, Mickey had developed a Zionist heart at Dachau. After having "stood in stunned silence before mountains of grotesquely-flung bodies...," he retired behind a barracks to weep. "Was this the climax to man's progress on earth?" he pondered. Two days later, his epiphany was complete; rolling through the moonlit countryside in a tank column, Mickey suddenly heard "a ragged, eerie chorus of voices from the nearby woods." Upon inspection, he saw a group of about fifty liberated Jewish prisoners—"gray skeletons with hollow faces eaten away from inside and out"—standing at attention and singing. Then he recognized the song, "Hatikvah!" "The prisoners didn't even know the words...," he related. "They were just singing 'la la la.' But that 'la la la' was pregnant with the enthusiasm of a people who had returned from the depths of hell to the land of the living." That moment pushed Mickey over the top, leaving him with a singular purpose: "[T]he door to Palestine must be kept open."[54] (Many Shoah survivors would live to fight, and die, in the 1948 War—"their Hitler concentration camp numbers burned into their arms."[55])

Thus, to Ben-Gurion's total surprise (and exhilaration), Mickey volunteered *himself.* As Captain Alfred Dreyfus motivated Herzl to begin the Zionist cause, Marcus would be the soldier of providence to inspire Ben-Gurion to complete the dream. Like Jefferson, Adams, Hamilton, and Jay before him, he would also abandon a promising law career to espouse a higher calling. In the spirit of General Tadeusz Kosciuszko (Cadet Marcus having passed his statue daily at "The Point"), who left his native Poland to fight as a volunteer for Washington, he too would join another's noble cause. As Haym Solomon had saved the day for America, Mickey would do the same for Israel's War of Independence. His only request was that he receive no salary.[56] While his superiors were stunned, the War Department reluctantly approved the highly irregular request, but with the caveat that Marcus, a reservist, use an alias. Thus, as *"the dragon stood before the woman which was ready to be delivered, for to devour her child as soon as it was born"* (Revelation 12:4), Colonel David Daniel (Mickey) Marcus—*nom de guerre* "Michael (Mickey) Stone"—arrived in Palestine in January 1948, two months into the Arab revolt.

MICKEY'S MEDALS

While *Mickey's* medals remained at home (he never wore them), they would more than match the "fruit salad" of his coming British adversary—*and in far less time*: Bronze Star; Army Commendation Ribbon; European Campaign Medal with Bronze Battle Star; American Defense Service Medal; Asiatic-Pacific Campaign Medal; World War II Victory Medal; Army of Occupation Medal; New York State Conspicuous Service Cross; et al.[57]

It is also noteworthy that Colonel Marcus had declined a sure promotion to brigadier general, choosing time with his wife over more assignments (ditto a Rhodes Scholarship at the cost of extended overseas study).[58] A few other awards bear mention. Mickey's most treasured wartime memento may have been the German Walther Model 9, 6.35 mm caliber pistol given to him by General George Patton (displayed at the West Point Museum). More seriously, Marcus received the coveted Distinguished Service Medal on May 18, 1945. Not only did the official citation note the recipient's "first-hand experience acquired in accompanying the 101st Airborne Division in the invasion of Normandy," but the Jewish Judge Advocate was also cited for his role in the "negotiation and drafting of the Italian Surrender Instrument" and—get *this*—the Instrument of Unconditional Surrender of Germany."[59] Thus, we see that Hitler was defeated by one Jew (Kauder), while *another* Jew drew up the surrender papers!

Finally, matching medal for medal, there was one decoration that both opposing commanders shared—the Order of the British Empire (available to non-British nationals for significant contributions to the

United Kingdom). This particular order of British chivalry comprises five classes in civil and military divisions. As noted, in 1925 Glubb received the OBE—*Officer* of the Most Excellent Order of the British Empire—level number *four* (in bragging rights). In one of the more humorous episodes in an otherwise dark period, on April 20, 1948, at the British Embassy in Washington, DC—while Mickey was home on a two-week leave (attending to his sick wife), having spent the last three months secretly leading the Jews as Michael Stone—the Jewish colonel was awarded the CBE, *Commander* of the Most Excellent Order of the British Empire, which just happens to be level number *three*.[60] The only thing funnier was when Glubb finally learned about Michael Stone—relating in his memoirs, "We were surprised to hear…that a Colonel in the United States Army, David Marcus, was commanding the Israeli forces which were attacking Latrun."[61]

CASTING A GIANT SHADOW

Ted Berkman was an American author, screenwriter, and journalist who also served in Army intelligence during World War II. In 1964, he wrote the definitive biography on Marcus entitled *Cast a Giant Shadow* (later made into a major motion picture by the same name). Berkman relates that Mickey hit the ground running, pursuing three immediate priorities: appraising the danger (theater by theater); designing an intricate command structure; and personally compiling (nearly all from memory) the requisite training manuals, covering such topics as communications, logistics, reserves, and multi-operations.

Mickey would have all of four months to do the impossible—unify Jews. Though the Haganah, Irgun, and Lehi had fought bravely as underground guerrillas, they had no experience as a national army. He would also have to do this incognito. Once, while barely passing himself off as a "foundry worker" at a British checkpoint, "Mike" realized that he was still wearing his ruby-stoned signet ring from West Point![62] Over the arduous days ahead, his signature exhortation was always: "You have to act with what you've got…David did it with a slingshot, didn't he?"[63] (Years later, Yitzchak Rabin would say of Mickey: "He brought with him the atmosphere of action."[64])

DAVID'S "MIGHTY MEN"

As with Glubb's pool of British officers, an initial array of over 200 Americans (with forty or so Canadians thrown in for good measure), mostly Jewish male WWII veterans, also joined the fracas. These enlistees, along with some 3,500 others from roughly fifty countries, were known as *Machalniks* ("Volunteers from Abroad"). Their timely aid to the embryonic Jewish state would prove inestimable.

I Chronicles 11:10 records, *"These also are the chief of the mighty men whom David had, who strengthened themselves with him...."* To highlight a few of *Mickey's* "mighty men" (as found in Jeff and Craig Weiss' book, *I Am My Brother's Keeper*), Bronx-born Lieutenant Paul Shulman, USN, was appointed the *first* commander-in-chief of the Israeli Naval Service.[65] USAF veteran Nat Cohen was the *first* head of IAF Intelligence.[66] Chalmers "Slick" Goodlin, of Pennsylvania, became Israel's *first* test pilot.[67] Marlin Levin (also from PA), helped crack Jordan's military code.[68] The IDF's *first* tank was commanded by Canadian Lionel Druker (not to be confused with fellow Canuck, Benjamin Dunkelman, commander of the 7th Armored Brigade, the nation's best-known tank unit).[69] Gideon "Giddy" Lichtman, USAF veteran from New Jersey, was credited with the *first* kill during aerial combat (a British-supplied/Egyptian-piloted Spitfire).[70] USN pilot Philip "Poppy" Marmelstein of Philadelphia was the *first* commander of 35 Flight (a squadron of AT-6 Harvard dive-bombers); when he left to be Israel's *first* military-trained flight instructor, his slot was filled by a Goy Machalnik, Ted Gibson—the son of a Baptist minister![71]

THE INITIAL PHASE OF FIGHTING

Mickey's original assignment was to create and advise the Israel Defense Force. The top native IDF commander (for all intents and purposes) was assistant chief of staff Lieutenant General Yigael Yadin, who served as head of operations throughout the war. On the surface, Yadin seemed a most unlikely candidate for serious military responsibility. The tall, prematurely balding thirty-year-old Israeli was a graduate student in archeology (doing his doctoral thesis on the translation of the Dead Sea Scrolls) who later became Israel's top archeologist.

However, when called upon by his nation, Yadin rose to the occasion, going on to make many vital decisions of the war.

Other key officers included: Yaakov Dori (Yadin's ailing superior); Yigal Allon (Palmach founder, considered the war's most famous general); Yitzhak Rabin (future prime minister); Yitzhak Sadeh (a.k.a. "The Old Man"); Chaim Laskov (Israel's first armored battalion commander); Moshe Carmel (fittingly, *Carmeli* Brigade commander); Shimon Avidan (Givati Brigade commander); Yosef Avidor (Northern Regional commander); and the legendary one-eyed Lieutenant Colonel Moshe Dayan (commander of IDF-controlled areas of Jerusalem).

The simultaneous multinational Arab invasion stretched Israel's geocentric vulnerabilities to the limit. In the opening Syrian offensive, a column of 200 armored vehicles, including 45 tanks, wound its way down to the defenseless string of Jewish settlements at the southern tip of the Sea of Galilee. After overrunning several sites, the enemy advanced toward Degania, the oldest kibbutz in Palestine. Moshe Dayan was the local commander. His "heavy artillery" consisted of a flamethrower and two antiquated howitzers, from the Franco-Prussian War era. As the convoy enveloped the covey, the first fieldpiece scored a direct hit on the lead tank. (Not bad for a guy with one eye.) Sachar writes, "[T]he armored vehicles swung around in their tracks and clattered back up the mountain road. They never returned."[72]

The enemy also sought to exploit the isolated Negev (twenty-two of the twenty-seven barbed wire-enclosed communes having fewer than thirty defenders). As two Egyptian brigades, supported by tanks and artillery, advanced from their positions in the eastern Sinai, Marcus initiated a series of hit-and-run tactics (mostly nocturnal), using thirty jeeps mounted with machine guns. Ultimately, all but one of the outmanned kibbutzim were able to repulse their attackers. The colonel's strategy, together with the settlers' stubborn defense, not only saved the Negev, but delayed the Egyptians' advance on Tel Aviv. Israel Carmi, a former Jewish Brigade officer, stated: "We didn't need Napoleon in the Negev. We needed Mickey Marcus."[73]

On May 20, 1948, the Czech government gave an entire airfield to the Jews which became Israel's principal base in Europe for "Dakota commuters" shuttling supplies to the front.[74] The IAF made a quick purchase of 25 Avia S-199 fighters from Kauder's friends, airlifting them to Israel by Curtis C-46 and Douglas C-54 transports. By May 29, four of the Avia S-199s had been uncrated, reassembled, and armed for action.[75] Ironically, not only was the Avia S-199 developed from the Messerschmitt Bf 109, the very aircraft flown by Göring's Luftwaffe, but the Jewish pilots who trained in Czechoslovakia wore coveralls left behind by the Nazis—which still bore swastikas.[76]

The aircraft took off that afternoon from Ekron, piloted by two Israelis and two Machalniks (an American and a South African). The first sortie in the history of the IAF could not have commenced too soon. The immediate threat was an Egyptian column of 500 vehicles, mostly tanks and artillery, which had advanced along the coastal road to within twenty-five miles of Tel Aviv—population, a quarter million. (Their only disruption was an evening counterattack from the rear.) In the ensuing raid, Eddy Cohen was killed by antiaircraft fire. After the other men got their meager payloads away (two 70 kg bombs apiece), they were unable to strafe the convoy as all three of their machine guns jammed. A second plane was damaged on landing. Yet, to everyone's surprise, the Egyptians must have suffered the same shock as the Japanese experienced when Doolittle's Raiders suddenly appeared over Tokyo. Author Leonard Slater writes: "The Egyptians, sobered by the sight of Israeli fighter planes, were digging in at Ashdod, apparently for a prolonged stay. They had not been destroyed. But they would not be in Tel Aviv...The Egyptians had been stopped. They would never get any farther."[77]

Meanwhile, an Iraqi division of one armored and two infantry brigades had entrenched in the Samarian locale called "The Triangle" (between Nablus, Jenin, and Tulkarm). After thwarting an assault on Netanya, the IDF counterattacked on May 29, capturing Jenin, though forced to retreat three days later. Further north, another stalemate was occurring between Syrian forces and the kibbutzim by Lake Tiberias. Though the Arabs attacked in superior number (an infantry brigade, mechanized battalion, artillery regiment, and tank company), they failed to press their advantage, withdrawing from their fleeting seizure of three settlements. The Lebanese Army was barely more effective. After taking the strategic village of Malkiya (Israel's eastern gateway) on May 15, only to be dislodged by the IDF three days later, they recaptured the site on June 6 with Syrian and ALA reinforcements.[78]

THE BATTLE FOR JERUSALEM

When Abdullah ordered Glubb to attack Jerusalem, the Brit became unnerved, relating that he had fallen on his knees and cried, "Oh God, I am not equal to these events. I entreat Thee to grant me Thy Help."[79] As to *which* "god" (Psalm 83:18) Glubb supplicated, the Associated Press reported: "He always carried Moslem prayer beads."[80]

By May 25, a tithe of 10,000 shells had rained upon the 100,000 Jews in Jerusalem.[81] Glubb's artillery ranged from six-pound anti-tank guns and eighteen-pound fieldpieces to cannons firing twenty-five-pound shells. Though denied by Bevin, at least four artillerists were British.[82] Dov Yosef, the city's military governor, wrote: "To have to sit helplessly while the Arabs cannonaded the city day after day and night after night…in the knowledge that we had no cannon with which to hit back, did more to undermine public morale than almost any other hardship."[83] Still, the Jews held firm, repelling repeated assaults, often, hand-to-hand—some, serving *without* a hand; Tova Goldberg, a sixteen-year-old courier, delivered her severed hand (the result of shrapnel) to the Haganah post, its fingers still clutching her dispatch.[84]

As the IDF turned to their 2,000 beleaguered brethren in the Jewish Quarter of the Old City, a nutty Irish Catholic priest, one "Father" Eugene, was seen manning the walls with his Muslim neighbors. Appeals for help flooded Amman, "Save us! Our ammunition is finished! We can hold on no longer! Where is the Arab Legion? Min shan Allah! (For God's Sake!) Save us!"[85] Ironically, the Jewish Quarter would be the only part of Jewish Jerusalem to fall. After ten days of fierce house-to-house resistance—only 36 of its 300 men able to stage a defense, their ammunition all but gone—the local Haganah commander had Rabbi Weingarten negotiate the surrender for May 28.[86] For the government's unconscionable sin of censoring God's name, the Quarter's restored autonomy had lasted all of two weeks!

The ancient enclave, cynosure of Orthodox Jewry, was looted, desecrated, and burned, the civilians evacuated through the wall, the Haganah men hauled to Transjordan captivity. (Unknown to the Arabs, the "ethnic cleansing" was documented through the lens of Life magazine reporter John Phillips.) Glubb's treatment of the Old City was in stark contrast to Allenby's reverent deportment in 1917. On a related note, Thomas C. Wasson, US Counsel General and a UN Truce Commission member, died at Hadassah Hospital after being shot near his office. His last act was to petition Glubb to stop shelling Hadassah.

Having halted the West Jerusalem offensive, the Jews would now have to survive the enemy's siege (a near-fatal crisis two months earlier). Food rationing hit nine hundred calories a day (two hundred more than at Bergen-Belsen). The coastal pipeline was cut, causing an acute water shortage. To minimize evaporation, the daily ration of two gallons per person was distributed at night. The gloom was epitomized by a mother who named her newborn daughter, "Reinforcements."[87]

The Arabs controlled the main supply route from Tel Aviv, having occupied the deserted British fortification at Latrun. The attendant east-west network of redoubts stretched along the ridge commanding the critical passage between *Sha'arHaGai* and *Al-Qastal.* On May 25, in the face of a blistering sirocco, augmented by repeated waves of tiny black mosquitoes (called *barkaches*), the IDF committed a hastily assembled brigade to a frontal assault of the heavily defended heights. The raw recruits, newly landed immigrants speaking eight different languages, were literally arriving from Tel Aviv in taxis and busses.[88] Though the battle dominated the Valley of Ayalon, where Joshua bade the moon stand still, the attack stalled, leaving hundreds of fallen Jews among the melons. (Another attempt five days later likewise failed.)

However, Arab assaults on the northern sector of New Jerusalem were increasingly futile as well. In retrospect, the *real* reason Glubb Pasha "got religion" when told to assault Jerusalem was because he knew this would be a twin debacle. His force was 100% mechanized and the *last* place it needed to deploy was in a constricted, urban area. Also, while bogged down in Abdullah's Stalingrad, Glubb would be unable to join the Iraqis in a vital westward pincer to sever Haifa Port from the south. Thus, to employ a second historical analogy, every day spent reducing the "Jewish Alamo" bought precious time for Ben-Gurion's pending arms arrival at Haifa. However, Sir John's greatest downer came on May 30 when his royal dream team of forty veteran British officers was scrapped due to US pressure.[89] Glubb described the evacuation order as a "shattering blow," writing: "They included all operational staff officers, both the brigade commanders and the C.O.s of three out of the four infantry regiments, and all the trained artillery officers. The British officers were the keystone to the whole edifice in 1948."[90] The *Great Arab Conquests* author would now get the same "reality check" experienced by Colonel T. E. Lawrence.

Meanwhile, Egyptian troops bolstered by the Moslem Brotherhood were attempting an alternative strike on Ramat Rachel (astride the entrance to southern Jerusalem). Sachar opines, "What followed was the single most furious encounter of the Palestine war. The little kibbutz changed hands five times during the next four days. Soldiers pressing forward in bayonet attack often had to climb over bodies piled on top of each other."[91] When the battle ended on May 26, the Israelis (mostly Etzel members) remained in control. Two days later, Glubb halted his stalled offensive. Like the Sennacherib Prism relates of King Hezekiah, "[H]imself, like a caged bird I shut up in Jerusalem, his royal city," Glubb would now consign *his* captives to a similar ordeal. Many were soon reduced to eating thistles and mulberry leaves.[92] And so, with the Holy City on life support, the time had come for an alternative solution—enter "Mike Stone, foundry worker."

"PAVING THE GOAT PATH"

On May 28, the provisional government issued the IDF Establishment Order (retaining the Haganah's general staff while disbanding the Irgun and Lehi). Up to now, the largest unit under a single commander had been a brigade. Under the new order, Prime Minister Ben-Gurion appointed the Manhattan-born Marcus as commanding general of the entire Jerusalem front. His official Hebrew title was the sacred rank of *Aluf* (Major-General), making him the first Jewish general since Judas Maccabaeus 2,000 years before! Mickey had finally gained his elusive star, only *this* one would be a *real* "Star of David."

His first priority was to relieve the starving masses in Jerusalem. Ironically, the greatest threat to the "City of Peace" was a UN *ceasefire* set for June 11. Because the terms required that all troop movement be frozen at the levels prevailing when the truce began, the fate of "populations under siege was not as yet spelled out."[93] At this critical juncture, Mickey took a giant leap of faith. If they could not use the existing road, they would simply have to build *another* artery. When his staff responded with incredulity, Mickey countered, with a smile:

"We made it across the Red Sea, didn't we?"[94] (Given the immediate particulars, re-parting the Red Sea might have been easier.)

To circumvent the blockade, a Jewish version of the "Burma Road" (named for the 750-mile route the Allies paved from Burma to China in WWII) would be laid atop an existing goat path of wild mustard, thyme, and cyclamen, penetrating a rocky, three-mile farrago of winding ravines, barren hills, and jagged cliffs, ending with a hair-raising, serpentine descent along the final stretch of sheer cliff. And to keep things interesting, the week-long project had to be done in secret, mostly at night, and in close proximity to the enemy. As Nehemiah 4:16 says, *"And it came to pass from that time forth, that the half of my servants wrought in the work, and the other half of them held both the spears, the shields, and the bows, and the habergeons...,"* Berkman describes the dramatic coalescence of middle-aged civilian workers, youthful military guards, and the one who cheered them on:

> Hammers clanged; engines roared; stonecutters grunted; foremen cursed. At strong points in the hills, sun-baked young riflemen crouched through the night, while behind them axes swung, donkeys brayed, and truck drivers coughed in the thick, persistent dust. Towering over the entire turbulent scene was the sturdy figure of the brigadier from America: organizing, coaxing, shaping the path hewn through rock and shellfire what was to be popularly hailed as the 'Marcus Road.' Mickey was everywhere...he never slackened his buoyant drive...Many men, including Shamir himself, were instrumental in building the Burma road; but Mickey was the magnetic rallying-point, the overlord of the front in fact as well as technically. He was in his own person a kind of Burma Road for the embattled and disenchanted Israelis: a link to the world of normalcy and good cheer, to the future and to hope...a single strand of apparently indestructible humanity.[95]

In the wee hours of June 6, less than a week from the time of its inception, the nearly complete "Burma/Marcus Road" was ready for its first trial run—four jeeps hauling a battery of four-inch mortars. Mickey discerned that the heavy guns would serve as a morale-boosting appetizer for the starving inhabitants, enabling them to "pay back the merciless Arab artillery in its own coin."[96] He personally led the spearhead convoy which arrived at dawn. As news raced through the streets—"Guns have arrived, guns for Jerusalem!"—ecstatic crowds mobbed the drivers, "pummeling, hugging, [and] kissing them." Mickey "stood smilingly aside. He had his reward in the smiling faces swarming around him. Jerusalem would no longer be helpless under the Arab onslaught."[97] Two nights later, as an incredible third futile assault on Latrun was drawing diversionary fire, a massive sixty-five-ton convoy rumbled across the former *goat* path (Job 39:1). The siege was finally broken by an uncanny fulfillment of the idiom—"paving the goat path." The Holy City was saved with three days to spare (a water pipeline tossed in as a bonus). A memorial attributes the miracle to "Our commander Mickey Marcus who came to us from afar, a fighting man who knew the souls of men."[98]

The fact that the epic nocturnal project received the sobriquet "Burma Road," would also serve as a reminder of that *other* renowned fighting man from afar—the British Zionist, General Orde Wingate, founder of the Palmach's Special Night Squads, who later became a hero in the Burma Campaign itself. Gershon Rivlin, editor of the Israeli Army weekly, *Maarahoth*, compared the two men accordingly: "Wingate was the perfect captain—an expert in plotting and carrying out the small, hard-hitting operation…What Wingate gave us on the tactical level, Marcus gave us on the strategic or at least the large-operational plane…Marcus forged our haphazard units into a regular army, capable of planning and mounting real offensives." He concludes: "Without Wingate, there would have been no foundation on which to build a Jewish Army. Without Marcus, that army might have remained a band of guerrillas."[99] The dynamic duo embodied the rare antithesis of Anglo-American anti-Semitism. (Sadly, Wingate's life was cut short at forty-one when he and nine others perished in the crash of a US Army Air Corps transport in India on March 24, 1944.)

"HABUB"

The UN ceasefire was scheduled for 10:00 a.m. on June 11. As central front commander, Mickey spent the last twenty-four hours cautioning his officers to be alert for any last-minute Arab surprises, putting special emphasis on the sentries.[100] Mickey and his officers were billeted in the abandoned monks' quarters of the Notre Dame Catholic monastery high atop the Christian Arab village of Abu Ghosh, eight miles west of Jerusalem. According to local tradition, this was the biblical Kirjathjearim, *"the house of Abinadab in the hill...,"* where the ark of the Lord abode for twenty years (I Samuel 7:1-2).

After attending a staff *kumsitz* ("evening festivity") to celebrate the imminent truce, Mickey and his aide-de-camp made a last-minute inspection of the sentry posts around 1:00 a.m. He then retired to his room. Unable to sleep, the restless general wrapped himself in a white sheet and went for a walk in the cool mountain air. Exchanging greetings with the sentinel, he slipped over the wall and vanished into the dark. The time was 3:35 a.m. When he returned fifteen minutes later, he was arrested by a different voice, both in tone and language. Whoever this man was, he was rattled and had challenged him in Hebrew ("*Mi sham?*" – "Who goes there?"). Unskilled in the native tongue (knowing only Yiddish), Mickey attempted to communicate in English. The man replied by firing a warning shot—*not* good!

Unknown to Mickey, the relief guard due at 4:00 a.m. had arrived early, while unknown to *him*, the unintelligible stranger advancing in a white shroud was his commanding general, the very one who had issued the heightened sentry alert. Thus, with Mickey back over the perimeter fence and failing to give the countersign *again*, eighteen-year-old Eliezer Linski (a one-year Palmach veteran) drew a bead on the intruder and fired from ten yards away. Berkman soberly notes:

> By the time Yigael Alon raced to the scene, Mickey lay lifeless in front of the low stone wall, a bullet through his heart...Mickey was struck down within a hundred feet of the spot where, two thousand years before, the immortal warrior-king for whom he was named had danced and sung in praise of the Lord. He fell at 3:50 A.M., six hours and ten minutes before the guns went silent...the last casualty before the truce on the Israeli side.[101]

Like the Confederacy's loss of *Stone*wall Jackson, "The citizen-soldiers of Israel were stunned as they had not been by five Arab Armies."[102] The body of "Aluf Stone" was placed in a plain coffin of rubbed white pine and flown from Tel Aviv to America by special military transport on June 30. Ben-Gurion and Dayan accompanied the flight. Tributes flowed in from around the world. Even Marshal Zhukov expressed grief at the loss of his friend.[103] When the draped casket landed in New York, the Star of David was replaced by the Stars and

Stripes before being lowered from the hold. An honor guard of twenty-five New York City policemen stood at attention, saluting.

After a memorial service at Brooklyn's Union Temple, Mickey's sixty-car cortege wound its way through streets thickly lined with mourners to City Hall where Mayor William O'Dwyer and various officials joined in a four-minute tribute of silence. Then it was time for Mickey's last ride—up the east bank of the Hudson to the Old Cadet Chapel at West Point. Here, the many dignitaries included Governor Thomas Dewey, Academy superintendent General H. Maxwell Taylor, and former Treasury Secretary Henry Morgenthau, Jr. Also attending was Yosef Hamburger, legendary Haganah commander of the *Exodus*.

The most poignant moment was when Prime Minister Ben-Gurion handed Mickey's anguished widow, Emma, the posthumously awarded Israeli Order of Independence—Mickey's *greatest* medal. (While a real-life adulterer, Kirk Douglas, portrayed Mickey in the star-studded Hollywood film, *Cast a Giant Shadow*, the infidelity ascribed to him was an inexplicable lie.) Ben-Gurion summarized the man's character in seven words—"He was the best man we had."[104] Ironically, the highest honor America bestowed on Marcus was his *grave*—the only plot in West Point Cemetery that marks the resting place of a soldier killed while fighting under a foreign flag! (Two years later, Orde Wingate received a related distinction when *his* remains, and those of his comrades, were moved from India to a common grave in Arlington National Cemetery.) Mickey's headstone reads simply: "Colonel David Marcus—*A Soldier for All Humanity*." Emma received the following eulogy from Eve Kirshner, a housewife in Tel Aviv:

> We all knew him but a short time. But he belonged to those rare people whose purity brings out the best in others from the first minute. He arrived here under the name of Stone. He left us as Mickey and 'Habub,' an endearing name our soldiers gave him, which means 'darling' in Arabic. I want you to know that when his men learned that Mickey was killed, they wept. Those boys, most of whom are but children, do not cry easily and death is a common, accepted thing with them…but this time they were not ashamed to cry. The day of his death will remain for us a day of mourning for as long as we live, and our children and grandchildren will be taught to love and admire the American soldier who came to our

> help in this desperate, difficult fight. Many could come, but he was the only one who came; and we will never forget it.[105]

Thus, despite *their* rejection of *Him*, Israel's "Rock" had saved *them* with a "Stone"—*"the stone of Israel"* (Genesis 49:24)—the same way David had delivered their *fathers* from Goliath (I Samuel 17:49). And by the way, according to Daniel 12:1, it just so happens that *Michael* is the archangel that will stand up for the Jewish people.

THE FIRST TRUCE

Many have said that the letters UN stand for "United Nuts." At the end of the first phase of Israel's life-and-death struggle against an array of Islamic invaders, the Security Council's four-week ceasefire actually stipulated that "movement of troops or war materials from one interested country to another, or closer to the borders of Palestine or to the fighting front in Palestine are prohibited during the period of the truce."[106] The envoy assigned to police this unrealistic joke was a blue-blooded Swede, Folke Bernadotte, Count of Wisborg. (The details of his proposal for yet another partition plan are not even worth reviewing apart from their utter rejection by both sides of the conflict.)

Suffice it to say that when the fighting ended on June 11, there were 60,000 active combatants in Palestine; when hostilities recommenced on July 9, that number had "remained" *up* to 100,000![107] During the much-needed respite (described by Moshe Carmel as "dew from heaven"), the Jews "out-procured" their Arab opponents considerably.[108] While Ben-Gurion secured more undetected weapons from Czechoslovakia, Meinertzhagen praised the IDF for employing some local chutzpah, noting in his diary on July 1, 1948: "The Jews, at the last moment, stole two Churchill tanks from the army…I'm delighted they got them. I wish it could have been a destroyer."[109]

THE ALTALENA AFFAIR

On a more dissonant note, to illustrate the albatross that Marcus endured while trying to get his fellow Jews to cooperate, another ceasefire was brokered on June 22—only *this* truce was between the State of Israel and the Begin-led Irgun! Nearly two millennia ago, the Apostle Paul described *his* kinsmen after the flesh as being *"contrary to* ALL *men...."* (I Thessalonians 2:15) The following story represents "one for the books" in the annals of Aliyah Bet catastrophes.

On the afternoon of June 20, 1948, a 4,000-ton cargo ship arrived at Kfar Vitkin beach in northern Israel. The *Altalena* (named after the *nom de plume* of the late Vladimir "Ze'ev" Jabotinsky[110]), purchased by the Irgun in France, was carrying 940 Machalniks, plus a large weapons cache (5,000 rifles, 450 machine guns, and millions of rounds).[111] While the fact that Radio London was already announcing that the operation violated the UN's arms embargo represented a political distraction for Ben-Gurion, the greater, *internal* problem concerned a stipulation in the standing Establishment Order requiring that the Irgun cease all independent arms acquisitions. (In Begin's defense, had the *Altalena* arrived by its original target date of May 15, the action would have merely violated British authority, while enabling the Irgun to skirt the May 28 IDF deadline as well; but then, everyone knows how unpredictable smuggling schedules can be, etc.)

Menachem had told Ben-Gurion that he would gladly transfer the consignment to the IDF—provided that his *own* stipulations were honored, i.e., that *his* men get "first dibs" (20%). The prime minister was aghast at his subordinate's audacity. When Ben-Gurion refused to authorize the unloading, Begin had his own men initiate the process. Meanwhile, those near-1,000 volunteers were whisked away to an IDF camp to be formally inducted. (Many must have been scratching their heads.) At an emergency cabinet session in Tel Aviv, Ben-Gurion thundered that there was only *one* state and only *one* army. He equated the illicit unloading as tantamount to civil war—creating "an army within an army."[112] The meeting ended with a resolution to empower the military to use force if needed to confiscate the *Altalena's* cargo.

On June 21, the Alexandroni Brigade, commanded by Dan Even, surrounded Begin and his men (still offloading the ship). After delivering an ultimatum, Even gave the Irgun leader ten minutes to stand down—or *else*. When his time was up, Menachem requested an extension. Dan's reply was not exactly what Begin had in mind. While Ben-Gurion's old pal, Harry Truman, would merely *fire* Douglas MacArthur for *his* insubordination, Israel's leader chose to fire *at* his upstart. In the ensuing battle, six Irgunists and two IDF members were killed. Begin and his men reboarded the *Altalena* and sped off for Tel Aviv, hoping to dialogue with the provisional government.[113]

However, when they docked at Tel Aviv the next day, all requests for parlays were denied and the ship was shelled! Dr. Jack L. Schwartzwald of Brown University writes: "As the vessel went up in flames, scores of Irgun fighters jumped into the sea. (It is reported that Begin had to be thrown overboard to keep him from going down with the ship.) Ten more Irgun men were killed – some being cut down in the water as they sought to swim ashore. The bulk of the cargo was lost (and with it, claim many Irgun supporters, Israel's best hope for retaking Jerusalem's Old City)."[114]

As for Begin, rather than ignite further internecine strife, the future prime minister yielded to the current officeholder and everyone got back to firing at the *real* enemy…well…sort of. Incredibly, with only eight days until the end of the truce, Ben-Gurion threatened to resign as both prime minister and minister of defense over *another* power struggle, a.k.a. "The Generals Revolt" (only resolved at the eleventh hour). Finally, according to Palmach veteran Aryeh Kaplan (naval base commander in Haifa), on Ben-Gurion's order in November 1948, the *Altalena* was refloated, towed fifteen miles out to sea and sunk.[115] (He makes no mention of any attempts to salvage her sunken cargo.)

THE FIGHTING RESUMES

The second phase of the war began on July 9 and lasted only ten days. Though Mickey was sadly gone, the fruit of his labor would be harvested directly. Having no one else but Arabs to work with, Glubb knew the jig was up. As he would dolorously sum up in his memoirs, the Arab Legion had "in reality shot their bolt. They had lost the momentum of their advance; it was obvious that [hereafter] the Arabs would grow weaker while the Jews would grow stronger."[116]

There were three main theaters of activity. In a five-day fight to the north, IDF units dislodged the Syrians from several villages, including the Arab stronghold of Nazareth, thus bringing Lower Galilee under Israeli control. The IAF also bombed Damascus for the first time. To the south, Egyptian forces under General Muhammad Naguib launched several costly attacks hoping to strengthen their blockade of the Negev. In the July 12 Battle of Negba, they suffered 300 casualties while the

IDF had 5 dead and 4 wounded. The assault on the village of Be'erot three days later was equally ruinous; 200 dead and wounded (compared to 32 Israeli casualties). Adding insult to injury, three heavy B-17 "Flying Fortresses" (Ben-Gurion's latest acquisition) bombed Cairo, El-Arish, and Gaza en route from America to Israel.[117]

The main IDF campaign, "Operation Danny," was directed by General Allon. (The mission was reputedly code-named "Operation Mickey" in honor of Marcus, but was changed at the last minute due to a security leak.) On July 9, Allon combined several brigades (totaling 8,000 troops) to assault the Legion-occupied Lydda-Ramle salient, which formed a wedge just eleven miles from Tel Aviv, threatening to divide the country. Two days later, Lydda and its international airport fell to Colonel Dayan's mechanized infantry. Over 450 Arabs were killed, compared to less than 10 Israelis. On July 12, IDF units took the adjacent town of Ramle as well. Tel Aviv was secure. Subsequent attempts to outflank Latrun were unsuccessful, however.

The Second Truce

The next UN ceasefire was as futile as the first, though lasting slightly longer (July 19 to October 15). Abdullah's first move was canning Sir John (under the guise of "badly needed R&R in Europe"). Jordanian children literally spat at Glubb's motorcade for losing Lydda and Ramle.[118] And his was not the only career to be terminated.

On September 16, the Count submitted still another plan to the UN. Once again, the proposal was rejected outright by Jews and Arabs alike. However, *this* time, as the allotted territory for the reconfigured Jewish state was even *less* than before—dividing the Negev between Egypt and Transjordan, with Arab Galilee going to the Jews as compensation, while also recommending that all future immigration be controlled by the UN—Israel rejected it a tad *more* brazenly. The following day, while being chauffeured through New Jerusalem, Folke Bernadotte was assassinated by a four-man Lehi hit squad.

THE FINAL CAMPAIGNS

When the second ceasefire commenced, 90,000 Israelis occupied some 620 sq. miles of new territory. It would now behoove Tel Aviv to end the war. Thus, as the UN rang the bell for round three on October 15, the IDF launched its most aggressive offensive.

In "Operation Yoav" (a.k.a. Ten Plagues), Allon led 30,000 troops, supported by a small air fighter squadron, on a two-week sweep of the northern Negev, restoring vital communication lines throughout the isolated kibbutzim. Over a dozen Arab villages were captured. An entire Egyptian brigade (4,000 men and equipment) became trapped in the now famous "Faluja Pocket." In a secondary battle on October 21 ("Operation Moses"), several brigades combined to overrun the sleepy Arab village of Beersheba, romantic capital of the Negev; 120 prisoners were taken. Israel's infant Navy sank the Egyptian flagship *Emir Farouq* off Gaza with 700 soldiers aboard. Thus, with Pharaoh on the ropes crying, "Let *my* people go," the Security Council came to the rescue, enforcing a local cessation of fighting on October 22.

The IDF then turned north after the last vestige of Syrian and Lebanese hostility. "Operation Hiram" began October 23, under Moshe Carmel and his Carmeli Brigade. In three days the entire Galilee region was secured, leaving some 400 Arabs dead (a similar number captured). By month's end, Hiram advance units were at the Litani River (five miles into Lebanon)—the Biblical stomping grounds of King Hiram himself. Thus, *another* UN ceasefire was abruptly ordered.[119] Then, as Egypt had repeatedly violated the October truce (the Israelis doing the same), the IDF launched "Operation Horev" on December 22, clearing out the demoralized remnants of Naguib's army of the Negev in five days. When the first fortress of al-Auja surrendered, their colonel was still in his PJs.[120] This would prove the most provocative campaign of the war. In an uncanny reversal of the original Exodus, Allon pushed the political envelope by pushing into the Sinai Peninsula, occupying Abu Ageila in the center and al-Arish in the north.[121] However, unlike Israel's incursion into Lebanon, Egypt had a big brother—in London.

NEW YEAR'S EVE ON GALILEE

Two years earlier, a newspaper article in *The West Australian*, dated May 2, 1946, sent reverberations throughout the Christian world. Under the heading "Galilee Lido," the piece ran as follows:

> LONDON, May 1.—In the course of its report the Anglo-American Committee on Palestine says: 'The Lido [a fashionable beach resort] with its dancing and swing music on the shore of the Sea of Galilee offends the susceptibilities of many Christians. Reports have come to our notice of other projects the completion of which would be equally objectable. Therefore we emphasise the necessity for close supervision of a strengthening of the law if necessary.' The Lido mentioned, where there is also mixed bathing and tennis courts, is in Tiberias. An official of the Zionist Federation in London told the 'Daily Mail' that it was started by the Arabs. An Arab Office official said it was started by a German and bought up a year or two ago by a number of Jews.[122]

Colonel Meinertzhagen wrote: "I am deeply shocked to see in the Report that there is a Lido complete with jazz band on the Sea of Galilee. However our Administration permitted such a sacrilege is beyond my comprehension. I consider this an insult to Christianity and brings shame on those who permitted it."[123] Well, it just so happens that on the evening of December 31, 1948, Ben-Gurion and his wife were staying in Tiberias when they received a high-profile visitor at their hotel. In fact, their guest had served on the six-man US delegation that produced the above-mentioned report. The VIP arrived by police escort, having made the 115-mile drive in two hours (often at 70 miles an hour, despite landmines and rugged terrain). He had a sober message to give the embattled Jewish leader on this normally festive Gentile occasion; though with a war on, there was no mention of any jazz band entertaining the "score or so of people" in the lobby.

In July 1948, Truman had appointed James Grover McDonald as the Special Representative of the United States to Israel (later becoming America's first ambassador to Israel). The dark subject of his communiqué concerned the presence of Israeli troops in Egypt. Representing the greatest psychological blow of the war, McDonald relates in his book, *My Mission to Israel*:

> At this critical juncture Washington instructed me to deliver immediately to the Israel authorities the substance of a cable which radically changed the whole situation. This was Great Britain's dramatic threat—it became public property a few days later—to invoke its obligations under its treaty of 1936 with Egypt to come to her aid (though Cairo had not requested it) and to enter into war with Israel unless the Israel troops withdrew from Egyptian soil.[124]

And, as if this was not bad enough, McDonald went on to confirm: "The United States, in transmitting this British demand, strongly supported the UN position forbidding offensive military operations in Palestine or in Egypt and declared sharply that Israel must withdraw its troops at once if the war were not to spread."[125]

Was it poetic justice that Israel's prime minister received such disheartening news in the same town where Jews would market a Lido for dancing beside the very lake where Jesus walked—and on the goy New Year's Eve (which also fell on Shabbat)? In any event, while vigorously articulating Israel's obvious moral right to defend herself, especially against a coalition of five aggressor states, Ben-Gurion reluctantly agreed to the Attlee-Bevin ultimatum. According to McDonald's diary, their ninety-minute talk ended close to midnight.[126] By January 2, nearly all IDF troops had quit the Sinai, despite the fact that Egypt was still occupying Gaza. That evening, Cairo showed its "appreciation" by bombing Jewish Jerusalem—the first time in history that *any* belligerent power dared to attack the Holy City by air.[127]

THE LAST "BATTLE"

The last battle of the first Arab-Israeli War was a two-phase aerial engagement over southern Palestine on January 7, 1949. Two days earlier, the Egyptian government had notified the UN of its willingness to accept a ceasefire and enter into negotiations with Israel. Consequently, a joint ceasefire was agreed upon to begin at 2 p.m. on January 7. As the final day dawned, both sides attempted last-minute blows. While Israeli Harvards dive-bombed Dir El-Ballah, one of their P-51 escorts destroyed a Royal Egyptian Air Force (REAF) fighter.[128]

Around noon, four menacing Spitfire FR18s buzzed an IDF convoy that had just been attacked by five Egyptian Spitfire LF9s. (The two

Spitfire models were similar in appearance.) In the ensuing anti-aircraft barrage, one plane was downed, and a second damaged. As the ground forces were being strafed, two British-built, Czech-supplied IAF Spitfire LF9s, flown by American Chalmers "Slick" Goodlin and Canadian John McElroy, arrived and took out all three remaining intruders. One pilot was killed, another rescued by Bedouins, while the other two were captured and taken to Tel Aviv for interrogation.[129]

Later that day, four more FR18s—escorted by *fifteen* Hawker Tempest fighters—returned to the scene. This time an IAF patrol of four LF9s roared in to intercept the mini armada. The Israeli formation was led by Ezer Weizman (legendary future IAF commander and seventh president of Israel). The other participants were Weizman's native wingman, Alex "Sandy" Jacobs, followed by Americans Bill Schroeder and Caesar Dangott. In the 23-plane melee, Schroeder got the only kill (a Hawker Tempest flown by David Tattersfield) while Ezer's plane and two "enemy" aircraft suffered minor damage. In two of the many uncanny incidents of the day, it was later discovered that over half of the Tempests had left Fayid field with their guns loaded, but in the *uncocked* position, while many of their external fuel tank cradle arms had also been over-tightened, preventing the pilots from attaining emergency maneuverability by jettisoning their drop tanks.[130]

Now about the time this dogfight was fixin' to become a turkey-shoot, the disabled airmen started waggling their wings as a signal to the Israelis that "something was *definitely* wrong with this picture." Fortunately, the frantic measure worked. The four IAF Spitfires promptly disengaged and returned to Hatzor Airbase. As things turned out, it was all one big mistake. The "enemy" planes were not R*E*AF; they were actually…*uh*…just—RAF. Apparently, the original four British FR18s were on a reconnaissance sortie along the border when they spotted the flaming IDF column and decided to reconnoiter. They were also unaware of the September 7 ceasefire. B. T. Williamson, a retired RAF squadron leader writes, "[D]ue to an astonishing foul-up in communications [a *third* freak occurrence] this information was never actually passed to the British forces in the Canal Zone."[131]

Thus, after being strafed by look-alike Spitfires, the IDF naturally tried to stop a recurrence. And why would British planes be violating Israeli sovereignty anyway?[132] After all, hadn't HMG just threatened to declare war on tiny Israel for having some of *her* troops on *Egyptian* soil? Williamson states: "The formation had been clearly briefed not to cross the frontier into Israel; however, it had also been made clear that any information they obtained if they 'accidentally' strayed over the border somewhere along the featureless desert, would be most welcome."[133] The former RAF officer then confirms: "Close [captured pilot] was allowed to talk to various press correspondents, who quoted him as saying the formation had crossed the frontier into Israel."[134]

The day after the attack, the Israeli pilots sent their Limey detractors the following generic olive branch apology: "Sorry about yesterday, but you were on the wrong side of the fence. Come over here and have a drink sometime. You will see many familiar faces."[135] To Israel's credit, the two captured pilots were later released to their superiors, appropriately enough—on a slow boat to Cyprus. Privately, the Brits must have been miffed as this was not their first embarrassing encounter with the IAF. On November 20, 1948, Wayne Peake, a non-Jewish, American WWII veteran, described as a "guitar-strumming Carolina hillbilly," downed a sophisticated, high-flying RAF de Havilland Mosquito PR34 surveillance aircraft as it flew toward Hazor in Upper Galilee.[136] Noting that these special planes spied on "various Middle East countries, including Palestine," Williamson went on to say: "The intelligence gathered from these missions helped inform a plan known as 'Barter' which entailed the UK going to the aid of Transjordan under the terms of the Anglo-Transjordan Treaty."[137] So, would anyone like to guess how much intel had gone to Glubb Pasha??

The bottom line of this surreal finale to the 1948 War is a four-point spiritual explanation that has *nothing* to do with any "fog of war" scenario: 1) Five days after Jerusalem was bombed by Britain's "ally," Britain lost five aircraft—equipment that theoretically would have augmented those ominous invasion plans announced on New Year's Eve; 2) The "mix-up" would never have happened had Britain refrained from supplying the REAF with over thirty Spitfires resembling her own planes; 3) At the end of the day (literally), the IAF pilots, outnumbered 4-1, were able to make it home safely because their adversaries had encountered a host of "technical difficulties"; 4) As with that second, unexplainable friendly-fire bombing of the British graves in Oświęcim, the tragic deaths of two RAF pilots on January 7, 1949, nonetheless represents *another* unsettling illustration of divine retribution. (As a gesture of reconciliation, when the body of David Tattersfield was laid to rest in the British War Cemetery at Ramleh on January 11, six members of the IAF carried his coffin.[138])

GENERAL ARMISTICE AGREEMENTS

On March 5, 1949, Israel launched "Operation Ovda," the last campaign of the war. Five days later, the IDF was at the Red Sea, taking Umm al-Rashrash without a battle. (Later renamed Eilat, the port would serve as Israel's lifeline through the Gulf of Aqaba and Straits of Tiran to markets in Africa and Asia.) A makeshift Israeli flag, fashioned from a white sheet inscribed with ink (a.k.a. the "Ink Flag") was raised to commemorate March 10, 1949, as the formal end of the 1948 War. After a gestation period lasting nine months, three weeks, and two days, Israel's newborn freedom had *finally* arrived!

By this time, formal armistice talks were underway (the precursor to the peace process). On January 13, 1949, Egyptian and Israeli diplomats began UN-brokered negotiations on the island of Rhodes. Six weeks later, on February 24, the first General Armistice Agreement (GAA) was signed by both parties officially ending hostilities. The Rhodes demarcation line reflected the existing military border with one exception; Israel had to forfeit the Gaza coastal strip. With King Farouk setting the pace, Lebanon reached a similar deal with Israel on March 23 after only three weeks of talks at the frontier town of Rosh HaNikrah. Sustaining a military coup in Damascus on March 30, Syria proved the least cooperative belligerent, maintaining a filibuster from April 5 to July 20 (in a Bedouin tent, no less) before acquiescing to the original borders—with one notable caveat; IDF troops could not replace departing Syrian forces, creating another series of demilitarized zones. The Kingdom of Iraq was a no-show, having authorized the Jordanian delegation as its representative.[139]

As expected, Abdullah I was the wiliest negotiator of all. Having held private talks with Israel since November 1948 (his front men at Rhodes simply going through the motions), the Emir made his *official* "concession" on April 3—eventually gaining most of the West Bank (central Palestine hill country). As the Palestinians rejected their UN portion in November 1947, why shouldn't the Hashemites scoop it up? In Abdullah's defense, he was only doing the "people's will" per the

Jericho Conference of December 1948, where a handful of handpicked pro-Jordanian Palestinian leaders had petitioned for annexation, later known as the "Unification of the Two Banks." (Ensconced on both sides of the river, the Kingdom would soon drop the "Trans.") Though unable to prevent Abdullah's land grab in the main, Israeli negotiators were successful in gaining a significant eastward extension of the Rhodes Armistice Demarcation Line, the so-called "Green Line" forming the de facto border between Israel and its new Arab neighbors (named after the green marker with which it was drawn).[140]

Overall, postwar Israel ended up with 8,000 square miles of Palestine, or 21% more territory than allotted under the UN plan. However, the new Jordanian jurisdiction over Jerusalem would constitute a major train wreck in the making. While New Jerusalem *technically* remained in Jewish hands, with the Old City (including the historic Jewish Quarter) remaining in Arab hands, Emir Abdullah had replaced HMG as the new landlord. The Jews were assured access to priority sites such as Hadassah Hospital, the Hebrew University on Mount Scopus, and the Jewish cemetery on Mount Olivet. However, as Sachar notes, "The convoluted nature of the Jerusalem settlement, with its precarious easements to educational sites and holy places, was too dependent on Arab goodwill to be inherently workable."[141] The same dangers would prevail with the Egyptian presence in Gaza and the Syrian perch atop the demilitarized Golan Heights.

Finally, though King Abdullah I bin al-Hussein of Transjordan had been duly upgraded to "King of All Palestine" by that sham conference (the official resolution adopted April 24, 1950, in a joint session of the Jordan House of Deputies and Notables), he would not have long to enjoy his new title. As the ground he claimed in Allah's name was already spoken for (Exodus 3:5 calling it "*holy* ground," i.e., belonging to *Israel's* God), the sixty-nine-year-old Muslim was fatally shot on Friday (Islam's "holy day"), July 20, 1951, while praying at Al-Aqsa Mosque. The assassin was a twenty-one-year-old fellow Mohammedan named Mustafa Ashi. (The exiled Mufti, Al-Husseini, was later implicated in the plot.)[142] The departed King was succeeded by his son, Talal bin Abdullah. However, since Talal was actually mentally ill, *his* son, Hussein bin Talal, took over on August 11, 1952.

SEEDS OF THE REFUGEE CRISIS

Israel's application for United Nations membership was approved by the Security Council on March 11, 1949. Sachar writes, "As the Israeli flag was ceremoniously hoisted in the plaza of the General Assembly building, Shertok, Eban, and other participants, together with the Jewish world at large, asked themselves whether only four years had passed since the Star of David had been identified primarily as the seal of doom worn by concentration camp inmates."[143] However, no sooner did the hard-fought political legitimacy of the nascent Jewish state finally appear to be up and running, than a new crisis arose—a skewed public relations albatross that continues to this day.

The most enduring postwar deception exploited by Palestinian mythologists concerns the so-called "mass *expulsion*" of innocent Palestinian civilians as ordered by the government of Prime Minister David Ben-Gurion. This lie has, in turn, spawned two other delusional mantras—the so-called "Palestinian Refugee Problem," compounded by the so-called "Palestinian Right of Return" (the latter involving an exponentially rising number of claimants). Amateur historian Alison Weir begins by stating: "Within months [of UN Resolution 181] the Zionists had forced out over 413,000 people."[144] Of course, she doesn't explain *how* this was pulled off given the ubiquitous British military presence that checked every Jewish irregularity.[145] The pro-Arab British proximity would also negate Weir's other baseless charge that the IDF perpetrated "at least 33 massacres of Palestinian villages, half of them before a single Arab joined the conflict."[146] She then writes, "[B]y the end of Israel's 'War of Independence' over 750,000 Palestinian men, women, and children were ruthlessly expelled."[147]

Also, how can Israel stand charged with "displacement of Arabs" in areas of western Palestine where there *were* no Jews, i.e., the West Bank? The only portion of "Palestine" that applies to the claim that Jews "displaced" Arabs is that sliver of western Palestine assigned *to* the Zionists. For instance, the Negev was 50% of the 70% of land in western Palestine originally allotted to Israel in 1948. The majority of Weir's inflated figures (and claims) represent Palestinians from *Arab* territory. There is also the rarely discussed imperceptible element in western Palestine known as "Arab In-Migration," positing that a sizeable percentage of the so-called "indigenous Palestinian Arab population," extant at the time of the Balfour Declaration, comprised recent arrivals, having neither land nor legacy. Dr. Carl H. Voss, then-chairman of the American Christian Palestine Committee, wrote in 1953: "The Arab population of Palestine was small and limited until Jewish resettlement restored the barren land and drew to it Arabs from neighboring countries. When organized Jewish colonization began in 1882, there were fewer than 150,000 Arabs in the land.[148]

Regarding Weir's original claim, note how the esteemed Jewish scholar, Dr. Avram Noam Chomsky, Professor Emeritus at Massachusetts Institute of Technology, a.k.a. "Father of Modern Linguistics," author of over 100 books, recipient of over forty honorary degrees, voted the "world's top public intellectual" in 2005—and *no friend of the modern State of Israel*—was prudent enough to add *one* little word to her statement in his *own* anti-Semitic work, *Fateful Triangle*: "About 700,000 Palestinians FLED (author's emphasis) or were expelled in the 1948 conflict."[149] (For what it's worth, Weir even contradicted herself in her own endnote documenting the initial assertion that 413,000 people had been "forced out," stating on page 173: "Dr. Benny Morris [another anti-Israel Jew], an Israeli historian, reports that 400,000 Palestinians FLED (author's emphasis) between November 29, 1947 and June 1, 1948."[150]) But then, even Chomsky left *his* readers deceived by the disingenuous way he employed that other word, implying that the Palestinians who *were* "expelled" were ejected by the IDF, when the great majority departed at the behest of their *own* leaders. (Like the drafters of Israel's Declaration, Noam's former employer, led by its Jewish president, L. Rafael Reif, barred God from the school's 2014 commencement benediction because of one critical op-ed—by a *Jewish* student.)

The historical record is clear, being affirmed by British and American officials alike. An MI6 report from April 1948 stated: "Jewish victories in Tiberias, Haifa, Jaffa and Qatamon have reduced Arab morale to zero and, following the cowardly example of their inept leaders, they are fleeing from the mixed areas in thousands."[151] That month the US consulate in Haifa confirmed that the "local Mufti-dominated Arab leaders urge all Arabs [to] leave [the] city and large numbers [are] going." (Haifa's Arab population of 65,000 was second only to Jaffa's 70,000.) Three days later, US assessment was more precise: "Reportedly [the] Arab Higher Committee [is] ordering all Arabs [to] leave." Writing on the same day to the colonial secretary in London, Sir Alan Cunningham,

High Commissioner of Palestine, was equally frank: "British authorities in Haifa have formed the impression that total evacuation is being urged on the Haifa Arabs from higher Arab quarters and that the townsfolk themselves are against it."[152]

The Arab Higher Committee (AHC) appeared to use the carrot-and-stick approach. While some Palestinian residents received threatening letters stating that unless they evacuated they would be "branded as traitors deserving of death,"[153] others were told that if they left *temporarily*, they would share in the postwar spoils.[154] Overall, the civilian population felt led to hit the road because of Arab perfidy. Sir Henry Gurney, chief secretary to the Palestine Mandate Government and a scathing critic of Zionism, recorded in his diary on May 5, 1948:

> The Arabs are rabbits...90% of the population of Jaffa have just run away...only some 5,000 remain. Yesterday the municipal engineer locked the pumping station, and walked off...The Mayor has gone, without even saying goodbye...the remnants of the Liberation army are looting and robbing. This is what the Palestine Arabs get from the aid provided by the Arab states.[155]

Conversely, while Arab leaders were working to eject their own, the Jews were trying to halt the stampede. In April 1948, the British district superintendant of police in Haifa noted: "Every effort is being made by the Jews to persuade the Arab population to stay and carry on with their normal lives, to get their shops and businesses open and to be assured that their lives and interests will be safe."[156] In an unprecedented act, the Haifa rabbinate even issued Jewish bakers a special dispensation to make extra bread during the Passover holiday for distribution among their hurting Arab neighbors.[157] The sincerity of these overtures was also corroborated by local American officials. On April 26, Vice-Consul Aubrey Lippincott informed Washington that the "Jews want them [to] remain for political reasons to show [the] democratic treatment they will get...." And in a follow-up cable three days later, he cited an Arab source accusing Jews of having "organized a large propaganda campaign to persuade [the] Arabs to return."[158]

In fact, the Jews' offer was *so* good, that the usually stoic Major-General Hugh Stockwell, Sixth Airborne Division Commander in Haifa, berated the Arabs for having rejected it: "You have made a foolish decision...Think it over, as you'll regret it afterward. You must accept the conditions of the Jews. They are fair enough. Don't permit life to be destroyed senselessly. After all, it was you who began the fighting, and the Jews have won."[159] Of course, the only "problem" with the general's approach was that it was *rational*; thus, the Muslims' brain-dead reply was: "We will not sign...All is already lost, and it does not matter if everyone is killed so long as we do not sign the document."[160] Furthermore, on April 27, 1950, the Arab Higher Committee of Haifa admitted in a memo to the Arab States: "The removal of the Arab inhabitants...was voluntary and was carried out at our request. The Arab delegation proudly asked for the evacuation of the Arabs and their removal to the neighboring Arab countries...."[161]

The evacuation scenario displayed by the two largest Arab population centers set the pace for the rest of Palestine. The Arab Liberation Army was also instrumental in displacing its citizens. Karsh writes, "Indeed, the deliberate depopulation of Arab villages and their transformation into military strongholds were marked corollaries of the Arab campaign from the onset of hostilities...At times there was no need to order an evacuation. The mere fear of ALA occupation was sufficiently alarming to spark flight...."[162]

The main, though infrequent, exception where Arab locals were evicted by Israeli troops was mandated by ad hoc battle zone security considerations (*another* rational approach).[163] Karsh cites the cities of Lydda and Ramle as being "the first, indeed the *only*, instance in the war where a substantial urban population [30,000] was driven out by Jewish or Israeli forces." Like the American GIs in Vietnam—after a hard-fought, tenuous victory, "the IDF felt unable to leave a potential hotbed of armed resistance at its rear which might disrupt the ongoing offensive at a time when the Legion was recuperating...."[164]

While Israel's critics would reject such a threat rationale toward Arab "friendlies," Attlee pushed the envelope by likening the timely arrival of Shoah survivor/volunteers to Nazis: "That was just Hitler's method. He put people in as tourists, but they were soon armed once they got in. The Jews would put them in as immigrants but they would soon become soldiers, and it was known that they were already being drilled and trained."[165] Thus, as the fighting continued, Tel Aviv grew increasingly resistant to the premature return of *any* Arab refugees, given the obvious threat of their becoming a Fifth Column.

PALESTINIAN RIGHT OF RETURN

As the Cold War replaced WWII, Israel was destined to experience her own protracted era of postwar tension, specifically over the repatriation issue, a.k.a. "Palestinian Right of Return." On December 11, 1948, the UNGA set the bar by passing Resolution 194 to recognize this so-called right. However, after nearly seven decades of debate in the court of public opinion, the problem remains unresolved.

As borne out by five subsequent wars (and two intifadas), the main reason for the impasse continues to center on Israel's basic right to exist. The trajectory was set early on. Addressing the UNGA's annual session in Paris on November 22, 1948, AHC delegate Henry Cattan, had the audacity to revisit Hitler's racist ideology, stating: "Arab opposition to the creation of a Jewish state in Palestine followed a law of nature which could be likened to the resistance of the human body to a cancerous growth," concluding defiantly, "That opposition would continue until the cancer was destroyed."[166] Having correctly assessed the situation, Israel's foreign minister, Moshe Shertok, articulated his nation's only option regarding Palestinian repatriation:

> The root cause of the present conflict – of which the mass flight of Arabs and their consequent suffering are mere corollaries – is the refusal of the Arab League to accept the State of Israel either as a matter of right or an accomplished fact...As long as this intransigence persists, any attempt to tear the problem of Arab refugees out of its context and treat it in isolation can only, as already stated, aggravate the issue...When the Arab States are ready to conclude a peace treaty with Israel, this question will come up for constructive solution as part of the general settlement."[167]

Ben-Gurion reiterated this rational approach, stating in September 1948, "Should we be able to have direct talks with the Arabs that will culminate in peace – we will return the refugees. Should the [postwar] settlement fall short of peace with the Arabs – we will not allow their return."[168] In 1949, Israel set the number of war-related refugees at between 550,000 and 600,000.[169] However, in the twenty-first century, the total number, including all "kinfolk," can range anywhere from a low of 5,000,000 to over 10,000,000, depending on what crackpot anti-Semitic source is cited, beginning with the corrupt United Nations

Relief and Works Agency for Palestine Refugees (UNRWA). And the *repatriation* figure only grows when coupled with the equally insane demand for financial *reparation*.

Though the world will never admit the truth whenever it favors Israel, let the record state that the entire crisis is a hypocritical sham for three obvious reasons. First, if conditions among the Israelis were so bad, why would the Arab powers want to force their Palestinian cousins back in? Meinertzhagen posed this contradiction in August 1948: "The Arab States, who have repeatedly stated that they are invading Palestine to save the Arabs from Jewish terror, now want to return the refugees to Israel."[170] Second, if the freedom-loving Palestinian refugees are so bent on regaining their "forfeited political sovereignty," why did they never protest once during the two decades they were annexed to neighboring Jordan? Third, not only did the Arab League *create* the refugee crisis by *starting* the war, then *prevent* its immediate end by *refusing* to recognize Israel, but most egregiously it has *perpetrated* the crisis by keeping the exiles in *perpetual* refugee status by *refusing* to absorb them into their *own* expansive territories.

Then, in the rare cases when asylum *is* afforded, the "hospitality" is usually limited to squalid camps, as citizenship is rarely offered—all while Israel stays condemned for *its* refugee policies in the West Bank! Decades of studies have confirmed the obvious societal advantages that Palestinian émigrés would gain by settling within the common culture of their "host" nations. The added fact that UN funds have never lacked only exacerbates the transgression. This untenable position has also elicited criticism from independent Arab spokesmen.

There is no end to the degree of "spin" incumbent upon Palestinian mythologists. For instance, why is it never mentioned that Israel had its *own* refugee crisis to confront—the hordes of Jews summarily evicted from *their* homes in Arab lands after November 1947? Christians normally equate Israel as a haven for Holocaust survivors. Yet, as early as 1918, nearly half of the total Jewish population in Jerusalem consisted of "Mizrahi/Oriental" Jews (i.e., hailing from the Middle East)—as opposed to "Ashkenazi" (European) or "Sephardi" (Iberian) Jewry—the majority of whom had fled Muslim persecution.

With all the UN scaremongering over the hoax of "global overpopulation," was it possible that Israel—one of the smallest countries in the world—was getting a tad cramped accepting her *own* exiles?

According to a March 7, 1951, report by President Truman's International Development Advisory Board: "Israel, occupying an area of 8,100 square miles, which in three years has been compelled to absorb 700,000 Jewish refugees—almost equivalent in number to the Arab refugee population, half of them in flight from Moslem countries of the Middle East and North Africa, cannot reabsorb the Arabs who fled its borders. But it can, and, indeed, has offered to contribute to a fund for Arab resettlement."[171] (According to some nutty State Department source cited by Weir, that fund amounted to "500 cases of oranges"[172]—as if Israel owed her defeated foes even one orange *peel.*)

As dictated by the Arab League agenda, the elusive "right of return" is the *only* "human right" the Palestinians will *ever* have. The bottom line is that they are simply too valuable as political bargaining chips and public relations tools for eliciting sympathy to *ever* be freed. Like one disgruntled refugee in Kuwait told *Forbes Magazine* editor James Cook in 1975, "They owe me citizenship. I've been here for nearly 20 years and I helped create this country's great wealth. I did. I haven't simply earned my citizenship, they owe it to me."[173] By keeping the refugee saga center court, a major shift in public perception has occurred—from the xenophobic and powerful Arab world opposing the tiny Jewish state—to a localized battle between the bully Zionist nuclear power and the tiny homeless "nation" of rock-throwing Palestinian exiles. (The publicized deaths of 2,000 Gaza "civilians" in the 2014 Israel-Hamas war is germane to this point.)

Behind all the rhetoric, Muslims believe that a fabricated "Arab Palestinian" identity, maintained at the cost of untold human suffering, is the new political panacea for attaining what they failed to accomplish through military might—the annihilation of the Zionist presence. Even Jordan's King Hussein was willing to finger his own, declaring in an Associated Press interview with the *Daily Star* in Beirut on January 19, 1960: "Since 1948 Arab leaders have approached the Palestine problem in an irresponsible manner...They have used the Palestinian people for selfish political purposes. This is ridiculous and, I could even say, criminal."[174] In the final analysis, every single *bit* of the blame for the Palestinian refugee crisis must rest squarely upon the Arabs themselves.

Perhaps the most succinct, post-game analysis of the 1948-49 Islamic disaster was provided by a Nablus-born Sunni Muslim named Muhammad Izzat Darwaza. The author of over thirty volumes, Darwaza divided his career choices between educator, historian, and politician. As a longtime sympathizer of Arab nationalism, as well as an outspoken opponent of the British Mandate, the pan-Arab intellectual joined the Arab Executive Committee in 1930, later becoming a principle organizer of the 1936-39 Arab Revolt. In 1946, he joined the Arab Higher Committee led by Haj Amin al-Husseini. However, after only one year, he resigned in disgust and promptly moved to Syria. In 1972, the Arab "Uncle Tom" rendered the following politically incorrect assessment, hinting (rather strongly) that the *al-Nakba* was—in reality—a *self-inflicted* catastrophe:

> The Arabs failed their fateful test not because of numerical or material inferiority – for the Jews had no edge in either category. They failed because of the spirit that had guided them for quite some time and continues to do so...A spirit of laziness, neglect, incompetence, indecision, divisiveness, delusion, humbug...lack of seriousness, willingness to sacrifice, and solidarity...and no true belief in the cause for which they are fighting.[175]

THE KEY TO THE CITY

On May 15, 2008, an event was held in Bethlehem to mark the sixtieth anniversary of *al-Nakba*, the great Palestinian displacement vis-à-vis the birth of the Jewish state. The main attraction was the unveiling of a monument erected adjacent to the Al Aida UNRWA refugee facility—a giant, two-ton, nine-meter-long steel *key* (reputedly the world's largest) resting atop a uniquely shaped mammoth keyhole (serving as the camp's entrance). The Arab folk symbol, made by refugees at the Aida Social Youth Center, was a militant reminder of the Palestinian Right of Return. (In 2012, the key was flown to Germany to appear at a public relations exhibit at the Berlin Biennale; how appropriate!)

Though far less imposing, another piece of "art," created by a local teenager, projects the same theme. "Resolution 194, a UN resolution," features four real keys from Palestinian families who left their houses in 1948, hanging in a keyhole-shaped niche behind a sliding face inscribed with the number "194." The obvious reference points to the feckless UN support for repatriation. Numerous variations of the "Key of Return" (most commonly a literal key hung around the refugee's neck or carried in the sleeve of his jellabiya) permeate the Palestinian world, representing the leading motif for the Right of Return shtick.

But there is only one problem with these Muslim "keys"—*they* will never work. As covered in the Introduction, the *only* key that matters in the Church Age, in Israel (or elsewhere), is a *Jewish* key, i.e., *"the key of David"* (Revelation 3:7; Isaiah 22:22). David secured his key, the original "key to the city," when he bought Araunah's threshing floor—*fifteen centuries before Mohammad's first birthday party* (II Samuel 24:24-25). The *only* "Right of Return" that matters is the one about to occur at the Eastern Gate (Ezekiel 44:1-3; Zechariah 14:4). No cement wall guarded by any Muslim cemetery is going to keep the Jewish Messiah from riding right into the Holy City (Revelation 19:11-16). The Lord Jesus Christ, King of Kings and Lord of Lords, is *more* than able to pass *through* graveyards and mortar, having *already* done so, albeit in reverse order (Matthew 27:66; John 20:15).

In the meantime, since Muslims *profess* to believe in the Jewish Old Testament, they would save themselves a lot of time and trouble by reading the book of Nehemiah. Facing the PLO of *his* day—a coalition of disgruntled locals boasting an independent *"army of Samaria"* (Nehemiah 4:2) who threatened the Jews with Jihad for rebuilding the walls and gates of Jerusalem (*despite* the fact that the region was under *Persian* jurisdiction)—Nehemiah, gave them the *final* prophetic "what for" on the so-called "Palestinian Problem":

> *"Then answered I them, and said unto them, The God of heaven, he will prosper us; therefore we his servants will arise and build: but ye have no* PORTION [East Jerusalem], *nor* RIGHT [Right of Return], *nor* MEMORIAL [Dome of the Rock], *in Jerusalem."*
> (Nehemiah 2:20)

15

Sinai: The Hundred-Hour War

"Hitler of the Nile"
(London *Daily Mail's* sobriquet for Nasser)

"Go choke on your fury."
(Nasser to the US, July 26, 1956)

"That terrible man."
(Eden's appraisal of John Foster Dulles)

THE BIBLE SAYS, *"Joshua made war a long time...."* (Joshua 11:18) The modern Jewish state would do the same. In just the first six decades of her tenuous existence, Israel would divert 20% of her resources to seven wars and two intifadas—one conflict every 6.66 years. The Scripture also says that the Jews' troubles began when many of Christ's disciples *"went back, and walked no more with him."* (John 6:66) Thankfully, as "Joshua" (Hebrew equivalent of Jesus) means "Jehovah saves," the "Rock of Israel" would *continue* to deliver His covenant nation—whether they acknowledged Him or not. As the last book in God's Word shows—her *ultimate* deliverance will be from the number 666 itself (Revelation 13:18).

PREWAR DEVELOPMENTS

Israel's second war in seven years was fought with Egypt in the fall of 1956. The main theaters were the Sinai Peninsula and the Suez Canal. Several salient events occurred during the opening prewar interlude.

The first national election was on January 25, 1949. The emergent republican polity (a British-Zionist hybrid) featured a prime minister and titular president working in tandem with a cabinet, parliament, and judiciary. The Knesset is a unicameral legislature, delimited to 120 seats elected by ballots cast for party lists rather than individual members. (The First Knesset in 1947 had 21 party lists.) To the surprise of many, the only democracy in the Middle East has never had a written constitution; a tri-tiered court guards the civil and religious rights of all citizens with special attention afforded to Arab minorities. The internecine cancer of Israeli politics has been *government by coalition*, described by historian George Kirk as separate entities "entwined in an inimical embrace like two fighting serpents."[1] Dr. Paul Eidelberg writes in *The Myth of Israeli Democracy*: "In Israel, the multiplicity of rival parties in the cabinet not only precludes coherent and resolute national policies; it also produces governments whose average duration is less than two years, thus making the pursuit of long-range national goals impossible."[2] (On May 14, 2015, Benjamin Netanyahu formed the nation's 34th government in sixty-seven years.)

The most significant bill enacted in the first year was the comprehensive Defensive Service Law. This vital security measure (patterned after the Swiss mobilization model), legalized Israel's citizen army, dividing every subject (both sexes) into regular and reserve IDF units. (Arabs and Orthodox Jews were exempted.) With the surrounding Arab populations eclipsing Israel forty to one, the need for an expanded military became the main impetus for the immigration boom of the foundational era. Approximately 340,000 Jews made aliyah in the first eighteen months after the Declaration of Independence. In July 1950, the First Knesset passed a "Jewish" Law of Return, affording Diaspora Jewry the legal right of immigration to Israel. Thus, between May 15, 1948, and June 30, 1953, the Jewish population in Israel doubled, then nearly tripled by 1957 to 1,667,000.[3]

The massive influx of émigrés caused a two-fold shock to the nascent state—cultural and economic. Surprisingly, the greatest amount of arrivals hailed from Moslem lands. While "Operation Magic Carpet" airlifted 47,000 Yemeni Jews, "Operation Ali Baba" delivered another 131,000 from Iraq.[4] (Additional masses hailed from Iran, Kurdistan, Afghanistan, Turkey, Libya, Syria, Lebanon, and Egypt.) Though Orientals comprised only 14% of immigration in 1948, the figure rose to 47% in 1949, then 92% in 1955 (the eve of the Sinai crisis). In 1948, Ashkenazi Jews accounted for 75% of Israel's population; by 1961 the number had fallen to 55%.[5] That this unanticipated flood of Eastern Jewry had little or no Zionist affinity was only slightly less vexatious than their indigent status (the malaise-impacted North Africans among the poorest). Their meager backwater possessions had equaled the "exact amount" of their exit visas (Reich Flight Tax). Thus, by 1951, 97,000 men, women, and children (10% of Israel) were "living" in 17,000 tents in 53 refugee camps (an unsettling experience not unlike the Jews' former subsistence at Atlit).

The year 1952 would represent a milestone for the fledgling Jewish state. Previously, on September 20, 1945, Weizmann had petitioned the victorious Allies for reparations on behalf of German Jewry. Seven years later, the prospect of direct negotiations with Berlin (West Germany's *de jure* capital 1949-90) precipitated a national crisis of conscience. Nonetheless, on September 10, 1952, the controversial Treaty of Luxembourg was formalized, assigning $820 million in goods and currency to Israel, spread over fourteen years. On November 9, Dr. Chaim Weizmann—world-renowned chemist, Zionist patriarch, and sitting first president of the State of Israel—died at 6:30 a.m. in his home at the Weizmann Institute of Science in Rehovot, eighteen days shy of his seventy-eighth birthday. (After Albert Einstein declined Ben Gurion's personal invitation to assume the presidency, Yitzhak Ben-Zvi followed, serving until 1963.) A glass-enclosed custom-built Ford Lincoln Cosmopolitan is displayed near Chaim's gravesite on the Institute campus. The luxury limo, a duplicate from the presidential fleet produced for Harry Truman, was presented to the Jewish leader in 1950 by none other than Henry Ford II (as a belated post-victory gift).

Also in November 1952, Republican Dwight D. Eisenhower defeated Democrat Adlai Stevenson to become the 42nd chief executive of the United States. Thus, the Jewish nation lost President Weizmann *and* her beloved President Truman just five days apart. Loftus and Aarons write: "The Israelis no longer had friends in the American government."[6] However, a third "changing of the guard" (occurring four months earlier) would prove the most telling prewar event of all.

THE COLONEL'S COUP

On July 22, 1952, eight disgruntled military officers overthrew Egypt's King Farouk in a near-bloodless, twenty-four-hour coup d'état. The key participant (after Muhammad Naguib, Egypt commander in 1948) was a young ambitious colonel named Gamal Abdel Nasser Hussein. Nasser's two main confidants were Muhammad Anwar El-Sadat (his future successor) and Abdel Hakim Amer. Michael Oren, former Israeli ambassador to the US, writes, "[T]he CIA had quietly assisted his coup...."[7] Burton Hersh adds: "[T]he Acheson State Department rubberstamped the fateful coup...."[8] Allen Dulles (by then CIA director) slipped the emerging strongman a prefatory $3,000,000 "get acquainted" gift.[9] Loftus and Aarons state that later perks included "Western arms and...intel against Israel...all part of a wider espionage war against the Jews...planned and executed by the Dulles brothers and their supporters in the Eisenhower administration, largely behind the president's back."[10]

The following June, Egypt was proclaimed a "republic." By November 1954, Nasser controlled the country, having evolved from prime minister to president by toppling General Naguib. The junta had three immediate goals: 1) impress the Ummah by antagonizing Israel; 2) cash in by forging a pan-Arab (i.e., Nasser-led) federation; 3) end British suzerainty (especially of the Suez Canal). Nasser's main competition was the Baghdad Pact of 1955, a British-inspired, Turkish-based Arab consortium, ostensibly formed to thwart Soviet hegemony. Also called the Central Treaty Organization (CENTO), the pact was eventually signed by Iraq, Iran, Turkey, Pakistan, and Britain.

When the State Department worsened matters by declining Egypt's request for weapons, Gamal turned to Moscow for a sympathetic ear. Upon Stalin's death on March 5, 1953, the Cold War baton passed to Nikita Sergeyevich Khruschev. By August 1955, the two nations concluded an unprecedented interest-free arms deal worth $320 million. For twelve years of cotton shipments, Egypt received 200 tanks, 150 artillery pieces, 120 MiGs, 50 jet bombers, 20 transport planes, 2 destroyers, 2 submarines, 15 minesweepers, a plethora of vehicles, plus thousands of rifles and machine guns.[11] Ironically, as the deal went down three years after Vladimír Clementis' execution, the arms came from Czechoslovakia. (To Israel's added dismay, Egypt's main coalition partner, Syria, also received a hefty weapons package.)

"HITLER OF THE NILE"

In 1939, Nasser called Hitler the "strongest man in Europe"[12] and collaborated with Nazi provocateurs during the war.[13] He also saw the creation of Israel as the "greatest international crime" in history.[14]

As Britain aided Abdullah, Nasser's neo-Fascist regime was progressively influenced by German personnel—supplied by the CIA. Hersh writes in *The Old Boys: The American Elite and the Origins of the CIA*: "For a number of months the political nutcutter in the office adjacent to Gamal Nasser was a CIA career man. To retrain the mildewed Egyptian Army, several hundred ex-Wehrmacht specialists reached Egypt; in addition fifty or so ex-SS intelligence officers [chief among them, Otto Scorzeny]."[15] Reinhard Gehlen, the former Nazi intel chief recruited by Dulles, affirmed: "We at Pullach did our best to inject life and expertise into the Egyptian secret service, supplying them with SS officers."[16] Richard Deacon states: "[I]t was somewhat of a shock to learn that, while some [Nazis] were bent solely on living anonymously in hiding in South America, others were once again pledged to attacking their old adversaries, the Jews...Egypt was engaging Germans not by the dozen, but by the score...."[17] Thankfully for Israel, her Mossad was able to penetrate Egypt's *Mukhabarat* (General Intelligence Directorate).[18]

In 1953, amidst rumors that Hitler was still alive, Cairo's leading weekly, *Al Musawwar*, asked a number of prominent Egyptians to submit a fantasy letter to the Führer. As everything rises and falls on leadership, Nasser's myrmidon, Colonel Sadat, penned the following: "My Dear Hitler, I congratulate you from the bottom of my heart. Even if you appear to have been defeated, in reality you are the victor." After a few more lines, he closes: "We will not be surprised if you appear again in Germany or if a new Hitler arises in your wake."[19] Three years later, the conservative London *Daily Mail* labeled Nasser, "Hitler of the Nile."[20] Whereas Churchill once called *Mein Kampf* the "new Koran of faith and war,"[21] Nasser's 1955 book, *The Philosophy of the Revolution*, was now being compared to *Mein Kampf*.[22]

Of his many anti-Semitic issues, the Nilotic "Hitler" had an old score to settle from the 1948 War. It was *his* 4,000-man brigade that was humiliated in the Faluja Pocket. Thus, in early 1954, Nasser initiated a series of Fedayun raids along Israel's frontier. Nearly 400 incidents were logged with the Egypt/Israeli Mixed Armistice Commission in just the first three months. Emboldened by UN incompetence, Palestinian terrorists extended their mayhem to the interior, destroying crops, bridges, roads, and pumping stations, while stealing everything that wasn't nailed down. Raiding parties murdered families in their sleep, planted mines along roads to schools, and tossed grenades into children's bedrooms.[23] Israeli cargo vessels (and ships bound for Israel) were also being stopped at the Suez Canal and the Straits of Tiran. By now, both Sadat and his minister of national guidance, Salah Salem, opposed *any* peace initiatives with Israel.[24]

After a record forty-five Palestinian sorties in February 1955, the IDF launched a major, brigade-sized strike on Gaza. Tensions reached postwar highs. With Israel out-gunned 6-1, Nasser's plans were hardly veiled (Luke 11:21-22). When Ben-Gurion petitioned America to attain emergency weapons parity, Ike piously declined, citing the 1952 NEACC Arms embargo. ("We already refused Egypt," etc.) However, as Oxford scholar Anthony Verrier writes: "Eisenhower was intent on his forthcoming election campaign, determined to become a peace-making President…'hasten slowly' was a good motto in election year. In deference to the far more powerful oil lobby, Eisenhower hastened with extreme slowness in supplying Israel with weapons: he supplied none."[25] Daniel Yergin adds, "The Suez Crisis of 1956, which truly marked the end of the road for the old European imperial powers, was as much about oil as about anything else."[26]

PERES TO PARIS

Fortunately for Israel, France was experiencing her own problems with Egypt, specifically Nasser's support of the escalating *Front de Libération Nationale* (FLN) insurgency in Algeria. Also, since 1949 Israeli nuclear scientists had been working at Saclay in the planning and construction of the French experimental reactor known as EL-2.[27]

Politics aside, however, French Prime Minister Guy Mollet could empathize with the Jews, having spent seven months in Buchenwald as a political prisoner.[28] Thus, in December 1954, France stepped up to the plate and approved an initial Israeli order for twelve Dassault Ouragon jet fighters. Building on this momentum, Shimon Peres, director-general of the ministry of defense, visited Paris in early 1955 to do some *serious* shopping. A second deal was closed in October for sixty additional Mystères.[29] Though Eisenhower tried to dissuade the sale—reminding Mollet that 1,700,000 Jews could never defeat forty million Arabs,[30] France was resolved to atone for the Dreyfus Affair.

In a bellicose address on June 19, 1956, Nasser declared: "We must be strong in order to regain the rights of the Palestinians by force."[31] His military commander, Abdel Hakim Amer, warned on July 5: "The hour is approaching when [we]...will stand in the front ranks of the battle against imperialism and its Zionist ally."[32] On September 29, 1956, Mollet came through once again, providing Israel with 100 Super-Sherman tanks, 200 armored personnel carriers, 300 six-by-six trucks, and 20 tank transporters.[33]

GAMAL'S CANAL

Nasser's main domestic priority was ameliorating Egypt's population explosion by enlarging her tillable acreage. This required dispersing the Nile's waters more efficiently over the uncultivated periphery of the valley. Consequently, Nasser proposed a High Dam three miles south of Aswan between the First Cataract and the Sudan frontier.

Though the construction budget was *high* (especially with the unplanted cotton crop mortgaged for weapons), Nasser got preliminary assurances for a $1 billion loan from the World Bank. However, after learning of the pending Soviet-bloc arms deal, the US (i.e., Secretary of State John Foster Dulles) withdrew its financial commitment ($56 million) on July 19, 1956. Following Britain's defection two days later, the loan was rescinded. The timing was uncanny; only a month earlier, the last British troops withdrew from the canal in accordance with an agreement negotiated by then-Foreign Minister Anthony Eden.

Less than one week later, Nasser stunned the world by cancelling the Anglo-French concession and nationalizing the Suez Canal Company. He made his brazen decree from Alexandria's Manchia Square on July 26 (fourth anniversary of Farouk's abdication). In his speech over live radio, Nasser told the West: "Go choke on your fury!"[34] If the "powers that be" would not *loan* him the capital, the wily colonel would *raise* the dough by charging *them* a toll to use "Gamal's Canal." With the passing of Ibn Saud on November 9, 1953, Nasser was now being nostalgically cast as the up-and-coming "Father of the Arab World." As biographer

Saïd Aburish wrote: "Soon his pictures were to be found in the tents of Yemen, the souks of Marrakesh, and the posh villas of Syria...He was giving Arabs a sense of being which had been denied them for most of the 20th century."[35]

While Nasser (in the spirit of II Duce) ended the historic day by slipping into the Metro Cinema to see Cyd Charisse in *Meet Me in Las Vegas* (a "picture" of the gamble *he* had just made), Harold Macmillan, England's chancellor of the exchequer, noted ominously in his diary: "There was last night and through today, the most violent gale I ever remember."[36] His "employer" owned 44% of the Suez Canal Company with most of the remaining stock held by private French investors.[37] (Slightly more intellectual than Nasser, Harold passed the first two weeks of the crisis reading thousands of pages of nineteenth-century novels, stating later that had he not done so, "I'd have gone barmy!"[38])

The new order was especially repugnant to Prime Minister Mollet, given the colossal 33-ft. bronze statue of Ferdinand Marie de Lesseps (the French diplomat who oversaw the decade-long project) situated at the waterway's entrance in Port Said. The figure's extended right hand, designed to welcome arriving ships, would now symbolize Gamal's high-handed shakedown. Yet, as Carroll Quigley notes: "There can be no doubt that Egypt had the right to nationalize an Egyptian corporation such as the Suez Canal Company, and the only concern of the outside world was the twofold one that the owners of record be adequately compensated and that the transit operations through the Canal be efficiently conducted for all shipping."[39] Thus, Nasser covered all the bases, "pledging" to reimburse all shareholders.

UNHINGED

For Prime Minister Anthony Eden, in office just over a year, the pressure was intense. Nearly 25% of the nation's imports passed through the Suez, 33% of the overall traffic traveling on British ships. With 66% of western Europe's petroleum utilizing the narrow 100-mile artery as well, James Bamford likened the canal to a "plasma tube [that] allowed vital oil shipments to pass from refineries in Saudi Arabia and elsewhere to storage tanks in England and France."[40]

The year 1956 also marked the twentieth anniversary of Hitler's remilitarization of the Rhineland. Yet, twenty-four Labor MPs warned in a joint statement on August 8 that forcing Nasser to denationalize the canal would violate the UN charter. The United States was notably resolute that it would *not* support a military strike against Egypt. (While Britain fretted over the canal, the White House and America's oil barons were more concerned with inflaming the Arab World.)

As a result, Prime Minister Eden was becoming more unhinged by the minute. Dulles family biographer Leonard Mosley writes:

> He had always had a sharp temper and now he was subject to fits of ungovernable rage…Whitehall and the diplomatic salons were rife with rumors about the volcanic nature of the prime minister's choler, and the almost Pavlovian frothing at the mouth that occurred when the name of Nasser was mentioned to him. A minister of state in the British cabinet, Anthony Nutting, was still metaphorically wiping the flecks of spittle out of his eyes after one encounter with Eden's growing fanaticism.[41]

When an attorney from the Foreign Office legal department presented Eden with a report confirming the legality of Nasser's position, the prime minister took the paper, read it through, tore it into pieces, and threw it in the lawyer's face.[42]

Her Majesty's Government (Elizabeth II having succeeded her father, George VI, in February 1952) was not *about* to be challenged by some "cheeky little wog" born in a mud-brick house on an unpaved street in the poverty-stricken Alexandrian suburb of Bacos, where his father was the postmaster. Quigley notes: "From the beginning the British took their stand…maintaining, incorrectly, that the company was not an Egyptian corporation but an international organization, that the Egyptians could not operate…and that the British would use force, if necessary, to prevent Nasser from obtaining control of the Canal."[43]

After inviting the esteemed military historian-theorist, Captain (Sir) Basil Henry Liddell-Hart (cited elsewhere in this volume), to a private conference at 10 Downing Street, Eden had another kerfuffle when his guest *dared* to patronize him following several highbrow challenges to *his solicited advice* on invasion strategy. However, as Mosley shares, *this* time Sir Anthony should have stuck to intimidating lawyers:

> There was a moment's silence. Eden's handsome face went first pale and then red. He looked across at the long, languid shape of

Captain Liddell-Hart, clad in a smart off-white summer outfit, then he reached out a hand, grasped one of the heavy, old-fashioned Downing Street inkwells, and flung it at his visitor. Another silence. Liddell-Hart looked down at the sickly blue stains spreading across his immaculate linen suiting, uncoiled himself, picked up a government-issue wastepaper basket, and jammed it over the prime minister's head before slowly walking out of the room.[44]

THE PROTOCOL OF SÈVRES

Eden finally crashed under the strain, spending October 5-8 in the hospital with a 106° fever. Something had to be done, and *quickly*. On October 22-24, senior British, French, and Israeli officials converged, incognito, on a private villa on the Rue Emanuel Girot in the Paris suburb of Sèvres. Brokered by Mollet's military deputy chief of staff, General Maurice Challe (i.e., "The French Connection"), the result of this top-secret meeting would constitute the *strangest* chapter in the Jews' erratic forty-year relationship with HMG. To save Eden's *hide*, Israel would take on the Biblical role of a scapegoat (Leviticus 16:10).

In a nutshell, the furtive plot envisioned the following: Having sustained repeated fedayun incursions, Israel would launch an overdue reprisal on Egyptian forces—*near the Suez Canal*; Nasser would naturally retaliate; Britain and France would then issue two differently worded "appeals" (ultimatums) for "both sides" to stand down within twelve hours; *assuming* that Egypt would fail to comply, an Anglo-French airborne force would then possess the casus belli to occupy the Canal Zone, ostensibly to separate the combatants and rescue the canal for posterity, etc.[45] (Nasser's ouster was a foregone conclusion.) After receiving assurances that Egypt's new air force would be bombed (to protect Jewish cities), Ben-Gurion committed his government.[46]

With the "gentlemen's agreement" set, David suggested (to his co-conspirators' anxiety) that a *written* record be compiled. Therefore, at 7 p.m. on October 24, three copies of a quickly typed seven-article document (drafted in French, the language of international diplomacy), a.k.a. "The Protocol of Sèvres," were signed by Christian Pineau, French foreign minister; Patrick Dean, assistant under-secretary at the British Foreign Office; and David Ben-Gurion.[47] The next day, officials from Egypt, Syria, and Jordan finalized their own pact under Colonel Nasser's lead. (On Gamal's insistence, Abdullah sent Glubb and his medals into *permanent* retirement.) The resultant eight-day imbroglio would be known by many names: Suez Canal Crisis, Sinai War, Suez War, Sinai-Suez Campaign, Second Arab-Israeli War, etc. From a logistical point, it could even be called The Hundred-Hour War. In deference to the *Quai d'Orsay*, the clandestine, tripartite expedition was privately code-named—"Operation Musketeer."[48]

THE THREE MUSKETEERS

Sachar identifies General Sir Charles Keightley as the commander of Operation Musketeer.[49] French Admiral Pierre Emile Marie Johannes Barjot was deputy commander, with Israel's Lieutenant General Moshe Dayan bringing up the rear. Though perhaps a tad strained, the "official" *esprit de corps* (for the moment, anyway) was the axiomatic mantra—"*One for all, and all for one!*" (It is not known if Dumas' novel was included in Macmillan's reading list.)

At 4:30 p.m. on Monday, October 29, a low-flying squadron of Israeli transport planes crossed the Sinai undetected by Egyptian radar. Three hours later, 400 paratroopers were already at the Mitla Pass, some thirty miles from the canal. Though Nasser and his advisors were clueless at the time, Musketeer was up and running on schedule. The stealth advantage was gained from rumors (circulated by the Mossad) of an imminent strike on Jordan. A retired IDF colonel told this author, "The trick was so effective that it managed to deceive all the people in Israel. For about a week, the IDF called thousands of reserves to come back to service and gathered most of them in Jerusalem, which was then a divided city. It was clear to all that the war was boiling up against Jordan and in Jerusalem. History has many twists."

Having finally gotten his act together around midnight, Nasser deployed an armored brigade toward the Suez. When he called on Syria and Jordan to jump in, both allies claimed they needed "more time" to get ready. Meanwhile, the IDF 202nd Paratroop Brigade was racing toward Mitla, led by its twenty-eight-year-old commander, Colonel Ariel Sharon. That morning's *Jerusalem Post* front-page headline read: "ARMY ATTACKS BASES IN HEART OF SINAI."[50] By midday, the Israeli and Egyptian ambassadors in London were told by their

British and French counterparts that both armies had twelve hours to withdraw to points ten miles east and west of the canal, respectively. The final line read: "If at the expiration of that time one or both governments have not undertaken to comply with the above requirements, the United Kingdom and French forces will intervene in whatever strength may be necessary to secure compliance."[51]

While Israel was happy to remain outside the buffer zone, Gamal thumbed his nose at the dictum. To Ben-Gurion's dismay, however, as the twelve-hour deadline passed, his promised air support was nowhere in sight. Finally, at 7 p.m. on October 31, over 200 British and French fighter bombers began eliminating Nasser's costly Slovak jets. But then the allies made *another* tactical delay—one that would cost them dearly. The climactic Anglo-French airborne assault on the canal did not begin until November 5, the seaborne landings following the day after. Nasser wasted no time exploiting the blunder. Dozens of ships filled with rocks, cement, even old beer bottles, were scuttled in the canal, blocking the waterway to any sizable tonnage. At Nasser's order, Syrian engineers delivered the *coup de grâce*, sabotaging the pumping stations along the pipeline of the Iraq Petroleum Company. Europe's lifeblood was gurgling away onto the hot desert sands.

OPERATION KADESH

Having fulfilled their phony, diversionary obligation, Dayan and company would now devote the next 100 hours pursuing *their* nation's military agenda. Dubbed "Operation Kadesh" after the Biblical site in northern Sinai, the epithet represented a powerful ethnoscape for the IDF. The *first* time Jews were in the area (known as Kadesh Barnea in 1490 BC), they refused to invade Canaan for fear of the giants (Numbers 13-14)—*this* time they would fight! Their two-fold mission objective was to punish the Gaza Strip, and secure the Straits of Tiran.

Shimon Peres (a key player at Sèvres) was the reputed mastermind behind the 1956 Sinai War.[52] Professor Quigley called the campaign "a brilliant military success."[53] It was practically over before it started. With Jewish "boots on the ground," Nasser hastened a general "exodus" from Sinai (to reinforce the canal), enabling roving IDF units to engage in "a high-speed, hit-and-run battle."[54] The first significant rout occurred near dawn on November 1 at the Abu Agheila hedgehog in central

Sinai. Rather than prolong a futile resistance before Israeli armor, 3,000 exhausted enemy troops fled wildly into the sand dunes, Sachar writing: "[T]he Egyptians had 'escaped' to a wretched fate in the desert, their throats cut and their bodies stripped by Bedouin."[55]

As Brigadier Chaim Bar-Lev's tank column proceeded along the main coastal road toward Suez, his advance was halted by a massive roadblock of 385 abandoned Egyptian vehicles, including forty heavy Soviet-built tanks. Thousands of Nasser's demoralized men were turning themselves in for food and water, resembling "an endless procession of pilgrims, their white underwear conspicuous against the background of the golden sand."[56] Quigley writes, "Individual Egyptians and small units often fought fiercely, but the command was incompetent, morale was almost totally absent, and training was equally bad. Whole units fled like sheep…."[57] After a two-day firefight, IDF armor captured the strategic city of Rafah, then rumbled into Gaza City where the entire garrison surrendered in confusion.

The vital campaign for Tiran ("Israeli Suez Canal") combined an airborne drop over the southwestern tip of the peninsula with a precarious march across southern Sinai, "a lunar surface of jagged peaks, impassable ridges, and rock-strewn slopes."[58] At dawn on October 31, some 1,800 farmer-reservists of Colonel Avraham Yoffe's 9th Brigade began their 700-mile trek to Tiran. When the men of the 202nd Brigade dropped at al-Tur, the winds were so strong that many were dragged across the sand for miles. By 9:30 p.m. on November 4, the two units coalesced at Sharm el-Sheikh at the bottom of the Sinai wedge. With the commander's surrender, Yoffe's troops were sent home in time to harvest their winter crops.[59] The Straits of Tiran were secure, ensuring renewed navigation into the Red Sea and the Indian Ocean. Sachar summarizes the remarkable feats of Operation Kadesh:

> At a cost of 180 men killed and 4 captured, of 20 planes and some 2,000 worn-out vehicles, Israel in essentially a hundred-hour campaign had occupied the whole of the Sinai Peninsula and the Gaza Strip, had shattered 3 Egyptian divisions, killed 2,000 of the enemy, and taken nearly 6,000 prisoners (a number that could have been far higher). Similarly, Israeli forces had captured war matériel valued at over $50 million, including 7,000 tons of ammunition, half a million gallons of fuel, 100 Bren carriers, 200 artillery pieces, 100 tanks, over 1,000 other vehicles, and an Egyptian frigate that had

been trapped off Haifa by a French destroyer, then rocketed into surrender by Israeli planes.[60]

THE END OF EDEN

The wake of Musketeer was catastrophic. Loftus and Aarons write: "Instead of the three musketeers, it was every man for himself."[61] An omen of things to come, on December 23, 1956, the despised statue of Ferdinand Marie de Lesseps at Port Said was blown off its pedestal with three consecutive charges of TNT before a howling mob of Muslims. (It now stands in a small garden in Port Fouad shipyard.) While Mollet was able to survive the political dynamite (only to have his government collapse the following June over Algeria), his fellow swashbuckler across the channel was destined to fare much worse.

On November 5—the day Eden's "paraboys" were finally landing at the canal—a UNGA resolution demanding an *immediate* ceasefire was already three days old. Abba Eban (who served concurrently as Israel's ambassador to America and the UN) likened the charged mood at the Security Council to Sam Goldwyn's famous line to his MGM executives: "Boys, I want a movie that begins with an earthquake and works its way up to a climax."[62] Eden never knew what hit him. While the NSA's British partner GCHQ (Government Communications Headquarters) had been passing along carefully selected intercepts from its western Europe and Middle East listening posts (exempting those between Paris and Tel Aviv),[63] Loftus and Aarons relate that Kim Philby, our old "friend" at MI6, "was, in fact, the second-in-command to the SIS point man for Operation Musketeer…."[64]

Kim naturally informed his boss, Premier Khrushchev, who, after exposing the whole charade at the UN (and, with plenty of attendant drama), gave the perpetrators his own ultimatum—get the "blank" *out* or get *nuked*.[65] To illustrate the scandal's overarching reach, Nikita (a goyim) was able to muster the chutzpah to condemn the "Three Musketeers" for *their* aggression at the canal, the very week *his* tanks were crushing Hungarians in Budapest. Touché! (For what it's worth, Hungary's precipitate uprising was triggered by false radio messages by Prince Turkul that American paratroopers were on the way.[66])

Then it was *America's* turn. In *The Three Musketeers*, the story's main character, the heroic D'Artagnan, becomes the fourth musketeer.

In 1956, this role *should* have been played by the US. However, when Sir Anthony asked Washington for help, John Foster Dulles—"that terrible man"—as Eden would later describe him,[67] threatened to devalue the sterling unless Britain imposed an immediate ceasefire. The popular London weekly, *Punch*, called Dulles "schizophrenic."[68] (Foster was also behind the November UN resolution.) And, of course, Eden might just as well have referred to CIA Director Allen Dulles as "that *other* terrible man," Loftus and Aarons relating, "According to a number of our sources in the intelligence community, the Arabs were, in fact, provided with excellent intelligence on the Israeli plans."[69]

For his part, Eisenhower was so livid, that when his first telephone call was patched through to 10 Downing Street, he cussed out a startled aide and hung up, assuming that he had just delivered his one-way tongue-lashing to Eden. (Robert Welch described his subsequent transatlantic beat downs as using "cavalry barracks language."[70]) Ike just couldn't fathom how Eden could invade Egypt—the day before *he* was up for reelection. Yergin writes: "[T]he last thing he wanted now was a military crisis that might frighten the electorate and threaten his campaign. In an appalling blunder, the British and French never really factored the calendar of the American Presidential election into their calculations."[71] Mosley saw it as "pure hypocrisy," opining, "[T]here was never a chance that Eisenhower would lose the election."[72]

Then it was the *Arabs'* turn. As Nasser held a grudge against the Jews over Faluja, he harbored an older animus against Churchill and his then-deputy Eden, for having replaced the pro-Axis cabinet of Prime Minister Ali Maher with an "emergency wartime government" under the quisling, Mustafa al-Nahas Pasha. The expulsion was so painful for Egypt, especially the army, that General Mohammad Saleh Harb (war minister 1939-40) only barely mentioned it in his memoirs as the "1942 Incident."[73] In *Europe and the Islamic World*, co-authors John Tolan, Gilles Veinstein, and Henry Laurens relate: "The Egyptian public felt a real national humiliation."[74] Thus, the Aboul-Enein brothers confirm: "[T]he seed of the 1952 revolution and Nasser's Free Officers Association that overthrew Farouk and established the Egyptian Republic was planted on February 4, 1942."[75]

The Ummah backed Nasser by slapping an immediate oil embargo on Britain. With her reserves down to weeks, Ike told his inner circle, "I'm inclined to think that those who began this operation should be left to work out their own oil problems—to boil in their own oil, so to speak."[76] Relieved to have *their* man back in the White House, the US oil lobby received an emergency executive pass to circumvent antitrust laws so they could "cooperate" in supplying Europe with petroleum. (The ensuing "Oil Lift" would replenish 90% of the diminished stock by spring 1957.[77]) "Sir Eden," as he was mockingly called by Nasser,[78] had no choice but to announce a ceasefire on November 6.

His "war" had lasted all of a day; his "conquest"—a sliver of sand twenty-three miles south of Port Said. The humbled Anglo-French Task Force also had to meet an abrupt withdrawal date of December 22 (so UN monitors could spend Christmas at the canal). Loftus and Aarons note: "The Americans had won, especially the Dulles brothers' oil friends."[79] Mosley concludes: "Three unlikely partners—Gamal Abdel Nasser, the Soviet Union, and John Foster Dulles—had made sure that the British lion had roared for positively the last time."[80]

Then it was the *Lord's* turn. At the height of the crisis, Eden suffered a physical and emotional breakdown requiring an extended convalesce in Jamaica (aptly, in a house owned by *James Bond* creator Ian Fleming).[81] His doctor's advice to resign represented a timely exit strategy. (A friend of this author who resides in New Zealand recalled that Eden was the laughing stock of the entire Commonwealth, derided in rugby parlance as the "dropkick prime minister.") Eden stepped down in January 1957 (replaced by Sir Harold Macmillan, the egghead who almost went "barmy"). Eden's health issues began in 1953 when, during a gall bladder operation, a negligent surgeon damaged his bile duct, which was only partly corrected by later operations, leaving the patient, as he once remarked—"with a largely artificial inside."[82]

There was more truth to this self-diagnosis than one might think. Sadly, during his first two (of three) terms as Secretary of State for Foreign Affairs (1935-38, 1940-45), Eden showed himself to be a "gutless wonder" regarding helping the Jews in WWII. The reader will recall the following quotes: In a private discussion in March 1943 with Roosevelt, Secretary of State Hull, and Under Secretary Wells, Eden advised his colleagues to "move very cautiously about offering to take all Jews out of a country." He then candidly warned, "Hitler might well take us up on any such offer, and there simply are not enough ships and means of transportation in the world to handle them." Then, as late as 1951—seven years *after* the liberation of Auschwitz—Eden wrote his private secretary: "If we must have preferences, let me murmur in your ear that I prefer Arabs to Jews," the secretary subsequently noting in his diary: "Unfortunately, A. E. is immovable on the subject of Palestine. He loves Arabs and hates Jews."

In keeping with the ongoing validation of Genesis 12:3 (Dunkirk evacuation, London blitz, Kriegie disinterment, RAF shoot-down, et al.)—with absolutely *no* regard for *any* comments from the peanut gallery of academia—the 1956 disaster represented the latest and greatest judgment of Almighty God upon HMG for its perpetual sin of afflicting the Jewish people. As Eden had abandoned Europe's Jews to the crematoria—feigning a shortage of ships—*Egyptian* ships became the ruinous blockade of *British* ships, ensuring his *political* abandonment. Yergin writes that Eden's reputation "was to be ignominiously scuttled with the ships that Nasser sent to the bottom of the canal."[83] Eban adds: "Britannia could no longer rule all the waves, or even most of them."[84] Youssef Aboul-Enein concludes: "British colleagues have told me in discussions that Eden went to war on a lie that undermined his purpose in forcibly removing Nasser, and that despite being Churchill's protégé, Eden ended as the least successful prime minister in twentieth-century British political history."[85]

For the record, as God is no respecter of persons, Eden was not the only anti-Semite who got smacked around at this time. After suffering a heart attack in 1955, Eisenhower was stricken with ileitis in June 1956. Then, while the front-page headline of the *Jerusalem Post* on November 4, 1956, announced, "SINAI BATTLE WON," the caption of a small article on the page's left side read, "DULLES TAKEN TO HOSPITAL." (Not unlike that missing gas van at Chelmno, the ambulance driver got lost between Foster's home and Walter Reed Army Hospital[86]). An incredible *third* article, immediately below the hospital story, stated: "Dulles Would Like Bonn To Halt Reparations" (i.e., those West German shipments for Israel as legally sanctioned by the 1952 Treaty of Luxembourg).[87] Diagnosed with terminal stomach cancer, the "terrible man" would go to his "reward" on May 24, 1959.

Finally, it was the *Jews'* turn. "On the British side, Anthony Eden bore the ultimate responsibility and received most of the opprobrium for the collusion with France and Israel," writes New Historian author, Avi Shlaim. "Eden was desperate for a pretext to go to war in order to get rid of Nasser, and the alliance with Israel was the price he reluctantly paid to procure such a pretext. The elaborate plot embodied in the protocol was so transparent that it is still difficult to understand how Eden could have believed that it would not be seen as such."[88]

Amidst the swirl of rumors about Musketeer, Eden added insult to injury by denying the whole affair. He had practically swallowed his tongue when Patrick Dean informed him about the written record of the Sèvres conference. As Keith Kyle writes in *Suez: Britain's End of Empire in the Middle East*, "Eden now knew that somewhere and at some time there would be a smoking gun."[89] While Christian Pineau acknowledged the conspiracy in 1976 (a year before Eden's death on January 14, 1977), thanks to Ben-Gurion's original prudence, the hard evidence would finally surface in 1996:

> To the end of his days Sir Anthony Eden, the driving force on the British side on the road to war, denied that there had been any collusion with Israel or even foreknowledge that Israel would attack Egypt. The Protocol of Sèvres tells a different story. The British copy was in fact destroyed on Eden's orders, the French copy was lost and the Israeli copy was kept under lock and key in the Ben-Gurion Archives…In 1996 permission was given to photocopy the protocol for a BBC documentary shown on the 40th anniversary of the Suez war. With the release of the protocol, the tripartite meeting at Sèvres became not only the most famous but also the best-documented war plot in modern history.[90]

REPROOF FOR ISRAEL

The Jewish state won a Pyrrhic victory in the Anglo-French conspiracy. After its hard-fought gains, the IDF had to quit Sinai by March 1957 to allow the worthless United Nations Emergency Force (UNEF) into Gaza and Sharm el-Sheikh. Conversely, Gamal Abdel Nasser emerged stronger than ever. Abba Eban would later write:

> The Sinai campaign was politically the most unplanned war in history. It was based on a complete lack of political appraisal. Exaggerated importance was attached to France and Britain. We appeared before the whole world as tools of the imperialists…it should have been a completely Israeli operation and we should have done it after the American election….[91]

Richard Deacon adds: "[T]he Suez débâcle created by the Anglo-French withdrawal from the Canal Zone after their abortive landings, taught Israel the lesson that in future she must go it alone and rely entirely on her own efforts."[92]

In his own book, *Heroes of Israel*, former President Chaim Herzog attempted a positive (though not dissimilar) spin on the 1956 War: "More than anything else, the Sinai Campaign increased Israel's self-confidence."[93] There is an element of irony in his assertion. That surge of "*self*-confidence" was commensurate with Israel's latest reality check—that she would *never* be accepted by the nations of this world—specifically, for being a unique people created *by* and *for* the very "Rock" they would continue to disavow (Numbers 23:9).

The new Jewish prime minister (standing 4 feet, 11 inches, seven inches shorter than Mussolini) naturally craved the acceptance of his political peers. Sèvres was Ben-Gurion's foray into the big leagues, his first *ever* invite to an international summit. Of course, the only problem *here* (like the joke about the golfing Rabbi's "hole-and-corner" hole-in-one on the Sabbath) was that the group's illicit agenda made any subsequent boasting a *serious* "no-no." Shlaim writes: "What he deeply longed for was a partnership between equals…Ben-Gurion hoped to meet Eden but the British prime minister did not want to be seen to be allied to him in any way…He badly wanted to join the great powers club and he found that subscribing to the Suez campaign at the end of October was the only way of doing it."[94]

Eden's stand-in at Sèvres, Secretary of State Selwyn Lloyd (with his aide, Donald Logan), remained similarly aloof. Dayan noted in his memoirs: "Britain's foreign minister may well have been a friendly man, pleasant, charming, amiable. If so, he showed near-genius in concealing these virtues. His manner could not have been more antagonistic. His whole demeanor expressed distaste – for the place, the company and the topic."[95] However, while deprived of normal shoulder rubbing, Israel's leader did receive his very own copy of the Protocol of Sèvres (albeit a *secret* one). "Although the document had to be ratified by all three governments, Ben-Gurion made no effort to conceal his excitement. He studied his copy of the document, folded it carefully and thrust it deep into the pocket of his waistcoat."[96]

The disdain which the British held for Ben-Gurion and his upstart nation throughout the trilateral talks can be illustrated by two closing subtleties. Shlaim writes: "Once the protocol had been signed, champagne was produced but there was little sparkle in the atmosphere and no comradely backslapping. The first to exit the rue Emanuel Girot were the British. They left, writes Dayan, 'mumbling as they went words of politeness tinged with humor and not quite comprehensible.'"[97] The second snub occurred afterwards:

> Ben-Gurion was under the impression that each government would send two letters, one to each partner, ratifying the protocol. But he was far from confident that a British letter would arrive. Ben-Gurion's suspicion was justified: he received no letter from Eden. Eden only wrote to Mollet to ratify the agreement reached at the tripartite meeting. The most charitable explanation of Eden's behaviour is that he followed the usual diplomatic practice of addressing ratification to the depository power, in this case France."[98]

To their credit, the French did send Ben-Gurion written confirmation of their pledge to provide aerial support.

In his original essay, *The Protocol of Sèvres, 1956: Anatomy of a War Plot*, Shlaim wrote of Ben-Gurion: "[H]e greatly resented the suggestion that Israel should be used as a prostitute in providing services for the great powers."[99] Though he may have resented the metaphor, Ben-Gurion committed his nation to the immoral role, nonetheless. And yet, this is *precisely* what the Jews have been indicted for throughout their rebellious existence (some 100 Old Testament passages, not to mention the entire book of Hosea, casting Israel as a whore). Ben-Gurion's problem (as with Herzl, Weizmann, et al.) was that he was too "intellectual" to make an unconditional surrender to the Tanakh (Hebrew Bible) as *the* supernatural book of Jehovah—otherwise, he might have caught the prophetic application of Ezekiel 23:3—*"And they committed* WHOREDOMS *in Egypt; they committed* WHOREDOMS *in their youth: there were their breasts pressed, and there they bruised the teats of their virginity."*

SAMSON IN GAZA

In a move of providence, "Israel's Rock" allowed at least one seminal benefit from the otherwise calamitous war. To the ire of the international community, the IDF maintains a policy called "nuclear opacity." Like that famous line in *Dirty Harry* when the wounded bank robber says to Detective Callahan, "Hey, I *gots* ta know," Israel's "Maybe vee *do*, maybe vee *don't*" approach (regarding persistent rumors of an atomic arsenal) has similarly kept 40,000,000 Muslims wondering, "Did he fire *six* shots or only *five*?" As Judges 16:1 says, *"Then went Samson into Gaza...,"* it is not without significance that Israel's nuclear program—dubbed by Norman Podhoretz as "The *Samson* Option" (i.e., "If *we* die, we bring the roof down on *everybody*...")[100]—was initiated on the eve of Operation Kadesh.

And so, to ensure that Israel would still be here when her Messiah *returns*, a last-minute deal was struck at that shady villa in Sèvres. Shimon Peres relates in his personal memoirs, *Battling for Peace*:

> Before the final signing, I asked Ben-Gurion for a brief adjournment, during which I met Mollet and [Minister of Defense] Bourgès-Maunoury alone. It was here that I finalized with these two leaders an agreement for the building of a nuclear reactor at Dimona, in southern Israel...and the supply of natural uranium to fuel it. I put forward a series of detailed proposals and, after discussion, they accepted them.[101]

The words "before the final signing" speak to Shimon's negotiating acumen, Shlaim adding: "[I]t reveals the full extent of the incentives that the French were prepared to give Israel in order to induce it to play the part assigned to it in the war plot against Egypt...."[102]

> The development of nuclear power was a subject dear to Ben-Gurion's heart. He saw in it a technological challenge which would help to transform Israel into an advanced industrial state. The negotiations with the French were about a small nuclear reactor for civilian purposes. Nothing was said at this stage about possible military applications of this nuclear technology. But that was Ben-Gurion's ultimate aim: to produce nuclear weapons. He believed that nuclear weapons would strengthen Israel immeasurably, secure its survival and eliminate any danger of another holocaust.
>
> Shimon Peres was the moving force behind the Israeli attempt to get French help in building a nuclear reactor...On 21 September 1956, a month before Sèvres, Peres reached an agreement with the French on the supply of a small nuclear reactor. He used the occasion of Sèvres to try to commit France at the political level...For Ben-

Gurion the high-level French political commitment to assist Israel in the nuclear field was one of the greatest achievements of the gathering at Sèvres.[103]

Upon Musketeer's collapse, Mollet was distraught over France's failure to carry out its pledge to Israel, an aide quoting him as saying, "I owe the bomb to them. I owe the bomb to them."[104] However, while his government would soon fall, Shlaim relates, "[I]n September 1957, when Bourgès-Maunoury was Prime Minister, France delivered to Israel a nuclear reactor which had twice the capacity previously promised."[105] As they say—"All's vell that ends vell!"

"And Samson took hold of the two middle pillars upon which the house stood, and on which it was borne up, of the one with his right hand, and of the other with his left. And Samson said, Let me die with the Philistines. And he bowed himself with all his might; and the house fell upon the lords, and upon all the people that were therein. So the dead which he slew at his death were more than they which he slew in his life."
(Judges 16:29-30)

16

The Six-Day War

"I have been a conspirator for
so long that I mistrust all around me."
(Nasser, *Time*, July 28, 1958)

"I have come to inform you
that we no longer have an air force."
(Egyptian aide to Nasser, June 5, 1967)

"Har ha-Bayit be-Yadenu."
"The Temple Mount is in our hands."
(Motta Gur's radio message, June 6, 1967)

"Caiaphas...said unto them...it is expedient for us, that one man should die for the people, and that the whole nation perish not...from that day forth they took COUNSEL *together for to put him to death."*
(John 11:49-50, 53)

IN LATE MAY 1967, a Jewish youth was finishing his senior year in a Philadelphia area high school. With summer break approaching, his classmates would be hitting the beach to catch a few rays. *This* seventeen-year-old would be skipping commencement to help defend his native land. Some fifty years later, Benjamin "Bibi" Netanyahu—who still speaks English with a distinct "Philly" accent—is the current, albeit embattled, prime minister of Israel.

1957-67

The last IDF troops withdrew from Sinai on March 11, 1957. Two weeks later, the Suez Canal reopened. With Israelis longing for peace, the intervening decade between the Hundred-Hour War and the Six-Day War would begin with a portentous *bang*.

On October 29, 1957 (three weeks after *Sputnik* blasted into space), a hand grenade exploded in the Knesset chamber (then located in Frumin House). Several members were sprayed with shrapnel, including David Ben-Gurion and Foreign Minister Golda Meir. Reminiscent of the failed shooting of Dr. Herzl's colleague by a deranged Jewish-Russian student, the perpetrator was Moshe Dwek, a 26-year-old Israeli mental patient from Yemen. Ironically, the incident was allegedly provoked by Moshe's inability to obtain government *health* insurance. That a War of Independence veteran would toss a bomb off the balcony of his own Knesset was unsettling enough; that the would-be assassin, turned wannabe politician, could go on to make a failed bid for that same body (in 1988), affords a profound insight into the prevailing internecine fabric of a people void of their "Rock."

While Colonel Nasser was "reloading," a myriad of domestic conflicts kept Israelis in perpetual agitation. The Lavon Affair was the defining political scandal of that time. The debacle arose from several failed sabotage missions in Egypt in 1954 that were vigorously denied by Ben-Gurion's government. On the cultural front, the debate over Jewish identity (sparked by prosaic registration problems) continued to elude a civil consensus; should the nagging question—"Who is a Jew?"—be applied primarily to citizenship, nationality, or religion? The persistent efforts of the Orthodox ("affectionately" known as "Penguins"), particularly the ultra-fanatical Neturei Karta, to impose rabbinical law on the public represented another domestic dilemma (e.g., how much infrastructure should close on Shabbat, especially public transportation in Jerusalem).

Conversely, having ignored God for so long, secular Israelis were becoming painfully aware that their non-religious children had "somehow" grown indifferent to Zionism as well. Abba Eban writes: "The word [Zionism] even became the target for condescending jokes…The phrase 'Espresso Generation' was coined to describe a youth that was prepared for sacrifice if necessary, but was insistent on living in ease and relative affluence if they were possible."[1] Though the Beatles were banned from performing in Israel in 1965, the cultural trajectory was plainly city *discos* over kibbutzim *discers*.

Due to sustained immigration levels, the 1950s and early '60s were called *Tekufat HaTzena* ("period of austerity"). Jews from this era rarely had cavities, as few could afford such luxuries as sugar or candy.[2] However, as Romans 11:29 states that *"the gifts and calling of God are without repentance,"* the divinely endowed nation would experience a number of technological perks *despite* her backslidden status. With adequate water deemed second only to civil defense, to the chagrin of Jordan and Syria, Israeli engineers created the National Water Carrier—an integrated aquatic distribution system running from the northwest corner of Lake Galilee to the northern Negev.

Unfortunately, this initiative would enable modern Israelis to bypass their historic providential dilemma. While Mrs. Meir upbraided Moses over oil, the nation's *real* problem was a dearth of H_2O. Lacking this natural resource, Jews had to look *up* for their drinking water (Deuternomy11:11), unlike the two major civilization centers along the Nile and the Tigris and Euphrates Rivers. Bible geographer Barry Beitzel writes: "In a word, this was a land that fostered faith...God prepared the promised land for His chosen people to the same degree that He prepared His chosen people for the Promised Land...it was a certain kind of land that was selected and prepared by God, positioned at a particular spot, and designed to elicit a specific and appropriate response."[3] To Golda's relief, a similar *land* canal for oil, utilizing pipelines forty-two inches in diameter, connected tankers and oilers from Eilat to Ashkelon. (According to Luke 16:24, Jews who reject Jesus Christ will find their *ultimate* water shortage in Hell.)

As Nazi scientists were assisting Egypt on missile development, Israel's first sounding rocket, *Shavit 2* ("Comet"), was launched into space by Rafael Advanced Defense Systems on July 5, 1961. (More recently, the company's "Iron Dome," a mobile all-weather air defense system, regularly intercepts Hamas rockets from Gaza.) Another milestone occurred in October 1966 when Shmuel Agnon received the Nobel Prize in Literature, becoming Israel's first Nobel laureate. As of 2013, Nobel Prizes have gone to 876 people and groups, with 20% being Jews (or of Jewish descent)—despite making up just 0.2% of the world's inhabitants. Conversely, though 20% of the population, a grand total of *ten* Nobel

Prize winners have been devotees of Allah—the late psychopath Yasser Arafat among them. (Some would add Barak Hussein Obama to the list.) Colonel Meinertzhagen wrote: "It has been said that the Jew is born educated; in no country in the world has education reached such a high standard as in Israel."[4] (Einstein's brain was secretly preserved in two Mason jars at Princeton for years.)

Two notable executions occurred during this time. In a joint Mossad/Shin Bet operation, Otto Adolf Eichmann (alias Ricardo Klement) was abducted off the street near his Buenos Aires home on May 11, 1960. After a lengthy trial (reaching the Supreme Court), the notorious "Desk Murderer" was condemned to hang in Ramleh. On the evening of May 31, 1962—Eichmann's last in this world—the Protestant-born Nazi spurned a Christian minister's offer to read the Bible with him; having only two hours to live, he simply had no "time to waste."[5] According to the *Jerusalem Post*, at 11:58 p.m.—as the trapdoor was about to spring—the pastor made a last plea for Otto to simply say "Jesus"; his reply was, "Long live Germany, Austria and the Argentine," after which he bid his wife, family, and friends a "poignant" farewell.[6] (Eichmann remains the only person to be civilly executed in Israel.) On May 18, 1965, the celebrated Mossad spy Elie Cohn (alias Kamel Tabet) was hanged from a hook before a rabid mob in Damascus' Martyrs' Square (Esther 5:14). The macabre execution, occurring at 3:35 a.m., was broadcast live on Syrian television.[7]

Israelis would also be challenged by a dual transition at the top of their government (in the same year). On April 23, 1963, Yitzhak Ben-Zvi, Israel's second president, died in office. His successor was Zalman Shazar. Of far weightier import, Prime Minister David Ben-Gurion resigned on June 26, having led the nation for nearly fourteen years (also serving as defense minister throughout). Levi Eshkol, the stodgy former minister of agriculture and finance, became the new prime minister. (Ben-Gurion would remain in politics for seven more years before leaving public service altogether at age eighty-four.)

COUNTDOWN TO WAR

Israel's third major conflict in eighteen years was fought June 5-10, 1967. The timing was hastened by a CIA leak to the Arabs that Israeli scientists were closing in on their first nuclear warhead. Other sources disclosed that the Egyptians (Nasser) had used chemical and biological weapons in Yemen.[8] The four main belligerents were Egypt (United Arab Republic or UAR, 1958-71), followed by Syria, Jordan, and Iraq. The Six-Day War was precipitated by *six* Arab provocations.

First, the infamous Palestine Liberation Organization (PLO) was formally hatched in 1964 at the inaugural Palestinian Congress in Cairo. Ahmed al-Shuqayri was the first chairman. Known in geopolitics as "politicide" (a gradual, systematic effort to exterminate a sovereign entity), the mission statement was simple: "[L]iquidate the Zionist and imperialist presence."[9] With the words "liberation" and "organization" representing serious misnomers, Fatah, the PLO's largest *splinter* group (led by its charismatic terrorist, Chairman Arafat) would ultimately *dominate* the rest. By spring 1967, Palestine Liberation Army guerillas (mostly local refugees) had led over 100 raids against helpless Israeli civilians. Abba Eban writes, "Residences had been blown up within a few hundred yards of the Knesset."[10]

Second, while Syria's army shelled Jewish settlements from the Golan Heights (augmenting ground incursions by Fatah), her fighter pilots extended the killing zone. In a stunning retaliatory strike on April 7, 1967, the IAF destroyed six Soviet-supplied SAF MiGs. Then, on May 15 (Israel's Independence Day), two Egyptian armored brigades brazenly entered the Sinai and began an ominous deployment along the frontier. Three days later, Syrian troops were amassed in the Golan while Iraqi brigades headed for Jordan.

Afterward, in back-to-back communiqués over May 16-17, Mr. U Thant, the milquetoast Burmese Secretary General of the United Nations, was abruptly apprised that Cairo had decided to "terminate the presence of the UN emergency force in Egypt and the Gaza Strip."[11] Thant reacted with a similar spontaneity—*terminating the ten-year DMZ mission in twenty-four hours*. Calling the sequence of events "the most astonishing days in the history of international institutions," veteran Israeli diplomat Eban ridiculed "U's UN U-ie" as "an umbrella which is taken away as soon as it begins to rain."[12] As the architect of the initial UNEF guarantees, Abba brooded: "Israelis were less likely to credit me with the decade of stability than to blame me for its termination."[13] (To Nasser's credit, a lingering controversy posits that his initial goal was to merely "redeploy" the peacekeepers *on the border* while his boyhood pal, the delusional commander-in-chief of the

Army, Marshal Abdel Hakim 'Amer, secretly ordered the "withdrawal" of every blue helmet *on Egyptian soil.*[14])

Next, while Thant, described by one of his closest advisers as "emotionless and moon-faced…rather simple-minded,"[15] was quick to order his peacekeepers *out*, he was a tad slow at getting his own carcass *in*, to forestall any further steps to war. With the world literally holding its breath, the cigar-sucking Buddhist delayed his "emergency" (face-saving) follow-up meeting with Nasser for three agonizing days—*solely on the basis of his daily horoscope.*[16] As the perfect illustration of Psalm 2:4, *"He that sitteth in the Heavens shall laugh…,"* on May 22, while "U" was in Paris en route to Cairo, he learned to his dismay that the Gulf of Aqaba, Israel's gateway to Africa and Asia, had closed that afternoon. (Guess how the Knesset reacted to U's follow-up solution to redeploy his UN troops to Israel.)

Finally, on May 26, Israel's top-secret nuclear site at Dimona got a surprise "photo-op" by four MiG-21s soaring at 55,000 feet. Though IAF Mirages were scrambled and Hawk missiles fired, Nasser's aerial paparazzi got away unscathed. The next day Walworth Barbour, US Ambassador to Israel, cabled Washington, citing the breach as "part of the 'conclusive' proof Israel pointed to 'that Nasser has "crossed the Rubicon" and surprise aerial attack expected any moment.'"[17] In his *New York Times* bestseller, *Six Days of War*, Michael Oren writes:

> The incident touched on one of Israel's darkest concerns, that its pursuit of nuclear power would impel Egypt to launch a conventional attack while it still had the chance…Thus, though Nasser never once cited Dimona as a motive for his decisions in May, Israeli commanders assumed it was and concluded they had to strike first. Israel's fear for the reactor—rather than Egypt's *of* it—was the greater catalyst for the war.[18]

Award-winning Israeli journalists Isabella Ginor and Gideon Remez contend that the intruders were cutting-edge MiG-25 "Foxbats" flown by *Soviet* pilots. Being designed for near-mach 3 speed and a ceiling of 70,000 feet would explain their ability to elude the IAF interceptors.[19]

AHLAN WA-SAHLAN

The "Hitler of the Nile" (like his departed namesake) was an expert at staccato bellicosity. His two favorite themes were: "Israel is the greatest crime in history" and "Ben-Gurion is the greatest war criminal in this century." To Colonel Nasser, Israel's very *existence* was a "stain," a "shame," a "disgrace," and a "bleeding wound."[20]

During a particular rant in Yemen's capital in 1964, Nasser reaffirmed his famous vow: "We swear to God that we shall not rest until we restore Arab nationalism to Palestine and Palestine to the Arab nation," reaffirming on March 8, 1965, "We shall not enter Palestine with its soil covered in sand. We shall enter it with its soil saturated in blood."[21] His strongest "in your face" taunt (similar to the 2003 Bush "Bring em' on!" bravado) was displayed before a group of delirious REAF pilots on May 22 (the day he closed the Tiran Straits):

> The Aqaba Gulf constitutes our Egyptian territorial waters. Under no circumstances will we allow the Israeli flag to pass through...The Jews threatened war. We tell them: *Ahlan Wa-sahlan* (You are welcome), we are ready for war. Our armed forces and all our people are ready for war, but under no circumstances will we abandon any of our rights. The water is ours.[22]

Oren confirms: "Similar elation was registered throughout the Arab world, where Nasser's *Ahlan Wa-sahlan* reverberated."[23]

10,000 GRAVES

With the proverbial "Rock of Israel" dismissed—*as usual*, the nation's blood pressure began to rise—*as usual*. Eshkol's chain-smoking, grizzled chief-of-staff, General Yitzhak Rabin (of whom US diplomat Dennis Ross wrote, "I never met a more secular Israeli"[24]), suffered an emotional breakdown on May 23.[25] Others were not far behind.

Israel's emergency measures spoke volumes: thousands of civilians digging trenches, filling sandbags and building shelters; children evacuated to Europe; blood drives; 14,000 hospital beds readied; antidotes stockpiled for gassings. The Rabbinate declared the crisis one of *pikuach nefesh* ("life or death"), issuing dispensations to labor on

Shabbat.[26] Historian Abraham Rabinovich writes: "Pervading the city was a feeling that if war came to Jerusalem it would be a bloody block by block battle in which no quarter would be given…widely envisioned was the image of the Warsaw Ghetto: buildings turned to rubble…The municipality secretly began to bulldoze a hillside near Mount Herzl to prepare grave sites"[27]; Oren puts the figure at 10,000.[28]

A local saying had a sign at the boarding gate at Lod Airport asking that the last one out of Israel turn off the lights.[29] Zeev Barkai, a young lieutenant in the elite Paratroop Battalion 71, said: "Remember the song 'The End,' by Jim Morrison and the Doors? It was popular then. There was a line that said something like 'This is the end, my friend, this is the end.' That's what those weeks felt like."[30] Concurrently, the number one hit on Radio Damascus was—"Cut Their Throats!"[31]

For many, Nasser's rhetoric was not the greatest concern. Similar to Senator Bentsen's slam dunk of Dan Quayle, "Senator, you're no Jack Kennedy," Israelis were becoming painfully aware that Ben-Gurion's successor was "no Ben-Gurion." The former prime minister himself wrote in his diary, "As long as Eshkol's in office we will plummet into the abyss."[32] On the brink of war, Eshkol's legendary indecisiveness was his least endearing trait, *especially* at $20 million per day in lost revenue due to mobilization[33] ($142 million in 2016 dollars). Oren writes, "One popular joke had Eshkol, asked by a waitress whether he wanted coffee or tea, hedging, 'half of both.'"[34] Abba Eban recalled: "He had few gifts of expression…to get at his precise meaning was like trying to grasp a cake of soap in a bath."[35]

The crisis peaked on May 28. In a live radio broadcast—meant to *inspire* the nation—Eshkol did the opposite by reading a stammering, rambling, incoherent monologue. At one point he was even heard to pause and ask someone, "What is *this* word?"[36] Listening with his reserve unit in the Sharon Plain, IDF commander Itzik Barnoach exclaimed: "My God, this schmuck is not only talking nonsense, he's stuttering."[37] The unsettling balagan was later attributed to fatigue, a chest cold, an illegible transcript, and, incredibly, "an artificial lens in one eye—the result of a recent cataract surgery—that kept shifting."[38]

Now if Israelis *had* to place their trust in an "ocularly challenged" defense minister, they might as well choose one with combat experience. Thus, on June 1, Eshkol was forced to relinquish his secondary charge to Moshe Dayan. Though lionized for his military prowess, the general's reputation was sullied by his philandering and pilfering of national antiquities.[39] Privately, Eshkol called him an *Abu Jildi*—"a scurrilous one-eyed Arab bandit."[40] In a risible anecdote, when missing archeological treasures pointed to the famed warrior, Yigael Yadin reputedly said: "I know who did it, and I am not going to say who it is, but if I catch him, I'll poke out his other eye, too."

Eshkol may have gotten the last laugh on Moshe, as he was able to appoint the retired Yadin as "special advisor" to the rookie defense minister—i.e., to personally keep "an eye" on him. (In an email to this author, a retired IDF officer recalled: "He was sure a very bright and probably a good military person…Did you know he was an advisor to the US army in Vietnam? I did not like him as a human being…He left his wife with 3 kids and had a love affair with a married woman who left her husband and kids for him…Not my type of LEADER.")

To worsen matters, a former Israeli ambassador to the US (Michael Oren) could apprise Gamal Nasser as: "A quiet man renowned for his attentiveness and humor, he lived frugally, faithfully with his wife and children, and, in a country notorious for graft, was by all accounts incorruptible."[41] Thus, as another celebrated Jewish adulterer testified in Psalm 18:35—*"thy right hand hath holden me up, and thy gentleness hath made me great"*—any subsequent victories (and attendant adulation) would occur in *spite* of General Moshe Dayan.

THE JADID JIHAD

Unlike 1956, Syria would now pose a serious threat to Israel's northern border. After years of political upheaval, the Ba'athist strongman, Colonel Salah Jadid, had emerged in February 1966 as the *de facto* head of the nation's military regime. (Nureddin al-Atassi was the titular president.) In this Syrian version of Egypt's 1952 "Colonel's Revolt," Jadid's main accomplice was air force commander and future president, Colonel Hafez al-Assad (a.k.a. "The Lion").

The Jadid-Assad junta vowed to continue resisting Israel's National Water Carrier (by attempting to divert the Jordan headwaters) while also impeding Israeli cultivation of the asymmetrical Demilitarized Zone. Oren states: "More than any other individual factor, the war would revolve around water."[42] (In "Arabic logic," increased *water* increased *irrigation*, which increased *immigration.*) Moscow, already covering Nasser's tab for the Aswan Dam (a major Cold War defeat for the US), was glad to aid Syria as well, giving al-Assad sixty MiG-21s. Russia's military "investments" in the Middle East since 1956 already totaled $2 billion—43% going to Egypt.[43]

Egypt and Syria signed a mutual defense pact on November 4, 1966. That deal would receive a foreboding test six months later. On May 13, Soviet intel alerted Cairo that "Israel has mobilized most of its reserves and...has concentrated the bulk of its forces on the Syrian border."[44] Though the report proved untrue, some believe it was the catalyst for Egypt's May 15 deployment. "There is no room for doubt that the 'information' supplied by the Soviet Union on May 13 was the proximate cause of the 1967 war," Abba Eban affirmed.[45] However, as Sachar notes: "Shams Badran, the former Egyptian war minister, said: 'General Mahmud Fawzi...found these assumptions...without foundation.' Nasser's decision to allow the crisis to escalate was based, rather, on other factors."[46] Having surveyed the border in a private plane himself, Defense Minister Fawzi told Nasser: "There is nothing there. No massing of forces. Nothing."[47] When Eshkol offered to personally escort Russia's ambassador to Israel, Leonid Chuvakhin, on an inspection tour of the Syrian border—the diplomat declined.[48]

A Word Concerning "Miracles"

When Fredrick the Great asked a Christian if he had any "proof" that the Bible was inspired, the humble believer gave a simple two-word answer—"The Jew." By now, some readers may be wondering when this book (especially this section, and particularly this chapter) will broach the many popular accounts of "divine intervention" on the battlefield (fifty-foot-tall angels popping up and smashing Egyptian tanks, etc.). To be frank, this will not occur for several reasons.

While Christians will instinctively embrace *any* supernatural event recorded in *Scripture*, they are never obligated to believe the professed experiences of *individuals*. (However, as Proverbs 21:11 relates, some unmistakable displays of divine judgment, like "The Great Hurricane of 1938" and "The Perfect Storm," *are* intended to warn the simple.) This is not to say that certain "unexplainable phenomena" (apart from everyday "normal" miracles, like timely answers to prayer and needful providential chastisement) cannot occur today, for Hebrews 13:2 cautions,

"...some have entertained angels unawares." The point is, that *if* and *when* such rare and personal moments *do* occur, the "beneficiary" is expected to have enough spiritual discernment to exercise reticence. When Moses brought the tablets down from Mount Sinai, he failed to cover his shining countenance, frightening the people as a result (Exodus 34:29-35). While the commandments were for the Jews, God's revelation of His person was for Moses alone.

The Bible states in Philippians 4:8, *"Finally, brethren, whatsoever things are true, whatsoever things are honest...think on these things."* Likewise, Romans 12:17 enjoins, *"Provide things honest in the sight of all men."* Believers are to avoid "spiritual hearsay," much less propagate the same (I John 4:1). While it is certainly possible that some perceptible supernatural events may have contributed to Israel's many miraculous victories, sadly, because the Holy Land has such an empyreal heritage, legions of legends (and not a few lies) abound, a.k.a. *"cunningly devised fables."* (II Peter 1:16)

For example, the *YouTube* video "The Miracle! God's Eyes in the Sky!" shows a cloud that *seems* to have two scary eyes peering out. An animated IDF soldier once told this author that the film was shot in Israel during a battle where the enemy was "miraculously scared off." However, another posting of the same video states that it was filmed in Kerch, Crimea, during a hurricane. (While this chapter was being written, one of many articles to go viral during the 2014 Israeli-Hamas crisis stated: "'Hand of God' prevents rocket from striking its target: Israeli Iron Dome Operator says sudden gust of wind blew missile into sea when defense system failed."[49])

One of the most enduring apocryphal stories from the Six-Day War claims that Israeli spy Elie Cohn (Cohen) convinced Syria's military leaders to plant eucalyptus trees around bunkers and artillery sites to offer both camouflage and shade. With the given assertion that "Cohen informed Israel's military intelligence," one evangelical writes, "[T]he information he provided before his death gave Israel the victory in the Six-Day War two years later," allegedly, because the "Israeli air force simply targeted the stands of newly planted eucalyptus trees – and they were able to easily destroy most of the Syrian military installations on the Golan Heights."[50] Alas, the romantic tale cannot be substantiated, scholars consigning it to fiction. When asked about the account, a retired IDF official e-mailed this author: "I simply do not know, and as you can imagine in such situations a lot of legends are a part of history…but I never saw it in 'real documents.'" (A more rational nexus between the "Cohn tree" and Israel's disproportionate edge in security matters would be the eucalyptus trees adorning a discrete block of buildings in the affluent Pitua district of Herzilya, believed by some to be the arcane headquarters of the Mossad itself.)[51]

In the finale of *The Man Who Shot Liberty Valance*, a reporter, upon learning that the "heroics" of a US Senator (James Stewart) were bogus, shreds his notes and utters his famous line: "This is the West, sir; when the legend becomes fact, print the legend." Eban writes:

> The supremacy of legends and ideas over transient facts has always impressed me as the key to the understanding of the Jewish journey. In March 1944 when I heard of Wingate's death in a plane crash near the Burmese-Indian border I felt, with all my grief, that he had always seen his life as a drama and…would probably have given wry approval to the manner of its end.[52]

Ironically, the 1967 Associated Press commemorative edition of *Lightning Out of Israel* made the fanciful claim: "Wingate's widow was later to drop the bible of this Lawrence of the Hebrews from a plane over a Jewish community besieged during the 1948 war."[53] Yet, a 1999 biography states that Lorna Wingate's flyover was denied for obvious safety issues, whereupon she inscribed the Bible and gave it to a group of women previously evacuated from the site (Kibbutz Ramot Naftali). The Bible was later donated to a museum in Ein Harod.[54]

Even an acclaimed researcher like Oren is not immune to fleeting naiveté. In *Six Days of War*, he writes: "In the south, Dayan surveyed Operation Nachshon I (after the *biblical* Nachshon ben Aminadav, *the first Hebrew to set foot in the freshly split Red Sea*) for the conquest of the Sinai front…."[55] (Author's emphasis) The Tanakh says *nothing* of the kind. To the contrary, Rabbi Patricia Karlin-Neumann relates: "[N]ot only is he [Nachshon] not singled out [in Exodus] at the Red Sea as a hero, he is not even mentioned! Yet the rabbis praise him for being the first in line to enter the water."[56] Another female rabbi, Debbie Young-Somers, traces the myth to the *Midrash*, which—contrary to Oren's claim that Nachshon was the first to "set foot in the freshly split Red Sea"—makes the inane and contradictory assertion that the water did not split *until* Nachshon waded out to nose depth![57]

THE UNSEEN HAND

While Oren committed the usual Jewish transgression of bypassing inspired Scripture for non-inspired rabbinical twaddle, he did cite a key timeline that shows a genuine miracle of the Six-Day War (albeit without the discernment to attribute it to divine providence).

Unknown to the IDF, Egypt was poised to begin "Operation Dawn" ('Amer's long-awaited invasion of Israel) on Saturday, May 27, fittingly, at first light. Thus, Israel's "Rock" would initiate His own preemptive strike. Just hours before the scheduled attack, Nasser was awakened by an emergency visit from the Soviet ambassador, Dmitri Pojidaev. As Gamal shook the cobwebs out of his head, Dmitri read a two-line communiqué from Premier Kosygin: "One hour ago, President Johnson informed me that Egyptian forces are preparing an attack on Israeli positions and that this attack is about to be launched. If such a thing happens, then the United States will consider itself freed from the commitments it gave the USSR to exercise restraint."[58] (The substance of this generic alert was initially cabled to Abba Eban directing him to apprise the president during their May 26 visit.)

Nasser was stunned! "For him, the crux of the cable was not that the Soviets might fail to aid Egypt, nor even that the Americans might intervene," Oren writes. "Rather, it was proof that Israel had accessed Egyptian secrets and compromised them."[59] Nasser raced off to Supreme Headquarters to cancel Dawn before sunrise. After protests from 'Amer, the stand-down order prevailed. The secularist Oren was left to deduce: "The Egyptian offensive was all but dead, struck down by a *chance* intervention just short of H-hour."[60] (Author's emphasis)

Adding insult to injury, while the *gist* of LBJ's alert to Kosygin (i.e., "an Egyptian surprise attack was expected"[61]) turned out to be correct, Eban denounced the affair as a "cheap trick" by his own government to justify an Israeli strike.[62] "I later learned that the hypochondriac cables reflected a gust of uncertainty that had come over our establishment. One of the causes was the nervous indisposition of the chief of staff, Yitzhak Rabin, through what was charitably defined as nicotine poisoning."[63]

But then, a *second* "coincidental" delay occurred the following day in Tel Aviv. After conducting a tempestuous all-night Cabinet meeting in the "Pit" (underground command bunker) located in the "Campus" (IDF General Staff HQ), Eshkol called a recess at 4:00 a.m. On the crucial subject of preemption, the Hawks were in the ascendency, Rabin reminding his colleagues: "The noose is closing around our necks."[64] The group was told to retire for some badly needed rest, then return later that day to vote. Eshkol's parting remark bears mention: "We must decide in whose hands we will place this generation, into fate's, America's, or Chuvakhin's [Russia's]."[65] While the officials were asleep, two top-secret telegrams arrived from Washington: the first reaffirmed Johnson's support for the so-called "Red Sea Regatta" plan (a pipe dream proposal for an international flotilla to challenge Nasser's blockade); the second cautioned restraint. Oren writes:

> The communications served to tilt the balance in the Cabinet when it reconvened on Sunday afternoon. Instead of a slight majority in favor of war, a straw poll revealed a deadlock...The government concluded its session by resolving to wait...By the thinnest of margins, war had been averted—a war that, whether started by Israel or Egypt, at that stage would have radically altered the subsequent history of the Middle East.[66]

From a purely spiritual perspective, there was a major divine cause for this eleventh-hour delay. Had the war begun "at that stage," Israel could *not* have recovered East Jerusalem. On the morning of May 28—the very *day* Eshkol's Cabinet would vote to postpone preemption—Hussein bin Talal (i.e., the Kingdom of Jordan; the West Bank; the Holy City; the Temple Mount; the Western Wall) told Egypt's ambassador to Jordan, Uthman Nuri, that he wanted a private sit-down with Nasser within forty-eight hours. Two days later, the Hashemite monarch, a .357 on his hip, piloted his own Caravelle jet to Cairo and promptly signed a defense pact with Egypt. When he returned to Amman his jubilant subjects (two-thirds being Palestinian "refugees") swamped his limousine, lifting it off the ground.[67]

Though subdued for political considerations, the Jews had the greater cause for joy. Now the bifurcated status of Israel's ancient capital *could* be terminated. (As a final kicker, Hussein's PTSD would only worsen later with the news that, despite his pact with Gamal, Dayan's last order had clarified that no action be taken against Jordan, including minor land grabs, *unless* they attacked first.)[68]

As I Corinthians 2:14 says, *"But the natural man receiveth not the things of the Spirit of God: for they are foolishness unto him: neither can he know them, because they are spiritually discerned,"* Mr. Oren, once again, would dismiss a divine aegis for these epic events, stating that the liberation of Jerusalem "came about largely through *chance*," while the "last-minute cancellation of Operation Dawn—Egypt's one *chance* to do to Israel what Israel would soon do to Egypt—poignantly illustrated the process's *randomness*."[69] (Author's emphasis)

"HIGH NOON"

With Jordan now affording a strategic land bridge to the nearing conflict, Baghdad joined the coalition on June 3. (Abdul Rahman Arif was Iraq's president in 1967, the Hashemite monarchy ending in 1958 with the assassination of Faisal II, grandson of Arab bigwig, Faisal I.) Other Muslim nations pledged their ancillary support as well. While Nasser's southern front was augmented by Morocco, Libya, Tunisia, and Saudi Arabia, Lebanon would have Syria's back. Hussein was also assured that Yemen, Sudan, and Algeria would heed the clarion call.

Of course, everyone knew that the Russian bear was the proverbial dark horse in the land of Arabian stallions. Still, privately Nasser understood that the sum total of atheistic Russia's fidelity could be deduced from the fatuous pledge by Defense Minister Andre Grechko to his Egyptian counterpart, Shams al-Din Badran: "There should be no doubt about the Soviet Union's commitments to give political and material aid to the Arabs…even to support them spiritually."[70]

Meanwhile, with Charles de Gaulle attempting an inauspicious comeback with the Muslims, Britain's Prime Minister Harold Wilson withdrawing from "Regatta," and Lyndon Johnson distracted by domestic and international headaches, Israel's military, diplomatic, and even psychological needs were being seriously neglected. Johnson flat out admits in his memoirs that Israel had a legitimate right to expect America to honor Eisenhower's prior commitments regarding Aqaba. "In the 1956 war Israeli troops overran the Sinai peninsula. They agreed to withdraw from the area for two reasons: first, a UN decision to put in a peacekeeping force…and, second, President Eisenhower's assurance that the Gulf of Aqaba…would remain open as an international waterway."[71] He then states that he asked Ike for his personal take on the issue: "General Eisenhower sent me a message stating his view that the

Israelis' right of access to the Gulf of Aqaba was definitely part of the 'commitment' we had made to them."[72]

And yet, despite LBJ's characterization of the UN as being a "zero," the only thing Eban took away from his May 26 Oval Office meeting was the president's mantra: "Israel will not be alone unless it decides to go it alone," sealed by a "Texas handshake" so strong that Abba doubted whether he "would ever regain the use of it."[73] Oren adds: "Though Johnson was not averse to bolstering Israel verbally, weapons were out of the question."[74] Lyndon (like Eden and all the rest) would pay a high price for leaving Israel in the lurch (post-Civil Rights Act "Long Hot Summer of 1967," unprecedented campus unrest, escalating Vietnam imbroglio, one-term presidency, etc.).

As the last grains in the hourglass trickled down, the IDF stood at 275,000 men, 1,100 tanks, and 200 planes,[75] while the Arab coalition comprised 500,000 men, 5,000 tanks, and 900 combat aircraft. Oren notes, "Added to this was immense political might. Arab oil producers had agreed to boycott any countries that assisted Israel, to nationalize their refineries and even destroy their pipelines."[76] At the end of the day, oil would once again prove the decisive factor. Dr. Hugh Smythe, US ambassador to Syria, put it bluntly, but accurately: "On the scales we have Israel, an unviable client state whose ties, value to US is primarily emotional, balanced with [a] full range [of] vital strategic, political, commercial/economic interests represented by Arab states."[77]

On May 21, Richard Nolte arrived in Cairo as the new American ambassador. The next day, the Gulf of Aqaba closed to Israeli ships. His suitcase barely unpacked, Nolte opined on May 26 that this was just "tit for tat" for 1956 and that the US was under no onus to ensure the security of any nation "established by force."[78] Two weeks later, Dick had to drag his bags out *again*, getting the boot in a "tête-à-tête" on June 10, stating, "Thus endeth my meteoric mission to Cairo."[79]

Eshkol convened his last prewar Cabinet "Pit stop" on Sunday morning, June 4. After General Aharon Yariv delivered his latest intel assessment on Israel's growing vulnerability (especially with Jordan now onboard), the prime minster gave his long-awaited endorsement: "I'm convinced that today we must give the order to the IDF to choose the time and the manner to act."[80] The formal approval was twelve votes to two. In his own imaginative appraisal of the final clash, Walt Whitman Rostow, LBJ's Jewish national security advisor, found a parallel in another iconic Western—anticipating that Israel (deserted as usual) would ultimately have to throw down "like a sheriff in High Noon, alone"—and using *whatever* force was "necessary to achieve not merely self-respect but respect in the region."[81]

DAY ONE: "WHERE ARE *OUR* PLANES?"

For Israel's "Gary Cooper" (Moshe Dayan favoring a pirate more than a lawman), "High Noon" would come a tad earlier. In base commander Shmuel Shefer's final operational meeting on Sunday evening, the colonel silently wrote on the blackboard in bold, stark strokes—07:45. Major Ran Ronen, leader of Mirage Fighter Squadron 119, recalled: "Shefer turns to face the room. No speech is necessary. The squadron commanders do not glance to one another. No one speaks a word."[82]

When the scramble order sounded at 7:10 a.m., sixteen 1950s-era Fouga Magister training jets, sporting newly-added rockets, took off from Hatzerim Airfield flying a routine patrol pattern. *This* departure constituted the *tachboulah* ("deception"). Five minutes later, two hundred state-of-the-art, French-built Ouragons, Vautours, Mirages, Mystères, and Super Mystères, low-slung with bombs and rockets—the *real* attack force comprising "Operation Moked" ("Focus")—roared out of multiple bases in staggered intervals, the more part heading due west over the Mediterranean. (The aircraft names would say it all—*Hurricanes*, *Vultures*, *Mirages*, and *Mysteries*.) Though flying barely fifty feet above water at 885-feet-per-second (Ronen describing the experience as "riding a rocket sled at the height of a clothesline"[83]), the unprecedented concentration of blips metastasized on Jordan's sophisticated British-built radar system atop Mount Ajlun.

However, in one of many *bona fide* miracles, when the prearranged codeword for war, *Inab* ("Grape"), was radioed to Cairo, it remained indecipherable, Gamal's technocrats having altered the encoding frequencies the day before without advising Amman.[84] After skirting Alexandria, the aerial armada hooked back in a wide, banking arch that brought them into Egypt from the west at roughly 7:45 a.m. (8:45 Egyptian time). With three years of planning, primarily coordinated by Captain Rafi Sivron,[85] it would all be over well before "High Noon."

The Associated Press described the war's opening scene accordingly: "By noon...Brigadier Mordechai Hod reported his jets had destroyed more than 400 Arab planes in the air and at 25 fields in four Arab countries."[86] (The mustachioed, cigar-smoking "Motti" Hod, IAF commander and future first president of El Al Airlines, was the overall architect of Focus.) Due to "near-perfect intelligence" providing the precise location of nearly all EAF aircraft, plus flight schedules at eleven target areas—even the pilots' names[87]—over 90% of the enemy planes were destroyed on the ground, over 200 in just the first thirty minutes. Reconnaissance photos revealed wreck after wreck with hardly a crater in the runways. (The IAF lost seventeen aircraft.) Convinced that an attack would only come at dawn, Nasser's pilots were eating breakfast at the time, having just returned from scouting patrols. Relieved (and rather humbled), Dayan later said: "All I can say is that the role of Intelligence had been all as important as that of the Air Force or the armored corps."[88] Dan Raviv and Yossi Melman write in *Every Spy a Prince*, "The lightning victory over Egypt, Jordan and Syria, was largely [Mossad chief] Meir Amit's triumph…."[89]

In another divine "coincidence," Egypt's key military personnel were not even present when the war began. Marshal 'Amer (traveling with several senior officers to conduct troop inspections) was literally airborne over Sinai during Monday's attack.[90] (Some contend that he had Egypt's air defense system deactivated to avoid being shot down by rebel forces.) General 'Abd al-Hamid al-Dugheidi, air force chief in Sinai, would lament: "It was the first war of its kind, where all the commanders were far away from their commands."[91] Finally, scholars Andrew and Leslie Cockburn state that on June 4 the CIA told Hussein that Israel would attack Egypt the next morning.[92] The king naturally tipped Gamal. However, in one of the *greatest* miracles, as Genesis 19:14 says of Lot's warning to his sons-in-law, *"he seemed as one that mocked,"* Hussein's eleventh-hour alert was ignored as a *joke*.[93]

The rout was *so* calamitous that for the first twenty-four hours 'Amer issued repeated radio bulletins announcing *Israel's* "imminent doom," etc. With his vice president hiding at home and his defense minister locked in his office, Nasser was in the dark as well. Not until 4:00 p.m., when he entered Supreme Headquarters—the spirit of the place described as "bedlam"—did Egypt's president receive the surreal news himself, a junior officer ("sacrificial lamb") gingerly updating him: "I have come to tell you that we no longer have an air force."[94] For his part, the "great" Field Marshal 'Amer was "either drunk or drugged or both…inconsolable and practically incoherent."[95]

Two hours later, the public would finally hear the "truth" over Cairo's "Voice of the Arabs" program—Egypt's air force was actually destroyed by American and British planes, etc. The phantom reports generated a sirocco of anti-Western sentiment across the Ummah, including severed diplomatic ties, sacked embassies, and a threatened oil embargo. (In retrospect, as Dayan knew that Russia and the UN would never initiate a ceasefire as long as they believed Nasser was winning, Egypt's duplicity, complimented by Israel's prudent radio silence, bought the IDF precious time to achieve its military priorities.)

Israel's ground thrust in Sinai, code-named "Sadin Adom" ("Red Sheet"), began at 8:15 a.m. with three columns of armor and mechanized infantry following their key recon jeeps and halftracks. As seen in 1956, the IDF manuals inculcate a blitzkrieg-style, advance-at-*any*-cost theory known as a "war of movement," the raison d'être conveyed by the Hebrew *en brea* ("no alternative"). Dayan relates:

> Warfare in Sinai is a campaign of roads. An armored column seeking to reach the Canal from the east can proceed by one of only three arteries: the coast highway from El Arish to Qantara, the central road via Bir Gafgafa to Ismailiya, or the southern route through the Mitla, Giddi, or Sudr Passes...If our forces can block the enemy's passage along these routes, we can trap them, bring them to battle, and destroy them.[96]

In the north, General Israel Tal's littoral route broke through the village of Khan Yunis (isolating the PLA in Gaza). A second tank brigade captured Rafah (a.k.a. the "Palestinian Mogadishu"), allowing Tal's main force to reach the outskirts of El-Arish (the main base of the Egyptian 7th Division) by late evening. The southern offensive, led by Brigadier General Ariel "Arik" Sharon, centered on the formidable Anglo/Soviet-fashioned Abu Ageila defense plexus along the Nitzana-Ismailia axis. At 10:00 p.m., Sharon's batteries, comprising 105 mm and 155 mm howitzers, fired a record 6,000 shells at Umm Qatef in 20 minutes. Meanwhile, a third force led by General Avraham Yoffe moved across the "impassable" terrain, splitting the two other theaters.

The dual strategy behind this three-fold pincer thrust would be readily apparent by Tuesday. With the IAF strafing and bombing Nasser's undefended convoys with impunity (piling up wrecks at each end, trapping the rest in between), 100,000 fleeing Egyptians would find their ratlines blocked by three IDF battalions. *Not* good! The debacle was typified by the one question on the parched lips of every Muslim solider—"Where are *our* planes? Where are *our* planes?"[97]

For all of Jadid's "boots on the ground" jingoism, the colonel made a last-minute decision to hunker down in the Heights, opting to hit Israeli border settlements with artillery and aerial attacks. According to one press release, his first confirmed "kill" was probably a *carp*: "The first Syrian artillery rounds fell in artificial ponds where the farmers were raising carp to process into gefüllte fish."[98] By late afternoon, two-thirds of al-Assad's air force (thirty-two MiG-21s, twenty-three MiG-17s, and three helicopters) had been obliterated by eighty-two IAF sorties. The Iraqi base at H-3 was also struck resulting in ten enemy planes destroyed. (Lesson: As further evidenced by then-Secretary of State Hillary Clinton's one-line "gefilte fish" email of March 5, 2010, "Where are we on this?"—Don't mess with the Jews' gefilte fish!)

As previously noted, of far greater significance from a prophetic view, the extent of Jordanian aggression would determine Israel's ability to legitimize its long-anticipated Seder chant: "Next year in Jerusalem." On Monday morning, 'Amer apprised Amman that 75% of the IAF was destroyed and that Egyptian tanks were already rumbling through Israel, etc. (II Kings 22:22) Hussein would candidly acknowledge later: "[W]e were misinformed about what had happened in Egypt when the Israelis attacked the UAR bases...These reports – fantastic to say the least – had much to do with our confusion and false interpretation of the situation."[99] Inveigled by these false claims, Jordan would accede to her ally's call to arms *despite* a last-minute communiqué from Eshkol transmitted via General Odd Bull, commander of UNSTO (United Nations Truce Supervision Organization), affirming that "Israel will not, repeat not, attack Jordan if Jordan maintains the quiet."[100]

At 10:00 a.m., Jordan's American-made 155 mm 'Long Tom' guns began pummeling targets from West Jerusalem to Tel Aviv, followed by 3-inch mortars and 106 mm recoilless rifle fire. Some 6,000 shells would ultimately hit Jerusalem, damaging 1,000 apartments, killing 20 civilians, and wounding 250. At 11:50 a.m., sixteen Jordanian Hawker Hunter jet fighters struck sites around Netanya. Still resolved to avoid a land incursion, Dayan chose the "measured response" of unleashing the IAF. At 12:30 (while the Hawkers were refueling), the first sortie rendered the airfields at Amman and Mafraq inoperable. Thirty minutes later—as Hussein and his two young sons watched from their backyard—

strike two wiped out the "entire" Royal Jordanian Air Force (twenty-eight planes). The Associated Press reported:

> The waves of Mirages and Mystères now ruled the air over Amman, flying lower than the minarets from which the muezzin call the devout to prayer. From the city's tallest minaret, a loudspeaker boomed: 'God is great. Come to pray and greet Mohammed the Prophet.' The voice was lost in the roar of Israeli jets banking over the city.[101]

Hussein's hapless operation (under the tacit command of Egypt's military chief-of-staff, General 'Abd al-Mun'im Riyad) appeared to react in knee-jerk fashion. At around 1:30 p.m., Jordan's 27th 'Isam bin Zayt Battalion, led by Major Badi 'Awad, still convinced—*along with Riyad himself*—that Israel was retreating, crossed over the Jerusalem armistice lines into the Demilitarized Zone, promptly occupying the UNSTO headquarters building, a.k.a. the Government House, former residence of the British High Commissioner.[102] (The snooping role of the United Nations was forecast in Jeremiah 4:14, *"Make ye mention unto the nations; behold, publish against Jerusalem that watchers come from a far country, and give voice against the cities of Judah."*)

For the Israelis, this was not just another provocation, it was an untenable security threat! The three-story compound was situated atop the easternmost locus of a ridgeline commanding the critical artery to Bethlehem and Hebron. Some of the most densely populated Jewish sprawl in New Jerusalem lay below the strategic rise known as *Jabel Mukaber*. Evan Wilson, the US minister-consul general in Jerusalem, remarked: "It was an open invitation to the Israelis to move in and it provided the latter with an essential base of operations to take the Old City."[103]

Around 2:30 p.m., Lieutenant Colonel Asher Drezin began a coordinated assault, the enormity of which was felt by all, IDF tank commander Major Aaron Kamara declaring over the intercom: "We're beginning to make history."[104] Government House was retaken directly, followed by a sweep of proximate secondary targets (Antenna Hill, Lonely House, and the Training Farm within the DMZ; the Sausage and the Bell inside Jordanian space). Calling the precipitous seizure "Hussein's gravest error," Sachar states, "He failed to detect in the unchallengeable power of Israeli air squadrons over Amman, at a time when Cairo was boasting that virtually all Israel's planes had been destroyed, the clue to what actually was happening in the Middle Eastern war."[105] Rabinovich adds: "Hussein had chosen to come into the game when the ultimate outcome could already be read in the columns of smoke rising over Egyptian airfields from Sinai to the pyramids."[106] The IDF would have all of southern Jerusalem by night.

For what it's worth, Nasser and Hussein were not the only ones to lose face on that "*Blue* Monday." To revisit our recurrent theme of poetic justice, General Odd Bull—described by Oren as "ill-disposed toward Israel"[107]—had one *very* humiliating day himself. First, as the Jordanians burst into his sacrosanct domain, the guard at the gate—*another* Burmese named U (U Than Aye)—dove under the table after being grabbed by his blue scarf.[108] Needless to say, Bull saw red! His memoirs state: "I do not remember ever having been as angry in my life."[109] Then, the peace-loving Norwegian got to watch his residence and automobile destroyed in the withering IDF counter-attack,[110] Rabinovich citing the soldiers' "undisguised joy in being able to fire at the white building symbolizing the UN presence."[111]

Next, as related by military historian Eric Hammel: "Toward dusk, the U.N. colors were struck and an Israeli flag was raised over Government House."[112] The Israelis then denied Odd's request for Jordanian repatriation (arranging for his ignoble return through Israel).[113] The air force general would also learn that he had lost his private plane in the IAF raid in Amman.[114]

Finally, on a *far* more sober note, while the climactic battle for the Old City and Temple Mount would continue for another two days, an uncanny correlation exists between the *epithet* of the ridge comprising Hussein's initial land grab (Jabel Mukaber) and the *cause* for the resultant debacle (i.e., 'Amer's *deceitful advice* to invade). The ground where Jordan's first (and short-lived) conquest occurred, just *happens* to be known as "The Hill of Evil Counsel"[115]—the traditional site of Caiaphas' palace where the Pharisees plotted to kill Jesus!

Regardless of the claim's archeological veracity (dating to the Byzantine era), the *infallible* New Testament account records that in "a council" (normally convened at the high priest's residence[116]), Caiaphas declares, *"[I]t is expedient for us, that one man should die for the people, and that the whole nation perish not...,"* followed by John's inspired commentary, *"[H]e prophesied that Jesus should die for that nation...from that day forth they took* COUNSEL *together for to put him to death."* (John 11:47-53) The fact that Caiaphas directly caused Christ's death also fulfilled the scriptural requirement that only a priest could offer a sacrificial lamb. (If anyone but the priest had slain Christ, the sacrifice would not have been accepted.)

Thus, it would appear that in a *second* display of divine mercy (the *first* being that twin delay of the war, allowing Jordan's participation), Israel's "Rock" ordained that the Jews' long-awaited recovery of *Yerushalayim* would be tied to the very *spot* where their ancestors, led by Judas Iscariot, betrayed their own Messiah (Matthew 26:3, 57; Luke 22:54). That this site remains the United Nations' headquarters in Israel, not only speaks to its infamous past but to a far greater evil to come: *"And it shall come to pass in that day, that I will seek to destroy all the* NATIONS *that come against* JERUSALEM*...For I will gather all* NATIONS *against* JERUSALEM *to battle...Then shall the LORD go forth, and fight against those* NATIONS, *as when he fought in the day of battle."* (Zechariah 12:9; 14:2-3)

DAY TWO: AMMUNITION HILL

On the diplomatic front, Israel's main "ally" was utterly feckless. State spokesman Robert McCloskey abruptly declared: "[O]ur position [on the war] is neutral in thought, word, and deed." (Republican Senator Everett Dirksen called it "snootral"—i.e., "sticking up your snoot at both sides.") Forced into spin mode from an immediate Jewish backlash, Dean Rusk clarified that "neutral, a great concept in international law, is not an expression of indifference."[117]

Meanwhile, *Pravda* declared: "[T]he Soviet Government remains loyal to its pledge to assist the victims of aggression."[118] Incredibly, President Johnson's first cable to Moscow begins: "Dear *Comrade* Kosygin...You may be assured we will exercise all our influence to bring hostilities to an end."[119] LBJ would write in his memoirs: "I have never concealed my regret that Israel decided to move when it did."[120]

President Nasser's propaganda regarding Anglo-American aerial intervention (dubbed "The Big Lie") ultimately backfired in two areas. While Johnson, unwilling to lend further credence to collusion, hesitated to influence Israel's military decisions (i.e., pressing for a precipitate ceasefire), Kosygin, briefed by Soviet intelligence that Israel had indeed acted alone, was compelled to rethink further commitments (i.e., avoiding certain embarrassment as the Mossad had secretly recorded Nasser's calls to Amman plotting the subterfuge). More significantly, Gamal's refusal to accept a UN-brokered ceasefire sealed Hussein's fate (i.e., forfeiture of the Temple Mount). Thus, with Egypt's air force "neutralized," Dayan would scramble to envelop 'Amer's ground troops while penetrating East Jerusalem and encircling the Old City. Apart from an anemic early morning feint (repulsed by local defenders), Nasser's northern "ally" would spend a second day ensconced atop the 3,000-foot Golan Heights, inspiring the Arab proverb: "Syria [is] willing to fight to the last Egyptian."[121]

In the spirit of Orde Wingate, Israel's "day" battles usually began after dark. Upon capturing the strategic junction at Bir Lahfan late Monday, General Yoffe waged a successful tank battle from 11 p.m. to 10 a.m. Encountering a statue of a Palestinian refugee pointing toward Israel, an Israeli Centurion leveled it with a blast.[122] Egypt's GHQ in Gaza City was taken by Tuesday morning. Reinforced by an unprecedented nocturnal helicopter landing of an entire paratroop brigade, three miles behind enemy artillery batteries, Arik launched his own nighttime tachboulah, engaging Egyptian armor from as close as ten yards. Umm Qatef (a.k.a. "The Death Trap") capitulated by first light. In his dawn reconnoiter of the "burning and totally destroyed" Egyptian revetments further west at Bir Hasana, an Umm Qatef survivor, 'Adel Mahjub, wrote—"It was like a journey to hell."[123]

Daylight only made things hotter. Already stifled by desert temperatures reaching 130 degrees (causing over 20,000 heatstroke deaths alone), thousands were incinerated by raining napalm (jellied gasoline). A "tactical fallback" ordered by Marshal 'Amer around noon morphed into a pell-mell retreat within hours. "Jammed on roads with thousands of vehicles, tens of thousands of men…became easy prey for marauding Israeli jets…The Egyptian army was running."[124]

Day two on the Jordanian front began with similar unearthly conditions. Hussein described those wee hours in a conundrum: "That night was hell. It was clear as day. The sky and the earth glowed with the light of the rockets and the explosions of bombs pouring from Israeli planes."[125] The decision to retaliate against Jordan would inch along five increasingly sensitive theaters: 1) East Bank airfields; 2) the West Bank; 3) East Jerusalem; 4) the Old City; 5) the Temple Mount. While a multiregional assault was being waged against the West Bank, nearly every Jewish soldier *knew* that the Temple Mount constituted the veritable epicenter (especially after losing it in 1948). Though Eshkol's cabinet would delay the political option as long as possible, the military had the onus of securing the Holy City's submission with minimal collateral damage. Mindful of the potential for international backlash, Dayan remarked, "I want none of that Vatican."[126]

At 2:10 a.m., Israeli batteries (guided by giant spotlights atop the Histadrut Building) unleashed a thirty-minute fusillade of artillery, tank, and mortar fire upon the East Jerusalem front (just north of the Old City). The next several hours were fraught with a myriad of challenges. Battalion 71 commander, Major Uzi Eilam, recalled: "Brigade 55... possesses no shortage of proven commanders and heroes...But no one has assaulted a city. None has fought house to house in a locality of this scale. And no one has thrown together a plan of attack in sixty minutes, then put it into action, at night, with virtually no supporting armor or heavy weapons, in an urban environment that is a maze and a mystery to most of his men."[127]

Colonel Mordecai "Motta" Gur, commander of the freshly arrived 55th Reserve Paratroop Brigade began his three-pronged pincer strike by sending Major Yosef "Yossi" Yoffe and his 66th Battalion across the no-man's land near Mandelbaum Gate (main crossing point between the two city sectors). The objective was to pierce the enemy's defenses and relieve the one-square-mile, UN-monitored Jewish enclave atop Mount Scopus—the key to isolating Old Jerusalem below. Yoffe's immediate target was the heavily fortified Jordanian Police Academy. On the 23rd anniversary of D-Day, Israeli troops were *also* found crawling through withering machine gunfire, detonating mines, and destroying barbed wire with Bangalore torpedoes. With the Academy breached by 3:00 a.m., Gur directed his remaining battalions against the major bulwark—a lethal labyrinth of deep interlocking trenches, bunkers, and concrete obstacles reinforced by mines and concertina wire—known as *Givat Hatachmoshet* ("Ammunition Hill"), named after the garrison where General Allenby stored his ordnance during WWI. The imposing redoubt was manned by a 140-man company of Jordan's crack 2nd al-Husseini Battalion.

The ensuing multifaceted attack (supported by French Shermans) waged on for two hours. The heroics were many (ten citations later awarded). Like the hedgerows at Normandy, each trench line, each fire bay, and each bunker had to be methodically taken, one by one—in the dark. Built on a slope, the circuitous earthworks were designed so that one trench would provide cover for another. Entering in single file, the point man was invariably killed. As Israelis burst through with Uzis and phosphorous grenades, Legionnaires shouting "Allahu Akbar" met them with blazing Bren machineguns. Jews and Arabs alike had their heads blown off at point-plank range. Ironically, much of the close order combat on *Ammunition* Hill devolved into hand-to-hand; Major Mansur Kranshur, the wounded Jordanian commander, lamented in his last radio message before retreating: "[A]mmunition is running low."[128] At 5:00 a.m., the Star of David was finally hoisted atop Ammunition Hill. Oren rates the epic battle as "one of the bloodiest in Arab-Israeli history."[129] (Seventy-one Legionaries were killed with forty-six wounded; thirty-five Israelis died.) As one of the Jordanian prisoners told his captor—"We fought well, but you fought better."[130]

In the meantime, the 71st Battalion emerged at Wadi Joz at the base of Mount Scopus, effectively severing the Old City from Jericho and East Jerusalem from Ramallah. The adjacent Rockefeller Archeology Museum fell to a detachment of the 28th Battalion around 7:30 a.m. While Gur's survivors took a well-deserved rest, elements of the 10th and 4th Brigades expedited mop-up operations. By midday a Jordanian military communiqué confirmed: "[T]he enemy has conquered all of Jerusalem except for the Old City."[131] (The full occupation of Scopus was deferred until Wednesday). In one of the day's lesser-known game changers, Squadron 147—a stopgap aerial armada of twenty-four lumbering, outdated Fouga Magisters—ravaged several Jordanian and Iraqi columns moving from the Jordan Valley to Jerusalem. According to IAF pilot Zvi "Kantor" Kanor, the unsung Jewish heroes "saved the city and the troops in it, and produced victory in the West Bank."[132]

When the Ministerial Defense Committee met at 2:00 p.m., Eshkol gave the long-awaited go-ahead to formalize the *fait accompli* the following morning; hopefully, the surrender of Old Jerusalem would be accepted (not forced). Tel Aviv would then provide high-profile assurances to the world's religious leaders regarding the safekeeping of their sacred sites. The second day of the war ended around 11:30 p.m. with King Hussein ordering a full-scale, every-man-for-himself, evacuation of the entire West Bank.[133] (Earlier that afternoon, while personally reconnoitering the Jordan Valley in a jeep, Hussein had observed his proud Legionnaires retreating from the north.[134])

Wednesday's *Jerusalem Post* headline would summarize the previous day's results: "SCOPUS ROAD OPENED, OLD CITY ENCIRCLED; 200 EGYPTIAN TANKS SMASHED; GAZA FALLS."[135]

Every Israeli child learns the patriotic folksong "Givat Hatachmoshet," retelling the epic battle. The focal line reads: "There were no questions—those who went first, just fell. You really needed a lot of luck on Givat Hatachmoshet." This recurrent emphasis on "chance" coincides with the impression gleaned by an American reporter who said of the soldiers: "[M]ost of them were not religious Jews, but the Old City of David and Solomon, of Isaiah and Jeremiah had an emotional appeal."[136] (The defense minister himself never had a bar mitzvah.[137]) Sadder yet, many secular Israelis were more than just "not religious." Having bluntly said, "I don't give a d--n about the Old City," Company B commander, Uzi Eilat remarked upon locating some lost munitions, "If I believed in God, I would thank him"; Yigal Talmi, an intel officer on the Sinai front and son of the noted atheist Emma Talmi, begrudgingly rationalized his acceptance of a rabbi's prayer card, stating, "[T]his is no time to p--s off the Big Guy."[138]

However, the evidence of that "unseen hand" was ubiquitous. For instance, what were *paratroopers* doing crawling through minefields on Ammunition Hill? Well—it just so *happened* that on Monday afternoon, someone at IDF headquarters phoned General Uzi Narkiss and asked "if he could use a battalion of paratroopers in Jerusalem." Strained for manpower, Narkiss replied that "he could use a whole brigade." Fifteen minutes later GHQ rang back and gave Uzi the entire 55th Brigade![139] The crusty brigadier unashamedly acknowledged: "The 55th dropped on us from Heaven."[140]

To connect the proverbial dots of divine providence, the original assignment of the 55th—a combined parachute drop and amphibious assault on El-Arish—was obviated by the unexpected acceleration of the Sinai offensive. The freed-up "red berets" were packed into buses and rushed off to Jerusalem.[141] The Sinai blitzkrieg was also arranged by the "Rock of Israel." As noted, Cairo had failed to advise Amman regarding the altered radar encoding frequency. Another factor enabling Narkiss to receive his badly needed reserves was that 'Amer had been deprived of *his*—70,000 troops sitting idle in Yemen (resulting from the 1962-67 Egyptian-Yemen War). And then, there were all those Soviet tanks that kept malfunctioning due to unsuitable desert conditions (albeit less dramatic than 50-ft. angels, etc). As airborne commander Colonel Rafael Eytan would remark after the war, "Apparently someone in heaven was watching over us. Every unintended action they [Egyptians] took and every unintended action we took always turned out to our advantage."[142]

Finally, Rabinovich relates that a Corporal Eylan used a hand grenade to blast several Legionnaires out of "a large cave set back from the main trench line…[that] contained Jewish tombs from the Second Temple period."[143] As the capture of Government House was tied to the spot of Christ's betrayal, it is not without significance that the victory on Givat Hatachmoshet occurred *less than a mile* north of the Garden Tomb (adjacent to Gordon's Calvary). In 1968, archeologists digging on *Givat Hamivtar* (near a former Jordanian fort where snipers fired on Israelis during Ammunition Hill) unearthed the first-century skeletal remains of a Jewish male (24-28 years old) identified as "Jehohanan, son of HGQWL" (Tomb 1, Chamber B, Ossuary 4). Of particular interest was "a right *calcaneum* (heel bone), still pierced by an 11.5 cm (4.5 inch) iron nail…with traces of wood at both ends," representing "the total physical evidence from the ancient world for crucifixion."[144] Thus, Psalm 22:16 (*cross*-referenced with Zechariah 12:10 and 13:6) provides the two most important (and least-known) Messianic signs—*"they pierced my hands and my feet."*

DAY THREE: "SOMETHING SPECIAL HAD HAPPENED"

With Dayan's upgraded approval to "induce" the *surrender* scenario, Israeli artillery began shelling the Muslim Quarter at 6:00 a.m. (the rules of engagement sparing the Dome of the Rock, al-Aqsa Mosque and Church of the Holy Sepulchre). Having cleared the Jordanian remnants from Scopus and the adjacent Augusta Victoria Ridge (the latter facilitated by napalm), Gur's men moved to the Mount of Olives.

Overlooking the Garden of Gethsemane, Motta radioed his famous directive to the battalion commanders: "We occupy the heights overlooking the Old City. In a little while we will enter it. The ancient city of Jerusalem which for generations we have dreamed of and striven for—we'll be first to enter it. The Jewish nation is awaiting our victory. Israel awaits our victory. Israel awaits this historic hour. Be proud. Good luck!"[145] Gur gave his order "in the clear," indicating that he sensed the moment was too eventful for code names, speaking "in plain Hebrew for all the world to hear"[146] (Habakkuk 2:2).

The plan was to enter Old Jerusalem via the Lion's Gate (also called St. Stephen's or Sheep)—on the *eastern* side. With the Holy City having fallen some forty times throughout its expanding 3,000-year history, the invading host inevitably made the primary thrust from the *north*.[147] The three exceptions to this rule would be: General Joab and his volunteers ascending through the *tsinnor* ("gutter" or "water system") below the east wall (II Samuel 5:8); Colonel Gur and his forces storming through the Lion's Gate; and, King Jesus *to* enter via the sealed Eastern Gate at the Second Advent (Ezekiel 44:1-3).

It is also noteworthy that Gur descended from Mount Olivet—just as the Jewish Messiah will do (Zechariah 14:4). Thus, at precisely 9:45 a.m., the forty-foot high, 750-year-old Lion's Gate, chosen for its proximity to the Temple Mount and still bearing the insignia of the Mamluk Sultan Baibars, was *blasted* open by a Sherman tank at point-blank range. (With matching *pairs* of sculpted lions facing one another on either side of the arch, the incorrect spelling of "*Lion's* Gate St." represents a conspicuous illustration of Israel's "*blindness in part.*") Encountering only minimal resistance, Israeli armor and airborne units swept through the breach. In *another* "coincidence," the *Via Dolorosa* (traditional route of Christ's passion) was situated straight ahead.

While other companies of the Jewish Brigade and 71st Paratroopers were converging on the Zion and Dung gates, Motta and his men raced to the Wailing Wall. Incredibly, they had to ask a mysterious old man for directions. In his bestselling non-fiction narrative, *The Lion's Gate*, Stephen Pressfield relates the following edited version of Sergeant Moshe Milo (Captain Yoram Zamosh's radioman):

> Now the craziest thing happens. To get to the Wall, we know, we must pass through Sha'ar Mughrabim, the Moroccan Gate [one of eleven outer gates to the walled Temple Mount]. None of us knows where this is or how hard it will be to break through. In fact, we are carrying explosives to blow the gate open once we locate it. Suddenly, out of nowhere emerges an ancient Arab man wearing a white robe, with a huge key that must weigh half a kilo hanging around his neck. Yair commands "A" Company's 1st Platoon. He dashes straight to this elderly gent, who is clearly confused, frightened, and bewildered. Yair asks him, in English, "Where is the Wailing

> Wall?" The old man is too scared to answer. Levanon speaks to him calmly, promising we will not hurt him. "That key around your neck? What is it for?"
>
> Apparently the man is in charge of the Mughrabim Gate. He's the gatekeeper. Haltingly he leads us there. It's a green wooden gate—a small door within a larger door. It's locked. Zamosh's second-in-command is Lieutenant Rafi Malka. He's speaking to the gatekeeper now in Arabic. One of our sergeants, Ze'ev Parnes, stands beside him. Parnes tells me later that the old man answered in Arabic, very calmly and without fear, referring to 1948 when the Jordanians drove the Israelis out of Old Jerusalem: "I have been waiting for you for nineteen years. I knew you would come." He hands Parnes the key and we open the gate. We cross through and there is the Wall.[148]

Unlike the broad, stone plaza of today, only a narrow, six-foot-wide alley separated the sixty-two-foot-high wall from the Arab tenements. Describing the IDF men "on their knees, weeping…looking on with dumbstuck eyes," author Richard Cohen relates, "It finally seemed that the Jews had a future, a place in the world. There was a sense of the miraculous; even the atheists felt it…The soldiers brushed the stones with their fingertips as you might brush the fur of a sleeping animal, thrilled and afraid."[149] Surveying the tree-lined pavilion, known to Muslims as *al-Haram al-Sharif* ("Nobel Sanctuary") and to Jews as *Har haBayit* ("Temple Mount"), intelligence officer Arik Achmon preserved the moment: "There you are, on a half track after two days of fighting, with shots still filling the air, suddenly you enter this wide open space that everyone has seen before in pictures, and though I'm not religious, I don't think there was a man who wasn't overwhelmed. Something special had happened."[150]

After a brief skirmish with Legionnaire regulars, Gur radioed Narkiss the climactic words—"*Har ha-Bayit be-Yadenu*" ("The Temple Mount is now in our hands"). The previous day, an elderly widow placed a faded, irregular-shaped Israeli flag into the hands of Captain Zamosh. "This I have kept," the grandmother tearfully related, "since my husband and I were driven from our home. It flew last in the Old City."[151] Standing before the Wall, Zamosh took a battered ballpoint pen and inscribed upon the sacred banner: "This flag of Israel was placed here by paratroopers of the 55th Brigade, 7 June, 1967, who have liberated the Old City." The Star of David was hoisted above the Kotel, a strong breeze holding it open. Upon Colonel Moshe Stempel's order, the soldiers fired three Uzi bursts into the air.[152] The impromptu ceremony ended with Gur's mesmerized warriors singing the "HaTikva," the final couplet resounding with closure: "To be a free people in our land. The land of Zion and Jerusalem." Later that evening, Naomi Shemer would compose the concluding stanza of her now epic anthem, "Jerusalem of Gold" (originally commissioned for the Independence Day celebration that very year)—"Back to the wells and to the fountains, within the ancient walls...."[153]

Meanwhile, after conveniently delaying Eshkol's visit to the Kotel over "security concerns," etc. (though at least one praying soldier *was* reportedly killed by a sniper[154]), Dayan, flanked by Rabin and Narkiss, "bravely" proceeded with his *own* choreographed victory stride, morphing from Gary Cooper to Douglas MacArthur. (Eshkol would eventually arrive by dusk.) Standing before the Wall, he declared: "We have unified Jerusalem, the divided capital of Israel. We have returned to the holiest of our holy places, never to depart from it again."[155]

Having ordered the removal of an Israeli flag from the Dome of the Rock, the politically sensitive Dayan assured one and all: "To our Arab neighbors we extend, at this time, a hand in peace. To members of other religions, Christians and Muslims, we promise faithfully to protect your full freedom and religious rights. We have not come to Jerusalem to conquer sites holy to others or to restrict the freedom of other religious groups...."[156] Then, in accord with Jewish tradition, the defense minister scribbled a note on a scrap of paper and inserted it into a crack between the stones. "What did you wish for?" a reporter asked. "Peace," was the one-word reply[157] (Haggai 2:7).

Shlomo Goren, the army's chief rabbi, represented the other extreme. Not content with blasting his shofar from atop a tank,[158] Shlomo lobbied unsuccessfully to hasten the messianic era by *blasting the Dome of the Rock!*[159] The epitome of appeasement rationale, Dayan and Eshkol overcompensated for such fanaticism by installing two contentious policies. First, control over the Temple Mount was awarded to the Jerusalem Islamic Waqf. Second (and more revolting to Israelis), Jews were literally forbidden to pray at the site itself. (The place remains a growing flashpoint between Jews and Muslims.)

The IDF lost 179 men in the battle for Jerusalem (compared to 330 Legionnaire deaths). Of some 900 casualties brought to Hadassah in fifty-six hours, major surgeries were performed on 300 with all but eleven surviving.[160] Much of the credit for this remarkable statistic was due to the celebrated courage of the battlefield medics. In just one well-directed enemy barrage, all ten medics of Battalion Eight, along with the battalion doctor, were thrown bleeding into the street.[161]

The rest of Wednesday's gains appear anticlimactic by comparison. The Straits of Tiran were reopened at noon. The Sinai Peninsula (23,000 sq. miles) was just about sealed, with hundreds of Egyptians fleeing barefooted into the desert.[162] Elements of the 4th Armored Division (one of the first to cross the Suez Canal) were already nearing Cairo. And, while Bethlehem was taken at dusk with barely a shot fired, Israeli troops proceeded to encounter a "menace" far greater than bullets—*Arab merchants in the souks hawking their souvenirs*.[163]

DAY FOUR: CHUTZPAH ON STEROIDS

General Avaraham Yoffe received a radio communiqué in mid-afternoon from the commander of an Israeli column in the far west theater: "Request permission to wash feet…."[164] Though initially taken aback at the unintelligible message, the HQ commander smiled as he finished reading—"in the Suez Canal!" This was how Israel learned its troops had reached Nasser's prized possession.[165] The June 23 front-page cover of *Life* magazine featured a smiling IDF lieutenant (Yossi Ben-Hanan), weapon in hand, cooling off in the Canal. However, the really big news that day would involve a *different* body of water.

At 2:05 p.m., three high-performance Israeli delta-wing Mirage fighters, followed moments later by two lighter Dassault Super Mystères, attacked an unarmed American ship, the USS *Liberty*, as it drifted thirteen miles off the Sinai coast. In twenty-two minutes of coordinated strafing runs, the squadron employed rocket, cannon, and machine-gun fire, along with thousand-pound bombs and napalm.[166] (Survivors testified that "bullets rained on the deck like hailstones."[167]) Immediately afterwards, three French-built, 62-ton Israeli motor torpedo boats (MTBs) arrived in attack formation, firing five 19-inch torpedoes, one scoring a direct hit to the starboard. The *Liberty* was picked completely out of the water by the force of the blast. Over the next forty minutes, the MTBs circled the now-listing vessel, machine-gunning all visible targets (reputedly, empty life rafts as well) with armor-piercing projectiles.[168] By 3:30 p.m., the assailants were gone.

Shortly after dawn, the US Naval destroyers *Davis* and *Massey* finally arrived. Helicopters evacuated the casualties, 34 killed (including Executive Officer Philip Armstrong) and 171 wounded (including Commander William L. McGonagle). The enraged Joint Chiefs of Staff (JCS) "proposed a quick, retaliatory airstrike on the Israeli naval base"[169] at Haifa, but were overruled by LBJ.[170]

Within hours of the attack, Israel's Cabinet "apologized" for the "tragic case of mistaken identity" (followed later by a pledge to make full restitution). President Johnson "graciously" accepted. Case closed (as in *slammed shut*). Limping into Malta on June 14, the *Liberty* displayed 821 separate holes on its hull and superstructure, including a 40-foot torpedo gash. A total news blackout was immediately imposed, the genesis of a permanent cover-up. The initial Navy Court of Inquiry at Valetta was chaired by Admiral Isaac Kidd, Jr.

According to the "official" (unclassified) JCS explanation, the USS *Liberty* AGTR-5—registered as a "General Technical Research Ship" ("to conduct technical research operations in support of U.S. Navy electronic research projects which include electromagnetic propagation studies and advanced communications systems"[171])—was *purportedly* sent into harm's way (unescorted) "to assist in relaying information concerning the evacuation of American dependents and other American citizens from the countries of the Middle East."[172] With Eban on record stating: "I categorically assert that the *Liberty* tragedy was not deliberate,"[173] Israel's "formal" (unclassified) spiel was that a massive explosion in El-Arish at 11:24 a.m. (later found to be an *onsite* blast) was initially claimed to have resulted from a naval barrage, with the "unidentified" *Liberty* purported to be one of two *Egyptian* ships doing the shelling, etc. (One of Dayan's major assets that would expedite "closure," at least on the diplomatic front, was the disturbing *fact* that "somehow" Washington had neglected to notify its ally that *any* USN vessel—much less some weird-looking, high-tech, electromagnetic, *whatever* kind of ship—would be *snooping* around in such volatile waters.[174])

In reality, the USS *Liberty* was classified in *Jane's Fighting Ships* as an "Electronic Intelligence Ship," known in naval parlance as a "Spook Ship," deployed to monitor, intercept, and record all radio transmissions in the ambient ether. Oren writes: "The Liberty was a spy ship, code-named Rockstar, and operating at the behest of the National Security Agency."[175] Essentially two vessels in one, the lower "off limits" area accommodated a detachment of SIGINT specialists from the highly classified Naval Security Group, superintending $10.2 million worth of cutting-edge, eavesdropping accoutrements, including high-powered radio-communication equipment (1,500-mile range) and computerized signals-analysis gear for deciphering monitored coded messages.[176] Some forty-five peculiar-shaped steel antennae, capped by a sixteen-foot dish-shaped moon-bounce unit (a.k.a. the "Big Ear") resting high atop the stern, graced the "normal" top half of the vessel.[177] Former JCS chairman Admiral Thomas Moorer said: "The *Liberty* was the ugliest, strangest looking ship in the U.S. Navy."[178]

As for her legitimate purpose, eleven days after the attack, *Newsweek* was already reporting that "the Liberty was no ordinary vessel but an intelligence-gathering ship on a 'ferret' mission. It carried elaborate gear to locate both Israeli and Egyptian radio and radar and to track and tape all military messages sent from command posts to the battlefield."[179] Sticking with his government's "tragic accident" story,[180] Oren seems to hedge on his own conspiracy theory: "Its exact mission, unknown even to the skipper, Commander William L. McGonagle, was probably to track the movements of Egyptian troops and their Soviet advisors in Sinai."[181] An *undated* NSA report (declassified in 2002) states: "The SIGINT tasking of the USS LIBERTY was directed at coverage of communications related to United Arab Republic (UAR) Air, Military and Naval Forces activity…known to use Soviet-provided equipment."[182] In 2007, former Defense Secretary Robert S. McNamara (age 91) rivaled Don Rumsfeld's "unknown unknowns" gaff, telling the *Chicago Tribune* he had "absolutely no recollection of what I did that day," except that "I have a memory that I didn't know at the time what was going on."[183]

Though ultimately impossible to prove why the *Liberty* was *really* attacked (like the mysterious disappearance of KAL 007), there were plenty of shenanigans to go around—on *both* sides. For instance, in *Body of Secrets*, James Bamford cites *five* emergency JCS evacuation orders that "somehow" failed to reach *Liberty—the number one communications ship in the world.*[184] Richard Deacon writes: "No explanation of this appalling muddle over top secret orders of great urgency ever seems to have been given."[185] Then, despite a Mayday signal that *did* reach the US Sixth Fleet, Oren confirms: "Help never arrived."[186] In his definitive work, *Assault on the Liberty*, survivor James Ennes, Jr., unintentionally shares an arresting *déjà vu*: "'Where are our jets?' we asked each other."[187] (Adding insult to injury, shortly after midnight, a Soviet guided missile destroyer appeared and offered assistance, the gesture being declined.[188])

Conversely, the same IAF pilots who were sharp enough on *Monday* to separate the real EAF planes from their dummy lookalikes parked nearby,[189] could make *nine* reconnaissance passes over *Liberty* on *Wednesday* (one within 200 feet, close enough to wave[190]), yet "somehow" fail to detect (in perfect visibility) a clearly identified, flag-flying, aerial-sprouting, $40,000,000, state-of-the-art SIGINT platform, from the Egyptian *El Quseir*—a decrepit, rusted out, Arabic-marked, decommissioned, docked in Alexandria, coastal horse cavalry transport, less than *half* the *Liberty's* size and projecting a radically different silhouette. (Admiral Moorer once compared the *Liberty*, with its multiple moving antennae, to a lobster.[191]) Both governments would dismiss these (and other) aberrations to incompetence. Bamford labeled them "a series of Keystone Kops foul-ups."[192]

As the Bible states in I Corinthians 14:33, *"God is not the author of confusion...,"* a mélange of conflicting conspiracy theories abound. And the more one tries to maneuver through this anti-Semitic quagmire, the more one can sense its satanic origin. Ennes believes his ship was attacked because the "spooks" were about to out Israel's plans to invade Syria.[193] Bamford (a former classmate of Mr. Loftus) posits that the IDF tried to silence *Liberty* for having honed in on the massacre of "as many as 1,000 Egyptian prisoners in the Sinai."[194] (Jim was "apparently" unaware that this story was debunked more than four years before *Body of Secrets* was published.)[195]

Then, according to the collated views of Deacon, former CIA station chief Wilbur "Bill" Eveland, and freelance correspondent and author Anthony Pearson, the CIA forged a plan with the Mossad that Israel could attack Egypt to expedite Nasser's ouster but with the caveat that no further aggression occur (i.e., toward Jordan or Syria). The paranoid Hussein was advised to play along.[196,197,198] The authors contend that Israel broke the agreement by tricking the Arabs into attacking *them* by "cooking the books," i.e., intercepting, altering, and re-routing Egyptian high-speed radio traffic to Jordan and Syria, asserting that *Egypt* had destroyed *Israel's* air force.[199,200] Eveland and Pearson further concur that a Polaris nuclear submarine (USS *Andrew Jackson*) had shadowed *Liberty*, conforming to a White House contingency pledge to Moscow that Israel's silos would be taken out should Dayan order ballistic missile strikes on Arab cities, or worse yet, trigger the "Samson Option."[201,202] Thus, the *Liberty*, ostensibly deployed to track Israel's movements—having successfully detected the electronic sabotage—was mauled to destroy the recorded data.[203]

The much-lauded 2002 BBC documentary, *USS Liberty: Dead in the Water* (followed by the 2003 book, *Operation Cyanide* by British author Peter Hounam), advanced the most audacious claim to date—that the US and Israel *conspired* to sink *Liberty*, accuse Nasser, then *nuke* Cairo![204] (Should we have expected less from the anti-Semitic British?) Supposedly brokered by CIA counter-intel chief James Jesus Angleton (a mole for Israel),[205] the plot was code-named "Operation Cyanide." The auxiliary role of a "spook sub" (some believe the USS *Amberjack*) is implied on a one-page document titled "Memorandum for the Record" (dated April 10, 1967). Purported to be the minutes of the "303 Committee" (a secret body described by former CIA director Richard Helms as "a device for examining covert operations…"), it cites "a sensitive DOJ project known as Operation Frontlet 615."[206]

In the most derelict manner (even eclipsing the former CNN pundit Piers Morgan), the BBC fantasy weaves snippets of partial and/or discrepant testimony (based mostly on memory and/or second-hand accounts), then makes its *own* pontifical decree. With a half-dozen versions floating around of when, how, and especially *why*, whatever aircraft were dispatched from the US Sixth Fleet *however* many times, then recalled *however* many times by *whoever*, the documentary makes the unsubstantiated claim that "Retaliation was ordered for the attack… Incredibly the US was about to launch a nuclear strike against Egypt, the *Liberty's* presumed attacker…[and that]…Cairo was about to be incinerated." Oh, *really?* Like an *admiral* would take it upon himself (on the spur of the moment, mind you) to employ WMD never even used in Korea or Vietnam against a *second*-rate nation merely "presumed" to be *Liberty's* attacker? (The only thing "funnier" was the ambiguous statement from Richard Parker, US political counsel in Cairo, that the American embassy was advised of the impending attack: "funny," as in *minutes* away; "ambiguous," as his scripted remark noticeably fails to specify a "nuclear" attack.)

For all their pious umbrage toward any who would question *their* biased pipedreams, Israel's detractors need to rethink a few things. While *Shin Bet* (Israeli Security Agency) certainly had the expertise to "cook" Jordan's inbound messages, the claim that they did so—on *this* occasion—is ludicrous! What possible motive would 'Amer have had (as *nutty* as he was) to try and entice Hussein (as *naive* as he was) to risk half his realm *by informing him that Egypt's air force was already annihilated?* (Was that the approach being used over Cairo radio?) Thus, to employ a Hebrew version of caveat emptor, technically, the only "deception" for which Israel could be faulted was allowing the Egyptian ruse to pass, i.e., when they *could* have cooked the lie to save Hussein. Similarly, what motive could Dayan have had (as *egotistical* as *he* was) to risk losing land legitimately reclaimed from Jordan on Wednesday by attempting to hasten Nasser's demise (much less ignite a nuclear clash with Russia) by sinking an American ship on Thursday—*three days* after Egypt's war-making capabilities were effectively neutralized? (Hello? The word here is, "Duh!")

Moreover, had the *Liberty* been sunk (as planned), do you suppose that any post-salvage, US investigation teams would have detected a slight ballistics "challenge" upon examining those 821 bullet pocks? How could Nasser become the fall guy when the facts would clearly show that the damage came from Israel's NATO-issued ammunition and *not* the Soviet-grade used by Egypt? Why hadn't Moshe thought to have his Mirages rearmed to fire *Russian* rockets, cannon shells, and machine gun bullets in his staged production?[207] And by the way, wasn't the EAF just a *memory* by Thursday? (The ballistics evidence would also have to reconcile that pesky torpedo, the assertion requiring the synchronized role of Egypt's navy as well—three days after 'Amer "lost it.") Finally, as Detective Columbo would have asked BBC producer Christopher Mitchell: "Oh Sir, *just one more thing*—given the lethal objective of "Operation Cyanide" as presented in your documentary, why did the Israelis break off their attack in the first place—leaving the ship afloat, i.e., *dead in the water*?"

The point is somehow missed that in their collective rush to judge Israel, the "experts" were forced to concede one critical point—America was definitely spying on her purported ally. Perry Fellwock was a naive twenty-one-year-old National Security Agency analyst stationed in Turkey during the Six-Day War. In an August 1972 interview with

Ramparts magazine, the man known today as the first NSA whistle blower stated (under the pseudonym of Winslow Peck):

> The whole idea of sending the "Liberty" in was that at that point, the U.S. simply did not know what was going on. We sent it in really close so that we could find out hard information about what the Israelis' intentions were...The Israelis shot at the "Liberty," damaged it pretty badly and killed some of the crew, and told it to stay away. After this it got very tense. It became pretty clear that the White House had gotten caught with its pants down.[208]

James Bamford makes a further big to-do about a Navy EC-121 ferret buzzing high over head.[209]

Captain Ernest Castle, USN attaché to Israel during the *Liberty* incident, gave an amazing statement in his report to Johnson: "[O]nly the Israeli Defense Force knows with certainty the exact sequence of events that led to the tragic incident."[210] He could have easily added, "And they're not talking." When former Israeli intelligence officer Rafi Eitan was queried in the BBC special about "Cyanide," he discretely replied: "I suggest we stop the interview here." When pressed on the issue, the seventy-five-year-old "spook" responsible for Adolf Eichmann's abduction, coolly replied: "I know exactly what I am able to tell you and I know where I stop, and here I stop."[211]

Now, although the Jews are wont to keep a tight lid on things, they have been known to share an occasional nugget with a proven Gentile friend (especially one with an intel background). Former Nazi-hunter John Loftus also holds the distinction of being the first Irish-Catholic president of the Florida Holocaust Museum. (Talk about a double anomaly!) In Mr. Loftus' magnum opus, *Secret War Against the Jews* (co-authored with fellow *mensch* Mark Aarons), the endnote section for the *Liberty* chapter features ninety-one authorities. Of these, thirty-nine are listed as "Confidential interviews," comprising multiple anonymous sources from deep within the Intelligence community (e.g., CIA, NSA, Naval Intelligence, British Military Intelligence)—sources *consistent* with John's preeminent professional credentials. Of this total, twenty-eight include references stating, "former Israeli military attaché; former Israeli military intelligence officers; former members, Israeli intelligence."[212]

Critics of Loftus, who would disregard such an incumbent national security accommodation, might want to screen the comments of their *own* crowd ("minor leaguers" in contrast). To cite one of Ennes' caveats, after admitting his inability to document that "nuclear-armed aircraft were sent to our defense and were prematurely recalled," he asserts matter-of-factly: "Because I trust the sources of this story, because it fits neatly into the known scenario, and because it helps to explain why *Liberty* was still without help more than three hours after first asking for it, I have reported the incident as fact—which I believe it is."[213] (He also cites the persistent, though similarly baseless, claim of certain crewmembers who supposedly read in the *National Enquirer* that "Jeane Dixon said the USS *Liberty* was going to sink."[214])

It is this author's opinion that Loftus and Aarons present the most logical explanation for the *premeditated* Israeli attack—one that sheds an entirely different light on the otherwise blatant anti-Semitic pile-on.

> According to our sources in the American intelligence community who talked to us about the *Liberty* incident, passing Israeli secrets to the Egyptians was the whole idea of stationing the ship off the Sinai coast. They believe that all the published versions of the *Liberty* incident—the crew's, the Israelis', the U.S. government's, Eveland's and Deacon's—are wrong. When the authors described what we already knew from Western sources, several Israelis reluctantly provided corroboration of the best kept secret of the Six Day War. Contrary to the Israel government's categorical denials, the assault on the *Liberty* had been deliberate, but it was an act of self-defense.[215]

To summarize a most elaborate contrivance, by late May, the Israeli embassy had alerted Washington of its plans to strike Egypt and Syria, getting a green light for both. The West Bank was to remain off limits, providing Hussein behaved himself. However, to Israel's later (and alarming) discovery, the White House had also been schmoozing with the Egyptians. With Lyndon "Texas Tea" Johnson being the consummate "erl man," certain powerbrokers within the US petroleum industry successfully prevailed to have Nasser offered a steady flow of intelligence regarding IDF activity—compliments of the USS *Liberty*—in exchange for Arab promises that *their* pipelines stay open. To ARAMCO's disappointment, Cairo was not impressed, correctly judging that the "flow" would be a dribble of insignificant data.

That all changed after June 5. Suddenly, a three-way pressure cooker was ready to blow: Nasser about to *lose* face in the Arab world; the

West (thanks to the "Big Lie") about to *face* a major oil embargo; and the IDF doing an *about-face* in the Sinai (to man a second front in the Golan). Thus, the *Liberty* was redeployed from Rota, Spain, into the "perfect storm." This time, however, the NSA would have to deliver some *serious* intel to appease Israel's oil-producing enemies. *Liberty* was assigned to monitor the precise electronic footprints of Dayan's mobile reserves as they withdrew from the desert.[216] Known as "raw intelligence," the compressed recordings—comprising walkie-talkie chatter, tank-radio dialogue, headquarters' telephone calls, even coded cable traffic—would then be transmitted for analysis and processing to the secret British base on Cyprus (GCHQ), one of the world's largest electronic listening posts. Loftus and Aarons write: "[T]he plan was for the British to hand the final product of the *Liberty's* intelligence haul to the Egyptians. The finished war map was a detailed order of battle intelligence report, or OB. It is the most useful information generals can have in time of war."[217]

Though the bootlegged electronic dust would not have caused an Israeli defeat, it *could* have enabled 'Amer's scattered remnants to regroup and (to quote a former CIA man) "thread their way through the holes in the southern front left by the withdrawal of the IDF."[218] The ensuing hit-and-run campaign against Negev kibbutzim might have afforded Nasser the time to force a stalemate, securing an eleventh-hour *diplomatic* victory. According to the "old spies" (as Loftus calls his former colleagues), "Israeli intelligence had discovered the *Liberty's* espionage mission before it even arrived off the coast."[219] After an IAF ferret ("flying boxcar") honed in on the intrusive vessel at dawn, Eshkol's cabinet (briefed in emergency session) concluded that the US and British were working in tandem with Egypt to undermine Israel's security.[220] The conviction was so pronounced that the Golan offensive, scheduled for 11:30 a.m., was postponed for twenty-four hours (ostensibly due to weather). Thus, forced to choose between sacrificing untold thousands of additional Israeli soldiers or silencing one American spook ship—oh well![221]

To Israel's credit, insiders confirm that the cabinet's order was to only disable *Liberty* with minimal loss of life (89% of the crew would survive). The pilots were also chosen on a volunteer basis, over half refusing consideration, many having family and friends in the States. (Ironically, two of the reluctant fliers were American-born Israelis.[222])

As expected, Loftus and Aarons incurred a measure of ridicule for their unique apologetic treatise. Reverdy Fishel (former *Liberty* Veterans Association member) called *The Secret War Against the Jews* "a collection of preposterous and demonstrably false theories and allegations."[223] After lambasting the authors for several "ludicrous statement[s]…concoctions…[and] other ridiculous claims…"[224] (in the *Liberty* chapter), Fishel attempts to discredit the generally accepted premise that the spook ship was spying on Israel, by insisting that there were no Hebrew linguists on board. However, according to three declassified NSA documents (posted on the USS *Liberty* Inquiry website, no less), at least *one* trained Hebrew speaker *was* on the mission. The same papers also express concern over a lack of Hebrew dictionaries.[225] But then, Fishel must have forgotten that the primary role of the *Liberty* was recording and transmission—*not translation.*

At the end of the day, the Loftus-Aarons thesis is the only cogent explanation for *all* of the following questions: 1) *Why* the Israelis struck in the first place; 2) *Why* they only *disabled* their target; 3) *Why* the US pilots were told to stand down; 4) *Why* Nasser kept on fighting, only to accept the ceasefire *after* the *Liberty* was *hors de combat*; 5) *Why* Israel chose a fabricated alibi to cover her ungrateful ally; 6) *Why* the White House stoically refused to challenge such a demonstrable fabrication; 7) *Why* both governments have remained silent to this day.

Ironically, the bottom line to these arresting realities was provided by one of Ennes's own unnamed sources. According to a *certain* Navy master chief petty officer, who was working on a *certain* sensitive task at Langley, a *certain* CIA employee told him in confidence: "Sending *Liberty* to Gaza was a calculated risk from the beginning. Israel had told us long before the war to keep our intelligence ships away from her coast. *Liberty* was sent anyway because we just didn't think they were serious…We didn't think they would really try to sink her."[226] The 2012 NSA report essentially implies the same: "[T]he position of the USS LIBERTY was operationally and technically proper from a SIGINT standpoint except in the hindsight of the rash Israeli act."[227]

Finally, as *this* book was written with an unabashed bias toward "*the* Book," once again, a closing spiritual remark is fitting. To revisit our politically incorrect (though *scripturally* correct) theme of anti-Semitism-incited Anglo-American comeuppance (American bombs falling on British graves; IAF pilots downing RAF planes; Forrestal's and Eden's mental problems; Foster Dulles's wild ambulance ride, etc.), let the record state that the listing *Liberty* fared a *whole* lot better than those numerous Aliyah Bet atrocities. While it is certainly regrettable that twenty-five unsuspecting American surrogates had to die from that torpedo (including at least one Jewish sailor, Bob Eisenburg of Minnesota)—over *thirty* times that number of defenseless men, women, and children perished when a single torpedo sunk the *Struma*. Bamford supplies the following unnerving scene:

> The torpedo struck dead center in the NSA spaces, killing nearly everyone inside...Frank Raven of G Group later talked to several of the few survivors from the NSA spaces. 'They told me that they saw the torpedo...in the room with them. The torpedo came right through the side of the ship before it exploded—they saw it before it exploded. They had the torpedo in the room with them. It came right through the side of the ship and they jumped behind desks and things of that sort and it went off.[228]

Proving once again that "truth is stranger than fiction"—as if to accommodate Ennes's Freudian slip regarding a "holocaust on the bridge,"[229] that 19-inch torpedo, fired by IN Motor Torpedo Boat 203 just *happened* to be made in—West *Germany*.[230]

DAY FIVE: SHOWDOWN ON THE GOLAN

Day five included several political harbingers. With the Jewish holiday of *Shavuot* less than two weeks away, the IDF proceeded to demolish the entire Mughrabi Quarter, situated thirteen feet from the Kotel. Whereas the narrow pavement was limited to 12,000 devotees a day, the expanded plaza could now accommodate 400,000. Some 100 Arab families lost their hovels in this inconvenient, though necessary, "urban renewal project." (For the record, the eviction was appropriate payback given Jordan's persistent disavowal of the 1949 armistice agreement allowing Jews access to the Wall; ditto the UN Government House mauling given *their* attendant refusal to enforce the agreement.)

Meanwhile, convinced that Washington had betrayed him, King Hussein reportedly grilled his CIA contact: "Didn't you tell me that Israel was not going to attack Jordan?" When the official agreed,

Hussein replied, "Have they not taken over half my country?" Again, he nodded. "Well," said the disillusioned Mohammedan—"what the [expletive] do I do now?"[231] Thousands of his subjects spent the Muslim holy day crossing *their* Rubicon to start life anew on the *East* Bank. An American reporter observed:

> Three miles out of Jericho, where the river narrowed between sandy banks, four Israeli paratroopers crouched behind a 50-caliber machine gun pointed…across the softly murmuring water. They were there to stop refugees from returning. A case of Gold Star beer, submerged in midstream but anchored to a tree, sparkled in the moonlight, just below a neatly painted sign that said in English: 'Traditional Site of the Baptism of Jesus.'[232]

After ending three days of seclusion on Thursday (sleeping with a gun under his pillow[233]), Gamal Nasser suddenly felt the "liberty" to accept the UN ceasefire. He then shocked the nation by announcing his "resignation," only to rescind the offer upon a "spontaneous burst of adulation" in Tahrir Square (busloads of political hacks). The charade was followed by a 360-0 "vote of confidence" in the National Assembly.[234] In the meantime, as his dehydrated troops were staggering homeward (some with empty canteens drinking their own urine[235]), 'Amer gave the callous order to blow the bridges spanning the canal, theoretically to hinder any further Israeli advance.[236] (Not surprisingly, while under house arrest three months later, Nasser's "pal" would replicate Erwin Rommel's ignominious end.)

With two theaters secure, Israel's last agonizing decision concerned the Golan Heights—700 sq. miles guarded by 70,000 Syrians. At stake were the perennial security concerns of the exposed kibbutzim from Upper Galilee to the Chula Valley, especially the border settlements, (known as the nation's "trip wire," or first line of defense). Politically, such an "unwarranted act of aggression" would be instantly denounced at the UN, especially by the pro-Arab Soviets. For its part, Washington appeared to be sending mixed signals. While LBJ's handpicked Jewish ambassador to the UN, Arthur Goldberg, cautioned Eban: "Israel must be careful not to push its advantage too far,"[237] National Security Advisor McGeorge Bundy told the same official "in a tentative voice, that it would seem strange that Syria—which had originated the war—might be the only one that seemed to be getting off without injury."[238]

At 6:00 a.m., throwing caution to the wind, Dayan opted to exploit the on-again-off-again ceasefire by commencing "Operation Hammer." Three hours later, an intense IAF campaign was underway (described by Radio Damascus as an Anglo-American effort to "save the Israelis from destruction"[239]). However, while inflicting sizable psychological damage, the hundreds of tons of explosives (including napalm) proved inadequate to penetrate the mass of underground pillboxes. Not unlike Ammunition Hill, the Golan's defenders were ensconced in a labyrinth of trenches and bunkers (8 feet deep by 3 feet wide) reinforced with cement and black volcanic rock, concealed with steel, dirt, and grass, strategically positioned to afford overlapping fields of fire—all behind dense mines and barbed wire. Syria's "mini Maginot line" stretched along a thirty-five-mile ridge from Galilee to Mount Hermon. Over ten miles deep, with an average elevation of 3,300 feet, the formidable redoubts comprised row upon row of gun emplacements, mortars, rocket launchers, dug-in tanks, tank traps, and antiaircraft batteries.

Major General David "Dado" Elazar, Northern Front commander, began the ground offensive by assaulting the northern Golan with two battle groups of the 8th Armored Brigade. The daunting column—bulldozers and sappers at the point, aged Sherman tanks in the middle, infantry at the rear—proceeded to scale the escarpment, crossing the border at 11:30 a.m. Two hours later, a second battle group from the 1st Golani Brigade entered the fray. Despite heavy losses, the divergent waves forged ahead, capturing Qala', Za'ura, and 'Ein Fit by 6:00 p.m. Tel 'Azzaziat (900 feet straight up) and Tel Fakhr (700 feet higher) required more hours and blood (including hand-to-hand combat) to subdue.[240] Other costly victories were won across the central front at Jalibna, Dradra, Tel Hilel, and Darbeshiya.[241]

As darkness fell, Dayan and Elazar consolidated their hard-fought gains. The Israelis held a decisive weapons advantage, the Uzi being more suited for close combat than the enemy's heavier, long-range AK-47s. Superior intelligence also played a vital role. Although the Cohn eucalyptus "story" was probably just that, his detailed reports on the Golan fortifications were spot-on. Leadership was another factor. While many Syrian officers deserted their own men, the well-known IDF philosophy of "leading from the front" inspired critical camaraderie (though also generating commensurate losses, the famed battalion commander Moshe "Musa" Klein being among them).

With the political clock now working against them, the exhausted yet adrenalized Jews would have to push on through the night to administer the coup de grâce on the morrow. However, in the midst of their euphoria, an isolated incident occurred that should have turned their attention to David's admonition in I Samuel 20:3, *"[T]here is but a step between me and death."* According to Dr. Mati Maizel, author of *The Golan Heights Campaign in the Six-Day War*, regiment number 129 of the 8th Armored Brigade took a wrong turn and entered a Syrian ambush. By the end of the battle, only 2 of its 26 tanks remained operational. The regiment commander was injured and his replacement killed. Total casualties were listed as 13 dead and 33 wounded.[242] The spiritual message is clear—but for the "Rock of Israel," the entire IDF could have experienced one *big* ambush via one *big* wrong turn!

DAY SIX: THE BOGUS BROADCAST

The IDF's main (and final) "Hammer" blow was upon Quneitra, an inland town of 80,000 serving as the Golan's administrative/military capital. However, in the morning, Dayan was surprised to learn that his army had already achieved their objective—*three hours before they would actually do so*. In a desperate move to pressure the UN to enforce a ceasefire, the Jadid regime had undermined its own army by having Radio Damascus broadcast the premature surrender of Quneitra. Later bulletins also "confirmed" that Israeli planes were bombing Syria's capital, a mere forty-five miles from the Quneitra junction.

The ruse resulted in a rout. Already deserted by their officers, the dispirited Syrian troops finally "lost it," dynamiting their own bunkers as they fled pell-mell—95,000 civilians behind them.[243] The calculated deception did, however, produce the desired objective of exacerbating global tensions. While Alexei Kosygin ratcheted up his veiled nuclear rhetoric over the Moscow-Washington Direct Communication Link (DCL), Johnson instructed McNamara to divert the Sixth Fleet to the eastern Mediterranean. With Israel being accused of genocide in Syria, the USSR and nine Communist bloc nations broke diplomatic ties with Tel Aviv. Worst of all, Eshkol's calls to the White House requesting military aid (should Russia intervene) were *not* being returned.[244]

Because the "real" Quneitra still required taking, Dayan would end the war by countering Syria's deceit with superior Israeli brinkmanship. At 10:00 a.m., the defense minister gave Dado his final number of hours—*four* more and *no* more—concluding: "Don't even ask for air cover after two o'clock."[245] Then, believe it or not, Colonel al-Assad *reversed* his radio propaganda, stating: "Our brave forces are still fighting in Quneitra…Great numbers of the enemy's tanks have been destroyed," a commentator adding, "Our victory in Quneitra today means victory in Tel Aviv tomorrow."[246] Notwithstanding, by 12:30 p.m., Syria's command center was taken without firing a shot. Like the amazing story in II Kings 7 when *another* Syrian army deserted its camp, leaving *their* supplies behind, the Golani Brigade (being the first to enter) found the town nearly empty, "their stores and markets full, lunches still hot on the table."[247] At the risk of giving the "Rock of Israel" *too* much "credit," II Kings 7:6 *does* note, *"For the LORD had made the host of the Syrians to hear a noise of chariots…Wherefore they arose and fled…."* Oren relates: "[D]riven by rumors of Israelis wielding nuclear weapons, some 4,000 Syrian soldiers sought refuge in Jordan, and 3,000 in Lebanon."[248]

While Elazar and his staff were raising "L'chaims" in the Syrian Officers' Club, General Bull finally caught up with Dayan in Tel Aviv at 3:00 p.m. With the resultant ceasefire promptly concluded, Sachar notes: "The Six Day War ended officially at 6:30 p.m., Israel time, on June 10."[249] In just twenty-seven hours, Syria lost 2,500 killed and 5,000 wounded, a third of their tanks, and half their artillery, not to mention the entire Golan plateau; Israel suffered 5% by comparison, 115 killed and 306 wounded.[250] Upwards of 15,000 Egyptians died, with thousands wounded. Jordan had 700 killed and 6,000 wounded or missing. Total IDF casualties were listed at 800 killed and 2,563 wounded—a 25-1 ratio.[251] Of course, for any Jewish mother, *one* loss is too many. Nehama Nissenbaum (mother of Benzi Nissenbaum) testified: "I survived the Holocaust, but my son did not survive the Six Day War. I visit the cemetery once every three weeks. I light a candle, leave a few flowers, and go home and think, If only he were still alive. But that is what life has given us, what fate has given us."[252]

MAHROUSS' MUTTERINGS

As dawn broke on day six, Corporal Kamal Mahrouss, with several of his bedraggled comrades, had just arrived at the canal after a grueling four-day, 150-mile homeward trek through the Sinai's ankle-deep, choking, velvet sand. Their final shame was a surprise IDF checkpoint.

After being interrogated, searched, and relieved of any last valuables, the soldiers were released. As the main swing bridge across the canal was out of commission (thanks to 'Amer's bombing order), Kamal had to wait for local transport, finally crossing on a small ferry. Standing on the far bank, the obdurate Arab turned and gazed across the watery divide. "'We'll be back,' he muttered. 'Soon.'"[253]

THE THREE RESOLUTIONS

On Sunday, June 11, 1967, Colonel Pinchas Noi of the 13th Golani Battalion, flew by helicopter to Mount Hermon and planted the Israeli flag atop the snow-capped 9,232-foot summit, described as "the eyes of the nation." The next day, Israel's government announced that it would *not* be withdrawing to the 1949 armistice line. (Colonel Richard Meinertzhagen died the next Saturday in London at the age of 89.)

Between 175,000 (Israeli estimates) and 250,000 (Jordanian estimates) Palestinians had fled the West Bank for Jordan, many being "second-time" refugees (leftovers from the unresolved 1948 crisis).[254] Once again, Israel's essential desideratum for peace stipulated that any resolution of this growing problem could only be achieved within the framework of a comprehensive treaty; once again, the Arabs rejected the proposal. Three subsequent political developments would coalesce to amplify Corporal Mahrouss's "muttering."

On June 19, 1967, Eshkol's cabinet agreed to: 1) exchange Sinai and the Golan for peace with Egypt and Syria; 2) annex the Gaza Strip; 3) defer action on the West Bank. The rancorous Resolution 563 passed by *one* vote. (The formal annexation of East Jerusalem was announced on June 28.) While Dayan was waiting for the phone call that never came, Nasser rendered his own opinion of the Israeli olive branch by initiating the vitriolic Khartoum Resolution on September 1. Known as the "Three No's of Khartoum," the collective mindset of the eight Arab leaders who attended the three-day African summit was as follows: 1) *no* peace with Israel; 2) *no* recognition of Israel; 3) *no* negotiations with Israel. (Scratch one Israeli cabinet resolution.)

Finally, on November 22, the "United Nuts" unanimously adopted its own "Fantasy Island" plan entitled "Resolution 242 Concerning Principles of a Just and Lasting Peace in the Middle East." The deliberately ambiguous text called for: "Withdrawal of Israeli armed forces from territories occupied in the recent conflict" along with "respect for and acknowledgment of the sovereignty, territorial integrity and political independence of every State in the area."[255] To jar Israel into compliance, U Thant chose Gunnar Jarring, another hapless Swede in the line of Count Bernadotte (both being the antithesis of Raoul Wallenberg) as a special envoy for the Middle East peace process. While Israel and Jordan reluctantly accepted Resolution 242, both nations would employ their own private interpretations. Tel Aviv would view the absence of the definite article "the" before "territories" as implying a pledge of less than full withdrawal. King Hussein was quick to pass the buck, telling his subjects, "If in the end you were not rewarded with glory, it was not because you lacked courage, but because it was the will of Allah."[256] Nasser, however, was another story. Having *appeared* to endorse the UNSC decision, in private he assured his generals: "[Y]ou don't need to pay any attention to anything I may say in public about a peaceful solution."[257]

WHAT'S IN A NAME?

Several names were proposed for the war's official title, e.g., War of Daring, War of Salvation, and War of the Sons of Light. (Muslims favored the Setback, Disaster, or the anodyne June, or Third Israeli-Arab War.) The cabinet gave its popular chief-of-staff, Yitzhak Rabin, the honor of making the final choice. He picked the least pretentious, Six-Day War—recalling the Genesis days of Creation.[258]

The obvious flaw in Rabin's well-intended model is that it's off by 24 hours, as the *sixth* day in Genesis 1:24-31 equates to Friday, while the *seventh* equates to Saturday, or Shabbat. However, there *is* a major truth embedded in this name. Ezekiel 11:17 represents one of many Old Testament promises that the Jew will eventually return to his land. *"Thus saith the Lord GOD; I will even gather you from the people, and assemble you out of the countries where ye have been scattered, and I will give you the land of Israel."* The Bible also gives an ETA for this marvelous event according to its own intrinsic formula: *"But, beloved, be not ignorant of this one thing, that one day is with the Lord as a thousand years, and a thousand years as one day."* (II Peter 3:8)

After nearly 4,000 years of Old Testament history—representing *four* prophetic days—Jesus Christ presented Himself to Israel as the nation's long-awaited Messiah. Betrayed on the "Hill of Evil Counsel," the Son of God was crucified, buried, and rose again. Less than a generation later, the Romans sacked Jerusalem, destroyed the Temple, and evicted the Jews from their land. The key cross-reference regarding Jacob's ultimate renewal is Hosea 6:1-2. *"Come, and let us return unto the LORD: for he hath torn, and he will heal us; he hath smitten, and he will bind us up. After* TWO DAYS *will he revive us: in the* THIRD DAY *he will raise us up, and we shall live in his sight."*

After nearly 2,000 years of being "torn" and "smitten" (*two* more prophetic days), the Jews are suddenly back where they started. This is what Jesus was referring to in Luke 21:24: *"And they shall fall by the edge of the sword, and shall be led away captive into all nations: and Jerusalem shall be trodden down of the Gentiles, until the times of the Gentiles be fulfilled."* Noting the instant euphoria felt by World Jewry following the Israeli victory, Sachar writes: "It was evident now that the peoples of Israel, on the ancestral soil and in the overseas hinterland alike, were rapidly being fused into a single people."[259]

So—why should any Jew be surprised that the "Rock of Israel" allowed His covenant people to recapture the Holy City in a *Six*-Day War? All that remains is for Jesus to return so Israel can be "raised up" and "live in His sight" on that glorious *third* day—her thousand-year Sabbatical rest (representing the *seventh* and *last* prophetic day).

"There remaineth therefore a rest to the people of God."
(Hebrews 4:9)

17

The Yom Kippur War

"As a Socialist, I, of course, do not believe in God;
I believe in the Jewish people."
(Golda Meir)

"The time has come for a shock."
(Anwar Sadat, April 1973)

"The best result would be if Israel came out
a little ahead but got bloodied in the process."
(Henry Kissinger, October 1973)

"For the life of the flesh is in the blood: and I have given it to you upon the altar to make an ATONEMENT *for your souls: for it is the blood that maketh an* ATONEMENT *for the soul...Also on the tenth day of this seventh month there shall be a day of* ATONEMENT*: it shall be an holy convocation unto you; and ye shall afflict your souls, and offer an offering made by fire unto the* LORD.*"*
(Leviticus 17:11; 23:27)

ISRAEL'S LIGHTNING VICTORY in the Six-Day War was nothing short of phenomenal. While history books speak of the Hundred Years and Thirty Years Wars, here—in less than *one* week—the tiny Jewish state captured *seven* strategic prizes: the Gaza Strip, Sinai Peninsula, West Bank, East Jerusalem, Old City, Temple Mount, and Golan Heights. The acquired territory more than tripled the area previously controlled (from 8,000 to 26,000 sq. miles). Truth be told, with a million-plus instant "Gibeonites" thrown in as well, it was *too* good (Joshua 9:25-27). As former Prime Minister Shimon Perez said: "The victory was too big, too fast, it intoxicated us."[1]

The lopsided conquest created a recipe for disaster in two areas. While the Jews succumbed to delusions of grandeur, the Arabs galvanized to avenge Allah's honor. The die was cast when a *Life* editorial on June 16, 1967, asked "an impolite but unavoidable question: 'What *is* the matter with the Arab armies? Was there ever a people so bellicose in politics, so reckless and raucous in hostility, and then so unpugnacious in pitched combat, as Nasser's Egyptians?'"[2]

Calling the Hebrew hubris "a mixture of conceit and complacency," Chaim Herzog, Israel's Irish-born sixth president, noted: "The very magnitude and decisiveness of the Arab defeat in June 1967, with its implications to Arab pride, self-respect and honour (the importance and significance of which had never been adequately appreciated by Israeli leaders), created the inevitability of the next war."[3] Oren adds: "Egypt had failed to appreciate the advantages of launching a first strike, had failed to gauge the enemy's power and his willingness to use it. Lulled into arrogance by these errors, the Israelis would repeat them six years later, in their next war with the Arabs."[4]

For the first time in her brief existence, Israel was in fine fettle, occupying strategic buffer zones on all three fronts (Sinai, West Bank, and Golan). Who would *dare* attack them now? The answer was preordained vis-à-vis the veracity of God's Holy Bible—*"Pride goeth before destruction, and an haughty spirit before a fall."* (Proverbs 16:18) Thus, as Joshua's supernatural conquest of Jericho anticipated Dayan's miraculous achievement in 1967, the Yom Kippur debacle became the modern-day atavism of the Jews' humiliation at Ai (Joshua 7:3-4). And the fact that Israel's "judgment" *happened* to fall on Yom Kippur—a *Shabbat Shabbaton* (Sabbath of Sabbaths), a High Holy Day, the DAY OF ATONEMENT—should have been a no-brainer.

Israeli author Arnold Sherman writes: "[N]o Jew is totally comfortable on Yom Kippur. As iconoclastic as he may be, there is the almost certain knowledge that God is peering over his shoulder…The Jewish atheist… even feels that the air is heavy with a religious scent that he cannot define, because it is undefinable, dolorous, frightening."[5] (As Hank Greenberg before him, legendary LA Dodger southpaw Sandy Koufax—a *non-religious* Jew—refused to pitch the opening game of the 1965

World Series because it fell on Yom Kippur.) Fortunately, Israel's successful counterattack in week two of the October conflict was likewise foreshadowed by the Second Battle of Ai (Joshua 8:1-29). The interim between the two wars was defined by two three-year periods: Nasser's last licks (a.k.a. War of Attrition) and Anwar Sadat's preparations for his own jihad against Jacob.

WAR OF ATTRITION

Nasser did not believe that Israel could sustain a protracted campaign because the IDF consisted mostly of reserves. He therefore resolved to create an Israeli version of America's "Vietnam fatigue" by draining the Jewish State physically, economically, and psychologically. While the Suez Canal afforded Israel a premium defensive barrier, it would now be used against them to shield an array of deadly surface-to-air missiles. The sheer length of the channel would also serve to detain an inordinate body of troops and patrol aircraft. The initial aim of Egypt's "limited war" was to force Israel to relinquish the Sinai Peninsula.

On July 1, 1967 (twelve days after Israel's cabinet privately voted to cede the Sinai for peace), Nasser began the first stage of his calculated harassment, deploying a force to Ras el' Ish, ten miles south of Port Said on the canal's eastern bank. The attendant artillery barrage killed Israel's senior commander, while injuring thirteen others. The IAF responded by attacking Egyptian batteries. With her own international image at stake, Moscow wasted no time rearming Egypt's depleted stores. Throughout the month, an armada of transport planes and ships delivered vast quantities of new weaponry. An ebb-and-flow clash of limited artillery duels and small-scale incursions ensued (some 104 incidents reported from June 1967 to June 1968[6]).

As an ominous precursor to the "War of the Day of Judgment," having neutralized the USS *Liberty* in better times, Israel's navy would now suffer twin maritime disasters within a four-month period. On October 21, 1967, an Egyptian missile ship sank the flagship INS *Eilat* off the Sinai coast, killing forty. (Three days later, 80% of Cairo's oil refineries were destroyed in retaliation.) In January, the INS *Dakar* (a modified T-class submarine purchased from Britain) disappeared with all hands during her maiden voyage from Birmingham to Haifa. While the *Dakar* was found (between Crete and Cyprus) and salvaged in 1999, the cause of her fate rivals *Liberty* for conspiratorial intrigue.

Israel's first television station (Channel 1) premiered May 2, 1968, just in time for the nation's 20th Independence Day parade. However, it would also funnel a strain of doom and gloom into the living rooms of an already paranoid populace. The opening story on June 6, was the assassination of Senator Robert Kennedy by Sirhan Sirhan, a 23-year-old Jordanian stable boy. The news on July 23 was an El-Al hijacking (en route from Rome) by agents of the Popular Front for the Liberation of Palestine (PFLP). Another El-Al plane was struck at Athens airport on December 26, followed by a third attempt in Zurich on February 8, 1969. The lead piece on February 4 concerned one, Mohammed Abd al-Rahman abd al-Rauf Arafat al-Qud al-Husseini—a short, balding, middle-aged, Egyptian-born terrorist and future Nobel peace laureate famously hidden behind dark glasses and a stubbly beard, sporting a "NASCAR checkered flag" (keffiyeh) on his head, a.k.a. Fatah founder Yasser Arafat—elected chairman of the Palestinian Liberation Organization (PLO) on that date. Ensconced in Jordan (against Hussein's druthers), Yasser's Muslim thugs would soon be averaging thirty terrorist attacks a month in Israeli towns and city centers.

BAR-LEV LINE

By October 1968, Nasser took his aggression to the next level, ordering a major spike in artillery strikes. On November 3, seventeen EAF fighters attacked Israeli forces, catching them unprepared and vulnerable. The IAF hit back with intensity. Resolved to "attriting the attritors,"[7] Israeli engineers began construction of the Bar-Lev Line (named for former chief of staff Lieutenant General Chaim Bar-Lev), an intricate forward security system using some twenty concrete and steel revetments stretching along the 100-mile east bank of the Suez.

The individual *maozim* ("small strongholds") were staggered roughly seven miles apart. Each redoubt, manned by fifteen soldiers, controlled one-half to one mile on each of its flanks, the remainder monitored by observation posts and roving patrols. Tanks were also stationed between the gaps, their guns positioned to provide enfilade fire along the canal. An ancillary network of roads, maintenance depots, airfields, and command posts ran parallel in the rear. The vital facade to the Bar-Lev Line was an imposing 70-ft-high wall of sand (equal to a three-story building). The IDF believed that an Egyptian invasion force would require twelve hours to blast through the sand, allowing ample time for reservists to arrive. Ironically, with over one billion Israeli Lira invested by 1970,[8] a serious debate continued to fester regarding the main purpose of the Bar-Lev Line (i.e., whether for an early warning system or a first line of defense). Herzog notes, "This lack of clarity was to exact its cost in the first hours of the fighting along the Canal."[9]

MRS. MEIR

In the midst of these turbulent events, Levi Eshkol succumbed to heart failure on February 26, 1969 (the first prime minister to die in office). Hastening to the foot of his fallen leader's bedside, Dayan cried, "Eshkol!" then fled away sobbing.[10] What occurred next was amazing.

As if driven by a national death wish, Israel's Labor Party called a 70-year-old, chain-smoking, grandmother (with a hidden six-year history of lymphoma) out of retirement to stabilize the crisis. While Ben-Gurion called Golda Meir "the best man in the government,"[11] Israelis *should* have heeded Solomon's warning, *"Give not thy strength unto women...."* (Proverbs 31:3) Averse to her God-given role of wife and mother (especially the stereotypical "Jewish mother"), Mrs. Meyerson (separated, though never divorced from her late husband) presumed to lead a nation, stating: "There are mothers who work only when they are forced to...But there is a type of woman who cannot remain home for other reasons. In spite of the place which her children and her family take up in her life, her nature and being demands something more; she cannot divorce herself from a larger social life. She cannot let her children narrow her horizon."[12]

In Golda's "defense," the former Milwaukee teacher was just a product of her times. On June 3, 1972, Sally Jane Priesand became the first female rabbi in America ordained by a rabbinical seminary, and only the second ordained woman in Jewish history (behind Auschwitz victim, Regina Jonas). Far more inscrutable (at least to *this* author), is the fact that while the self-deprecating Meir once remarked, "Not being beautiful forced me to develop my inner resources," Israel's premier female premier was actually accused of having "slept her way to power," acquiring the salacious sobriquet, "The Mattress."[13]

But why would the Tanakh mean anything to a typical secular Jew? (The reader will recall Meir's famous quip against the nation's founder regarding oil.) The outspoken, grey-bunned feminist even surprised the radical, German-born agnostic Hannah Arendt, declaring: "You will understand that, as a Socialist, I, of course, do not believe in God; I believe in the Jewish people"[14] (see Matthew 3:9). This cutesy remark was bound to resonate in Heaven—*especially* on October 6, 1973—for Solomon also wrote: *"When a man's ways please the LORD he maketh even his enemies to be at peace with him."* (Proverbs 17:7)

On March 8, 1969, *one day after Golda's nomination* (her formal installation occurring March 17), Nasser launched the mailed fist of his Attrition War—employing over 1,000 artillery pieces against the Bar-Lev Line. Sustaining heavy losses, the IDF returned fire, killing General Abdul Munim Riad, Egypt's chief of staff. Six weeks later, a chain of Soviet S-125 surface-to-air missile pods were positioned along the canal. Between 10,000 and 14,000 Russian "advisors" were also in Egypt at this time, supported by a sixty-vessel flotilla off the coast. Soviet pilots were flying reconnaissance missions as well.[15] On May 13, Sergeant Benjamin Netanyahu, Israel's future prime minister, was wounded twice in a firefight in the dark waters of the Suez. (Inducted into the army two months after the end of the Six-Day War, "Bibi" had also returned from MIT to fight in the Yom Kippur War.)

Thus, on July 20, the IAF began bombing runs inside Egypt. A major Syrian offensive was repelled in the Golan at the end of July. (Hafez al-Assad would also be a major beneficiary of Soviet largesse, hosting 15,000 Red Army personnel himself.) In August, 1,000 combat sorties were flown against Egyptian targets alone. On at least one occasion, IAF pilots downed Soviet-supplied, Soviet-flown "Egyptian" MiGs.[16] Consequently—like that memorable Nazi flight with Il Duce at the controls—Israelis would now get to experience the "wit" of their senior prime minister, who once said: "Old age is like a plane flying through a storm. Once you're aboard, there's nothing you can do."[17]

MR. SADAT

The year 1970 began with the IAF's first deep foray into Egyptian airspace, hitting bases in the Nile Delta on January 3. By June, Russia handed Cairo a cutting-edge system of interlocking SAM SA-3 missile sites. With the pressure ratcheting up, various peace proposals were bandied about, though with little to no success. Finally, on August 7, 1970, Secretary of State William Rogers brokered a ninety-day ceasefire along the canal. Nasser violated the agreement before sundown, using the truce to reposition his newly arrived mobile SAMs from behind the Canal Zone to the bank of the channel itself. With a range of thirty-three miles, the new "missile wall" would now enable Egyptian forces to seize a bridgehead across the Suez, safe from IAF intrusion.

Closer to home, a civil war broke out in Jordan the following month, pitting Arafat and his PLO (assisted by Syria) against the Jordanian Armed Forces loyal to the Hashemite dynasty. The term "Black September" would henceforth define both the ten-month insurrection (ending with Yasser's relocation to Lebanon) and its offshoot terror cell, the Black September Organization (BSO).

To Israel's surprise (and considerable relief), the unstable ceasefire was providentially sustained when Gamal Abdel Nasser also suffered a fatal heart attack on September 28, 1970. (His run-up to Yom Kippur had claimed 600 Israeli lives with 2,000 wounded, his own nation sustaining nearly 10,000 casualties.) The Ummah was stunned at the news, their revered leader being only fifty-two years of age. (Like Golda's cancer, Gamal's long-standing diabetes was also a military secret.) The funeral procession through Cairo on October 1 was attended by over five million mourners. As the cortege passed by, Yasser Arafat cried and Libya's Muammar Gaddafi fainted, *twice.*[18] (How touching!) Of far greater significance, 75,000 Arabs rampaged through the Old City of Jerusalem, shouting, "Nasser will never die!" On October 15, Muhammad Anwar El-Sadat, Egypt's vice president, was installed as the new "Hitler of the Nile." The following month his future partner in crime, Hafez al-Assad, seized power in Damascus.

THE THREE-YEAR INTERLUDE

The State of Israel would now have to hold its breath while Anwar got his ducks in order. Though willing to dispense with his predecessor's crypto-socialism, his initial remarks to the nation on September 28 left little to the imagination: "No words suffice to console us for the death of Gamal Abdel Nasser. The only thing that will show him just recompense and recognition is a patient, steadfast, courageous and able attitude by the whole Arab nation until the victory—for which the great son of Egypt, the hero, man and leader of this people lived and died as a martyr—has been achieved."[19]

For the sake of prudence, the new president was also less vocal of his private admiration of Hitler,[20] the Mossad being well aware of his prior efforts to collaborate with Nazi Germany on behalf of the Mufti.[21] Sadat was jailed by the British twice, during and after the war; the latter eighteen-month stint in Cairo's Central Prison engendered his chimerical spiritual epiphany in "Cell 54" (about as serious an experience as officer Gunther Toody's escapades in "Car 54").

Given the added failure of Nasser's War of Attrition, Sadat would face even more pressure to restore Arab self-esteem. Yet he was no dummy. Convinced of Israel's military superiority, Anwar stunned Egypt's parliament on February 4, 1971, announcing his willingness to reopen the Suez Canal in exchange for a *partial* withdrawal of Israeli troops on the east bank, to be realized "as a first step in a timetable to be laid down with a view to implementing the other provisions of the Security Council Resolution [242]."[22] Defense Minister Dayan even favored a unilateral, limited withdrawal.[23] However, given her well-known "penchant for inflexibility,"[24] Meir's reply was harsh. Gideon Rafael recalled: "I had strongly urged Golda to respond. In the Knesset on 9 February she extended a finger to him—not a hand."[25] (As she was wont to say: "'Intransigent' was to become my middle name."[26])

Describing Meir's impetuous reaction as "singularly inflexible, unresponsive, and unimaginative," Michael Sterner, director of Egyptian Affairs at the US State Department, represented many who felt that war could have been averted, arguing that Cairo had shown signs of pliability.[27] Sadat's eventual decision to invade would be cemented on February 24 and 25, 1973, after three secret meetings between his defense minister and Henry Kissinger confirmed Nixon's reluctance to dissuade Israel from her diplomatic "intransigence."[28]

Meanwhile, Egypt would not be the Jews' only distraction throughout the ensuing thirty-six-month interim. On January 12, 1971, Israel's three-millionth citizen arrived from the USSR. With housing at a premium, Dayan gave a major speech on August 20, 1971, advising the government to "create facts" (i.e., construct Jewish settlements) in the so-called occupied territories.[29] The Labor party's "bulldozer diplomacy" was highly resented throughout the Arab world. Thus, on September 5, 1972, the nation's record population was dramatically *decreased* by eleven at the Munich Olympic Games. Nearly the entire Israeli delegation was slaughtered by a cadre of Black September terrorists, aided by German neo-Nazis. (Yossef Romano, the heroic champion weightlifter who tried to save his friends, was *castrated* for his efforts.) Four days earlier, the Jewish athletes had made an eerie tour of Dachau, prompting legendary sports announcer Jim McKay (ABC's event anchor) to remark that the presence of an Israeli team at an Olympiad hosted by Germany showed how "the world has come a long way…since the Holocaust."[30]

The callous tragedy was enflamed on October 29, 1972, when the Brandt government freed the three surviving gunmen, ostensibly for a hijacked Lufthansa jetliner. Within ten months, the Mossad would exact vengeance on a dozen Palestinians linked to Black September.[31] (Four decades later, a universal petition to observe a minute of silence at the 2012 London Olympics in memory of the murdered Israelis was denied by the International Olympic Committee, though the same body *did* allow a video tribute to the fifty-two people who were killed in the London transit system the day after the city won the Games in 2005. Fulfilling Galatians 6:7, on July 22, 2016, a German-Iranian yelling "Allahu Akbar" slaughtered nine people in a Munich shopping mall.)

On November 1, 1972 (less than twelve months to *Egypt's* D-Day), Moscow agreed to replenish Sadat's depleted air defense system. The year would end with the mother of all harbingers as marathon negotiations were finalized permitting the Saudis to purchase 25% of Aramco. On January 16, Golda became the first major Israeli to meet with a Pope (Paul VI). She then went to the White House on March 1 to confer with Nixon. Three weeks later, Sadat proclaimed himself military governor of Egypt, declaring martial law. By late summer, Egypt and Syria each possessed the ultimate left-right combination—Soviet state-of-the-art SAM-6 missile technology to shield advancing Arab forces from IAF attacks *and* surface-to-surface missiles poised at Israeli cities to deter long-range bombing of their own civilian centers.

Around this same time, Emir Feisal assured Sadat that he would back the latest war with the biggest weapon of all—a Saudi oil embargo—*guaranteed* to turn all industrialized nations against Israel. In mid-September, the two leaders privately set October 6 (Assad's 43rd birthday) for the invasion date. Like Japan's "peace" legation was received in Washington on December 7, 1941, talks between the Arabs and American oil executives were set to begin in Vienna on October 6.

At T-minus 23 days and counting, the IAF killed thirteen Syrian MiG-21s in a dogfight off the coast of Syria. (One Israeli plane was lost, the pilot later rescued.) However, the tide was about to turn. In an earlier, prescient interview on April 23, 1973, Sadat told *Newsweek* editor, Arnaud de Borchgrave: "The time has come for a shock…All West Europeans are telling us that everybody has fallen asleep over the Middle East crisis. But they will soon wake up to the fact that America has left us no other way out. Everything is now being mobilized in concert for the resumption of the battle which is inevitable."[32] Herzog notes: "Seldom has a leader of a country bent on war enunciated so clearly his intentions to the world and to all parties concerned."[33]

To Israel's loss, GHQ blew it off as Arab hyperbole. On September 25, Hussein secretly flew his own helicopter to a Mossad facility outside Tel Aviv where he personally assured Meir that a preemptive strike was coming.[34] Dr. Assaf David of Hebrew University writes: "Hussein's mysterious source was Abboud Salem, an Iraqi pilot who defected to Jordan in the early 1960s and became a Jordanian intelligence officer."[35] In a desert déjà vu scenario, just like Nasser's disregard of Hussein's eleventh-hour warning of an Israeli strike in 1967, the hapless Jordanian was ignored *again*—this time by "Granny Golda." David states: "Israel did not heed the king's vague warning."[36]

On Wednesday, October 3, Dayan held a meeting at Mrs. Meir's home to assess the latest developments. While they spoke, a Soviet reconnaissance satellite was launched into space and proceeded to fly over the Sinai, the Canal, the Galilee region, and the Syrian-Israeli border.[37] Similar telltale reports confirmed that the wives and children of Soviet staff in Egypt and Syria were being hastily evacuated. Still, the threat consensus remained "low," Meir recalling: "Nobody in the meeting thought that it was necessary to call up the reserves, and nobody thought that war was imminent."[38] (In stereotypical fashion, *money* played a major role in the Jews' reluctance to mobilize, a false alarm that spring having cost the Treasury a whopping $35 million.[39]) Yet, clouds of doubt would hover over the next forty-eight hours. As a last-minute precaution, on Friday, October 5, Chief of Staff General "Dado" Elazar, sent the 460th Armored Brigade to the Sinai and the 7th Armored Brigade to the Golan. Herzog writes, "That night the political and military leaders of Israel went to sleep with an uneasy feeling, but few dreamt that the country was facing an imminent attack."[40]

JUDGMENT DAY

At 4:00 a.m. on Saturday, October 6, the phones began to ring off the hook. Apparently, Major General Eli Zeira, chief of AMAN (Israel's Military Intelligence Directorate, analogous to the NSA), *now* believed an attack *was* certain, and that H-hour would be at 6:00 p.m. that very evening. (The infallible "tip" came from a covert meeting in London with the Mossad's "most reliable" source.) Hearing the news, Meir moaned in Yiddish: *"Nor dos felt mir!"*[41] ("That's all I needed!").

Incredibly, Golda's first move at her 8:05 a.m. "Kitchen Cabinet" (inner circle) meeting in the Kirya was to deny Elazar's request—not only for a first strike against Syria (the smaller, though greater, proximate threat)—but for a nearly full mobilization as well. (Having requested 200,000 to 250,000 reserves, Dado received less than half that number.) The defense minister concurred with both decisions. (To clarify protocol, Dayan's jurisdiction was political, while operational commands had to come from the chief of staff.) Rabinovich writes:

> It was admittedly bizarre to have two generals, veteran warhorses at the pinnacle of Israel's military establishment, bringing their differences over vital military matters to a seventy-five-year-old grandmother…Mrs. Meir made no pretense of understanding military matters. She would confess to her military aide, General Yisrael Lior, that she had no idea what a division was.[42]

Her primary reasoning here was realpolitik; Nixon and Kissinger had already clarified that an Israeli first strike would not be condoned. According to Golda's long-classified testimony before the Agranat

Commission, released in 2013, the prime minister acknowledged: "My heart was drawn to a preemptive strike, but I was scared."[43]

For the few privy to the imminent scourge, the emotional paralysis must have resembled David's resignation in I Chronicles 21:16, *"And David lifted up his eyes, and saw the angel of the LORD stand between the earth and the heaven, having a drawn sword in his hand stretched out over Jerusalem."* When Golda asked her defense minister to brief the cabinet at 12:30 p.m., only four hours after he had opposed Elazar, Rabinovich notes, "[T]here appeared to be a tremor in Dayan's voice. He looked like a man whose certainties had suddenly crumbled."[44]

Unlike Alfred E. Newman (fictitious mascot of *Mad* magazine, popularized by two Jews, Harvey Kurtzman and Al Feldstein), "Jacob" had *plenty* to "worry" about. Egypt's force alone numbered 600,000 men, 2,000 tanks, 2,300 artillery pieces, 160 SAM missile batteries, and 550 combat planes. The combined might of the big four—Egypt, Syria, Iraq, and nominally committed Jordan—comprised a population of 55 million, standing armies of 538,000 troops, 970,000 reserves, 4,740 tanks, 4,700 armor-plated vehicles (halftracks, bulldozers, bridging tanks), 1,222 aircraft, 318 helicopters, and 149 warships.

In addition, Saudi Arabia, Kuwait, Morocco, Tunisia, Algeria, Libya, Sudan, and Uganda had pledged troops and/or munitions. Uganda's dictator, Idi Amin, a reputed cannibal (i.e., "Eaty" Amin), offered to join his men.[45] Twenty-nine Black African States broke ties with Israel in 1973.[46] Unknown to most, a smidgen of North Koreans even got in on the coalition, piloting Sadat's Soviet-built MiGs (two being downed in the war's last days.)[47] Finally, a brigade of Castro's anti-Semitic Cubans was stationed in Syria during 1973 (though it remains unclear if they participated in any combat missions).[48]

At 2:00 p.m. on Saturday, October 6, 1973—while Israel's Jewish population was preoccupied with Yom Kippur solemnities—"Sadat's shock" arrived *four hours early*, vis-à-vis an opening 1,300-gun, thirty-minute fusillade upon the entire Bar-Lev Line! Egypt's version of the Battle of San Jacinto ("Remember the Alamo") was on. After three years of seething inactivity, tempered only by meticulous planning, 10,000 shells were unleashed in the first minute alone (175 explosions per second). Unlike June 5, 1967, 200 EAF supersonic MiGs and Sukhois ruled the skies, raining death and destruction on IDF positions along the east bank of the Suez and across the Sinai. Ironically (as noted in Sadat's diary), the president's younger half-brother, Atef el-Sadat, died "in the first strike"[49] when his SU7 was downed (likely in the battle cited by Shlomo Aloni in *Israeli Mirage and Nesher Aces*[50]).

Meanwhile, in relative coordination (Arab misnomer), Syrian aircraft began pounding Israel's northern border at about the same time. After an hour-long accompanying barrage from 700 artillery pieces, two armored divisions of 800 tanks and three infantry divisions in armored personnel carriers (AMPs), started crossing over the ceasefire line. Israeli planes arriving at either front were deterred by SAMs and Russian self-propelled quadruple 23-mm AA cannons (the latter proving more lethal).[51] "It was like flying through hail...," one Skyhawk pilot recalled.[52] (One-eighth of the entire IAF—forty-nine planes—would be lost in the first four days alone.[53]) Thus began the fourth, and most precarious, Arab-Israeli War in twenty-five years.

ALLAHU AKBAR!

Within fifteen minutes of the opening salvo, 4,000 Egyptian troops and engineers began crossing the 180-yard-wide channel in 720 rubber dinghies under covering smoke. (The previous night, combat divers blocked the underwater pipes on the opposite bank to prevent Israelis from dispelling oil into the canal and igniting it.) As the initial volley subsided, the shell-shocked Jews (some clutching Torah scrolls) were arrested by an even more ominous sound—fifty loudspeakers leading the charging Muslims in chants of *Allahu Akbar* ("God is Greater")![54]

The symbolic crossing (code-named *Badr*) was intended as a two-fold religious psych-out; October 6 was also the 10th day of Ramadan, the date in AD 624 when Mohammed began preparations for the Battle of Badr, eventuating his triumphant entry into Mecca six years later.[55] Sadat's modern invaders stormed ashore with a virulent anti-Semitism instilled by their training. According to the indoctrination primer, *Instructions in Moral Guidance for the Training Year in 1969*:

> Mankind has never known and will never know a brutal enemy like the Jews. They can only damage, plan conspiracies, place traps before justice and create disturbances. From their mother's womb they have the lowest form of character which they pass on from generation to generation...They have spread out throughout the

world in order to poison mankind...They joined the conspiracy against Jesus in order to kill him.[56]

Then, to the Israelis' further surprise, eighty elite sapper units began scouring holes in the giant sand barriers with a secret weapon stronger than dynamite—*water* cannons! Egyptian engineers employed 150 German-made, turbine-driven pumps (T.S.T. 40/7s) capable of sucking 1,000 gallons of canal seawater per minute, then ejecting it through hoses under high pressure to degrade the berms.[57] Thus, the IDF's twelve-hour security window (based on dynamite) was watered down to four, the first of sixty breaches completed by 6:30 p.m.[58] (In a wild prophetic parallel, as seen in Revelation 12:15, with Job 40:23, Isaiah 59:19, and Daniel 9:26, Satan will try to drown the Jewish remnant in the Tribulation by using his own *mouth* as a water cannon!)

With the bridgeheads secured, eight heavy-duty Russian PMP floating bridges and four lighter pontoons attached the two continents. Over 23,000 Muslims crossed in the first two hours. Needless to say, the 450 *jobniks* (reservists doing their annual stint) manning less than half of the redoubts, were bypassed with ease. Of the fortunate ones able to surrender (many at the wrong end of a flamethrower), several made their Arab TV "debut" on Tuesday as humbled POWs.[59]

Six miles rearward, Israel's second line of defense sprang into action. However, deployed without standard reconnaissance and aerial cover, her tanks were ambushed with impunity by sallies of infantry (a.k.a. "creepy crawlies") firing shoulder-held RPG-7s (300-yd. range) and portable SA-3 "SAGGER" anti-tank missiles (3,000-yd. range). Moving at 450 feet per minute, wire-guided Saggers would pierce a Centurion, igniting a 1,000-degree blast, the ensuing fireball incinerating the crew. Nearly 66% of Division Commander Albert Mandler's 290 tanks were killed in the process, some at fifty paces.[60] Others met their end in the marshes. The driver of one mauled tank was seen fleeing with the torso of his dead commander hanging out of the turret.[61] (Scores of Arab commandos, landed by helicopter behind Israeli lines after dark, further impeded incoming reservists.)

By Sunday afternoon, five Egyptian divisions, comprising 100,000 troops and 1,000 Soviet-built T-55 battle tanks had crossed along the length of the entire canal.[62] Arnold Sherman opines, "Perhaps the greatest surprise of the war was the swiftness with which the canal was spanned and the durability of the structures."[63] Sadat's chief of staff,

General Saad el-Shazly, was an obvious improvement over ‘Amer. Fewer than 200 Egyptians died in the start of *Badr*. As for “Allah’s” role, Mohammed Heikal writes in *The Road to Ramadan*, “[A] great deal was owed to that fickle ally, General Luck.”[64]

An Israeli pushback on Monday (on Zangwill plain astride the Havraga maozim) proved disastrous, being “marred by excruciating errors of judgment and abysmal battlefield management.”[65] General Sharon’s unauthorized attempt to rescue Bar-Lev defenders the next day likewise failed. (Having fought in all Israeli wars to date, Arik’s legendary scorn for his superiors would peak during Yom Kippur.)

“COULD *THIS* BE THE IDF?”

The scene on Israel’s northern front was no less deleterious. The “Golan Bar-Lev” was a picket of seventeen redoubts, each manned by fifteen to twenty soldiers, supported by one armored platoon, two infantry battalions, and four artillery batteries.[66] Not unlike the Battle of the Bulge, when the fighting erupted, Syria’s Army was deployed with three full infantry divisions, some 50,000 men, 600 gunnery sites, and 540 tanks (including the Russian T-62), augmented by two armored divisions of 460 tanks, with 500 in reserve for a total of 1,500—all under their “Red umbrella” surface-to-air missile system.[67]

Arrayed against this Muslim onslaught were roughly 175 Israelis (two light infantry regiments, many “lightheaded” from fasting), a few cannons, and 177 tanks (along with 11 support batteries).[68] The telltale sign of imminent danger came around noon when the Mount Hermon observatory reported that the Syrians were removing the camouflage nets from their artillery. The reader can take it from here…

The first twenty-four hours consisted of one horrific David-and-Goliath clash after another, the giants mostly prevailing (especially along the flatter southern flank). “I never knew there were so many tanks in the world,” a stunned Israeli commander remarked.[69] Near Tel Aksha, 60 tanks of the Barak Brigade squared off against 600 Syrian tanks; by late Saturday the numbers stood at 15-450. Lieutenant Zvi Greengold (a.k.a. “Force Zwicka”) launched his now epic all-night personal grudge match at 50-1 odds. For the 1st Syrian Armored Division opposing Barak’s 2nd Battalion, the ratio was slightly better at 80-6.[70]

Isolated platoons were fending off whole battalions (sometimes brigades), the enemy pouring through the breaches by sheer mass.

Turning the tables on IDF tradition, the Syrians were also able to capitalize on the dark as their Soviet T-55 tanks (unlike the older Israeli Centurions) had infrared night-fighting equipment (detecting targets up to 4,000 feet). Blum describes a typical surreal encounter: "[Battalion Commander Lieutenant Colonel Avigdor] Kahalani searched the ridge with his night vision binoculars and he saw the shining eyes of a beast of prey. A pair of infrared lights stared back at him."[71] Adding to Dayan's woes, Britain's historical "pro-Arab neutrality" was evidenced by their banning Centurion replacement parts to Israel while supplying the Saudis with *their* hardware and training.[72] On a rare positive note, as the Syrians had "inexplicably" placed their bridge tanks in the rear, numbers of enemy armor drove straight into Israel's anti-tank ditches, being picked off in the process.

The pressing crisis was that the Syrian bulge threatened to overrun all of northern Israel. By first light on Sunday, Syria's 47th Tank Brigade was staring down in awe at the Sea of Galilee. Across the tranquil sheen lay their first inviting conquest—Tiberias (site of that sacrilegious, Jewish-owned Lido). Enemy forces near the Kuzabia crossroads were poised within six miles of the Jordan River. At the height of the crisis, Lieutenant Colonel Pinie, deputy commander of the Brigade District, viewed a rare, pell-mell IDF retreat. Herzog says:

> On the road he saw sights that horrified him and aroused the nighttime memories of his childhood in war-torn Europe. Could this be the IDF? Here before him straggled units of a defeated army. He stopped one unit…by standing in the middle of the road and pointedly reminding the officer in charge what the penalty for cowardice in the face of the enemy was even in the IDF. It was clear…that the Israeli Army was at a loss when withdrawing.[73]

Perhaps the most emblematic reversal of that first untoward day was the fall of *Jabal al-Shaykh* ("Mount Hermon"). Described as the "eyes of the nation," Israel's highest peak rises thirteen times in Scripture (Psalm 133:3 the most familiar text). After gaining the prize in 1967, the IDF built a radar/observation post (code-named *Mutzav 104*) on a spur at 6,600 feet, housing sensitive electronic equipment. The adjacent area also served as the nation's premier ski resort.

On Yom Kippur, fifty-five Israeli troops and intelligence staff were perched in the strategic aerie. At 2:45 p.m., the first shells struck the site. Fifteen minutes later, three Soviet-built Mi-8 helicopters landed a crack battalion of Syrian commandos. In the ensuing firefight (lasting hours), eleven Israelis managed to escape, the rest being killed or captured. According to former IDF intelligence officers, shortly thereafter, Soviet advisors arrived and began dismantling their treasure trove of classified spoils spread throughout seven underground levels.[74] Two days later, a hasty counterattack was repelled. Abraham Rabinovich writes: "The fall of the Hermon was for Israel the single most humiliating episode of the Yom Kippur War."[75] Ironically, the nation's key *listening* post had been captured in a *surprise* attack.

SHOCK THERAPY

The first day of fighting ended with Prime "Spin Meister" Meir giving her live "cover-your-tuchas" broadcast to the nation:

> Citizens of Israel: At around 14:00 today the armies of Egypt and Syria launched an offensive against Israel…They hoped to surprise the citizens…on the Day of Atonement while many were praying in the synagogues…But we were not surprised…Our forces were deployed as necessary to meet the danger….[76]

The defense minister came on next, boasting: "We shall smite the Egyptians hip and thigh…We have had losses, but, relatively speaking, this was what we estimated to be in the first day of fighting…."[77] Off camera, however, things were not so calm. When Dayan, who by now was already prepared to give up the canal, offered to resign,[78] Meir replied, "God forbid"![79] Golda was actually too busy pondering her *own* "departure" to process the gesture. Blum writes, "[H]er personal secretary, Lou Kadar, had given her a bottle of pills. Two were all she would need. She put the bottle in her bag. When the time came, she would rather die than witness the destruction of the Jewish state."[80]

In his personal analysis of Israel's charismatic defense minister, Chaim Herzog observed, "The *shock* of the war caused something to snap in Dayan."[81] Giving the Devil his due, as Sadat had promised a "shock," Carly Beckerman-Boys, of the University of Birmingham, relates, "'Trauma' is a word often associated with the October War."[82] Howard Sachar notes, "[T]his was Israel's first war in which doctors treated numerous *shock* cases."[83] When Colonel Ben Porat, commander of IDF electronic signal intelligence unit 848, first learned of the Egyptian attack, he "began shaking" in front of his men. Blum writes, "He dropped to his knees, and then started to crawl. But he could not stop shaking. Finally he lay down, stretched flat out, convulsing. Someone yelled for a stretcher."[84] Rabinovich adds:

> Apart from the psychological *shock*, mental circuits were thrown out of kilter as commanders tried to simultaneously grasp what was happening, how it could have happened, and what needed to be done…A brigade commander would later say that for officers in his category it generally took two days before the *shock* wore off and they returned to themselves….[85]

As Sachar notes, the noncombatant was even less prepared: "[T]he Israeli public was *shocked* to its depths."[86] Rabinovich elaborates: "For civilians too, the abrupt switch from tranquility and national self-confidence on Yom Kippur afternoon to all-encompassing war and existential alarm—without what psychologists would call 'the positive process of anticipatory fear'—was a *shock* that would not quickly heal."[87] Israelis have defined their national defibrilation as a *mehdal* ("unnecessary shortcoming"). Dr. Jacob Eriksson of the University of York concludes: "Although it ended in Israeli victory, the October War was nonetheless a national trauma with immense political ramifications."[88] Thus, it appears that in a morbid sort of way, Egypt's "*shock* jock" president had conformed to the "holiday spirit"—the ten days between Rosh Hashanah and Yom Kippur being known as the "Days of *Awe*."

Reflecting on the cavernous gloom among the war cabinet, Air Force commander Benny Peled renamed the Kirya's Pit, the "Holocaust Basement."[89] Rabinovich renders a humbling conclusion:

> Virtually every assumption by the Israeli command about the nature of the coming war had proven wrong—that AMMAN would provide ample warning, that the air force could save the day, that the IDF could get by with limited artillery and infantry, that 'armor *shock*' would stampede the enemy, that the Arab soldier was a pushover and the Arab military command inept.[90]

SUNDAY MORNING QUARTERBACKING

On October 7, Moshe Dayan was heard muttering at sunrise, "The Third Temple is in danger,"[91] a metaphorical reference to the destruction of Jerusalem's Temple, first by the Babylonians, then by the Romans (both precipitating the Jews' ejection from Eretz Yisrael). "We had all the information but were blind," a Yom Kippur veteran told this author. "There is an account in the Bible where God hit the land with blindness—that is what we had." Co-authors Dan Raviv and Yossi Melman write: "The Yom Kippur surprise was similar to what American historians have written about the Japanese attack on Pearl Harbor in 1941. The information was there, but intelligence chiefs either chose to ignore it or wrongly analyzed it."[92]

True to the adage, "Victory has many fathers, but failure is an orphan," Israel's "blame game" started posthaste. The main theory for the unprecedented security lapse on October 6 was attributed to Eli Zeira's slavish addiction to his own National Intelligence Estimate (NIE) for 1973, a long-term threat assessment known as *Ha-Konseptzia* ("The Concept"). According to this paradigm, Syria would *never* attack Israel without Egypt, and Egypt would *never* attack without Soviet-supplied SAMs and, more importantly, long-range fighter bombers—the former to deter intruding IAF sorties, the latter to threaten Israeli airfields and cities.[93] While "Comrade" Brezhnev delivered the missiles, he deferred on the bombers, ostensibly to avoid harming detente talks with Washington. Thus, without the possibility of preempting Israel's superior air power, Sadat would *never* send his infantry and armor beyond Egypt's limited surface-to-air missile cover, etc. All the IDF had to do was monitor Egypt's ports and airfields for evidence that the weapons had arrived; simple enough.

Meanwhile, swelling troop numbers were dismissed as standard maneuvers. Constituting one of several ploys designed by a special inter-ministerial committee for deception, starting in January 1973, Egyptian reservists were mobilized for training and then released some twenty times.[94] Between war games, Shazly had members of his code-named "Lazy Unit" appear unarmed in casual clothes along the canal bank, fishing, loafing, even playing soccer. Tens of thousands of Egyptian troops and supplies would routinely amass along the Bar-Lev Line only to disengage and go home—*the* fatal exception, *Tahrir*

("Liberation") 41—occuring October 1-6. (The parallel proliferation on the Golan was deemed related to the aerial battle of September 13.)

General Zeira's unshakable belief in the Concept was augmented by its unique source—the man many regarded as Israel's greatest spy. Recruited in 1970, Ashraf Marwan was not just *any* Egyptian—he was Nasser's son-in-law (married to his third daughter, Mona), then chief of President Sadat's Information Bureau. Known in Mossad parlance as a "walk-in," Dr. Marwan volunteered his services, claiming he "believed in the ultimate triumph of the Zionists" and felt "ashamed of the disgraceful performance of the Arabs in the last war."[95] True to Proverbs 27:20, *"the eyes of man are never satisfied,"* filthy lucre seems to have been the *real* motive, his own wealth notwithstanding.[96] Marwan received 100,000 British pounds sterling, delivered in cash, at each face-to-face rendezvous with his handler, Dubi Asherov. As the Marwans spent considerable time in London (occasioned by Ashraf's pursuit of a Master's degree and occasional medical treatments), a safe house was arranged in the fashionable neighborhood of Dorchester.

The consummate sleuth, Ashraf Marwan had two code names: "In-Law" and "Angel" (the latter after the hit British TV series, *The Saint*, rendered in Israel, "The Angel"). Over the next four years, the Mossad invested a staggering $20 million to finance the operation.[97] As Blum relates, Israel's leaders agreed that it was money well spent: "No spy in the history of Israel ever delivered such intelligence."[98] The Concept (considered the ultimate dividend) was predicated upon two documents purloined by Marwan—a transcript of a talk Nasser had with the Russian general staff in Moscow on January 22, 1970, and a confidential letter written by Sadat to Soviet leader, Leonid Brezhnev. Both attest to Egypt's need for missiles *and* long-range bombers as a prerequisite for attacking Israel.[99] (It was the "In-Law" who apprised Mossad Director Zvi Zamir in their London meeting on October 5 that Egypt and Syria would attack Israel the following day at sunset.)

Solomon wrote in Proverbs 14:12, *"There is a way which seemeth right unto a man, but the end thereof are the ways of death."* Although the Concept was *initially* correct, Sadat was not about to sit still and do nothing (even if it meant betraying al-Assad). Besides, recovering the *entire* Sinai (and Golan) was never the paramount goal; restoring Arab pride was. Losing the Six-Day War was humiliating enough; a protracted no-peace-no-war stalemate only exacerbated matters. Dr. Yoram Meital of Ben-Gurion University writes, "During the summer of 1972, Sadat came to the conclusion that, as a matter of principle, the status quo needed to be broken by a military operation."[100] Sadat told King Hussein's political advisor, Zaid Rifa'i, that he intended to "start a war '*harb taharik mish harb tahrir*'—a war for movement, not a war for liberation. 'For me, I shall cross the canal and stop.'"[101]

The code name for the catalytical strategy was *Operation Spark*.[102] General Shazly, Egypt's chief of staff, submitted the following threefold answer to the Concept: 1) cross the canal in spectacular, ego-building fashion; 2) reoccupy a sliver of Israeli-held Egyptian territory, five to six miles inland being deemed adequate; 3) secure the standard UN-Soviet induced "emergency" cease-fire (before being expelled *again*). And, should everything go according to plan, the international recoil might even force the Jews back to the 1967 lines.

The only drawback was that al-Assad would never risk a first strike if his Cairo counterpart was unwilling to a make a full commitment. Keeping Israel engaged in the desert was necessary to ensure a commensurate reduction of IDF pressure in the Golan. Sadat overcame this challenge with standard Arab mendacity; he simply "assured" his Muslim brother that once his army regrouped it would *definitely* proceed to drive the Israelis out of Sinai, etc.[103] Shazly would write in his biography, "I was sickened by the duplicity."[104]

COUNTERATTACK

Although the Syrian army was much smaller than Egypt's military, GHQ gave the Golan Heights priority over the southern theater, mainly owing to geographic issues. Whereas the 23,000-sq.-mile Sinai Peninsula provided a minimum 150-mile-wide security buffer, no such strategic depth shielded Israeli citizens along the northern frontier. (On a more sinister note, to revisit the theme of Sadat's perfidy with Damascus, Assad biographer Patrick Seale hints that many Syrians believed that he probably told Israel of his limited territorial goals.)[105]

Despite this hard reality, Israel's "defense" minister—losing his nerve *again*—advised a major withdrawal in the Golan. Dayan believed that "nowhere in the world, including the Soviet Union and Vietnam, was there such a dense deployment of modern Soviet weaponry."[106] Fortunately, Meir entrusted the final call to her former chief of staff,

Chaim Bar-Lev (then-Minister of Trade and Industry), who, after personally reconnoitering the front on Sunday night, calmly overruled Dayan's phobia, ordering an immediate counterattack.[107] General Moshe Peled later opined, "On that evening Bar-Lev became one of the real heroes."[108] In Golda's follow-up briefing with Chaim, resting her right elbow on the table, she flopped her upright arm from side to side, stating: "The great Moshe Dayan! One day like this. One day like that!"[109] Dayan's scheduled Monday TV slot was abruptly scrubbed for morale's sake, General Aharon Yariv replacing him.[110]

The stellar IDF feat in the opening phase of the resurgence was the epic stand of the 7th Armored Brigade at Quneitra led by Colonel Avigdor "Yanosh" Ben-Gal (Israel's George A. Custer). The four-day, non-stop (i.e., no sleep) battle was joined when Ben-Gal's greatly reduced band of 40 tanks clashed with over 500 Syrian tanks (including the elite Republican Guard Brigade led by the president's brother, Major General Rifaat al-Assad). It ended with 260 enemy tanks and hundreds of AMPs strewn across the Valley of Tears.[111]

Battalion commander Lieutenant Colonel Yosef "Yossi" Ben Hanan, a major participant in the engagement, was wounded four times in three days. Sustaining his last injury when a Sagger literally blew him out of his cupola, Yossi was rescued by Yonatan Netanyahu, older brother of Bibi Netanyahu. (Considered a vital "national treasure," Yossi was the soldier on that famous cover of *Life* showing him after the Six-Day War, jubilantly clutching his weapon in the Suez.) Brigadier General Rafael "Raful" Eitan, 36th Armored Division commander, lauded the 7th Brigade over the radio: "You have saved the people of Israel."[112] (Seven is the Bible number for completion.)

The destruction on October 9 of over 200 Syrian tanks in the tiny hamlet of Hushniya was the major IDF victory in the southern Golan. The following day the enemy was pushed back over the Purple Line (i.e., the initial ceasefire partition in 1967). Of the original 1,400 tank invasion force, 867 were left behind, along with thousands of AMPs, anti-tank vehicles, guns, and sundry equipment.[113] The miraculous reversal was attributed to the expeditious, albeit piecemeal, arrival of various reserve brigades. Their main contribution was preventing the Syrians from occupying the strategic Jordan River bridges.

By late Wednesday, GHQ agreed that the Muslims should be chased across the northern frontier for at least a dozen miles. With the war cabinet's approval, Elazar's sector commander, Major General Yitzhak "Haka" Hofi, scheduled the pursuit for 11:00 a.m. the next morning. Meanwhile, King Hussein, sharing in the general consensus among his peers that the latest Arab-Israeli war was "a piece of jackassery by Sadat and Assad,"[114] had maintained a "Thanks-but-no-thanks" attitude toward repeated Arab entreaties to join in the fight, *again*—Tunisia's President Bourguiba calling it "the chance of a lifetime."[115] However, by October 8, Hussein's mood was described as "incoherent."[116] Three days later, the king finally caved, committing two armored brigades to fight (under Syrian authority), along with a "pledge" to block Israel from entering Syria via his turf. (Yeah, right!)

To cover his tracks, Hussein sent Mrs. Meir a letter, explaining his dilemma and asking that Israel "refrain from attacking this unit if at all possible."[117] His prime minister, Samir al-Rifa'i, confided to US Ambassador Dean Brown: "What is required is that there be Jordanian martyrs."[118] In a meeting with Henry Kissinger, Golda described the royal petition as "touching."[119] As for her reply, the Hashemite was advised "not to move the unit."[120] Kissinger remarked in his memoirs: "Only in the Middle East is it conceivable that a belligerent would ask its adversary's approval for engaging in an act of war against it."[121]

Over the next week, the IDF would take out retreating Syrians, the Moroccan and Iraqi Expeditionary Forces, and, yes, King Hussein's token (sacrificial) 40th Armored Brigade. Jordan lost twenty-seven dead, fifty wounded, and fourteen tanks.[122] Adding insult to injury, when Saudi Arabia's 3,000-man 20th Armored Brigade got lost in the desert (sustaining minimal battle casualties as a result), Hussein had to send *camels* to rescue them.[123] His Highness *did* receive at least one "neighborly" (profit-motivated) comp: On Dayan's order the bridges connecting Jordan and the West Bank remained open during the war.

By October 18, Moshe Peled's 146th Reserve Armored Division occupied the expanse reaching the suburbs of Damascus only twenty-two miles away (ironically, the general locale where Saul met Jesus in Acts 9:3). Syria's panic stretched all the way to Moscow. Finally, on October 21, paratroopers arriving by helicopter joined with ground forces to retake Mount Hermon. One by one, the defenders were dislodged from their sangars. Within thirty-six hours, the nation's "eyesight" was restored—but not without a price. Colonel Avraham Ayalon, a veteran of the Givati Brigade in the War of Independence, would find the lifeless body of his eldest son upon the conquered mount.[124] When Syria capitulated on October 23, the IDF controlled the entire Golan Heights, including the newly acquired enclave comprising 150 square miles.

THE STORYBOOK ENDING

In the war's opening week, Soviet transports delivered 1,000 tons of supplies to Egypt and Syria in nonstop shuttle operations, employing a fleet of Antonov-12 cub transports (each hauling ten to twelve tons of cargo), augmented by Antonov-22 oversized freighters (sporting fifty-ton payloads).[125] Israel suffered 724 soldiers killed in just the first 48 hours of fighting—more than were lost in the entire Six-Day War.[126]

Now, according to the history books, in the ongoing drama of "patrons and proxies," Israel was saved by a beneficent emergency airlift sanctioned by President Richard Milhous Nixon, working in concert with his providentially appointed secretary of state, the Jewish, German-born Holocaust survivor, Dr. Henry "Heinz" Alfred Kissinger. As related in the Preface, Christians are particularly enamored to learn that this eleventh-hour intervention was supposedly motivated by a prophecy uttered by Nixon's Quaker grandmother that "one day he would rescue the Jews from destruction."

On October 9, Nixon authorized Kissinger to resupply Israel's depleted munitions. After three days of "logistical" delays (i.e., Henry's insistence that commercial charters be used), Israel's US ambassador, Simcha Dinitz, threatened to go directly to Congress.[127] Defense Secretary James Schlesinger was subsequently ordered to expedite the ordnance in American military planes (C-5 Galaxies and C-141 Starlifters). Code-named *Operation Nickel Grass*, 22,000 tons of tanks, trucks, artillery, ammunition and miscellaneous supplies would arrive in Israel over the next month, spanning 567 missions.[128] The Organization of Arab Petroleum Exporting Countries (OAPEC) countered with a total oil embargo on America and the Netherlands (the latter being the only European country to avail its airfields for the airlift). With the war's price tag of $10 million an hour sending Israelis into "sticker *shock*"[129] (Haggai 1:6), Congress authorized an emergency $2.2 billion supplemental appropriations bill as well.

ISRAELI "AFRIKA KORPS"

Assured of US supplies, the Sinai resurgence developed in several stages. Deemed incompetent, General Shmuel "Shmulik" Gonen, chief of the Southern Command, was replaced by Bar-Lev.[130] Given the greater Syrian priority (plus a desperate need to regroup), Dado Elazar was compelled to maintain a stopgap containment near the strategic mountain passes. To al-Assad's horror, Egypt's chief of staff appeared to cooperate by employing his own "operational halt," apparently content with the six-mile-wide stretch of sand he had "liberated." Over the next five days, Egyptian forces probed Israel's lines with a "creeping defense" (wary of moving beyond its missile coverage).[131]

By October 11, Syria was in check. Thus, Southern Command was directed to end the stalemate by preparing a covert canal-crossing operation. Division Commander General Avahram "Bren" Adan (the man in that other iconic photo hoisting the "Ink Flag" at Eilat in 1949) gave the enemy fair warning over the radio: "Oh, Egyptians! If you are listening to us, then listen carefully, you sons of b-----s: your turn is coming!"[132] Sadat, meanwhile, under intense pressure from Damascus (and against the protest of General Shazly), also relented to break the impasse. At 6:20 a.m. on Sunday, October 14, the Egyptian 21st Armored Division inaugurated the mission's third operational phase, the critical breakthrough from the bridgehead eastward.

The Battle of the Sinai—the largest tank duel in history apart from the WWII Battle of Kursk—was joined with over 2,000 tanks engaged along the length of the entire front. Over the next twelve hours, Egypt suffered a decisive beatdown, losing 264 tanks (not counting those eliminated by air) compared to only six Israeli tanks destroyed.[133] (As the reader will discover, the timely arrival of America's latest secret weapon played a critical role in the victory.) A relieved Bar-Lev phoned Meir, "It has been a good day. Our forces are themselves again and so are the Egyptians."[134] (Emotions were tempered by the loss of General Avraham "Albert" Mendler, who died on the eve of the fight when his armored vehicle took a direct hit; the revered Sinai Commander was supposed to take over the Israeli Armored Corps on October 7, but refused to abandon his men with the outbreak of war.)

In another providential act, the rout was *so* bad that Egypt's Second Army commander, Lieutenant General Mohammed Saad Mamoun, suffered a severe heart attack, requiring his immediate replacement. Major Richard Owen, USMC, relates, "After the war, this change in command was noted by the Egyptians as a factor contributing to the lack of decisiveness shown by the Army commanders during this period."[135] British historian Edgar O'Ballance adds, "[I]t was later deduced that the commander's absence had stopped the flow of infantry across the canal."[136] Thus, when Sadat ordered his disoriented remnants to fall back and form defensive positions, a critical "seam" was left between the Second Army and the Great Bitter Lake. Though less spectacular than the Red Sea parting, Israel's modern army would gratefully "shoot the gap" for their surprise comeback return to Egypt.

At 5:00 p.m. on October 15, Sharon launched his boldly conceived incursion with a diversionary attack at Talia and Televisia (just north of the intended staging area at Matsmed). Code-named *Abirei-Lev* ("Operation Valiant"), the IDF's threefold plan was to drive a wedge between the Second and Third Armies, securing their flank against the former while eventually encircling the latter. Unnerving Cairo (guarded by Egypt's First Army) was a bonus. The most intense fighting developed near the agricultural research station known as the Chinese Farm (an extended area marked by several dry irrigation ditches). Here, the outnumbered Israelis not only faced a heavily reinforced Egyptian infantry division, but a fully armored one as well.

To secure the crucial turning point on the Suez front (by opening the roads for bridging equipment to pass), the horrific four-day, round-the-clock fight would take 450 Israeli lives, leaving 1,200 wounded. "I saw hundreds and hundreds of burned and twisted vehicles," Sharon would remark upon viewing the aftermath at the Tirtur-Lexicon crossroads. "Here and there Israeli and Egyptian tanks had destroyed each other at a distance of a few metres barrel to barrel…Inside those tanks and next to them lay their dead crews…No picture could capture the horror of the scene."[137] Colonel Amnon Reshef of the 14th Armored Brigade said, "There is no better description like 'the real hell.'"[138]

In the crammed war room at Southern Command HQ, General Yariv reflected: "I don't remember a night this fateful in all our wars," to which Elazar, studying the large wall map, replied: "If the history of how we pulled this off is ever written, it will be seen as the height of chutzpa."[139] The following Tuesday, at 1:25 a.m. (not unlike General Washington's nocturnal crossing of the Delaware), the IDF morphed into an Israeli version of Rommel's "Afrika Korps," the advance wave of Colonel Danny Matt's 247th Reserve Paratrooper Brigade stealthily paddling across the Suez Canal just north of the Great Bitter Lake. Moments after Platoon Commander Eli Cohen became the first man ashore, Matt reported, "Acapulco!"—the prearranged signal, meaning "We have a hold on the west bank." Encountering zero resistance, the bridgehead was secured just east of Deversoir (opposite Matsmed). The commandos then proceeded to stake out a second disembarkation point with an overall perimeter three miles wide by one mile deep.

The entire brigade of 750 paratroopers was safely over by 5:00 a.m. However, a serious problem developed when Israel's monster Roller Assault Bridge (RAB) failed to arrive at the pre-positioned, brick-surfaced marshalling area (a.k.a. "The Yard"). Requiring 16 tanks to transport (12 for towing, 4 for braking), the 400-ton, 200-yard-long pre-constructed span, comprising 100 metal drums of polyurethane, broke down while negotiating a series of shallow slopes and had to be repaired. Known in military jargon as "Clausewitzian Friction" (Prussian version of "Murphy's Law"), the ancillary uni-float (iron cube) pontoons were also running late due to twelve miles of unforeseen bumper-to-bumper congestion, exacerbated by sporadic ambuscades. (The first casualty in Bren Adan's division, Major Oded Hermony, died in a highway accident while rushing to the front.[140])

Though marooned on the tropical African bank without conventional armored protection, the paratroopers would soon be reinforced. By first light, a crucial (albeit not much for looks) "Yankee" provision was underway; twenty-seven tanks and seven APCs were being ferried across the canal via eighteen obsolete US Army Amphibious River Crossing Equipment (ARCE), self-propelled, inflatable rafts known as Gilowas. Rabinovich astutely notes: "Israel's major strategic move in the war, on the verge of being abandoned, was literally being kept afloat by recycled junk."[141] Despite the incongruous conditions (three Gilowas for every tank), Arik had his officers shave in preparation for their historic crossing.[142]

While Sharon's brigade commander, Colonel Haim Erez took off with twenty-one tanks in search of missile pods, yet another "miracle" occurred. The reader will recall how Nasser had dismissed Hussein's warning of an Israeli strike in 1967, and how the king was similarly ignored by Meir on Yom Kippur eve. Well, now it would be Sadat's turn. If you can believe it, as Matt's paratroopers were literally hiding in the weeds on Tuesday, Israel's "Grandmother-in-chief," longing to give her people some positive news, publicly announced: "Right now as we convene in the Knesset, an IDF task force is operating on the west bank of the Suez Canal." Dayan and Dado nearly collapsed at the security breach! Yet, thanks to Israel's "Rock," Egypt's president blew it off as a "television operation,"[143] using "psychological warfare."[144]

Delivering his own speech to the People's Council in Cairo that same afternoon, Sadat was unaware that puzzling snippets of an Israeli incursion were already trickling into the underground Operations Room of Third Army Field HQ (a.k.a. "Chapter Ten"). Unwilling to believe his own reports, Egypt's sycophant defense minister, General Ahmed Ismail Ali, declined to notify his commander-in-chief. Ali also refused to issue a standard alert, fearing that any negativity might stampede the army (as in 1967).[145] Haim's roving tank platoons were subsequently able to pounce on several unsuspecting convoys and bases, destroying four surface-to-air missile pods along the way.[146]

With Akavish Road finally clear, the first pontoon splashed into the Suez Canal at 7:15 a.m. on Wednesday. Unfortunately, so did the first artillery rounds. Now in panic mode (due to Soviet satellite images), Egypt's military would concentrate tens of thousands of shells on the Yard throughout the rest of the war.[147] While FROG surface-to-surface missiles rained down, Egyptian frogmen were repelled by paratroopers laying along the edge of the bridge, periodically tossing hand grenades into the water.[148] As suicide helicopter missions added barrels of napalm to the deadly payload, brave Israeli engineers (led by General Dan Even) finished the pontoon bridge by 4:00 p.m. Over 100 Israelis were killed in the process, many buried alive in their own foxholes. Hundreds more were wounded, including General Sharon—Arik's "head bandage" soon rivaling the fading glory of Dayan's signature eye patch. (The long-lost caterpillar span eventually arrived via the Tirtur axis, becoming operational on October 19.)

WAR COUNCIL IN THE DUNES

While GHQ had issued the order to "*prepare* a crossing operation," the final details (in particular, which division would cross first) were still unresolved by October 17. At this critical junction, once again the hand of providence intervened, at least according to the opinion of General Adan, the first head of Israel's Armored Corps:

> No one had decided that a commanders' conference would be held by my forward command post. It was as though an unseen hand had assembled, at the right time and the right place, the minister of defense, the chief of staff, the commander of the front, and the two division commanders. And so it was that what later gained fame as the 'war council in the dunes' was held...The fact that a council of war was being held just as a shift became evident in the battlefield stalemate lent it supreme importance.[149]

As General Adan goes on to explain, the "Big Three" (Dayan, Elazar, and Bar-Lev) just *happened* to drop in on Sharon and him to stabilize an extremely fluid situation. Bar-Lev ultimately directed Arik to continue expanding the corridor while Bren crossed first. Sharon would follow, but only after completing his task.[150] However, before he could initiate the exercise, Bren's division would have to check a massive threat from the south—Third Army's 25th Armored Brigade. The elite unit, led by Colonel Ahmed Badawi Hassan, fielded nearly 100 Soviet T-62 tanks and 40 AMPs. Conforming to the previously cited Second Battle of Ai, the modern Hebrew victory would also employ a tactical ambush (Joshua 8:2-22). After little more than an hour, sixty enemy tanks plus scores of support vehicles littered the sandy plain north of Bitter Lake. One of Adan's Centurions even downed an Egyptian MiG carrying napalm. Israeli losses amounted to all of three tanks, two hit by mines, the other disabled by a Sagger.[151]

By 5:15 a.m. the next morning (October 18), Adan's 162nd Reserve Armored Division, comprising two brigades of seventy tanks each, plus a self-propelled artillery brigade, had refueled and trundled over the bridge into the land of Ham (Psalm 105: 23, 27). With the ensuing crossings of Sharon's 143rd Division and the truncated division of General Kalman Magen (Mandler's successor), things were starting to look up. "They have lost the battles, and now we are here," a resuscitated Dayan declared.[152] Sherman observes, "The Egyptians were apparently totally unprepared for the Israeli lunge into the country, nor did they understand the scale of the Israeli assault...Faced with an unclear set of parameters, the Egyptian war chiefs responded apathetically. It was the psychological turning point of the war in the south."[153] Rabinovich

The *Exodus 1947* after deadly British takeover twenty nautical miles off the coast of Palestine, July 18, 1947

The *Af-Al-Pi-Chen* ("Nevertheless") at the Clandestine Immigration and Naval Museum, Haifa *(Author's Collection)*

Child Holocaust survivors detrain at Atlit Detention Camp south of Haifa; internment of the "illegal immigrants" included guard towers, barbed wire, corrugated wooden barracks, and roll calls—all within Eretz Yisrael *(Zoltan Kluger/Israel Government Press Office)*

Disinfection chamber and showers in Atlit, eerily reminiscent of Auschwitz-Birkenau *(Author's Collection)*

King David Hotel, bombed by the Irgun, July 22, 1946 *(Hugo Mendelson/Israel Government Press Office)*

Gallows in Acre Prison *(Author's Collection)*

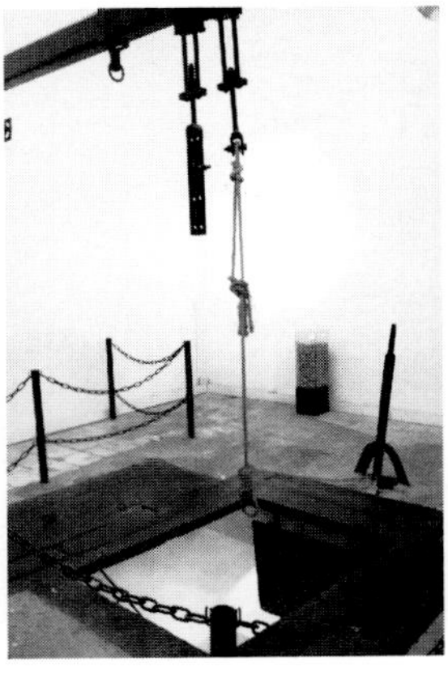

Damage from prison break at Acre, May 4, 1947

UN General Assembly taking final vote on Partition of Palestine, November 29, 1947; Resolution 181 passed 33-13, with 10 abstentions *(UN Photo/MB)*

Hadassah Hospital convoy attacked by Arabs, leaving seventy-eight dead, including doctors, nurses, students, patients, and several soldiers, April 13, 1948

Standing under Herzl's portrait, David Ben-Gurion reads the Declaration of the Establishment of the State of Israel over KOA radio at Dizengoff House, Tel Aviv, May 14, 1948 *(Reuters)*

Israelis dancing in the street to celebrate the landmark Partition vote creating separate Jewish and Arab states

British soldiers departing Palestine, May 1948, their strategic redoubts "abandoned" to the Arabs *(Reuters)*

Jewish citizens of the nascent state cheer across the street as the Declaration is read *(Reuters)*

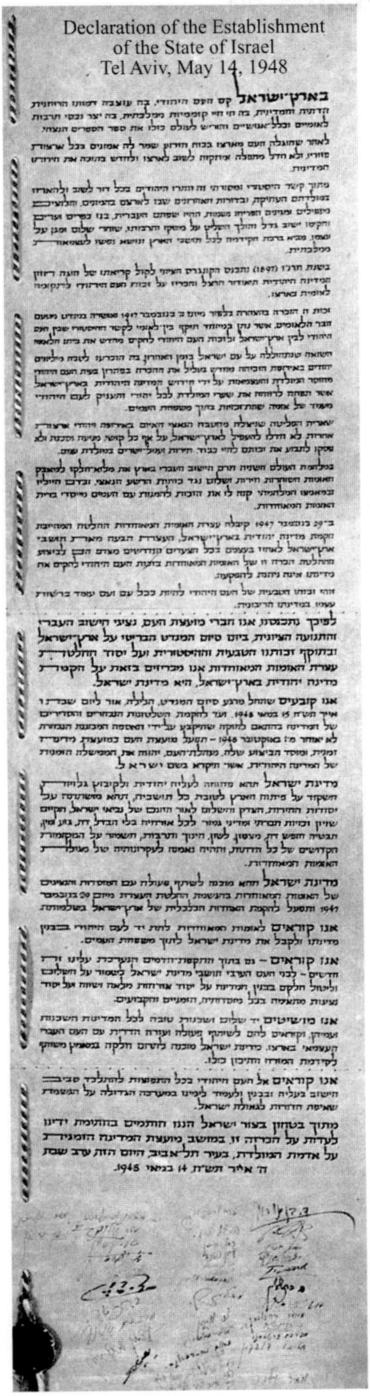

Declaration of the Establishment
of the State of Israel
Tel Aviv, May 14, 1948

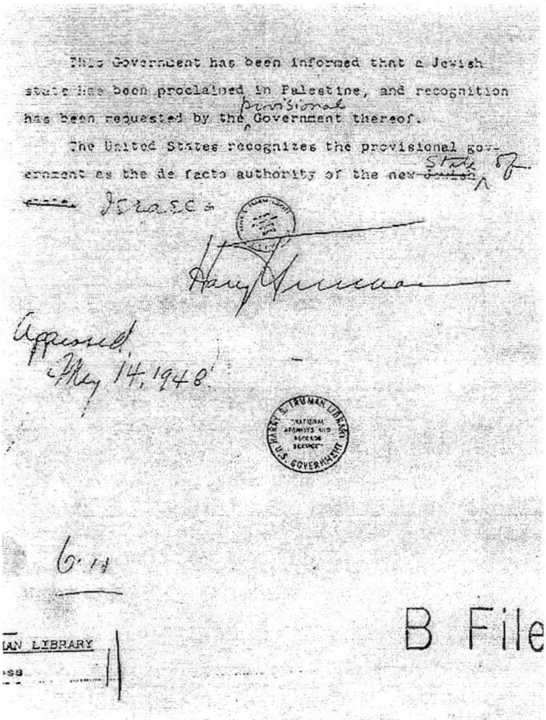

This Government has been informed that a Jewish state has been proclaimed in Palestine, and recognition has been requested by the provisional Government thereof.

The United States recognizes the provisional government as the de facto authority of the new ~~Jewish~~ State of Israel.

Harry Truman

Approved, May 14, 1948.

6.11

B File

Surprise press release by President Truman (a.k.a. "The man from Independence"), giving de facto recognition to the State of Israel, May 14, 1948; recorded at 6:11 p.m. EST, eleven minutes after midnight Israel time *(Harry S. Truman Presidential Museum and Library/Charlie Ross Papers)*

Statuette that led to America's recognition of the State of Israel; Oval Office replica of Charles Keck's statue of Harry's hero, Andy Jackson, cited by his Jewish friend, Eddie Jacobson, when asking for an executive confab with Chaim Weizmann *(Harry S. Truman Presidential Museum and Library)*

Colonel David "Mickey" Marcus (alias Michael Stone), Israel's first modern general (Aluf) and chief military advisor, pictured here during "Burma Road" campaign, June 1948 *(Israel Government Press Office)*

Haganah troops engage enemy near an Arab village in the Galilee region during opening phase of the War of Independence *(Reuters)*

President Truman receives a Torah scroll from Dr. Weizmann, May 25, 1948, followed by an election surprise, "I will bless them that bless thee…" *(Harry S. Truman Presidential Museum and Library)*

"Aluf Stone" headed for home at "The Point" in a plain white pine casket *(Robert Capa/Magnum)*

IDF in Eilat affix Ink Flag at end of war, March 10, 1949 *(Perry Micha/ Israel Government Press Office)*

Memorial to David Marcus near Abu Ghosh *(Fritz Cohen/Israel Government Press Office)*

Egypt's President Gamal Abdel Nasser (a.k.a. "Hitler of the Nile") sparked global outrage by nationalizing the Suez Canal on July 26, 1956, inciting the Sinai "Hundred-Hour War"

British Prime Minister Anthony Eden countered by authorizing "Operation Musketeer," a covert tripartite alliance between Britain, France, and Israel, proposing (as recorded in the Protocol of Sèvres) a casus belli invasion and occupation of the Suez Canal Zone

Israeli paratrooper at Mitla Pass (thirty miles from the Suez Canal) during initial phase of "Operation Musketeer," October 29, 1956; surprise drop achieved by rumors circulated by Mossad of an imminent attack on Jordan

Upon Nasser's predictable unwillingness to heed an Anglo-French ultimatum to stand down following IDF diversionary strike at the canal, Colonel Ariel Sharon (upraised hand) begins "Operation Kadesh" (Numbers 13-14) during the Sinai Crisis to punish Gaza and secure the Straits of Tiran *(Reuters)*

Royal Marine Commandos being shuttled over to Port Said from the HMS *Theseus*, November 5; "Musketeer" dissolves after Nasser obstructs canal and Soviet mole in MI6 (Kim Philby) tips Khrushchev, who threatens nukes; Anglo-French relinquish one-day "conquest" (a sliver of sand some twenty-three miles south of Canal Zone); Prime Minister Eden experiences nervous breakdown and resigns; meanwhile, Ben-Gurion prevails, the IDF retaking Straits of Tiran *(Imperial War Museum)*

Meeting privately with French Prime Minister Mollet and Defense Minister Bourgès-Manoury (prior to the Sèvres signing), Shimon Peres, Director-General of the Ministry of Defense, secured a promise to build a reactor at Dimona. Here, Peres and Golda Meir tour the Soreq Nuclear Research Center, 1958

Jordan's King Hussein and President Nasser sign a defense treaty in Cairo, May 30, 1967. Hussein's subsequent commitment of his army (against the UN Government House) afforded a providential justification for Israel's historic capture of Jerusalem and the West Bank in the Six-Day War. *(Calvert/Associated Press)*

Colonel Mordechai "Motta" Gur (bareheaded, turning with field phone) addressing his battalion commanders from the Mount of Olives prior to their assault on the Old City of Jerusalem, June 7 *(Israel Government Press Office)*

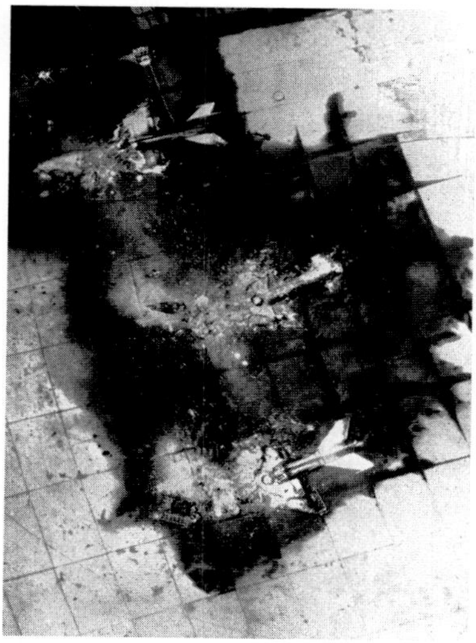

Egyptian MiG-21s destroyed on tarmac by an IAF preemptive strike, 7:45 a.m., June 5, 1967. A junior officer reports to Nasser: "I have come to inform you that we no longer have an air force." *(Israel Government Press Office)*

IDF soldiers approach the Lion's Gate (a.k.a. St. Stephen's Gate) blasted open by a Sherman tank at point-blank range *(Fondation Gilles Caron/Gamma-Rapho/Getty Images)*

"Har ha-Bayit be-Yadenu." ("The Temple Mount is now in our hands.") Paratroopers fastening the national flag to iron fence on the Temple Mount above the Western Wall *(Israel Government Press Office)*

Minister of Defense Moshe Dayan, flanked by General Uzi Narkiss (left) and Chief of Staff Yitzhak Rabin, enter Old City through Lion's Gate, June 7 *(Ho New/ Reuters)*

"Something special had happened." Soldiers stand in awe of the Western Wall following hard-fought battle *(Ho New/Reuters)*

IAF Super Mystère fighter makes attack run to destroy communication antennae during surreal assault on the USS *Liberty* (a USN technical research ship), June 8 *(Photo 1123755/ United States Navy)*

Aerial photograph taken on eve of war showing Government House compound (center wooded area), located in demilitarized zone atop "Hill of Evil Counsel," Ground Zero of the Battle for Jerusalem *(American Jewish Historical Society) Inset:* A disconsolate Hussein faces international press following rout of his Legionnaires

President Nixon, National Security Advisor Kissinger, and Prime Minister Golda Meir, meet in Oval Office, March 1, 1973. By October 4, the NSA knew Egypt and Syria would strike Israel in 48 hours (on Yom Kippur), yet Nixon refused to warn Meir until the morning of the attack. Henry later told Defense Secretary Schlesinger, "The best result would be if Israel came out a little ahead, but got bloodied in the process, and if the US stayed clean." *(National Archives and Records Administration)*

Inset: President Anwar Sadat: "The time has come for a shock," April 1973 *(Israel Government Press Office)*
Egyptian sapper units employ water cannons to degrade 70-ft-high sand berm along Bar-Lev Line on Israeli bank of Suez Canal during opening phase of Yom Kippur War, October 6

After withstanding a parallel preemptive strike in the north by 50,000 Syrian troops, the IDF launched its celebrated counterattack on October 9 (eventually threatening the Damascus suburbs). Defense Minister Dayan observes the enemy's crumbling line from bunker in the Golan Heights *(Associated Press)*

Israeli armor advancing under air cover during Battle of the Sinai, October 14 *(Israeli Government Press Office)*

Sharon (with bandage), joined by Bar-Lev (facing him), Adan (left foreground), Dayan, and Elazar, "...as though assembled by an unseen hand..." *(Israel Government Press Office)*

Following "war council in the dunes," Adan's and Sharon's armored divisions morphed into an Israeli "Afrika Korps," crossing the Suez on roller-bridges, leading to encirclement of Egyptian Third Army *(Israel Government Press Office)*

Chief of Staff Alexander "Al" Haig, the real hero of the Yom Kippur War *(Richard Nixon Presidential Library)*

Modern IDF Humvee with BGM-71 TOW missile tube, the mystery weapon that Haig covertly deployed to Israel (contrary to US policy) on the eve of the decisive Battle of the Sinai *(Matanya)*

Egyptian-born PLO chairman and Nobel Peace Prize laureate Mohammed Yasser Abdel Raouf Arafat al-Qudwa, a.k.a. "The Father of Modern Terrorism" *(www.comunismulinromania.ro/)*

One of eight "Black September" Palestinian terrorists peers over balcony at Munich Olympic village during police standoff following torture killing of two Israeli athletes and kidnapping (later, murder) of nine others, September 5, 1972—four days after the team made a poignant visit to Dachau Concentration Camp *(Russell McPhedran/Getty Images)*

Crowd gathers to mourn five members of the Ehud Fogel family, slain in their beds, March 11, 2011, by two teenage Palestinian cousins in the West Bank settlement of Itamar *(Baz Ratner/Reuters)* *(Inset)* Three-month-old Hadas, the youngest victim, was decapitated "for the glory of Allah"; three other siblings escaped harm.

Courageous IDF soldiers, like those on the right conducting an operation in the Gaza Strip, hazard their lives daily to minimize the carnage and "neutralize" the perpetrators. *(Author's Collection)*

Former Gush Katif resident Moshe Saperstein and author visit in his government-issued communal bomb shelter—a 6 ft. x 12 ft. concrete sewer pipe—known in resettlement parlance as a "sewervilla"

Author at Kerem Shalom Border Crossing (between Israel and the Gaza Strip), just northeast of their triangular convergence with Egypt

Intel-gathering balloons (equipped with hi-def cameras and meteorological sensors) provide the IDF with 24/7, 360-degree view *(Author's Collection)*

Jonathan Pollard, civilian US Naval intel analyst, convicted in 1987 of spying for Israel; expecting only two-four years from a plea bargain, he would serve nearly three decades

Prime Minister Yitzhak Rabin, assassinated, November 4, 1995, by a right-wing extremist, Yigal Amir, who rejected the Oslo Accords *(Ya'acov Sa'ar/Israel Government Press Office)*

Ilan Ramon, Israel's first (and only) astronaut, died with six fellow crew members in space shuttle *Columbia* tragedy, February 1, 2003 (his son, Asaf, died in 2009 when his F-16 crashed during a training exercise)

President Obama meets with Prime Minister Netanyahu in the Oval Office November 9, 2015. Obama's true regard for Bibi was exposed in a hot mic incident when French President Sarkozy whispered to him, "I cannot bear Netanyahu, he's a liar," whereupon Barack answered, "You're fed up with him, but I have to deal with him even more than you." *(Lamarque/Reuters)*

Obama's broken-down limo, "The Beast," as it's towed after being filled with wrong fuel during his first visit to Israel, March 2013 *(Associated News 24)*

“When She Was Good, She Was Very, Very Good…”

Haym Solomon, “America’s Banker”; financed American Revolution for Congress

Benjamin Disraeli, only Jewish-born Prime Minister of United Kingdon; served two terms

Emma Lazarus, penned the words, “Give me your tired, your poor, your huddled masses…”

Julius Rosenwald, Sears co-owner; philanthropist, funded 5,000 schools for black children in South

Samuel Cohen (with author), Manhattan Project physicist; invented neutron bomb in 1958 to ease civilian misery by eliminating collateral damage (vis-à-vis “Just War Theory”); received “Medal of Peace” from Pope John Paul II

Albert Einstein, awarded Nobel Prize in Physics; developed the theory of relativity ($E=mc^2$)

Irving Berlin, prolific composer; wrote “God Bless America,” his mother having inspired the theme

John “Johnnie” von Neumann, a.k.a. “world’s smartest man”; seminal thinker, polymath

Dr. Jonas Salk, virologist; invented one of the first successful polio vaccines, saving countless lives

"...But When She Was Bad, She Was Horrid"

Sigmund Freud, a.k.a. "Father of Psychoanalysis": "We are bringing them [America] the plague."

Samuel "Red" Levine; an observant hitman for Murder, Inc.; refused to kill on the Sabbath *(NYPD)*

Anton LaVey; founder of the Church of Satan; author of *The Satanic Bible (Bettman/Getty Images)*

Jerry Springer, TV's Smut King; one-time Cincinnati mayor; outed for writing check to hooker *(Reuters)*

Over 25,000 march in Pride Parade in central Jerusalem, July 30, 2015 ("Oy vey, I'm gay!); six participants stabbed by ultra-Orthodox Jew despite strict security *(Amir Cohen/Reuters)*

Howard Stern, "shock jock" pioneer; rated highest-paid media personality by *Forbes* in 2015 *(Reuters)*

Gene Simmons, "The Demon"; Israeli-born co-founder of KISS *(Belanger/Reuters)*

Sarah Silverman, "I hope the Jews did kill Christ...I'd [f-----g] do it again in a second." *(Cassese/Reuters)*

Anthony Weiner, sexting a minor on his device ultimately led to Hillary's election loss *(Reuters)*

With 40,000,000 viewers as witnesses, Tiny Tim wed Victoria "MissVicki" Budinger on the *Tonight Show*, December 17, 1969 *(Reuters)*

"There goes the neighborhood": Rodney Dangerfield's gravestone in a Los Angeles cemetery epitomizes his famed "I don't get no respect" self-deprecating shtick

Israeli Elvis impersonators posing before world's tallest Elvis statue (16 ft.) at the Elvis Inn, a '50s-style diner filled with Elvis memorabilia, Neve Ilan, Israel, one mile outside Jerusalem *(Emilio Morenatti/AP)*

Matthew Paul Miller, a.k.a." Matisyahu," an Orthodox reggae/hip-hop/rock "artist" from Pennsylvania, no longer sports a beard or Hasidic clothes *(Mario Anzuoni/Reuters)*

Russian-Jewish musician making a "joyful noise" with his bizarre hybrid instrument outside Jaffa Gate, Old City, Jerusalem *(Author's Collection)*

Holy Land Tattoo Parlor inside Old City (now Sam's Tattoo and Beauty Clinic, New Gate), offers tourists a "lasting memory" of their visit *(Author's Collection)*

McDonald's restaurant in Tiberias, located just steps away from the Sea of Galilee (visible in background) *(Photo Courtesy of Rebecca Storie)*

John Nelson Darby (1800-1882), Anglo-Irish, Spirit-led, Plymouth Brethren Bible teacher who pioneered pretribulational, premillennial interpretation of Scripture based on the "seventy weeks" of Daniel 9

Cyrus Ingerson Scofield (1843-1921), Confederate Civil War veteran; former US District Attorney for Kansas; converted drunk; Congregationalist pastor; incorporated Darby's notes in his 1909 Reference Bible

Clarence Larkin (1850-1921), mechanical engineer/architect, turned Baptist minister; spread Darby's discovery through his visual classic, *Dispensational Truth: God's Plan and Purpose in the Ages* (1919); regarded as the standard on premillennial dispensationalism (over 100 charts and illustrations)

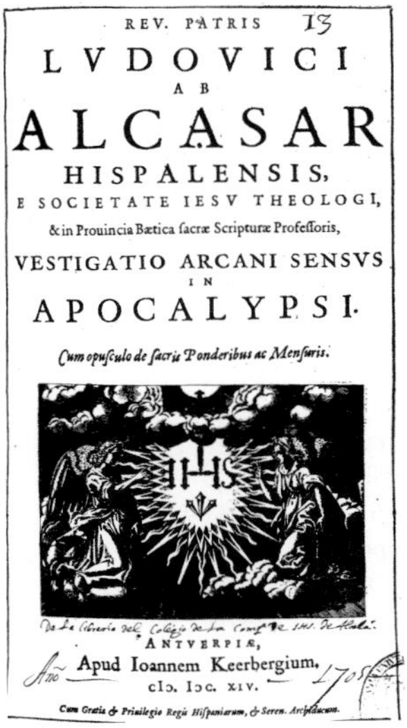

REV. PATRIS

LVDOVICI

AB

ALCASAR

HISPALENSIS,

E SOCIETATE IESV THEOLOGI,

& in Prouincia Bætica sacræ Scripturæ Professoris,

VESTIGATIO ARCANI SENSVS

IN

APOCALYPSI.

Cum opusculo de sacris Ponderibus ac Mensuris.

ANTVERPIÆ,

Apud Ioannem Keerbergium,

cIↃ. IↃC. XIV.

Cum Gratia & Priuilegio Regis Hispaniarum, & Seren. Archiducum.

Title page from the *Vestigatio* by Spanish Jesuit theologian Luis del Alcázar (1614); seminal heretical work on preterism positing that John's prophecies in Revelation 1-19 were fulfilled by first century, with Ancient Israel morphing into the Christian Church at fall of Jerusalem in 70 AD

Olive wood NIV "Bible" displayed in Garden Tomb gift shop, Jerusalem, near Gordon's Calvary; deletes *only* scriptural reference *to* Calvary, Luke 23:33 *(Author's Collection)*

A. B. Warner (1827-1915), godly, patriotic Christian; blessed several generations of Sunday School children; given unique posthumous military honor

Pope Francis (the first Jesuit pope) continues Rome's deceptive end-day rapprochement with Israel, visiting Auschwitz on July 16, 2016; for the record, Hitler and 90% of his SS thugs were Roman Catholic *(Reuters)*

The end of an era: September 30, 2016, state funeral at Mount Herzl national cemetery for Shimon Perez, the last living patriarch who was present with David Ben-Gurion at Israel's birth *(Baz Ratner/Reuters)*

"And don't forget about *me*!" *Moveon.org* donor, atheist billionaire George Soros, lurking in the shadows *(Reuters)*

Despite President Trump's landmark reforms, many are as nervous about *him* at the controls as Hitler's guests were of Mussolini (right of the Führer's personal pilot, Hans Baur) flying *them* back to Berlin. *(Ullstein Bild/Getty)*

Though providentially saving America from Hillary Clinton, "The Donald," seen here nine days after his inauguration on the telephone with Saudi King Salman (his *Jewish* son-in-law and top advisor Jared Kushner at hand), will NEVER be able to make the *ultimate* "deal"—a true and lasting Middle East peace (Haggai 2:7-9) without the Prince of Peace (John 15:5). Pray that the First Family gets born again. *(Ernst/Reuters)*

Atlantico, II Duce's prized stallion, provides a perfect, twofold illustration for God's people in these perilous times. In *his* last days he was never idle. After hauling tourists around Rome he finished his career by accepting *any* payload (like the hay in the picture). Christians likewise need to remain in *their* harnesses, *"paw[ing] in the valley..."* (Job 39:21) till we are called home prior to His renewed focus on Israel. Atlantico also reminds us of the white horses we will return upon. *(Geneva Daily Times)*

adds: "With the crossing of the canal, the Israeli high command had begun to think about the finish line. As General Tal put it at a meeting in the Pit on Thursday morning, October 18, the war-of-survival stage had ended for Israel. The IDF now had to determine where it wanted to be when the shooting stopped."[154]

On a related note, Israel's defense minister came close to missing the finish line altogether. Dayan had visited Bren's forward command post that first Thursday morning. When the antiquities aficionado later wandered off to scan the ground for ancient shards,[155] Adan cautioned the aide-de-camp, "Keep an eye on your boss. There may still be Egyptian soldiers around."[156] Suddenly, two Egyptian helicopters swooped down at treetop level dropping barrels of napalm, one hitting within sixty feet of where Moshe was standing! For some "unknown reason," the incendiaries failed to ignite. Both helicopters, however, *did* explode—Bren's indignant troops having blasted them to smithereens in an "unbelievable spectacle."[157]

ENCIRCLEMENT OF EGYPT'S THIRD ARMY

The apogee of Adan's five-day, trans-canal incursion was the expeditious flanking and encirclement of Egypt's Third Army Corps. His race against the clock anticipated the standard UN Security Council ploy of drafting "emergency" cease-fire resolutions whenever the Jews' enemies were on the ropes. Such last-minute posturing would enhance Israel's postwar negotiations, ensuring that a 600-sq.-mile enclave on the west bank more than offset Arab gains in Sinai.

While Sharon turned north in a failed bid to isolate Second Army at Ismailia, Adan (with Magen) hastened southwest, then southeast towards Suez City (the canal's terminus). The 162nd Division had three tactical goals. The first was to destroy anti-aircraft and surface-to-air missile batteries. (Thirty sites were promptly eliminated, facilitating a timely reengagement by the IAF.) The next priority was severing the arteries and junctions between Cairo and the canal to forge necessary lines of supply, communication, and evacuation (while denying them to the enemy). Bren's initial success was the defensive position at Tsach, astride the Havit-Sakranut axis. Further south, Sarag Road (Highway 12), which linked the capital to Suez City, was the linchpin to his largest task—slipping in between Egypt and her Third Army.

The burden of command was enormous. On October 21 (the eve of the final surge), Bren met with General Bar-Lev and his old Palmach commander, Yigal Allon: "Before he and Bar-Lev left, he gave me a pat on the shoulder and asked whether I was aware that the fate of the entire campaign rested to a large extent with me."[158]

At 10:00 p.m. that evening, Dayan was summoned to the Kirya where Meir told him that the UN Security Council would be voting on a ceasefire in five hours. Sadat's nerve had finally cracked two days earlier during a state visit by Soviet Premier Kosygin. The Russians relayed Egypt's "request" to the White House, whereupon Secretary of State Kissinger flew to Moscow the following day to formulate the proposal. Assad was understandably torqued by his ally's defection, Sadat having told his generals that "this was not a war for the Palestinians or for the other Arabs; it was for Egypt."[159] After three hours of debate, the diplomats in New York decreed that the ceasefire would go into effect on Monday, October 22, at 6:52 p.m. Israeli time.

Bren Adan had twelve hours to earn that pat on the shoulder. His original plan was to seal Highway 12 (halting the flow of enemy supplies), then sprint for the flat strip between the Geneifa Hills and the canal, deploying his armor along the east bank directly behind the 7th and 19th Egyptian Divisions stranded on the west side. The looming truce now forced him to divert his full energies to reaching Suez City. By nightfall, however, having met alternating sallies of enemy diehards firing their weapons, along with thousands of desperate men eager to surrender, the 162nd fell short of its mandate.

No worry; having stopped off at Tel Aviv on his way back from Moscow, Kissinger assured Meir: "You won't get violent protests from Washington if something happens during the night, while I'm flying. Nothing can happen in Washington until noon tomorrow." When her generals confirmed that they would need two or three extra days to destroy the enemy, Henry was even more amenable: "Two or three days? That's all? [wink-wink] Well, in Vietnam the ceasefire didn't go into effect at the exact time that was agreed on."[160] (Henry's philosophy on diplomacy was defined by his famous quote, "The illegal we do immediately; the unconstitutional takes a little longer.") Abraham Rabinovich writes, "He saw the importance of stopping the war, but not before Israel had advanced far enough to at least even the score with the Arabs strategically. On the other hand, it would not do to let the Israelis advance so far as to humiliate the Arabs."[161]

In any event, Egypt's own truce violations gave the "kitchen cabinet" ample justification to sanction the requisite extension.[162] Bren ultimately split the difference: "About an hour after dark the encirclement of the Third Army was complete."[163] The following morning, Israeli ships entered Adabiya Port, adding a blockade to the Third Army's predicament. Officially, the guns fell silent at 5:00 p.m. on that Wednesday, October 24. However, Sadat's army refused to give up, making a last futile effort on Friday to blast their way out.

Thus, to Israel's dismay, the war would end the way it began. GHQ's "last-minute, grab-what-you-can" order for Adan's weary men, *particularly* to "capture Suez City, if it does not become a Stalingrad situation,"[164] would drag for two more days (October 24-25), resulting in a decisive Egyptian victory. IDF casualties were shocking—80 killed or missing with 120 wounded.[165] Still, Israel's overall postwar position was strong. When the Security Council passed Resolution 340 on October 25, Israeli tanks were parked within sixty miles of Cairo.

With UN observers deployed, three matters required prompt action: 1) a POW exchange (8,300 Egyptians for 230 Israelis); 2) coordinates for the final ceasefire line; 3) the fate of Egypt's Third Army Corps (30,000 men). Adan comments on the dire straits of the Third Army:

> We knew that there were some two thousand casualties there as a result of our air strikes of the past few days. We had cut off their water and fuel pipelines. We had taken huge reservoirs of fuel and ammunition. They were besieged! Unquestionably, we held the power of life and death over the entire Third Army. That was a real bargaining card![166]

KILOMETER 101

Golda was initially against emergency aid for Egypt's beleaguered troops, insisting that Sadat taste the "full flavor of his defeat."[167] Kissinger recalled his own frustration at having failed to dissuade the angry senior: "My ultimate responsibility was as secretary of state of the United States, not as a psychiatrist to the government of Israel."[168] The impasse was ended when Egypt's humbled president agreed to direct Egyptian-Israeli talks as a *quid pro quo* for saving his army.

At 1:00 a.m. on October 28, disengagement talks began in the bitter cold on an inauspicious wooden table beneath a camouflage canopy stretched between four tanks at "Kilometer 101" (the IDF checkpoint on the Cairo-Suez Road, located 101 kilometers from Cairo). Major General Aharon Yariv represented Israel; Lieutenant General Abdel Ghani el-Gamasy spoke for Egypt. Emory University Professor Kenneth Stein writes: "The pending Egyptian-Israeli talks were unique in their countries' respective belligerent relationship: Egyptian and Israeli military officials were about to negotiate the separation of their forces without the United States or another party in a mediation role, and with the United Nations relegated to a mere gopher status."[169] Egyptian Foreign Ministry deputy Omar Surry, remarked: "No one understood the political significance of what we were doing."[170]

With discussions underway, UN staff manned all check points. A ceasefire was signed (in the tent) on November 11, 1973 (the 55th anniversary of the WWI armistice). Four days later, a POW swap was arranged. Other treaties resulted from Dr. Kissinger's famous shuttle diplomacy. The Sinai Separation of Forces Agreement was ratified at Kilometer 101 on January 18, 1974. The pact (Sinai I) decreed a juxtaposition of forces on both banks, with a UN Emergency Force stationed between (the latter costing Israel twelve miles of the eastern side). On May 31, 1974, Israeli and Syrian diplomats in Geneva reached the Agreement on Disengagement, legally ending the 1973 Arab-Israeli War. Under this belated pact, Israel returned to the Purple Line, accepting another UN mission. On June 5, 1975, the Suez Canal reopened. The Sinai Interim Agreement (Sinai II) was secured three months later. Finally, building on the 1976 Camp David Accords, Israel and Egypt signed their historic peace agreement in Washington, DC, on March 26, 1979. (There is still no peace treaty between Israel and Syria.) This concludes our "storybook ending" as reputedly played out by America's Quaker president and Jewish secretary of state.

THE *REST* OF THE STORY

As previously noted, the front-page headline of the *Honolulu Advertiser* of November 30, 1941—one full week *before* Japan's "sneak" attack on Pearl Harbor—read as follows: "Japanese May Strike Over Weekend"; a byline stated, "Hawaii Troops Alerted."[171] The "surprise" attack on October 6, 1973, was no less conspiratorial in origin.

On October 1, fewer than a dozen Egyptians knew that their latest "training exercise" would be the real thing by week's end. Two days later, General Ismail flew to Damascus to coordinate the invasion with Syria's minister of defense, General Mustafa Tlas. H-Hour was set for 2:05 p.m. on October 6.[172] Russia's consulates in Cairo and Damascus were duly notified (which explains the flight of Soviet dependents). However, when the emissaries cabled their coded reports to Moscow, the National Security Agency was listening.[173] "By October 4 the NSA knew beyond a shadow of a doubt that an attack on Israel would take place on the afternoon of October 6," Loftus and Aarons affirm. "According to several of our sources among the former intelligence officers, the Nixon White House ordered the NSA to sit on the information…To cover the Nixon White House from political fallout, word of the NSA's warning would be leaked to Israel—but only on the morning of the attack, a few hours before the Arab onslaught."[174]

THE JEW ROOM

In the early 1970s, Bruce Brill was an NSA "Special Arabic" analyst. On October 23, 1992, the *Jerusalem Post* ran an exposé by Brill titled, "One Man's Agony After The Fact." The whistleblower revealed: "I learned of the planned October 6, 1973, invasion of Israel by Syria and Egypt – 30 hours before the US notified Israel. Upper-echelon Agency personnel knew of the planned attack hours, if not days, prior to that. Not passing this vital information along in time resulted in the unnecessary death and maiming of thousands of young Israelis."[175]

As Loftus and Aarons relate, the moral ramifications were appalling! "Six years later, in 1973, the NSA got their payback for the *Liberty*, by waiting until the very last moment before telling Israel that the Arabs were planning a surprise attack on Yom Kippur…It was, the 'old spies' say, Nixon's way of teaching them a lesson."[176] Brill then gave a second arresting disclosure:

> The US intelligence community's anti-Israel policy has until now been successfully kept secret, even at the Agency itself, since the 'need to know' rule governing such policies is strictly applied only to select non-Jews. It was, therefore, quite by accident that I discovered the existence of chambers at NSA that are off-limits to Jews, US citizens with the highest security clearances, simply because they are Jews. Clearly, efforts toward Israel's demise are made here. These Agency inner sancta are so totally immune from any monitoring, that such unconstitutional goings on continue.[177]

According to Loftus and Aarons, the "chamber" in question is known as—the "Jew Room."[178]

"Bloodied In The Process"

The prevailing consensus among Washington insiders is that Richard Nixon had two motives for undermining Israel. The first was to curry favor with the Arabs (Saudi "oil pressure" being the obvious incentive).[179] The other was to weaken Soviet hegemony.[180] In May 1971, Secretary of State William Rogers, accompanied by Assistant Secretary of State Joseph Sisco, arrived in Cairo to discuss the stalemate. Herzog writes: "In their meeting with Sadat, Rogers and Sisco had implied that the United States would be prepared to do a deal at Israel's expense in return for the Egyptians doing a deal at the Soviet Union's expense."[181] To Israel's dismay, two years later, Nobel Peace laureate Dr. Henry Kissinger was poised to facilitate that "deal."

Reared in Nazi Germany, young "Heinz" was often harassed for being a Jew. According to the popular Paul Harvey story, "The Bully and The Boy," having taken beatings for years, one day (around age eleven) Kissinger discovered the art of *talking* his way out of trouble, setting the trajectory for his career. Of course, the future envoy would not have *had* a life, had his family not fled to America in 1938. But then, how quickly they forget! As later revealed on secret Oval Office tapes, after Mrs. Meir had requested US intervention for Soviet Jewry, Henry (his Anglicized, "non-Jewish" sounding name) callously remarked to President Nixon on March 1, 1973: "The emigration of Jews from the Soviet Union is not an objective of American foreign policy. And if they put Jews into gas chambers in the Soviet Union, it is not an American concern. Maybe a humanitarian concern."[182]

Henry Kissinger was the only man to serve (concurrently) as both US National Security Advisor and Secretary of State (appointed to the latter on September 22, 1973). However, America's top diplomat was hindered by two main flaws. While peerless in the geopolitical arena, Henry's naiveté in military matters[183] was surpassed only by his insatiable ego[184]—a deadly combination given Israel's tenuous security concerns. "Many of the American comments about Kissinger [from the intel community] are unprintable," Loftus and Aarons write. "The gist of the Israeli comments is that Kissinger's religious affiliation should be changed from 'Jewish' to 'self-promotion'...by 1973, few Israelis were prepared to believe anything he said."[185]

The definitive illustration of such distrust occurred during one of Kissinger's visits with Mrs. Meir. According to an American eyewitness, Henry attempted to clear the air: "First, I am an American; second, I am the secretary of state of the United States of America; third, I am a Jew." The prime minister replied, without missing a beat: "That's alright, sonny, we read from right to left."[186] (Though beyond Golda's grasp at the time, nearly all major cultures *west* of Golgotha write left-to-right, while those to the *east* are right-to-left, illustrating that *both* hemispheres, like the two thieves, point to the Cross of Christ. Likewise, in Acts 26:26, Paul reminds a Jewish king that *"this thing was not done in a corner,"* the Messiah's Resurrection having occurred at the junction of Europe, Asia, and Africa.)

Behind Meir's back, "sonny boy" devised and enacted a three-step plan to help Israel's enemies regain their manhood: 1) delay giving Tel Aviv adequate warning for the attack; 2) insist that Israel absorb the first strike while limiting mobilization; 3) hamper the emergency airlift. As Seymour Hersh confirms, this was no conspiracy theory:

> There was widespread rage inside the Israeli cabinet at the Nixon White House—aimed especially at Henry Kissinger—over what was correctly perceived in Israel as an American strategy of delaying the resupply in an attempt to let the Arabs win some territory, and some self-respect, and thus set up the possibility of serious land-for-peace bargaining.[187]

Heinz summarized his "battlefield stalemate" approach during a chilling conversation with Jim Schlesinger during the first weekend of the war: "The best result would be if Israel came out a little ahead but got bloodied in the process, and if the U.S. stayed clean."[188]

"CAIRO, DAMASCUS—POOF! *GONE!*"

America's foremost cerebral statesman was a consummate neophyte in military strategy. Loftus and Aarons state: "He just did not understand the drastic consequences of delaying mobilization, nor did he appreciate the logistical implications of a seven-day ammunition stock...The unwitting Kissinger, intent on letting the Jews bleed a little, had opened up an artery instead."[189] Unknown to the world, October 8, 1973, was a watershed in human history, as Dayan's catchword, "Temple," was also Israel's codeword for *nukes*.[190]

Concerning the go-for-broke counterattack in the Golan Heights, Rabinovich writes: "According to an account published abroad, the inner cabinet met on Monday, October 8, and decided to arm Israel's nuclear arsenal for fear the army might collapse."[191] Thirty years later, the Israeli press would confirm that Yisrael Tal told a secret forum in 1974 that the General Staff had proposed "extreme measures" against the Arabs.[192] Seymour Hersh adds in the *Samson Option*: "Sometime early in 1968, Dimona finally was ordered into full-scale production and began turning out four or five warheads a year—there were more than twenty-five bombs in the arsenal by the Yom Kippur War...."[193]

Thus, on Grandma Meir's order, "the nuclear missile launchers at Hirbat Zachariah, as many as were ready, would be made operational, along with eight specially marked F-4s that were on twenty-four-hour alert at Tel Nof, the air force base near Rehovot. The initial target list included the Egyptian and Syrian military headquarters near Cairo and Damascus."[194] As the director at Dimona, Dr. Shalheveth Freier phrased it: "If they push us into the sea, they will find out they have nothing to return to. Cairo, Damascus—poof! *Gone!*"[195]

While Israel was certainly prepared to go the "Sum of All Fears" route as a weapon of last resort, Hersh opines that her preferred objective was to apply political "blackmail" to the Soviets and Americans alike. On the former, "to urge their allies in Egypt and Syria to limit their offensive and not attempt to advance beyond the pre-1967 borders"; on the latter, to "force the United States to begin an immediate and massive resupply of the Israeli military."[196] Tel Aviv University Professor Eyal Zisser notes that various analysts explain the "premature standstill" of Syrian forces—just miles from the strategic Jordan River passages—was because "they were afraid Israel would use the nuclear weapons in its possession...."[197]

Herman F. Eilts, US ambassador to Egypt, recalls: "Henry threw in that there was concern that the Israelis might go nuclear. There had been intimations that if they didn't get military equipment, and quickly, they might go nuclear."[198] Columnist Jack Anderson wrote on March 10, 1980: "Locked in secret Pentagon files is startling evidence that Israel maneuvered dangerously near the edge of nuclear war after the 1973 Arab assault...This was the most compelling reason, according to the secret papers, that the United States rushed conventional weapons to Israel."[199] With America's commitment in place, Dayan's "Temple" weapons were put on "safety," freeing the IAF to launch its attack on Tuesday by dropping "normal" bombs on Damascus. The meager damage report was offset by the psychological benefit. (Israeli pilots would conduct 6,000 sorties on the Golan front.)

"HAS PRESIDENT NIXON GONE CRAZY?"

As truth is stranger than fiction, there is an incredible postscript to the Israeli "doomsday machine" scenario. When Golda decided to take Henry's advice to grab a few more kilometers of turf (despite the UN-imposed ceasefire), Brezhnev reacted by rattling *his* nuclear saber.

At 7:05 p.m. on October 24, Russian ambassador Anatoly Dobrynin phoned Kissinger to say that Moscow would support a joint US-Soviet peacekeeping force in the region *if* the UN's non-aligned members were to sanction one. He rang back to mention that his government was considering sponsoring such a resolution; Dobrynin then called Henry a third time at 9:35 p.m. to read a "very urgent" cable he had just received from Brezhnev for the American president. Having "invited" Nixon to help him "compel observance of the ceasefire without delay" (i.e., with armed troops), the Russian leader added, "I will say it straight that if you find it impossible to act jointly with us in this matter, we should be faced with the necessity urgently to consider the question of taking appropriate steps unilaterally."[200]

According to biographer Walter Isaacson, "Kissinger had a chance to discuss the issue with Nixon directly, but decided not to…Nixon's mood [distraught over impeachment talk] made it unwise to present him with a serious foreign policy matter."[201] Deputy National Security Advisor William Quandt said, "Kissinger quickly relayed the message to [White House chief of staff, Alexander] Haig for Nixon."[202] Haig affirms that the president rejected the Brezhnev demarche.[203] Leaving the volatile situation to his advisors, Nixon reputedly "retired" for the evening. In his other role as National Security Advisor, Henry convened an ad hoc session of the National Security Council (NSC) and the Washington Special Actions Group (WSAG) in the White House Situation Room. Getting a consensus near midnight, he had JCS Chairman Admiral Thomas Moorer order the military to DEFCON 3 (Defense Condition)—the highest stage of peacetime readiness.[204]

Dr. Asaf Siniver of Birmingham University explains *why* Henry was running the show: "There are multiple sources suggesting that the president was intoxicated during this episode and was in no condition to chair this crucial meeting…According to Quandt, Nixon was so unstable that Defense Secretary Schlesinger ordered the military to ignore any presidential orders which might come during that night…."[205] Treasury Secretary George Shultz attributed Nixon's clinical paranoia to a greater, overall combination of single-malt Scotch, Seconal, Dilantin, and amphetamines.[206]

To say that the president was momentarily distracted by other matters would be an understatement. "For the duration of the war, Nixon was preoccupied with Watergate," Isaacson states.[207] In the now-famous "Saturday Night Massacre" (just four days earlier), Nixon fired Archibald Cox, abolished the office of special prosecutor, and accepted the resignations of Attorney General Elliot Richardson and Deputy Attorney General William Ruckelshaus. Haig phoned Henry in Moscow, informing him—"All H--l has broken loose!"[208]

Ironically, while *Nixon* was musing (as early as 1970) as to whether *Henry* was the one needing "psychiatric care,"[209] an article in the October 27, 1973, *Washington Star* asked: "Has President Nixon Gone Crazy?" Three days after the Yom Kippur War ended, syndicated columnist Carl Rowan rattled his readers by positing, "[I]n the face of a vote to impeach he might try, as 'commander-in-chief,' to use military forces to keep himself in power."[210]

On August 27, 1974, the *Washington Post* revealed that Schlesinger had placed a second, unparalleled kibosh on Nixon's executive authority: "Defense Secretary James Schlesinger requested a tight watch in the military chain of command to ensure that no extraordinary orders went out from the White House during the period of uncertainty (and) that no commanders of any forces should carry out orders which came from the White House, or elsewhere, outside the normal military channels."[211] According to *New York Times* bestselling author Anthony Summers, the word on Pennsylvania Avenue was that the paranoid president might actually call the USMC to save him! As Schlesinger wrote: "The last thing I wanted was to have the marines ordered to the White House and then have to bring the Army to confront the marines. It would have been a bloody mess...."[212] (When a research assistant for this author contacted the Richard Nixon Presidential Library and Museum for information on these widespread allegations, they replied: "We were not able to locate any documents or any other evidence to verify these scenarios."[213])

The defining illustration of what happens to a man's brain when he messes with Israel is revealed in the following excerpt from Summers' book, *The Arrogance of Power: The Secret World of Richard Nixon*:

> His [Schlesinger's] attention had been drawn to the president's state of mind by a phone call a few months earlier from Joseph Laitin, the Public Affairs spokesman of the Office of Management and Budget, based in the Executive Office Building, just across from the White House. In an interview with the author, Laitin vividly recalled the encounter with Nixon in the spring of 1974 that prompted him to call Schlesinger. 'I was on my way over to the West Wing of the White House to see Treasury Secretary Shultz,' Laitin said. 'I'd reached the basement, near the Situation Room. And just as I was about to ascend the stairway, a guy came running down the stairs two steps at a time. He had a frantic look on his face, wild-eyed, like a madman. And he bowled me over, so I kind of lost my balance. And before I could pick myself up, six athletic-looking young men leapt over me, pursuing him. I suddenly realized that they were Secret Service agents, that I'd been knocked over by the President of the United States.' Laitin was so shocked at Nixon's appearance that he postponed the meeting with Shultz and returned to his office.[214]

"A FATE OF BIBLICAL PROPORTIONS"

On Sunday morning, October 14 (the day after Nickel Grass began), Nixon made a telling statement to Kissinger. "We have to squeeze the Israelis when this is over, and the Russians have got to know it. We have to squeeze them [g-----n] hard"[215] (Exodus 20:7). For the sin of allowing Jacob's bleeding on his watch, Dick Nixon would become the only president in history to be *squeezed* out of office (just missing "*Jail* to the Chief")—joining his second-in-command, Spiro *"Nolo contendere"* Agnew as the only vice president forced to resign as well.

But for the mercy of God, America's nightmare could have been worse. In his memoir, *Inner Circles*, General Haig devotes an entire chapter to the possibility of an unprecedented "double impeachment" opening the door to what special White House Counsel J. Fred Buzhardt described as a "coup d'état with the Legislative Branch taking over the Executive Branch under the cover of the Constitution. The Speaker of the House [a Democrat] would become President."[216] As portrayed in Oliver Stone's bizarre 1995 film, *Nixon*, the definitive scene of the Nixonian denouement occurs in the Lincoln Sitting Room the night before the president's resignation. In their farewell meeting, Kissinger laments to his outgoing boss, "To be undone by a third-rate burglary is a fate of biblical proportions." (Ironically, Henry actually did make this statement, though at a later date.[217])

When the two were about to part company the condemned chief executive stopped Henry in his tracks with a sudden last request. "Nixon then asked his secretary of state to kneel and pray with him. It was, for Kissinger, an awkward request; even as a child, back when he was religiously inclined, prayers did not involve kneeling. Nevertheless, tentatively bending one knee, then the other, he knelt down and prayed with the president."[218] With a 1972 poll of Hugh Hefner's harlots naming Heinz as their top choice for a date (no less believable than Golda's "mattress" moniker), Isaacson's follow-up rings more insightfully: "Given the surreal and tragic circumstances, prayer seemed to Kissinger to be as appropriate as anything. His only problem was that no prayers came into his head at that moment, only what he later described as 'a deep sense of awe which seemed its own meaning.'"[219] Back in his office, his shirt drenched with sweat, Kissinger unloaded to Brent Scowcroft: "Nothing I have been through has ever been so traumatic."[220] (The reader is left to conjecture as to the greater cause for Henry's anguish of soul—watching the former Quaker quake or finding *himself* quaking on his *own* knees.)

ISRAEL'S "TAKE-CHARGE GUY"

Despite Nixon's rabid anti-Semitism (confirmed on his own secret audio recordings), the disgraced former president once said: "Ch---t, if it weren't for me, there wouldn't be any Israel. They know that in Israel."[221] Though the Nixon administration believed its "better-late-than-never" airlift would help Israel persevere, the munitions scarcity grew more ominous with each 24-hour delay. This *would* have kept the Samson Option alive were it not for the providential intervention of the man John Loftus calls "The Real Hero of Yom Kippur."

While President Reagan was having surgery after being shot on March 30, 1981, Secretary of State Haig made a well-intended, though constitutionally inaccurate, remark to the press: "As of now, I'm in control here, pending the return of the vice president." In his memoirs, Haig posits that his assertive declaration, interpreted in context with his other statement—"There are absolutely no alert measures that are necessary at this time"—was spoken to assure the Soviets that they were not suspected in the plot.[222] Though the retired four-star general was never able to outlive those fourteen dramatic words, few Americans realize that the State of Israel was able to survive the Yom Kippur War (specifically, Kissinger's near-fatal "logistical" delays) largely due to the same man exercising that same take-charge spirit.

Within minutes of the October 6 attack—Henry having taken a hegira to his thirty-fifth-floor suite at the Waldorf Astoria—Nixon's combat veteran (Distinguished Service Cross, Defense Distinguished Service Medal, Army Distinguished Service Medal, Silver Star, Legion of Merit, Distinguished Flying Cross, Bronze Star, Purple Heart, etc.) chief of staff made a bold flanking maneuver around the secretary of state. (Isaacson's kid-glove biography, *Kissinger*, describes Nixon's future prayer partner as being "jolted awake" by the news.[223]) Loftus and Aarons write: "On Saturday, October 6, Alexander Haig told Israeli intelligence that there was a new weapon that could stop the Arab tank onslaught. If they could get a team to the United States, he would give it to them."[224] (Haig—a lifetime Roman Catholic and from *Philadelphia*, no less—represents another *key* providential exception to the rule of Rome's historical anti-Semitism.)

While Mr. Loftus' detractors will often challenge his assertions based on their anonymous nature, on *this* occasion the source was John himself! On that Saturday evening in 1974, *Lieutenant* Loftus just happened to be the assigned duty officer on hand at the 5th Battalion headquarters of the Infantry Officer Candidate School in Fort Benning, Georgia (where the US Army trains its own officers as well as those of allied nations). On the opening night of the war, John's commanding officer gave him a highly sensitive order:

> A CIA plane is en route from Israel with about 40 Israeli field-grade commanders. They will arrive after midnight. You are to hide them in one of the empty barracks. You will give them an orientation on the TOW missile system and answer any questions they have. The Israelis will be here…for training, while we ship every TOW we have over there. If the press calls and asks if we are supplying Israel with a classified weapon, you are neither to confirm or deny."[225]

Developed in 1970, the BGM-71 is a highly sophisticated, made-in-America, Anti-Tank Guided Weapon (ATGW), the acronym TOW standing for tube-launched, optically tracked, and wire-guided. It had only been shared with Britain and West Germany. In flight, the winged missile unreels (tows) two miles of thin cable connected to a steering telescope. Fitted with Command to Line of Sight guidance (CLOS), the gunner simply has to keep the cross-hairs of his sight on the target until the missile impacts. The "kill ratio" for the TOW is roughly 97%.

The Israelis arrived in the middle of the night, looking, as Loftus recalls, more like hippies than military officers (long hair, mustaches, mod-style civilian clothes, etc.).[226] This firsthand account mirrors Sachar's reference to the IDF's "erosion of discipline since 1967, which was revealed most flagrantly during the alert called only hours before the outbreak of the Yom Kippur War…Soldiers went into action improperly dressed."[227] While the officers spent the next week training under the future co-author of *The Secret War Against The Jews*, General Haig was busy commandeering every available TOW in the US and Europe and rushing them to Israel via Galaxy cargo planes.

By October 14, John's "grads" were back in Israel, deployed along the southern front with 4,000 of Al's TOWs—*just in time to impact the decisive Battle of the Sinai.* "The opening of the final Egyptian assault on Israel turned into a rout as the Arabs' tank force was cut to ribbons."[228] Because Tel Aviv had kept Haig's unsanctioned "tourniquet" a military secret, Cairo and Moscow were dumbfounded at such unanticipated losses. At first they assumed the tanks were destroyed from the air; however, later action reports confirmed that they were hit on the side, which is consistent with BGM-71 damage.[229]

According to historian Simon Dunstan, the Israelis were not the only ones who kept the covert airlift under wraps: "Israeli infantry knocked out many Egyptian tanks with American-supplied TOW missiles (although the US has always maintained that no TOW missiles were supplied to Israel before the last days of the war)."[230] In a recently declassified October 15, 1973, State Department Action Memorandum itemizing Israel's refurbishment "wish list," Politico-Military Bureau Affairs director Seymour Weiss distinctly informs Henry: "A number of TOW missiles and launchers has already been delivered." And, the TOWs already *in* Israel are clearly distinguished from the "16,000 LAW's [Light Anti-tank Weapon] now in the airlift system en route to Israel."[231] While some would deny the TOWs' participation, much less their effectiveness, in the Battle of the Sinai, the eminent British military academic, Major Edgar O'Ballance (author of over forty books) writes in *No Victor, No Vanquished*:

> On the fourteenth the Israelis had their mechanised infantry mortars, and antitank weapons forward with their leading tanks...The Israelis denied they had TOWs at this stage, but later General Sharon admitted his division had been issued them the previous day, the thirteenth, when he had taught his men to use them. Only four hours practice was required to attain reasonable proficiency in their use...It is now clear that the Israelis had ample numbers of the TOW and used them. In fact, they used and relied upon their missiles far more than they cared to admit. Heikal [Egyptian historian] writes that the 'accurate fire from a variety of French SS antitank missiles, and also from newly arrived TOW missiles...stopped the Egyptian armour about twelve to fifteen kilometres from its starting point'....

> Later I discussed this battle at length with General Ismail...As General Ismail anticipated, on the morning of the fifteenth the Israelis attacked...and the Great Tank Battle, or rather series of battles, continued...The Israelis claim that by the seventeenth they had destroyed another 100 Egyptian tanks, and there was no doubt that they had suddenly become plentifully equipped with U.S. TOWs, which took a heavy toll.[232]

At the end of the day (quite literally), the timing of Haig's feat cannot be emphasized enough. Loftus and Aarons conclude:

> The American arms authorized by Kissinger had arrived too late to help with the defense of the pass [Mitla]. In fact, before the first official U.S. airlift had even started to unload weapons on Sunday, October 14, the crucial defensive battle in the Sinai was all but over. It is no coincidence that the Israelis put their atomic bombs back in to storage on October 14, the day the TOWs were first tried out in Israel.[233]

The TOW's ultimate role notwithstanding, General Haig's selfless undertaking undoubtedly contributed to an expedient psychological stimulus. As Major O'Ballance relates: "The Israelis were convinced that they had a won a great armoured battle against the Egyptians. Israeli morale rose."[234] The man branded by the press as a "power-hungry war-monger" never even hinted at the clandestine procurement in his memoirs, naming *Nixon* as the one who "had saved Israel."[235] Wherever else he may have erred in his long career, on that second week in October 1973, Al Haig was *Israel's* "take-charge guy."

AFTERSHOCKS

Proverbs 30:33 says, *"Surely...the wringing forth of the nose bringeth forth blood."* Enshrined as "a war of fathers and sons," Israel lost 2,500 soldiers killed and over 3,000 wounded in eighteen days of fighting. The tiny nation drew little consolation in knowing that Egyptian and Syrian deaths were 7,700 and 3,500, respectively. The economic cost of the war has been estimated as high as $7 billion—the equivalent of Israel's Gross National Product for an entire year.

The "win" was a classic Pyrrhic victory. While the Arabs regained their pride, the Jews lost a sizable measure of theirs. With their head of state known for her snide remark, "Don't be so humble, you're not that great," the *politicians* were humbled by Nasser; the *intelligence* by Marwan; the *generals* by Shazly; the *pilots* by SAMs; and the *tankers* by Saggers. Her perceived invincibility shattered, Israel would never be the same. The transition was eerily marked on November 18 when David Ben-Gurion suffered a cerebral hemorrhage at his desert kibbutz of Sde Boker. As he lay dying in Tel Aviv's Sheba Medical Center, his grandson, Alon, a paratrooper in the war, was hospitalized as well, being treated for shrapnel wounds.[236] The veritable "Father of the Nation" passed away on December 1, 1973, at the age of eighty-seven. The government honored Ben Gurion's request to be interred in his beloved Negev (rather than in Jerusalem like Israel's other leaders).

Several, however, were not as "fortunate," having to *live* to face the repercussions of their deeds. Dr. Shimon Agranat, the American-born president of Israel's Supreme Court, was appointed to chair a national investigation of the intel failures that precipitated the war. On April 2, 1974, the Agranat Commission concluded its inquiry. AMAN director Major General Eli Zeira, was dubbed the main "scapegoat" for the October 6 fiasco. He and three of his key deputies were promptly sent "into the wilderness" (Leviticus 16:10). Dado Elazar and Shmuel Gonen lost their posts as well. Outraged by the whitewash, the public demanded Golda's hide. The illogical acquittal of Israel's *defense* minister was also resented. Meir, one of twenty-four signatories on the Declaration of Independence, duly "retired" nine days later, Dayan bowing out (with the rest of the Labor government) on June 3, 1974.

Raviv and Melman write: "Precisely how the Israeli intelligence bureaucracy handled – or mishandled – the signals of war remains a mystery, with retired officials still vehemently defending their honor."[237] In true "Spy vs. Spy" fashion, Zeira spent the rest of his days accosting Zamir over the credibility of his "too-good-to-be true" walk-in recruit. (As late as 2013, the two octogenarian intel legends traded barbs at a Tel Aviv conference marking the 40th anniversary of the surprise attack.) Known as the "Marwan Affair," many now believe that the "Angel" was, in fact, a *fallen* angel—a double agent planted by Egypt to feed Israel false info, culminating in the Concept (more specifically, the suppression of its cancelation). After all, given

Marwan's proven access to Cairo's inner sanctum, how could he *not* have known about Nasser's altered policy *long* before October 4?[238]

In a dramatic reversal of fortune—revisiting the "Hill of Evil Counsel"—having placed all of her eggs in one basket, the explanation for Israel's "intelligence failure" was prerecorded by her greatest warrior king in the first verse of the first Psalm of the Hebrew Scriptures: *"Blessed is the man that walketh not in the counsel of the ungodly...."* In December 2002, Ahron Bregman, an Israeli writer in London, put to rest one of the war's most enduring mysteries, unmasking Dr. Marwan (a billionaire industrialist by then) as the "In-law" of Mossad fame. Around 1:00 p.m. on June 27, 2007, the Angel "fell" to his death from the fifth floor window of his London flat in Carlton House Terrace.

As usual, the war's guiltiest parties got away scot-free. As early as summer 1973, the US petroleum industry was apprised that trouble was brewing in the Middle East. On August 27, Saudi Oil Minister Ahmed Yamani "sounded a warning" to Aramco that a two-million-barrel-per-day reduction was likely.[239] Beltway cronies would be caught talking out of both sides of their mouths. While Quandt insisted that "Pro-Arab groups and oil companies played no role in Nixon's decisions to press Israel to accept a cease-fire on October 12 or to save the Third Army Corps," the former Deputy Security Advisor was *also* careful to list, as his second priority after keeping Israel from being "driven to desperation," that "Sadat should not be humiliated."[240]

As former Lieutenant Loftus reveals, the full extent of Aramco's acquiescence was nothing short of treason!

> To implement the embargo, the company had to act against the interests of the U.S. government, including cutting off all oil supplies to the military. As usual, profit triumphed over principle and Aramco cut off oil to the U.S. Navy. Washington actually had to turn to London to ask if it could supply the Sixth Fleet....[241]

QUE SERA, SERA

According to Jewish tradition (Colossians 2:8), three books are opened in Heaven on Rosh Hashanah, the start of the Jewish New Year: 1) for the completely righteous; 2) for the completely wicked; and, 3) for those stuck in between. On that solemn day, the names of the righteous are inscribed in the "Book of Life," the wicked are logged in the "Book of Death," with the fate of the rest (the majority) suspended until Yom Kippur. Those who "turn over" enough "new leaves" during the intervening "Ten Days of Penitence" are sealed in the "Book of Life"; the ones who don't, *well*—you know where *their* names go…

Thus, the timing of the October 6 invasion was wrought with heavy liturgical overtones. On Yom Kippur eve, with war looming in the air, a restless Dado Elazar left his generals with the customary holiday greeting: "May you be well inscribed in the Book of Life."[242] Arnold Sherman entitled his eyewitness account of the war, *When God Judged and Men Died.* The following *piyyut* ("liturgical poem"), *Unetanah Tokef* ("We shall ascribe holiness to this day"), is recited on Rosh Hashanah and Yom Kippur to remind the candidates of the contrasting sets of possibilities awaiting them in the coming year:

> On Rosh Hashana their decree is inscribed,
> and on Yom Kippur it is sealed.
> How many shall pass away, and how many shall be created;
> Who shall live, and who shall die;
> Who shall come to his timely end, and who to an untimely end;
> Who shall perish by fire, and who by water;
> Who by the sword, and who by the beast;
> Who by hunger, and who by thirst;
> Who by earthquake, and who by the plague;
> Who by strangling, and who by stoning;
> Who shall be at rest, and who shall wander about;
> Who shall have serenity, and who shall be confused;
> Who shall be tranquil, and who shall be tormented;
> Who shall become poor, and who shall become wealthy;
> Who shall be brought to a low state, and who shall be uplifted….[243]

With all due respect, this Jewish version of "Que Sera, Sera" was not taken from the Tanakh. Rather, its legendary composition is generally attributed to a rabbi, Amnon of Mayence (Maintz).[244] Over twenty-six centuries before Amnon was born, Moses conveyed the Lord's personal warning to Israel regarding the use of *any* religious authority apart from inspired Scripture: *"Ye shall not add unto the word which I command you, neither shall ye diminish ought from it, that ye may keep the commands of the LORD your God which I command you."* (Deuteronomy 4:2)

In the third book of the Torah, Moses recorded God's *precise* instructions for the Day of Atonement. It has *nothing* to do with books, repentance, or incantations, while it has *everything* to do with the vicarious sacrifice of an innocent victim! *"Also on the tenth day of this seventh month there shall be a day of atonement: it shall be an holy convocation unto you; and ye shall afflict your souls, and offer an offering made by fire unto the LORD."* (Leviticus 23:27)

With *Kissinger's* "bloodletting" to begin on Yom Kippur, the Jewish diplomat could not have chosen a more malapropos metaphor—*"for it is the* BLOOD *that maketh an atonement for the soul."* (Leviticus 17:11) About the only resemblance to the biblical Day of Atonement in the rabbinical aberration is the concept of a ten-day grace period. The Hebrew word for *atonement* means a "covering," as in a *temporary*, year-to-year "covering" of the nation's transgressions—*"For it is not possible that the blood of bulls and of goats should take away sins."* (Hebrews 10:4)

A Shocking Perspective

While composing the current chapter, this author engaged a highly regarded American-born Israeli political scientist (who also regards himself as a religious Jew) on the inseparable scriptural theme of mankind's innate sinfulness (Genesis 5:1-3, 6:5; Job 14:4; Psalm 14:1-3; 51:5; 58:3; Isaiah 64:6) and the divine *sine qua non* of propitiation by blood (Genesis 3:21; 4:4; 8:20; 15:9-10; 17:10-11, 23; 22:13; Exodus 12:13; Leviticus 4:27-31; 16:14, Hebrews 9:22, et al.). His response from Jerusalem follows:

> Bill…You surely know that Jews do not believe they are born in sin. The Jewish sages say we are born with a good inclination and bad inclination, and that we should use the bad inclination for good ends. The Zohar speaks of egoism and altruism, and that we need to overcome the former for the sake of the latter. But the Rabbis are very commonsensical about the "bad inclination," because that may be one reason why the Creation Narrative ends with "very good." Egoism is an essential part of creation; the question is what is done

with it. On the issue of blood sacrifices, Jews are very wary about blood, and there is a question about such sacrifices in connection with the yet to be constructed Third Temple, but I am not qualified to address this subject.

In a follow-up email, the religious egghead added:

> Jews don't believe in sin per se. They regard sin as a mistake or an error. This is also the case of idolatry which Onkelos translates as a mistake, and no translation of the Bible equals that of Onkelos, according to the Talmud. Perhaps this is why Jews, according to Nietzsche, brought reason to mankind, and why Jewish monotheism is so cheerful as well as the source of science (although Whitehead, my favorite modern philosopher might disagree). In any event, one must be careful about reading any translation of the Bible, of which only Jews learned in the Hebrew alphanumeric alphabet can have an adequate understanding. For this purpose, allow me to recommend Yitzchak Ginsburgh (The Hebrew Letters), a rabbi conversant in quantum mechanics and general relativity. Also, there is the polymath Rabbi David Toledano, who is also learned in neurology, psychology and Kabbalah, and perhaps has no equal. So far as I know, none of these rabbis discourse on 'sin'. Best.

Given the Bible's supernatural content, the greatest Jewish "sage" of the first century "emailed" the following *inspired* warning to his Gentile converts at the Church of Colossi: *"Beware lest any man spoil you through* PHILOSOPHY *and* VAIN DECEIT, *after the* TRADITION OF MEN, *after the* RUDIMENTS OF THE WORLD, *and not after* CHRIST.*"* (Colossians 2:8) The former "Saul of Tarsus" likewise cautioned a young pastor: *"O Timothy, keep that which is committed to thy trust, avoiding profane and vain babblings, and oppositions of* SCIENCE FALSELY SO CALLED.*"* (I Timothy 6:20)

Concerning that amazing concession that "Jews are very wary of blood," the word "blood" is repeatedly used in the Tanakh—eighty-eight times in the book of Leviticus alone. For all the Jews' focus on the Kotel, do you suppose any of them have a clue as to how *much* blood flowed around the Temple Mount in Israel's heyday? According to I Kings 8:63, *"And Solomon offered a sacrifice of peace-offerings, which he offered unto the LORD, two and twenty thousand oxen, and an hundred and twenty thousand sheep."* Veterinarians tell us that the amount of blood in all animals is 9% of its live body weight. Based on standard blood volume charts, a sheep has 60 ml/kg and a cow 55 ml/kg. Thus, a sheep weighing 150 lbs. will have 1.268 gallons of blood and a 1,500 lb. ox will have about 9.9 gallons.

Now if this author's "polymath" is correct, the amount of blood in Solomon's sacrifice would equal about 369,960 gallons. To gain some perspective, a 48-foot-long commercial tanker truck holds roughly 9,000 gallons of fuel. The total quantity of blood at I Kings 8:63 would fill forty-two of these vehicles. Parked bumper-to-bumper, the caravan would stretch for over *half a mile*. And that is just for *one* sacrifice. Little wonder that the nation of Israel required an entire tribe just to keep the blood flowing! In conclusion, the reason why Jews are "wary" about blood must undoubtedly relate to their ancestors' blood-curdling cry before Pontius Pilate: *"His* BLOOD *be on us, and on our children."* (Matthew 27:25) And when He returns, the crimson flow will reach *"even unto the horse bridles...."* (Revelation 14:20)

A HUMBLE SYNOPSIS

In contrast to all that "babbling" from Israel, the author received a different email from a humble Lebanese Christian, born amidst the shelling of the 1982 Lebanon War, who pastors a small Arabic-speaking Baptist Church in Montreal, Canada. As the *professor's* profile was prerecorded in II Timothy 3:7, *"Ever learning, and never able to come to the knowledge of the truth,"* the *preacher's* perspective bears powerful witness to the prayer of Jesus Christ in Matthew 11:25, *"I thank thee, O Father, Lord of heaven and earth, because thou hast hid these things from the wise and prudent, and hast revealed them unto babes."*

Without the aid of a single work on general relativity, quantum mechanics, philosophy, neurology, psychology, polymath, the Hebrew alphanumeric alphabet, or the Kabbalah, the King James Bible believer was able to conceptualize 2,000 years of anti-Semitism in one succinct statement: "Jesus Christ is the scapegoat of Israel. He bore the sins of Israel. Israel rejects that truth. Therefore Israel has become the scapegoat of the Gentiles!" And, as Jews routinely dismiss the Christian doctrine of Christ's Son-ship (citing Exodus 4:22), the man of God added in his own follow-up email: "Both are sons of God. If Israel won't have the

Son of God bare the sins of the world, it (the next son of God in line) will have to bear them. 'His blood be on US'...and the rest is history."

THE FINAL WORD ON YOM KIPPUR

The fact that Israel was *blindsided* (i.e., "brought to a low state") on the uncanny date of Yom Kippur constituted a major wake-up call that her people were celebrating their Old Testament holy day in spiritual *blindness* (Romans 11:25), pursuing a manmade ritual, void of a blood sacrifice, away from the Temple Mount—and, most importantly of all—two thousand years after their *divine* Messiah had already offered up His *own* body and blood as the *permanent* sacrifice for man's sin (Genesis 22:8; Acts 20:28; Hebrews 10:11-14). Until the Jews acknowledge Jesus Christ as the Son of God, they will *continue* to bleed—as they have been doing so for some 2,000 years—"FOR IT IS THE BLOOD THAT MAKETH AN ATONEMENT FOR THE SOUL." (Leviticus 17:11)

"IT IS FINISHED."
(John 19:30)

18

Fightings Without, Fears Within

"And I will bring again the captivity of my people of Israel...And I will plant them upon their land, and they shall no more be pulled up out of their land which I have given them, saith the LORD thy God."
(Amos 9:14-15)

"Throughout the Middle East, we seek a stable and enduring settlement. We've not defined what this means...Nevertheless, we believe territorial compromise is essential for peace."
(President Bush, Madrid, October 1991)

"For Gaza shall be forsaken...."
(Zephaniah 2:4)

"They have said, Come, and let us cut them off from being a nation; that the name of Israel may be no more in remembrance...So persecute them with thy tempest, and make them afraid with thy storm."
(Psalm 83:4, 15)

AN ARTICLE IN the *Jerusalem Post* commemorating the fortieth anniversary of the Yom Kippur War stated: "Forty years on, the war that cost 2,522 Israeli fatalities, traumatized a generation and profoundly impacted the Jewish state's society, politics, economy and psyche, refuses to go away."[1] While no Arab coalition has invaded Israel since that tent at Kilometer 101 was struck (i.e., Samson Option), a different form of bloodletting has defined the ensuing four decades. Faced by the growing potential of "oppressed" Palestinian terrorists at home inciting her nuclear neighbors to Jihad, Israel would enter the 21st century under the very conditions her ancestors had inflicted upon the Apostle Paul 2,000 years before—*"but we were troubled on every side; without were fightings, within were fears."* (II Corinthians 7:5)

KIRYAT SHMONA (1974)

Israel's new "fears within" were felt on April 11, 1974 (five months to the ceasefire date). As Mrs. Meir was announcing her resignation in Tel Aviv, eighteen civilians—over half of them women and children—were being *hacked* to death in their apartment building in the northern Galilee town of Kiryat Shmona. Another fifteen were wounded.

The carnage was inflicted by three members of the Popular Front for the Liberation of Palestine (PFLP) who slipped into Israel from Lebanon. The Muslim killers originally entered the Janusz Korczak Middle School but found the place empty due to the Passover holiday. When Israeli soldiers arrived at the housing project, the cowards blew themselves up. After another twenty-two children and four adults were slain on May 15 in a second school shooting in Ma'alot, the PLO was "rewarded" with UN observer status on November 22, 1974.

UNGA RESOLUTION 3379 (1975)

On November 10, 1975—the 37th anniversary of Kristallnact—United Nations General Assembly Resolution 3379, adopted by a vote of 72 to 35 (with 32 abstentions), concluded that "Zionism is a form of racism and racial discrimination."

Standing at the podium, Israel's ambassador to the United Nations (and future president), Chaim Herzog, tore the infamous document to shreds. Daniel Patrick Moynihan, Herzog's American diplomatic counterpart, labeled it *another* "date which will live in infamy." (The resolution would require sixteen years to be revoked.)

OPERATION THUNDERBOLT (1976)

The nation's "fightings without" commenced 2,500 miles away. On June 27, 1976, an Air France Airbus, en route from Tel Aviv to Paris, was seized in Athens by a German couple and two PFLP members The flight crew and 256 passengers were flown to Entebbe via a refueling stop in Libya. Uganda's genocidal, syphilis-infected (flesh-eating?) dictator, Idi Amin (a.k.a. "Big Daddy"), arrived by helicopter with his eight-year-old son to welcome the criminals to his African sanctuary (described by a US official as "racist, erratic, unpredictable, brutal, inept, bellicose, irrational, ridiculous, and militaristic"[2]).

The dazed travelers were taken to the old terminal building of the Entebbe International Airport. The hijackers (joined by six embedded Palestinians) moved the Israelis to a separate room where Amin taunted them by waving and shouting: "Shalom, Shalom." When a young mother addressed Idi as "Mr. President," the meshuggener growled: "I am His Excellency, Field Marshal Doctor Idi Amin Dada, appointed by God Almighty to be your savior."[3] Over the next two days, the 148 Gentiles on hand were "selected" for release, revisiting scenes of the Shoah. The remaining 108 Jews (plus the twelve-member crew) were detained as bargaining chips to eventuate the release of 53 Palestinians held in Israel and elsewhere. The captors also threatened to execute the hostages one by one if their demands were not met.

The UN remained mute through the crisis. Thus, after evaluating several options, Golda's successor, Yitzhak Rabin, approved a daring rescue mission by the elite reconnaissance unit, Sayeret Matkal. In the providence of God (here we go *again*, folks), the Mossad was able to obtain architectural blueprints of the disused terminal, as it just so happened that the structure was built by an Israeli firm when Kampala had diplomatic relations with Tel Aviv. On the uncanny date of July 4, 1976, four 70-ton IAF Hercules C-130H propjets ended their seven-hour, storm-tossed flight, landing 100 commandos and 200 support troops in Entebbe around 1:00 a.m. local time. (The armada included an escort of F-4 Phantoms and two Boeing 707s, one serving as a forward command post, the other as an airborne hospital.) As no Israeli had ever landed a C-130 in the dark, Brigadier General Dan Shomron (architect and commander of "Operation Thunderbolt"), made a perfect touchdown on a fully lit runway, having timed his arrival with the refueling stop of a British Airways airliner.

As depicted in the 1977 made-for-TV film, *Raid on Entebbe*, the first vehicle out of the lead Hippo (followed by two Land Rovers) was a black Mercedes limousine configured to resemble Amin's staff car, even sporting twin Ugandan flags and an "official" diplomatic license plate (UGN 35620).[4] As the sham convoy carrying Lieutenant Colonel Jonathan "Yoni" Netanyahu and his ten-man team (disguised in black Ugandan uniforms) rolled by the main checkpoint, the two saluting guards were shot with assault pistols fitted with silencers.[5] The main operational phase (securing the lounge area) took approximately 90 seconds; the entire extraction was completed in as many minutes.

When the smoke cleared, the ten terrorists lay dead, plus forty-five Ugandan troops. All but four of the hostages were safely airlifted to Tel Aviv. Prior to the raid, Dora Bloch was taken to Mulago Hospital in Kampala. The next day, the 73-year-old grandmother was dragged from her sick bed and executed by Idi's thugs. Her body was later discovered in a sugar plantation, exhibiting severe burns to the face.[6]

Before the commandos left, Omer Bar-Lev's unit decided to teach "Big Daddy" a parting lesson—wasting eight of his Russian-built MiGs (one-third of the "Ugandan Air Force"). Five Israelis were wounded in the tour de force strike. Ironically, the sole fatality was the thirty-year-old assault leader, Yoni Netanyahu (older brother to Bibi Netanyahu), known to his troops by the ancient Hebrew expression, "Man of the sword and the Bible."[7] (The mission would later be renamed "Operation Yonatan" in his honor.) Howard Sachar notes: "Once news of the rescue was announced, Israel's entire population all but exploded with pride and relief. The reaction manifestly was a psychological compensation after the trauma of the Yom Kippur War, of endless economic crises, and unrelieved Arab hostility."[8]

CAMP DAVID I (1978)

Once again, things appeared to be looking *up* in Eretz Yisrael. While Idi Amin boasted that one day Uganda would put a man on the *moon*,[9] exactly one week after the Entebbe raid, Rina Messinger became the first (and only) Israeli to be crowned "Miss *Universe*." That renewed optimism would peak with the historic Israeli-Egyptian peace treaty.

In April 1977, Prime Minister Rabin resigned in the wake of a financial scandal. On May 17, Menachem Begin's Likud won the Knesset elections by a landslide. The rebel who nearly went down with the *Altalena* in 1948 became the horn-rimmed bespectacled sixth prime minister of the State of Israel. (Moshe Dayan got the nod for foreign minister.) Stranger yet, the former Irgun commander would be Anwar Sadat's "partner for peace." Intent on inviting Sadat to Israel, Begin wooed his prospective guest by literally saving his life—alerting him to a Libyan assassination plot uncovered by the Mossad.[10]

Determined to achieve a *modus vivendi* with Tel Aviv, Egypt's grateful president became the first Arab leader to visit the Jewish state, deplaning at Ben-Gurion Airport on November 19, 1977. Hafez al-Assad proclaimed a national day of mourning on behalf of the Arab world for Egypt's tacit recognition of Israel. Although the 36-hour state visit was primarily superficial—IAF fighter escort for Sadat's presidential jet; 21-gun salute on a red-carpeted tarmac; IDF band playing Egypt's national anthem; motorcades and 10,000 security personnel; ubiquitous Egyptian flags; resplendent receptions; King David Hotel royal suite; prayer in Al-Aqsa mosque; inscription in Yad Vashem's guest book; ceremonial entrance into a packed Knesset, amidst trumpet blasts; radio microphones to broadcast the landmark address live; dozens of photo-ops with attendant world-wide headlines; not to mention hospital operating rooms put on emergency alert with specific blood reserves matching Sadat and his delegation—an unprecedented door of opportunity had unquestionably opened.

When Begin made his reciprocal visit on December 25, 1977 (the Muslim Sadat's birthday, no less), the mood was anything *but* "jolly."[11] Conspicuously barred from Cairo, Israel's prime minister was whisked to Ismailia to confer with Sadat at one of his many mansions. Historian Paul Merkley writes: "There was no official reception, no playing of national anthems. Egyptian flags were everywhere; Israeli flags were nowhere. Welcome signs did appear along the streets of Ismailia; but they all addressed only to 'Sadat, bringer of Peace!' Begin's name did not appear in public."[12] With Egypt's president catching "Holy Jahannam" across the ummah for his "Journey to Jerusalem," the one-day summit collapsed due to Sadat's insistence that any resolution between Cairo and Tel Aviv over the Sinai must also include "self-determination" for the Palestinians in the "occupied territories" (Golan Heights, Gaza Strip, and West Bank).

The peace baton was then passed to James Earl "Jimmy" Carter, Jr. (a.k.a. "The Man From Plains"). Once so unobtrusive that in 1973 he could sign in as the mystery guest on *What's My Line?* as Georgia's governor, *President* Carter was now on the world stage poised to host the epic Camp David Accords. Having agreed to accept Carter's offer to mediate their disputes, the two Middle Eastern leaders (accompanied by their aides) arrived separately on September 5, 1978, at the presidential retreat in Maryland's Catoctin Mountains. Jimmy's staff tried to think of everything. All guests were encouraged to dress casually. The two factions were deliberately lodged in alternate cabins to "encourage chance informal encounters."[13] However, the first six days were more reminiscent of *Close Encounters of the Third Kind.*

With Sadat's chopper idling on the helipad, and Israel's prime minster ready to depart as well, a breakthrough occurred on September 12. Induced by Carter's last-minute assurances of Western capital for Egypt's failing economy, Sadat caught Dayan's eye by not mentioning the Palestinian issue in his "final" proposal. Begin quickly agreed to a full-scale, three-year incremental withdrawal from the Sinai, including settlements and military bases (the president having promised *him* two replacement air fields in the Negev). Egypt's face-saving caveat was Begin's added pledge to a separate accord entitled a "Framework for Peace in the Middle East." The three-stage, convoluted "fig leaf" envisioned: 1) Israel, Egypt, and Jordan negotiating the ground rules to establish a "self-governing authority" in the West Bank and Gaza; 2) a transitional five-year period for Israel to terminate its military government and redeploy its soldiers to restricted security locations; and, 3) joint discussions between the three nations with an elected Palestinian authority to resolve the permanent status of the territories while brokering a peace treaty between Tel Aviv and Amman.

On December 8, 1978, Israelis mourned the passing of Golda Meir (having succumbed to lymphatic cancer in Jerusalem at age 80). Two days later, Begin and Sadat regained the spotlight by sharing the Nobel Peace Prize. *Finally*—after months of procedural glitches, including a dramatic eleventh-hour impasse over linkage (requiring Carter's own pilgrimage to the area)—Israel's prime minster and Egypt's president affixed their signatures to a formal peace treaty at a special White

House ceremony on March 26, 1979. Sadat concluded his remarks by exhorting all to "work together until the day comes when they beat their swords into plowshares and their spears into pruning hooks…."[14] Menachem, wearing a black kippah, closed his address by reciting Psalm 126.[15] Egypt thus became the first Arab nation to officially recognize the State of Israel (a full thirteen years before the Vatican State).

Appropriately, Carter was denied a second term in office by the *Iranian* Hostage debacle. The anti-Semitic, liberal, Southern Baptist Sunday School teacher would divide the rest of his time between championing Arab grievances (as presented in his book *Palestine: Peace Not Apartheid*) and hammering nails for Habitat for Humanity.

On the telltale date of October 6, 1981, while reviewing Cairo's annual parade observing the Yom Kippur War, Anwar Sadat was assassinated on live television by four of his own military officers. According to Sadat's nephew, the Nobel laureate had refused a bullet-proof vest, stating: "I am among my sons" (Genesis 16:12). As Talaat El Sadat told *CNN*: "The president thought the killers were part of the show when they approached the stands firing, so he stood saluting them."[16] Sadat's sixty-two-year-old, bullet-riddled, comatose body was transported to Maadi Hospital where a medical bulletin attributed his death at 2:40 p.m. to "violent nervous SHOCK and internal bleeding in the chest cavity…."[17] (Author's emphasis) Wounded in the same attack, Hosni Mubarak became Egypt's fourth president. Ten days later, Moshe Dayan passed away from a heart ailment.

OPERATION OPERA (1981)

In 1975, fickle France made a $200 million secret deal with Iraq to build a nuclear "research" reactor at Baghdad's Al Tuwaitha Nuclear Center. Saddam Hussein named his new toy "Tammuz" (after the Arabic month when the Ba'th Party took over in a 1968 coup.)[18] While nuclear energy was the last thing Iraq needed, Saddam was intent on securing three nuclear bombs to vaporize the Jews in Eretz Yisrael.

After diplomacy failed to deter the sprawling construction project, Prime Minister Begin resorted to "other measures." In the ensuing months, over a dozen Iraqi scientists began turning up dead (II Kings 19:35). Nonetheless, by June 1, 1981, the French press reported that the Osirak 40 megawatt light-water reactor was now complete. As the facility would go "hot" within months, Begin was compelled to give the final go ahead for Israel's contingency plan, "Operation Opera."

On Sunday, June 7, 1981, eight heavily armed F-16 Fighting Falcons (flanked by six F-15s) departed Etzion Air Force Base in the Negev headed for Baghdad (600 miles eastward). As the low-level raiding party entered Jordanian air space over the Gulf of Aqaba, who do you suppose was vacationing down below on his luxurious royal yacht? According to author Rodger Claire, the wooden planks under King Hussein's feet "trembled" as the Israeli pilots streaked overhead at less than one hundred feet.[19] Truth really *is* stranger than fiction. And, just as that other old idiom says, "The third time's a charm," incredibly—while the Hashemite issued yet *another* warning, this time to his namesake in Iraq—*somehow* the communiqué went astray.[20]

Having recovered from their own astonishment at happening upon the hapless monarch, the strike force encountered another surprise at Baghdad. As the modified F-16s approached the target area with literally no defenses (added fuel tanks replacing jamming ports), for some "inexplicable" reason, the Iraqis had neglected to activate their radar.[21] In the ensuing moments, all but two of the sixteen 2,000-lb Mark 84 unguided delay-action bombs hit the reactor dome, *blasting* it back to the "Stone Age."[22] While the pilots made their escape, not a single surface-to-air missile was launched. All eight planes landed safely in Israel, their fuel tanks nearly spent. (Ilan Ramon, youngest of the Osirak flyers, would later become Israel's first astronaut, only to perish in the Space Shuttle Columbia tragedy on February 1, 2003.)

When National Security Advisor Richard Allen broke the news to Ronald Reagan, the president stammered—"They did *what*?" After he repeated his statement, Ronnie replied, "You know…Boys will be boys!"[23] The mood was less jovial when the National Security Council convened in the Oval Office to formulate an official response. Allen states that all but one of the men expressed outrage at the Israelis, Vice President Bush and Chief of Staff Baker being the most "vitriolic," both demanding "punitive action." When the rancor subsided, the sole dissenter went on record, stating: "Before this is over we'll be on our knees thanking God Israel did what it did."[24] It wouldn't take long for Al Haig's prophecy to be fulfilled. After the successful conclusion of the Gulf War in 1991, the US Secretary of Defense gave IAF Commander David Ivry a satellite photograph of the destroyed reactor, inscribed with the message: "With thanks and appreciation. You made our job easier in Desert Storm. Dick Cheney."[25]

FIRST LEBANON WAR (1982-85)

As the heroes of Operation Opera were taking their well-deserved curtain calls, the nation was already pursuing its "new normal," post-Yom Kippur trajectory, this time, "*fightings without.*" Like the colloquialism, "It ain't over 'til the fat lady sings," implies, Yasser Arafat would personify Israel's latest "fat lady."

In April 1982, the IDF ended its phased withdrawal from Sinai. The new threat had shifted north to Lebanon where Israel's smallest neighbor was embroiled in a deadly fifteen-year civil war (1975-90). After being ejected from Jordan in 1971, the PLO had ensconced itself in southern Lebanon, brutalizing the local Maronite (Eastern Catholic) population, subsidizing (exploiting) 300,000 destitute Sunni refugees, and disrupting upper Galilee and beyond. Between July 1981 and June 1982, some 270 attacks were staged along the Lebanese and Jordanian borders, throughout Israel proper, and in the West Bank and Gaza.

When Israel's ambassador to Britain, Shlomo Argov, was permanently disabled in an assassination attempt in London on June 3, 1982, Begin directed his new defense minister, Ariel Sharon, to begin an immediate aerial bombardment of southern Lebanon. That the failed hit was actually traced to the Abu Nidal terror cell (begun by Arafat's nemesis, Sabri al-Banna) was of little consequence.[26] Three days later, the IDF launched "Operation Peace for Galilee," striking PLO strongholds with 80,000 sets of boots on the ground. The defined (and limited) expedition to create a "twenty-five-mile security zone" got off to a precipitate start. Thirty-seven years to the day that American paratroopers scaled Pointe du Hoc in Normandy, a company of Israeli commandos climbed the 1,200-ft. cliff face of Beaufort Castle, a Crusader fortress serving as a PLO firing base.

However, upon neutralizing the immediate threat, Arik's *expanded* plan—"Operation Big Pines"—called for entering Beirut to eradicate Arafat's quasi-government, centered in the city's western sector.[27] The strategic objective of the semi-secret mission was to pave the way for Bashir Gemayel, commander of the Phalangist militia, to become the nation's duly elected "Christian" president. Sharon's vision stemmed from a false "assumption" (based on Bashir's tacit "assurance") that a new and grateful Lebanon would reciprocate by ratifying a treaty with Israel, thereby forming, with Egypt, a "triangle of peace" providing open borders.[28] The precise text of Sharon's agenda was to "change the map of power and authority in the Middle East by creating a new political order."[29] Israeli journalists Ze'ev Schiff and Ehud Ya'ari, described by Abba Eban as "two of the most respected political and military commentators,"[30] write: "Born of the ambition of one willful, reckless man, Israel's 1982 invasion of Lebanon was anchored in delusion, propelled by deceit, and bound to end in calamity."[31]

By mid-June, the Jews had ghettoized 6,000-9,000 PLO and Syrian fighters embedded in the heavily populated West Beirut suburbs. Over the next two months (a worthless US-brokered truce notwithstanding), four hundred Israeli tanks and one thousand artillery pieces pulverized the PLO nerve center (killing thousands of civilians in the process). After absorbing 127 IAF sorties in one ten-hour period alone on August 4, Yasser finally called it quits. With the aid of Philip Habib, US ambassador to Lebanon, the PLO chief relocated his headquarters to Tunisia, while his thugs were farmed out to Syria, Iraq, and good ol' King Hussein. The exodus was monitored by a global peacekeeping force (including contingents of the US Army, Marines, and Navy SEALS). On August 23, 1982, Bashir Gemayel was elected president of Lebanon by a margin of fifty-seven votes to five blanks.[32]

The following week Bashir met with Begin and Sharon in Nahariya in northern Israel. Instead of a peace treaty, the wily Phalangist, aware of his multicultural constituency, offered only a non-aggression pact. When Begin—on the verge of plotzing—reminded his guest of the formidable IDF presence in his country, Bashir extended both arms to Sharon and cried: "Put the handcuffs on! I am not your vassal."[33] And that was that. However, two weeks later Lebanon needed a new leader. On September 14, the president-elect was assassinated by a bomb blast as he spoke at a meeting of the Phalangist Party in Ashrafiye.

While most believe that the killer was a pro-Syrian dissident, the root cause for Bashir's death (along with the ongoing demise of his country) can be traced to the *original* geo-political pact between Israel and Lebanon. According to the Tanakh, God punished the ancient kingdom of Tyrus for selling Jews to their worst enemies—the half-breed Edomites. The key phrase is the specific indictment that Bashir's ancestors *"remembered not the brotherly covenant."* (Amos 1:9) This expression relates to David's uniquely sanctioned rapport with Hiram, King of Tyre (II Samuel 5:11). After David's death, Hiram passed his bond of devotion on to King Solomon (I Kings 5:1). The term "brotherly covenant" is a key cross-reference to I Kings 9:13 where Hiram addresses Solomon as *"my brother."*

Following the hit, hundreds of Phalangist militiamen perpetrated a wholesale massacre on September 16-17 in the Sabra and Shatila shantytowns. On September 20, a grisly scene rivaling Jonestown appeared on the front page of the *Jerusalem Post*; the article stated: "Correspondents reported seeing what appeared to be entire families shot to death inside their homes...."[34] The remains of over 2,300 Palestinian men, women, and children were initially found.[35] The "pogrom" went down in clear view of an IDF post less than 100 yards away, the men reportedly "lounging about...reading magazines and listening to Simon and Garfunkel."[36] Chomsky writes, "Throughout Thursday night, Israeli flares lighted the camps while the militias went about their work, methodically slaughtering the inhabitants."[37]

The "international community" recoiled with predictable rage (Genesis 34:30). The IDF admitted to approving the "Aktion" (Sharon even giving a charge to the commanders), but only because the camps were "supposedly" harboring some 2,000 PLO stalwarts, plus caches of weapons, etc. To the contrary, Ze'ev Schiff states that an "authorized investigation" confirmed that it was *not* a "revenge killing" but rather "a premeditated attack which was designed to cause a mass flight of Palestinians from Beirut and from the whole of Lebanon."[38] According to Pulitzer Prize-winning author David Shipler, as early as mid-June, "Israeli officials were speaking privately of a plan, being considered by Defense Minister Ariel Sharon, to allow the Phalangists to go into west Beirut and the camps against the PLO."[39]

The military's official spin before the Kahan Commission, that the Christian Phalangists "had simply lost control of their men,"[40] did not bode well before the Judge of the Universe. Described in Acts 10:34 as *"no respecter of persons,"* Israel's God was equally unimpressed with Begin's dismissive retort that "gentiles kill gentiles and everybody blames the Jews."[41] The culprits obviously missed the chance to learn from their fathers' sin as found in Habakkuk 2:17, *"For the violence of Lebanon shall cover thee"* (a reference to the Chaldeans' destruction of Lebanon's forests, cited in Isaiah 37:24). Thus, on November 12, *another* front-page photo appeared in the *Post*, the charred debris of the IDF headquarters after being *blown to bits* by a "previously unknown group called The Armed Struggle Organization."[42] With over 100 casualties leading historian Samuel Katz to label it "the worst single disaster in Israeli military history,"[43] should any be surprised that the blast just *happened* to occur in Tyre?

There were other dark milestones as well. Beirut became the only Arab capital to be occupied by the IDF. Among the many fallen, Major General Yekutiel Adam was the highest-ranking officer to ever die in battle. The Lebanon War was the first conflict in Israel's history when military members refused to obey orders for conscience' sake.[44] This, in turn, prompted the first wartime peace movement, called "Soldiers Against Silence"; civilians expressed their disdain for the unpopular war through the "Peace Now" movement. On September 24, 1982, a combined rally of both groups drew 400,000 Israelis to Tel Aviv's Municipality Square, the largest protest in the country's existence. Begin could only scratch his head as countless Jewish volunteer groups raised funds and supplies for the *Arab* victims of *his* invasion.[45]

Even the United States would earn a mark for evil. With the arrival of 1,000 Iranian Revolutionary Guards having spawned the Hezbollah network, 241 US Marines died in Beirut on Sunday morning, October 23, 1983, when Hezbollah terrorists drove an explosive-laden truck into their barracks. *CBS News* later called it "the deadliest terrorist attack on Americans prior to September 11."[46] Begin's chief of staff, General Rafael Eitan, remarked, "This is the first war in which the war's ends were determined from beginning to end in the General Staff master plan…"[47] (reflecting Sharon's perfidy). Finally, all of these watershed events ironically resulted from the same "expedition" described by Dr. Howard Sachar as "the most thoroughly prepared campaign in Israel's history."[48]

Ariel Sharon stepped down as defense minister on February 14, 1983. Lauded as "King Arik" after Yom Kippur, his legacy subsequent to Big Pines would devolve to the epithet, "Arik's War." On May 17, 1983, Lebanon's new president, Amine Gemayel (Bashir's neophyte sibling), signed a pseudo peace treaty with Israel, only to rescind the "brotherly covenant" in March 1984. In hindsight, Sharon's lack of discernment is revealed by the very *tree* he used for the mission name. Had Arik read the Bible he would have known that Solomon built the Temple with *cedars of Lebanon* supplied by King Hiram (I Kings 5:6).

After hanging on for a few more months, Israel's embattled prime minister resigned as well, leaving office on October 10, 1983. (Begin would spend his retirement in relative seclusion, even heading off a state funeral for his death on March 10, 1992.) Inheriting Menachem's mess, Israel's seventh prime minister, Yitzhak Shamir, passed it off to Shimon Peres less than a year later. The new coalition government promptly voted to quit Lebanon, doing so on May 31, 1985. A token force of 1,000 was deployed in a narrow security zone extending eight miles inland to protect Israel's northern frontier and to reinforce the South Lebanese army. In the three-year incursion, the IDF lost over 1,200 killed, with twice that number wounded. The protracted military occupation was deemed a major albatross. Israel would finally withdraw all of its troops in May of 2000.

IRAN-CONTRA (1985-87)

Barely out of Lebanon, Israel's government made a fatal decision to cooperate with Washington in a most bizarre machination. Having bested Jimmy Carter in the original Iranian hostage crisis (1979-81), Ronald Reagan had his own debacle in 1985 when several Americans were abducted by Hezbollah agents in Beirut. (Some 100 persons from twenty-plus nations were systematically kidnapped in Lebanon between 1982 and 1992.) The victims' families naturally exerted considerable pressure on the White House to secure their release.

When the Ayatollah Khomeini ran low on guns during his "holy war" against Iraq (then in its fifth year), National Security Advisor Robert McFarlane convinced Reagan that an "arms-for-hostages" swap might be arranged with Iranian moderates eager to restore ties with the US. No matter that Defense Secretary Rumsfeld had *already* given Saddam Hussein everything from firecrackers to WMD.[49] To circumvent the congressional arms ban, McFarlane arranged to launder the shipments through Tel Aviv. The Israelis would sell "their" weapons to Iran, then refurbish their depleted stores from America. Khomeini's *quid pro quo* translated to exit visas for Iran's ninety thousand Jews. The fact that the arms would be used against Iraq, the closer belligerent to Israel's eastern borders, was an added incentive.

The Persians pursued the standard Middle Eastern "demand everything/concede-nothing" approach. After over 500 TOW anti-tank missiles were purchased and delivered in back-to-back shipments in August and September 1985, only *one* American was freed (Reverend Benjamin Weir). A third shipment comprising 100 Hawk anti-aircraft missiles failed to free a single detainee, Iran claiming the stuff was "obsolete." To keep the pressure on, after four Palestinian militants seized the Italian cruise liner *Achille Lauro* on October 7, the disciples of Allah murdered one of their captives, an elderly disabled American Jew named Leon Klinghoffer, then gave him a burial at sea—dumping his blood-stained body overboard while still in his wheelchair!

Things quickly deteriorated. Not content with directing *one* volatile connivance, McFarlane, aided by Colonel Oliver North, convinced "The Gipper" to do *another* end-run around Capitol Hill—*this* time by having the Israelis channel their Iranian profits (via Swiss banks) to Nicaragua's right-wing Contra guerrillas, engaged in a fight against Daniel Ortega's Communist regime. ("Ollie" would press the envelope by securing most of his *contra*band from the "bad guys.") For a while, everything seemed to be going smoothly. Three more hostages were even traded for another 500 TOWs. But then the inevitable "leak" hit the Lebanese press, launching the Iran-Contra hearings in the Senate.

Of course, there was more to the story than meets the eye. To summarize a complex narrative, among other intrigues, Israel would become the fall guy for Skull and Bones alumnus George Bush's own hostage crisis. According to Loftus and Aarons, unbeknown to the American people (including Congress and the CIA), the vice president's office had its own counterterrorist cabal—the Special Situation Group (SSG), augmented by the Crisis Pre-Planning Group (CPPG). During a 1984 botched attempt to kidnap Lebanese terrorists, CPPG agent Bill Buckley was seized by the Islamist Jihad. At Bush's request, MI6 agreed to help ransom Buckley by opening the greater "Second Channel" to Tehran (after Israel's token "First Channel" was closed by CIA head William Casey). British mercenary Leslie Aspin contacted the notorious global gunrunner, Monzer Al-Kassar, who signed on to funnel arms to Khomeini's crazies for Buckley's release.

Ultimately, the $42 million scheme crashed and burned: Monzer procured most of his cache from Communist munitions plants, piggybacking significant quantities to the PLO in South Yemen;

Buckley was tortured and killed by Soviet agents, his 400-page signed confession used to blackmail Bush into further illicit transactions; Israel was ultimately blamed for providing the illegal weapons at both ends of the Iran-Contra affair.[50] Yitzhak Shamir could only say: "Everything attributed to Israel has no basis in reality."[51]

JONATHAN POLLARD (1986)

Ironically, in the midst of the Iran-Contra fiasco, Israel got embroiled in *another* debilitating scandal. Jonathan Jay Pollard was employed as a civilian American Naval research analyst at the Navy's Field Operations Intelligence Office in Suitland, Maryland (specifically the Threat Analysis Division in the Anti-Terrorist Alert Center). The Texas-born, Indiana-bred, Stanford University alumnus became the classic exception to the aforementioned "Jew Room" proscription. His story represents another stark example for the subtitle of this book.

Pollard discovered that many critical intel reports were not being shared with Tel Aviv as per the 1981 US-Israel Memorandum of Understanding. This was unacceptable to Pollard, described by his family and friends as a "passionate Zionist."[52] Having lost over seventy relatives in the Shoah, Jonathan had already visited Dachau *and* made aliya while still in his early teens. His protests at Naval Intelligence were scorned. On the subject of Israeli concerns over Arab WMD, his supervisor said, "Jews are too sensitive about gas."[53]

Determined to circumvent the illegal interdict, Pollard volunteered his "services" to Rafael Eitan, director of Israel's Office of Scientific Liaison (LAKAM). Over the next eighteen months, Pollard transmitted scores of classified documents, graphs, and satellite images, primarily pertaining to Middle East weapons systems and storage facilities. Unfortunately, he compromised his testimony by accepting money from Israel. His enhanced lifestyle then attracted the FBI. On the advice of his handlers, Pollard and his wife, Anne, went to the Israeli embassy in Washington, expecting to be flown to Israel. To their dismay, however, they were remanded to waiting federal agents.

Three words define the evolving Pollard saga—*unprecedented*, *disproportionate*, and *inexcusable*. In lieu of a formal trial, Jonathan took a plea bargain, sparing both governments added embarrassment. After nine months of polygraph tests, the FBI concluded that despite the compensation, his motives were primarily altruistic.[54] On June 4, 1986, Pollard plead guilty to *one* count of conspiracy to deliver national defense information to a foreign government. The maximum penalty for such a mitigable offense is ten years (the median two to four). On March 5, 1987, Judge Aubrey Robinson handed Pollard a *life* sentence. (His ailing wife received five years). At no time in US history has any citizen received life for divulging classified intel to an *ally*.[55] By comparison, in 2010, *ten* Russian sleeper spies arrested in New York City (a.k.a. "Illegals Program") were sentenced to "time served"—eleven days—then promptly deported back to Moscow, Anna Chapman becoming an instant celebrity. (One American and three Soviet double agents were released in the Obama-era "swap.")

The day before the draconian verdict, Defense Secretary Caspar W. Weinberger (an assimilated Jew on his father's side) submitted a forty-six-page *classified* dossier to the US District Court in Washington, DC, purporting to justify the punishment as commensurate with the full extent of Pollard's *greater* crimes. As the story went, Shabtai Kalmanovich was a Russian mole in the Mossad who exposed over forty CIA assets in the USSR. Of course, Pollard was his American source, etc. In Caspar's opinion, Pollard should have been shot as a traitor![56] (The word "traitor" would imply that Israel was *not* a US ally.) However, in 1994, Aldrich Ames (an alcoholic CIA agent) was arrested as the real culprit who had "outed" many of his friends for cash, framing Pollard in the process. Resolved that Pollard *must* have disclosed the others, the "rat" would continue to rot. But then, in February 2001, a senior FBI official, Special Agent Robert Hanssen, confessed that *he* had given up the remaining spies.[57]

Despite a formal apology from Tel Aviv, the intercession of five former Israeli prime ministers, joined by forty US congressmen and numerous senior officials (including former CIA chief James Woolsey and three secretaries of state: Kissinger, Shultz, even Caspar himself), plus a petition signed by 1.5 million American and Israeli citizens—political prisoner #09185-016 would *remain* in the Federal Correctional Complex in Butner, North Carolina. For the ultimate hypocrisy of widespread US snooping on Israel, Esther Pollard (Jonathan's prison bride), claimed that the man who fingered her husband was Andrzej "Angie" Kielcynski (alias Joseph Barak), a member of Ariel Sharon's Foreign Intelligence Committee, *and* a double agent for the CIA.[58] In a

March 27, 2001, interview broadcast over Kol Yisrael Radio, Kielcynski admitted betraying Israel's nuclear secrets along with various persons—*including* Mr. Pollard.[59]

John Loftus came to believe that Pollard may have incurred the greatest wrath for giving Israel the names of all Saudi and other Arab intelligence operatives who were known to the CIA as of 1984. Their identities (in the so-called "Blue Book") prove beyond question that the US intelligence community understood the Saudi-terrorist nexus—*seventeen years before 9/11*.[60] Meanwhile, on March 12, 2013 (just eight days before his state trip to Israel), President Obama said in a televised interview with Israel's Channel 2: "I have no plans for releasing Jonathan Pollard immediately…As the president, my first obligation is to observe the law here in the United States…I've got to make sure that every individual is treated fairly and equally"[61] (Isaiah 59:14). In November 2015, after three decades of confinement, Jonathan Pollard, age 61, in failing health, received his mandatory probation, though soured by a five-year travel restriction (with ankle bracelets, no less). Barack "Executive Order" Obama would leave office a year later having refused to lift Jonathan's final indignity.

FIRST INTIFADA (1987-93)

On December 8, 1987, an Israeli civilian truck driver lost control of his vehicle near the crowded Gaza refugee camp of Jabaliya. The rig hit an oncoming car filled with local Arabs, killing four. Within hours, the first *intifada* (Arabic for "shaking off," "awakening," or "uprising" when applied to the perennial tension), had spontaneously erupted throughout the Palestinian Territories. The prolonged encounter would become the most embarrassing military crisis in Israel's brief history.

Ironically, the PLO leadership in Tunis and the Israeli intelligence community were both caught off guard by the grassroots revolt. They quickly adjusted; the former to hijack and direct the movement, the latter to suppress it. The initial stage exhibited massive protests and unprecedented rioting. Troops confronted mobs of knife- and ax-wielding Palestinian "youths" hurling rocks, Molotov cocktails, even hand grenades. Traffic was snarled by barricades and burning tires. Israelis were stunned as their neighborhoods morphed into war zones. Routine acts, such as riding a bus, driving to work, hitchhiking to an army base, or taking children to school were suddenly life-threatening experiences. Then things *really* got crazy.

With Egypt no longer at odds with Israel, Yasser Arafat saw his chance to put the Palestinian agenda on the front burner. He also was desperate to reinvent himself after his latest eviction, this time from Lebanon. He thus decided upon a revolutionary strategy (no pun intended). As the liberal press was just a phone call away, Yasser would garner sympathy on the world stage by augmenting the chaos with civil disobedience. The "peace-loving" PLO chairman would become a mutant version of Mahatma Gandhi and Martin Luther King.

Knowing his enemy well, Arafat focused on Israel's purse strings first. Crippling strikes were staged by the commuting West Bank and Gaza work forces (sixty-thousand laborers). Agriculture, construction, and tourism suffered accordingly. Palestinian businessmen closed their shops intermittently and ceased paying taxes. Arabs boycotted Israeli products. With over ten thousand troops deployed to the Territories, the increased workload impacted the military budget. The total cost of the intifada on Israel's economy (1988-89) was estimated at $1 billion, or 2-2.5% of the nation's GDP.[62] (The commensurate drop in the Gaza-West Bank economies only made a bad situation worse.)

The government was never able to get out in front of this new humiliating technique. Every reprisal was caught on film. Second-hand furniture and personal items were hauled away for delinquent taxes. As farming permits were suspended, soldiers found themselves busting Palestinian mothers for planting kitchen gardens. Six years after taking out Saddam's nuclear reactors, the IDF was now reduced to barring Arab children from illegal home schools, the Knesset in its "wisdom" having temporarily stopped public education (affecting nearly 300,000 students). The arts were also banned as PLO "freedom fighters" drew inspiration from patriotic songs and dances. Scores of Palestinians were jailed for various "crimes": violating curfew; waving Palestinian flags; refusing to carry mandatory identification cards. Meanwhile, as punishment for intifada activities, over 3,000 Palestinian homes were demolished under a law that also prohibited them to rebuild.[63]

Like in the Lebanon War, many Israeli soldiers suffered a crisis of conscience. While the Mossad's 1988 Tunis assassination of Arafat loyalist "Abu Jihad" (with seventeen of his cohorts) was certainly justified, the May 20, 1990, Oyoun Qarra massacre (a.k.a. "Bloody

Sunday") and Temple Mount riots of October 8, 1990 (a.k.a. "Bloody Monday") were self-defeating disasters. According to the Swedish branch of Save the Children, between 23,600 and 29,000 children required medical treatment for *beating* injuries in the first two years of the uprising.[64] Data from *B'Tselem* (Israeli Information Center for Human Rights in the Occupied Territories) confirmed that 1,265 deaths occurred during that period, nearly 90% Palestinian.[65]

The public sector was conflicted as well. Arafat was obviously a ruthless killer. According to a special commission led by Judge Meir Shamgar, president of the Israeli Supreme Court, Arab acts of mayhem during the five years of chaos included: 150,000 stoning incidents; 5,655 Molotov cocktails tossed; 3,000 knifings and assaults; 281 shootings; and 256 hand-grenade attacks—resulting in 64 Israeli deaths, with 4,000 injured.[66] And yet, the majority of ordinary Palestinians were perceived as the unfortunate dupes of a fourfold, irremediable dilemma: exploited by the PLO (intent on Israel's demise); excluded from the Arab world; barred from citizenship by the reality of demographics; and, defrauded by the pipedream of a two-state solution.

A controversial rabbi once said: *"He that is without sin among you, let him first cast a stone...."* (John 8:7) With the stereotypical image of stone-throwing Palestinian youths defining the intifada, one bold Hebrew University professor reputedly slung a stone of his own:

> The phenomenon of children throwing stones did not begin with the Intifada, but with Haredi (ultra-Orthodox) children stoning cars driving on the Sabbath. Those in Israel now calling for shooting Palestinian children who throw stones, arguing that stones are deadly weapons, would of course never dare to propose shooting the Haredi children. They are, after all, Jewish, and in Israel this is the difference that makes the difference.[67]

MADRID PEACE CONFERENCE (1991)

With the intifada in full swing, Israel also had to face over two dozen Scud missile attacks from western Iraq during the six weeks of "Operation Desert Storm," January 17 to February 25, 1991. (When an air raid siren spread panic during an Israeli Philharmonic concert, Isaac Stern so calmed the audience with a movement of Bach, that the grateful patrons donned gas masks, refusing to budge.) By fall, Yitzhak Shamir (having reclaimed the mess from Peres) was constrained to engage his Palestinian counterparts at the Madrid peace conference (hosted by Spain and cosponsored by the US and USSR).

In his opening address at the Royal Palace on October 30, President Bush introduced his now-famous buzz phrase fantasy for securing a permanent solution to the Israeli-Palestinian conflict ("Land for Peace"): "Throughout the Middle East, we seek a stable and enduring settlement. We've not defined what this means. Indeed, I make these points with no map showing where the final borders are to be drawn. Nevertheless, we believe territorial compromise is essential for peace."[68] However, like the five-day summit itself, the "magic bullet" speech was a *blank*. The real action that night was elsewhere.

While Bush was speaking in Spain, a portentous atmospheric phenomenon was listening in the North Atlantic Ocean. A powerful storm packing sustained winds of 73 mph was spotted off the coast of Nova Scotia. This was quite unusual, as most hurricanes originate in the tropics (after forming off the western coast of Africa). And while the normal gale pattern for North America is west to east, *this* storm would travel over a thousand miles in the *opposite* direction. You might say it had a mind of its own. The following day (October 31), the storm decided to do some "trick-or-treating," abruptly smashing its way into New England with waves in excess of one hundred feet—the highest on record! The "thing" was initially called a "monster," as it was literally hundreds of miles wide. It then proceeded down the coast all the way to Florida, causing $200 million in "tricks."

The meteorologists were stunned by their own data. The extremely rare weather patterns that coalesced to form this "Halloween Monster" only happen about once every century. They concluded that it was one of the most powerful storms ever. These findings resulted in a book followed by a Hollywood film, both entitled *The Perfect Storm*. The front-page headlines of the *New York Times* and *USA Today* had the Madrid Peace Conference and the Perfect Storm stories right next to each other. The adjacent articles in *USA Today* were titled: "One-on-one peace talks next" and "East Coast hit by rare storm."[69]

As with the Great Hurricane of 1938, the Scripture that explains this surreal display is Psalm 83:4,15: *"They have said, Come, and let us cut them off from being a nation; that the name of Israel may be no more in remembrance...So persecute them with thy* TEMPEST*, and make them afraid with thy* STORM*."* The great coalition builder behind Desert Storm got so spooked by the Perfect Storm that he blew out of Madrid early to check on his beloved turn-of-the-century mansion in Kennebunkport, Maine. The Associated Press reported: "The president said he couldn't believe the extent of the damage, 'and I've been around the ocean a long time. Most who have lived around here all their lives have never seen anything like it.'"[70] This author interviewed a contractor who helped repair the president's vacation home. When asked for his outstanding recollection of the damage, the man recalled how everyone was shocked that the storm surge had wiped out the massive 3-4 ft. thick, 15-20 ft. high retaining wall (including the submerged foundation) designed to protect the property. His second-most vivid memory was that the ocean had swept through half the house, leaving seaweed, sand, and other debris in its wake.[71]

While this was no doubt just a "freak coincidence," on August 23, 1992—the very day President Bush reconvened the Madrid fiasco in Washington—Hurricane Andrew obliterated southern Florida.

OSLO ACCORDS (1993-95)

William Jefferson Clinton followed one-term George Bush on January 20, 1993. Like his predecessor, Clinton would learn that siding with Israel's foes was not the healthiest idea. On January 16, 1994, Clinton met with Syria's President Hafez Assad in Geneva to discuss more "land for peace" deals. This time Israel would have to return the Golan Heights to Syria. Less than twenty-four hours later, a 6.0 earthquake pulverized southern California. The seismic convulsion, centered in Northridge (ground zero for America's pornography industry), became the second-most deadly "natural" disaster to come against America.

Bill's biggest error would be pressing Israel over the Oslo Accords. Having surmounted his earlier financial scandals, Yitzhak Rabin regained the prime minister's office on July 13, 1992. Following a series of secret back channel talks in Oslo, Norway, Clinton announced on September 1, 1993, that he would meet with Arafat and Rabin to begin the Oslo Accords. (After nearly a week of meandering in the Atlantic, Hurricane Emily struck North Carolina on this day.)

An historic exchange of official correspondence ("Letters of Mutual Recognition") took place between Tel Aviv and the Palestine Liberation Organization on September 9, 1993. Arafat's opening pledge stated: "The PLO recognizes the right of the State of Israel to exist in peace and security." Prime Minister Rabin replied: "I wish to confirm to you that, in light of the PLO commitments included in your letter, the Government of Israel has decided to recognize the PLO as the representative of the Palestinian people and commence negotiations with the PLO within the Middle East peace process."[72]

On September 13, 1993, PLO negotiator Mahmoud Abbas and Israeli Foreign Minister Shimon Peres signed the Oslo I Accord ("Declaration of Principles On Interim Self-Government Arrangements") at a special White House ceremony hosted by President Clinton. The stated purpose of this first of two interim agreements was to secure a peace treaty (within five years) based on UN Security Resolutions 242 and 338—predicated on the "right of the Palestinian people to self determination." While the end goal of Camp David was to "secure the final status of the West Bank and Gaza" through a pact between Israel and Jordan, Oslo I involved Israel and the Palestinians. (On October 26, 1994, King Hussein *finally* made the right move, the Hashemite Kingdom of Jordan becoming the second Arab country, after Egypt, to sign a formal peace treaty with Israel.)

Naturally, not all Jewry was singing "Kumbaya," particularly as Arab violence accelerated in the wake of Oslo I.[73] Elyakim Haetzni, an Israeli attorney and settlement activist announced: "We are loyal to the covenant with God, we are not loyal to Oslo."[74] Thus, on February 25, 1994, Baruch Goldstein, a Brooklyn-born Israeli physician, murdered twenty-nine innocent Palestinians and wounded 125 in a ninety-second shooting spree in the Ibrahimi Mosque at the Cave of the Patriarchs in the West Bank city of Hebron. (Dr. Goldstein's weapon of choice was his army-issued Galil assault rifle.) The thirty-seven-year-old Messianic fanatic was subdued and beaten to death by the survivors. One of Goldstein's pals, Moshe Feiglin, felt that the doctor had acted to avert "a clear and palpable danger" to Hebron's Jewish enclave.[75]

Another "wet blanket" event in 1994 eroding the Palestinian illusion of "self-determination" was the massive two-year security barrier project begun along the Gaza Strip border. Palestinians would now be limited to only five entry/exit points into Israel and Egypt: two pedestrian crossing locations—northern Erez into Israel and southern Rafah into Egypt; plus three cargo crossing sites for commercial traffic—the eastern Karni, northern Sufa, and southern Kerem Shalom.

Yitzhak Rabin and Yasser Arafat signed the Oslo II Accord in Taba, Egypt, on September 28, 1995. This highly complex treaty divided the West Bank into three non-contiguous administrative categories, giving Palestinians greater autonomy, though falling short of statehood. According to Phase I of this bureaucratic monstrosity (entwined with an equally bewildering schedule of troop withdrawals, known as "Further Redeployments" or FRDs), Area A, comprising 3% of the West Bank (excluding East Jerusalem), would afford the Palestinian Authority (PA) full civil *and* security power over all seven major Palestinian cities (Nablus, Jenin, Tulkarem, Qalqilya, Ramallah, Bethlehem, plus 80% of Hebron) and their immediate locales; Area B, at 23-25%, would combine Palestinian civil control with joint Israeli-Palestinian security control over 440 scattered Palestinian villages and their environs; Area C, at 72-74%, would place its roughly 110,000 Jewish settlers under full Israeli civil and security jurisdiction.)[76]

RABIN ASSASSINATION (1995)

Oslo II was as contentious in Israel as Camp David was in Egypt. Consequently, on November 4, 1995—thirty-seven days after affixing his signature alongside that of Yasser Arafat—Yitzhak Rabin became the first prime minister of the State of Israel to be assassinated. And, just as Anwar Sadat's assailants were Egyptians, Rabin's shooter was a fellow Israeli. Of course (not that anyone cares), the so-called West Bank of Eretz Yisrael was not within the scriptural jurisdiction of *any* politician to begin parceling out to Mohammed's crowd (Joel 3:2).

Rabin was gunned down at 9:30 p.m. as he was leaving a "peace" rally at Kings of Israel Square in Tel Aviv. The perpetrator was an ultranationalist fanatic named Yigal Amir. As Rabin descended the steps of City Hall toward the open door of his limo, Amir fired three shots at him with a Beretta 84F .380 ACP semi-automatic pistol. The assassin was immediately taken into custody while the prime minister was rushed to Ichilov Hospital. The seventy-three-year-old patient expired on the operating table from blood loss and a punctured lung. Ironically, the blood-soaked Hebrew lyrics to the popular song *Shir*

LaShalom ("Song of Peace") were found in Rabin's pocket.[77] The following week, the British newspaper, *European*, ran a photograph of the macabre song sheet, perforated by one of the bullets.[78] The scope of the ensuing conspiracy theories would rival the JFK assassination.[79]

THE RISE AND FALL OF BIBI (1996-2000)

In the closing years of the second millennium, Israel would continue to experience "fightings without and fears within." According to one database, 53 terrorist attacks occurred between January 6, 1996, and September 29, 2000, killing 53 while injuring 803. (The totals from Oslo I, through November 27, 1995, were 74 and 495, respectively.)[80]

The slain prime minister was followed by fellow Labor member Shimon Peres (his second term) on November 22, 1995 (ironically, the anniversary date of the Kennedy shooting). Several notable events occurred during his brief six-month tenure. On January 6, 1996, the notorious Hamas bomb-maker, Yehiya Ayyash (a.k.a. "The Engineer"), was blown away in Gaza, by a booby-trapped cell phone activated by Shin Bet agents. (Ayyash was connected to the deaths of 150 Israelis and the injuring of 500 others.[81]) President Clinton visited Israel on March 14 and 15. On April 11, the IDF launched "Operation Grapes of Wrath" in retaliation for Hezbollah strikes in northern Israel. The sixteen-day bombing campaign in Lebanon resulted in heavy civilian casualties. On May 4, 1996, Jerusalem celebrated its 3,000-year anniversary as the capital of Israel. Likud's Benjamin Netanyahu won the nation's first direct election for prime minister on May 29, 1996. (At forty-six, Bibi became the youngest prime minister in Israel's history as well as the first native-born office holder.)

While Israeli envoys spent 1997 forging ties with the Vatican, Bibi made three pilgrimages to America, meeting with President Clinton in February and April. In 1998, Israel celebrated her golden anniversary. On October 23, Netanyahu and Arafat signed the Wye River Memorandum before Clinton and King Hussein and at a special White House ceremony (the agreement essentially revitalizing Oslo II). Four months later, King Hussein bin Talal of Jordan died of lymphoma on February 7, 1999. (The sixty-three-year-old Hashemite monarch was the longest serving executive head of state in the world.)

In the July 6, 1999, election for prime minister, Netanyahu was unseated by Labor candidate Ehud Barak. The span of conjecture over his defeat ranged from charges of political corruption to the cumulative toll of the "Moshe Dayan Syndrome." Sadly, Bibi cheated on both his *first* wife, Miriam (while she was pregnant), and his *third* wife, Sara (whom he married only *after* she got pregnant); Fleur, the partner in his *first* affair (who became his *second* wife), was a non-Jewish Brit, while Ruth (the partner in his *second* affair) was his "public relations" director, no less (Proverbs 7:26).

CAMP DAVID II (2000)

The year 2000 got off to a "whoop-dee-do" start. On January 5, Israel shifted (to the Palestinians) 3% of the land in Area "C" to Area "B", and 2% from "B" to "A." (About 99% of rank-and-file Israelis grow increasingly baffled at their government's post-Oslo, "alphabet soup" diplomacy.) While Pope John Paul popped in for a visit on March 21, Hafez al-Assad departed this world on June 10 (succumbing to a heart attack in Damascus), with no impending Israeli treaty. However, the year's biggest shindig would be the much-anticipated July 11-25 Camp David II, hosted by another folksy southern Democratic president.

Ostensibly, the goal of the two-week summit was to secure a *final* settlement of the Israeli-Palestinian dispute vis-à-vis the Oslo Accords. In a nutshell, the entire thing flopped because of one "nut job"—President Yasser Arafat. (On November 15, 1988, the PLO chairman became the first elected president of the PA.) To illustrate his unstable mental condition (ironically, Yasser means "easy going" in Arabic), renowned international military and threat analyst Yossef Bodansky relates: "He never moved without his 'emergency button'—an electronic buzzer that activated an elaborate security system."[82] (According to an eyewitness who observed the subject during another meeting between Israeli and Palestinian officials, "When Arafat was momentarily separated from his emergency button he went crazy."[83])

Normally, Secretary of State Madeline Albright would blame the Israelis for Yasser's frequent "mood swings," asking: "What are you doing to our Arafat?"[84] However, the daily stonewalling, especially his refusal to offer counterproposals, drove Clinton to activate his *own* emergency button. The president's ire was worsened by the fact that

Barak was practically giving away the store. In a landmark proposal, essentially entailing quasi-Palestinian statehood, Israel was now willing to evacuate the Gaza Strip *and* nearly *all* of the West Bank.

Barak's chief spokesman, Israeli Foreign Minister Shlomo Ben-Ami, kept a detailed diary of the proceedings. (The point is germane to the ongoing controversy over the fact that the main proposal was not made in writing.) Conforming to the "12-88 map" (tacitly endorsed in May 2000 at Stockholm), Israel's sole demand amounted to annexing just 12% of the West Bank (comprising the highly populated settlement blocs of Etzion, Ariel, and the Jerusalem area, home to roughly 80% of Israeli homesteaders), plus an essential security corridor in the Jordan Valley.[85] Abu Ala, Arafat's mouthpiece, gave a "Thanks-but-no-thanks" response. (Giving Abu the benefit of the doubt, the main sticking point was that the deal would split the territories into four non-contiguous cantons; yet, on the other hand, the PLO continued to withhold any serious counteroffer.) Ben-Ami notes that Clinton got red in the face and started "shouting terribly" at the Arab, then walked out in a huff. (Abu was so rattled, he did little else but drive around the lawns in a golf cart the rest of his stay.)[86]

Finally, after Israel made a further epic concession with East Jerusalem (the outer envelope of Arab neighborhoods placed under Palestinian sovereignty, the inner under functional autonomy), Arafat privately informed Clinton on July 16 that he could live with 8-10% remaining under Israeli control. After the apparent breakthrough caused renewed optimism with the Israelis, "Easy Going" abruptly retracted his offer. (Meanwhile 200,000 Jews had filled Tel Aviv Square to protest Barak's treacherous betrayal.) On the last night of the meeting, Clinton was pressing Arafat over the extremely generous position on Jerusalem. Predictably, the PLO guru thumbed his nose at the proposal and went home—taking his emergency buzzer with him.

Team Clinton was aghast! In his post-flop press conference, the president placed the blame squarely on Yasser. However, with his legacy at stake, Bill hustled the two leaders back to the White House in December for a last-ditch effort before he and Hillary moved out. This time—with the Second Intifada entering its fourth month—the Israelis pared their counter offer down to just 4-6%. Barak was even willing to cede East Jerusalem and parts of the Old City, along with partial Temple Mount sovereignty as well.[87] However, once again, the Palestinian president passed. In January 2001 (as Clinton was cleaning out his desk, etc.), Arafat called him and said in a flattering tone: "You are a great man," to which he replied: "The h--l I am, I'm a colossal failure and you made me one."[88] (For the record, back on January 21, 1998—the very time Clinton was about to meet Yasser in the Oval Office—the Monica Lewinsky scandal broke, leaving him the dubious distinction of being only the second US president to be impeached.)

SECOND INTIFADA (2000-05)

On Friday morning, September 29, 2000, Ariel Sharon, Barak's minister of housing (and ideological nemesis), made a provocative, forty-five minute "visit" to the Temple Mount as the Moslems were assembling for "worship" at Al-Aqsa Mosque. Suddenly, a gang of Palestinian youths began stoning Sharon's police escort. With the arrival of reinforcements, a general riot ensued. While Sharon did not attempt to enter al-Aqsa (or the Dome of the Rock), he did venture noticeably close to the new entrance of the sunken mosque beneath Al-Aqsa. Arik's parting statement to the press was classic: "I think we can live together with the Palestinians. I came to see what was going on here…I have not committed any act of provocation."[89] When the tumult settled after several hours, four Arabs were dead and 164 wounded; 25 policemen were also injured. Here we go *again*.

"Impromptu" protests erupted across Gaza and the West Bank. Two PA officials (not to mention Arafat's widow), would later acknowledge that the uprising had been planned ever since Camp David.[90] That the supposed spark was struck at a "holy" site would lend a religious fervor to this second rebellion (the Al-Aqsa Intifada). Soon the entire nation was being traumatized by roadside snipers and improvised explosive devices (IEDs). Many Israelis died under the most horrific circumstances. On October 12, 2005, two IDF reservists who accidentally entered Ramallah were beaten, stabbed to death, and disemboweled. (One of the bodies was also set on fire.)

Qassam rockets debuted in April 2001 (though the first direct hit on an Israeli city was not until March 2002). Some 4,561 high-trajectory sorties were launched against Israel during the Second Intifada (mostly from Gaza).[91] Martyrdom bombers were introduced that summer. Six deaths and 100 injuries resulted from a May 15 suicide bombing at a shopping mall in Netanya. Two weeks later, twenty-one young people were killed and 120 maimed at a disco near Tel Aviv. On August 9, a Sbarro Pizzeria blast in the Holy City left fifteen dead and 130 hurt.

According to Israel's Ministry of Foreign Affairs, 1,084 Israelis died in 405 separate acts of Palestinian violence from September 29, 2000, through the end of 2005; the injured numbered 6,264.[92] Four telling events would unfold during the grisly five-year Second Intifada.

"BROTHER BUSH" & "BANDAR BUSH" VS. THE "BURNING BUSH" (2001)

During his 2000 election campaign, George W. Bush stated in a debate with Al Gore, "I want everyone to know, should I be the president, Israel's going to be our friend. I'm going to stand by Israel."[93] In what *should* have served as a spiritual harbinger, America barely escaped a Constitutional crisis when a 5-4 Supreme Court decision gave Bush the presidency. After land for a US embassy in Jerusalem was given to Washington in 1991, Congress authorized the relocation from Tel Aviv. Yet, Bill Clinton refused to make the change. In another campaign promise, Bush assured Jewish voters that *he* would move the embassy if elected president. Was anyone *really* holding their breath?

On June 6, 2001, President Bush (a Billy Graham "convert") sent CIA Director George Tenet to Israel to broker a cessation of building projects in the disputed settlements. (Bush was going to "stand by Israel," etc.) Well, a funny thing happened out in the Gulf of Mexico while George was en route to Tel Aviv; Tropical Storm Allison formed within a day and headed off to the president's home state. Allison had never heard the expression, "Don't mess with Texas"; she was more familiar with the concept, "Don't mess with Israel." One of the heaviest rains in US history drenched numerous portions of Texas June 5-11. More than two feet of water closed George Bush Intercontinental Airport for nearly two days. Houston received over twenty-eight inches in a single 24-hour period. The city was forced to shut down for three days. Some 25,000 homes and businesses were damaged or destroyed, as well as 50,000 automobiles and trucks.[94]

Allison's ten-day "visit" left Texas in shambles. Twenty-eight counties were declared a disaster area (along with fourteen Louisiana parishes). The price tag for Bush's attempt to "stand by Israel" was $3 billion in Houston and another $4 billion statewide. As with his father's Perfect Storm encounter, the two stories shared front-page coverage. In the June 13, 2001, *New York Times*, one article was entitled: "Flood Tunneled into Houston's Cultural Heart"; the adjacent title read, "Two Sides in Mideast Accept U.S. Plan for a Cease-Fire."[95] But this was mere child's play compared to what happened later.

On March 7, 2001, Islam's worst nightmare occurred—Ariel Sharon (a.k.a. "The Bulldozer") became Israel's eleventh prime minster. Less than six months later, Saudi Arabia's Crown Prince Abdullah blew a gasket on August 23 when he saw Bush make a rare pro-Israel comment on CNN. The "incendiary" blip was: "The Israelis will not negotiate under terrorist threat…I strongly urge Mr. Arafat to put one hundred percent effort into stopping terrorist activity…." The potentate promptly phoned his billionaire ambassador to the US, Prince Bandar bin Sultan, at his $36 million Rocky Mountain retreat in Aspen, Colorado. Bandar was told to confront Bush accordingly.

The Saudi oil prince was so close to "Bush 41" that First Lady Barbara affectionately called him "Bandar Bush."[96] However, as "business is business," the time had come for the "bramble bush" (Judges 9:14) to give G. W. a Middle Eastern rude awakening. With "43" on a month-long vacation at his Crawford ranch (ultimately taking 977 vacation days for an incredible 33% of his two-term stint), Bandar met with National Security Advisor Condoleezza Rice at her White House office on August 27. Using a twenty-five-page script from Abdullah, Bandar began: "This is the hardest message I've had to deliver between our two countries since I started working in this country in 1983." He then shifted to the bottom line: "We believe there has been a strategic decision by the US that its national interest in the Middle East is 100% based on Israeli prime minister Ariel Sharon." Bandar's missive ended with a threat: "Starting from today, you're from Uruguay, as they say. You Americans, go your way; I, Saudi Arabia, go my way. From now on we will protect our national interests, regardless of where America's interests lie in the region."[97]

Condi, a future oil executive herself (Chevron later naming an oil tanker in her honor[98]), assured Bandar that there had been no change in American policy. According to Craig Unger's highly documented *New York Times* best seller, *House of Bush, House of Saud: The Secret Relationship Between the World's Two Most Powerful Dynasties*:

> For his part Bush still had no intention of getting involved in the sticky Middle East peace process. Nevertheless, Bush was so stunned by the Saudi threat that he immediately did an about-face. Within thirty-six hours, Bandar returned to Riyadh with a groundbreaking proposal written by the president to mollify Abdullah.[99]

After beginning innocently enough—"I am troubled and feel deeply the suffering of ordinary Palestinians in their day to day life and I want such tragedies and sufferings to end"—the president crossed the line, declaring: "I firmly believe that the Palestinian people have a right to self-determination and to live peacefully and securely in their own state in their own homeland."[100] As Unger notes, "Bush was not just getting involved. For the first time, he was publicly supporting a Palestinian state—and he had done it in writing."[101]

Apparently, *Brother* Bush feared *Bandar* Bush more than the *Burning* Bush:

> Abdullah had played the game well. He had banged his fist and the United States had jumped. He was so thrilled with his victory…that he proudly showed off his correspondence—Bush's two-page letter and the long message he had given Bandar—as trophies to Arab leaders in Syria, Egypt, and Jordan…At Abdullah's invitation, Yasir Arafat came all the way from South Africa to Riyadh especially to read it.[102]

Bandar was then sent back to Washington to convince Bush to make public his commitment to Palestinian statehood.

On Friday, September 7, Bandar met with Bush, Rice, Cheney, and Colin Powell, telling his American friends "how happy he was to discover that he had misinterpreted the White House's policy toward the Middle East."[103] The Bush administration "reiterated its desire to pursue new peace initiatives immediately."[104] Unger writes:

> Many questions were unresolved about how to pursue such initiatives, but suddenly there was enough goodwill that discussions continued between the two countries over the weekend of September 8 and 9. At issue was whether Colin Powell or President Bush should make the speech announcing the new plans. Bush was even willing to meet with Arafat at the UN—a prospect that pleased the Saudis immensely.[105]

As Proverbs 29:25 warns, *"The fear of man bringeth a snare,"* America was now in mortal danger for aligning with Islam to divide God's "Holy Ground." To the dismay of the "religious" world, the first mention of the word "holy" in Scripture is found in Exodus 3:5, the venerated object being—"dirt." (Even one of Hafez al-Assad's ancestors grasped this truth, as shown in II Kings 5:17.) The bottom line that guarantees judgment for messing with this "holy dirt" is Psalm 132:13, *"For the LORD has chosen Zion; he hath desired it for his habitation."* Thus, the secular, Harvard-educated Unger concludes:

> And so, on that Monday night, Prince Bandar bin Sultan bin Abdul Aziz was, in his own words, "the happiest man in the world." As he told the *Washington Post*, he decided to relax in the indoor swimming pool of his lavish McLean residence, smoking a cigar. He had been back and forth between Saudi Arabia and Washington with the Bush response and then the Saudi response. He had worked through the entire weekend, until three or four o'clock in the morning, and then had worked all day Monday. He deserved a rest, so he called his office. He told them he was taking Tuesday off—Tuesday, September 11, 2001.[106]

Isaiah 26:5 declares that *"he bringeth* DOWN *them that* DWELL ON HIGH*; the* LOFTY CITY*, he layeth it* LOW*, even to the* GROUND*; he bringeth it even to the* DUST.*"* (And if you're into "Bible codes," don't miss the untold subtle nuggets in the *English* text of the King James Bible, the first mention of a satanically inspired lethal implosion appearing in—Job 1:19.)

OPERATION DEFENSIVE SHIELD (2002)

The first mention of a "shield" in Scripture is found in Genesis 15:1, "After these things the word of the LORD came unto Abram in a vision, saying, Fear not, Abram: I am thy SHIELD, and thy exceeding great reward." As the Jews continued to relegate the God of their fathers to a geological substance, they would also have to issue their own shield against a never-ending array of threats—both from within and without.

"Operation Defensive Shield" was a counterinsurgency push that sought to reassert IDF control over the Palestinian cities in Area "A."

(So much for the "wisdom" of Oslo II and all future two-state solution security guarantees.) The impetus for the month-long incursion was a new wave of Islamic terrorism. Rehavam Ze'evi, Israel's tourism minister, was killed at the Jerusalem Hyatt by PFLP assassins on October 17, 2001. A spike in suicide bombings followed in March, (a.k.a. "Black March"); 131 deaths in fifteen explosions (averaging one attack every two days). The main perpetrators were Hamas, Islamic Jihad, Tanzim, and the Al-Aqsa Martyrs' Brigades. On March 9, eleven people were killed and fifty-four injured when a terrorist detonated himself in the trendy Café Moment coffee shop in downtown Jerusalem, a mere soccer field removed from the prime minister's residence. The final straw was the infamous March 27 Park Hotel "Passover Massacre" in Netanya. Of the 250 (mostly elderly) guests attending the Seder meal, twenty-two were killed instantly (eight dying afterward) with 150 wounded, a 72% casualty rate!

Authorized by Prime Minister Sharon and directed by IDF Chief of Staff Shaul Mofaz, Defensive Shield became the largest West Bank operation since 1967. On March 29, infantry, armor, and combat bulldozers, supported by helicopter gunships, entered Ramallah and promptly surrounded Arafat's mukataa ("headquarters"), trapping the PA CEO in the process. Scores of incriminating documents were uncovered. With Yasser under wraps, the IDF occupied the rest of the city, killing 30, arresting 700, and seizing large caches of weapons.

This was not the first time Arafat had been cornered like a rat. On October 3, 2000, with Camp David still smoldering, he apparently had another "anxiety attack" in a meeting with Secretary Albright at the US embassy in Paris. As the native Egyptian wild man suddenly jumped up and took off for home, Bodansky relates: "Albright literally ran after him, shouting to the Marine guards, 'Shut the gates!'"[107] Effectively contained in the compound, "Easy" returned to the room, but refused to cooperate. (It is not known if he set off his buzzer.)

That morning Israeli troops entered Bethlehem, the city of Christ's birth. The campaign's nadir was the five-week siege of the Church of the Nativity, 200 barricaded Muslim terrorists having converted the 1,500-year-old "Christian" shrine into their own Defensive Shield. On day three of the standoff, Samir Ibrahim Salman, the forty-five-year-old bell-ringer, was shot in the crossfire, bleeding to death in Manger Square. (Both sides deny firing the fatal round.) Described by Reuters as a "simple man" (other accounts ranging from "mentally impaired" to "retarded") who walked with his "back slightly bent,"[108] the real-life "Hunchback of Notre Dame," unlike Quasimodo, was "beloved of the town,"[109] having "served as caretaker at the church for more years than his friends could recall, [ringing] its bell daily, announcing worship services, weddings or funerals to the residents."[110]

Thus, no matter how many priests and nuns were being held, there was no way the Jews could escape from this publicity disaster. And to make matters worse, like the original "no room in the inn" scenario for Joseph and Mary, there was "no room in the morgue" for Salman, his bullet-riddled corpse being kept "in an empty hospital room, where two small fans straining on the highest setting circulated the air."[111]

The last strongholds were subdued with minimal effort. Tulkarm and Qalqilya surrendered on April 1. Jenin, the main PLO base, folded the following day (though not without more bad press; reports of 500 civilians massacred in the local refugee camp were later refuted by a UN investigation). Nablus, the largest and second-most dangerous city (8,000 thugs and 13,000 "ordinary" Palestinians), fell on April 4.

Defensive Shield concluded on May 3. The IDF lost thirty men (twenty-three in Jenin alone, including three lieutenants, one captain, and two majors), plus 120 wounded; 240 terrorists died, with over 4,000 detained. Some 4,600 weapons and hundreds of explosives were confiscated. Unfortunately, the well-fought mission would prove to be just another bandage on an incurable wound. Hamas apologist, Beverley Milton-Edwards of Queens University, concludes: "The unequivocal victory eventually proved elusive and the Israelis and Palestinians resumed a variety of forms of low intensity warfare with each other."[112]

SECURITY BARRIER (2002)

In June 2002, the Knesset endorsed Prime Minister Sharon's request to build a security barrier (a.k.a. the "Apartheid Wall") to segregate the West Bank territories from Israel proper. Though generally depicted as an imposing replica of the Berlin Wall,[113] over 95% of the projected 422-mile circuitous route is actually a high-tech, electrified, 10-ft. high chain-link fence, flanked by paved pathways, rolled barbed wire, and 6-8 ft. deep vehicle barrier trenches monitored by drones, cameras, censors, and thermal imaging. In most locations, the average width of the area is 160 feet. (The more familiar 30-ft. high concrete walls are used in urban areas to thwart snipers.)

Despite Robert Frost's verse, "Good fences make good neighbors," the contentious impediment continues to push the envelope between the two disparate cultures. By September 2013, ninety-nine checkpoints existed through which Palestinians were required to pass when moving from one West Bank town to another. (Most of these "flashpoints" are run by privatized security firms with little regard for political correctness.) Representing another problem, according to B'Tselem, when the wall is completed, 9.5% of the West Bank (containing sixty settlements) will be situated on the Israeli side.[114]

Amidst growing criticism, Israel simply cited the data. In 2002, there were 457 deaths attributed to PLO insurgents, most slipping across the Green Line at will. Brigadier General Eival Gilady reported: "[O]n seven different occasions during 2002, suicide bombers stayed overnight at a 'terrorist bed-and-breakfast' in Anin, a Palestinian village in the northwest corner of the West Bank, before walking into Israel to perpetrate the mass murder of innocents."[115] By 2008, the fatality count was down to eight. Par for the course, after condemning Israel's barrier, the hypocritical UN announced plans to build its own security fence in Manhattan.[116] On the tenth anniversary of the Knesset vote, the project's chief architect, Colonel Danny Tirza, reflected, "I would have gladly done without the fence. Yet, we had no choice but to build it in order to protect our lives and our children's lives."[117]

As of 2014, over 20% of the wall was unfinished. At $2 million per kilometer, "Arik's fence" constitutes the largest infrastructure project in Israel's history, costing $260 million annually for maintenance alone. Someone should have called "The Donald." (While some see Ezekiel 38:11-12 implying that Israel will have dismantled her walls in a glaring security concession to implement her Tribulation covenant with Antichrist, the context, specifically verse 22 as cross-referenced with Revelation 20:8-9, may apply to Gog's latter-day attack on Jerusalem at the end of the Millennium.)

GUSH KATIF (2005)

On June 24, 2002, Bush made his long-overdue speech endorsing a "peaceful and democratic state alongside Israel." At a follow-up Rose Garden ceremony on March 14, 2003, the president added that he would unveil a "roadmap" for peace once a Palestinian prime minster with "real authority" was installed. Five days later, Arafat nominated Mahmoud Abbas ("Abu Mazen") as the first prime minister of the PA.

Though Sharon had long been in tow, the public felt stunned and betrayed. On April 30, 2003, the touted Roadmap (officially titled: *A Performance-Based Roadmap to a Permanent Two-State Solution to the Israeli-Palestinian Conflict*) arrived at the Knesset. The next day three Israelis were killed and twenty injured in a blast at Mike's Place, a Tel Aviv pub. Nevertheless, the political stage was set for Israel to implement the greatest disaster of her brief modern existence.

On December 18, 2003, Prime Minister Sharon, praising the Bush Roadmap as a "clear and reasonable plan," made his first speech broaching the volatile Gaza "Disengagement Plan." The Roadmap represented a unique geo-political approach, including pioneering a defined set of chronological goals, leading to a Palestinian State in 2005. To meet this schedule, the specifics of the unilateral disengagement were released the following April—the evacuation and redeployment of all civilian and military personnel (apart from a security detachment on the Egypt-Gaza border), followed by their redeployment outside the Strip, as well as a plan to relocate four isolated West Bank settlements in Northern Samaria (providing territorial contiguity for Palestinians).

On October 26, 2004, the Knesset approved the plan 67 to 45 (with one abstention and one absentee). Fate seemed to condone the deed with Arafat's "sudden" death on November 11, 2004, from "unknown causes," the leading theories being poison, alcoholism, or AIDS. After a second vote on February 16, 2005, to underwrite the resettlements, Sharon signed the historic disengagement order four days later. ("Rachel," bar the door!)

The pending removal triggered *great* distress within the targeted communities along with unparalleled dissention throughout the nation. Ground Zero for Sharon's edict was the Gush Katif bloc, comprising twenty-one settlements (mostly along the southwestern edge of the Strip). The betrayal was particularly bitter to the 8,600 residents (many of them Orthodox Jews), for their precarious existence (dating from 1968) had served as a strategically positioned *civilian* bulwark to thwart future invasions from Egypt, or use of the area as a staging ground for fedayeen attacks. On August 15, 2005, the IDF distributed eviction notices telling the patriots that they had forty-eight hours to leave their homes.

On August 16, some 40,000 IDF troops began the historic, highly charged expulsion of their fellow citizens—a blatant violation of Amos 9:15, *"And I will plant them upon their land, and they shall* NO MORE BE PULLED UP OUT OF THEIR LAND WHICH I HAVE GIVEN THEM, *saith the LORD thy God."* The last holdouts were forcibly "pulled up" on August 23, with the last of their West Bank counterparts ousted the next day. All told, over 10,000 Israelis were homeless within a week. Every building was promptly leveled, except for twenty-one synagogues and several large greenhouses (the latter left as a naive goodwill gesture). The final indignity was the gruesome exhumation of forty-eight graves, a macabre reenactment of the Shoah. Ironically, one of the bodies was a female survivor of Auschwitz.[118]

Now it just so *happened* that on that very day that the last Jew in Samaria was ejected (August 24), Tropical Depression 12 (Israel's number) formed over the Bahamas, then upgraded to Tropical Storm Katrina (meaning "to purify"). By August 29, Katrina had intensified to a Category 5 (death) hurricane, *smashing* ashore with a tidal surge of nearly 35 feet (the highest on record). The rest is history—over 1,700 killed; 500,000 homes destroyed or seriously damaged; $100 billion in losses with 1.3 million *Americans* left "homeless" in its wake (a 130-1 ratio)—all courtesy of the "Bush Peace Plan." An online *CBS News* story read, "Katrina Leaves Toxic Bathtub,"[119] a fitting metaphor given the expellees' future degrading experience with government-issued sewer pipe air-raid shelters.

For the record, after documenting twenty instances of divine judgment on America linked to political policies hostile to Israel, the opening chapter of volume one in this series (published in January 2005) concluded with the following subliminal prophecy:

> If you're still undecided about standing with the Lord, just start watching the Weather Channel before retiring each night. (As the humanistic advertisement for the program *StormWatch* puts it, 'Experience people at their best and Nature at its worst.') Then pull

> those covers snugly against your chin. You won't have to worry about anything stirring out there in the dark—*until* the next mile marker is reached on the 'Road Map to Peace.' *Nighty-night!*

Six-and-a-half-years later, the June 6, 2011, front cover of *Newsweek* featured a foreboding tornado funnel with the words: "WEATHER PANIC – THIS IS THE NEW NORMAL (AND WE'RE HOPELESSLY UNPREPARED)."

Apart from the general threat posed by the disengagement, the exit of Israeli forces along the Gaza-Egyptian border was a source of particular alarm. On September 1, 2005, Israel and Egypt signed the "Agreed Arrangements Regarding the Deployment of a Designated Force of Border Guards Along the Border in the Rafah Area." Under the terms, *Hosni Mubarak* would now be "responsible" for watching Israel's back along the narrow, eight-mile weapons smuggling route (lately reinforced with a mammoth 23-ft. high concrete wall). As an intriguing connection to the Introduction of *Holy Ground*, this *cordon sanitaire*—faithfully guarded by the IDF for over three decades—just *happens* to be named the "Philadelphia Corridor" (the lengthy title of the abrogation pact also being known as the Philadelphi Accord).

At 7:00 a.m. on Monday, September 12, 2005, IDF officials locked the main gate at the Kissufim Crossing, effectively ending thirty-eight years of Israeli presence in Gaza. Brigadier General Aviv Kochavi was the last Jew to leave, unwittingly fulfilling the prophecy in Zephaniah 2:4, *"For Gaza shall be forsaken...."* The new "residents" promptly destroyed the lucrative greenhouses (real "bright" move) and torched the synagogues (sparing one of the latter for a terrorist museum). Four months later, Prime Minister Ariel Sharon suffered a hemorrhagic stroke (remaining in a coma till his death on January 11, 2014).

The relocation and "compensation" of the Gush Katif settlers is a separate tragedy all its own. In June 2014, this author interviewed one of the more outspoken expellees (an American-born, disabled Yom Kippur veteran) at his government-provided *caravilla* (a flimsy, plasterboard, modular box-house) in the overcrowded, refuse-strewn, refugee camp in Nitzan (halfway between Ashdod and Ashkelon). The highlight of the visit was "touring" the communal "bomb shelter"—a filthy 6 ft. x 12 ft. concrete sewer pipe "affectionately" known as a "sewervilla." The drainpipe sanctuary (located within "puking distance" of the man's front door) represents a sick double entendre, for the

Gush Katif residents had been constantly told that their tenuous existence in the Strip had become a "*drain* on the military budget."

Unable to withstand a direct hit, the pipe's main function is to shield the occupants from the periodic "shrapnel showers" from rockets exploded by Iron Dome. While Defense Ministry officials insist that the drainpipes are really *muganiyots* ("teensy weensy shelters"), to Shoah survivors they are a cruel reminder of those subterranean escape routes in the Warsaw Ghetto. When asked for a summary statement for the tragedy of Gush Katif, the one-armed, cigar-smoking native New Yorker gruffly replied: "We told you what would happen if we were forced out. You refused to believe it. It has happened exactly as we said. And *still* no one gives a d--n!"

SECOND LEBANON WAR (2006)

Ehud Olmert, one-time mayor of Jerusalem, became Israel's twelfth prime minister on April 14, 2006. (Formerly of Likud, Olmert aligned with the new Kadima party, which split off Likud over Gaza.) Israel's first "benefit" after disengaging in the south, was a Katyusha barrage from the north. The 2006 Lebanon War was a futile month-long scrap between the IDF and Hezbollah in Lebanon and the Golan Heights.

Upon Israel's withdrawal in May 2000, the Iranian-inspired Islamic revolutionary cell, Hezbollah ("Party of God"), ensconced itself in Southern Lebanon, creating a "state within a state." Enter five years of terrorist strikes against northern Israel. On July 12, 2006, while a diversionary rocket fusillade was menacing the Israeli town of Shlomi, Hezbollah fighters made a cross-border raid near Zar'it, killing eight IDF soldiers, wounding six, and capturing two. Over the next ten days Israel responded with air strikes and artillery. On July 23, an ambitious ground campaign was reluctantly launched, ostensibly to rescue the two soldiers (more realistically, to force Hezbollah across the Litani).

The Litani Offensive comprised four hectic engagements in thirty-four days: Maroun al-Ras, Bint Jbeil, Ayta ash-Shab, and Wadi Saluki. Despite several exemplary efforts, the Second Lebanon War became another no-win quagmire for Tel Aviv. When the UN truce took effect on August 14, "God's Party" had already fired 3,790 rockets into Israel, striking 901 cities and towns, killing 42 civilians and injuring

4,262. In a "blast from the past," 2,773 other civilians had to be treated for "shock and anxiety."[120] The post-war Winograd Commission Report concluded: "The IDF was not ready for this war."[121] Benjamin Lambeth, a Senior Research Associate for the RAND Corporation adds: "Israel's second Lebanon war ended up being the most inconclusive performance by the IDF in its many trials by fire since 1948, in that it represented the first time that a major confrontation ended without a clear-cut military victory on Israel's part."[122]

Ironically, the campaign was both doomed and defined by its very name: "Operation Change of Direction." According to Lieutenant Colonel Ron Tira, chief IAF planner, the main flaw was Israel's "over-zealous embrace of the American effects-based operations (EBO) idea."[123] As he relates, this involved a basic *change* in tactic—from breaking the enemy's *back* (via ground forces) to severing his *head* (via aerial strikes). "EBO's aim is to paralyze the enemy's operational ability, in contrast to destroying its military force. This is achieved by striking the headquarters, lines of communications, and other critical junctions in its military force."[124] Alas, this is just what the IAF/IDF did *not* do: "Israel failed on the strategic, operational, and tactical levels. Israel did not succeed in generating decapitation, paralysis, blindness, or any other effect that substantially harms the will or functioning of the organization's command and control echelon."[125]

A 2006 war vet (and friend of this author) concurred with Tira's analysis, stating: "They thought air control would determine the result. They wanted a small, smart, and advanced army which would include smaller infantry units. Infantry units and reserves were barely training and maintaining their goals. Battle equipment was lacking bad. The war was not organized by any means and intelligence failed its job, costing many lives." When asked about the Litani Offensive, the sniper specialist recalled: "The whole war from beginning to end was very intensive and aggressive, involving deep strikes in Lebanon." Between 600-800 Hezbollah guerrillas were killed, plus some 1,200 Lebanese civilians. The IDF lost 120 dead, with over 600 wounded. The number of KIAs represents a shocking 400% increase over the First Lebanon War, where 1,200 soldiers died in thirty-six months. Included among the fatalities were Ehud Goldwasser and Eldad Regev, the two hostages. At the time of their abduction, both were reservists on their last day of duty. On July 16, 2008, their remains were returned to Eretz Yisrael via a morbid (though standard) corpse swap.

OPERATION ORCHARD (2007)

On the heels of her latest debacle, Israel rebounded to yet another precarious plateau. In July 2000, Bashar al-Assad succeeded his father to become Syria's new president. A "chip off the old block," the medical doctor—turned murderous dictator—had *no* intention of signing any treaty with Israel. To the contrary, by 2007, Syria already had a top-secret, nearly completed plutonium nuclear reactor named al-Kibar. The facility was located in the desert region of Deir ez-Zor (less than a mile from the prophetically relevant Euphrates River, cited in Revelation 9:14 and 16:12). On the evening of September 6, 2007, Bashar's pride and joy went the way of Saddam's Osirak reactor.

Now, as for what actually happened, no one knows "officially." While Damascus has remained too mortified for comment, the Israelis have prudently reciprocated. (When this author broached the subject with a reserve IDF officer, the normally cooperative source replied with a winsome reticence: "It wasn't us. ☺") According to a September 2012 *New Yorker* article, Mossad agents broke into the Vienna residence of Ibrahim Othman, the head of Syria's Atomic Energy Commission. (Othman was in town for the International Atomic Energy Agency's board of governors.) The Israelis extracted some three dozen photos and other incriminating documents from Othman's hard drive confirming that Assad's reactor was developed from its Korean prototype in Yongbyon. (An earlier version of this story in the November 2009 German magazine, *Der Spiegel*, has the agents in a London hotel, hacking the laptop of an unnamed "senior Syrian government official" with a "Trojan Horse" program).[126]

The revelation posed a red line for Tel Aviv. Further confirmation was supplied by contaminated soil samples from Deir ez-Zor retrieved by Shaldag operatives (an elite IAF commando unit). After a full CIA briefing, President Bush declined to get involved, primarily on Condi's advice.[127] However, he did give Olmert a tacit nod for a preemptive strike. The top-secret mission, codenamed "Operation Orchard," would be led by IAF Major General Eliezer Shkedy.

The sketchy "off the record" version of Israel's second swing at a foreign nuclear reactor in twenty-five years began on September 5, when, according to Dr. Gilbert, "[A] team of elite Israeli Special Force commandos reached the site the day before, to mark the target with laser beams."[128] At 8:45 p.m. the next evening, ten US-made F-15I *Ra'am* fighter jets (with an escort of F-16I *Sufas*) roared off from Ramat David Air Force Base south of Haifa. (Three of the F-15Is were abruptly released for an in-flight reserve.) Crossing into Syrian airspace, the formation leader dropped his first bomb, taking out a radar station in Tall al-Abuad.[129] Twenty minutes later—with X marking the spot—seventeen *tons* of laser-guided AGM-65 bombs fell on al-Kibar, smoking the facility along with ten Korean technicians.

On a personal note, while traveling with a private tour of IDF bases in October 2007, this author was privileged to visit in the home of a popular rabbi, the father of twelve children, one of whom is the pilot who painted his laser beam on the Syrian reactor. (The man had a beautiful olive garden and gave each guest a bottle of olive oil, the label reading in Hebrew—"Not touched by Arab hands.")

ANNAPOLIS CONFERENCE (2007)

On November 27, 2007, George Bush convened the Annapolis Conference at the United States Naval Academy in Annapolis, Maryland. The two major players were Prime Minister Ehud Olmert and President Mahmoud Abbas. (Some forty international guests were also on hand). The stated purpose for the one-day public relations gathering was to revive the Israeli-Palestinian dialogue to implement the Roadmap before December 2008 (the end of Bush's second term).

President Bush began his opening address, stating: "We meet to lay the foundation for the establishment of a new nation—a democratic Palestinian state that will live side by side with Israel in peace and security."[130] Of course, this latest attempt to inaugurate "Peace on Earth" *without* the "Prince of Peace"—not to mention the *third* successive meeting in a place indirectly named for the Vatican "goddess," Mary[131] (i.e., "Mary land," formally dubbed after the fanatically Popish Queen, Henrietta Maria[132])—was destined to go *nowhere* fast! (For the record, Annapolis is located sixty miles from the oldest Roman Catholic Church in America, St. Francis Xavier in Leonardtown, Maryland, the county seat of "St. Mary's County.")

A synopsis of the otherwise futile forum can help one gain a working knowledge of the intricacies incumbent upon the negotiators. The four core issues of the elusive Roadmap remain: definable borders;

national security; the final status of Jerusalem (the PA insisting that East Jerusalem be renamed Al-Quds as its official capital); and the return (and/or compensation) of the so-called Palestinian refugees. Israel's long-held demand for political recognition was *technically* met by Yasser Arafat after the epic Palestinian Declaration of Independence on November 15, 1988. The resultant "Historic Compromise" issued by the Palestine National Council (PNC) rendered implicit legitimacy to the Jewish State by endorsing the "two-*state* solution." The key to Arafat's landmark concession (i.e., forfeiting 78% of the "historic" Palestinian homeland, etc.) was that the new Palestinian State would accept nothing less than the total acreage within the 1967 borders (a.k.a. the "Green Line").

The obvious glitch was that a sizable number of Moshe Dayan's "facts" had eventuated in the West Bank between 1967 and 1988 with many others following. The *good* news (from Tel Aviv's perspective) was that most of these settlements existed along the Green Line (the old Area "C" of Oslo II), and could therefore be easily absorbed within Israel proper. (Many viewed Sharon's security barrier as having rendered the proposal a *fait accompli.*) The *bad* news (from Ramallah's perspective) was that "a deal is a deal," i.e., not one "zig" or "zag" beyond the 1967 borders would be countenanced.

Unfortunately, 375,000 Israelis were living in nine of the twelve largest "illegal" settlements (East Jerusalem, Modi'in Illit, Beitar Illit, Ma'ale Adumim, Elkana Bloc, Giv'at Ze'ev, Etzion Bloc, Efrat, and Alfei Menashe). As they were not about to be uprooted or abandoned, the only viable solution was a mutually agreeable cross-border land swap. And *that* was the central focus at Annapolis. The alternating percentage offers that transpired over the ensuing bi-weekly sessions were beyond mindboggling. Olmert's opening bid was 5.2% of Eretz Yisrael to annex 5.9% of the West Bank (encompassing 426,800 of the half million settlers); Abbas counter-offered 1.6% (only 310,000 Jews) for 2.0% of contiguous "holy dirt."[133] While 69% of Israelis initially supported Annapolis, only 17% deemed it a success afterward.[134] As if to mock the absurd affair, Mother Nature "barely" showed up. According to Bill Koenig, "only" two back-to-back, billion-dollar disasters hit the US in December (the largest flood in the history of Washington state and a massive ice storm in Oklahoma).[135]

President Bush concluded his formal greeting, saying:

> The day is coming when the terrorists and extremists who threaten the Israeli and Palestinian people will be marginalized and eventually defeated. When that day comes, future generations will look to the work we began here in Annapolis. They will give thanks to the leaders who gathered on the banks of the Chesapeake for their vision, their wisdom and courage to choose a future of freedom and peace. Thanks for coming. May God bless their work.[136]

Do you suppose that any of those august envoys "gathered on the banks of the Chesapeake" realized that their conference coincided with two important milestones in modern Israeli history? The "foundation" for the new "democratic Palestinian State" was laid on November 27—the birthday of Israel's first president, Dr. Chaim Weizmann (1874-1952). The year itself marked the 60th anniversary of the ill-fated voyage of the Aliya Bet transport, *Exodus 1947* (formerly the *USS President Warfield*), an American-made, steel-hulled passenger steamer, originally commissioned as a ferry—on the *Chesapeake Bay*.

THE GAZA WARS (2007-14)

Less than five months after Gush Katif's Jews were evicted, their prescient warnings started coming to pass. On January 25, 2006, the Hamas proxy party, "Change and Reform" (the former National Islamic Salvation Party), won a landslide victory in the new Palestinian parliament, trouncing the incumbent Fatah Party of President Mahmoud Abbas. Thus, a Muslim terror cell won 76 of the 132 seats, giving the party at war with Israel the legal right to form the next cabinet under Abbas. Most telling, UN observers "agreed that the process had been democratic and transparent with no corruption."[137]

On March 28, while Israelis were going to their *own* voting booths, the first Katyusha was launched into Israel from Gaza. According to the Israel Security Agency, 1,247 rockets were fired in 2006 (compared to "only" 286 in 2005, a 436% increase).[138] Adding insult to injury, many of the Gaza exiles now found themselves in the direct line of fire, while their urban brethren in Tel Aviv and Haifa sipped lattes and espressos well beyond harm's way. On June 25, Gilad Shalit, a nineteen-year-old soldier, was captured by Hamas militants on the Israeli side of the Kerem Shalom Crossing. Three days later, the army was redeployed to Gaza. The IDF conducted "Operation Summer Rains" (June 28 to November 26), reinforced by "Operation Autumn Clouds" (October 31 to November 7). In the "lopsided" match (pitting 3,000 Israelis against 9,000 bad guys), the IDF lost 7 killed and 38 wounded, compared to 1,400 Palestinian casualties, including 117 civilian deaths. (Corporal Shalit would remain a convenient bargaining chip until his 2011 high-profile trade for 1,027 Hamasites.)

The main Gaza campaign was the "Six-Day" Muslim civil war between Hamas and Fatah (June 10-15, 2007). The insurgents easily defeated Fatah's National Security Forces. While President Abbas dissolved the Palestinian-Hamas hybrid on June 14, Prime Minister Ismail Haniyeh "stayed on" as the disputed head of the de facto Hamas "government." Over the next months, some fifty "Talibanization" attacks were made against various non-Muslim soft targets (the Holy Bible Association, the YMCA library, Greek Orthodox churches and schools, even barber shops, music stores, and a UN school where boys and girls played sports together).[139] Sharia courts became the main organs of Gaza "justice." The liberal Human Rights Watch agency called the acts "serious violations of international humanitarian law, in some cases amounting to war crimes."[140] Dr. Jonathan Schanzer wrote, "The few, reluctant steps toward liberalization that the PA had taken during its 13-year rule in Gaza—small advances in press and political freedoms, for example—had been wiped out in a matter of days."[141]

As the renewed rocket attacks and cross-border incursions began their natural escalation, *courtesy of the Israeli-created terrorist enclave*, many settlers in the outlying areas suffered a commensurate rise of emotional strain. One study revealed that in Sderot (the closest town to Gaza, thus, the most frequently targeted), "between 75% and 94% of children aged 4-18 showed symptoms of post-traumatic stress, and 28% of adults, and 30% of children in Sderot have post-traumatic stress disorder (PTSD)."[142] Indicia range from diaper regression to youths sleeping with their shoes on. Mitchell Bard, Executive Director of the American-Israeli Cooperative Enterprise (AICE) writes:

> To put the impact in more concrete terms, people living in Sderot limit their showers to less than a minute for fear they will literally be caught with their pants down if a warning siren sounds. They also have stopped wearing seat belts so they can get out of their

cars more quickly. Some Israelis are afraid to listen to music because they might not hear the siren.[143]

Faced with such "rocket science" realities, the IDF was drawn into a demoralizing cycle of house-to-house search and destroy missions, all within the world's most densely populated city (1.7 million people). While the end of any one operation was generally signaled by a ceasefire, the start of the next would be occasioned by the inevitable rupture of the same. The new era would also be hindered by the ongoing historic protest from within the IDF itself (as documented in the controversial 2012 release, *Our Harsh Logic: Israeli Soldiers' Testimonies from the Occupied Territories, 2000-2010*).

The first such endeavor was "Operation Hot Winter" (February 28 to March 3, 2008). While 450 enemy fighters and civilians were killed in the five-day period (the IDF losing only three soldiers), some 200 rockets chased Israeli citizens into their "sewervillas," nonetheless.

The next mission was "Operation Cast Lead" (December 27, 2008, to January 18, 2009). Nearly 1,400 Palestinians (mostly civilians) were killed in the twenty-two-day fight. Cast Lead proceeded in two phases: a week of massive aerial sorties involving F-16 fighter jets, Apache helicopters, and unmanned drones, followed by a two-week combined air and ground assault. With Israel forced to answer the non-stop rocket attacks against its own people (600 during the operation), the civilian population of Gaza was caught in the middle, as usual. While the IDF broadcast radio warnings, dropped leaflets, and even made 150,000 phone calls to minimize non-combatant casualties, Hamas utilized apartment buildings and schools as launching pads for rockets and storage areas for munitions. One Hamas official would later admit what everyone already knew—that the religious fanatics had "created a human shield of women, children, and the elderly."[144] As Mrs. Meir famously said, "We can forgive the Arabs for killing our children, but we can never forgive them for forcing us to kill their children."

Israel's *third* no-win Gaza fiasco was "Operation Returning Echo" (March 9-14, 2009). The IAF flew thirty-seven sorties against targets such as weapons storage facilities, rocket launch sites, and training bases. More significantly, by month's end, Benjamin Netanyahu was poised to make a *return* of his own. On March 31, 2009, less than two years after Annapolis, it was "anchors aweigh" for Ehud Olmert, Israel's embattled leader. With Olmert's administration awash in corruption, the ever-resilient Bibi was promptly elected to his second term as prime minister. (An August 30, 2009, indictment brought about Ehud's conviction in July 2012 on one count of breach of trust, followed by a second conviction in March 2014 for bribery; after a lengthy appeal, his six-year term was reduced to eighteen months.)

For the record, as Proverbs 6:27 asks, *"Can a man take fire in his bosom and his clothes be not burned?"* in December 2010, the time of the Mount Carmel forest fire (the nation's greatest natural disaster), former Israeli president Moshe Katsav (2000-2007) was convicted on two counts of forcible rape. Sadly, the moral stain occurred in 1998 when Katsav was Netanyahu's minister of tourism—as the saying goes, "Everything rises and falls on leadership."

Now lest the reader get the impression that all was peaceful elsewhere, one of the most horrific crimes in Israel's history occurred on March 11, 2001, in the West Bank Jewish settlement of Itamar (Area "C"). As a classic testimony to the "Beauty of Islam," two Palestinian teenage cousins murdered five members of a Jewish family as they slept in their own beds (on Sabbath night, no less). While parents Ehud and Ruth Fogel, along with their two older children, Yova, age eleven, and Elad, four, were "merely" *knifed* to death, their three-month-old baby girl, Hadas, was *beheaded* for Allah's "glory." (The Fogels' three other children avoided the attack.) According to a poll by the Harry S. Truman Research Institute for the Advancement of Peace, one-third of PA Arabs (Israel's so-called "Roadmap to peace partners") expressed their *support* for the heinous slaughter.[145]

On May 31, 2010, Netanyahu made his foray into Gaza's quicksand with "Operation Sea Breeze," the naval boarding raid on the "Gaza Freedom Flotilla" sixty miles off the Gaza coast in international waters. The six-vessel Turkish convoy had intended to breach Israel's blockade of the Gaza Strip as a public relations stunt. Nine activists were killed and several wounded in the hour-long, predawn engagement; ten "Shayetet-13" commandos (IN special forces) were injured. As expected, Molotov cocktails, detonators, clubs, and other contraband were discovered among the "humanitarian supplies."[146] The 700-plus passengers from 38 nations were promptly deported. The Freedom Flotilla has come to represent a cause célèbre among global activists and non-governmental organizations (NGOs.)[147]

Bibi's next challenge was "Operation Pillar of Defense" (November 14-21, 2012). The week-long incursion was precipitated by a spike in rocket attacks after an IAF drone smoked Hamas strongman, Ahmed Jabari. On the second day of fighting, three Israeli citizens were killed when a Qassam hit their residence in Kiryat Malachi. On day three, the first air-raid sirens heard in Jerusalem for a rocket attack shared the airwaves with the Muslim sundown chant. (Falling outside the Holy City, the winged projectile from Gaza was later described as an "upgraded Qassam."[148]) While 1,456 rockets were fired *at* Israel during Pillar of Defense (the great majority either veering wildly off course or destroyed by Iron Dome), over 1,500 targets *in* Gaza (primarily rocket launch-pads and weapons caches) *were* struck, and, with deadly accuracy. Hamas officials claimed 133 Palestinian deaths, 53 being civilians. The IDF suffered six killed and 240 injured.[149]

On June 2, 2014, Prime Minister Abbas—apparently having deemed Hamas adequately contrite—welcomed the terror party back into the fold. The new Palestinian "unity" government was facilitated by a pact between the Fatah and Hamas parties. Ten days later, three Jewish teenagers were abducted off the street in the West Bank Israeli settlement of Alon Shvut in Gush Etzion. The IDF immediately swept the area, arresting scores of Palestinians, including nearly the entire Hamas leadership. Between June 12 and July 5 the IDF launched 80 raids against Hamas targets in Gaza. The enemy retaliated with 117 rockets.[150] On June 30, 2014, the missing boys' corpses were discovered in a field near Hebron. Within forty-eight hours a sixteen-year-old Palestinian boy was kidnapped in Arab East Jerusalem. His remains were found a few hours later in Jerusalem Forest. (The autopsy revealed that the youth had been beaten and burned *alive*.[151])

Prime Minister Netanyahu subsequently authorized "Operation Protective Edge" (July 8 to August 26, 2014) to punish the small but deadly hell-hole yet again. However, in addition to standard Hamas targets (e.g., rocket launchers, command bunkers, terrorists' houses, weapons-making facilities, and ammo depots), the main objective focused on an elaborate labyrinth of underground tunnels. Described by the IDF as "arteries of terror,"[152] the subterranean passages served as the key source of contraband, weapons smuggling, and cross-border assaults and kidnappings. (In late April 2014, this author visited several IDF staging areas outside the Gaza Strip, unknown at the time to be astride active tunnel openings.) In the ensuing fifty-day campaign, beginning with extended artillery and air strikes, followed by a ground incursion, Israel struck 5,263 targets, destroying thirty-four tunnels in the process. Despite the onslaught, Hamas managed to fire 4,564 rockets back at the Israelis.[153] Over 80,000 reservists were activated, with 64 killed and 469 wounded. Nearly 2,200 Palestinians died, including 1,400 civilians, 600 of whom were children.

The following account, relayed to this author by a veteran of Protective Edge, is included to give this otherwise dreary section a reflective ending. (It also represents the nearest thing to a "divine intervention" in this book.) The opening infantry attack (Thursday, July 17) was a multi-pronged sequential thrust along the length of the Gaza Strip, conducted under cover of early morning darkness. The subject's unit was assigned to attack the southern-most city of Rafah (population 150,000). Major Sharon Feingold assured Human Rights Watch—this would be no cakewalk: "Rafah and the Philadelphi route is the most dangerous, violent area of the whole conflict."[154] Known as the "Gaza Mogadishu," Rafah is also the key facilitator of smuggling tunnels, being situated within 2.5 miles of the Philadelphi(a) Corridor.

In a rare case, the meticulously timed attack was delayed for over two hours, taking a serious psychological toll on what is known in IDF parlance as "battlefield synergy" (the intuitive need to compensate for smaller numbers by maximizing resourcefulness, precision, and cohesion). As the soldiers would now have to make their steep advance across open ground in broad daylight, severe casualties were a foregone conclusion. However, as the lieutenant went on to relate, "a thick fog suddenly descended out of nowhere." While literally feeling their way toward the enemy, the men could barely see where they were going. When they finally reached the perimeter of strongly fortified houses, the heavy mist lifted as quickly as it had fallen. The startled defenders were subsequently overwhelmed by the equally awe-inspired assault team. Dozens of Hamas fighters were killed with over 100 taken prisoner, giving new meaning to the phrase "fog of war." The greatest part of the story is that this author's congregation had specifically prayed for the young man's safety during their Wednesday night Church service—just *hours* before the battle (Jeremiah 33:3)!

THE BIBI-BARACK WARS (2009-17)

While the tiny Jewish State continued to confront one Islamic threat after another, the sole Middle Eastern democracy was also forced to deflect a steady barrage of rockets from "Christian" America (specifically, *political* projectiles from the White House). On January 20, 2009, Barack Hussein Obama (a.k.a. Barry Soetoro) was sworn into office as the 44th President of the United States. (See Spirit-led forecast of said event in volume one of this series, April 2005.)[155] Exactly ten weeks later, Benjamin "Bibi" Netanyahu was returned as the prime minister of Israel (one of only twelve Israelis to serve in that capacity). The next eight years—*culminating in the 100th anniversary of the Balfour Declaration*—would constitute the tragic denouement in a century of Anglo-American anti-Semitism (1917-2017).

In the middle of America's so-called "War on Terrorism," with two hot wars being fought simultaneously in two Islamic countries, an anti-Semitic, Indonesian-bred (some would add, Kenyan-born), closet Muslim with three Middle Eastern Islamic names was elected to the highest office in the land! While Proverbs 19:10, 29:2, 30:21-22, and Ecclesiastes 10:16 show that God's people are spiritually programmed to loathe the acts of wicked rulers, counterbalancing verses such as Romans 13:1-7, Colossians 1:16, I Timothy 2:1-3, I Peter 2:13-17, II Peter 2:10-12, and Jude 8-10 enjoin the believer to *respect* "the office" (including underlings). Thankfully, Christians are *not* required to "love" *any* politician, I Peter 2:17 stating, *"Love the brotherhood...Honor the king."* In reality, the litany of Barack's depravities is derived from the *greater* sin of Laodicean Christians *locking Jesus Christ out of His own Church* (Revelation 3:14-22).

Then-Senator Obama campaigned on the theme of "change" (just as Daniel 7:25 says the anti-Christ will do). Like it or not, can anyone deny that his promise was *more* than kept? However, the many changes that were foisted upon the nation's shrinking conservative minority would rate as mere "*chump* change" when compared to Obama's unprecedented breach with the State of Israel. While this book has indicted previous administrations for undermining Israel, Barack Obama is the first chief executive to wage a *public* war against America's sacrosanct ally. In fact, the president's un-statesmanlike conduct has given rise to a new national buzzword—"petulant" (defined by *Oxford Dictionary* as "childishly sulky or bad-tempered").

In Obama's first term, the slights were nominal. Five months into office the new president bypassed Israel for a Muslim dais at Cairo University. Once again, Barack was most transparent, entitling his speech, "A New Beginning." The SRO crowd cheered as America's top leader criticized Tel Aviv for building settlements on the West Bank. When Joe Biden paid Bibi a "courtesy" visit on March 8, 2010, he likewise denounced the latest construction in East Jerusalem.

Two weeks later, Netanyahu flew to Washington for an audience with the president. Upon arriving, he was rudely slipped in through a side door with no photos taken. Obama immediately pressed his guest with a list of thirteen demands designed to end their escalating feud. When Bibi stalled, POTUS rose from his seat and announced: "I'm going to the residential wing to have dinner with Michelle [FLOTUS] and the girls."[156] (His parting remarks roughly translated to: "Consider the errors of your ways," etc.) *Such treatment is without historical precedent.* Not even Israel's attack on the USS *Liberty* could evoke a rebuke from President Johnson. As Netanyahu was unrepentant when Obama returned—over an hour later—America's sole ally in the volatile Middle East was escorted out through the same side door.

Back in Zion, the rebuffed leader spent April 19 with his fellow countrymen celebrating Israel's sixty-second Independence Day. That evening, FOX News posted a stunning article: "Obama and Israel: Showdown at the UN?"[157] The gist involved an expected "statement" (threat) by US Ambassador Susan Rice that automatic vetoes on anti-Israel resolutions *might* be ending. So, what do you suppose happened next? As the "snub heard 'round the world" would ultimately relate to Wall Street's suicidal addiction to Muslim oil in the *Persian* Gulf, an oil spill in *America's* Gulf began *the very next day* with the catastrophic explosion of the British Petroleum "Deepwater Horizon" offshore drilling rig, forty miles southeast of the Louisiana coast.

Nearly five million barrels of oil (205 million gallons) eventually spewed out of the ruptured well. Jonathan Ramseur, a specialist in environmental policy, states: "In its 2010 financial statement, BP estimated the combined oil spill costs—cleanup, natural resource and economic damages, potential Clean Water Act (CWA) penalties, and other obligations—will be approximately \$41 billion."[158] For the record, according to a *60 Minutes* special that outlined the sequence of events, the *initial* damage to the blowout preventer that triggered the failure on April 20 occurred on March 23—the *exact* day that Mr. Netanyahu was left twiddling his thumbs in the Roosevelt Room.[159]

Moving right along, in September 2010, Obama hosted his own Peace Summit with Prime Minister Netanyahu and President Abbas. The meeting bombed. (Yawn.) In May 2011, another icy White House encounter occurred between Bibi and Barack. Then, there was that awkward "hot mic" snafu at the November G-20 summit in Cannes where former French President Nicolas Sarkozy whispered to Obama, "I cannot bear Netanyahu, he's a liar," whereupon Obama replied, "You're fed up with him, but I have to deal with him even more often than you."[160] When Bibi requested time with Obama during their upcoming appearance at the UNGA in September 2012, the president declined, citing "schedule conflicts." Some of Barry's more pressing "Big Apple" stops included a fundraiser hosted by Jay-Z and Beyonce and the taping of his *seventh* appearance on the *Late Show with David Letterman.*[161] When Obama made his long-awaited trip to Israel on March 20, 2013, the *Washington Times* headline reported: "President Obama's limo breaks down at Israeli airport."[162] Apparently, Obama's "Caddie" (appropriately known as "The Beast") was filled with the wrong fuel.

The low point of the rift between the Philadelphia-reared Israeli prime minister and the African-American president occurred in March 2015. When Mr. Netanyahu accepted the invitation of House Speaker Boehner to address a joint session of Congress (his third appearance, matched only by Winston Churchill), Obama refused to see him, *again.* By the time Bibi delivered his speech (a riveting, eye-opening warning regarding a nuclear-armed Iran), Vice President Biden and fifty-five "honorable" members of Congress had also felt led to boycott the guest speaker. Their collective alibi was that the visit was "inappropriate" due to Israel's upcoming elections. (No matter that Israel is the *only* Middle East country that even *has* legal elections.)

As the contest neared, reports circulated that a team of five American political strategists—led by Obama's former national field director, Jeremy Bird—had been flown to Israel (by the US tax-exempt group "One Voice") to run the anti-Netanyahu campaign.[163] Bibi's opponents were seen grasping at every possible "Windy City" shenanigan, the *craziest* being "Bottlegate"—a lingering controversy accusing Israel's first lady, Sara Netanyahu, of misappropriating government pop-bottle deposits (Psalm 56:8).[164]

Upon Netanyahu's stunning come-from-behind landslide victory, Obama surprised even his closest supporters by refusing to congratulate the Prime Minister-elect. After stalling for two days, Barack phoned his regards—a warning that the US would be "reassessing its approach to Israeli-Palestinian peace."[165] Then, with Jonathan Pollard *still* rotting in prison, the White House accused Israel of spying on the US–Iran nuclear talks and giving the intelligence to unnamed US lawmakers![166] Finally, on March 25, 2015, the Israeli news source *Arutz Sheva 7* made the following chilling claim:

> In a development that has largely been missed by mainstream media, the Pentagon early last month quietly declassified a Department of Defense top-secret document detailing Israel's nuclear program, a highly covert topic that Israel has never formally announced to avoid a regional nuclear arms race, and which the US until now has respected by remaining silent. But by publishing the declassified document from 1987, the US reportedly breached the silent agreement to keep quiet on Israel's nuclear powers for the first time ever, detailing the nuclear program in great depth…The 386-page report entitled 'Critical Technological Assessment in Israel and NATO Nations' gives a detailed description of how Israel advanced its military technology and developed its nuclear infrastructure and research in the 1970s and 1980s….[167]

For the record, according to a September 15, 2016, article in the *Times of Israel*, a hacked Colin Powell email (dated March, 3, 2015), revealed that the former Secretary of State told Democratic Party donor Jeffery Leeds that Israel has some 200 nukes.[168]

On July 14, 2015, a Joint Comprehensive Plan of Action (JCPOA) was reached between the Islamic Republic of Iran and the P5+1 group (America, Britain, France, China and Russia plus Germany). After the predictable, pusillanimous, veto-sustaining support by 150 Congressional Democrats, crippling sanctions were progressively lifted upon the "assurance" of the International Atomic and Energy Agency (IAEA) that Iran had restricted its sensitive nuclear activities. While a mushroom cloud of ambiguity hovers over the details (centrifuge and enriched uranium reduction, IAEA inspections, research and development monitoring, breakout time estimates, et al.,) the world's largest state sponsor of terror was essentially given $160,000,000,000 in "mad money" (thawed assets and renewed oil revenues)—*over four times the highly touted record $38 billion US military aid package to Israel.* The president's *Shiite* Muslim father, the late Barack Hussein Obama, Sr., would have been proud of his boy's unwavering support for Israel-hating *Shiite* Iran. (Akin to his Irish cousin, Henry Healy, "Barry O'bama's" senior advisor, Valerie Jarrett, is an Iranian born, "African-American," whose paternal great-grandfather was Jewish.)

Then, between Obama's funeral snubs of Supreme Court Justice Antonin Scalia and former First Lady Nancy Reagan, Joe Biden made another nugatory visit to Israel in March 2016. While he was "speaking out" against terrorism and the threat of a nuclear-armed Iran, an American university student was stabbed to death in Jaffa by a Palestinian and Iran test-fired two ballistic missiles, one inscribed with the phrase, "Israel should be wiped off the earth."

All of this was happening while Israelis were fleeing to their "sewervillas," Soviet troops were deploying in neighboring Syria, and ISIS was turning the Arab Spring into an Arab Blizzard (five million Egyptians living in five Cairo cemeteries, not to mention the protracted Sinai insurgency, defined by the October 31, 2015 downing of Metrojet Flight 9268, killing all 224 aboard). This last point—that ISIS (and other jihadists) could wreak unrestrained havoc throughout the ummah (i.e., 1,274 Islamic attacks in 50 countries through the first 6½ months of 2016 alone, rendering 11,774 deaths and 14,303 injuries[169])—represents the latest proof that the so-called "Great Arab Revolt" was, and remains, a feckless "Great Arab Myth." Ironically, as Martin Luther King, Jr.'s, famous line, "Let my people go," was originally spoken by a *Jew* to an *Egyptian*, the "Bibi-Barack Wars" occasioned a bizarre déjà vu encounter where *another* Jew was being forced to make the *same* petition to *another* dark-skinned, bi-racial potentate who reveled in *his* Hamitic roots.

Obama's parting shot was his "Happy Hanukkah," one-two punch of the December 23 US abstention on UNSC Resolution 2334 (condemning Israeli West Bank settlement expansion) administered by America's Irish-born, Roman Catholic, UN Ambassador, Samantha Power, followed five days later by a seventy-minute, anti-Israel diatribe by the Skull and Bones, Roman Catholic, US Secretary of State, John Kerry. (For what it's worth, John's Austrian grandfather, Fritz Kohn, was a Jew who changed his name to Frederick Kerry and "converted" to Catholicism, several of his relatives later dying in the Holocaust).[170] Finally, just hours before leaving office on Friday, Obama quietly slipped the Palestinian Authority a cool $221 million "love gift," funds that the GOP Congress had been blocking.

TEMPLE MOUNT TRAJECTORY

On October 29, 2014, a motorcycle rider who spoke with a "thick Arab accent" pulled up alongside a Jewish man in Jerusalem and shot him in the chest four times at point-blank range. The shooter, identified as Mutaz Hijazi, a member of the Islamic Jihad Movement in Palestine, was later killed by police. The victim, Yehuda Joshua Glick, miraculously survived the attempted assassination, spending nearly a month in Shaare Zedek Medical Center.

Glick is an American-born Israeli rabbi and current Member of the Knesset (Likud Party) who campaigns for expanded Jewish access to the Temple Mount. He is also chairman of the Temple Mount Heritage Foundation. The Brooklyn native is considered the up-and-coming lightning rod for future Arab–Israeli contention. A wave of random shootings in and around Jerusalem in the wake of his recovery and renewed activism attest to his formidable presence. (Some have called him the "Donald Trump of Israel.")

The core rub of Glick's growing protest movement is simple: While Muslims *are* allowed to pray on the Temple Mount, Jews are *not*. The policy, known as the "status quo," is cautiously endorsed by Prime Minister Netanyahu (the leader of Glick's party). The big problem, however, is that the "equal prayer" agenda is no longer a fringe movement but is gaining momentum within the mainstream of Israeli society. Thus, the current Temple Mount trajectory (not to mention the pro-Israel Trump Administration) is sure to move the Jewish people closer to the final section of *Holy Ground*—Salvation from Statehood.

PART III

Salvation from Statehood

19

Beloved Enemies

"As concerning the gospel, they are enemies for your sakes: but as touching the election, they are beloved for the fathers' sakes."
(Romans 11:28)

"A false balance is an abomination to the LORD...."
(Proverbs 11:1)

"I'm not trying to convert the Jewish people to the Christian faith…trying to convert Jews is a 'waste of time'…They (already) have a faith structure."
(John Hagee, 1988)

"Jesus himself was not and is not a 'Jew.'"
(Texe Marrs, 2013)

THE READER WILL now discern the climactic double-entendre embodied in the subtitle, *"A Scriptural View of the True History of the* STATE *of Israel"*—the imperative shift from the *State* of Israel to the *state* of Israel (Genesis 43:7). The premise of this final section—that Israel will ultimately experience "salvation *from* statehood"—posits that the Jews' current status among the "community of nations" is a non-kosher, political aberration. That this restoration will correlate with a spiritual revival also confirms that the Jewish people are out of fellowship with the God of their fathers.

To broach this dual assessment will evoke cries of anti-Semitism from Jews; to expand upon the latter, *especially* the unsettling particulars of this apostasy, will often generate similar umbrage from evangelical Christians. Nevertheless (to invoke the *Aliyah Bet* mantra), as this book has consistently asserted, the A.V. 1611 remains *the* final authority in all matters of faith and practice. Thus, while Isaiah 40:17 states, *"All nations before him are as nothing,"* the singular exception in Numbers 23:9 constitutes the last word on Jacob's pre-ordained, *sui generis* destiny—*"the people shall dwell alone,* AND SHALL NOT BE RECKONED AMONG THE NATIONS.*"*

This truth was graphically illustrated in a September 22, 1999, full-page ad in the *New York Times*, placed by the American Jewish Committee. Split into two parallel columns, the left heading reads: "Countries eligible to sit on the United Nations Security Council"; 187 nations, from Afghanistan to Zimbabwe, appear below. The opposite legend states: "Countries not eligible to sit on the United Nations Security Council"; surrounded by a sea of white, Israel is the sole nation listed. (The discriminatory practice, engineered via a political maneuver by the Arab bloc, ended in 2000.)

The designation "State of Israel" contains thirteen letters, the Bible number for rebellion. The LORD *never* called His covenant people to co-exist "*among* the nations" (i.e., as just one more secular entity), as the Jews' eternal station is "*above* the nations." Isaiah 2:2-3 states:

> *And it shall come to pass in the last days, that the mountain of the LORD'S house shall be established in the top of the mountains, and shall be exalted above the hills; and all nations shall flow unto it. And many people shall go and say, Come ye, and let us go up to the mountain of the LORD, to the house of the God of Jacob; and he will teach us of his ways, and we will walk in his paths: for out of Zion shall go forth the law, and the word of the LORD from Jerusalem.*

The global conditions that result from this Judeocentric rule are given in verse four: *"And he shall judge among the nations, and shall rebuke many people: and they shall beat their swords into plowshares, and their spears into pruninghooks: nation shall not lift up sword against nation, neither shall they learn war anymore."* In typical hypocrisy, as the text reads on the "Isaiah Wall" at the United Nations building in New York, it negates God's rebuke on the UN by starting at "they," giving man credit for "peace on earth." The address was also cut to lift the message from its negative context. (Note how the reverse order in

Joel 3:10, *"Beat your plowshares into swords and your pruninghooks into spears,"* would be the more fitting text for a "Joel Wall," the UN having sponsored some 100 wars since its inception.)

Jacob's exclusive geo-political status in the Millennium is also presented in Zechariah 8:22-23: *"Yea, many people and strong nations shall come to seek the LORD of hosts in Jerusalem, and to pray before the LORD. Thus saith the LORD of hosts; In those days it shall come to pass, that ten men shall take hold out of all languages of the nations, even shall take hold of the skirt of him that is a Jew, saying, We will go with you: for we have heard that God is with you."* Gentiles who refuse to make their mandatory annual pilgrimage to Jerusalem will be punished accordingly. *"And it shall be, that whoso will not come up of all the families of the earth unto Jerusalem to worship the King, the LORD of hosts, even upon them shall be no rain."* (Zechariah 14:21) Because these (and many other) unique prophecies have yet to occur, the Jews having missed the time of their visitation at the First Advent, and as Numbers 23:19 says that God cannot lie—Israel obviously must have a national restoration at the Second Advent (Romans 11:26).

A FALSE BALANCE

Unfortunately, not all Christians agree on these matters. Proverbs 11:1 says, *"A false balance is abomination to the LORD: but a just weight is his delight."* While the context (interpreted by the cross-references in Leviticus 19:35-36, Deuteronomy 25:13-14, and Amos 8:5) applies to a man who carries two sets of weights for cheating people on the scales, the verse can also be used for *any* "false balance."

In the closing days of Laodicea, the majority of professing believers generally lean toward one of two extremes regarding Israel. While one side is overly enamored with "all things Jewish," the other is consumed with "Christian anti-Semitism." For starry-eyed Christian Zionists, the Jew can do no wrong. Replacement theology advocates find *their* fulfillment in assailing dispensational Premillennialism, promoting Holocaust denial, rejecting the ethnicity of modern Israelis, and perpetuating the bogus Russian *Protocols of the Elders of Zion*. Ironically, the point men for these antipodean ideologies are both headquartered in Texas (about an hour apart). At the *far* right is

John C. Hagee, founder and senior pastor of Cornerstone Church in San Antonio. His Charismatic credentials include a BS from Southwestern Assemblies of God in Waxahachie, Texas, and an Honorary Doctorate from Oral Roberts University. (Oral was the crackpot televangelist who claimed he saw a 900-ft. Jesus.) In 2006, Hagee founded Christians United for Israel (CUFI), described on his website as "a grass roots national association through which every pro- Israel Christian ministry, para-church organization, or individual in America can speak and act with one voice in support of Israel and the Jewish people."[1] David Brog, an American Jew, is the Executive Director. Hagee is *so* "pro-Israel" that he doesn't believe Jews need to be saved like everyone else in this age, telling the *Houston Chronicle*:

> I'm not trying to convert the Jewish people to the Christian faith…trying to convert Jews is a waste of time…They (already) have a faith structure…The Jewish people have a relationship to God through the law of God as given through Moses. I believe that every Gentile person can only come to God through the cross of Christ. I believe that every Jewish person who lives in the light of the Torah, which is the word of God, has a relationship with God and will come to redemption.[2]

Even the press noted Hagee's aberration (a.k.a. "Dual Covenant" theology): "John Hagee, fundamentalist pastor from San Antonio and friend of Israel, is truly a strange fish. Although a Christian minister, he celebrates Passover and the Feast of Tabernacles…He also believes that Jews can come to God without going through Jesus Christ."[3] While Hagee has done some serious *crawfishing* (Southern colloquialism for *spin*) over these "purported" remarks, this author is unaware of any retractions by the *Chronicle* (nor any libel damages awarded to the "Rev"). What *cannot* be contested are John's own words in his promo video for his 2007 book, *In Defense of Israel*:

> I'm delighted to present my latest book, *In Defense of Israel*. This book will expose the sins of the fathers and the vicious abuse of the Jewish people. *In Defense of Israel* will shape Christian theology. It scripturally proves that the Jewish people, as a whole, did *not* reject Jesus as Messiah. It will also prove that Jesus did *not* come to earth to *be* the Messiah. It will prove that there was a Calvary conspiracy between Rome, the High Priest, and Herod to execute Jesus as an

> insurrectionist too dangerous to live. Since Jesus refused, by word and deed, to claim to be the Messiah, *how* could the Jews be blamed for rejecting what was *never* offered?[4]

When a *Jerusalem Post* reporter asked the International Christian Embassy Jerusalem if they were missionaries to Jews, Director Jan Willem van der Hoeven, replied, "Not so. The Zionist Christians are different. Our objectives are not as you describe...We don't believe in conversion, we don't want to make the Jews into Christians."[5] Dr. Margaret Brearley of the Church of England, concurs with this view:

> Because the Jewish people do in some mysterious way bear God's name and witness to his existence and ethical demand...Christianity was clearly not designed to replace Judaism...Christians need to learn from observant Jews...The Church, God's Gentile worshippers, vitally needs God's Jewish worshippers; for together we are the 'household of God.'[6]

Of course, such pacifism can also serve as a convenient hiding place, as Jews are not the easiest sinners to pigeonhole. In a 2006 article in *Haaretz*, American-born Israeli journalist Bradley Burston bluntly told Jews for Jesus, "Believe whatever you want. Practice whatever you preach. Just stay the h--l away from us."[7]

Hagee is a typical shallow Pentecostal who wouldn't know "right division" from a "right hook" (II Timothy 4:3-4). As for Christ-rejecting Jews entertaining some esoteric bond with God if they "live in the light of the Torah," Jesus excoriated His detractors to the contrary: *"For had ye believed Moses, ye would have believed me: for he wrote of me. But if ye believe not his writings, how shall ye believe my words?"* (John 5:46-47) Regarding Hagee's notion that Jews can bypass *"the door"* and enter the sheepfold by climbing up *"some other way"* (John 10:1), Jesus told his disciples, *"I am* THE WAY, *the truth, and the life:* NO MAN *cometh unto the Father, but by me."* (John 14:6) He likewise informed Nicodemus, *"Except a man be born again, he* CANNOT *see the kingdom of God."* (John 3:3)

Jesus was condemned by the Jewish leaders for telling them the *opposite* message that Hagee gives their descendants today: *"I said therefore unto you, that ye shall die in your sins: for if ye believe not that I am he, ye shall die in your sins."* (John 8:24) Peter shucked the same "intolerant" corn after Pentecost: *"Neither is there salvation in any other: for there is* NONE *other name under heaven given among men, whereby we must be saved."* (Acts 4:12) If the Jews are exempt from the new birth, somebody should have told Paul, for Luke records that he routinely *"reasoned with the Jews"* (Acts 17:2, 17; 18:4, 19).

At the other ideological periphery is Texe W. Marrs, founder and director of Power of Prophecy in Austin. This guy (in the spirit of Wilhelm Marr) is *so* eaten up with anti-Semitism, he cannot even *conceive* of Jesus being a Jew. Worse than nut-job Jeremiah Wright, who claimed that Jesus was a Palestinian, Texe piously writes in *DNA Science and the Jewish Bloodline*:

> Now, while Jesus came in the flesh first to the Jews, and the bearer (Mary) of the Christ child was of the tribe of Judah, Jesus himself *was not* and *is not* a "Jew"...I have even had Christian pastors and evangelists assert to me that Jesus is in Heaven today, bodily as a Jew. This is sacrilege. This is the desacralizing of the Son of God....I for one am angered at such diabolism, even when the offending party is sincere.[8] [Author's emphasis]

One would think that a former college professor with over forty books to his credit could read simple English: Gabriel informs Mary that God will give her son *"the throne of his father David,"* from which He is to *"reign over the house of Jacob for ever."* (Luke 1:32-33) The next chapter cites the definitive proof, Jesus' *circumcision* eight days after His birth, conforming to Leviticus 12:3. (See: *Christ Circumcised*, by Andrew S. Jacobs.) The Magi ask Herod: *"Where is he that is born King of the Jews?"* (Matthew 2:2); Nicodemus, *"a ruler of the Jews,"* called Jesus *"Rabbi"* (John 3:2). Jesus avowed His own ethnicity when He told the Samaritan woman, *"Ye worship ye know not what: we know what we worship: for salvation is of the Jews."* (John 4:22) Four verses later, He claimed to be the Messiah. Even Rome declared Him *"THE KING OF THE JEWS."* (Mark 15:26)

To suggest that Jesus does not have a Jewish identity affixed to His glorified human body is more sanctimonious sophistry. Mary called her resurrected Lord, *"Rabboni"* (John 20:16). One of the twenty-four elders in Heaven described Him as *"the Lion of the tribe of Judah, the Root of David."* (Revelation 5:5) Jesus, as a *"Lamb,"* appears with 144,000 ascended Jews on Mount Sion (Revelation 14:1). The Song of

Moses is sung in Heaven (Revelation 15:3). Jesus calls the Tribulation Jews *"brethren."* (Matthew 25:40) At the Second Advent, the title *"KING OF KINGS AND LORD OF LORDS"* is written on Christ's vesture and thigh. (Revelation 19:16) Having taught his converts to "rightly divide" between Jew, Gentile, and the church of God, Paul calls Jesus *"the blessed and only Potentate, the King of kings, and Lord of lords."* (I Corinthians 10:32; I Timothy 6:15) At the risk of sounding overly simplistic, there are no "kings" in the polity of a local church; Paul lists only two *offices*—"bishop" and "deacon" (I Timothy 3:1, 8). In short, if *"the man Christ Jesus"* does not return as a "*Jewish* king," why does He rule from David's throne in Jerusalem for 1,000 years? (I Timothy 2:5; Revelation 20:4, 6) Must we *really* go on???

For what it's worth, on page 128 in the same comic book (*DNA Bloodline*), Marrs features a "clandestine" photograph of David Ben-Gurion and another man handing an object to a smiling Harry Truman. The caption reads: "Abraham Feinberg (center), Jewish spy, secretly gave President Truman (left) a bribe to recognize Israel as a State. David Ben-Gurion, Israel's first Prime Minister, is on right." Actually, in a series of photos documenting the same iconic scene—as recorded on the Harry S. Truman Presidential Library and Museum website—the so-called "Jewish spy" is none other than "H. E. Abba Eban, Ambassador of Israel." The same website identifies the "bribe" as Israel's official state gift for Truman—a Menorah.

SPIRITUAL CONUNDRUM

As the world becomes increasingly transfixed on the volatile "Middle East" (i.e., Israel), the attendant theological debate over Zionism will only foster a commensurate rise of declension among Christians and ridicule by nonbelievers. With the Church in disarray, four versions of Israel's history are now in play: 1) Palestinian mythology; 2) Israel's own subjective history; 3) Christian Judeophilia (ignoring Israel's evil); 4) Christian Judeophobia (ignoring Israel's election). Thus, the need of the hour is for God's people at both abominable peripheries to move toward the center—no matter *what* their individual gurus say.

The main text to help end-day believers achieve this desperately needed equilibrium is Romans 11:28, *"As concerning the gospel, they are enemies for your sakes: but as touching the election, they are beloved for the fathers' sakes."* This verse constitutes an amazing spiritual conundrum. (*Oxford Dictionary* defines "conundrum" as "a confusing and difficult problem or question"; synonyms include riddle, quandary, and puzzle.) For instance, if someone broke into *your* home, would you categorize the intruder as an "enemy" or "beloved"? The answer is obvious (Exodus 22:2 sanctioning lethal force as well).

The two concepts are also mutually exclusive; how can one be simultaneously an enemy *and* beloved? Yet, according to Romans 11:28, this is the precise relationship that the Church has with the Jew: *"concerning the gospel...*ENEMIES *for your sakes"; "touching the election...*BELOVED *for the fathers' sakes."* Thus, in God's wisdom, the Jew has become the Christian's "beloved enemy." However, the twain shall never *begin* to meet until believers in both factions reach a "true balance" on this divisive issue. While philo-Semitic Christians need to acknowledge the Jew as their "beloved *enemy*," anti-Semitic Christians need to embrace the Jew as their "*beloved* enemy."

"*ENEMIES* FOR YOUR SAKES"

Most born-again Christians fall into the pro-Israel category, the main core comprising independent Baptists, evangelical Protestants, and non-denominational Charismatics. (Messianic Jews remain in their own orbit, falling under Luke 9:50.) Some of the more high-profile faces in this group would include: Pat Robertson, Franklin Graham, Jerry Falwell Jr., Tim LaHaye, Hal Lindsey, John MacArthur, Chuck Missler, Jack Van Impe, Mike Evans, Perry Stone, and others. David Barton, a graduate of Oral Roberts University, has extended the "right hand of fellowship" to Glen Beck, a Mormon, as other compromisers have done to the Roman Catholic, Sean Hannity (II Corinthians 6:14).

While most of these Christian Zionists do not ascribe to Hagee's heresy (exempting Jews from the new birth), the movement as a whole exhibits a conspicuous hesitation to confront Jews with the gospel (analogous to a physician hiding a cancer diagnosis from a patient to avoid upsetting the person). Exceptions to the rule notwithstanding (e.g., the late Zvi Kalisher's bold witness in Jerusalem), the innocuous mission statement printed in every issue of the enormously popular evangelical bi-monthly publication, *Israel My Glory*, reads: "The

Friends of Israel *Gospel* Ministry Inc. is a worldwide Christian ministry communicating biblical truth about Israel and the Messiah while fostering solidarity with the Jewish people." (Author emphasis) David Brickener, a converted Jew, states:

> Some Christian Zionists are so eager to be for Israel that they seem to care little about Jews being for Jesus. They are so in love with the idea of Jewish people being in the Land that they don't think of the implications of those same people being outside of Christ...God is no more willing to pass over the sins of disobedient Israel today than He was on that first Passover Eve...Without the blood of the Lamb on the doorposts of their hearts, modern Israelites are destined for judgment, too. This means that the majority of the people of Israel are in jeopardy...There is no automatic pass. Only in Christ is there assurance of lasting safety and peace for the Jewish nation.[9]

The explanation for this will astound you. The main reason why Christians have an instinctive awe of Jews in general, and Israel in particular, is because *they have a Jew living inside of them.* Colossians 1:27 states, *"To whom God would make known what is the riches of the glory of this mystery among the Gentiles; which is* CHRIST IN YOU, *the hope of glory...."* This also explains why believers are mesmerized by Hebrew. The Bible reveals that Hebrew is the language of Heaven. Before God confused the tongues at Babel, *"the whole earth was of one language, and of one speech."* (Genesis 11:1) That language was undoubtedly Hebrew, as all Hebrew roots are tri-consonantal (i.e., they come from a *Trinity*). When Paul gave his testimony to Agrippa, he declared, *"I heard a voice speaking unto me, and saying in the* HEBREW TONGUE, *Saul, Saul why persecutest thou me?"* (Acts 26:14) When Heaven's saints rejoice over Rome's demise, they shout "ALLELUIA" three times (Revelation 19:3-6). The word ("hallelujah" in English) is Hebrew for, "Praise ye Jehovah (the LORD)." In the Millennium, human speech will revert to pre-Babel uniformity. *"For then will I turn to the people a* PURE LANGUAGE.*"* (Zephaniah 3:9) That "pure language" will be Hebrew.[10]

Now, while this "coziness" for "Jewishness" was designed to be a blessing, like anything else, it can become detrimental if one fails to see the whole picture (i.e., Jacob's historical "baggage"). Thus, not only will unenlightened believers feel "unworthy" when witnessing to one of "God's chosen people," but they will also hesitate to consider, much less believe, that much of what anti-Semites proclaim is *true*—that the Jew *has* been the enemy of New Testament evangelism and Christian morality. To illustrate, *Haaretz* reported in January 2012:

> Israel's LGBT community has a reason to be proud: It has officially been proclaimed the best gay travel destination of 2011 [the 400th anniversary of the King "Jacob" Bible, no less]. In a world-wide survey conducted by GayCities.com and American Airlines, 43% of voters cast their ballot in favor of the White City, followed by New York City with 14%, Toronto with 7%....[11]

Noting that "5,000 gay tourists were recorded as visiting Tel Aviv last June for the annual Gay Pride Parade – 25% more than in 2010," the article concludes, "Now that it's been voted best city, Tel Aviv can probably expect even more visitors this June."[12] In June 2014, *Haaretz* stated: "More than 100,000 people are taking part in the Gay Pride Parade in Tel Aviv on Friday...culminating in a huge beach party in Charles Clore Park...some 30,000 tourists were expected to take part, according to the organizers...."[13] As for the Christian Zionists' core mantra, "God Bless America," the story adds, "for the first time the rainbow flag was hoisted this year alongside the U.S. flag outside the American embassy in the city."[14] The new Eretz Yisrael is now defined by its brazen tee shirt—"Oy Vey, I'm gay"; so much for the Tanakh's warning that its Author *incinerated* two cities for this very sin (Genesis 19:24). Thus, in the time of "Jacob's trouble," Jerusalem *"spiritually is called* SODOM *and Egypt...."* (Revelation 11:8)

"Contrary To All Men"

The previous chapters have frequently verified the subtitle, *A Century of Anglo-American Anti-Semitism*. Contrary to the misguided mindset of Christian Zionists, the catalyst for this worldwide phenomenon was revealed 2,000 years ago in I Thessalonians 2:14-16: *"For ye, brethren... have suffered like things of your own countrymen, even as they have of the Jews: Who both* KILLED THE LORD JESUS, *and their own prophets, and have* PERSECUTED US; *and they please not God, and are* CONTRARY TO ALL MEN: *Forbidding us to speak to the Gentiles that they might be saved, to fill up their sins alway:* FOR THE WRATH IS COME UPON THEM TO THE UTTERMOST.*"*

Thus, it would appear that much (though not all) of recorded anti-Semitic "wrath" has been *self-inflicted*—the result of pervasive asocial agitation. On February 8, 1920, Winston Churchill (then-Secretary of State for War and Air) submitted a carefully worded article for the *Illustrated Sunday Herald*. His theme was an appeal to the Jews of Russia (and elsewhere) to choose between Zionism and Bolshevism. An excerpt from the Philo-Semitic paragon follows:

> Some people like Jews and some do not, but no thoughtful man can doubt...that they are beyond all question the most formidable and the most remarkable race which has ever appeared in the world...The conflict between good and evil which proceeds unceasingly in the breast of man nowhere reaches such intensity as in the Jewish race. The dual nature of man is nowhere more strongly or more terribly exemplified...[T]his same astounding race may at the present time be in the actual process of producing another system of morals and philosophy, as malevolent as Christianity was benevolent, which, if not arrested, would shatter irretrievably all that Christianity has rendered possible. It would almost seem as if the gospel of Christ and the gospel of Antichrist were destined to originate among the same people; and that this mystic and mysterious race had been chosen for the supreme manifestations, both of the divine and the diabolical.[15]

Paul wrote in I Corinthians 6:12, *"[A]ll things are lawful for me, but I will not be brought under the power of any."* Warm and fuzzy feelings notwithstanding, a Christian is the last person who should shrink from the truth, no matter *how* disturbing. Should our love for Jews be lessened because the historical record happens to corroborate their prophetic profile? The great teaching of Romans 11:28 is that a spirit-filled believer will love the Jews—*in spite of all they have done.* To deny or repress these negative realities is to evoke charges of ignorance and or naiveté from "Christian" anti-Semites. Simply put, as the progenitor of the twelve tribes had two names, *Jacob* ("trickster") and *Israel* ("Prince with God"), the Jew is personified by Longfellow's "little girl with the little curl"—"When she was good, she was very, *very* good [Barry Goldwater]. And when she was bad she was *horrid* [Bernie Sanders]."

TORAH VS. TALMUD

Christian Zionists are also generally unaware of the "spiritual" authority of religious Jews. Louis Finkelstein writes in his definitive four-volume set, *The Jews: Their History, Culture, and Religion*, "[A]ny decision regarding the Jewish Religion must be based on the Talmud...."[16] Immanuel Jakobovitz, former Chief Rabbi of the British Commonwealth, echoes this sentiment: "The true character of Judaism cannot be appreciated except by an intimate acquaintance with the Oral Law...What makes us and our faith distinct and unique is the oral tradition as the authentic key to an understanding of the written text we call the Torah."[17] In *The Tradition of the Jews* (regarded as one of the rarest books among antiquarian collectibles), Johann Eisenmenger quotes another famous rabbi: "Do not imagine that the *Written* Law is the foundation or groundwork; for, on the contrary, the *Oral* Law is the foundation; and on this Law the Covenant was made."[18]

Exodus 32:9 states, *"And the LORD said unto Moses, I have seen this people, and, behold, it is a* STIFFNECKED *people...."* On the eve of the Babylonian exile, the rabbis developed a separate, oral tradition, ostensibly the laws and legal interpretations that Moses did *not* include in the Torah (or *Pentateuch*, meaning "five books"). This was a clear violation of Isaiah 8:20, *"To the law and to the testimony: if they speak not according to this word, it is because there is no light in them."* The transition continued in the 400-year intertestamental era (along with the institution of the synagogue and the two sects known in the Gospels as the Pharisees and Sadducees). By the First Advent, the recorded Mosaic authority was eclipsed by the verbal commentary of Rabbinic Judaism. Thus, as referenced by the familiar phrase, *"Ye have* HEARD *that it hath been* SAID*...,"* Jesus declares, *"This people draweth nigh unto me with their mouth, and honoureth me with their lips; but their heart is far from me. But in vain they do worship me, teaching for doctrines the commandments of men."* (Matthew 5:33, 38, 43; 15:8-9)

Through the ensuing centuries (following the Temple's destruction in AD 70), the "Oral Torah" morphed into a two-part (Mishnah-Gemara) written series, spanning twenty-plus volumes, called the Babylonian *Talmud* ("learning"). Michael Brown, a Messianic Jew, writes: "What makes this all the more ironic is that the Talmud stated that the written Torah was not to be transmitted orally and the oral Torah was not to be transmitted in writing."[19] Thus, while Joshua 1:8 and Psalm 1:2 exhort Israelites to meditate on the Torah, the Talmud states in Erubin 21b, "My son, be more careful in the observance of the words of the Scribes than in the words of the Torah."[20] Will Durant adds: "For 1400 years the Talmud was the core of Jewish education. Seven hours a day, through seven years, the Hebrew youth pored over it, recited it, sank it into his memory by sound and sight; and like the Confucian classics similarly memorized, it formed mind and character by the discipline of its study and the deposit of its lore."[21] (Thus, in one of the closing scenes of *Schindler's List*, the *Schindlerjuden* present their benefactor with a gold ring, engraved with the Talmud text, "Whoever saves one life, saves the world.")

For the record, apart from a survey of the "Holy" Koran (and/or the history of Freemasonry), the quickest route to the loony bin is to hazard a study of the Talmud, described by Philip Schaff as a "chaos of Jewish learning, wisdom, and folly, a continent of rubbish…[which, despite occasional]…hidden pearls of true maxims and poetic parables…[remains]…the Old Testament misinterpreted and turned against the New…a rabbinical Bible without inspiration, without the Messiah [and] without hope."[22] Far worse than the Talmud's chaotic structure is its vitriolic, anti-Christian tone. The ultimate example depicts Jesus' fate in the "Netherworld" as "sitting forever in boiling excrement."[23] The contemporary manifestation of this ancient blasphemy is the infamous photograph of a crucifix in a container of urine, entitled, "P--s Christ," exhibited in the Whitney Museum, headed by Leonard Lauder (a friend of Ariel Sharon).[24]

Its next most prevalent theme deals with cheating the goyim out of every last dollar (primarily by usury), disrupting their government in the process. Goldwin Smith, Regius Professor of Modern History at Oxford (1853-1866), characterized Europe's Jewish money lenders as "alien invaders, without bowels of compassion for the Gentiles, [who] come among a simple peasantry, strip the peasant by usury of all he has, and reduce him to the slavery of debt."[25] The secular Catholic historian, Will Durant (assisted by his Jewish co-author/wife, Ariel), wrote that certain Jews "waxed rich through usury, and all were hated by it."[26] No less of an authority than Theodore Herzl chided his brethren as "leeches" and "a money-worshipping people incapable of understanding that a man can act out of other motives than money."[27]

However, while this mercenary practice was bound to incite a pogrom or two, by the late fourth century the *visible* "Church" was a *long* way from its prototype in the book of Acts, Durant concluding: "[H]ere and there, in these twenty volumes, we find words of hatred for Christianity; but they were for a Christianity that had forgotten the gentleness of Christ."[28] Dr. Schaff concurs: "Unfortunately, this people, still remarkable even in its tragical end, was in many ways cruelly oppressed by the Christians after Constantine, and thereby only confirmed in its fanatical hatred of them."[29] The truth is, the Talmud's evolving hostility against Christianity was a "hybrid" hatred—*initiated* against the early Church, *exacerbated* by latent Catholicism and Protestantism.

AN "ATHEIST GENE"

Christian Zionists often fail to realize that Gospel-rejecting Jews are spiritually incapable of understanding their own Hebrew Bible (I Corinthians 2:14). Thus, the Talmud became the expedient proxy; ditto the Jews' empirical addiction to education, literature, music, and the Arts. (Albert Einstein supposedly said, "I never let my schooling interfere with my education.")

However, when the rabbis led their congregants to embrace the Talmud over the Torah, it was only a matter of time before the greater part of Jewry would choose secularism over Judaism. The wisest man in history wrote, *"The fool hath said in his heart, There is no God."* (Psalm 14:1) A "Who's Who" among Jewish fools (with a few agnostics thrown in for good measure) would include: Baruch Spinoza, Emma Goldman, Moses Hess, David Ben-Gurion, Ayn Rand, Golda Meir, Carl Sagan, Moshe Dayan, Albert Einstein, Robert Oppenheimer, Yitzhak Rabin, Hans Bethe, Stanislaw Ulam, Arthur Miller, John von Neumann, Stanley Kubrick, Stan Lee, Stephen Pinker, Eli Wiesel, Norman Finkelstein, Mark Zuckerberg, and, last but not least, David Silverman—*president* of the American Atheists!

In 1956, Prime Minster Ben-Gurion stated: "In Israel, in order to be a realist you must believe in miracles."[30] Yet, according to a 2009 survey by the Guttman Center, 46% of Israeli Jews identified as secular. A 2012 Gallup poll conducted in fifty-seven countries (excluding Israel) found Jews to be the *least* religious, only 38% of world Jewry considering itself religiously inclined.[31] On September 17, 2011, a Jewish-American voyeur, Spencer Tunick, photographed 1,000 naked Israelis in the *Dead* Sea (how appropriate). In the 2014 PBS special, *The Story of the Jews*, several spaced-out Israeli youths remark: "Jerusalem is *too* heavy – no beaches." (In a reference to the anti-Christ, Revelation 13:1 shows *"a beast rise up out of the* SEA.*"*)

On September 26, 2011, a *USA Today* article entitled "Judaism Without God" revealed that over half of American Jews doubt God's existence. "Atheism and Judaism are not contradictory, so to have an atheist in a Jewish congregation isn't an issue or a challenge or a problem," explains (spins) Berkeley alumnus, Maxim Schrogin. "It is par for the course. That is what Judaism is. It is our tradition to question God from top to bottom."[32] In his 2009 *Ynet* article, "Why So Many Jews Are Atheists," Rabbi Levi Brackman cites the famous Jewish infidel, Christopher Hitchens, who suggested that "Jews carry an atheist gene." He then makes the inevitable link to the Talmud:

> Now, it is undeniable...that Jews have traditionally been deeply analytical questioners. One has only to study the Talmud...to recognize this. In fact the entire genre of rabbinic literature is full of questions, arguments and intellectual query. For thousands of years Jews have been taught to question and delve deeper to uncover the truth inherent in any discussion...One might argue that the entire literature of Jewish mysticism, otherwise known as the Kabbalah, is based on a single existential question pertaining to the meaning of the famous biblical phrase, "Hear O' Israel the Lord our God the Lord in One" (Deuteronomy 6:4). The Jewish mystics wanted to understand what the Bible meant when it said that God is one. They question how one unified God was able to create a universe so fragmented. The question of why a God would care what humans do (or don't do) is a question that Jewish mystics prominently ask. These are questions that atheists also ask. It is fair to say that most Jewish metaphysicians were skeptics at heart. They doubted the simplistic way of understanding the Bible."[33]

Alan Dershowitz is a Harvard Law professor and civil libertarian attorney. In his 1997 book, *The Vanishing American Jew*, the self-described "borderline agnostic" stated: "I think about God only infrequently, and then mostly as an intellectual conundrum. God is not central to my particular brand of Jewishness."[34] Thus, his 2000 bestseller, *The Genesis of Justice*, begins: "Would you give a young person a book whose heroes cheat, lie, steal, murder—and get away with it? Chances are you have. The book, of course, is Genesis…Even the God of Genesis can be seen as an imperfect God, neither omniscient, omnipotent, nor even always good."[35] Ironically, Mr. Dershowitz is best known as a member of the "Dream Team" for O. J. Simpson—*the veritable poster child for getting away with murder.*

The nadir of Jewish impiety was shown at the September 7, 2014, funeral of Joan Rivers at Temple Emanu-El (landmark synagogue on New York's Fifth Avenue where the 81-year-old degenerate comedienne was a member). The imbecilic Jewish journalist, Geraldo Rivera, told Reuters: "It really was so funny. [Proverbs 14:9] Howard Stern opened with an X-rated joke. Cindy Adams, the columnist, followed shortly after. The rabbi was burying his head as the F-bombs were launched. And then Hugh Jackman nailed it with a great Broadway song. So it was a real New York show. It was exactly like Joan would have wanted it."[36]

While Jews may not have "atheist genes," many, *especially* in the Knesset, do possess "*pharisaical* genes," for while Jews who dump Judaism for secularism (or any number of other "isms," Hinduism, Buddhism, even Satanism) get to retain *their* Jewish standing—based *solely* on ethnicity—those who accept Christianity are denied *their* Jewishness, despite identical racial claims. According to a 1989 Israeli Supreme Court ruling, the 1950 Law of Return guarantees all Jews their "*Rock of Israel*-given right" to make aliya—unless, of course, they happen to embrace *Jesus* as their "Rock." Justice Menachem Elon wrote (as cited by the Israeli press), "Messianic Jews attempt to reverse the wheels of history by 2,000 years…But the Jewish people has decided during the 2,000 years of its history [that Messianic Jews] do not belong to the Jewish nation and have no right to force themselves on it. Those who believe in Jesus are, in fact, Christians."[37]

INTERNATIONAL JEWRY

It rarely occurs to students of history that the greatest collection of anti-Semitic "hate literature" was originally composed in Hebrew—by the *Jewish* authors of the Tanakh itself! (Exodus 32:7-10; Leviticus 26:14-39; Numbers 16:19-49; 21:5-6; Deuteronomy 28:15-68; Isaiah 5:24-30; Jeremiah 5:13-25; 6:8, 11-12, 19; Ezekiel 6:1-14; 9:1-11; et al.) After Samuel told Saul that *"rebellion is as the sin of witchcraft,"* Israel's first king visits the witch of Endor (I Samuel 15:23; 28:7). Thus, Isaiah 30:9 states, *"[T]his is a rebellious people, lying children, children that will not hear the law of the LORD...."*

The classic case of Jewish obstinacy is the rich man's reply in Luke 16:30—*"NAY, father Abraham: but if one went unto them from the dead, they will repent."* Even while burning in Hell, the Jew thinks he knows more than God! Jesus indicted his religious adversaries accordingly: *"Ye are of your father the devil, and the lusts of your father ye will do."* (John 8:44) After demanding a king early (I Samuel 8:1-7), the Jews later reject the very ruler they *should* have accepted (Matthew 21:5, John 19:15). With their subsequent eviction from Eretz Yisrael, would Jews have been *less* inclined to foment rebellion in a *foreign* land? Do the words *"contrary to all men"* apply?

In his 1927 study, *The Jew As Radical*, Jewish author Maurice Hindus opined: "Jews had a predisposition to radicalism that stemmed from their ancient heritage, a predisposition that could be stimulated to action by certain conditions."[38] Even Wiesel, the sacrosanct voice of the Shoah, reputedly said: "We have to make revolution, because God told us to. God wants us to become communists."[39] Like their presumptuous ancestors at Kadesh-barnea who forged ahead *without* God's presence (Numbers 14:44), the Jew *remains* committed to a "kingless kingdom." (As for Churchill's vatic remark about the "gospel of the Antichrist," Daniel 11:37 reveals that the "son of perdition" will be a narcissistic sodomite Jew.)

The 1960 film *Spartacus* portrayed the Thracian gladiator who led a failed slave revolt against Rome. It won four academy awards and became the biggest money maker in Universal's history (until surpassed by *Airport* in 1970). It was apropos that the lead role went to a *Jew*, Kirk Douglas (born Issur Danielovitch), with another Hebrew heavy, Tony Curtis (Bernard Schwartz), co-starring as Antonius, for history confirms that International Jewry (as opposed to assimilated Jewry) has exerted a disproportionate influence on war and revolution. Hebrew University professor Gideon Shimoni writes: "In the modern history of most Jewish communities not only in Europe but in countries of the New World, and not least of all the US, Jews have been ubiquitously prominent in radical leftist movements, particularly communism...."[40] When Dr. Adam Weishaupt (believed by many to have Jewish ancestry) founded the Secret Order of the Illuminati in 1776 in Ingolstadt, Germany, he chose the pseudonym *Spartacus*.

Sir Martin Gilbert of Oxford University is the official biographer of Winston Churchill (fifteen of his eighty-eight books dealing with that genre). In *Churchill and the Jews: A Lifelong Friendship*, Dr. Gilbert comments on the Churchill article of 1920:

> In his determination to see Bolshevism crushed in Russia, Churchill studied the nature and organization of the Bolshevik government in Moscow. He was familiar with the names and origins of all its leaders: Lenin was almost the only member of the Central Committee who was not of Jewish origin. Neither Churchill nor his colleagues, nor the Jews, knew that Lenin's paternal grandfather was a Jew.[41]

This is a stunning assessment, as Jews represented just 4.2% of Russia's population in 1900.[42]

After Churchill commends the assimilated Jews who, "dwelling in every country throughout the world, identify themselves with that country…and, while adhering faithfully to their own religion, regard themselves as citizens in the fullest sense of the State which received them…," he addresses the more destructive International faction (Jews who supported Red reign within Russia and Red revolt without):

> In violent opposition to all this sphere of Jewish effort rise the schemes of the International Jews. The adherents of this sinister confederacy are mostly men reared up among the unhappy populations of countries where Jews are persecuted on account of their race. Most, if not all, of them have forsaken the faith of their forefathers, and divorced from their minds all spiritual hopes of the next world.[43]

In the article section entitled "Terrorist Jews," Churchill said that there was "no need to exaggerate the part played in the creation of Bolshevism and in the actual bringing about of the Russian Revolution, by these international and for the most part atheistical Jews."[44] He then opines that their purpose "is certainly a very great one; it probably outweighs all others. With the notable exception of Lenin, the majority of the leading figures are Jews. Moreover, the principle inspiration and driving power comes from the Jewish leaders."[45] Relating that Jews fulfilled similar roles in the Hungarian and German upheavals (Bela Kun and Rosa Luxemburg), he states that although in these countries "there are many non-Jews every whit as bad as the worst of the Jewish revolutionaries, the part played by the latter in proportion to their numbers in the population is astounding."[46]

Regrettably (especially for naive Christians), Winston's assertions are spot on. The Communist ideology was birthed by the Jewish-born philosopher, Karl Marx, the pagan famously labeling religion "the opium of the people."[47] With Jewish blood in his veins and goy blood on his hands, Vladimir Lenin said: "Every religious idea, every idea of God, even flirting with the idea of God, is unutterable vileness…."[48] Lenin's "left-hand" man, Leon Trotsky, was also a Jew. The Jewish American financier, Jacob Schiff, invested $20 million in the Russian Revolution.[49] The three-century-old Romanov dynasty was ended by a Bolshevik hit squad, led by a "Lutheran Jew," Yakov Yurovsky. In 1990, Russian scholar Edvard Radzinksy revealed that Lenin's sub-rosa order to kill Nicholas and his family was countersigned by his key advisor, Yakov Sverdlov, *another* Jew.[50] Professor Niall Ferguson of Harvard documents that Jews kept a ubiquitous presence within the evolving Bolshevik terror organs (Cheka, GPU, OGPU, NKVD, KGB, MGB), sending multiplied millions to Stalin's gulag—or *worse*.[51] Convicted Cold War spies Julius and Ethel Rosenberg represent the only married couple to be executed in US history. (Sixty-three-years later, Bernie Sanders—a *Socialist*—gave Hillary Clinton coughing fits, capturing *twenty-three* contests in the 2016 Democratic primary race before being sabotaged by fellow Jew, Debbie Wasserman Schultz.)

To be fair, as related to this author by Sam Cohen, Jews often devote their lives to achieving what they were discretely taught from childhood—that their exceptional racial endowments (what Bible believers discern as "wired-to-rule Millennial genes") were meant to help improve the world for everyone. Of course, by the time they grow up, societal conditions are *worse*. Thus, Jews wind up being their own best clients on the psychiatric couch. This reality check relates to a Jewish joke about a certain Rabbi Morris Feinberg who spent sixty years in front of the Western Wall praying for world peace. When a CNN reporter asked the man, "How do you feel after doing this for sixty years?" Feinberg replied—"Like I'm talking to a wall!"

MANIFOLD MAYHEM

In Deuteronomy 4:5-6, Moses told the Jews that God expected them to be an example to the heathen: *"Behold, I have taught you statutes and judgments, even as the LORD my God commanded me, that ye should do so in the land whither ye go to possess it. Keep therefore and do them; for this is your wisdom and your understanding in the sight of the nations, which shall hear all these statutes, and say, Surely this great nation is a wise and understanding people."*

Sadly, though, as forecast by Jacob's lament to his sons in Genesis 34:30, *"Ye have troubled me to make me stink among the inhabitants of the land,"* his posterity would perpetuate the unholy stench. (A Jewish friend once shocked this author with a "Holocaust joke," stating that the reason Hitler shot himself was because he saw the gas bill!)

While Ephesians 5:12 says *"it is a shame even to speak of those things which are done of them in secret"* (i.e., sinners in general, the *"children of disobedience"* in verse 6), the greater, disproportionate ills of world Jewry have been showcased to all. In the 1920s, Maurice Samuel, a Romanian-born British-American intellectual, novelist, and lecturer, brashly proclaimed: "We Jews, we, the destroyers, will remain the destroyers forever. Nothing that you (Gentiles) will do will meet our needs and demands. We will forever destroy because we need a world of our own, a God-world, which it is not in your nature to build."[52] In 2010, former Sephardi Chief Rabbi of Israel Yosef Ovadia opined similarly: "Gentiles were born only to serve us. Without that they have no place in the world – only to serve the People of Israel."[53]

In a gross perversion of Israel's Messiah having *"done all things well"* (Mark 7:37), His obstreperous, yet gifted, people would exhibit an equally diverse propensity—though for *evil*—the Talmud's subversive spirit impacting nearly every aspect of human experience. This 2,000-year phenomenon of inordinate influence has permeated end-day American culture, running the gamut from the fictitious Mickey Goldmill (Rocky Balboa's manager) to Jonathan Goldsmith, a.k.a. "the world's most interesting man." The following sections include a smattering of mischlings, "half-Jews" like Paul Newman who self-identified as Jewish "because it's more of a challenge."[54]

MURDER: "IS THIS THE END OF RICO?"

As typed by Edward G. Robinson, born Emanuel Goldenberg (a.k.a. "Rico" in *Little Caesar*), a number of legitimate Jewish mobsters were "living" legends in their day. A "Top Ten" list would include: beer baron Dutch Schultz (born Arthur Simon Flegenheimer); millionaire Arnold "The Brain" Rothstein (reputed fixer of the 1919 Black Sox Scandal, mentor to Charles "Lucky" Luciano); Meyer Lansky (a.k.a. "The Mob's Accountant"); Louis "Lepke" Buchalter ("Murder Inc." CEO responsible for 1,000 contract killings); Abe "Kid Twist" Reles (Lepke's "top gun"); Jake "Greasy Thumb" Guzik (Al Capone's political "greaser"); Benjamin "Bugsy" Siegel ("unlucky" founder of the Flamingo Casino); Morris "Moe" Dalitz (a.k.a. "Mr. Las Vegas"); professional gambler, Frank "Lefty" Rosenthal (portrayed by Robert De Niro in Martin Scorsese's 1995 film, *Casino*); and Samuel "Red" Levine (orthodox hit man who refused to break the *fourth* commandment by breaking the *sixth* commandment on the Sabbath).

Despite the enduring Sicilian Mafioso stereotype ("I'm gonna make him an offer he can't refuse," etc.), America's original "godfathers" were *Jews*. Drawing on their hereditary bent for turning a fast buck, the Jewish mob served as the inspiration for goy gangsters like Charlie Luciano's National Crime Syndicate.[55] Jewish director Stanley Kubrick believed that Francis Ford Coppola's *The Godfather* may have been the greatest movie in history.[56] Produced by a Jew, Al Rudy, three of the main characters in the mafia trilogy (a.k.a. the "Jewish Star Wars") were played by Jews: James Caan (Santino "Sonny" Corleone), Abe Vigoda (Salvatore Tessio), and Lee Strasberg (Hyman Roth); Alex Rocco, an Italian-American actor, portrayed the fictional Jewish gangster Mo Green (based on Bugsy Siegel). *The Godfather* held its 1972 world premier at the landmark Loew's State Theater, founded by Marcus Loew, the son of Polish Jewish immigrants.

As depicted in Scorsese's other blockbuster crime film, *Goodfellas*, the FBI's Brooklyn-born, Irish-Sicilian gangster-turned-informant, Henry Hill (played by Catholic Ray Liotta), converted to Judaism to marry Jewess, Karen Friedman (played by Gentile Lorraine Bracco), spawning the Mafia princess reality show *Mob Wives*. On the flip-flop, goy Chuck Low portrayed Morris "Morrie" Kessler, based on Martin Krugman, the Russian Jewish bookie who provided the critical tip for the 1978 record-setting $6 million Lufthansa heist at JFK Airport. Finally, in the award-winning HBO series *The Sopranos*, Jewish actor Jerry Adler played Herman "Hesh" Rabkin, the unofficial Jewish consigliere for the fictional Italian-American crime boss, Tony "Bada Bing" Soprano; Jewish actress, Jamie-Lynn Sigler portrayed his naive daughter Meadow; with Bracco slipping in for her second mob role as Dr. Jennifer Melfi, the Don's fellow paisano psychiatrist.

On February 15, 2012, the Jewish mayor of Las Vegas, Carolyn Goodman, emceed the gala opening of the "Las Vegas Mob Museum," a glitzy $42 million, 17,000 sq. foot, 3-stories-high, interactive facility to honor La Cosa Nostra (including many of the aforementioned sons of Abraham). Board member and attorney Oscar Goodman (Carolyn's husband and mayoral predecessor) personally represented scores of "wise guys" throughout his Sin City career, including Meyer Lansky and "Lefty" Rosenthal. Sadly, as with Hollywood, the Jews (led by Bugsy Siegel, the penultimate pioneer of Las Vegas) used their divine endowments to steal the Millennial promise, *"the desert shall rejoice, and blossom as the rose."* (Isaiah 35:1)

On the amateur front, two wealthy (spoiled) University of Chicago prodigies, Nathan Freudenthal Leopold, Jr., and Richard Albert Loeb (a.k.a. "Leopold and Loeb") received life terms for the 1924 abduction and murder of Robert "Bobby" Franks, Loeb's fourteen-year-old cousin. Convinced of their intellectual superiority, the dynamic duo resolved to "achieve immortality by committing the perfect crime."[57] Instead, their heinous act (committed with a *chisel*) was widely described as the "Crime of the Century." Nearly forty years later, strip club owner Jack Ruby (born Jacob Rubenstein) attained *his* fifteen minutes of fame by shooting Lee Harvey Oswald on live television.

In August 1977, David Richard Berkowitz (a.k.a. "Son of Sam") was indicted for murdering six New Yorkers and wounding nine others (eleven victims being women) during a thirteen-month crime spree. As depicted in the 1999 film *Summer of Sam* (and the anticipated 2017 40th anniversary, Blum/Fox six-part miniseries, *Son of Sam*), the "city that never sleeps" had experienced a nightmare. At his arraignment, Berkowitz claimed to have acted alone, taking orders from a demon-possessed dog owned by his neighbor, *Sam* Carr. However, he later revealed that five other shooters were involved, including two women, comprising the core assassins of a satanic criminal enterprise called "The Process Church of Final Judgment." Though complicit in all of the shootings, David, heavily immersed in the occult (II Timothy 2:26), was the triggerman in only two of the attacks, resulting in three homicides.[58]

During the 1990s, investment maven Bernie Madoff "made off" with $20 billion of his clients' funds (his record $65 billion Ponzi scheme ripping off more Jews than any scam since the Reich Flight Tax). Meanwhile, "back at the kibbutz," Ronnie Leibowitz (a.k.a. the "Motorcycle Bandit") became a folk hero after pulling 21 Tel Aviv-area bank jobs in 1990, absconding on his Italian-made Moto Guzzi. (Israel's "John Dillinger" served eight years in prison.) On July 11, 2011, Levi Aron, a Brooklyn-born Orthodox Jew, abducted, murdered, and dismembered an eight-year-old Hasidic boy named Leiby Kletzky. Then there's Detroit reality TV star Leslie "Les" Gold who runs the nation's most intimidating pawn shop, American Jewelry and Loan.

On a positive note, while "The Dutchman" converted to Catholicism shortly before the Hebrew hatchet man, Emanuel "Mendy" Weiss, had him whacked in the Palace Chophouse toilet in 1935—"Son of Sam" became a "Son of Hope" in a prison cell in 1987,[59] faithfully spreading the Gospel of his personal Saviour and Messiah Jesus Christ! (In a private interview with this author, Berkowitz, who was adopted, confirmed that his birth parents—Betty Falco, née Broder, and Joseph Kleinman—were Jewish as well.)

MONEY: "JESUS SAVES; MOSES INVESTS"

The Bible says, *"He that hastenth to be rich hath an evil eye...For the love of money is the root of all evil...."* (Proverbs 28:22; I Timothy 6:10) It is noteworthy that Jesus began *and* ended His ministry by bouncing Jewish "bankers" out of the Temple (John 2:13-17; Matthew 21:12-17). To their enduring shame, Jacob's descendants have remained oblivious to the scriptural truth that their undeniable fiscal acumen (i.e., j-e-w-elry) is a prescient God-given racial edge to ensure their national survival (especially through the Diaspora):

> *Beware that thou forget not the LORD thy God...Lest when thou hast eaten and art full, and hast built goodly houses, and dwelt therein...thou say in thine heart, My power and the might of mine hand hath gotten me this wealth.* But thou shalt remember the *LORD thy God:* FOR IT IS HE THAT GIVETH THEE POWER TO GET

> WEALTH, *that he may establish his covenant which he sware unto thy fathers, as it is this day.* (Deuteronomy 8:11-18)

Sadly, determined instead to *"consume it upon* [their] *lusts"* (James 4:3), the blasphemous Jewish adage goes—"Jesus saves, but Moses invests."

Concerning high finance, of the various central bankers, the House of Rothschild became the dominant financial dynasty in Europe. As previously cited, Heinrich Heine said, "Money is the God of our times, and Rothschild is his prophet."[60] The "Old Man" (Mayer Amschel Rothschild) was wont to boast, "Let me issue and control a nation's money and I care not who writes the laws."[61] Family biographer Frederic Morton concludes: "[T]hose five incredible sons…conquered the world more thoroughly, more cunningly, and much more lastingly than all the Caesars before or all the Hitlers after them."[62]

In 2015, ten Jews were among the Forbes Top 50 Billionaires, including tech giant Larry Ellison ($54.2), Michael Bloomberg ($35.5), Mark Zuckerberg ($33.4), Google co-founders Sergey Brin ($29.2) and Larry Page ($29.7), George Soros ($24.2), Carl Icahn ($23.5), and Michael Dell ($19.2).[63] Conservative New Yorkers recall Bloomberg as the "Republican" mayor who opposed 64-oz. soft drinks while backing a mosque at Ground Zero, along with Hillary's 2016 run for president. One online poll rated atheist billionaire George Soros "the single most destructive leftist demagogue in the country."[64] Five Jewesses made the full "1,826 Billionaires Club": Shari Arison, Karen Pritzker, Lynn Schusterman, Doris Fisher, and Sheryl Sandberg, as did the founder and CEO of Rockstar energy drinks, Russ Weiner, son of maverick talk show host Michael Savage (born Michael Alan Weiner). The last three economists to head the Federal Reserve Board have been Jews: Alan Greenspan (1987-2006); Ben Bernanke (2006-14); and Obama appointee, Janet Yellen, the first woman chair. (Janet's vice chairman is former Bank of Israel Governor Stanley Fischer.) Jacob Joseph "Jack" Lew was Obama's Treasury Secretary, 2013-17.

In 2007, Nathan Burstein of the *Jerusalem Post* wrote an eye-opening article entitled, "Jewish Power Dominates at Vanity Fair." Confirming the saying that "money equals power," Burstein acknowledges that of the world's most influential people, "100 of the bankers and media moguls, publishers and image makers who shape the lives of billons… more than half…are Jewish."[65] In a conspiracy-hardened culture, he describes the cabal as "an exclusive, insular club, one whose influence stretches around the globe but is concentrated strategically in the highest corridors of power"[66] (Luke 4:6).

MACHINATION: "PERCEPTION IS REALITY"

In 2017—the 100th anniversary of the Balfour Declaration—three of the nine US Supreme Court Justices are Jews: all are *liberal*; two are *female*, Ruth Bader Ginsburg and Obama appointee, Elena Kagen (the latter persistently rumored to be a lesbian). Thus, while constituting less than 2% of the population, leftist Jews control 33% of the highest court in the land (a whopping 1,500% over-representation).

Confirming that *"[a] little leaven leaveneth the whole lump"* (Galatians 5:9), this is the same court that on Friday, June 26, 2015 (half-way between Fathers' Day and the 4th of July), overturned millennia of history by legalizing sodomite "marriage." (Ditto the two pro-Affordable Care Act decisions in 2012/2015). Now we know why the cancer-stricken, 82-year-old Justice Ginsburg (a.k.a. "Notorious RBG")—seven years senior to Golda's age in 1973—refused to step down. (In July 2016, "Notorious" slammed Donald Trump in three interviews, an open violation of Canon 5 of the Code of Conduct for United States Judges, evoking a cutesy defense by fellow Jew, Noah Feldman, Felix Frankfurter Professor of Law at Harvard University, "Doesn't *everyone* have an outspoken Jewish grandmother?")

After Obama's *Amazing Grace* solo at Rev. Pinckney's funeral that morning, and his afternoon congratulatory call to same-sex plaintiff Jim Obergfell—the first black man to occupy the White House retired inside an "in-your-face" rainbow-lit mansion. In July 2016, Obama declined a request to light the White House in blue to support the fallen police officers in Dallas, Texas. For what it's worth, Chicago's corrupt Jewish mayor, Rahm Emanuel—Barack's former chief of staff—blames the city's soaring murder rate on police officers "going fetal." Meanwhile, 73-year-old Judith Sheindlin (a.k.a. "Judge Judy") rules the arbitration-based reality court show airwaves with a rod of iron. ("I'm not here because I'm pretty; I'm here because I'm smart!")

Richard Harris, a Jewish American diplomat, has been president of the powerful 4,000-member Council on Foreign Relations since 2003. Such political clout is no accident. Niccolò Machiavelli (1469-1527), a reputed closet Philo-Semitic, was the foremost political theorist of the Italian renaissance. His definitive work, *The Prince*, covers various methods from fraud to religion by which ascendant rulers could retain control over the masses ("perception is reality"). Medievalist scholar Laurent Guyénot writes: "Just as we speak of the 'Christian Right' as a political force in the US, we could also therefore speak of the neoconservatives as representing the 'Jewish Right'...Neoconservatism is essentially a modern Jewish version of Machiavelli's political strategy. What characterizes the neoconservative movement is not as much Judaism as a religious tradition, but rather Judaism as a political project, i.e. Zionism, by Machiavellian means."[67]

In a January 6, 2006, article in *The Forward* (America's oldest Jewish weekly), Gal Beckerman reaffirmed that that the Neocon lobby was birthed by radical Jews in the 1930s:

> If there is an intellectual movement in America to whose invention Jews can lay sole claim, neoconservatism is it. It's a thought one imagines most American Jews, overwhelmingly liberal, will find horrifying. And yet it is a fact that as a political philosophy, neoconservatism was born among the children of Jewish immigrants and is now largely the intellectual domain of those immigrants' grandchildren.[68]

Gal labels New York intellectual and former Trotskyite Irving Kristol (1920-2009) as the "godfather of Neoconservatism." In a piece titled, "The Neoconservative Persuasion," Kristol acknowledges: "One can say that the historical task and political purpose of neoconservatism would seem to be this: to convert the Republican party, and American conservatism in general, against their respective wills, into a new kind of conservative politics suitable to governing a modern democracy."[69]

What this translates to is that "*new* conservatives" were dedicated to gutting traditional conservatism (both economically and culturally), which is based on the Christian model known as White Anglo-Saxon Protestant (WASP). Thus, the GOP's recent desertion of numerous morals-based planks. Jewish scholar Murray Friedman writes: "Jewish groups had come to play a critical role in the 'de-Christianization' of American culture."[70] J. J. Goldberg, editor-at-large of the *Forward*, concurs: "Jews were overwhelmingly against permitting public-school prayer or allowing religious symbols—*any* religious symbols—on government property. Other Americans were strongly in favor of both."[71] Jewish sociologist Stephen Cohen drily adds, "We have thus the curious phenomenon of far more gentiles than Jews expressing a readiness to accept the public display of a menorah."[72]

On the foreign policy front, author Gary Dorrien writes:

> In the waning months of the cold war, shortly before an expiring Soviet Union finally disintegrated, a group of neoconservative policy makers and intellectuals began to argue that the moment had come to create an American-dominated world order. Some… called it 'the unipolarist imperative.' Instead of reducing military spending, they contended, the US needed to expand its military reach to every region of the world, using America's tremendous military and economic power to create a new Pax Americana.[73]

In a word, neoconservatism is an ultra hawkish ideology. More specifically, nearly all neocons are strongly committed to the State of Israel (in stark contradistinction to much of American Jewry). Par for the course, when "Bush 43" (Iraq War II) asked "Bush 41" (Iraq War I) to describe a neocon, Senior replied, "I'll give it to you in one word: Israel."[74] Russell Kirk, the well-known political strategist has opined: "[W]hat really animates the neoconservatives, especially Irving Kristol, is the preservation of Israel. That lies in the back of everything."[75] Regrettably for the US, the Iraq War of 2003-11 was included in this "everything"—4,500 soldiers killed, 32,200 wounded, all financed by $1 trillion in "funny money" (a staggering 1/18 of the national debt as of 2015), confirming the adage, "clash equals cash."

Dr. Guyénot makes a compelling case for comprehensive, neocon complicity in the debacle, indicting twenty key Jewish agitators: William Kristol, Paul Wolfowitz, Richard Perle, Elliott Abrams, Douglas Feith, David Wurmser, Lewis Libby, Charles Krauthammer, Joseph Lieberman, Eliot Cohen, William Safire, Norman Podhoretz, Kenneth Adelman, Philip Zelikow, Robert Kagan, Bernard Lewis, David Frum, Albert Wohlstetter, Oded Yinon, and Bibi Netanyahu.[76] Although a substantial number of prominent neocons are Jewish, some of the leading ones are not, such as John Bolton, James Woolsey, William Bennett, and Dick Cheney.[77] Karl Rove, chief White House advisor for George W. Bush, is widely regarded as a "Machiavelli aficionado."[78] [Note: Though this author's 2005 prediction that Iraq would be a no-win albatross[79] proved accurate, the material would have been strengthened by a survey of Jewish neocon influence.]

In their 2007 bestseller, *The Israel Lobby and U.S. Foreign Policy*, co-authors John J. Mearsheimer and Stephen M. Walt posit: "U.S. support for Israel was a significant source of anti-Americanism in the Middle East and a source of tension with key strategic allies..." and that "pro-Israel groups and lobbies were a major influence on U.S. foreign policy in this vital region...."[80] The writers substantiate their thesis by attributing Israel's unprecedented, exclusive US aid (military and economic) to a vast network of influence peddlers and think tanks.

A shortlist, led by the American Israel Public Affairs Committee (AIPAC), would include: Project for the New American Century (PNAC), Jewish Institute for National Security Affairs (JINSA), Jewish Council for Public Affairs (JCPA), Washington Institute for Near East Policy (WINEP), Zionist Organization of America (ZOA), American Jewish Committee (AJC), Hudson Institute, Foundation For Defense of Democracies (FDD), American Enterprise Institute (AEI), Center for Security Policy (CSP), Conference of Presidents of Major American Jewish Organizations (CoP), Religious Action Center of Reform Judaism (RAC), Americans for a Safe Israel (AFSI), American Jewish Congress (AJC), Pro-Israel Political Action Committees (PACs), American Israel Education Foundation (AIEF), Israel Policy Forum (IPF), Simon Wiesenthal Center (SWC), Middle East Forum (MEF), Anti-Defamation League (ADL), International Fellowship of Christians and Jews (IFCJ), and Christians United for Israel (CUFI).

To illustrate the power of this Jewish bloc, journalist Michael Massing relates that a pro-Israel congressional staffer informed him, "We can count on well over half the House—250 to 300 members—to do reflexively whatever AIPAC wants."[81] Likewise, former AIPAC foreign policy director Steve J. Rosen illustrated AIPAC's influence to J. J. Goldberg by placing a napkin in front of him and stating: "In twenty-four hours, we could have the signatures of seventy senators on this napkin."[82] Yet, in fairness to Israel, unlike the methods employed by "Greasy Thumb" Guzik, even Mearsheimer and Walt concede:

> Like the efforts of other ethnic lobbies and interest groups...the Israel lobby's various elements are legitimate forms of democratic political participation, and they are for the most part consistent with America's long tradition of interest group activity...Jewish Americans

> are no different from their fellow citizens in this regard. The Israel lobby is not a cabal or conspiracy or anything of this sort. It is engaged in good old-fashioned interest group politics, which is as American as apple pie.[83]

Goldberg adds: "[T]here is an entity called the Jewish community made up of a group of organizations and public figures that's part of the political rough and tumble. There's nothing wrong with playing the game like everybody else."[84]

Concerning Israel's "favored nation" status, Mearsheimer and Walt write: "Because this level of support is rarely questioned today, it is easy to forget that the 'special relationship' that now exists did not emerge until several decades after Israel's founding."[85] Noting that the "sea change" in *real* support began after the 1967 War, they confirm:

> After averaging roughly $63 million annually from 1949 to 1965 (more than 95% of which was economic assistance and food aid), average aid increased to $102 million per year from 1966 to 1970. Support soared to $634.5 million in 1971 (roughly 85% was military assistance) and more than quintupled after the 1973 Yom Kippur War. Israel became the largest annual recipient of U.S. foreign assistance in 1976, a position it has retained ever since.[86]

In keeping with the subtitle of *Holy Ground*, the truth is that America's volte-face was contrived by the Jews having "won at the goys' game." Thus, it would appear that the anti-Israel lobby is fueled by "sour grapes." (Once again: "The main reason that Gentiles hate Jews is because Gentiles love money and Jews know how to make it.")

MORALS: "WE ARE BRINGING THEM THE PLAGUE"

On May 20, 2015, two bizarre stories were breaking at the same time. *CNN* ran a headline, "Girl Scouts welcome transgender girls,"[87] while *The Daily Beast* stated, "Adopted 'Father' and 'Son' to Marry."[88] By Christmas, the NYC Commission on Human Rights had expanded its shelter of the LGBTQ community to *thirty-one* gender groups. Fines totaling $250,000 could now be leveled at employers/landlords who refuse to use an employee/tenant's preferred name, pronoun, or title

(Revelation 13:17). The new list includes, "Ze," "Hir," "Two-Spirit," "Third Sex," "Gender Bender," "Trans Person," and "Androgynous."

Though highly unpalatable for Christians to consider, while Professor Earle Cairns wrote that "Judaism may be thought of as the stalk on which the rose of Christianity was to bloom,"[89] much of America's moral decline can be traced to that same stalk! The most famous burlesque chain in US history was peddled by four Jewish brothers in New York City from 1912 to 1937: Abe, Morton, Billy, and Herbert Minsky. The most famous stripper of the Minskys' brand was Rose Louise Hovick (a.k.a. "Gypsy Rose Lee"). According to author Stacey Wolf, "The real Rose Lee [Gypsy's mother, Rose Thomas Hovick] was both Jewish and a lesbian."[90] To help perpetuate the sin, William Friedkin directed *The Night They Raided Minsky's*, while fellow Jew, Mervyn LeRoy, directed *Gypsy*.

Jewish historian Edward Bristow affirms that Germany's negligible Hebrew population was the largest ethnic class to profit from white slavery and prostitution.[91] Not that the coming demon-possessed Adolf Hitler would need any *further* impetus to persecute Jews (ditto today's neo-Nazi agenda), Dr. Magnus Hirschfeld, hailed as the "Einstein of Sex" for his "theory of sexual relativity," was already transforming the Weimar Republic into a cesspool of iniquity.[92] Culminating in the phenomenon known as "sexual magic," the schtick was a "scientific" pretention to promote *anything* and *everything* from pornography and sodomy to pedophilia, incest, sadomasochism, and bestiality. Jewish scholar Mel Gordon adds "urine drinkers" and "high heel stompers" to the list, describing Berlin as "one of the most faithless—or heathen—cities in the Western world."[93] (Berlin's erotic climate was captured in the film *Cabaret*, starring Liza Minnelli as "Sally Bowles.") Gerhard "Gad" Beck (1923-2012), author of *An Underground Life: Memoirs of a Gay Jew in Nazi Germany*, would keep the torch "burning" (Romans 1:27), representing one of Jewry's last sodomite Holocaust survivors. (See *Torch Song Trilogy*, by Jewish sodomite Harvey Fierstein.)

In 1959, the German sex toy known as "Lilli" became the prototype for Barbie, America's first girl toy to reveal breasts (a great perk for inquisitive little brothers). The driving force behind this taboo-busting watershed was Jewish businesswoman Ruth Handler, president of Mattel, Inc. In 2016, Mattel released a Barbie version of the lesbian US soccer star, Abby Wambach, complete with her distinctive cropped sidecut.

Moving right along, American philosopher Dr. Paul Kurtz was known as the "Father of Secular Humanism."[94] In 1966, Howard Stanton "Anton" LaVey founded the "Church" of Satan in San Francisco. (David Berkowitz was birthed into the occult by LaVey's Satanic Bible.[95]) Film executive Roman Polanski was arrested and convicted of raping a thirteen-year-old girl in 1977, spurring a thirty-two-year exile in France. (His 8½-month-pregnant Catholic wife, actress Sharon Tate, was murdered in 1969, by the quasi neo-Nazi Charles Manson "family.") New York's acerbic three-term mayor Ed Koch, *a lifetime bachelor*, consistently refused to discuss his "sexuality," fueling rumors that he was "gay." When Koch ran for mayor in 1977, anonymous flyers flooded the streets urging New Yorkers to "Vote for Cuomo, Not the Homo."[96] Harvey Milk became California's first open sodomite elected to public office, winning a seat on the San Francisco Board of Supervisors in 1977. After passing a strict gay rights ordinance, Milk and Mayor George Moscone were killed on November 27, 1978, by Dan White, a disgruntled former city official. Sean Penn portrayed Milk in the 2008 film, *Milk*. Obama posthumously awarded Harvey the Presidential Medal of Freedom in 2009. The Navy named a ship after him in 2016. (Moscone's successor, Diane Feinstein, is one of the most liberal members of Congress.)

Heywood "Woody" Allen (born Allan Konigsberg) made headlines in 1992 when word leaked that the fifty-six-year-old actor, writer, director, comedian, and playwright was fornicating with twenty-one-year-old Soon-Yi Previn, the adopted daughter of Mia Farrow, his "shack-up" of over ten years and his leading "lady" in thirteen films. (The famous atheist has spent years dodging claims that he also molested his seven-year-old adopted daughter, Dylan Farrow—the assault confirmed by Dylan herself.) In the 1990s, Heidi Fleiss (a.k.a. "Hollywood Madame") was America's foremost purveyor of whores for the rich and famous. New York Governor Eliot Spitzer resigned in March 2008 due to his patronage of a prostitution ring. Representative Anthony Weiner (D-NY) quit in 2011, due to a sexting scandal. That same year, Isaac Mizrahi (the "Jewish Versace") and his partner of six years, Arnold Germer, were "married" in a civil ceremony in New York City Hall. (To Isaac's credit, he *does* oppose "man buns.") Finally, retired US Representative Barnett "Barney" Frank (D-MA) is considered the senior "gay" politician in America. As Barney once said, "I'm used to being in the minority.

Hey, I'm a left-handed gay Jew. I've never felt, automatically, a member of any majority."[97]

Joy Ladin (born Jay Ladin) is the first openly transgender professor at an Orthodox institution. (Dr. "It" holds the David and Ruth Gottesman Chair in English at Stern College, the undergraduate *women's* college of arts and sciences of Yeshiva University, located at the school's campus in Manhattan.) Meanwhile, back in the "Holy Land," with Israel the capital of cannabis research, the press reported in September 2014 that police busted a "messianic prostitution sect" allegedly using drugs and alcohol to brainwash Jewish girls into believing that "having sex with non-Jews would hasten redemption of the Jewish people."[98]

The celebrated Jewish Viennese neurologist, Dr. Sigmund Freud (a.k.a. the "Father of Psychoanalysis"), is regarded as having laid the foundation for America's "erotic emancipation." Conjoined to his central crackpot thesis of *id*, *ego*, and *superego*—Freud's magnum opus for perversion—his so-called "Oedipus complex" hypothesized that incestuous desires (i.e., son/mother, daughter/father) are healthy childhood instincts. Freud biographer Mark Edmundson wrote, "'We are bringing them the plague,' Freud reportedly said when he and Jung and Ferenczi disembarked in New York in 1909. 'We're bringing them the plague, and they don't even know it.'"[99]

Freud's main protégé was his younger cousin and fellow sham psychoanalyst, William Reich. Banned from the "Reich" for preying on the Hitler youth, Dr. Reich followed Freud to America where *New Yorker* magazine called him the "Father of the Sexual Revolution."[100] Historian Christopher Turner states that Reich offered the "tantalizing suggestion that sexual emancipation would lead to positive social change."[101] Reich was such a good con man, he actually invented and marketed a gizmo called the "Orgone Energy Accumulator," a crucible resembling a telephone booth, lined with metal sheeting and steel wool, where his patients sat "hoping to dissolve the toxic dangers of conformity…."[102] According to Turner, Bill deemed his product "an almost magical device that could improve its users' 'orgastic potency' and by extension their general, and above all, mental health."[103] He even claimed that the "mysterious currents" could help cure cancer.[104]

Though Albert Einstein denounced the "Orgone Box" as a hoax, and Reich was later investigated by the Food and Drug Administration and sent to prison, his liberating lunacy had opened the flood gates. Biographer Myron Sharaf wrote, "Reich was well aware that he was a 'fury on earth' and of the fate meted out to such furies. Indeed, this very problem preoccupied him during the last years of his life…."[105] Upon Reich's death behind bars in 1957, his physician, Dr. Elsworth Barker, compared his tragic denouement to "The Murder of Christ."[106]

Four worldly-wise Jewess counseling experts followed in Reich's wake. The most famous was Karola Ruth Siegel Westheimer (a.k.a. "Dr. Ruth"). The 4-foot-7-inch, German-born Shoah survivor was profiled in the *New York Times* as "the Sorbonne-trained psychologist who became a kind of cultural icon in the 1980s" [who] "ushered in the new age of freer, franker talk about sex on radio and television…."[107] (In the 2004 film, "Meet the Fockers," the Jewish family comprises a male nurse, Gaylord "Greg" Focker, played by Ben Stiller; his eccentric father, Bernie, played by Dustin Hoffman; and Barbra Streisand as the equally bizarre mother, Rozalin, a sex therapist for elderly couples.) The more discreet Dr. Joyce Brothers, lauded by the *New York Times* as offering "nonthreatening advice on sex, relationships, family and all manner of decent behavior…,"[108] was eulogized by the *Washington Post* as "The face of American psychology"[109] (Psalm 1:1; Jeremiah 10:2; Romans 12:2; Colossians 2:8; I John 2:15).

Identical twins Ann Landers (Esther "Eppie" Lederer) and Dear Abby (Pauline Phillips), a.k.a. Abigail Van Buren, were rated in *Time* as "arguably the most famous advice columnists" in America.[110] (Though the sisters could advise everyone else, behind their pennames they conducted a bitter rivalry for nearly half-a-century.) One sample Q&A (September 3, 1986) will serve to illustrate Paul's words, *"hath not God made foolish the wisdom of this world?"* (I Corinthians 1:20):

> Dear Abby: I am writing because I need some advice about my present employment in relation to how I feel about myself spiritually. You see, I am a topless dancer and I also consider myself to be a good Christian. I don't want to change my job because I am a single parent and make a good living for myself and my family. Also, I love to dance. This job allows me to spend time with my children, take classes at the university, and live a respectable lifestyle. I will eventually get my degree and pursue a career. I believe in God, and live a clean and virtuous life. I go straight home after work at the club and do not accept invitations from customers. Abby, do you think a person can dance topless and believe in God? Concerned and Praying:

Dear Concerned: Obviously a person can dance topless and believe in God, because you do.[111]

MUSIC: "TIPTOE THROUGH THE TULIPS WITH ME"

According to Ezekiel 28:13-14, musical instruments were originally built into the body of Satan. An old Jewish joke illustrates the supernatural power of music: When Billy Graham sang *All I Want is Jesus*, 5,000 Catholics became Protestants. When the Pope sang *Ava Maria*, 10,000 Protestants converted to Rome. When Pat Boone sang *There's a Gold Mine in the Sky*—100,000 Jews joined the Air Force!

Ironic to many (though predictably subtle to Bible believers), the "Happy Hanukkah" crowd wrote (or composed) some of the most enduring Christmas songs in history. However, the "holiday" hits were decidedly secular, as in "diversionary" from the *real* "reason for the season" (e.g., "Rockin' Around the Christmas Tree," "Santa Baby," "Rudolf the Red-Nosed Reindeer," "Run, Rudolf, Run," "Silver Bells," "I'll Be Home For Christmas," "It's the Most Wonderful Time of the Year," "Winter Wonderland," "Sleigh Ride," "The Christmas Song," "The Christmas Waltz," "Let it Snow! Let it Snow! Let it Snow!," "You're a Mean One, Mr. Grinch," and America's all-time favorite, "White Christmas"). The *rest* of the story is less abstruse.

Whereas Christian composers like Johann Bach said, "The aim and final end of all music should be none other than the glory of God and the refreshment of the soul"[112] (e.g., Katherine Davis' "Little Drummer Boy"), *Jacob's* seed marched to the beat of a *different* drum. Leonard Bernstein, acclaimed director of the New York Philharmonic Orchestra, was an openly sodomite communist. His protégé, Aaron Copland (a.k.a. "Dean of American Composers"), was another gay Red. Mel "The Velvet Fog" Tormé pioneered "African-American" jazz. Bernard "Buddy" Rich was billed as "The World's Greatest Drummer." Benjamin David "Benny" Goodman was dubbed "King of Swing." Artie Shaw was regarded as one of the finest jazz clarinetists. Husband and wife duo, Steve Lawrence (born Sidney Liebowitz) and Eydie Gormé helped advance big band, swing, and traditional pop. Promoter George Wein launched the Newport Jazz Festival in 1954 and the Newport Folk Festival in 1959. Chicago drug dealer and jazz aspirant, Milton "Mezz" Mezzrow (the original Rachel Dolezal), was so enamored with jungle musicians (like "Satchmo" Armstrong, one of his best pot clients), he married a black gal, moved to Harlem, adopted a "jazz-jive" lingo, and declared himself a "voluntary negro."[113]

Songwriters/production partners Jerome "Jerry" Leiber and Mike Stoller handed Elvis Presley some of his greatest hits ("Hound Dog," "Jail House Rock," "Love Me," "Loving You," "King Creole," and "Don't"). Hal Wallis, described as "the Paramount Producer who reigned over Elvis Presley's film career," made nine of his movies.[114] According to J. J. Goldberg's 2014 *Forward* article, "On Elvis' Yahrzeit [death anniversary], His Not So Secret Jewish History," just as with the *real* Mob, Presley's famed inner circle, the "Memphis Mafia," included several prominent Jews: Alan Fortas (nephew of Supreme Court Justice Abe Fortas), disc jockey George Klein ("elder statesman of Memphis rock 'n' roll"), Marty Lacker (Elvis's "personal sounding board"), and Larry Geller (his hairdresser and spiritual guru).

Citing his interview with Klein, J. J. said: "He explained to me that Elvis's great-great-grandmother had been Jewish and Elvis was very proud of it…He told me that Elvis had put a Star of David on his mother's gravestone…at Memphis' Park Forrest Cemetery."[115] After his own death and a foiled grave robbery, mother and son were reinterred at Graceland, though "the new gravestone, lacking Elvis's active attention, didn't get a star."[116] The *Wall Street Journal* states: "According to 'Elvis and Gladys,' a 1985 book by Elaine Dundy, Elvis's maternal great-great-grandmother Nancy Tackett was Jewish…So, according to Jewish law which stipulates that Jewish identity is passed on matrilineally, Mr. Presley was Jewish."[117] Graceland official Todd Morgan affirmed: "We know there is Jewish heritage in Elvis's family going a few generations back. It was something Elvis was aware of and certainly was sensitive to."[118] (Some believe Elvis was *melungeon*, tri-racial descendants of 17th-century crypto-Jewish traders from Scotland who settled in Appalachia.)[119]

Also, his parents gave him the middle name of "Aron" after Moses' brother, the first High Priest in Israel (later changing it to the more Biblical spelling, "Aaron").[120] And while his so-called *Christian* name, "Elvis," is supposedly an Anglicization of the Irish "Saint" Ailbhe of Munster,[121] it's hard to miss the *Hebrew* nomenclature in "El."

According to Daniel Hartal (a.k.a. "Elvis Schmelvis"), reputedly "the world's only Orthodox Elvis impersonator": "Elvis had a special *neshama* (soul). You don't see followers of John Lennon or Jim Morrison behaving the same way Elvis fans do. There was something special beyond the man. His spirit, his music, his connection."[122] (El's female fans bombing him with their "unmentionables" being the obvious exception, etc.) Finally, should any further "proof" be needed, the world's largest graven image to the "King of Rock and Roll" sits just outside Abu Ghosh (where David Marcus died). The "Elvis Inn," a gas station-eatery moonlighting as a shrine to Elvis, proudly displays (according to *JNS.org*, August 26, 2005) a sixteen-foot-high brass statue of the Jewish idol (I John 5:21).

The early '60s sound can be defined by four Brooklyn Jews. WABC's "Cousin Brucie" (Bruce Morrow, born Bruce Meyerowitz), was the most famous disc jockey on the East Coast. John "Jay" Traynor was the *lead* "J" in the all-Jew band, "Jay and the Americans." Carole King (Carol Joan Klein) wrote "Up On The Roof" (the "Big Apple" getaway known as "Tar Beach"). Leslie Gore (Leslie Sue Goldstein), famous for such "normal" heterosexual tween themes as "It's My Party" and "Judy's Turn to Cry" (her third album entitled, "Boys, Boys, Boys"), was a lifelong closet lesbian. ("You Don't Own Me" *should* have been a clue.)

Having stated, "If there hadn't been an Elvis there wouldn't have been the Beatles,"[123] John "Imagine There's No Heaven" Lennon and his fellow mop tops were led to *their* fame and fortune by Brian Epstein, a neurotic, pill-popping sodomite. On April 2, 1970, the Beatles' last album, "Let It Be," was tweaked by the Grammy-winning music wizard, Phil Spector; on April 13, 2009, the wig aficionado was convicted of second-degree murder in the 2003 shooting death of actress Lana Clarkson at his sprawling California mansion. Paul's first wife was Jewish—Linda Louise, Lady McCartney (née Eastman).

Following the British invasion, a fifth column of "Hebrew homies" kept the destruction going. *Rolling Stone* magazine (a.k.a. "The Bible of Rock and Roll music") was founded in 1967 by Jewish entrepreneur Jann Wenner (the same also helping launch Cleveland's Rock and Roll Hall of Fame Museum). Unable to *"sing the LORD'S song in a strange land"* (Psalm 137:4), a "Who's Who" of the old guard comprised such patriarchs as Arlo Guthrie; Neil Sedaka; William "Billy" Joel ("Piano Man"); Paul Simon and Art Garfunkel; Manfred Mann; Norman ("Spirit in the Sky") Greenbaum; and "former" born-again Christian, Bob Dylan (born Robert Allen Zimmerman).

Some of the more mellow appearing artists included: Neil Diamond (a.k.a. "The Jewish Elvis"); Burt Bacharach; Barry Manilow; Herb Albert (Tijuana Brass); "Mama" Cass Elliot; Peter Yarrow (Peter, Paul, and Mary); Kenneth Bruce Gorelick ("Kenny G"); and Ed Ames (a.k.a. "Mingo") and his famous tomahawk. Led by Leslie Gore and inspired by proselyte Helen "I Am Woman" Reddy, Gloria Steinem's satanic "feminazi" cause was driven by insurgents like Carly Simon; Carole King; Dinah Shore; Phoebe Snow; Bette Midler; Julie Gold; Janis Ian; Victoria Shaw; Marcy Levy; and the undisputed, verklempt-inducing Jewess of all time—Barbra Joan "Babs" Streisand (a.k.a. "First Lady of Entertainment," "Mother of Divas," "Diva of Divas").

There was even a noted Jewish influence on the jungle beat of soul music. A June 2015 article in *My Jewish Detroit*, "Motown Mensches Live," attributes much of Berry Gordy, Jr.'s, success to "the talents of many Jewish producers, advisors, agents and writers."[124] Al Abrams, Gordy's first full-time employee, became the firm's critical National Promotion Director. The Handleman Company was Motown Records' earliest distributor. Gordy's legal/accounting team consisted of Harold and Sidney Noveck. Dearborn deejay Robin Seymour (WKNR) and Windsor-based radio station director Paul Drew (CKLW) were two of the key early record spinners credited with pushing the Motown label. Several Motown hits came from Jewish writers (e.g., Carole King and the Leiber-Stoller team). Finally, in 1959, four young Jewish males calling themselves "The Valadiers" (Stuart Avig, Jerry Light, Marty Coleman, and Art Glasser) made music history, crossing the color line (in reverse) as the first *white* vocal group signed to Motown Records.

The "Woodstock Music & Art Fair" of August 1969 was one of the greatest counterculture watershed events in American music history. Unbeknown to many, the "concert" (500,000 strung-out flower children) was staged by Jews. As Nate Bloom relates in his article *Woodstock: The Jewish Connection*, the four horsemen behind the apocalyptic gathering were impresarios Michael Lang and Artie Kornfeld, along with investors Joel Rosenman and John Roberts. The venue that the team eventually secured was a dairy farm near Bethel, New York, owned by a successful Jewish farmer, Max Yasgur. It was fitting that the heavily Jewish rural area, once known as the "Borscht Belt," sits in the Catskill Mountains where countless Jews began their showbiz careers. The Monticel Jewish Community Center represents the most "far out" Hebrew link to

Woodstock for making hundreds of sandwiches to abate the "munchies" of the beset revelers.[125]

As Douglas Fairbanks, Sr., astutely said in 1919, "The Semitic race seemed to be the only people who have the combination of financial acumen and artistic sense,"[126] a slate of Jewish performers also made their mark on the three-day epic fest. The list includes soloists Bob Dylan, Arlo Guthrie, and Bert Sommer (whose locks appeared on the playbill for *Hair*); Alan Malarowitz, Sweetwater; Jorma Kaukonen and Marty Balin, Jefferson Airplane; Leslie West, Mountain; Alan Cooper, Henry Gross, and Eliot Cahn, Sha-Na-Na; Bobby Robertson, The Band; plus, Mark Kapner and Doug Meltzer with "Country Joe" McDonald (*half* Jew) and Barry "The Fish" Melton (*full* Jew).[127]

The iconic R&B band, Blood, Sweat and Tears ("Spinning Wheel," "You've Made Me So Very Happy," "And When I Die," et al.) began their hour-long set (minus founder, Al Kooper) around 1:30 a.m. on August 18, the festival's last day. According to *Tablet Magazine*:

> One particularly intense night at Café Au Go Go in Greenwich Village, Al Kooper bled all over his organ keyboard. He'd just formed a new band after leaving the Blues Project…this incident inspired their name. Blood, Sweat and Tears was comprised of Kooper, Blues Project guitarist Steve Katz, and four other Jewish musicians: Bobby Colomby on drums, Randy Brecker and Jerry Weiss on trumpet, and Fred Lipsuis on sax and piano."[128]

The Bible states of God's Son in the Garden of Gethsemane, *"And being in an* AGONY *he prayed more earnestly: and his* SWEAT *was as it were great drops of* BLOOD *falling down to the ground."* (Luke 22:44) Ironically (in view of Isaiah 7:14), the article ends, "'Child is Father to the Man' remains their greatest creative endeavor."

The bottom fell out after Woodstock via Hebrew headbangers like Israeli native Gene Simmons (born Chaim Witz), a.k.a. "The Demon," and Paul Stanley of KISS; David Lee "Diamond Dave" Roth; The Doors' Robbie Krieger ("The End"); Jay Jay French, Twisted Sister; Mickey Hart, Grateful Dead; Keith Reed and Gary Brooker, Procol Harum ("A Whiter Shade of Pale"); Joey Kramer, Aerosmith; Peter Green, Fleetwood Mack; Michael Bolton, Blackjack; David Bryan, Bon Jovi; Chris Stein, Blondie; and Rush's Gary "Geddy Lee" Weinrib (son of Dachau and Bergen-Belsen survivors).

The "Punk Pioneers" were next: Thomas Erdelyi and Jeffrey Ross Hyman (a.k.a. Tommy and Joey "Ramone"), followed by Brits Marc Bolan of T. Rex, and Sex Pistol Malcolm McLaren (a.k.a. "The Godfather of Punk"). Haifa native Hilel Slovak landed in Los Angeles as an original member of the Red Hot Chili Peppers (OD'd on heroin). Lenny Kravitz's multifaceted genres encompass rock, *funk* rock, *hard* rock, *soul* rock, neo-soul and neo-psychedelia (whatever all *that* garbage means). "Honorable" mention goes to Mr. Herbert Khaury, the 1970s one-hit-wonder and ukulele virtuoso "professionally" known as "Tiny Tim," for "Tiptoe Through the Tulips With Me."

A legion of aspiring artists crossed into the 21st century: Thomas Jacob "Jack" Black; Paula Abdul; Dan Bern; Evan and Jaron; Adam Noah Levine; Alecia Beth "Pink" Moore; Lisa Loeb; Marc Cohn; and the late, great British star, Amy *Wine*house, dead at twenty-seven from *alcohol* poison. Representing the "You Can't Make This Stuff Up" genre, not to be eclipsed by the 6-foot-3-inch bearded orthodox rapper Matisyahu, in a 2011 *Forbes Magazine* article by (get *this* name) Zack *O'Malley* Greenberg titled "Hip-Hop-Hanukkah," Adam Yauch, Mike Diamond and Adam Horovitz (a.k.a. "The Beastie Boys") were listed as "The best Jewish hip-hop act of all time."[129] Then we have *Schmekel*, the Brooklyn-based, all-transgender, all-Jewish, klezmer-core punk band, whose name means "little penis." The 2013 Tony-winning Broadway Musical *Kinky Boots* (enough said) was produced by two Jews, Hal Luftig and Daryl Roth (the book written by Harvey Fierstein). *Texas Monthly* described country-western anomaly Richard "Kinky" Friedman (and his "Texas Jewboys") as "the only recording star in Nashville who buys his clothes at the Hadassah Thrift Shop."[130]

Finally, in a 2013 *Times of Israel* article, "Just your typical 6' 1" African American Yiddish singer," Anthony Mordechai Tzvi Russell, a Texas-born, Baptist-bred, "well versed in the Bible," home-schooled, Navy brat (lately from Oakland, California),[131] was featured as "a Jew by choice, an opera singer by training, and a Yiddish singer by calling [who wows fans with]…his expressive interpretation of Yiddish folk songs and Hassidic *niggunim* (wordless melodies)."[132] And if you thought that the one-eyed "Rat Pack" member, Sammy Davis, Jr. ("The black Moshe Dayan"), and his blonde Swedish actress wife, May Britt (both converts to Judaism), were a tough act to follow, the story adds *this* "touching" tidbit about Tony and *his* special someone: "After moving in with his boyfriend, Rabbi Michael Rothbaum (whom he had met on a blind date to a Mets baseball game), in Nyack, New York, in 2009, Russell started going to a local Conservative synagogue and celebrating Jewish holidays."[133] ("Beam me up Scotty—quick!")

MOVIES: "YOU OUGHT TO BE IN PICTURES"

When the Jews were preparing to enter the Promised Land, the Lord had Moses deliver a critical directive: *"When ye are passed over Jordan into the land of Caanan; Then ye shall drive out all the inhabitants of the land from before you, and destroy all their* PICTURES*...."* (Numbers 33:51-52) Not only did Israel fail to obey this order, but they embraced the sin as well. Regarding the proverbial "Hole in the Wall" (i.e., "Hell-hole"), God gave Ezekiel a vision of this evil, along with a prophetic picture of the modern movie theater:

> *And he brought me to the door of the court; and when I looked, behold a* HOLE IN THE WALL. *Then said he unto me, Son of man, dig now in the wall: and when I had digged in the wall, behold a door. And he said unto me, Go in, and behold the wicked abominations that they do here. So I went in and saw; and behold every form of creeping things, and abominable beasts, and all the idols of the house of Israel,* POURTRAYED *upon the wall round about...Then said he unto me, Son of man, hast thou seen what the ancients of the house of Israel do in the* DARK, *every man in the chambers of his* IMAGERY? *for they say, the LORD seeth us not; the LORD hath forsaken the earth.* (Ezekiel 8:7-12)

Thus, it was fitting that the "chosen people"—having cut their teeth in vaudeville from the Catskills (a.k.a. "Jewish Alps") to Broadway (e.g., Fanny Brice, Sophie Tucker, Al Jolson, Irving Berlin, George and Ira Gershwin, Groucho, Harpo, Chico, and Zeppo Marx, George Burns, Milton Berle, Jack Benny, Phil Silvers, and Danny Kaye, along with Louis Feinberg, Moses, Jerome, and Samuel Horowitz, a.k.a. Larry, Moe, Curly, and Shemp of "The Three Stooges")—would now journey westward to perfect their craft in the new "Holy Land" of Hollywood. Numerous books have documented how the Jews moved from "Tin Pan Alley" to "Tinsel Town," becoming the premier actors, writers, producers, studio moguls, and distributors of the fledgling industry. (See: *The American Jewish Story Through Cinema*, Eric Goldman; *Hollywood's Chosen People*, Daniel Bernardi; *An Empire of Their Own: How the Jews Invented Hollywood*, Neal Gabler, et al.)

The noted philo-Semitic scholar, Paul Johnson, states, "[T]he movie industry…was almost entirely put together by Jews…."[134] Stephen Silbiger concurs, "The Jewish involvement in motion pictures is more than a success story; it is the basis of the disproportionate influence that Jews have had in shaping American popular culture."[135] Famed Jewish silent film star, Douglas Fairbanks, Sr., was crowned the original "King of Hollywood." The first "talkie," Warner Brothers' *The Jazz Singer*, centers on a liberated rabbi's son (Al Jolson), culminating in his acclaimed rendition of "Mammy." In his joke about the impatient mugger's demand, "I *said*, 'Your money or your *life*,'" Jack Benny's reply—"I'm thinking! I'm thinking!"—is considered the greatest punch line in showbiz history. Bernardi comments on the Eastern European Jews who converted Edison's kinetoscope reels into a "revolutionary cultural tool that transformed popular consciousness":

> Indeed, the names of these immigrants turned studio bosses are now common historical reference points in film history books: Harry Cohn (of Columbia), William Fox (born Vilmos Fried, of Fox Pictures, later merged into Twentieth Century-Fox), Samuel Goldwyn (born Samuel Gelbfisz) of Goldwyn Pictures, later merged into Metro-Goldwyn-Mayer, Carl Laemmle (of Universal), Louis B. Mayer (of Metro), Jack and Harry Warner (born Wonskolaser, two of the Warner brothers), and Adolph Zukor (of Paramount). Each contributed to building a Hollywood entertainment industry that remained at the center of cultural production throughout the first half of the twentieth century.[136]

A survey of the top Jewish producers, writers, and directors—the human agents who helped spread Freud's plague via a slate of benchmark films—must begin with Melville Shavelson, the producer and director of *Cast A Giant Shadow*, who *cast a giant shadow* on the marital fidelity of David Marcus. Mel's cohorts would include: Ernst Lubitsch (*Heaven Can Wait*, *Ninotchka*); Mervyn LeRoy (*Wizard of Oz*, *Little Caesar*); David O. Selznick (*Gone With The Wind*); Michael Curtiz (*Casablanca*, *White Christmas*); Otto Preminger (*Laura*, *Exodus*); Sam

Zimbalist (*Quo Vadis*, "starring" Atlantico); Billy Wilder (*Some Like it Hot*, *The Seven Year Itch*); Sidney Lumet (*12 Angry Men*, *Network*); William Wyler (*The Best Years of Our Lives*, *Ben-Hur*); Stanley Kubrick (*Lolita*, *A Clockwork Orange*); Harry Saltzman (nine "James Bond" films); Robert Earl Wise (*The Sand Pebbles*, *Westside Story*, *The Sound of Music*); Joseph E. Levine (*The Carpetbaggers*, *Harlow*); Mike Nichols (*Who's Afraid of Virginia Woolf?*, *The Graduate*, *Carnal Knowledge*); Stanley Kramer (*Guess Who's Coming to Dinner*); Arthur P. Jacobs (*Planet of the Apes*); John Schlesinger (*Midnight Cowboy*); Paul Mazursky (*Bob & Carol & Ted & Alice*); Norman Lear (*All in the Family*, *The Jeffersons*, *Sanford and Son*, *Maude*); Mel Brooks (*Blazing Saddles*, *History of the World, Part 1*); Woody Allen (*Hannah and Her Sisters*); Marvin Chomsky (*Roots*); Roman Polanski (*Rosemary's Baby*); Bill Friedkin (*The Boys in the Band, The Exorcist*); Richard Donner (*The Omen*); Miloš Forman (*The People vs. Larry Flynt*); Ivan Reitman (*Ghostbusters I & II*); George Cukor (*My Fair Lady*); Sydney Pollack (*Tootsie*); Joel and Ethan Coen (*Fargo*, *Oh Brother, Where Art Thou?*); James Schamus (*Brokeback Mountain*); Bruce Cohen (*Milk*); Sam Raimi (*Spider-Man, Drag Me to Hell*); and Sherry Lansing of Twentieth Century-Fox, the industry's first female studio head (*Indecent Proposal*, *Fatal Attraction*).

Two Hollywood Hebrews warrant a paragraph of their own. Steven Spielberg is one of the most influential director/producers in cinematic history. His acclaimed titles are: *Jaws*; *Close Encounters of the Third Kind*; *Raiders of the Lost Ark*; *E.T., the Extra-Terrestrial*; *Amistad*; *Saving Private Ryan*; *War of the Worlds*; *Munich*; *Schindler's List*; *A.I. Artificial Intelligence*; and, *the Jurassic Park*, *Poltergeist*, and *Indiana Jones* series. Conversely, Canadian David Cronenberg has been called "The King of Venereal Horror" and "The Baron of Blood." The most grotesque of *his* twenty-plus films (constituting the "heebie-jeebies" genre) include: *Rabid*; *The Brood*; *Scanners*; *Videodrome*; *The Fly*; *Naked Lunch*; *Crash*; *Spider*; and, *A Dangerous Method*. In a *Rolling Stone* interview on February 6, 1992, the Hell-bound auteur said, "The minute you say evil, I think Christianity."[137]

An attendant "short list" of the Jewish actors, actresses, and/or comedians who actually *infected* the masses would comprise: Zsa Zsa, Eva, and Magda Gabor (twenty husbands); Larry King (eight wives, including a Playboy bunny—two more than Henry VIII); Henny Youngman ("Take my wife…please!"); Eddie Fisher (sex, gambling, and amphetamine addict whose first daughter, Carrie Fisher, declared on the release of his second tell-all memoir, *Been There, Done That*, "That's it; I'm having my DNA fumigated"); Dame Joan Collins (*Dynasty's* "Alexis Carrington," America's foremost soap opera slut); Peter Lorre (trademark creepiness from early role of a serial killer preying on little girls); Bess Meyerson (*first* and *only* Jewish "Miss America," 1945); Goldie Hawn ("Sock-it-to-me baby!"); Sarah Jessica Parker (*Sex in the City*); Judy Gold (lesbian comic); George Burns *(Oh, God!)*; Lewis Black (*Nothing's Sacred*); Mel Brooks (profane Last Supper scene in *History of the World, Part I*); Dustin Hoffman (seduced in *The Graduate* by Mel's Gentile wife, Anne Bancroft); Joan Rivers (said of model Heidi Klum: "The last time a German looked this hot was when they were pushing Jews into the ovens").

Then, we have Jennifer Grey (*Dirty Dancing*, a.k.a. "The Most Jewish Film Ever"); Bobby Saget (*Dirty Daddy: The Chronicles of a Family Man Turned Filthy Comedian*); Daniel Jacob Radcliffe (*Harry Potter*); Jacob Benjamin "Jake" Gyllenhaal (*Brokeback Mountain*); Maury Povich and Ricki Lake (lowlife tabloid talk show hosts); David Copperfield (a.k.a. "Most commercially successful magician in history," *Forbes*); Sandra Bernhard (lesbian, a.k.a. "America's scariest entertainer"); Sarah Silverman (2005 special, *Jesus is Magic*); shock jock Howard Stern (mocks Christ by wearing crown of thorns); Minnesota Senator Alan Stuart "Al" Franken (*Saturday Night Live*); London-born former Cincinnati mayor, Gerald Norman "Jerry" Springer ("exposed" for writing prostitute a personal check); and, Jackie Mason (a.k.a. "The Ultimate Jew"), whose contract with *The Ed Sullivan Show* was cancelled for allegedly giving Ed the finger during his October 18, 1964, performance.[138]

Other "*stars* of David" include: Lee J. Cobb (born Leo Jacob); Jill St. John (Jill Arlyn Oppenheim); Don Rickles (a.k.a. "Mr. Warmth"); Rodney Dangerfield ("No Respect"); Paul Newman (*Cat on a Hot Tin Roof*); Zero Mostel (*Fiddler on the Roof*); Jerry Lewis (original *Nutty Professor*); Peter Sellers (*Dr. Strangelove*); Rod Serling (*The Twilight Zone*); Gene Wilder (*Young Frankenstein*); Jeff Goldblum (*The Fly*); William Shatner and Leonard Nimoy ("Captain Kirk" and "Mr. Spock"); Peter Falk ("Lt. Columbo"); Brad Garrett ("Lt. Robert Barone"); Lorne Green and Michael Landon ("Ben and 'Little Joe' Cartwright"); Ed Asner ("Lou Grant"); Tony Randall and Jack Klugman (*The Odd Couple*); Bea Arthur (*Maude*, *Golden Girls*); Harrison Ford (*Star Wars*, *Indiana*

Jones); Tom Bosley and Henry Winkler (*Happy Days*); Carl and Rob Reiner ("Saul Bloom" and "Michael 'The Meathead' Stivic"); Adrien Brody (*The Pianist*); Fran "*The Nanny*" Drescher (quintessential "New *Yawker*"); Natalie Portman (Jerusalem-born); Eli Roth ("The Bear Jew"); Roseanne Barr (mangled *The Star Spangled Banner*); Jamie-Lynn Sigler ("Meadow Soprano"); Sir Daniel-Day Lewis (*Gangs of New York*); John Bernthal, Lauren Cohan, and Michael Zegen (*The Walking Dead*).

Also on the red carpet are: Joaquin, Rain, and River Phoenix; Kirk and Michael Douglas; Tony and Jamie Lee Curtis; Sid Caesar; Totie Fields; Harvey Korman; Alan Arkin; Harvey Keitel; Billy Crystal; Buddy Hackett; Alan King; Red Buttons; Walter Matthau; Hedy Lamar; Suzanne Pleshette; Shelley Winters; Elliott Gould; Jeff Chandler; Richard Dreyfuss; Jerry Seinfeld; Jon Stewart; Mandy Patinkin; Sean Penn; George Segal; Steven Seagal; Jerry and Ben Stiller; Noah Wyle; David Duchovny; Mila Kunis; Rashida Jones; Zachary Israel Braff; Chelsea Handler; Gwyneth Paltrow; Scarlett Johansson; Scott Caan; Logan Lerman, Jon Favreau; Sacha Baron Cohen; Sarah Michelle Gellar; Rachel Weisz; Seth Green; Seth Rogen; Eugene Levy; Andy Samberg; Adam Goldberg; Adam Brody; Adam "The Zohan" Sandler; and, lastly, Gilbert Gottfried—one *weird* "duck"—fired as the quacking Aflac voice for tweeting jokes about the 2011 earthquake in Japan, where Aflac does 75% of its business.

Mae West (*Frankie and Johnnie*) reputedly had a Jewish mother.[139] Philo-Semitic Madonna Louise Ciccone is a Kabbalah devotee. Other famous *Christ-rejecting* proselytes to Judaism would include Marilyn Monroe (JFK affair); Carol Baker (*Baby Doll*); Anne Meara; Polly Bergen; Helen Reddy; Mary Hart; Elizabeth Banks; Connie Chung; Nell Carter; "Dr. Laura" Schlessinger; Dame Elizabeth Taylor (seven husbands); and the ever popular Mrs. Ivanka Kushner, a.k.a. "Ivanka Trump."

Some of the worst satanic filth and violence is produced by American Movie Classics (AMC). True to its slogan, "Something More," a sample of past weekly perversion includes: *The Walking Dead*; *Mad Men*; *Hell on Wheels*; *Breaking Bad*; *Kendra on Top*; *The Killing*; *Making of the Mob*; and *Humans*. At the time of this writing, AMC's front office was crawling with Jewish executives, led by President and General Manager Charles "Charlie" Collier.[140] The same degree of Jewish penetration exists across the entire entertainment spectrum, the nadir being Comedy Central's *South Park* cartoon of Jesus Christ (voiced by co-producer Matt

Stone amidst the related characters' four-letter-word laden dialogue). Discover America's *Exorcism Live* debuted on October 30, 2015, followed by FOX Network's (Luke 13:32) epoch-making January 2016 television series release—*Lucifer*.

THE "SEEDIER COUSIN"

The trillion-dollar, X-rated film genre has been called "Hollywood's seedier cousin." Jewish Professor Nathan Abrams writes:

> ...there's no getting away from the fact that secular Jews have played (and still continue to play) a disproportionate role throughout the adult film industry in America. Jewish involvement in pornography has a long history in the United States, as Jews have helped to transform a fringe subculture into what has become a primary constituent of Americana. These are the 'true blue Jews'.[141]

One of the pioneers of silent porn was the famed French director, Albert Kirchner. His first release, a seven-minute clip, *Le Coucher de la Mariee*, appeared in 1896. Jay A. Gertzman, Jewish author of *Bootleggers and Smuthounds: The Trade in Erotica, 1920-1940*, wrote: "Jews were preponderant as distributors of *gallantiana* [erotic-themed fiction, dirty joke books, and ballads], avant-garde sexually explicit novels, sex pulps, sexology, and the most flagitious materials."[142] In postwar America, Reuben Sturman was lauded as the "Walt Disney of Porn." Abrams relates, "Sturman did not simply control the adult-entertainment industry; he *was* the industry."[143] More recently, Steven Hirsch has been dubbed the "Donald Trump of Porn."[144] Herschel Savage was *the* leading man during the "Golden Age of Porn" (1970s-80s). The *New York Post* cites Ron Jeremy as making the Guinness Book of World Records for "Most Appearances in Adult Films" (2,000 titles). According to the story, a 2013 near-fatal aortic dissection "made the observant Jew feel the Lord was 'sending him a message.'"[145] Dr. Annie Sprinkle and Nina Hartley are two of the main female practitioners of this sin (Sprinkle relishing her occult and drug expertise, portrayed God in her 1996 release *Bubbles Galore*).[146] Bryan Matthew *Sevilla* (a.k.a. "James Deen") is the lead smut rebel in the "sewervilla" business. (Jews, like *Girls Gone Wild* producer Joe Francis, also control the soft-core industry.)

Dr. Abrams then makes the vital connection to insurrection: "Is there a deeper reason, beyond the mere financial, as to why Jews in particular have become involved in porn? There is surely an element of rebellion in Jewish X-rated involvement. Its very taboo and forbidden nature serves to make it attractive...Jews in America have been sexual revolutionaries."[147] And the main target of this resistance is Christianity. "Pornography thus becomes a way of defiling Christian culture...."[148] Alvin "Al" Goldstein (*Screw* founder/publisher), made the definitive nexus between the two. Unfortunately, even worse than "toilet mouth" Sarah Silverman's F-bomb-laced "comedy" lines ("I hope the Jews did kill Christ; I'd do it again. I'd [f-----g] do it again in a second"[149]), Al's comment is too blasphemous to even partially reconstruct.[150] Abrams concludes: "The adult entertainment business required something that Jews possessed in abundance—*chutzpah*."[151]

THE *REAL* DANGER OF MOTION PICTURES

Now while Jacob's kinfolk certainly *created* Hollywood, Bernardi was careful to reject the "stereotype that they also 'controlled' it" as "an argument that smacks of traditional anti-Semitism...," concluding: "Hollywood is too complex to be controlled by a handful of people, and Jews are hardly now, and were hardly then, a unified group that shared a singular goal of domination."[152] Yet, J. J. Goldberg says: "In a few key sectors of the media, notably Hollywood studio executives, Jews are so numerically dominant that calling these businesses Jewish-controlled is little more than a statistical observation."[153]

Regardless of how much Jewish "control" existed, the point is that Ezekiel's "Hell-hole" was up and running for *all* money-hungry flesh merchants, Jews and Gentiles alike. (While Humphrey Bogart was an Episcopalian, his fourth wife, Lauren Bacall, was Jewish.) Jonas Alexis (an "African-American" Judaphobe Christian who teaches math in South Korea) implies that the movie racket was once a decent entity, "[W]hen Hollywood film industries were overtaken by Jewish revolutionaries, they began to implement communist and sexual ideologies in their films."[154] Alexis cites Neal Gabler, who relates, "[W]hen sound movies commanded the industry, Hollywood was invaded by a battalion of Jewish writers, mostly from the East...."[155] Having taught church history on a college level for ten years, this author can assure Jonas that

America's "old-time religion" preachers drew *no* distinction between "good" and "bad" films, duly blasting *all* "picture shows" (including *The Ten Commandments*).

"THE GODS ARE COME...IN THE LIKENESS OF MEN"

Israel's God declared, *"I am the LORD: that is my name: and my glory will I not give to another."* (Isaiah 42:8) The first commandment says: *"I am the LORD thy God, which have brought thee out of the land of Egypt, out of the house of bondage. Thou shalt have no other gods before me."* (Exodus 20:2-3) When Satan tempted Eve he knew what button to push: *"For God doth know that in the day ye eat thereof, then your eyes shall be opened, and ye shall be as gods, knowing good and evil."* (Genesis 3:5) Our first parents suffered Paradise Lost for the same reason the Devil was booted from Heaven (Isaiah 14:12-14).

By Noah's day, the sin of "man worship" was epidemic. Serious Bible teachers hold that the *"sons of God"* (in Genesis 6) were fallen angels (Job 1:6; 2:1; 38:7) that cohabited with women. (The case that angels cannot reproduce comes from deleting *"in heaven"* at Matthew 22:30 and then misdefining angels as "sexless.") The mutant offspring, labeled in verse four as "MIGHTY MEN *which were of old,* MEN OF RENOWN," became the catalyst for the vice in verse five: *"And GOD saw that the wickedness of man was great in the earth, and that every imagination of the thoughts of his heart was only evil continually."*

While some of the more "cultured" brethren find this doctrine repulsive, they might pause to consider that whatever occurred "back yonder" made God mad enough that He drowned the entire world (save eight). Though ignored in most Christian circles, the subject of "gods" is often mentioned in Scripture (e.g., Psalm 82:1, 6; Jeremiah 10:11; John 10:34; Acts 12:22, 14:11; I Corinthians 8:5; I John 5:20). As noted in Alexander Hislop's Two Babylons, it has also appeared in secular history (e.g., Ulysses, Apollo, Venus, Aphrodite, Tammuz, Ashtoreth, Baal, Diana, Jupiter, Thor, Zeus, Atlas, Mercury).

This topic is germane, as Jesus prophesied, *"But as the days of Noe were, so shall also the coming of the Son of man be."* (Matthew 24:37) Thus, one of the key end-day signs will be *"mighty men...men of renown"*; enter Hollywood, located (get this) in the "City of Angels," the world's foremost maker of "human gods"—duly known as "stars." In the words of the ancient Lycaonians when awed by the miracles of Paul and Barnabas, *"The* GODS *are come down to us in the likeness of men."* (Acts 14:11) If you doubt whether Hollywood celebrities are filled with the satanic power seen in Luke 4:6, just note what happens when "mere mortals" come into their presence. Have you ever gotten to meet a "real live star?" If so, what was your first reaction? Does the robotic buzz phrase "Oh My God!" ring any bells? (See Exodus 20:7)

The shocking bottom line regarding the hellish "entertainment" industry is that a select group of mortals get to spend their entire lives receiving worship that belongs to God alone! Paul references this abomination in Romans 1:25: *"[W]ho changed the truth of God into a lie, and worshipped and served the creature more than the Creator, who is blessed forever. Amen."* Thus, the most popular American president in the twentieth century was a former movie star, Ronald Reagan. (Ditto his astrology-driven First Lady, Nancy.)

But, there is more. Because Satan knows that only a few aspirants will make it to the "Big Time" ("Midnight Train to Georgia"; "Do you Know the Way to San Jose?"), he fixed it so that nearly anyone can qualify. Thus, the modern accelerated process of "self-worship" has run the gamut from karaoke, through American Idol, culminating with YouTube and the entire end-day religion of social media (especially Instagram and Snapchat). Could Scripture be more accurate, having predicted in II Timothy 3:2 that men would be *"lovers of their own* SELVES*"*? (Oxford Dictionary's 2013 word of the year was "selfie.")

And don't think that the KJV failed to foresee the end-time electronics revolution, Paul writing in II Corinthians 2:11, *"Lest Satan get an advantage over us: for we are not ignorant of his* DEVICES,*"* along with John's allusion in Revelation 3:17 to the ever-expanding power of the panacean "App" to supply your every need *"and have* NEED OF NOTHING.*"* Ditto every other modern perversion—from test tube babies and genetic stem cell research to transgender surgery and marketing aborted babies' brains—covered by Romans 1:30, *"inventors of evil things."* Talk about Satan getting in your face, the very logo for Apple Inc. depicts the eponymous fruit of an apple with a bite taken out of it (Genesis 3:6). (The relevant verses for social media obsession would be, first and foremost, Luke 16:15, followed by Job 32:21-22; Ecclesiastes 5:1-3; John 1:22-23; 5:44; 7:18; I Corinthians 3:7; II Corinthians 4:5; Galatians 6:14 and Philippians 2:7.)

THE SILVER LINING IN THE SILVER SCREEN

One of the most profound and least understood reasons why America is kaput—i.e., why a national revival is impossible—is because *the great majority of prospects have rendered themselves unreachable by their willful addiction to the cult of god making.* For instance, why should a sinner listen to some "religious fanatic" preach about some *invisible* God (with plenty of intolerant "hang-ups" to boot) when he or she is already enchanted with a pantheon of *visible* "deities?"

While there was a time when souls could be saved by telling them that Jesus Christ is the one who *"giveth* LIFE*"* as *"the resurrection, and the* LIFE,*"* and thus *"the way, the truth, and the* LIFE*"* (John 6:33; 11:25; 14:6), the *silver* screen (Proverbs 25:11) would now *project* mere mortals as "*bigger* than life." With "silver" as a major type of *redemption* in Scripture, America's new saviors would be "leading men" like: Errol Flynn (fornicator); Gary Cooper (adulterer); Rock Hudson (sodomite); Spencer Tracey (adulterer); Clint Eastwood (fornicator); Randolph Scott (sodomite); Leonardo DiCaprio (fornicator); Arnold Schwarzenegger (adulterer); Cary Grant (sodomite); Brad Pitt (adulterer); George Clooney (fornicator); Marlon Brando (sodomite). And it wouldn't matter if they were Jew *or* Gentile "gods" (George Burns or George Scott; John Garfield or John Wayne, Jack Klugman or Jack Nicholson, James Caan or James Stewart.)

When the *Rolling Stone* reporter asked David Cronenberg, "Are you positing 'art against death'?" the producer admitted: "I'm positing art as a means of coming to terms with death. Yes. I'm putting art in opposition to religion - or as a replacement of religion, in the sense that if religion is used to allow you to come to terms with death, and also to guide you how to live your life, then I think that art can do the same thing. But in a much less schematic way, in a much less rigid and absolute way. Which is why it appeals to me and religion doesn't."[156] Dave's brethren in the lucrative superhero movie and comic book genre (Will Eisner, Jack Kirby, Bob Kane, Stan Lee, Joe Simon, Marvin Wolfman, et al.) are also helping to replace Christianity.[157]

And so, as the preaching has waned in Laodicea, don't blame the Jews for giving money-waving goys what they want. The truth is that the Body of Christ determines how many potential customers the smut merchants will get. After all, Evangelist (and closet anti-Semite) Billy

Graham *was* the first "preacher" to be honored with his own star in the Hollywood Walk of Fame! Like the manacled prisoner being guarded by the sheriff near the campfire, the aspiring Jewish entrepreneur cannot harm society unless the Church falls asleep on the job.

As forecast in II Timothy 3:1-13, the sole *up*lifting truth about our vile culture is that it's just about over. Regarding that harbinger trait of *"fierce"* (verse 3), it seems that the US will be going out with a bang, especially in movie theaters. On July 20, 2012, a mass shooting inside a Century 16 cinema in Aurora, Colorado, during a midnight screening of *The Dark Knight Rises*, caused twelve deaths and seventy injuries (including a four-month-old baby shot at point-blank range). The trilogy's co-producer, Charles Roven, is Jewish, while the original DC Comics superhero, Batman, was created by another Jew, Bob Kane. With several patrons having fled the smoke-filled darkness in their Batman costumes, the shooter, James Holmes—a bug-eyed, twenty-four-year-old, former PhD candidate in neuroscience—allegedly told police he was the Joker. (Incidentally, after Heath Ledger won an Oscar for his chilling portrayal of the demonic "Joker" in *The Dark Knight*, the number four highest-grossing film of all time, the twenty-eight-year-old Gentile from "Down Under" *went* "down under," dying from an overdose of prescription medications on January 22, 2008.)

Three years later, the nation's second theater shooting (two dead and nine injured) went down on July 23, 2015, in Lafayette, Louisiana, under *another* portentous title, *Trainwreck* (produced *and* directed by a Jew, Judd Apatow, with Jewess Amy Schumer as the script writer and lead actress.) Twelve days later, a hatchet-wielding ticket holder in a surgical mask attacked an audience in Nashville, Tennessee, during a *Mad Max: Fury Road* screening. Among other "new normal" developments, in the next month alone, four psychos, one waving a gas-powered leaf blower, faked a chainsaw attack at a Newport Beach, California, cinema showing *The Gift*, while unprecedented numbers of security guards were posted in theaters nationwide for the screening of the anti-police "gangsta rap" flick, *Straight Out of Compton*.

One of the Bible's deepest prophecies sits unnoticed in the story of the Flood. (You could call it the silver lining in the silver screen.) As Jesus said in Matthew 24:37, *"But as the days of Noe were, so shall also the coming of the Son of man be,"* the pertinent cross-reference is Genesis 6:3, the time when those *first* "stars" appear on earth, *"And the LORD said, My spirit shall not always strive with man, for that he also is flesh: yet his days shall be* AN HUNDRED AND TWENTY YEARS.*"* After years of honing Edison's Kinetoscope technology (1887-94)—a peep-show device housed in a cabinet (Ezekiel 8:7)—the first silent film with a story, "The Great Train Robbery," debuted in 1903. So do the math, as in 1903 plus 120 years, a good indicator of the era we are fast approaching. And don't miss Isaiah 2:16 where the Messiah destroys *"all pleasant* PICTURES... *"* in the Millennium.

"*BELOVED* FOR THE FATHERS' SAKES"

Most end-day believers are oblivious to spiritual matters. While Paul warned Timothy, *"For the time will come when they will not endure sound doctrine,"* John told Laodicea's locksmiths to *"anoint thine eyes with eyesalve, that thou mayest see."* (II Timothy 4:3; Revelation 3:18) Having apprised the naive pro-Israel majority, the following section will address the shallowness of the nasty anti-Israel minority.

The biggest error that Judaphobic Christians make is missing the words *"they* ARE *beloved for the fathers' sakes."* This inspired text, penned twenty-seven years *after* the Jewish deicide, is in the *present* tense! If God expects the killers of His own Son to be loved, i.e., *now*, one might want to be careful about running one's mouth against said individuals (Ecclesiastes 10:20 and Psalm 94:11 adding one's *thoughts* as well). With Jeremiah 17:9 stating, *"The heart is deceitful above all things, and desperately wicked: who can know it?"* and I Timothy 6:10, *"For the love of money is the root of all evil,"* the true cause for anti-Semitism (both heathen and Christian alike) is *avarice.* Note how Mearsheimer and Walt show their hand: "Although the US has derived a number of benefits from its support for Israel and from Israel's undeniable achievements, it has given far more than it has gained."[158]

Like "Mother Rome," Protestantism has also focused on lands and "stuff." (See "Thirty Years' War," 1618-48.) Thus, Baptists and Evangelicals make up the Heavenly-minded branch of "Christendom." When incensed *idolaters* (Colossians 3:5) like Jonas Alexis moan that "trillions of dollars have been spent for wars when they could have helped reboot the economy,"[159] Bible believers yawn, resting in the words, *"a man's life consisteth not in the abundance of the* THINGS *which he possesseth."* (Luke 12:15) Grasping the depth of the Pauline addendum, *"all* THINGS *are yours"* (I Corinthians 3:21), they are free to love the Jews—no matter *how* badly their worst representatives have behaved—the same Apostle testifying in Philippians 3:7-8, *"what* THINGS *were gain to me, those I counted loss for Christ. Yea doubtless, and I count all* THINGS *but loss for the excellency of the knowledge of Christ Jesus my Lord: for whom I have suffered the loss of all* THINGS, *and do count them but dung, that I may win Christ."*

The main reason why Gentiles should love Jews is revealed in a second conundrum found in Romans 11:28—*"enemies* FOR YOUR SAKES.*"* Spoiled American Christians are so busy blaming Jacob's line for their *decline* (i.e., "financial portfolios") that they fail to discern an incredibly subtle truth. The very fact that Jewry became the Gentiles' *temporal* enemy has worked to *their* eternal gain: *"For if the casting away of them be the reconciling of the world, what shall the receiving of them be, but life from the dead?"* (Romans 11:15) Thus, instead of denouncing the poor spiritually bankrupt Jews, stupid goys should be shouting *hallelujahs*, for as Paul writes, *"The branches were broken off,* THAT I MIGHT BE GRAFFED IN.*"* (Romans 11:19)

The Jewish Apostle to the Gentiles then gives the natural, practical admonition: *"But now I go unto Jerusalem to minister unto the saints. For it hath pleased them of Macedonia and Achaia to make a certain contribution for the poor saints which are at Jerusalem. It hath pleased them verily;* AND THEIR DEBTORS THEY ARE. *For if the Gentiles have been made partakers of their spiritual things, their* DUTY *is also to minister unto them in carnal things."* (Romans 15:25-27) Though the reference is to *saved* Jews (i.e., the "saints in Jerusalem") as opposed to *unsaved* Israel, the scriptural principle is that the Jews should at least have an edge over all other unsaved races and nations (like the baseball rule that a tie goes to the runner). This certainly applies in the Tribulation where surviving Gentiles will be judged according to their treatment of the Jews, described by Jesus as including *"the* LEAST *of these my brethren...."* (Matthew 25:40)

"How Shall I Give Thee Up, Ephraim?"

Blinded by greed, Texe and his ideological hacks—henceforth referred to as "The Posse" (1975 Paramount Pictures, starring *and* produced by Kirk Douglas), e.g., Jonas Alexis, Gary Burge, Gary DeMar, Sami

Awad, Tony Campolo, Hank Hanegraaff, Mrs. Bill (Lynne) Hybles, Paul Wittenberger, and one *really* loose cannon, Westboro Baptist Church wannabe and "film producer extraordinaire," Pastor Steven Anderson—are *totally* clueless regarding God's true feeling for His wayward covenant nation. While Hagee avoids witnessing to Jews, Stevie's idea of "soul winning" is saturating the Ummah with his anti-Semitic DVD, *Marching To Zion* (in Arabic, *The Jews and their Lies*). One of his nutty internet disciples once accused this author, in his own church parking lot, of being unsaved for preaching repentance.

Because this crowd stays fixated on the object of their wrath, they cannot escape the laughable result of appropriating the very traits they despise. Due to their delusions, born-again "Pharisees" cannot discern between the *letter* and the *spirit* of the Law. The Bible is replete with examples of God's enduring love for Israel, along with warnings to her potential foes, *especially* professing Christians (Luke 12:48). Joseph is the greatest type of Christ in Scripture. Notice the demeanor he feigns compared to his true affection when providentially reunited with those who had *"conspired against him to slay him."* (Genesis 37:18; Matthew 12:14) The scene opens in Genesis 42:7: *"Joseph saw his brethren, and he knew them, but made himself strange unto them, and spake* ROUGHLY *unto them; and he said unto them, Whence come ye?"* Then the Lord pulls the curtain back in Genesis 43:29-31; 45:1-3.

> *And he lifted up his eyes, and saw his brother Benjamin, his mother's son, and said, Is this your younger brother, of whom ye spake unto me? And he said, God be gracious unto thee, my son. And Joseph made haste; for his* BOWELS DID YEARN *upon his brother: and he sought where to* WEEP*; and he entered into his chamber, and* WEPT *there. And he washed his face, and went out, and refrained himself...Then Joseph could not refrain himself before all them that stood by him; and he cried, Cause every man to go out from me. And there stood no man with him, while Joseph made himself known unto his brethren. And he* WEPT *aloud...And Joseph said unto his brethren, I am Joseph....*

David is the second-most recognized Old Testament picture of Jesus. His encounter with the Amalekite provides another insightful example of Jehovah's disposition toward backslidden Israel. Though Saul was *"rejected...from reigning over Israel..."* (I Samuel 16:1) and David already anointed as his successor (the change provoking three attempts on his life), the one described by the LORD as *"a man after mine own heart..."* (Acts 13:22) threw a holy fit in II Samuel 1:14-16 upon learning that the young man had given Saul the deathblow.

> *And David said unto him, How wast thou not afraid to stretch forth thine hand to destroy* THE LORD'S ANOINTED? *And David called one of the young men, and said, Go near, and fall upon him. And he smote him that he died. And David said unto him, Thy blood be upon thy head; for thy mouth hath testified against thee, saying, I have slain* THE LORD'S ANOINTED.

Though *"Wisdom is too high for a fool..."* (Proverbs 24:7), the lesson is simple to spiritual believers: While *individual* Jews are Hell-bound sinners like anyone else, as a *race* they remain God's *anointed* nation despite their *temporary* estrangement (Romans 11:23-25).

Moses records a chilling prophecy in Deuteronomy 28:63: *"And it shall come to pass, that as the LORD rejoiced over you to do you good, and to multiply you; so* THE LORD WILL REJOICE OVER YOU TO DESTROY YOU, *and to bring you to nought; and ye shall be plucked from off the land whither thou goest to possess it."* Proverbs 1:25-28 repeats this theme: *"But ye have set at nought all my counsel, and would none of my reproof:* I ALSO WILL LAUGH *at your calamity;* I WILL MOCK *when your fear cometh...Then shall they call upon me, but I will not answer...."* Yet, by Ezekiel 18:23, the *same* LORD asks rhetorically: "HAVE I ANY PLEASURE AT ALL *that the wicked should die?...and not that he should return from his ways, and live?"*

In Hosea 4:17, God says: "EPHRAIM *is joined to idols:* LET HIM ALONE." Like the bureaucrats who pressed Darius over his decree in Daniel 6:9, Ephraim's modern detractors would hold God's feet to the fire on this verse as well. However, by Hosea 11:8, Jehovah is already lamenting—"HOW SHALL I GIVE THEE UP, EPHRAIM?*...mine heart is turned within me, my repentings are kindled together."*

"WHOA!"

The context of the book of Hosea itself (augmented by several verses in Isaiah and Jeremiah) represents the *scariest* implication for Israel's critics. While Proverbs 6:34 says, *"For jealousy is the rage of a man,"* I Corinthians 11:7 adds, *"the woman is the glory of the man."*

According to the Old Testament, Texe and his cohorts are vehemently reproaching the former wife of Jehovah! And as the LORD is not *about* to remain a *divorcee* forever, the Posse is also messing with the woman He is planning to *remarry* someday—"Whoa!" Whereas the LORD confirms in Jeremiah 3:8 that when *"backsliding Israel committed* ADULTERY, *I had put her away, and given her a* BILL OF DIVORCE,*"* He then affirms in Hosea 2:14, 19: *"behold,* I WILL ALLURE HER... *and speak comfortably unto her...*AND I WILL BETROTH THEE UNTO ME FOREVER.*"* Isaiah 54:4-8 adds:

> *Fear not; for thou shalt not be ashamed...*THY MAKER IS THINE HUSBAND*; the LORD of hosts is his name; and thy Redeemer the Holy One of Israel; The God of the whole earth shall he be called. For the LORD hath called thee as a woman forsaken and grieved in spirit, and a wife of youth, when thou wast refused, saith thy God. For a small moment have I forsaken thee; but with great mercies will I gather thee. In a little wrath I hid my face from thee for a moment; but with everlasting kindness will I have mercy on thee, saith the LORD thy Redeemer.*

And as every good husband will provide for his bride, initiating his commitment by carrying her over the threshold, Isaiah 62:4 depicts Jehovah as marrying the Holy Land (as Revelation 21:2, 9-10 has Jesus marrying the Holy City).

BETTER LISTEN TO "TINY"

Because of these sober realities, it would obviously behoove certain brethren to reconsider slamming their Father's future wife—the one He plans to "allure." (Should further motivation be needed, chapter twelve of Revelation also portrays the woman/Israel as Jesus' mother!) Frankly, the Posse would do well to take their cue from "Tiny Tim."

While Tiny's 6-foot-one-inch beanpole frame, stringy red-orange hair, and signature falsetto-vibrato voice might have made him appear more like a "giant mashugana" (though his December 17, 1969, wedding to "Miss Vickie" on the *Tonight Show* did draw a record 40,000,000 viewers), the screeching ukuleleist looked like Al Einstein compared to pseudo intellectuals like Texe Marrs, Jonas Alexis, and Steve Anderson. Recognizing Jewry's historic rebellion is one thing; constantly denouncing them is something else. As I Corinthians 13:6 says, *"Charity rejoiceth not in iniquity,"* the rule of thumb for just citing Israel's "indiscretions" would be to—"tiptoe through the tulips."

The Bible gives several examples of this discretion (known, even among heathens, as "not airing one's dirty laundry"). Though Noah was drunk and naked, his two discerning sons (Japheth and Shem), refusing to view the scene, *tiptoed* in backward to cover their father's body (Genesis 9:23). Though Moses unwisely married an Ethiopian woman, Miriam got leprosy for *not* tiptoeing around her brother's situation, the Lord asking her, *"Wherefore...were ye not afraid to speak against my servant Moses?"* (Numbers 12:8) Upon Absalom's revolt, David had to defend himself against his own child. As his army left Mahanaim for the final battle, the King uttered a sensitive order to his commanders: *"Deal gently for my sake with the young man, even with Absalom."* (II Samuel 18:5) With Israel also typed as Jehovah's son in Exodus 4:23 and Hosea 11:1, David's inconsolable grief at Absalom's death gives yet another glimpse of *God's* grief over the Jews' perennial rebellion, and attendant suffering (II Samuel 18:33).

ENDLESS GENEALOGIES

Texe and his gang are a strange bunch indeed. When they are not blaming "*the* Jews" for the world's ills, they will inevitably say that the *same* folks are not "*real* Jews" after all. News flash, people—You can't have it both ways! To say that Ashkenazi Israelis are pseudo-Jews genetically descended from the *Khazars*, an eleventh-century semi-nomadic Turkic people, is hypocritical, illogical, and unscriptural quackery.[160] (See D. M. Dunlop's *The History of the Jewish Khazars*, the so-called definitive work on this mess.)

Par for the course, two self-loathing Jews gave the racist theory renewed international focus, supposedly to extricate the poor Palestinians from the fraudulent land claims of counterfeit Ashkenazi Jewry. In 2008, Professor Shlomo Sand, of Tel Aviv University, published *The Invention of the Jewish People*,[161] while Johns Hopkins University post-doctoral researcher Eran Elhaik, an Israeli molecular geneticist, later challenged the longstanding findings of several reputable geneticists encapsulated in the 2012 book, *Legacy: A Genetic History of the Jewish People*, by Harry Ostrer, professor of pathology and genetics at Yeshiva University's Albert Einstein College of Medicine.[162] In 2013, Shaul Stampfer, professor of Soviet and East European Jewry at Hebrew University, exposed the lack of *credible* proof for Sand's thesis of a Khazarian Jewish diaspora.[163]

The Posse's other nonsense that true Jews only came from the two *southern* tribes is revealed by Paul's words to Peter in Galatians 2:5, "WE *who are Jews by nature...*" (i.e., according to John 1:44, Pete was a Yank). The Bible-blockhead thesis that bona fide Jews could not have migrated *to* Israel *from* Europe (Japheth's ethnoscape as per Genesis 9:27) is discredited by Deuteronomy 28:64—*"And the LORD shall scatter thee* AMONG *ALL* PEOPLE, FROM THE ONE END OF THE EARTH EVEN UNTO THE OTHER...." (And what about Israel's 1.4 million *Sephardic* Jews?) Any doubt about the ten northern tribes is eliminated by the opening verse of the New Testament (chronologically speaking)—*"James, a servant of God and of the Lord Jesus Christ,* TO THE TWELVE TRIBES WHICH ARE SCATERED ABOUT." (James 1:1)

For the Church to embrace this genetic thesis is particularly telling. Only four verses into his first pastoral epistle, Paul warns Timothy, *"Neither give heed to fables and* ENDLESS GENEALOGIES, *which minister questions."* Titus received the same advice as well (Titus 3:9). As for basing the anti-Semitic theory on DNA, the "antiquated" KJV was prescient as usual, exclusively translating Paul's other caution in I Timothy 6:20, *"avoiding...oppositions of* SCIENCE FALSELY SO CALLED...."

If Ashkenazi Jews are really Gentiles in disguise, how does one account for their peerless fiduciary skills conforming to Deuteronomy 8:18? In any event, Satan's crowd sure seemed to know who *they* were after. Though Hitler later gave up "race tracing," he kept his genocide alive by taking the Jews' word about their *own* ethnicity. The Führer grasped a concept too simple for the Posse, i.e., the apologetic method for Jesus' resurrection, that alleged eye-witnesses would not have died for a lie. So, why would *other* humans submit to centuries of needless persecution? God Himself must have endorsed Eurasian Jewry, considering all their pain to date. After all, *some* group had to fulfill I Thessalonians 2:16. All doubt departs by cross-referencing Proverbs 16:7,

"When a man's ways PLEASE *the LORD, he maketh even his enemies to be at peace with him,"* with I Thessalonians 2:15, *"and they* PLEASE *not God."* (Christian martyrs were slain by *God's* foes.)

Ironically, religious Jews would love for DNA to locate a direct descendant of David. Susan Roth, founder of the *Eshet Chayil* ("A Woman of Valor") Foundation in Union, New Jersey, envisions a royal House of David juxtaposed with the current Israeli government:

> Just like in England, where there is a queen who is a figurehead, there could be a king of Israel who is a figurehead. A king would be taken seriously and signify that Jews have been in Israel for over 3,000 years. The Knesset could run the country but there would be a royal house that would bring legitimacy. The royal House of David could be a light unto the nation. It would bring about peace, harmony, and everything the world is waiting for, because the world is in a terrible shape right now.[164]

Roth's associate, Yisroel Cohen, adds, "My greatest hope is for us to produce a king like King David today."[165]

Not that it would matter, Jewry being averse to its own Tanakh, but even if they *could* find a Davidic scion, he would still be *cursed* from being their King; Jeremiah 22:30 says of *Coniah* (a form of *Jeconiah*), *"Thus saith the LORD, Write ye this man childless, a man that shall not prosper in his days: for no man of his seed shall prosper, sitting upon the throne of David, and ruling any more in Judah."* (Thus, Joseph could *not* have been Christ's father, as Matthew 1:11-16, the Jews' last infallible genealogy, has Mary's husband descending from Coniah.)

Finally, God is "so worried" about such things that He lists four *Gentile* women (including a harlot) in His Messianic line: Tamar, a *Canaanite* (Genesis 38:1-6; Matthew 1:3); Rahab, an *Amorite* (Joshua 5:1, 6:25, 7:7; Matthew 1:5); Ruth, a *Moabite* (Ruth 1:22; Matthew 1:5); and, Naamah, an *Ammonite* (I Kings 14:21, 31; Matthew 1:7).

SEVEN LAWS FOR LOVING JEWS

There is a third related conundrum to be considered. While Romans 11:28 states, *"they* ARE *beloved for the fathers' sakes"* (i.e., in the Church Age), these very recipients of divine affection are also under the simultaneous judgment of God, the same Apostle writing, *"for the wrath* IS *come upon them to the uttermost."* (I Thessalonians 2:16)

If the Holy Ghost could inspire the words in Proverbs 31:6, *"Give strong drink unto him that is ready to perish, and wine unto those that be of heavy hearts,"* how much *more* should blood-washed, Bible-believing Christians love the Jewish people who languish on *Satan's* Death Row? (John 3:18, 36) The following "Seven Laws of Love" will find application within both camps on the current debate over Jewry:

1) Love them with selflessness. How *you* fare is irrelevant. Jesus said, *"Ye have heard that it hath been said, Thou shalt love thy neighbor, and hate thine enemy. But I say unto you, Love your enemies, bless them that curse you, do good to them that hate you, and pray for them which despitefully use you, and persecute you...For if ye love them which love you, what reward have ye? do not even the publicans the same?"* (Matthew 5:43-44, 46) God loves *unconditionally* (Jeremiah 31:3; Romans 5:8; 8:35, 38-39; I Corinthians 13:1-13; Ephesians 3:17-19; I John 4:19).

2) Love them with knowledge. Reaching out to Jews—despite their contrary ways—will magnify the believer's motive. The only "rose-colored glasses" one needs is the vantage point of the "Rose of Sharon" (Song of Solomon 2:1; Matthew 9:36; John 2:24).

3) Love them with evangelism. While there is a Biblical motive for tangible benevolence to Israel—whether political, financial, or military (Genesis 12:3)—giving Jews the "good news" of the Gospel is the greatest "good" you can share (Matthew 16:26).

4) Love them with deliberation. Born-again believers should only give financial aid to Jewish causes as the Holy Spirit leads, *never* under coercion (Romans 8:14). As with many a Holy Land tour guide (Jew and Arab alike) who gets "saved" by the end of the *trip* (i.e., before the *tip*), it is spiritually demeaning to allow typical Jewish ministries, like schnorrer Rabbi Eckstein's International Fellowship of Christians and Jews, to "put the arm" on "soft-hearted" (and/or "-headed") members of Christ's Body.

5) Love them with separation. As II Corinthians 6:14 says, *"Be ye not unequally yoked together with unbelievers,"* God's people should never *join* so-called "Christian-Jewish" alliances (any more than they should pray with Catholics at abortion clinics). The same applies to Bible-believing Baptists going off the deep end, calling

Jesus "Yahshua," observing Jewish feasts, conducting Seders, blowing shofars, donning tallits, practicing Messianic/Davidic dancing, searching for "spiritual nuggets" in various Jewish scams (e.g., Rabbi Daniel Lapin's *Ancient Jewish Wisdom* TV program), and other unscriptural eccentricities (Galatians 5:1, Colossians 2:16-17).

6) Love them with humility. Paul warned the Gentiles, *"And if some of the branches be broken off, and thou, being a wild olive tree, wert graffed in among them, and with them partakest of the root and fatness of the olive tree; Boast not against the branches. But if thou boast, thou bearest not the root, but the root thee. Thou wilt say then, The branches were broken off, that I might be graffed in. Well; because of unbelief they were broken off, and thou standest by faith. Be not highminded, but fear: For if God spared not the natural branches, take heed lest he also spare not thee."* (Romans 11:17-21)

7) Love them with mercy. Jesus' parable on forgiveness will help the Church avoid getting an uppity spirit toward His Covenant Nation: *"Then his lord, after that he had called him, said unto him, O thou wicked servant, I forgave thee all that debt, because thou desiredst me: Shouldest not thou also have had compassion on thy fellowservant, even as I had pity on thee?"* (Matthew 18:32-33) One must always remember that the Jews are a *handicapped* race. The context of Romans 11:28 provides a fitting end to this chapter. While verse 25 says *"blindness in part is happened to Israel,"* verses 30-31 conclude, *"For as ye in times past have not believed God, yet have now obtained mercy through their unbelief: Even so have these also now not believed, that through your mercy they also may obtain mercy."*

"O the depth of the riches both of the wisdom and knowledge of God! how unsearchable are his judgments, and his ways past finding out!"
(Romans 11:33)

20

The Shoah in the Scriptures

"Ephraim shall bring forth his children to the MURDERER.*"*
(Hosea 9:13)

"...for the WRATH *is come upon them to the uttermost."*
(I Thessalonians 2:16)

"Behold therefore the goodness and SEVERITY
of God: on them which fell, SEVERITY*...."*
(Romans 11:22)

"This is not a sanatorium, but a German concentration camp.
There is only one exit—through the crematorium chimney."
(SS Captain Karl Fritzsch at Auschwitz)

SITUATED BETWEEN THE LORD'S rebuke in Hosea 4:17, *"Ephraim is joined to idols: let him alone,"* and His later cry in Hosea 11:8, *"How shall I give thee up, Ephraim?"* is the chilling prophecy in Hosea 9:13—*"Ephraim shall bring forth his children to the* MURDERER.*"* Jesus called Satan *"a* MURDERER *from the beginning."* (John 8:44) While the Antichrist (666) will be the Jews' worst nightmare in the Tribulation, Adolf Hitler (555) will undoubtedly be the chief murderer of Ephraim's children this side of the Rapture. The Shoah must therefore represent the greatest empirical evidence for Jehovah's 2,000-year censure of Israel (Proverbs 16:7).

Thus, to heed Paul's admonition to "BEHOLD *therefore the goodness and* SEVERITY *of God: on them which fell,* SEVERITY*..."* (Romans 11:22), this chapter will revisit the most surreal crime scene in history to examine the Holocaust in the light of the A.V. 1611. The cross-reference here is I Samuel 12:24, *"Only fear the LORD, and serve him in truth with all your heart:* FOR CONSIDER HOW GREAT THINGS HE HATH DONE FOR YOU*"*—i.e., the greatest "thing" God ever did *for* you being the "thing" He did not do *to* you!

As typified by the 1961 film *Town Without Pity* (starring Kirk Douglas, produced and directed by the German-born Jew, Gottfried Reinhardt), the lucre-driven Posse remains heartless to Jewry's suffering. In his second volume, Jonas Alexis undermines the Shoah by including an entire chapter entitled, "Challenging the Uniqueness Doctrine."[1] He contends that mainline Jewish historians have routinely exploited the tragedy by insisting that "no atrocity will ever quite compare to the Nazi Holocaust of the Jews."[2] Abraham Foxman is quoted accordingly: "The Holocaust is something different. It is a singular event. It is not simply one example of genocide but a nearly successful attempt on the life of God's chosen children and, thus, on God himself."[3] While Winston Churchill called it "the greatest and most horrible crime ever committed in the whole history of the world," Jonas opines (citing the higher victim totals from the Red holocausts of Stalin and Mao), "Historically and intellectually, this 'uniqueness' doctrine is an abomination...But ideologically it is useful, since it puts Jewish suffering above any other suffering in human history, giving Jews a power no other ethnic group has."[4]

Anti-Semitic Jewish celebrities, like Jerusalem-born Natalie Portman, are quick to concur, the American actress/director telling *The Independent* in a September 15, 2015, interview:

> I think a really big question the Jewish community needs to ask itself, is how much at the forefront we put Holocaust education. Which is, of course, an important question to remember and to respect, but not over other things...We need to be reminded that hatred exists at all times and reminds us to be empathetic to other people that have experienced hatred also. Not used as a paranoid way of thinking that we are victims.[5]

To be fair, there is no question (as verified in Norman Finkelstein's 2000 book, *The Holocaust Industry*) that certain Jews have indeed played the "H" card, manipulating their collective tragedy for ulterior motives. Sadder still is the related "can't win for losing" stigma that apparently *no* amount of victims can elicit a commensurate degree of genuine sympathy from Gentiles, in contrast to the seemingly endless number of "pedophilia passes" the Vatican receives. In June 2016, a fleeting app-based "game" posted on Google Play let users "live like a real Jew in Auschwitz Concentration Camp." On July 12, 2016, the *Washington Post* featured "A Doduo in the Pokemon Go app found in the Holocaust Museum in D.C.," prompting the pathetic appeal "Holocaust Museum to visitors: Please stop catching Pokemon here. " What the Jew does not get is that the LORD has decreed that not even the genocide of 6,000,000 *humans* could trump *their* unique crime of *deicide* (killing God) along with its attendant penalty, *"who*...KILLED THE LORD JESUS...*for* THE WRATH IS COME UPON THEM TO THE UTTERMOST. *"* (I Thessalonians 2:15-16)

Yet, despite this egregious abuse, any number of coalescent factors could easily categorize the Jewish Holocaust as an unparalleled phenomenon (ideological devotion, deleterious cost, breadth of reach, sadistic ferocity, deception employed, industrialized methodology, et. al.). However, these all pale in comparison to the fact that several specific facets of this horrific event were prerecorded in Scripture.

ANNE FRANK

As previously related, the British troops that liberated Bergen-Belsen initially encountered the stench of 10,000 unburied corpses, many in advanced decomposition. (The shocking memory no doubt contributed to those 10,000 graves dug on the eve of the Six-Day War.)

Israel's God declared in Jeremiah 14:16, *"and they shall have* NONE TO BURY THEM, *them, their wives, nor their sons, nor their daughters: for I will pour their wickedness upon them."* Conversely, when others were cast *"down into the pit"* (Psalm 143:7), the ground's unforeseen heaving required their disinterment and incineration, conforming in type to Leviticus 20:22, *"Ye shall therefore keep all my statutes, and all my judgments, and do them: that the land, whither I bring you to dwell therein,* SPUE YOU NOT OUT.*"*

Laying somewhere in that acre of carnage were the bloated, emaciated remains of a fifteen-year-old girl destined to become the veritable face of the Holocaust. Because the sheer magnitude of the

Shoah demands an equally breathtaking cause, Annelies Marie "Anne" Frank—as one of those 10,000 bodies—would also come to represent an eerie statistical reminder that her people killed the very One described in the Jews' own Scriptures as *"the chiefest among* TEN THOUSAND.*"* (Song of Solomon 5:10)

LUKE 19:41-44

Josephus wrote that one million Jews died in the siege of Jerusalem in AD 70 (Matthew 22:7). Jesus detailed the future calamity accordingly:

> *And when he was come near, he beheld the city, and wept over it, Saying, If thou hadst known, even thou, at least in this thy day, the things which belong unto thy peace! but now they are hid from thine eyes. For the days shall come upon thee, that thine enemies shall* CAST A TRENCH *about thee,* and COMPASS THEE ROUND, *and keep thee in on every side, And shall lay thee even with the ground, and thy children within thee; and they shall not leave in thee one stone upon another; because thou knewest not the time of thy visitation.* (Luke 19:41-44)

Twenty centuries later, six million Jews would die under similar conditions, *their* enemies casting a trench about *them*, compassing *them* round on every side vis-à-vis Heydrich's communiqué regarding the "concentration of the Jews from the countryside into the larger cities." The Nazis called this a *Judenjagd* ("Jews hunting"), fulfilling Jeremiah 16:16, *"and after will I send for many* HUNTERS, *and they shall* HUNT *them from every mountain, and from every hill, and out of the holes of the rocks."* And the cause for this judgment would remain the same—European Jewry knowing not the time of *their* visitation.

Thus, it is not without significance that the Shoah lasted forty-two months—from June 1941 (Operation Barbarossa) to December 1944 (Auschwitz crematoria dismantlement)—matching the Jews' rejection of Christ's 3½-year public ministry. Therefore, the reader might take *another* look at that inconspicuous numeric address—Luke 19:41-44.

GOMER

In the Old Testament book of Hosea, the prophet's adulterous wife is named Gomer. In the related typology, Gomer represents fornicating Israel. It is noteworthy that most Bible scholars identify the *other* Gomer in Ezekiel 38:6 with the modern nation/state of Germany—the greatest scourge of Jehovah's unfaithful spouse.

When Jesus saw the multitudes, Matthew 9:36 says that *"he was moved with compassion on them, because they fainted, and were scattered abroad, as* SHEEP HAVING NO SHEPHERD.*"* After Pilate asked the Jews, *"Shall I crucify your King?"* the mob replied, *"We have no king but* CAESAR.*"* (John 19:15) Two thousand years later, their descendants got *their* Roman (Catholic) demigod, Adolf Hitler. And, of course, it *just so happens* that Adolf means—"Noble WOLF."

The German people expressed their undying devotion to the Führer by returning his signature *sieg heil* ("hail victory") salute, snapping their right arms in an elevated trajectory. (Jews were forbidden to do so.) Ezekiel 20:33 states, *"As I live, saith the Lord GOD, surely with a mighty hand, and* WITH A STRETCHED OUT ARM, *and with fury poured out, will I rule over you."* An astute preacher friend emailed this author, "That is just what happened during the Holocaust; God ruled over Israel with fury poured out *through Hitler's stretched out arm*." The cross-reference is Psalm 17:13-14, where the context is Israel's rescue from the Antichrist (prefigured by Hitler): *"Arise, O LORD, disappoint him, cast him down: deliver my soul from the wicked, which is thy sword:* FROM MEN WHICH ARE THY HAND, O LORD.*"* (Incidentally, Pontius and Adolf both committed suicide.)

PO LIN

To the humanists' ire, the exact conditions of the Jewish Diaspora were laid out in the Torah itself: *"because thou wouldest not obey...*THE LORD SHALL SCATTER THEE AMONG ALL PEOPLE...*And among these nations shalt thou find no ease, neither shall the sole of thy foot have* REST....*"* (Deuteronomy 28:62-65) If one were to actually take God seriously, *His* usage of the word "rest" is in sharp contrast to the fanciful Jewish tale that eleventh-century refugees, having fled to present-day Poland from pogroms in western Europe, heard a voice from Heaven say in Hebrew—"Po lin"—meaning "Rest here."[6]

Though initially welcomed for their skills, if the Shoah illustrates *anything*, "rest" was the *last* thing that Jews ultimately found in Poland. As the Bible warns in I John 4:1, *"Beloved, believe not every spirit, but try the spirits whether they are of God...,"* the relevant Old Testament waymark that Jacob *should* have followed is Micah 2:10, *"Arise ye, and depart;* FOR THIS IS *NOT* YOUR REST*: because it is polluted, it shall* DESTROY *you, even with a sore* DESTRUCTION.*"* With first-century Jewry having rejected *their* Heaven-sent *Pauline* revelation in the Hebrew tongue (Acts 21:40; 28:25-28), their descendants' "Po lin" revelation would remain a fantasy. Thus, all six death camps were constructed on Polish soil. (For the record, Poland's name, "Polska," is derived from the word "Polanie," literally, "people of the *fields*," i.e., *killing* fields for Abraham's physical *seed*.)

As multitudes of former weary souls (like David Berkowitz) can now affirm through experience, *true* rest can only be found in the accuracy of God's infallible Book. Nearly 3,400 years before the first roll call at Konzentrationslager Auschwitz, the Holy Spirit led Moses to summarize the prisoners' daily routine with remarkable precision:

> *[B]ut the LORD shall give thee there a trembling heart, and failing of eyes, and sorrow of mind: and thy life shall hang in doubt before thee; and thou shalt fear day and night, and shalt have none assurance of thy life: in the morning thou shalt say, would God it were even! and at even thou shalt say, would God it were morning!* (Deuteronomy 28:65-67)

OŚWIĘCIM

The name "Auschwitz" is the Germanized form of *Oświęcim*. Ironically, in view of its now-infamous legacy, Oświęcim means "enlightened place," or "place that is made holy." Indeed, the ancient Polish town existed as a spiritual center for Judaism from 1549. However, the region's later economic expansion was built upon a manufacturing base of "strong drink," the vanguard Vodka & Liquor Factory being established by the Jacob Haberfeld family in 1804.

As a progressive Jew, Jacob would have dismissed any notion that his "product" had placed Oświęcim under a divine curse according to Habakkuk 2:15, *"WOE unto him that giveth his neighbour drink, that puttest thy bottle to him, and makest him drunken also...."* In early 1941, the town's entire Jewish population of 7,000 was scattered to area ghettos in Sosnowiec, Będzin, and Chrzanów. Over 90% of them were later gassed at Auschwitz-Birkenau. Sadly, Haberfeld's two-year-old great-granddaughter, Franciszka Henryka, was among the victims.[7] (On a related note, while the identity of the person who revealed the hiding place of Anne Frank's family remains a mystery, the going reward was fifty guilders—the equivalent of a bottle of Dutch Gin.)

RAISING THE BAR

The Jews cried out before Pilate, *"His blood be on us, and our* CHILDREN.*"* (Matthew 27:25) Little Franciszka was one of over 1,000,000 boys and girls who would perish in Hitler's Final Solution.

Reference has been made to an eyewitness report from Auschwitz that children were forced to participate in a morbid SS version of the "Limbo Rock" (the bar for life set at 4 feet, 3 inches). God warned Israel in Ezekiel 20:37, *"And I will cause you to* PASS UNDER THE ROD.*"* (Gentiles who survive the Tribulation will face their own *selection* at the Judgment of the Nations [Matthew 25:31-46]; only *this* time it will be Dr. Jesus, a.k.a. "The Angel of *the Lord*," deciding who goes *left* and who goes *right*, based on their treatment of His brethren.)

"THE GLORY IS DEPARTED..."

When the Russians entered Auschwitz they discovered seven tons of women's hair bagged for shipment to the Reich's upholstery industry (4,000 pounds remain on exhibit at the Auschwitz State Museum). This macabre fact holds particular scriptural relevance.

Paul wrote that it was *"a shame for a woman to be shorn"* because a woman's *"long hair...is a* GLORY *to her: for her hair is given her for a covering."* (I Corinthians 11:6, 15) As revealed in the context, because man was not *"created for the woman; but the woman for the man,"* the lengthy locks in question represent her husband's *"power on her head."* This explains the stereotypical "dyke haircuts" sported by in-your-face lesbians like MSNBC anchor, Rachel Maddow (not to mention the glaring disparity of natural baldness between the genders).

At the time of Israel's nascent apostasy, Eli's dying daughter-in-law (Phinehas' wife) named her newborn son *Ichabod* ("inglorious" or "where is the honor?"), lamenting, "THE GLORY IS DEPARTED FROM ISRAEL: *because the ark of God was taken."* (I Samuel 4:21) Consequently, on the eve of the Babylonian captivity, Jehovah had Jeremiah rebuke His rebellious/divorced wife accordingly:

> *But thou shalt say unto them, This is a nation that obeyeth not the voice of the LORD their God, nor receiveth correction:* TRUTH *is perished, and is* CUT OFF *from their mouth.* CUT OFF THINE HAIR, O JERUSALEM, *and cast it away...for the LORD hath rejected and forsaken the generation of his wrath. For the children of Judah have done evil in my sight....* (Jeremiah 7:28-30)

With the further edict in Jeremiah 14:11, *"Pray not for this people for their good"* (not unlike the startling words in John 17:9), reciting the Kadesh at the crematoria would become a sad exercise in futility. The first-century ideal was the Jewess—Mary of Bethany—who wiped the feet of the Jews' Messiah with her hair. (John 12:3)

HOLY TATTOOS

One of the Holy Land's more bizarre tourist sites (likened to the Elvis Inn) is the 300-year-old Razzouk Tattoo parlor located in the Christian Quarter of Old Jerusalem. (The Razzouks are Coptic.) Their website states, "Tattoos of religious symbols provide a memorable mark for travelers to the Old City Jerusalem."[8] (Local "competition" includes Sam's Tattoo and Beauty Clinic, formerly Holy Land Tattoos.)

While the selection ramp at Auschwitz was designed for Jews, all prisoners received a personal registration number. Initially sewn on the uniform, beginning in 1943 the numeric was tattooed on the inmate's left forearm (a process unique to Auschwitz). This would have been an added stigma for religious Jews, as Leviticus 19:28 enjoins, *"Ye shall not...print any marks upon you: I am the LORD.*") This satanic mark of ownership will return in the Tribulation (Revelation 13:16-18).

VERNICHTUNG DURCH ARBEIT

As noted earlier, Heydrich alluded to "Annihilation through Labor" in Wannsee, saying: "As part of the development of the final solution the Jews are now to be put to work...as road-builders, in the course of which, no doubt, a large number will be lost by natural wastage."

Jehovah alluded to this concept in eternity past, stating: *"Because they rebelled against the words of God, and contemned the counsel of the most High: Therefore he brought down their heart with* LABOUR; *they fell down* [like the Muselmänner], *and there was none to help."* (Psalm 107:11-12)

"ANUS MUNDI"

As previously cited, Leon Szalet testified that inmates were ordered to drink out of unflushed toilet bowls, and when they only pretended to drink, the block-führers forced the men's heads deep into the bowls until their faces were covered with excrement (many losing their minds). While this is no doubt true—giving added meaning to Heinz Thilo's indelicate metaphor regarding Auschwitz as the "anus mundi" ("anus of the world")—rather than pursue further abstract theories relating excreta to the Shoah (Paul Ricoeur, Julia Kristeva, et al.[9]), once again, the ultimate insight is found in the Jews' own Scriptures.

The God of Israel declared in Malachi 2:3, *"Behold, I will corrupt your seed, and* SPREAD DUNG UPON YOUR FACES...." You can't get much clearer than *that* folks! Jeremiah 8:1-2 further states that the disinterred corpses of Israel's prophets, priests, and kings, along with those of the princes and the inhabitants of Jerusalem, would be *"for* DUNG *upon the* FACE *of the earth."*

In Deuteronomy 23:13, Moses wrote, *"And thou shalt have a paddle upon thy weapon; and it shall be, when thou wilt ease thyself abroad, thou shalt dig therewith, and shalt turn back and* COVER THAT WHICH COMETH FROM THEE." The next verse provides the obvious reason: *"For the LORD thy God walketh in the midst of thy camp."* Thus, uncovered excrement—a type of unconfessed sin—symbolized a barrier of defilement to a Holy God. The related word "execration" is defined as "something cursed or detested," being evidenced by Jehovah's warning to the Jews in Jeremiah 42:18, *"For thus saith the LORD of hosts, the God of Israel...*YE SHALL BE AN EXECRATION.*"* (The fourth-century North African heretic, Arius, hemorrhaged to death inside a Constantinople latrine, collapsing in a mire of blood, intestines, and excrement.[10]) As shown on the cover of this volume, God told Moses to *"put off thy shoes from off thy feet, for the place whereon thou standest is* HOLY GROUND.*"* (Exodus 3:5)

This represents the scriptural take on Libusa Breder's remark that Auschwitz had "such horrible conditions that God decided not to go there," or, as that elderly rabbi told Eli Wiesel, "It's over. God is no longer with us."[11] While the Talmud would consign Jesus Christ to eternal boiling excrement, the Apostle Paul, a former rabbi who spent his life pointing Jews to their only *true* Rabbi, wrote, *"But what things were gain to me, those I counted loss for Christ. Yea doubtless, and I count all things but loss for the excellency of the knowledge of Christ Jesus my Lord: for whom I have suffered the loss of all things, and do count them but* DUNG, *that I may win Christ."* (Philippians 3:7-8)

J. A. TOPF UND SÖHNE

David wrote, *"Thou shalt make them as a* FIERY OVEN *in the time of thine anger: the LORD shall swallow them up in his wrath, and* THE FIRE SHALL DEVOUR THEM.*"* (Psalm 21:9) As stated previously, the hefty and highly negotiated contract for building the crematoria at Birkenau was ultimately awarded to J. A. Topf *und Söhne* ("and Sons"), manufacturers of heating equipment in Erfurt, Germany.

A dual etymological/historical aside bears mention. First, it was at the University of Erfurt that Martin Luther imbibed the anti-Semitism articulated in his vitriolic verbal pogrom, *On the Jews and their Lies* ("We are at fault for not slaying them"). Second, *Topf* is nearly identical (in spelling) to the Hebrew *toph* ("drum"), the instrument used to mute the cries of Jewish children being burned *alive* by the priests of Molech: *"And they have built the high places of* TOPHET, *which is in the valley of the son of Hinnom, to burn their sons and their daughters in the fire...."* (Jeremiah 7:31) Wiesel testified about "infants thrown into fiery ditches."[12] Significantly, as confirmed in I Kings 11:7, the genocide was sanctioned by Israel's own backslidden monarch, King Solomon. Hence, Tophet appears as an Old Testament reference for "Hell" in Isaiah 30:33. In the Millennium, the LORD will give His restored covenant nation *"beauty for* ASHES.*"* (Isaiah 61:3)

THE JESUS-AUSCHWITZ NEXUS

In retrospect, the New Testament (primarily the Gospels) contains many uncanny parallels between the rejected Jewish Messiah and the resultant Jewish Holocaust. Consider the following sample of "coincidental comparisons" between *Jesus* and *Auschwitz*:

- Jesus' birth was identified by a shining star (Matthew 2:2); Jews were identified by bright yellow stars.
- Jesus heard a hymn before his death (Matthew 26:30); Jews heard orchestra music before *their* deaths.
- Jesus was betrayed by Judas (Luke 22:48); Jews were betrayed by sonderkommandos.
- Jesus entered Jerusalem from the east, via the Golden Gate (Luke 22:54); Jews entered Birkenau from the east, via the Death Gate.
- Jesus was condemned by a Roman Governor (Luke 23:24); Jews were condemned by a Roman Catholic (Adolf Hitler).
- Jesus suffered *"without the camp"* (Hebrews 13:13); Jews suffered *within* the camps.
- Jesus was spurned as the *"good shepherd"* (John 10:11); Jews were met by German Shepherds.
- Jesus endured selection at the judgment seat (Matthew 27:17); Jews endured selection at the Judenrampe.
- Jesus warned the women: *"weep not for me, but weep for yourselves, and for your children. For, behold, the days are coming, in the which they shall say, Blessed are the barren, and the wombs that never bare, and the paps which never gave suck"* (Luke 23:28-29); Jewish mothers arriving with infants and/or small children were sent directly to the gas chambers.
- Jesus was falsely accused, beaten, and mocked; (Matthew 27:12, 26-31); Jews were falsely accused, beaten, and mocked.

- Jesus was *"numbered with the transgressors"* (Isaiah 53:12); Jews were numbered with tattoos.
- Jesus was denounced for professing His deity (John 5:18); Jews were further branded with triangles.
- Jesus was pressed for *"signs"* (Matthew 12:38); Jews encountered many signs: "To the Baths"; "Halt! Stój!"; "WARNING! DANGER OF DEATH!" (the latter two depicting a skull and crossbones).
- Jesus wore a crown of thorns (Matthew 27:29); Jews were encircled with barbed wire.
- Jesus' ordeal was monitored by Satan, who is described as "lightning" (II Corinthians 4:4; Luke 10:18; Ephesians 2:2); Jews' ordeal was secured by electrified fences.
- Jesus was *"brought as a lamb to the slaughter"* (Isaiah 53:7); Jews were brought to their captors similarly.
- Jesus was sold for thirty pieces of silver (Matthew 26:15); Jews were sold by God Himself (Deuteronomy 32:30 stating, *"How should one chase a thousand, and two put ten thousand to flight, except* THEIR ROCK HAD SOLD THEM?*"*).
- Jesus' clothing was confiscated by Roman soldiers (John 19:23); Jews' clothing was confiscated by German soldiers.
- Jesus suffered amidst three crosses (Matthew 27:38); Jews suffered amidst three camps (Auschwitz I, II, & III).
- Jesus was murdered at *"The place of a skull"* (Mark 15:22); Jews' murderers sported "Death's Head" skull insignias.
- Jesus' last view was from a cross (John 19:25-26); Jews' last view *was* a cross (Red Cross trucks parked by the crematoria, the benevolent organization itself ironically founded by a Christian Zionist, Jean Henri Dunant).
- Jesus cried, *"It is finished"* (John 19:30); Jews cried throughout the "*Final* Solution."
- Jesus died on a tree (Acts 5:30); Jews died in a place named after a tree ("Birkenau").
- Jesus died naked (John 19:23); Jews died naked.
- Jesus was laid in a sealed tomb (Matthew 27:66); Jews arrived in sealed boxcars and left in sealed gas chambers.
- Jesus suffered from asphyxiation (John 19:31-33); Jews succumbed *to* asphyxiation.

- Jesus told the Jews to carry their enemies' belongings (Matthew 5:41); some 58,000 Jews compelled to carry Nazis' baggage in forced death march retreat from Auschwitz.
- Jesus dismissed His spirit at 3:00 p.m. (Matthew 27:46-50); Jewish survivors were liberated by Russians at 3:00 p.m.
- Jesus declared, *"If the* SON *therefore shall make you* FREE, *ye shall be* FREE INDEED*"* (John 8:36); Jews, *"going about to establish their own righteousness"* (Romans 10:3), dropped into Hell beneath the banner, *"ARBEIT MACHT FREI"*—"WORK SETS YOU FREE."

"TRUTH OR CONSEQUENCES"

Once again, the Bible clearly affirms that God would judge Israel for rejecting His Son (Psalm 2:12). The definitive case is the parable of the householder demanding fruit from his vineyard. With the murdered heir picturing Christ, the passage ends, *"When the lord therefore of the vineyard cometh, what will he do unto those husbandmen? They say unto him, He will miserably* DESTROY *those wicked men, and will let out his vineyard unto other husbandmen, which shall render him the fruits in their seasons."* (Matthew 21:40-41) Thus, I Thessalonians 2:16 states, "WRATH *is come upon them to the* UTTERMOST*."*

Though rarely considered, much of the Jews' suffering—the Shoah representing the nadir of "Jacob's Trouble" *this* side of the Rapture—can also be attributed to the stereotypical dilemma of a defenseless widow/divorcée (not to mention a woman that Satan was determined to destroy) having to suddenly fend for herself. Such is the theme of the book of Hosea (Hosea 2:7). The ultimate application of this *truth*, along with the implied *consequences* of Israel's resultant repudiation, can be found in another statement Jesus made (six chapters after His parable of judgment):

> *O Jerusalem, Jerusalem, thou that killest the prophets, and stonest them which are sent unto thee,* HOW OFTEN WOULD I *have gathered thy children together, even as a hen gathereth her chickens under her wings,* AND YE WOULD NOT! *Behold, your house is left unto you desolate. For I say unto you, Ye shall not see*

me henceforth, till ye shall say, Blessed is he that cometh in the name of the Lord. (Matthew 23:37-39)

The Tanakh says in I Samuel 15:23, *"For rebellion is as the sin of witchcraft,"* implying that a wife who denies her husband's authority will open herself up to direct contact with evil spirits. Paul adds that those who refuse to acknowledge the truth *"are taken captive by him* [the devil] *at his will."* (II Timothy 2:23-26) Thus, while Scriptures such as Amos 3:2 state that the LORD will chasten His own, the Shoah was not so much God's punitive knee-jerk reaction against Israel for rejecting His Son as it was the Jews' *own* doing for having spurned *the* one who longed to guard *them* from Satan. This idea would approach the theological construct known as theodicity—reconciling God's nature with the evidential presence of evil. (Psalm 51:4; Romans 3:4)

REHEARSAL FOR THE TRIBULATION

As the UN is acutely aware, the Jewish State has become a formidable military power (her "nuclear opacity" notwithstanding). On September 4, 2003, the IAF made a compelling statement to this effect when three F-15 jets, piloted by descendants of Shoah survivors, circled over the Auschwitz-Birkenau complex as a tribute to the Jewish victims.

With some 200 IDF soldiers standing at attention, the jets streaked by (the blue Star of David clearly visible on the fuselage). Speaking in Hebrew, Brigadier General Amir Eshel issued a dramatic cockpit transmission: "We the pilots of the Israeli Air Force flying in the skies above the camp of horrors, arose from the ashes of the millions of victims and shoulder their silent cries, salute their courage and promise to be the shield of the Jewish people and its nation Israel."[13] He then bade a symbolic farewell to his grandmother who died in the camp. The exhibit ended with a moving rendition of "HaTikvah." The Catholic administrators at the Auschwitz-Birkenau State Museum labeled "the demonstration of Israeli military might…an entirely inappropriate way to commemorate the victims."[14] In August 2015, the Museum "sparked a red-hot controversy" itself, installing "misting stations" (sprinkler *showers*) to cool off visitors.[15]

Now despite Israel's uncontested military prowess, the fact remains that her firepower will fall woefully short against a global coalition led by the Beast. But then the forces of Antichrist will pale in contrast to the purging "anti-Semitic" wrath of Israel's "Rock" (Job 19:21; Psalm 35:6). For example, in Ezekiel 9:1-11, six angels brandishing *"slaughter weapons"* descend on Jerusalem to slay every man, woman, and child who fails to *"sigh and cry for all the abominations that be done in the midst thereof."* (A female Jewish tour guide in Israel once told this author that she thought Ezekiel was on drugs when he wrote his book.)

The rest of the time won't be much better. In the camps, Jews had to contend with *beastly* men; in the Tribulation, they (and their tormentors alike) will face *literal* beasts of a supernatural constitution (Revelation 9:3-10). In the camps, Jews could end their ordeal by "going to the wire." In the Tribulation, suicide will be a physiological impossibility (Revelation 9:6). Other unparalleled events will include: demonic activity; oceanic and ecological disturbances; falling stars; one hundred-pound hailstones; darkness; heat; boils; fire; drought; earthquakes; nuclear wars; torture; genocide; famine; cannibalism; and a "little" pestilence thrown in for good measure. Jesus summed it up in Matthew 24:21: *"For then shall be great tribulation, such as was not since the beginning of the world to this time, no, nor ever shall be."*

The key "sign" to discern is that the Jews' 42-month Holocaust was sandwiched between the 42-month public ministry of Jesus Christ and the 42-month latter half of Daniel's 70th week (distinguished as the "*Great* Tribulation"). Thus, as the Jews chose the Law over the One Who *fulfilled* the Law (Matthew 5:17), the LORD will deal with Israel as Israel dealt with His Son—42 months of rejection and persecution for 42 months of rejection and persecution (i.e., *"an eye for an eye"*).

CONCLUDING OBSERVATIONS

Dr. Jonathan Webber is a contributing editor to the definitive pictorial treatise, *Auschwitz: A History in Photographs*. In his essay "What does Auschwitz mean today?" he writes, "The historians and survivors can tell us what happened at Auschwitz, but sociologists and theologians have yet to explain adequately why Auschwitz happened at all."[16]

Before one can *understand* something, he or she must first *believe* that it exists. In his book, *The Terrible Secret*, Walter Laqueur opines that the Final Solution "touches on wider cognitive questions: what is the meaning of 'to know' and 'to believe'?"[17] At a private meeting during the war, recently arrived Polish envoy Jan Karski briefed Associate Justice Felix Frankfurter on the growing genocide in Europe. "Frankfurter told Karski that he did not believe him. When Karski protested, Frankfurter explained that he did not imply that Karski had in any way not told the truth, he simply meant that he could not believe him – there was a difference."[18]

Dr. Laqueur (who is Jewish) tells how he was "preoccupied" by the disconnect between the questions "What was known?" and "Why was it not believed?" He explains his own protracted fixation as follows:

> First, because it is still one of the riddles making the understanding of the catastrophe so difficult; secondly, because it is, of course, directly connected with a more general issue, that of the denial of reality, the psychological rejection of information which for one reason or another is not acceptable…Men freely believe, as Julius Caesar and many others have noted, that which they desire, and there is enormous resistance against accepting what is highly undesirable… What is the reason for the inclination among otherwise normal, even highly intelligent, human beings to deny reality, however glaring?…Whatever the reason, such behavior is still mysterious and the mystery deepens if the issues at stake are…very real dangers to the survival of one's group or oneself.[19]

One would think that the widest "cognitive" question *should* be, "What light does the *Bible* shed on the murder of six million people?" After all, the words "THOU SHALT NOT KILL" (taken from Exodus 20:13) appear in three languages (Hebrew, Polish, and English) across the imposing memorial at the former Radegast Train Station in Łódź (from which 180,000 Jews embarked to their *deaths* at Chelmno and Auschwitz). Far from a *sociological* issue, the *Shoah* is not even a *theological* issue; it is a *scriptural* issue. As for "matters mysterious," Moses wrote in the Torah, *"The* SECRET *things belong unto the LORD our God."* (Deuteronomy 29:29) Connecting the dots, Amos 3:7 adds, *"Surely the Lord GOD will do nothing, but he revealeth his* SECRET *unto his servants the prophets."* Thus, if you *really* want to know *why* men repress "undesirable" things (i.e., "grapple" with the Holocaust)—don't ask a socialist or a theologian—find a prophet!

According to God's final authority (KJV), the main problem with the Final Solution, is that it reveals a dark truth about human nature, one that is about as "undesirable" as you can get. This truth was articulated over 2,700 years ago by the prophet Isaiah: *"But we are all as an unclean thing, and all our righteousnesses are as filthy rags...."* (Isaiah 64:6) Jeremiah, another "negative" prophet, concurs: *"The heart is deceitful above all things, and desperately wicked: who can know it?"* (Jeremiah 17:9) Interpreting this text by the airhead clichés of our modern culture, one could say that Hitler and his goons were merely "following their hearts," etc. The nation's *ultimate* Prophet (whose coming was foretold in Deuteronomy 18:15) wound up nailed to a cross, having shared similar politically incorrect sentiments: *"For from within, out of the heart of men, proceed evil thoughts, adulteries, fornications, murders, Thefts, covetousness, wickedness, deceit, lasciviousness, an evil eye, blasphemy, pride, foolishness: All these evil things come from within, and defile the man."* (Mark 7:21-23)

As nearly all theologians are Bible critics in one form or another, Webber rightly alludes that the professional minister is as clueless as everyone else. For instance, the Protestant intellectual and first World Council of Churches secretary, Dr. W. A. Visser 't Hooft, was well aware of Nazi crimes, having passed the war years in Switzerland. Yet, when writing about these events thirty years later, he acknowledged that it took several months before the information he received was able to penetrate his consciousness. This led him to posit: "It is possible to live in a twilight between knowing and not knowing."[20]

Conversely, as the author of *this* tome is a Bible-believing Baptist preacher, he will automatically surpass any mere scholar (Isaiah 28:9; Matthew 11:25). The problem *with* (and reason *for*) man's *professed* "inability" to handle the Holocaust is simple—self-righteous humans reject the only "religious" book in history that foretells their *own* history with 100% accuracy! And it doesn't matter *how* many times its flawless predictions can be confirmed (Ecclesiastes 1:11), it just *has* to be dismissed, as the same book condemns *all* men as SINNERS, thus requiring them to turn to God in repentance and faith (Acts 20:21).

Take the premise that the Shoah is an "unbelievable" phenomenon. The Tanakh clearly warns that this is the very thing its divine author specializes in (i.e., creating "unbelievable" scenarios); "unbelievable" that is, to those who refuse to humble themselves before Him. Prior to the judgment on Eli's sons, the LORD said unto Samuel, *"Behold, I will do a thing in Israel, at which* BOTH THE EARS OF EVERY ONE THAT HEARETH IT SHALL TINGLE.*"* (I Samuel 3:11) Then later, He stated: *"Behold ye among the heathen, and regard, and wonder marvelously: for I will work a work in your days,* WHICH YE WILL NOT BELIEVE, *though it be told you."* (Habakkuk 1:5) Here, the foretold event was the brutal Babylonian invasion of Israel.

Thus, at the end of the day—while *Gentiles* were unwilling to accept the *reality* of the Holocaust revealed by their own *photographs*, because it indicted human nature—*Jews* were equally unwilling to accept the *reason* for the Shoah revealed by their own *prophets*, because it fingered *them*. And while history has indicted Adolf Hitler the undisputed monster of all time, as chapter ten reveals, the Führer was *also* the proverbial "fall guy" (Matthew 18:7) who was willing to do the dirty work of an unseen collage of Anglo-American cohorts. (The postwar scam would begin with a "shocked" General Eisenhower forcing German citizens to tour various camps, followed by the hypocritical show trials at Nuremberg.) For the record, concerning the unsettling theme of God's human instruments of judgment (Hitler obviously making the list), three times the LORD personally called Nebuchadnezzar "my servant" (Jeremiah 25:9; 27:6; and 43:10).

To revisit Sherman's maxim that "truth is not always palatable," while the Axis and Allied powers were locked in a death struggle, they were also aligned against a common *ideological* foe, the Jew. Given the intensity of prewar anti-Semitism in Britain and America, the only difference between Hitler and many in the West was that *he* acted as *they* thought. This assertion is borne out by the respective acts of the major belligerents near the end of the war.

Two weeks before Germany's epic Stalingrad surrender, Himmler rushed the Reich Minister of Transport a letter regarding "the removal of Jews" from occupied territories. In tandem with Matthew 12:26 (*"if Satan cast out Satan, he is divided against himself"*), he states, "I need your help and support. If I am to wind things up quickly I must have more trains for transports...I know very well how taxing the situation is for the railways and what demands are constantly made of you. Just the same, I must make this request of you: help me get more trains."[21] (On August 17, 1942, the budget office advised the Finance Ministry that 18 France to Auschwitz trains had cost RM 515,000.[22])

Then, as previously shown, with the Reich on the run, the Allies refused to preempt Himmler's onslaught by their repeated demoralizing flyovers of the camps. Thus, during the very window when American air power was at its peak in Upper Silesia, nearly 40% of all the Jewish deaths at Auschwitz would occur. David Wyman rightly observes the irony: "To kill the Jews, the Nazis were willing to weaken their capacity to fight the war. The United States and its allies, however, were willing to attempt almost nothing to save them."[23]

THE MOST SURREAL SCRIPTURE OF ALL!

Once again, not only did Deuteronomy 28 foretell the *fact* of the Diaspora, but the attendant *fallout* as well. Karl Fritzsch is credited with performing the landmark experiment employing the Zyklon B pesticide on humans. (He was also the sadist who laid dead prisoners under the camp's lighted Christmas tree.)

In his "welcoming" speech to new arrivals, Fritzsch would say, "This is not a sanatorium, but a German concentration camp. There is only one exit: through the crematorium chimney."[24] As previously noted, "going up the chimney" was the defining metaphor in death camp parlance. Do you suppose Herr Fritzsch realized that he was citing *the* most applicable Old Testament verse regarding the Shoah?

After the LORD "vents" in Hosea 13:2 regarding backsliding Ephraim, *"And now they sin more and more, and have made them molten images,"* He goes on in the very next verse to foretell a most precise detail concerning their future destiny: *"Therefore they shall be...*AS THE SMOKE OUT OF THE CHIMNEY.*"* Job, the greatest type of the Jew in the Great Tribulation, adds:

> *"I am become like dust and ashes...*THOU LIFTEST ME UP TO THE WIND*; thou causest me to ride upon it, and dissolvest my substance."*
>
> (Job 30:19, 22)

21

The New Covenant

"The church does not replace Israel—the church is Israel."
(Jonas Alexis, 2013)

"But thou, O Daniel, shut up the words, and seal the book, even to the time of the end: many shall run to and fro, and knowledge shall be increased."
(Daniel 12:4)

"I say then, Hath God cast away his people? God forbid... blindness in part is happened to Israel, until the fulness of the Gentiles be come in. And so all Israel shall be saved...."
(Romans 11:1, 25-26)

"Behold, the days come, saith the LORD, that I will make a new covenant with the house of Israel, and with the house of Judah...."
(Jeremiah 31:31)

"[A]nd the name of the city from that day shall be, The LORD is there."
(Ezekiel 48:35)

PAUL WROTE THAT the Jewish people are *"beloved for the* FATHERS' *sakes."* Like the misspelling of *Lion's* Gate Street in Old Jerusalem, Bible students often misread "Father's" for "fathers'." The main reason why Jews are beloved is because of the unconditional covenant God made with their patriarchal "fathers"—

Abraham, *Isaac*, and *Jacob* (Romans 15:8). The pledge, designated for Jacob's *physical* progeny, constitutes a land grant stretching from *"the river of Egypt unto the great river, the river Euphrates."* (Genesis 15:18) The Bible records this solemn oath in no fewer than *five* separate texts (Genesis13:14-17; 15:18; 17:8; 22:15-17; 24:7). To reinforce this pledge, *fifty-eight* passages in the fifth book of Moses alone affirm that Palestine was divinely deeded to Jewry. (Deuteronomy 1:8, 21, 25, 35-39; 2:12, 24; 3:2, 20; 4:1, 21, 38, 40; 5:16, 31, 33; 6:10, 18, 23; 7:13; 8:1, 7-10; 9:5-6; 10:11; 11:9, 17, 21, 31; 12:1, 10; 15:4, 7; 16:20; 17:2, 14; 18:9; 19:1-3, 8, 10, 14; 20:16; 21:1, 23; 24:4; 25:15, 19; 26:1-3, 9-10, 15; 27:2-3; 28:8, 11, 52; 30:20; 31:7, 20-21, 23; 32:52; 34:4)[1]

Now despite this voluminous record of the covenant's inviolability (likened in Jeremiah 33:24-26 to the solar system itself), the Vatican has insisted over the centuries that God is *finished* with the Jew for having committed the "unpardonable sin" of deicide. Subject to this purported dissolution, every Pope has called Rome the New Jerusalem (a.k.a. Augustine's *City of God*), expropriating all of Jehovah's promises to the Jews. Thus, Rome's "replacement" of Israel has come to be known as *replacement theology* (or supersessionism from the English verb "supersede"). Note how this eventuality was veiled in the KJV's "archaic" rendering of John 11:48 (the Pharisees' paranoid prophecy uttered atop the Hill of Evil Counsel), *"If we let him thus alone, all men will believe on him: and the* ROMANS *shall come and take away both our* PLACE *and nation."* In time, the sixteenth-century Protestant Reformation (like its East/West Orthodox precursor in AD 1053) was the finale of John's prophetic profile of Roman Catholicism in Revelation 17:5, **"MYSTERY, BABYLON THE GREAT, THE MOTHER OF HARLOTS AND ABOMINATONS OF THE EARTH"**—*thirteen* bolded uppercase words for triple emphasis.

Not only is Rome a filthy slut for fornicating with the *"kings of the earth"* (Revelation 2:20-21; 17:2; 18:3), but she is also a "MOTHER *of harlots"* for birthing two bastard lines which have replicated her novel church-state "evangelism" methods (i.e., *literal* "swords of the Lord"). Thus, the historic Catholic/Orthodox/Protestant animus towards Jews (not to mention Islam's ire), has focused on a single, *non*-religious issue—dirt—the *"holy ground"* of Exodus 3:5.[2] Even Hollywood got it right when 20th Century Fox titled their 2005 Crusader film, *Kingdom of Heaven*—the scriptural title for Israel's future, visible, *earthly* domain (i.e., earth being located *in* the heavens) versus the Church's present, invisible, *empyrean* domain, known as the *Kingdom of God.*

This unscriptural land grab is the core of ecumenical Judeophobia. And, like Hagee's overreach on the right, certain southpaws are wilder than others. While "*replacement* theology" is bad enough, Jonas Alexis writes, "In a nutshell, the church—which is composed of both ethnic Jews and Gentiles—is the true Israel. The Israel of the flesh is not and cannot be the true Israel at all...The church does not replace Israel—the Church is Israel. As Gary DeMar rightly points out, Gentiles were simply grafted into an already existing church."[3]

Of course, the *fact* that the word "church" does not even appear in Romans 11:17 (the subject being an "olive tree") means nothing to these agenda-driven heretics. Nor does it matter that the same inspired Apostle taught the Body of Christ to avoid this very error by rightly dividing itself away from both Jews and Gentiles alike (I Corinthians 10:32). While Acts 7:38 employs the word in its purely grammatical (i.e., non-theological) meaning of an "assembly" when describing pre-Canaan Israel as the *"church in the wilderness,"* the proverbial "church in the wildwood" is an altogether different entity, one that was obviously *future* when Jesus said in Matthew 16:18, *"Thou art Peter, and upon this rock* I *WILL* BUILD MY CHURCH.*"*

"BROTHER" JONAS

Mr. Jonas E. Alexis (an "African-American," Judeophobe who teaches math in South Korea), appears to be the latest attack dog in the growing phenomenon of "Christian anti-Semitism." His "stellar" literary achievement is a three-volume set entitled *Christianity and Rabbinic Judaism.* (The "Jekyll and Hyde" author also maintains a toxic Jew-bashing website/blog, *Veterans Today*, where he exhibits all the vile *ad hominem* tactics he so piously decries in his books.[4])

Upon receiving an unsolicited, complimentary copy of Volume I (from Alexis himself), this author read the full text (later purchasing and reading Volume II, the final installment of the proposed trilogy being incomplete at the time). The opening book sets the pace. While Jonas piously dedicates his work to "the Glory of God and His Son Jesus Christ," *the first authority he cites* is the celebrated sodomite Greek philosopher Plato.[5] It's all downhill from there, folks. His most telling *faux pas* is the following inane statement:

> Central to dispensationalist eschatology is a clear distinction between Israel and the Church, a distinction which can be found nowhere in the New Testament and even classical historical theology...If the distinction between the church and Israel is so vital to dispensationalism, why is it not so clear in Scripture, most specifically in the New Testament?[6]

"Brother" Jonas must have missed I Corinthians 10:32—*"Give none offence, neither to the* JEWS, *nor to the* GENTILES, *nor to the* CHURCH OF GOD.... *"* As all of the standard anti-Semitic positions are represented in his compendium, the ensuing observations will illustrate the Posse's overall "credibility."

EL PAPA'S MEA CULPA KVITLE

Being a good modern-day Protestant (i.e., ecumenical), Brother Jonas is careful to tacitly link his whore Vatican matriarch to legitimate Bible-believing Christianity, *repeatedly* projecting the single greatest killer of both Jews *and* Christians in a positive light.[7,8]

Naturally, he identifies the harlot of Revelation 17-18 as Israel, specifically, Jerusalem, despite the fact that Revelation was written some thirty years *after* the city's destruction.[9] His logic is short of astounding. To exonerate the Roman "Church," he writes "[B]oth the Old and New Testaments address the harlotry issue very clearly, and it has never referred to false religions but to nations...."[10] Someone should enlighten the brother that his native government holds formal diplomatic relations with the "Vatican City State"—a wall-enclosed, 110-acre, sacerdotal/monarchal city-state, internationally recognized as the world's smallest sovereign nation—replete with its own flag, coat of arms, national anthem, diplomatic corps, passports, minted Euros, postage stamps, and a halberd-wielding mercenary army.

For what it's worth, the American people were "blessed" to host the "Apostolic Journey of Pope Francis to the United States," September 22-27, 2015. As the chartered Alitalia jet taxied down the runway at Joint Base Andrews in Washington, DC, Vatican and US flags were displayed from the cockpit. When Francis was formally received at the White House the next day, the outdoor ceremony began with the USMC band playing *Inno e Marcia Pontificale*, "The Pontifical Anthem and March"—the national anthem of the Vatican City State. On Thursday, the "religious leader" proceeded to lecture America's *political* leaders in the first-ever papal address before a joint session of Congress (the Catholic Vice President and Catholic Speaker of the House seated behind him, the Catholic Secretary of State and five Catholic Supreme Court Justices before him). During the one-hour "papal 'bull' session," Francis promoted (illegal) immigration and climate control, while decrying the evils of "misdirected capitalism" (previously referring to it as the "Dung of the Devil"[11]).

When he spoke at the UN on the seventieth anniversary of the General Assembly—addressing the largest collection of global leaders in the history of that satanic cesspool—the Vatican Flag was flying aloft, while the Pope's "peeps" observed from their designated non-member *state* section behind the impressive digital sign marked "Holy See." (If you're wondering how the first *Jesuit* Pope was able to pull all this off, the answer is contained in your dictionary, the word "Jesuit" being defined as "one given to intrigue or equivocation.")

Next, noting that Israel was often charged with fornication, Jonas relates, "Rome never committed 'fornication' in a theological sense because Rome was never a bride in the first place."[12] To interject a personal word: If Jonas requires a spouse for the Vatican ("Holy Mother Church"), this former cassock-wearing Catholic altar boy has *no* problem positing that *"that great city"* in Revelation 17:18 ("The Eternal City"), which sits on "*seven mountains*" in Revelation 17:9 ("The City of Seven Hills"), is the swinger wife of the equally promiscuous Lucifer himself (*The Bride of Frankenstein*). And my, my, don't they just make the perfect couple, *"the god of this world"* ruling alongside his glorious, sitting *"queen"* (II Corinthians 4:4; Revelation 18:7; Jeremiah 44:19)?

In another "excursion to cloudland" (as Dean John Burgon would say), Alexis cites the "humble spirit" of "St. Anthony" of Egypt (AD 251-356),[13] a.k.a. "Anthony of the Desert"—a masochistic anchorite who "obeyed" the Great Commission by investing the majority of his life *sequestered in a sepulcher* (later "moving on up" to the ruins of a castle.)[14] Continuing his "survey of monks' contributions to Western civilization," Alexis cites Oxford historian George Holmes who lauds the Catholic Church as "a distinct elite corporation whose institutional and sacramental structure was intended to lead man to salvation."[15]

While attempting to whitewash the Holy See's "Unholy Sea" of Jewish blood (except when popes needed loans), Alexis states in passing, "Although Protestants and Catholics disagree on several key theological issues [the understatement of history], when faced with the persecution of the Jews by Nazi Germany, both were on the same side, fighting to save as many Jews as possible."[16] He then quotes the compromising Jewish British historian, Cecil Roth: "The truth is that the popes and the Catholic Church from the earliest days of the Church were never responsible for physical persecution of Jews and only Rome, among the capitals of the world, is free from having been a place of Jewish tragedy."[17] (Apparently, Dr. Roth does not consider the deportation of the city's 1,000 Jews to Auschwitz a "tragedy.")

Conversely, Jewish author and former Harvard associate professor, Daniel Jonah Goldhagen, affirms in *A Moral Reckoning*, his 2003 exposé of Vatican-Nazi complicity: "The Catholic Church was a source of an enormous amount of antisemitism and acted badly toward Jews in many ways."[18] Jonas then makes the following asinine assessment regarding ratlines: "Building on G. S. Graber's book *The History of the SS*, [Dave] Hunt writes that 'Tens of thousands of the worst Nazi war criminals—most of them Catholics—would travel the secret "Ratlines" to a new life. The principle agent in their escape would be the Vatican.' Nothing could be further from the truth."[19]

In any event, John Paul II (a.k.a. "*Saint* Pope John Paul II" as of 2014), was obviously unaware of the sources cited by Roth, Alexis, and other Vatican apologists, as the *kvitle* ("written prayer") he stuck in the Kotel on March 12, 2000, contained the following "half-a-loaf is better than none" historic mea culpa: "God of our fathers, you chose Abraham and his descendants to bring your name to the nations. We are deeply saddened by the behavior of those who in the course of history have caused these children of yours to suffer, and asking your forgiveness we wish to commit ourselves to genuine brotherhood with the people of the covenant."[20] Cardinal Edward Cassidy's antecedent concession was more specific, seeking absolution for "sins committed by not a few of their number against the people of the covenant."[21] (The pontifical petition, signed "Joannes Paulus II" and stamped with the Vatican seal, was later put on display at the *Yad Vashem* museum.

Thus, the rule of thumb for illustrations of Rome *assisting* Jews in the Shoah merely illustrates the adage, "The exception proves the rule."

SATANIC SEMANTICS

Alexis writes: "The Apostle Paul challenged his younger brother in Christ Timothy to 'study to shew thyself approved unto God, a workman that needeth not to be ashamed, rightly dividing the word of truth' (2 Timothy 2:15). Many Christians largely ignore this warning…."[22] The Bible dunce then gives the following contradiction: "The distinction between the Church and Israel certainly makes things ambiguous and theologically shallow."[23] Unable (or unwilling) to rightly divide between *"Jews…Gentiles* [and] *the Church of God,"* Brother Jonas and company are forced to employ *semantic subterfuge* to market their Jesuit-spawned replacement theology.

While Hosea 2:14 says that the LORD desires to *"*ALLURE *her* [Israel], *and bring her into the wilderness, and speak comfortably unto her,"* Peter illuminates the Posse's similar approach for evil: *"And through covetousness shall they with* FEIGNED WORDS *make merchandise of you…For when they speak* GREAT SWELLING WORDS OF VANITY, *they* ALLURE *through the lusts of the flesh, through much wantonness, those that were clean escaped from them who live in error."* (II Peter 2: 3, 18) By *"doting about questions and* STRIFES OF WORDS*"* (I Timothy 6:4), they mislead their fatuous followers into believing that the Church has become the "New Israel of God" with Christians as the "New Israelites."

The purported "proof text" for this nonsensical nomenclature is Galatians 6:15-16: *"For in Christ Jesus neither circumcision availeth any thing, nor uncircumcision, but a new creature. And as many as walk according to this rule, peace be on them, and mercy, and upon the* ISRAEL OF GOD.*"* Alexis writes: "The true Israel is therefore the Church, which is composed of both ethnic Jews and Gentiles."[24] However, a careful grammar read shows that God's peace and mercy are meant for *two* uniquely related groups, separated by a comma and a conjunction: *"as many as walk according to this rule* [an obvious reference to saved Gentiles], *peace be on them, and mercy,* AND *upon the Israel of God"* [an equally plain reference to saved Jews]. Thus, the title "Israel of God" is Jehovah's personal moniker for His Jewish remnant in the Church Age, referenced in Romans 11:5, *"Even so then at this present time also there is a remnant according to the election of grace."* (Now if Texe can't handle *this* explanation, he'll have to content himself with being a "Jewish Gentile," an extraordinary concession for a guy who doesn't even believe that *Jesus* was a Jew.)

Another favorite watering hole for the Posse is Ephesians 2:11-13:

> *Wherefore remember, that ye being in time past Gentiles in the flesh, who are called Uncircumcision by that which is called the Circumcision in the flesh made by hands; That at that time ye were without Christ, being aliens from the* COMMONWEALTH OF ISRAEL, *and strangers from the covenants of promise, having no hope, and without God in the world: But now in Christ Jesus ye who sometimes were far off are made nigh by the blood of Christ.*

Anti-Semitic Christians posit that the Church, as the Israel of God, is the *new* Commonwealth of Israel (the essence of replacement theology). Marrs writes with great sanctimony:

> What a lover of all mankind is our Saviour, Jesus! Once, before they were born again, Christians were of two separate types in the flesh, "Gentiles and Jews," [b]ut no longer. The blood of Jesus has changed us through faith in Him, so that all who believe in Christ Jesus, all who are born again, are now one. We are all of the commonwealth of Israel. We are together the Israel of God, the People of God. The wall between Jews and Gentiles is broken down."[25]

While Texe correctly says that saved Jews and Gentiles are one in Christ, note that he (like Jonas) misidentifies the Church as *"the Israel of God."* News flash for the Posse: A "commonwealth" is not a "church"—it's a "commonwealth!" The word (appearing only once in the KJV) is described in *Webster's 1828 American Dictionary of the English Language* as: "An established form of government, or civil polity; or more generally, a state." Interestingly, Jewish historians date the period 1000 BC to 586 BC as the First Commonwealth, with the years 530 BC to AD 70 assigned to the Second Commonwealth. As Romans 11:16 depicts ethnic Israel as the original *root* of God's olive tree, believing Jews *this* side of Calvary (i.e., the *spiritual* "Israel of God") represent Church Age *figureheads* of the "Commonwealth of Israel" (in temporary exile). Continuing with *Webster's* definition, "This term is applied to the government of Great Britain, which is of mixed character," *commonwealth* is simply the clearest English word to convey the reality that Gentile and Jewish believers may now *share* a "common wealth." (Metaphorically, the scenario resembles an exclusive Jewish club that suddenly opens its membership to goys.)

Notice how this kibbutz-style Christianity portrayed the embryonic Jewish church at Jerusalem: *"And all that believed were together, and had all things common; And sold their possessions and goods, and parted them to all men, as every man had need."* (Acts 2:44-45) Though ultimately a preemptive effort (in view of Israel's second rejection of Christ at Stephen's execution), that early communal spirit provides a holy glimpse of the commonwealth in action. Thus, while saved Jews join saved Gentiles to enjoy spiritual blessings in the "Body of Christ" during the present Church Age (conforming to the Kingdom of God), saved Gentiles will join saved Jews to enjoy earthly blessings in the "Commonwealth of Israel" during the future Millennial Age (conforming to the Kingdom of Heaven). For now, it is *"the common salvation"* (Jude 3) based on *"the common faith"* (Titus 1:4); when faith turns to sight (Hebrews 11:1), the commonwealth will act as Webster concludes: "The word signifies strictly, the common good or happiness; and hence, the form of government supposed best to secure the public good." Paul therefore reminds the Gentiles, *"if the casting away of them be the reconciling of the world, what shall the receiving of them be, but life from the dead?"* (Romans 11:15)

Romans 2:28-29 is another sleight-of-hand reference: *"*FOR HE IS NOT A JEW, WHICH IS ONE OUTWARDLY*; neither is that circumcision, which is outward in the flesh:* BUT HE IS A JEW, WHICH IS ONE INWARDLY*; and circumcision is that of the heart, in the spirit, and not in the letter; whose praise is not of men, but of God."* According to Jonas, "Once again it is quite clear that Paul here is not dealing with an ethnic term but a theological term, one that has several implications."[26] The intended scam is that *saved Gentiles* have somehow morphed into "spiritual Israelites." However, the context shows that the verse is addressed to *ethnic Jews* who are hiding behind their Old Testament trappings. *"For the name of God is blasphemed among the Gentiles through* YOU*, as it is written. For circumcision verily profiteth, if thou keep the law: but if thou be a breaker of the law, thy circumcision is made uncircumcision."* (Romans 2:24-25)

Paul is basically telling these self-righteous Jews that the Law is *not* their passport to Heaven. In the Church Age (again, the "Church of God" being set apart from Gentiles and ethnic Jews in I Corinthians 10:32), sinners who trust the *"gospel of the grace of God"* (Acts 20:24; I Corinthians 15:3-4) are placed into the Body of Christ by the Holy Spirit (I Corinthians 12:13). The Church is *not* a physical nation or race—it is a *spiritual relationship.* And in that spiritual context Galatians 3:28 states, *"There is neither* JEW NOR GREEK [offset by 2:15]...*neither bond nor free...male nor female: for ye are all one in Christ Jesus."* Incredibly, Jonas says that Paul actually wrote this "in reference to the Old Testament."[27] When the Holy Spirit indwells the New Testament believer (Jew and Gentile alike), He circumcises them on the *inside.* In contrast to *"the Circumcision in the flesh* MADE WITH HANDS*"* (Ephesians 2:11), Colossians 2:11 states: *"In whom also ye are circumcised with the circumcision* MADE WITHOUT HANDS, *in putting off the body of the sins of the flesh by the circumcision of Christ."* (Believe it or not, some anti-Semitic nuts go so far as to use Galatians 3:28 to argue that *Jews no longer exist*; of course, they always avoid the *"neither male nor female"* part.)

Jonas and his cohorts will then try to twist Romans 9:6-7, *"Not as though the word of God hath taken none effect.* FOR THEY ARE NOT ALL ISRAEL, WHICH ARE OF ISRAEL*: Neither, because they are the seed of Abraham, are they all children: but, In Isaac shall thy seed be called."*[28] Here, the context is Paul's burden for his *"kinsmen according to the flesh"* to trust Christ. (Romans 9:3) The attendant subjects are the individual *"children of the flesh,"* not the collective *nation* of Israel. (Romans 9:8) As there were lost Israelites in the Old Testament who still counted as *ethnic* Israel, the big, bad phrase at issue—*"they are not all Israel, which are of Israel"*—is no different than saying, "they are not all Church, which *are* of the Church." The same would apply to Revelation 2:9 and 3:9 (verses which could also be employed against the New Israelites, replacement theology heretics *"which say they are Jews, and are not"*).[29]

"YE CHOSEN SEED OF ISRAEL'S RACE"

By far, the greatest amount of religious skulduggery concerns Abraham's seed (fourteen references to the subject in *Christianity and*

Rabbinic Judaism alone). Jonas writes, "When the Jews keep telling Jesus that 'we be Abraham's seed' and that 'Abraham is our father,' Jesus has a different answer for them: 'If ye were Abraham's children, ye would do the works of Abraham.' (John 8:33, 39)."[30] The truth is, Jesus had *two* answers for them. His first was in verse 37: *"I know that ye are Abraham's seed."* The obvious contrast is between the *natural* and the *spiritual* posterity of Abraham, the former without the latter meaning nothing *in the Church Age*. Stephen certainly understood this theological dichotomy when he addressed the Jews who were about to murder him in Acts 7:2, *"And he said, Men,* BRETHREN, *and fathers, hearken; The God of glory appeared unto* OUR FATHER ABRAHAM, *when he was in Mesopotamia...."*

Even Jonas says, "Jesus here implied that by not demonstrating the faith of Abraham, the Pharisees could not have been Abraham's spiritual seed, even though they were *ethnically* Jewish."[31] No credible dispensationalist would posit that Christ-rejecting, Hell-bound, Church Age Jews can be classified as Abraham's *spiritual* seed. The critical issue, however, involves the *future* status of Abraham's *physical* seed. Bible believers hold to the post-Tribulation, premillennial Restoration of Israel, while replacement theology advocates reject this doctrine.

The Posse is *so* dense they cannot grasp how the Jews can *remain* God's "chosen *people*" despite their *apparent* disenfranchisement, their glorious *future* reconciliation confirming their status as a "people *chosen*" for an *ultimate* purpose. The trick is to deny the scriptural reality that God would naturally have two distinct sets of promises for Abraham's two distinct lines of descendants. Thus, the main goal of the "geometry teacher" is to blur these two "lines" into one (i.e., the "New Israel of God"). Alexis states about Galatians 3:28-29, "As one commentator explains this passage, 'Not lineal descent from Abraham, but spiritual kinship to him through a faith like his, determines whether we are heirs of THE PROMISE [i.e., the *only* promise] made to him.'"[32] (Author's emphasis) Yet, the context in verse 16 clearly states, *"Now to Abraham and his seed were* THE PROMISES *made."*

The *first* set of "promises" that Jehovah made to Abraham concern his *physical* progeny. Genesis 12:1-3 confirms:

> *Now the LORD had said unto Abram, Get thee out of thy country, and from thy kindred, and from thy father's house, unto a land that I will shew thee: And I will make of thee a great nation, and I will*

> *bless thee, and make thy name great; and thou shalt be a blessing: And I will bless them that bless thee, and curse him that curseth thee: and in thee shall all families of the earth be blessed.*

Here, God implies that the seventy-five-year-old, childless Bedouin will one day bequeath a great nation to the benefit of all mankind. The prophetic precursors would include Arabians from Ishmael taking the Old Testament throughout Persia, Turkey, Arabia, North Africa, and Spain (Genesis 21:13), along with Abraham's great-grandson feeding the world's starving families from Egyptian granaries (Genesis 41:56-57). Hence, Laban told Jacob, *"I have learned by experience that the LORD hath* BLESSED *me for thy sake."* (Genesis 30:27) Built into this high calling is an *unconditional* pronouncement of attendant blessings or curses upon those who would intersect with this line. Regarding the Posse's objection that this promise no longer applies,[33] note how the provision remains in force regardless of Israel's *spiritual* status—from Balaam's verbatim chant in Numbers 24:9 to the Messiah's paraphrase in Matthew 25:31-46, at the end of "Jacob's Trouble."

Abram's name appears in Genesis 11:31, the first Scripture where the phrase *"land of Canaan"* shows up. As this opening narrative unfolds, the key promise to Abraham's *physical* line is *land* (the obvious corollary for "seed").

> *So Abram departed, as the LORD had spoken unto him...And Abram took Sarai his wife, and Lot his brother's son, and all their substance that they had gathered, and the souls that they had gotten in Haran; and they went forth to go into the* LAND *of Canaan... And Abram passed through the* LAND *unto the place of Sichem, unto the plain of Moreh. And the Canaanite was then in the* LAND. *And the LORD appeared unto Abram, and said,* UNTO THY SEED WILL I GIVE THIS LAND. (Genesis 12:4-7)

The next stage of the promise involved land that Abram could *see*:

> *And the LORD said unto Abram, after that Lot was separated from him, Lift up now thine eyes, and look from the place where thou art northward, and southward, and eastward, and westward:* FOR ALL THE LAND WHICH THOU SEEST, TO THEE WILL I GIVE IT, AND TO THY SEED FOR EVER. *And I will make thy seed as the dust of the earth: so that if a man can number the dust of the earth,*

> *then shall thy seed also be numbered. Arise, walk through the* LAND *in the length of it and in the breadth of it; for I will give it unto thee.* (Genesis 13:14-17)

The third stage began with God testing Abram's faith:

> *And he brought him forth abroad, and said, Look now toward heaven, and tell the stars, if thou be able to number them: and he said unto him, So shall thy seed be. And he believed in the LORD; and he counted it to him for righteousness. And he said unto him, I am the LORD that brought thee out of Ur of the Chaldees,* TO GIVE THEE THIS LAND TO INHERIT IT. (Genesis 15:5-7)

He then gives Abram the actual boundaries of this unconditional, pre-circumcision, pre-Law land grant (comprising roughly 300,000 sq. miles): *"In the same day the LORD made a covenant with Abram, saying,* UNTO THY SEED HAVE I GIVEN THIS LAND, FROM THE RIVER OF EGYPT UNTO THE GREAT RIVER, THE RIVER EUPHRATES.*"* (Genesis 15:18) Whereas the LORD had said on the two previous occasions, *"I will give,"* He now says, *"I have given,"* a *covenant* favoring a more binding, formalized agreement.

Following the birth of Isaac, Ishmael fades off the radar as the LORD assures Abraham that *"in Isaac shall thy seed be called."* (Genesis 21:12) He later confirms this promise to Isaac personally:

> *Sojourn in this* LAND, *and I will be with thee, and will bless thee;* FOR UNTO THEE, AND UNTO THY SEED, I WILL GIVE ALL THESE COUNTRIES, AND I WILL PERFORM THE OATH WHICH I SWARE UNTO ABRAHAM THY FATHER; *And I will make thy seed to multiply as the stars of heaven...and in thy seed shall all the nations of the earth be blessed.* (Genesis 26:3-4)

After Jacob sows the seed for his own future victimization (via replacement theology) by hijacking the patriarchal blessing from Esau—specifically, that notable clause, *"cursed be every one that curseth thee, and blessed be he that blesseth thee"* (Genesis 27:29)—the LORD transfers the entire land package to the *goniff* at Bethel:

> *And, behold, the LORD stood above it, and said, I am the LORD God of Abraham thy father, and the God of Isaac:* THE LAND

> WHEREON THOU LIEST, TO THEE WILL I GIVE IT, AND THY SEED; *And thy seed shall be as the dust of the earth, and thou shalt spread abroad to the west, and to the east, and to the north, and to the south: and in thee and in thy seed shall all the families of the earth be blessed.* (Genesis 28:13-14)

Finally, twenty-eight years later the LORD reassures Jacob in Genesis 35:9-12 that the promise will pass to his twelve sons:

> *And God appeared unto Jacob again, when he came out of Padan-aram, and blessed him. And God said unto him, Thy name is Jacob: thy name shall not be called any more Jacob, but Israel shall be thy name: and he called his name Israel. And God said unto him, I am God Almighty: be fruitful and multiply; a nation and a company of nations shall be of thee, and kings shall come out of thy loins;* AND THE LAND WHICH I GAVE ABRAHAM AND ISAAC, TO THEE I WILL GIVE IT, AND TO THY SEED AFTER THEE WILL I GIVE THE LAND.

This exclusive, multigenerational, unconditional, perpetual real estate transfer is beautifully summarized in Psalm 105:6-11:

> *O ye seed of Abraham his servant, ye children of Jacob his chosen. He is the LORD our God: his judgments are in all the earth. He hath remembered his covenant for ever, the word which he commanded to a thousand generations. Which covenant he made with Abraham, and his oath unto Isaac; And confirmed the same unto Jacob for a law, and to Israel for an everlasting covenant: Saying,* UNTO THEE WILL I GIVE THE LAND OF CANAAN, THE LOT OF YOUR INHERITANCE.

Now while the Posse will condemn Jacob for his chicanery, casting him as the model for all of Jewry, etc., these professing Christian Israelites (or *whatever* they consider themselves), would attempt to *steal* the designated 300,000 sq. mile tract for themselves. (Ditto Herbert W. and Garner Ted Armstrong's British Israelism, and the moronic Mormons claiming the promise of Genesis 12:3 for English-speaking people.) The ploy is to *spiritualize* God's *non-spiritual* promise to Abraham's *physical* descendents in Genesis 12:1-3 (the promise to Abraham's *spiritual* children does not show up until six chapters later). Paul wrote in Galatians 3:13-14, *"Christ hath redeemed us from the curse of the law, being made a curse for us: for it is written, Cursed is every one that hangeth on a tree: That the* BLESSING OF ABRAHAM *might come on the Gentiles through Jesus Christ; that we might receive the* PROMISE OF THE SPIRIT THROUGH FAITH.*"* The *spiritual "blessing of Abraham"* constitutes the believer's imputed righteousness of verse 6 and justification of verse 8, both related to the indwelling work of the Holy Spirit promised by Jesus Christ in Luke 24:49, Luke 7:38-39, and Acts 1:4.

Galatians 3:8-9 is the Posse's key text in their misguided attempt to connect the *spiritual* blessing of Abraham to God's original promise in Genesis 12:1-3 regarding *material* blessings (specifically land) to Abraham's *physical* descendants: *"And the scripture, foreseeing that God would justify the heathen through faith, preached before the gospel unto Abraham, saying,* IN THEE SHALL ALL NATIONS BE BLESSED. *So then they which be of faith are blessed with faithful Abraham."* Based on that one phrase—*"in thee shall all the* NATIONS *be blessed"*—Alexis comments accordingly: "In other words, the prophecy in Genesis [12:3] cannot be applied in our time *outside of the faith in Jesus Christ.*"[34]

As only the Holy Spirit can do, just as that *other* notorious anti-Semite Haman wound up swinging *"from the gallows that he had prepared for Mordecai"* (Esther 7:9), Brother Jonas has been hoisted by his own petard—*semantics*. Having criticized John Hagee for "not put[ting] Scripture with Scripture"[35] while backhanding another for not "harmonizing Scripture with Scripture"[36] and still another for not "interpreting Scripture with Scripture,"[37] Jonas neglects to do the same, *discrediting his entire thesis in the process*. Contrary to popular opinion, Paul is *not* quoting Genesis 12:3 in Galatians 3:8. According to the inspired text of the A.V. 1611, Genesis 12:3 says, *"and in thee shall all* FAMILIES *of the earth be blessed,"* while Galatians 3:8 says, *"In thee shall all* NATIONS *be blessed."* (Uh, duh, "families" and "nations" are two entirely *distinct* entities.)

The verse Paul quotes to the Galatians is Genesis 18:18, *"Abraham shall surely become a great and mighty nation, and all the* NATIONS *of the earth shall be blessed in him."* As usual, the key to the exegesis is the context. Here, the LORD has just informed Abraham that Sarah will have a son (Genesis 18:10). Isaac, as Abraham's *literal* seed, will represent the major type of Christ through whom the *spiritual* blessing of

Abraham will flow (Galatians 3:16). Paul describes this in Romans 11:15 as *"the reconciling of the world."* Thus, the back-to-back revelations in Genesis 12 and 18 conform to the inspired order in I Corinthians 15:46, *"Howbeit that was not first which is spiritual, but that which is natural; and afterward that which is spiritual."*

Any scoffers who would label this classic case of right division a "textual coincidence" are referred to Genesis 22:17-18 for another. After Abraham passed his test on Mount Moriah, God praised him: *"That in blessing I will bless thee, and in multiplying I will multiply thy seed as the stars of the heaven, and as the sand which is upon the sea shore; and thy seed shall possess the gate of his enemies; And in thy seed shall all the* NATIONS *of the earth be blessed."* The gate is slammed in Genesis 26:3-4 with a matching pledge to Isaac himself:

> *Sojourn in this land, and I will be with thee, and will bless thee; for unto thee, and unto thy seed, I will give all these countries, and I will perform the oath which I sware unto Abraham thy father; And I will make thy seed to multiply as the stars of heaven, and will give unto thy seed all these countries; and in thy seed shall all the* NATIONS *of the earth be blessed.*

When the land grant passes to Jacob, the father of the twelve tribes of Israel, notice how the Holy Spirit rightly divides between Isaac and his son—preserving the *former* as the major type of Christ through whom the *spiritual* blessings will come:

> *I am the* LORD *God of Abraham thy father, and the God of Isaac: the land whereon thou liest, to thee will I give it, and to thy seed; And thy seed shall be as the dust of the earth, and thou shalt spread abroad to the west, and to the east, and to the north, and to the south: and in thee and in thy seed shall all the* FAMILIES *of the earth be blessed.* (Genesis 28:13-14)

With Abraham's descendants forged into a nation at Mount Sinai in Exodus 19:8, the LORD reaffirms His land grant before Moses in Deuteronomy 34:1-4, the eve of Israel's crossing into Canaan:

> *And Moses went up from the plains of Moab unto the mountain of Nebo, to the top of Pisgah, that is over against Jericho. And the* LORD *shewed him all the land of Gilead, unto Dan, And all*

> *Naphtali, and the land of Ephraim, and Manasseh, and all the land of Judah, unto the utmost sea, And the south, and the plain of the valley of Jericho, the city of palm trees, unto Zoar. And the LORD said unto him,* THIS IS THE LAND WHICH I SWARE UNTO ABRAHAM, UNTO ISAAC, AND UNTO JACOB, SAYING, I WILL GIVE IT UNTO THY SEED*: I have caused thee to see it with thine eyes, but thou shalt not go over thither.*

Throughout the ensuing centuries, the split lineage of *ethnic* and *spiritual* seed would continue via the immoral majority and the godly minority (the latter depicted in I Kings 19:18 as *"seven thousand in Israel, all the knees which have not bowed unto Baal"*). Crossing into the New Testament, upon Stephen's murder (Acts 7:58-60), the greater mass of Abraham's *physical* children are blinded (II Corinthians 3:14), while Abraham's *spiritual* children move on to join their Gentile brethren *in* the Body of Christ (Ephesians 3:6). Many of Abraham's blinded offspring continue to bless Earth's *families* via medical research, technology, and other humanitarian advancements. (Ironically, Adolf Hitler's family doctor was a Jew, Eduard Bloch.)

Finally, to the Posse's consternation, all *ethnic* Jews who survive the Tribulation will morph into *spiritual* Jews at the Second Advent, Paul writing in Romans 11:26, "AND SO ALL ISRAEL SHALL BE SAVED*: as it is written, There shall come out of Sion the Deliverer, and shall turn away ungodliness from Jacob."*

Thus, while *"all the* FAMILIES *of the earth" will be* blessed *by* and *with* Abraham's *physical* seed, vis-à-vis Israel's *future* restoration in the Millennium (their *material* inheritance obtained as "joint-heirs"), *"all the* NATIONS *of the earth" are being* blessed with and by Abraham's *spiritual* seed, vis-à-vis the imputed righteousness and justification resulting from Christ's Gospel in the *present* Church Age (their *spiritual* inheritance obtained through "faith"). At the end of the day (i.e., the "LORD'S Day"), God's plan for the Ages incorporates two lines of seed, with two sets of promises, resulting in two kinds of inheritances. With Jacob's name changed to Israel in Genesis 32:28, the prophetic/patriarchal order becomes: Abraham/Old Testament; Isaac/Church Age; Jacob/Tribulation; and Israel/Millennium. As the enduring hymn *All Hail the Power of Jesus' Name* puts it:

YE CHOSEN SEED OF ISRAEL'S RACE,
Ye ransomed from the fall,
Hail Him who saves you by His Grace,
And crown Him Lord of all.

THE RESTORATION OF ISRAEL

The main problem with the "math whiz" in South Korea (exemplified by the glaring misnumbered page count in his index), is that he cannot seem to handle that 1 + 1 = 2. While Jonas writes, "Yes, God did promise the Restoration of Israel in the Old Testament, and He kept His promise by bringing the people back to the land from Babylon,"[38] the Bible delineates *two* distinct physical restorations for the Jews; one for each of their *two* historical dispersions (586 BC and AD 70).

The *first* restoration was forecast in Isaiah 44:28 where Jehovah named the unborn Persian facilitator some 175 years *before* the event: *"That saith of* CYRUS, *He is my shepherd, and shall perform all my pleasure: even saying to Jerusalem, Thou shalt be built; and to the temple, Thy foundation shall be laid."* Observe next how the same prophet in Isaiah 11:10-12 records the climactic *second* restoration (inaugurated by Dr. Theodore Herzl) following the Great Tribulation:

> *And in that day there shall be a root of Jesse, which shall stand for an ensign of the people; to it shall the Gentiles seek: and his rest shall be glorious. And it shall come to pass in that day that the Lord shall set his hand* AGAIN THE SECOND TIME *to recover the remnant of his people which shall be left...and shall assemble the outcasts of Israel, and gather together the dispersed of Judah from the FOUR* CORNERS OF THE EARTH.

Whereas the *first* return was from Persia, the *second* will hail from *"the four corners of the earth."* Thus, dispensationalist Dr. Oswald J. Smith wrote, "None of it [Isaiah 11:1-13] was fulfilled at the first advent, and none of it can be spiritualized, for it has no fulfillment in the Church, in spite of what the great commentators say. God did not see fit to enlighten them."[39] Brother Jonas (apparently deficient in basic reading skills also) introduced Smith's quote with: "Smith went so far as to say that the prophecy of Isaiah 11:1-13, a passage which clearly talks about the coming of Jesus Christ, was not fulfilled."[40]

Amos 9:13-15 also details a second, final return: *"Behold, the days come, saith the LORD, that the plowman shall overtake the reaper, and the treader of grapes him that soweth seed; and the mountains shall drop sweet wine, and all the hills shall melt. And I will bring* AGAIN *the captivity of my people of Israel, and they shall build the waste cities and inhabit them...."* While this end-day remnant will be fulfilling the prophecy to *"plant vineyards, and drink the wine thereof...make gardens, and eat the fruit of them,"* the LORD will be doing a little tinkering with the soil Himself: "AND I WILL PLANT *THEM* UPON THEIR LAND, *and they shall* NO MORE *be pulled up out of their land which I have given them, saith the LORD thy God."* How could anyone but a mathematician confuse this pledge of permanency with the Jews' brief stay between Cyrus and Vespasian?

In Ezekiel 37 the Lord transports Ezekiel to the famous "Valley of Dry Bones" to illustrate the coming physical restoration. (The Mount of Olives Jewish cemetery is the most ancient cemetery in Jerusalem.)

> *And he said unto me, Son of man, can these bones live? And I answered, O Lord GOD, thou knowest. Again he said unto me, Prophesy upon these bones, and say unto them, O ye dry bones, hear the word of the LORD. Thus saith the Lord GOD unto these bones; Behold, I will cause breath to enter into you, and ye shall live: And I will lay sinews upon you, and will bring up flesh upon you, and cover you with skin, and put breath in you, and ye shall live; and ye shall know that I am the LORD. So I prophesied as I was commanded....* (Ezekiel 37:3-7)

The key for interpreting the vision is found in verses 11-12:

> *Then he said unto me, Son of man,* THESE BONES ARE THE WHOLE HOUSE OF ISRAEL: *behold, they say, Our bones are dried, and our hope is lost: we are cut off for our parts. Therefore prophesy and say unto them, Thus saith the Lord GOD;* BEHOLD, O MY PEOPLE, I WILL OPEN YOUR GRAVES, AND CAUSE YOU TO COME UP OUT OF YOUR GRAVES, AND BRING YOU INTO THE LAND OF ISRAEL.

After ending his sermon to the skeletons, the prophet is then instructed to preach another message to another unusual congregation. To illustrate the gravity of the greater, second restoration, the LORD has Ezekiel reaffirm His pledge—to the very ethnoscape itself.

> *Also, thou son of man, prophesy unto the mountains of Israel, and say...hear the word of the LORD...Because the enemy hath said against you, Aha, even the ancient high places are ours in possession... Because they have made you desolate, and swallowed you up on every side...Therefore, ye mountains of Israel, hear the word of the Lord GOD...I have lifted up mine hand, Surely the heathen that are about you, they shall bear their shame. But ye, O mountains of Israel, ye shall shoot forth your branches, and yield your fruit to my people of Israel;* FOR THEY ARE AT HAND TO COME. *For, behold, I am for you, and I will turn unto you, and ye shall be tilled and sown:* AND I WILL MULTIPLY MEN UPON YOU, ALL THE HOUSE OF ISRAEL, EVEN ALL OF IT...YEA, I WILL CAUSE MEN TO WALK UPON YOU, EVEN MY PEOPLE ISRAEL; *and they shall possess thee, and thou shalt be their inheritance, and thou shalt no more henceforth bereave them of men.* (Ezekiel 36:1-12)

The main difference between the two restorations is that the *latter* is followed by a spiritual one as well; again, after the Biblical order in I Corinthians 15:46, *"first...that which is natural; and afterward that which is spiritual."* The physical restoration is Israel to the land; the spiritual is Israel to the LORD. Having given God's pledge to Eretz Yisrael, Ezekiel elucidates the two-stage second return: *"For I will take you from among the heathen, and gather you out of all countries, and will bring you into your own land.* THEN *will I sprinkle clean water upon you, and ye shall be* CLEAN*: from all your filthiness, and from all your idols, will I cleanse you."* (Ezekiel 36:24-25) The order is clear: physical restoration *first*; spiritual conversion *second*. This is the main scriptural justification for Christian Zionism.

The Old Testament reveals that Israel's end-day deliverance will be even *more* glorious than her former deliverance from Pharaoh.

> *Therefore, behold, the days come, saith the LORD, that it shall no more be said, The LORD liveth, that brought up the children of Israel out of the land of Egypt; But, The LORD liveth, that brought*

up the children of Israel from the land of the north, and from all the lands whither he had driven them: and I will bring them again into their land that I gave unto their fathers. (Jeremiah 16:14-15)

So, which of the two scenarios will eclipse the Jews' original exodus from Egypt: Their three-part piecemeal return from Persia (536-446 BC); or, their three-part aliyah from *"*ALL THE LANDS *whither he had driven them"—commencing* with the "Balfour DECLARATION" (AD 1917), *continuing* through the "DECLARATION of Independence" (AD 1948), and *culminating* with her glorious national conversion at the Second Advent, constituting the symbolic fulfillment of Esther 10:2—*"the* DECLARATION *of the greatness of Mordecai* (a type of Israel), *whereunto the king advanced him"*?

The Jews' post-Tribulation revival will be triggered by a surreal encounter with their Messiah, for *"they shall look upon me whom they have* PIERCED.... *"* (Zechariah 12:10) Jonas disagrees; using *more* absurd exegesis, he cites John 19:36-37 to "prove" that "Zechariah 12:10... was accomplished when Christ died at the cross."[41] While he asks with indignation, "Why doesn't this plain reading of Scripture become obvious?"[42] the more pertinent question is, do he and his fellow Posse members *really* believe that the *"spirit of grace and of supplications"* was poured out *"upon the inhabitants of Jerusalem"*—when Christ was on the cross—like the context states in verse 10? Did the *"house of David...mourn for him, as one mourneth for his only son"* in AD 33? (Try selling *that* one to Stephen, James, and the other protomartyrs.) The answer is a no-brainer for Bible believers; the same Apostolic writer gives Zechariah's forecast its consummate fulfillment in Revelation 1:7, *"Behold, he cometh with clouds; and* EVERY EYE SHALL SEE HIM, *and they also which* PIERCED *him: and all kindreds of the earth shall wail because of him."* With the context set at the Second Advent, Zechariah 13:6 reads: *"And one shall say unto him, What are these* WOUNDS IN THINE HANDS*? Then he shall answer, Those with which I was wounded in the house of my friends."*

Finally, should the Posse want additional verses on Israel's future restoration, this author would suggest the following "shortlist": Isaiah 1:25-27; 2:1-5; 4:2-6; 11:11-13; 25; 26:1,2, 12-19; 27:13; 29:18-24; 30:18-26; 32:15-20; 33:13-24; 35; 37:31,32; 40:2,9; 41:27; 44; 49:13-23; 51; 52:1-12; 60; 61:4-9; 62; 66:5-22; Jeremiah 3:14-18; 4:3-18; 12:14-16; 23:3; 24:1-7; 29:1-14; 30:3-22; 32:36-44; 33; 44:28; Ezekiel 14:22-23;

16:60-63; 20:40, 41; 36:1-38; 37:12, 21; Daniel 11:30-45; 12:1; Joel 3; Amos 9:9-15; Obadiah 17-21; Micah 2:12, 13; 5:3; Zephaniah 2:7; Zechariah 1:14-21; 2; 8; 10:5-12; 12:1-14; 13; 14:3-21; Malachi 3:4; Romans 11; II Corinthians 3:16; and Revelation 7:5.[43]

DANIEL'S SEVENTIETH WEEK

All serious Bible students know that the books of Daniel and Revelation complement one another. The great key to understanding that God is *not* through with Israel is the prophetic timetable revealed in Daniel 9:20-27. The key to interpreting the passage, known as the "seventy weeks of years," is the cross-reference in Genesis 29:27. Here "a week" equals a period of seven *years* (rather than seven *days*). Thus, when Gabriel begins by saying, *"Seventy weeks are determined upon thy people,"* the Holy Spirit is announcing that the sequence He is about to rightly divide concerning Daniel's people (Israel) is 490 years in duration ("seventy sevens" at 360 days per year).

> SEVENTY WEEKS *are determined upon thy people and upon thy holy city, to finish the transgression, and to make an end of sins, and to make reconciliation for iniquity, and to bring in everlasting righteousness, and to seal up the vision and prophecy, and to anoint the most Holy. Know therefore and understand, that from the going forth of the commandment to restore and to build Jerusalem unto the Messiah the Prince shall be seven weeks, and threescore and two weeks: the street shall be built again, and the wall, even in troublous times. And after threescore and two weeks shall Messiah be cut off, but not for himself: and the people of the prince that shall come shall destroy the city and the sanctuary; and the end thereof shall be with a flood, and unto the end of the war desolations are determined.* AND HE SHALL CONFIRM THE COVENANT WITH MANY FOR ONE WEEK*: and in the midst of the week he shall cause the sacrifice and the oblation to cease, and for the overspreading of abominations he shall make it desolate, even until the consummation, and that determined shall be poured upon the desolate.* (Daniel 9:24-27)

This complex appearing 490-year span is split into three sequential stages. The first, starting around 450 BC with Artaxerxes' decree *"to restore and to build Jerusalem"* runs seven weeks (forty-nine years), during which the Holy City is rebuilt by Nehemiah. (Note the two English nuggets, *"to* RESTORE,*"* relating to the *first* "restoration," and the allusion to a schedule in Nehemiah 2:6, *"So it pleased the king to send me; and I set him a* TIME.*"*) The second interval extends sixty-two weeks (434 years), ending with the Messiah being *"cut off"* at Calvary in AD 33. Georges Antonius writes in *Unsealing Daniel*, "This is possibly the clearest Old Testament scriptural prophecy that Israel's Messiah must first die before he can reign. The Jews, unfortunately, were and are blind to this truth."[44] It is at this point (more precisely, after Stephen's murder), that the Jews are "cut off" for an indeterminate time (the Church Age, cited in Ephesians 3:1-12).

Following the Rapture ("catching away") of the Body of Christ in I Thessalonians 4:16-17, God's prophetic clock begins to tick again as He resumes His dealings with Israel by inaugurating the final week—the horrific, two-part, seven-year Tribulation described in Daniel 9:26-27. In the book of Job (the main Old Testament picture of this event), Job suffers *"upon the ground* SEVEN DAYS *and* SEVEN NIGHTS.*"* (Job 2:13) With the close of Daniel's Seventieth Week at the Second Advent, Israel's restoration will usher in *"everlasting righteousness."* Once again, the question of Jewish viability is reduced to simple math (i.e., *simple* for most); *this* time, subtraction, 490 – 483 = 7.

The right interpretation of Daniel 9:24-27 will produce two related eschatological doctrines. The first is the *pre*-Tribulation Rapture of the Church (as opposed to the *mid-* or *post*-Tribulation view), positing that Jesus removes His Church from the earth *before* the seven-year Tribulation begins (John 14:3; I Corinthians 15:51-52; I Thessalonians 4:16-17; 5:9). The second is the premillennial Advent of Christ (as opposed to the postmillennial or amillennial view), that Jesus returns to the earth with His Church *before* the Millennium begins (Revelation 19:11; 20:6). Incredibly, Jonas holds that *premillennialists* are the anti-Semites for "prophesying another persecution of the Jews."[45]

The opposing position, known as *preterism* (from the Latin prefix *praeter*, denoting that which is "past"), insists that all or most of the Old Testament prophesy regarding Israel was fulfilled by AD 70 (i.e., the destruction of Jerusalem and the Temple *was* the "Tribulation" and the "abomination of desolation"). Of course, the problem is always a lack of corroboration (no extant account that General Vespasian sat down in the *"temple of God showing himself that he is God,"* as mandated by II Thessalonians 2:4). Sir Robert Anderson wrote in *The Coming Prince*, "History contains no record of events to satisfy the predicted course of the seventieth week."[46] Naturally, the preterist heresy was developed by a sixteenth-century Jesuit, Luis de Alcasar, as a ratline for "Mother Rome's" escape from Revelation 17.[47]

The reality that Jesus Christ will rule on the Earth for 1,000 literal years is presented six times in six consecutive verses in Revelation 20:2-7. (The *English* nugget here is that 6,000 years of history will occur before the Devil is bound, conforming to the prophetic timetable in II Peter 3:8.) Still, Brother Jonas warns: "Right now 'the salt has lost his savor' among many evangelical Christians because they are being held captive by the falsehood of eschatological premillennialism…."[48] The pedagogue's only explanation is that "King Jesus" is *already* ruling over the earth, albeit—invisibly.

> Lewis Sperry Chafer, a champion of the dispensationalist camp, declares that 'one needs only to search the Scriptures to discover the fact that He [Jesus] is never mentioned as King of the church, nor even king of the nations until He comes again as "KING OF KINGS, AND LORD OF LORDS" (Revelation 19:16).' If He is not King of the nations [i.e., now], who is in charge then?[49]

The answer to this vacuous question is Satan, a.k.a. *"the god of this world"* (e.g., Job 9:24, Luke 4:6, John 18:36, and II Corinthians 4:4).

One should always remember that when New Israelites oppose a literal thousand-year Millennium, their main contention is not just with "any" kingdom *per se*, but with the scriptural rub that the only "thousand-year game in town" is a *Jewish* theocracy with a *Jewish* potentate ruling by *Jewish* law from a *Jewish* throne in a *Jewish* city, having a *Jewish* temple with *Jewish* sacrifices officiated by *Jewish* priests.[50] As Jonas wastes so much ink denying a future temple in Jerusalem ("Why is there not a single verse in the New Testament that even remotely makes a suggestion of a rebuilt Temple?"[51]), he may want to read—in addition to II Thessalonians 2:4—Ezekiel 40-48 where *nine* chapters involve the Millennial Temple. The vast material includes a priestly restriction against wearing *"any thing that causeth sweat"* (Ezekiel 44:18), as *"the last Adam"* (I Corinthians 15:45) has already done all the sweating *for* us (Genesis 3:19; Luke 22:44).

Clarence Larkin rightly concludes, "No such building as Ezekiel so minutely describes has ever yet been built, and so the prophecy cannot refer to either Zerubbabel's or Herod's Temple, and as there is to be no Temple in the New Jerusalem, it must be a description of the Temple that is to be on the earth during the Millennium."[52] (To head the Posse off at the pass at Hebrews 10:10-14, concerning the one effectual sacrifice of Christ, Ezekiel 45:17 clarifies that the Millennial sacrifices are not for *individual* salvation, but to *"make reconciliation for* THE HOUSE OF ISRAEL.*"*) Israel's "Christian" antagonists might also want to read the last verse in the book, as the Holy Ghost's appellation for future earthly Jerusalem would make a great title for Pastor Anderson's next movie—*"and the name of the city from that day shall be,* THE LORD IS THERE.*"* (Ezekiel 48:35)

In summary, while the Zionist movement obviously constitutes the tail end of Israel's rebellious efforts to "go it alone," spirit-filled believers discern that the miracle of 1948 was a prophetic epoch—one that should garner praise and thanksgiving as it confirms the nearness of the Rapture and the glorious restoration of the Jewish people. Such is the essence of a "*true* balance" in the ongoing debate over Zionism.

THE KJV'S UNIQUE PREMILLENNIAL ORDER

As previously noted, the specific order of II Chronicles, Ezra, and Nehemiah is unique to the A.V. 1611. The main events of these three Old Testament books foreshadow their modern antitypes accordingly: King Nebuchadnezzar's destruction of Jerusalem (II Chronicles), anticipating Jerusalem's destruction under Titus; the proclamation of Cyrus (Ezra), a type of the Balfour Declaration under King George V; and the returning remnant (Nehemiah), representing post-1948 Israel. (It is not without significance that Nehemiah has thirteen chapters, the Bible number for rebellion.) But why stop here? The next three books build on this inspired record of *future* history by affirming the twin doctrines of the pre-Tribulation Rapture and the premillennial return of Christ.

With the Rapture as the next major event on God's schedule, the book of Esther follows accordingly: Vashti, a *feminist* GENTILE bride, is replaced by Esther, a *submissive* JEWISH bride—the *former* unwilling to come in (Esther 1:12); the *latter* unwilling to stay out (Esther 5:1). Then, revealing that the Body of Christ goes up before the start of Daniel's Seventieth Week, Esther is followed by Job, the greatest Old Testament type of Israel in the Tribulation: Job suffers for *seven* days and nights; the book has 42 chapters, one for each month of the *Great* Tribulation; "Job" means "one persecuted"; Satan afflicts Job as he will afflict Israel (Revelation 12:13); Job's trial occurs in Edom (Lamentations 4:21), where the Jewish remnant will hide in the Tribulation (II Kings 14:7; Isaiah 63:1); finally, *"the LORD turn[s] the captivity of Job"* in the 42nd chapter (verse 10)—the *exclusive* KJV phrase equating to the turning of *Israel's* captivity in *her* 42nd month (Deuteronomy 30:3; Psalm 14:7; 85:1; 126:4; Jeremiah 32:44; 33:7, 11; Hosea 6:11; Joel 3:1; Amos 9:14; Zephaniah 3:20).

And so, with Israel's captivity turned, who do you think shows up? (Hint: Psalm 2:6 says, *"Yet have* I SET MY KING UPON MY HOLY HILL OF ZION,*"* the location of the "Dome of the Rock"). The book of Psalms, positioned *after* Job, represents an advanced revelation in the A.V. 1611 confirming that the Second Advent will occur at the *end* of Job's *week*-long ordeal—i.e., immediately *before* the Millennium begins. (One need only compare the KJV order of II Chronicles, Ezra, Nehemiah, Esther, Job, and Psalms with the Masoretic Text: Psalms, Proverbs, Job, Song of Songs, Ruth, Lamentations, Ecclesiastes, Esther, Daniel, Ezra, Nehemiah, I Chronicles, II Chronicles.)

THE "POWER OF POSITIVE THINKING"

The first word that Satan uttered to the first human beings in history was *"Yea"* (Genesis 3:1). Someone has said that the Devil is positive about mankind and negative about God's word, while the Lord is just the opposite—positive about the Bible (Psalm 138:2) and negative about humanity (Psalm 39:5).

As Scripture depicts those who deny Israel's future restoration as being *"wise in [their] own conceits"* (Romans 11:25), it is easy to see why so many of them deny dispensational premillennialism. Blinded by pride, deceived by naïveté, and fueled by positive thinking, the Posse can't take Paul's *negative* forecast of the end days (II Timothy 3:1-13; 4:3-4)—conditions *so* bad that only God can straighten them out. While numerous brain-dead American teens are now reverting to wearing diapers during marathon gaming sessions, in October 2015, an

8-year-old Tennessee (Bible Belt) girl was killed by a 12-gauge shotgun blast to the chest—her 55-pound, 11-year-old male assailant having pulled the trigger over an argument involving her puppy.

While God says that *"evil men and seducers shall wax* WORSE AND WORSE*"* (II Timothy 3:13) as they near His certain judgment (II Thessalonians 1:7-10; II Peter 3:10-12), note the humanistic hint by Jonas that Western culture could feasibly continue without King Jesus on the scene. Commenting on America's Christian foundation, he writes, "If those principles are deconstructed and thrown out as rubbish—as we are beginning to see—then America, like Rome and other great civilizations of ancient history, will soon become a heap of ashes."[53] He then shows surprise at what *real* Christians were told to watch for *and* expect in II Timothy 4:1-6: "Christianity, as we shall see, is one of the main pillars of Western Culture, and if it can be undermined, then the West will eventually crumble."[54]

His next gem is a real doozy (note the first word). "If the West is going to survive, it has to repudiate any movement that is not based on reason...."[55] Finally, while Paul affirms in Romans 8:7-8 that *"the carnal* MIND is *enmity against God: for it is not subject to the law of God, neither indeed can be,"* the worldly-wise Jonas assures us:

> As we have seen, in the mind of the Western world, a group is welcome in Western society as long as it does not seek to denigrate or subvert values inherent in Christianity and in the intellectual traditions that uphold the West. The Western mind, as E. Michael Jones points out, 'is traditionally born into a world that is radically reasonable, radically logical, because that world mirrors the mind of God, who behaves in ways that sometimes go beyond what human reason can comprehend but never in ways that contradict that reason.[56]

Somebody needs to inform "Jonas & Jones" that while Japheth has certainly experienced his predicted "enlargement" as the superior race (Genesis 9:27),[57] 90% of the Western world remains *non*-Christian (Matthew 7:13-14), with absolutely *no* recourse to the "mind of God" (I Corinthians 2:14-16; Philippians 2:5). In addition to her perennial anti-Semitism, as forecast in John 15:18-20 (and confirmed in *Foxe's Book of Martyrs*), the West's 2,000-year track record of persecuting Bible-believing Christians constitutes a serious indictment for the

Posse: *"Ye adulterers and adulteresses, know ye not that the friendship of the world is enmity with God? whosoever therefore will be a friend of the world is the enemy of God."* (James 4:4) Thus, the Bible affirms that in the Millennium, *every* UN member state will serve Israel while simultaneously submitting to the authority of the King's glorified Bride (Isaiah 14:2; 49:23; 60:10-12; Jeremiah 3:17; Joel 3:6-8; Matthew 25:21; II Timothy 2:12; Revelation 5:10; 19:15).

DARBY, SCOFIELD, AND LARKIN

Because the prophetic linchpin in Daniel 9 has enabled Christians to discern end-day events, it has naturally evoked a barrage of satanic attacks. Much of the abuse has fallen upon the three diverse pioneers of this edifying truth: John Nelson Darby (1800-1882), the Anglo-Irish Plymouth Brethren Bible teacher who received the Holy Spirit's initial leading in 1830; Cyrus Ingerson Scofield (1843-1921), the former Civil War veteran and US District Attorney for Kansas turned Congregationalist pastor, who incorporated Darby's teaching in his famous reference Bible in 1909; and Clarence Larkin (1850-1921), the mechanical engineer and architect-turned-Baptist pastor, who proliferated Darby's discovery through his classic 1919 publication, *Dispensational Truth: God's Plan and Purpose in the Ages.*

Mr. Darby is accused of fomenting needless discord over his "radical" views. "With Darby's pompous ideas, it was inevitable that he split the Plymouth Brethren into two,"[58] Jonas writes. While Larkin is often challenged over his lack of formal "theological training," even *Wikipedia* was willing to state: "His intricate and influential charts provided readers with a visual strategy for mapping God's action in history and for interpreting complex biblical prophecies."[59] Yet, "Larkin's charts" are despised by the Posse. For instance, Jeremiah 30:7 states: *"Alas! for that day is great, so that none is like it: it is even the time of Jacob's trouble, but he shall be saved out of it."* Note how Jonas takes the *preterist* position, assailing Larkin in the process.

> Nearly all Dispensationalists view Jeremiah 30:7 as something that will occur in the future. This idea was popularized at the beginning of the twentieth century by famous dispensationalist Clarence Larkin, most specifically in his book *Dispensational Truth.* Are

these dispensationalists prophesying another persecution of the Jews? (Most secular scholars would view this as anti-Semitic.)[60]

If Alexis is crazy enough to believe that Jeremiah 30:7 is past, how does he reconcile all of the obviously *pending* events listed in the ongoing context, starting with Israel's *permanent* rescue in verse 8?

The assaults against C. I. Scofield are mostly personal, accusations of business and political corruption in his *pre-conversion* years, along with his later divorce from the former Leontine Cerrè, a French Roman Catholic debutante from St. Louis. Rather than rejoice in the amazing providence that delivered an unsaved youth from eighteen Civil War battles (including Antietam, the bloodiest single-day action in US history) to produce his namesake reference work, Christian gossipmongers will revert to fake news: "*It is said* [author's emphasis] that in the church where Scofield was a pastor at the time, there is 'no mention of the divorce....'"[61] The Posse's logic is "unassailable": Christians should boycott the foremost study Bible that correlates the doctrinal significance of Jehovah's Old Testament *divorce* from Israel with the New Testament epistles of a converted *mass murderer* because the editor was a *divorced man* with a *checkered past.* Hello? As the adage goes, "The best of men are men at best"; God only *has* flawed vessels to use (II Corinthians 4:7). Having worn out a dozen Scofield Study Bibles since trusting Christ in 1974 (and in Clarence Larkin's home church, no less), this author joins countless others in rendering the spot-on testimony of John 9:25—*"Whether he be a sinner or no, I know not: one thing I know, that, whereas I was blind, now I see."*

THE IRON HORSE

The major objection to Daniel's Seventieth Week continues to be its recent exegesis. Jonas asks:

> [If] the dispensationalist teaching is so important, why has it escaped godly men through the centuries? Why has it escaped men such as Ignatius of Antioch, Polycarp, Irenaeus, John Chrysostom, and Athanasius? Many of these people do not even discuss the study of last things...Jonathan Edwards, William Tyndale, John Wycliffe, John Knox, Roger Williams, John Wesley, and even A. W. Tozer in

> the twentieth century, knew nothing about these dispensationalist teachings.[62]

That Darby's teaching not only surfaced in the Philadelphia Church Age, but in the nascent years of Zionism as well, should have caused spiritual people to notice. Dr. Charles Ryrie writes:

> The fact that something was taught in the first century does not make it right (unless taught in the canonical Scriptures), and the fact that something was not taught until the 19th century does not make it wrong, unless, of course, it is unscriptural…After all, the ultimate question is not, Is dispensationalism—or any other teaching—historic? but, Is it scriptural?[63]

Brother Jonas then cites dispensationalist Dr. H. A. Ironside, who confirms the protracted dormant status of the pre-Tribulation Rapture:

> Ironside challenged anyone who doubted his statement [i.e., that Darby's teaching 'is scarcely to be found in a single book or sermon through the period of sixteen hundred years!'] to study the writings of the early church, as he had done, to see if his statement could not be verified, and said, 'he will find the "mystery" conspicuous by its absence.'[64]

Well, it just so happens that the Apostle Paul, having written in I Corinthians 4:1, *"Let a man so account of us, as of the ministers of Christ, and stewards of the* MYSTERIES *of God,"* lists the Rapture of the Church *and* the Restoration of Israel—the corollary doctrines of Daniel's Seventieth Week—as two of ten major New Testament mysteries: *"Behold, I shew you a* MYSTERY*; We shall not all sleep, but we shall all be changed, In a moment, in the twinkling of an eye, at the last trump: for the trumpet shall sound, and the dead shall be raised incorruptible, and we shall be changed"* (I Corinthians 15:51-52); and, *"For I would not, brethren, that ye should be ignorant of this* MYSTERY, *lest ye should be wise in your own conceits; that blindness in part is happened to Israel,* UNTIL THE FULNESS OF THE GENTILES BE COME IN. *And so all Israel shall be saved…."* (Romans 11:25-26) Israel's blindness will end with the Gentiles' subjugation at the conclusion of Daniel's Seventieth Week:

> *But in the days of the voice of the seventh angel, when he shall begin to sound, the* MYSTERY OF GOD *should be finished, as he hath declared to his servants the prophets...And the seventh angel sounded; and there were great voices in heaven, saying,* THE KINGDOMS OF THIS WORLD ARE BECOME THE KINGDOMS OF OUR LORD, AND OF HIS CHRIST*; and he shall reign for ever and ever.* (Revelation 10:7; 11:15)

The Bible labels any who would deny Israel's restoration as being *"wise in [their] own conceits."* This has particular application to the Posse for sticking their noses into God's business (dictating how and when He should reveal His mysteries). In some cases, the revelation is the doctrine itself. Concerning the "Mystery of Christ" (the union of Jews and Gentiles in Christ's Body, the Church), Paul wrote:

> *For this cause I Paul, the prisoner of Jesus Christ for you Gentiles, If ye have heard of the dispensation of the grace of God which is given me to you-ward: How that by revelation he made known unto me the* MYSTERY*; (as I wrote afore in few words, Whereby, when ye read, ye may understand my knowledge in the* MYSTERY *of Christ*) WHICH IN OTHER AGES WAS NOT MADE KNOWN UNTO THE SONS OF MEN, *as it is* NOW *revealed unto his holy apostles and prophets by the Spirit; That the Gentiles should be fellowheirs, and of the same body, and partakers of his promise in Christ by the gospel....* (Ephesians 3:1-6)

However, at other times, the revelation is the "revelation *of* the revelation," often called "illumination," though more acutely tied to "inspiration" (the "breadth of the breath" as seen in Job 32:8, *"But there is a spirit in man: and the* INSPIRATION *of the Almighty giveth them* UNDERSTANDING*"*).[65] While man has all of the inspired Scripture God wants him to have, he does not have all of the spiritual understanding he needs. Though David could pen Psalm 23—the most familiar text in the Bible—even he had to pray, *"Open thou mine eyes, that I may behold wondrous things out of thy law."* (Psalm 119:18)

Sometimes these petitions went unanswered. And herein lies the scriptural vindication for Darby's so-called "pompous ideas." With the ink still wet on Daniel's original, the prophet was told to *"shut up the words, and seal the book,"* prompting the exchange: *"And I heard, but I understood not: then said I, O my Lord, what shall be the end of these things? And he said, Go thy way, Daniel:* FOR THE WORDS ARE CLOSED UP AND SEALED TILL THE TIME OF THE END.*"* (Daniel 12:4, 8-9) The same chapter then includes the two critical signs that will usher in the end-time comprehension of these prophetic utterances: *"But thou, O Daniel, shut up the words, and seal the book, even to the time of the end: many shall* RUN TO AND FRO, *and* KNOWLEDGE SHALL BE INCREASED.*"* (Daniel 12:4)

The *first* prophecy, accelerated transportation, began to unfold in the early 19th century with the railroad. The epic invention (a.k.a. "The Iron Horse") marked the first time that humans could travel faster than Adam and Eve (25-50 miles per day by horseback). America's first steam locomotive debuted at 18 mph in 1830, circa "Darby's Delayed Discovery." The most obvious sign, the creation of the Jewish State, was sandwiched between the breaking of the sound barrier in 1947 and the fulfillment of Daniel's *second* prophecy, the dawn of the modern computer age in 1951! While IAF F-15 and F-16 fighter jets can reach speeds of 1,500-1,650 mph, the country is less than 300 miles long (affording only about a ten-minute flight). Over twenty-five centuries after the double prophecy was made, its uncanny fulfillment is known by the internet metaphor—"Information Highway."

THE NEW COVENANT

The key reason that the Posse remains clueless about Israel's restoration is their inability to identify the "New Covenant." All replacement theology nuts confuse the New Covenant with the New Testament, the former belonging to Israel, the latter to the Church. Alexis writes:

> When Christ died on the cross, the age of ritualistic commandments was over, and the New Covenant—represented by those who accept Christ—has reigned ever since...The New Testament makes it quite clear that Jesus has established His new covenant, and outside of Jesus Christ there is no remission of sins. Therefore, we can reject the conclusion that God will bless nations if they happen to bless Israel.[66]

As usual, Brother Jonas is full of prunes. The specifics of the New Covenant are clearly laid out in Jeremiah 31:31-34, the LORD saying:

> *Behold, the days come...that I will make a new covenant with* THE HOUSE OF ISRAEL, *and with* THE HOUSE OF JUDAH: *Not according to the covenant that I made with their fathers in the day that I took them by the hand to bring them out of the land of Egypt; which my covenant they brake...But this shall be the covenant that I will make with the house of Israel; After those days...I will put my law in their inward parts, and write it in their hearts; and will be their God, and they shall be my people. And they shall teach no more every man his neighbour, and every man his brother, saying, Know the* L*ORD*: *for they shall all know me, from the least of them unto the greatest of them...for I will forgive their iniquity, and I will remember their sin no more.*

An honest exegesis reveals four points: First, God will make His New Covenant with the same people with whom He made the Old—*"*THE HOUSE OF ISRAEL*"* and *"*THE HOUSE OF JUDAH*"* (verse 31). It has *nothing* to do with the Church, the Israel of God, or spiritual Jews. Second, whereas the laws of the First Covenant were inscribed in tablets of stone when the Hebrews left Egypt, the laws of the New Covenant will be put in the their *"inward parts"* and written *"in their hearts"* when they exit the Great Tribulation (verse 33). Third, *every* Jew alive at that time will be saved (verse 34), pursuant to Romans 11:25-27.

> *For I would not, brethren, that ye should be ignorant of this mystery, lest ye should be wise in your own conceits; that blindness in part is happened to Israel, until the fulness of the Gentiles be come in. And so* ALL ISRAEL SHALL BE SAVED*: as it is written, There shall come out of Sion the Deliverer, and shall turn away ungodliness from Jacob:* FOR THIS IS MY COVENANT UNTO THEM, WHEN I SHALL TAKE AWAY THEIR SINS.

Last, Israel's revival will be so widespread that witnessing will be literally outlawed in the Millennium (Isaiah 11:9; Jeremiah 31:34) and may even be a capital offense as well (Zechariah 13:3).

Not *one* of these conditions has occurred to date, not even with the "Christian Israelites." As Romans 11:27 shows, when the New Testament was written, the New Covenant was still seen as a *future* event for *Israel* with *no* allusion that it was somehow "transferred" to the Church upon Christ's death. Yet, the Posse insists that the New Covenant has definitely arrived, etc.; of course, the only reason you can't actually *see* it is because it's invisible. Protestant apologist Hank Hanegraaff gives an excellent example of how his cronies *spiritualize* Jehovah's *physical* promises to Abraham's *physical* seed (via an article by Stephen Sizer on his Christian Research Institute website):

> The process of redemptive history has yielded a dramatic movement, from shadow to substance. The land that God once constrained to the specific place of His redemptive purpose He then expanded to the entire breadth of the created cosmos, through the New Covenant. The exalted Christ rules sovereign over the entire world, from the heavenly Jerusalem.[67]

The snag for these racists is Jesus' words: *"For this is my blood of the* NEW TESTAMENT, *which is shed for many for the remission of sins."* (Matthew 26:28) *Webster's 1828 Dictionary* defines testament as: "A solemn authentic instrument in writing, by which a person declares his will as to the disposal of his estate and effects after his death. This is otherwise called a will. A testament, to be valid, must be made when the testator is of sound mind, and it must be subscribed, witnessed and published in such manner as the law prescribes."

As B. R. Lakin would say, "Hold my mule while I shout!" On the eve of His death, Jesus Christ, "being of sound mind," declared *His* Last Will and Testament before twelve witnesses in the upper room. Regarding the "disposal of his estate," having testified in Luke 9:58, *"Foxes have holes, and birds of the air have nests; but the Son of man hath not where to lay his head,"* His only possessions were the souls God had given Him: *"Father,* I WILL *that they also, whom thou hast given me, be with me where I am...."* (John 17:24) This "final expense" would be *covered* by the *"blood of the New Testament."*

And it's all totally legit, as Matthew and John wrote it down *and* recorded it in a publication called—you got it—*The New Testament*. In book 19 of this 27-volume set, is a copy of the New Covenant from Jeremiah 31 (Hebrews 8:8-12), a reference to the *original* testament involving animal blood as a *temporary* covering (Hebrews 9:20), and the central legal requirement to confirm a valid Will and Testament:

> *And for this cause he is the mediator of the* NEW TESTAMENT, *that by means of death, for the redemption of the transgressions that were under the* FIRST TESTAMENT, *they which are called*

> *might receive the promise of eternal inheritance.* FOR WHERE A TESTAMENT IS, THERE MUST ALSO OF NECESSITIY BE THE DEATH OF THE TESTATOR. *For a testament is of force after men are dead: otherwise it is of no strength at all while the testator liveth.* (Hebrews 9:15-17)

Consequently, far from being the *same*, the New Testament and the New Covenant are *two* agreements, the *latter* predicated on the *former*. The blood of the New *Testament* not only offers salvation for all mankind, but a New *Covenant* for the reunited houses of Israel and Judah as well! In the meantime, soul winning is far from outlawed, for the resurrected Christ said on His way back to glory: *"Go ye into all the world and preach the gospel to every creature."* (Mark 16:15)

22

Naomi's Sojourn

"No one yet knows what awaits the Jews in the 21st century,
but we must make every effort to ensure that it is
better than what befell them in the twentieth,
the century of the Holocaust."
(Benjamin Netanyahu, 2000)

JOHN BUNYAN'S CLASSIC allegory, *The Pilgrim's Progress*, is generally regarded as the most influential book in the history of English literature, second only to the A.V. 1611 (Charles H. Spurgeon read it over 100 times). Published in 1678, *Pilgrim's Progress* has never been out of print. As Christian's *literal* pilgrimage winds to its close in the final days of the Church Age, a most bizarre transition is playing out (well beyond the creative genius of Bunyan himself).

At the end of the day, the "locksmiths of Laodicea" are seen to include both extremes in the Zionist debate. While one camp despises the Lord's "Jewishness," the other makes an idol of His "*Jewish* key" (many exchanging their fidelity to the KJV for Christian Zionism). In contrast to the transitional first-century pattern of witnessing *"to the Jew first"* (Romans 1:16), Hagee doesn't even believe that Jews need the Gospel, while Anderson concentrates on evangelizing Muslims at the Jews' expense. Thus, to close the Baptist minister's story in a purely allegorical (non-dogmatic) genre, the parallel climactic denouement of *Naomi's Sojourn* (the Hebrew version of *Pilgrim's Progress*—a.k.a. "The Wandering Jew"), will focus on a surreal chain of providential events that coalesce in the New Covenant.

RUTH AND BOAZ

The book of Ruth, known as the "romance of redemption," is one of only two Bible books that are named after a woman. While the Jewess Esther is a type of Israel, the restored Wife of Jehovah, the Gentile Ruth is a type of the Church, the espoused Bride of Christ. As the Bride passes the time of her betrothal on *earth*, represented in Scripture by the number four, we note that there are four letters in Ruth's name, her spouse's name, and her child's name, and four chapters in the book itself.

Seen by the words, *"the LORD hath brought me home* AGAIN *empty"* (Ruth 1:21), Naomi pictures modern Israel, returning to *her* land after a period of divine chastisement (Judges 2:15; Amos 4:6-11). With Naomi comprising *five* letters, the death number, we find the deaths of her husband and *two* sons (i.e., Israel and Judah) in Ruth 1:5. With Luke 21:24 implying that the Jews' ultimate aliyah can only be made after *"the times of the Gentiles be fulfilled,"* Naomi reappears in Ruth 1:4-6 after a ten-year "sojourn" in a Gentile land, *ten* being the Gentile number. Naomi's son Mahlon pictures the Law, as his death freed Ruth to be *"married to another"*; in type, *"even to him that is raised from the dead."* (Romans 7:4) Just as Romans 8:3 depicts the Law as *"weak through the flesh,"* the name Mahlon happens to mean "sickly." Then, as a *"wild olive tree"* cannot *"[partake] of the root and the fatness"* of the natural tree unless *"some of the branches be broken off,"* Naomi's entire line had to die so that Ruth the Moabitess could be *"graffed in."* (Romans 11:17)

Our hero makes his debut in chapter two: *"And Naomi had a kinsman of her husband's, a mighty man of wealth, of the family of Elimelech; and his name was Boaz."* As a type of Christ, Boaz is a Judean Jew from the tribe of Judah, born in Bethlehem, and related to Naomi. Within one verse of his name, the word *"grace"* appears (2:2). After Ruth is introduced to Boaz by an unnamed *"servant"* (a type of the Holy Spirit/John 16:13), the Gentile *"bowed herself to the ground,"* addressing Boaz as *"my lord"* (2:10, 13). Her confession, *"I am a* STRANGER...*not like unto one of thine handmaidens"* (2:10, 13), was a holy precursor to Paul's words in Ephesians 2:12, *"That at that time ye were without Christ, being aliens from the commonwealth of Israel, and* STRANGERS *from the covenants of promise, having no hope, and without God in the world."*

The main focus of the book is the manner in which Boaz and Ruth are brought together as husband and wife. The procedure that governed

Naomi's need for a "kinsman redeemer" was based on local tradition, particularly the custom of Levirate marriage (Deuteronomy 25:7-9). Thus, to simplify a complicated story, whenever a widow was constrained by poverty to sell the property of her late husband, a relative of the deceased could "redeem" the land on her behalf (either by purchasing it *from* her, or buying it back from another *for* her). If the widow was childless and still young enough to conceive, the kinsman would also be expected to marry her so that a male heir could be raised up to re-enter the family of the first husband, in order to perpetuate the patriarchal name, inheriting the land in the process.

Being past the age of fertility, Naomi counsels her daughter-in-law to pursue Boaz as her own kinsman redeemer, as the estate would eventually pass to her anyway (3:1-6; 4:3). While Ruth's subsequent nocturnal visit to Boaz may appear inappropriate, it was not so when judged by prevailing social mores. The key doctrinal application is that Ruth *initiated* the final stage of their relationship (Romans 10:13). As our Saviour promised in John 6:37, *"him that cometh to me* I WILL *in no wise cast out,"* Boaz likewise assured Ruth, *"And now, my daughter, fear not;* I WILL *do to thee all that thou requirest."* (3:11)

In the interim, whatever sustenance Naomi receives (like the *"six measures of barley"* in 3:17) can *only* come through Ruth, reflecting how Jews in the Church Age (the *"present time"* of Romans 11:5) can *only* be saved by trusting Christ, forming that *"remnant according to the election of grace."* That the Bible-believing Christian is the Jew's "BFF" is revealed by the meaning of Ruth's name—"friendship" (1:16-17). Yet, as Amos 3:3 asks rhetorically, *"Can two walk together, except they be agreed?"* Ruth and Naomi are shown to walk together no further than *Bethlehem*, a picture of Israel's historic rejection of the Virgin Birth.

As prefigured in 1:21-22, and prophesied in II Timothy 3:1, the final leg of their journey will spell doubt and danger for both. But then, *suddenly* (*"in the twinkling of an eye,"* Boaz meaning "quickness"), the pair will be parted by the words, *"So Boaz took Ruth"* (4:13; I Corinthians 15:52). Reflecting Ruth's eleventh-hour rapture, Lamentations 4:17 implies that Israel, deprived of *her* anemic evangelical lobby, will no longer be able to count on the USA: *"As for us, our eyes as yet failed for our vain help: in our watching we have watched for a nation that could not save us."* (Based on a revisited exegesis of Daniel 7, some posit that the three global-phobic kings/horns—prolonged by God in verse 12, to be subdued by Antichrist in verses 8, 20, and 24—are the "Brexit Britain" griffin of verse 4, the ravenous Russian bear of verse 5, and the multicultural American leopard of verse 6, making the NATO-leery "Trump of God's" rapprochement with the ultranationalist Vladimir Putin and choice of Theresa May as his first foreign visitor eerily significant.)

Meanwhile, a potential impediment surfaces that leads to yet another powerful truth. Although Boaz was a kinsman of Elimelech, he was not the *nearest* of kin. Thus, he would have to offer "the deal" (which included Ruth) to the *"kinsman nearer than I."* (3:12) When the presentation is formally made before the elders (numbering ten, as Christ's Bride would be mostly Gentile in nature), a startling reply is given by the *unnamed* nearer redeemer. While initially willing to accept the offer on behalf of Naomi, he was forced to decline when Ruth entered the arrangement: *"And the kinsman said, I cannot redeem it for myself,* LEST I MAR MINE OWN INHERITENCE: *redeem thou my right to thyself; for I cannot redeem it."* (4:6) Here, we find the *nearest* of kin being a type of God the Father, who already has His inheritance: *"For the LORD'S portion is his people;* JACOB IS THE LOT OF HIS INHERITANCE.*"* (Deuteronomy 32:9)

Though technically related to the Moabitess through creation (Ruth being the *"offspring of God"* depicted in Acts 17:29), Jehovah was not *about* to violate His own principal of "right division" by sanctioning Jew and Gentile as one *prior* to Calvary; only "Boaz" could do this, *"For* HE *is our peace,* WHO HATH MADE BOTH ONE, *and hath broken down the middle wall of partition between us."* (Ephesians 2:14) Thus, we discern the greatest decree affirming Boaz as a picture of Christ: *"Moreover Ruth the Moabitess, the wife of Mahlon,* HAVE I PURCHASED *to be my wife."* (4:10) Paul would exhort the Ephesian elders to *"feed the church of God, which* HE HATH PURCHASED *with his own blood."* (Acts 20:28) Then, as Naomi had assured Ruth that *"the man will not be in rest, until he hath* FINISHED *the thing this day"* (3:18), we see the import of John 19:30, *"It is* FINISHED,*"* and that He *also* finished before the end of the day. (John 19:31-33)

Finally, the purchase encompassed far more than the property of Ruth the Gentile (including her Hebrew in-laws as well): *"And Boaz said unto the elders, and unto all the people, Ye are witnesses this day, that I have bought* ALL THAT WAS ELIMELECH'S, AND ALL THAT WAS CHILION'S AND MAHLON'S, *of the hand of Naomi."* (4:9) And, as the *greater* "Boaz"—after being *"raised* UP*" from* the dead (Acts 2:24)—would *"ascend* UP" *with* the dead (Ephesians 4:8), transporting all the Old Testament saints from Paradise *"far above all heavens"* (Ephesians 4:10), we have that holy postscript: *"Moreover Ruth...have I purchased to be my wife, to raise* UP *the name of the dead upon his inheritance,* THAT THE NAME OF THE DEAD BE NOT CUT OFF FROM AMONG HIS BRETHREN.*"* (4:10)

"BLIND LEADERS OF THE BLIND"

But, alas, this beautiful scene represents God's *ideal.* The more accurate antitype for Ruth would be the Philadelphia-minded *remnant* faithfully gleaning in the closing shadows of Laodicea (Revelation 3:10-12). As covered in the Introduction, Revelation 3:20 depicts Boaz as locked out of His own church on the cusp of the Rapture.

Whereas Jehovah's wife was deemed unfaithful because of her idolatry, the end-day representatives of the Bride of Christ are not much better. In Revelation 3:17 Jesus rebukes the church of Laodicea for saying, *"I am rich, and increased with goods, and have need of nothing."* The cross-reference is Colossians 3:5, where covetousness is equated with idolatry. Ironically, the ultimate picture of this spiritual defection can be seen literally within steps of the Garden Tomb in Jerusalem (superintended by the Church of England). Among the various souvenirs for sale at the onsite Christian bookstore is an olive wood New International Version "Bible"—famous for deleting the only scriptural reference to the word "Calvary" (Luke 23:33).

The larger part of this end-day majority—the less-informed of the pro-Israel right (as opposed to the Posse)—is unconsciously acting out a prophecy in Matthew 15:14. Directing his words at the Pharisees, Jesus told his disciples, *"Let them alone: they be blind leaders of the blind. And if the blind lead the blind, both shall fall into the ditch."* As prefigured by the locksmiths of Laodicea, with Jesus on the wrong side of the door, the resultant loss of salt in "Christian" America has triggered a commensurate rise of global anti-Semitism (i.e., *secular* locksmiths). This, in turn, has led apostate Laodicea (specifically described as "blind" in Revelation 3:17) to *overcompensate* by making Israel (specifically described in Romans 11:7 as "blinded" also) its vicarious, feel-good pet project (i.e., the previously examined false balance of *worshiping* Jews without *witnessing* to them).

Thus, given Jacob's decided edge in the "cunning" department (Psalm 137:5), the present-day scenario is uncanny—blind *Jews* leading blind *Christians*; the former out for all the shekels they can hustle, the latter, only too willing to ante up. (As previously noted, "professing" Christians like Dr. Bryan Mark Rigg, traded his Baptist heritage for a kippah.) For an excellent case in point, consider the following "inspirational anecdote" concerning Moshe Dayan as featured on *Jerusalem-news.net* for April 4, 2012.[1] Entitled "Moshe Dayan and the Nazarene," the site accurately quotes a well-respected pro-Israeli American author[2] accordingly:

> I recently read an amazing statement from General Moshe Dayan as he lay on his death bed in 1981. A Hebrew-language newspaper in Jerusalem reported some of his last words: "All my life," the dying general said, "it seems that someone has been following me; and that someone was the Nazarene." Apparently Jesus of Nazareth significantly occupied Dayan's thoughts during his lifetime. We know there are many Jewish people like him who have heard about Yeshua and continue to wonder about Him.[3]

Any red-blooded Christian who loves Israel would certainly rejoice at such an amazing revelation. Given the aura of Dayan (at least in his better days), the imagery is striking. As Ruth Dayan recounted about her ex-husband's trademark profile, "[T]he eye patch was a symbol of the country at that time."[4] (In 2005, ninety years after Moshe saw the light of day as the second baby born on Israel's first kibbutz, his iconic eye patch was trading on eBay for $75,000![5]) From a spiritual view, who could better represent an entire race afflicted by *"blindness* IN PART*"*? (Romans 11:25) Of course, the only problem with this *story* is that there doesn't appear to be any proof. (Unable to elicit a return email from the writer, this author hired an Israeli researcher who also came up empty.) And yet, should this account prove false (as with those other unsourced tales from chapter sixteen), it would *still* be true that the one-eyed general was followed by the "Rock of Israel," I Corinthians 10:4, stating, *"for they drank of* THAT SPIRITUAL ROCK *that* FOLLOWED *them*: *and* THAT ROCK WAS CHRIST.*"*

A second, less familiar application of "blind Jews" leading "blind Christians" exists between certain Messianic groups and local Baptist congregations. While it is indeed a blessing to see unprecedented numbers of Jews finding Jesus Christ in the contemporary Messianic movement, especially in Eretz Yisrael (Sam Cohen once telling this author how "Jews for Jesus" had made a lasting impression on him), Independent Baptists must be careful to preserve their historic scriptural identity. After describing the coming Laodicean apostasy, Paul concludes by exhorting his pastoral protégé, *"But* CONTINUE *thou in the things which thou hast learned...."* (II Timothy 3:14)

Applying this charge to the closing days of the 400-year A.V. 1611 era, the scattered remnants of the Philadelphia Church Age need to continue *their* legacy of "keeping" the Holy Ghost-sanctioned English text of the Protestant Reformation (Revelation 3:8, 10). When New Testament Baptist churches start searching for God's truth in Hebrew codes, Shemitahs, Blood Moons, or any other esoteric, Kabbalah-styled revelation, it's time to hit the restart button—quick! And if certain Messianic leaders prefer the title "Rabbi," despite the proscription in Matthew 23:8, the scriptural answer would be, *"Forbid him not."* (Luke 9:50) But don't YOU go around calling them Rabbi, etc. (And remember, nobody goes to Heaven for simply accepting Jesus as *Messiah*; they get there for accepting Jesus as their *Saviour*.)

The specific warning regarding the blind leading the blind is that *"both shall fall into the* DITCH.*"* The cross-reference here is Proverbs 23:27, *"For a* WHORE *is a deep* DITCH*...."* With the Holy Spirit employing two chapters in Revelation to expose the Vatican WHORE, the application is clear—*both* groups will be adversely affected by Rome. Most end-day Christian Zionists have fallen into the ditch by *ditching* their A.V. 1611s for any number of satanic Bibles traced to a Catholic manuscript named after the Papal crib itself (Codex B, a.k.a. Codex *Vaticanus*). In the most subtle manner, an excessive focus on "Israel" has replaced the age-old veneration for the King James Bible. (Ironically, as if things could not get any more incongruous, many Posse members, led by Texe himself, are quasi-KJV advocates; Steven Anderson, the whack-job pastor of "Faithful Word" Baptist Church in Tempe, Arizona, spends considerable time promoting the Authorized Version while Brother Jonas quotes exclusively from the same.)

Also, many evangelicals, inspired by Rick Warren and other lucre-driven apostates, are currently headed back to Mother Rome at light speed.[6] On May 13, 2008, Pastor Hagee apologized to Catholics for criticizing their "church," primarily for having "emphasized the darkest chapters in the history of Catholics and Protestant relations with the Jews."[7] The erratic Christian Zionist who doesn't believe in evangelizing Jews whimpered: "Out of a desire to advance a greater unity among Catholics and evangelicals in promoting the common good, I want to express my deep regret for any comments that Catholics have found hurtful."[8] The Harlot's contempt for the Philadelphia Church Age remnant in America was shown when Pope Francis ended his historic 2015 pilgrimage with a Sunday Mass in the *City of Brotherly Love.* As an added dig, at Independence Hall he spoke from the same lectern that Abe Lincoln used in the Gettysburg Address. (See: *Rome's Responsibility for the Assassination of Abraham Lincoln* by General Thomas Harris, esteemed member of the nine-man military tribunal which tried and sentenced the conspirators.)

The spadework for Israel's fall into the ditch is the growing historic rapprochement between Tel Aviv and Vatican City. On March 15, 2013, the *Huffington Post* ran an article titled: "Pope Francis Reaches Out to the Jews." Ronald Lauder, president of the World Jewish Congress, said he feels that Francis will "speak out against all forms of anti-Semitism both within and without the Catholic Church, that he will take action against clerics who deny or belittle the Holocaust and that he will strengthen the Vatican's relations with Israel."[9] During his US pilgrimage, Fran sent America's Jews a special Yom Kippur greeting. After literally falling flat on his face in his own "ditch" during a mass in Poland in July 2016, the Argentine "Vicar of Christ" visited Auschwitz-Birkenau (the third consecutive pontiff to employ the prophetically relevant stunt). In an August 29, 2016, private audience, tech icon Mark Zuckerberg gave Francis a toy drone. (Three days later, his $150 million Facebook satellite exploded on the launch pad.)

The Jews will ultimately hit *their* ditch during *"the time of Jacob's trouble."* (Jeremiah 30:7) As prefigured in the main Old Testament book foreshadowing the Tribulation, Job laments, *"Yet shalt thou plunge me in the* DITCH.*"* (Job 9:31) Much of that future intrigue will undoubtedly involve the Pope's "service" as an interlocutor between the Jews and Antichrist. That Israel will find herself *in* the Roman Whore's DITCH is indicated by the LORD'S directive in Revelation 18:4 (recorded thirty years *after* Jerusalem is destroyed): *"*COME *OUT* OF HER, MY PEOPLE, *that ye be not partakers of her sins...."*

"HEDGED UP"

To digress, while most Bible believers are passionate in their support of the State of Israel, few understand the unique dilemma that the Jewish people face regarding the so-called "Road Map" to peace. Simply put, from a geo-political standpoint Israel is "hedged up."

Once again, as with Ruth and Boaz, this scenario was forecast over 2,700 years ago in the Lord's rebuke over Gomer's unfaithfulness to Hosea, a type of Israel's own spiritual adultery. *"I will hedge up thy way with thorns, and make a wall, that she shall not find her paths."* (Hosea 2:6) Having presented their Messiah with a crown of *thorns*, the Jews would experience nothing *but* thorns in a perennial "hedged up" existence ("hedge" being defined in *Webster's* as "to obstruct in any manner; to enclose for preventing escape").

Because of Israel's unwillingness to accept their *new* covenant, Jehovah literally "fixed things" so they would be unable to obey the commandments of the *first* covenant—by *evicting* them from their covenant land—*the very place where they were obligated to worship.* Henceforth, the Jew would be snared by the words of Deuteronomy 12:11, "THEN THERE SHALL BE A PLACE *which the LORD your God shall choose to cause his name to dwell there;* THITHER SHALL YE BRING ALL THAT I COMMAND YOU*; your burnt offerings, and your sacrifices, your tithes, and the heave offering of your hand, and all your choice vows which ye vow unto the LORD."* (This "place" was purchased by King David in II Samuel 24:18-25.)

In Hosea 3:4 the specifics of the approaching "Catch-22" are recorded: *"For the children of Israel shall abide many days without a king, and without a prince,* AND WITHOUT A SACRIFICE, *and without an image, and without an ephod, and without teraphim."* The preliminary stage of Israel's separation from her land was the seventy-year Babylonian captivity that began in 586 BC, vicariously described through Jeremiah's pen in Lamentations 3:7, *"He hath* HEDGED *me about, that I cannot get out."* Psalm 137:4 epitomizes their predicament: *"How shall we sing the LORD'S song in a strange land?"*

The second phase was inaugurated by the siege and destruction of Jerusalem by the Roman general, Titus, in AD 70. This was the "hedging" up that Jesus foretold in Luke 19:43 and 21:20. The view from the city wall in the closing days left no doubt as to what the word "hedge" meant.

History records that 500 Jews a day were being caught and summarily crucified,[10] Josephus adding, "till owing to the vast numbers there was no room for the crosses, and no crosses for the bodies"[11] (an eerie fulfillment of their own prophecy in Matthew 27:25, *"His* BLOOD *be on us, and on* OUR CHILDREN,*"* uttered only a *generation* earlier). With the eventual expulsion of the survivors, the really heavy judgments (and "rejoicing") of Deuteronomy 28:63 would begin.

Then, after twenty centuries of being "hedged up" in a worldwide Diaspora of pogroms and genocide, a Jewish remnant miraculously found itself back in the land—though as "hedged up" as ever. About the size of New Jersey, the modern State of Israel is bordered by four Arab nations, with the Mediterranean Sea to her back. And with "Allah's" flunkies in charge of the Temple Mount, Israel *still* cannot pursue her ancient worship. However, her greatest quandary has now become the focus of relentless international scrutiny.

Christians find it disconcerting that *any* Israeli (much less many) would endorse a two-state solution for the contrived Palestinian "problem." For example, in a July 7, 2010, interview on *Larry King Live*, Israeli Prime Minister Benjamin Netanyahu said that he spends an hour-and-a-half every Sabbath reading "from the Bible" with his younger son, gaining "enormous reservoirs of strength and relaxation." (Earlier that year, fifteen-year-old Avner Netanyahu won the prestigious National Bible Quiz for youth, stating: "The Bible is the very essence and foundation of the existence and spirit of the Jewish people.") And yet, the prime minister has consistently endorsed (albeit with conditions) a Palestinian state *within the historic boundaries of Israel*. Ironically, one of the many pertinent texts that this famous father and son would have encountered is Joel 3:2, where Israel's God explains that one day He will wipe out most of the world (including millions of Jews) for the unpardonable sin of having *"parted my land."*

Should Israel go with the "Road Map," her national security would be compromised even further by another demand that is never discussed by the liberal media. In his first address to the United Nations General Assembly on September 22, 2009, President Obama called for a "viable, independent Palestinian state with *contiguous* territory." What this translates to is that Gaza and the West Bank would have to be joined by a meaningful corridor, or easement. Thus, not only would the sole Jewish state in the world be downsized to a land mass smaller than

Rhode Island, but the remaining territory would be split in half, effectively creating *two* separate cantons.

Now, the reason why this untenable concession is practically inevitable is because "Gomer" is "hedged up" even further. The way the Lord has arranged things this time is simple: The Knesset has only three possible options: She can reject a two-state solution and continue the status quo—denying citizenship to the 4.2 million "Palestinians" in the West Bank and Gaza. However, this would only accelerate the already widening international condemnation from *without*, as the "crisis" is perceived as Middle East apartheid. Her second choice would be to reject a two-state solution while granting citizenship to her Arab residents. However, this would invite destruction from *within*, as Israel's continued existence as a "Jewish State" relies upon a sustained Jewish demographic majority. Of Israel's 8.5 million citizens (as of 2016), approximately 74.8% are Jewish; 20.8% are Arabs; and those identified as "others" (non-Arab Christians, Baha'i, etc.) make up 4.4% of the population. However, if everyone were suddenly lumped together into one big "happy" family, Israel's "voter edge" would drop to about 52% to 48%, a tenuous margin, indeed. Furthermore, all the experts agree that the non-Jewish population will definitely tip the scale in the immediate future. Then, as we have previously noted, the satanic United Nations wants to exacerbate matters by including *another* 4-5 million Palestinian "refugees" from outside of the country, vis-à-vis the "Right of Return" mandate in Resolution 194, specifically—"Article 11" (how appropriate). The realpolitik dilemma was articulated by Secretary of State John Kerry's adage, "If the choice is one state, Israel can either be Jewish or democratic; it cannot be both."

Thus, we can discern why Israel will come to believe that her only choice is option number 3—accepting a two-state solution; eliminating threats from both *within* and *without* in the process. Unfortunately, the only problem is that this time the destruction will come from *above*. In 586 BC, the Jews were *taken* out of their land; in AD 70, they were *thrust* out of their land; however, in 20??, they will *walk* out of their land—*voluntarily*—for perceived self-preservation. Consequently, we see God "hedging up" His own people for the final slaughter described in Ezekiel 9 and Revelation 4-19. As the greatest type of Israel in the Tribulation, we now understand the significance of Job's dilemma when he lamented, *"Why is light given to a man whose way is hid, and whom God hath* HEDGED *in?"* (Job 3:23)

MARRIED, DIVORCED, AND WIDOWED

The crux of the New Covenant in allegorical form is that Jehovah likens His original covenant with Israel to a marriage contract:

> *Behold, the days come, saith the LORD, that I will make a new covenant with the house of Israel, and with the house of Judah: Not according to the covenant that I made with their fathers in the day that* I TOOK THEM BY THE HAND [as any normal groom would do] *to bring them out of the land of Egypt;* WHICH MY COVENANT THEY BRAKE, ALTHOUGH I WAS AN *HUSBAND* UNTO THEM, *saith the LORD.* (Jeremiah 31:31-32)

Upon her symbolic, proxy betrothal in Genesis 15:18, Abraham's physical seed pledged her marital fidelity (as any normal bride would do) with a collective vow on Mount Sinai: *"All that the LORD hath* spoken WE WILL DO.*"* (Exodus 19:8) Notice the veiled reference to exclusive *intimacy* in Amos 3:2 (similar to Matthew 1:25 and Luke 1:34): *"You only have* I KNOWN *of all the families of the earth."* Unfortunately, in the process of time, Israel received a "BILL OF DIVORCE" for having *"treacherously departed from her* HUSBAND.*"* (Jeremiah 3:8, 20) The record of Israel's unfaithfulness (described in Isaiah 54:4 as *"the* SHAME *of thy youth"*) is particularly degrading. While Ezekiel 16:10-13 reveals that Jehovah would have given His bride any blessings she desired, verses 30-33 show that she preferred the services of a *gigolo* instead:

> *How weak is thine heart, saith the LORD GOD, seeing thou doest all these things, the work of an* IMPERIOUS WHORISH WOMAN*; In that thou buildest thine eminent place in the head of every way, and makest thine high place in every street; and hast not been as an harlot, in that thou scornest hire; But as a wife that committeth adultery, which taketh strangers instead of her husband! They give gifts to all whores:* BUT THOU GIVEST THY GIFTS TO ALL THY LOVERS, AND HIREST THEM, *that they may come unto thee on every side for thy whoredom.*

Another intriguing twist is the LORD'S reference to his *former* wife, specifically, *"the reproach of thy* WIDOWHOOD.*"* (Isaiah 54:4) Having received a *"bill of divorce"* from Jehovah (Jeremiah 3:8) Israel was permitted under the Law to *"be another man's wife."* (Deuteronomy 24:2) While Lamentations 1:1 states that the Babylonian captivity had caused Israel to become *"*AS *a widow,"* Hosea 2:7 implies that she became a widow through the *desertion* and *disappearance* of her subsequent significant others—*"and she shall seek them,* BUT SHALL NOT FIND THEM*: then shall she say, I will go and return to my* FIRST HUSBAND.*"* The underlying principle here is that while *ceremonial* marriage is standard (John 2:1-12), "marriage" per se, as established by the *first* marriage in Genesis 2:24, is actuated by "flesh joining flesh" (Deuteronomy 21:13; Matthew 19:4-6; Mark 10:6-8; I Corinthians 6:13-16; Ephesians 5:31). In any event, three separate scriptures, Jeremiah 3:8, Hosea 2:7, and Isaiah 54:4, describe Israel as *divorced*, *remarried*, and *widowed*.

Then, as Acts 3:19-21 shows, *had* Israel repented and accepted her Messiah, the LORD would have gladly reclaimed her *"when the times of refreshing shall come,"* following the seven-year Tribulation that *would* have begun after the Crucifixion and Resurrection. However, with Stephen's death, the New Covenant is put on temporary hold. (In the Church Age, the New Testament represents an interim spiritual application of the New Covenant to *all* believers, Jew and Gentile alike—similar to the parables of *"the mysteries of the kingdom of heaven"* in Matthew 13, illustrating the Kingdom of Heaven in its mystery form in the Church Age.) As previously indicated, it has rarely occurred to many that the lion's share of ensuing Jewish pain—the Holocaust representing the nadir of "Jacob's Trouble" *this* side of the Rapture—can be attributed to the stereotype of a defenseless divorcée/widow now having to fend for herself (not to mention one whom Satan is *determined* to destroy).

SATAN DIVORCES ROME FOR ISRAEL

Isaiah 28:15 states: *"Because ye have said,* WE HAVE MADE A COVENANT WITH DEATH, AND WITH HELL *are we at agreement; when the overflowing scourge shall pass through, it shall not come unto us: for we have made lies our refuge, and under falsehood have we hid ourselves."* When Israel enters the Tribulation, she will do the absolute unthinkable! (Better put your seat belt on for *this* allegorical finale.)

According to Daniel 9:27, the Beast makes a seven-year peace treaty with Israel: *"he shall confirm the* COVENANT *with many for one week."* More precisely (in the spirit of Leopold Amery), being a Jew himself (Daniel 11:37), *"he shall* CONFIRM *the covenant with many"* (render unprecedented diplomatic recognition to the historic Abrahamic Covenant). Thus, while the previous sins of Jehovah's imperious "ex" were confined to "hiring lovers," to attain her elusive goal of renewed spousal security (Hosea 2:7), Israel will *formally* "tie the knot" a second time, only now—*with the Devil himself.* (Satan may well be planning to lure persecuted World Jewry to Israel so he can turn the country into one big ghetto for the *final* Final Solution.)

Incumbent upon the use of proxies, the ghastly union will pair the acting Israeli prime minister with the Man of Sin (a Jew), who, as the antitype of Judas Iscariot, will also be indwelt by Satan (Luke 22:3; John 6:70; 13:27). And to make Israel feel even more secure, her new "hero" will resemble a coupling of the nation's two greatest military icons. While Yosef Trumpeldor and Moshe Dayan lost their left arm and eye, respectively, Zechariah 11:17, with Revelation 13:12-14, implies that Antichrist will lose his right eye *and* one of his arms.

But things get crazier yet. The reader will recall that the one who muses in Revelation 18:7, *"I sit a* QUEEN,*"* represents the ideal swinging spouse for the *"god of this world."* However, to marry Israel "right and proper like," the Devil will have to "officially" divorce his Vatican wife ("the lady of kingdoms" in Isaiah 47:5). Here, the Pope represents the spurned wife. To complicate matters, many Bible teachers hold that the "Holy Father" will be the infamous *second* Beast ("the false prophet" in Revelation 16:13). Should this be the case, then things would prove even wilder. John reveals that Beast number two will play the more powerful, behind-the-scenes role that the popes have traditionally exploited, handing the *political* aspirant his official *religious* endorsement, *"And he exerciseth all the power of the first beast before him, and* CAUSETH *the earth and them which dwell therein* TO WORSHIP THE FIRST BEAST*...."* (Revelation 13:12)

As Hebrews 7:7 says, *"And without all contradiction, the less is blessed of the better,"* all European kings have historically resented this inescapable handicap (the classic case occurring when Pope Leo III surprised Charlemagne on Christmas Day, AD 800, by crowning him Emperor of the Holy Roman Empire). The inherent power of the Vatican ho' is seen by her profile in Revelation 17, depicted in the title of Dave Hunt's bestseller, *The Woman Rides the Beast* (Revelation 17:3, 7, 9). In any event, Revelation 17:16 affirms that the Antichrist's political confederation *"shall* HATE THE WHORE, *and shall make her desolate and naked, and shall* EAT HER FLESH [an ironic dose of political justice for centuries of pagan transubstantiation], AND BURN HER WITH FIRE*"* (more reaping for her historic *auto-da-fés*).

The two beasts in the flesh, as the surrogate spouses of Satan and Rome, will also represent the model "gay couple." As noted previously, Daniel 11:37 says of the Antichrist: *"Neither shall he regard the God of his fathers* [showing that he is a Jew], *nor the* DESIRE OF WOMEN [showing that he is a sodomite], *nor regard any god* [showing that he is an atheist]*."* With "Holy Mother Church" paying *millions* of bucks to *thousands* of litigants in *countless* pedophilia lawsuits, is it *really* necessary to argue that "celibacy" is *against* nature? (Not to mention that I Timothy 3:2 lists marriage as one of the Biblical qualifications for a bishop.) In a July 29, 2013, *US News and World Report* article, "Catholic Priests: It's 'Imperial Fact' That Many Clergy Are Gay," Elizabeth Flock says of the author of *The Changing Face of the Priesthood*: "Rev. Donald B. Cozzens suggested that the priesthood was increasingly becoming a gay profession. Cozzens estimated that as much as 58% of priests were gay, and that percentages were even higher for younger priests."[12]

In the spirit of "Cardinal Franny" Spellman, Pope Francis is on record asking, "If someone is gay and he searches for the Lord and has good will, who am I to judge?"[13] (Illustrating Rome's unmitigated hypocrisy, while the same tolerant Pontiff reputedly voiced righteous indignation over Obama inviting several Catholic transgender activists to his 2015 welcome ceremony at the White House,[14] CBS correspondent Mo Rocca, an open sodomite, began the "Holy Father's" Madison Square Garden Mass with a Scripture reading!)

Requiring far less spiritual conjecture, Daniel 9:27 reveals that Israel's high-profile marriage of expediency lasts all of 42 months. Whereas Jacob fulfilled Rachel's "week" *twice* (Genesis 29:28), Antichrist breaks *his* week after just three-and-a-half prophetic "days": *"And he shall confirm the* COVENANT *with many for one week:* AND IN THE MIDST OF THE WEEK *he shall cause the sacrifice and the oblation to cease, and for the overspreading of* ABOMINATIONS *he shall make it* DESOLATE, *even until the consummation, and that determined shall be poured upon the* DESOLATE.*"* Note the cross-reference in Matthew 24:15-21, *"When ye therefore shall see the* ABOMINATION OF DESOLATION, *spoken of by* DANIEL *the prophet, stand in the holy place...Then let them which be in Judaea flee into the mountains...For then shall be* GREAT TRIBULATION, *such as was not since the beginning of the world to this time, no, nor ever shall be."* In Paul's account of this act, describing the *"son of perdition"* as one who *"opposeth and exalteth himself above all that is called God, or that is worshipped,"* he adds, "SO THAT HE AS GOD SITTETH IN THE TEMPLE OF GOD SHEWING HIMSELF THAT HE IS GOD." (II Thessalonians 2:4)

Rescuing the Mother-in-Law

For the next forty-two months, Satan writes the book on restraint order violations (Revelation 12:13-17). But then, when it's *just about over*, the greatest *ending* to the greatest *love story* in history will occur.

In what will also be the consummate "apocalyptic-apoplectic" encounter for whatever Posse members actually make it to Heaven via the pre-Tribulation Rapture (a doctrine most didn't even believe)—after giving an account of their asinine anti-Semitic "ministries" at the *"judgment seat of Christ"* (II Corinthians 5:10), followed by their participation in the *"marriage of the Lamb"* (Revelation 19:7), they, along with the rest of the *"armies which were in heaven"* (Revelation 19:14), will mount their *"white horses,"* wearing their wedding dresses, no less (Revelation 19:8), to follow their bridegroom back to Earth to rescue their Father's "former" wife, a.k.a. *their* future mother-in-law (as typed by Ruth and Naomi), from the clutches of the real "Snidely Whiplash," the world's ultimate villain—Lucifer himself!

Now, the reason why "former" is highlighted is because Jehovah never really *did* accept that *"bill of divorce"* stuff. Do you recall when He said in Jeremiah 3:8, *"for all the causes whereby backsliding Israel committed adultery I had put her away, and given her a bill of divorce"*? Well, only six verses later, He says something totally different: *"Turn, O backsliding children, saith the LORD;* FOR I AM MARRIED UNTO YOU*...and I will bring you to Zion."* (Ditto for that *"she is* NOT *my wife"* comment in Hosea 2:2). You see, when you're the *"blessed and only* POTENTATE*"* (I Timothy 6:15), you basically get to do *whatever* you want, *whenever* you want, etc. Note how this applies to the following relevant proscription in the Torah:

> *"When a man hath taken a wife, and married her, and it come to pass that she find no favour in his eyes, because he hath found some uncleanness in her: then let him write her a bill of divorcement, and give it in her hand, and send her out of his house. And when she is departed out of his house, she may go and be another man's wife. And if the latter husband hate her, and write her a bill of divorcement, and giveth it in her hand, and sendeth her out of his house; or if the latter husband die, which took her to be his wife;* HER FORMER HUSBAND, WHICH SENT HER AWAY, MAY *NOT* TAKE HER AGAIN TO BE HIS WIFE, AFTER THAT SHE IS DEFILED; FOR THAT IS ABOMINATION BEFORE THE LORD: AND THOU SHALT NOT CAUSE THE LAND TO SIN*...."* (Deuteronomy 24:1-4)

This would certainly *appear* to disqualify Jehovah from ever remarrying Israel after her several "incidental indiscretions," capped by her 42-month legitimized marriage to Satan. But again, as Jeremiah 3:1 shows, when you're "THE LORD," you do as you please: "THEY SAY, *If a man put away his wife, and she go from him, and become another man's, shall he return unto her again? shall not that land be greatly polluted? but thou hast played the harlot with many lovers;* YET RETURN AGAIN TO ME, SAITH THE LORD*."* Can't you just see those New Israelites who make it to the Judgment Seat? "But Lord, I *know* that I read in John 8:44—in my KJV, no less—where you told those sorry Jews they were *"of their father the devil,"* etc., and *now* you're telling me you're gonna take them back??? *"Wilt thou be altogether unto me as a liar?"* (Jeremiah 15:18)

Jude 14 says, *"Behold the Lord cometh with ten thousands of his saints,"* and what an exhilarating ride that will be! While Revelation 19:11 has the Lord leading on a white steed, because verse 16 adds that He is "KING OF KINGS AND LORD OF LORDS," don't be surprised if King Jesus kind of stands out from the rest. According to Psalm 18:10, the Lord *and* his horse may actually descend upon the back of a majestic heavenly cherub! In any event, contrary to the teaching of KJV-denying evangelicals, Jesus and his armies do not go *directly* to the Mount of Olives (this is where He *ultimately* arrives and dismounts, as per Zechariah 14:4). As the Bible contains roughly 1,800 individual prophecies on 700-plus subjects in over 8,350 verses (representing 27% of some 31,100 total verses), an amazing string of prophetic chain references imply an extensive and detailed itinerary (a.k.a. "The Path of the Second Advent").

Coming from *"the north"* (Isaiah 14:31) to *"Damascus"* (Isaiah 17:1), the Heavenly Expeditionary Force (HEF)—*totaling every single person who was ever saved in the Church Age*—seems to proceed as follows: Marching through Syria (Amos 1:5), then over to Tyre (Amos 1:10), the Lord *storms* into Armageddon (Zechariah 12:11; Judges 5:19); next, it's down the ancient Gaza Strip to annihilate the modern Philistines, arriving in Egypt for more devastation (Isaiah 19:1); the campaign then reverses course at Mt. Sinai (Deuteronomy 33:1-3) to shadow the Old Testament route of the Holy Ark, advancing into Edom southeast of the Dead Sea (Amos 1:11),*"leaping upon the mountains"* (Song of Solomon 2:8), specifically, Mt. Seir, Mt. Teman, and Mt. Paran (Judges 5:4-5; Habakkuk 3:3, 8-16; Psalm 45:1-8; 68:1-4, 8-9; Song 2:8, 3:6;); then, over to Bozrah (Isaiah 63:1), up the King's Highway (Numbers 20:14-17; 21:22), and on through to Moab (Jeremiah 48); here, the incursion turns west over the Jordan where Joshua and the Ark, as well as David, Elijah, and Elisha crossed, no doubt at the very site where Jesus' was later baptized; *finally*, after passing through a fissure in Mt. Olivet (Zechariah 14:4), it's over a Muslim cemetery and through the cemented Eastern Gate (Ezekiel 44:1-2) into the City of David itself (Zechariah 12:8).[15]

JEWS IN THE TRIBULATION

Now, it would be natural to assume that Jesus' dramatic arrival in Jerusalem would be the climax of His return. However (as alluded to by the actual mission objective), an earlier scene could very well top even that (at least from God the Father's perspective).

While some prophecies are easily discerned, many are shrouded in a spiritual mist (I Corinthians 13:12). Comparing Scripture with Scripture, the Jews in the Tribulation appear divided into three categories. One group, numbering 144,000 male virgins, is sealed on Earth in Revelation 7:4-8, then viewed in Heaven in Revelation 14:1-4, indicating a mid- or post-Tribulation rapture to attend the Marriage of the Lamb (Esther 2:2; Psalm 45:14; Song of Solomon 1:3, 6:8; Matthew 25:1-13; Revelation 19:7).

Unlike the Church, described as a *"chaste virgin"* (singular) *"espoused... to Christ"* in II Corinthians 11:2, the virgins (plural) in Matthew 25:1-13 do not *marry "the bridegroom,"* they go to *meet* Him at His marriage to another, i.e., "the Church" (Luke 12:35-37). Of course, their sudden appearance (accompanied by Moses and Elijah) will represent one *more* shock for the Posse to absorb as they prepare to mount their chargers. As the Christian soldiers on *"white horses"* in Revelation 19:14 (described as *"terrible as an army with banners"* in Song of Solomon 6:13) cross-referenced with the Jewish riders on *"white asses"* in Judges 5:10 appear to imply—the 144,000 just might constitute the ultimate fulfillment of the Zion Mule Corps!

Apart from this supernatural body of globetrotting evangelists (i.e., the *real* Jehovah's witnesses), the Tanakh indicates that two-thirds of the rest of World Jewry will perish, while one-third will survive:

> *And it shall come to pass, that in all the land, saith the LORD, two parts therein shall be cut off and die; but the third shall be left therein. And I will bring the third part through the fire, and will refine them as silver is refined, and will try them as gold is tried: they shall call on my name, and will I will hear them: I will say, It is my people: and they shall say, The LORD is my God.* (Zechariah 13:8-9)

The one-third that survives further divides into two parts. One group *endures* and then *believes* at the Second Advent (Zechariah 12:10-14; 13:6; Romans 11:1; 25-26). According to Mark 13:27 (with Matthew 8:11; 24:31), these eleventh-hour converts shall be gathered together *"from the* UTTERMOST *part of the earth to the* UTTERMOST *part of heaven"*—no doubt having been harbored by God-fearing Gentiles who learned about the Judgment of the Nations from the 144,000 (Matthew 25:31-46). The applicable cross-reference here reveals that although I Thessalonians 2:16 rightly predicts *"wrath is come upon them to the* UTTERMOST," Hebrews 7:25 affirms, *"Wherefore he is able to save them to the* UTTERMOST *that come unto God by him...."* The highlight of this world-wide harvest will be the reaping of the vital symbolic core under siege in Jerusalem (Zechariah 12:1-14; 14:1-7).

However, as Jesus said in John 20:29, *"[B]lessed are they that have not seen, and yet have believed,"* the second group, acting in reverse, *believes* (the preaching of the 144,000, reinforced by the two witnesses), then *endures* in *"her place"* of refuge (Revelation 12:14) to await the return of the Lord from His marriage to the Church (Luke 12:35-37). *"And I will bring you out from the people, and will gather you out of the countries wherein ye are scattered, with a mighty hand, and with a stretched out arm, and with fury poured out. And I will bring you into the* WILDERNESS *of the people, and there will I plead with you face to face. Like as I pleaded with your fathers in the wilderness of the land of Egypt...."* (Ezekiel 20:34-36)

Thus, we see that the Jews who survive, do so in three areas: "the world" (the uttermost part of the Earth); "the land" (Eretz Yisrael); and "their place" (Petra). This third group is the faithful remnant that represents the figurative "mother-in-law" to be rescued by the Church.

"ROCK OF AGES"

The aforementioned foray into Edom will provide a different take on that "Rock of Israel" business. The "scholarly" exposition for the word *Selah* (meaning "rock") is usually limited to "a musical notation indicating an intended place for pause and meditation," etc. However, II Kings 14:7 reveals that Selah was a fortress city in Edom conquered by King Amaziah. Today, that mountainous site is known as *Petra*. Notably, as seen by Léon De Laborde's 19th-century steel engraving, the *Ruinen von Selah Petra* ("Ruins of Selah Petra"), the rock-walled city of Petra was once called by its *full* name—Selah Petra.

Premillennial believers usually hold that Mount Petra is the refuge that Jesus was referring to in Matthew 24:16: *"Then let them which be in Judaea flee into the mountains."* Group three repairs here in the Tribulation, where God feeds them miraculously like He did ancient Israel in the wilderness (Psalm 74:14; Micah 7:14; Revelation 12:14). This was forecast in Exodus 33:22 where the LORD told Moses (one of the two witnesses in the Tribulation): *"And it shall come to pass, while my glory passeth by,* THAT I WILL PUT THEE IN A CLIFT OF THE ROCK, *and will cover thee with my hand while I pass by."*

In 1763, British hymnist Augustus Toplady composed the immortal lines, *"Rock of Ages cleft for me, let me hide myself in thee."* (Legend says that he wrote the lyrics while taking shelter from a storm in the gorge of Burrington Combe in the Mendip Hills of England.) Thus, wherever "Selah" shows up in the Old Testament (especially in the Psalms), the context is always the Second Advent. (Pause and meditate on *that*!)

By way of an interesting aside, in the early 1970s, an elite IDF anti-terrorism group (known only as "a recon unit of the GHQ"), had an uncanny initiation rite—a *voluntary* thirty-mile, four- to five-day trek from the Israeli border across a perilous stretch of Jordanian desert to Petra. The main threat was that the route traversed several damp wadis where unavoidable footprints would alert Bedouin patrols, a picture of what the Antichrist will do to the Jewish remnant. (Inductees who declined the challenge would be passed over for critical missions.)[16]

The harbinger buzzword ("Selah") appears thrice in Habakkuk, chapter three, alone (3:3, 9, 13). The action picks up at verse 12: *"Thou didst march through the land in indignation, thou didst thresh the heathen in anger"* (the area named in verse 2 as Teman and Paran). According to the unfolding scenario, the King and his armies will sweep in and save the Jewish remnant in Selah Petra. (Contrary to popular opinion, *this* is the "day" prophesied in Isaiah 66:8, not May 15, 1948.) We therefore perceive that Israel—*saved by a stone* in the War of Independence—will be *rescued in a rock* in the Great Tribulation!

Jesus then torches the entire locale (Obadiah 15-21), where it continues to burn throughout the Millennium (Isaiah 34). As cited in chapter six, cross-referencing Isaiah 34:9 with Revelation 14:11 further indicates that the smoldering region will morph into man's worst nightmare—the literal fulfillment of his oft-repeated flippant remark about undergoing "Hell on earth," only *this* time, he will get the whole enchilada—the "Lake of Fire" itself! In the LORD'S Millennial *"rod of iron"* justice (Revelation 19:15), whoever repudiates the Sermon on the Mount will be tossed *alive* into the streams of burning pitch in the land of Idumea (Isaiah 34:6-9; 66:24; Matthew 5:22, 29-30; 10:28; Mark 9:43-48).

Christian reader, can *you* visualize *your* participation in this dramatic eleventh-hour rescue of the Father's Bride? It is the arch-fulfillment of every stereotypical martial raid in history (from Douglas MacArthur's immortal, "I have returned," to "Yonni" Netanyahu's daring "Operation Thunderbolt"). Like the believer's subliminal affinity for Hebrew, it's the main reason why your spirit resonates at the cadence of a *military* parade—*especially* one that incorporates "the pipes." Can you *even* imagine riding down with angelic bagpipers playing "Amazing Grace"? It also explains why you can hardly hold back the tears when singing hymns like "Hold The Fort" and "Keep on the Firing Line." (The tactical details of this coming rescue are scattered throughout the English text of an A.V. 1611 Old Testament; Joel 2:1-11 will get you started.)

WHATEVER HAPPENED TO "NANA NAOMI?"

To end our Jewish version of *The Pilgrim's Progress* where we began, the great love story in Ruth concludes with Boaz and his bride living "happily ever after." But what of Ruth's mother-in-law; how did *she* spend *her* golden years? The last glimpse we have of "Nana Naomi" shows her caring for Obed (4:16), the royal grandfather of King David. Thus, the fullest extent of her *"restoration of life"* and *"nourishment in old age"* must be left to spiritual speculation (4:15). However, while we cannot know what happened to the *historical* Naomi—as we have previously seen—the Bible *does* reveal what *will* happen to her great *antitype*, the nation of Israel. The LORD will eventually *"allure her into the wilderness and speak comfortably unto her,"* thrice vowing specifically, *"I will* BETROTH *thee unto me."* (Hosea 2:14, 19-20)

Now if Israel's *literal* remarriage to the LORD were to be applied back to the original types of our narrative—*for the sake of illustration alone*—a most remarkable event "would have" occurred. With the widow Naomi as a type of *Israel*, and the nearer kinsman-redeemer a type of *Jehovah*, we understand that *their* eventual reconciliation "would have" constituted the *ultimate* "Rest of the Story"! (Remember that this unnamed kinsman had initially agreed to rescue Naomi's parcel, declaring, *"I will redeem it,"* declining only when Ruth the *Gentile* entered the picture.) Thus, if we "read in the white" (i.e., between the lines), Elimelech "would have" actually represented Naomi's *second* husband—the one responsible for that costly sojourn in Moab. While no type plays out in *every* particular, the inspiring truth to "glean" from this purely allegorical scenario is that the *Church's* marriage to *Jesus* will be followed by *Israel's re*marriage to *Jehovah*. (Moral of the story: Replacement Theology is out of Hell!)

WAITING FOR THE SHOE TO DROP...

The final type in our allegory constitutes a solitary *shoe*. When the kinsman-redeemer waived his right of redemption, he removed his shoe and gave it to Boaz as a means of solemnizing the transaction.

> *Now this was the manner in former time in Israel concerning redeeming and concerning changing, for to confirm all things;* A MAN PLUCKED OFF HIS SHOE, AND GAVE IT TO HIS NEIGHBOUR*: and this was a testimony in Israel. Therefore the kinsman said unto Boaz, Buy it for thee.* SO HE DREW OFF HIS SHOE. (Ruth 4:7-8)

According to the similar rite of Levirate marriage in Deuteronomy 25:10, the declining kinsman *"shall be called in Israel, The house of him that hath his* SHOE LOOSED.*"* The custom in Ruth's day probably began with the idea that the right to "tread the soil" belonged *solely* to the owner. Thus, the transfer of a sandal would serve as an appropriate object lesson for the relinquishment of this right. (Moses was told to remove *his* shoes when standing on *Jehovah's* mountain.)

Once again, the related typology is profound. As the antitype for the nearer redeemer, God the Father would also have to remove *His* shoe as the symbolic deferring to Jesus Christ, the antitype of Boaz. And, in this holy supposition we are not left without cross-references, for *twice* the LORD declares in Psalms 60:8 and 108:9, "MOAB *is my washpot;* OVER EDOM WILL I CAST OUT MY SHOE.*"* (Note the distinct allusion to Ruth, the Moabitess, and Edom, the specific site of the rescue.) According to the context in both passages, the Father will kick off His shoe somewhere over Edom in the Tribulation, just in time for those Heavenly festivities described by John in Revelation 19:7: *"Let us be glad and rejoice, and give honour to him: for the marriage of the Lamb is come, and his wife hath made herself ready."* Meanwhile, as *we* await that glorious day, may we glean *our* fields with patience, being mindful of that classic pledge of selfless fidelity:

"And Ruth said, Intreat me not to leave thee, or to return
from following after thee: for whither thou goest, I will go;
and where thou lodgest, I will lodge: thy people shall be my people,
and thy God my God: Where thou diest, will I die, and there
will I be buried: the LORD do so to me, and more also,
if ought but death part thee and me."
(Ruth 1:16-17)

23

Three Graves

"For God so loved the world, that he gave his only begotten Son, that whosoever believeth in him should not perish, but have everlasting life."
(John 3:16)

THE STATE OF Israel was born three years after the Holocaust. As previously noted, Ted Berkman wrote the definitive work on the life of Colonel David "Mickey" Marcus. The opening line of *Cast a Giant Shadow* follows: "High above the tranquil Hudson, where the grounds of the United States Military Academy dip toward the shadowed folds of Storm King Mountain, stands the West Point Military Cemetery."[1] The author then proceeds to enumerate several of the famous Americans buried within the stone-walled enclosure (General George A. Custer, Lieutenant General Winfield Scott, et al.).

Berkman then writes, "In this gallery of military immortals, one grave is unique. It stands near the cemetery entrance, a few yards from the shrub-lined path that winds west from the Old Cadet Chapel. Here an American soldier was laid to rest on a warm early summer's day in 1948."[2] After citing the many dignitaries who attended the interment, he concludes:

> What chiefly sets this burial plot apart, however, is not the tributes paid that day, nor the cluster of battlefield and public glory that attaches to it. It is the only one, of all the three thousand-odd graves at West Point, that marks the resting place of a soldier killed fighting under a foreign flag.

> The headstone is wedge-shaped and solid, as was the man who lies beneath it. The inscription it carries might justly have read, 'Here lies a man who, after long and devoted service to his city and his country, felt democracy had unfinished business overseas. Like Lafayette before him, he carried his fight for human dignity to a struggling young republic far away, helping to shape a citizens' army. In the teeth of the enemy he carved out of naked mountainside the unseen road that saved the people of besieged Jerusalem, then fell at the city's gates, the first to hold the rank of General in the Army of Israel since biblical times.' The gravestone bears instead, in letters chiseled deep to withstand snow and wind and rain, the quiet legend: 'Colonel David Marcus—A Soldier for All Humanity.'[3]

Three thousand years before Berkman employed the word "shadow" in the first sentence of his biography, Mickey's namesake penned the word in what has become the most recognized chapter of the entire Bible: *"Yea, though I walk through the valley of the* SHADOW *of death, I will fear no evil...."* (Psalm 23:4) Indeed, David Marcus *cast a giant shadow* for World Jewry by sacrificing his own life to provide his battered race with a refuge in Eretz Yisrael. Though doctrinally applicable to the LORD alone, in a vicarious sense, Marcus made it possible for Shoah survivors (and their descendants) to proclaim: *"Under his* SHADOW *we shall live among the heathen,"* for they *"that dwell under his* SHADOW *shall return...."* (Lamentations 4:20; Hosea 14:7)

However, while Berkman is *technically* correct that the Marcus burial plot is indeed unique among the "military immortals," there is *another* headstone in the West Point Military Cemetery that is even *more* unique than that. This other grave—located about "a *stone's* throw away"—belongs to the realm of "*non*-military immortals."

ANNA BARTLETT WARNER

On January 22, 1915 (five years before David entered West Point), the academy's most distinguished civilian neighbor passed away at the age of eighty-seven. Since childhood, Anna Bartlett Warner and her older sister Susan had lived in a fine Manhattan townhouse with their widowed father, Henry Whiting Warner, a prominent attorney and real-estate speculator. (His older brother, Thomas, entered the ministry and served as West Point Chaplain from 1828 until 1838.)

In 1836, Henry purchased Constitution Island (located on the east side of the Hudson River opposite West Point), hoping to build an elegant resort and hotel. (The strategic 282-acre isle is the site of the earliest Revolutionary War fortifications in the Hudson Valley, specifically the "Great Chain.") However, the Panic of 1837 devastated his finances, forcing him to relocate his family to a primitive farmhouse on the new island property. As temporal tragedies will often trigger spiritual breakthroughs, both sisters were subsequently converted to Christianity (joining New York's Mercer Street Presbyterian Church in 1841).

By 1849, Mr. Warner's portfolio had little improved. Anna and her sister began writing poems and short stories to supplement the household income. After their father's death in 1875, the two unmarried siblings struggled to keep the bills paid, their goal being to keep Constitution Island, by then the prized target of numerous commercial investors. With Susan's passing in 1885, Anna fought on alone, selflessly refusing one lucrative offer after another, resolved to save the historic locale for "The Point." Finally, in 1908 (aided by philanthropist Margaret Sage), Anna was able to donate Constitution Island to the United States of America. In gratitude, the sisters were posthumously honored as the only non-military-related civilians interred at West Point Cemetery.

While the world would dismiss Anna and Susan as a couple of religious spinsters, many West Point graduates would disagree. On Sundays, Christian cadets would routinely row out to the island for Bible studies with the sisters. In *Constitution Island*, Ronnie Coffey adds, "Aside from Bible class, small groups of cadets were regularly invited to dinner or afternoon tea."[4] However, the *main* inspiration for their visits will surprise you. They wanted to meet Anna, the one who had written the most famous hymn of their childhood—"Jesus Loves Me."

Thus, while the subtitle of Berkman's book is *The Story of Mickey Marcus Who Died to Save Jerusalem*, Anna wrote about the *One Who died to save Mickey Marcus* and the *rest* of the world as well!

JESUS LOVES ME

Jesus loves me! This I know,
For the Bible tells me so;
Little ones to Him belong;
They are weak, but he is strong.

REFRAIN:
Yes, Jesus loves me!
Yes, Jesus loves me!
Yes, Jesus loves me!
The Bible tells me so.

Jesus loves me! He who died
Heaven's gate to open wide;
He will wash away my sin,
Let his little child come in.

REFRAIN

Jesus loves me! He will stay
Close beside me all the way;
Thou has bled and died for me.
I will henceforth live for Thee.

REFRAIN

Postscript: In 1995, a baby girl was born blind, then diagnosed with cerebral palsy. Before she could talk, the child was humming Warner's nineteenth-century classic, "Jesus Loves Me," and playing the piano by age two. Fast-forwarding to January 21, 2017—with half-a-million anti-God, pro-abortion, Trump-hating feminists fulminating outside—Marlana VanHoose sang "How Great Thou Art" in the Washington National Cathedral Inaugural Prayer Service, moving the tearful First Lady, Melania Trump, to lead a standing ovation for the Christian prodigy; *"...and their works do follow them."* (Revelation 14:13)

Mickey Marcus
Headstone
(Brittany Stein)

The Garden Tomb
(Author's Collection)
"He is not here: for he is risen...."
(Matthew 28:6)

Anna B. Warner
Headstone
(Brittany Stein)

Epilogue

"And they come to Jesus, and see him that was possessed with the devil, and had the legion, sitting, and clothed, and in his right mind: and they were afraid."
(Mark 5:15)

IT SHOULD COME as no surprise that *Holy Ground* was written to help point Jews to Jesus Christ as their Saviour, Lord, and Messiah. The last person to call on Jesus in His earthly ministry was an unnamed, condemned Jewish criminal—a.k.a. "The thief on the cross" (Matthew 27:38-44; Mark 15:27-28; Luke 23:32-43; John 19:18, 32). That the Messiah would die among the dregs of society was specifically prophesied in the Tanakh: *"And he made his grave with the wicked... and he was numbered with the transgressors...."* (Isaiah 53:9, 12)

And yet, there is more. Not only does God specialize in saving the so-called "hard cases" (Genesis 18:14; Jeremiah 32:27), but He will also employ them in His service (Acts 9:15-16). For instance, He used three murderers to write nineteen books of the Holy Bible—Moses, David, and Paul. The latter constitutes the quintessential case of divine mercy. Having produced—as Saul of Tarsus—the *worst* track record of any *prospect* in Scripture (Acts 8:3; 26:9-11; Galatians 1:13; Ephesians 3:8; and I Timothy 1:15), the Apostle Paul produced the *most* tangible results of any *convert* in Scripture (II Corinthians 11:5, 22-33; Galatians 1:15-24; Ephesians 3:1-12).

As an addendum to his Damascus Road experience (Acts 9:1-31; 22:1-16; 26:9-18), Paul relates in I Timothy 1:12-16 that he made his proverbial way "from the *guttermost* to the *uttermost*" to serve as the ultimate plumbline of God's long-suffering:

And I thank Christ Jesus our Lord, who hath enabled me, for that he counted me faithful, putting me into the ministry; Who was before a blasphemer, and a persecutor, and injurious: but I obtained mercy, because I did it ignorantly in unbelief. And the grace of our Lord was exceeding abundant with faith and love which is in Christ Jesus. This is a faithful saying, and worthy of all acceptation, that Christ Jesus came into the world to save sinners; of whom I am chief. Howbeit for this cause I obtained mercy, that in me first Jesus Christ might shew forth all longsuffering, for a PATTERN *to them which should hereafter believe on him to life everlasting.*

Ironically, with "HaTikvah" (meaning "The Hope," taken from II Kings 22:14 and Ezra 10:15) as the national anthem of Israel, the Jews have been singing about Jesus Christ for decades, albeit unknowingly, for Paul—the converted murderer-turned-preacher—refers to the spurned Jewish Messiah accordingly: *"Looking for that blessed* HOPE, *and the glorious appearing of the great God and our Saviour Jesus Christ."* (Titus 2:13) Consequently, the following surreal testimony of *another* converted Jewish murderer-turned-soul winning Christian who found "hope" in Jesus—having committed *his* crimes in ignorance and unbelief as well—is reprinted (by permission of the author) in the sincere *hope* that it will give YOU hope!

SON OF HOPE
THE TESTIMONY OF DAVID BERKOWITZ

My name is *David Berkowitz* and I am a prison inmate who has been incarcerated since 1977. I have been sentenced to prison for the rest of my life. I was the notorious murderer known as "*Son of Sam.*"

It was in 1987, when I was living in a cold and lonely prison cell, that God got hold of my life. Here is my story of *hope*.

CHILDHOOD

Ever since I was a small child, my life seemed to be out of control. I was like a wild and destructive animal. My mother had no control over me. My father had to pin me to the floor until I calmed down.

When I was in public school, I was so violent and disruptive that a teacher had to grab me in a headlock and throw me out of his classroom. I got into a lot of fights. Sometimes I started screaming for no reason. I was plagued with bouts of severe depression. Eventually my parents were ordered by the school officials to take me to a child psychologist or else I would be expelled. I had to go to the psychologist once a week for two years, yet the therapy sessions had no effect on my behavior.

THOUGHTS OF SUICIDE

Thoughts of suicide often came into my mind. Sometimes I spent time sitting on a window ledge with my legs dangling over the side. We lived on the 6th floor of an old apartment building. When my dad saw me doing this he would yell at me to get back inside. I had no idea what to do and neither did my parents. They had me talk to a Rabbi, teachers, and school counselors, but nothing worked.

THE DEATH OF MY MOTHER

When I was 14, my mother was stricken with cancer. Within several months she was dead. I had no brothers or sisters, so it was just my dad and me. He had to work 10 hours a day, six days a week. We spent very little time together.

For the most part, my mother had been my source of stability. With her now gone, however, my life quickly went downhill. I was filled with anger at the loss of my mom. I felt hopeless, and my periods of depression were more intense than ever. I also became even more rebellious and began to cut out of school.

My dad tried to help as best he could. He managed to push me through high school. The day after I graduated, I went into the Army. Even in the service I had trouble coping, though I did manage to finish my three-year enlistment.

INVOLVEMENT IN THE OCCULT

I got out of the service in 1974 to start life again as a "civilian." All my friends that I knew before had either married or moved away. So I found myself living alone in New York City.

In 1975 I met some guys at a party who, I later found out, were heavily involved in the occult. I had always been fascinated with witchcraft, Satanism, and occult things since I was a child. When I was growing up, I watched countless horror and Satan-type movies, some of which totally captivated my mind.

Now I was 22 and the forces of Satan were becoming more and more evident in my life. I felt as if something was trying to take control of my life. I began to read the Satanic Bible by the late Anton LaVey who founded the Church of Satan in San Francisco in 1966. I began, innocently, to practice various occult rituals and incantations.

I am utterly convinced that something satanic had entered into my mind and, looking back at all that happened, I realize that I had been slowly deceived. I did not know that bad things were going to result from all this, yet over the months the things that were wicked no longer seemed to be such. I was headed down the road to destruction and I did not know it. Maybe I was at a point where I just didn't care.

THE HORROR BEGINS

Eventually, I crossed that invisible line of no return. After years of mental torment, behavioral problems, deep inner struggles, and my own rebellious ways, I began committing horrible crimes. Looking back, it was all an awful nightmare and I would do anything if I could undo everything that happened. Six people lost their lives. Many others suffered at my hand and will continue to suffer for a lifetime. I am sorry for this.

In 1978 I was sentenced to about 365 consecutive years, virtually burying me alive behind prison walls. When I first entered the prison system I was placed in isolation. I was then sent to a psychiatric hospital because I was declared temporarily insane. Eventually I was sent to other prisons including the infamous "Attica."

HOPE APPEARS

Ten years into my prison sentence, when I was feeling despondent and without hope, another inmate came up to me as I was walking the prison yard one cold winter evening. He introduced himself and began to tell me that Jesus Christ loved me and wanted to forgive me. Although I knew he meant well I mocked him because I did not think that God would ever forgive me or that He would want anything to do with me. Still this man persisted, and we became friends. His name was Rick, and we would walk the yard together. Little by little he would share with me about his life and what Jesus had done for him. He kept reminding me that no matter what a person did, Christ stood ready to forgive if that individual would be willing to turn from the bad things he was doing and would put his full faith and trust in Jesus Christ and what He did on the cross—dying for our sins. He gave me a Gideon Pocket Testament and asked me to read the Psalms. I did. Every night I would read from them. It was at this time the Lord was quietly melting my stone-cold heart.

A NEW LIFE BEGINS

One night I was reading Psalm 34. I came upon the 6th verse which says, *"This poor man cried, and the LORD heard him, and saved him out of all his troubles."* It was at this moment, in 1987, that I began to pour out my heart to God. Everything seemed to hit me at once—the guilt of what I had done and the disgust at what I had become. Late that night in my cold cell I got down on my knees and began to cry to Jesus Christ.

I told Him that I was sick and tired of doing evil. I asked Jesus to forgive me for all my sins. I spent a good while on my knees praying to Him. When I got up it felt as if a heavy but invisible chain that had been around me for so many years was broken. A peace flooded over me. I did not understand what was happening. In my heart I just knew that somehow my life was going to be different.

FREEDOM!

More than 27 years have gone by since I had that first talk with the Lord. So many good things have happened in my life since. Jesus Christ has allowed me to start an outreach ministry right here in the prison where I have been given permission by prison officials to work in the "Special Needs Unit." This is where men who have various emotional and coping problems are housed. I can pray with them as we read our Bibles together. I get the chance to show them a lot of brotherly love and compassion. And sometime I get the opportunity to teach or preach in the chapel.

In addition, my story has since gone into countless prisons and youth facilities in America and abroad. Friends have also set up a website where one can view my story on video or read my journal. In 2012 I was invited to be the keynote speaker during the city of Suffolk, Virginia's National Day of Prayer gathering. About 400 people, many of them military personnel and government officials, attended this event as I addressed them via video. I have also been able to tell millions around the world, via television programs such as Larry King Live, what Jesus has done for me.

THERE IS HOPE FOR YOU, TOO

One of my favorite passages of Scripture is *Romans 10:13*. It says, *"Whosoever shall call upon the name of the Lord shall be saved."* Here it is clear that God has no favorites. He rejects no one, but welcomes all who call upon Him.

I know that God is a God of mercy who is willing to forgive. He is perfectly able to restore and heal our hurting and broken lives. I have discovered from the Bible that Jesus Christ died for our sins. He took our place on the cross. He shed His blood as the complete payment God required for our sins.

The Bible says, *"All have sinned, and come short of the glory of God"* (Romans 3:23). Furthermore, it says, *"The wages of sin is death; but the gift of God is eternal life through Jesus Christ our Lord"* (Romans 6:23). These passages make it clear that everyone has sinned. Some like myself, are worse sinners than others, but *all* have sinned. Therefore, we must all acknowledge our sins before God, own that we deserve God's judgment for eternity, and realize that we are *lost*!

When we reach the point of realizing that we are *lost*, guilty, ruined sinners, then we will be ready to accept the Savior whom God has provided for us. Who is this Savior? He is the Lord Jesus Christ who is the Creator of the universe and the eternal Son of God who came into this world as a Man. As perfect, sinless Man, he suffered and died on the cross for our sins (I Corinthians 15:3; I Peter 2:24; 3:18). Then He was buried and on the third day He rose again in victory, for death could not hold Him. If you realize you are lost and need a Savior, then place your full, undivided faith and trust in the Lord Jesus Christ who died for *your* sins. *"He was wounded for* OUR *transgressions, He was bruised for* OUR *iniquities: the chastisement of* OUR *peace was upon Him; and with His stripes,* WE *are healed"* (Isaiah 53:5). Have you put *your* name in this verse? To reject the Lord Jesus Christ and His work on the cross is to reject God's perfect and only gift of salvation and eternal life.

HERE IS YOUR OPPORTUNITY

Friend, here is your opportunity to get things right with God. The Bible says, "If thou shalt confess with thy mouth the Lord Jesus, and shalt believe in thine heart that God hath raised him from the dead, thou shalt be saved. For with the heart man believeth unto righteousness; and with the mouth confession is made unto salvation" (Romans 10:9, 10). So believe in your heart that these words from the Bible are true and apply to you. Please consider what I am saying. I beg you with all my heart to place your faith in Christ right now! Do not be ashamed to do this! Do not wait for a more convenient time! Tomorrow is promised to no one. Do not wait for your death bed, for you may not have one! "Behold, NOW is the accepted time; behold, NOW is the day of salvation" (II Corinthians 6:2).

WHAT DIFFERENCE WILL IT MAKE?

Once you place your trust in Jesus Christ as your Savior and Lord, the Holy Spirit will start a life-long work of transformation in your life

(Romans 12:1, 2) so that you will begin, finally, to do works and deeds that are pleasing to God (Ephesians 2:8-10; Titus 2:14). With some this work may proceed more rapidly than with others, or may be intermingled with failures and setbacks. But the more your focus is on Christ your Savior, the more the Holy Spirit will help you to get the victory over the sin patterns in your life (Romans 6-8). Best of all, you now have the assurance of eternal life with Christ (John 3:16; I Thessalonians 4:15-17) in heaven.

CONCLUDING COMMENTS

I am not sharing this message simply to tell you an interesting story. Rather I want you to taste the goodness of God in the life of a man who was once a Satan-worshiper and a murderer, to show you that Jesus Christ can bring about forgiveness, hope, and change.

I was involved in the occult and I got burned. I became a cruel killer and threw away my life as well as destroying the lives of others. Now I have discovered that Christ is my answer and my hope. He broke the chains of sin, self-will, and depression that had me bound. He has turned me from a path leading to eternal damnation in the lake of fire to the blessed assurance of eternal life in heaven. God has miraculously transformed "Son of Sam" into "Son of Hope." He wants to perform the same kind of transformation in your heart and life today!

Thank you for reading this. May God bless you.
Love in Christ, David Berkowitz

[This testimony is available in tract form from Moments with The Book, PO Box 322, Bedford, Pennsylvania. You may also visit David's website at www.AriseAndShine.org.]

Appendix 1

Why Many Jews Accept Jesus Christ as their Saviour and Messiah

"...and now the Lord GOD, and his Spirit, hath sent me."
(Isaiah 48:16)

"In the beginning was the Word, and the Word was with God, and the Word was God. The same was in the beginning with God...And the Word was made flesh, and dwelt among us, (and we beheld his glory, the glory as of the only begotten of the Father,) full of grace and truth."
(John 1:1-2, 14)

"For there are three that bear record in heaven, the Father, the Word, and the Holy Ghost: and these three are one."
(I John 5:7)

IN THE SOUTHWEST extension of modern Jerusalem, stands the Shrine of the Book (a wing of the Israel Museum), home to the famed Dead Sea Scrolls, discovered in Qumran on the eve of Israel's Independence. (The reader will recall that Yigal Yadin did his doctoral thesis on the leather scrolls.) The enigmatic white-domed, cave-simulated structure, designed as one of the fifty pottery jar covers found in Cave I, is considered a benchmark of twentieth-century museum architecture.

Centered directly beneath the dome is a giant cylinder, over twenty-five feet in circumference, displaying the feature exhibit—The Great Isaiah Scroll (1QIsa[a])—one of the seven original Qumran Scrolls. Dated from 125 BC (some 1,000 years earlier than the oldest extant Hebrew manuscripts, yet validating the Masoretic Traditional text which underlies the A.V. 1611), it is the largest and best preserved of all the biblical scrolls, and the only one that is nearly complete.

Unbeknown to 99.9% of the Jewish patrons who gaze at this indigenous ancient treasure, the "Rock of Israel" has positioned the single greatest proof for the deity of Jesus Christ *right before their very eyes*. Unfortunately, the same scroll states at Isaiah 29:10, *"For the LORD hath poured out upon you the spirit of deep sleep, and hath* CLOSED YOUR EYES...." Lord willing, the following essay will reveal this *spiritual* treasure to Jews who long to know the truth about their Messiah, for the scroll also reads at Isaiah 44:3, *"For I will pour water on him that is thirsty, and floods upon the dry ground...."*

"HEAR, O ISRAEL: THE LORD OUR GOD IS ONE LORD."

When Jesus Christ visited His boyhood village of Nazareth He entered the synagogue on the Sabbath and stood up to read from the Tanakh. The inspired New Testament account relates what happened next:

> *And there was delivered unto him the book of the prophet Esaias. And when he had* OPENED THE BOOK, *he found the place where it was written, The Spirit of the Lord is upon me, because he hath anointed me to preach the gospel to the poor;* HE HATH SENT ME *to heal the brokenhearted, to preach deliverance to the captives, and recovering of sight to the blind, to set at liberty them that are bruised, To preach the acceptable year of the Lord. And he* CLOSED THE BOOK, *and he gave it again to the minister, and sat down. And the eyes of all them that were in the synagogue were fastened on him. And he began to say unto them, This day is this scripture fulfilled in your ears.* (Luke 4:17-21)

The young rabbi startled his former neighbors by declaring that the material he had just read in Isaiah 61:1-2 was specifically written about Him. As the source of right division (II Timothy 2:15), the Messiah conspicuously ended His reading at the *comma* in verse two, signifying that the remainder of the text, *"and the day of vengeance of our God; to comfort all that mourn,"* applies to His Second Advent at the end of the Tribulation. Any Jew familiar with the book would recognize the earlier cross-reference at Isaiah 42:1-4:

> *Behold my servant, whom I uphold; mine elect, in whom my soul delighteth;* I HAVE PUT MY SPIRIT UPON HIM*: he shall bring forth judgment to the Gentiles. He shall not cry, nor lift up, nor cause his voice to be heard in the street. A bruised reed shall he not break, and the smoking flax shall he not quench: he shall bring forth judgment unto truth. He shall not fail nor be discouraged, till he have set judgment in the earth: and the isles shall wait for his law.*

Jesus claimed this prophecy as well (Matthew 12:18-21). The salient truth here is that the second person of the Godhead is visible in the Old Testament. For the Christian, this bears intrinsic witness to the Trinity (Latin: Trinitas, lit. "triad," from trinus, "threefold")—that the man Christ Jesus is "very God of very God," along with the Father and the Holy Spirit—matching I John 5:7, *"For there are three that bear record in heaven, the Father, the Word, and the Holy Ghost: and these three are one."* Yet, "on the other hand" (as Tevye would often say), the Jews, being a stiff-necked people, will insist on more precise evidence (their ancestors' Δ tattoos notwithstanding).

The most sacred verse in the Tanakh is Deuteronomy 6:4, the famous *Shema*: *"Hear, O Israel: The LORD our God is* ONE *LORD."* Much debate rages over whether the mystical Jewish book *Zohar* interprets the Hebrew "one" as a "united one." In any event, many religious Jews, their rabbis' rhetoric notwithstanding, are privately troubled by the conundrum of a "unity in plurality," starting with the unique grammatical construction in the opening verse of the Torah: *"In the beginning God created the heaven and the earth."* (Genesis 1:1) According to the corresponding note in the *Scofield Study Bible*, "*Elohim* (sometimes *El* or *Elah*), English form 'God,' the first of the three primary names of Deity, is a uni-plural noun formed from *El* = strength, or the strong one, and *Alah* to swear, to bind oneself by an oath, so implying faithfulness."

The first shocking affirmation of this holy doctrine appears only twenty-five verses later: *"And* GOD *said, Let* US *make man in* OUR *image, after* OUR *likeness,"* followed by, *"So* GOD *created man in* HIS *own image, in the image of* GOD *created* HE *him; male and female created* HE *them."* (Genesis 1:26-27) The Apostle Paul wrote, *"And the very God of peace sanctify you wholly; and I pray God your whole* SPIRIT *and* SOUL *and* BODY *be preserved blameless unto the coming of our Lord Jesus Christ."* (I Thessalonians 5:23) Thus, man is a *tripartite* being, reflecting his *triune* Creator. The State of Israel unknowingly displays this bedrock Christian truth vis-à-vis the dual triangles (the Star of David) in her national flag—Jehovah depicted by the upward-pointing triangle, man's fallen nature by the downward-pointing triangle.

Many other references to Jesus Christ abound in the Tanakh. When Jesus was communing with the two disciples on the road to Emmaus, He gave them a *personal* Bible study: *"And beginning at Moses and all the prophets, he expounded unto them in all the scriptures the things concerning* HIMSELF.*"* (Luke 24:27) Psalms 2:7 and 12, and Proverbs 30:1-4, reveal that that God has a Son. When He appears as *"the angel of the LORD"* in Judges 13:16, Manoah asks Him, *"What is thy name?"* only to be told, *"Why askest thou thus after my name, seeing it is secret?"* (Proverbs 30:4; Revelation 19:13). Other striking examples include, the LORD raining brimstone and fire from the LORD out of Heaven in Genesis 19:24; God anointing God in Psalm 45:7; the LORD talking to the Lord in Psalm 110:1; et. al.

A devoted pastor's wife in New York, who suffers from serious health issues (Psalm 119:71), asked this author to review a number of "Jesus sightings" that she discovered in her private study of Isaiah. The "shocking" result of this analysis is as follows…

THE ISAIAH 48 SHOCK TEXT

Only six chapters into Isaiah, the prophet sets the stage by declaring at verse *three*: "HOLY, HOLY, HOLY, *is the* LORD *of hosts"* (i.e., one identical title for each member of the Trinity). With this precursor in place, the "uni-plural" God of Genesis 1:1 and 26 reappears at verse eight, *"Also I heard the voice of* THE LORD, *saying, Whom shall* I *send, and who will go for* US*…?"* (Note, "I"/"Us" = "the Lord.")

The prophet then tells Israel to look for a *virgin-born* Messiah (no less of a miracle than Sarah having Isaac at age ninety), *"Therefore the Lord himself shall give you a sign; Behold, a* VIRGIN *shall conceive, and bear a son, and shall call his name* IMMANUEL.*"* (Isaiah 7:14) For the record, the Lord's appointed Hebrew name just *happens* to mean, *"God with us."* (Matthew 1: 23)

In chapter *nine* (fruit-bearing number), the Scripture rightly divides between the human Messiah, *born* in time, and the divine Son of God, *given* from all eternity. *"For unto us a* CHILD IS BORN, *unto us a* SON IS GIVEN*: and the government shall be upon his shoulder: and his name shall be called Wonderful, Counsellor*, THE MIGHTY GOD, THE EVERLASTING FATHER, *The Prince of Peace."* (Isaiah 9:6) The promised child/Son, Jesus, is also called both God *and* Father.

Fast forwarding to chapter forty-seven, the One doing the talking (i.e., He who promises to *"take vengeance"* in verse three) slips in a most disturbing twist at verse four: *"As for* OUR *redeemer, the* LORD *of hosts is his name, the Holy One of Israel."* (Hint: The "our" here is *not* referring to Isaiah and his brethren/see Genesis 1:26) While this aberration was disconcerting enough, the "Isaiah Shock" in chapter forty-eight will make the "Sadat Shock" of Yom Kippur appear like a rap on the funny bone in comparison. After reading Jehovah's words in the previous chapter, the Jews (then *and* now) would naturally *assume* that they were still following the same speaker. The LORD'S commentary begins naturally enough:

> *Hear ye this, O house of Jacob, which are called by the name of Israel, and are come forth out of the waters of Judah, which swear by the name of* THE LORD, *and make mention of* THE GOD OF ISRAEL, *but not in truth, nor in righteousness. For they call themselves of the holy city, and stay themselves upon* THE GOD OF ISRAEL; THE LORD OF HOSTS *is his name. I have declared the former things from the beginning; and they went forth out of my mouth, and I shewed them; I did them suddenly, and they came to pass.* (Isaiah 48:1-3)

However, after twelve more verses of thinking they are still listening to Jehovah, the *ultimate* "Oy Vey!" reality check bursts upon them: The "shock text"—Isaiah 48:16 (as it appears within Isaiah 47:11-49:4 in Column XL behind the museum's glass-enclosed, soft-lighted case)—translates into English:

> *Come ye near unto me, hear ye this;* I HAVE NOT SPOKEN IN SECRET FROM THE BEGINNING; FROM THE TIME THAT IT WAS, THERE AM I: AND NOW THE LORD GOD, AND HIS SPIRIT, HATH *SENT* ME.

Note the double cross-reference to this divine commission (the former—as preserved in the Great Isaiah Scroll, being hidden soon after the latter, recited by Jesus in the synagogue, was recorded by the "beloved physician"), *"he hath* SENT *me to bind up the brokenhearted..."* (Isaiah 61:1); *"he hath* SENT *me to heal the brokenhearted..."* (Luke 4:18).

This same truth is revealed in Zechariah 2:8-9, *"For thus saith the* LORD *of Hosts; After the glory* HATH HE SENT ME *unto the nations which spoiled you: for he that toucheth you toucheth the apple of his eye. For, behold, I will shake mine hand upon them...and ye shall know that the* LORD *of hosts* HATH SENT ME.*"*

As the Jews discover that the speaker—i.e., the "One" who was there *"from the beginning"* (eliminating Isaiah as the source)—was *not* the "Lord GOD," but rather, was SENT *by* "THE LORD GOD *AND* HIS SPIRIT" (the natural thing for the other two persons of the Godhead to do, based on that *"*OUR *redeemer"* construction in Isaiah 47:4), the LORD JESUS CHRIST continues: *"Thus saith* THE LORD, *thy* REDEEMER, *the* HOLY ONE OF ISRAEL; I AM THE LORD THY GOD *which teacheth thee to profit, which leadeth thee by the way that thou shouldest go."* (Isaiah 48:17) Thus, the "Holy ONE" of Israel is none other than the "united ONE" of Genesis 1:1.

Notice further how that key ancillary word—"beginning"—debuted in Genesis 1:1 and manifested in Isaiah 48:16, was used to introduce Jesus Christ as "the Word" in John 1:1-2, *"In the* BEGINNING *was the Word, and the Word was with God, and the Word was God. The same was in the* BEGINNING *with God."*

You say—"Dr. Grady, GOOD NIGHT, this is some H-E-A-V-Y stuff!" (You got *that* right; about as heavy as the "ROCK of Israel.") When Jesus said, *"I and my Father are* ONE*"* (John 10:29), He wasn't using figurative speech. No matter what the "penguins" say about "intrusive vowel points" (and other rabbinical rope-a-dope), the linchpin rendering of Isaiah 48:16 remains faithfully represented across the entire spectrum of reputable Hebrew-English translations. Note the following sample beginning with the first serious effort in the 19th century.

> Come ye near unto me, hear ye this; never from the beginning have I spoken in secret; from the time that it occurred, was I there. And now the Lord Eternal hath sent me, and his Spirit. (*The Twenty-Four Books of the Holy Scriptures*, 1853)

> Come ye near unto Me, hear ye this: From the beginning I have not spoken in secret; from the time that it was, there am I; and now the L-rd GOD hath sent me, and His spirit. (Jewish Publication Society *Tanach*, 1917)
>
> Come close to me, and listen to this: since the beginning I have not spoken in secret, since the time things began to be, I have been there; and now *Adonai ELOHIM* has sent me and his Spirit. (*Complete Jewish Bible*, 1998)
>
> Draw near to me, hear this; I have not spoken in secret from the beginning; from the time that it was, I was there: and now the Lord YHWH, and his Spirit, has sent me. (*The Translation of the Great Isaiah Scroll*, Fred P. Miller, 2001)
>
> Draw near to Me and hear this: From the beginning, I did not speak in secret; From the time anything existed, I was there. 'And now the Lord God has sent me, endowed with His spirit.' (*The Jewish Study Bible*, 2014)

With no chapter and verse divisions in the original manuscripts, "the Word" (John 1:1-3) continues to speak in the beginning of chapter forty-nine. Note the clear second cross-reference to His virgin birth.

> *Listen, O isles, unto me...The* LORD *hath called me from the* WOMB*; from the* BOWELS *of my mother hath he made mention of my name. And he hath made my mouth like a sharp sword; in the shadow of his hand hath he hid me, and made me a polished shaft; in his quiver hath he hid me; And said unto me, Thou art my servant, O Israel, in whom I will be glorified.* (Isaiah 49:1-3)

While Orthodox Jewry will strain to make this servant the nation of Israel (as it *appears* to read), Jacob was *not* named before he was born (as verse one requires)—Jesus *was* (Luke 1:30-32). And besides, the Israel in verse three (Jesus, depicted here as a *spiritual* form of Israel) could not *possibly* be Eretz Yisrael, because *this* Israel is specifically called to *"restore the* PRESERVED OF ISRAEL*"* to God in verse six.

The rabbis will then cite Exodus 4:22, Deuteronomy 32:18 and Jeremiah 31:9 to argue that Israel was God's Son. While Israel is indeed the LORD'S firstborn Son—in a *national* sense—Jesus is God's only *begotten* Son (Psalm 2:7; John 1:14, 18, 3:16; Hebrews 1:4-9), *for He was the only human to experience a physical conception by the Holy Spirit* (Luke 1:35). And because all Christians will ultimately be conformed to Christ's image (Romans 8:29; I John 3:1-3), Hebrews 1:6 causes the added conundrum that God's *"only begotten"* Son is also God's *"firstbegotten"* Son.

Thus, with the LORD and *"his servant"* Jesus Christ existing from eternity past as separate, yet one (not to mention the Holy Spirit), many passages where God *seems* to be utilizing two titles, may also be referring to both persons. Consider the following intriguing sample:

> *Woe to them that go down to Egypt for help; and stay on horses, and trust in chariots, because they are many; and in horsemen, because they are very strong; but they look not unto the Holy One of Israel,* NEITHER *seek the LORD!* (Isaiah 31:1)
>
> *Fear not, thou worm Jacob, and ye men of Israel; I will help thee, saith the LORD,* AND *thy redeemer, the Holy One of Israel.* (Isaiah 41:14)
>
> *That they may see, and know, and consider, and understand together, that the hand of the LORD hath done this,* AND *the Holy One of Israel hath created it.* (Isaiah 41:20)
>
> *For thy Maker is thine husband; the LORD of hosts is his name;* AND *thy Redeemer the Holy One of Israel; The God of the whole earth shall he be called.* (Isaiah 54:5)
>
> *Surely the isles shall wait for me, and the ships of Tarshish first, to bring thy sons from far, their silver and their gold with them, unto the name of the LORD thy God,* AND *to the Holy One of Israel, because he hath glorified thee.* (Isaiah 60:9)

And if you go back to Deuteronomy 6:4, you might want to count the number of divine titles employed in the Shema: *"Hear, oh Israel:* THE LORD (1), OUR GOD (2), is ONE LORD (3)*."*

There is also a notable contrast between Isaiah 48:12 and Isaiah 41:4. In the former (four verses before our shock text), Jesus Christ declares: *"Hearken unto me, O Jacob and Israel, my called; I am he;* I AM THE FIRST, I ALSO AM THE LAST*."* Christians will recognize the cross-references in Revelation 1:8, 17 and 22:13 where Jesus says, *"I am Alpha and Omega, the beginning and the ending...Fear not;* I AM THE FIRST AND THE LAST*."* However, note the nuance in Isaiah 41:4 where God the Father is talking: *"Who hath wrought and done it, calling the generations from the beginning? I the LORD,* THE

FIRST, AND *WITH* THE LAST*; I am he."* While Jehovah was the *first* member of the Godhead to reveal His name to Israel (Exodus 3:13-14), Jesus Christ was the *last* revelation (John 1:31; Hebrews 1:1-3;). And since Jesus declared in John 10:30, *"I and my Father are one,"* either "One" can be Alpha, Omega—even *both*—simultaneously. (John 3:13; 5:18; 14:7-9)

Meanwhile, back in Isaiah 49, Jehovah God returns to the inspired dais at verse seven to advance a key trait about His Son (i.e., Israel's "Redeemer" and *His* "Holy One"). *"Thus saith the LORD, the Redeemer of Israel, and his Holy One,* TO HIM WHOM MAN DESPISETH, *to whom the nation abhorreth...."* This explains Sarah Silverman's rant, "I hope the Jews did kill Christ; I'd do it again. I'd f-----g do it again in a second." Significantly, *two* specific cross-references to the Messiah being "despised" appear in Isaiah 53:3.

The watershed depiction of a *suffering* Messiah in Isaiah 53 begins with His Father's introduction in the closing portion of the previous chapter: *"Behold,* MY SERVANT *shall deal prudently, he shall be exalted and extolled, and be very high. As many were astonied at thee;* HIS VISAGE WAS SO MARRED MORE THAN ANY MAN, *and his form more than the sons of men:"* (Isaiah 52:13-14) The historical corroboration is the torturous scourging Jesus endured by the Romans (Matthew 27:26; Mark 15:15; John 19:1).

WARNING: The following detailed account in Isaiah 53 of the life and death of Jesus Christ has been *dodged*, *denied*, and *misapplied* to the Nation of Israel by every Hell-bound rabbi since AD 33. (The New Testament fulfillment of these prophecies appear in brackets.)

> [1]*Who hath believed our report?* [John 12:37-38] *and to whom is the arm of the LORD revealed?* [2]*For he shall grow up before him as a tender plant, and as a root out of a dry ground: he hath no form nor comeliness; and when we shall see him, there is no beauty that we should desire him* [Matthew 13:54-57; Philippians 2:7-8]. [3]*He is* DESPISED [Luke 4: 28-29] *and rejected of men* [Matthew 27:21-23]*; a man of sorrows, and acquainted with grief* [Matthew 26:37-38]*: and we hid as it were our faces from him* [Mark 14:50-52]; *he was* DESPISED, *and we esteemed him not.* [4]*Surely he hath borne our griefs, and carried our sorrows* [I Peter 2:24; 3:18]*: yet we did esteem him stricken, smitten of God* [Matthew 27:46], *and afflicted.* [5]BUT HE WAS WOUNDED FOR OUR TRANSGRESSIONS, HE WAS BRUISED FOR OUR INIQUITES [Matthew 26:28]*: the*

chastisement of our peace was upon him; and with his stripes [Matthew 27:26] *we are healed* [Ephesians 2:13-18]. [6]*All we like sheep have gone astray; we have turned every one to his own way;* AND THE LORD HATH LAID ON HIM THE INIQUITY OF US ALL (I John 4:10]. [7]*He was oppressed, and he was afflicted* [Matthew 27:27-31], *yet he opened not his mouth: he is brought as a lamb to the slaughter* (John 1:29), *and as a sheep before her shearers is dumb, so he openeth not his mouth* [Matthew 27:12]. [8]*He was taken from prison* [Matthew 26:47-27:31] *and from judgment* [John 18:13-22; Matthew 26:57-66, 27:11-14, 22-24; Luke 23:11; Romans 3:3-4]: *and who shall declare his generation?* FOR HE WAS CUT OFF OUT OF THE LAND OF THE LIVING; FOR THE TRANSGRESSION OF MY PEOPLE WAS HE STRICKEN [John 3:16; I John 2:2]. [9]*And he made his grave with the wicked and with the rich in his death* [Matthew 27:57-60]; *because he had done no violence* [John 18:38], *neither was any deceit in his mouth* [I Peter 2:21-22]. [10]YET IT PLEASED THE LORD TO BRUISE HIM; *he hath put him to grief* [Romans 3:23-26]: *when thou shalt make his soul an offering for sin* ; [Ephesians 5:2], *he shall see his seed, he shall prolong his days* [Mark 16:16; Revelation 1:17-18], *and the pleasure of the LORD shall prosper in his hand* [Matthew 28:18]. [11]*He shall see of the travail of his soul, and shall be satisfied* [John 12:27]: *by his knowledge shall my righteous servant justify many;* FOR HE SHALL BEAR THEIR INIQUITIES [Romans 5:18-19]. [12]*Therefore will I divide him a portion with the great, and he shall divide the spoil with the strong; because he hath poured out his soul unto death: and he was numbered with the transgressors* [Luke 23:32]; AND HE BARE THE SIN OF MANY [II Corinthians 5:21], *and made intercession for the transgressors* [Luke 23:34].

THE POOL OF SILOAM

During the Lord's earthly ministry He was adamant about the fact that He had been "sent" to the Jews by His Heavenly Father (thereby conforming to the great prophecy in Isaiah 48:16). Having read Isaiah 61:1 in the synagogue, He would reemphasize this point *forty-one times* in the Gospel of John alone.

The classic case is found in chapter nine where a blind Jew is cured at the pool of Siloam. The Lord begins by declaring in verse four, *"I must work the works of him that* SENT *me, while it is day: the night cometh, when no man can work."* After anointing the man's eyes with clay and spittle, Jesus instructs him, *"GO, wash in the pool of Siloam...."* In a "holy coincidence," visitors to the Shrine of the Book can see this pool cited (with its Old Testament spelling) in Isaiah 8:6, *"this people refuseth the waters of* SHILOAH *that go softly"* (symbolic of the rejected Davidic monarchy enthroned upon Zion compared to the turbulent Euphrates, depicting the current world power). But the *really* wild thing is the meaning of the name Siloam: *"Go, wash in the pool of Siloam, (which is by interpretation,* SENT.*)"* As the man obeys, the text ends: *"He went his way therefore, and washed, and came* SEEING.*"*

David Berkowitz had *his* sight restored at the "Pool of Siloam/Sent" in 1987. The onetime ".44 Caliber Killer" was then able to be *sent* once again—this time, as a witness for his Saviour and Messiah. When Jesus commissioned His apostles ("sent ones") He told them, *"Peace be unto you: as my Father hath* SENT *me, even so* SEND *I you."* (John 20:21) As the hymn, "Footprints of Jesus" states, "Though they lead o'er the cold, dark mountains, Seeking His sheep, Or along by *Siloam's* fountains, Helping the weak: Footprints of Jesus, that make the pathway glow! We will follow the steps of Jesus where'er they go."

In December 2015, David *sent* me a lovely Christmas card. Seven Jews are shown on the front cover praying before the Western Wall, with excerpts from Isaiah 53 superimposed on the stones. It was signed, "With love in the Lord Jesus, our Savior and Messiah. Bro. David Berkowitz." I have never seen "Keeping Up with the Kardashians"; yet, "somehow" I *have* to believe that the reality show has nothing on an old-time Baptist preacher getting a Christmas greeting from a Jewish serial killer serving 365 *years* in a maximum security prison!

In closing, I beseech my Jewish readers, let Jesus *send* YOU to the "Pool of Siloam." It may be that His deity—like the Great Isaiah Scroll that lay dormant for 2,000 years—may come to light in *your* life as well (John 1:9). But, whatever you do, don't send *Him* away, for He is not just God's only "begotten" Son and His "firstbegotten" Son, but His "beloved" Son as well (Matthew 3:17). So, *"Kiss the Son..."* (Psalm 2:12) while you can; His promise remains the same today...

"And this is the will of HIM *that* SENT *me, that every one which seeth the Son, and believeth on him, may have everlasting life: and I will raise him up at the last day."*
(John 6:40)

Shrine of the Book

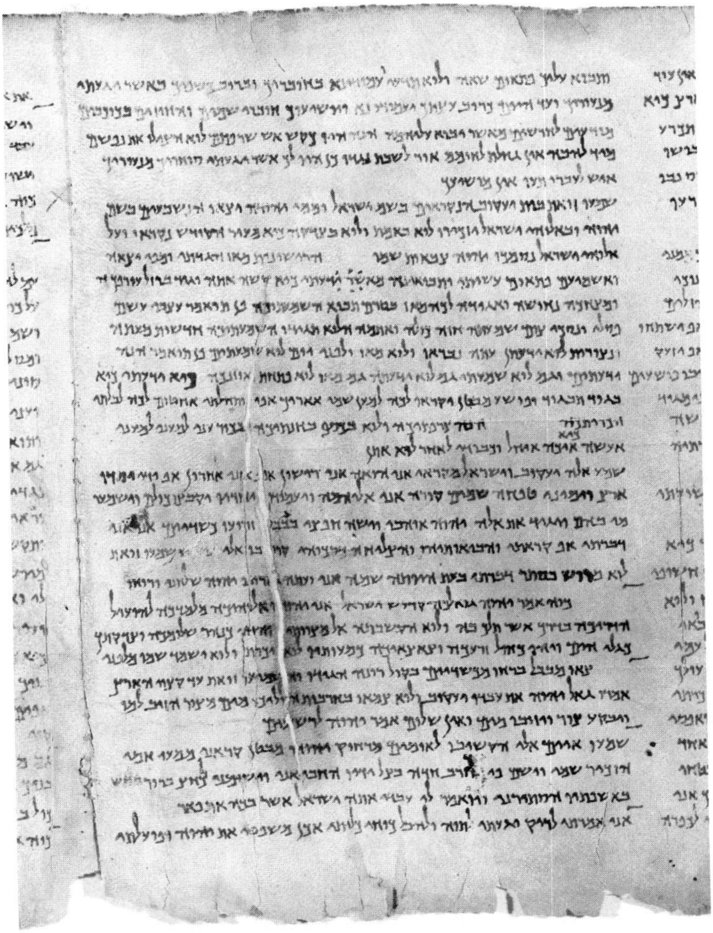

The Great Isaiah Scroll, Column XL – Isaiah 47:11 - 49:4
For English readers, Isaiah 48:16 is on lines 20 and 21.
(Ardon Bar-Hama/The Israel Museum, Jerusalem)

Appendix 2

Gracious Words

"Jesus answered them, and said, My doctrine is not mine, but his that sent me. If any man will do his will, he shall know of the doctrine, whether it be of God, or whether I speak of myself."
(John 7:16-17)

"And ye shall know the truth, and the truth shall make you free… If the Son therefore shall make you free, ye shall be free indeed."
(John 8:32, 36)

THE NEW TESTAMENT states about Jesus Christ, *"And the common people heard him gladly."* (Mark 12:37). The reason for His strong appeal among the rank and file of Judaism was given in John 7:46, *"Never man spake like this man."* Two other verses elaborate on this explanation: Matthew 7:28-29 declares, *"the people were astonished at his doctrine: For he taught them as one having authority, and not as the scribes"*; Luke 4:32 adds, *"they were astonished at his doctrine: for his word was with power."*

This growing popularity was both a rebuke and a threat to the Jewish leaders. *"The Pharisees therefore said among themselves, Perceive ye how ye prevail nothing? behold* THE WORLD IS GONE AFTER HIM.*"* (John 12:19) As a result, their only option was to keep the people from *hearing* the powerful rabbi, for Romans 10:17 says, *"So then faith cometh by hearing, and hearing by the word of God."* Jesus excoriated them accordingly: *"But woe unto you, scribes and Pharisees, hypocrites! for ye shut up the kingdom of heaven against men: for ye neither go in yourselves, neither suffer ye them that are entering to go in."* (Matthew 23:13)

Very little has changed in the past 2,000 years. The rabbis are *still* working overtime to keep Jewish men, women, and children from experiencing what their ancestors did in that Nazareth synagogue: *"And all bare him witness, and wondered at the* GRACIOUS WORDS *which proceeded out of his mouth."* (Luke 4:22) They want to keep you confined in a ghetto of spiritual ignorance.

When accosted by the Pharisees, the parents of the man who was healed at the pool of Siloam replied, *"We know that this is our son, and that he was born blind: But by what means he now seeth, we know not; or who hath opened his eyes, we know not:* HE IS OF AGE; ASK HIM: *he shall speak for himself."* (John 9:20-21) I will therefore conclude this volume by applying the spirit of their answer to my precious Jewish readers. While the rabbis would likewise shut *you* out from giving Jesus Christ a personal hearing, with all due respect I say—YOU are of age, ask Him! The following three chapters are from the Gospel of Matthew. (And the Messiah won't even mind if you read them under the covers with a flashlight!)

THE SERMON ON THE MOUNT
MATTHEW 5

[1]*And seeing the multitudes, he went up into a mountain: and when he was set, his disciples came unto him:* [2]*And he opened his mouth, and taught them, saying,* [3]*Blessed are the poor in spirit: for their's is the kingdom of heaven.* [4]*Blessed are they that mourn: for they shall be comforted.* [5]*Blessed are the meek: for they shall inherit the earth.* [6]*Blessed are they which do hunger and thirst after righteousness: for they shall be filled.* [7]*Blessed are the merciful: for they shall obtain mercy.* [8]*Blessed are the pure in heart: for they shall see God.* [9]*Blessed are the peacemakers: for they shall be called the children of God.* [10]*Blessed are they which are persecuted for righteousness' sake: for their's is the kingdom of heaven.* [11]*Blessed are ye, when men shall revile you, and persecute you, and shall say all manner of evil against you falsely, for my sake.* [12]*Rejoice, and be exceeding glad: for great is your reward in heaven: for so persecuted they the prophets which were before you.*

13 Ye are the salt of the earth: but if the salt have lost his savour,
wherewith shall it be salted? it is thenceforth good for nothing, but to
be cast out, and to be trodden under foot of men. 14 Ye are the light of
the world. A city that is set on an hill cannot be hid. 15 Neither do men
light a candle, and put it under a bushel, but on a candlestick; and it
giveth light unto all that are in the house. 16 Let your light so shine before
men, that they may see your good works, and glorify your Father which
is in heaven.

17 Think not that I am come to destroy the law, or the prophets: I am
not come to destroy, but to fulfil. 18 For verily I say unto you, Till heaven
and earth pass, one jot or one tittle shall in no wise pass from the law,
till all be fulfilled. 19 Whosoever therefore shall break one of these least
commandments, and shall teach men so, he shall be called the least in
the kingdom of heaven: but whosoever shall do and teach them, the
same shall be called great in the kingdom of heaven. 20 For I say unto
you, That except your righteousness shall exceed the righteousness of
the scribes and Pharisees, ye shall in no case enter into the kingdom of
heaven. 21 Ye have heard that it was said of them of old time, Thou shalt
not kill; and whosoever shall kill shall be in danger of the judgment:
22 But I say unto you, That whosoever is angry with his brother without
a cause shall be in danger of the judgment: and whosoever shall say to
his brother, Raca, shall be in danger of the council: but whosoever
shall say, Thou fool, shall be in danger of hell fire. 23 Therefore if thou
bring thy gift to the altar, and there rememberest that thy brother hath
ought against thee; 24 Leave there thy gift before the altar, and go thy
way; first be reconciled to thy brother, and then come and offer thy
gift. 25 Agree with thine adversary quickly, whiles thou art in the way
with him; lest at any time the adversary deliver thee to the judge, and
the judge deliver thee to the officer, and thou be cast into prison.
26 Verily I say unto thee, Thou shalt by no means come out thence, till
thou hast paid the uttermost farthing. 27 Ye have heard that it was said
by them of old time, Thou shalt not commit adultery: 28 But I say unto
you, That whosoever looketh on a woman to lust after her hath committed
adultery with her already in his heart. 29 And if thy right eye offend
thee, pluck it out, and cast it from thee: for it is profitable for thee that
one of thy members should perish, and not that thy whole body should
be cast into hell. 30 And if thy right hand offend thee, cut it off, and cast
it from thee: for it is profitable for thee that one of thy members should
perish, and not that thy whole body should be cast into hell.

31 It hath been said, Whosoever shall put away his wife, let him give
her a writing of divorcement: 32 But I say unto you, That whosoever
shall put away his wife, saving for the cause of fornication, causeth her
to commit adultery: and whosoever shall marry her that is divorced
committeth adultery. 33 Again, ye have heard that it hath been said by
them of old time, Thou shalt not forswear thyself, but shalt perform
unto the Lord thine oaths: 34 But I say unto you, Swear not at all;
neither by heaven; for it is God's throne: 35 Nor by the earth; for it is
his footstool: neither by Jerusalem; for it is the city of the great King.
36 Neither shalt thou swear by thy head, because thou canst not make
one hair white or black. 37 But let your communication be, Yea, yea;
Nay, nay: for whatsoever is more than these cometh of evil. 38 Ye have
heard that it hath been said, An eye for an eye, and a tooth for a tooth:
39 But I say unto you, That ye resist not evil: but whosoever shall smite
thee on thy right cheek, turn to him the other also. 40 And if any man
will sue thee at the law, and take away thy coat, let him have thy cloak
also. 41 And whosoever shall compel thee to go a mile, go with him twain.
42 Give to him that asketh thee, and from him that would borrow of thee
turn not thou away. 43 Ye have heard that it hath been said, Thou shalt
love thy neighbour, and hate thine enemy. 44 But I say unto you, Love your
enemies, bless them that curse you, do good to them that hate you, and
pray for them which despitefully use you, and persecute you; 45 That ye
may be the children of your Father which is in heaven: for he maketh
his sun to rise on the evil and on the good, and sendeth rain on the just
and on the unjust. 46 For if ye love them which love you, what reward
have ye? do not even the publicans the same? 47 And if ye salute your
brethren only, what do ye more than others? do not even the publicans
so? 48 Be ye therefore perfect, even as your Father which is in heaven
is perfect.

MATTHEW 6

1 Take heed that ye do not your alms before men, to be seen of them:
otherwise ye have no reward of your Father which is in heaven.
2 Therefore when thou doest thine alms, do not sound a trumpet before
thee, as the hypocrites do in the synagogues and in the streets, that
they may have glory of men. Verily I say unto you, They have their

reward. 3 *But when thou doest alms, let not thy left hand know what thy*
right hand doeth: 4 *That thine alms may be in secret: and thy Father*
which seeth in secret himself shall reward thee openly. 5 *And when*
thou prayest, thou shalt not be as the hypocrites are: for they love to
pray standing in the synagogues and in the corners of the streets, that
they may be seen of men. Verily I say unto you, They have their reward.
6 *But thou, when thou prayest, enter into thy closet, and when thou hast*
shut thy door, pray to thy Father which is in secret; and thy Father
which seeth in secret shall reward thee openly. 7 *But when ye pray, use*
not vain repetitions, as the heathen do: for they think that they shall be
heard for their much speaking.

8 *Be not ye therefore like unto them: for your Father knoweth what*
things ye have need of, before ye ask him. 9 *After this manner therefore*
pray ye: Our Father which art in heaven, Hallowed be thy name. 10 *Thy*
kingdom come, Thy will be done in earth, as it is in heaven. 11 *Give us*
this day our daily bread. 12 *And forgive us our debts, as we forgive our*
debtors. 13 *And lead us not into temptation, but deliver us from evil:*
For thine is the kingdom, and the power, and the glory, for ever. Amen.
14 *For if ye forgive men their trespasses, your heavenly Father will also*
forgive you: 15 *But if ye forgive not men their trespasses, neither will*
your Father forgive your trespasses.

16 *Moreover when ye fast, be not, as the hypocrites, of a sad*
countenance: for they disfigure their faces, that they may appear unto
men to fast. Verily I say unto you, They have their reward. 17 *But thou,*
when thou fastest, anoint thine head, and wash thy face; 18 *That thou*
appear not unto men to fast, but unto thy Father which is in secret: and
thy Father, which seeth in secret, shall reward thee openly.

19 *Lay not up for yourselves treasures upon earth, where moth and*
rust doth corrupt, and where thieves break through and steal: 20 *But*
lay up for yourselves treasures in heaven, where neither moth nor rust
doth corrupt, and where thieves do not break through nor steal: 21 *For*
where your treasure is, there will your heart be also. 22 *The light of the*
body is the eye: if therefore thine eye be single, thy whole body shall be
full of light. 23 *But if thine eye be evil, thy whole body shall be full of*
darkness. If therefore the light that is in thee be darkness, how great is
that darkness! 24 *No man can serve two masters: for either he will hate*
the one, and love the other; or else he will hold to the one, and despise
the other. Ye cannot serve God and mammon.

25 Therefore I say unto you, Take no thought for your life, what ye
shall eat, or what ye shall drink; nor yet for your body, what ye shall
put on. Is not the life more than meat, and the body than raiment?
26 Behold the fowls of the air: for they sow not, neither do they reap,
nor gather into barns; yet your heavenly Father feedeth them. Are ye
not much better than they? 27 Which of you by taking thought can add
one cubit unto his stature? 28 And why take ye thought for raiment?
Consider the lilies of the field, how they grow; they toil not, neither do
they spin: 29 And yet I say unto you, That even Solomon in all his glory
was not arrayed like one of these. 30 Wherefore, if God so clothe the
grass of the field, which to day is, and to morrow is cast into the oven,
shall he not much more clothe you, O ye of little faith? 31 Therefore
take no thought, saying, What shall we eat? or, What shall we drink?
or, Wherewithal shall we be clothed? 32 (For after all these things do
the Gentiles seek:) for your heavenly Father knoweth that ye have need
of all these things. 33 But seek ye first the kingdom of God, and his
righteousness; and all these things shall be added unto you. 34 Take
therefore no thought for the morrow: for the morrow shall take thought
for the things of itself. Sufficient unto the day is the evil thereof.

MATTHEW 7

1 Judge not, that ye be not judged. 2 For with what judgment ye judge,
ye shall be judged: and with what measure ye mete, it shall be measured
to you again. 3 And why beholdest thou the mote that is in thy brother's
eye, but considerest not the beam that is in thine own eye? 4 Or how
wilt thou say to thy brother, Let me pull out the mote out of thine eye;
and, behold, a beam is in thine own eye? 5 Thou hypocrite, first cast
out the beam out of thine own eye; and then shalt thou see clearly to
cast out the mote out of thy brother's eye. 6 Give not that which is holy
unto the dogs, neither cast ye your pearls before swine, lest they trample
them under their feet, and turn again and rend you.

7 Ask, and it shall be given you; seek, and ye shall find; knock, and it
shall be opened unto you: 8 For every one that asketh receiveth; and he
that seeketh findeth; and to him that knocketh it shall be opened. 9 Or what
man is there of you, whom if his son ask bread, will he give him a stone?
10 Or if he ask a fish, will he give him a serpent? 11 If ye then, being evil,
know how to give good gifts unto your children, how much more shall

your Father which is in heaven give good things to them that ask him?
12 *Therefore all things whatsoever ye would that men should do to you,*
do ye even so to them: for this is the law and the prophets.
13 *Enter ye in at the strait gate: for wide is the gate, and broad is the*
way, that leadeth to destruction, and many there be which go in thereat:
14 *Because strait is the gate, and narrow is the way, which leadeth unto*
life, and few there be that find it.
15 *Beware of false prophets, which come to you in sheep's clothing,*
but inwardly they are ravening wolves. 16 *Ye shall know them by their*
fruits. Do men gather grapes of thorns, or figs of thistles? 17 *Even so*
every good tree bringeth forth good fruit; but a corrupt tree bringeth
forth evil fruit. 18 *A good tree cannot bring forth evil fruit, neither can a*
corrupt tree bring forth good fruit. 19 *Every tree that bringeth not forth*
good fruit is hewn down, and cast into the fire. 20 *Wherefore by their*
fruits ye shall know them.
21 *Not every one that saith unto me, Lord, Lord, shall enter into the*
kingdom of heaven; but he that doeth the will of my Father which is in
heaven. 22 *Many will say to me in that day, Lord, Lord, have we not*
prophesied in thy name? and in thy name have cast out devils? and in
thy name done many wonderful works? 23 *And then will I profess unto*
them, I never knew you: depart from me, ye that work iniquity.
24 *Therefore whosoever heareth these sayings of mine, and doeth*
them, I will liken him unto a wise man, which built his house upon a
rock: 25 *And the rain descended, and the floods came, and the winds*
blew, and beat upon that house; and it fell not: for it was founded upon
a rock. 26 *And every one that heareth these sayings of mine, and doeth*
them not, shall be likened unto a foolish man, which built his house
upon the sand: 27 *And the rain descended, and the floods came, and the*
winds blew, and beat upon that house; and it fell: and great was the
fall of it. 28 *And it came to pass, when Jesus had ended these sayings,*
the people were astonished at his doctrine: 29 *For he taught them as*
one having authority, and not as the scribes.

So—what do you think? Do you sense an unsettling conviction in your soul (John 6:44)? By now you should certainly realize that *real* Bible-believing Christianity (with a few nutty exceptions) should *never* be confused with Roman Catholicism. At least *ten* ancient Christians have succumbed to the "Bloody Whore" for every one Jewish victim. I often tell Jews that the Church is not looking for a Christian pastor/pope to return in the clouds; we are looking for a Jewish King. To sum it up, your born-again stand-ins are longing to turn the reins back over to you! The only reason Christianity came on the scene in the first place is because your ancestors missed the time of their visitation (Luke 19:44).

Dear friend, if the Lord's words in the Sermon on the Mount have moved *you* to accept Him as *your* Saviour and Messiah, just follow the example of the penitent Jewish tax collector in Luke 18:13...

"And the publican, standing afar off, would not lift up so much as his eyes unto heaven, but smote upon his breast, saying, God be merciful to me a sinner." (Luke 18:13)

Gordon's Calvary

"And he bearing his cross went forth into a place called the place of a skull, which is called in the Hebrew Golgotha: Where they crucified him...." (John 19:17-18)

The most gracious words of all:
"Then said Jesus, Father, forgive them, for they know not what they do." (Luke 23:34)

Endnotes

PROLOGUE

[1] Daniel Gordis, "Israel Wonders What Happens When Its Fathers Are Gone," *Bloomberg View*, Bloomberg LP, 28 Sept. 2016, Web, 03 Dec. 2016.

[2] Anita Fuentes, dir. "Netanyahu Congratulates Trump Victory" *YouTube*, YouTube, 09 Nov. 2016, Web, 03 Dec. 2016.

[3] Stephen Dinan, "Obama Admin. Sent Taxpayer Money to Oust Netanyahu," *The Washington Times*, The Washington Times, 12 July 2016, Web, 27 Dec. 2016.

[4] Garry Manaraze, "Listen to the Trumpets," 13 Nov. 2016, Heritage Bible Baptist Church, Greenwood, DE, morning sermon.

[5] Ron Kampeas, "Top 5 Donors to Hillary Clinton Campaign Are All Jewish," *The Forward*, The Forward Assn., 26 Oct. 2016, Web, 27 Dec. 2016.

[6] Nathan Guttman, "Presidential Aide Valerie Jarrett Discloses Her Jewish Roots," *The Forward*, The Forward Assn., 07 Mar. 2011, Web, 27 Dec. 2016.

[7] Benjamin Netanyahu, *A Durable Peace: Israel and its Place Among the Nations*, Rev. ed. (New York: Warner, 2000), xxiii.

[8] Dennis Ross, *Doomed to Succeed: The U.S.-Israel Relationship from Truman to Obama* (New York: Farrar, 2015), xii.

PREFACE

[1] William Tecumseh Sherman, *Memoirs of General William T. Sherman* (1875; reprint, Bedford, Mass.: Applewood, n.d.), 176.

[2] Avraham Ziv-Tal, *Enigma Named Max*, trans. Rena Bar-David (Rishon Lezion, Israel: n. p., 2013), back jacket flap.

[3] John Loftus and Mark Aarons, *The Secret War Against the Jews: How Western Espionage Betrayed the Jewish People* (New York: St. Martin's, 1994), 511.

[4] Ibid., 12.

[5] Ibid., 302.

INTRODUCTION

[1] William Grimes, "The Man Who Rendered Jesus For the Age of Duplication," *The New York Times*, The New York Times, 11 Oct. 1994, Web, 05 Nov. 2015.

[2] Cathy Lynn Grossman, "More Americans Tailoring Religion to Fit Their Needs," *USATODAY.COM*, Gannett, 13 Sept. 2011. Web, 05 Nov. 2015.

[3] Ibid.

[4] William P. Grady, *Understanding the Times*, vol. 1: *How Satan Turned America Against God* (Knoxville, Tenn.: Grady, 2005), 899.

[5] Eugene E. Narrett, *World War III: The War on the Jews and the Rise of the World Security State* (Springdale, Ark.: Lightcatcher, 2007), 2.

[6] (From a letter to F. A. Van der Kemp [Feb. 16, 1808] Pennsylvania Historical Society).

[7] Peter Knight, ed., *Conspiracy Theories in American History: An Encyclopedia*, vol. 1 (Santa Barbara: ABC-CLIO, 2003), 81.

[8] Richard Meinertzhagen, *Middle East Diary: 1917-1956* (New York: Thomas Yoseloff, 1959), 171.

[9] Esco Foundation for Palestine, *Palestine: A Study of Jewish, Arab, and British Policies*, vol. 1 (New Haven, Conn.: Yale UP, 1947), 545.

[10] Doreen Ingrams, *Palestine Papers, 1917-1922: Seeds of Conflict* (London: Eland, 2009), 175.

[11] Narrett, *World War III*, 2.

[12] David Kaufmann, "Every Jew a Canny Yankee," *The Forward*, The Forward Assn., 15 Apr. 2005, Web, 06 Nov. 2015, Updated, 14 Apr. 2015.

[13] Esco, *Palestine*, 1:149.

[14] Meinertzhagen, *Middle East Diary*, 185.

[15] Ibid., 23.

[16] Ibid., 21-22.

CHAPTER 1

Palestinian Mythology

[1] Rory Miller, "The Other Side of the Coin: Arab Propaganda and the Battle against Zionism in London, 1937-48," in *Israel: The First Hundred Years,* vol. 1: *Israel's Transition from Community to State*, ed. Efraim Karsh (London: Frank Cass, 2000), 216.

[2] Esco Foundation for Palestine, *Palestine: A Study of Jewish, Arab, and British Policies,* vol. 1 (New Haven, Conn.: Yale UP, 1947), 510.

[3] Richard Meinertzhagen, *Middle East Diary: 1917-1956* (New York: Thomas Yoseloff, 1959), 141.

[4] Carroll Quigley, *The Anglo-American Establishment: From Rhodes to Cliveden* (New York: Books in Focus, 1981), 171.

[5] Meinertzhagen, *Middle East Diary*, 246-47.

[6] "Lawrence of Arabia: Lowell Thomas," PBS.org, Devillier Donegan Enterprises, October 2003, Web, 15 June 2012.

[7] Michael Korda, *Hero: The Life and Legend of Lawrence of Arabia* (New York: Harper, 2010), back inside flap.

[8] Meinertzhagen, *Middle East Diary*, 27, 30.

[9] Ibid., 41-42.

[10] Ibid., 39.

CHAPTER 2

Eretz Yisrael

[1] Robert John and Sami Hadawi, *1914-1945; Britain's Involvement*, vol. 1 of *The Palestine Diary* (New York: New World, 1970), xiii-xiv.

[2] Esco Foundation for Palestine, *Palestine: A Study of Jewish, Arab, and British Policies*, vol. 1 (New Haven, Conn.: Yale UP, 1947), 430.

[3] Nigel Maslin, "Palestine," *History Workshop Journal* 9.1 (1980): 184-88, *Oxfordjournals.org*, Web, 07 July 2015.

[4] *World Book Encyclopedia*, 2003 ed., vol. P, *s.v.* "Palestine."

[5] Bernard Lewis, "The Palestinians and the PLO," *Commentary*, 1 Jan. 1975: n. pag., *Commentarymagazine.com*, Web, 25 June 2015.

[6] Palestine Royal Commission, *Palestine Royal Commission Report* (London: His Majesty's Stationery Office, 1937), 6.

[7] George F. Gilder, *The Israel Test: Why the World's Most Besieged State is a Beacon of Freedom and Hope for the World Economy* (New York: Encounter, 2012), 39.

[8] Carl Hermann Voss, *The Palestine Problem Today: Israel and Its Neighbors* (Boston: Beacon, 1953), 13.

[9] Alphonse de Lamartine, *A Pilgrimage to the Holy Land: Comprising Recollections, Sketches and Reflections, Made During a Tour in the East, in 1832 - 1833*, vol. 1 (Philadelphia: Carey, Lea & Blanchard, 1835), 255, 296.
[10] Mark Twain, *The Innocents Abroad* (Hartford, Conn.: American, 1869), 396-97.
[11] Efraim Karsh, *Essential Histories*, vol. 28, *The Arab-Israeli Conflict: The Palestine War 1948* (Oxford: Osprey, 2002), 14.
[12] Esco, *Palestine*, 1:428.
[13] Ibid.
[14] Ibid., 428-29.
[15] Ibid., 429.
[16] Francis M. Deng, *War of Visions: Conflict of Identities in the Sudan* (Washington, D.C.: Brookings Inst., 1995), 4.
[17] Philip Khuri Hitti, *The Arabs: A Short History* (1943; reprint, Washington, D.C.: Regnery-Eagle, 1996), 97, 105.
[18] Mu'assasat al-Dirāsāt al-Filasṭīnīyah, Jāmi'at al-Kuwayt, *International Documents on Palestine* (Beirut: Inst. for Palestine Studies, 1981), 419.
[19] P. J. Vatikiotis, *Nasser and His Generation* (London: Croom Helm, 1978), 254.
[20] Palestine Royal Commission, *Report*, 6.
[21] Anne Sinai and Allen Pollack, *The Syrian Arab Republic: A Handbook* (New York: American Acad. Assn. for Peace in the Middle East, 1976), 147.
[22] Ruth Kark and Joseph B. Glass, "The Jews in Eretz-Israel/Palestine: From Traditional Peripherality to Modern Centrality," in *Israel: The First Hundred Years*, vol. 1: *Israel's Transition from Community to State*, ed. Efraim Karsh (London: Frank Cass, 2000), 74.
[23] Minutes of the Supreme Council, in David Hunt Miller, *My Diary at the Conference of Paris*, 22 vols. (New York: 1924), vol. 14, p. 405.
[24] *Encyclopaedia Britannica*, 11th ed., *s.v.* "Palestine: Population."
[25] Kark and Glass, "Jews in Eretz-Israel/Palestine," 89.
[26] Palestine Royal Commission, *Report*, 2-5, 7-9, 11.
[27] James Parkes, *Whose Land?: A History of the Peoples of Palestine* (New York: Taplinger, 1949), 266.
[28] John Loftus and Mark Aarons, *The Secret War Against the Jews: How Western Espionage Betrayed the Jewish People* (New York: St. Martin's, 1994), 32.
[29] Palestine Royal Commission, *Report*, 11-12.
[30] Esco, *Palestine*, 1:228-29.
[31] Ernst Frankenstein, *Justice For My People* (New York: Dial, 1944), 86-87.
[32] Ibid., 89.
[33] Richard Meinertzhagen, *Middle East Diary: 1917-1956* (New York: Thomas Yoseloff, 1959), 171.
[34] Palestine Royal Commission, *Report*, 11.
[35] Esco, *Palestine*, 1:150.
[36] Meinertzhagen, *Middle East Diary*, 168.
[37] Ibid., 202.
[38] Palestine Royal Commission, *Report*, 11.
[39] Anthony D. Smith, "Sacred Territories and National Conflict," in *Israel: The First Hundred Years*, vol. 1: *Israel's Transition from Community to State*, ed. Efraim Karsh (London: Frank Cass, 2000), 16.
[40] Ibid., 15.
[41] Ibid., 17.
[42] "50th Anniversary Gettysburg Reunion," *Our History - Order of the Arrow, Boy Scouts of America*, Boy Scouts of America, n.d., Web, 10 Nov. 2015.
[43] Ibid., 19-20.
[44] Leonard Slater, *The Pledge* (New York: Simon, 1970), 299.
[44] Irene L. Gendzier, ed., *A Middle East Reader* (New York: Pegasus, 1969), 357.
[46] Eugene E. Narrett, *World War III: The War on the Jews and the Rise of the World Security State* (Springdale, Ark.: Lightcatcher, 2007), 18.

CHAPTER 3
Diaspora to Zionism

[1] Bernard Lewis, *The Arabs in History*, Rev. ed. (New York: Harper-Colophon, 1966), 40.
[2] E. J. Brill, *First Encyclopaedia of Islam 1913-1936* (1927; reprint, Leiden, The Netherlands: n.p., 1987), 184.
[3] *The Koran*, trans. N. J. Dawood (New York: Penguin, 2006), Web, 13 June 2015, 295.
[4] Ibid., 85.
[5] Martin Gilbert, *Jerusalem: Rebirth of a City* (London: Chatto & Windus-Random, 1985), 14.
[6] Palestine Royal Commission, *Palestine Royal Commission Report* (London: His Majesty's Stationery Office, 1937), 8.
[7] Ibid.
[8] Ibid., 8-9.
[9] *Catholic Encyclopedia*, 1912 ed., *s.v.* "Torquemada."
[10] Palestine, Royal Commission, *Report*, 9.
[11] Ibid.
[12] "Jewish Massacre Denounced," *The New York Times*, 28 April 1903, 6.
[13] Peter Wrangel, *The Memoirs of General Wrangel: The Last Commander-in-Chief of The Russian National Army*, trans. Sophie Goulston (London: Duffield & Co., 1930), 239.
[14] Ibid.
[15] Ibid., 28-29.
[16] Ernst Frankenstein, *Justice For My People* (New York: Dial, 1944), 14.
[17] Esco Foundation for Palestine, *Palestine: A Study of Jewish, Arab, and British Policies*, vol. 1 (New Haven, Conn.: Yale UP, 1947), 8.
[18] Ernst Pawel, *The Labyrinth of Exile: A Life of Theodor Herzl* (New York: Farrar, 1989), 205.
[19] Alex Bein, *Theodore Herzl: A Biography*, trans. Maurice Samuel (Philadelphia: The Jewish Publication Society of America, 1945), 160.
[20] "Napoleon and the Jews," *Project Gutenberg Self-Publishing*, World Public Library Assn., n.d., Web, 10 Nov. 2015.
[21] Esco, *Palestine*, 1:9.
[22] Chaim Herzog, *Heroes of Israel: Profiles of Jewish Courage* (Boston: Little, 1989), 97- 98.
[23] Devin Sper, *The Future of Israel* (Scottsdale, Ariz.: Sy, 2004), 240.
[24] Esco, *Palestine*, 1:392.
[25] Ibid., 505, 507.
[26] Ibid., 440.
[27] Bein, *Herzl*, 174.
[28] Leon Pinsker, *Auto-Emancipation: An Admonition to His Brethren by a Russian Jew*, trans. D. S. Blondheim (1882; reprint, New York: Maccabaean, 1906), 1.
[29] Ibid., 2.
[30] Ibid., 2-3.
[31] Ibid., 4-6.
[32] Ibid., 8.
[33] Bein, *Herzl*, 35-36.
[34] Ibid., 9.
[35] Ibid., 12, 15-16.
[36] Jonas E. Alexis, *Christianity and Rabbinic Judaism, vol. 1, Surprising Differences, Conflicting Visions, and Worldview Implications from the Early Church to our Modern Time* (Bloomington, Ind.: WestBow, 2012), 257.

CHAPTER 4
Thedor Herzl

[1] Ernst Pawel, *The Labyrinth of Exile: A Life of Theodor Herzl* (New York: Farrar, 1989), 11.
[2] Ibid., 12.
[3] Alex Bein, *Theodore Herzl: A Biography*, trans. Maurice Samuel (Philadelphia: The Jewish Publication Society of America, 1945), 37.
[4] Mordecai Newman, comp., *Theodor Herzl: Excerpts From His Diaries*, trans. Joel Lipsky (New York: Scopus, 1941), 1.
[5] Bein, *Herzl*, 40.
[6] Ibid., 42.
[7] Ibid., 67.
[8] Pawel, *Labyrinth*, 137.
[9] Bein, *Herzl*, 70.
[10] Pawel, *Labyrinth*, 210.
[11] Ibid., 183.
[12] Bein, *Herzl*, 82.

[13] Pawel, *Labyrinth*, 214.
[14] Ibid., 199.
[15] Ibid., 212.
[16] Ibid., 244.
[17] Bein, *Herzl*, 113.
[18] Jonas E. Alexis, *Christianity and Rabbinic Judaism,* vol. 1: *Surprising Differences, Conflicting Visions, and Worldview Implications from the Early Church to our Modern Time* (Bloomington, Ind.: WestBow, 2012), 163.
[19] Bein, *Herzl*, 115-16.
[20] Mitchell Bard and Moshe Schwartz, *1,001 Facts Everyone Should Know about Israel* (Lanham, Md.: Rowman, 2005), 2.
[21] Pawel, *Labyrinth*, 209.
[22] Bein, *Herzl*, 123.
[23] Ibid., 126.
[24] Ibid., 127.
[25] Ibid., 164.
[26] Newman, *Excerpts*, 1.
[27] Bein, *Herzl*, 127.
[28] Ibid., 136.
[29] Ibid., 137.
[30] Alison Weir, *Against Our Better Judgment: The Hidden History of How the U.S. Was Used to Create Israel* (Lexington, Ken: CreateSpace, 2014), 99.
[31] Herzl, Theodor, *The Jewish State: An Attempt at a Modern Solution of the Jewish Question*, trans., Sylvie D'Avigdor, 4th ed. (London: Rita Searl, 1946), 14-15.
[32] Ibid., 28.
[33] Ibid., 79.
[34] Bein, *Herzl*, 195.
[35] Pawel, *Labyrinth*, 261.
[36] Ibid., 303-04.
[37] Ibid., 305-06.
[38] Ibid., 307.
[39] Bein, *Herzl*, 208-09.
[40] Ibid., 209.
[41] Pawel, *Labyrinth*, 307.
[42] Bein, *Herzl*, 209-10.
[43] Ibid., 210.
[44] Pawel, *Labyrinth*, 269.
[45] Bein, *Herzl*, 210.
[46] Pawel, *Labyrinth*, 313.
[47] Ibid., 319.
[48] Bein, *Herzl*, 281.
[49] Ibid., 214.
[50] Ibid., 229.
[51] Ibid., 231.
[52] Ibid., 231-32.
[53] Ibid., 232-34.
[54] Ibid., 234.
[55] Ibid., 235.
[56] Ibid., 239.
[57] Ibid., 241.
[58] Ibid., 242.
[59] Bard and Schwartz, *1,001 Facts*, 63.
[60] Bein, *Herzl*, 243.
[61] Ibid.
[62] Ibid., 266.
[63] Ibid., 243.
[64] Ibid., 296.
[65] Ibid., 298.
[66] Ibid., 300-01.
[67] John Loftus and Mark Aarons, *The Secret War Against the Jews: How Western Espionage Betrayed the Jewish People* (New York: St. Martin's, 1994), 33.
[68] Pawel, *Labyrinth*, 384.
[69] Bein, *Herzl*, 302.
[70] Ibid., 304-05.
[71] Ibid., 313.
[72] Pawel, *Labyrinth*, 309.
[73] Bein, *Herzl*, 329.
[74] Ibid., 334.
[75] Ibid., 14.
[76] Pawel, *Labyrinth*, 430.
[77] Bein, *Herzl*, 341.
[78] Ibid., 346.
[79] Ibid.
[80] Ibid., 347.
[81] Pawel, *Labyrinth*, 259.
[82] Ibid., 445.
[83] Ibid., 311.
[84] Bein, *Herzl*, 369.
[85] Pawel, *Labyrinth*, 300.
[86] Bein, *Herzl*, 363.
[87] Ibid., 349.
[88] Ibid., 351.
[89] Ibid., 377.
[90] Ibid., 385.
[91] Ibid., 387.
[92] Ibid.
[93] Ibid.
[94] Ibid., 346.
[95] Ibid., 390-91.
[96] Ibid., 388-89.
[97] Ibid., 389.
[98] Pawel, *Labyrinth*, 481.
[99] Bein, *Herzl*, 453.
[100] Richard Meinertzhagen, *Middle East Diary: 1917-1956* (New York: Thomas Yoseloff, 1959), 2.
[101] Newman, *Excerpts*, 116.
[102] Ibid., 120.
[103] Bein, *Herzl*, 490.
[104] Ibid., 499-500.
[105] Ibid., 501.
[106] Pawel, *Labyrinth*, 528.
[107] Bein, *Herzl*, 503.
[108] Pawel, *Labyrinth*, 525.
[109] Amos Elon, *Herzl* (New York: Holt, 1975), 400-01.
[110] Pawel, *Labyrinth*, 252.
[111] Bein, *Herzl*, 505.
[112] Ibid.
[113] Pawel, *Labyrinth*, 531.
[114] Ibid., 520.
[115] Bein, *Herzl*, 94-95.
[116] Ibid., 516.
[117] Ibid., 69.
[118] Pawel, *Labyrinth*, 313.
[119] Ibid., 272.
[120] Bein, *Herzl*, 100.
[121] "Nonfiction Book Review: Labyrinth of Exile by Ernst Pawel, Author," *PublishersWeekly.com*, PWxyz, LLC., n.d., Web, 13 Nov. 2015.
[122] Pawel, *Labyrinth*, 48.
[123] Ibid., 125.
[124] Ibid., 529.
[125] Bein, *Herzl*, 518.
[126] Pawel, *Labyrinth*, 64-65.
[127] Arthur Francis Day, *Our Friends, the Jews: Or, the Confessions of a Proselytizer* (Kent, Eng.: Burns, Oates and Washbourne Limited, 1943), 19.
[128] Pawel, *Labyrinth*, 535.
[129] Martin Gilbert, *The Holocaust: A History of the Jews of Europe During the Second World War* (New York: Holt, 1985), 551.
[130] Pawel, *Labyrinth*, 245.
[131] Ibid., 181.
[132] Ibid., 31.
[133] Ibid., 37-38.
[134] Ibid., 461.
[135] Bein, *Herzl*, 136.
[136] Pawel, *Labyrinth*, 531-32.

CHAPTER 5

The Balfour Declaration

[1] Ernst Pawel, *The Labyrinth of Exile: A Life of Theodor Herzl* (New York: Farrar, 1989), 525.
[2] Esco Foundation for Palestine, *Palestine: A Study of Jewish, Arab, and British Policies*, vol. 1 (New Haven, Conn.: Yale UP, 1947), 52-54.

[3] Efraim Karsh and Inari Karsh, *Empires of the Sand: The Struggle for Mastery in the Middle East 1789-1923* (Cambridge: Harvard UP, 1999), 249.
[4] Howard M. Sachar, *A History of Israel: From the Rise of Zionism to Our Time*, 3rd Rev. ed. (New York: Knopf, 2007), 113.
[5] Richard Meinertzhagen, *Middle East Diary: 1917-1956* (New York: Thomas Yoseloff, 1959), 120.
[6] Peter S. Ruckman, *The Books of Ezra, Nehemiah, Esther,* The Bible Believer's Commentary Series (Pensacola: BB Bookstore, 2004), 7.
[7] Chaim Weizmann, *Trial and Error: The Autobiography of Chaim Weizmann* (New York: Schocken, 1949), 179.
[8] Ibid., 180.
[9] Ibid.
[10] Ibid., 181.
[11] Ibid., 181-82.
[12] Ibid., 180.
[13] Weizmann, *Trial and Error*, 182-83.
[14] Ibid., 110-11.
[15] Ibid., 176.
[16] Ronald Sanders, *The High Walls of Jerusalem: A History of the Balfour Declaration and the Birth of the British Mandate for Palestine* (New York: Holt, 1984), 325.
[17] Alison Weir, *Against Our Better Judgment: The Hidden History of How the U.S. Was Used to Create Israel* (Lexington, Ken: CreateSpace, 2014), 11.
[18] Mark Raider, *The Emergence of American Zionism* (New York: New York UP, 1998), 152.
[19] Esco, *Palestine*, 1:87.
[20] Ibid., 90.
[21] John and Hadawi, *Palestine Diary*, 1:75-76.
[22] Michael J. Cohen, *Britain's Moment in Palestine: Retrospect and Perspectives, 1917-1948* (New York: Routledge-Taylor, 2014), 31.
[23] Weizmann, *Trial*, 152.
[24] Carroll Quigley, *Tragedy and Hope: A History of the World in Our Time* (New York: Macmillan, 1966), 246.
[25] Meinertzhagen, *Middle East Diary*, 205.
[26] Arthur Koestler, *Promise and Fulfilment: Palestine 1917-1948* (London: Macmillan, 1949), 4.
[27] Weizmann, *Trial*, 133-34.
[28] Saul David, "How Germany lost the WWI arms race," BBC News Magazine, 15 Feb. 2012, Web, 05 Apr. 2013.
[29] Weizmann, *Trial*, 173.
[30] Quigley, *Tragedy*, 231.
[31] David Lloyd George, *War Memoirs of David Lloyd George: 1915-1916*, vol. 2 (Madison, Wis.: Little, 1933), 50.
[32] Weizmann, *Trial*, 150.
[33] Ibid.
[34] Sachar, *History of Israel*, 99.
[35] Esco, *Palestine*, 1:115.
[36] Ibid., 57.
[37] Karsh and Karsh, *Empires*, 199.
[38] Esco, *Palestine*, 1:81.
[39] Ibid.
[40] David Lloyd George, *The Truth about the Peace Treaties*, vol.2 (London: Victor Gollancz, 1938), 1121.
[41] Ibid.
[42] Paul Kennedy, *The Rise and Fall of the Great Powers: Economic Change and Military Conflict from 1500 to 2000* (New York: Random, 1987), 278.
[43] Quigley, *Tragedy*, 228-29.
[44] Lloyd George, *War Memoirs,* 2:431.
[45] S.L.A. Marshall, *World War I*, 1964, Intro. David Kennedy (New York: Mariner-American Heritage, 2001), 236.
[46] Ibid., 237.
[47] Weir, *Against Our Better Judgment*, 9-10.
[48] Ibid., 13.
[49] John and Hadawi, *Palestine Diary*, 1:69.
[50] Doreen Ingrams, *Palestine Papers, 1917-1922: Seeds of Conflict* (London: Eland, 2009), 8.
[51] Ibid., 16.
[52] John Loftus and Mark Aarons, *The Secret War Against the Jews: How Western Espionage Betrayed the Jewish People* (New York: St. Martin's, 1994), 517.
[53] Ibid., 29.
[54] Ibid.
[55] Ibid., 517.
[56] Ibid., 29.
[57] John and Hadawi, *Palestine Diary*, 1:79.
[58] Ibid., 90.
[59] Samuel Landman, *Great Britain, the Jews and Palestine* (London: New Zionist, 1936), 6.
[60] Kennedy, *Rise and Fall*, 279.
[61] Quigley, *Tragedy*, 256.
[62] Texe Marrs, *Circle of Intrigue: The Hidden Inner Circle of the Global Illuminati Conspiracy* (Austin, Tex.: Living Truth, 1995), 49.
[63] Palestine Royal Commission, *Palestine Royal Commission Report* (London: His Majesty's Stationery Office, 1937), 23.
[64] John and Hadawi, *Palestine Diary*, 1:91.
[65] Ibid., 62-63.
[66] Ibid., 63.
[67] Ibid.
[68] Ibid.
[69] Ibid., 78.
[70] Ingrams, *Palestine Papers*, 19.
[71] Palestine Royal Commission, *Report*, 23.
[72] John and Hadawi, *Palestine Diary*, 1:90-91.
[73] Ibid., 78.
[74] Ibid.,76.
[75] Esco, *Palestine*, 1:58.
[76] Ibid.
[77] Weizmann, *Trial*, 151.
[78] Meinertzhagen, *Middle East Diary*, 66.
[79] Ibid., 59.
[80] Weizmann, *Trial*, 178.
[81] Ibid.
[82] Sachar, *History of Israel*, 98-99.
[83] Esco, *Palestine*, 1:115.
[84] Meinertzhagen, *Middle East Diary*, 202.
[85] Esco, *Palestine*, 1:75.
[86] Ingrams, *Palestine Papers*, 5.
[87] Esco, *Palestine*, 1:116.
[88] Sachar, *History of Israel*, 106-07.
[89] Esco, *Palestine*, 1:116.
[90] Ibid., 117.
[91] Carroll Quigley, *The Anglo-American Establishment: From Rhodes to Cliveden* (New York: Books in Focus, 1981), 169.
[92] Ibid.
[93] William D. Rubinstein, "The Secret of Leopold Amery," *Historical Research* 73, 181 (June 2000), 175-96.
[94] Ingrams, *Palestine Papers*, 7.
[95] Quigley, *Tragedy*, 950.
[96] Ibid.
[97] Quigley, *Anglo-American Establishment*, vii.
[98] William Jasper, *Global Tyranny...Step By Step* (Appleton, Wis.: Western Island, 1993), 53.
[99] Dennis Laurence Cuddy, *Secret Records Revealed: The Men, the Money, and the Methods Behind the New World Order* (Oklahoma City, Okla.: Hearthstone, 1994), 13.
[100] Quigley, *Anglo-American Establishment,* 172.
[101] Ibid.
[102] Ibid., 171.
[103] Ibid., 172.
[104] Ibid., 170.
[105] Ibid., 170.
[106] Weizmann, *Trial*, 171.

CHAPTER 6

Little Wrongs

[1] Chaim Weizmann, *Trial and Error: The Autobiography of Chaim Weizmann* (New York: Schocken, 1949), 208.
[2] Ibid.
[3] Richard Meinertzhagen, *Middle East Diary: 1917-1956* (New York: Thomas Yoseloff, 1959), 141.
[4] Doreen Ingrams, *Palestine Papers, 1917-1922: Seeds of Conflict* (London: Eland, 2009), 169.
[5] Ibid., 73.

[6] Efraim Karsh and Inari Karsh, *Empires of the Sand: The Struggle for Mastery in the Middle East 1789-1923* (Cambridge: Harvard UP, 1999), 186.
[7] Ibid., 204-05.
[8] Ibid., 207.
[9] Ibid., 211.
[10] Ibid., 207-08.
[11] John Loftus and Mark Aarons, *The Secret War Against the Jews: How Western Espionage Betrayed the Jewish People* (New York: St. Martin's, 1994), 29.
[12] Karsh and Karsh, *Empires*, 216-17.
[13] Ibid., 217.
[14] Ibid., 218.
[15] Ibid., 211.
[16] Ibid., 220.
[17] Ibid., 220-21.
[18] Esco Foundation for Palestine, *Palestine: A Study of Jewish, Arab, and British Policies*, vol. 1 (New Haven, Conn.: Yale UP, 1947), 74.
[19] Karsh and Karsh, *Empires*, 274.
[20] Michael Yardley, *Backing into the Limelight: Biography of T. E. Lawrence* (London: Harrap, 1985), 103.
[21] Denis Brian, *The Seven Lives of Colonel Patterson: How an Irish Lion Hunter Led the Jewish Legion to Victory* (Syracuse, N.Y.: Syracuse UP, 2008), 87.
[22] Ibid.
[23] Ibid., 94.
[24] Ibid., 93.
[25] Ibid., xiii.
[26] Ibid., 87.
[27] Ibid., 110.
[28] Esco Foundation for Palestine, *Palestine: A Study of Jewish, Arab, and British Policies,* vol. 1 (New Haven, Conn.: Yale UP, 1947), 209.
[29] Brian, *Seven Lives*, 107.
[30] John Henry Patterson, *With the Judeans in the Palestine Campaign* (New York: Macmillan, 1922), 33.
[31] Brian, *Seven Lives*, 118.
[32] Patterson, *With the Judeans*, 52.
[33] Ibid., 241.
[34] Ibid., 46.
[35] Ibid., vii.
[36] Richard Meinertzhagen, *Middle East Diary: 1917-1956* (New York: Thomas Yoseloff, 1959), 48.
[37] Patterson, *With the Judeans*, 58.
[38] Ibid., viii.
[39] Ibid., 59.
[40] Ibid., 59-60.
[41] Ibid., 82-83.
[42] Ibid., 99.
[43] Ibid., 86, 99.
[44] Ibid., 117.
[45] Ibid., 155.
[46] Ibid., 99.
[47] Brian, *Seven Lives*, 176.
[48] Patterson, *With the Judeans*, 100.
[49] Ibid., 80-81.
[50] Ibid., 113.
[51] Ibid., 74.
[52] Brian, *Seven Lives*, 131.
[53] Ibid., 122-23.
[54] Patterson, *With the Judeans*, 120.
[55] Ibid., 179.
[56] Ibid., 183.
[57] Ibid., 181-82.
[58] Sachar, *History of Israel*, 115.
[59] Brian, *Seven Lives*, 232.
[60] Ibid., 19.
[61] Sachar, *History of Israel*, 93.
[62] Karsh and Karsh, *Empires*, 274.
[63] Ibid., 217.
[64] Ibid., 188.
[65] Meinertzhagen, *Middle East Diary*, 7.
[66] Karsh and Karsh, *Empires*, 189-90.
[67] Ibid., 206-07.
[68] Ibid., 207.
[69] Ibid., 275.
[70] Meinertzhagen, *Middle East Diary*, 86-87.
[71] Karsh and Karsh, *Empires*, 191-92.
[72] Ibid., 191.
[73] Esco, *Palestine*, 1:207.
[74] Karsh and Karsh, *Empires*, 191.
[75] Ibid., 193-95.
[76] Ibid., 197.
[77] Ibid., 196.
[78] Ibid., 198.
[79] Esco, *Palestine*, 1:68-69.
[80] Ingrams, *Palestine Papers*, 2.
[81] Efraim Karsh, *Rethinking the Middle East* (Portland, Ore.: Frank Cass, 2003), 62.
[82] Ibid., 166.
[83] Carroll Quigley, *Tragedy and Hope: A History of the World in Our Time* (New York: Macmillan, 1966), 246.
[84] Karsh, *Rethinking Middle East*, 63.
[85] Karsh and Karsh, *Empires*, 228.
[86] Ibid., 221.
[87] Howard Grief, *The Legal Foundation and Borders of Israel under International Law: A Treatise on Jewish Sovereignty over the Land of Israel* (Jerusalem, Israel: Mazo, 2008), 26.
[88] Karsh and Karsh, *Empires*, 225.
[89] Ibid.
[90] Esco, *Palestine*, 1:60.
[91] Grief, *Legal Foundation*, 25.
[92] Karsh and Karsh, *Empires*, 251.
[93] Ibid., 212-13, 229.
[94] Sachar, *History of Israel*, 95-6.
[95] Karsh and Karsh, *Empires*, 252.
[96] Ibid.
[97] Sachar, *History of Israel*, 101.
[98] Karsh and Karsh, *Empires*, 248.
[99] Ibid.
[100] Ibid., 213.
[101] Sachar, *History of Israel*, 98.
[102] "Sykes-Picot Agreement," Jewish Virtual Library, Web, accessed 14 June 2013.
[103] Karsh and Karsh, *Empires*, 250.
[104] Sachar, *History of Israel*, 101.
[105] Ibid.
[106] Karsh and Karsh, *Empires*, 250.

CHAPTER 7

Towards a Mandate

[1] Doreen Ingrams, *Palestine Papers, 1917-1922: Seeds of Conflict* (London: Eland, 2009), 8-9.
[2] Ibid., 101.
[3] Ibid., 147.
[4] Ernst Frankenstein, *Justice For My People* (New York: Dial, 1944), 198.
[5] Esco Foundation for Palestine, *Palestine: A Study of Jewish, Arab, and British Policies*, vol. 1 (New Haven, Conn.: Yale UP, 1947), 266.
[6] Palestine Royal Commission, *Palestine Royal Commission Report* (London: His Majesty's Stationery Office, 1937), 33.
[7] Esco, *Palestine*, 1:111.
[8] Richard Meinertzhagen, *Middle East Diary: 1917-1956* (New York: Thomas Yoseloff, 1959), 8-9.
[9] Ingrams, *Palestine Papers*, 174.
[10] Meinertzhagen, *Middle East Diary*, 68.
[11] Ingrams, *Palestine Papers*, 20.
[12] Ibid., 21.
[13] Ibid., 22.
[14] Ibid., 23.
[15] Ibid., 24.
[16] Ibid., 21.
[17] Chaim Weizmann, *Trial and Error: The Autobiography of Chaim Weizmann* (New York: Schocken, 1949), 217-18.
[18] Ingrams, *Palestine Papers*, 55.
[19] Efraim Karsh and Inari Karsh, *Empires of the Sand: The Struggle for Mastery in the Middle East 1789-1923* (Cambridge: Harvard UP, 1999), 268.
[20] Ibid.

[21] Alison Weir, *Against Our Better Judgment: The Hidden History of How the U.S. Was Used to Create Israel* (Lexington, Ken: CreateSpace, 2014), 25.
[22] Ibid., 139-40.
[23] Esco, *Palestine*, 1:218.
[24] Ibid., 221.
[25] Ibid., 145-46.
[26] Karsh and Karsh, *Empires of the Sand*, 284.
[27] John Henry Patterson, *With the Judeans in the Palestine Campaign* (New York: Macmillan, 1922), 259.
[28] Denis Brian, *The Seven Lives of Colonel Patterson: How an Irish Lion Hunter Led the Jewish Legion to Victory* (Syracuse, N.Y.: Syracuse UP, 2008), 140.
[29] Patterson, *With the Judeans*, 253.
[30] Ibid., 253-54.
[31] Ibid., 261.
[32] Meinertzhagen, *Middle East Diary*, 79-80.
[33] Ibid., 83.
[34] Weizmann, *Trial*, 258-59.
[35] John Loftus and Mark Aarons, *The Secret War Against the Jews: How Western Espionage Betrayed the Jewish People* (New York: St. Martin's, 1994), 26.
[36] Ibid., 30-31.
[37] Weizmann, *Trial*, 260.
[38] Howard Grief, *The Legal Foundation and Borders of Israel under International Law: A Treatise on Jewish Sovereignty over the Land of Israel* (Jerusalem, Israel: Mazo, 2008), 18.
[39] Esco, *Palestine*, 1:148-49.
[40] Meinertzhagen, *Middle East Diary*, 87.
[41] Esco, *Palestine*, 1:259.
[42] Meinertzhagen, *Middle East Diary*, 92.
[43] Ibid., 88.
[44] Esco, *Palestine*, 1:226.
[45] Grief, *Legal Foundation*, 45.
[46] Gideon Biger, "The Boundaries of Mandatory Palestine: How the Past Influences the Future," in *Israel: The First Hundred Years*, vol. 1: *Israel's Transition from Community to State*, ed. Efraim Karsh (London: Frank Cass, 2000), 112.
[47] Grief, *Legal Foundation*, 47.
[48] Ingrams, *Palestine Papers*, 77.
[49] Grief, *Legal Foundation*, 54.
[50] Ibid.
[51] Meinertzhagen, *Middle East Diary*, 96.
[52] William Manchester, *The Last Lion, Winston Spencer Churchill*, vol. 1: *Visions of Glory, 1874-1932* (New York: Dell-Bantam Doubleday, 1983), 703.
[53] Ibid.
[54] Ibid., 704-05.
[55] Esco, *Palestine*, 1:267.
[56] Howard M. Sachar, *A History of Israel: From the Rise of Zionism to Our Time,* 3rd Rev. ed. (New York: Knopf, 2007), 126.
[57] Karsh and Karsh, *Empires*, 323.
[58] Ibid., 324.
[59] Esco, *Palestine*, 1:267.
[60] David Garnett, ed., *The Letters of T. E. Lawrence of Arabia* (London: Jonathan Cape, 1938), 333.
[61] Ingrams, *Palestine Papers*, 121.
[62] Palestine Royal Commission, *Report*, 51.
[63] Meinertzhagen, *Middle East Diary*, 50.
[64] Ibid., 134.
[65] Ibid., 97.
[66] Ibid., 100.
[67] Ingrams, *Palestine Papers*, 139.
[68] Ibid., 144.
[69] Esco, *Palestine*, 1:476.
[70] Larry Collins and Dominique Lapierre, *O Jerusalem!* (New York: Simon, 1972), 92.
[71] Manchester, *Last Lion*, 1:700.
[72] Ernst Frankenstein, *Justice For My People* (New York: Dial, 1944), 105-06.
[73] Palestine Royal Commission, *Report*, 38.
[74] "Zionist Organization Statement on Palestine, Paris Peace Conference, February 3, 1919," Jewish Virtual Library, Web, accessed 02 July 2013.
[75] Ingrams, *Palestine Papers*, 43.
[76] Grief, *Legal Foundation*, 311.
[77] Weizmann, *Trial*, 219-20.
[78] Meinertzhagen, *Middle East Diary*, 86.
[79] "Chaim Weizmann the Scientist," The Chaim Weizmann Laboratory, Web, accessed 07 July 2013.
[80] Grief, *Legal Foundation*, 311-12.
[81] Ibid., 351.
[82] League of Nations, *Official Journal,* November 1922, 1188-89.
[83] Weizmann, *Trial*, 290.
[84] Esco, *Palestine*, 1:284.
[85] Frankenstein, *Justice*, 105.
[86] Grief, *Legal Foundation*, 310-11.
[87] Ibid., 312.
[88] Frankenstein, *Justice*, 105.
[89] Ibid.
[90] King Abdallah of Jordan, *My Memoirs Completed: "Al-Takmilah"* (Washington: Near Eastern Translation Program, 1954), 96-97.
[91] Weizmann, *Trial*, 292.
[92] Ibid., 293.
[93] Meinertzhagen, *Middle East Diary*, 134.

CHAPTER 8
The First Decade

[1] Esco Foundation for Palestine, *Palestine: A Study of Jewish, Arab, and British Policies*, vol. 1 (New Haven, Conn.: Yale UP, 1947), 409.
[2] Ruth Kark and Joseph B. Glass, "The Jews in Eretz-Israel/Palestine: From Traditional Peripherality to Modern Centrality," in *Israel: The First Hundred Years*, vol. 1: *Israel's Transition from Community to State*, ed. Efraim Karsh (London: Frank Cass, 2000), 98.
[3] Howard M. Sachar, *A History of Israel: From the Rise of Zionism to Our Time*, 3rd Rev. ed. (New York: Knopf, 2007), 161.
[4] Chaim Weizmann, *Trial and Error: The Autobiography of Chaim Weizmann* (New York: Schocken, 1949), 303.
[5] Esco, *Palestine*, 1:368.
[6] Ibid., 368-69.
[7] Eyal Chowers, *The Political Philosophy of Zionism: Trading Jewish Words for a Hebraic Land* (New York: Cambridge UP, 2012), 148.
[8] Chaim Herzog, *Heroes of Israel: Profiles of Jewish Courage* (Boston: Little, 1989), 105.
[9] Sachar, *History of Israel*, 151.
[10] Esco, *Palestine*, 1:380-81.
[11] Sachar, *History of Israel*, 143.
[12] Weizmann, *Trial*, 266.
[13] Ibid., 272,
[14] Esco, *Palestine*, 1:381.
[15] Ibid., 383-84.
[16] Ibid., 385.
[17] Michael Brenner, *A Short History of the Jews*, trans. Jeremiah Riemer (Princeton, N.J.: Princeton UP, 2010), 314.
[18] Esco, *Palestine*, 1:384-85.
[19] Ibid., 386.
[20] Sachar, *History of Israel*, 157.
[21] Esco, *Palestine*, 1:387-88.
[22] Ibid., 394-95.
[23] Ibid., 397-98.
[24] Ibid., 403-04.
[25] Sachar, *History of Israel*, 154.
[26] Yossi Katz, "Zionism and Jerusalem - the Conflict of Priorities: Changes in Zionist Settlement in the Jerusalem Vicinity, 1937-48, " in *Israel: The First Hundred Years*, vol. 1: *Israel's Transition from Community to State*, ed. Efraim Karsh (London: Frank Cass, 2000), 121.
[27] Ibid., 123.
[28] Ibid., 125.
[29] Ibid., 127.
[30] Ibid., 125, 128.
[31] Ibid., 126.
[32] Ernst Frankenstein, *Justice For My People* (New York: Dial, 1944), 148-49.

[33] Denis Brian, *The Seven Lives of Colonel Patterson: How an Irish Lion Hunter Led the Jewish Legion to Victory* (Syracuse, N.Y.: Syracuse UP, 2008), 139.
[34] Doreen Ingrams, *Palestine Papers, 1917-1922: Seeds of Conflict* (London: Eland, 2009), 96.
[35] Frankenstein, *Justice*, 149.
[36] John Loftus and Mark Aarons, *The Secret War Against the Jews: How Western Espionage Betrayed the Jewish People* (New York: St. Martin's, 1994), 32-33.
[37] Ibid., 34.
[38] Ibid.
[39] Ibid.
[40] Robin Leonard Bidwell et al., *British Documents on Foreign Affairs-Reports and Papers from the Foreign Office Confidential Print: The Pilgrimage in the Reign of Ibn Saud, 1927-1939* (Lanham, Md.: University Publications of America, 1989), xi-xiii.
[41] Ibid., 35.
[42] Ibid.
[43] Ibid.
[44] Daniel Yergin, *The Prize: The Epic Quest for Oil, Money, and Power* (New York: Touchstone-Simon, 1992), 286-87.
[45] Loftus and Aarons, *Secret War Against Jews*, 35-36.
[46] Albert Marrin, *Black Gold: The Story of Oil in Our Lives* (New York: Knopf, 2012), 69.
[47] Esco, *Palestine*, 1:295.
[48] Ibid., 296.
[49] Esco Foundation for Palestine, *Palestine: A Study of Jewish, Arab, and British Policies*, vol. 2 (New Haven, Conn.: Yale UP, 1947), 602.
[50] Ibid., 604.
[51] Ibid., 605.
[52] Ibid.
[53] Ibid., 605-06.
[54] Ibid., 608.
[55] Daniel Greenfield, "Remembering the 65th Anniversary of the Hadassah Medical Convoy Massacre," 15 Mar. 2013, Front Page Mag, 07 Mar. 2014.
[56] Palestine Royal Commission, *Palestine Royal Commission Report* (London: His Majesty's Stationery Office, 1937), 68.
[57] Esco, *Palestine*, 2:614-15.
[58] Ibid., 615.
[59] Ibid., 617.
[60] Ibid., 621.
[61] Ibid., 622.
[62] Ibid., 624-25.
[63] Ibid., 625.
[64] Ibid.
[65] Ibid., 629.
[66] Weizmann, *Trial*, 332.
[67] Esco, *Palestine*, 2:633.
[68] Ibid., 635.
[69] Ibid., 637.
[70] Ibid., 638.
[71] Sachar, *History of Israel*, 176.
[72] Ibid.
[73] Ibid.
[74] Esco, *Palestine*, 2:648.
[75] Ibid., 648-49.
[76] Sachar, *History of Israel*, 177.
[77] Esco, *Palestine*, 2:649.
[78] Sachar, *History of Israel*, 178.
[79] Ibid.
[80] Esco, *Palestine*, 2:660.
[81] Sachar, *History of Israel*, 178.
[82] Klaus Michael Mallmann and Martin Cüppers, *Nazi Palestine: The Plans for Extermination of the Jews in Palestine*, trans. Krista Smith (New York: Enigma, 2005), 15-16.
[83] Alison Weir, *Against Our Better Judgment: The Hidden History of How the U.S. Was Used to Create Israel* (Lexington, Ken: CreateSpace, 2014), 43.

CHAPTER 9

Prelude to War

[1] Antony C. Sutton, *Wall Street and the Rise of Hitler: The Astonishing True Story of the American Financiers Who Bankrolled the Nazis* (West Sussex: Clairview, 2010), 11.
[2] John Loftus and Mark Aarons, *The Secret War Against the Jews: How Western Espionage Betrayed the Jewish People* (New York: St. Martin's, 1994), 38.
[3] Anthony Gallea, *Bulls Make Money, Bears Make Money, Pigs Get Slaughtered: Investment Wisdom that Stands the Test of Time* (New York: New York Inst. of Finance, 2002), front dust jacket.
[4] Ibid., 55.
[5] Ibid., 39.
[6] Carroll Quigley, *Tragedy and Hope: A History of the World in Our Time* (New York: Macmillan, 1966), 305-06.
[7] Ibid., 307.
[8] Ibid., 308.
[9] Ibid., 309.
[10] Ibid., 308.
[11] Leo Haber, ed., "Zionism," *Midstream* 1995, Web, 12 June 2015, 33.
[12] Glen Yeadon and John Hawkins, *The Nazi Hydra in America: Suppressed History of a Century: Wall Street and the Rise of the Fourth Reich* (Joshua Tree, Calif.: Progressive, 1999), 85.
[13] Ibid., 57.
[14] Ibid.
[15] Quigley, *Tragedy*, 309.
[16] Sutton, *Wall Street and Hitler*, 21.
[17] Ibid., 15-16.
[18] Robert Engler, *The Politics of Oil: A Study of Private Power and Democratic Directions* (Chicago: Phoenix-U of Chicago P, 1961), 102.
[19] Sutton, *Wall Street and Hitler*, 21.
[20] Ibid., 22.
[21] Max Wallace, *The American Axis: Henry Ford, Charles Lindbergh, and the Rise of the Third Reich* (New York: St. Martin's, 2003), 54.
[22] Ibid., 2.
[23] Reinhold Billstein et al., "1945. How the Americans Took Over Cologne–and Discovered Ford Werke's Role in the War," in *Working for the Enemy; Ford, General Motors, and Forced Labor in Germany during the Second World War*, ed. Nicholas Levis (New York: Berghahn, 2000), 111.
[24] Raul Hilberg, *The Destruction of the European Jews*, 3rd ed., 3 Vols. (New Haven: Yale UP, 2003), 3:1034.
[25] Shlomo Venezia, *Inside the Gas Chambers: Eight Months in the Sonderkommando of Auschwitz*, ed. Jean Mouttapa, trans. Andrew Brown (Malden, Mass.: Polity, 2009), 41.
[26] Sutton, *Wall Street and Hitler*, 21.
[27] Engler, *Politics of Oil*, 100.
[28] Daniel Yergin, *The Prize: The Epic Quest for Oil, Money, and Power* (New York: Touchstone-Simon, 1992), 330.
[29] Ibid.
[30] Engler, *Politics of Oil*, 102.
[31] Ibid.
[32] Quigley, *Tragedy*, 510.
[33] Yergin, *The Prize*, 331.
[34] Burton Hersh, *The Old Boys: The American Elite and the Origins of the CIA* (St. Petersburg, Fla.: Tree Farm, 2002), 62.
[35] Yergin, *The Prize*, 333.
[36] Quigley, *Tragedy*, 513.
[37] Yergin, *The Prize*, 333.
[38] Sutton, *Wall Street and Hitler*, 21-22.
[39] Engler, *Politics of Oil*, 103-04.
[40] Sutton, *Wall Street and Hitler*, 33.
[41] Ibid., 35.
[42] Yergin, *The Prize*, 333, 344.
[43] Ibid., 345.
[44] Ibid., 345-46.
[45] Ibid., 346.
[46] Ibid., 284.
[47] Ibid., 287-88.
[48] Ibid., 292.

[49] Ibid., 301.
[50] Loftus and Aarons, *Secret War Against Jews*, 44.
[51] Engler, *Politics of Oil*, 182.
[52] Ibid., 182, 199.
[53] Loftus and Aarons, *Secret War Against Jews*, 68.
[54] Ibid., 39-40.
[55] Ibid., 38.
[56] Ibid., 61, 63.
[57] Antony C. Sutton, *America's Secret Establishment: An Introduction to The Order of Skull & Bones* (Billings, Mont.: Liberty House, 1986), 172.
[58] *John Loftus, America's Nazi Secret: An Insider's History of How the United States Department of Justice Obstructed Congress* (Walterville, Ore.: TrineDay, 2011), 7.
[59] Loftus and Aarons, *Secret War Against Jews* , 63-64.
[60] Ibid., 64.
[61] Ibid., 64-70.
[62] Ibid., 528.
[63] Esco Foundation for Palestine, *Palestine: A Study of Jewish, Arab, and British Policies*, vol. 2 (New Haven, Conn.: Yale UP, 1947), 766, 787.
[64] Klaus Michael Mallmann and Martin Cüppers, *Nazi Palestine: The Plans for Extermination of the Jews in Palestine*, trans. Krista Smith (New York: Enigma, 2005), 23.
[65] Ibid.
[66] Ibid., 22, 24.
[67] Ibid., 20.
[68] Howard M. Sachar, *A History of Israel: From the Rise of Zionism to Our Time*, 3rd Rev. ed. (New York: Knopf, 2007), 200.
[69] Esco, *Palestine*, 2:795.
[70] Ibid.
[71] Ibid., 797.
[72] "Pre-State Israel: The 1936 Arab Riots (April - November 1936)," *Jewish Virtual Library*, American-Israeli Cooperatve Enterprise, n.d. Web, 13 June 2015.
[73] Esco, *Palestine*, 2:797.
[74] Ibid., 826.
[75] Palestine Royal Commission, *Palestine Royal Commission Report* (London: His Majesty's Stationery Office, 1937), 131.
[76] Esco, *Palestine*, 2:829.
[77] Palestine Royal Commission, *Report*, 300.
[78] Ibid., 394.
[79] Mallmann and Cüppers, *Nazi Palestine*, 19.
[80] Peter Longerich, *Holocaust: The Nazi Persecution and Murder of the Jews* (New York: Oxford UP, 2010), dust jacket front flap.
[81] Ibid., 5.
[82] Hilberg, *Destruction of Jews*, 1:64.
[83] Longerich, *Holocaust*, 65.
[84] Ibid., 30, 71.
[85] Ibid., 33, 38-41.
[86] Hilberg, *Destruction of Jews*, 1:68-9.
[87] Longerich, *Holocaust*, 99.
[88] Hilberg, *Destruction of Jews*, 1:176.
[89] Hilberg, 2:701.
[90] Hilberg, 1:130.
[91] Ibid., 129.
[92] David S. Wyman, *The Abandonment of the Jews: America and the Holocaust, 1941-1945* (New York: Pantheon-Random, 1985), 5.
[93] Arthur D. Morse, *While Six Million Died: A Chronicle of American Apathy* (New York: Random, 1968), 210.
[94] Ibid., 212.
[95] Ibid., 214.
[96] Ibid., 219.
[97] Ibid., 221.
[98] Ibid.
[99] Golda Meir, *My Life* (New York: Putnam's, 1975), 158.
[100] Bernard Wasserstein, *Britain and the Jews of Europe: 1939-1945* (New York: Oxford UP, 1979), 28.
[101] Wyman, *Abandonment of Jews*, 6.
[102] Morse, *While Six Million Died*, 217.
[103] Ibid., 224.
[104] Richard Meinertzhagen, *Middle East Diary: 1917-1956* (New York: Thomas Yoseloff, 1959), 170-71.
[105] Wyman, *Abandonment of Jews*, 9.
[106] Morse, *While Six Million Died*, 189.
[107] Richard Sandomir, "FILM; He Batted for the Tigers, Himself and American Jews," *New York Times*, 09 Jan. 2000, Web, 05 Nov. 2013.
[108] Howard Megdal, "Religion Aided a Home Run Chase, and May Have Led to its Failure," *The New York Times*, 20 Mar. 2010, Web, 05 Nov. 2013.
[109] Ibid.
[110] John P. McTernan, *As America Has Done to Israel* (N.p.: Xulon, 2006), 47-48.
[111] Ibid., 48.
[112] Ibid., 49-50.
[113] Ibid., 48.
[114] Ibid., 51.
[115] R. A. Scotti, *Sudden Sea: The Great Hurricane of 1938* (New York: Little, 2003), 242.
[116] Aram Goudsouzian, *The Hurricane of 1938* (Beverly, Mass.: Commonwealth Editions, 2004), 21.
[117] McTernan, *As America*, 40.
[118] Goudsouzian, *Hurricane of 1938*, 72.
[119] Peter Longerich, *The Unwritten Order: Hitler's Role in the Final Solution* (Gloucestershire: Tempus, 2001), 64-65.
[120] Wasserstein, *Britain and the Jews*, 6.
[121] Morse, *While Six Million Died*, 236-37.
[122] Ibid., 234.
[123] Mallmann and Cüppers, *Nazi Palestine*, 27.
[124] Graham Macklin, *Chamberlain* (London: Haus, 2006), 52.
[125] Richard Breitman, *Official Secrets: What the Nazis Planned, What the British and Americans Knew* (New York: Hill and Wang-Farrar , 1998), 182.
[126] Martin Gilbert, *In Ishmael's House: A History of Jews in Muslim Lands* (Toronto: McClelland & Stewart, 2010), 174.
[127] "British White Paper of 1939," *The Avalon Project*, Yale Law School Lillian Goldman Law Library, 2008, Web, 12 June 2015.
[128] Esco, *Palestine*, 2:902.
[129] Wasserstein, *Britain and the Jews*, 17.
[130] Esco, *Palestine*, 2:911.
[131] Wasserstein, *Britain and the Jews*, 21.
[132] Ibid.
[133] Morse, *While Six Million Died*, 291.
[134] Ibid., 288.
[135] Ibid., 300.

CHAPTER 10

The Real "Final Solution"

[1] Monty Noam Penkower, *Decision on Palestine Deferred: America, Britain and Wartime Diplomacy,* 1939-1945 (Portland, Ore.: Frank Cass, 2002), 7.
[2] Ibid.
[3] Chaim Weizmann, *Trial and Error: The Autobiography of Chaim Weizmann* (New York: Schocken, 1949), 414.
[4] Bernard Wasserstein, *Britain and the Jews of Europe: 1939-1945* (New York: Oxford UP, 1979), 40.
[5] Ibid., 43.
[6] Walter Laqueur, *The Terrible Secret: Suppression of the Truth about Hitler's 'Final Solution'* (Boston: Little, 1980), 1.
[7] Raul Hilberg, *The Destruction of the European Jews*, 3rd ed., 3 Vols. (New Haven: Yale UP, 2003), 3:1054.
[8] Laqueur, *Terrible Secret*, 2.
[9] Hilberg, *Destruction of Jews*, 2:423-24.
[10] "Instructions by Heydrich on Policy and Operations Concerning Jews in the Occupied Territories, September 21, 1939," Shoah Resource Center, Web, accessed 18 Feb. 2014.
[11] Robert L. Baker, *Oil, Blood, and Sand* (New York: D. Appleton-Century, 1942), 40.
[12] Peter Longerich, *Holocaust: The Nazi Persecution and Murder of the Jews* (New York: Oxford UP, 2010), 153.
[13] Hilberg, *Destruction of Jews*, 2:426.
[14] Leslie Alan Horvitz and Christopher Catherwood, *Encyclopedia of War Crimes and Genocide* (New York: Facts on File-Infobase, 2006), 139.
[15] Arthur D. Morse, *While Six Million Died: A Chronicle of American Apathy* (New York: Random, 1968), 317.

[16] Laqueur, *Terrible Secret*, 12.
[17] Hilberg, *Destruction of Jews*, 3:1086-87.
[18] Bernard Wasserstein, *Britain and the Jews of Europe: 1939-1945* (New York: Oxford UP, 1979), 136.
[19] Ibid.
[20] Hilberg, *Destruction of Jews*, 1:34.
[21] Hilberg, 2:410.
[22] Wasserstein, *Britain and the Jews*, 42.
[23] Ibid., 43-44.
[24] Hilberg, *Destruction of Jews*, 1:136.
[25] Bryan Mark Rigg, *Hitler's Jewish Soldiers: The Untold Story of Nazi Racial Laws and Men of Jewish Descent in the German Military* (Lawrence, Kans.: UP of Kansas, 2002), 16.
[26] Peter Longerich, *The Unwritten Order: Hitler's Role in the Final Solution* (Gloucestershire: Tempus, 2001), 32.
[27] Ibid., 156.
[28] Nora Levin, *The Holocaust: The Destruction of European Jewry 1933-1945* (New York: Crowell, 1968), 314.
[29] Hilberg, *Destruction of Jews*, 3:1097.
[30] Hitler, Adolf, *Mein Kampf*, trans. James Murphy (1939; reprint, N.p.: Bottom of the Hill, 2010), 58.
[31] Hilberg, *Destruction of Jews*, 2:411.
[32] Longerich, *Holocaust*, 124.
[33] Ibid.
[34] Longerich, *Unwritten Order*, 92.
[35] Longerich, *Holocaust*, 163.
[36] Wasserstein, *Britain and the Jews*, 43.
[37] Hilberg, *Destruction of Jews*, 2:414.
[38] Wasserstein, *Britain and the Jews*, 43.
[39] Longerich, *Holocaust*, 68.
[40] Hilberg, *Destruction of Jews*, 1:139.
[41] Hilberg, 2:412.
[42] Wasserstein, *Britain and the Jews*, 45.
[43] Hilberg, *Destruction of Jews*, 2:418.
[44] Longerich, *Holocaust*, 275.
[45] Hilberg, *Destruction of Jews*, 2:418.
[46] Hilberg, 1:224.
[47] Ibid., 4.
[48] Hilberg, 2:423.
[49] Ibid., 424.
[50] Hilberg, 1:50-52.
[51] Hilberg, 2:413.
[52] Ibid.,412.
[53] Ibid.
[54] Longerich, *Holocaust*, 125.
[55] Hilberg, *Destruction of Jews*, 2:680.
[56] David S. Wyman, *The Abandonment of the Jews: America and the Holocaust, 1941-1945* (New York: Pantheon-Random, 1985), 183.
[57] Elie Wiesel, *Night*, trans., Marion Wiesel (New York: Hill and Wang-Farrar, 2006), 81.
[58] Wasserstein, *Britain and the Jews*, 166-67.
[59] Ibid., 167.
[60] Ibid., 96.
[61] Ibid., 52.
[62] Ibid., 54.
[63] Ibid., 74.
[64] Ibid., 58.
[65] Wyman, *Abandonment of Jews*, 218.
[66] Yehuda Bauer, *American Jewry and the Holocaust: The American Jewish Joint Distribution Committee, 1939-1945* (Detroit: Wayne State UP, 1981), 353.
[67] Wasserstein, *Britain and the Jews*, 60-61.
[68] Ibid., 69.
[69] Ibid., 76.
[70] Ibid., 144.
[71] Arthur D. Morse, *While Six Million Died: A Chronicle of American Apathy* (New York: Random, 1968), 321.
[72] Wasserstein, *Britain and the Jews*, 156.
[73] Ibid., 154.
[74] Morse, *While Six Million Died*, 202.
[75] Ibid.
[76] Wyman, *Abandonment of Jews*, 8.
[77] Ibid., 10.
[78] US Bureau of the Census, *Statistical Abstract of the United States: 1970,* 91st ed. (Washington, DC: 1970), 91.
[79] Morse, *While Six Million Died*, 98.
[80] Wyman, *Abandonment of Jews*, 136.
[81] Ibid.
[82] Ibid., 126.
[83] Ibid., 127.
[84] Morse, *While Six Million Died*, 141-42.
[85] Wyman, *Abandonment of Jews*, 133.
[86] Ibid., 137.
[87] Morse, *While Six Million Died*, 154.
[88] Irene Zoech, "Named: the baby boy who was Nazis' first euthanasia victim," *The Sunday Telegraph*, October 12, 2003, Web, 25 February 2014.
[89] Longerich, *Holocaust*, 136.
[90] Trevor Ravenscroft, *The Spear of Destiny: The Occult Power Behind the Spear Which Pierced the Side of Christ* (York Beach, Maine: Samuel Weiser, 1982), 8-9.
[91] Longerich, *Unwritten Order*, 81.
[92] Longerich, *Holocaust*, 138.
[93] Giuliana S. Bullard, ed., "More CIA Name Files Released," November 2002, Disclosure, Web, 27 February 2014.
[94] Henry Friedlander, *The Origins of Nazi Genocide: From Euthanasia to the Final Solution* (Chapel Hill: UNC P, 1995), 139.
[95] Hilberg, *Destruction of Jews*, 3:963.
[96] Longerich, *Holocaust*, 139-42.
[97] Ibid., 140-42.
[98] Ibid., 145.
[99] Wasserstein, *Britain and the Jews*, 134.
[100] Wyman, *Abandonment of Jews*, 4.
[101] Hilberg, *Destruction of Jews*, 1:283.
[102] Longerich, *Holocaust*, 182.
[103] Hilberg, *Destruction of Jews*, 1:287.
[104] Ibid., 288.
[105] Longerich, *Holocaust*, 183.
[106] Ibid., 247.
[107] Hilberg, *Destruction of Jews*, 1:293.
[108] Hilberg, 3:1084-85.
[109] Longerich, *Holocaust*, 189.
[110] Ibid., 190.
[111] Ibid.
[112] Ibid., 191.
[113] Ibid., 192.
[114] Ibid., 203.
[115] Ibid., 207.
[116] Ibid.
[117] Hilberg, *Destruction of Jews*, 3:1095.
[118] Longerich, *Holocaust*, 244.
[119] Ibid., 201.
[120] Longerich, *Unwritten Order*, 117.
[121] Longerich, *Holocaust*, 221.
[122] Hilberg, *Destruction of Jews*, 1:294.
[123] Longerich, *Holocaust*, 239.
[124] Ibid., 196.
[125] Ibid., 238.
[126] Wasserstein, *Britain and the Jews*, 138.
[127] Hilberg, *Destruction of Jews*, 1:323.
[128] Longerich, *Holocaust*, 230.
[129] Wasserstein, *Britain and the Jews*, 137.
[130] Charles Lawliss, *...and GOD CRIED: The Holocaust Remembered* (North Dighton, Mass.: JG, 1994), 73.
[131] Martin Gilbert, *The Holocaust: A History of the Jews of Europe during the Second World War* (New York: Henry Holt, 1985), 155.
[132] Warren I. Cohen, *Profiles in Humanity: The Battle for Peace, Freedom, Equality, and Human Rights* (Lanham, Md.: Rowman & Littlefield: 2009), 149.
[133] Wyman, *Abandonment of Jews*, 3-4.
[134] Gilbert, *Holocaust*, 178.
[135] Hilberg, *Destruction of Jews*, 1:300.
[136] Hilberg, 2:517.
[137] Hilberg, 1:311-89.
[138] Ibid., 405.
[139] Ibid., 392.

[140] John Loftus and Mark Aarons, *The Secret War Against the Jews: How Western Espionage Betrayed the Jewish People* (New York: St. Martin's, 1994), 498.
[141] Wyman, *Abandonment of Jews*, 20.
[142] Gilbert, *Holocaust*, 203.
[143] Ibid., 420-22.
[144] Ibid., 422.
[145] Ibid.
[146] Ibid., 423.
[147] Ibid., 424.
[148] Hilberg, *Destruction of Jews*, 1:353.
[149] Longerich, *Unwritten Order*, 23.
[150] Ibid., 149.
[151] Longerich, *Holocaust*, 181.
[152] Ibid., 292-93.
[153] Ibid., 293.
[154] Ibid.
[155] Ibid., 318.
[156] Ibid., 305.
[157] Ibid., 306.
[158] Ibid., 307.
[159] Ibid., 308.
[160] Ibid., 309.
[161] Ibid., 308.
[162] Longergich, *Unwritten Order*, 173.
[163] Longerich, *Holocaust*, 309-10.
[164] Longergich, *Unwritten Order*, 154.
[165] Hilberg, *Destruction of Jews*, 3:958.
[166] Gilbert, *Holocaust*, 502.
[167] Hilberg, *Destruction of Jews*, 3:1080.
[168] Ernst Klee, Willi Dressen, and Volker Riess, *"The Good Old Days": The Holocaust as Seen by Its Perpetrators and Bystanders*, trans. Deborah Burnstone (Old Saybrook, Conn.: Konecky & Konecky, 1991), 163.
[169] Ibid., 167.
[170] Christopher Simpson, *Blowback: America's Recruitment of Nazis and Its Effects on the Cold War* (New York: Weidenfeld & Nicolson,1988), 25.
[171] Hilberg, *Destruction of Jews*, 2:546.
[172] Jürg Amann, ed. *The Commandant: The Rudolf Hoess Text* (New York: Peter Mayer-Overlook Duckworth, 2012), 71.
[173] Hilberg, *Destruction of Jews*, 1:337.
[174] Ibid., 1:345.
[175] Longerich, *Holocaust*, 278, 339.
[176] Lucja Pawlicka-Nowak, ed., *The Extermination Center for Jews in Chelmno-On-Ner in the Light of the Latest Research*, trans. Arkadiusz Kamiński and Katarzyna Krawczyk (Lodz, Poland: Oficyna Bibliofilów, 2004), 93.
[177] Gilbert, *Holocaust*, 260.
[178] Pawlicka-Nowak, *Extermination Center for Jews*, 50.
[179] Konnilyn G. Feig, *Hitler's Death Camps: The Sanity of Madness* (New York: Holmes & Meier, 1979), 270.
[180] Longerich, *Holocaust*, 138.
[181] Pawlicka-Nowak, *Extermination Center for Jews*, 50.
[182] Feig, *Hitler's Death Camps*, 270.
[183] Hilberg, *Destruction of Jews*, 3:1041.
[184] Feig, *Hitler's Death Camps*, 270.
[185] Gilbert, *Holocaust*, 248, 266, 269.
[186] Feig, *Hitler's Death Camps*, 270.
[187] Gilbert, *Holocaust*, 722.0
[188] Ibid., 447.
[189] Patrick Montague, *Chelmno and the Holocaust: A History of Hitler's First Death Camp* (London: Tauris, 2012), 123.
[190] Hilberg, *Destruction of Jews*, 2:515.
[191] Pawlicka-Nowak, *Extermination Center for Jews*, 49.
[192] Gilbert, *Holocaust*, 260.
[193] Ibid., 246.
[194] Feig, *Hitler's Death Camps*, 271.
[195] Miroslaw Zbigniew Wojalski, *The Jewish Cemetery in Lodz*, trans. Guido Schreiber (Lodz, Poland: Widzewska Oficyna Wydawnicza ZORA, 2001), 5.
[196] Ibid., 20, 65.
[197] Hilberg, *Destruction of Jews*, 3:961.
[198] Longerich, *Holocaust*, 430.
[199] Callum MacDonald, *The Killing of Reinhard Heydrich: The SS "Butcher of Prague"* (Cambridge: Da Capo, 1998), 181.
[200] Ibid.
[201] Ibid., 182.
[202] Longerich, *Holocaust*, 332.
[203] Ibid., 431.
[204] Ibid., 340.
[205] Morse, *While Six Million Died*, 207.
[206] Hilberg, *Destruction of Jews*, 3:981.
[207] Laqueur, *Terrible Secret*, 99.
[208] Hilberg, *Destruction of Jews*, 3:1211-13.
[209] Robert Furmanczuk and Lidia Kelly, "Ravensbrueck Letters Written in Urine Gifted to Polish Museum," *Reuters*, Ed. Tom Heneghan, Thomson Reuters, 20 Feb. 2017, Web, 04 Mar. 2017.
[210] Laqueur, *Terrible Secret*, 138-39.
[211] Wasserstein, *Britain and the Jews*, 167.
[212] Laqueur, *Terrible Secret*, 93.
[213] Ibid., 136-37.
[214] Ibid., 73-74.
[215] Hilberg, *Destruction of Jews*, 3:1202.
[216] Laqueur, *Terrible Secret*, 99.
[217] Ibid., 32.
[218] Ibid., 83.
[219] Wyman, *Abandonment of Jews*, 42-43, 362.
[220] Morse, *While Six Million Died*, 9.
[221] Ibid.
[222] Laqueur, *Terrible Secret*, 80.
[223] Morse, *While Six Million Died*, 23.
[224] Wyman, *Abandonment of Jews*, 23.
[225] Ibid., 24-25.
[226] Morse, *While Six Million Died*, 26.
[227] Wasserstein, *Britain and the Jews*, 169.
[228] Morse, *While Six Million Died*, 20.
[229] Wyman, *Abandonment of Jews*, 51.
[230] Nancy Scott Anderson and Dwight Anderson, *The Generals* (New York: Knopf, 1988), 399.
[231] Wyman, *Abandonment of Jews*, 72.
[232] Ibid.
[234] Wasserstein, *Britain and the Jews*, 172-73.
[235] Ibid., 173.
[236] Ibid.
[237] Ibid.
[238] Ibid., 174.
[239] Morse, *While Six Million Died*, 55.
[240] Wasserstein, *Britain and the Jews*, 189.
[241] Ibid., 191.
[242] Wyman, *Abandonment of Jews*, 115.
[243] Morse, *While Six Million Died*, 55.
[244] Wyman, *Abandonment of Jews*, 113.
[245] Wasserstein, *Britain and the Jews*, 184.
[246] Morse, *While Six Million Died*, 45.
[247] Ibid., 53-54.
[248] Ibid., 57.
[249] Wyman, *Abandonment of Jews*, 119.
[250] Ibid., 105.
[251] Wasserstein, *Britain and the Jews*, 188.
[252] Ibid.
[253] Ibid., 189.
[254] Wyman, *Abandonment of Jews*, 114.
[255] Ibid., 189.
[256] Wasserstein, *Britain and the Jews*, 248.
[257] Ibid., 221.
[258] Ibid., 252.
[259] Morse, *While Six Million Died*, 61.
[260] Danuta Czech, *Auschwitz Chronicle: 1939-1945* (New York: Tauris, 1990), 429.
[261] Wasserstein, *Britain and the Jews*, 205.
[262] Ibid., 201.
[263] Ibid., 202.
[264] Wyman, *Abandonment of Jews*, 141.
[265] Morse, *While Six Million Died*, 237.
[266] Ibid., 65.
[267] Wyman, *Abandonment of Jews*, 98.
[268] Ibid., 336.
[269] Morse, *While Six Million Died*, 99.
[270] Wyman, *Abandonment of Jews*, 98.
[271] Ibid., 137.

[272] Ibid., 122.
[273] Ibid.
[274] Wasserstein, *Britain and the Jews*, 202.
[275] Laqueur, *Terrible Secret*, 90.
[276] Lyn Smith, *Remembering: Voices of the Holocaust* (New York: Carroll & Graf, 2005), 105.
[277] Gilbert, *Holocaust*, 129-30.
[278] Hilberg, *Destruction of Jews*, 1:248-49.
[279] Ibid., 226.
[280] Laqueur, *Terrible Secret*, 110.
[281] Ibid., 43.
[282] Hilberg, *Destruction of Jews*, 1:219.
[283] Ibid., 1:253.
[284] Ibid., 1:263.
[285] Ibid., 2:557.
[286] Ibid., 1:263.
[287] Longerich, *Holocaust*, 154.
[288] Hilberg, *Destruction of Jews*, 1:273.
[289] Levin, *Holocaust: Destruction of European Jewry*, 326.
[290] Wladyslaw Szpilman, *The Pianist*, trans. Anthea Bell (New York: Picador, 1999), 95-6.
[291] Lawliss, *...and GOD CRIED*, 98.
[292] Katarzyna Puchalska, ed., *The 70th Anniversary of the Warsaw Ghetto Uprising*, trans. by Barbara Herchenreder (Warsaw: Centrum Uslug Wspolnych, 2013), 30.
[293] Lawliss, *...and GOD CRIED*, 99.
[294] Wyman, *Abandonment of Jews*, 123.
[295] Lawliss, *...and GOD CRIED*, 100.
[296] Ibid.
[297] Simhah Rotem, *Memoirs of a Warsaw Ghetto Fighter*, trans. Barbara Harshav (New Haven: Yale UP, 1994), 50.
[298] Gilbert, *Holocaust*, 564-65.
[299] Puchalska, *70th Anniversary Warsaw Ghetto Uprising*, 31.
[300] Morse, *While Six Million Died*, 66.
[301] Wasserstein, *Britain and the Jews*, 304.
[302] Gilbert, *Holocaust*, 564.
[303] Puchalska, *70th Anniversary Warsaw Ghetto Uprising*, 36.

CHAPTER 11

The Camps

[1] Daniel Jonah Goldhagen, *Hitler's Willing Executioners: Ordinary Germans and the Holocaust* (New York: Vintage-Random, 1997), 167.
[2] Eric Lichtblau, "The Holocaust Just Got More Shocking," *The New York Times*, March 1, 2013, Web, 01 April 2014.
[3] Barbie Zelizer, ed., *Visual Culture and the Holocaust* (New Brunswick, N.J.: Rutgers UP, 2001), 275-76.
[4] Doris L. Bergen, *War & Genocide: A Concise History of the Holocaust* (Lanham, Md.: Rowman, 2003), 175.
[5] Peter Longerich, *The Unwritten Order: Hitler's Role in the Final Solution* (Gloucestershire: Tempus, 2001), 179.
[6] Raul Hilberg, *The Destruction of the European Jews*, 3rd ed., 3 Vols. (New Haven: Yale UP, 2003), 3:1065.
[7] Konnilyn G. Feig, *Hitler's Death Camps: The Sanity of Madness* (New York: Holmes & Meier, 1979), 277.
[8] Arthur D. Morse, *While Six Million Died: A Chronicle of American Apathy* (New York: Random, 1968), 50-51.
[9] Feig, *Hitler's Death Camps*, 286.
[10] Martin Gilbert, *The Holocaust: A History of the Jews of Europe During the Second World War* (New York: Henry Holt, 1985), 546.
[11] Feig, *Hitler's Death Camps*, 287.
[12] Bergen, *War and Genocide*, 94.
[13] Hilberg, *Destruction of Jews*, 3:970.
[14] Ibid., 971.
[15] Yisrael Gutman and Michael Berenbaum, eds. *Anatomy of the Auschwitz Death Camp* (Bloomington, Ind.: Indiana UP, 1994), 55.
[16] Filip Müller, *Eyewitness Auschwitz: Three Years in the Gas Chambers* (Chicago: Ivan R. Dee, 1979), 142.
[17] Miriam Novitch, *Sobibor, Martyrdom and Revolt: Documentaries and Testimonies* (Madison: UWP, 1980), 75.
[18] Feig, *Hitler's Death Camps*, 288.
[19] Ibid., 289.
[20] Hilberg, *Destruction of Jews*, 3:971.
[21] Ibid., 3:963.
[22] Daniel Schorn, "Revisiting the Horrors of the Holocaust," CBS News, CBS Interactive, 14 Dec. 2006, Web, 05 Apr. 2014.
[23] Roy Barak, "Auschwitz Inmate Who Survived by Boxing Dies Aged 86," *Haaretz.com.*, Haaretz Daily Newspaper Ltd., 30 Apr. 2009, Web, 10 Dec. 2015.
[24] Associated Press, "Israel archaeologist digs into Sobibor death camp in search of Nazi killing machines," *Haaretz*, 21 Aug. 2012, Web, 08 Apr. 2014.
[25] Müller, *Eyewitness Auschwitz*, 59, 161.
[26] Feig, *Hitler's Death Camps*, 292.
[27] Thomas Toivi Blatt, *From the Ashes of Sobibor: A Story of Survival* (Evanston: Northwestern UP, 1997), 231.
[28] Feig, *Hitler's Death Camps*, 286.
[29] Ibid., 293.
[30] Ibid., 296.
[31] Ibid., 299.
[32] Ibid., 299-300.
[33] Charles Lawliss, *...and GOD CRIED: The Holocaust Remembered* (North Dighton, Mass.: JG, 1994), 116.
[34] Hilberg, *Destruction of Jews*, 3:964.
[35] Feig, *Hitler's Death Camps*, 300.
[36] Hilberg, *Destruction of Jews*, 3:937.
[37] Ibid., 3:1040.
[38] Feig, *Hitler's Death Camps*, 302.
[39] Ibid., 306.
[40] Ibid., 279.
[41] Ibid., 306.
[42] Ibid., 310.
[43] Bergen, *War and Genocide*, 181.
[44] Gilbert, *Holocaust*, 499.
[45] Ibid., 655.
[46] Feig, *Hitler's Death Camps*, 313.
[47] Gilbert, *Holocaust*, 627.
[48] Hilberg, *Destruction of Jews*, 2:561.
[49] Ibid., 2:557.
[50] Ibid., 2:569, 571.
[51] Ibid., 3:1079.
[52] Gilbert, *Holocaust*, 629-30.
[53] Franciszek Piper and Teresa Świebocka, eds., *Auschwitz: Nazi Death Camp*, trans. Douglas Selvage (Oświęcim, Poland: Auschwitz-Birkenau State Museum, 1996), 195.
[54] Gutman and Berenbaum, *Anatomy*, 195.
[55] Taduesz Borowski, *This Way for the Gas, Ladies and Gentlemen*, trans. Barbara Vedder (New York: Penguin, 1967), 23.
[56] Gilbert, *Holocaust*, 722.
[57] Ibid., 438.
[58] Ibid., 452.
[59] Müller, *Eyewitness Auschwitz*, 38.
[60] Shlomo Venezia, *Inside the Gas Chambers: Eight Months in the Sonderkommando of Auschwitz*, ed. Jean Mouttapa, trans. Andrew Brown (Malden, Mass.: Polity, 2009), 36.
[61] Gutman and Berenbaum, *Anatomy*, 93.
[62] "Auschwitz: Inside the Nazi State," Episode 4: "Corruption," PBS.org, Devillier Donegan Enterprises, early 2005, Web, 10 Apr. 2014.
[63] Teresa Świebocka, ed., *Auschwitz: A History in Photographs*, trans. Jonathan Webber and Connie Wisack (Bloomington: Indiana UP, 2011), 145.
[64] Ibid., 283.
[65] Bergen, *War and Genocide*, 182.
[66] Hermann Langbein, *People in Auschwitz*, trans. Harry Zorn (Markham, Ont.: Fitzhenry and Whiteside, 2005), 3.
[67] Ibid., 65.
[68] Elie Wiesel, *Night*, trans., Marion Wiesel (New York: Hill and Wang-Farrar, 2006), xiii-iv.
[69] Nora Levin, *The Holocaust: The Destruction of European Jewry 1933-1945* (New York: Crowell, 1968), 315.
[70] Borowski, *This Way for the Gas*, 84.
[71] Wiesel, *Night*, 40.
[72] Gutman and Berenbaum, *Anatomy*, 162.
[73] Borowski, *This Way for the Gas*, 38.
[74] Gutman and Berenbaum, *Anatomy*, 261.
[75] Feig, *Hitler's Death Camps*, 334.

[76] Hilberg, *Destruction of Jews*, 3:1031.
[77] Ibid., 3:1032.
[78] Walter Laqueur, *The Terrible Secret: Suppression of the Truth about Hitler's 'Final Solution'* (Boston: Little, 1980), 23.
[79] Hilberg, *Destruction of Jews*, 3:1030-31.
[80] Feig, *Hitler's Death Camps*, 333.
[81] Gutman and Berenbaum, *Anatomy*, 93.
[82] Auschwitz and Birkenau Memorial and Museum News, State Museum of Auschwitz-Birkenau in Oświęcim, *Christmas Eve in Auschwitz as Recalled by Polish Prisoners*, 23 December 2005, Web, 16 Aug. 2016.
[83] Gutman and Berenbaum, *Anatomy*, 148.
[84] Ibid., 401.
[85] Hilberg, *Destruction of Jews*, 3:996.
[86] Ibid., 3:1040.
[87] Feig, *Hitler's Death Camps*, 346.
[88] Gilbert, *Holocaust*, 688.
[89] Langbein, *People in Auschwitz*, 405.
[90] Wiesel, *Night*, 48.
[91] Gutman and Berenbaum, *Anatomy*, 6.
[92] Peter Longerich, *Holocaust: The Nazi Persecution and Murder of the Jews* (New York: Oxford UP, 2010), 307.
[93] Piper and Świebocka, *Auschwitz*, 145.
[94] Gutman and Berenbaum, *Anatomy*, 5.
[95] Primo Levi, *Survival in Auschwitz: The Nazi Assault on Humanity* (New York: Touchstone-Simon, 1996), 55.
[96] Ibid., 27.
[97] Gutman and Berenbaum, *Anatomy*, 5.
[98] Ibid., 8-9.
[99] Ibid., 19.
[100] Ibid., 139.
[101] Piper and Świebocka, *Auschwitz*, 144-45, 150.
[102] Gutman and Berenbaum, *Anatomy*, 128-31.
[103] Ibid., 131-33.
[104] Auschwitz-Birkenau Memorial and Museum, State Museum of Auschwitz-Birkenau in Oświęcim, "Testimonies Fond," vol. 110, p. 46, Web, 2013.
[105] Jürg Amann, ed. *The Commandant: The Rudolf Hoess Text* (New York: Peter Mayer-Overlook Duckworth, 2012), 61.
[106] Gisella Perl, *I Was a Doctor in Auschwitz* (1948; reprint, North Stratford, N.H.: Ayer, 1997), 32-3.
[107] Bergen, *War and Genocide*, 183.
[108] Hilberg, *Destruction of Jews*, 3:975.
[109] Gilbert, *Holocaust*, 682.
[110] Levi, *Survival in Auschwitz*, 40.
[111] Müller, *Eyewitness Auschwitz*, 6.
[112] Gutman and Berenbaum, *Anatomy*, 130.
[113] Ibid.
[114] Gilbert, *Holocaust*, 682.
[115] Borowski, *This Way for the Gas*, 92.
[116] Piper and Świebocka, *Auschwitz*, 83.
[117] Levi, *Survival in Auschwitz*, 51.
[118] Borowski, *This Way for the Gas*, 94,114.
[119] Venezia, *Inside the Gas Chambers*, 75.
[120] Piper and Świebocka, *Auschwitz*, 82.
[121] Ibid., 83.
[122] Świebocka, *Auschwitz: History in Photographs*, 119.
[123] Auschwitz and Birkenau Memorial and Museum News, *Christmas Eve in Auschwitz*.
[124] Hilberg, *Destruction of Jews*, 3:976.
[125] Perl, *Doctor in Auschwitz*, 39-40.
[126] Piper and Świebocka, *Auschwitz*, 143.
[127] Świebocka, *Auschwitz: History in Photographs*, 109.
[128] Piper and Świebocka, *Auschwitz*, 72, 74.
[129] Świebocka, *Auschwitz: History in Photographs*, 18.
[130] Wiesel, *Night*, 34.
[131] Borowski, *This Way for the Gas*, 130.
[132] John Frank, "Holocaust Testimonies Project," Interview by Steve Gonzer and Rose Magel, Special Collections, University of Delaware Library, (1995): Tape 23.
[133] Venezia, *Inside the Gas Chambers*, 47.
[134] Gutman and Berenbaum, *Anatomy*, 123.
[135] Ibid., 126.
[136] Ibid., 93-4.
[137] Hilberg, *Destruction of Jews*, 3:955.
[138] Amann, *The Commandant*, 69.
[139] Feig, *Hitler's Death Camps*, 355.
[140] Hilberg, *Destruction of Jews*, 3:951, 955.
[141] Piper and Świebocka, *Auschwitz*, 167.
[142] Amann, *The Commandant*, 70.
[143] Gilbert, *Holocaust*, 134.
[144] Świebocka, *Auschwitz: History in Photographs*, 24.
[145] Ibid., 154.
[146] Gutman and Berenbaum, *Anatomy*, 146, 178.
[147] Amann, *The Commandant*, 90.
[148] Hilberg, *Destruction of Jews*, 3:942.
[149] Feig, *Hitler's Death Camps*, 357.
[150] Amann, *The Commandant*, 89.
[151] Venezia, *Inside the Gas Chambers*, 178-79.
[152] Gutman and Berenbaum, *Anatomy*, 170.
[153] Levin, *Holocaust: Destruction of European Jewry*, 316.
[154] Gutman and Berenbaum, *Anatomy*, 163.
[155] Ibid., 170.
[156] Gilbert, *Holocaust*, 452-53.
[157] Venezia, *Inside the Gas Chambers*, 65, 72.
[158] Ibid., 64-65.
[159] Ibid., 71.
[160] Müller, *Eyewitness Auschwitz*, 110-11.
[161] Ibid., 112.
[162] Ibid., 113.
[163] Ibid., 113-14.
[164] Ibid., 117-18.
[165] Gutman and Berenbaum, *Anatomy*, 171, 258.
[166] Hilberg, *Destruction of Jews*, 3:1032-33.
[167] Gutman and Berenbaum, *Anatomy*, 171-74.
[168] Lyn Smith, *Remembering: Voices of the Holocaust* (New York: Carroll & Graf, 2005), 162.
[169] John C. Zimmerman, "Body Disposal at Auschwitz: The End of Holocaust Denial," The Holocaust History Project, 12 July 2009. Web, 03 Apr. 2017.
[170] Hilberg, *Destruction of Jews*, 1:13-14.
[171] "Anti-Semitism: Martin Luther - 'The Jews & Their Lies,'" Jewish Virtual Library, Web, accessed May 29, 2014.
[172] Ibid.
[173] Hilberg, *Destruction of Jews*, 1:5.
[174] Ibid., 1:13.
[175] Ibid., 3:1150.
[176] Ibid., 3:1136.
[177] Paul Seabury, *The Wilhelmstrasse: A Study of German Diplomats Under the Nazi Regime* (Berkeley: U of California P, 1954), 126.
[178] Youssef Aboul-Enein and Basil Aboul-Enein, *The Secret War for the Middle East: The Influence of Axis and Allied Intelligence Operations during World War II* (Annapolis, Md.: Naval Inst. P, 2013), 108.
[179] John Frank, "Holocaust Testimonies Project."
[180] Gilbert, *Holocaust*, 722.
[181] Borowski, *This Way for the Gas*, 43.
[182] Gutman and Berenbaum, *Anatomy*, 26.
[183] Ibid., 253-260.
[184] Venezia, *Inside the Gas Chambers*, 40, 48, 108-09, 123, 181.
[185] Borowski, *This Way for the Gas*, 11, 29, 46, 105-06, 108, 128, 146, 156.
[186] Müller, *Eyewitness Auschwitz*, 2, 16, 20, 22, 30, 46, 65, 72, 136-138.
[187] Piper and Świebocka, *Auschwitz*, 155-56.
[188] Müller, *Eyewitness Auschwitz*, 69.
[189] Ibid., 70.
[190] Ibid.
[191] Ibid., 70-71.
[192] Ibid., 71.
[193] David S. Wyman, *The Abandonment of the Jews: America and the Holocaust, 1941-1945* (New York: Pantheon-Random, 1985), 160.
[194] Ibid., 147.
[195] Ibid., 200.
[196] Ibid., 148.
[197] Ibid., 152.
[198] Ibid., 175.
[199] Ibid., 209.
[200] Ibid., 215.
[201] Ibid., 190.

[202] Morse, *While Six Million Died*, 349.
[203] Wyman, *Abandonment of the Jews*, 214.
[204] Ibid., 221.
[205] Hilberg, *Destruction of Jews*, 2:860.
[206] Longerich, *Holocaust*, 406.
[207] Ibid., 400.
[208] Hilberg, *Destruction of Jews*, 2:854.
[209] Wyman, *Abandonment of the Jews*, 236.
[210] Morse, *While Six Million Died*, 368.
[211] Walter Laqueur, *The Terrible Secret: Suppression of the Truth about Hitler's 'Final Solution'* (Boston: Little, 1980), 55.
[212] Morse, *While Six Million Died*, 14.
[213] Hilberg, *Destruction of Jews*, 2:898.
[214] Mark Aarons and John Loftus, *Unholy Trinity: The Vatican, the Nazis, and Soviet Intelligence* (New York: St. Martin's, 1991), 179-80.
[215] Ibid., 180.
[216] Morse, *While Six Million Died*, 382.
[217] Hilberg, *Destruction of Jews*, 2:898.
[218] Bergen, *War and Genocide*, 213.
[219] Gutman and Berenbaum, *Anatomy*, 463.
[220] Gilbert, *Holocaust*, 675.
[221] Morse, *While Six Million Died*, 367.
[222] Gutman and Berenbaum, *Anatomy*, 464.
[223] Perl, *Doctor in Auschwitz*, 74.
[224] Bergen, *War and Genocide*, 213.
[225] Morse, *While Six Million Died*, 369.
[226] Hilberg, *Destruction of Jews*, 3:1219.
[227] Ibid., 3:1220.
[228] Morse, *While Six Million Died*, 370.
[229] Wyman, *Abandonment of the Jews*, 247-49.
[230] Ibid., 268.
[231] Morse, *While Six Million Died*, 389.
[232] Wyman, *Abandonment of the Jews*, 241.
[233] Morse, *While Six Million Died*, 390-91.
[234] Ernst Pawel, *The Labyrinth of Exile: A Life of Theodor Herzl* (New York: Farrar, 1989), 242.
[235] Martin Gilbert, *Auschwitz and the Allies: A Devastating Account of How the Allies Responded to the News of Hitler's Mass Murder* (New York: Holt, Rinehart and Winston, 1981), 291.
[236] Bernard Wasserstein, *Britain and the Jews of Europe: 1939-1945* (New York: Oxford UP, 1979), 271.
[237] Ibid., 259.
[238] Wyman, *Abandonment of the Jews*, 290.
[239] John Loftus and Mark Aarons, *The Secret War Against the Jews: How Western Espionage Betrayed the Jewish People* (New York: St. Martin's, 1994), 102.
[240] Hilberg, *Destruction of Jews*, 3:1217.
[241] Wasserstein, *Britain and the Jews*, 313.
[242] Wyman, *Abandonment of the Jews*, 296.
[243] Ibid., 299.
[244] Wasserstein, *Britain and the Jews*, 319.
[245] Michael Beschloss, "FDR's Auschwitz Secret," *Newsweek*, IBT Media, 13 Oct. 2002, Web, 03 Feb. 2015.
[246] Ringelheim, Joan, dir., "Benjamin Ferencz Oral History Interview, Part 1," *America History TV*, C-SPAN3, N.d., *C-SPAN.org*, Web, 07 Jan. 2016.
[247] Gilbert, *Auschwitz and the Allies*, 315.
[248] Jeffrey S. Gurock, ed., *American Jewish History*, Vol. 7, *America, American Jews, and the Holocaust* (New York: Routledge, 1998), Web, 06 June 2014, 18.
[249] Wyman, *Abandonment of the Jews*, 303.
[250] Wiesel, *Night*, 60.
[251] Wyman, *Abandonment of the Jews*, 303.
[252] Hilberg, *Destruction of Jews*, 3:1217.
[253] Wyman, *Abandonment of the Jews*, 305.
[254] Hilberg, *Destruction of Jews*, 3:978.
[255] Gene A. Plunka, *Staging Holocaust Resistance* (New York: Palgrave Macmillan, 2012), 97.
[256] Hilberg, *Destruction of Jews*, 3:1067.
[257] Piper and Świebocka, *Auschwitz*, 270-72.
[258] Wiesel, *Night*, 85.
[259] Piper and Świebocka, *Auschwitz*, 276.
[260] Ibid., 274.
[261] Hilberg, *Destruction of Jews*, 3:1048-49.
[262] Venezia, *Inside the Gas Chambers*, 181.
[263] Piper and Świebocka, *Auschwitz*, 279.
[264] Ibid., 280.
[265] Wiesel, *Night*, viii.
[266] David Fraser, *The Jews of the Channel Islands and the Rule of Law, 1940-1945: 'Quite Contrary to the Principles of British Justice'* (Portland, Ore.: Sussex Acad. P, 2000), 14.
[267] Ibid., 212.
[268] Joseph Robert White, "'Even in Auschwitz… Humanity Could Prevail': British POWs and Jewish Concentration-Camp Inmates at IG Auschwitz, 1943-1945," *Holocaust and Genocide Studies*, 15 (2001): 270, California State University, Web, 10 June 2014.
[269] Ibid., 282-83.
[270] Colin Rushton, *Spectator in Hell: A British Soldier's Story of Imprisonment in Auschwitz* (Gretna, La.: Pelican, 2010), 111-13.

CHAPTER 12

The Jews and WWII

[1] Jon Latimer, *Alamein* (Cambridge: Harvard UP, 2004), 55.
[2] John Bierman and Colin Smith, *War Without Hate: The Desert Campaign of 1940-1943* (New York: Penguin, 2004), 200.
[3] Klaus Michael Mallmann and Martin Cüppers, *Nazi Palestine: The Plans for Extermination of the Jews in Palestine*, trans. Krista Smith (New York: Enigma, 2005), 200-01.
[4] Chaim Herzog, *Heroes of Israel: Profiles of Jewish Courage* (Boston: Little, 1989), 162.
[5] Mark Aarons and John Loftus, *Unholy Trinity: The Vatican, the Nazis, and Soviet Intelligence* (New York: St. Martin's, 1991), 107.
[6] "Russians Captured With Nazis Riot at Fort Dix; 3 Commit Suicide," *The New York Times*, 29 June 1945, Web, 13 June 2014.
[7] Robert L. Baker, *Oil, Blood, and Sand* (New York, D. Appleton-Century Co., 1942), 27.
[8] Mallmann and Cüppers, *Nazi Palestine*, 74.
[9] Youssef Aboul-Enein and Basil Aboul-Enein, *The Secret War for the Middle East: The Influence of Axis and Allied Intelligence during World War II* (Annapolis, Md.: Naval Inst. P, 2013), 32.
[10] Mallmann and Cüppers, *Nazi Palestine*, 52-3.
[11] Ibid., 38.
[12] Ibid., 67.
[13] Aboul-Enein and Aboul-Enein, *Secret War for Middle East*, 60.
[14] Adolf Hitler, "Führer Directive 30," *World War II Database*, NJ: Lava Development, LLC, n.d., 13 June 2014.
[15] Mallmann and Cüppers, *Nazi Palestine*, 74.
[16] Ibid., 75.
[17] Hitler, "Führer Directive 30."
[18] Adolf Hitler, "Führer Directive 32," *World War II Database*, NJ: Lava Development, LLC, n.d., 13 June 2014.
[19] Ibid.
[20] Ibid.
[21] Ibid.
[22] Ibid.
[23] Efraim Karsh, *Palestine Betrayed* (New Haven: Yale UP, 2010), 67.
[24] Mallmann and Cüppers, *Nazi Palestine*, 89.
[25] Aboul-Enein and Aboul-Enein, *Secret War for Middle East*, 26.
[26] Ibid., 30.
[27] Mallmann and Cüppers, *Nazi Palestine*, 96-97.
[28] Ibid., 97.
[29] Aboul-Enein and Aboul-Enein, *Secret War for Middle East*, 27.
[30] Mallmann and Cüppers, *Nazi Palestine*, 95.
[31] Ibid., 99-100.
[32] Ibid., 34.
[33] Aboul-Enein and Aboul-Enein, *Secret War for Middle East*, 29.
[34] Mallmann and Cüppers, *Nazi Palestine*, 132.
[35] Ibid.
[36] Aboul-Enein and Aboul-Enein, *Secret War for Middle East*, 37.
[37] Robert Lee Baker, *Oil, Blood, and Sand* (New York: D. Appleton-Century, 1942), 97-114.
[38] Ibid., 133.
[39] Aboul-Enein and Aboul-Enein, *Secret War for Middle East*, xiv.
[40] Mallmann and Cüppers, *Nazi Palestine*, 133-34.

[41] Ibid., 30.
[42] John Loftus, *America's Nazi Secret: An Insider's History of How the United States Department of Justice Obstructed Congress* (Walterville, Ore.: TrineDay, 2011), 14.
[43] Aboul-Enein and Aboul-Enein, *Secret War for Middle East*, 7.
[44] Mallmann and Cüppers, *Nazi Palestine*, 100.
[45] Ibid., 32.
[46] Ibid., 103.
[47] Ibid., 104.
[48] Ibid., 106.
[49] Aboul-Enein and Aboul-Enein, *Secret War for Middle East*, 168.
[50] Ibid., 162-63.
[51] Mallmann and Cüppers, *Nazi Palestine*, 109.
[52] Pierre van Paassen, *The Forgotten Ally* (New York: Dial, 1943), 187-90.
[53] Daniel Yergin, *The Prize: The Epic Quest for Oil, Money, and Power* (New York: Touchstone-Simon, 1992), 340-41.
[54] Van Paassen, *Forgotten Ally*, 179.
[55] Mallmann and Cüppers, *Nazi Palestine*, 141.
[56] Ibid., 147.
[57] Ibid., 138.
[58] Ibid., 140.
[59] Ibid., 147.
[60] Ibid., 118.
[61] Ibid., 124-25.
[62] Howard M. Sachar, *A History of Israel: From the Rise of Zionism to Our Time*, 3rd Rev. ed. (New York: Knopf, 2007), 229.
[63] Mallmann and Cüppers, *Nazi Palestine*, 117.
[64] Ibid., 155.
[65] Ibid., 162.
[66] Ibid., 186.
[67] Ibid.
[68] Ibid., 187.
[69] Ibid., 163.
[70] Tom Reiss, *The Orientalist: Solving the Mystery of a Strange and Dangerous Life* (New York: Random, 2005), xii.
[71] Avraham Ziv-Tal, *Enigma Named Max*, trans. Rena Bar-David (Rishon Lezion, Israel: n. p., 2013) 200.
[72] Thomas Newdick, ed., *Air Warfare from World War I to the Present: Air/Land/Sea Warfare* (San Diego: Thunder Bay-Advantage, 2008), 105.
[73] B. H. Liddell Hart, *History of the Second World War* (New York: Putnam, 1970), 256.
[74] Aboul-Enein and Aboul-Enein, *Secret War*, 177.
[75] Mallmann and Cüppers, *Nazi Palestine*, 189.
[76] Ibid., 190-92.
[77] Aboul-Enein and Aboul-Enein, *Secret War for Middle East*, 27.
[78] Ibid., 28.
[79] John Loftus and Mark Aarons, *The Secret War Against the Jews: How Western Espionage Betrayed the Jewish People* (New York: St. Martin's, 1994), 25.
[80] Yergin, *The Prize*, 340-43.
[81] Winston S. Churchill, *The Second World War,* vol. 4: *The Hinge of Fate* (New York: Houghton, 1950), 541.
[82] William Manchester and Paul Reid, *The Last Lion: Winston Spencer Churchill,* vol. 3: *Defender of the Realm, 1940-1965* (2012; reprint, New York: Random, 2013), 159.
[83] Raul Hilberg, *The Destruction of the European Jews*, 3rd ed., 3 Vols. (New Haven: Yale UP, 2003), 2:688.
[84] Mallmann and Cüppers, *Nazi Palestine*, 174.
[85] Van Paassen, *Forgotten Ally*, 227.
[86] Mallmann and Cüppers, *Nazi Palestine*, 143.
[87] Sachar, *History of Israel*, 230.
[88] Mallmann and Cüppers, *Nazi Palestine*, 145.
[89] Ibid., 148.
[90] Ibid., 150.
[91] Sachar, *History of Israel*, 233.
[92] Mallmann and Cüppers, *Nazi Palestine*, 150.
[93] Sachar, *History of Israel*, 233.
[94] Van Paassen, *Forgotten Ally*, 197-98.
[95] Ibid., 230.
[96] Sachar, *History of Israel*, 230.
[97] Mallmann and Cüppers, *Nazi Palestine*, 145.
[98] Van Paassen, *Forgotten Ally*, 232.
[99] Ibid., 232-34.
[100] Julian Richards, "Signals Intelligence," *Routledge Companion to Intelligence Studies*, Robert Dover, Michael S. Goodman, and Claudia Hillebrand, eds. (Abingdon: Routledge-Taylor, 2014), 90.
[101] F. H. Hinsley and Alan Stripp, *Code Breakers: The Inside Story of Bletchley Park* (Oxford: Oxford UP, 1993), 5.
[102] Ibid.
[103] Christine Large, "Some Human Factors in Codebreaking," October 2003, 18 July 2014.
[104] Benjamin Ginsburg, *How the Jews Defeated Hitler: Exploding the Myth of Jewish Passivity in the Face of Nazism* (Lanham, Md.: Rowman, 2013), 74.
[105] Richard Deacon, *The Israeli Secret Service* (New York: Taplinger, 1977), 37.
[106] Martin Sugarman, "Breaking the Codes; Jewish personnel at Bletchley Park in WW2," *Journal of the Jewish Historical Society of England*, November 2005.
[107] Ibid.
[108] Christopher Simpson, *Blowback: America's Recruitment of Nazis and Its Effect on the Cold War* (New York: Weidenfeld & Nicolson, 1988), 28.
[109] Ginsburg, *How the Jews Defeated Hitler*, 75.
[110] John Loftus, *The Belarus Secret*, Nathan Miller, ed. (New York: Knopf, 1982), 48.
[111] Sam Cohen, *Shame: Confessions of the Father of the Neutron Bomb* (Bloomington, Ind.: Xlibris, 2000), 29.
[112] Ibid., 50.
[113] Ibid., 50-51.
[114] Ibid., 53-54.
[115] Ralph Berger, "Moe Berg," *The Baseball Biography Project*, n.d., The Society for American Baseball Research, 22 July 2014.
[116] "'Moe' Berg: Sportsman, Scholar, Spy," 10 July 2014, Central Intelligence Agency News and Information, 22 July 2014.
[117] "The Shrine of the Eternals 2000 Electees: Morris 'Moe' Berg," n.d., The Baseball Reliquary, 22 July 2014.
[118] Ziv-Tal, *Enigma*, 338.
[119] Ibid., 10-12.
[120] Ibid., 56.
[121] Ibid., 60.
[122] Ibid., 127.
[123] Ibid., 144.
[124] Aarons and Loftus, *Unholy Trinity* (1991 ed.), 167.
[125] Ibid., 158.
[126] Ibid., 166.
[127] Stuart D. Goldman, *Nomonhan, 1939: The Red Army's Victory That Shaped World War II* (Annapolis: Naval Inst. P, 2012), 175-76.
[128] Hart, *History of the Second World War*, 169.
[129] Aarons and Loftus, *Unholy Trinity* (1991 ed.), 160.
[130] Ibid., 168.
[131] Ziv-Tal, *Enigma*, 405.
[132] Ibid., 209.
[133] Ibid., 277.
[134] Ibid., 293-97.
[135] Ibid., 299.
[136] Ibid., 319.
[137] Aarons and Loftus, *Unholy Trinity* (1991 ed.), 160.
[138] Ziv-Tal, *Enigma*, 329.
[139] Aarons and Loftus, *Unholy Trinity* (1991 ed.), 184.
[140] Walter Schellenberg, *The Labyrinth: Memoirs of Walter Schellenberg, Hitler's Chief of Counterintelligence*, trans. Louis Hagen (New York: Harper, 1956), 263.
[141] Loftus and Aarons, *Secret War Against Jews*, 135-36.
[142] Ziv-Tal, *Enigma*, 410.
[143] Michael Bar-Zohar, *Beyond Hitler's Grasp: The Heroic Rescue of Bulgaria's Jews* (Holbrook, Mass.: Adams Media Corporation, 1998), front jacket flap.
[144] Avraham Ziv-Tal, "Lest we Forget," n.d., Enigma Named Max, 05 August 2014.
[145] Avraham Ziv-Tal, *Enigma Named Max*, trans. Rena Bar-David (Rishon Lezion, Israel: n. p., 2013), 383-84.
[146] Hilberg, *Destruction of Jews*, 3:1136.
[147] "Suitland Federal Center," n.d., United States Census Bureau, 25 July 2014.

[148] John Loftus, *America's Nazi Secret*, 7.
[149] Simpson, *Blowback*, 179.
[150] Ibid.
[151] Aarons and Loftus, *Unholy Trinity* (1991 ed.), xi.
[152] Ibid., 88.
[153] John Loftus, *America's Nazi Secret*, unnumbered page 3 of Author's Note.
[154] Aarons and Loftus, *Unholy Trinity* (1991 ed.), 211.
[155] Ibid., 161.
[156] Loftus and Aarons, *Secret War Against Jews*, 89.
[157] Aarons and Loftus, *Unholy Trinity* (1991 ed.), 215.
[158] Ibid., 37-39.
[159] Avro Manhattan, *The Vatican's Holocaust* (Ozark: Springfield, Mo., 1986), 136.
[160] Aarons and Loftus, *Unholy Trinity* (1991 ed.), 39-40.
[161] Ibid., 26-29.
[162] Simpson, *Blowback*, 249.
[163] Aarons and Loftus, *Unholy Trinity* (1991 ed.), 29.
[164] Ibid., 116.
[165] Simpson, *Blowback*, 185.
[166] Loftus, *America's Nazi Secret*, 28.
[167] Simpson, *Blowback*, 180.
[168] William P. Grady, *What Hath God Wrought!: A Biblical Interpretation of American History* Knoxville, Tenn.: Grady, 1996), 434.
[169] Aarons and Loftus, *Unholy Trinity* (1991 ed.), 111.
[170] Manhattan, *Vatican's Holocaust*, 87.
[171] John Cornwell, *Hitler's Pope: The Secret History of Pius XII* (New York: Penguin-Random, 1999), 254.
[172] Manhattan, *Vatican's Holocaust*, 35.
[173] Aarons and Loftus, *Unholy Trinity* (1991 ed.), 86.
[174] Walter Isaacson and Evan Thomas, *The Wise Men: Six Friends and the World They Made* (New York: Touchstone-Simon, 1986), 448.
[175] Simpson, *Blowback*, 102.
[176] Ibid., 146-55.
[177] John Loftus, *America's Nazi Secret*, 21.
[178] Simpson, *Blowback*, 171.
[179] Loftus and Aarons, *Secret War Against Jews*, 506.
[180] Ibid., 507.
[181] Loftus, *Belarus Secret*, 152-53.
[182] Ibid., 30.
[183] Simpson, *Blowback*, 89.
[184] Ibid., 171.
[185] Aarons and Loftus, *Unholy Trinity* (1991 ed.), 196.
[186] Simpson, *Blowback*, 91.
[187] Avro Manhattan, *Catholic Imperialism and World Freedom* (London: Watts & Co., 1952), 202.
[188] Robert I. Gannon, *The Cardinal Spellman Story* (New York: Doubleday & Co., 1962), 154.
[189] Ibid., 180.
[190] John Cooney, *The American Pope: The Life and Times of Francis Cardinal Spellman* (New York: Times, 1984), 109.
[191] Loftus and Aarons, *Secret War Against Jews*, 79, 82.
[192] Aarons and Loftus, *Unholy Trinity* (1991 ed.), 52.
[193] Loftus and Aarons, *Secret War Against Jews*, 79, 80.
[194] Jack Epstein, "Argentina Tracks Trail Of Stolen Nazi Wealth: Government and private efforts search for bank ties," 30 April 1997, Web, 13 June 2015.
[195] Mark Aarons and John Loftus, *Unholy Trinity: The Vatican, the Nazis, and the Swiss Banks*, Rev. ed. (New York: St. Martin's Griffin, 1998), 289, 300.
[196] Ibid., 123.
[197] Ibid., 289.
[198] Simpson, *Blowback*, 262.
[199] Ibid., 63.
[200] Ziv-Tal, *Enigma*, 345-46.
[201] Simpson, *Blowback*, 54, 65.
[202] Loftus, *America's Nazi Secret*, 33.
[203] Aarons and Loftus, *Unholy Trinity* (1991 ed.), xiv.
[204] Loftus, *Belarus Secret*, 83.
[205] Aarons and Loftus, *Unholy Trinity* (1991 ed.), 205.
[206] Ziv-Tal, *Enigma*, 420.
[207] Loftus, *America's Nazi Secret*, 33.
[208] Simpson, *Blowback*, 288.
[209] Ibid.
[210] Ibid., 212-13.
[211] William P. Grady, *Understanding the Times*, vol. 1: *How Satan Turned America Against God* (Knoxville, Tenn.: Grady, 2005), 230.
[212] Antony C. Sutton, *The Best Enemy Money Can Buy* (Billings, Mont.: Liberty House, 1986), 200- 01.
[213] Loftus and Aarons, *Secret War Against Jews*, 128.
[214] Simon Dunstan and Gerrard Williams, *Grey Wolf: The Escape of Adolf Hitler* (New York: Sterling, 2011), v. (Publisher's Note).
[215] Knappe, Siegfried and Ted Brusaw, *Soldat: Reflections of a German Soldier, 1936-1949* (New York: Dell-Random, 1992), 51.
[216] Peter Longerich, *The Unwritten Order: Hitler's Role in the Final Solution* (Gloucestershire: Tempus, 2001), 213.
[217] Margherita Marchione, *Yours Is a Precious Witness: Memoirs of Jews and Catholics in Wartime Italy* (Mahwah, N.J.: Paulist, 1997), 65.
[218] Cornwell, *Hitler's Pope*, 327.
[219] Ibid., 152.
[220] Ibid., 292.
[221] Ibid., 292-93.
[222] Ibid., 273.
[223] Hilberg, *Destruction of Jews*, 2:703.
[224] Cornwell, *Hitler's Pope*, 304.
[225] Ibid., 305.
[226] Ibid., 308-10.
[227] Ibid., 356.
[228] Ibid., 357.
[229] Aarons and Loftus, *Unholy Trinity* (1991 ed.), 86.
[230] Cornwell, *Hitler's Pope*, 271.
[231] Ibid., 358.
[232] Aarons and Loftus, *Unholy Trinity* (1991 ed.), 126.
[233] *Schooled in Hate: Anti-Semitism On Campus*, Anti-Defamation League, 1997, Jewish Virtual Library, 02 August 2014.
[234] Aleksandr Solzhenitsyn, *The Gulag Archipelago*, vol. 1 (New York: Harper, 1973), 85.
[235] Nicholas Bethell, *The Last Secret: The Delivery to Stalin of Over Two Million Russians by Britain and the United States* (New York: Basic Book, 1974), 31.
[236] Sven Steenberg, *Vlasov*, trans. Abe Farbstein (New York: Alfred A. Knopf, 1970), 21.
[237] Antony Beevor, *Stalingrad: The Fateful Siege, 1942-1943* (New York: Penguin-Putnam, 1998), xii.
[238] Steenberg, *Vlasov*, 37.
[239] B. H. Liddell Hart, ed., *The Red Army* (New York: Harcourt, 1956), 96.
[240] Nikolai Tolstoy, *The Secret Betrayal* (New York: Scribner's, 1977), 46-47.
[241] Bethell, *Last Secret*, 33.
[242] Tolstoy, *Secret Betrayal*, 371.
[243] Ibid., 409.
[244] Catherine Andreyev, *Vlasov and the Russian Liberation Movement: Soviet Reality and Émigré Theories* (New York: Cambridge UP, 1987), 133-36.
[245] Bethell, *Last Secret*, 34.
[246] Tolstoy, *Secret Betrayal*, 51-52.
[247] George Fischer, *Soviet Opposition to Stalin: A Case Study in World War II* (Cambridge: Harvard UP, 1952), 119.
[248] "Interview with Dr. Heinrich Pichler." Personal interview.
[249] "Interview with Ataman Alexander Pewnew." Personal interview.
[250] Tolstoy, *Secret Betrayal*, 186.
[251] Nikolai Tolstoy, *The Minister and the Massacres* (London: Century Hutchinson, 1986), 259.
[252] Johann Andritsch, ed., *Judenburg 1945 in Augenzeugenberichten* (Judenburg, Austria: Verlag des Museumsvereins Judenburg, 1994), 38 (translated page in author's file).
[253] Tolstoy, *Secret Betrayal*, 327.
[254] Julius Epstein, *Operation Keelhaul: The Story of Forced Repatriation from 1944 to the Present* (Old Greenwich, Conn.: Devin-Adair, 1973), 104.
[255] Tolstoy, *Secret Betrayal*, 326.
[256] Epstein, *Operation Keelhaul*, 51.

[257] Aboul-Enein and Aboul-Enein, *Secret War for Middle East*, 167.
[258] Hilberg, *Destruction of Jews*, 2:703.
[259] David Stahel, *Kiev 1941: Hitler's Battle for Supremacy in the East* (New York: Cambridge UP, 2012), 135.
[260] Santi Corvaja, *Hitler and Mussolini: The Secret Meetings* (New York: Enigma, 2008), 194.
[261] Bradley Lightbody, *The Second World War: Ambitions to Nemesis* (New York: Routledge-Taylor, 2004), 142-43.
[262] Aboul-Enein and Aboul-Enein, *Secret War for Middle East*, 25.
[263] "How Have the Mighty Fallen" (photo caption), *Geneva Daily Times*, 01 August 1952, Web, 09 Aug. 2014.
[264] "In Brief: Mussolini's horse remembered…Jewels on the skin…Witch doctor's convention," *The Sydney Morning Herald*, 22 Oct. 1950, Web, 09 Aug. 2014.

CHAPTER 13

Statehood

[1] Robert Baer, *Sleeping With the Devil: How Washington Sold Our Soul for Saudi Crude* (New York: Three Rivers-Random, 2003), 83.
[2] Michael Oren, *Power, Faith, and Fantasy: America in the Middle East, 1776 to the Present* (New York: Norton, 2007), 471.
[3] Howard Grief, *The Legal Foundation and Borders of Israel under International Law: A Treatise on Jewish Sovereignty over the Land of Israel* (Jerusalem, Israel: Mazo, 2008), 630-31.
[4] Herbert Parzen, "The Roosevelt Palestine Policy, 1943-1945: An Exercise in Dual Diplomacy," *American Jewish Archives*, April 1974: 31-65, Web, 18 June 2015, PDF.
[5] Martin Gilbert, *Churchill and the Jews: A Lifelong Friendship* (New York: Holt, 2007), 234.
[6] Michael T. Benson, *Harry S. Truman and the Founding of Israel* (Westport, Conn.: Praeger-Greenwood, 1997), 27.
[7] Bernard Postal and Henry W. Levy, *And the Hills Shouted for Joy: The Day Israel Was Born* (New York: D. McKay, 1973), 303.
[8] David McCullough, *Truman* (New York: Simon, 1992), 595.
[9] Howard M. Sachar, *A History of Israel: From the Rise of Zionism to Our Time*, 3rd Rev. ed. (New York: Knopf, 2007), 249.
[10] Geoffrey Wigoder, *The Holocaust* (Danbury, Conn.: Grolier, 1997), 104.
[11] Sachar, *History of Israel*, 249-50.
[12] Robert S. Wistrich, ed., *Terms of Survival: The Jewish World Since 1945*, (New York: Routledge, 1995), 263.
[13] Raul Hilberg, *The Destruction of the European Jews*, 3rd ed., 3 Vols. (New Haven: Yale UP, 2003), 3:1243.
[14] Ibid., 1173-94.
[15] Ibid., 1157.
[16] Ibid., 1159.
[17] Ibid., 1172.
[18] Ibid., 1241.
[19] Ibid., 1158.
[20] Ibid., 1246.
[21] Robert John and Sami Hadawi, *1945-1948; United States, United Nations Intervention*, vol. 2 of *The Palestine Diary* (New York: New World, 1970), 7.
[22] McCullough, *Truman*, 595-97.
[23] Rudiger Dornbusch, Wilhelm Nölling, and Richard Layard, eds., *Postwar Economic Reconstruction and Lessons for the East Today* (Cambridge: MIT, 1993), 117.
[24] Peter Duignan, Lewis H. Gann, *The Rebirth of the West: The Americanization of the Democratic World, 1945-1958* (Lanham, Md.: Rowman, 1992), 312.
[25] John and Hadawi, *Palestine Diary*, 2:9.
[26] W. F. Abboushi, *The Angry Arabs* (Philadelphia, Penn.: Westminster, 1974), 241.
[27] Peter Weiler, *Ernest Bevin* (Manchester: Manchester UP, 1993), 170.
[28] Efraim Karsh, *Palestine Betrayed* (New Haven: Yale UP, 2010), 73.
[29] William Roger Louis, *The British Empire in the Middle East, 1945-1951: Arab Nationalism, the United States, and Postwar Imperialism* (New York: Oxford UP, 1984), 389.
[30] John and Hadawi, *Palestine Diary*, 2:30.
[31] Sachar, *History of Israel*, 260.
[32] John and Hadawi, *Palestine Diary*, 2:33.
[33] Michael Robert Marrus, *The Unwanted: European Refugees from the First World War Through the Cold War* (Philadelphia: Temple UP, 2002), 334.
[34] Anglo-American Committee of Inquiry, "Chapter 1 - Recommendations and Comments: Refugee Immigration Into Palestine," *The Avalon Project*, Yale Law School Lillian Goldman Law Library, 2008, Web, 16 June 2015.
[35] Ibid., "Principles of Government: No Arab, No Jewish State."
[36] Francis Williams, *Ernest Bevin: Portrait of a Great Englishman* (London: Hutchinson, 1952), 260.
[37] McCullough, *Truman*, 600.
[38] Michael R. Beschloss, *Presidential Courage: Brave Leaders and How They Changed America 1789-1989* (New York: Simon, 2007), 201.
[39] David Ralph Shibley, *Ernest Bevin and the Arab League* (Stanford: Department of History, Stanford University, 1957), 9.
[40] Alison Weir, *Against Our Better Judgment: The Hidden History of How the U.S. Was Used to Create Israel* (Lexington, Ken: CreateSpace, 2014), 68-70.
[41] Barbie Zelizer, ed., *Visual Culture and the Holocaust* (New Brunswick: Rutgers P, 2001), 204.
[42] Mordecai Naor, *The Atlit Camp: A Story of a Time and Place*, Gavriel Fiske, ed. (Mikveh Israel, Israel: Yehuda Dekel Library/Society for Preservation of Israel, 2010), 41-42.
[43] Dan Stone, *The Liberation of the Camps: The End of the Holocaust and Its Aftermath* (New Haven: Yale UP, 2015), 186.
[44] Ronnie S. Landau, *The Nazi Holocaust: Its History and Meaning* (New York: Tauris, 2006), 250.
[45] Sachar, *History of Israel*, 270.
[46] John and Hadawi, *Palestine Diary*, 2:10.
[47] Sachar, *History of Israel*, 264-65.
[48] John Loftus and Mark Aarons, *The Secret War Against the Jews: How Western Espionage Betrayed the Jewish People* (New York: St. Martin's, 1994), 198.
[49] Sachar, *History of Israel*, 265.
[50] Shaul Zadka, "Jewish Armed Struggle in Palestine in the 1940s: Its Impact on British Morale and Public Opinion," in *Israel: The First Hundred Years*, vol. 1: *Israel's Transition from Community to State*, ed. Efraim Karsh (London: Frank Cass, 2000), 181-82.
[51] Ibid., 183.
[52] Sachar, *History of Israel*, 271.
[53] "41 Dead, 53 Injured, 52 Missing, in Terrorist Attack on Secretariat," *The Palestine Post*, July 23, 1946, late ed., sec. A.
[54] Ibid.
[55] "Attackers Outlawed by Jewish Heads," *The Palestine Post*, July 23, 1946, late ed., sec. A.
[56] "Tel Aviv's 200,000 Being Checked by Two Divisions," *The Palestine Post*, July 31, 1946, late ed., sec. A.
[57] Harry S. Truman, *1946-52 Years of Trial and Hope, Memoirs: Volume 2* (N.p.: New Word City, 2014), Web, 16 June 2015.
[58] Sachar, *History of Israel*, 273.
[59] John B. Judis, *Genesis: Truman, American Jews, and the Origins of the Arab/Israeli Conflict* (New York: Farrar, 2014), 245.
[60] Chaim Weizmann, *Trial and Error: The Autobiography of Chaim Weizmann* (New York: Schocken, 1949), 443.
[61] Ibid., 442.
[62] Ibid., 443.
[63] Richard Meinertzhagen, *Middle East Diary: 1917-1956* (New York: Thomas Yoseloff, 1959), 217.
[64] "4 Hanged in Secret At Acre; Funeral at Safad," *The Palestine Post*, April 17, 1947, late ed., sec. A.
[65] Jerry A. Grunor, *Let My People Go: The trials and tribulations of the people of Israel, and the heroes who helped in their independence from British colonization* (New York: iUniverse, 2005), 187.
[66] Richard Pierce Greenfield and Irving A. Greenfield, *The Life Story of Menachem Begin* (New York: Manor, 1977), 163.
[67] Meinertzhagen, *Middle East Diary*, 219.

[68] Ruth Gruber, *Exodus 1947: The Ship that Launched a Nation* (New York: Sterling, 1948), 53.
[69] Ibid., 51.
[70] Ibid., 107.
[71] "Refugees Refuse to Leave the Ships," *The Palestine Post*, July 30, 1947, late ed., sec. A.
[72] "Refugees Forced to Land at Hamburg," *The Palestine Post*, Sept. 9, 1947, late ed., sec. A.
[73] *Official Records of the General Assembly, Second Session, Supplement No. 11*, vol. I (A/364).
[74] Karsh, *Palestine Betrayed*, 152, 212.
[75] *Official Records of the General Assembly, Second Session, Supplement No. 11*, vol. I (A/364).
[76] Jonathan Steele, *Soviet Power: The Kremlin's Foreign Policy - Brezhnev to Chernenko* (New York: Touchstone-Simon, 1984), 186.
[77] Sachar, *History of Israel*, 292.
[78] Harry S. Truman, *Memoirs: Year of Decisions* (Cambridge: Da Capo, 1986), 69.
[79] Sachar, *History of Israel*, 287.
[80] Terry Tamminen, *Lives Per Gallon: The True Cost of Our Oil Addiction* (Washington, D.C.: Island 2009), 82.
[81] Walter Isaacson and Evan Thomas, *The Wise Men: Six Friends and the World They Made* (New York: Touchstone-Simon, 1986), 452.
[82] McCullough, *Truman*, 597.
[83] Weir, *Against Our Better Judgment*, 45.
[84] Ibid., 50.
[85] Loftus and Aarons, *Secret War Against Jews*, 159.
[86] Robert J. Donovan, *Conflict and Crisis: The Presidency of Harry S. Truman, 1945-1948* (1977, reprint; Columbia: U of Missouri P, 1996), 322.
[87] Loftus and Aarons, *Secret War Against Jews*, 164.
[88] John and Hadawi, *Palestine Diary*, 2:262-63.
[89] Loftus and Aarons, *Secret War Against Jews*, 163.
[90] Ibid., 164.
[91] Ibid., 165.
[92] Priscilla Mary Roberts, ed., *World War II: The Essential Reference Guide* (Santa Barbara: ABC-CLIO, 2012), 164.
[93] Charles Higham, *The Films of Orson Welles* (Berkley: UCP, 1970), 85.
[94] Loftus and Aarons, *Secret War Against Jews*, 167.
[95] Charles Higham, *Trading with the Enemy: An Exposé of the Nazi-American Money Plot 1933-1949* (New York: Delacorte, 1983), 62.
[96] Loftus and Aarons, *Secret War Against Jews*, 168-69.
[97] Ibid., 169.
[98] Ibid., 169-70.
[99] John and Hadawi, *Palestine Diary*, 2:263.
[100] United Nations General Assembly, "Resolution 181: Part IV - Capitulations," *The Avalon Project*, Yale Law School, 1996, Web, 19 June 2015.
[101] Loftus and Aarons, *Secret War Against Jews*, 170.
[102] John and Hadawi, *Palestine Diary*, 2:257.
[103] Sachar, *History of Israel*, 294.
[104] John and Hadawi, *Palestine Diary*, 2:266-67.
[105] Loftus and Aarons, *Secret War Against Jews*, 171.
[106] Efraim Karsh, *Essential Histories*, vol. 28, *The Arab-Israeli Conflict: The Palestine War 1948* (Oxford: Osprey, 2002), 8.
[107] James Rothrock, *Live by the Sword: Israel's Struggle for Existence in the Holy Land* (Bloomington, Ind.: WestBow, 2011), 7.
[108] Karsh, *Palestine Betrayed*, 100.
[109] Karsh, *Arab-Israeli Conflict*, 33.
[110] Karsh, *Palestine Betrayed*, 103.
[111] Philip Mattar, *Encyclopedia of the Palestinians*, Rev. ed. (New York: Facts on File, 2005), 51.
[112] Larry Collins and Dominique Lapierre, *O Jerusalem!* (New York: Simon, 1972), 103.
[113] Karsh, *Arab-Israeli Conflict*, 38.
[114] Ibid., 44.
[115] Sachar, *History of Israel*, 333.
[116] Daniel Greenfield, "Remembering the 65th Anniversary of the Hadassah Medical Convoy Massacre," 15 Mar. 2013, Front Page Mag, 07 March 2014.
[117] Karsh, *Palestine Betrayed*, 163-64.
[118] Collins and Lapierre, *O Jerusalem!*, 140.
[119] Richard Meinertzhagen, *Middle East Diary: 1917-1956* (New York: Thomas Yoseloff, 1959), 222-23.
[120] John and Hadawi, *Palestine Diary*, 2:306.
[121] Loftus and Aarons, *Secret War Against Jews*, 199.
[122] Ibid., 152-53.
[123] Ibid., 153.
[124] John and Hadawi, *Palestine Diary*, 2:311-12.
[125] Loftus and Aarons, *Secret War Against Jews*, 173-74.
[126] Weizmann, *Trial and Error*, 472.
[127] John Snetsinger, *Truman, the Jewish Vote, and the Creation of Israel* (Stanford: Hoover Inst. P, 1974), 75.
[128] McCullough, *Truman*, 606-07.
[129] Ibid., 604.
[130] Ibid.
[131] Ibid., 608.
[132] Weizmann, *Trial and Error*, 472.
[133] Karsh, *Palestine Betrayed*, 192.
[134] McCullough, *Truman*, 610-11.
[135] Ibid., 611.
[136] Ibid., 612.
[137] Sachar, *History of Israel*, 311-12.
[138] Joseph B. Schechtman, *The United States and the Jewish State Movement: The Crucial Decade, 1939-1949* (New York: Herzl, 1966), 287.
[139] Spencer C. Tucker., ed., *The Encyclopedia of the Arab-Israeli Conflict: A Political, Social, and Military History*, vol. 1, A-H (Santa Barbara: ABC-CLIO, 2008), 404.
[140] Isaacson and Thomas, *Wise Men*, 452.
[141] McCullough, *Truman*, 615.
[142] Clark Clifford and Richard Holbrooke, *Counsel to the President: A Memoir* (New York: Random, 1991), 13.
[143] McCullough, *Truman*, 616.
[144] Ibid.
[145] Collins and Lapierre, *O Jerusalem!*, 10-11.
[146] Jerry L. Jennings, *Stella's Secret: A True Story of Holocaust Survival* (Bloomington, Ind.: Xlibris Corporation, 2005), 73.
[147] Hugh A. Mulligan et al., eds., *Lightning Out of Israel: The Arab-Israeli Conflict* (Englewood Cliffs, N.J.: Prentice-Hall, 1967), 40.
[148] Clifford and Holbrooke, *Counsel to the President*, 19.
[149] Ibid., 20.
[150] John Acacia, *Clark Clifford: The Wise Man of Washington* (Lexington: UP of Kentucky, 2009), 112.
[151] Vera Weizmann and David Tutaev, *The Impossible Takes Longer: The Memoirs of Vera Weizmann as told to David Tutaev* (New York: Harper, 1967), 234.
[152] McCullough, *Truman*, 618.
[153] Stanley Meisler, *United Nations: The First Fifty Years* (New York: Atlantic Monthly, 1995), 48.
[154] Truman, *Years of Trial and Hope*, n.p.
[155] John and Hadawi, *Palestine Diary*, 2: 377-78.
[156] "Egyptian Air Force Spitfires Bomb Tel Aviv; One Shot Down," *The Palestine Post*, May 16, 1948, daily ed., sec. A.
[157] Weir, *Against Our Better Judgment*, 171-73.
[158] Michael Richards, *Destiny's Consul: America's Ten Greatest Presidents* (Lanham, Md.: Rowman, 2012), 307.
[159] Evan M. Wilson, *A Calculated Risk: The U.S. Decision to Recognize Israel* (1979; reprint, Cincinnati: Clerisy, 2008), 281.
[160] Arnold A. Rogow, *James Forrestal: A Study of Personality, Politics, and Policy* (New York: Macmillan, 1963), 307.
[161] Ibid., 214.
[162] Weir, *Against Our Better Judgment*, 163-64.
[163] "Welcome to the finest aircraft carrier in the fleet!," n.d., U.S. Navy, 23 Oct. 2014.
[164] McCullough, *Truman*, 83.
[165] Robert H. Ferrell, ed., *The Letters from Harry to Bess Truman, 1910-1959* (Columbia: U of Missouri P, 1983), 24.
[166] Weiler, *Ernest Bevin*, 4.
[167] McCullough, *Truman*, 620.
[168] Clifford and Holbrooke, *Counsel to the President*, 25.

CHAPTER 14

War of Independence

1 Eliezer Segal, *Sanctified Seasons* (Calgary, Ont.: Dept. of Religious Studies, U of Calgary, 2008), 46.
2 Ibid., 47.
3 Larry Collins and Dominique Lapierre, *O Jerusalem!* (New York: Simon, 1972), 410, 413.
4 Noah J. Efron, *A Chosen Calling: Jews in Science in the Twentieth Century* (Baltimore: Johns Hopkins UP, 2014), 93.
5 John Loftus and Mark Aarons, *The Secret War Against the Jews: How Western Espionage Betrayed the Jewish People* (New York: St. Martin's, 1994), 200.
6 Richard Meinertzhagen, *Middle East Diary: 1917-1956* (New York: Thomas Yoseloff, 1959), 228.
7 Loftus and Aarons, *Secret War Against Jews*, 235.
8 Alison Weir, *Against Our Better Judgment: The Hidden History of How the U.S. Was Used to Create Israel* (Lexington, Ken.: CreateSpace, 2014), 56, 58.
9 Ibid., 176.
10 Walter Isaacson and Evan Thomas, *The Wise Men: Six Friends and the World They Made* (New York: Touchstone-Simon, 1986), 452.
11 David McCullough, *Truman* (New York: Simon, 1992), 615.
12 Daniel Gavron, *The Kibbutz: Awakening from Utopia* (Lanham, Md.: Rowman &b Littlefield, 2000), 194.
13 Leonard Slater, *The Pledge* (New York: Simon, 1970), 34.
14 Howard M. Sachar, *A History of Israel: From the Rise of Zionism to Our Time*, 3rd Rev. ed. (New York: Knopf, 2007), 329.
15 Loftus and Aarons, *Secret War Against Jews*, 198.
16 Richard Deacon, *The Israeli Secret Service* (New York: Taplinger, 1977), 41.
17 Slater, *The Pledge*, 21-28.
18 Ibid., 13-17.
19 Weir, *Against Our Better Judgment*, 64, 1582-83.
20 Alexander Zvielli, "Teddy Kollek and his life-long dedication," *Jerusalem Post*, 02 Jan. 2007, Web, 29 Oct. 2014.
21 Avraham Ziv-Tal, *Enigma Named Max*, trans. Rena Bar-David (Rishon Lezion, Israel: n. p., 2013), 353.
22 Radomir Luza and Christina Vella, *The Hitler Kiss: A Memoir of the Czech Resistance* (Baton Rouge: Louisiana State UP, 2002), 211.
23 Ziv-Tal, *Enigma*, 355-61.
24 Loftus and Aarons, *Secret War Against Jews*, 202-03.
25 Mark Aarons and John Loftus, *Unholy Trinity: The Vatican, the Nazis, and Soviet Intelligence* (New York: St. Martin's, 1991), 217-18.
26 Loftus and Aarons, *Secret War Against Jews*, 205-07.
27 Ibid., 206-07.
28 Ibid., 207.
29 Deacon, *Israeli Secret Service*, 41.
30 Ziv-Tal, *Enigma*, 355-61.
31 Michael C. Desch, *Power and Military Effectiveness: The Fallacy of Democratic Triumphalism* (Baltimore: Johns Hopkins UP, 2008), 122.
32 Loftus and Aarons, *Secret War Against Jews*, 208.
33 Sachar, *History of Israel*, 323.
34 "How Israel Won Her Greatest Victories By Defying U.S. Pressure," 11 Aug. 2004, JTF.org, 30 Oct. 2014.
35 Benny Morris, *The Road to Jerusalem: Glubb Pasha, Palestine and the Jews* (London: Tauris, 2002), 239.
36 Meinertzhagen, *Middle East Diary*, 228.
37 Ibid., 225.
38 Ted Berkman, *Cast A Giant Shadow: The Story of Mickey Marcus Who Died to Save Jerusalem* (New York: Pocket, 1962), 217.
39 Efraim Karsh, *Palestine Betrayed* (New Haven: Yale UP, 2010), 200.
40 Ibid., 195.
41 Ibid., 196.
42 Ibid.
43 Meinertzhagen, *Middle East Diary*, 233.
44 Berkman, *Giant Shadow*, 120.
45 Ibid., 188-89.
46 Ibid., 132.
47 Ibid., 196-99.
48 Ibid., 24.
49 Ibid., 14.
50 David T. Zabecki, "David 'Mickey' Marcus," *Military History*, Apr. 1998: n. pag., HISTORYnet.com, Web, 31 Oct. 2014.
51 Lawrence J. Epstein, *A Treasury of Jewish Inspirational Stories* (Northvale, N.J.: Jason Aronson, 1993), 121.
52 Berkman, *Giant Shadow*, 34-40.
53 Ibid., *Giant Shadow*, 59.
54 Ibid., 197-98.
55 Ibid., 79.
56 Ibid., 60.
57 Ibid., 160.
58 Ibid., 44, 140.
59 Ibid., 40, 196.
60 Ibid., 160.
61 Ibid., 283.
62 Ibid., 5.
63 Ibid., 237.
64 Ibid., 96.
65 Jeffrey Weiss and Craig Weiss, *I Am My Brother's Keeper: American Volunteers in Israel's War for Independence 1947-1949* (Atglen, Penn.: Schiffer, 1998), 23.
66 Ibid., 20.
67 Ibid., 224.
68 Ibid., 20.
69 Ibid.
70 Ibid., 96.
71 Ibid., 257.
72 Sachar, *History of Israel*, 319.
73 Berkman, *Giant Shadow*, 241.
74 Elinor Slater and Robert Slater, *Great Moments in Jewish History* (Flushing, N.Y.: Jonathan David, 1998), 37.
75 Shlomo Aloni, *Osprey Combat Aircraft*, vol. 23, *Arab-Israeli Air Wars 1947-1982*, ed. Tony Holmes (Oxford: Osprey, 2001), 10.
76 Slater, *The Pledge*, 297.
77 Ibid., 304.
78 Efraim Karsh, *Essential Histories*, vol. 28, *The Arab-Israeli Conflict: The Palestine War 1948* (Oxford: Osprey, 2002), 60.
79 Sachar, *History of Israel*, 323.
80 Hugh A. Mulligan et al., eds., *Lightning Out of Israel: The Arab-Israeli Conflict* (Englewood Cliffs, N.J.: Prentice-Hall, 1967), 23.
81 Chaim Herzog and Shlomo Gazit, *The Arab-Israeli Wars: War and Peace in the Middle East* (New York: Vintage-Random, 2004), 45.
82 Meinertzhagen, *Middle East Diary*, 230.
83 Berkman, *Giant Shadow*, 254.
84 Collins and Lapierre, *O Jerusalem!*, 548.
85 Robert John and Sami Hadawi, *1945-1948; United States, United Nations Intervention*, vol. 2 of *The Palestine Diary* (New York: New World, 1970), 377.
86 Collins and Lapierre, *O Jerusalem!*, 435, 444, 519.
87 Ibid., 257.
88 Berkman, *Giant Shadow*, 250.
89 Ibid., 283.
90 Ibid., 249.
91 Sachar, *History of Israel*, 324.
92 Berkman, *Giant Shadow*, 141.
93 Ibid., 284.
94 Ibid., 290.
95 Ibid., 295-96.
96 Ibid., 299.
97 Ibid., 301.
98 Ibid., 305.
99 Ibid., 156.
100 Ibid., 314.
101 Ibid., 319.
102 Ibid., 320.
103 Ibid., 201-02, 321.
104 Ibid., 320.
105 Ibid.
106 Folke Bernadotte, "S/1025 of 5 October 1948," n.d., United Nations Security Council, 08 November.
107 Karsh, *Arab-Israeli Conflict*, 64.

[108] Larry Collins and Dominique Lapierre, *O Jerusalem!* (New York: Simon, 1972), 566.
[109] Meinertzhagen, *Middle East Diary*, 239.
[110] Joseph B. Schechtman, *The Life and Times of Vladimir Jabotinsky: Rebel and Statesman* (1956; reprint, Silver Spring, Md.: Eshel Books-Information Dynamics, n.d.), 58.
[111] Deborah Hart Strober and Gerald S. Strober, *Israel at Sixty: An Oral History of a Nation Reborn* (Hoboken, N.J.: Wiley, 2008), 85.
[112] Jack L. Schwartzwald, *Nine Lives of Israel: A Nation's History Through the Lives of Its Foremost Leaders* (Jefferson, N.C.: McFarland, 2012), 55-56.
[113] Ibid.
[114] Ibid.
[115] Aryeh Kaplan, *This Is the Way It Was*, Israel: Palyam.org, n.d. PDF.
[116] Berkman, *Giant Shadow*, 314.
[117] Aloni, *Arab-Israeli Air Wars*, 14.
[118] Michael Doran, *Pan-Arabism Before Nasser: Egyptian Power Politics and the Palestine Question* (New York: Oxford UP, 1999), 170.
[119] Karsh, *Arab-Israeli Conflict*, 68.
[120] Sachar, *History of Israel*, 343-45.
[121] Karsh, *Arab-Israeli Conflict*, 68.
[122] "Galilee Lido," *The West Australian*, 02 May 1946, accessed 18 Nov. 2014.
[123] Meinertzhagen, *Middle East Diary*, 207.
[124] James Grover McDonald, *My Mission In Israel, 1948-1951* (New York: Simon, 1951), 116.
[125] Ibid., 116-17.
[126] Ibid., 121.
[127] Meinertzhagen, *Middle East Diary*, 326.
[128] Aloni, *Arab-Israeli Air Wars*, 22.
[129] B. T. Williamson, "Caught in the Middle: Air Combat between Israel and the RAF," *The Royal Air Force Air Power Review*, vol. 8, no. 2, 2005: 79-83, accessed 20 Nov. 2014.
[130] Ibid., 83-85.
[131] Ibid., 79.
[132] Ibid., 80.
[133] Ibid., 79-80.
[134] Ibid., 86.
[135] Ibid., 85.
[136] Ibid., 77-78.
[137] Ibid., 77.
[138] Ibid., 86.
[139] Sachar, *History of Israel*, 348-49.
[140] Spencer C. Tucker et al., eds., *The Encyclopedia of the Arab-Israeli Conflict: A Political, Social, and Military History*, vol. 1, A-H (Santa Barbara: ABC-CLIO, 2008), 404.
[141] Sachar, *History of Israel*, 350.
[142] Youssef Aboul-Enein and Basil Aboul-Enein, *The Secret War for the Middle East: The Influence of Axis and Allied Intelligence Operations during World War II* (Annapolis: Naval Inst., 2013), 31.
[143] Sachar, *History of Israel*, 353.
[144] Weir, *Against Our Better Judgment*, 56.
[145] Karsh, *Palestine Betrayed*, 237.
[146] Weir, *Against Our Better Judgment*, 58.
[147] Ibid.
[148] Carl Hermann Voss, *The Palestine Problem Today: Israel and Its Neighbors* (Boston: Beacon, 1953), 13.
[149] Noam Chomsky, *Fateful Triangle: The United States, Israel, and the Palestinians*, updated ed. (Cambridge: South End, 1999), 96.
[150] Weir, *Against Our Better Judgment*, 173.
[151] Karsh, *Palestine Betrayed*, 176.
[152] Efraim Karsh, *Rethinking the Middle East* (Portland, Ore.: Frank Cass, 2003), 146-47.
[153] Ibid., 145.
[154] Meinertzhagen, *Middle East Diary*, 272.
[155] Karsh, *Palestine Betrayed*, 157-58.
[156] Ibid., 124.
[157] Karsh, *Rethinking Middle East*, 142.
[158] Karsh, *Palestine Betrayed*, 139.
[159] Karsh, *Rethinking Middle East*, 140-41.
[160] Ibid. 141.
[161] Shlomo Sharan and Dāwid Bûqay, *Crossovers: Anti-Zionism and Anti-Semitism* (New Brunswick, N.J.: Transaction, 2010), 33.
[162] Karsh, *Palestine Betrayed*, 182-83.
[163] Ibid., 237, 322 (endnote 23).
[164] Ibid., 216-117, 318 (endnote 20).
[165] Ibid., 200.
[166] Ibid. 227.
[167] Ibid., 223-24.
[168] Ibid., 225.
[169] Karsh, *Rethinking Middle East*, 165.
[170] Meinertzhagen, *Middle East Diary*, 234.
[171] Hobson Dewey Anderson, *The Arab Refugee Problem: How it Can be Solved; Proposals Submitted to the General Assembly of the United Nations* (n.p.: n.p., December 1951), 8-9.
[172] Weir, *Against Our Better Judgment*, 83.
[173] Bertie Charles Forbes, "Biggest Little Superpower in the World," *Forbes*, August 1, 1975, xcvi.
[174] Shmuel Bar, "Palestine or Peace? A 1960 Jordanian Peace Initiative: Reexamining History," *Middle East Quarterly* Summer 2006: 59-66, *The Middle East Quarterly*. The Middle East Forum, Web, 22 Nov. 2014.
[175] Karsh, *Palestine Betrayed*, 230.

CHAPTER 15

The Hundred-Hour War

[1] George Kirk, *The Middle East 1945-1950: Survey of International Affairs* (London: Oxford UP, 1954), 246.
[2] Paul Eidelberg, *The Myth of Israeli Democracy: Toward a Truly Jewish Israel* (Fullerton, Calif.: Davidson, 2007), 29.
[3] Isaac Alteras, *Eisenhower and Israel: U.S.-Israeli Relations, 1953-1960* (Gainesville, Fla.: UP of Florida, 1993), 103.
[4] Sachar, *History of Israel*, 398-99.
[5] Ibid., 403.
[6] John Loftus and Mark Aarons, *The Secret War Against the Jews: How Western Espionage Betrayed the Jewish People* (New York: St. Martin's, 1994), 228.
[7] Michael B. Oren, *Six Days of War: June 1967 and the Making of the Modern Middle East* (New York: Presidio-Random, 2003), 8.
[8] Burton Hersh, *The Old Boys: The American Elite and the Origins of the CIA* (St. Petersburg, Fla.: Tree Farm, 2002), 310.
[9] Ibid.
[10] Loftus and Aarons, *Secret War Against Jews*, 233.
[11] Sachar, *History of Israel*, 473-74.
[12] Youssef Aboul-Enein and Basil Aboul-Enein, *The Secret War for the Middle East: The Influence of Axis and Allied Intelligence Operations during World War II* (Annapolis: Naval Inst. P, 2013), 32.
[13] Mati Alon, *Holocaust and Redemption* (Victoria, BC: Trafford, 2003), 208.
[14] Daniel Yergin, *The Prize: The Epic Quest for Oil, Money, and Power* (New York: Touchstone-Simon, 1992), 281.
[15] Hersh, *Old Boys*, 310.
[16] Ibid.
[17] Richard Deacon, *The Israeli Secret Service* (New York: Taplinger, 1977), 131-35.
[18] Ibid., 131-38.
[19] Paul Eidelberg, *An American Political Scientist in Israel: From Athens to Jerusalem* (Lanham, Md.: Lexington-Rowman, 2010), 19-20.
[20] Cole C. Kingseed, *Eisenhower and the Suez Crisis of 1956* (Baton Rouge: Louisiana State UP, 1995), 43.
[21] Winston S. Churchill, *The Second World War*, vol. 1: *The Gathering Storm* (1948; reprint, New York: Houghton, 1985), 50.
[22] John Melady, *Pearson's Prize: Canada and the Suez Crisis* (Toronto: Dundurn, 2006), 51.
[23] Steven Pressfield, *The Lion's Gate: On the Front Lines of the Six Day War* (New York: Penguin, 2014), 64.
[24] Benny Morris, *Righteous Victims: A History of the Zionist-Arab Conflict, 1881-2001* (New York: Vintage-Random, 2001), 266.
[25] Anthony Verrier, *Through the Looking Glass: British Foreign Policy in the Age of Illusions* (London: Cape, 1983), 130.

[26] Yergin, *The Prize*, 14.
[27] Seymour M. Hersh, *The Samson Option: Israel's Nuclear Arsenal and American Foreign Policy* (New York: Random, 1991), 39.
[28] Yergin, *The Prize*, 487.
[29] Hersh, *Samson Option*, 42.
[30] Sachar, *History of Israel*, 483.
[31] Baylis Thomas, *How Israel was Won: A Concise History of the Arab-Israeli Conflict* (Lanham, Md.: Lexington, 1999), 121.
[32] Ibid., 121-22.
[33] Simon C. Smith, ed., *Reassessing Suez 1956: New Perspectives on the Crisis and its Aftermath* (Aldershot: Ashgate, 2008), 104.
[34] Peter Golden, *O Powerful Western Star!: American Jews, Russian Jews and the Final Battle of the Cold War* (Jerusalem: Gefen, 2012), 133.
[35] Saïd K. Aburish, *Nasser: The Last Arab* (New York: Dunne-St. Martin's, 2004), 108.
[36] Yergin, *The Prize*, 483.
[37] Golden, *Western Star!*, 133.
[38] Yergin, *The Prize*, 486.
[39] Carroll Quigley, *Tragedy and Hope: A History of the World in Our Time* (New York: The Macmillan Co., 1966), 1076.
[40] James Bamford, *Body of Secrets: Anatomy of the Ultra-Secret National Security Agency From the Cold War Through the Dawn of A New Century* (New York: Doubleday-Random, 2001), 40.
[41] Leonard Mosley, *Dulles: A Biography of Eleanor, Allen, and John Foster Dulles and Their Family Network* (New York: Dial-Wade, 1978), 405, 408.
[42] Ibid., 406.
[43] Quigley, *Tragedy and Hope*, 1076.
[44] Mosley, *Dulles*, 409.
[45] Avi Shlaim, "The Protocol of Sèvres, 1956: Anatomy of a War Plot," in *The 1956 War: Collusion and Rivalry in the Middle East,* ed. David Tal, (2001; reprint, Abingdon: Routledge-Taylor, 2013), 119.
[46] Ibid., 138.
[47] Ibid., 119.
[48] Sachar, *History of Israel*, 487.
[49] Howard M. Sachar, *Israel and Europe: An Appraisal in History* (New York: Vintage-Random, 1998), 30.
[50] "Army Attacks Bases in Heart of Sinai," *Jerusalem Post*, October 30, 1956, daily ed., sec. A.
[51] Steven Z. Freiberger, *Dawn Over Suez: The Rise of American Power in the Middle East 1953-1957* (Chicago: Ivan R. Dee, 1992), 262.
[52] "Shimon Peres," Jewish Virtual Library, accessed 06 Dec. 2014.
[53] Quigley, *Tragedy and Hope*, 1078.
[54] Sachar, *History of Israel*, 499.
[55] Ibid., 499-500.
[56] Barry Turner, *Suez 1956: The Inside Story of the First Oil War* (London: Hodder and Stoughton, 2006), Web, 20 June 2015, n. p.
[57] Quigley, *Tragedy and Hope*, 1078.
[58] Sachar, *History of Israel*, 501.
[59] Ibid.
[60] Ibid.
[61] Loftus and Aarons, *Secret War Against Jews*, 253.
[62] Abba Eban, *Personal Witness: Israel Through My Eyes* (New York: Putnam's, 1992), 264.
[63] Bamford, *Body of Secrets*, 40.
[64] Loftus and Aarons, *Secret War Against Jews*, 249.
[65] Alfred M. Lilienthal, *The Zionist Connection: What Price Peace?* (New York: Dodd, Mead and Co., 1978), 537.
[66] Loftus and Aarons, *Secret War Against Jews*, 250-52.
[67] Peter L. Hahn, *The United States, Great Britain, and Egypt, 1945-1956: Strategy and Diplomacy in the Early Cold War* (Chapel Hill: U of North Carolina P, 1991), 223.
[68] Robert Welch, *The Politician* (Belmont, Mass.: Belmont, 1963), 166.
[69] Loftus and Aarons, *Secret War Against Jews*, 236.
[70] Welch, *Politician*, 165.
[71] Yergin, *The Prize*, 484.
[72] Mosley, *Dulles*, 417.
[73] Aboul-Enein and Aboul-Enein, *Secret War for Middle East*, 174.
[74] John Tolan, Gilles Veinstein, and Henry Laurens, *Europe and the Islamic World: A History* (Princeton: Princeton UP, 2013), 388.
[75] Aboul-Enein and Aboul-Enein, *Secret War for Middle East*, 176.
[76] Yergin, *The Prize*, 491.
[77] Ibid., 495.
[78] Ibid.
[79] Loftus and Aarons, *Secret War Against Jews*, 251.
[80] Mosley, *Dulles*, 425.
[81] Yergin, *The Prize*, 495-96.
[82] Ibid., 489.
[83] Ibid., 495.
[84] Eban, *Personal Witness*, 260.
[85] Aboul-Enein and Aboul-Enein, *Secret War for Middle East*, xv.
[86] Mosley, *Dulles*, 427.
[87] Alexander Zvielli, comp., *Front Page Israel: Modern Israel's Extraordinary History as Captured on the Front Pages of The Jerusalem Post* (Jerusalem: *Jerusalem Post*, 2008), 114.
[88] Shlaim, "Protocol of Sèvres: *1956 War*," 138.
[89] Keith Kyle, *Suez: Britain's End of Empire in the Middle East* (New York: Tauris, 2011), 331.
[90] Shlaim, "Protocol of Sèvres: *1956 War*," 119-20.
[91] Sachar, *History of Israel*, 513.
[92] Deacon, *Israeli Secret Service*, 119.
[93] Chaim Herzog, *Heroes of Israel: Profiles of Jewish Courage* (Boston: Little, 1989), 244.
[94] Shlaim, "Protocol of Sèvres: *1956 War*," 123, 125, 139.
[95] Ibid., 126.
[96] Ibid., 132.
[97] Ibid., 136.
[98] Ibid., 137.
[99] Shlaim, "Protocol of Sèvres: *1956 War*," 509-530.
[100] Hersh, *Samson Option*, 137.
[101] Shimon Peres, *Battling for Peace: A Memoir* (New York: Random, 1995), 130.
[102] Shlaim, "Protocol of Sèvres: *1956 War*," 134.
[103] Ibid., 133-34.
[104] Hersh, *Samson Option*, 43.
[105] Shlaim, "Protocol of Sèvres: *1956 War*," 134.

CHAPTER 16

The Six-Day War

[1] Abba Eban, *Personal Witness: Israel Through My Eyes* (New York: Putnam's, 1992), 350.
[2] Steven Pressfield, *The Lion's Gate: On the Front Lines of the Six Day War* (New York: Penguin, 2014), 8.
[3] Barry J. Beitzel, *The Moody Atlas of Bible Lands* (Chicago: Moody, 1985), 27.
[4] Richard Meinertzhagen, *Middle East Diary: 1917-1956* (New York: Yoseloff, 1959), 357.
[5] Hannah Arendt, *Eichmann in Jerusalem: A Report on the Banality of Evil* (1963; reprint, New York: Penguin, 1992), 252.
[6] "Eichmann Hanged," *The Jerusalem Post*, June 1, 1962, early morning ed., sec. A.
[7] Eli Ben-hanan, *Our Man in Damascus: Elie Cohn* (Bnei Brak, Israel: Steimatzky, n.d.), 137.
[8] C. Gus Martin, ed., *The SAGE Encyclopedia of Terrorism*, 2nd ed. (Los Angeles: Sage, 2011), 129.
[9] United Nations Security Council, "Documents Officiels, Volume 31" (New York: United Nations Security Council, 1977), 12, Web, 20 June 2015.
[10] Eban, *Personal Witness*, 346.
[11] Ibid., 357.
[12] Ibid., 357, 416.
[13] Michael B. Oren, *Six Days of War: June 1967 and the Making of the Modern Middle East* (New York: Presidio-Random, 2003), 101.
[14] Ibid., 66-67.
[15] Brian Urquhart, *A Life in Peace and War* (New York: Norton, 1987), 190.

[16] Oren, *Six Days of War*, 75.
[17] Isabella Ginor and Gideon Remez, *Foxbats Over Dimona: The Soviets' Nuclear Gamble in the Six-Day War* (Grand Rapids, Mich.: Integrated Publishing Solutions, 2007), 129.
[18] Oren, *Six Days of War*, 75-76.
[19] Ginor and Remez, *Foxbats*, 130.
[20] Eban, *Personal Witness*, 328-29.
[21] Yehoshafat Harkabi, *Arab Attitudes to Israel* (New York: Halstead-Wiley, 1974), 4, 38.
[22] Oren, *Six Days of War*, 84.
[23] Ibid.
[24] Dennis Ross, *The Missing Peace: The Inside Story of the Fight for Middle East Peace* (New York: Farrar, 2004), 91.
[25] Ibid., 93.
[26] Abraham Rabinovich, *The Battle for Jerusalem: June 5-7, 1967* (New York: The Jewish Publication Society of America, 1972), 54.
[27] Ibid., 57-58.
[28] Oren, *Six Days of War*, 136.
[29] Tom Segev, *1967: Israel, the War and the Year that Transformed the Middle East* (New York: Metropolitan, 2005), 15.
[30] Pressfield, *Lion's Gate*, 4-5.
[31] Ibid., 33.
[32] Oren, *Six Days of War*, 134.
[33] Rabinovich, *Battle for Jerusalem*, 59.
[34] Oren, *Six Days of War*, 50.
[35] Eban, *Personal Witness*, 318.
[36] Pressfield, *Lion's Gate*, 34.
[37] Ibid., 35.
[38] Oren, *Six Days of War*, 132.
[39] Ibid., 148.
[40] Ibid.
[41] Ibid., 38.
[42] Ibid., 2.
[43] Ibid., 27.
[44] Ibid., 55.
[45] Eban, *Personal Witness*, 354.
[46] Sachar, *History of Israel*, 622.
[47] Oren, *Six Days of War*, 64.
[48] Yehuda Lukacs and Abdalla M. Battah, eds., *The Arab-Israeli Conflict: Two Decades of Change* (Boulder, Colo.: Westview, 1988), 15.
[49] "'Hand of God' Prevents Rocket from Striking Its Target: Israeli Iron Dome Operator Says Sudden Gust of Wind Blew Missile into Sea When Defence System Failed," *Jews News*. N.p., 06 Aug. 2014, Web, 20 Jan. 2015.
[50] Michael Youssef, *You Want Me to Do What?: Get Off Your Blessed Assurance and Do Something* (New York: Faith Words-Hachette Book Group, 2009), 27-28.
[51] Daniel Smith, *100 Places You Will Never Visit: The World's Most Secret Locations* (London: Quercus, 2012), 162.
[52] Eban, *Personal Witness*, 46.
[53] Hugh A. Mulligan et al., eds., *Lightning Out of Israel: The Arab-Israeli Conflict* (Englewood Cliffs, N.J.: Prentice-Hall, 1967), 35.
[54] John Bierman and Colin Smith, *Fire in the Night: Wingate of Burma, Ethiopia, and Zion* (New York: Random, 1999.
[55] Oren, *Six Days of War*, 168.
[56] Patricia Karlin-Neumann, "Crossing into 2012: Exodus 13:1-22, Psalms 114," sermon text (01 Jan. 2012), Web, 22 Jan. 2015, 2.
[57] Debbie Young-Somers, "Crossing the Reed Sea," Rabbi Debbie Young-Somers, 24 Apr. 2011, par. 1.
[58] Michael Karpin, *The Bomb in the Basement: How Israel Went Nuclear and What That Means for the World* (New York: Simon, 2006), 282.
[59] Ibid., 120.
[60] Ibid., 121.
[61] Eban, *Personal Witness*, 382.
[62] Oren, *Six Days of War*, 122.
[63] Eban, *Personal Witness*, 382.
[64] Oren, *Six Days of War*, 122.
[65] Ibid., 123.
[66] Ibid., 123-24.
[67] Ibid., 129-31.
[68] Ibid., 167.
[69] Ibid., 312.
[70] Ibid., 118.
[71] Lyndon Baines Johnson, *The Vantage Point: Perspectives of the Presidency, 1963-1969* (New York: Holt, 1971), 288-89.
[72] Ibid., 291.
[73] Oren, *Six Days of War*, 113-15.
[74] Ibid., 51.
[75] Ibid., 168.
[76] Ibid., 164.
[77] Jonathan Colman, *The Foreign Policy of Lyndon B. Johnson: The United States and the World, 1963-1969* (Edinburgh: Edinburgh UP, 2010), 149.
[78] Oren, *Six Days of War*, 143.
[79] United States Department of State, Office of the Historian, *Foreign Relations of the United States, 1964-1968, Volume XIX, Arab-Israeli Crisis and War, 1967, Document 178*, "Telegram From the Embassy in the United Arab Republic to the Department of State."
[80] Oren, *Six Days of War*, 157.
[81] Ibid., 165.
[82] Pressfield, *Lion's Gate*, 133.
[83] Ibid., 146.
[84] Oren, *Six Days of War*, 170-71.
[85] Pressfield, *Lion's Gate*, 103-09, 111-14.
[86] Mulligan et al., *Lightning*, 55.
[87] Richard Deacon, *The Israeli Secret Service* (New York: Taplinger, 1977), 185.
[88] Ibid., 167.
[89] Dan Raviv and Yossi Melman, *Every Spy a Prince: The Complete History of Israel's Intelligence Community* (Boston: Houghton, 1990), 152.
[90] Oren, *Six Days of War*, 171.
[91] Ibid., 166-67.
[92] Andrew Cockburn and Leslie Cockburn, *Dangerous Liaison: The Inside Story of the U.S.-Israeli Covert Relationship* (New York: Harper, 1991), 149.
[93] Avi Shlaim and William Roger Louis, eds., *The 1967 Arab-Israeli War: Origins and Consequences* (New York: Cambridge UP, 2012), 112.
[94] Glenn Frankel, *Beyond the Promised Land: Jews and Arabs on the Hard Road to a New Israel* (New York: Touchstone-Simon, 1994), 33.
[95] Oren, *Six Days of War*, 209.
[96] Pressfield, *Lion's Gate*, 331-32.
[97] Mulligan et al., *Lightning*, 70.
[98] Ibid., 62.
[99] King Hussein of Jordan, *Hussein of Jordan: My War with Israel*, trans. Vick Vance and Pierre Lauer (New York: William Morrow, 1969), 65-65.
[100] Oren, *Six Days of War*, 184.
[101] Mulligan et al., *Lightning*, 54.
[102] Oren, *Six Days of War*, 177, 189.
[103] Sachar, *History of Israel*, 644-45.
[104] Rabinovich, *Battle for Jerusalem*, 125.
[105] Sachar, *History of Israel*, 644.
[106] Rabinovich, *Battle for Jerusalem*, 122.
[107] Oren, *Six Days of War*, 184.
[108] Rabinovich, *Battle for Jerusalem*, 115-17.
[109] Odd Bull, *War and Peace in the Middle East: The Experiences and Views of a UN Observer* (Barnsley: Leo Cooper, 1976), 115.
[110] Oren, *Six Days of War*, 191.
[111] Rabinovich, *Battle for Jerusalem*, 128.
[112] Eric Hammel, *Six Days in June: How Israel Won the 1967 Arab-Israeli War* (Pacifica: Pacifica Military History, 1992), 300.
[113] Ibid., 299.
[114] Oren, *Six Days of War*, 188.
[115] Sachar, *History of Israel*, 644.
[116] H. D. M. Spence and Joseph S. Exell, *The Pulpit Commentary*, vol. 17: *Gospel of John* in two volumes (N.d.; reprint, Grand Rapids: Eerdmans, 1978), 2:97.
[117] Oren, *Six Days of War*, 198.
[118] Ibid., 251.
[119] Ibid., 197.

[120] Johnson, *Vantage Point*, 297.
[121] Norman G. Finkelstein, *Image and Reality of the Israel-Palestine Conflict*, 2nd ed. (New York: Verso-New Left, 2003), 194.
[122] Mulligan et al., *Lightning*, 83.
[123] Oren, *Six Days of War*, 212.
[124] Ibid., 215.
[125] Simon Sebag Montefiore, *Jerusalem: The Biography* (New York: Knopf, 2001), 517.
[126] Oren, *Six Days of War*, 232.
[127] Pressfield, *Lion's Gate*, 268.
[128] Oren, *Six Days of War*, 222.
[129] Ibid.
[130] Rabinovich, *Battle for Jerusalem*, 379.
[131] Oren, *Six Days of War*, 224.
[132] Pressfield, *Lion's Gate*, 315.
[133] Shlaim and Louis, *1967 Arab-Israeli War*, 118-19.
[134] Montefiore, *Jerusalem*, 517.
[135] "Scopus Road Opened, Old City Encircled; 200 Egyptian Tanks Smashed; Gaza Falls," *Jerusalem Post*, June 7, 1967, daily ed., sec. A.
[136] Mulligan et al., *Lightning*, 73.
[137] Pressfield, *Lion's Gate*, 7.
[138] Ibid., 232, 272, 275.
[139] Hammel, *Six Days in June*, 321.
[140] Simon Dunstan, *The Six Day War 1967: Jordan and Syria* (New York: Osprey, 2009), 51.
[141] Hammel, *Six Days in June*, 321.
[142] Sholom Gold, *Touching History: From Williamsburg to Jerusalem* (Jerusalem: Gefen, 2015), Web, 25 June 2015, n. pag.
[143] Rabinovich, *Battle for Jerusalem*, 236.
[144] James Riley Estep, "Archeological Insights into the Crucifixion of Jesus," in *My Father's World: Celebrating the Life of Reuben G. Bullard*, John D. Wineland, Mark Ziese, and James Riley Estep, eds. (Eugene, Ore.: Wipf and Stock, 2011), 75.
[145] Montefiore, *Jerusalem*, 518.
[146] Pressfield, *Lion's Gate*,309.
[147] Ibid., 316.
[148] Ibid., 321-23.
[149] Rich Cohen, *Israel is Real: An Obsessive Quest to Understand the Jewish Nation and Its History* (New York: Picador-Farrar, 2009), 264.
[150] Ibid.
[151] Pressfield, *Lion's Gate*, 303.
[152] Rabinovich, *Battle for Jerusalem*, 426.
[153] Avi Tsur, ed., *Landmarks: Resource Material, Poetry, Songs, Games and Activities* (Jerusalem: Israeli Ministry of Education, Culture and Sport, 1998), 103.
[154] Mulligan et al., eds., *Lightning*, 105.
[155] Aba Gefen, *Israel at a Crossroads* (Jerusalem: Gefen, 2001), 137.
[156] Kobi Cohen-Hattab and Noam Shoval, *Tourism, Religion, and Pilgrimage in Jerusalem* (New York: Routledge, 2015), 135.
[157] Pressfield, *Lion's Gate*, 336.
[158] Rabinovich, *Battle for Jerusalem*, 433.
[159] Montefiore, *Jerusalem*, 518-19.
[160] Rabinovich, *Battle for Jerusalem*, 352.
[161] Ibid., 298.
[162] Hammel, *Six Days in June*, 269.
[163] Oren, *Six Days of War*, 255.
[164] W. Cleon Skousen, *Fantastic Victory: Israel's Rendezvous with Destiny*, 2nd ed. (New York: C & J Investments, 2011), 77.
[165] Mulligan et al., *Lightning*, 119-20.
[166] James Bamford, *Body of Secrets: Anatomy of the Ultra-Secret National Security Agency From the Cold War Through the Dawn of A New Century* (New York: Doubleday-Random, 2001), 214.
[167] Anthony Pearson, *Conspiracy of Silence: The Attack on the U.S.S. Liberty* (London: Quartet, 1978), 41.
[168] Bamford, *Body of Secrets*, 218-19.
[169] Patrick J. McGarvey, *CIA.: The Myth and the Madness* (New York: Saturday Review, 1972), 17.
[170] Pearson, *Conspiracy of Silence*, 57.
[171] James M. Ennes, Jr., *Assault on the Liberty: The True Story of the Israeli Attack on an American Intelligence Ship*, 5th ed. (New York: Random, 1979), 8.
[172] Ibid., 126.
[173] Eban, *Personal Witness*, 422.
[174] Pearson, *Conspiracy of Silence*, 68.
[175] Oren, *Six Days of War*, 142.
[176] Pearson, *Conspiracy of Silence*, 34.
[177] Bamford, *Body of Secrets*, 207.
[178] America's Highest Ranking Naval Officer, Admiral Thomas Moorer (1912 - 2004), Former Chief of Naval Operations and Chairman, Joint Chiefs of Staff Rejects the Israeli Excuse," *USS Liberty Memorial*. James M. Ennes, Jr., n.d. Memorandum, 08 June 1997, Web, 05 Feb. 2015.
[179] Ennes, *Assault*, 141.
[180] Oren, *Six Days of War*, 262-71.
[181] Ibid., 142.
[182] National Security Agency, *Report to the Director NSA, USS Liberty (AGTR-5), 23 May - 8 June 1967* [Washington, DC], National Security Agency, n.d. Declassified document, p. 2.
[183] John Crewdson, "New revelations in attack on American spy ship," *Chicago Tribune*, 02 Oct. 2007.
[184] Bamford, *Body of Secrets*, 199.
[185] Deacon, *Israeli Secret Service*, 182.
[186] Oren, *Six Days of War*, 267.
[187] Ennes, *Assault*, 91.
[188] Ibid., 116.
[189] Ibid., 37.
[190] Kyle Munson, "Liberty Sailor Honored despite Bitterness over Attack," The Des Moines Register, 11 Nov. 2014: n. pag. USA Today, Gannett Satellite Information Network, 11 Nov. 2014, Web, 10 Mar. 2015.
[191] Moorer, Memorandum.
[192] Bamford, *Body of Secrets*, 198.
[193] Ennes, *Assault*, 211-13.
[194] Bamford, *Body of Secrets*, 202.
[195] Alex Safian, "False Israeli 'Massacre' Story Resurrected," Committee for Accuracy in Middle East Reporting in America, 04 Mar. 2007, Web, 06 Feb. 2015.
[196] Deacon, *Israeli Secret Service*, 178-79.
[197] Wilbur Crane Eveland, *Ropes of Sand: Americas Failure in the MIddle East* (New York: Norton, 1980), 323.
[198] Pearson, *Conspiracy of Silence*, 15-16.
[199] Deacon, *Israeli Secret Service*, 180-81.
[200] Pearson, *Conspiracy of Silence*, 31, 93, 116.
[201] Ibid., 28, 38, 118, 159, 162.
[202] Eveland, *Ropes of Sand*, 324-25.
[203] Deacon, *Israeli Secret Service*, 182.
[204] Peter Hounam, *Operation Cyanide: Why the Bombing of the USS Liberty Nearly Caused World War III* (London: Vision-Satin, 2003), 3-4, 267-68, 303.
[205] Raviv and Melman, *Every Spy*, 90-92, 198.
[206] *USS Liberty: Dead in the Water*, dir. Christopher Mitchell, DVD, BBC, 2002.
[207] Pearson, *Conspiracy of Silence*, 164-65.
[208] Peter Collier et al., eds., "U.S. Electronic Espionage: A Memoir" *Ramparts*, 02 Aug. 1972, 43.
[209] Bamford, *Body of Secrets*, 212-16.
[210] Ennes, *Assault*, 164.
[211] *USS Liberty*, DVD.
[212] Loftus and Aarons, *Secret War Against the Jews*, 568-72.
[213] Ennes, *Assault*, 218-19.
[214] Ibid., 14.
[215] Loftus and Aarons, *Secret War Against the Jews*, 267.
[216] Ibid., 281.
[217] Ibid., 271.
[218] Ibid., 272.
[219] Ibid., 274.
[220] Ibid., 274-75.
[221] Ibid., 275.
[222] Zaki Shalom, *The Role of US Diplomacy in the Lead-up to the Six Day War: Balancing Moral Commitments and National Interests* (Portland, Ore.: Sussex Acad. P, 2012), 1.

[223] Reverdy S. Fishel, "The Attack on the Liberty: An 'Accident'?" *International Journal of Intelligence and Counter Intelligence*, 8.3, 1995, *The USS Liberty Memorial Website*. Ussliberty.org., Web, 02 Feb. 2015.
[224] Ibid.
[225] K. J. Halliwell, "Were Hebrew Linguists Aboard USS Liberty?" *USS Liberty Inquiry*, 25 Oct. 2007, Web, 02 Feb. 2015, Essay 18.
[226] Ennes, *Assault*, 206-07.
[227] NSA, *Report to the Director*, Introduction, p. ii.
[228] Bamford, *Body of Secrets*, 217.
[229] Ennes, *Assault*, 87.
[230] Bamford, *Body of Secrets*, 216.
[231] Cockburn and Cockburn, *Dangerous Liaison*, 151.
[232] Mulligan et al., *Lightning*, 139.
[233] Robert Henry Stephens, *Nasser: A Political Biography* (New York: Simon, 1971), 513.
[234] Mulligan et al., *Lightning*, 134.
[235] Ibid., 133.
[236] Oren, *Six Days of War*, 273.
[237] Ibid., 271.
[238] Eban, *Personal Witness*, 423.
[239] Oren, *Six Days of War*, 280.
[240] Ibid., 282.
[241] Mulligan et al., *Lightning*, 130.
[242] Mati Maizel, *The Golan Heights Campaign in the Six-Day War* (Tel Aviv: IDF History Department,1999), trans. in emails from Maor Levi, Tour Director, Yad La-Shiryon Museum, 06-11 Nov. 2014, 216, 219.
[243] Oren, *Six Days of War*, 301.
[244] Ibid., 298-99.
[245] Ibid., 300.
[246] Ibid.
[247] Ibid., 302.
[248] Ibid., 300.
[249] Sachar, *History of Israel*, 658.
[250] Ibid.
[251] Oren, *Six Days of War*, 305.
[252] Pressfield, *Lion's Gate*, 372.
[253] Mulligan et al., *Lightning*, 153.
[254] Oren, *Six Days of War*, 306.
[255] Sachar, *History of Israel*, 664.
[256] James D. Lunt, *Hussein of Jordan: Searching for a Just and Lasting Peace* (New York: Morrow, 1989), 106.
[257] Nigel J. Ashton, ed., *The Cold War in the Middle East: Regional Conflict and the Superpowers 1967-73* (New York: Routledge, 2007), 93.
[258] Ibid., 309.
[259] Sachar, *History of Israel*, 715.

CHAPTER 17

The Yom Kippur War

[1] Paul Jenkins, dir. "Israel's Generals - Moshe Dayan" *YouTube*, YouTube, 22 Feb. 2014, Web, 24 Feb. 2015.
[2] Howard Blum, *The Eve of Destruction: The Untold Story of the Yom Kippur War* (New York: Harper, 2003), 14.
[3] Chaim Herzog, *The War of Atonement: October 1973* (Boston: Little, 1975), 13.
[4] Michael B. Oren, *Six Days of War: June 1967 and the Making of the Modern Middle East* (New York: Presidio-Random, 2003), 311.
[5] Arnold Sherman, *When God Judged and Men Died: A Battle Report of the Yom Kippur War* (New York: Bantam, 1973), 2.
[6] Ibid., 31.
[7] Avi Kober, *Israel's Wars of Attrition: Attrition Challenges to Democratic States* (New York: Routledge-Taylor, 2009), 59.
[8] Ibid., 102.
[9] Herzog, *War of Atonement*, 12.
[10] Oren, *Six Days of War*, 317.
[11] Hela Crown-Tamir, *Israel, History in a Nutshell: Highlighting the Wars and Military History* (Jerusalem: Tsur Tsina, 2012), 137.
[12] Luci Swindoll, *Notes to a Working Woman: Finding Balance, Passion, and Fulfillment in Your Life* (Nashville: W-Thomas Nelson, 2004), 75.
[13] Elinor Burkett, *Golda* (New York: Harper, 2008), 68.
[14] Elisabeth Young-Bruehl, *Hannah Arendt: For Love of the World* (Binghamton, N.Y.: Vail-Ballou, 1982), 332.
[15] Donald J. McCarthy, Jr., *The Sword of David: The Israeli Air Force at War* (South Yorkshire: Pen & Sword, 2013), 16-17.
[16] W. Andrew Terrill, "Escalation and Intrawar Deterrence During Limited Wars in the Middle East," *Strategic Studies Inst.* (16 Sept. 2009). The US Army War College, PDF file.
[17] Joseph M. Demakis, ed., *The Ultimate Book of Quotations* (Charleston, S.C.: CreateSpace, 2012), 5.
[18] Saïd K. Aburish, *Nasser: The Last Arab* (New York: Dunne-St. Martin's, 2004), 315-16.
[19] "Anwar El Sadat's Statement to the Nation, September 28, 1970," *The Anwar Sadat Chair for Peace and Development* (2006). The University of Maryland, PDF file.
[20] Abraham Rabinovich, *The Yom Kippur War: The Epic Encounter That Transformed the Middle East* (New York: Schocken-Random, 2004), 13.
[21] David G. Dalin and John F. Rothman, *Icon of Evil: Hitler's Mufti and the Rise of Radical Islam* (New York: Random, 2008), 87.
[22] Asaf Siniver, *The Yom Kippur War: Politics, Legacy, Diplomacy* (New York: Oxford UP, 2013), 34.
[23] Ibid., 215.
[24] Ibid., 31.
[25] Ibid., 2558.
[26] Jack L. Schwartzwald, *Nine Lives of Israel: A Nation's History through the Lives of Its Foremost Leaders* (Jefferson, N.C.: McFarland, 2012), 111.
[27] Siniver, *Yom Kippur War*, 35.
[28] Ibid., 52, 86.
[29] Daniel Dishon et al., eds., *Middle East Record: Volume Four, 1968* (Jerusalem: Israeli Universities P, Wiley, 1973), 258.
[30] Susan Kone, dir. "Moment of Silence to Remember the Munich 11/Universal Prayer for Peace," *YouTube*, YouTube, 05 Sep. 2014, Web, 04 Mar. 2015.
[31] Dan Raviv and Yossi Melman, *Every Spy a Prince: The Complete History of Israel's Intelligence Community* (Boston: Houghton, 1990), 186.
[32] Siniver, *Yom Kippur War*, 216.
[33] Herzog, *War of Atonement*, 26.
[34] Blum, *Eve of Destruction*, 94-95.
[35] Siniver, *Yom Kippur War*, 122.
[36] Ibid.
[37] Herzog, *War of Atonement*, 48.
[38] Uri Bar-Joseph, *The Watchman Fell Asleep: The Surprise of Yom Kippur and Its Sources* (Albany: State U of New York P, 2005), 129.
[39] Blum, *Eve of Destruction*, 139.
[40] Herzog, *War of Atonement*, 51-52.
[41] Blum, *Eve of Destruction*, 152.
[42] Rabinovich, *Yom Kippur War*, 89-90.
[43] Mitch Ginsburg, "Golda Meir: 'My Heart Was Drawn to a Preemptive Strike, but I Was Scared,'" *The Times of Israel*, 12 Sept. 2013, Web, 07 Mar. 2015.
[44] Rabinovich, *Yom Kippur War*, 94.
[45] Joel Peters, *Israel and Africa: The Problematic Friendship* (New York: St. Martin's, 1992), 36.
[46] Ibid., 37.
[47] "Peled; North Korean Pilots Flew for Egypt During Yom Kippur War," *JTA*, 31 Oct. 1975, Web, 07 Mar. 2015.
[48] Jaime Suchlicki, ed., *The Cuban Military Under Castro* (Piscataway, N.J.: Transaction, 1989), 41.
[49] Anwar El Sadat, R. Israeli, ed., *The Public Diary of President Sadat, Part 1* (Leiden: Brill, 1979), 1232.
[50] Shlomo Aloni, *Osprey Aircraft of the Aces,* Vol. 59, *Israeli Mirage and Nesher Aces*, eds. Tony Holmes and Bruce Hales-Dutton (Oxford: Osprey, 2004), 67-68.
[51] Blum, *Eve of Destruction*, 234.
[52] Sherman, *When God Judged*, 37.
[53] Rabinovich, *Yom Kippur War*, 261.
[54] Blum, *Eve of Destruction*, 133-34.
[55] Herzog, *War of Atonement*, 33.
[56] Ibid., 34.
[57] Blum, *Eve of Destruction*, 89.
[58] Rabinovich, *Yom Kippur War*, 103.
[59] Ibid., 277.

60 Ibid., 125.
61 Avraham Adan, *On the Banks of the Suez: An Israeli General's Personal Account of the Yom Kippur War* (New York: Presidio, 1980), 22.
62 Uri Joseph Fisher, *Military Entrepreneurship and War Duration* (Ann Arbor: ProQuest, 2007), 230.
63 Sherman, *When God Judged*, 67.
64 Mohamed Heikal, *The Road to Ramadan* (New York: The New York Times, 1975), 15.
65 Rabinovich, *Yom Kippur War*, 252.
66 Sachar, *History of Israel*, 756.
67 Herzog, *War of Atonement*, 61-63.
68 Blum, *Eve of Destruction*, 157.
69 Ibid., 167.
70 Herzog, *War of Atonement*, 78, 84, 85, 89.
71 Blum, *Eve of Destruction*, 181.
72 Sherman, *When God Judged*, 57, 102.
73 Herzog, *War of Atonement*, 94.
74 Seymour M. Hersh, *The Samson Option: Israel's Nuclear Arsenal and American Foreign Policy* (New York: Random, 1991), 238.
75 Rabinovich, *Yom Kippur War*, 155.
76 Sachar, *History of Israel*, 763.
77 Ibid.
78 Rabinovich, *Yom Kippur War*, 220.
79 Blum, *Eve of Destruction*, 203.
80 Ibid., 228-29.
81 Herzog, *War of Atonement*, 280.
82 Siniver, *Yom Kippur War*, 11.
83 Sachar, *History of Israel*, 762.
84 Blum, *Eve of Destruction*, 153.
85 Rabinovich, *Yom Kippur War*, 119.
86 Sachar, *History of Israel*, 762.
87 Rabinovich, *Yom Kippur War*, 221.
88 Siniver, *Yom Kippur War*, 45.
89 Rabinovich, *Yom Kippur War*, 259.
90 Ibid., 125.
91 Gershom Gorenberg, *The Accidental Empire: Israel and the Birth of the Settlements 1967-1977* (New York: Times-Holt, 2006), 256.
92 Raviv and Melman, *Every Spy a Prince*, 211.
93 Rabinovich, *Yom Kippur War*, 48.
94 Herzog, *War of Atonement*, 38.
95 Blum, *Eve of Destruction*, 36.
96 Siniver, *Yom Kippur War*, 198.
97 Blum, *Eve of Destruction*, 36.
98 Ibid., 32.
99 Ibid., 36-37.
100 Siniver, *Yom Kippur War*, 52.
101 Ibid., 217.
102 Terrill, "Escalation and Intrawar Deterrence," 13.
103 Rabinovich, *Yom Kippur War*, 45.
104 Ibid.
105 Siniver, *Yom Kippur War*, 74.
106 Rabinovich, *Yom Kippur War*, 270.
107 Herzog, *War of Atonement*, 116-17.
108 Ibid., 117.
109 Ibid., 118.
110 Adan, *Banks of the Suez*, 174.
111 Herzog, *War of Atonement*, 107-13.
112 Trevor N. Dupuy, *Elusive Victory: The Arab-Israeli Wars, 1947-1974* (Garden City, N.Y.: Military Book Club, 2002), 459.
113 Herzog, *War of Atonement*, 127.
114 Siniver, *Yom Kippur War*, 125.
115 Sherman, *When God Judged*, 69.
116 Siniver, *Yom Kippur War*, 126.
117 Ibid., 129.
118 Ibid., 130.
119 Ibid., 287.
120 Ibid., 129.
121 Henry Kissinger, *Years of Upheaval: The Second Volume of His Classic Memoirs* (1982, reprint, New York: Simon, 2011), 506.
122 Siniver, *Yom Kippur War*, 133.
123 Ibid., 131.
124 Sachar, *History of Israel*, 787.
125 Sherman, *When God Judged*, 82.
126 Siniver, *Yom Kippur War*, 90.
127 Ibid., 92.
128 P. R. Kumaraswamy, ed., *Revisiting the Yom Kippur War* (Portland, Ore.: Cass, 2000), 117.
129 Sherman, *When God Judged*, 112.
130 Adan, *Banks of the Suez*, 154-56, 173-74.
131 Ibid., 232.
132 Ibid., 227.
133 Herzog, *War of Atonement*, 206.
134 Ibid.
135 Richard L. Owen, "Operation Valiant: Turning of the Tide in the Sinai, 1973 Arab-Israeli War," *GlobalSecurity.org*, 01 Apr. 1984, Web, 24 Mar. 2015.
136 Edgar O'Ballance, *No Victor, No Vanquished: The Yom Kippur War* (San Rafael: Presidio, 1978), 166.
137 Simon Dunstan, *The Yom Kippur War 1973 (2): The Sinai* (Oxford: Osprey, 2003), 76.
138 Odysseas Socrates, dir. "Greatest Tank Battles 1973 Yom Kippur War - Battle for the Sinai," *YouTube*, YouTube, 11 Sep. 2013, Web, 24 Mar. 2015.
139 Rabinovich, *Yom Kippur War*, 366.
140 Adan, *Banks of the Suez*, 15.
141 Ibid., 380.
142 Ibid.
143 Herzog, *War of Atonement*, 231.
144 Rabinovich, *Yom Kippur War*, 393.
145 Herzog, *War of Atonement*, 233.
146 Ibid., 238.
147 Ibid., 229.
148 Rabinovich, *Yom Kippur War*, 418.
149 Adan, *Banks of the Suez*, 298.
150 Ibid., 299.
151 Ibid., 302-03.
152 Sherman, *When God Judged*, 139.
153 Ibid., 106-07.
154 Rabinovich, *Yom Kippur War*, 421-22.
155 Adan, *Banks of the Suez*, 325.
156 Rabinovich, *Yom Kippur War*, 425.
157 Adan, *Banks of the Suez*, 325.
158 Ibid., 369.
159 Siniver, *Yom Kippur War*, 217.
160 Ibid., 90.
161 Rabinovich, *Yom Kippur War*, 435.
162 Adan, *Banks of the Suez*, 400.
163 Ibid., 407.
164 Ibid., 411, 427.
165 Ibid., 422.
166 Ibid., 425.
167 Sachar, *History of Israel*, 784.
168 Walter Isaacson, *Kissinger: A Biography* (New York: Simon, 1992), 536.
169 Siniver, *Yom Kippur War*, 221.
170 Ibid., 220.
171 William P. Grady, *Understanding the Times*, vol. 1: *How Satan Turned America Against God* (Knoxville, Tenn.: Grady, 2005), 907.
172 Herzog, *War of Atonement*, 33.
173 John Loftus and Mark Aarons, *The Secret War Against the Jews: How Western Espionage Betrayed the Jewish People* (New York: St. Martin's, 1994), 580.
174 Ibid., 308-09.
175 Bruce Brill, "One Man's Agony After The Fact," *Jerusalem Post* 23 Oct. 1992: n. pag., Jonathanpollard.org., Web, 02 Apr. 2015.
176 Loftus and Aarons, *Secret War Against Jews*, 286, 309.
177 Brill, "One Man's Agony."
178 Loftus and Aarons, *Secret War Against Jews*, 193-94, 550.
179 Daniel Yergin, *The Prize: The Epic Quest for Oil, Money, and Power* (New York: Touchstone-Simon, 1992), 595-96, 604.
180 Herzog, *War of Atonement*, 23-24.
181 Ibid., 20.
182 Menachem Rosensaft, "Our Long National Fascination With Henry Kissinger Is Over," The Huffington Post, 17 Dec. 2010, Web, 02 Apr. 2015.

183 Siniver, *Yom Kippur War*, 91.
184 Nick Thimmesch, "How Kissinger Fooled Us All," *New York Magazine* 04 June 1973: 48-59, Web, 03 Apr. 2015.
185 Loftus and Aarons, *Secret War Against Jews*, 313-14.
186 Hersh, *Samson Option*, 230.
187 Ibid., 227.
188 Isaacson, *Kissinger*, 514.
189 Loftus and Aarons, *Secret War Against Jews*, 315.
190 Hersh, *Samson Option*, 226.
191 Rabinovich, *Yom Kippur War*, 269.
192 Ibid.
193 Hersh, *Samson Option*, 179.
194 Ibid., 225.
195 Blum, *Eve of Destruction*, 228.
196 Hersh, *Samson Option*, 227.
197 Siniver, *Yom Kippur War*, 76.
198 Hersh, *Samson Option*, 230.
199 Ibid., 236.
200 William B. Quandt, *Peace Process: American Diplomacy and the Arab-Israeli Conflict Since 1967*, Rev. ed. (Washington, DC: Brookings Inst., 2001), 121.
201 Isaacson, *Kissinger*, 530.
202 Quandt, *Peace Process*, 121.
203 Alexander M. Haig, Jr. and Charles McCarry, *Inner Circles: How America Changed the World: A Memoir* (New York: Warner, 1992), 415.
204 Siniver, *Yom Kippur War*, 98.
205 Ibid., 97.
206 Anthony Summers and Robbyn Swan, *The Arrogance of Power: The Secret World of Richard Nixon* (New York: Penguin, 2000), 331-33.
207 Isaacson, *Kissinger*, 514.
208 Yergin, *The Prize*, 609.
209 Siniver, *Yom Kippur War*, 97.
210 David Allen Rivera, *Final Warning: A History of the New World Order* Rev. ed. (Oakland: InteliBooks, 2004), 36.
211 Ibid., 37.
212 Summers and Swan, *Arrogance of Power*, 508.
213 Jack Minor, "Question about Rumors 82nd Airborne Might Have Removed Nixon from Office," message to the author, 20 Mar. 2015, e-mail.
214 Summers and Swan, *Arrogance of Power*, 506.
215 Isaacson, *Kissinger*, 522.
216 Haig and McCarry, *Inner Circles*, 350-51.
217 Isaacson, *Kissinger*, 598.
218 Ibid., 599.
219 Ibid.
220 Ibid.
221 David G. Dalin and Alfred J. Kolatch, *The Presidents of the United States & The Jews* (Middle Village, N.Y.: Jonathan David, 2000), 223.
222 Haig and McCarry, *Inner Circles*, 416.
223 Isaacson, *Kissinger*, 512.
224 Loftus and Aarons, *Secret War Against Jews*, 315-16.
225 Ibid., 316.
226 Ibid.
227 Sachar, *History of Israel*, 746.
228 Loftus and Aarons, *Secret War Against Jews*, 317.
229 Ibid.
230 Dunstan, *Yom Kippur War 1973 (2)*, 67.
231 Seymour Weiss, Top Secret, *Action Memorandum* George Washington University. 07 Apr. 2015.
232 Edgar O'Ballance, *No Victor, No Vanquished: The Yom Kippur War* (San Rafael: Presidio, 1978), 161-67.
233 Loftus and Aarons, *Secret War Against Jews*, 317.
234 O'Ballance, *No Victor, No Vanquished*, 166.
235 Haig and McCarry, *Inner Circles*, 417.
236 Nadine Brozan, "Chronicle: Alon Ben-Gurion," *The New York Times*, 04 Apr. 1997, sec. Style, Web, 25 June 2015.
237 Raviv and Melman, *Every Spy a Prince*, 210.
238 Siniver, *Yom Kippur War*, 203-04.
239 Yergin, *The Prize*, 597.
240 Quandt, *Peace Process*, 126-27.
241 Loftus and Aarons, *Secret War Against Jews*, 319.
242 Rabinovich, *Yom Kippur War*, 79.
243 Blum, *Eve of Destruction*, ix.
244 Ronald H. Isaacs, *Every Person's Guide to the High Holy Days* (Northvale, N.J.: Jason Aronson, 1999), 78-79.

CHAPTER 18

Fightings Within - Fears Without

1 Amotz Asa-El, "Middle Israel: The Last War," *Jerusalem Post*, Jpost, 13 Sept. 2013, Web, 10 July 2015.
2 Simon Dunstan, *Entebbe: The Most Daring Raid of Israel's Special Forces* (New York: Rosen, 2011), 16.
3 Eyal Sher, dir., *Operation Thunderbolt: Entebbe Documentary (2000)*, perf. Michel Bacos et al., Globus Group, 2014, YouTube.
4 Iddo Netanyahu, *Yoni's Last Fight: The Rescue at Entebbe, 1976* (Jerusalem: Gefen, 2002), 90.
5 William Stevenson, *90 Minutes at Entebbe* (New York: Bantam, 1976), 112.
6 Robert Verkaik, "Revealed: The Fate of Idi Amin's Hijack Victim," *The Independent*, Independent Digital News and Media, 13 Feb. 2007, Web, 14 July 2015.
7 J. P. Fonté, *The Lure of the Lion* (Bloomington, Ind.: Xlibris, 2003), 166.
8 Howard M. Sachar, *A History of Israel: From the Rise of Zionism to Our Time*, 3rd Rev. ed. (New York: Knopf, 2007), 830.
9 Stevenson, *90 Minutes*, 33.
10 Joseph Finklestone, *Anwar Sadat: Visionary Who Dared* (London: Cass, 1996), xiv.
11 David Reynolds, *Summits: Six Meetings that Shaped the Twentieth Century* (New York: Basic-Perseus, 2007), 299.
12 Paul Charles Merkley, *American Presidents, Religion, and Israel: The Heirs of Cyrus* (Westport: Praeger-Greenwood, 2004), 116.
13 David Landau, "Togetherness Under the Trees Planned by Camp David Hosts, " *Jerusalem Post*, September 6, 1978, daily ed., sec. A.
14 Harry Hurwitz and Yisrael Medad, eds., *Peace in the Making: The Menachem Begin-Anwar El-Sadat Personal Correspondence* (Jerusalem: Gefen, 2011), 128.
15 Ibid., 131.
16 Mohamed Fadel Fahmy, "30 Years Later, Questions Remain over Sadat Killing, Peace with Israel-CNN.com," *CNN*, Cable News Network, 06 Oct. 2011, Web, 14 July 2015.
17 William E. Farrell, "Sadat Assassinated at Army Parade as Men Amid Ranks Fire Into Stands; Vice President Affirms 'All Treaties': At Least 8 Killed; Speaker of Parliament Is Interim President - Election in 60 Days," *New York Times* 06 Oct. 1981, Late City Edition ed., sec. A: 1, *The New York Times On the Web Learning Network: On This Day*, Web, 07 July 2015.
18 "Osiraq/Tammuz I," *Fas.org*, Federation of American Scientists, 09 Oct. 2000, Web, 16 July 2015.
19 Rodger W. Claire, *Raid on the Sun: Inside Israel's Secret Campaign that Denied Saddam the Bomb* (New York: Broadway-Random, 2004), 174.
20 "Israel's Wars & Operations: Operation Opera - Raid on Iraqi Nuclear Reactor (June 7, 1981)," *Jewish Virtual Library*, American-Israeli Cooperative Enterprise, n.d., Web, 16 July 2015.
21 Claire, *Raid*, 210-11.
22 Benjamin S. Lambeth, *The Transformation of American Air Power* (Ithaca: Cornell UP, 2000), 78.
23 Richard V. Allen, "Reagan's Secure Line," *The New York Times*, 07 June 2010, ed., sec. A:23.
24 Military Channel Documentary, "Israeli Raid on Iraqi Reactor," *YouTube*, You Tube, n.d., Web, 23 Apr., 2015.
25 Claire, *Raid*, 240.
26 Saïd K. Aburish, *Arafat: From Defender to Dictator* (New York: Bloomsbury, 1998),170 .
27 Mark Tessler, *A History of the Israeli-Palestinian Conflict* (Bloomington: Indiana UP, 1994), 580-82.
28 Sachar, *History of Israel*, 908, 911-12.
29 Abba Eban, *Personal Witness: Israel Through My Eyes* (New York: Putnam's, 1992), 604.
30 Ibid., 608.
31 Ze'ev Schiff and Ehud Ya'ari, *Israel's Lebanon War*, ed. and trans. Ina Friedman (New York: Simon, 1984), 301.

[32] Marius Deeb, *Syria's Terrorist War on Lebanon and the Peace Process* (New York: Palgrave Macmillan, 2003), 78.
[33] Ahron Bregman and Jihan El-Tahri, *The Fifty Years' War: Israel and the Arabs* (New York: TV, 1999), 212.
[34] "Hundreds Brutally Massacred in W. Beirut Refugee Camps, " *Jerusalem Post*, September 20, 1982, daily ed., sec. A.
[35] Sachar, *History of Israel*, 914.
[36] Noam Chomsky, *Fateful Triangle: The United States, Israel, and the Palestinians*, updated ed. (Cambridge: South End, 1999), 366.
[37] Ibid., 364.
[38] Ibid., 370.
[39] Ibid.
[40] Neil James Mitchell, *Democracy's Blameless Leaders: From Dresden to Abu Ghraib, How Leaders Evade Accountability for Abuse, Atrocity, and Killing* (New York: New York UP, 2012), 123.
[41] Gerald Cromer, *A War of Words: Political Violence and Public Debate in Israel* (New York: Cass, 2004), 52.
[42] Charles Hoffman, Joshua Brilliant, et al., "Dozens Killed, Wounded in Massive Tyre Blast," *Jerusalem Post*, 12 November 1982, daily ed., sec. A.
[43] Samuel M. Katz, *Guards Without Frontiers: Israel's War Against Terrorism* (London: Arms & Armour, 1990), 117.
[44] Ruth Linn, *Conscience at War: The Israeli Soldier as a Moral Critic* (Albany: State U of New York P, 1996), 9.
[45] Sachar, *History of Israel*, 913.
[46] Jarrett Murphy et al., "Beirut Barracks Attack Remembered," *CBSNews*, CBS Interactive, 23 Oct. 2003, Web, 17 July 2015.
[47] Eban, *Personal Witness*, 610-11.
[48] Sachar, *History of Israel*, 903.
[49] William Lowther, "Rumsfeld 'helped Iraq Get Chemical Weapons,'" *Mail Online*, Associated Newspapers, n.d., Web, 18 July 2015.
[50] John Loftus and Mark Aarons, *The Secret War Against the Jews: How Western Espionage Betrayed the Jewish People* (New York: St. Martin's, 1994), 407-408, 412, 415-422, 481-482.
[51] Jonathan Marshall, Peter Dale Scott, and Jane Hunter, *The Iran-Contra Connection: Secret Teams and Covert Operations in the Reagan Era* (Cheektowaga, N.Y.: Black Rose, 1987), 168.
[52] Elliot Goldenberg, *The Spy Who Knew Too Much: The Government Plot to Silence Jonathan Pollard* (New York: S.P.I.-Shapolsky, 1993), xix.
[53] Ibid., 52.
[54] Hillel Fendel, "Handcuffs and Prayers at Pollard Rally This Week," *Arutz Sheva*, Israelnational news.com, 20 Nov. 2005, Web, 18 July 2015.
[55] Mati Alon, *The Return to Zion* (Bloomington, Ind.: Trafford, 2011), 118.
[56] Mark Shaw, *Miscarriage of Justice: The Jonathan Pollard Story* (St. Paul: Paragon House, 2001), 168.
[57] John Loftus, "The Truth About Jonathan Pollard," *Aish.com*. Yeshivat Aish Hatorah, n.d., Web, 21 July 2015. (This article originally appeared in *Moment* magazine, June 2003.)
[58] "Israeli Cabinet Minister Spied for U.S. - New U.S. Docs Reveal," *Jonathanpollard.org*, Jonathanpollard.org, n.d., Web, 21 July 2015. (This article originally appeared in *Hamodia*, June 23, 2004, under the title, "Was There An American Spy In the Israeli Government?")
[59] "Interview of Kielczynski, Israeli Spy for CIA," *Foreign Affair Journal*, Kol Yisrael Radio, Reshet Bet, Jerusalem. 27 Mar. 2001, Web, Transcript.
[60] Loftus, "Truth About Pollard."
[61] Matthew Lee and Josef Federman, "AP Source: US Talking with Israel on Spy Release," *Yahoo! News*, Yahoo, 31 Mar. 2014, Web, 21 July 2015.
[62] Robert O. Freedman, *The Intifada: Its Impact on Israel, the Arab World, and the Superpowers* (Gainesville: UP of Florida, 1991), 384.
[63] Chomsky, *Fateful Triangle*, 475.
[64] Constance Hilliard, *Does Israel Have a Future?: The Case for a Post-Zionist State* (Dulles, Va.: Potomac, 2009), 35.
[65] C. Gus Martin, ed., *The SAGE Encyclopedia of Terrorism*, 2nd ed. (Los Angeles: Sage, 2011), 292.
[66] Jerold S. Auerbach, *Hebron Jews: Memory and Conflict in the Land of Israel* (Lanham, Md.: Rowman, 2009), 121.
[67] M. Clement Hall, *Intifada* (Raleigh, N.C.: Lulu, 2009), 85.
[68] George H. W. Bush, "Remarks at the Opening Session of the Middle East Peace Conference in Madrid, Spain, 10-30-1991," *Public Papers*, George Bush Presidential Library and Museum, n.d., Web, 23 July 2015.
[69] John McTernan and Bill Koenig, *Israel: The Blessing or the Curse* (Oklahoma City: Hearthstone, 2002), 63.
[70] Tom Raum, "Bush surveys storm damage to home," *Maine Sunday Telegraph*, 03 November 1991, pp. 1B and 12B.
[71] William P. Grady, *Understanding the Times*, vol. 1: *How Satan Turned America Against God* (Knoxville, Tenn.: Grady, 2005), 4.
[72] Yasser Arafat and Yitzhak Rabin, "Israel-PLO Recognition - Exchange of Letters between PM Rabin and Chairman Arafat/Arafat Letter to Norwegian FM (Non-UN Documents) (09 Sept. 1993)," *Unispal.u.org*, United Nations, n.d., Web, 23 July 2015.
[73] Auerbach, *Hebron Jews*, 125.
[74] Ibid., 139.
[75] Ibid.
[76] Ilan Bijaoui, *The Economic Reconciliation Process: Middle Eastern Populations in Conflict* (New York: Palgrave Macmillan, 2014), 29.
[77] Yoram Peri, *The Assassination of Yitzhak Rabin* (Stanford: Stanford UP, 2000), 353.
[78] Jeremy Sutton, *Painter 8 Creativity: Digital Artist's Handbook* (Burlington, Mass: Focal-Elsevier, 2003), 259.
[79] Barry Chamish, *Who Murdered Yitzhak Rabin?* (Brookline, Mass.: Brookline, 2000), entire book.
[80] William Robert Johnston, "Chronology of Terrorist Attacks in Israel, Part IV: 1993-2000," *Johnston's Archive*, William Robert Johnston, 18 May 2013, Web, 23 July 2015.
[81] Samuel Katz, *The Hunt for the Engineer: How Israeli Agents Tracked the Hamas Master Bomber* (New York: Fromm, 1999), ix.
[82] Yossef Bodansky, *The High Cost of Peace: How Washington's Middle East Policy Left America Vulnerable to Terrorism* (Roseville, Calif.: Prima-Random, 2002), 122.
[83] Ibid.
[84] Ibid., 214.
[85] Ari Shavit, "End of a Journey," *Haaretz.com*, Haaretz Daily Newspaper, 13 Sept. 2001, Web, 25 July 2015.
[86] Ibid.
[87] Idith Zertal and Akiva Eldar, *Lords of the Land: The War Over Israel's Settlements in the Occupied Territories, 1967-2007*, trans. Vivian Eden (New York: Nation-Avalon, 2007), 178.
[88] Barry Rubin and Judith Colp Rubin, *Yasir Arafat: A Political Biography* (New York: Oxford UP, 2003), 213.
[89] Charles Enderlin, *Shattered Dreams: The Failure of the Peace Process in the Middle East, 1995-2002*, trans. Susan Fairfield (New York: Other, 2002), 287.
[90] Mitchell Bard, "Myths & Facts: The Palestinian War (Al-Aqsa Intifada, 2000-2005)," *Jewish Virtual Library*, American-Israeli Cooperative Enterprise, n.d., Web, 27 July 2015.
[91] "Rocket Launching," *Israeli Security Agency*, Shabak.gov.il, n.d., Web, 27 July 2015.
[92] "Victims of Palestinian Violence and Terrorism since September 2000," *Israel Ministry of Foreign Affairs*, Mfa.gov.il, n.d., Web, 27 July 2015.
[93] McTernan and Koenig, *Israel: Blessing or Curse*, 151.
[94] Ibid., 93.
[95] Ibid., 94-95.
[96] Craig Unger, *House of Bush, House of Saud: The Secret Relationship Between the World's Two Most Powerful Dynasties* (New York: Scribner, 2004), 145.
[97] Ibid., 242-45.
[98] Kevin Phillips, *American Dynasty: Aristocracy, Fortune, and the Politics of Deceit in the House of Bush* (New York: Viking, 2004), 150.
[99] Unger, *House of Bush, House of Saud*, 243.
[100] Ibid., 243-44.
[101] Ibid., 244.
[102] Ibid.
[103] Ibid.

[104] Ibid.
[105] Ibid., 245.
[106] Ibid.
[107] Bodansky, *High Cost*, 357.
[108] Reuters News Staff, "Sniper Kills Bethlehem Church Bell-Ringer," *Rense.com*, Jeff Rense, n.d., Web, 28 July 2015.
[109] Rick Marschall, "The Bethlehem Bell Ringer," *Monday Morning Music Ministry*, Rick Marschall, 12 Dec. 2010, Web, 28 July 2015.
[110] "Palestinian Bell-ringer for Church of Nativity Killed," *Smh.com.au*, Sydney Morning Herald, 05 Apr. 2002, Web, 28 July 2015.
[111] Ibid.
[112] Beverley Milton-Edwards, *The Israeli- Palestinian Conflict: A People's War* (New York: Routledge, 2009), 158.
[113] Mohammad A. Chaichian, *Empires and Walls: Globalization, Migration, and Colonial Domination* (Leiden: Brill, 2014), 246.
[114] "The Separation Barrier," *Separation Barrier*. B'Tselem, The Israeli Information Center for Human Rights in the Occupied Territories, 01 Jan. 2011, Web, 28 July 2015.
[115] David Makovsky, "How to Build a Fence: Partition without Partnership," *Foreign Affairs*, Council on Foreign Affairs, 28 Jan. 2009, Web, 28 July 2015.
[116] Mitchell Bard, "West Bank Security Fence: Background & Overview," *Jewish Virtual Library*. American-Israeli Cooperative Enterprise, n.d., Web, 28 July 2015. Updated, April 2015.
[117] Danny Tirza, "Israeli Security Fence Architect: Why The Barrier Had to Be Built," *Al-Monitor*, Jamal Daniel, 01 July 2012, Web, 28 July 2015.
[118] Giulio Meotti, *A New Shoah: TheUntold Story of Israel's Victims of Terrorism* (New York: Encounter, 2009), 211.
[119] Christine Lagorio, "Katrina Leaves Toxic Bathtub," *CBSNews*, CBS Interactive, 1 Sept. 2005, Web, 30 July 2015.
[120] Matt M. Matthews, *We Were Caught Unprepared: The 2006 Hezbollah-Israeli War* (Darby, Penn.: Diane, 2011), 61.
[121] Ibid.
[122] Benjamin S. Lambeth, *Air Operations in Israel's War Against Hezbollah: Learning from Lebanon and Getting It Right in Gaza* (Santa Monica: RAND Corporation, 2011), xiii.
[123] Matthews, *Caught Unprepared*, 61.
[124] Ibid., 62.
[125] Ibid., 61.
[126] Erich Follath and Holger Stark, "The Story of 'Operation Orchard': How Israel Destroyed Syria's Al Kibar Nuclear Reactor," Der Spiegel, 02 Nov. 2009, Web, 31 July 2015.
[127] Condoleezza Rice, *No Higher Honor: A Memoir of My Years in Washington* (New York: Crown-Random, 2011), 708.
[128] Martin Gilbert, *The Routledge Atlas of the Arab-Israeli Conflict*, 12th ed. (New York: Routledge, 2012), 209.
[129] Yaakov Katz and Yoaz Hendel, *Israel vs. Iran: The Shadow War* (Dulles, Va.: Potomac, 2012), 79.
[130] George W. Bush, "Israel, Palestine, and the Prospect of Peace: Remarks at the Annapolis Conference," Annapolis Conference, United States Naval Academy, Annapolis, Maryland, 27 Nov. 2007, *Presidentialrhetoric.com.*, Web, 31 July 2015.
[131] Katy Carl, "Catholics Give Thanks to God in Maryland: St. Francis Xavier Church Celebrates 350 Years of Faith," *National Catholic Register*, EWTN News, 21 Nov. 2012, Web, 31 July 2015.
[132] Henrietta Haynes, *Henrietta Maria* (New York: Putnam, 1912), 129.
[133] Zvika Krieger, "Transcript for 'Is Peace Possible?' Chapter 1: Borders," *The Atlantic*. Atlantic Media Co., 25 Oct. 2011, Web, 31 July 2015.
[134] Eytan Gilboa and Efraim Inbar, eds., *US-Israeli Relations in a New Era: Issues and Challenges After 9/11* (New York: Routledge, 2009), 68.
[135] Bill Koenig, "US Sponsored Israeli-Palestinian Meetings Coincided with Two Major Record US Disasters in December," *World Watch Daily*, William Koenig, n.d., Web, 31 July 2015.
[136] Bush, "Remarks at the Annapolis Conference."
[137] Krista Eileen Wiegand, *Bombs and Ballots: Governance by Islamist Terrorist and Guerrilla Groups* (Surrey: Ashgate, 2010), 135.
[138] Israel, Security Agency, *Rocket Launching*, Israel Security Agency, n.d., Web, 01 Aug. 2015.
[139] Jonathan Schanzer, *Hamas vs. Fatah: The Struggle For Palestine* (New York: Palgrave Macmillan, 2008), 111-12.
[140] "Gaza: Armed Palestinian Groups Commit Grave Crimes," *Human Rights Watch*, Human Rights Watch, 12 June 2007, Web, 01 Aug. 2015.
[141] Schanzer, *Hamas vs. Fatah*, 110.
[142] Mitchell G. Bard, *Death to the Infidels: Radical Islam's War Against the Jews* (New York: Palgrave Macmillan, 2014), 105.
[143] Ibid.
[144] Daniel Byman, *A High Price: The Triumphs and Failures of Israeli Counterterrorism* (New York: Oxford UP, 2011), 196.
[145] Zvi Ben Gedalyahu, "One-Third of PA Arabs Support Massacre of Fogels," *Arutz Sheva*, IsraelNationaNews.com, 04 June 2011, Web, 01 Aug. 2015.
[146] Carol Migdalovitz, *Israel's Blockade of Gaza, the "Mavi Mamara" Incident, and Its Aftermath* (Darby, Penn.: Diane, 2010), 3.
[147] John Baylis, Steve Smith, and Patricia Owens, eds., *The Globalization of World Politics: An Introduction to International Relations* (Oxford: Oxford UP, 2013), 27.
[148] "Rocket Fire Slows after Day of Clashes That Saw Hamas Target Jerusalem, Tel Aviv," *The Times of Israel*, The Times of Israel, 16 Nov. 2012, Web, 04 Aug. 2015.
[149] Stuart Casey-Maslen, ed., *The War Report: 2012* (New York: Oxford UP, 2013), 112.
[150] Anthony Best, Jussi M. Hanhimäki, Joseph A. Maiolo, and Kirsten E. Schulze, *International History of the Twentieth Century and Beyond*, 3rd ed. (New York: Routledge-Taylor, 2015), 493.
[151] Ibid.
[152] Fred Abrahams, Marc E. Garlasco, Darryl Li, *Razing Rafah: Mass Home Demolitions in the Gaza Strip* (New York: Human Rights Watch, 2004), 38.
[153] Best, et al., *International History*, 493.
[154] Abrahams, et al., 38.
[155] William P. Grady, *Understanding the Times*, vol. 1: *How Satan Turned America Against God* (Knoxville, Tenn.: Grady, 2005), 879.
[156] Adrian Blomfield, "Obama Snubbed Netanyahu for Dinner with Michelle and the Girls, Israelis Claim," *The Telegraph*, Telegraph Media Group, 25 Mar. 2010, Web, 07 Aug. 2015.
[157] Ben Evansky, "Obama and Israel: Showdown at the UN?" *Liveshots*, Fox News Network, 19 Apr. 2010, Web, 07 Aug. 2015.
[158] Jonathan Ramseur, *Liability and Compensation Issues Raised by the 2010 Gulf Oil Spill* (Darby, Penn.: Diane, 2011), 1.
[159] William P. Grady, *Given By Inspiration: A Multifaceted Study on the A.V. 1611 with Contemporary Analysis* (Swartz Creek, Mich.: Grady, 2010), 253.
[160] Katie Zezima, "A Short History of Awkward Encounters between Obama and Netanyahu," *The Washington Post*, The Washington Post, 01 Oct. 2014, Web, 07 Aug. 2015.
[161] David Jackson, "Obama Snubs Netanyahu to Hang with Jay-Z, Letterman," *Fox Nation*, Fox News Network, 18 Sept. 2012, Web, 07 Aug. 2015.
[162] Dave Boyer, "President Obama's Limo Breaks down at Israeli Airport," *Washington Times*, The Washington Times, 20 Mar. 2013, Web, 07 Aug. 2015.
[163] John Fund, "Obama Operatives Try to Sway Israel's Election," *Newsmax*, Newsmax Media, 18 Mar. 2015, Web, 07 Aug. 2015.
[164] "Weinstein to Rule on Possible Criminal Probe against Sara Netanyahu in 'Bottlegate' Affair," *The Jerusalem Post*, Jpost, 02 Feb. 2015, Web, 07 Aug. 2015.
[165] "Obama Finally Calls Netanyahu, Says US Rethinking Palestinian Policy," *The Times of Israel*, The Times of Israel, 19 Mar. 2015, Web, 07 Aug. 2015.
[166] Adam Entous, "Israel Spied on Iran Nuclear Talks With U.S.," *The Wall Street Journal*, Dow Jones, 23 Mar. 2015, Web, 07 Aug. 2015.

[167] Ari Yashar and Matt Wanderman, "US Declassifies Document Revealing Israel's Nuclear Program," *Arutz Sheva*, Arutz Sheva, 25 Mar. 2015, Web, 07 Aug. 2015.
[168] Judah Ari Gross, "In Leaked Emails, Colin Powell Says Israel Has 200 Nukes," *The Times of Israel*, 15 Sept. 2016, Web, 30 Dec. 2016.
[169] "List of Islamic Terror." *The Religion of Peace*. The Religion of Peace, n.d. Web. 16 July 2016.
[170] Michael Kranish, "Ten Years Later, Revelation of John Kerry's Ancestry Has a New Chapter," *BostonGlobe.com*, 13 Oct. 2013, Web, 30 Dec. 2016.

CHAPTER 19

Beloved Enemies

[1] "Pastor John C. Hagee: Senior Pastor Cornerstone Church," *John Hagee Ministries*, John Hagee Ministries, n.d., Web, 11 Aug. 2015.
[2] Julia Duin, "San Antonio Fundamentalist Battles Anti-Semitism," *Houston Chronicle* 30 Apr. 1988, 2 Star ed., sec. 6:1. Print.
[3] Ibid.
[4] "John Hagee Denies Jesus Christ as Messiah," *Vimeo*, Vimeo LLC, 2012, Web, 02 Sept. 2015.
[5] Michael P. Prior, ed., *Speaking the Truth: Zionism, Israel, and Occupation* (Northampton, Mass.: Olive Branch, 2005), 109.
[6] Jonas E. Alexis, *Christianity and Rabbinic Judaism*, vol. 1: *A History of Conflict Between Christianity and Rabbinic Judaism from the Early Church to our Modern Time* (Bloomington, Ind.: WestBow, 2013), 217.
[7] Jonas E. Alexis, *Christianity and Rabbinic Judaism*, vol. 2: *A History of Conflict Between Christianity and Rabbinic Judaism from the Early Church to our Modern Time* (Bloomington, Ind.: WestBow, 2013), 71.
[8] Texe Marrs, *DNA Science and the Jewish Bloodline* (Austin, Tex.: RiverCrest, 2013), 184-87.
[9] Stephen Sizer, *Christian Zionism: Road-map to Armageddon?* (Nottingham: Inter-Varsity, 2004), 144.
[10] Peter S. Ruckman, *Minor Prophets*, vol. 2: *Habakkuk-Malachi* (Pensacola: BB Bookstore, 2011), 189-91.
[11] "Tel Aviv Declared World's Best Gay Travel Destination," *Haaretz.com.*, Haaretz Daily Newspaper, 11 Jan. 2012, Web, 22 Aug. 2015.
[12] Ibid.
[13] Ilan Lior, "Tel Aviv Gay Pride Parade Draws 100,000 - National," *Haaretz.com*. Haaretz Daily Newspaper, 13 June 2014, Web, 22 Aug. 2015.
[14] Ibid.
[15] Martin Gilbert, *Churchill and the Jews: A Lifelong Friendship* (New York: Holt, 2007), 38.
[16] Louis Finkelstein, *The Jews: Their History, Culture, and Religion*, vol. 2, 3rd ed. (New York: Harper, 1960), 1744.
[17] Michael L. Brown, *What Do Jewish People Think about Jesus?: And Other Questions Christians Ask about Jewish Beliefs, Practices, and History* (Grand Rapids: Chosen-Baker, 2007), 32.
[18] Johann Andreas Eisenmenger, *The Traditions of the Jews*, ed. John Peter Stehelin (1748, reprint, Coeur d'Alene, Ida.: Independent History & Research, 2006), 166.
[19] Brown, *What Jewish People Think*, 33.
[20] Alexis, *Christianity and Rabbinic Judaism*, 1:259.
[21] Will Durant, *The Story of Civilization*, vol. 4: *The Age of Faith: A History of Medieval Civilization (Christian, Islamic, and Judaic) from Constantine to Dante, A.D. 325 - 1300* (New York: Simon, 1950), 365.
[22] Philip Schaff, *History of the Christian Church*, vol. 2: *Ante-Nicene Christianity, A.D. 100-325* (1910: reprint, Grand Rapids: Eerdmans, 1973), 39.
[23] Peter Schäfer, *Jesus in the Talmud* (Princeton: Princeton UP, 2007), 13.
[24] Israel Shamir, *Pardes: An Etude in Cabbala* (N.p.: BookSurge, 2005), 150.
[25] Durant, *Story of Civilization*, 4:392.
[26] Paul T. Phillips, *The Controversialist: An Intellectual Life of Goldwin Smith* (Westport: Praeger-Greenwood, 2002), 136.
[27] Kevin B. MacDonald, *Separation and Its Discontents: Toward an Evolutionary Theory of Anti-Semitism* (Westport: Praeger-Greenwood, 1998), 48.
[28] Durant, *Story of Civilization*, 4:364.
[29] Schaff, *History of the Christian Church*, 2:39.
[30] Robert Andrews, *The Columbia Dictionary of Quotations* (New York: Columbia UP, 1993), 477.
[31] "New Poll Shows Atheism on Rise, With Jews Found to Be Least Religious," *Haaretz.com*, Haaretz Daily Newspaper, 20 Aug. 2015, Web, 25 Aug. 2015.
[32] Kimberly Winston, "Judaism without God? Yes, Say American Atheists," *USA Today*, Gannett, 26 Sept. 2011, Web, 25 Aug. 2015.
[33] Levi Brackman, "Why so Many Jews Are Atheists," *Ynetnews.com*, Yedioth Internet, 25 Nov. 2009, Web, 25 Aug. 2015.
[34] Alan M. Dershowitz, *The Vanishing American Jew: In Search of Jewish Identity for the Next Century* (New York: Little, 1997), 180.
[35] Alan M. Dershowitz, *The Genesis of Justice: Ten Stories of Biblical Injustice that Led to the Ten Commandments and Modern Morality and Law* (New York: Warner, 2000), 1-2.
[36] Christine Kearney, "Family, Friends Remember Joan Rivers in Poignant, Funny Funeral," *Reuters.com*, Thomson Reuters, 07 Sept. 2014, Web, 27 Aug. 2015.
[37] "Israeli Court Rules Jews for Jesus Cannot Automatically Be Citizens," *The New York Times*, The New York Times, 27 Dec. 1989, Web, 27 Aug. 2015.
[38] Alan M. Wald, *The New York Intellectuals: The Rise and Decline of the Anti-Stalinist Left from the 1930s to the 1980s* (Chapel Hill: U of North Carolina P, 1987), 46-47.
[39] E. Michael Jones, *The Jewish Revolutionary Spirit: And Its Impact on World History* (South Bend: Fidelity, 2008), 752.
[40] Gideon Shimoni, *Community and Conscience: The Jews in Apartheid South Africa* (Waltham, Mass.: Brandeis UP, 2003), 75.
[41] Gilbert, *Churchill and the Jews*, 37.
[42] Richard Pipes, *The Russian Revolution* (New York: Vintage-Random, 1991), 53.
[43] Gilbert, *Churchill and the Jews*, 39-40.
[44] Ibid., 40.
[45] Ibid.
[46] Ibid., 41.
[47] Karl Marx, *Critique of Hegel's 'Philosophy Of Right' (Cambridge Studies in the History and Theory of Politics)*, trans. Annette Jolin and Joseph O'Malley (New York: Cambridge UP, 1970), 131.
[48] Paul Gabel, *And God Created Lenin: Marxism Vs Religion in Russia, 1917-1929* (Amherst, N.Y.: Prometheus, 2005), 21.
[49] G. Edward Griffin, *The Creature from Jekyll Island: A Second Look at the Federal Reserve* (Appleton, Wis.: American Opinion, 1994), 265.
[50] Edvard Radzinsky, *The Last Tsar: The Life and Death of Nicholas II*, trans. Marian Schwartz (New York.: Doubleday-Random, 1992), 327, 344-46.
[51] Niall Ferguson, *The War of the World: Twentieth-Century Conflict and the Descent of the West* (New York: Penguin, 2006), entire book.
[52] Maurice Samuels, *You Gentiles*, ed. Edward Hurst, 3rd ed. (1924, North Charleston, S.C.: CreateSpace, 2014), 62.
[53] Sam A. Cohen, *Future of the Middle East, United Pan-Arab States: Divided by Imperialism, United by Destiny* (Bloomington, Ind.: AuthorHouse, 2014), 199-200.
[54] Earl Blackwell, *Celebrity Register* (New York: Harper, 1986), 366.
[55] Richard Cohen, *Tough Jews: Fathers, Sons, and Gangster Dreams* (New York: Simon, 1998), entire book.
[56] Michael Herr, "Kubrick," *Vanity Fair*, Condé Nast, Apr. 2000, Web, 29 Aug. 2015.
[57] Irving Stone, *Clarence Darrow Attorney for the Defense: A Biography*, (reprint;1941, New York: Bantam, 1958), 256.
[58] A&E: Investigative Reports, "Son Of Sam Speaks," *YouTube*, YouTube, 17 Jan. 2013, Web, 03 Sept. 2015.
[59] Ed Mazza, "'Son Of Sam' David Berkowitz Denied Parole, But Says Jesus Has Forgiven Him," *The Huffington Post*, TheHuffingtonPost.com, 13 May 2014, Web, 30 Aug. 2015.

[60] Niall Ferguson, *The Ascent of Money: A Financial History of the World* (New York: Penguin, 1985), 85.
[61] Andrew P. Napolitano, *It Is Dangerous to Be Right When the Government is Wrong: The Case for Personal Freedom* (Nashville: Thomas Nelson, 2011), 205.
[62] Frederic Morton, *The Rothschilds: A Family Portrait* (Philadelphia: Curtis, 1961), 21.
[63] Gabe Friedman, "10 Jews in Forbes Top 50 Billionaires," *The Times of Israel*, The Times of Israel, 03 Mar. 21, Web, 31 Aug. 2015.
[64] "George Soros: Top 10 Reasons He Is Dangerous, *Human Events*, Eagle, 2 Apr. 2011, Web, 31 Aug. 2015.
[65] Nathan Burstein, "Jewish Power Dominates at 'Vanity Fair'" *The Jerusalem Post*, Jpost, 11 Oct. 2007, Web, 31 Aug. 2015.
[66] Ibid.
[67] Laurent Guyénot, "The Machiavellian Threefold Game of the Neoconservatives," *My Catbird Seat*, My Catbird Seat, 31 May 2013, Web, 31 Aug. 2015.
[68] Gal Beckerman, "The Neoconservative Persuasion: Examining the Jewish Roots of an Intellectual Movement," *Gal Beckerman*, Gal Beckerman, 06 Jan. 2006, Web, 31 Aug. 2015.
[69] Stephen J. Sniegoski, Paul Findley, and Paul Gottfried, *The Transparent Cabal: The Neoconservative Agenda, War in the Middle East, and the National Interest of Israel* (New York: Enigma Editions, 2008), 42.
[70] Murray Friedman, *The Neoconservative Revolution: Jewish Intellectuals and the Shaping of Public Policy* (New York: Cambridge UP, 2005), 25.
[71] J. J. Goldberg, *Jewish Power: Inside the American Jewish Establishment* (New York: Basic-Perseus, 1996), 26.
[72] Ibid.
[73] Gary Dorrien, *Imperial Designs: Neoconservatism and the New Pax Americana* (New York: Routledge, 2004), 1.
[74] Andrew Cockburn, *Rumsfeld: His Rise, Fall, and Catastrophic Legacy* (New York: Scribner, 2007), 219.
[75] William F. Buckley, *In Search of Anti-Semitism* (New York: Continuum, 1992), 78.
[76] Guyénot, "Machiavellian Game."
[77] John J. Mearsheimer and Stephen M. Walt, *The Israel Lobby and U.S. Foreign Policy* (New York: Farrar, 2007), 240.
[78] Kevin Phillips, *American Dynasty: Aristocracy, Fortune, and the Politics of Deceit in the House of Bush* (New York: Viking, 2004), 345.
[79] William P. Grady, *Understanding the Times*, vol. 1: *How Satan Turned America Against God* (Knoxville, Tenn.: Grady, 2005), 731-39.
[80] Mearsheimer and Walt, *Israel Lobby*, vii.
[81] Ibid., 10.
[82] Ibid.
[83] Ibid., 5, 13.
[84] Ibid., 14.
[85] Ibid., 26.
[86] Ibid.
[87] Katia Hetter, "Girl Scouts Welcomes Transgender Girls - CNN.com," *CNN*, Cable News Network, 20 May 15, Web, 01 Sept. 2015.
[88] "Adopted 'Father' and 'Son' to Marry," *The Daily Beast*, Newsweek/The Daily Beast, 20 May 2015, Web, 01 Sept. 2015.
[89] Earle E. Cairns, *Christianity Through the Centuries: A History of the Christian Church*, 3rd ed., rev. and expanded (Grand Rapids: Zondervan, 1996), 44.
[90] Stacy Ellen Wolf, *A Problem Like Maria: Gender and Sexuality in the American Musical* (Ann Arbor: U of Michigan P, 2002), 107.
[91] Edward J. Bristow, *Prostitution and Prejudice: The Jewish Fight Against White Slavery, 1870-1939* (New York: Schocken, 1983), 52-53.
[92] Alexis, *Christianity and Rabbinic Judaism*, 2:338-342.
[93] Ibid., 339-340.
[94] Ibid., 257.
[95] David Berkowitz, "My Testimony," *AriseandShine*, AriseandShine.org, n.d., Web, 03 Sept. 2015.
[96] Jonathan Soffer, *Ed Koch and the Rebuilding of New York City* (New York: Columbia UP, 2010), 140.
[97] Kurt F. Stone, *The Jews of Capitol Hill: A Compendium of Jewish Congressional Members* (Lanham, Md.: Scarecrow-Rowman, 2011), 378.
[98] "Police Bust 'messianic' Prostitution Ring Active across Israel," *The Times of Israel*, The Times of Israel, 07 Sept. 2014, Web, 03 Sept. 2015.
[99] Mark Edmundson, The Death of Sigmund Freud: Fascism, Psychoanalysis and the Rise of Fundamentalism (London: Bloomsbury, 2007), 32.
[100] Ariel Levy, "Novelty Acts," *The New Yorker*, Condé Nast, 19 Sept. 2011, Web, 03 Sept. 2015.
[101] Christopher Turner, *Adventures in the Orgasmatron: How the Sexual Revolution Came to America* (New York: Farrar, 2011), 6.
[102] Ibid.
[103] Ibid., 5.
[104] Ibid.
[105] Myron Sharaf, *Fury on Earth: A Biography of Wilhelm Reich* (reprint; 1983, Boston: Da Capo, 1994), 13.
[106] Ibid., 3.
[107] James Barron, "Some Things Never Age. Just Ask Dr. Ruth," *The New York Times*, The New York Times, 12 Dec. 1998, Web, 04 Sept. 2015.
[108] Margalit Fox, "Dr. Joyce Brothers, On-Air Psychologist Who Made TV House Calls, Dies at 85," *The New York Times*, The New York Times, 13 May 2013, Web, 04 Sept. 2015.
[109] Martin Weil, "Dr. Joyce Brothers, 85; TV Psychologist and Columnist," *The Washington Post*, The Washington Post, 13 May 2013, Web, 04 Sept. 2015.
[110] Terri Pous, "Double Vision: Top 10 Famous Twins - Ann Landers and Dear Abby," *NewsFeed Double Vision Top 10 Famous Twins Comments*, Time, 03 Jan. 2013, Web, 04 Sept. 2015.
[111] Abigail Van Buren, "Dancer Can Go Topless And Believe In God, Too," *Chicago Tribune*, Chicago Tribune, 03 Sept. 1986, Web, 04 Sept. 2015.
[112] Gregory Wilbur, *Glory and Honor: The Musical and Artistic Legacy of Johann Sebastian Bach*, ed. David Vaughan (Nashville: Cumberland House, 2005), 1.
[113] Seth Rogovoy, "The Original Rachel Dolezal Was a Jew Named Mezz Mezzrow," *The Forward*, The Forward Assn., 16 June 2015, Web, 05 Sept. 2015.
[114] Alan Hanson, "Hal Wallis - The Paramount Producer Who Reigned Over Elvis Presley's Film Career," *BLOGINROLL*, Blogspot, 19 Feb. 2012, Web, 05 Sept. 2015.
[115] J. J. Goldberg, "On Elvis' Yahrzeit, His Not So Secret Jewish History," *The Forward*, The Forward Assn., 30 Jan. 2014, Web, 05 Sept. 2015.
[116] Ibid.
[117] Joshua Harris Prager, "All Shook Up in the Holy Land: Pilgrims Honor Elvis's Yahrzeit," *The Wall Street Journal*, Dow Jones, 17 Aug. 1998, Web, 05 Sept. 2015.
[118] Ibid.
[119] Donald N. Panther-Yates, *Old Souls in a New World: The Secret History of the Cherokee Indians* (Phoenix: Panther's Lodge, 2013), 33-42.
[120] Heart Lanier Shapré , *Why Elvis Left the Building: Revealing Seven Lost Years: The Child, the Man, the Truth* (Durham, Conn.: Strategic, 2011), 3.
[121] Iseabail Macleod and Terry Freedman, comps., *The Wordsworth Dictionary of First Names: A Concise and Useful Guide to the Origins and Meanings of Over 2000 Names* (Hertfordshire: Wordsworth, 1995), 68.
[122] Richard Rabkin, "Was Elvis Presley Jewish?" *Aishcom*, Aish.com, n.d., Web, 05 Sept. 2015.
[123] Steve Templeton, *Elvis Presley: Silver Screen Icon* (New York: Overmountain, 2002), 144.
[124] Vivian Henoch, "Motown Mensches Live," *My Jewish Detroit*, Jewish Federation of Metropolitan Detroit, n.d., Web, 08 Sept. 2015.
[125] Nate Bloom, "Woodstock - The Jewish Connection," *Jewish Standard*, Jewish Standard, 14 Aug. 2009, Web, 08 Sept. 2015.
[126] Ibid.
[127] Nate Bloom, "Woodstock - Confirmed Jewish Musicians at Woodstock," *Jewish Standard*, Jewish Standard, 14 Aug. 2009, Web, 08 Sept. 2015.

[128] "Music - The Jews Who Rock Wiki," *Jewcy*, Jewcy Media, 15 Nov. 2006, Web, 08 Sept. 2015.
[129] Zack O'Malley Greenberg, "The Best Jewish Rappers of All Time," *Forbes*, Forbes Magazine, 22 Dec. 2011, Web, 10 Sept. 2015.
[130] Kaye Northcott, "Kinky Friedman's First Roundup," *Texas Monthly*, Texas Monthly, 20 Jan. 2013, Web, 10 Sept. 2015.
[131] Renee Ghert-Zand, "Just Your Typical 6'1" African-American Yiddish Singer," *The Times of Israel*, The Times of Israel, 27 Apr. 2013, Web, 12 Sept. 2015.
[132] Ibid.
[133] Ibid.
[134] Paul Johnson, *A History of the Jews* (New York: Harper Perennial-Harper, 1987), 463.
[135] Steve Silbiger, *The Jewish Phenomenon: Seven Keys to the Enduring Wealth of a People* (Lanham, Md.: Longstreet, 2000), 108.
[136] Daniel Bernardi, Murray Pomerance, and Hava Tirosh-Samuelson, eds., *Hollywood's Chosen People: The Jewish Experience in American Cinema* (Detroit: Wayne State UP, 2013), 5-6.
[137] David Breskin, "David Cronenberg. The Rolling Stone Interview," *David Cronenberg Rolling Stone, February 1992*, Davidcronenberg.de, 6 Feb. 1992, Web, 17 Sept. 2015.
[138] "Top 5 Most Controversial Performances From The Ed Sullivan Show," *Ed Sullivan Show*, SOFA Entertainment, n.d., Web, 18 Sept. 2015.
[139] Emily Wortis Leider, *Becoming Mae West* (Cambridge: Da Capo, 1997), 23-24.
[140] Joel Stein, "Who Runs Hollywood? C'mon, " *Los Angeles Times*, Los Angeles Times, 19 Dec. 2008, Web, 21 Sept. 2015.
[141] Nathan Abrams, "Triple-exthnics," *The Jewish Quarterly*, The Jewish Quarterly, n.d., Web, 21 Sept. 2015.
[142] Jay A. Gertzman, *Bookleggers and Smuthounds: The Trade in Erotica, 1920-1940* (Philadelphia: U of Pennsylvania P, 1999), 124.
[143] Abrams, "Triple-exthnics."
[144] Ibid.
[145] Reed Tucker, "How Almost Dying Renewed Ron Jeremy," *New York Post*, NYP Holdings, 02 May 2015, Web, 21 Sept. 2015.
[146] Alexis, *Christianity and Rabbinic Judaism*, 1:202.
[147] Abrams, "Triple-exthnics."
[148] Ibid.
[149] Vic975, dir. "Sarah Silverman Says 'I Would Kill Christ Again,'" *YouTube*, YouTube, 24 Apr. 2011, Web, 21 Sept. 2015.
[150] Abrams, "Triple-exthnics."
[151] Ibid.
[152] Bernardi, *Hollywood's Chosen People*, 8.
[153] Goldberg, *Jewish Power*, 280.
[154] Alexis, *Christianity and Rabbinic Judaism*, 2:98.
[155] Alexis, *Christianity and Rabbinic Judaism*, 1:140.
[156] Breskin, "David Cronenberg.
[157] Alexis, *Christianity and Rabbinic Judaism*, 1:249.
[158] Mearsheimer and Walt, *Israel Lobby*, 48.
[159] Alexis, *Christianity and Rabbinic Judaism*, 2:34.
[160] Paul Wexler, *Two-Tiered Relexification in Yiddish: Jews, Sorbs, Khazars and the Kiev-Polessian Dialect*. (New York: Mouton de Gruyter, 2002), 536.
[161] Ofer Aderet, "Why Ashkenazi Jews Are Not Descended From Khazars - and What It Means," *The Forward*, The Forward Assn., 25 June 2014, Web, 01 Sept. 2016.
[162] Rita Rubin, "'Jews a Race' Genetic Theory Comes Under Fierce Attack by DNA Expert," *The Forward*, The Forward Assn., 07 May 2013, Web, 23 Aug. 2016.
[163] Stroum Jewish Studies, "The Myth of the Khazar Conversion - Shaul Stampfer," *YouTube*, YouTube, 07 Jan. 2013, Web, 01 Sept. 2016.
[164] Nadine Epstein, "King David's Genes," *Moment Magazine*, Center for Creative Change, 04 Mar. 2014, Web, 05 Oct. 2015.
[165] Ibid.

CHAPTER 20

The Shoah in the Scriptures

[1] Jonas E. Alexis, *Christianity and Rabbinic Judaism, vol. 2: A History of Conflict Between Christianity and Rabbinic Judaism from the Early Church to our Modern Time* (Bloomington, Ind.: WestBow, 2013), 293-304.
[2] Ibid., 381.
[3] Ibid., 293.
[4] Ibid., 298.
[5] Kaleem Aftab, "Natalie Portman Interview: Black Swan Actress Talks Anti-semitism, Learning Hebrew and Directorial Debut A Tale of Love and Darkness," *The Independent*, Independent Digital News and Media, 21 Aug. 2015, Web, 24 Oct. 2015.
[6] "Museum of the History of Polish Jews to Open," *World Jewish Congress*, World Jewish Congress, 16 Apr. 2013, Web, 26 Oct. 2015.
[7] Szyndler, Artur, *Oshpitzin: Guide to Jewish History of Oświęcim*, trans. Maciek Zabierowski (Oświęcim, Poland: Auschwitz Jewish Center, 2011), 5, 30.
[8] Wassim Razzouk, "Welcome," *Razzouk Tattoo*, Razzouk Tattoo, n.d., Web, 26 Oct. 2015.
[9] Yisrael Gutman and Michael Berenbaum, eds. *Anatomy of the Auschwitz Death Camp* (Bloomington: Indiana UP, 1994), 130.
[10] Will Durant, *The Story of Civilization*, vol. 4: *The Age of Faith: A History of Medieval Civilization (Christian, Islamic, and Judaic) from Constantine to Dante, A.D. 325 - 1300* (New York: Simon, 1950), 5.
[11] Elie Wiesel, *Night*, trans., Marion Wiesel (New York: Hill and Wang-Farrar, 2006), 76.
[12] Ibid., xiii.
[13] Henrik Alstad, dir., "Yadvashem.org: IAF Israeli Air Force Fly over Auschwitz," *YouTube*, YouTube, 11 Oct. 2007, Web, 27 Oct. 2015.
[14] "IAF Pilots Perform Fly-over at Auschwitz Death Camp," *Haaretz.com*, Haaretz Daily Newspaper, 4 Sept. 2003, Web, 27 Oct. 2015.
[15] Ed Payne, "Auschwitz 'Showers' Offend Some Visitors to the Former Nazi Camp," *CNN*, Cable News Network, 01 Sept. 2015, Web, 27 Oct. 2015.
[16] Teresa Świebocka, ed., *Auschwitz: A History in Photographs*, trans. and ed., Jonathan Webber and Connie Wisack (Oświęcim, Poland: Auschwitz-Birkenau State Museum, 1993), 283.
[17] Walter Laqueur, *The Terrible Secret: Suppression of the Truth about Hitler's 'Final Solution'* (Boston: Little, 1980), 3.
[18] Ibid.
[19] Ibid., 3-4.
[20] Ibid., 100.
[21] Martin Gilbert, *The Holocaust: A History of the Jews of Europe During the Second World War* (New York: Henry Holt, 1985), 526.
[22] Raul Hilberg, *The Destruction of the European Jews*, 3rd ed., 3 Vols. (New Haven: Yale UP, 2003), 2:685.
[23] David S. Wyman, *The Abandonment of the Jews: America and the Holocaust, 1941-1945* (New York: Pantheon-Random, 1985), 5.
[24] Świebocka, et al., *Auschwitz: A History*, 79.

CHAPTER 21

The New Covenant

[1] Peter S. Ruckman, ed., *The Ruckman Reference Bible* (Pensacola: BB Bookstore, 2009), 1829.
[2] Peter S. Ruckman, *Israel: A Deadly Piece of Dirt* (Pensacola: BB Bookstore, 2001), xxv.
[3] Jonas E. Alexis, *Christianity and Rabbinic Judaism*, vol. 2: *A History of Conflict Between Christianity and Rabbinic Judaism from the Early Church to our Modern Time* (Bloomington, Ind.: WestBow, 2013), 219-20.
[4] Jonas E. Alexis, *Christianity and Rabbinic Judaism*, vol. 1: *Surprising Differences, Conflicting Visions, and Worldview Implication—From the Early Church to our Modern Time* (Bloomington, Ind.: WestBow, 2012), 89-94.
[5] Ibid., 1:1.

6 Ibid., 2:202, 205.
7 Ibid., 1:116, 180, 182, 286, 288, 374.
8 Ibid., 2:5, 20, 32, 85, 122-128, 163, 383-384.
9 Ibid., 2:45-46.
10 Ibid., 2:48.
11 Daniel Burke, "Pope Calls Greed 'the Devil's Dung,'" *CNN*, Cable News Network, 07 July 2015, Web, 09 Oct. 2015.
12 Alexis, *Christianity and Rabbinic Judaism*, 2:46.
13 Ibid., 126.
14 Philip Schaff, *History of the Christian Church,* vol. 3: *Nicene and Post-Nicene Christianity, A.D. 311-600* (1910, reprint, Grand Rapids: Eerdmans, 1973), 183.
15 Alexis, *Christianity and Rabbinic Judaism*, 2:124.
16 Ibid., 2:377.
17 Ibid., 2:385.
18 Daniel Jonah Goldhagen, *A Moral Reckoning: The Role of the Church in the Holocaust and Its Unfulfilled Duty of Repair* (New York: Vintage-Random, 2003), 13.
19 Alexis, *Christianity and Rabbinic Judaism*, 2:380.
20 Hugh Fogelman, *Christianity Uncovered: Viewed Through Open Eyes*, 2nd ed. (Bloomington, Ind.: AuthorHouse, 2012), 216.
21 Sarah Delaney, "Pope Asks Pardon for Sins of Church," *The Washington Post*, 13 Mar. 2000, Web, 06 June 2016.
22 Alexis, *Christianity and Rabbinic Judaism*, 1:125.
23 Ibid., 2:204.
24 Ibid., 2:523.
25 Texe Marrs, "Scriptures Disprove Jewish Fables," *Power of Prophecy*, Texe Marrs, n.d., Web, 10 Oct. 2015.
26 Alexis, *Christianity and Rabbinic Judaism*, 2:522.
27 Ibid., 2:198.
28 Ibid., 2:231.
29 William P. Grady, *Given By Inspiration: A Multifaceted Study on the A.V. 1611 with Contemporary Analysis* (Swartz Creek, Mich.: Grady, 2010), 7.
30 Alexis, *Christianity and Rabbinic Judaism*, 2:526.
31 Ibid., 1:42.
32 Ibid., 2:198-99.
33 Ibid., 1:387.
34 Ibid.
35 Ibid., 2:195.
36 Ibid., 2:215.
37 Ibid., 2:526.
38 Ibid., 2:232.
39 Ibid., 2:207.
40 Ibid.
41 Ibid., 206.
42 Ibid.
43 Orville J. Nave, ed., *Nave's Topical Bible: A Digest of the Holy Scriptures* (Nashville: Nelson, 1979), 646.
44 Georges Antonius, *Unsealing Daniel* (Montreal: Self Published, 2016), 216.
45 Alexis, *Christianity and Rabbinic Judaism*, 2:205.
46 Robert Anderson, *The Coming Prince* (Grand Rapids: Kregel, 1984), 76.
47 Stephen P. Bohr, *Futurism's Incredible Journey: The Change of the Times and its Implications for Seventh-day Adventist Apocalyptic Interpretation* (Roseville, Calif.: Amazing Facts, 2009), 58-59.
48 Alexis, *Christianity and Rabbinic Judaism*, 2:514.
49 Ibid., 2:203.
50 Clarence Larkin, *Dispensational Truth or God's Plan and Purpose in the Ages*, 3rd Rev. ed. (1920; reprint, Glenside, Penn.: Clarence Larkin, 1918, 94.
51 Alexis, *Christianity and Rabbinic Judaism*, 2:210.
52 Larkin, *Dispensational Truth*, 94.
53 Alexis, *Christianity and Rabbinic Judaism*, 1:127.
54 Ibid., 1:253.
55 Ibid., 1:371.
56 Ibid., 2:255.
57 William P. Grady, *Understanding the Times*, vol. 1: *How Satan Turned America Against God* (Knoxville, Tenn.: Grady, 2005), 53-96.
58 Alexis, *Christianity and Rabbinic Judaism*, 2:201.
59 Wikipedia contributors, "Clarence Larkin," *Wikipedia, The Free Encyclopedia*, Wikipedia, The Free Encyclopedia, 27 Apr. 2015, Web, 17 Oct. 2015.
60 Alexis, *Christianity and Rabbinic Judaism*, 2:205.
61 Ibid., 2:197.
62 Ibid., 2:201.
63 Charles C. Ryrie, *Dispensationalism*, Rev. ed. (Chicago: Moody, 2007), 70.
64 Alexis, *Christianity and Rabbinic Judaism*, 2:195-96.
65 William P. Grady, *Given By Inspiration: A Multifaceted Study on the A.V. 1611 with Contemporary Analysis* (Swartz Creek, Mich.: Grady, 2010), 85-108.
66 Alexis, *Christianity and Rabbinic Judaism*, 1:133, 387.
67 Stephen Sizer, "Modern Israel in Bible Prophecy: Promised Return or Impending Exile?" *Christian Research Inst.*, Christian Research Inst., 03 July 2012, Web, 17 Oct. 2015.

CHAPTER 22

Naomi's Sojourn

1 David Davis, "Moshe Dayan and the Nazarene," *Jerusalem-news.net*, Jerusalem-news.net, 04 Apr. 2012, Web, 19 Oct. 2015.
2 Elwood McQuaid, *II Peter: Standing Fast in the Last Days* (Bellmawr, N.J.: Friends of Israel Gospel Ministry, 2001), 55.
3 Davis, "Dayan and Nazarene."
4 All About Israel, "Israel's Generals - Moshe Dayan - Documentary," *YouTube*, YouTube, 15 June 2015, Web, 19 Oct. 2015.
5 Galya Yemini, "Moshe Dayan's Eye Patch Ends up for Sale on EBay for $75,000," *Haaretz.com*, Haaretz Daily Newspaper, 25 July 2005, Web, 19 Oct. 2015.
6 Mark Woods, "Rick Warren on Roman Catholicism: 'We Have More in Common than What Divides Us,'" *Christian Today*, Christian Media Corporation, 05 Dec. 2014, Web, 21 Oct. 2015.
7 Jim Kuhnhenn, "Televangelist John Hagee Apologizes to Catholics," *USATODAY.com*, Gannett, 13 May 2008, Web, 21 Oct. 2015.
8 Ibid.
9 Josh Fleet, "Pope Francis Reaches Out To Jews," *The Huffington Post*, TheHuffingtonPost.com, 15 Mar. 2013, Web, 21 Oct. 2015.
10 Victor Duruy, *History of Rome and the Roman Empire: From Its Origin to the Establishment of the Christian Empire*, Ed. J. P. Mahaffy, vol. 4. pt. 1, rev. ed. (London: K. Paul, Trench & Co., 1885), 633.
11 Flavius Josephus, *The Jewish War*, Ed. G. A. Williamson (1959, reprint, London: Penguin, 1970), 293.
12 Elizabeth Flock, "Catholic Priests: It's 'Empirical Fact' That Many Clergy Are Gay," *US News*, U.S. News & World Report, 29 July 2013, Web, 22 Oct. 2015.
13 Rachel Donadio, "On Gay Priests, Pope Francis Asks, 'Who Am I to Judge?'" *The New York Times*, The New York Times, 29 July 2013, Web, 22 Oct. 2015.
14 Francis X. Rocca, "Vatican Disputes White House Guest List for Papal Visit," *The Wall Street Journal*, Dow Jones, 17 Sept. 2015, Web, 22 Oct. 2015.
15 Peter S. Ruckman, ed., *The Ruckman Reference Bible* (Pensacola: BB Bookstore, 2009), 338, 384-385, 935.
16 David B. Tinnin, *To Those Who Trusted* (New York: Dell, 1977), 58-59.

CHAPTER 23

Three Graves

1 Ted Berkman, *Cast A Giant Shadow: The Story of Mickey Marcus Who Died to Save Jerusalem* (New York: Pocket, 1962), 1.
2 Ibid.
3 Ibid., 2.
4 Ronnie Clark Coffey, *Constitution Island*, Images of America Series (Charleston, S. C.: Arcadia, 2008), 89.

Bibliography

AARONS, MARK AND JOHN LOFTUS. *Unholy Trinity: The Vatican, the Nazis, and Soviet Intelligence*. New York: St. Martin's, 1991.

_____. *Unholy Trinity: The Vatican, the Nazis, and the Swiss Banks*. Rev. ed. New York: St. Martin's, 1998.

ABBOUSHI, W. F. *The Angry Arabs*. Philadelphia: Westminster, 1974.

ABDALLAH, KING OF JORDAN. *My Memoirs Completed: "Al-Takmilah"* Washington, D.C.: Near Eastern Translation Program, 1954.

ABRAHAMS, FRED, MARC E. GARLASCO, AND DARRYL LI. *Razing Rafah: Mass Home Demolitions in the Gaza Strip*. New York: Human Rights Watch, 2004.

ABOUL-ENEIN, YOUSSEF AND BASIL ABOUL-ENEIN. *The Secret War for the Middle East: The Influence of Axis and Allied Intelligence Operations during World War II*. Annapolis: Naval Inst. P, 2013.

ABURISH, SAÏD K. *Arafat: From Defender to Dictator*. New York: Bloomsbury, 1998.

_____. *Nasser: The Last Arab*. New York: Thomas Dunne-St. Martin's, 2004.

ACACIA, JOHN. *Clark Clifford: The Wise Man of Washington*. Lexington, Ken.: UP of Kentucky, 2009.

ADAN, AVRAHAM (BREN). *On the Banks of the Suez: An Israeli General's Personal Account of the Yom Kippur War*. New York: Presidio, 1980.

ALDINGTON, RICHARD. *Lawrence of Arabia: A Biographical Enquiry*. 1955. Reprint. London: Collins, 1969.

ALEXIS, JONAS E. *Christianity and Rabbinic Judaism*. Vol. 1, *Surprising Differences, Conflicting Visions, and Worldview Implications—From the Early Church to our Modern Time*. Bloomington, Ind.: WestBow, 2012.

_____. *Christianity and Rabbinic Judaism*. Vol. 2: *A History of Conflict Between Christianity and Rabbinic Judaism from the Early Church to our Modern Time*. Bloomington, Ind.: WestBow, 2013.

AL-FILASṬĪNĪYAH, MU'ASSASAT AL-DIRĀSĀT AND JĀMI'AT AL-KUWAYT. *International Documents on Palestine*. Beirut: Inst. for Palestine Studies, 1981.

ALON, MATI. *Holocaust and Redemption*. Victoria, BC: Trafford, 2003.

_____. *The Return to Zion*. Bloomington, Ind.: Trafford, 2011.

ALONI, SHLOMO. *Arab-Israeli Air Wars, 1947-1982*. Ed. Tony Holmes. Vol. 23. Oxford: Osprey, 2001. Print. Osprey Combat Aircraft.

_____. *Israeli Mirage and Nesher Aces*. Eds. Tony Holmes and Bruce Hales-Dutton. Vol. 59. Oxford: Osprey Limited, 2004. Print. Osprey Aircraft of the Aces.

ALTERAS, ISAAC. *Eisenhower and Israel: U.S.-Israeli Relations, 1953-1960*. Gainesville: UP of Florida, 1993.

AMANN, JÜRG, ed. *The Commandant: The Rudolf Hoess Text*. New York: Peter Mayer-Overlook Duckworth, 2012.

Anderson, Hobson Dewey. *The Arab Refugee Problem: How it Can be Solved; Proposals Submitted to the General Assembly of the United Nations*. N.p.: N.p., December, 1951.

ANDERSON, NANCY SCOTT AND DWIGHT ANDERSON. *The Generals*. New York: Knopf, 1988.

ANDERSON, ROBERT. *The Coming Prince*. Grand Rapids: Kregel Publications, 1984.

ANDREWS, ROBERT. *The Columbia Dictionary of Quotations*. New York: Columbia UP, 1993.

ANDREYEV, CATHERINE. *Vlasov and the Russian Liberation Movement: Soviet Reality and Émigré Theories*. New York: Cambridge UP, 1987.

ANTONIUS, GEORGES. *Unsealing Daniel*. Montreal: Self Published, 2016.

ARENDT, HANNAH. *Eichmann in Jerusalem: A Report on the Banality of Evil*. 1963. Reprint. New York: Penguin, 1992.

ASHTON, NIGEL J., ed. *The Cold War in the Middle East: Regional Conflict and the Superpowers 1967-73*. New York: Routledge, 2007.

AUERBACH, Jerold S. *Hebron Jews: Memory and Conflict in the Land of Israel*. Lanham, Md.: Rowman & Littlefield, 2009.

BAER, ROBERT. *Sleeping With the Devil: How Washington Sold Our Soul for Saudi Crude*. New York: Three Rivers-Random, 2003.

BAUER, YEHUDA. *American Jewry and the Holocaust: The American Jewish Joint Distribution Committee, 1939-1945*. Detroit: Wayne State UP, 1981.

BAKER, ROBERT L. *Oil, Blood, and Sand*. New York: D. Appleton-Century, 1942.

BAMFORD, JAMES. *Body of Secrets: Anatomy of the Ultra-Secret National Security Agency From the Cold War Through the Dawn of A New Century*. New York: Doubleday-Random, 2001.

BARD, MITCHELL AND MOSHE SCHWARTZ. *1,001 Facts Everyone Should Know about Israel*. Lanham: Rowman & Littlefield, 2005.

BAR-JOSEPH, URI. *The Watchman Fell Asleep: The Surprise of Yom Kippur and Its Sources*. Albany, N.Y.: SUNY P, 2005.

BAR-ZOHAR, MICHAEL. *Beyond Hitler's Grasp: The Heroic Rescue of Bulgaria's Jews*. Holbrook, Mass.: Adams Media, 1998.

BAYLIS, JOHN, STEVE SMITH, AND PATRICIA OWENS, eds. *The Globalization of World Politics: An Introduction to International Relations*. Oxford: Oxford UP, 2013.

BEEVOR, ANTONY. *Stalingrad: The Fateful Siege, 1942-1943*. New York: Penguin, 1998.

BEIN, ALEX. *Theodor Herzl: A Biography*. Trans. Maurice Samuel. Philadelphia: The Jewish Publication Society of America, 1945.

BEN-HANAN, ELI. *Our Man in Damascus: Elie Cohn*. Bnei Brak, Israel: Steimatzky House, n.d.

BENSON, MICHAEL T. *Harry S. Truman and the Founding of Israel*. Westport, Conn.: Praeger-Greenwood, 1997.

BERGEN, DORIS L. *War & Genocide: A Concise History of the Holocaust*. Lanham: Rowman and Littlefield, 2003.

BERKMAN, TED. *Cast A Giant Shadow: The Story of Mickey Marcus Who Died to Save Jerusalem*. New York: Pocket, 1962.

BERNARDI, DANIEL, MURRAY POMERANCE, AND HAVA TIROSH-SAMUELSON, eds. *Hollywood's Chosen People: The Jewish Experience in American Cinema*. Detroit: Wayne State UP, 2013.

BESCHLOSS, MICHAEL. *Presidential Courage: Brave Leaders and How They Changed America 1789-1989*. New York: Simon, 2007.

BEST, ANTHONY, JUSSI M. HANHIMÄKI, JOSEPH A. MAIOLO, AND KIRSTEN E. SCHULZE. *International History of the Twentieth Century and Beyond*. 3rd ed. New York: Routledge-Taylor, 2015.

BETHELL, NICHOLAS. *The Last Secret: The Delivery to Stalin of Over Two Million Russians by Britain and the United States*. New York: Basic, 1974.

BIDWELL, ROBIN LEONARD ET AL. *British Documents on Foreign Affairs - Reports and Papers from the Foreign Office Confidential Print: The Pilgrimage in the Reign of Ibn Saud, 1927-1939.* Lanham: UP of America, 1989.
BIERMAN, JOHN AND COLIN SMITH. *Fire in the Night: Wingate of Burma, Ethiopia, and Zion.* New York: Random, 1999.
_____. *War Without Hate: The Desert Campaign of 1940-1943.* New York: Penguin, 2004.
BIGER, GIDEON. "The Boundaries of Mandatory Palestine: How the Past Influences the Future." In *Israel: The First Hundred Years.* Vol. 1, *Israel's Transition from Community to State.* Ed. Efraim Karsh. London: Frank Cass, 2000.
BIJAOUI, ILAN. *The Economic Reconciliation Process: Middle Eastern Populations in Conflict.* New York: Palgrave Macmillan, 2014.
BILLSTEIN, REINHOLD. "1945. How the Americans Took Over Cologne–and Discovered Ford Werke's Role in the War." In *Working for the Enemy: Ford, General Motors, and Forced Labor in Germany during the Second World War.* Ed. Nicholas Levis. New York: Berghahn, 2000.
BLACKWELL, EARL. *Celebrity Register.* New York: Harper, 1986.
BLUM, HOWARD. *The Eve of Destruction: The Untold Story of the Yom Kippur War.* New York: Harper, 2003.
BOHR, STEPHEN P. *Futurism's Incredible Journey: The Change of the Times and its Implications for Seventh-day Adventist Apocalyptic Interpretation.* Roseville, Calif.: Amazing Facts, 2009.
BOROWSKI, TADUESZ. *This Way for the Gas, Ladies and Gentlemen.* Trans. Barbara Vedder. New York: Penguin, 1967.
BREAKING THE SILENCE, COMP. *Our Harsh Logic: Israeli Soldiers' Testimonies from the Occupied Territories, 2000-2010.* New York: Metropolitan-Holt, 2012.
BREGNAN, AHRON AND JIHAN EL-TAHRI. *The Fifty Years' War: Israel and the Arabs.* New York: TV, 1999.
BREITMAN, RICHARD. *Official Secrets: What the Nazis Planned, What the British and Americans Knew.* New York: Hill and Wang-Farrar, 1998.
BRENNER, MICHAEL. *A Short History of the Jews.* Trans. Jeremiah Riemer. Princeton.: Princeton UP, 2010.
BRIAN, DENIS. *The Seven Lives of Colonel Patterson: How an Irish Lion Hunter Led the Jewish Legion to Victory.* Syracuse, NY: Syracuse UP, 2008.
BRILL, E. J. *First Encyclopaedia of Islam 1913-1936.* 1913-1936. 9 Vols. Reprint. Leiden, The Netherlands: N.p., 1987.
BRISTOW, EDWARD J. *Prostitution and Prejudice: The Jewish Fight Against White Slavery, 1870-1939.* New York: Schocken, 1983.
BROWN, MICHAEL L. *What Do Jewish People Think about Jesus?: And Other Questions Christians Ask about Jewish Beliefs, Practices, and History.* Grand Rapids: Chosen-Baker, 2007.
BUCKLEY, WILLIAM F. *In Search of Anti-Semitism.* New York: Continuum, 1992.
BULL, ODD. *War and Peace in the Middle East: The Experiences and Views of a UN Observer.* Barnsley, Eng.: Leo Cooper, 1976.
BURKETT, ELINOR. *Golda.* New York: Harper, 2008.
BYMAN, DANIEL. *A High Price: The Triumphs and Failures of Israeli Counterterrorism.* New York: Oxford UP, 2011.
CAIRNS, EARLE E. *Christianity Through the Centuries: A History of the Christian Church.* 3rd ed., rev. and expanded. Grand Rapids: Zondervan, 1996.
CARTER, JIMMY. *Palestine: Peace Not Apartheid.* New York: Simon, 2006.
CASEY-MASLEN, STUART, ed. *The War Report: 2012.* New York: Oxford UP, 2013.
CHAICHIAN, MOHAMMAD A. *Empires and Walls: Globalization, Migration, and Colonial Domination.* Leiden, The Netherlands: Brill, 2014.
CHAMISH, BARRY. *Who Murdered Yitzhak Rabin?* Brookline, Mass: Brookline, 2000.
CHIGER, KRYSTYNA AND DANIEL PAISNER. *The Girl in the Green Sweater: A Life in Holocaust's Shadow.* New York: St. Martin's, 2008.
CHOMSKY, NOAM. *Fateful Triangle: The United States, Israel, and the Palestinians.* Updated ed. Cambridge: South End, 1999. Print.
CHOWERS, EYAL. *The Political Philosophy of Zionism: Trading Jewish Words for a Hebraic Land.* New York: Cambridge UP, 2012.
CHURCHILL, WINSTON S. *The Second World War.* Vol. 1, *The Gathering Storm.* 1948. Houghton, 1985.
_____. *The Second World War.* Vol. 4, *The Hinge of Fate.* 1950. New York: Houghton, 1985.
CLAIRE, RODGER W. *Raid on the Sun: Inside Israel's Secret Campaign that Denied Saddam the Bomb.* New York: Broadway-Random, 2004.
CLIFFORD, CLARK AND RICHARD HOLBROOKE. *Counsel to the President: A Memoir.* New York: Random, 1991.
COCKBURN, ANDREW. *Rumsfeld: His Rise, Fall, and Catastrophic Legacy.* New York: Scribner, 2007.
_____ AND LESLIE COCKBURN. *Dangerous Liaison: The Inside Story of the U.S.-Israeli Covert Relationship.* New York: Harper, 1991.
COFFEY, RONNIE CLARK. *Constitution Island.* Charleston, S. C.: Arcadia, 2008. Print. Images of America Series.
COHEN-HATTAB, KOBI AND NOAM SHOVAL. *Tourism, Religion, and Pilgrimage in Jerusalem.* New York: Routledge, 2015.
COHEN, MICHAEL J. *Britain's Moment in Palestine: Retrospect and Perspectives, 1917-1948.* New York: Routledge, 2014.
COHEN, RICH. *Israel is Real: An Obsessive Quest to Understand the Jewish Nation and Its History.* New York: Picador-Farrar, 2009.
COHEN, RICHARD. *Tough Jews: Fathers, Sons, and Gangster Dreams.* New York: Simon, 1998.
COHEN, SAM A. *Future of the Middle East, United Pan-Arab States: Divided by Imperialism, United by Destiny.* Bloomington, Ind.: AuthorHouse, 2014.
COHEN, SAM T. *Shame: Confessions of the Father of the Neutron Bomb.* Bloomington, Ind.: Xlibris, 2000.
COHEN, WARREN I. *Profiles in Humanity: The Battle for Peace, Freedom, Equality, and Human Rights.* Lanham: Rowman & Littlefield, 2009.
COLLINS, LARRY AND DOMINIQUE LAPIERRE. *O Jerusalem!* New York: Simon, 1972.
COLMAN, JONATHAN. *The Foreign Policy of Lyndon B. Johnson: The United States and the World, 1963-1969.* Edinburgh: Edinburgh UP, 2010.
COONEY, JOHN. *The American Pope: The Life and Times of Francis Cardinal Spellman.* New York: Times, 1984.
CORNWELL, JOHN. *Hitler's Pope: The Secret History of Pius XII.* New York: Penguin, 1999.
CORVAJA, SANTI. *Hitler and Mussolini: The Secret Meetings.* New York: Enigma, 2008.
CROMER, GERALD. *A War of Words: Political Violence and Public Debate in Israel.* New York: Frank Cass, 2004.
CROWN-TAMIR, HELA. *Israel, History in a Nutshell: Highlighting the Wars and Military History.* Jerusalem: Tsur Tsina, 2012.
CUDDY, DENNIS LAURENCE. *Secret Records Revealed: The Men, the Money, and the Methods Behind the New World Order.* Oklahoma City: Hearthstone, 1994.
DALIN, DAVID G. AND JOHN F. ROTHMAN. *Icon of Evil: Hitler's Mufti and the Rise of Radical Islam.* New York: Random, 2008.
_____ AND ALFRED J. KOLATCH. *The Presidents of the United States & The Jews.* Middle Village, N.Y.: Jonathan David, 2000.
DAY, ARTHUR FRANCIS. *Our Friends, the Jews: Or, the Confessions of a Proselytizer.* Kent, Eng.: Burns, Oates and Washbourne Limited, 1943.
DEACON, RICHARD. *The Israeli Secret Service.* New York: Taplinger, 1977.
DEEB, MARIUS. *Syria's Terrorist War on Lebanon and the Peace Process.* New York: Palgrave Macmillan, 2003.
DEMAKIS, JOSEPH M., ed. *The Ultimate Book of Quotations.* Charleston, S.C.: CreateSpace, 2012.
DENG, FRANCIS M. *War of Visions: Conflict of Identities in the Sudan.* Washington, D.C.: The Brookings Inst., 1995.
DERSHOWITZ, ALAN M. *The Genesis of Justice: Ten Stories of Biblical Injustice that Led to the Ten Commandments and Modern Morality and Law.* New York: Warner, 2000.
_____. *The Vanishing American Jew: In Search of Jewish Identity for the Next Century.* New York: Little, 1997.
DISHON, DANIEL ET AL., eds. *Middle East Record: Volume Four, 1968.* Jerusalem: Israeli Universities P, Wiley, 1973.

DONOVAN, ROBERT J. *Conflict and Crisis: The Presidency of Harry S. Truman, 1945-1948.* 1977. Reprint. Columbia, Mo.: U of Missouri P, 1996.
DORAN, MICHAEL. *Pan-Arabism Before Nasser: Egyptian Power Politics and the Palestine Question.* New York: Oxford UP, 1999.
DORNBUSCH, RUDIGER, WILHELM NÖLLING, AND RICHARD LAYARD, eds. *Postwar Economic Reconstruction and Lessons for the East Today.* Cambridge: MIT P,1993.
DORRIEN, GARY. *Imperial Designs: Neoconservatism and the New Pax Americana.* New York: Routledge, 2004.
DUIGNAN, PETER AND LEWIS H. GANN. *The Rebirth of the West: The Americanization of the Democratic World, 1945-1958.* Lanham: Rowman & Littlefield, 1992.
DUNLOP, D. M. *The History of the Jewish Khazars.* 1954. Reprint. New York: Schocken, 1967.
DUNSTAN, SIMON. *Entebbe: The Most Daring Raid of Israel's Special Forces.* New York: Rosen, 2011.
_____. *The Six Day War 1967: Jordan and Syria.* Oxford: Osprey, 2009.
_____. *The Yom Kippur War 1973 (2): The Sinai.* Oxford: Osprey, 2003.
_____ AND GERRARD WILLIAMS. *Grey Wolf: The Escape of Adolf Hitler.* New York: Sterling, 2011.
DUPUY, TREVOR N. *Elusive Victory: The Arab-Israeli Wars, 1947-1974.* Garden City, N.Y.: Military Book Club, 2002.
DURANT, WILL. *The Story of Civilization.* Vol. 4: *The Age of Faith: A History of Medieval Civilization (Christian, Islamic, and Judaic) from Constantine to Dante, A.D. 325 - 1300.* New York: Simon, 1950.
DURUY, VICTOR. *History of Rome and the Roman People: From Its Origin to the Establishment of the Christian Empire.* Ed. J. P. Mahaffy. Comp. and Arr. Kelly and Co. Vol. 4, Pt. 1. Rev. Ed. London: K. Paul, Trench & Co., 1885
EBAN, ABBA. *Personal Witness: Israel Through My Eyes.* New York: Putnam's, 1992.
EDMUNDSON, MARK. *The Death of Sigmund Freud: Fascism, Psychoanalysis and the Rise of Fundamentalism.* London: Bloomsbury, 2007.
EFRON, NOAH J. *A Chosen Calling: Jews in Science in the Twentieth Century.* Baltimore: Johns Hopkins UP, 2014.
EIDELBERG, PAUL. *The Beginning and End of American Exceptionalism: A Theo-Political Analysis.* Springdale, Ark.: Lightcatcher, 2013.
_____. *The Myth of Israeli Democracy: Toward a Truly Jewish Israel.* Fullerton, Calif.: Davidson, 2007.
EISENMENGER, JOHANN ANDREAS. *The Traditions of the Jews.* Ed. John Peter Stehelin. 1748. Reprint. Coeur d'Alene, Ida.: Independent History & Research, 2006.
ELON, AMOS. *Herzl.* New York: Holt, 1975.
ENDERLIN, CHARLES. *Shattered Dreams: The Failure of the Peace Process in the Middle East, 1995-2002.* Trans. Susan Fairfield. New York: Other, 2002.
ENGLER, ROBERT. *The Politics of Oil: A Study of Private Power and Democratic Directions.* Chicago: Phoenix-U of Chicago P, 1961.
ENNES, JAMES M., JR. *Assault on the Liberty: The True Story of the Israeli Attack on an American Intelligence Ship,* 5th ed. New York: Random, 1979.
EPSTEIN, JULIUS. *Operation Keelhaul: The Story of Forced Repatriation from 1944 to the Present.* Old Greenwich, Conn.: Devin-Adair, 1973.
EPSTEIN, LAWRENCE J. *A Treasury of Jewish Inspirational Stories.* Northvale, N.J.: Jason Aronson, 1993.
ESCO FOUNDATION FOR PALESTINE. *Palestine: A Study of Jewish, Arab, and British Policies,* Vols. 1 & 2. New Haven: Yale UP, 1947.
ESTEP, JAMES RILEY. "Archeological Insights into the Crucifixion of Jesus." In *My Father's World: Celebrating the Life of Reuben G. Bullard.* Eds. John D. Wineland, Mark Ziese, and James Riley Estep, 72-85. Eugene, Ore.: Wipf and Stock, 2011.
FEIG, KONNILYN G. *Hitler's Death Camps: The Sanity of Madness.* New York: Holmes & Meier, 1979.
FERGUSON, NIALL. *The Ascent of Money: A Financial History of the World.* New York: Penguin, 1985.
_____. *The War of the World: Twentieth-Century Conflict and the Descent of the West.* New York: Penguin, 2006.
FERRELL, ROBERT H., ed. *The Letters from Harry to Bess Truman, 1910-1959.* Columbia: U of Missouri P, 1983.
FIERSTEIN, HARVEY. *Torch Song Trilogy: Three Plays.* New York: Villard, 1979.
FINKELSTEIN, LOUIS. *The Jews: Their History, Culture, and Religion.* Vol. 2. 3rd ed. New York: Harper, 1960.
FINKELSTEIN, NORMAN G. *Image and Reality of the Israel-Palestine Conflict.* 2nd ed. New York: Verso-New Left, 2003.
_____. *The Holocaust Industry: Reflections on the Exploitation of Jewish Suffering.* London: Verso-New Left, 2000.
FINKLESTONE, JOSEPH. *Anwar Sadat: Visionary Who Dared.* London: Frank Cass, 1996.
FISHER, URI JOSEPH. *Military Entrepreneurship and War Duration.* Ann Arbor: ProQuest Information and Learning Co., 2007.
FOGELMAN, HUGH. *Christianity Uncovered: Viewed Through Open Eyes.* 2nd ed. Bloomington, Ind.: AuthorHouse, 2012.
FONTÉ, J. P. *The Lure of the Lion.* Bloomington, Ind.: Xlibris, 2003.
FRANKEL, GLENN. *Beyond the Promised Land: Jews and Arabs on the Hard Road to a New Israel.* New York: Touchstone-Simon, 1994.
FRANKENSTEIN, ERNST. *Justice For My People.* New York: Dial, 1944.
FRASER, DAVID. *The Jews of the Channel Islands and the Rule of Law, 1940-1945: 'Quite Contrary to the Principles of British Justice.'* Portland, Ore.: Sussex Acad. P, 2000.
FREEDMAN, ROBERT O. *The Intifada: Its Impact on Israel, the Arab World, and the Superpowers.* Gainesville: UP of Florida, 1991.
FREIBERGER, STEVEN Z. *Dawn Over Suez: The Rise of American Power in the Middle East 1953-1957.* Chicago: Ivan R. Dee,1992.
FRIEDLANDER, HENRY. *The Origins of Nazi Genocide: From Euthanasia to the Final Solution.* Chapel Hill: UNC P, 1995.
FRIEDMAN, MURRAY. *The Neoconservative Revolution: Jewish Intellectuals and the Shaping of Public Policy.* New York: Cambridge UP, 2005.
GABEL, PAUL. *And God Created Lenin: Marxism Vs Religion in Russia, 1917-1929.* Amherst, N.Y.: Prometheus, 2005.
GABLER, NEAL. *An Empire of their Own: How the Jews Invented Hollywood.* New York: Anchor-Random, 1989.
GALLEA, ANTHONY. *Bulls Make Money, Bears Make Money, Pigs Get Slaughtered: Investment Wisdom that Stands the Test of Time.* New York: New York Inst. of Finance, 2002.
GANNON, ROBERT I. *The Cardinal Spellman Story.* New York: Doubleday, 1962.
GARNETT, DAVID, ed. *The Letters of T. E. Lawrence of Arabia.* London: Jonathan Cape, 1938.
GEFEN, ABA. *Israel at a Crossroads.* Jerusalem: Gefen, 2001.
GENDZIER, IRENE L., ed. *A Middle East Reader.* New York: Pegasus, 1969.
GERTZMAN, JAY A. *Bookleggers and Smuthounds: The Trade in Erotica, 1920-1940.* Philadelphia: U of Pennsylvania P, 1999.
GILBERT, MARTIN. *Auschwitz and the Allies: A Devastating Account of How the Allies Responded to the News of Hitler's Mass Murder.* New York: Holt, 1981.
_____. *Churchill and the Jews: A Lifelong Friendship.* New York: Holt Paperbacks, 2007.
_____. *In Ishmael's House: A History of Jews in Muslim Lands.* Toronto: McClelland & Stewart, 2010.
_____. *Jerusalem: Rebirth of a City.* London: Chatto & Windus-Random, 1985.
_____. *The Holocaust: A History of the Jews of Europe During the Second World War.* New York: Holt, 1985.
_____. *The Routledge Atlas of the Arab-Israeli Conflict.* 12th ed. New York: Routledge, 2012.
GILBOA, EYTAN AND EFRAIM INBAR, EDS. *US-Israeli Relations in a New Era: Issues and Challenges After 9/11.* New York: Routledge, 2009.
GILDER, GEORGE F. *The Israel Test: Why the World's Most Besieged State is a Beacon of Freedom and Hope for the World Economy.* New York: Encounter, 2012.

GINOR, ISABELLA AND GIDEON REMEZ. *Foxbats Over Dimona: The Soviets' Nuclear Gamble in the Six-Day War*. Grand Rapids: Integrated Publishing Solutions, 2007.
GINSBURG, BENJAMIN. *How the Jews Defeated Hitler: Exploding the Myth of Jewish Passivity in the Face of Nazism* (Lanham: Rowman & Littlefield, 2013.
GOLD, SHOLOM. *Touching History: From Williamsburg to Jerusalem*. Jerusalem: Gefen, 2015.
GOLDBERG, J. J. *Jewish Power: Inside the American Jewish Establishment*. New York: Basic-Perseus, 1996.
GOLDENBERG, ELLIOT. *The Spy Who Knew Too Much: The Government Plot to Silence Jonathan Pollard*. New York: S.P.I.-Shapolsky, 1993.
GOLDHAGEN, DANIEL JONAH. *A Moral Reckoning: The Role of the Church in the Holocaust and Its Unfulfilled Duty of Repair*. New York: Vintage-Random, 2003.
_____. *Hitler's Willing Executioners: Ordinary Germans and the Holocaust*. New York: Vintage-Random, 1997.
GOLDMAN, ERIC A. *The American Jewish Story through Cinema*. Austin: UT P, 2013.
GOLDMAN, STUART D. *Nomonhan, 1939: The Red Army's Victory That Shaped World War II*. Annapolis: Naval Inst. P, 2012.
GORENBERG, GERSHOM. *The Accidental Empire: Israel and the Birth of the Settlements 1967-1977*. New York: Times-Holt, 2006.
GOUDSOUZIAN, ARAM. *The Hurricane of 1938*. Beverly, Mass.: Commonwealth Editions, 2004.
GRADY, WILLIAM P. *Given By Inspiration: A Multifaceted Study on the A.V. 1611 with Contemporary Analysis*. Swartz Creek, Mich.: Grady Publications, 2010.
_____. *Understanding the Times*. Vol. 1, *How Satan Turned America Against God*. Knoxville: Grady Publications, 2005.
_____. *What Hath God Wrought!: A Biblical Interpretation of American History*. Knoxville: Grady Publications, 1996.
GREENFIELD, RICHARD PIERCE AND IRVING A. GREENFIELD. *The Life Story of Menachem Begin*. New York: Manor, 1977.
GRIEF, HOWARD. *The Legal Foundation and Borders of Israel under International Law: A Treatise on Jewish Sovereignty over the Land of Israel*. Jerusalem: Mazo, 2008.
GRIFFIN, G. EDWARD. *The Creature from Jekyll Island: A Second Look at the Federal Reserve*. Appleton, Wis.: American Opinion, 1994.
GRUNOR, JERRY A. *Let My People Go: The trials and tribulations of the people of Israel, and the heroes who helped in their independence from British colonization*. New York: iUniverse, 2005.
GUROCK, JEFFREY S., ed. *American Jewish History*. Vol. 7, *America, American Jews, and the Holocaust*. New York: Routledge, 1998. Web. 06 June 2014.
GUTMAN, YISRAEL AND MICHAEL BERENBAUM, eds. *Anatomy of the Auschwitz Death Camp*. Bloomington: Indiana UP, 1994.
HAHN, PETER L. *The United States, Great Britain, and Egypt, 1945-1956: Strategy and Diplomacy in the Early Cold War*. Chapel Hill: UNC P, 1991.
HALL, M. CLEMENT. *Intifada*. Raleigh, N.C.: Lulu, 2009.
HAMMEL, ERIC. *Six Days in June: How Israel Won the 1967 Arab-Israeli War*. Pacifica: Pacifica Military History, 1992.
HARDING, THOMAS. *Hanns and Rudolf: The True Story of the German Jew Who Tracked Down And Caught the Kommandant of Auschwitz*. New York: Simon, 2013.
HARKABI, YEHOSHAFAT. *Arab Attitudes to Israel*. New York: Halstead-John Wiley, 1974.
HARRIS, THOMAS M. *Rome's Responsibility for the Assassination of Abraham Lincoln*. Pittsburgh: Williams, 1897.
HART, B. H. LIDDELL. *History of the Second World War*. New York: Putnam's, 1970.
_____, ed. *The Red Army*. New York: Harcourt, 1956
HAYNES, HENRIETTA. *Henrietta Maria*. New York: Putnam's, 1912.
HEIKAL, MOHAMED. *The Road to Ramadan*. New York: Times, 1975.
HERSH, BURTON. *The Old Boys: The American Elite and the Origins of the CIA*. St. Petersburg, Fla.: Tree Farm, 2002.
HERSH, SEYMOUR M. *The Samson Option: Israel's Nuclear Arsenal and American Foreign Policy*. New York: Random, 1991.
HERZL, THEODOR. *The Jewish State: An Attempt at a Modern Solution of the Jewish Question*. Trans. Sylvie D'Avigdor. 4th ed. London: Rita Searl, 1946.
HERZOG, CHAIM. *Heroes of Israel: Profiles of Jewish Courage*. Boston: Little, 1989.
_____. *The War of Atonement: October 1973*. Boston: Little, 1973.
_____ AND SHLOMO GAZIT. *The Arab-Israeli Wars: War and Peace in the Middle East*. New York: Vintage-Random, 2004.
HIGHAM, CHARLES. *The Films of Orson Welles*. Berkeley: U of California P, 1970.
_____. *Trading with the Enemy: An Exposé of the Nazi-American Money Plot 1933-1949*. New York: Delacorte, 1983.
HILBERG, RAUL. *The Destruction of the European Jews*. 3rd ed. Vols. 1-3. New Haven: Yale UP, 2003.
HILLIARD, CONSTANCE. *Does Israel Have a Future?: The Case for a Post-Zionist State*. Dulles, Va.: Potomac, 2009.
HINSLEY, F. H. AND ALAN STRIPP. *Code Breakers: The Inside Story of Bletchley Park*. Oxford: Oxford UP, 1993.
HIRSCHMAN, ELIZABETH CALDWELL AND DONALD N. PANTHER-YATES. When Scotland Was Jewish: DNA Evidence, Archeology, Analysis of Migrations, and Public and Family Records Show Twelfth Century Semitic Roots. Jefferson, N.C.: McFarland, 2007.
HISLOP, ALEXANDER. *The Two Babylons: Or, The Papal Worship Proved to be the Worship of Nimrod and His Wife*. 4th ed. 1929. Reprint. London: S.W. Partridge, 1959.
HITLER, ADOLF. *Mein Kampf*. Trans. James Murphy. 1939. Reprint. N.p., Bottom of the Hill, 2010.
HITTI, PHILIP KHURI. *The Arabs: A Short History*. 1943. Reprint. Washington, D.C.: Regnery-Eagle, 1996.
HORVITZ, LESLIE ALAN AND CHRISTOPHER CATHERWOOD. *Encyclopedia of War Crimes and Genocide*. New York: Facts on File-Infobase, 2006.
HOUNAM, PETER. *Operation Cyanide: Why the Bombing of the USS Liberty Nearly Caused World War III*. London: Vision-Satin, 2003.
HURWITZ, HARRY AND YISRAEL MEDAD, eds. *Peace in the Making: The Menachem Begin-Anwar El-Sadat Personal Correspondence*. Jerusalem: Gefen, 2011.
ISAACS, RONALD H. *Every Person's Guide to the High Holy Days*. Northvale, N.J.: Jason Aronson, 1999.
ISAACSON, WALTER. *Kissinger: A Biography*. New York: Simon, 1992.
_____ AND EVAN THOMAS. *The Wise Men: Six Friends and the World They Made*. New York: Touchstone-Simon, 1986.
JACOBS, ANDREW S. *Christ Circumcised: A Study in Early Christian History and Difference*. Philadelphia: U of Pennsylvania P, 2012.
JASPER, WILLIAM. *Global Tyranny...Step By Step*. Appleton: Western Island, 1993.
JENNINGS, JERRY L. *Stella's Secret: A True Story of Holocaust Survival*. Bloomington: Xlibris, 2005.
JOHN, ROBERT AND SAMI HADAWI. *The Palestine Diary*. Vols. 1 & 2. New York: New World, 1970.
JOHNSON, LYNDON BAINES. *The Vantage Point: Perspectives of the Presidency, 1963-1969*. New York: Holt, 1971.
JOHNSON, PAUL. *A History of the Jews*. New York: Harper Perennial-Harper, 1987.
JONES, E. MICHAEL. *The Jewish Revolutionary Spirit: And Its Impact on World History*. South Bend: Fidelity, 2008.
JOSEPHUS, FLAVIUS. *The Jewish War*. Ed. G. A. Williamson. 1959. Reprint. London: Penguin, 1970.
JUDIS, JOHN B. *Genesis: Truman, American Jews, and the Origins of the Arab/Israeli Conflict*. New York: Farrar, 2014.
JULIUS, ANTHONY. *Trials of the Diaspora: A History of Anti-Semitism in England*. New York: Oxford UP, 2010.
KARAS, JOŽA. *Music in Terezin, 1941-1945*. Hillsdale, NY: Pendragon, 1985.
KARK, RUTH AND JOSEPH B. GLASS. "The Jews in Eretz-Israel/Palestine: From Traditional Peripherality to Modern Centrality." In *Israel: The First Hundred Years*. Vol. 1, *Israel's Transition from Community to State*. Ed. Efraim Karsh. London: Frank Cass, 2000.
KARPIN, MICHAEL. *The Bomb in the Basement: How Israel Went Nuclear and What That Means for the World*. New York: Simon, 2006.

KARSH, EFRAIM. *Essential Histories*. Vol. 28, *The Arab-Israeli Conflict: The Palestine War 1948*. Oxford: Osprey, 2002.
_____, ed. *Israel: The First Hundred Years*. Vol. 1, *Israel's Transition from Community to State*. London: Frank Cass, 2000.
_____. *Palestine Betrayed*. New Haven: Yale UP, 2010.
_____. *Rethinking the Middle East*. Portland, Ore.: Frank Cass, 2003.
_____ AND INARI KARSH. *Empires of the Sand: The Struggle for Mastery in the Middle East 1789-1923*. Cambridge: Harvard UP,1999.
KATZ, SAMUEL M. *Guards Without Frontiers: Israel's War Against Terrorism*. London: Arms & Armour, 1990.
_____. *The Hunt for the Engineer: How Israeli Agents Tracked the Hamas Master Bomber*. New York: Fromm International, 1999.
KATZ, YAAKOV AND YOAZ HENDEL. *Israel vs. Iran: The Shadow War*. Dulles, Va.: Potomac, 2012.
KATZ, YOSSI. "Zionism and Jerusalem - the Conflict of Priorities: Changes in Zionist Settlement in the Jerusalem Vicinity, 1937 -48." In *Israel: The First Hundred Years*. Vol. 1, *Israel's Transition from Community to State*. Ed. Efraim Karsh, 120-143. London: Frank Cass, 2000.
KENNEDY, PAUL. *The Rise and Fall of the Great Powers: Economic Change and Military Conflict from 1500 to 2000*. New York: Random, 1987.
KIRK, GEORGE. *The Middle East 1945-1950: Survey of International Affairs*. London: Oxford UP, 1954.
KISSINGER, HENRY. *Years of Upheaval: The Second Volume of His Classic Memoirs*. 1982. Reprint. New York: Simon, 2011.
KLEE, ERNST, WILLI DRESSEN, AND VOLKER RIESS. *"The Good Old Days": The Holocaust as Seen by Its Perpetrators and Bystanders*. Trans. Deborah Burnstone. Old Saybrook, Conn.: Konecky & Konecky, 1991.
KNAPPE, SIEGFRIED AND TED BRUSAW. *Soldat: Reflections of a German Soldier, 1936-1949*. New York: Dell-Random, 1992.
KNIGHT, PETER, ed. *Conspiracy Theories in American History: An Encyclopedia*, Vol. 1. Santa Barbara: ABC-CLIO, 2003.
KOESTLER, ARTHUR. *Promise and Fulfilment: Palestine 1917-1948*. London: Macmillan, 1949.
KYLE, KEITH. *Suez: Britain's End of Empire in the Middle East*. New York: Tauris, 2011.
LAMARTINE, ALPHONSE DE. *A Pilgrimage to the Holy Land: Comprising Recollections, Sketches and Reflections, Made During a Tour in the East, in 1832 - 1833*. Vol. 1. Philadelphia: Carey, Lea & Blanchard, 1835.
LAMBETH, BENJAMIN S. *Air Operations in Israel's War Against Hezbollah: Learning from Lebanon and Getting It Right in Gaza*. Santa Monica: RAND Corporation, 2011.
_____. *The Transformation of American Air Power*. Ithaca: Cornell UP, 2000.
LANDAU, RONNIE S. *The Nazi Holocaust: Its History and Meaning*. New York: Tauris, 2006.
LANDMAN, SAMUEL. *Great Britain, the Jews and Palestine*. London: New Zionist, 1936.
LANGBEIN, HERMANN. *People in Auschwitz*. Trans. Harry Zorn. Markham, Ont.: Fitzhenry and Whiteside, 2005.
LAQUEUR, WALTER. *The Terrible Secret: Suppression of the Truth about Hitler's 'Final Solution.'* Boston: Little, 1980.
LARKIN, CLARENCE. *Dispensational Truth or God's Plan and Purpose in the Ages*. 3rd Rev. ed. 1920. Reprint. Glenside, Penn.: Clarence Larkin, 1918.
LATIMER, JON. *Alamein*. Cambridge: Harvard UP, 2004.
LAWLISS, CHARLES. *...and GOD CRIED: The Holocaust Remembered*. North Dighton, Mass.: JG, 1994.
LEIDER, EMILY WORTIS. *Becoming Mae West*. New York: Da Capo, 1997.
LEVI, PRIMO. *Survival in Auschwitz: The Nazi Assault on Humanity*. New York: Touchstone-Simon, 1996.
LEVIN, NORA. *The Holocaust: The Destruction of European Jewry 1933-1945*. New York: Crowell, 1968.
LEWIS, BERNARD. *The Arabs in History*. Rev. ed. New York: Harper, 1966.
LIGHTBODY, BRADLEY. *The Second World War: Ambitions to Nemesis*. New York: Routledge, 2004.
LILIENTHAL, ALFRED M. *The Zionist Connection: What Price Peace?* New York: Dodd, 1978.
LINN, RUTH. *Conscience at War: The Israeli Soldier as a Moral Critic*. Albany: SUNY P, 1996.
LLOYD GEORGE, DAVID. *The Truth about the Peace Treaties*. Vol. 2. London: Victor Gollancz, 1938.
_____. *War Memoirs of David Lloyd George: 1915-1916*. Vol. 2. Madison: Little, 1933.
LOFTUS, JOHN. *America's Nazi Secret: An Insider's History of How the United States Department of Justice Obstructed Congress*. Walterville, Ore.: TrineDay, 2011.
_____. *The Belarus Secret*. Ed. Nathan Miller. New York: Knopf, 1982.
_____ AND MARK AARONS. *The Secret War Against the Jews: How Western Espionage Betrayed the Jewish People*. New York: St. Martin's, 1994.
LONGERICH, PETER. *Holocaust: The Nazi Persecution and Murder of the Jews*. New York: Oxford UP, 2010.
_____. *The Unwritten Order: Hitler's Role in the Final Solution*. Gloucestershire, Eng.: Tempus, 2001.
LORCH, NETANEL. *The Edge of the Sword: Israel's War of Independence, 1947-1949*. New York: Putnam's, 1961.
LOUIS, WILLIAM ROGER. *The British Empire in the Middle East, 1945-1951: Arab Nationalism, the United States, and Postwar Imperialism*. New York: Oxford UP, 1984.
LUKACS, YEHUDA AND ABDALLA M. BATTAH, eds. *The Arab-Israeli Conflict: Two Decades of Change*. Boulder: Westview, 1988.
LUNT, JAMES D. *Hussein of Jordan: Searching for a Just and Lasting Peace*. New York: William Morrow, 1989.
LUZA, RADOMIR AND CHRISTINA VELLA. *The Hitler Kiss: A Memoir of the Czech Resistance*. Baton Rouge: LSU P, 2002.
MACDONALD, CALLUM. *The Killing of Reinhard Heydrich: The SS "Butcher of Prague."* Cambridge: Da Capo, 1989.
MACDONALD, KEVIN B. *Separation and Its Discontents: Toward an Evolutionary Theory of Anti-Semitism*. Westport: Praeger-Greenwood, 1998.
MACLEOD, ISEABAIL AND TERRY FREEDMAN, COMPS. *The Wordsworth Dictionary of First Names: A Concise and Useful Guide to the Origins and Meanings of Over 2000 Names*. Hertfordshire: Wordsworth Editions, 1995.
MACKLIN, GRAHAM. *Chamberlain*. London: Haus, 2006.
MALLMANN, KLAUS MICHAEL AND MARTIN CÜPPERS. *Nazi Palestine: The Plans for Extermination of the Jews in Palestine*. Trans. Krista Smith. New York: Enigma, 2005.
MANCHESTER, WILLIAM. *The Last Lion: Winston Spencer Churchill*. Vol. 1, *Visions of Glory, 1874-1932*. New York: Dell-Bantam, 1983.
_____ AND PAUL REID. *The Last Lion: Winston Spencer Churchill*. Vol. 3, *Defender of the Realm, 1940-1965*. 2012. Reprint. New York: Random, 2013.
MANHATTAN, AVRO. *Catholic Imperialism and World Freedom*. London: Watts, 1952.
_____. *The Vatican Billions*. Rancho Cucamonga: Chick, 1983.
_____. *The Vatican's Holocaust*. Springfield, Mo: Ozark, 1986.
MARCHIONE, MARGHERITA. *Yours Is a Precious Witness: Memoirs of Jews and Catholics in Wartime Italy*. Mahwah: Paulist, 1997.
MARRIN, ALBERT. *Black Gold: The Story of Oil in Our Lives*. New York: Knopf, 2012.
MARRS, TEXE. *Circle of Intrigue: The Hidden Inner Circle of the Global Illuminati Conspiracy*. Austin, Tex.: Living Truth, 1995.
_____. *DNA Science and the Jewish Bloodline*. Austin, Tex.: RiverCrest, 2013.
MARRUS, MICHAEL ROBERT. *The Unwanted: European Refugees from the First World War Through the Cold War*. Philadelphia: Temple UP, 2002.
MARSHALL, JONATHAN, PETER DALE SCOTT, AND JANE HUNTER. *The Iran-Contra Connection: Secret Teams and Covert Operations in the Reagan Era*. Cheektowaga, N.Y.: Black Rose, 1987.
MARSHALL, S.L.A. *World War I*. 1964. Intro. David Kennedy. New York: Mariner-American Heritage, 2001.

MARTIN, C. GUS, ed. *The SAGE Encyclopedia of Terrorism*. 2nd ed. Los Angeles: Sage, 2011.
MARX, KARL. *Critique of Hegel's 'Philosophy Of Right' (Cambridge Studies in the History and Theory of Politics)*. Trans. Annette Jolin and Joseph O'Malley. New York: Cambridge UP, 1970.
MATTAR, PHILIP. *Encyclopedia of the Palestinians*. Rev. ed. New York: Facts on File, 2005.
MATTHEWS, MATT M. *We Were Caught Unprepared: The 2006 Hezbollah-Israeli War*. Darby, Penn.: Diane, 2011.
MCCARTHY, DONALD J., JR. *The Sword of David: The Israeli Air Force at War*. South Yorkshire: Pen & Sword, 2013.
MCCULLOUGH, DAVID. *Truman*. New York: Simon, 1992.
MCGARVEY, PATRICK J. *CIA.: The Myth and the Madness*. New York: Saturday Review, 1972.
MCTERNAN, JOHN P. *As America Has Done to Israel*. N.p.: Xulon, 2006.
_____ AND BILL KOENIG. *Israel: The Blessing or the Curse*. Oklahoma City: Hearthstone, 2002.
MEARSHEIMER, JOHN J. AND STEPHEN M. WALT. *The Israel Lobby and U.S. Foreign Policy*. New York: Farrar, 2007.
MEINERTZHAGEN, COLONEL RICHARD. *Middle East Diary: 1917-1956*. New York: Thomas Yoseloff, 1959.
MEIR, GOLDA. *My Life*. New York: Putnam's, 1975.
MEISLER, STANLEY. *United Nations: The First Fifty Years*. New York: Atlantic Monthly, 1995.
MELADY, JOHN. *Pearson's Prize: Canada and the Suez Crisis*. Toronto: Dundurn, 2006.
MEOTTI, GIULIO. *A New Shoah: The Untold Story of Israel's Victims of Terrorism*. New York: Encounter, 2009.
MERKLEY, PAUL CHARLES. *American Presidents, Religion, and Israel: The Heirs of Cyrus*. Westport: Praeger-Greenwood, 2004.
MIGDALOVITZ, CAROL. *Israel's Blockade of Gaza, the "Mavi Mamara" Incident, and Its Aftermath*. Darby, Penn.: Diane, 2010.
MILLER, DAVID HUNT. *My Diary at the Conference of Paris*. 22 Vols. New York: 1924.
MILLER, RORY. "The Other Side of the Coin: Arab Propaganda and the Battle against Zionism in London, 1937-48." In *Israel: The First Hundred Years*. Vol. 1, *Israel's Transition from Community to State*. Ed. Efraim Karsh, 198-228. London: Frank Cass, 2000.
MILTON-EDWARDS, BEVERLEY. *The Israeli-Palestinian Conflict: A People's War*. New York: Routledge, 2009.
MITCHELL, NEIL JAMES. *Democracy's Blameless Leaders: From Dresden to Abu Ghraib, How Leaders Evade Accountability for Abuse, Atrocity, and Killing*. New York: New York UP, 2012.
MONTAGUE, PATRICK. *Chelmno and the Holocaust: A History of Hitler's First Death Camp*. London: Tauris, 2012.
MONTEFIORE, SIMON SEBAG. *Jerusalem: The Biography*. New York: Knopf, 2001.
MORRIS, BENNY. *Righteous Victims: A History of the Zionist-Arab Conflict, 1881-2001*. New York: Vintage-Random, 2001.
_____. *The Road to Jerusalem: Glubb Pasha, Palestine and the Jews*. London: Tauris, 2002.
MORSE, ARTHUR D. *While Six Million Died: A Chronicle of American Apathy*. New York: Random, 1968.
MOSLEY, LEONARD. *Dulles: A Biography of Eleanor, Allen, and John Foster Dulles and Their Family Network*. New York: Dial/James Wade, 1978.
MORTON, FREDERIC. *The Rothschilds: A Family Portrait*. Philadelphia: Curtis, 1961.
MÜLLER, FILIP. *Eyewitness Auschwitz: Three Years in the Gas Chambers*. Trans. and Ed. Susanne Flatauer. Chicago: Ivan R. Dee, 1979.
MULLIGAN, HUGH A. ET AL., eds. *Lightning Out of Israel: The Arab-Israeli Conflict*. Englewood Cliffs: Prentice-Hall, 1967.
NAOR, MORDECAI. *The Atlit Camp: A Story of a Time and Place*. Ed. Gavriel Fiske. Mikveh Israel: Yehuda Dekel Library/Society for Preservation of Israel, 2010.
NAPOLITANO, ANDREW P. *It Is Dangerous to Be Right When the Government Is Wrong: The Case for Personal Freedom*. Nashville: Thomas Nelson, 2011.
NARRETT, EUGENE E. *World War III: The War on the Jews and the Rise of the World Security State*. Springdale, Ark.: Lightcatcher, 2007.
NAVE, ORVILLE J., ed. *Nave's Topical Bible: A Digest of the Holy Scriptures*. Nashville: Thomas Nelson, 1979.
NETANYAHU, BENJAMIN. *A Durable Peace: Israel and its Place Among the Nations*. 1993. Rev. ed. New York: Warner, 2000.
NETANYAHU, IDDO. *Yoni's Last Fight: The Rescue at Entebbe, 1976*. Jerusalem: Gefen, 2002.
NEWDICK, THOMAS, ed. *Air Warfare from World War I to the Present: Air/Land/Sea Warfare*. San Diego: Thunder Bay-Advantage, 2008.
NEWMAN, MORDECAI, comp. AND JOEL LIPSKY, trans. *Theodor Herzl: Excerpts From His Diaries*. New York: Scopus, 1941.
NOVITCH, MIRIAM. *Sobibor, Martyrdom and Revolt: Documentaries and Testimonies*. Madison: UWP, 1980.
O'BALLANCE, EDGAR. *No Victor, No Vanquished: The Yom Kippur War*. San Rafael, Calif.: Presidio, 1978.
OREN, MICHAEL. *Power, Faith, and Fantasy: America in the Middle East, 1776 to the Present*. New York: Norton, 2007.
_____. *Six Days of War: June 1967 and the Making of the Modern Middle East*. New York: Presidio-Random, 2003.
PALESTINE ROYAL COMMISSION. *Report*. London: HMSO, 1937.
PANTHER-YATES, DONALD N. *Old Souls in a New World: The Secret History of the Cherokee Indians*. Phoenix: Panther's Lodge, 2013.
PARKES, JAMES. *Whose Land? A History of the Peoples of Palestine*. New York: Taplinger, 1949.
PATTERSON, JOHN HENRY. *With the Judeans in the Palestine Campaign*. New York: Macmillan, 1922.
PAWEL, ERNST. *The Labyrinth of Exile: A Life of Theodor Herzl*. New York: Farrar, 1989.
PAWLICKA-NOWAK, LUCJA, ed. *The Extermination Center for Jews in Chelmno-On-Ner in the Light of the Latest Research*. Trans. Arkadiusz Kamiński and Katarzyna Krawczyk. Lodz, Poland: Oficyna Bibliofilów, 2004.
PEARSON, ANTHONY. *Conspiracy of Silence: The Attack on the U.S.S. Liberty*. London: Quartet, 1978.
PENKOWER, MONTY NOAM. *Decision on Palestine Deferred: America, Britain and Wartime Diplomacy, 1939-1945*. Portland, Ore.: Frank Cass, 2002.
PERES, SHIMON. *Battling for Peace: A Memoir*. New York: Random, 1995.
PERL, GISELLA. *I Was a Doctor in Auschwitz*. 1948. Reprint. North Stratford, N.H.: Ayer, 1948.
PERI, YORAM. *The Assassination of Yitzhak Rabin*. Stanford: Stanford UP, 2000.
PETERS, JOEL. *Israel and Africa: The Problematic Friendship*. New York: St. Martin's, 1992.
PHILLIPS, KEVIN. *American Dynasty: Aristocracy, Fortune, and the Politics of Deceit in the House of Bush*. New York: Viking, 2004.
PHILLIPS, PAUL T. *The Controversialist: An Intellectual Life of Goldwin Smith*. Westport: Praeger-Greenwood, 2002.
PINSKER, LEON. *Auto-Emancipation: An Admonition to His Brethren by a Russian Jew*. Trans. D. S. Blondheim. 1882. Reprint. New York: Maccabaean, 1906.
PIPER, FRANCISZEK AND TERESA ŚWIEBOCKA, eds. Trans. Douglas Selvage. *Auschwitz: Nazi Death Camp*. Oświęcim, Poland: Auschwitz-Birkenau State Museum, 1996.
PIPES, RICHARD. *The Russian Revolution*. New York: Vintage-Random, 1991.
PLUNKA, GENE A. *Staging Holocaust Resistance*. New York: Palgrave MacMillan, 2012.
POSTAL, BERNARD AND HENRY W. LEVY. *And the Hills Shouted for Joy: The Day Israel Was Born*. New York: McKay, 1973.
PRESSFIELD, STEVEN. *The Lion's Gate: On the Front Lines of the Six Day War*. New York: Penguin, 2014.
PRIOR, MICHAEL P., ed. *Speaking the Truth: Zionism, Israel, and Occupation*. Northampton, Mass.: Olive Branch, 2005.
PUCHALSKA, KATARZYNA, ed. *The 70th Anniversary of the Warsaw Ghetto Uprising*. Trans. Barbara Herchenreder. Warsaw: Centrum Uslug Wspolnych, 2013.
QUANDT, WILLIAM B. *Peace Process: American Diplomacy and the Arab-Israeli Conflict Since 1967*. Rev. ed. Washington: Brookings Inst., 2001. Print.
QUIGLEY, CARROLL. *The Anglo-American Establishment: From Rhodes to Cliveden*. New York: Books in Focus, 1981.
_____. *Tragedy and Hope: A History of the World in Our Time*. New York: Macmillan, 1966.
RABINOVICH, ABRAHAM. *The Battle for Jerusalem: June 5-7, 1967*. New York: Jewish Publication Soc. of America, 1972.

_____. *The Yom Kippur War: The Epic Encounter That Transformed the Middle East.* New York: Schocken-Random, 2004.
RADZINSKY, EDVARD. *The Last Tsar: The Life and Death of Nicholas II.* Trans. Marian Schwartz. New York.: Doubleday-Random, 1992.
RAIDER, MARK. *The Emergence of American Zionism.* New York: New York UP, 1998.
RAVENSCROFT, TREVOR. *The Spear of Destiny: The Occult Power Behind the Spear Which Pierced the Side of Christ.* York Beach, Maine: Samuel Weiser, 1982.
RAVIV, DAN AND YOSSI MELMAN. *Every Spy a Prince: The Complete History of Israel's Intelligence Community.* Boston: Houghton, 1990.
REYNOLDS, DAVID. *Summits: Six Meetings that Shaped the Twentieth Century.* New York: Basic-Perseus, 2007.
RICCARDS, MICHAEL. *Destiny's Consul: America's Ten Greatest Presidents.* Lanham: Rowman & Littlefield, 2012.
RICE, CONDOLEEZZA. *No Higher Honor: A Memoir of My Years in Washington.* New York: Crown-Random, 2011.
RICHARDS, JULIAN. "Signals Intelligence." In *Routledge Companion to Intelligence Studies.* Eds. Robert Dover, Michael S. Goodman, and Claudia Hillebrand. Abingdon: Routledge, 2014.
RIGG, BRYAN MARK. *Hitler's Jewish Soldiers: The Untold Story of Nazi Racial Laws and Men of Jewish Descent in the German Military.* Lawrence, Kans.: UP of Kansas, 2002).
RIVERA, DAVID ALLEN. *Final Warning: A History of the New World Order.* Rev. ed. Oakland: InteliBooks, 2004.
ROBERTS, PRISCILLA MARY, ed. *World War II: The Essential Reference Guide.* Santa Barbara: ABC-CLIO, 2012.
ROGOW, Arnold A. *James Forrestal: A Study of Personality, Politics, and Policy.* New York: Macmillan, 1963.
ROSS, DENNIS. *Doomed to Succeed: The U.S.-Israel Relationship from Truman to Obama.* New York: Farrar, 2015.
_____. *The Missing Peace: The Inside Story of the Fight for Middle East Peace.* New York: Farrar, 2004.
ROTEM, SIMHAH. *Memoirs of a Warsaw Ghetto Fighter.* Trans. Barbara Harshav. New Haven: Yale UP, 1994.
ROTHROCK, JAMES. *Live by the Sword: Israel's Struggle for Existence in the Holy Land.* Bloomington: WestBow, 2011.
RUBIN, BARRY AND JUDITH COLP RUBIN. *Yasir Arafat: A Political Biography.* New York: Oxford UP, 2003.
RUCKMAN, PETER S. *The Books of Ezra, Nehemiah, Esther.* Pensacola, Fla.: BB Bookstore, 2004.
_____. *The Minor Prophets.* Vol. 2, *Habakkuk-Malachi.* Pensacola, Fla.: BB Bookstore, 2011.
RUSHTON, COLIN. *Spectator in Hell: A British Soldier's Story of Imprisonment in Auschwitz.* Gretna, La.: Pelican, 2010.
RYRIE, CHARLES C. *Dispensationalism.* Rev. ed. Chicago: Moody, 2007.
SACHAR, HOWARD M. *A History of Israel: From the Rise of Zionism to Our Time.* 3rd Rev. ed. New York: Knopf, 2007.
_____. *Israel and Europe: An Appraisal in History.* New York: Vintage-Random, 1998.
SADAT, ANWAR EL. *The Public Diary of President Sadat, Part 1.* Ed. R. Israeli. Leiden, Netherlands: Brill, 1979.
SAMUELS, MAURICE. *You Gentiles.* Ed. Edward Hurst. 3rd ed. 1924. Reprint. North Charleston, S.C.: CreateSpace, 2014.
SAND, SHLOMO. *The Invention of the Jewish People.* Trans. Yael Lotan. Brooklyn: Verso-New Left, 2009.
SANDERS, RONALD. *The High Walls of Jerusalem: A History of the Balfour Declaration and the Birth of the British Mandate for Palestine.* New York: Holt, 1984.
SCHÄFER, PETER. *Jesus in the Talmud.* Princeton: Princeton UP, 2007.
SCHAFF, PHILIP. *History of the Christian Church.* Vol. 2. *Ante-Nicene Christianity, A.D. 100-325.* 1910. Reprint. Grand Rapids: Eerdmans, 1973.
_____. *History of the Christian Church.* Vol. 3. *Nicene and Post-Nicene Christianity, A.D. 311-600.* 1910. Reprint. Grand Rapids: Eerdmans, 1973.
SCHANZER, JONATHAN. *Hamas vs. Fatah: The Struggle For Palestine.* New York: Palgrave Macmillan, 2008.
SCHECHTMAN, JOSEPH B. *The Life and Times of Vladimir Jabotinsky: Rebel and Statesman.* 1956. Reprint. Silver Spring, Md.: Eshel-Information Dynamics, n.d.
_____. *The United States and the Jewish State Movement: The Crucial Decade, 1939-1949.* New York: Herzl P, 1966.
SCHELLENBERG, WALTER. *The Labyrinth: Memoirs of Walter Schellenberg, Hitler's Chief of Counterintelligence.* Trans. Louis Hagen. New York: Harper, 1956.
SCHIFF, ZE'EV AND EHUD YA'ARI. *Israel's Lebanon War.* Ed. and trans. Ina Friedman. New York: Simon, 1984.
SCHWARTZWALD, JACK L. *Nine Lives of Israel: A Nation's History Through the Lives of Its Foremost Leaders.* Jefferson, N.C.: McFarland, 2012.
SCOTTI, R. A. *Sudden Sea: The Great Hurricane of 1938.* New York: Little, 2003.
SEABURY, PAUL. *The Wilhelmstrasse: A Study of German Diplomats Under the Nazi Regime.* Berkeley: U of California P, 1954.
SEGAL, ELIEZER. *Sanctified Seasons.* Calgary: Dept. of Religious Studies, U of Calgary P, 2008.
SEGEV, TOM. *1967: Israel, the War, and the Year That Transformed the Middle East.* Trans. Jessica Cohen. New York: Metropolitan, 2007.
SHALOM, ZAKI. *The Role of US Diplomacy in the Lead-Up to the Six Day War: Balancing Moral Commitments and National Interests.* Portland, Ore.: Sussex Acad. P, 2012.
SHAMIR, ISRAEL. *Pardes: An Etude in Cabbala.* N.p.: BookSurge, 2005.
SHAPRÉ, HEART LANIER. *Why Elvis Left the Building: Revealing Seven Lost Years: The Child, the Man, the Truth.* Durham, Conn.: Strategic Book Group, 2011.
SHARAF, MYRON. *Fury on Earth: A Biography of Wilhelm Reich.* 1983. Reprint. Boston: Da Capo, 1994.
SHARAN, SHLOMO AND DĀWID BÛQAY. *Crossovers: Anti-Zionism and Anti-Semitism.* New Brunswick: Transaction, 2010.
SHAW, MARK. *Miscarriage of Justice: The Jonathan Pollard Story.* St. Paul: Paragon House, 2001.
SHERMAN, ARNOLD. *When God Judged and Men Died: A Battle Report of the Yom Kippur War.* New York: Bantam, 1973.
SHERMAN, WILLIAM TECUMSEH. *Memoirs of General W. T. Sherman.* 1875. Reprint. Bedford, Mass.: Applewood, n.d.
SHIBLEY, DAVID RALPH. *Ernest Bevin and the Arab League.* Stanford: Department of History, Stanford UP, 1957.
SHIMONI, GIDEON. *Community and Conscience: The Jews in Apartheid South Africa.* Waltham, Mass.: Brandeis UP, 2003.
SHLAIM, AVI. *The Iron Wall: Israel and the Arab World.* New York: Norton, 2001.
_____. "The Protocol of Sèvres, 1956: Anatomy of a War Plot." In *The 1956 War: Collusion and Rivalry in the Middle East.* Ed. David Tal, 119-139. 2001. Reprint. Abingdon: Routledge, 2013.
_____ AND WILLIAM ROGER LOUIS, eds. *The 1967 Arab-Israeli War: Origins and Consequences.* New York: Cambridge UP, 2012.
SILBIGER, STEVE. *The Jewish Phenomenon: Seven Keys to the Enduring Wealth of a People.* Lanham, Md.: Longstreet, 2000.
SIMPSON, CHRISTOPHER. *Blowback: America's Recruitment of Nazis and Its Effect on the Cold War.* New York: Weidenfeld & Nicolson-Wheatland, 1988.
SINAI, ANNE AND ALLEN POLLACK. *The Syrian Arab Republic: A Handbook.* New York: American Acad. Assn. for Peace in the Middle East, 1976.
SINIVER, ASAF. *The Yom Kippur War: Politics, Legacy, Diplomacy.* New York: Oxford UP, 2013.
SIZER, STEPHEN. *Christian Zionism: Road-map to Armageddon?* Nottingham: Inter-Varsity, 2004.
SKOUSEN, W. CLEON. *Fantastic Victory: Israel's Rendezvous with Destiny.* 2nd ed. New York: C&J Investments, 2011.
SLATER, ELINOR AND ROBERT SLATER. *Great Moments in Jewish History.* Flushing, N.Y.: Jonathan David, 1998.
SLATER, LEONARD. *The Pledge.* New York: Simon, 1970.
SMITH, ANTHONY D. "Sacred Territories and National Conflict." In *Israel: The First Hundred Years.* Vol. 1, *Israel's Transition from Community to State.* Ed. Efraim Karsh, 13-31. London: Frank Cass, 2000.
SMITH, DANIEL. *100 Places You Will Never Visit: The World's Most Secret Locations.* London: Quercus, 2012.

SMITH, LYN. *Remembering: Voices of the Holocaust*. New York: Carroll & Graf, 2005.
SMITH, SIMON C., ed. *Reassessing Suez 1956: New Perspectives on the Crisis and its Aftermath*. Aldershot, Eng.: Ashgate, 2008.
SNETSINGER, JOHN. *Truman, the Jewish Vote, and the Creation of Israel*. Stanford: Hoover Inst. P, 1974.
SNIEGOSKI, STEPHEN J., PAUL FINDLEY, AND PAUL GOTTFRIED. *The Transparent Cabal: The Neoconservative Agenda, War in the Middle East, and the National Interest of Israel*. New York: Enigma Editions, 2008.
SOFFER, JONATHAN. *Ed Koch and the Rebuilding of New York City*. New York: Columbia UP, 2010.
SOLZHENITSYN, ALEKSANDR. *The Gulag Archipelago*. Vol. 1. New York: Harper, 1973.
SPENCE, H. D. M. AND JOSEPH S. EXELL. *The Pulpit Commentary*. Vol. 17, *Gospel of John*, n.d. Reprint. Grand Rapids: Eerdmans, 1978.
SPER, DEVIN. *The Future of Israel*. Scottsdale, Ariz.: Sy, 2004.
STAHEL, DAVID. *Kiev 1941: Hitler's Battle for Supremacy in the East*. New York: Cambridge UP, 2012.
STEELE, JONATHAN. *Soviet Power: The Kremlin's Foreign Policy - Brezhnev to Chernenko*. New York: Touchstone-Simon, 1984.
STEENBERG, SVEN. *Vlasov*. Trans. Abe Farbstein. New York: Knopf, 1970.
STEPHENS, ROBERT HENRY. *Nasser: A Political Biography*. New York: Simon, 1971.
STEVENSON, WILLIAM. *90 Minutes at Entebbe*. New York: Bantam, 1976.
STONE, DAN. *The Liberation of the Camps: The End of the Holocaust and Its Aftermath*. New Haven: Yale UP, 2015.
STONE, IRVING. *Clarence Darrow Attorney for the Defense: A Biography*. 1941. Reprint. New York: Bantam, 1958.
STONE, KURT F. *The Jews of Capitol Hill: A Compendium of Jewish Congressional Members*. Lanham, Md.: Scarecrow Rowman & Littlefield, 2011.
STROBER, DEBORAH HART AND GERALD S. STROBER. *Israel at Sixty: An Oral History of a Nation Reborn*. Hoboken: Wiley, 2008.
SUCHLICKI, JAIME, ed. *The Cuban Military Under Castro*. Piscataway: Transaction, 1989.
SUMMERS, ANTHONY AND ROBBYN SWAN. *The Arrogance of Power: The Secret World of Richard Nixon*. New York: Penguin, 2000.
SUTTON, ANTONY C. *America's Secret Establishment: An Introduction to The Order of Skull & Bones*. Billings, Mont.: Liberty House, 1986.
_____. *The Best Enemy Money Can Buy*. Billings, Mont.: Liberty House, 1986.
_____. *Wall Street and the Rise of Hitler: The Astonishing True Story of the American Financiers Who Bankrolled the Nazis*. West Sussex: Clairview, 2010.
ŚWIEBOCKA, TERESA, ed. *Auschwitz: A History in Photographs*. Trans. and ed., Jonathan Webber and Connie Wisack. Oświęcim, Poland: Auschwitz-Birkenau State Museum, 1993.
SWINDOLL, LUCI. *Notes to a Working Woman: Finding Balance, Passion, and Fulfillment in Your Life*. Nashville: W-Thomas Nelson, 2004.
SZPILMAN, WLADYSLAW. *The Pianist*. Trans. Anthea Bell. New York: Picador, 1999.
SZYNDLER, ARTUR. *Oshpitzin: Guide to Jewish History of Oświęcim*. Trans. Maciek Zabierowski. Oświęcim, Poland: Auschwitz Jewish Center, 2011.
TAL, DAVID, ed. *The 1956 War: Collusion and Rivalry in the Middle East*. 2001. Reprint. Abingdon: Routledge, 2013.
TAMMINEN, TERRY. *Lives Per Gallon: The True Cost of Our Oil Addiction*. Washington: Island, 2009.
TEMPLETON, STEVE. *Elvis Presley: Silver Screen Icon*. New York: Overmountain, 2002.
TESSLER, MARK. *A History of the Israeli-Palestinian Conflict*. Bloomington: Indiana UP, 1994.
THOMAS, BAYLIS. *How Israel was Won: A Concise History of the Arab-Israeli Conflict*. Lanham: Lexington, 1999.
TINNIN, DAVID B. *To Those Who Trusted*. New York: Dell, 1977.
TOLSTOY, NIKOLAI. *The Minister and the Massacres*. London: Century Hutchinson, 1986.
_____. *The Secret Betrayal*. New York: Scribner, 1977.
TRUMAN, HARRY S. *1946-52 Years of Trial and Hope, Memoirs: Volume 2*. N.p.: New Word City, 2014. Web. 16 June 2015.
_____. *Memoirs: Year of Decisions*. Cambridge: Da Capo, 1986.
TSUR, AVI, ed. *Landmarks: Resource Material, Poetry, Songs, Games and Activities*. Jerusalem: Israeli Ministry of Education, Culture and Sport, 1998.
TUCKER, SPENCER C. ET AL., eds. *The Encyclopedia of the Arab-Israeli Conflict: A Political, Social, and Military History*. Vol. 1, A-H. Santa Barbara: ABC-CLIO, 2008.
TURNER, BARRY. *Suez 1956: The Inside Story of the First Oil War*. London: Hodder and Stoughton, 2006.
TURNER, CHRISTOPHER. *Adventures in the Orgasmatron: How the Sexual Revolution Came to America*. New York: Farrar, 2011.
TWAIN, MARK. *The Innocents Abroad*. Hartford, Conn.: American, 1869.
UNGER, CRAIG. *House of Bush, House of Saud: The Secret Relationship Between the World's Two Most Powerful Dynasties*. New York: Scribner, 2004.
Urquhart, Brian. *A Life in Peace and War*. New York: Norton, 1987.
VAN PAASSEN, PIERRE. *The Forgotten Ally*. New York: Dial, 1943.
VATIKIOTIS, P. J. *Nasser and His Generation*. London: Croom Helm, 1978.
VENEZIA, SHLOMO. *Inside the Gas Chambers: Eight Months in the Sonderkommando of Auschwitz*. Ed. Jean Mouttapa. Trans. Andrew Brown. Malden, Mass.: Polity, 2009.
VERRIER, ANTHONY. *Through the Looking Glass: British Foreign Policy in the Age of Illusions*. London: Jonathan Cape, 1983.
VOSS, CARL HERMANN. *The Palestine Problem Today: Israel and Its Neighbors*. Boston: Beacon, 1953.
WALD, ALAN M. *The New York Intellectuals: The Rise and Decline of the Anti-Stalinist Left from the 1930s to the 1980s*. Chapel Hill: UNC P, 1987.
WALLACE, MAX. *The American Axis: Henry Ford, Charles Lindbergh, and the Rise of the Third Reich*. New York: St. Martin's, 2003.
WASSERSTEIN, BERNARD. *Britain and the Jews of Europe: 1939-1945*. New York: Oxford UP, 1979.
WEILER, PETER. *Ernest Bevin*. Manchester, Eng.: Manchester UP, 1993.
WEIR, ALISON. *Against Our Better Judgment: The Hidden History of How the U.S. Was Used to Create Israel*. Lexington, Ken.: CreateSpace, 2014.
WEISS, JEFFREY AND CRAIG WEISS. *I Am My Brother's Keeper: American Volunteers in Israel's War for Independence 1947-1949*. Atglen, Penn.: Schiffer, 1998.
WEIZMANN, CHAIM. *Trial and Error: The Autobiography of Chaim Weizmann*. New York: Schocken, 1949.
WEIZMANN, VERA AND DAVID TUTAEV. *The Impossible Takes Longer: The Memoirs of Vera Weizmann as told to David Tutaev*. New York: Harper, 1967.
WELCH, ROBERT. *The Politician*. Belmont, Mass.: Belmont, 1963.
WEXLER, PAUL. *Two-Tiered Relexification in Yiddish: Jews, Sorbs, Khazars and the Kiev-Polessian Dialect*. New York: Mouton de Gruyter, 2002.
WIEGAND, KRISTA EILEEN. *Bombs and Ballots: Governance by Islamist Terrorist and Guerrilla Groups*. Surrey: Ashgate, 2010.
WIESEL, ELIE. *Night*. Trans. Marion Wiesel. New York: Hill and Wang-Farrar, 2006.
WIGODER, GEOFFREY. *The Holocaust*. Danbury, Conn.: Grolier Ed., 1997.
WILBUR, GREGORY. *Glory and Honor: The Musical and Artistic Legacy of Johann Sebastian Bach*. Ed. David Vaughan. Nashville: Cumberland House, 2005.
WILLENS, LILIANE. *Stateless in Shanghai*. Hong Kong: Earnshaw, 2009.
WILLIAMS, FRANCIS. *Ernest Bevin: Portrait of a Great Englishman*. London: Hutchinson, 1952.
WILSON, EVAN M. *A Calculated Risk: The U.S. Decision to Recognize Israel*. 1979. Reprint. Cincinnati: Clerisy, 2008.

WISTRICH, ROBERT S., ed. *Terms of Survival: The Jewish World Since 1945*. New York: Routledge, 1995.
WOJALSKI, MIROSLAW ZBIGNIEW. *The Jewish Cemetery in Lodz*. Trans. Guido Schreiber. Lodz, Poland: Widzewska Oficyna Wydawnicza ZORA, 2001.
WOLF, STACY ELLEN. *A Problem Like Maria: Gender and Sexuality in the American Musical*. Ann Arbor: U of Michigan P, 2002.
WRANGEL, PETER. *The Memoirs of General Wrangel: The Last Commander-in-Chief of the Russian National Army*. Trans. Sophie Goulston. London: Duffield, 1930.
WYMAN, DAVID S. *The Abandonment of the Jews: America and the Holocaust, 1941-1945*. New York: Pantheon-Random, 1985.
YARDLEY, MICHAEL. *Backing into the Limelight: Biography of T. E. Lawrence*. London: Harrap, 1985.
YEADON, GLEN AND JOHN HAWKINS. *The Nazi Hydra in America: Suppressed History of a Century: Wall Street and the Rise of the Fourth Reich*. Joshua Tree, Calif.: Progressive, 1999.
YERGIN, DANIEL. *The Prize: The Epic Quest for Oil, Money, and Power*. New York: Touchstone-Simon, 1992.
YOUNG-BRUEHL, ELISABETH. *Hannah Arendt: For Love of the World*. Binghamton, N.Y.: Vail-Ballou, 1982.
YOUSSEF, MICHAEL. *You Want Me to Do What? Get Off Your Blessed Assurance and Do Something*. New York: Faith Words-Hachette, 2009.
ZELIZER, BARBIE, ed. *Visual Culture and the Holocaust*. New Brunswick, N.J.: Rutgers UP, 2001.
ZERTAL, IDITH AND AKIVA ELDAR. *Lords of the Land: The War Over Israel's Settlements in the Occupied Territories, 1967-2007*. Trans. Vivian Eden. New York: Nation-Avalon, 2007.
ZIV-TAL, AVRAHAM. *Enigma Named Max*. Trans. Rena Bar-David. Rishon Lezion, Israel: n. p., 2013.

Other Sources Cited

"4 Hanged in Secret At Acre; Funeral at Safad." *The Palestine Post*, 17 Apr. 1947, Late ed., sec. A.
"41 Dead, 53 Injured, 52 Missing, in Terrorist Attack on Secretariat." *The Palestine Post*, July 23, 1946, Late ed., sec. A.
"50th Anniversary Gettysburg Reunion." *Our History - Order of the Arrow, Boy Scouts of America*. Boy Scouts of America, n.d. Web. 10 Nov. 2015.
ABRAMS, NATHAN. "Triple-exthnics." *The Jewish Quarterly*. The Jewish Quarterly, n.d. Web. 21 Sept. 2015.
A&E: Investigative Reports. "Son Of Sam Speaks." *YouTube*. YouTube, 17 Jan. 2013. Web. 03 Sept. 2015.
ADERET, OFER. "Why Ashkenazi Jews Are Not Descended From Khazars - and What It Means." *The Forward*. The Forward Assn. 25 June 2014. Web. 01 Sept. 2016.
"Adopted 'Father' and 'Son' to Marry." *The Daily Beast*. Newsweek/Daily Beast, 20 May 2015. Web. 01 Sept. 2015.
AFTAB, KALEEM. "Natalie Portman Interview: Black Swan Actress Talks Anti-semitism, Learning Hebrew and Directorial Debut A Tale of Love and Darkness." *The Independent*. Independent Digital News and Media, 21 Aug. 2015. Web. 24 Oct. 2015.
ALL ABOUT ISRAEL. "Israel's Generals - Moshe Dayan - Documentary." *YouTube*. YouTube, 15 June 2015. Web. 19 Oct. 2015.
ALLEN, RICHARD V. "Reagan's Secure Line." *The New York Times* 7 June 2010, Today's Paper ed., sec. A:23. Print.
ALSTAD, HENRIK, dir. "Yadvashem.org : IAF Israeli Air Force Fly over Auschwitz." *YouTube*. YouTube, 11 Oct. 2007. Web. 27 Oct. 2015.
"America's Highest Ranking Naval Officer, Admiral Thomas Moorer (1912-2004), Former Chief of Naval Operations and Chairman, Joint Chiefs of Staff Rejects the Israeli Excuse." *USS Liberty Memorial*. James M. Ennes, Jr., n.d. Web. 5 Feb. 2015. Memorandum, June 8 1997.
ANDRITSCH, JOHANN, ed. *Judenburg 1945 in Augenzeugenberichten*. Judenburg, Austria: Verlag des Museumsvereins Judenburg, 1994. Translated page in author's file.
Anglo-American Committee of Inquiry. "Chapter 1 - Recommendations and Comments." *The Avalon Project*. Yale Law School Lillian Goldman Law Library, 2008. Web. 16 June 2015.
"Anti-Semitism: Martin Luther - 'The Jews & Their Lies.'" Jewish Virtual Library. 29 May 2014.
"Anwar El Sadat's Statement to the Nation, September 28, 1970." The Anwar Sadat Chair for Peace and Development (2006). The University of Maryland, PDF file.
ARAFAT, YASSER, AND YITZHAK RABIN. "Israel-PLO Recognition - Exchange of Letters between PM Rabin and Chairman Arafat/Arafat Letter to Norwegian FM (Non-UN Documents) (9 September 1993)." *Unispal.u.org*. United Nations, n.d. Web. 23 July 2015.
"Army Attacks Bases in Heart of Sinai." *Jerusalem Post*, Oct. 30, 1956, Daily ed., sec. A.
ASA-EL, AMOTZ. "Middle Israel: The Last War." *Jerusalem Post*. Jpost, 13 Sept. 2013. Web. 10 July 2015.
ASSOCIATED PRESS. "Israeli archaeologist digs into Sobibor death camp in search of Nazi killing machines." 21 August 2012. Haaretz.com, 08 April 2014.
"Attackers Outlawed by Jewish Heads." *The Palestine Post*, July 23, 1946, Late ed., sec. A.
AUSCHWITZ AND BIRKENAU MEMORIAL AND MUSEUM NEWS. State Museum of Auschwitz-Birkenau in Oświęcim. December 23, 2005. *Christmas Eve in Auschwitz as Recalled by Polish Prisoners*. Web. 16 Aug. 2016.
"Auschwitz: Inside the Nazi State." Episode 4: "Corruption." PBS.org. Devillier Donegan Enterprises, early 2005. Web. 10 April 2014.
BAR, SHMUEL. "Palestine or Peace? A 1960 Jordanian Peace Initiative: Reexamining History." *Middle East Quarterly* Summer 2006: 59-66. *The Middle East Quarterly*. The Middle East Forum. Web. 22 Nov. 2014.
BARAK, ROY. "Auschwitz Inmate Who Survived by Boxing Dies Aged 86." *Haaretz.com*. Haaretz Daily Newspaper Ltd., 30 Apr. 2009. Web. 10 Dec. 2015.
BARD, MITCHELL. "Myths & Facts: The Palestinian War (Al-Aqsa Intifada, 2000-2005)." *Jewish Virtual Library*. American-Israeli Cooperative Enterprise, n.d. Web. 27 July 2015.
_____. "West Bank Security Fence: Background & Overview." *Jewish Virtual Library*. American-Israeli Cooperative Enterprise, n.d. Web. 28 July 2015. Updated, Apr. 2015.
BARRON, JAMES. "Some Things Never Age. Just Ask Dr. Ruth." *The New York Times*. The New York Times, 12 Dec. 1998. Web. 04 Sept. 2015.
BECKERMAN, GAL. "The Neoconservative Persuasion: Examining the Jewish Roots of an Intellectual Movement." *Gal Beckerman*. Gal Beckerman, 6 Jan. 2006. Web. 31 Aug. 2015.
BERGER, RALPH. "Moe Berg." N.d. The Society for American Baseball Research. Web. 22 July 2014.
BERKOWITZ, DAVID. "My Testimony." *AriseandShine*. AriseandShine.org, n.d. Web. 03 Sept. 2015.
BERNADOTTE, FOLKE. "S/1025 of 5 October 1948." *S/1025 of 5 October 1948*. United Nations Security Council, n.d. Web. 08Nov. 2014.
BESCHLOSS, MICHAEL. "FDR's Auschwitz Secret." *Newsweek*. IBT Media, 13 Oct. 2002. Web. 03 Feb. 2015.

BLOMFIELD, ADRIAN. "Obama Snubbed Netanyahu for Dinner with Michelle and the Girls, Israelis Claim." *The Telegraph*. Telegraph Media Group, 25 Mar. 2010. Web. 07 Aug. 2015.
BLOOM, NATE. "Woodstock - Confirmed Jewish Musicians at Woodstock." *The Jewish Standard*. The Jewish Standard, 14 Aug. 2009. Web. 08 Sept. 2015.
_____. "Woodstock - The Jewish Connection." *The Jewish Standard*. The Jewish Standard, 14 Aug. 2009. Web. 08 Sept. 2015.
BOYER, DAVE. "President Obama's Limo Breaks down at Israeli Airport." *Washington Times*. The Washington Times, 20 Mar. 2013. Web. 07 Aug. 2015.
BRACKMAN, LEVI. "Why so Many Jews Are Atheists." *Ynetnews.com*. Yedioth Internet, 25 Nov. 2009. Web. 25 Aug. 2015.
BRESKIN, DAVID. "David Cronenberg. The Rolling Stone Interview." *David Cronenberg Rolling Stone, February 1992*. Davidcronenberg.de, 06 Feb. 1992. Web. 17 Sept. 2015.
BRILL, BRUCE. "One Man's Agony After The Fact." *Jerusalem Post* 23 Oct. 1992. Web. 2 Apr. 2015.
"British White Paper of 1939." *The Avalon Project*. Yale Law School Lillian Goldman Law Library, 2008. Web. 12 June 2015.
BROZAN, NADINE. "Chronicle: Alon Ben-Gurion." *New York Times* 04 Apr. 1997, sec. Style, The New York Times Co. Web. 25 June 2015.
BULLARD, GIULIANA S., ed. "More CIA Name Files Released." November 2002, Disclosure. Web. 27 Feb. 2014.
BURKE, DANIEL. "Pope Calls Greed 'the Devil's Dung.'" *CNN*. Cable News Network, 07 July 2015. Web. 09 Oct. 2015.
BURSTEIN, NATHAN. "Jewish Power Dominates at 'Vanity Fair'" *The Jerusalem Post*. Jpost, 11 Oct. 2007. Web. 31 Aug. 2015.
BUSH, GEORGE H. W. "Remarks at the Opening Session of the Middle East Peace Conference in Madrid, Spain, 10-30-1991." *Public Papers*. George Bush Presidential Library and Museum, n.d. Web. 23 July 2015.
BUSH, GEORGE W. "Israel, Palestine, and the Prospect of Peace: Remarks at the Annapolis Conference." Annapolis Conference. United States Naval Academy, Annapolis, Maryland. 27 Nov. 2007. *Presidentialrhetoric.com*. Web. 31 July 2015.
CARL, KATY. "Catholics Give Thanks to God in Maryland: St. Francis Xavier Church Celebrates 350 Years of Faith." *National Catholic Register*. EWTN News, 21 Nov. 2012. Web. 31 July 2015.
CARROLL, RORY. "Pope Says Sorry for Sins of Church." *The Guardian*. 13 Mar. 2000. Web. 09 Oct. 2015.
"Chaim Weizmann the Scientist." The Chaim Weizmann Laboratory. N.d. Web. 07 July 2013.
COLLIER, PETER ET AL., eds. "U.S. Electronic Espionage: A Memoir." *Ramparts* 02 Aug. 1972: 35-56. Print.
CREWDSON, JOHN. "New Revelations in Attack on American Spy Ship." *Chicago Tribune*. Chicago Tribune, 02 Oct. 2007. Web. 05 Feb. 2015.
DAVID, SAUL. "How Germany lost the WWI arms race." 15 Feb. 2012. BBC News Magazine. 05 April 2013.
DAVIS, DAVID. "Moshe Dayan and the Nazarene." *Jerusalem-news.net*. Jerusalem-news.net, 04 Apr. 2012. Web. 19 Oct. 2015.
DAWOOD, N. J., trans. *The Koran*. New York: Penguin, 2006. Web. 13 June 2015.
DELANEY, SARAH. "Pope Asks Pardon for Sins of Church." *The Washington Post*, 13 Mar. 2000. Web. 06 June 2016.
DINAN, STEPHEN. "Obama Admin. Sent Taxpayer Money to Oust Netanyahu." *The Washington Times*. The Washington Times. 12 July 2016. Web. 27 Dec. 2016.
DONADIO, RACHEL. "On Gay Priests, Pope Francis Asks, 'Who Am I to Judge?'" *The New York Times*. The New York Times, 29 July 2013. Web. 22 Oct. 2015.
DUIN, JULIA. "San Antonio Fundamentalist Battles Anti-Semitism." *Houston Chronicle* 30 Apr. 1988, 2 Star ed., sec. 6:1. Print.
EDITORS. "Drawing an Israel-Palestine Border: Is Peace Possible? Chapter 1: Borders." *The Atlantic*. Atlantic Media Co., 25 Oct. 2011. Web. 31 July 2015.
"Egyptian Air Force Spitfires Bomb Tel Aviv; One Shot Down." *The Palestine Post*, 16 May 1948, Daily ed., sec. A.
"Eichmann Hanged." *Jerusalem Post*, 01 June 1962, Early Morning ed., sec. A.
ENTOUS, ADAM. "Israel Spied on Iran Nuclear Talks With U.S." *The Wall Street Journal*. Dow Jones, 23 Mar. 2015. Web. 07 Aug. 2015.
EPSTEIN, JACK. "Argentina Tracks Trail Of Stolen Nazi Wealth: Government and private efforts search for bank ties." 30 Apr. 1997. Web. 13 June 2015.
EPSTEIN, NADINE. "King David's Genes." *Moment Magazine*. Center for Creative Change, 04 Mar. 2014. Web. 05 Oct. 2015.
EVANSKY, BEN. "Obama and Israel: Showdown at the UN?" *Liveshots*. Fox News Network, 19 Apr. 2010. Web. 07 Aug. 2015.
FARRELL, WILLIAM E. "Sadat Assassinated at Army Parade as Men Amid Ranks Fire Into Stands; Vice President Affirms 'All Treaties': At Least 8 Killed; Speaker of Parliament Is Interim President - Election in 60 Days." *The New York Times* 06 Oct. 1981, Late City Ed., sec. A:1. *The New York Times On the Web Learning Network: On This Day*. Web. 07 July 2015.
FENDEL, HILLEL. "Handcuffs and Prayers at Pollard Rally This Week." *Arutz Sheva*. Israelnationalnews.com, 20 Nov. 2005. Web. 18 July 2015.
FISHEL, REVERDY S. "The Attack on the Liberty: An 'Accident'?" *International Journal of Intelligence and CounterIntelligence* 8.3 (1995): 345-52. *The USS Liberty Memorial Website*. Ussliberty.org. Web. 02 Feb. 2015.
FLEET, JOSH. "Pope Francis Reaches Out To Jews." *The Huffington Post*. TheHuffingtonPost.com, 15 Mar. 13. Web. 21 Oct. 2015.
FLOCK, ELIZABETH. "Catholic Priests: It's 'Empirical Fact' That Many Clergy Are Gay." *US News*. U.S. News & World Report, 29 July 2013. Web. 22 Oct. 2015.
FOLLATH, ERICH AND HOLGER STARK. "The Story of 'Operation Orchard': How Israel Destroyed Syria's Al Kibar Nuclear Reactor." *SPIEGEL ONLINE*. Der Spiegel, 02 Nov. 2009. Web. 31 July 2015.
FOX, MARGALIT. "Dr. Joyce Brothers, On-Air Psychologist Who Made TV House Calls, Dies at 85." *The New York Times*. The New York Times, 13 May 2013. Web. 04 Sept. 2015.
FRANK, JOHN. "Holocaust Testimonies Project." Interview by Steve Gonzer and Rose Magel. Special Collections, University of Delaware Library. (May 1995): Tape 23.
FRIEDMAN, GABE. "10 Jews in Forbes Top 50 Billionaires." *The Times of Israel*. The Times of Israel, 03 Mar. 21. Web. 31 Aug. 2015.
FUENTES, ANITA, dir. "Netanyahu Congratulates Trump Victory" *YouTube*. YouTube, 09 Nov. 2016. Web. 03 Dec. 2016.
FUND, JOHN. "Obama Operatives Try to Sway Israel's Election." *Newsmax*. Newsmax Media, 18 Mar. 2015. Web. 07 Aug. 2015.
FURMANCZUK, ROBERT, AND LIDIA KELLY. "Ravensbrueck Letters Written in Urine Gifted to Polish Museum." *Reuters*. Ed. Tom Heneghan. Thomas Reuters, 20 Feb. 2017. Web. 04 Mar. 2017.
"Galilee Lido." *The West Australian*. 02 May 1946. Web. 18 November 2014.
"Gaza: Armed Palestinian Groups Commit Grave Crimes." *Human Rights Watch*. Human Rights Watch, 12 June 2007. Web. 01 Aug. 2015.
GEDALYAHU, ZVI BEN. "One-Third of PA Arabs Support Massacre of Fogels." *Arutz Sheva*. IsraelNationaNews.com, 04 June 2011. Web. 01 Aug. 2015.
"George Soros: Top 10 Reasons He Is Dangerous." *Human Events*. Eagle, 02 Apr. 2011. Web. 31 Aug. 2015.
GHERT-ZAND, RENEE. "Just Your Typical 6'1" African-American Yiddish Singer." *The Times of Israel*. The Times of Israel, 27 Apr. 2013. Web. 12 Sept. 2015.
GINSBURG, MITCH. "Golda Meir: 'My Heart Was Drawn to a Preemptive Strike, but I Was Scared.'" *The Times of Israel*. The Times of Israel, 12 Sept. 2013. Web. 07 Mar. 2015.
GOLDBERG, J. J. "On Elvis' Yahrzeit, His Not So Secret Jewish History." *The Forward*. The Forward Assn., 30 Jan. 2014. Web. 05 Sept. 2015.
GORDIS, DANIEL. "Israel Wonders What Happens When Its Fathers Are Gone." *Bloomberg View*. Bloomberg LP, 28 Sept. 2016. Web. 03 Dec. 2016.
GREENBERG, ZACK O'MALLEY. "The Best Jewish Rappers of All Time." *Forbes*. Forbes Magazine, 22 Dec. 2011. Web. 10 Sept. 2015.

GREENFIELD, DANIEL. "Remembering the 65th Anniversary of the Hadassah Medical Convoy Massacre." 15 March 2013. Front Page Mag. 07 Mar. 2014.
GRIMES, WILLIAM. "The Man Who Rendered Jesus For the Age of Duplication." *The New York Times*. The New York Times, 11 Oct. 1994. Web. 05 Nov. 2015.
GROSS, JUDAH ARI. "In Leaked Emails, Colin Powell Says Israel Has 200 Nukes." *The Times of Israel*. The Times of Israel. 15 Sept. 2016, Web. 30 Dec. 2016.
GROSSMAN, CATHY LYNN. "More Americans Tailoring Religion to Fit Their Needs." *USATODAY.COM*. Gannett, 13 Sept. 2011. Web. 05 Nov. 2015.
GUTTMAN, NATHAN. "Presidential Aide Valerie Jarrett Discloses Her Jewish Roots." *The Forward*. The Forward Assn. 07 Mar. 2011. Web. 27 Dec. 2016.
GUYÉNOT, LAURENT. "The Machiavellian Threefold Game of the Neoconservatives." *My Catbird Seat*. My Catbird Seat, 31 May2013. Web. 31 Aug. 2015.
HABER, LEO, ed. "Zionism." *Midstream* 1995. Web. 12 June 2015.
HALLIWELL, K. J. "Were Hebrew Linguists Aboard USS Liberty?" *USS Liberty Inquiry*. Sites.google.com, 25 Oct. 2007. Web. 02 Feb. 2015. Essay 18.
"'Hand of God' Prevents Rocket from Striking Its Target: Israeli Iron Dome Operator Says Sudden Gust of Wind Blew Missile into Sea When Defence System Failed." *Jews News*. N.p., 06 Aug. 2014. Web. 20 Jan. 2015.
HANSON, ALAN. "Hal Wallis - The Paramount Producer Who Reigned Over Elvis Presley's Film Career." *BLOGINROLL*. Blogspot, 19 Feb. 2012. Web. 05 Sept. 2015.
HENOCH, VIVIAN. "Motown Mensches Live." *My Jewish Detroit*. Jewish Federation of Metropolitan Detroit, n.d. Web. 08 Sept. 2015.
HERR, MICHAEL. "Kubrick." *Vanity Fair*. Condé Nast, Apr. 2000. Web. 29 Aug. 2015.
HETTER, KATIA. "Girl Scouts Welcomes Transgender Girls - CNN.com." *CNN*. Cable News Network, 20 May 15. Web. 01 Sept. 2015.
HITLER, ADOLF. "Führer Directive 30." *World War II Database,* NJ: Lava Development, LLC, n.d. Web. 13 June 2014.
_____. "Führer Directive 32." *World War II Database,* NJ: Lava Development, LLC, n.d. Web. 14 June 2014.
HOFFMAN, CHARLES, JOSHUA BRILLIANT, ET AL. "Dozens Killed, Wounded in Massive Tyre Blast." *Jerusalem Post* 12 Nov. 1982, Daily ed., sec. A:1-2. Print.
"How Have the Mighty Fallen." *Geneva Daily Times*. 01 August 1952. 09 August 2014.
"How Israel Won Her Greatest Victories By Defying U.S. Pressure." 11 Aug. 2004. JTF.org. 30 October 2014.
"Hundreds Brutally Massacred in W. Beirut Refugee Camps." *Jerusalem Post* 20 Sept. 1982, Daily ed., sec. A:1-2. Print.
"IAF Pilots Perform Fly-over at Auschwitz Death Camp." *Haaretz.com*. Haaretz Daily Newspaper Ltd., 04 Sept. 2003. Web. 27 Oct. 2015.
"In Brief: Mussolini's horse remembered…Jewels on the skin…Witch doctor's convention." *The Sydney Morning Herald*. 22 Oct. 1950. 09 Aug. Web. 2014.
"Instructions by Heydrich on Policy and Operations Concerning Jews in the Occupied Territories, September 21, 1939." Shoah Resource Center. 18 Feb. 2014.
"Interview of Kielczynski, Israeli Spy for CIA." *Foreign Affair Journal*. Kol Yisrael Radio, Reshet Bet, Jerusalem. 27 Mar. 2001. Web. Transcript.
"Interview with Ataman Alexander Pewnew." Personal interview.
"Interview with Dr. Heinrich Pichler." Personal interview.
ISRAEL. Security Agency. *Rocket Launching*. Israel Security Agency, n.d. Web. 01 Aug. 2015.
"Israeli Cabinet Minister Spied for U.S. - New U.S. Docs Reveal." *Jonathanpollard.org*. Jonathanpollard.org, n.d. Web. 21 July 2015. This article originally appeared in *Hamodia*, June 23, 2004, under the title, "Was There An American Spy In the Israeli Government?"
"Israeli Court Rules Jews for Jesus Cannot Automatically Be Citizens." *The New York Times*. The New York Times, 27 Dec. 1989. Web. 27 Aug. 2015.
"Israel's Wars & Operations: Operation Opera - Raid on Iraqi Nuclear Reactor (June 7, 1981)." *Jewish Virtual Library*. American-Israeli Cooperative Enterprise, n.d. Web. 16 July 2015.
JACKSON, DAVID. "Obama Snubs Netanyahu to Hang with Jay-Z, Letterman." *Fox Nation*. Fox News Network, 18 Sept. 2012. Web. 07 Aug. 2015.
JENKINS, PAUL, "Israel's Generals - Moshe Dayan," *YouTube*. YouTube, 22 Feb. 2014. Web. 26 Feb. 2015.
"Jewish Massacre Denounced." *New York Times*. April 28, 1903, p. 6.
"John Hagee Denies Jesus Christ as Messiah." *Vimeo*. Vimeo LLC, 2012. Web. 02 Sept. 2015.
JOHNSTON, WILLIAM ROBERT. "Chronology of Terrorist Attacks in Israel, Part IV: 1993-2000." *Johnston's Archive*. William Robert Johnston, 18 May 2013. Web. 23 July 2015.
KAMPEAS, RON. "Top 5 Donors to Hillary Clinton Campaign Are All Jewish." *The Forward*. The Forward Assn. 26 Oct. 2016. Web. 27 Dec. 2016.
KAPLAN, ARYEH. *This Is the Way It Was*. Israel: Palyam.org, n.d. PDF.
KARLIN-NEUMANN, PATRICIA. "Crossing into 2012: Exodus 13:1-22, Psalms 114." Sermon Text (2012): 1-5. Web. 22 January 2015.
KAUFMANN, DAVID. "Every Jew a Canny Yankee." *The Forward*. The Forward Assn., 15 Apr. 2005. Web. 06 Nov. 2015 Updated, 14 Apr. 2015.
KEARNEY, CHRISTINE. "Family, Friends Remember Joan Rivers in Poignant, Funny Funeral." *Reuters.com*. Thomson Reuters, 07 Sept. 2014. Web. 27 Aug. 2015.
KLEIMAN, SHELLEY. "The State of Israel Declares Independence." 27 Apr. 1999. Israel Ministry of Foreign Affairs. Web. 18 Oct. 2014.
KOENIG, BILL. "US Sponsored Israeli-Palestinian Meetings Coincided with Two Major Record US Disasters in December." *World Watch Daily*. William Koenig, n.d. Web. 31 July 2015.
KONE, SUSAN, dir. "Moment of Silence to Remember the Munich 11/Universal Prayer for Peace," *YouTube*. YouTube, 05 Sept. 2014. Web. 04 Mar. 2015.
KRANISH, MICHAEL. "Ten Years Later, Revelation of John Kerry's Ancestry Has a New Chapter." *BostonGlobe.com*. Boston Globe Media Partners, 13 Oct. 2013. Web. 30 Dec. 2016.
KRIEGER, ZVIKA. "Transcript for 'Is Peace Possible?' Chapter 1: Borders." *The Atlantic*. Atlantic Media Co., 25 Oct. 2011. Web. 31 July 2015.
KUHNHENN, JIM. "Televangelist John Hagee Apologizes to Catholics." *USATODAY.com*. Gannet. 13 May 2008. Web. 21 Oct. 2015.
LAGORIO, CHRISTINE. "Katrina Leaves Toxic Bathtub." *CBSNews*. CBS Interactive, 01 Sept. 2005. Web. 30 July 2015.
LANDAU, DAVID. "Togetherness Under the Trees Planned by Camp David Hosts." *The Jerusalem Post*, Sept. 6, 1978, Daily ed., sec. A.
LARGE, CHRISTINE. "Some Human Factors in Codebreaking." *FAS.org*. R&T Organization, Oct. 2003. Web. 18 July 2014.
"Lawrence of Arabia: Lowell Thomas." PBS.org. Devillier Donegan Enterprises: Oct. 2003. Web. 15 June 2012.
LEAGUE OF NATIONS. *Official Journal*. November 1922.
LEE, MATTHEW AND JOSEF FEDERMAN. "AP Source: US Talking with Israel on Spy Release." *Yahoo! News*. Yahoo, 31 Mar. 2014. Web. 21 July 2015.
LEVY, ARIEL. "Novelty Acts." *The New Yorker*. Condé Nast, 19 Sept. 2011. Web. 03 Sept. 2015.
LEWIS, BERNARD. "The Palestinians and the PLO." *Commentary*, 01 Jan. 1975. *Commentarymagazine.com*. Web. 25 June 2015.

LICHTBLAU, ERIC. "The Holocaust Just Got More Shocking." 01 Mar. 2013. *The New York Times*. 01 April 2014.
LIOR, ILAN. "Tel Aviv Gay Pride Parade Draws 100,000 - National." *Haaretz.com*. Haaretz Daily Newspaper Ltd., 13 June 2014. Web. 22 Aug. 2015.
"List of Islamic Terror." *The Religion of Peace*. The Religion of Peace, n.d. Web. 16 July 2016.
LOFTUS, JOHN. "The Truth About Jonathan Pollard." *Aish.com*. Yeshivat Aish Hatorah, n.d. Web. 21 July 2015. This article originally appeared in *Moment* magazine, June 2003.
LOWTHER, WILLIAM. "Rumsfeld 'helped Iraq Get Chemical Weapons.'" *Mail Online*. Associated Newspapers, n.d. Web. 18 July 2015.
MACALISTER, ROBERT A. S. "Palestine: Population." *Encyclopaedia Britannica*. 11th ed. 1911. *Archive.org*. Internet Archive, 05 Jan. 2010. Web. 26 June 2015.
MAIZEL, MATI. *The Golan Heights Campaign in the Six-Day War*. Tel Aviv: IDF History Department, 1999. Trans. in emails from Maor Levi, Tour Director, Yad La-Shiryon Museum, 06-11 November 2014.
MAKOVSKY, DAVID. "How to Build a Fence." *Foreign Affairs*. Council on Foreign Affairs, 28 Jan. 2009. Web. 28 July 2015.
MANARAZE, GARRY. "Listen to the Trumpets." 13 Nov. 2016, Heritage Bible Baptist Church, Greenwood, DE. Morning sermon.
MARRS, TEXE. "Scriptures Disprove Jewish Fables." *Power of Prophecy*. Texe Marrs, n.d. Web. 10 Oct. 2015.
MARSCHALL, RICK. "The Bethlehem Bell Ringer." *Monday Morning Music Ministry*. Rick Marschall, 12 Dec. 2010. Web. 28 July 2015.
MASLIN, NIGEL. "Palestine." *History Workshop Journal* 9.1 (1980): 184-88. *Oxfordjournals.org*. Web. 07 July 2015.
MAZZA, ED. "'Son Of Sam' David Berkowitz Denied Parole, But Says Jesus Has Forgiven Him." *The Huffington Post*. TheHuffingtonPost.com, 13 May 2014. Web. 30 Aug. 2015.
MEGDAL, HOWARD. "Religion Aided a Home Run Chase, and May Have Led to its Failure," 20 Mar. 2010, *New York Times*, 05 Nov. 2013.
Military Channel Documentary. "Israeli Raid on Iraqi Reactor." *YouTube*. You Tube, n.d. Web. 23 Apr. 2015.
MINOR, JACK. "Question about Rumors 82nd Airborne Might Have Removed Nixon from Office." Message to the author. 20 Mar. 2015. E-mail.
"'Moe' Berg: Sportsman, Scholar, Spy." 17 Jan. 2013. Central Intelligence Agency News and Information. Web. 22 July 2014.
MUNSON, KYLE. "Liberty Sailor Honored despite Bitterness over Attack." The Des Moines Register 11 Nov. 2014: n. pag. *USA Today*. Gannett Satellite Information Network. 11 Nov. 2014. Web. 10 Mar. 2015.
MURPHY, JARRETT ET AL. "Beirut Barracks Attack Remembered." *CBSNews*. CBS Interactive, 23 Oct. 2003. Web. 17 July 2015.
"Museum of the History of Polish Jews to Open." *World Jewish Congress*. World Jewish Congress, 16 Apr. 2013. Web. 26 Oct. 2015.
"Music - The Jews Who Rock Wiki." *Jewcy*. Jewcy Media LLC, 15 Nov. 2006. Web. 08 Sept. 2015.
"Napoleon and the Jews." *Project Gutenberg Self-Publishing*. World Public Library Assn., n.d. Web. 10 Nov. 2015.
"New Poll Shows Atheism on Rise, With Jews Found to Be Least Religious." *Haaretz.com*. Haaretz Daily Newspaper Ltd., 20 Aug. 2015. Web. 25 Aug. 2015.
"Nonfiction Book Review: Labyrinth of Exile by Ernst Pawel, Author." *PublishersWeekly.com*. PWxyz, LLC., n.d. Web. 13 Nov. 2015.
NORTHCOTT, KAYE. "Kinky Friedman's First Roundup." *Texas Monthly*. Texas Monthly, 20 Jan. 2013. Web. 10 Sept. 2015.
"Obama Finally Calls Netanyahu, Says US Rethinking Palestinian Policy." *The Times of Israel*. The Times of Israel, 19 Mar. 2015. Web. 07 Aug. 2015.
Official Records of the General Assembly, Second Session, Supplement No. 11, vol. I (A/364).
Operation Thunderbolt: Entebbe Documentary (2000). Dir. Eyal Sher. Perf. Michel Bacos et al. Globus Group, 2014. YouTube.
"Osiraq/Tammuz I." *Fas.org*. Federation of American Scientists, 09 Oct. 2000. Web. 16 July 2015.
OWEN, RICHARD L. "Operation Valiant: Turning of the Tide in the Sinai, 1973 Arab-Israeli War." GlobalSecurity.org. 01 Apr. 1984. 24 Mar. 2015.
"Palestinian Bell-ringer for Church of Nativity Killed." *Smh.com.au*. Sydney Morning Herald, 05 Apr. 2002. Web. 28 July 2015.
PARZEN, HERBERT. "The Roosevelt Palestine Policy, 1943-1945: An Exercise in Dual Diplomacy." *American Jewish Archives* Apr. 1974: 31-65. Web. 18 June 2015. PDF.
"Pastor John C. Hagee: Senior Pastor Cornerstone Church." *John Hagee Ministries*. John Hagee Ministries, n.d. Web. 11 Aug. 2015.
PAYNE, ED. "Auschwitz 'showers' Offend Some Visitors to the Former Nazi Camp." *CNN*. Cable News Network, 01 Sept. 2015. Web. 27 Oct. 2015.
"Peled; North Korean Pilots Flew for Egypt During Yom Kippur War." *JTA*. Jewish Telegraphic Agency, 31 Oct. 1975. Web. 07 Mar. 2015.
"Police Bust 'messianic' Prostitution Ring Active across Israel." *The Times of Israel*. The Times of Israel, 07 Sept. 2014. Web. 03 Sept. 2015.
POUS, TERRI. "Double Vision: Top 10 Famous Twins - Ann Landers and Dear Abby." *NewsFeed Double Vision Top 10 Famous Twins Comments*. Time, 03 Jan. 2013. Web. 04 Sept. 2015.
PRAGER, JOSHUA HARRIS. "All Shook Up in the Holy Land: Pilgrims Honor Elvis's Yahrzeit." *WSJ*. Dow Jones, 17 Aug. 1998. Web. 05 Sept. 2015.
"Pre-State Israel: The 1936 Arab Riots (April - November 1936)." *Jewish Virtual Library*. American-Israeli Cooperative Enterprise, n.d. Web. 13 June 2015.
RABKIN, RICHARD. "Was Elvis Presley Jewish?" *Aishcom*. Aish.com, n.d. Web. 05 Sept. 2015.
RAUM, TOM. "Bush surveys storm damage to home." *Maine Sunday Telegraph*, 03 Nov. 1991, pp. 1B and 12B.
"Refugees Forced to Land at Hamburg." *The Palestine Post*, Sept. 9, 1947, Late ed., sec. A.
"Refugees Refuse to Leave the Ships." *The Palestine Post*, July 30, 1947, Late ed., sec. A.
RAZZOUK, WASSIM. "Welcome." *Razzouk Tattoo*. Razzouk Tattoo, n.d. Web. 26 Oct. 2015.
Reuters News Staff. "Sniper Kills Bethlehem Church Bell-Ringer." *Rense.com*. Jeff Rense, n.d. Web. 28 July 2015.
RINGELHEIM, JOAN, dir. "Benjamin Ferencz Oral History Interview, Part 1." *American History TV*. C-SPAN3. N.d. *C-SPAN.org*. Web. 07 Jan. 2016.
ROCCA, FRANCIS X. "Vatican Disputes White House Guest List for Papal Visit." *WSJ*. Dow Jones, 17 Sept. 2015. Web. 22 Oct. 2015.
"Rocket Fire Slows after Day of Clashes That Saw Hamas Target Jerusalem, Tel Aviv. " *The Times of Israel*. The Times of Israel, 16 Nov. 2012. Web. 04 Aug. 2015.
"Rocket Launching." *Israeli Security Agency*. Shabak.gov.il, n.d. Web. 27 July 2015.
ROGOVOY, SETH. "The Original Rachel Dolezal Was a Jew Named Mezz Mezzrow." *The Forward*. The Forward Assn., 16 June 2015. Web. 05 Sept. 2015.
ROSENSAFT, MENACHEM. "Our Long National Fascination With Henry Kissinger Is Over." The Huffington Post. TheHuffingtonPost.com, 17 Dec. 2010. Web. 2 Apr. 2015.
RUBIN, RITA. "'Jews a Race' Genetic Theory Comes Under Fierce Attack by DNA Expert." *The Forward*. The Forward Assn., 07 May 2013. Web. 23 Aug. 2016.
RUBINSTEIN, WILLIAM D. "The Secret of Leopold Amery." *Historical Research*, 73, 181 June 2000: 175-96.
RUCKMAN, PETER S., ed. *The Ruckman Reference Bible*. Pensacola, Fla.: BB Bookstore, 2009.
"Russians Captured With Nazis Riot at Fort Dix; 3 Commit Suicide," *The New York Times* 29 June 1945: 1+. Web. 13 June 2014.
SAFIAN, ALEX. "False Israeli 'Massacre' Story Resurrected." Committee for Accuracy in Middle East Reporting in America. CAMERA.org, 04 Mar. 2007. Web. 06 Feb. 2015.
SANDOMIR, RICHARD. "FILM; He Batted for the Tigers, Himself and American Jews." 09 January 2000. *New York Times*. 05 Nov. 2013.
SCHORN, DANIEL. "Revisiting the Horrors of the Holocaust." CBS News. CBS Interactive: 14 Dec. 2006, Web. 05 Apr. 2014.
"Scopus Road Opened, Old City Encircled; 200 Egyptian Tanks Smashed; Gaza Falls." *Jerusalem Post*, June 07, 1967, Daily ed., sec. A.

SHAVIT, ARI. "End of a Journey." *Haaretz.com*. Haaretz Daily Newspaper Ltd., 13 Sept. 2001. Web. 25 July 2015.
"Shimon Peres." Jewish Virtual Library. 06 December 2014.
SHLAIM, AVI. "The Protocol of Sèvres,1956: Anatomy of a War Plot." *International Affairs*, 73:3 (1997), 509-30.
SIZER, STEPHEN. "Modern Israel in Bible Prophecy: Promised Return or Impending Exile?" *Christian Research Inst*. Christian Research Inst., 03 July 2012. Web. 17 Oct. 2015.
SOCRATES, ODYSSEAS, dir. "Greatest Tank Battles 1973 Yom Kippur War - Battle for the Sinai," *YouTube*. YouTube, 11 Sep. 2013. Web. 24 Mar. 2015.
STEIN, JOEL. "Who Runs Hollywood? C'mon." *Los Angeles Times*. Los Angeles Times, 19 Dec. 2008. Web. 21 Sept. 2015.
STROUM JEWISH STUDIES. "The Myth of the Khazar Conversion - Shaul Stampfer." *YouTube*. YouTube, 07 Jan. 2013. Web. 01 Sept. 2016.
"Suitland Federal Center." N.d. United States Census Bureau. Web. 25 July 2014.
"Sykes-Picot Agreement." Jewish Virtual Library. 14 June 2013.
"Tel Aviv Declared World's Best Gay Travel Destination." *Haaretz.com*. Haaretz Daily Newspaper Ltd., 11 Jan. 2012. Web. 22 Aug. 2015.
"Tel Aviv's 200,000 Being Checked by Two Divisions." *The Palestine Post*, July 31, 1946, Late ed., sec. A.
TERRILL, W. ANDREW. "Escalation and Intrawar Deterrence During Limited Wars in the Middle East." *Strategic Studies Inst.* (16 Sept. 2009). The US Army War College. PDF file.
"The Separation Barrier." *Separation Barrier*. B'Tselem, The Israeli Information Center for Human Rights in the Occupied Territories, 01 Jan. 2011. Web. 28 July 2015.
"The Shrine of the Eternals 2000 Electees: Morris 'Moe' Berg." N.d. The Baseball Reliquary. Web. 22 July 2014.
THIMMESCH, NICK. "How Kissinger Fooled Us All." *New York Magazine* 04 June 1973: 48-59. Web. 03 Apr. 2015.
TIRZA, DANNY. "Israeli Security Fence Architect: Why The Barrier Had to Be Built." *Al-Monitor*. Jamal Daniel, 01 July 2012. Web. 28 July 2015.
"Top 5 Most Controversial Performances From The Ed Sullivan Show." *Ed Sullivan Show*. SOFA Entertainment, n.d. Web. 18 Sept. 2015.
TUCKER, REED. "How Almost Dying Renewed Ron Jeremy." *New York Post*. NYP Holdings. 02 May 2015. Web. 21 Sept. 2015.
United Nations. General Assembly. "Resolution 181: Part IV - Capitulations." *The Avalon Project*. Yale Law School, 1996. Web. 19 June 2015.
United Nations. Security Council. "Documents Officiels, Volume 31." New York: United Nations, 1977. Web. 20 June 2015.
United States. Bureau of the Census. *Statistical Abstract of the United States: 1970*. 91st Edition. Washington, 1970.
United States. Department of State. Office of the Historian. *Foreign Relations of the United States, 1964-1968, Volume XIX, Arab-Israeli Crisis and War, 1967, Document 178*. "Telegram From the Embassy in the United Arab Republic to the Department of State." Web. 23 June 2015.
United States. National Security Agency. *Report to the Director NSA, USS Liberty (AGTR-5), 23 May - 8 June 1967*. [Washington, DC] National Security Agency. N.d. Declassified document.
USS Liberty: Dead in the Water. Dir. Christopher Mitchell. 2002. DVD. BBC.
VAN BUREN, ABIGAIL. "Dancer Can Go Topless And Believe In God, Too." *Chicago Tribune*. Chicago Tribune, 03 Sept. 1986. Web. 04 Sept. 2015.
VERKAIK, ROBERT. "Revealed: The Fate of Idi Amin's Hijack Victim." *The Independent*. Independent Digital News and Media, 13 Feb. 2007. Web. 14 July 2015.
Vic975, dir. "Sarah Silverman Says 'I Would Kill Christ Again.'" *YouTube*. YouTube, 24 Apr. 2011. Web. 21 Sept. 2015.
"Victims of Palestinian Violence and Terrorism since September 2000." *Israel Ministry of Foreign Affairs*. Mfa.gov.il, n.d. Web. 27 July 2015.
WEIL, MARTIN. "Dr. Joyce Brothers, 85; TV Psychologist and Columnist." *Washington Post*. The Washington Post, 13 May 2013. Web. 04 Sept. 2015.
"Weinstein to Rule on Possible Criminal Probe against Sara Netanyahu in 'Bottlegate' Affair." *The Jerusalem Post*. Jpost, 02 Feb. 2015. Web. 07 Aug. 2015.
WEISS, SEYMOUR. Top Secret. *Action Memorandum* George Washington University. 07 Apr. 2015.
"Welcome to the finest aircraft carrier in the fleet!" n.d. U.S. Navy. Web. 23 October 2014.
WHITE, JOSEPH ROBERT. "'Even in Auschwitz…Humanity Could Prevail': British POWs and Jewish Concentration-Camp Inmates at IG Auschwitz, 1943-1945." *Holocaust and Genocide Studies*. 15 (2001): 266-295. *California State University*. 10 June 2014.
WIKIPEDIA CONTRIBUTORS. "Clarence Larkin." *Wikipedia, The Free Encyclopedia*. Wikipedia, The Free Encyclopedia, 27 Apr. 2015. Web. 17 Oct. 2015.
WILLIAMSON, B. T. "Caught in the Middle: Air Combat between Israel and the RAF." *The Royal Air Force Air Power Review* Summer 8.2 (2005): 79-83. *Air Power Studies*. Royal Air Force. Web. 20 Nov. 2014.
WINSTON, KIMBERLY. "Judaism without God? Yes, Say American Atheists." *USA Today*. Gannett, 26 Sept. 2011. Web. 25 Aug. 2015.
WOODS, MARK. "Rick Warren on Roman Catholicism: 'We Have More in Common than What Divides Us.'" *Christian Today*. Christian Media Corporation, 05 Dec. 2014. Web. 21 Oct. 2015.
YASHAR, ARI AND MATT WANDERMAN. "US Declassifies Document Revealing Israel's Nuclear Program." *Arutz Sheva*. Arutz Sheva, 25 Mar. 2015. Web. 07 Aug. 2015.
YEMINI, GALYA. "Moshe Dayan's Eye Patch Ends up for Sale on EBay for $75,000." *Haaretz.com*. Haaretz Daily Newspaper, 25 July 2005. Web. 19 Oct. 2015.
YOUNG-SOMERS, DEBBIE. "Crossing the Reed Sea." Web blog post. *Rabbi Debbie Young-Somers*. Blogger, 24 Apr. 2011. Web. 22 Jan. 2015.
ZABECKI, DAVID T. "David 'Mickey' Marcus." *Military History* Apr. 1998: n. pag. HISTORYnet.com. Web. 31 Oct. 2014.
ZEZIMA, KATIE. "A Short History of Awkward Encounters between Obama and Netanyahu." *Washington Post*. The Washington Post, 1 Oct. 2014. Web. 07 Aug. 2015.
ZIMMERMAN, JOHN C. "Body Disposal at Auschwitz: The End of Holocaust Denial." *Body Disposal at Auschwitz: The End of Holocaust Denial*. The Holocaust History Project, 12 July 2009. Web. 03 Apr. 2017.
"Zionist Organization Statement on Palestine, Paris Peace Conference, February 3, 1919." Jewish Virtual Library. Accessed 02 July 2013.
ZIV-TAL, AVRAHAM. "Lest we Forget." n.d. Enigma Named Max. Web. 05 August 2014.
ZVIELLI, ALEXANDER, comp. *Front Page Israel: Modern Israel's Extraordinary History as Captured on the Front Pages of The Jerusalem Post*. Jerusalem: Jerusalem Post, 2008.
_____. "Teddy Kollek and his life-long dedication." *Jerusalem Post*, Jan. 2, 2007.
ZOECH, IRENE. "Named: the baby boy who was Nazis' first euthanasia victim." 12 October 2003. The Sunday Telegraph. 25 Feb. 2014.

Index

Maps

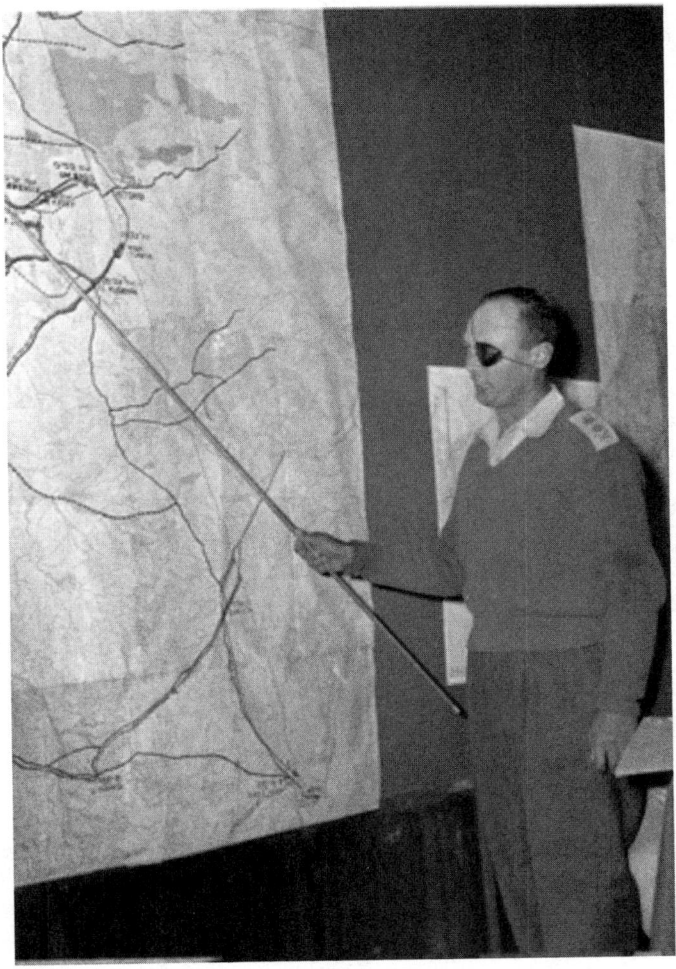

Moshe Dayan explaining Sinai campaign
(Israel Government Press Office)

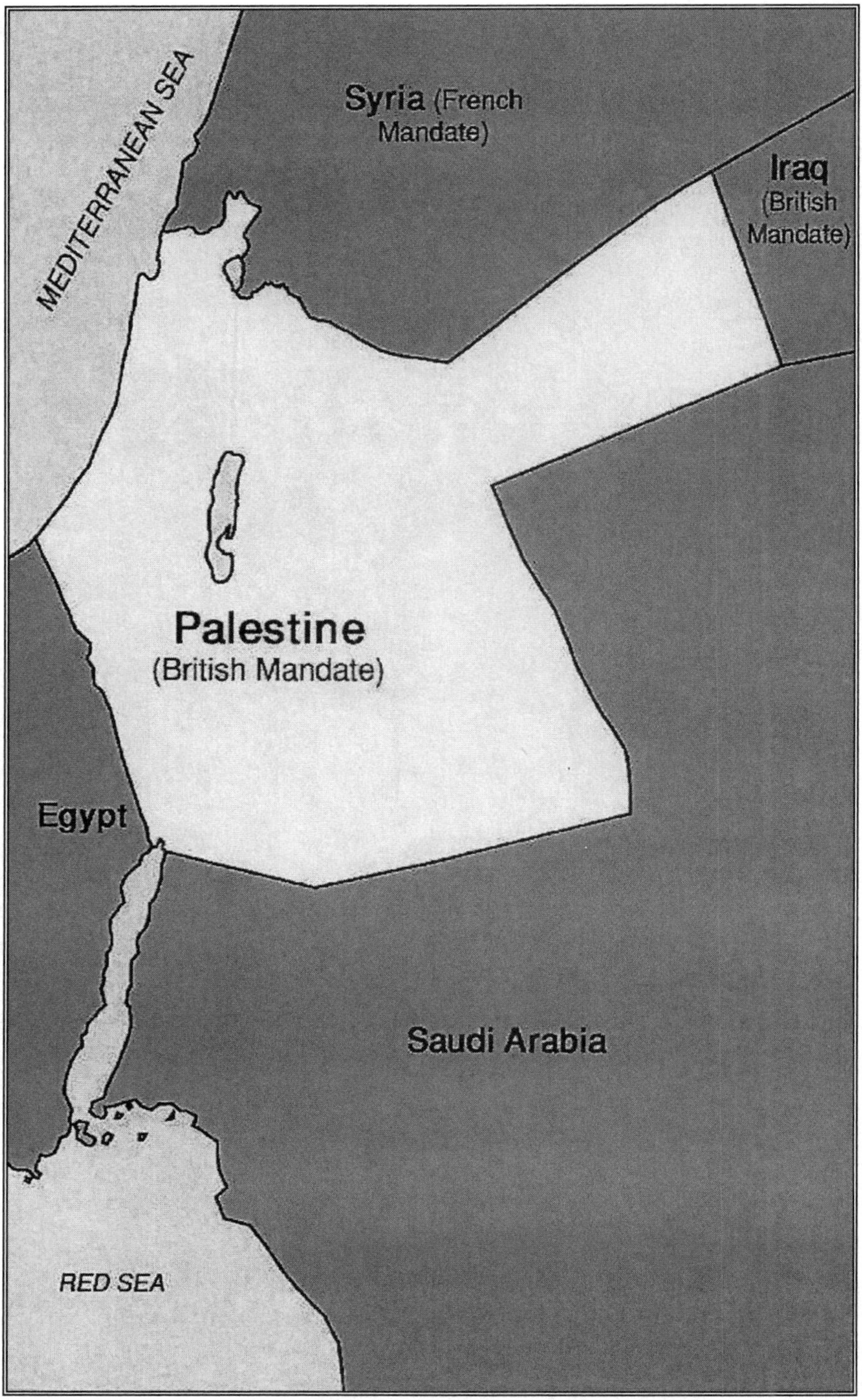

British Mandate of Palestine at 1920 San Remo Conference

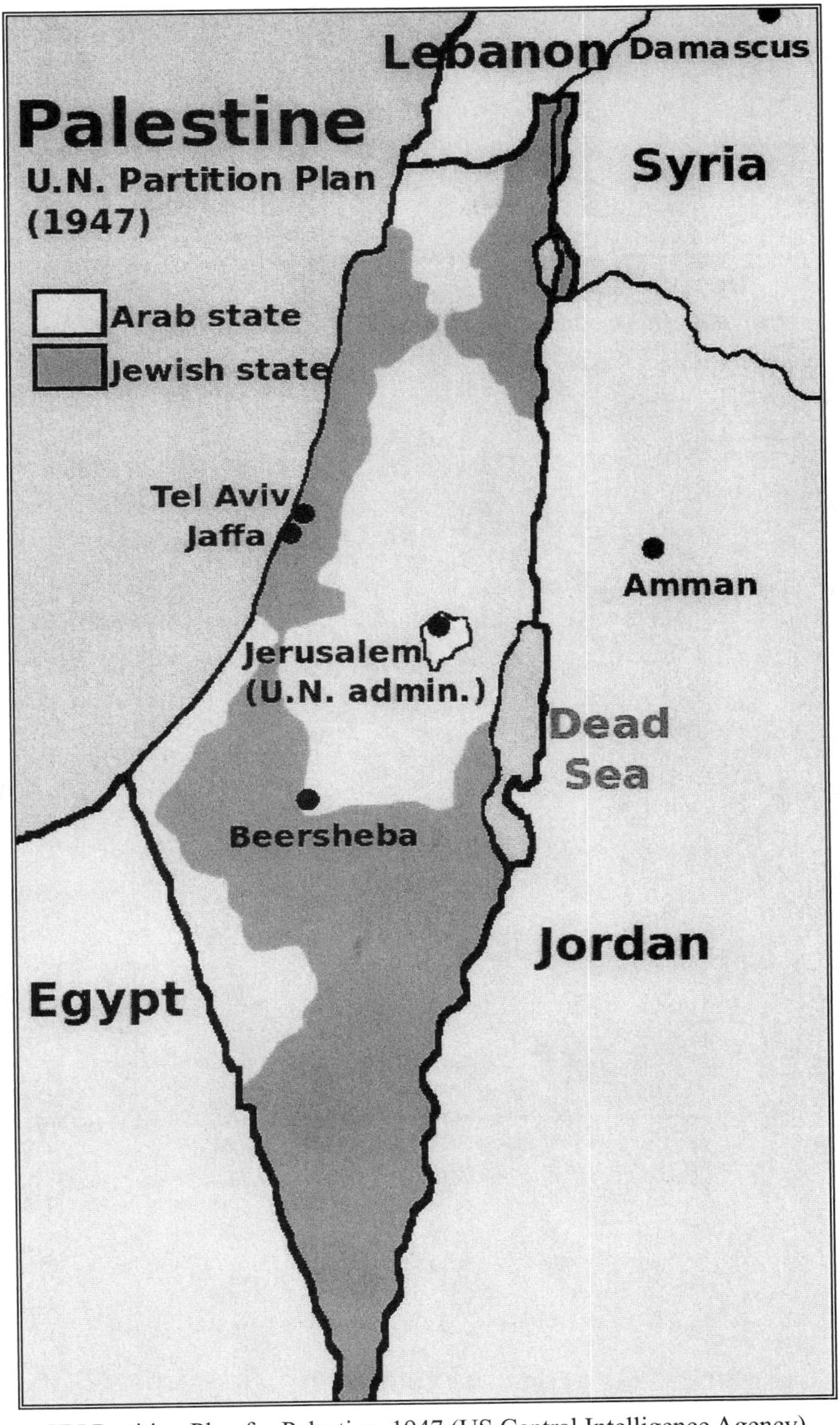

UN Partition Plan for Palestine, 1947 (US Central Intelligence Agency)

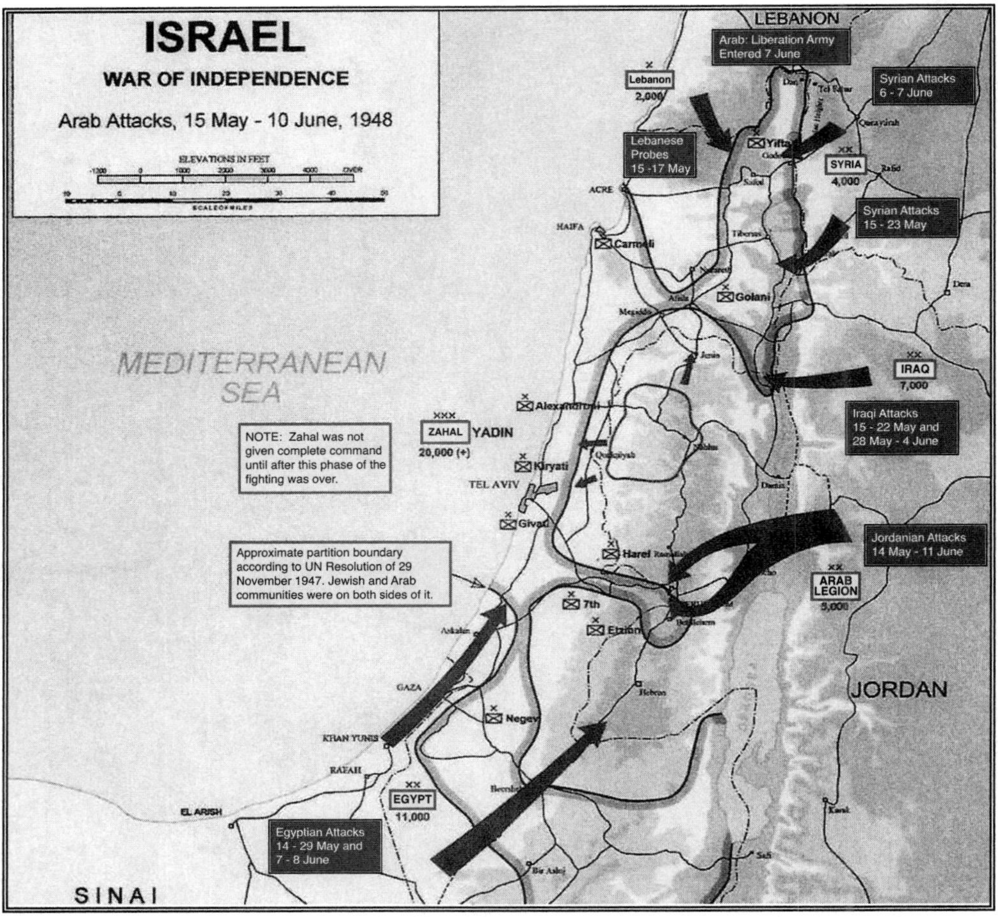

The 1948 Arab – Israeli War, May 15 - June 19
(Department of History, US Military Academy)

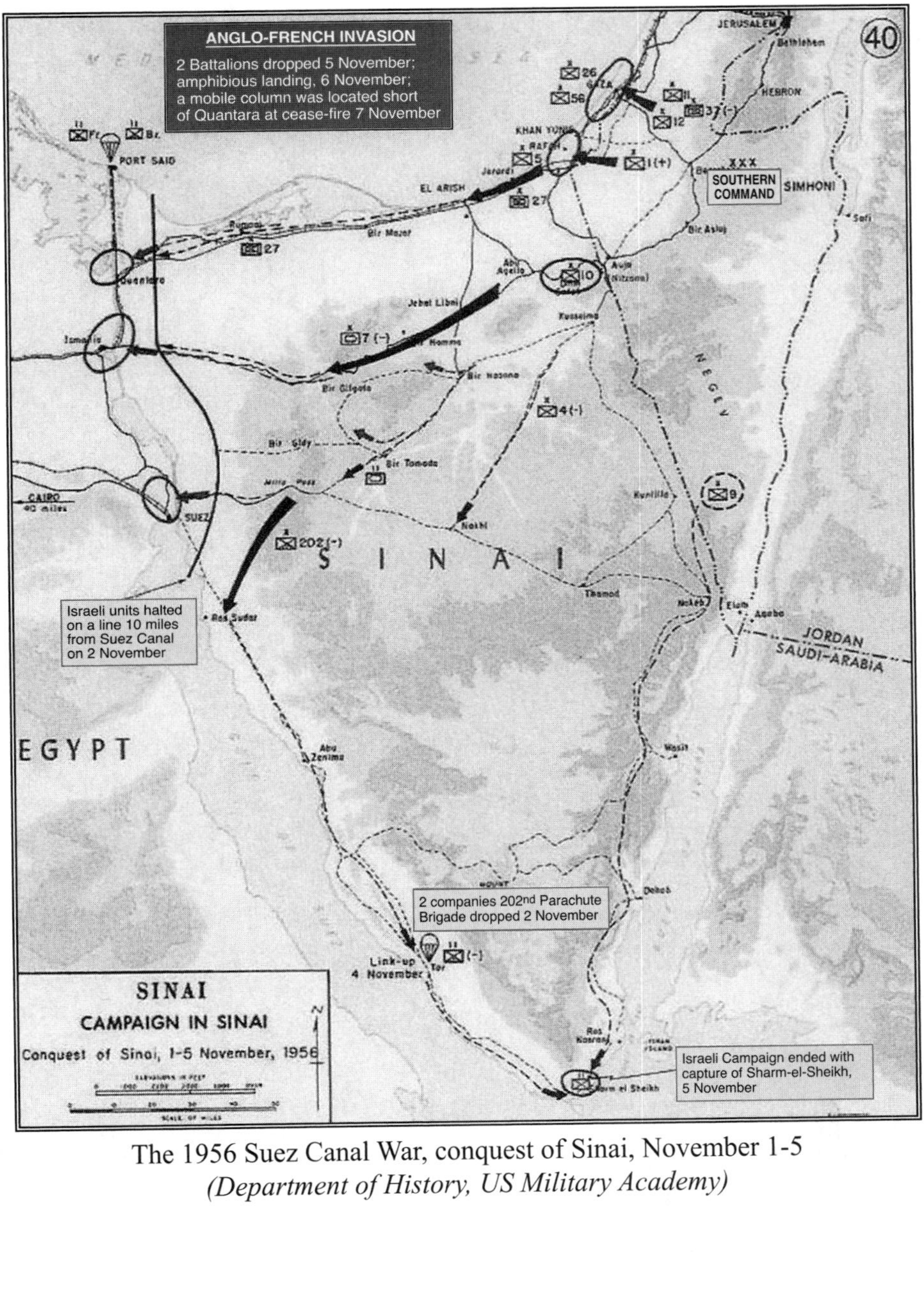

The 1956 Suez Canal War, conquest of Sinai, November 1-5
(Department of History, US Military Academy)

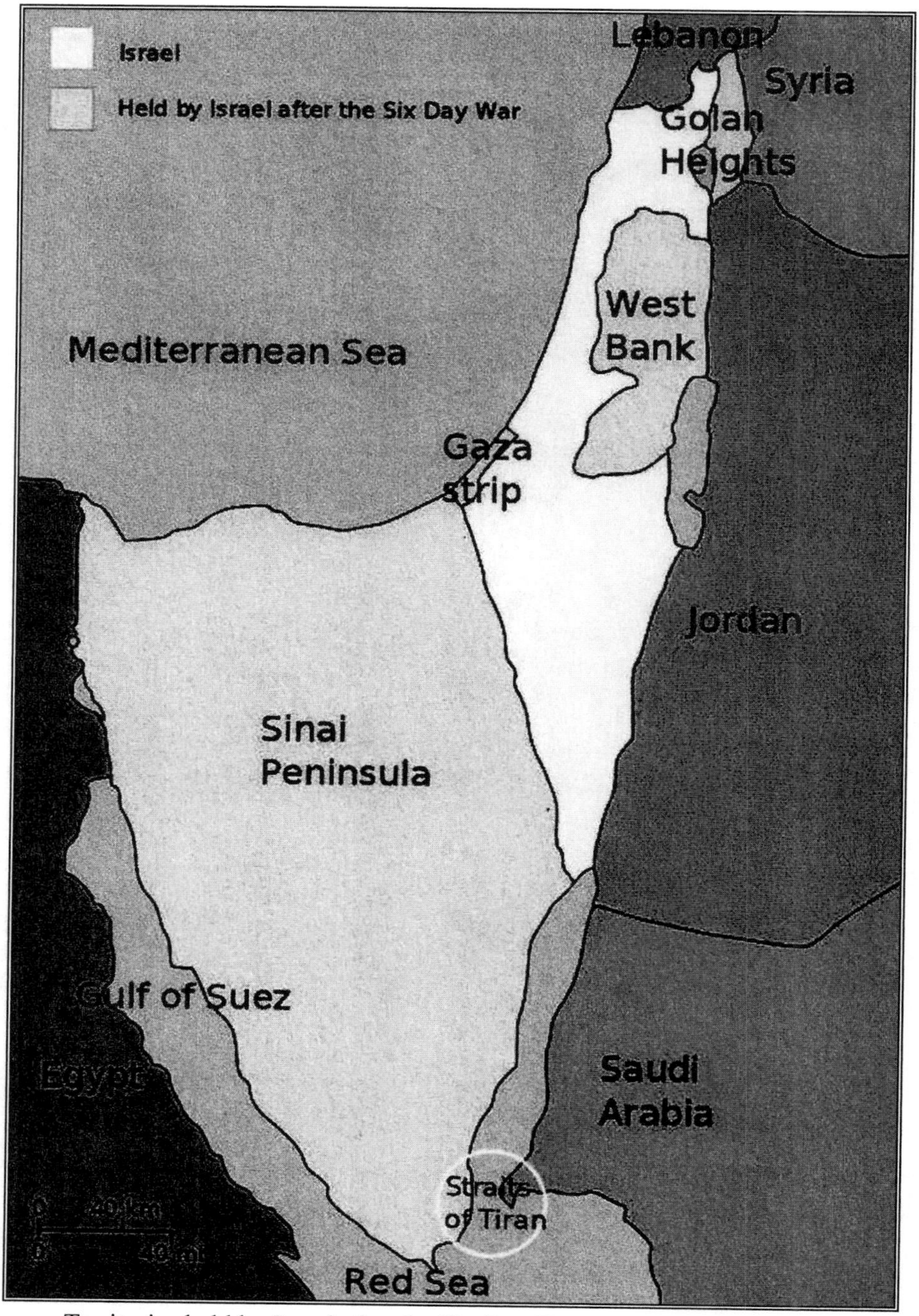

Territories held by Israel after the Six-Day War, June 1967 *(Ling Nut)*

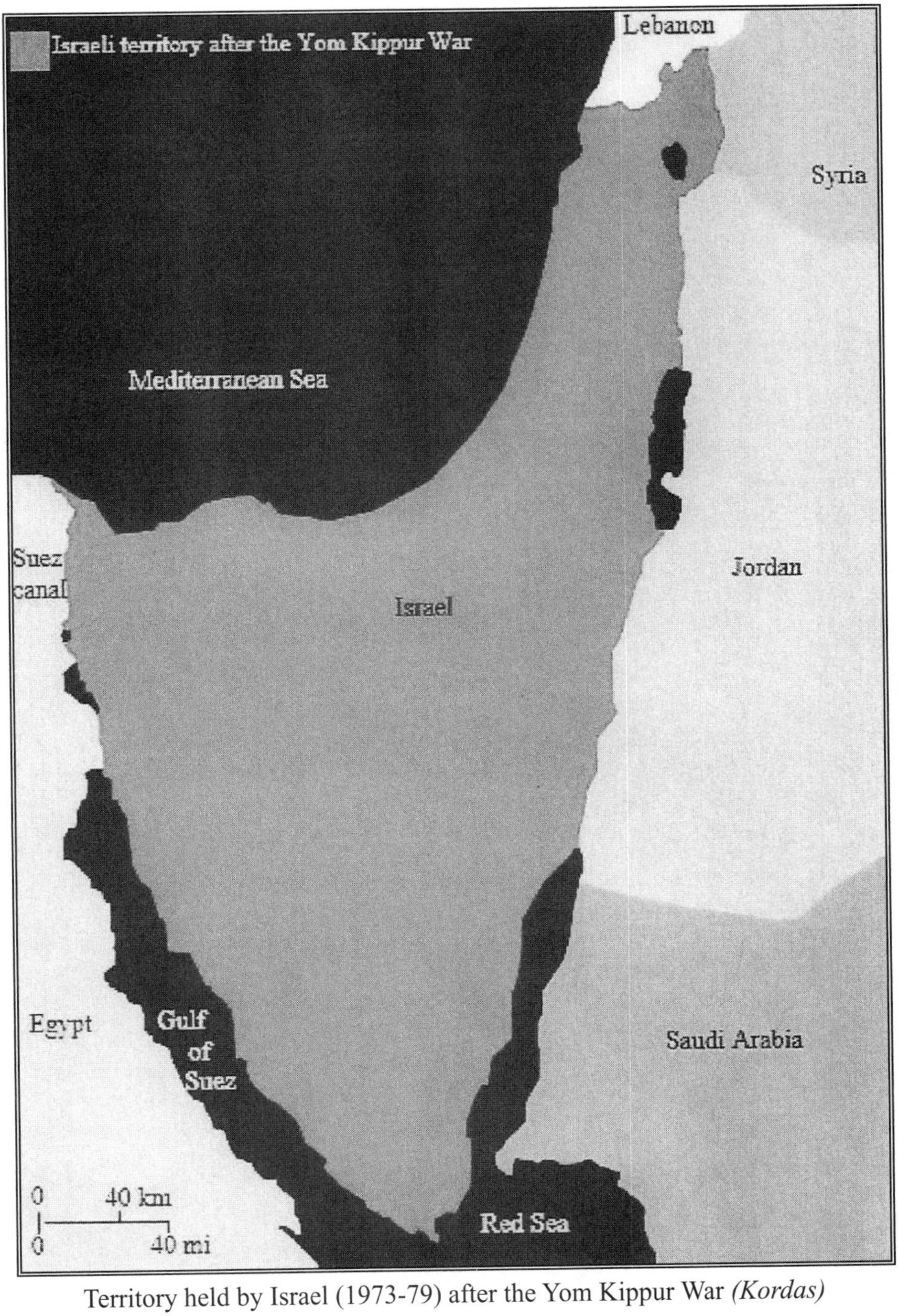

Territory held by Israel (1973-79) after the Yom Kippur War *(Kordas)*

About the Author

William P. (Bill) Grady was born on Manhattan's Upper East Side and reared as a strict Roman Catholic. His grade school diploma was signed by Cardinal Francis Spellman. In 1970, he graduated from Salesianum School in Wilmington, Delaware, the largest parochial high school in the state. (Ironically, at the close of his freshman year, a seventeen-year-old senior at Cheltenham High School, some thirty miles away in Wyncote, Pennsylvania, was compelled to skip his *own* commencement to return to his native land to enlist in the IDF at the outbreak of the Six-Day War—future Israeli Prime Minister Benjamin "Bibi" Netanyahu.)

After selling office equipment in the Delaware Valley for two years, Bill accepted a marketing position with British Airways in New York City. Following a promotion to Philadelphia in 1974, he was saved, baptized, and called to preach at the historic Marcus Hook Baptist Church (home church to Clarence Larkin). Apart from his ministerial degrees (which include a Ph.D. in History from the former Baptist International Seminary, Oxon Hill, Maryland), he also studied business and history at the University of Delaware, Goldey-Beacom College, and the University of Tennessee. As a minister of the Gospel, he founded and pastored two churches, taught Bible and history for ten years on the college level, and preached in over 1,000 churches as a full-time evangelist.

Dr. Grady's best-selling books have been featured in numerous venues, including *USA Today*, *Southwest Radio Church*, and the legendary *Barry Farber Show*, maintaining high reviews on Amazon and Barnes & Noble. (His 1993 classic, *Final Authority*, is currently in its fourteenth printing.) Bill's lifetime of travel, preaching, and research has spanned forty countries on four continents (including three trips to Asia, five to the Middle East, and eleven to Europe and Russia).

The Lord has also enhanced his writing by affording him unusual favor with several eyewitnesses to history, e.g., Mrs. Nathalie Basilevsky, daughter of Baron Lieutenant-General Pyotr Wrangel, Commander-in-Chief of the anti-Bolshevik White Army; Samuel T. Cohen, Manhattan Project physicist, "Father of the Neutron Bomb"; UNESCO Goodwill Ambassador, Kim Phuc (a.k.a. "the girl in the picture"); World War II fighter aces, Brigadier General Robert Lee Scott, Jr. (author of *God is My Co-pilot*) and Brigadier General David Lee "Tex" Hill (portrayed by John Wayne in *The Flying Tigers*); and Mei-ling Soong, (a.k.a. Madame Chiang Kai-shek), former First Lady of the Republic of China. (Having produced a short documentary on Madame Chiang's life, emphasizing her exemplary Christian testimony, Dr. Grady was honored to attend her 2003 Manhattan funeral at the invitation of Ambassador Andrew Kao, current Director-General of the Taipei Economic & Cultural Office.)

Among the many highlights of Dr. Grady's forty-two year ministry, in October 2007, Colonel Eyal Rozen, then-Commander of the IDF Givati Brigade (Special Forces) training camp in the Golan Heights, had the base flag struck and presented to him for his devotion to Israel.

Bill and his wife Linda have been blessed with forty-two years of marriage, producing three children and sixteen grandchildren. He currently serves as an evangelist out of Fellowship Baptist Church in Maryville, Tennessee, Pastor Tom Hatley.

Back in his Michigan church with his prized gift